LEGAL ISSUES in nursing

LEGAL ISSUES in nursing

Cynthia E. Northrop, R.N., M.S., J.D.

Admitted, Maryland Bar
Adjunct Associate Professor, Teachers College,
Columbia University, New York, N.Y.
Past President, The American Association of Nurse Attorneys

Mary E. Kelly, R.N., B.S.N., J.D.

Admitted, Illinois and California Bars
Private Practice, Los Angeles
Adjunct Professor, Southwestern University School of Law, Los Angeles
Instructor, California State University, Long Beach, Health Care Administration
Past President, The American Association of Nurse Attorneys

The C. V. Mosby Company

ST. LOUIS • WASHINGTON, D.C. • TORONTO 1987

A TRADITION OF PUBLISHING EXCELLENCE

Editor: Tom Lochhaas
Assistant editor: Laurie Sparks
Editing supervisor: Karen Edwards
Manuscript editors: Jennifer Collins, Roger McWilliams, Cheryl Whatley
Book design: Elizabeth Fett
Production: Jennifer Collins

Printed in the United States of America

The C.V. Mosby Company
11830 Westline Industrial Drive, St. Louis, Missouri 63146

Library of Congress Cataloging-in-Publication Data

Northrop, Cynthia E.
Legal issues in nursing.

Includes bibliographies and index.
1. Nursing—Law and legislation—United States.
I. Kelly, Mary E., (Mary Elizabeth) II. Title.
[DNLM: 1. Jurisprudence—United States—nurses' instruction. 2. Legislation, Nursing—United States.
WY 33 AA1 N76L]
KF2915.N8N67 1987 344.73'0414 86-33281
ISBN 0-8016-3720-1 347.304414

GW/VH/VH 9 8 7 6 5 4 3 02/C/217

Contributing nurse attorneys

ELIZABETH A. BOWYER, B.S., J.D.

Loss Prevention/Underwriting Representative,
Risk Management Foundation, Harvard Medical Institutions,
Boston, Massachusetts;
Admitted, Massachusetts Bar

NANCY J. BRENT, B.S., M.S., J.D.

Solo Practitioner of Law,
and Associate Professor of Nursing Graduate Program,
St. Xavier College, Chicago, Illinois;
Admitted, Illinois Bar

SHERYL A. FEUTZ, B.S.N., M.S.N., J.D.

Associate, Shughart, Thompson, and Kilroy,
Kansas City, Missouri;
Adjunct Professor, University of Missouri-Columbia,
School of Nursing, Columbia, Missouri;
Admitted, Missouri Bar

ANN BALDWIN MECH, A.A., B.S.N., M.S., J.D.

University of Maryland Medical System,
Department of Nursing,
Quality Assurance and Legal Affairs,
Baltimore, Maryland;
Admitted, Maryland Bar

ELLEN K. MURPHY, B.S., M.S., J.D., C.N.O.R.

Associate Professor, University of Wisconsin,
School of Nursing, Milwaukee, Wisconsin;
Admitted, Wisconsin Bar

KATHERINE J. POHLMAN, B.S.N., M.S., J.D.

Associate, Law Offices of Snyder and Sweeney,
Boston, Massachusetts;
Admitted, Massachusetts Bar

JO ANN SMITH, B.A., J.D.

Senior Attorney, Health-Allied Services
Beverly Enterprises
Pasadena, California;
Admitted, California Bar

DIANE TRACE WARLICK, B.S.N., J.D.

Associate, Law Offices of R. Eric Moore,
Christiansted, St. Croix, U.S. Virgin Islands;
Admitted, Massachusetts and U.S. Virgin Islands Bars

First Nurse Attorney

Mary Eleanor McGarvah

In 1985 I began a quest for the first book on nursing and the law and was greatly pleased not only to find it, but, more importantly, to discover the first nurse attorney. Eleanor McGarvah, R.N., Member of the Michigan Bar, collaborated in the authorship of *Jurisprudence for Nurses,* of which there were three editions in 1931, 1939, and 1945. It is to Mary Eleanor McGarvah, first nurse attorney, that Mary E. Kelly and I dedicate this book, all of which was written by nurse attorneys who have followed in her footsteps and zest for nursing and law. Ms. McGarvah's life and career was full, committed, involved, and exemplary.

I did most of my research for this book at Columbia University, School of Law Library, one of the oldest law schools in the country. It happens that the Law Library is just two blocks from where I am an adjunct associate professor at Teachers' College, Columbia University, one of the oldest nursing education programs. It was there that I found *Jurisprudence for Nurses.*

In the preface and foreword to the second edition, Ms. McGarvah stated: "As a first volume exclusively devoted to laws as they affect nurses, *Jurisprudence for Nurses* was received by the nursing and legal professions with considerable interest . . . [it] was a newborn babe in the world of nursing texts. . . . Prior to its appearance and use, nurses first became aware of their legal responsibilities in the school of sad experience."

The book's title page held the only clue to finding out more about Eleanor McGarvah, a reference to the Michigan Bar. I contacted the State Bar of Michigan in Lansing. Their Executive Director, Michael Franck, sent me a copy of Ms. McGarvah's obituary. Born in 1886, Mary Eleanor McGarvah was a graduate of the Farrand Training School of Nursing and had a bachelor of law degree from the University of Detroit. She served as the Director of the Division of Special Investigation for the Detroit Department of Health. She died in 1979 at the age of 92. The newspaper headline reads "Mary McGarvah, 92, retired attorney, nurse."

I have often thought, if only I had been looking for the *oldest* nurse attorney *first* as I began in 1977 looking for other nurse attorneys to start The American Association of Nurse Attorneys, I could have met and talked with Eleanor McGarvah. I have learned a deep-felt lesson of life and how priorities are set.

My public health nursing background told me the next step was to call the Director of Public Health Nursing, Detroit Department of Health. Cornelia Ford, R.N., M.P.H., was most helpful and sent me copies of Ms. McGarvah's writings, some in her own hand, her picture, articles the Health Department had saved, and a list of PHNs who were Ms. McGarvah's colleagues and friends.

Ms. McGarvah held badge number 2 at the Health Department, joining as a school nurse on July 1, 1914. The next year she became a supervisor of infant welfare and midwives, maternity homes, and boarding homes. In June, 1929, she graduated from the University of Detroit with a law degree and aided the Health Commissioner in legal matters. From 1946 until her retirement in 1955, she served as the department's Director of the

Division of Special Investigations. In total, she served the Health Department for 41 years.

I then turned my attention to the Farrand Training School and received great assistance from Lucy D. Germain. An outstanding and respected nursing leader, Ms. Germain was at one time Director of the Harper Hospital School of Nursing (formerly, Farrand Training School) in Detroit. She sent me a copy of the *History of the Farrand Training School for Nurses,* written in 1936. On p. 198 Nellie McGarvah is listed as a 1911 graduate. On p. 142 a section discussing registration of nurses and the passage of the Michigan nursing licensure law in 1909 states: "In recent years efforts have been made to revise the law. Eleanor McGarvah, a graduate of Farrand Training School, and a practicing attorney on the staff of the Bureau of Special Investigations of the Detroit Department of Health, has aided in this work."

Bernard Dobranski, Dean, and Mary Barden, Assistant Dean, University of Detroit, School of Law, also were helpful. They confirmed that Mary McGarvah graduated in 1929. Although they had no other information, they provided me with a list of classmates to whom I have written.

I've had long conversations and correspondence with two colleagues and friends of Ms. McGarvah. Both PHNs, Jessie Good and Phyllis G. Corwin, were extremely interested and so enthusiastic about Ms. McGarvah. Ms. Corwin wrote me:

"Miss McGarvah was readily available . . . fair and understanding. There was, as she often stated, one way to do things . . . the right way. She always found time to listen . . . She had a great sense of humor and a very ready laugh. Miss McGarvah was deeply religious . . . and very family oriented."

Her career involved public health laws and regulations. She is credited with gaining licensure for midwives, massage parlors, and schools, with regulation of boarding homes, and with being the author of the original Michigan regulations governing convalescent homes and homes for the aged. She was responsible for enforcing communicable disease laws, which at that time were largely statutes dealing with tuberculosis.

The research into Mary Eleanor McGarvah's life continues. Through Phyllis Corwin, I have made contact with two of Ms. McGarvah's nieces. The American Association of Nurse Attorneys Foundation and The American Associaton of Nurse Attorneys plan to officially recognize her as the first nurse attorney.

It is with deep respect that Mary E. Kelly and I dedicate this book to the first nurse attorney, Mary Eleanor McGarvah.

Cynthia E. Northrop

Preface

Our objectives as nurse attorneys are to educate nurses about law, become experts in this area of health law, and to publish. These, by the way, are similar to goals of The American Association of Nurse Attorneys (TAANA) and The American Association of Nurse Attorneys Foundation in which we have been so actively involved. We see this book as a step toward these goals. We hope through this book to make a substantial contribution to the professional development of nursing and nurse attorneys.

This book is intended for nurses and nursing students in all areas of practice, including nursing education, nursing administration, and nursing research. Nurse attorneys and other attorneys will also find this book relevant to their practice. It is a comprehensive text focused upon issues in all areas of nursing, beginning with general principles and systems, sources, and types of law. Issues for the nurse defendant in the hospital, community, federal government, education, research, and advanced practice settings are included. Strategies for managing legal risks in these settings are discussed. Areas in which nurses are, and should to a greater degree, assert their rights as plaintiffs are described, including employment claims, collective action, and control of practice. Other highlights include the topics of licensure, criminal law, and nursing businesses.

Chapters on nursing settings follow a similar format: an overview of the practice area; identification of legal issues for the nurse within the practice area; application of specific case law and legislation; discussion of standards of care; and recommendations and trends. Each chapter has its own references (endnotes) and most have additional reading lists.

In addition, this book was reviewed by an external panel of experts, including nurse attorneys. Their comments were vital to the development and comprehensiveness of the book.

Unique attributes of the book include the following:

1. It was written by nurse attorneys, individuals who have practiced nursing in clinical areas and who have practiced law in areas affecting nursing and the issues addressed in the book. Uniquely prepared as nurses and as attorneys, we have practiced nursing and practiced law, taught nursing and law courses and continuing education programs, and researched legal issues in nursing. Nursing law is our area of law practice.

2. The book is expansive in scope and coverage, and it includes extensive, comprehensive documentation and substantiation, covering all currently recognized areas in which nurses work and concluding with future direction of nursing into entrepreneurial roles.

3. The book maintains throughout that not only for the nurse defendant *but also* for the nurse plaintiff, asserting legal rights is just as important as defending them.

4. We have identified legal issues and factors important to the selection of legal counsel; this better prepares the reader not to solve legal problems, but to seek legal advice.

5. The book emphasizes *nursing* standards of care and assists the reader in meeting the standard of care.

We and our contributors have been leaders in TAANA and its Foundation. Three of us have been TAANA Presidents: Cynthia Northrop, Diane Trace Warlick, and Mary E. Kelly. Katherine Pohlman, the president in 1987, has also been TAANA Vice-President; Diane Trace Warlick, Mary E. Kelly, and Elizabeth Bowyer have been TAANA Recording Secretaries. Most of us have held committee membership and leadership, including Ann Baldwin Mech, who co-chairs the Task Force on Expert Nurse Witnesses.

This book carries with it a caveat. Each state jurisdiction is unique. Each state is bound by its own precedent—the decisions of its own courts. We have each applied laws of the states in which we are licensed to practice law and at least one other state. United States Supreme Court cases and other federal court cases and legislation are applied where relevant. As a result many states and cases have been covered, yet some have not. This reinforces the need to obtain legal advice for the particular jurisdiction in question. Our purpose is to point out the issues, not to itemize all state and federal laws. Given all of this, and because each court decision is unique to the facts of that decision, we intend Chapter 3 to be a resource to our readers for seeking legal advice.

The material in this book is not meant to be and should not be used as a substitute for legal advice. Laws and statutes have been checked as current through February, 1986.

Cynthia E. Northrop
Mary E. Kelly

December, 1986

Acknowledgements

I want to acknowledge the love and support of my husband, Harvey Cary Dzodin, my parents, Francis Merle Northrop and Marjorie Wion Northrop, and my brother, David.

I also want to express deep gratitude to Mary Kelly. I've learned so much from her and have appreciated so much working with her. (I'd do it again, without question!)

Cynthia E. Northrop

I would like to acknowledge my loving spouse, Thomas Garrick, for his many hours of assistance and support, my parents, Edward and Laurette Kelly, and all my brothers and sisters for their enthusiasm and encouragement, and most of all, my colleague and dear friend, Cynthia Northrop, for fostering my professional and personal growth. I, too, would do it all again.

Mary E. Kelly

We would like to acknowledge Marie Snyder, nurse attorney, Snyder & Sweeney, Boston, who greatly assisted us as expert and reviewer. We would also like to thank several nurse attorney colleagues who helped and supported us: Virginia Trotter Betts; D.-M. Boulay; Pamela Ames; and Sarah D. Cohn, M.S.N., J.D., Associate Counsel, Medicolegal Affairs, Yale New Haven Hospital, for her contribution to Chapter 29. We thank each of the contributors for their support, interest, and excellent effort.

Contents

UNIT VII
NURSING BUSINESSES

Appendixes

LEGAL ISSUES in nursing

UNIT I

Overview

Chapter 1

Introduction to federal and state systems of government

Mary E. Kelly

The respective powers of the federal and state governments and the rights of individuals are established by the United States Constitution, which is the supreme law of the land.[1] The Constitution grants to the federal government specific powers and reserves to the states all powers not expressly given to the federal government.[2]

In dividing powers and functions, the framers of the Constitution followed the general principle that matters of national concern requiring uniform policies were to be delegated to the national government. Two types of powers were delegated to the federal government by the Constitution: express and implied powers. The states possess reserve powers—those powers not expressly delegated to the federal government. Accordingly, the various states have established court systems and enacted constitutions and statutes similar to those of the federal system.

Express powers are those functions expressly delegated to the federal government in the Constitution; implied powers, authorized by the Constitution under the Necessary and Proper Clause, in effect allow Congress to utilize the method most useful and convenient for carrying into effect one of the expressly delegated powers. Exclusive powers of the federal government include the power to declare war, to conduct foreign relations, to coin money, to establish post offices, and to enter into treaties. Examples of the states' reserve powers include the power to tax and spend money, to regulate persons and property to promote health and safety, to maintain law and order, and to regulate domestic relations and intrastate commerce.

In addition to establishing the powers of the state and federal governments over individuals, the Constitution's Bill of Rights guarantees individuals certain rights that are protected from governmental intrusion. These rights serve as a limitation on federal and state government action. Although none of these rights is absolute, governmental action that interferes with any of these rights must be strictly justified.

The tripartite system of government

Under the doctrine of separation of powers, the processes of government are broken into three component parts and are exercised by three corresponding branches of government. The United States Constitution and state constitutions define three separate branches of the federal or state government: the judicial branch, the executive branch, and the legislative branch.

The framers of the Constitution were concerned about the concentration of power in one person or one arm of government. To achieve a balance of power, they devised a system of government that gives each branch of government distinct and separate functions and powers, the exercise of which is supposed to restrain the other branches. This tripartite system of government serves to operate as a system of checks and balances and to guard against autocratic abuses of authority.

Article III of the Constitution establishes the powers

of the judicial branch of government. Article I defines the legislative branch and Article II concerns the powers of the executive branch. The various state governments also follow this tripartite system. Because each branch of government has an impact on the legal issues confronting nurses, an analysis of the three branches' respective powers and functions follows.

The judicial branch: powers and limitations

The United States Constitution defines the judiciary's power to decide cases or controversies concerning particular subjects. State constitutions also establish the power of state courts. Each state may vary in detail as to that state court's power; however, most are patterned after the federal system.

FEDERAL COURT JURISDICTION

Article III of the United States Constitution provides that the judicial power shall be vested in one Supreme Court and in such inferior courts as Congress may establish. The lower federal courts created by Congress under Article III authority, sometimes referred to as Article III courts, include: (1) United States District Courts, which in general are the trial courts of the federal system and (2) the various circuit courts for the United States Court of Appeals, which have authority to review and alter the decisions of the district courts under them. The box (right) illustrates the twelve circuits' court of appeals under which the district courts are organized.

SUMMARY OF THE TWELVE JUDICIAL CIRCUITS

- District of Columbia Circuit
  - Washington, D.C.
- First Circuit
  - Maine
  - New Hampshire
  - Massachusetts
  - Puerto Rico
- Second Circuit
  - New York
  - Vermont
  - Connecticut
- Third Circuit
  - Pennsylvania
  - New Jersey
  - Delaware
  - Virgin Islands
- Fourth Circuit
  - Maryland
  - Virginia
  - West Virginia
  - North Carolina
  - South Carolina
- Fifth Circuit
  - Louisiana
  - Mississippi
  - Texas
- Sixth Circuit
  - Ohio
  - Michigan
  - Kentucky
  - Tennessee
- Seventh Circuit
  - Illinois
  - Indiana
  - Wisconsin
- Eighth Circuit
  - Minnesota
  - Iowa
  - Missouri
  - Arkansas
  - Nebraska
  - South Dakota
  - North Dakota
- Ninth Circuit
  - California
  - Oregon
  - Alaska
  - Hawaii
  - Nevada
  - Idaho
  - Washington
  - Montana
  - Guam
- Tenth Circuit
  - Wyoming
  - Utah
  - New Mexico
  - Kansas
  - Oklahoma
  - Colorado
- Eleventh Circuit
  - Alabama
  - Georgia
  - Florida

The Supreme Court, in turn, has authority to review the circuit courts' decisions, but Article III makes the Court's appellate authority subject to limitation by Congress. Some cases, such as those between two governments, are directly reviewed by the Court. Most cases, however, are reviewed by the Court on request of the losing party, known as a petition for *certiorari*. With few exceptions, the Court may choose which cases it will review. Although the requests for review number in the thousands, the Court hears only a couple of hundred per year.[3]

Article III limits the judiciary's power to resolving "cases or controversies." This in essence means that the judicial branch of the federal government has the power only to determine disputes presented in an adversary context and in a form historically viewed as proper for the judiciary to resolve.[4]

In addition, Article III defines the subject matter of the controversies and cases that federal courts have power to decide. This is known as subject matter jurisdiction. If the lawsuit is not a "case or controversy" or the federal court lacks subject matter jurisdiction, the case must be dismissed or the district court's decision on the merits will be reversed on appeal to a higher court. Because these concepts are fundamental to the court's exercise of power, each is discussed more fully below.

Case Or Controversy Limitations. Article III provides that the federal judiciary's power extends to "cases or controversies." The Supreme Court has interpreted this language as a limitation on the kinds of issues that Article III courts may resolve. The issue in a given lawsuit must be presented in an adversarial context, and the party bringing the lawsuit must have a sufficient personal stake in the outcome of the litigation.

Some of the case or controversy limitations established by the Court are grounded in the Constitution; others are judicially created. The significance of the source of the limitation is that Congress has the power to alter judicially created limitations on the court's power to hear a given case, but it may not do so if the limitation is grounded in the Constitution.

No Political Questions. Cases involving political questions or political in nature are examples of the kind of cases that federal courts may not properly decide. While the judicial branch has the power to decide whether a particular law is in violation of the United States Constitution[5] and to decide the rights of individuals, it may not inquire as to how the executive or legislative branches perform duties in which each has discretion.[6] The doctrine of separation of powers prevents the courts from deciding cases that would require interference with powers committed to the legislative and executive branches of government.

Thus, if the Constitution or a statute commits certain acts to the legislative or executive branches, then the courts will not inquire as to how those acts, discretionary in nature, should be performed. Rather, the courts will only determine if the statute or the Constitution provides that the action in question is one committed to the legislative or executive branch.[7]

No Advisory Opinions. The courts will not decide the issues in a lawsuit if there is no real controversy; that is, the courts will not render advisory opinions.[8] Thus, if Congress enacted a statute allowing the Supreme Court to advise Congress of the propriety of beginning war, the Court would refuse to hear such a case since it would violate separation of powers principles and require the Court to issue an advisory opinion.

In this example, only the government would be a party, and it would not be interested in a particular outcome or the result of the Court's decision. A request for advice presents an abstract question for the courts to resolve because it does not arise in an adversary factual context. A factual context is essential to the correct formulation of legal issues, and an adversary contest is essential for a credible determination of the facts for the courts to decide.

Only Ripe Issues. The courts also will not decide an issue if it is not "ripe" for review.[9] Thus, if the injury is something that could occur in the future, but has not yet happened, the courts will not resolve the issue because it is not ripe.

No Moot Issues. A related concept is that of mootness. If the issue has become "moot"; that is, the issue is no longer alive because of, for example, the passage of time, the courts will not decide the issue.[10]

There is an exception to the mootness limitation. If the issue is one that is likely to be repeated, yet it is also capable of avoiding review by the court, the court will hear the case. *Roe v. Wade,*[11] the decision legalizing abortion, illustrates the exception. There, the injury complained of was the inability to obtain a legal abortion. By the time the Supreme Court heard the case, the woman bringing the suit was no longer pregnant and thus no longer needed the abortion.

Under these circumstances, the injury—inability to obtain a legal abortion—was rendered moot by the passage of time. But the Court was faced with the practical problem that the appeal process is longer than gestation. The issue then would never be reviewed by the court because inevitably the child would be born before the Court had an opportunity to hear the case. The Court applied the exception and agreed to hear the case because the issue was one that was capable of repetition yet might never be reviewed by the Court if it treated the issue as moot.

Only Parties with Standing. In addition to limitations on the nature of cases that the courts will resolve, there is a requirement that the party bringing the lawsuit have a sufficient personal stake in the litigation. This is the concept of "standing" to bring a lawsuit.[12]

Under this doctrine, the injury complained of must be specific to the person bringing the lawsuit. Thus, taxpayer suits present standing problems. An example is a case in which a plaintiff who opposes a statute that gives money to religious schools and who wishes the money to go elsewhere wants the law declared unconstitutional. The plaintiff in this case is an "ideological plaintiff," someone who is attempting to espouse a personal ideology, not someone who is seeking to vindicate a wrong or to get back money wrongfully taken.

Generally speaking, standing will not present a problem where individual wrongs are being litigated. The more problematic areas, as the example above illustrates, are challenges to governmental statutes. The plaintiff must show a specific (threatened or actual) personal injury from the operation of the statute and a substantial likelihood that the remedy requested by the plaintiff will eliminate the injury in fact suffered.[13]

A party's standing to bring a lawsuit is distinct from whether the issue itself is properly before the court. Consequently, a party may have standing in a particular case, but the federal court may nevertheless refuse to hear the case because, for example, it presents a political question.

On the other hand, while the court may properly hear a lawsuit challenging the validity of a particular statute, the party bringing the action must be injured by its operation or the court will refuse to decide the case.[14] In other words, the issue must be one that is properly before the court and the party bringing the action must have standing to bring the action.[15]

There is an exception to the rule that the party bringing the action—not someone else—must be injured. Under certain circumstances, third persons may assert the injuries of others not before the court. So long as the person representing the third party satisfies certain requirements, that person may assert the rights of others. The courts require proof that the third person's right is bound to the activity that the representative party wishes to pursue or to challenge. The courts also consider the ability of the third person to assert his or her own rights.[16] Thus, in *Roe v. Wade* the court allowed doctors to bring the lawsuit on behalf of their female pregnant patients even though those patients were not before the court.

In sum, the judiciary is limited to resolving cases and controversies. The courts will not pass judgment on discretionary acts of the executive branch or invade the province of the legislature. The courts may interpret laws created by the legislature, or may determine whether nondiscretionary executive action is proper under a particular statute or the Constitution, so long as the case does not fall within the limitations outlined above.

State ex rel Nebraska Nurses Association v. State of Nebraska Board of Nursing[17] illustrates several of these principles. There, an individual registered nurse and the Nebraska State Nurses Association brought an action seeking to require the state attorney general (AG) to file an action to determine the constitutionality of a statute. The lower court granted the request, and ordered the attorney general to initiate an action to determine the validity of the act. The attorney general appealed, and the court reversed.

The controversy concerned the State Board of Nursing's rules implementing advanced nursing practice. Nebraska had amended its statutes concerning the practice of nursing, requiring the Board of Nursing, in cooperation with the Board of Examiners in Medicine and Surgery, to develop rules and regulations governing the expanded role of the professional nurse and to implement such rules and regulations. These rules and regulations were to provide for the kind of functions the nurse would be able to perform, under what circumstances the function could be performed, and the necessary educational and clinical preparation needed to do so.[18]

The Board of Nursing drafted a set of general rules regulating the practice of nurses in expanded roles and held public hearings on the proposed rules. As required under state administrative procedure, these general rules were submitted to the AG for consideration as to the statutory authority and constitutionality of such rules and his approval and disapproval. By letter, the AG returned the rules without approval. His office had concluded that the Board did not have authority to make the rules. In the AG's view, the legislature had erroneously delegated its legislative function—determining what the law should be—to an administrative agency.

Because the rules were not approved by the AG, the Board did not file them with the secretary of state, and they did not become effective. The lower court found that the Board of Nursing had failed to implement the rules and regulations because of the AG's opinion that the statute was unconstitutional. The court also determined that under applicable law, the AG had a duty to file an action to determine the validity of the rules.

At the time of the challenge, Nebraska law provided that when the AG issued a written opinion that a statute was unconstitutional and any state officer charged with implementing the act relied on this opinion and refused to implement the statute, the AG had to file an action in court to determine the validity of the act.[19]

On appeal, the court held that neither the state nurses association nor the individual had standing to maintain the action forcing the AG to file a lawsuit to determine the validity of the statute.[20] The party who had standing to bring the suit was the Board of Nursing, but the Board was named a defendant together with the AG. Thus, the Board and the AG were not adversaries.

The court also noted that it was not permitted to give an advisory opinion; courts will not decide questions of constitutionality unless they have been raised by a litigant whose interests are adversely affected. A court has no power to summarily pass on the constitutionality of an act of legislature; it only has the power to decide justiciable disputes. The power of the court to decide the constitutionality of a law arises only when that law affects the right of a litigant in a case. Since the Board of Nursing and the AG were joint defendants in the case and not adversaries, and there was no showing as to how the rights of the individual nurses or the state nursing association were affected by the law, there was no justiciable lawsuit. The Nebraska Supreme Court ordered the case remanded with directions that it be dismissed.

Limitations on Subject Matter Jurisdiction. The federal courts are courts of limited jurisdiction. In addition to the case and controversy requirements, there must be subject matter jurisdiction. This latter element concerns the power of the court to decide the issues in a case involving a particular subject matter. Federal courts have the power, exclusive of the states, to decide certain kinds of cases. This is known as exclusive jurisdiction.

In cases involving other subject matter areas, the federal and state courts share the power to hear the same case. In this instance, the party bringing the lawsuit may present the claim in either the federal or state court, assuming other requirements are met, because the courts have concurrent jurisdiction. Where a claim involves purely state law issues, the federal courts will not hear the case, absent some other basis for federal jurisdiction.

Article III of the United States Constitution provides that the federal judiciary's power extends to all cases arising under the Constitution, the laws of the United States, and any treaties. Cases affecting ambassadors and other public ministers and consuls, cases of admiralty and maritime jurisdiction, and controversies in which the United States is a party are also included. In addition, controversies between two or more states, a state and a citizen of another state, citizens of different states, as well as controversies between a state or its citizens and a foreign state, citizen, or subject are within the judiciary's Article III powers.[21]

Article III also provides Congress with the authority to limit or to regulate federal court subject matter jurisdiction in accordance with the Constitution. The types of federal court jurisdiction are outlined more fully below. In general, federal courts hear three types of cases. Criminal cases involving violations of federal criminal statutes are the exclusive jurisdiction of federal courts. Civil cases involving federal questions (federal question jurisdiction) or parties from different states (diversity of jurisdiction) also may be brought in federal court. Diversity jurisdiction additionally requires that the amount in controversy exceed $10,000.

Congress has authorized a civil defendant sued in state court to remove the case to federal court if either federal question or diversity jurisdiction exists. This is known as removal jurisdiction.

In addition, Congress, in creating a right under a particular federal statute, may also authorize federal court jurisdiction for its enforcement. The National Labor Relations Act is an example of this type of exclusive federal jurisdiction.

Although there may be a basis for federal court jurisdiction, the federal court may nevertheless abstain from hearing a civil case because it could be resolved by a state court. Under these circumstances, state court resolution of the claim may avoid the need for the federal court to pass on a question of a statute's constitutionality. In the event that the state proceedings do not resolve the issue, then the claim may be presented to the federal court for resolution.

Federal Question Jurisdiction. By statute,[22] the United States District Courts have subject matter jurisdiction over civil claims that involve federal questions. "Federal questions" are presented when the civil claim arises under the laws, Constitution, or treaties of the United States. That is, federal question jurisdiction is satisfied if the civil claim involves a federal statute, federal regulation, a constitutional provision, or a federal treaty.

Diversity Jurisdiction. By statute,[23] federal district courts have jurisdiction to hear all civil actions where the amount in controversy is in excess of $10,000 and where (1) the suit is between citizens of different states; (2) the suit is between citizens of a state and a foreign state or its citizens or subjects; or (3) citizens of different states and foreign states or its subjects or citizens are additional parties. So long as any of the adverse parties are not co-citizens, diversity jurisdiction is proper.[24]

Diversity jurisdiction, thus, is *not* dependent upon whether a federal issue is involved in the lawsuit, and most often such cases involve application of state law. The requirements are that the adverse parties be citizens of different states and that the matter in contest exceed $10,000. For purposes of diversity jurisdiction, a corporation is deemed a citizen of any state in which it is incorporated, as well as the state where it has its principal place of business.[25]

Removal Jurisdiction. Congress, by statute, has provided a remedy for defendants who are sued in a state court for a civil claim that could have been brought in federal court. If federal jurisdiction would have existed had the claim been brought in federal court, then the defendant may remove the claim from state court to federal court.[26] The case is removed to the district court where the state action is pending.

Removal jurisdiction generally is based either on federal question jurisdiction or diversity jurisdiction. Where the basis for removal is that the claim involves the laws of the United States, its treaties, or the Constitution, removal is proper without regard to the parties' citizenship. If, however, removal is sought because the parties are citizens of different states, then removal is proper only where none of the defendants is a citizen of the state in which the action is brought.

The Doctrine of Abstention. Under certain circumstances, a federal court will abstain from resolving a claim, even though it involves a federal question, because the claim could be decided on state grounds by a state court. This is an equitable doctrine, representing a sound respect for the independence of state action. The rationale for the doctrine is that conflicts in the interpretation of state law, dangerous to the success of state policies, would be almost certain to result from the intervention of federal courts in matters of state concern.[27]

To avoid this result, the federal court, exercising its discretion, restrains its authority because of scrupulous regard for the rightful independence of the state governments and the smooth working of the federal judiciary.[28] The doctrine is said to further the harmonious relation between state and federal authority without the need for congressional restriction of those powers. Thus, unless the party can show to the court that there is no method to obtain a definitive ruling from the state courts, the district court will abstain from ruling.[29]

STATE COURT JURISDICTION

The state court systems follow a hierarchy similar to that of the federal system, with trial courts at the bottom level and a supreme court at the highest level. Depending on the population of the state, the state may have an intermediate appellate court. A large city in a populated state is likely to have many different trial and appellate courts.

The great majority of criminal and civil cases are brought in state court because they involve state constitutions, state regulations or statutes, and state common law.[30] State constitutions may also provide greater rights to state residents than does the United States Constitution. State constitutions, however, may not restrict the rights guaranteed under the United States Constitution, since this is the supreme law of the land.

By statute, Congress has prohibited federal courts from enjoining or restraining state court proceedings except under specific circumstances.[31] If the case involves a subject matter area over which federal courts have exclusive jurisdiction, for example a labor dispute, and the dispute is presented in state court, the state court must dismiss the action because it has no power to hear a labor case. If the state court made a decision on the merits of the labor dispute, its decision would be void, and the case would be reversed by a higher court if appealed. A party may attack a court's decision for lack of subject matter jurisdiction for the first time at any time, even after the court has made its decision on the merits or after the case has been appealed.

Most states have statutes or constitutions establishing the jurisdictional requirements for each particular court tier within the state system. For example, monetary restrictions may prohibit claims under a certain amount from being heard in superior court; the amount claimed may require that the plaintiff bring the suit in small claims court or municipal court.

Municipal courts, or inferior courts, generally handle minor disputes and traffic or misdemeanor offenses. In rural areas, inferior courts are justice-of-the-peace courts. Some large cities, such as Los Angeles and Chicago, have specialty courts for family law, probate, and juvenile cases. In some jurisdictions, separate criminal and civil courts may exist; other jurisdictions may follow the federal example, where both civil and criminal cases are handled by the same court.[32]

The procedure for appeals varies with each state. In Illinois, for example, there is a lower trial court, called a circuit court; an intermediate court of appeals to which all criminal cases by statute may be appealed as of right; and a supreme court that accepts cases for review by *certiorari* or, as in capital cases, is the court to which a case is directly appealed, bypassing the appellate court.

California has a similar system, but the trial courts are called superior courts or municipal courts. A ruling of a municipal court, where all criminal cases originate, may be challenged in the superior court. Thus in California the superior court acts as a trial court and an appellate court. Intermediate appellate courts hear appeals from civil and criminal cases, except in capital death cases, where the case is directly appealed to the California Supreme Court.

The legislative branch: power and limitations

In general, the function of both federal and state legislatures is to enact laws. In dividing powers and functions, the framers of the Constitution followed the general principle that matters of national concern requiring uniform policies were to be delegated to the national government. The states possess reserve powers. Thus, in some instances the federal government has exclusive powers; in others the states and the federal government share powers.

THE FEDERAL LEGISLATURE

The Constitution provides that the legislative power shall be vested in a House and a Senate. The powers expressly delegated to Congress, set forth in Article I, Section 8, include the following:

- Assess and collect taxes, pay debts, and borrow money
- Provide for the general welfare
- Regulate commerce among the states (interstate commerce clause power) and foreign commerce
- Coin money
- Establish post offices
- Establish courts inferior to the Supreme Court
- Define and punish offenses against the law of nations
- Declare war and enter into treaties
- Raise and maintain the army and the navy
- Call forth the militia to execute the law of the union, suppress insurrection, and repel invasions
- Exercise exclusive legislation over the District of Columbia
- Make all laws that are necessary and proper to execute the foregoing powers and all other powers vested by the Constitution in the government or in any department or officer of the government (Necessary and Proper Clause)
- Amend the Constitution whenever two thirds of both the House and Senate deem it necessary[33]

The Senate has the additional power not given to the House of Representatives to approve or disapprove of certain presidential appointments by majority vote and to concur in treaties by a two thirds vote.

There are two types of delegated powers reflected in the list outlined above: powers expressly delegated to the federal government and implied powers authorized by the necessary and proper clause of Article I, Section 8. An early landmark decision of the Supreme Court, *McCulloch v. Maryland,*[34] established that the necessary and proper clause delegated to the federal government broad implied powers as well as expressed powers. The necessary and proper clause gives Congress the power to adopt any means, consistent with the Constitution, convenient and useful for carrying into effect one of the expressly delegated powers outlined before.

The courts have interpreted the provisions of Article I, Section 8 to include a wide variety of federal powers and activities. The Supreme Court has held that Article I of the Constitution confers upon Congress the power to create "legislative" courts or Article I courts—courts that exercise legislative or administrative functions.[35] Territorial courts, courts of the United States' owned territories, and administrative law courts are examples of legislative courts.[36] The District of Columbia is an example of a court that exercises both Article I and Article III powers.[37]

The Court has justified federal authority in the health field on the basis of the congressional power to promote the general welfare, to regulate interstate commerce, and to provide spending power. These provide the legal basis for congressional action in health care.[38]

Limitations on the Legislative Power. Article I, Section 9 imposes limitations on Congress' power. These limitations include prohibitions against passing titles of nobility and withdrawals of money from the United States Treasury unless appropriations are made by law. No *ex post facto* law[39] or bill of attainder[40] may be passed, and the privilege of *habeas corpus*[41] cannot be suspended unless there is an invasion or rebellion and safety requires its suspension. In addition, the ports of one state cannot be given preference over those of another state.

The rights guaranteed to individuals under the Constitution also serve as a limitation on the kinds of restrictions a statute may impose. For example, the legislature could not enact a statute restricting speech unless there was a compelling reason to do so.

The Legislative Process. The work of preparing and considering legislation is done largely by committees of both houses of Congress. Each bill and resolution is usually referred to the appropriate committee. The committee may report a bill in its original form, indicate that the committee favors or does not favor the bill or resolution, recommend amendments, or allow the bill or resolution to die in the committee without any action. All bills and joint resolutions must pass both houses.

There are, of course, limitations on the legislature's power. One restriction is that all bills and joint resolutions that pass both houses must be signed by the President. The act does not become law until the President signs it. If the President vetoes the act, Congress may override the President's veto by a two thirds vote. If the act is passed by a two thirds vote, it becomes law. The box on p. 10 illustrates the legislative process and the role of the executive in law making. Note that the President's signature is *not* required on proposed amendments to the Constitution.

The judiciary also operates as a check on the legis-

THE LEGISLATIVE PROCESS

Original Bill or Resolution

1. Study by specific committee of Senate or House of Representatives, then either:
   a. Bill or resolution dies without further action
   b. Bill or resolution is reported in original form or with recommended amendments, and committee indicates approval or disapproval
2. House of Representatives and Senate vote whether to pass and:
   a. If does not pass either the Senate or House of Representatives, bill or resolution dies
   b. If passes both Senate and House of Representatives, bill or resolution is submitted to the President
3. President considers bill or resolution and either:
   a. signs the bill or resolution, and it becomes law
   b. vetoes the bill or resolution
4. House of Representatives and Senate vote on vetoed bill or resolution and:
   a. If bill or resolution fails to pass by a two thirds vote, the bill or resolution does not become law
   b. If bill or resolution passes by two thirds vote of the Senate and the House of Representatives, bill or resolution becomes law

lative power. No law will be upheld by the courts if it violates the Constitution.[42]

THE STATE LEGISLATURES

Representatives of the original states that gathered to draft a national convention were determined that the new federal government should not become so powerful that it could usurp state sovereignty or trample on individual freedoms.[43] The resulting government, reflected in the Bill of Rights and throughout the Constitution, is known as federalism: the national government and the states each have their own areas of supremacy. Many of the constitutional law cases have been devoted to defining and redefining this relationship and settling conflicts.

The Constitution prohibits the states from entering into treaties, imposing any duties on imports or exports except those absolutely necessary for executing inspection laws, and engaging in war without the consent of Congress.[44] These powers, among others, are expressly delegated to the federal government. All powers not expressly delegated to the federal government in the Constitution are, under the Tenth Amendment to the Constitution, reserved to the states. The determination of which legislative acts are exclusively Congress' domain and which are shared with the states is a subject of continuing development that began with *McCulloch v. Maryland,*[45] the Supreme Court's landmark decision for federalism.

In *McCulloch,* the Court held that the United States Constitution and the federal law enacted by Congress in accordance with it are supreme and control a state's law or constitution. When the states became members of the Union under the Constitution, they surrendered certain of their powers of sovereignty and agreed, in essence, to be bound by the Constitution.

The doctrine of preemption stems from this principle. That doctrine holds that where the federal government preempts a field by passing a law in a particular area, the states are precluded from legislating in the same area.

Whether Congress intends to preempt an area when it passes legislation that covers only a portion of the field is not clear.[46] For example, both federal and state legislatures have enacted a variety of health-related laws that have been upheld. No clear-cut lines can be drawn to define precisely when the doctrine of preemption will be invoked by the courts; any attempt to predict is made difficult by the Supreme Court's case-by-case analysis.

Nevertheless, the Court has outlined certain of the powers possessed by the states that were not surrendered when they became members of the Union under the Constitution. Perhaps the most important of these is the police power. In the *License Cases,*[47] the Supreme Court described these powers as "the powers of government inherent in every sovereignty to the extent of its dominions . . . the power to govern [persons] and things within the limits of its dominion."[48]

Although the Court has consistently refrained from any attempt to define the limits of this power,[49] the Court has recognized that it includes the authority to enact health laws of every description. In addition, all laws that relate to matters completely within a state's territory that do not affect the people of other states,[50] such as laws that protect the public and public safety,[51] are included in the police power.

As noted earlier, the Constitution and federal laws limit the power of the states to enact laws under their police powers. This concept of supremacy includes those individual liberties guaranteed by the Constitution, and thus the states cannot eliminate the individual liberties or fundamental rights guaranteed by the Constitution. States may give greater rights to their residents than are provided by the federal Constitution, but no state may restrict the rights protected by the Constitution.

The executive branch: powers and limitations

Article II provides that the executive power shall be vested in a president and that it is the President's duty to see that the laws are faithfully executed. The Supreme Court has characterized this power as a broad administrative power over those subordinates who assist in the execution of the laws.[52] The President is authorized by the Constitution to require the principal officer of each executive department to provide a written opinion on any subject relating to the duty of the office.

Although Senate advice and consent is constitutionally needed for nominations and appointments of ambassadors, other public ministers, consuls, officers, and judges of the Supreme Court, the Supreme Court has held that the President has exclusive power to remove purely executive officers.[53] Thus, if the officer is the head of a quasi-legislative agency (that is, an agency created by an act of Congress as opposed to the President's cabinet), the power of removal does not exclusively belong to the President.[54]

The Constitution makes the President the commander in chief of the army and navy and authorizes presidential pardons for offenses against the United States, except in cases of impeachment. The President may also recommend legislation and inform the Senate of the state of the Union.

Clearly, the President's actions in executing the laws are subject to the Constitution since it is the supreme law of the land. Thus, the Supreme Court has held that there is no Constitutional authority for executive orders that, like statutes, require that certain policies be followed as if these policies are law.[55] Such executive orders are unconstitutional unless an act of Congress delegates such lawmaking authority to the President. To hold otherwise, the Court reasoned, would subject the lawmaking prerogative of Congress to presidential supervision and control, in violation of the separation of powers doctrine.

The respective powers, functions, and limitations of each branch of government are expected to achieve a balance of power. By virtue of exercising these powers, each branch has contributed to formation of the law. In the next chapter, each branch's contribution to the law is examined.

Endnotes

1. *See generally, Marbury v. Madison,* 1 Cranch 137 (1803).
2. U.S. CONST. amend. X.
3. W. LOUTHAN, THE POLITICS OF JUSTICE 53-55 (1979).
4. *Flast v. Cohen,* 392 U.S. 83 (1968).
5. *Marbury v. Madison,* 1 Cranch 137 (1803).
6. *Id.*
7. *Id.*
8. *Muskrat v. United States,* 219 U.S. 346 (1911).
9. *Warth v. Sedlin,* 95 S.Ct. 2197 (1975).
10. *DeFunis v. Odegard,* 94 S.Ct. 1704 (1974).
11. 410 U.S. 113 (1973).
12. *Id.*
13. *See, e.g., Simon Eastern Kentucky Welfare Rights Organization,* 96 S. Ct. 1917 (1976); *Warth v. Sedlin,* 95 S. Ct. 2197 (1975).
14. *Tyler v. The Judges of the Court of Registration,* 179 U.S. 405 (1900).
15. *Flast v. Cohen,* 392 U.S. 83 (1968); *Warth v. Sedlin,* 95 S. Ct. 2197 (1975). Consequently, persons wishing to challenge a particular statute simply because they are taxpayers and not because they are injured by the operation of a statute do not have standing to bring the action.
16. *Roe v. Wade,* 410 U.S. 113 (1973).
17. 290 N.W.2d 453 (Neb. 1980).
18. *Id,* at 454, citing NEB. REV. STAT. §71-1,132.11(15), as amended, NEB. REV. STAT. §71-1,132.11(1)-(11) (1981). This portion has been deleted from the amended statute.
19. NEB. REV. STAT. §84-215 (Supp. 1978).
20. 290 N.W. 2d at 456.
21. U.S. CONST. art. III, §2.
22. *E.g.,* 28 U.S.C. §1331 (1982).
23. *E.g.,* 28 U.S.C. §1332 (1982).
24. *State Farm Fire & Casualty Co. v. Tashmire,* 386 U.S. 523 (1967).
25. 28 U.S.C. §1332 (c) (1984).
26. *E.g.,* 28 U.S.C. §1441 (1982).
27. *Burford v. Sun Oil Co.,* 319 U.S. 315 (1943).
28. *Railroad Commission of Texas v. Pullman Co.,* 312 U.S. 496 (1941).
29. *Id.*
30. T. CRISTOFFEL, HEALTH AND THE LAW 24 (1982) (hereinafter cited as *Christoffel*).
31. *E.g.,* 28 U.S.C. §2283. Two explicit exceptions where the district court must issue an injunction halting the state court proceedings are where necessary to aid its jurisdiction or to protect one of its judgments.
32. *Christoffel, supra* note 30, at 24.
33. If two thirds of the state legislatures demand changes in the Constitution, it is the duty of Congress to call a constitutional convention. The proposed amendment is valid when ratified by the legislatures or conventions of three fourths of the states.
34. 4 Wheat 316 (1819).
35. *Palmore v. United States,* 411 U.S. 389 (1973).
36. *See id.*
37. *Id.*
38. Northrop, *Government and Legal Influences on the Practice of Community Health Nursing,* in M. STANHOPE & J. LANCASTER, COMMUNITY HEALTH NURSING (1985); *Christoffel, supra* note 30, at 51.
39. Black's Law Dictionary, citing *Andrus v. McCauley,* 21 F. Supp. 70 (D.C. Wash. 1942), defines an *ex post facto* law as a law which provides punishment for an activity which was considered innocent when the person committed the activity or a law which aggravates a crime or establishes a greater punishment than the punishment which was provided for at the time the crime was committed by

the person or alters the situation of the accused to his disadvantage. BLACK'S LAW DICTIONARY 663 (4th ed. 1968) (hereinafter cited as *Black's*).

40. A "bill of attainder" is defined as a legislative act, directed against a designated person, pronouncing him or her guilty of an alleged crime, usually treason or some serious felony, without trial or conviction according to the ordinary course of judicial proceedings, and passing a sentence, such as death, for the crime. *Black's, supra* note 39, at 162.
41. In Latin, the phrase means "you have the body." *Black's supra* note 39, at 837. Legally, it is a procedure or petition directed at a person, such as a prison warden, who is detaining or holding another person, commanding the warden to produce the body of the detainee, or prisoner, in court and submit to the ruling of the court on the petition. *Id.; see also id. at 837*. Currently, a petition for *habeas corpus* (called a writ of *habeas corpus* in some states) does not require that the prisoner actually be produced in court but rather that the warden answer the petition and abide by the court's decision on the merits of the petition.
42. *Marbury v. Madison,* 1 Cranch 137 (1803).
43. *See* M. PARENTI, DEMOCRACY FOR THE FEW (3rd ed. 1980); A. MILLER, DEMOCRATIC DICTATORSHIP: THE EMERGENT CONSTITUTION OF CONTROL (1981).
44. U.S. CONST. art. I, §10.
45. 4 Wheat 316 (1819).
46. See, e.g., *Huron Portland Cement Co. v. City of Detroit,* 362 U.S. 440 (1959) where the Court determined that a city's smoke abatement ordinance and the federal government's system of ship inspection and licensing, which was concerned with the ship's overall seaworthiness, were laws which regulated different things and thus neither law prevailed; the Court concluded that they could exist simultaneously.
47. 46 U.S. (5 How.) 504 (1847).
48. *Id.* at 582 (footnote omitted).
49. *Jacobson v. Massachusetts,* 197 U.S. 11 (1905).
50. *Id.*
51. *Id.*
52. *See Meyers v. United States,* 272 U.S. 52 (1926).
53. *Id.*
54. *Humphreys' Executor v. United States,* 295 U.S. 602 (1935); *See also Weiner v. United States,* 357 U.S. 349 (1958) (President has no power to remove a member of the War Claims Commission because it serves a judicial function.)
55. *Youngstown Sheet & Tube Co.,* 343 U.S. 579 (1952).

Chapter 2

Sources of the law

Mary E. Kelly

Although similarities exist among the various state and federal systems, such as the tripartite system of governing, each of the 50 states, the District of Columbia, and the federal system has its own structure and rules. The result is "a complex and voluminous set of laws."[1] Yet general principles about the sources and classifications of law, which impact on nursing practice, may be made. This chapter provides an overview of these sources and classifications.

Sources of the law

The three branches of government each "create" law in some fashion, and these, in addition to the Constitution, are sources of law. Common law, statutory law, and administrative law respectively reflect the influences of the judicial, legislative, and executive branches.

THE COMMON LAW

Common law is, in essence, law made by a judge as opposed to a law created by the legislature or a regulation created by an agency. The common law derives from earlier decisions of the court (legal precedent), custom, and tradition. Tort law, including the theory of negligence, and contract law, were developed from the common law. In recent years, these areas of law have been codified, but still reflect common law principles. The common law is an important source of law, and the common law tradition has important ramifications for nursing practice.

Crucial to the development of the common law is the concept of *stare decisis* or precedent. The gist of this doctrine, which dates back centuries in English law, is that prior decisions should be followed and settled points should not be disturbed where the same points arise in litigation.[2] Past decisions of the courts—precedent—become law and should should be followed when a court confronts the same question in a new case.

The development of American common law relied on English common law but also proceeded on an ideal universal body of rational principles that combines custom, usage, and procedural form.[5] Thus the doctrine of *stare decisis,* while important to developing an enduring and consistent common law, was not absolute.[3]

The American courts have never been reluctant to overrule an earlier decision if it is mistaken.[4] The "lessons of experience and the force of better reasoning" may convince the court to overrule a mistaken precedent; "the question is not whether an earlier decision should ever be overruled, but whether a particular decision ought to be."[5]

Every state has its own body of common law, developed independently by its own courts' decisions. A few states, such as Louisiana and Texas, have been influenced by the European civil law system, which emphasizes a statutory code system. This code system is arranged into chapters and indexed to make a complete body of laws designed to regulate completely the subjects to which they relate, such as health, education, criminal law, and the like.[6] Some states, like California, use both the code system and the common law developed by the courts of the state.

The English common law distinction between law and equity has been retained in federal and state legal systems. Equitable actions and defenses are based on principles of fairness. For example, injunctions, which seek to restrain or to compel certain conduct, are equitable actions that remedy imminent irreparable harm that is occurring or is about to occur. Estoppel is an equitable defense that may be asserted against someone because that person has been unjustly enriched or has committed a fraud. The Seventh Amendment to the Constitution authorizes jury trials in actions at law, not actions seeking equitable relief.

Interpretation of Laws vs. Creation of Remedies. Judicial decision making involves the process of interpreting law—common law (case law), statutes, codes, or regulations—and applying it to the factual situation presented in a case. Courts examine the factual setting of the case and analyze relevant earlier decisions. If the issues and the factual context are similar, the precedent or legal principles from the earlier case are applied to the present case, unless there exists a basis for overruling or modifying the earlier ruling. Occasionally, new law is made in areas where none exists.

To convince the court that an earlier decision should be overruled, modified, or considered inapplicable, lawyers focus on the reasoning of the earlier decision and present arguments why those reasons do not apply to the present case. If the earlier case contains statements unfavorable to the success of the present case, lawyers try to limit the impact of these statements by characterizing them as "dicta"—gratuitous remarks unnecessary to the court's decision. Such statements are not precedent because they were not a necessary part of the rationale for the particular decision.

Lawyers often argue that precedent should not be applied because of factual differences between the earlier case and the present case. Factual differences may make a case distinguishable from another, thereby minimizing its value as precedent. Occasionally, the court is asked to overrule precedent that has no meaning today or is unjust.

Sometimes there will be no existing precedent to resolve a case and the court will expand legal principles to cover the existing legal problem. New inventions, new discoveries, and different kinds of businesses shape the development of law. Courts must grapple with these realities when confronting new and different injuries or wrongs. For example, when confronted with injuries caused by defective products from industrial technology, the courts created a new theory of recovery, products liability.

The common law methodology may persuade a court to accept expanded views of nursing practice by broadly interpreting practice acts. Judicial decisions from other jurisdictions where courts have favorably interpreted nursing practice acts[7] may be cited to the court as persuasive precedent.

The fact that a particular court's decision may rest in part on the state's particular practice act,[8] does not render the precedent or the methodology useless. The process of judicial review requires the court to engage in interpretation; this interpretation may be influenced by what other jurisdictions have decided. Indeed, such precedent may provide the court with the authority necessary to interpret a particular phrase in a certain way that supports independent nursing practice. Judicial precedent enables a court to take a more active role because there is a legal basis for the court's action.

Moreover, courts do not exclusively rely on nursing practice acts as precedent for independent nursing practice. A 1979 California case demonstrates that the common law methodology is alive and well. In upholding independent nursing practice, the court cited the historical fact that "[t]oday's nurses are held to strict standards of knowledge and performance."[9] Without a single reference to the nursing practice, the court noted that an increased emphasis on high standards for nurses was occurring: "those with superior education and experience often exercise independent judgment as to the care of patients whether in a hospital setting or elsewhere."[10]

Congress and the state legislatures may overrule common law precedent or incorporate it by enacting a statute. For example, tort law, contract law, and property law were developed by the courts and a large body of common law in these areas still exists in many jurisdictions. Many states have enacted statutes covering these areas, especially property law. Once a statute is passed overruling or modifying existing common law, the courts are bound to follow the statute so long as it does not conflict with United States Constitution or the state's constitution.

Judicial Restraint vs. Judicial Activism. In conducting judicial review some courts have been more willing to protect individual freedoms and invalidate restrictive laws; other courts defer to the state legislatures that create the laws. The two different approaches have been described as judicial activism and judicial restraint.

The scholarly debate about the court's role in a democratic society has led to the development of these two theories of judicial review. Judicial restraint is the view that the court, in reviewing a statute, should always choose the narrowest ground for its decision. This view is based on due regard for separation of powers and the nature of the judicial process as the ultimate authority in interpreting the Constitution.[11]

Judicial activism reflects the philosophy that when substantial rights are at stake which the legislative process cannot or will not vindicate, the task of doing so passes to the courts.[12] The desegration of schools mandated by the Supreme Court in *Brown v. Board of Education*[13] is one example of this process.

These two philosophies have shaped the way in which the courts undertake their job of reviewing law and applying it to a given factual dispute. Different courts, of course, adopt different philosophies—after all, judges are human. Historical differences in judicial decisions are largely the result of the application of these two philosophies. Consequently, the courts occasionally break tradition with precedent and *stare decisis* and reverse earlier decisions.

Early in the development of this country's judicial system, the Supreme Court declared that where the law gives a right and that right is violated, the courts will recognize a remedy for that wrong even though the statute is silent as to what that remedy should be.[14] The Court held that it is the judiciary's role and duty to say what the law is and whether it is in violation of the Constitution.[15]

This power of substantive review is a tremendous one, and the concept of judicial supremacy has been criticized.[16] The basis for the criticism is that the judiciary is not a representative body chosen by the public to act in their behalf and it does not have the fact-finding machinery that the legislature possesses.[17] Since the justices of the Supreme Court are appointed for life, there is no way for the citizenry to choose them as their representative.

The process of interpreting existing legal principles or case law to new and different fact situations is dynamic. Variations of the old law are either made to fit or expanded to meet a new factual context. As will be demonstrated throughout this book, negligence law as applied to nurses is a good example of how precedent develops as roles and relationships in society change.

CONSTITUTIONAL LAW

In addition to defining the functions, powers, and limits of the three branches of government, the Constitution guarantees to the people certain basic fundamental liberties. The judiciary interprets the Constitution and the Supreme Court's interpretation cannot be overruled by statute.[18] Constitutional law defines the relationship between governmental authority and individual freedoms.

All powers not granted explicitly to the federal government by the Constitution are retained by the state governments or the people of the country. The state's power to govern is generally known as police power.[19] This power includes reasonable laws necessary to preserve the public order, the public's health, safety, welfare, and morals.

The Constitution limits the exercise of police powers by the state governments. The state cannot exercise powers in a way that the Constitution prohibits or that conflicts with a power granted to the federal government by the Constitution. Neither the states nor the federal government can exercise their powers in a way that unreasonably restricts the constitutionally protected rights secured by the United States Constitution.

States' constitutions may give individuals greater rights than those afforded in the federal Constitution, but they cannot eliminate the rights guaranteed by the federal Constitution. This is because the federal Constitution is the supreme law of the land.

Procedural and Substantive Rights. The Bill of Rights to the federal Constitution contains the rights of individuals referred to as civil liberties. These rights are not absolute and the government under certain circumstances may impose reasonable restrictions on them. The Constitution protects fundamental individual liberties against arbitrary governmental action.

Some suggest that these individual rights fall into two basic categories: procedural and substantive rights.[20] Procedural due process guarantees fairness in the process the government undertakes when it attempts to deprive a person of life, liberty, or property. The due process clause applies to the federal government (Fifth Amendment) and to the states (Fourteenth Amendment). Additional procedural rights protect those accused of crime,[21] and these are discussed in Chapter 24, "The Nurse as Criminal Defendant."

Substantive rights are those rights primarily found in the Bill of Rights, including the due process clause. Substantive due process protects an individual's liberty and privacy interests. The application of these to health providers is discussed in the civil rights section in Chapter 5. Challenges to health care activity or the lack of health care have also been made on the First, Fourth, Fifth, and Eighth Amendments.

The First Amendment's guarantees of freedom of religion and speech have been invoked by persons seeking to refuse treatment on religious grounds cases. The right to privacy, which emanates from various provisions of the Bill of Rights, including the Fourth Amendment's proscription against unreasonable governmental searches,[22] has also been invoked in cases involving refusal of treatment. The Eighth Amendment ban on cruel and unusual punishment may be claimed in prison cases where health care is denied.

STATUTORY LAW

A statute is a law enacted (codified) by the legislative branch. The legislatures of the federal and various state governments have codified laws relevant to health care. In the federal system, these statutes are published in the United States Code; in the states, they are published under the particular state's code.

State and federal governments have broad powers to legislate for the general welfare. In contrast to the federal government's explicit powers contained in the Constitution, the states have broad inherent powers to act. The states may exercise all powers inherent in government itself, except where the Constitution reserves the power to the federal government. The state's power to govern, or "police power" has never been explicitly and specifically delineated.[23] As one author notes:

> In the broadest usage of the term, the courts have defined the police powers to be all of the legitimate functions of government. Other courts have added some specificity, defining the police powers of the state as the powers inherent in the state to prescribe, within the limits of the state and federal constitutions, reasonable laws necessary to preserve the public order, health, safety, welfare and morals.[24]

Public health laws exemplify the breadth of police powers. As discussed in the next section, the courts have almost always upheld these laws as proper exercises of state authority so long as they could somehow be justified as necessary for the public's health. Protection of the individual and the public at large are also proper justifications. Particularly where individual action would risk the health or safety or welfare of others, and sometimes even where that action would harm the individual himself or herself, the state may act.

The states also have the power to act in place of a parent, known as *in loco parentis,*[25] and to act as guardian over people with disability, known as *parens patriae.*[26] Both terms really refer to the state's inherent police power to act as a parent to neglected or disabled persons.

Federal vs. State Health Authority. The federal and state relationship vis-à-vis health care largely is the product of the development of social welfare programs in the United States.[27] In 1965, Medicare and Medicaid were established by amendments to the Social Security Act. Social Security has been described as a federal insurance program for disabled or retired former workers, their dependents, and survivors, and Medicaid has been characterized as the basic welfare program that the states administer.[28]

Both state and federal governments have attempted a variety of programs intended to control the quality, distribution, and costs of health facilities. Most of these programs postdate World War II.[29] The first government-sponsored programs were established when Congress enacted the Hill-Burton program,[30] a hospital construction financing program, which was intended to respond to a perceived shortage of hospital facilities.

Hill-Burton authorized federal funds for each state to survey the need and develop state plans for the development of hospital facilities. It also provided matching funds and loans for public or nonprofit facilities to assist in construction projects to meet the needs identified in the state Hill-Burton plan. Funded projects had to comply with a number of requirements, including the provision of a reasonable amount of uncompensated care and community service.[31] Eventually the program was expanded to authorize the funding of nursing homes and other health facilities.[32]

Hospital licensing laws are largely the creature of the Hill-Burton program. States were required, as a condition of receiving federal Hill-Burton funds for construction of hospitals, to enact hospital licensing laws.[33] While the scope of licensing laws and the facilities regulated vary from state to state, virtually all states now require that hospitals, nursing homes, and some other health facilities be licensed.[34]

Estimates of the success of the Hill-Burton program are that in the first 20 years of the program over half the hospitals nationwide received federal assistance.[35] Nevertheless the program had its shortcomings, chiefly in that it had no authority to curb unnecessary projects. In the 1960s, federal efforts were made to encourage planning a "more rational distribution of health care resources."[36] States also began to directly regulate the health care industry, principally through certificate-of-need legislation.

Certificate-of-need programs authorize a state agency

to regulate the construction or expansion of institutional health facilities.[37] The state laws vary in their administrative structure, methods for appeal and review, and their relationship to various other state and local health planning activities.[38] Nevertheless, "all states cover hospital and nursing home construction; some include outpatient and other facilities . . . [c]ertain specified categories of projects or capitol expenditures above a minimum dollar cost are subject to review to determine the necessity of the project, by comparison with either various criteria or a developed state plan."[39] In general, if a proposal is found unnecessary, the project cannot be licensed.

States also license individual health care providers, including nurses, under the authority of protecting the welfare of the public. Although a review of each state's nursing practice act is beyond the scope of this book, the appendix to the book contains the statutory citation to every state nurse practice act.

Judicial Review of Constitutional Challenges to Laws. The power of the legislature to create laws, is, as noted earlier, not without limitation. The Fifth and Fourteenth Amendments prohibit the legislatures of the federal and state governments from creating a law that deprives someone of life, liberty, or property without due process of law. The Fourteenth Amendment also includes a prohibition that state shall not deny to any person within its jurisdiction the equal protection of the law. This latter limitation provides a basis to challenge, on equal protection grounds, a law that discriminates against a particular class.

Generally, due process challenges to state or federal government laws may be procedural or substantive in nature. Procedural challenges involve unfair procedures taken by the state or federal government in depriving persons of their liberty or property. The denial of procedural due process is a frequent constitutional challenge to criminal statutes and civil commitment laws.

Occasionally laws are characterized as denying substantive due process—the rights to liberty, property, and more recently, the rights to free speech and or privacy. The gist of such challenges is that the exercise of the legislative power either unduly restricts individual rights or unreasonably discriminates against a certain class of persons.

In general, every law involves some singling out of a group or class of people. Similarly, many laws restrict the exercise of constitutional rights. While the Constitution protects against unreasonable intrusions on these rights and prohibits certain forms discrimination against suspect classes (classifications based on race or alienage), it does not ban all restrictions or classifications.

Constitutional substantive due process challenges and equal protection challenges based on the Fourteenth Amendment require the Court to balance competing interests—the state's interest or purpose in the law and the importance of the individual's constitutional right at stake. The state denies equal protection of the laws only where the law invidiously discriminates. That in turn depends on the interest at stake—whether economic or constitutional in nature.

Lochner v. New York,[40] a 1905 case, has come to symbolize a period in the Supreme Court's history where the Court engaged in substantive review of economic legislation on Fifth and Fourteenth Amendment grounds, and held certain economic statutes unconstitutional on the grounds that they denied persons of property or liberty to contract without due process of law. The effect of this review was to blunt state and federal legislation initially designed to deal with exploitation of workers in industry and later to deal with the Depression.[41]

From the 1930s to the present time, however, this type of challenge—economic substantive due process—has typically been rejected by the courts.[42] For example, in reviewing laws that regulate businesses or industrial concerns, the Court has refused to engage in substantive review, and instead defers to the legislature. In 1955, the Court upheld a law that outlawed any person except a licensed optometrist or ophthalmologist to fit lenses to a face, absent a prescription. The law was challenged by opticians claiming a deprivation of property. The Court noted "The day is gone when this Court uses the Due Process Clause of the Fourteenth Amendment to strike down state laws, regulatory of business and industrial conditions, because they may be unwise, improvident, or out of harmony with a particular school of thought."[43]

Nevertheless in the area of criminal procedure, First Amendment rights, privacy rights, and equal protection challenges, the Court has actively intervened, exercising substantive review of laws that are noneconomic in nature (dubbed noneconomic substantive due process review). "This has produced a double standard of Fifth and Fourth Amendment protection and with it the notion that some freedoms such as speech and privacy are more preferred than others such as property and contract."[44]

Depending on the interest involved, the Court engages in what some describe as a two-tier or three-tier review. The "tier" refers to the level of scrutiny the Court gives the law on review. If the law (1) restricts the exercise of a fundamental right, such as speech, liberty, privacy, or freedom to travel—all interests protected by the Constitution—or (2) impacts on a suspect class—race, national origin, or alienage—the Court closely scrutinizes the law.

The strict scrutiny test of review requires the state to establish a compelling state interest that justifies the law and demonstrates that the challenged classification or distinction in the law is necessary to further its purpose. The law must be the least restrictive means of accomplishing the compelling state interest. If the state can achieve the law's objective without impacting on these interests or impacting in a less intrusive manner, the Court will find the statute unconstitutional.

At the other end, the lowest tier of review, are economic interests in property and social and economic welfare legislation. Where these interests are at stake, the Court has exercised restraint in its review of the law. The Court has given the law a sort of "presumption of constitutionality,"[45] requiring only that the classifications drawn by the statute bear some rational relationship to a conceivable legitimate state purpose.

In the area of economic and social welfare legislation, the legislature may take one step at a time, eliminating a problem in one field and neglecting problems in other fields. If the law has a rational relationship to its stated objective, there is no denial of equal protection.[46] In contrast, the strict scrutiny test outlined above requires that the state establish that it has compelling interest that justifies the law and that the classification is necessary to further the law's purpose.

A third or middle tier has been identified in the review of laws that contain classifications based on gender[47] and illegitimacy.[48] The court examines the law to see if it is substantially related to a legitimate state interest.

Judicial Deference to the Legislature in Health Matters. The courts generally defer to the legislature in matters of social and economic welfare, and this includes health matters. Thus, licensure laws have been upheld against challenges that these laws deny deprive an individual of property or equal protection of the laws.[49]

Similarly laws requiring compulsory vaccinations for adults, medical examinations, and vaccines for children have been upheld as a valid exercise of the power to legislate for the public safety.[50] The Supreme Court has noted that health laws of every description are included in the state's police power which embraces all reasonable regulations that protect public health and safety. The only limitations are (1) where the law interferes with a power of the federal government, or (2) where the law infringes on a constitutional right.[51]

With respect to the latter limitation the Court has noted that there is a sphere within which the individual may assert the supremacy of his or her own will and dispute the authority of the government. Nevertheless, "the liberty secured by the Constitution . . . does not import an absolute right in each person to be, at all times, and in all circumstances, wholly freed from restraint."[52] Rather there are restraints to which every person is necessarily subject for the common good.

This case aptly demonstrates that the constitutional right to exercise a fundamental freedom guaranteed by the Constitution is not absolute. Thus, medical care provided to children over the objection of their parents has been upheld in spite of religious beliefs such as those of Jehovah's Witnesses. In general, the courts will not intervene unless the potential harm to the child is immediate and life threatening.[53]

While the state has broad power to legislate for the public welfare and safety, and an individual's constitutional rights are not absolute, the state must legislate in a way that minimally impacts on freedoms guaranteed by the Constitution. Where a law restricts constitutional rights—as opposed to impacting on economic or social interests—the state is required to have a compelling reason to do so. The courts will strictly or closely scrutinize such laws. If the state could achieve the law's objective in a less restrictive way, one that did not interfere so greatly with an important constitutional interest, the law will be held unconstitutional.

For example, the Court has invalidated a law requiring compulsory sterilization of a third time felon. The Court held that the law violated equal protection because it authorized sterilization of anyone who had committed three successive felonies, but it exempted white collar crimes, such as embezzlement, and political offenses.[54]

The right to privacy generally has been held to be a restriction on government regulation of sexual conduct and family planning. In *Roe v. Wade,* this right formed the basis for a successful challenge to a state felony criminal law outlawing abortion except where necessary to save the mother's life.[55] The state argued that the law's prohibition against all but medically necessary abortions was a valid exercise of police power relating to public health.

The constitutional challenge to the statute was reviewed by the Court by analyzing both the state's purpose in enacting the law and the nature of the individual's interest affected by the law. In examining the statute and its purpose, the Court noted that two valid purposes could restrict decisions concerning abortion—to protect the mother from risk of danger to her health or to protect prenatal life.

With respect to the individual interest at stake, the Court held that the zones of privacy secured by the Constitution includes the woman's right to terminate her pregnancy. Thus, the law did indeed impact on a constitutionally protected right.

The Court reasoned that the state's interests in preserving the health of the mother and in protecting the potentiality of life grow substantially as the woman approaches term and become compelling at approximately the end of the first trimester, the point of viability. Consequently, from this point, the state may regulate the abortion procedure to the extent that the regulation reasonably relates to the preservation and protection of maternal health—licensing requirements and the like. Prior to this compelling point, the physician, "in consultation with his patient, is free to determine, without regulation by the State, that, in his medical judgment, the patient's pregnancy should be terminated. If that decision is reached the judgment may be effectuated by an abortion free of interference by the State."[56]

The strict scrutiny review, however, has not been applied in the area of public funding of abortions. The Court has generally applied the lower tier type or review, only requiring a rational basis for the law. The Court has upheld the constitutionality of state-imposed restrictions on Medicaid funding for abortions,[57] as well as federal funding restrictions.[58] These decisions demonstrate that equal protection challenges in the area of governmental spending will be upheld under the rational basis standard.[59]

In deciding to undergo or to forgo medical treatment however, the right to privacy has eroded the state's power to compel treatment of competent and incompetent adults. This topic is discussed in Chapter 5. The Fourteenth Amendment's prohibition against deprivations of freedom without due process of law has also been held to restrict the states' commitment powers.[60]

ADMINISTRATIVE LAW

Certain statutes delegate authority to administrative agencies to promulgate regulations that will implement a particular statute. A regulation must be adopted by an agency according to a specific process that is generally defined (1) in the statute that delegates the authority to the agency or (2) in the state or federal administrative procedures act.[60] The primary purpose of such acts is to regulate the processes of rule-making and the manner in which judicial review of agency action is to be conducted.[61] Certain rules may require advance publication of the proposed regulation to allow public comment prior to adoption of the regulation.

Administrative regulations allow the legislature to delegate administrative authority to an administrative agency that has expertise in a particular area of law.[63] For example, state boards of nursing are frequently authorized by nursing practice acts to promulgate specific regulations governing practice.

Attorney General opinions, another kind of administrative law, are issued from the office of the Attorney General, generally in response to a request from someone or an agency as to the interpretation of a law. These are the Attorney General's opinions and, as such, are not binding on the courts.

Judicial Review of Administrative Regulations. The rule-making authority of an agency, whether the rule is substantive or procedural, is determined primarily by interpreting the legislation that authorizes the agency to adopt rules and regulations. Where a regulation is challenged as an improper exercise of delegated authority, the first issue is whether the regulation is authorized by the rule-making power delegated by the legislature to the agency.[64]

This in turn necessitates analyzing the language of the statute. The statute may delegate to the agency broad-rule making authority, and a particular regulation may be found implicitly authorized under this broad grant of authority.[65] Even though a statute does not explicitly delegate a specific action, if there is broad-rule making authority granted, the courts must uphold the regulation unless "there are compelling indications that it is wrong."[66] The regulation is proper so long as it conforms to the fundamental objective of the act and rationally complements its remedial scheme.

The courts do not inquire into the propriety of the particular regulation—the substance of the regulation. So long as the regulation is reasonably related to the purposes of the enabling legislation, the courts will uphold the regulation.[67]

With respect to whether the proper procedure was followed in implementing the regulation, the courts again look to the legislation authorizing the agency to issue regulations. If a particular procedure is outlined, it must be followed by the agency. If a particular procedure is not set forth, then, in general, the agency is required to follow the state's administrative procedure act, unless some exception applies.[68] A regulation is invalid if the agency fails to follow the procedures required by the Administrative Procedure Act.[69]

Of course, a challenge to a regulation can be based on the constitution. When this occurs, the courts employ the same constitutional analysis that is used in reviewing constitutional challenges to statutes.[70] For example, if an administrative regulation imposes substantial economic and penal sanctions, the regulation must give fair warning of what is prohibited or required and it must set forth a reasonable standard of culpability.[71]

Occasionally, the courts refuse to exercise jurisdiction over a particular case because an agency ruling on the issue may obviate the need for judicial resolution. This is known as the primary jurisdiction doctrine. This doctrine enables the courts to defer to administrative agencies and require the agency to first rule on a disputed issue prior to judicial review.[72]

Exhaustion of administrative remedies, another prerequisite to judicial review, may either be required by a particular statute or be invoked on a discretionary basis by the court. In other words, whatever procedure is established by the agency, it must be exhausted first before bringing a court action. This prevents the courts from hearing challenges to agency action until relevant administrative proceedings have been concluded, thereby allowing the agency to develop a factual record.[73] An exception exists where the administrative remedy is inadequate or where proceeding within the administrative process would be futile or serve no purpose.[74] The courts are the final arbiters of agency action.[75]

Classifications of the law: substantive and procedural

There are two basic classifications or types of law: substantive law and procedural law. Substantive law, which defines the substance of law, may be further classified as civil, administrative, and criminal. Procedural law, which governs the procedure or rules employed to create, implement, or enforce the substantive law, may vary according to the type of substantive law at issue.

The substantive law defines various rights or prohibits certain conduct. Claims based on these laws are thus made up of various elements. Lawsuits brought to remedy violations of these laws must eventually prove the existence of the elements that make up the claim.

Lawsuits are adversarial proceedings governed by various procedures believed to determine the truth. This adversarial process can generally be divided into three stages: pretrial proceedings, the trial, and appeal.

The following discussion presents an overview of the procedural aspects of the litigation process in civil case and brief definitions of the types of substantive civil law. The procedural overview of a criminal proceeding and the substantive elements of crimes are extensively reviewed in Chapter 24. Finally, various aspects of administrative law are discussed in the next section.

PROCEDURAL OVERVIEW

The Anatomy of a Civil Lawsuit. In civil cases, litigation is commenced by filing a complaint. The person filing the complaint or claim that is based on substantive law is called the plaintiff. The person against whom the claim or complaint is filed is referred to as the defendant.

The complaint contains numerous factual statements, referred to as allegations, which the plaintiff must ultimately prove. Once the complaint has been served on the defendant, the litigation process commences.

Pretrial Proceedings. After the defendant has been served with the complaint, there is a certain amount of time within which he or she can respond. The defendant may make a motion to dismiss the claim because the court lacks subject matter jurisdiction. Another basis for dismissal is that the plaintiff failed to properly serve the defendant and therefore the court has no jurisdiction or power over the defendant's person. In either instance, if the court grants the motion to dismiss, the case is over.

The defendant may also argue that the case should be dismissed because it fails to state any claim under the law. Dismissing an action for this reason, as opposed to the court lacking power to hear the case, is extremely harsh since the court has not had the benefit of considering any evidence.

Consequently, in reviewing the allegations of the claim to determine if they state a claim for relief or a cause of action (which is determined by the substantive law), the court is required to accept as true all of the allegations in the complaint. If, even accepting these allegations as true, the court concludes that no legally recognizable claim is stated, the case is dismissed. The court may dismiss the complaint with or without prejudice, which means that the case is either ended (with prejudice) or the plaintiff may amend the complaint to try to state a proper claim (without prejudice). If the court dismisses the action with prejudice, the plaintiff has no recourse except appeal.[76]

If the court refuses to dismiss the case, the defendant

must file an answer to the charges either denying them or asserting some defense or excuse. If the defendant fails to do either, a default judgment may be entered. The plaintiff then wins the lawsuit by default.

Occasionally, the defendant has a claim against the plaintiff that arises out of the same transaction as that alleged in the plaintiff's complaint. The defendant may then, at the time he or she files an answer to the complaint, file a counterclaim against the plaintiff.

Sometimes the defendant believes that another person caused the harm to the plaintiff or the defendant has an indemnification agreement with a third party who has promised to be responsible for the claim. The defendant may sue this third person, thereby bringing him or her into the lawsuit. This is known as third party practice, and the defendant is referred to as the third party plaintiff.

Hospital liability based on nursing negligence may give rise to a claim for indemnification. The hospital may sue the nurse after an unfavorable judgment is rendered against it for the nurse's negligence. The hospital may also bring the nurse into the plaintiff's lawsuit. The nurse then may counterclaim against the hospital claiming that the hospital, not the nurse, is liable for some reason, such as inadequate staffing. With the current cost consciousness of hospitals, the potential for hospitals seeking indemnification poses serious concerns about conflict of interest that are discussed throughout this book.

Before the trial begins, the parties attempt to discover from each other what evidence exists to substantiate the respective claims and defenses. There are various procedural rules that govern the discovery process. Discovery devices include (1) interrogatories, which are written questions to the opposing side; (2) depositions, which are out of court examinations of the parties or experts, under penalty of perjury, that are transcribed by a court reporter and can be used at trial to impeach a person's testimony if is different than that given at the deposition; (3) requests to produce documents; (4) requests for admissions of fact; and (5) requests for an independent medical examination of the plaintiff.

A party may object to discovery requests on the grounds that they are unduly burdensome, the party seeks privileged information, or the requests are part of the attorney's work product.[77] The scope of discovery is, however, quite broad in civil cases. Any information that would lead to the discovery of relevant admissible[78] evidence may be discoverable.

A civil trial necessarily implies that the parties dispute facts that are material to a claim or defense. If after conducting discovery, it seems that there are no disputed facts, there is no need for a trial. Where there are no disputed facts, the issue is purely a legal question that may be determined by the court in a summary proceeding.

Either or both parties may request (move) the court to issue a summary judgment before trial because there are no disputed facts to be decided. The party opposing the motion must show the court that there is evidence demonstrating a factual dispute.

Summary judgment motions are sometimes referred to as trial by affidavit. This is especially true in malpractice actions, where the essence of the claim requires expert testimony to establish negligence. The opposing party must present the affidavit of an expert to refute the expert of the moving party.

Certain kinds of claims cannot be resolved by summary judgment because an element of the claim is factual in nature and thus there necessarily is a dispute as to a material fact. Intent is virtually always a question of fact. Thus, whenever intent is an element of a claim, for example, in a fraud claim or formation of contract dispute, summary judgment is improper and the case generally must go forward to trial.

The Trial. The trial begins with jury selection. After the jury is selected, the parties' counsel generally give opening statements outlining what they believe the evidence will show the jury.

The plaintiff has both the burden of production and persuasion. The burden of production means that the plaintiff must introduce evidence of each element of the claim. If the plaintiff fails to do so, the defendant may ask the court to direct a verdict in his or her favor, and the court must grant the motion.

The burden of persuasion refers to the plaintiff's burden to prove the claim by a preponderance of the evidence. This burden remains with the plaintiff throughout trial.

Once the plaintiff has introduced evidence of each element of the claim, the burden shifts to the defendant to dispute this evidence or offer affirmative evidence showing a defense or excuse. After the defense has put on its evidence, the plaintiff may ask the court to direct a verdict in its favor if the defense evidence is insufficient to establish a valid defense. If the court denies the motion, the plaintiff may introduce evidence to rebut the defense evidence.

At the conclusion of this evidence, requests for directed verdicts by both sides may be made. If they are denied, the court instructs the jury on the law (the parties request the jury instructions most favorable to their case and the judge decides which to give). The jury then retires to a secluded room to deliberate and decide the case. If the plaintiff has waived his or her right to a jury trial, the court decides the case.

The Appeal. When a party believes that the final decision of the court or jury is in error, that person may appeal the decision to a higher court.[79] This person is known as the appellant. The person defending the decision is known as the appellee. The appellate court then determines whether an error has been made, and if so, whether this error requires reversal of the decision. In making this determination, the appellate court only considers the record as it existed at the trial level.

The losing party may attempt to overturn the unfavorable verdict on appeal based on a variety of errors that occurred either during the trial or before trial. For example, the exclusion or admission of evidence at trial, under certain circumstances, may require reversal where it has substantially prejudiced the fairness of the trial.[80] The appellant may also charge that the jury's verdict was not supported by substantial evidence. With respect to this latter error, however, the appellate court reviews the evidence in a light most favorable to upholding the judgment. Cases are not frequently reversed on this ground. Jury instructions may also be the basis of an appeal, if they are prejudicial.

The appellate courts have their own body of procedural rules that must be followed. Strict time limits govern the jurisdiction of the appellate court; if the appeal is not timely filed, the court loses jurisdiction. Once the appeal is filed, the trial court loses jurisdiction over the case and cannot rule on any motions.

SUBSTANTIVE CATEGORIES

Civil Law

Tort Law. Tort law seeks to compensate a person and make him or her whole. There are a few causes of action for economic injury–related torts, such as intentional interference with contractual damages and interference with prospective advantage. The law of defamation seeks to protect a person's interest in his or her reputation. The law of negligence and the law of strict liability enable an injured person to recover for personal injuries.

Intentional torts also allow a plaintiff to recover damages for personal injury, although this is not an element of the claim. Intentional torts require, as their name implies, an element of intent. Because of this element of intent, punitive damages—damages that seek to deter future intentional conduct—are recoverable. Intentional torts include assault, battery, false imprisonment, and the like. These are discussed in Chapter 5.

Negligence law, largely developed from the common law, is not concerned with intent. The actor may be very well intentioned but nevertheless expose another person to an unreasonable risk of harm. If he or she does, and personal injury results from the conduct, an action for negligence may be maintained. Generally, everyone owes everyone a duty to act reasonably. This is known as the reasonably prudent person standard of care. This is the standard in an ordinary negligence case.

Unlike the intentional tort, a negligence action requires as an element of the claim that the plaintiff suffer some personal injury. A professional negligence claim additionally requires the testimony of an expert that the defendant professional's conduct fell below that of other professionals and caused the injury to the plaintiff. The requirement of an expert in professional malpractice cases is because the jury has no expertise in the practice of the professional, and thus has no way to judge the professional's conduct. Chapter 4 analyzes the nurse's liability for professional negligence.

Strict liability law also developed from the common law. Originally a mixture of tort and contract, strict liability evolved to remedy injuries from products. Many jurisdictions have adopted the Restatement of Torts definition of strict liability, commonly referred to as Section 402A.[81]

Section 402A applies to sellers of products, and it imposes liability without regard to fault. Strict liability is not concerned with intent, and liability may be imposed even though the actor intended no harm and a risk of danger was not foreseeable.[82] Strict liability for injuries occurring from products used in the delivery of health care is discussed in Chapter 33.

Contract Law. A contract is an agreement to do or not to do a certain thing that gives rise to an obligation or legal duty that is enforceable.[83] A contract requires four elements: (1) that the parties have the capacity to contract—that is, they are not incompetent or infants; (2) an offer; (3) an acceptance of the offer; and (4) consideration.

An offer must be certain and definite; it is not an invitation to negotiate. An offer may be revoked at any time prior to acceptance by communicating notice of the revocation. If the offer is not accepted within the time prescribed, it is automatically revoked. If no time is set forth, the offer is revoked after the lapse of a reasonable time. What is reasonable is a question of fact that depends on the circumstances.

Acceptance of the offer must be communicated. If the offer prescribes a particular form or manner of acceptance, then acceptance must occur in that manner to be binding. Improper manner of acceptance creates a counter offer, and there is no contract unless the person making the original offer accepts the counter offer.[84]

Consideration has been described in a number of ways: *quid pro quo;* a promise to do this in exchange for that; and something that is bargained for—generally the exchange of a promise for another is promise or a promise in exchange for another's agreement to do an act or not do an act, such as file a lawsuit. Past consideration—acts done in the past—cannot be consideration for a new promise. Thus, modifications of contracts generally require new consideration.

Similarly, promises to do that which a person is already legally obligated to do cannot be sufficient consideration. Promises to do something illegal also cannot provide sufficient consideration. There must be some legitimate exchange; a mutuality of assent between the parties to enter into a contract.[85] Each party's promise to rescind the contract is generally sufficient to terminate the contract.

If any of the four necessary elements to a contract are missing, a lawsuit based on a contract will fail. In addition, in virtually all states, the statute of frauds requires that certain contracts be in writing.[86] The statute of frauds is an affirmative defense that must be raised in the defendant's answer or it is waived. There are certain exceptions to the statute of frauds, such as where one party has performed and should be estopped from asserting the defense.

Other defenses include fraud, undue influence, duress, and illegality.[87] In addition, where the parties have unequal bargaining positions, the contract may be unenforceable as a contract of adhesion.

On occasion, parties enter into a contract intending to benefit a third person. This is known as a third party beneficiary contract. The third party may enforce the contract before the parties rescind it.

One may be a third party beneficiary to a contract although the contract calls for payment to another person. In *Arata v. Bank of America,*[88] a woman gave birth to a child whose father was not her husband. While she was pregnant, she agreed to live with the man, at his request, and to give the child his family name. The man agreed to pay her not less than $500.00 a month for support of the child until majority. A similar contract was made for the support of a second child. When the man died, the two children sued his estate to enforce the contract.

The court held that the children were third party beneficiaries to the contract between their mother and their father, even though the promise was to pay the mother. The children were clearly the intended beneficiaries of the contract.

Antitrust Law. Antitrust laws seek to promote competition. Various states have enacted antitrust laws that are modeled after the federal antitrust laws. These antitrust laws and their application to the health care setting are discussed in Chapter 33.

The federal antitrust laws, the Sherman and Clayton Acts,[89] prohibit concerted activities (two or more persons acting together) that restrain trade and attempts to monopolize any part of trade or commerce. Certain other practices are also illegal if they substantially lessen competition or tend to create a monopoly. These are (1) price discrimination, which is a practice where the seller charges different prices to different buyers for the same product; (2) tying arrangements, where the seller requires the buyer to buy an additional product to get one product; (3) exclusive dealing contracts, where the buyer is prohibited from dealing with the seller's competitors; and (4) corporate mergers among competitors. Treble damages may be recovered if injury to business or property can be shown to be the result of anything forbidden in the federal antitrust laws.

There is no doubt that the antitrust laws apply to health care professionals.[90] The courts' inquiry into particular practice arrangements—whether they are "preferred provider arrangements, cost cutting contracts, joint efforts to share services, or to plan expansion"[91]—will be to determine what impact they have on competition in the market. If the effect on competition is an unreasonable restraint of trade, liability may be found.

Additional Civil Laws. In addition to these laws, employment discrimination laws that seek to remedy racial, sexual, and age discrimination exist. These are discussed in Chapters 30 and 33. Labor laws, which protect workers' right to bargain collectively and outlaw unfair labor practices, are discussed in Chapter 31.

Criminal Law. In marked contrast to civil law, criminal law seeks to punish, deter, and rehabilitate those who violate the criminal laws. The various states and the federal government have statutes that define the substance of crimes.

There are procedural differences between civil and criminal cases that chiefly relate to the deprivation at stake in each: in civil cases, parties are generally fighting about money, property, or personal injuries; in criminal cases, a person's liberty and, in some cases, his or her life are at stake. Thus the process by which the government deprives one of life or liberty is much more stringent than that employed when it takes someone's property.

The discovery rules are also different than those applicable in the civil arena. The government's right of discovery in criminal cases is limited and exists only by statute. The defendant is under no obligation to reveal his or defenses, except that some states and the federal government require notice of an alibi. The federal rules governing criminal procedure do provide for reciprocal discovery from the defendant of certain documentary evidence such as scientific reports.[92]

Certain rules of evidence apply in criminal proceedings that are not applicable to civil proceedings. For example, the Sixth Amendment right to confront witnesses prohibits the introduction of a ledger found in the defendant's presence where the author of the ledger is unknown and the defendant's signature or fingerprint does not appear anywhere.[93] The right to confrontation is also implicated in certain forms of hearsay evidence (out of court statements).

The defendant also has a Sixth Amendment right to counsel throughout the criminal proceedings. If the defendant cannot afford private counsel, an attorney will be appointed to represent him or her free of charge. In contrast, in the civil system, there is no right to appointed counsel.

The burden of proof is also greater in criminal cases than in civil actions. The government is required to prove beyond a reasonable doubt every element of the crime. The burden of proof remains with the government; it does not shift to the defendant. The defendant is not required to offer any defense; if the state fails to prove the elements of the crime, the defendant should be found not guilty.

The appellate process is also different than that in civil cases. There is a right to appointed counsel if the defendant cannot afford an attorney. In addition, certain errors, especially constitutional errors, are more closely scrutinized on review. This again is because of the interest at stake.

Administrative Law. In addition to legislative functions, such as rule making and promulgating regulations, administrative agencies may act in adversary proceedings. They may investigate and subpoena persons to hearings; they may also issue interpretive opinions or decisions about the meaning of their regulations. For example a state licensing board investigates violations of the licensing laws, and it also promulgates substantive regulations defining conduct that violates the licensing law. Hearing officers or administrative law judges who preside over these quasijudicial proceedings exercise quasijudicial powers.[94]

The rules of evidence in administrative proceedings are more relaxed than those in criminal cases. For example, administrative law judges may consider hearsay (out-of-court statements) so long as admission of the statement is fair.[95]

In conducting an investigation or adjudicating a determination, an agency is authorized to issue administrative subpoenas. The test to determine the relevancy of the subpoena is whether the information sought by the subpoena is reasonably relevant to the agency's inquiry. The subpoena may be enforced by the courts, but the proceedings to enforce the subpoena must provide an adequate opportunity to raise objections to the subpoena.[96]

Substantive administrative law, as outlined above, is promulgated by agencies. Licensure laws, such as nursing practice acts, seek to protect the public by regulating the qualifications of those who practice. These laws define unprofessional conduct, establish penalties for the same, and outline the scope of practice. Chapter 25 thoroughly discusses these issues.

Recommendations and trends

The sources and classifications of law define, in large measure, the government's authority to control individual activity. Litigation to challenge a law is a lengthy and costly process. While new remedies are developed through the common law, expansion of individual rights often depends on a particular judge's philosophy. Thus, a combination of litigation, legislative, and administrative efforts may best further the autonomy of the nursing profession.

Endnotes

1. Greene, *The Development of the Doctrine of Stare Decisis and the Extent to Which It Should Be Applied,* 15 ILLINOIS LAW REVIEW 35 & n.1 (1946) (hereinafter cited as *Stare Decisis*).
2. *Stare Decisis, supra* note 1, at 45.
3. *Id.* at 46.
4. *United States v. South-Eastern Underwriters Assn.*, 322 U.S. 533, 579 (1944) (Stone, C.J., dissenting).
5. T. CRISTOFFEL, HEALTH AND THE LAW 19 (1982).
6. *See, e.g., Sermchief v. Gonzales,* 660 S.W.2d 683 (Mo. 1983) (en banc); *Fraijo v. Hartland Hospital,* 160 Cal. Rptr 246 (Cal. App. 1979).
7. *E.g., Sermchief v. Gonzales,* 660 S.W.2d 683 (Mo 1983) (en banc).
8. *Fraijo v. Hartland Hosp.*, 160 Cal. Rptr. 246, 252 (Cal. App. 1979).

9. *Id.*
10. *Id.*
11. *Youngstown Sheet & Tube Co. v. Sawyer,* 343 U.S. 579 (1952).
12. Wright, *The Role of the Supreme Court in a Democratic Society—Judicial Activism or Restraint?* 54 CORNELL LAW REVIEW, I (1968) (hereinafter cited as *Wright*).
13. 347 U.S. 483 (1954).
14. *Marbury v. Madison,* 1 Cranch 137 (1803).
15. *Id.*
16. M. PERTERSON, THE PORTABLE JEFFERSON 562-63 (1975).
17. *Wright, supra* note 10.
18. *Marbury v. Madison,* 1 Cranch 137 (1803).
19. K.R. WING, THE LAW AND THE PUBLIC'S HEALTH 19 (1985) (hereinafter cited as *Wing*).
20. *Id.* at 21.
21. Due process of law has been interpreted by the Supreme Court to include various procedural protections, including notice and an opportunity to be heard. The Fifth and Sixth Amendments contain important protections for those accused of criminal wrongdoing. For example, every person has the right against self-incrimination and the right to confront and cross-examine witnesses. In addition, the right to counsel and to compulsory process for obtaining favorable witnesses is guaranteed in criminal cases.
22. *See, e.g., Griswold v. Connecticut,* 381 U.S. 479 (1965).
23. *Wing, supra* note 17, at 19.
24. *Id.*
25. *Id.* at 30.
26. *Id.*
27. *See id.* at 97-101.
28. *Id.* at 101.
29. *Id.* at 120.
30. 60 Stat. 1041 (1946), as amended, 42 U.S.C. 291 (1982).
31. *Id.* at §291d.
32. *Id.* at §291.0(h).
33. *Id.* at §291c.
34. *Wing, supra* note 17, at 120.
35. *Id.* at 124.
36. *Id.* at 124.
37. *Id.* at 126.
38. *Id.*
39. *Id.*
40. 198 U.S. 45 (1905).
41. R.C. TURKINGTON & J.M. SHAMAN, CASES AND MATERIALS ON THE CONSTITUTIONAL PROCESS 267 (1976) (hereinafter cited as *Turkington*).
42. *Id.*
43. *Williamson v. Lee Optical Co.,* 348 U.S. 483, 487 (1955).
44. *Turkington, supra* note 40, at 267-68.
45. *Sail'er Inn, Inc., v. Kirby,* 95 Cal. Rptr. 329 (Cal. 1971).
46. *Williamson v. Lee Optical Co.,* 348 U.S. 483 (1955).
47. *Weinberger v. Wiesenfeld,* 95 S. Ct. 1225 (1975); *Stanton v. Stanton,* 95 S. Ct. 1373 (1975).
48. *Levy v. Louisiana,* 391 U.S. 68 (1968).
49. *Bowland v. Municipal Court,* 134 Cal. Rptr 630 (Cal. 1977) (en banc).
50. In 1905, the Supreme Court rejected a constitutional challenge to a state law requiring compulsory small pox vaccinations for all adults. *Jacobsen v. Massachusetts,* 197 U.S. 11 (1905). The plaintiff argued that compulsory vaccination was an unreasonable and arbitrary interference with his right to liberty. The Court noted that the states authority to enact this type of statute was the police power—a power the State did not give up when it became a part of the United States.
51. *Id.*
52. *Id.* at 26.
53. *See, e.g., In re Martin Seiferth,* 127 N.E.2d 820 (N.Y. 1955) (12-year-old boy who together with his parents did not want corrective surgery for a disfiguring harelip and cleft palate in spite of the County Health Department's insistence that treatment be instituted; the court rejected the county's petition, noting that there was no serious risk of harm to the boy, no emergency, and no serious threat to his life).
54. *Oklahoma v. Skinner,* 316 U.S. 535 (1942).
55. 410 U.S. 113 (1973).
56. *Id.* at 118.
57. *See, e.g., Beal v. Doe,* 432 U.S. 438 (1977) and *Maher v. Roe,* 432 U.S. 464 (1977).
58. *Harris v. McRae,* 448 U.S. 297 (1980).
59. It should be noted, however, that the right to travel, a fundamental right, has been successfully applied to certain state welfare restrictions, notably those requiring that a resident live in the state for a specified time prior to being eligible for welfare. *E.g., Shapiro v. Thompson,* 394 U.S. 618 (1969).
60. *See, e.g., O'Connor, v. Donaldson,* 422 U.S. 563 (1975).
61. *See, e.g.,* 5 U.S.C. §551-701, which is the federal Administrative Procedure Act. This act does not apply to state agencies. *West Penn Power Co. v. Train,* 522 F.2d 302 (6th Cir. 1975).
62. *See, e.g., Kroden v. United States Justice Department,* 564 F.2d 228 (7th Cir. 1977).
63. *See, e.g., American Trucking Assn. v. United States,* 344 U.S. 298 (1953) (Congress creates regulatory agencies so that they will bring to their work the expert's familiarity with industry conditions that delegating legislatures cannot be expected to possess).
64. *See FCC v. Schreiber,* 381 U.S. 279 (1965).
65. *See, e.g., Balelo v. Baldrige,* 724 F.2d 753 (9th Cir. 1984) (en banc).
66. *Haig v. Agee,* 453 U.S. 280, 291 (1981).
67. *See, e.g., Mourning v. Family Publications Service, Inc.,* 411 U.S. 356 (1973).
68. *See generally,* K. DAVIS, ADMINISTRATIVE LAW TEXT (3d ed. 1972).
69. *See, e.g., Buschmann v. Schweiker,* 676 F.2d 352 (9th Cir. 1982).
70. *See, e.g., Balelo v. Baldridge,* 724 F.2d 753 (9th Cir. 1984) (en banc).
71. *See, e.g., Shawgo v. Spradlin,* 701 F.2d 470 (5th Cir. 1983).
72. *See, e.g., Casey v. Federal Trade Commission,* 578 F.2d 793 (9th Cir. 1978).
73. *See, e.g., Association of National Advertisers, Inc. v. F.T.C.,* 627 F.2d 1151 (D.C. Cir. 1979).
74. *See, e.g., American Federation of Government Employees, Local 1668 v. Dunn,* 561 F.2d 1310 (9th Cir. 1977).
75. *See, e.g., West Helena Savings and Loan Assn. v. Federal Home Loan Bank Bd,* 417 F.Supp. 220, aff'd 553 F.2d 1175.
76. Various cases discussed throughout this book are appeals from dismissals of cases. It should be remembered that appeals from pretrial rulings do not involve a jury determination of liability. What the court in essence is stating if it reverses a case and remands it to the trial court for a trial is that if the plaintiff can prove what is stated in the complaint, then the jury, if it believes the evidence, may find him or her liable.

77. Generally, information relayed to an attorney by a party is protected by the attorney client privilege. Privileges are defined by state law and may vary. Some states recognize a marital privilege, protecting communications made during the marital relationship. The patient-physician privilege also protects communications made by a patient to a physician. This privilege, as with all privileges, may be waived by the patient. If the patient is suing for personal injuries, the privilege with respect to these injuries is generally deemed to be waived. It should be noted that the patient-physician privilege does not extend to communications between the nurse and the patient.
78. Relevancy refers to evidence that has any tendency to make a fact important to the lawsuit more or less probable. See, e.g., FED. R. EVID. 401. Even evidence that is relevant is sometimes excluded because of concern that it is unreliable or untrustworthy. An example is hearsay evidence. Absent a specific exception, such evidence is inadmissible at trial. See, e.g., FED. R. EVID. 801. Another example is evidence that is relevant and probative but its value as such is outweighed by the danger of unfair prejudice, confusion of issues, or misleading the jury, or by considerations of undue delay, waste of time, or needless presentation of cumulative evidence. See, e.g., FED. R. EVID. 403.
79. In certain limited situations, a party may appeal an order of the court before the litigation has ended.
80. FED. R. EVID. 103.
81. RESTATEMENT (SECOND) OF TORTS §402 A.
82. Certain exceptions apply. In the area of drug liability, an exception has been created in most jurisdictions that makes a drug manufacturer liable for failing to warn of known adverse consequences or those harms about which it reasonably should have known. *See, e.g.*, Kelly, *The Relevancy of Drug Efficacy Evidence in Strict Liability Actions: Needham v. White Laboratories, Inc.*, 14 JOHN MARSHALL LAW REVIEW 629 (1981).
83. B.E. WHITKIN, SUMMARY OF CALIFORNIA LAW, VOL. 1 §2 (8th ed. 1973) (hereinafter cited as Whitkin).
84. *Id.* at §131.
85. *Id.* at §144-162.
86. *Id.* at §180-192. In general, contracts that cannot be performed within 1 year and contracts for the sale of land must be in writing.
87. *Id.* at §244-315.
88. 35 Cal. Rptr. 703 (Cal. App. 1963).
89. *See, e.g.*, 15 U.S.C. §1-40.
90. *See, e.g.*, *Arizona v. Maricopa County Medical Society*, 457 U.S. 332 (1982).
91. *Wing, supra* note 17, at 191.
92. FED. R. CRIM. PRO. 16 (b).
93. *See, e.g.*, *United States v. Ordonez*, 737 F.2d 793 (9th Cir. 1984).
94. *See, e.g.*, *Snow v. Nevada Dept. of Prisons*, 543 F.Supp. 752 (D.Nev. 1982).
95. *See, e.g.*, *Baliza v. I.N.S.*, 709 F.2d 1231 (9th Cir. 1983).
96. *See, e.g.*, *F.T.C. v. Atlantic Richfield Co.*, 567 F.2d 96 (D.C. Cir. 1977).

Chapter 3

Selecting legal representation

Diane Trace Warlick

When and how to get legal representation? These questions are facing nurses more often today than ever before. This phenomenon is the result of at least two developments in the nursing profession over the last decade. First, as the general public and legal profession have begun to recognize the professionalism and independent legal accountability of nurses, nurses have increasingly become the target of malpractice lawsuits. Second, as discussed in other chapters, changes in the scope of nursing practice and expansion into what the medical profession has traditionally viewed as the exclusive realm of medicine have exposed individual nurses and nursing associations to both legislative and judicial confrontations.[1] Disciplinary proceedings and labor disputes also continue to raise the issue of legal representation for the practicing nurse. Unfortunately, a lawyer is frequently not consulted until much later than the optimal time period.

Once the need for legal assistance is recognized, it may be difficult to identify the most appropriate attorney to handle the particular problem. The purpose of this chapter is to help individual nurse practitioners and state nursing associations learn how to recognize when legal representation is required and how to select the best legal representation for the specific legal need.

Recognizing legal problems

The nature of legal problems that may face the individual nurse differs from those problems that may confront a state nurses' association. This is due to the inherent differences in the nature and role of the organization vis-à-vis the individual nurse in the nursing profession. The major legal issues facing each group are discussed below. This is not an exhaustive list, however, because the development of new legal issues by the courts, the passage of legislation, and creative lawyers represent a continual process.

INDIVIDUAL NURSES

There are three major areas of an individual nurse's professional practice in which legal representation is most likely to become necessary: employment disputes, disciplinary proceedings, and malpractice lawsuits. It should be emphasized at the outset that it is never harmful to consult an attorney too early in the development of a legal problem. The only potentially negative impact might be a financial one if the attorney charges for the initial consultation whether or not any action is necessary.

It is generally suggested that initial contact be made with a lawyer as soon as it becomes apparent that a professional situation with legal implications is developing. Preventive legal action may be as important to one's legal health as preventive health care is to one's physical well-being. At a minimum, when a potential legal risk arises, the careful practitioner will document events in sufficient detail to preserve the facts for future reference if legal representation becomes necessary.[2]

Employment Disputes. Despite the recent emergence of opportunities for independent nursing practice, most nurses are still employees of hospitals, other health care facilities, physicians, or educational institutions. This very large percentage of nurse employees are therefore exposed to legal ramifications from disputes with their employers.[3] These may arise from conflicts with supervisors, coworkers, administrators, or personnel the nurse is supervising or from disagreements with other health care professionals.

The nurse may dispute a procedure or regulation and be given a choice by his or her employer to comply, to resign, or to be fired. Disputes may center around working conditions or employee benefits. In these or other situations where legal proceedings may become inevitable, the nurse should keep a record of all events and retain all written documents.

If any active measures are taken against the nurse by the employer, coworker, or other health care professional, an attorney should be consulted immediately. Examples of measures that might trigger the need for legal assistance include demotion, loss of seniority, involuntary transfers, or discharge. In these situations, the nurse is more likely to be the plaintiff, seeking reinstatement and back pay or restoration of position, benefits, or seniority. An attorney will be able to advise the nurse on the active measures necessary to protect his or her position, actions to avoid, and remedies available, if any.

A nurse who is a member of a union or otherwise represented by a collective bargaining unit should contact the union representative and attorney. The union may provide legal counsel, or the union contract may involve the benefit of prepaid legal services.

Disciplinary Proceedings. Any disciplinary proceeding by a licensing board against a nurse has a potential impact on the nurse's license and ability to practice. Many nurses do not know their rights in disciplinary proceedings or how to assert them. Many of these rights as discussed in Chapter 25 are constitutionally mandated. The complexity of the issues and the potential severity of the result require the nurse to seek legal advice as soon as he or she becomes aware that a complaint has been filed.

A single consultation with an attorney may be all that is required under particular circumstances, or it may advisable to have an attorney monitor proceedings and provide ongoing legal representation. If the tribunal initiates formal disciplinary proceedings, the nurse should certainly be represented by an attorney throughout the proceedings. By electing to represent oneself, the nurse is highly likely to inadvertently waive rights or make errors that cannot be corrected later.

Malpractice Lawsuits. In some instances, the nurse may become aware very early in the nurse-patient relationship that the patient or family is a potential litigant. There may be specific threats to sue a particular individual or health care facility, or the patient or family may be openly critical of the medical or nursing service.

The cardinal rule regarding documentation applies here as in the two situations previously described. The nurse should begin to keep a detailed personal record of events as soon as alerted to a potential malpractice lawsuit. While his or her memory is fresh, the nurse should make notes of all previous events related to the patient's care.

A nurse must obtain legal representation as soon as notice that a lawsuit has been filed is received.[4] This rule applies even where the nurse feels the suit is totally frivolous and without merit. First notice may be a summons and complaint that initiates court proceedings, or it may be notice that a complaint has been presented to a malpractice tribunal or arbitration panel in those states that have prelitigation review proceedings.

The nurse who carries an individual professional liability insurance (malpractice) policy must notify the insurance company immediately when notice of a lawsuit is received. The insurance carrier has a duty under the policy to defend any lawsuits that fall within the terms of the insurance coverage. Consult Chapter 27 for further information on insurance.

The nurse who does not carry malpractice or professional liability insurance may still be covered by his or her employer. The nurse should check with the supervisor or employer immediately on receipt of notice of suit to determine whether there is coverage under the employer's insurance policy. The nurse who has private malpractice insurance coverage should also determine whether he or she is covered under the employer's policy.

STATE NURSES' ASSOCIATIONS

There are four primary areas of activity engaged in by the majority of state nurses' associations in which the legal expertise of an attorney may be required. Each of these categories, as with those discussed in reference to individual nurses, represents a distinct area of law with its own particular rules and procedures. The four primary substantive areas of law with which state nurses' associations are concerned in their day-to-day operations are labor relations, government relations, practice issues, and the organization and operation of the association.

Since state nurses' associations generally retain counsel to provide ongoing representation at all times, it is not necessary to elaborate on the timing for hiring coun-

STEPS FOR SELECTING LEGAL COUNSEL

Step one: Evaluate your legal requirements.
- Identify type of legal problem.
- Evaluate level of services desired.
- Determine type of counsel preferred.

Step two: Utilize tools available to identify prospective legal counsel.
- Refer to the *Martindale-Hubbell Directory of Attorneys* and other local, state, or national law directories if applicable.
- Check with friends, colleagues, and professional associations.
- Use bar associations and other lawyer referral services if applicable.

Step three: Interview prospects.
- Be attuned to the level of rapport between yourself and the lawyer.
- Discuss what services the lawyer feels may be necessary, the services he or she is willing to perform, and the amount of time available to perform them.
- Establish the fee structure, payment terms, and estimated total cost (approximate).

sel. The association and its agent responsible for retaining and working with the lawyer should be aware that not all lawyers have expertise in all of these fields. It may, therefore, be necessary to retain more than one attorney to handle legal matters for the association.

As new issues arise, it is recommended that the association review its current legal representation to determine whether additional representation is required or whether the matter can be handled by counsel previously retained. Specific criteria for evaluating the kind of legal services required and the expertise necessary for an attorney to competently handle the legal matter are discussed in the following section.

Selecting counsel

Careful evaluation during the selection process is important for the individual nurse and for the state nurses' association. Counsel should be selected on the basis of the type and level of services required, ability to communicate, and financial and other criteria. Each of these areas will be discussed below. The steps for selecting counsel are listed below (see the box above).

EVALUATION OF LEGAL REQUIREMENTS

Each legal question that arises will not require the same depth of analysis or degree of expertise or experience to address it competently. To select the best lawyer to handle the matter, the nurse or association must first identify the specific type of legal problem and the substantive area of law involved. The level of service required should be evaluated and an initial determination of the type of legal representation required should be made. The actual selection and hiring of an attorney should follow only after these initial steps have been taken.

Level of Services. The level of legal services required depends on the frequency with which the legal problem arises, the complexity of the issue, and the kind of legal action that may be necessary. Although the complexity of the issue may only be determined after initial legal consultation, the individual nurse or association should have a basic idea of what kind of legal assistance or result is desired. The answers to the following questions assist in determining the level of services required:

1. Is the problem recurring, or is this the only time it has developed?
2. Do you need a legal interpretation of a statute, regulation, or potential liability, or is legal representation required for purposes of defending or initiating a lawsuit, job action, or disciplinary matter?
3. Do you know whether other nurses or state nurses' associations have had similar problems?
4. If so, how long did it take to resolve the matter and how much time did the attorney spend on it?

The answers to these questions will provide some guidance in determining the level of services and type of counsel required.

Types of Counsel. Two basic factors must be considered in determining the type of counsel desired: (1) size of firm and (2) degree of specialization. Law offices range in size from single practitioners to hundreds of lawyers. Representation by a firm will generally provide a broader range of legal services since it can bring the combined expertise of each of the firm members and associates to the matter at hand. Because a firm will do a larger volume of business, it may also be able to offer the more specialized knowledge of firm members who limit their practice to particular legal issues or proceedings.

Representation by an individual attorney may be more personalized, and, in the case of associations, may provide a perspective that can only be gained by a broad focus on all the legal issues facing the organization. It is more critical when hiring an individual attorney to ascertain that he or she has expertise in the specific area of law at issue, particularly where there are no partners or associates with experience in the field available for consultation.

If an attorney has not practiced regularly or recently in the particular field, he or she will probably need to do more research and preparation to competently advise or represent his or her client. Although more experience is generally better, it is only one factor to consider along with the ability to communicate with the client, time available to devote to the problem, fees, the number of years in practice, and expertise with similar or related areas of law.

CRITERIA FOR SELECTION: TAANA GUIDELINES

The American Association of Nurse Attorneys (TAANA) is an association whose membership includes individuals who are educated and qualified to practice in both the nursing and legal professions.[5] As dual professionals, the association membership is dedicated to the education of nurses in the legal aspects of professional nursing practice, among other goals. TAANA members are actively involved in providing legal representation to nurses and other health care professionals. In 1983 the TAANA board of directors adopted the following general policy statements that should govern the selection of legal counsel:

1. The attorney selected should have the requisite knowledge to address the legal issue presented; and,
2. The attorney selected to handle an issue related to nursing practice should be learned and experienced in nursing practice.

The selection process

Although it may be easy to locate an attorney who will handle the case, it may not be so easy to find the best attorney for the particular nurse or association and the specific legal problem. Sufficient time and consideration should be given to the selection process to permit an informed decision to be made. There are a number of tools available for identifying prospective counsel. Once identified, the interview becomes a very important tool in the selection process. This will be discussed further below.

TOOLS FOR SELECTION

It is recommended in accordance with the TAANA guidelines that individual nurses and state nurses' associations seriously consider retaining a nurse attorney to represent them whenever feasible, particularly where the issue involves some aspect of nursing practice. Nurse attorneys will have an insight into the legal and practical problems nurses face in their practice and the scientific knowledge essential to understand practice issues. Referrals to nurse attorneys in specific areas of the country may be obtained by writing to TAANA, 113 W. Franklin Street, Baltimore, Maryland 21201 or calling (301) 752-3318.

The most comprehensive source of information on attorneys throughout the country is the MARTINDALE-HUBBELL DIRECTORY OF ATTORNEYS.[6] This directory can be found in most public and law libraries. It may also be found at the local courthouse and bar association. The directory lists virtually all attorneys in the country both alphabetically and geographically by state and city or town. The directory should be used in conjunction with one or more other information resources and to confirm the professional biographical data. The American Bar Association (ABA) recognizes that an individual seeking legal counsel "is best served" by an informed and disinterested recommendation.[7]

One of the best resources for locating an attorney is through friends, colleagues, or professional associations. Another nurse or health care professional who has had a similar problem in the past will know the length of time required to resolve the issues and how much it cost and will have insight into the professional style of the attorney. Professional nursing associations may be able to provide names of attorneys who practice in areas of health law. Local bar associations frequently have referral services, but generally the only information given is the name and area of practice.

The interview should be the final step in the selection process. It is the only means of determining whether one is comfortable with the attorney's professional style and whether the attorney has a basic understanding of the issues. Do not be afraid to interview more than one attorney before making a final decision. Explain the problem briefly and do not hesitate to ask questions. The attorney should respond to questions willingly and should not be hesitant to admit any limitations to the representation he or she is competent to give. Sample questions that one could ask an attorney during the interview are listed below (see the box on p. 31, upper left).

Fees should be discussed in the first interview. Try to get an estimate of the anticipated total cost to resolve the issues. As in all professional relationships, communication is a critical element. Be attuned to the rapport that develops during the interview. The attorney selected must be sensitive to his or her client's identified concerns

SAMPLE QUESTIONS TO ASK AT THE INTERVIEW

Before a lawyer can respond to questions, he or she must know what the problem is. Be prepared to fully explain the problem and then ask questions.

*Sample questions:**

Have you handled this kind of legal matter before? How frequently?

What was the result?

What can I expect?

What will I have to do?

Will you handle the matter or do you expect to bring in another lawyer to assist?

How long will it take to resolve?

Would you explain the legal issues?

*Questions regarding legal fees are found in the box on p. 32.

and interests and be able to integrate and translate them into legal issues that can be addressed and resolved in the most expedient and least expensive manner. It is equally important that the attorney be willing to work *with* as well as *for* the client.

THE INITIAL CONSULTATION

The initial consultation may be a continuation of the interview where the decision to retain the attorney is made, or it may take place at a subsequent time. The timing may also depend on the following factors:

1. The availability of necessary documentation
2. Whether the attorney needs to do any preliminary research
3. The nature and present status of the legal problem
4. The availability of sufficient time

At least an hour should be allowed for the initial consultation.

Prepare for the initial consultation by reviewing all available documents and any personal notes kept of the facts involved in the case. It is also helpful to prepare a brief written chronology of events that provides a quick overview of the circumstances that lead to the need for legal representation. These items should be taken to the initial consultation and copies left with the attorney for study and future reference. If a practice issue is involved, a copy of any written policy, guideline, regulation, or standard protocols that may be applicable should also be taken. A curriculum vitae may also be very helpful. When the appointment is made, the nurse should inquire whether there are any additional items that should be brought to the consultation.

IS THE LAWYER'S FEE REASONABLE?

These factors should be considered in evaluating the "reasonableness" of an attorney's fee:

1. Amount of time and labor required
2. Novelty and difficulty of the questions involved
3. Level of skill required to perform the legal service properly
4. Likelihood that the acceptance of the particular employment will preclude other employment by the lawyer (must be apparent to the client)
5. Fee customarily charged in the locality for similar legal services
6. Amount involved and the results obtained
7. Time limitations imposed by the client or by the circumstances
8. Nature and length of the professional relationship with the client.
9. Experience, reputation, and ability of the lawyer or lawyers performing the services
10. Whether the fee is fixed or contingent

Data from American Bar Association, MODEL CODE OF PROFESSIONAL RESPONSIBILITY DR 2-106(b) (1969, as amended to 1980). The same criteria have been incorporated into the MODEL RULES OF PROFESSIONAL CONDUCT Rule 1.5 (1983).

FEES

The amount an attorney charges for his or her services and the manner in which fees are calculated are a matter of contract; in other words, whatever that attorney and client agree to, subject only to limitations imposed by legislatures or the courts.[8] This issue should be discussed when interviewing prospective counsel and confirmed when the attorney is retained. Fees vary widely between and within various geographical locations but generally take one of four forms: (1) fee for service, (2) hourly billing, (3) retainer fee, and (4) contingency fee. Factors to consider in determining the reasonableness of a fee are listed in the box above. Reduced fees for senior citizens are often available.

Fee for service is a set fee for a particular service, regardless of the amount of time involved. This type of fee is generally reserved for specific, well-defined legal procedures that require only a limited amount of individualized attention or for which the amount of time required to handle the case can be accurately estimated in advance.

Nursing practice issues are unlikely to be included as a fee for service. Most defense attorneys and those who handle administrative or disciplinary proceedings,

SAMPLE QUESTIONS TO ASK AN ATTORNEY ABOUT HOURLY FEES

1. How much do you charge per hour?
2. Are secretarial services included?
3. How much will I be billed for time of associates, law clerks, or paralegals?
4. What can I expect to be billed for that is not included in the hourly fee?
5. How much will court costs be?
6. How much will I be charged for photocopying expenses?
7. Will you advance any costs or expenses?
8. When can I expect to be billed?
9. Can I pay over an extended period of time?

labor relations, and other matters that may require court appearances generally have an hourly rate and bill the client for the actual amount of time spent on the matter. The hourly rate usually does not include costs. Costs are fees charged by the courts for specific services, such as fees for filing official documents with the court and charges for obtaining transcripts of court proceedings. The hourly rate will also generally not include the necessary out-of-pocket expenses that are incurred by the attorney in handling the case. These include, for example, long-distance telephone calls, photocopying, and travel expenses. Be sure to ask what is and is not included in the hourly rate. Sample questions for obtaining information necessary to assess hourly rates are listed in the box above.

A retainer is basically a prepaid fee for services. The attorney should explain exactly what services will be provided for this fee and what additional fees can be anticipated. A contingency fee is a fee arrangement utilized almost exclusively in civil litigation by attorneys representing plaintiffs.[9] It is an agreement to represent an individual in a lawsuit in exchange for a percentage of the amount of money recovered for the client at the end of the litigation. The attorney essentially provides his or her services free of charge during the litigation in anticipation of making a substantial fee at the conclusion of the litigation. The attorney risks the possibility that his or her client will not prevail. In this event, the attorney will not be entitled to any fee, but the client will be required to reimburse him or her for expenses and court costs. The usual contingency fee is 33⅓% of the amount the plaintiff receives but may be limited by law in malpractice litigation to a smaller percentage.

Once the amount of the fee is established, billing arrangements should be discussed. An attorney may bill weekly, monthly, or at the conclusion of the particular matter. Do not hesitate to express a preference. It may be possible to arrange installment payments or credit in some circumstances. Remember, this is a contract and should be in writing to protect both parties. If the attorney has not prepared a written fee agreement, a letter of confirmation stating the client's understanding of the terms of the agreement can be written by the client and will serve the same purpose. A copy should be kept for the client's records.

The professional relationship

Because results depend on the effectiveness of legal representation, several additional aspects of the attorney-client relationship should be given consideration by the nurse. Termination of the legal representation raises many questions. Differences of opinion regarding level of communication and client involvement in the legal process may create strains in the professional relationship. Each of these will be discussed below.

COMMUNICATION AND INVOLVEMENT IN THE LEGAL PROCESS

The client and attorney should determine the degree of involvement the client will have in the legal process, the frequency of written reports to the client, if any, and other documentation the client should expect to receive. As was stressed in the preceding sections, good communication is the heart of the attorney-client relationship.

The attorney should be accessible and willing to discuss the client's concerns, explain the proceedings, and keep the client up to date on the developments in the case.[10] The attorney should return phone calls within 24 hours whenever feasible. It is generally reasonable to expect the attorney to respond to correspondence within a week. If the attorney is unavailable for any reason, the client should be informed and advised when the attorney anticipates being available for a substantive discussion.

Notwithstanding other clients, the attorney is expected to review documents on receipt and be prepared to advise the client of their significance and potential impact within a reasonable time.[11] What constitutes a reasonable time will depend on the nature of the case and the complexity of the documents. Since most court proceedings are subject to specific time limits, the client is entitled at a minimum to expect the attorney to respond in sufficient time to discuss the issues and take necessary action within the time permitted by statute or court rules. The client is entitled and should expect to be permitted to express his or her opinion on any matter affecting the case, before any action is taken. However, it should be remembered that many decisions involve professional judgment and should be made by the attorney.

A final word of caution: Do not retain an attorney whose advice you are not prepared to accept. Be candid, and provide the attorney with all available information on the pending matter; then trust his or her judgment on how the matter should be handled, or start looking for other legal representation.[12]

TERMINATING REPRESENTATION

The attorney-client relationship, as with other professional relationships, is a contractual one. The terms of the agreement may be negotiated by the parties. The terms agreed on by both parties will govern the relationship. If the client becomes dissatisfied with the attorney or the legal representation at any time, the client may terminate the relationship by so advising the attorney. On termination, the client is entitled to a complete copy of the file, including pleadings, discovery, and correspondence.

Although the client may unilaterally terminate the attorney-client relationship at any time, this is not always true for the attorney.[13] If litigation or other court action is pending, the attorney may withdraw from representation of the client only with the client's consent or with the permission of the court. The attorney must have "good cause" to withdraw from a case and must generally continue to represent the client for a sufficient period of time to permit the client to locate another attorney who is competent and willing to take over the case. Where it would be detrimental to the client for the attorney to continue acting on his or her behalf, the court can be asked to enter a stay of the proceedings until new counsel can be hired.

Standards for legal representation

Like medicine and nursing, the legal profession is self-regulated and establishes its own standards of practice. Somewhat different from other professions, standards of the legal profession are enforced by the courts, which determine who may and may not practice law. The courts have been guided by the "Canons of Professional Ethics" first adopted by the ABA in 1908. As has been referred to already, the most recent version, adopted in some form in most jurisdictions, is the 1969 ABA MODEL CODE OF PROFESSIONAL RESPONSIBILITY (Model Code). The ABA began consideration in August 1982 of a new code that substantially changes the format of the rules but does not contain any major revisions in the substantive rules. In an introductory note to the MODEL RULES OF PROFESSIONAL CONDUCT (Model Rules), the chairman of the ABA Commission on Evaluation of Professional Standards succinctly stated their purpose: "to serve as a national model . . . of enforceable standards of conduct governing the practice of law."[14]

The Model Rules and the 1969 code contain standards for prohibited conduct, the violation of which will subject a lawyer to disciplinary proceedings. They also establish standards for professionally responsible conduct in daily law practice. For example, both codes contain standards governing a lawyer's conduct in conflict of interest situations, safeguarding client property, pro bono service, organization and operation of law firms, confidentiality of client communications, and fees. The "Canons of Professional Conduct" in the ABA's Model Code are listed above. These canons express the basic tenents of professional conduct from which the disciplinary rules and ethical considerations are derived.

Conflict of interest situations are a potential pitfall in the attorney-client relationship of which the client should be aware. Both the Model Code and the Model Rules address conflicts of interest and prohibit lawyers from representing clients where a potential conflict may develop except in certain specified circumstances.

CANONS OF PROFESSIONAL CONDUCT

CANON 1: A Lawyer should assist in maintaining the integrity and competence of the legal profession.

CANON 2: A Lawyer should assist the legal profession in fulfilling its duty to make legal counsel available.

CANON 3: A Lawyer should assist in preventing the unauthorized practice of law.

CANON 4: A Lawyer should preserve the confidences and secrets of a client.

CANON 5: A Lawyer should exercise independent professional judgment on behalf of a client.

CANON 6: A Lawyer should represent a client competently.

CANON 7: A Lawyer should represent a client zealously within the bounds of the law.

CANON 8: A Lawyer should assist in improving the legal system.

CANON 9: A Lawyer should avoid even the appearance of professional impropriety.

Adapted from American Bar Association, MODEL CODE OF PROFESSIONAL RESPONSIBILITY (1969, as amended to 1980).

The Model Code requires a lawyer to refuse employment if "the exercise of his professional judgment on behalf of his client will be or reasonably may be affected by his own financial, business, property or personal interests."[15] A lawyer may not represent a client in litigation in which the lawyer may be a witness except under limited circumstances.[16] A lawyer may not enter into business transactions in which he or she is representing a client where the lawyer has "differing interest" unless he or she fully explains the interest and obtains the client's consent to the continuing representation.[17]

The Model Rules address conflicts of interest in a more direct manner than the Model Code, although the intent and basic rules are unchanged. Rule 1.8 lists nine prohibited transactions in conflict of interest situations.

Nurses involved in malpractice litigation are most likely to be faced with potential conflicts of interest where the defense attorney is representing more than one defendant. This situation frequently occurs where the defendants are insured by the same malpractice insurance carrier which selects one attorney to represent all of its insured health care providers. This is not an uncommon situation and is permissible as long as there is no potential conflict between the defendants.

The lawyer may not represent multiple defendants, however, where there is a substantial discrepancy between their testimony or differences in the possibilities of settlement of claims. The lawyer is also prohibited from representing more than one defendant where the position of one client is incompatible with or adverse to the position of another client. The nurse defendant should be particularly alert to the possibility of conflicts in the latter situation because he or she may discern this type of conflict long before the attorney. If the attorney is not well versed in the fields of health care, nursing, or medicine, he or she may not be aware of incompatible positions until advised of them. Should a potential conflict develop after undertaking multiple representation in litigation, the attorney must withdraw from representing one of the parties to the conflict.

If problems develop in an attorney-client relationship, the nurse should discuss the problem with the attorney in an effort to resolve it. If the nurse is uncertain whether particular conduct is appropriate, the Model Code or Model Rules should provide guidance. These documents should be available at the local courthouse, bar association, or law library. If a problem cannot be resolved to the nurse's satisfaction, the professional relationship may be terminated. An exception to this may be in malpractice litigation where the attorney is selected and paid by the insurance company. This is discussed in a later chapter on insurance. Any violations of the standards of conduct applicable in the jurisdiction should be reported to the disciplinary committee for the bar association.

Recommendations and trends

Selection of legal counsel should be approached in a thoughtful and carefully considered manner. Effective legal representation is as important to one's legal well-being as proper health care is to one's physical well-being. Litigation may be protracted and will require close cooperation between attorney and client; therefore it is essential that communication be open and a two-way process.

Endnotes

1. For examples of recent disputes, see the following news articles in the AMERICAN JOURNAL OF NURSING: *Delaware RN's win 7-year battle for NP Role, Practice Standards,* 83 A.J.N. 119 (August 1983); *Missouri NP's win appeal in Medical Practice Suit,* 84 A.J.N. 111 (January 1984); *Delaware MDs attack standing orders,* 84 A.J.N. 1052 (August 1984); *NPs Battle to expand practice: Connecticut gets reimbursement,* 84 A.J.N. 1424 (November 1984); *Top Arkansas Court balks MDs move to curb Nurse Practitioners,* 85 A.J.N. 228 (March 1985); *Massachusetts MDs move to clamp limits on NPs,* 85 A.J.N. 315 (March 1985).
2. Any writings made contemporaneously or shortly after events at issue may be used in legal proceedings to refresh one's recollection and may also be received as evidence in some instances. Fed. R. Evid. 612, and 803(5).
3. American Nurses' Association, THE REGISTERED NURSE POPULATION, AN OVERVIEW, NATIONAL SAMPLE SURVEY OF REGISTERED NURSES (November 1980). The characteristics of the employed RN population included place of employment as Hospitals (65.6%), Nursing Homes (8%), Community Health (6.6%), Physician's Offices (5.7%), Nursing Education (3.5%), Occupational Health (2.3%), Private Duty Nursing (1.6%), Other (1.7%), Not Reported (.6%). There are more than 1.7 million registered nurses in the U.S.; 96% are female; the median age is 38.4 years. The median staff nurse salary is $18,708. Close to 1500 schools provide education programs for RNs. Three-year programs prepare 43.5%; associate programs prepare 34.4% and 20.7% have bachelor's degrees from 4-year colleges; 7% have masters' and doctors' degrees.
4. *See* Chapter 4 for further discussion of this topic.
5. The American Association of Nurse Attorneys (TAANA) was incorporated in 1982. TAANA's aims and purposes are to better nurse attorneys and to educate the public on matters of nursing, health care, and law. TAANA presently has over 300 members. The American Association of Nurse Attorneys Foundation begun in 1984 exists to educate the public and members of the legal and health professions about the impact of legal decisions and legislation upon the health care delivery system and its participants. For further information or referral to a practicing nurse attorney member, contact TAANA Headquarters, 113 W. Franklin Street, Baltimore, Maryland 21201 or call (301) 752-3318. *See, e.g.,*

TAANA, GUIDELINES FOR THE SELECTION OF COUNSEL FOR THE STATE NURSE'S ASSOCIATION (1985).

6. MARTINDALE-HUBBELL LAW DIRECTORY (1985); *See, also,* AMERICAN BAR ASSOCIATION, THE AMERICAN LAWYER—HOW TO CHOOSE AND USE ONE (1978); DIRECTORY OF BAR ASSOCIATION (current ed.); LAW AND BUSINESS DIRECTORY OF CORPORATE COUNSEL (current ed.); LAW AND BUSINESS DIRECTORY OF MAJOR U.S. LAW FIRMS (1984-85); and WHO'S WHO IN AMERICAN LAW (current ed.).
7. MODEL CODE OF PROFESSIONAL RESPONSIBILITY EC 2-8 (1969, as amended to 1980). (hereinafter cited as MODEL CODE) The disciplinary rules prohibit attorneys from personally soliciting employment or compensating a third party to solicit clients. MODEL CODE DR 2-103.
8. MODEL CODE, *supra,* note 7, DR 2-106 states that lawyers shall not ''charge or collect an illegal or clearly excessive fee.'' ''Clearly excessive'' is defined as a fee that ''when after'' review of the facts, a lawyer of ordinary prudence would be left with a definite and firm conviction that the fee is in excess of a reasonable fee.'' The box on p. 31 lists the factors that the MODEL CODE states must be considered in evaluating the reasonableness of a fee.
9. MODEL CODE, *supra,* note 7, EC 2-20.
10. In its new formulation of standards of professional conduct, the American Bar Association has officially recognized the attorney's affirmative duty to communicate with his or her client. MODEL RULES OF PROFESSIONAL CONDUCT Rule 1.4 (1983, as amended 1984) states: (a) A lawyer shall keep a client reasonably informed about the status of a matter and promptly comply with reasonable requests for information. (b) A lawyer shall explain a matter to the extent reasonably necessary to permit the client to make informed decisions regarding the representation. The comment directs that a ''lawyer may not withhold information to serve the lawyer's own interest or convenience.'' (hereinafter cited as MODEL RULES).
11. MODEL CODE, *supra,* note 7, DR 6-101(A)(3) requires that a lawyer not ''neglect a matter entrusted to him.'' MODEL RULES, *supra,* note 12, Rule 1.3 requires a lawyer to ''act with reasonable diligence and promptness in representing a client.''
12. Information revealed in confidence to one's attorney in the course of the professional relationship is confidential and may not be disclosed without the client's consent. MODEL CODE, *supra,* note 7, DR 4-101. Under very limited circumstances, generally related to the commission of a crime, a lawyer is permitted to disclose otherwise confidential information.
13. A lawyer is required to withdraw from representing a client if the client discharges him or her. MODEL CODE, *supra,* note 7, DR 2-110(B)(4). The lawyer is also required to withdraw where the client is attempting to use legal process to harass or injure another and if continued employment would result in violation of another disciplinary rule or the lawyer is physically or mentally incapacitated. DR 2-110(B)(1) to (B)(3).
14. MODEL RULES, *supra,* note 10.
15. MODEL CODE, *supra,* note 7, DR 5-101(A).
16. MODEL CODE, *supra,* note 7, DR 5-101(B).
17. MODEL CODE, *supra,* note 7, DR 5-104.

UNIT II

Civil Claims

Chapter 4

Professional negligence overview

Mary E. Kelly

This chapter provides an overview of negligence law applicable to the nurse acting in a professional capacity. The elements of a professional negligence claim and the methods of proof are first addressed. Next, special doctrines of negligence law and defenses to negligence actions against nurses are examined. Cases are analyzed throughout the chapter to illustrate these principles. Subsequent chapters apply these principles to particular practice areas.

The elements of a professional negligence claim

To establish a claim of professional negligence against the nurse, the plaintiff must introduce proof of the existence of the four elements necessary for a professional negligence action: duty, breach, proximate cause, and damages.[1] If any one of these elements is not established by the plaintiff, the negligence claim may be dismissed.

Proof of the nurse's standard of care is crucial to establishing the required elements of duty, breach of duty, and proximate cause. Professional negligence cases require expert testimony as to the duty of care, its breach, and its causal relationship to the injury. In ordinary negligence cases, expert testimony is not required to prove any of these elements.

Thus, the requirement of expert testimony is a buffer against baseless claims. The test of whether a nurse's conduct was, under the circumstances, sound nursing practice will be measured by the standards of the nursing professional and the judgment of the nurse's professional peers. The nurse is not afforded this protection when his or her negligent conduct is characterized as ordinary negligence.

Characterizing nursing negligence as professional negligence also brings the nurse within the protection of time limits placed on filing a malpractice claim. Ordinary negligence actions generally provide the plaintiff with a longer time to bring a claim against the defendant than is the case in professional malpractice cases. The limitations period or statute of limitations for malpractice claims has been shortened in several jurisdictions, thereby restricting, often to 1 year, the time within which an injured patient can sue. If the nurse is held to an ordinary negligence standard, this shorter malpractice or professional negligence statute of limitations would not apply.

Perhaps the most significant lost protection belongs to the patient; failure to recognize nursing malpractice as professional negligence may lead nurses to believe that they lack responsibility to act in certain situations where there is a professional duty to act. As the discussion of case law throughout this book clearly demonstrates, the courts expect nurses to fulfill a professional duty of care to the patient. For example, courts have taken a dim view of the nurse's defense that the physician "ordered me to do it,"[2] and they condemn a nurse's failure to report substandard care.

THE NURSE'S DUTY OF CARE TO THE PATIENT

The law imposes a higher duty of care upon those who hold themselves out as professionals. While a few jurisdictions may treat nursing malpractice as ordinary negligence[3] the recent trend is to hold the nurse to a professional standard of care.[4] This trend reflects the growing independence of the nursing profession.

Thus, one who undertakes to perform the services of a professional nurse—whether gratuitously[5] or for money—is under a legal duty to use that reasonable degree of skill, knowledge, and care ordinarily possessed by nurses acting under similar circumstances. In *Fraijo v. Hartland Hospital*[6] the California Appellate Court approved the following instruction setting forth the duty of a professional nurse with respect to the care of a patient[7]:

> It is the duty of one who undertakes to perform the service of a trained or graduate nurse to have the knowledge and skill ordinarily possessed, and to exercise the care and skill ordinarily used in like situations, by trained and skilled members of the nursing profession practicing their profession in the same or similar circumstances.

The Professional Standard of Care. This instruction reflects the legal principle that a nurse has the duty to perform nursing services according to a professional nursing standard of care. Under this standard, the adequacy of a nurse's performance is tested with reference to the performance of other nurses.[8]

> Today's nurses are held to strict professional standards of knowledge and performance, although there are still varying levels of competence relating to education and experience. . . . [There is] an increasing emphasis on higher standards for nurses; those with superior education often exercise independent judgement as to the care of patients whether in a hospital setting or elsewhere. While nurses traditionally have followed the instructions of attending physicians, doctors realistically have long relied on nurses to exercise independent judgment in many situations.[9]

The California Supreme Court recently affirmed this view in *Fein v. Permanente Medical Group.*[10] Noting recent amendments to the California Nurse Practice Act (NPA),[11] the Court held that "'examination' or 'diagnosis' of a patient cannot in all circumstances be said as a matter of law—to be a function reserved to physicians, rather than registered nurses or nurse practitioners."[12] Thus, the court stated, a professional nursing standard of care, not a physician standard of care, is the yardstick against which to measure a nurse's conduct.

Where, however, the nurse's conduct exceeds the scope of practice authorized by the NPA, the nurse may be held to the higher standard of care required to perform a particular function, even if registered nurses do not typically perform that function.[13] For example, in *Thompson v. Brent,*[14] the nurse's removal of a cast with a Stryker saw that resulted in injury was judged by the applicable standard recommended for this procedure because the nurse assumed this duty and performed it in a negligent fashion.

This case underscores the principle that nurses who assume responsibility for tasks that require more skill and education must have the requisite skill and education to perform the task according to a professional standard of care. Although the performance of that task will be measured against that of a reasonably prudent nurse,[15] the reasonably prudent nurse is expected to know the limits of his or her experience, skill, and education.[16] As the Missouri Supreme Court stated in *Sermchief v. Gonzales*[17]:

> The broadening of the field of practice of the nursing profession authorized by the legislature and here recognized by the Court carries with it the profession's responsibility for continuing high educational standards and the individual nurse's responsibility to conduct herself or himself in a professional manner. The hallmark of a professional is knowing the limits of one's professional knowledge.

Proof of the Standard of Care. Since the reasonably prudent nurse is the yardstick against which the defendant nurse's conduct is measured,[18] in order to win a case against the nurse, the plaintiff, as a general rule, must introduce proof of this standard of care at trial. In other words, the patient must prove what duty of care was owed by the nurse. There are exceptions to this rule. The methods of proof and the instances where such proof is not required are summarized in the box on p. 41.

Methods of Expert Proof. Where a professional standard of care must be proven, there are various methods used in conjunction with expert testimony. These methods are examined next.

Expert Testimony. In general, the standard of care in a professional nursing negligence action must be established by expert testimony.[19] This does not necessarily mean that a nurse must testify to the standard of care. In some jurisdictions, physicians may properly testify to the proper standard of nursing care.[20] In other jurisdictions, the opposite rule exists.[21]

At least one case holds that a nurse may be an expert in nonnursing malpractice cases. In *Maloney v. Wake*

EXPERT PROOF	
Methods of Expert Proof	*Where Expert Proof is Unnecessary*
Expert testimony	Legal duty imposed by court
Documentary evidence: journals and treatises	Nontechnical injury within the jury's common knowledge
Statutes, administrative codes, and hospital policy/regulation	Jurisdiction does not recognize nursing negligence as professional negligence

Hospital System, Inc.[22] the North Carolina Appellate Court reversed a judgment because the trial court had refused to allow a nurse to testify as an expert in intravenous (IV) therapy. The trial court reasoned that a nurse lacks a medical license. On appeal, the court of review rejected this reasoning, and ruled that a nurse who possesses experience in IV therapy may testify on the subject as an expert witness. The appellate court found that, "[t]he role of the nurse is critical in providing a high standard of health care in modern medicine. [The nurse's] expertise is different from, but no less exalted than that of the physician."[23]

As the case law throughout the chapters illustrates, physicians frequently testify to the nurse's standard of care. The better practice, and a position adopted by The American Association of Nurse Attorneys, is that professional nurses should be the expert witness who testifies to the standard of professional nursing care in a nursing malpractice case.

The competency of an expert witness to testify as to his or her opinion is tested by the sufficiency of the witness's knowledge of the subject matter. Once the trial court has determined that the witness is competent to testify as an expert on a subject, the witness' testimony is admitted at trial; the degree or depth of the expert's knowledge only affects how much weight or credence the jury should give the testimony.[24]

Whether the expert must come from the same locality, a similar locality, or anywhere in the nation depends on the jurisdiction. Early cases held that allowance had to be made for the type of communication in which a provider carries on his or her practice. Consequently, a country physician could not be expected to have the same library or facilities or opportunities for learning as those practicing in large cities.[25]

This "same locality" rule eventually was deemed too narrow due to improved facilities of communication, literature, and the like, and the courts allowed the expert to testify to the standard in a similar community. Some courts have held that a national standard of care applies because certification of the practitioner depends on nationwide standards. An expert qualified in the specialty may testify to the standard of another practitioner in the same specialty even though the expert resides elsewhere.[26]

Although obtaining an expert nurse witness may be difficult for the plaintiff, the failure to have expert testimony will not necessarily mean that a nursing negligence action will fail. In many jurisdictions, the plaintiff may be able to call the defendant nurse as a "hostile" or adverse witness.[27] The defendant nurse may then be questioned about textbooks or learned treatises in nursing, and if the nurse's answer is in conflict with the text, the text may be read by the opposing attorney to the jury to impeach the defendant nurse's testimony. In this manner, the standard of care will be established by the defendant nurse's own testimony.

Documentary Evidence. Documentary evidence may also tend to establish the nurse's standard of care. The American Nurses' Association's Standards of Practice, the Joint Commission on the Accreditation of Hospitals' standards, the hospital's own policy and protocol, and nursing journal articles are examples of such evidence.[28] In *Czubinsky v. Doctors Hospital,*[29] the court looked to the hospital's written policy to determine the reasonableness of a surgical nurse's conduct in leaving a patient unattended.

Statutes and Administrative Codes. The standard of care of a reasonable nurse may also be determined by reference to a given state's NPA.[30] In addition, reporting statutes, such as mandatory child abuse reporting laws, and administrative codes or regulations may establish the nurse's standard of care.[31]

Instances Where Expert Proof is Not Necessary. Expert testimony and other methods of proving the standard of care of a nurse are not always necessary. The instances in which such proof is not necessary are examined next.

Legal Duty. On occasion, the courts have determined, as a matter of law, that a duty to perform a particular treatment or test exists. The court balances the burden of preventing the injury against the severity of the injury and the likelihood that the injury would occur without the preventative treatment or test. If, on balance, the risk of injury without the test or treatment is substantial, the injury itself is severe, and the burden of preventing it by the test or treatment is small, the court may determine that the provider has an absolute or legal duty to perform the treatment or test. When this occurs, the plaintiff does not need expert testimony to prove the provider's duty or breach.

Helling v. Carey[32] illustrates this rule. The Washington Supreme Court held that an ophthalmologist has a duty, as a matter of law, to test for glaucoma even though the patient was in her early twenties. The patient plaintiff complained of nearsightedness repeatedly. Eventually it was determined that she had glaucoma. The court ruled that even though expert testimony established that the risk of a patient in her twenties developing glaucoma is rare and therefore ophthalmologists only test for glaucoma in patients much older, the physician was liable as a matter of law. Since testing for glaucoma is relatively easy and not costly, and the disease has serious consequences, the court determined that a legal duty to test for glaucoma should be imposed.

Similarly, in *Call v. Kezirian,*[33] the court held that an attending physician is under a legal duty to test a middle-aged woman's fetus for Down's syndrome and to advise her of the results of the test. The decision to seek an abortion or permit the fetus to develop to term must be left to the mother.

Nontechnical Injury. Another instance where expert testimony is not required is when the injury is nontechnical and within the layperson's—the members of the jury—common knowledge. If, however, the negligence relates to a professional skill, then expert testimony is needed to establish the duty of care.[34] For example, in *Cramer v. Theda Clark Memorial Hospital,*[35] the court held that there was no need for expert testimony on the need for restraints where a postoperative patient broke a hip after a nurse had loosened his restraints so that he could eat.

In *Karrington v. Nazareth Covenant & Academy,*[36] the court held that expert testimony is not required where a practitioner's lack of skill is manifest to the lay observer or when the acts complained of could be regarded as negligent by applying common knowledge. *Karrington* involved a patient who, after removal of a drain from the site of gallbladder surgery, complained of pain 13 times throughout a 10½ hour period and asked the defendant nurse to notify the physician. The patient also requested the presence of a priest because he believed he was dying. When the physician arrived, the patient was in critical condition.

Because there was evidence of only one contact between the patient and the nurse, the hospital was found negligent. The court ruled that although expert testimony is normally required, the rule did not apply where, as in *Karrington*, the medical procedures or lack of skills are manifest to the lay observer, or when acts complained of can be regarded as negligent by applying common knowledge and experience.

The Illinois Appellate Court has determined that an injury resulting from a nurse's alleged negligence in injecting a hypodermic needle is such an instance. The court held that expert testimony would be required in the case.[37]

Presumption of Negligence. Another instance when expert testimony is not required is when a presumption of negligence is applicable. There are two principal presumptions in the health care context: violation of statute and *res ipsa loquitor* both of which are more fully discussed under the Special Doctrines in Negligence section of this chapter.

When either of these presumption applies, the need for the plaintiff to introduce expert testimony is eliminated, unless the defendant introduces expert testimony as a defense. In this instance, the plaintiff may either choose to rest on the presumption or to introduce expert testimony to refute the defense testimony. The factual issue as to whose evidence is more persuasive is then decided by the jury.

Nonprofessional Status. In those jurisdictions that do not recognize nursing negligence as professional negligence, expert testimony will not be necessary.[38]

BREACH OF THE NURSE'S DUTY OF CARE

Professional negligence is the failure to do what the reasonably prudent nurse would do under the same or similar circumstances.[39] Thus, an act or omission of the nurse may constitute a breach of the standard or duty of care.

Whether a duty has been breached depends on whether the risk of injury from acting in a certain way or failing to act in a given situation was foreseeable.[40] If the risk of injury was foreseeable, the conduct, to be negligent, must be unreasonable. Virtually all human acts carry some recognizable but remote possibility of harm to another. This does not mean that the action taken was unreasonable. Actions that must be guarded against are those that society, in general, considers sufficiently great to demand caution.[41]

This in turn depends on the gravity of possible harm when balanced against the burden of precaution necessary to prevent it. As the risk of harm increases, conduct that risks that harm becomes more unreasonable, especially if the burden of guarding against it is relatively minimal. The courts also consider the utility of the conduct and alternative courses open to the nurse.[42]

A nurse exercising independent judgment under certain circumstances will not be liable simply because his or her efforts prove unsuccessful or an error in judgment is made.[43] Similarly, where more than one nursing intervention is recognized and none of them is used exclusively and uniformly by all nurses of good standing, a nurse is not liable if, in exercising his or her best judgment, the nurse selected one of the approved methods that later turns out to be a wrong selection or one not favored by certain other nurses.[44]

The breach of a nurse's standard of care is proven in the same manner as is the duty of care. Expert testimony, written hospital procedures, and standards of practice may be evidence of a breach of the standard of care. For example, in the *Czubinsky* case mentioned earlier, the circulating room nurse left her patient unattended to assist the surgeon with another surgery. The patient suffered cardiac arrest. The court found the nurse's actions to be abandonment and in direct violation of the hospital's written policy, which required the circulating nurse to remain with the patient. The fact that the surgeon insisted that she leave the patient was no defense.[45]

Although a hospital's rules, regulations, and policies may establish a breach of the nurse's duty of care, evidence that these were followed does not necessarily establish that the defendant met the proper standard of care. In *Vanstreenburg v. Lawrence & Memorial Hospital,*[46] the court rejected the defendant hospital's argument that its policies alone established the proper standard of care. The hospital had no psychiatric unit and admitted a psychiatric patient to a private room. The patient seemed to improve, but on the third day, she jumped or fell from a window.

The plaintiff argued she should have been placed in a security room with mesh on the window. The hospital attempted to prove it was proper to place the patient in a private room by introducing its own rules, but the court rejected its position. The court's ruling is logical because otherwise a defendant could avoid liability by establishing compliance with rules that fall below the accepted standard of practice. In other words, a nurse does not meet his or her standard of care simply by following hospital policy; moreover, there is no duty to follow an unsound policy or procedure.

When the nurse's alleged negligent conduct involves professional skill, expert testimony is generally required to establish that the nurse breached a duty of care to the patient.[47] When expert testimony is necessary in a nursing malpractice action, the better practice is for a nurse expert witness to testify to the breach of the duty of care. This is the position taken by the The American Association of Nurse Attorneys.[48]

There are exceptions to the expert testimony requirement even where professional skill is questioned. For example, the defendant nurse's own testimony may establish the standard of care and the fact that it was not met.[49] Expert testimony as to the breach of the standard of care also is not necessary where the presumption of negligence is applicable.

In addition, certain types of injuries do not require expert testimony because the kind of injury and how it occurs is within the layperson's common knowledge. Different jurisdictions have reached different conclusions as to what injuries are common and need not be proven by expert testimony.

Carter v. Anderson Memorial Hospital[50] illustrates the South Carolina Appellate Court's approach. A student nurse caused a portable x-ray machine to fall on a patient's abdomen and left hand after he had been hospitalized for hemorrhage and had 10% of his stomach surgically removed.

After the accident, the patient began again to hemorrhage, which necessitated a second surgery. The patient testified that he felt fine after his first surgery, but that after the accident he felt pain and weakness and again began vomiting blood. The medical and nursing experts testified that the second surgery was not necessitated by the accident. They attributed the new bleeding to abdominal distress caused by removal of the nasogastric tube. Although the x-ray film seemed to confirm this fact, the jury found for the patient.

On appeal, defendants argued that the plaintiff had failed to meet his burden of proof because he had no expert testimony linking the accident to the injury. The appellate court disagreed, stating that it only took common sense to deduce cause and effect where a patient is fine before an accident and complains of a condition on the day of the accident and that it occurred as a result of the accident. Under such circumstances, expert testimony was not necessary.

Forlano v. Hughes[51] illustrates the Massachusetts Supreme Court's different approach. The court ruled that expert testimony was necessary in a case involving myelography. The court reversed a plaintiff's verdict because there was no evidence that if the dye entered the wrong area, it did so because of the defendant's negligence. The court cautioned that only the exceptional case will warrant an instruction that the jury may rely on its common knowledge and experience without the aid of expert testimony to determine whether a nurse's or physician's conduct is in violation of the special duty the law imposes.

New York also seems to follow this view. In *DeFalco v. Long Island College Hospital,*[52] the appellate court affirmed the trial court's setting aside of a jury verdict for a 75-year-old man who lost an eye after cataract surgery. Both the surgeon and the hospital were found liable by the jury. The hospital's liability is discussed in the Proximate Cause section that follows.

The plaintiff called the surgeon who performed the cataract surgery as his only expert witness. The surgeon noted that the surgery was uneventful except for a drop of blood that remained in the eye, a condition known as hyphema, which is a normal risk of surgery. Generally the hyphema is absorbed in 1 or 2 days. The court held that the sophisticated science of cataract surgery is beyond the ken of ordinary laypersons, and to prove that the hyphema caused the eye loss would require expert testimony. Thus the trial court properly set aside the jury verdict against the surgeon.

Tennessee has also refused to apply the common knowledge rule except in cases with the most obvious form of negligence. In *Tucker v. Metro Gov. of Nashville,*[53] the court of appeals held that expert testimony was required to establish negligence in a case where a man who had been placed unrestrained on a stretcher while in a catatonic state bolted out of the emergency room. He was killed by an automobile. The court reasoned that the proper treatment of a patient with serious mental problems who is in a catatonic state is not within the ordinary knowledge of the jury.

PROXIMATE CAUSE

The plaintiff must also introduce proof that the nurse's alleged negligent conduct was the proximate cause of his or her injury. In essence, proximate cause is a two-pronged analysis: is the conduct the cause-in-fact of the injury; and is the conduct so closely connected with the result and of such significance that the law is justified in imposing liability.[54]

Cause-in-fact is a matter of what actually happened. An act or omission is not regarded as a cause of an injury if the injury would have occurred without the act or omission. There are two principal formulations of the cause-in-fact test: the ''but-for'' test and the ''substantial factor'' test.

The but-for test of causation requires that the injury could not have occurred but for the defendant's conduct. In other words, ''[t]he defendant's conduct is not a cause of an event if the event would have occurred without it.''[55] This formulation of the cause-in-fact test works well when a single actor or cause operates to bring about an event.

Where, however, two persons cause an injury and either one of them standing alone would have been sufficient to cause the result, the but-for test is an inadequate cause-in-fact test. Consequently, some jurisdictions, such as Kansas,[56] have adopted the substantial factor test. Under this formulation the defendant's conduct is the cause of an event if it is a material and substantial factor in bringing about the injury.[57]

The second prong of proximate cause is really a question of ''whether the policy of the law will extend responsibility for the conduct to the consequences which in fact have occurred.''[58] Limits must be placed upon how far causation will be extended back in time for purposes of imposing liability because ''in a philosophical sense, the consequences of an act go forward to eternity, and the causes of an event go back to the discovery of America and beyond.''[59]

Foreseeability of risk of injury is the test employed to determine where to draw the proximate cause line. This, in turn, is connected to whether the defendant was under a duty to protect the patient against the injury that did in fact occur and whether that injury was foreseeable. Although this formulation of the test may seem incomprehensible, perhaps an illustration will demystify the verbiage.

A nurse has difficulty catheterizing a female patient prior to a surgeon's examination of her abdominal wound. This delays the examination by the surgeon. Upon examination, the surgeon realizes that the catheter has been inserted into the patient's anus. Angered, the surgeon clasps the tubing and pulls the catheter out, dragging the tubing across the wound of the patient. The patient later develops a serious infection.

Is the nurse the cause-in-fact of the infection? Under both the but for and the substantial factor formulations of the cause-in-fact test, the nurse's conduct is a cause in the patient's infection. But for the negligent placement of the catheter, the infection would not have occurred.

The nurse's conduct also can be characterized as a material and substantial factor in producing the infection.

Nevertheless, the proximate cause analysis does not stop with a determination of cause-in-fact. The concepts of duty and foreseeability must be addressed. Was the nurse under a legal duty to protect the patient from the harm that thereby resulted—that is, protect the patient from the event that did in fact occur? Stated another way, was it reasonably foreseeable that if the nurse wrongly inserted the catheter, then the surgeon would drag the tubing across the patient's abdominal wound? Although one may be able to attribute the nurse's conduct as a cause in fact of the injury, legal policy—foreseeability—the second prong of the proximate cause analysis, limits liability in this context.

Some jurisdictions would characterize the surgeon's conduct as an intervening supervening cause and would impose liability on the surgeon. Others would hold that the nurse's conduct was not the proximate cause of the injury. Still others might apportion fault between the two actors.

In general, expert testimony is required to prove proximate cause in a malpractice claim. For example, in *Lenger v. Physician's Hospital, Inc.*,[60] the court held that a registered nurse was not liable for a patient's condition that had worsened in the absence of evidence that the nurse's conduct had proximately caused the worsening of the patient's condition. The nurse, in violation of physician's orders that the patient should not have oral intake, gave the patient solid food. A second surgery 8 days after the abdominal surgery showed the patient's condition was worsening. There was no evidence, however, to establish that the feeding made the patient's condition worsen, and the nurse was deemed not liable.

Another example is *Plutshock v. University of Minnesota Hospital*.[61] The court held that a nurse was not negligent for holding a child in a flexed position while the physician performed lumbar puncture to diagnose meningitis. The child afterwards suffered a cardiac arrest and brain damage. The plaintiff failed to introduce expert testimony indicating that the nurse's conduct could have directly caused the child's injuries.

Occasionally, the courts hold that the injury and its cause are within the jury's common knowledge and thus no expert testimony on this issue is necessary. Once again, the jurisdictions reach different conclusions as to when proximate cause must be proven by expert testimony. *DeFalco v. Long Island College Hospital*[62] illustrates New York's approach.

In *DeFalco*, the plaintiff was a 75-year-old man suing for the loss of his eye following cataract surgery. In spite of drug therapy, the patient developed an infection, which was discovered 7 days after surgery. The infection was caused by enterobacteria, found in the gastrointestinal tract, and *Staphylococcus aureus*, an airborne organism. The plaintiff based his claim against the hospital on the alleged negligence of a nurse who dropped an eye patch on the floor but nevertheless applied the patch directly to the eye. He argued that it is a matter of common knowledge that such an act is unsanitary and obviously not in accordance with good nursing practice.

The court acknowledged that the act of placing a presumably soiled eye patch over the patient's eye, "by its very nature, bespeaks improper treatment and malpractice."[63] The plaintiff, however, offered no expert testimony that the presumably unsterile eye patch was the cause-in-fact of the injury. Expert testimony, the court stated, was needed to prove that the presumably soiled eye patch carried enterobacteria and *S. aureus* germs from the floor to the patient's eye, which in turn caused the infection. Since the plaintiff failed to establish the causal connection between the nurse's act and the plaintiff's injury by competent expert testimony, he could not win his case against the hospital.

DAMAGES

An essential element of every professional negligence action is proof of actual loss or damage that is proximately caused by the professional's negligent conduct.[64] The threat or possibility of future harm is not sufficient and would result in a defense verdict.[65] Injured persons and, under certain circumstances, their family members may recover damages.

The time when damage manifests itself is important for purposes of the statute of limitations. In general, the limitations period—the time within which the plaintiff must bring a suit or lose the claim forever—does not begin running until the damage has occurred.[66]

Of course, if there is no damage, there can be no recovery under a negligence theory. Expert testimony as to the damage element is not necessary, although it may be helpful. In *Capelouto v. Kaiser Foundation Hospitals*,[67] the California Supreme Court held that an infant plaintiff can recover damages for pain and suffering as the result of a negligently caused injury. Lay testimony may be admitted and may provide evidence of pain and suffering in infants, as well as in adults. Even if there is no specific evidence of pain and suffering, the jury may infer that there was pain and suffering, so long as the injury is such that the jury, in its common experience, knows that such an injury is normally accompanied by pain.

The Injured Patient's Damages. Property loss and personal injury are both recoverable in negligence actions. These damages seek to compensate the victim and make him or her whole for pain and suffering and economic losses resulting from an injury. In some jurisdictions, a plaintiff may recover for loss of earning capacity even though he or she has not been employed for a number of years.[68] Generally, compensatory damages are now largely a creature of statute.

In addition, certain family members witnessing another family member's injuries may recover damages for the negligent infliction of emotional distress.[69] Several courts require, however, that the person asserting a claim for negligent infliction of emotional distress manifest some physical symptoms of injury as a result of witnessing the incident. Other jurisdictions, such as California, have abandoned this requirement.[70]

Since 1946, courts have recognized a child's right of recovery for injuries caused in the uterus as long as the child is born alive.[71] By statute, California permits a child to recover damages for prenatal injuries, including medical malpractice, if the child is born alive.[72]

The Noninjured Person's Right To Recover Damages. The death of an injured person may terminate the existing claim and prevent recovery by that person's estate or personal representative.[73] On the other hand, the cause of action or claim may survive the person's death and pass to that person's estate. Several states have "survival statutes," which provide that certain claims survive the injured person's death.[74]

Some states provide by statute for survival of certain actions and additionally have, by statute, created a new cause of action for the members of the victim's family for loss of economic benefits (future economic earnings) and loss of affection. These are called "wrongful death" statutes.[75]

Virtually all states provide a cause of action for prenatal injuries resulting in the wrongful death of a child born alive.[76] More recently, courts have expanded the right to recover for the wrongful death of a stillborn child.[77]

Apportionment Of Damages. Where two persons negligently cause another's injury, and the damage attributable to each is divisible, damages will be apportioned between them.[78] For example, if the nurse's negligence causes a patient a knee injury and a physician's negligence causes an arm injury, the damages from each injury are somewhat easily ascertainable. Because the damage from each is divisible, damages may be apportioned so that the nurse pays for the damage to the knee and the physician pays for the damage to the arm.

Where, however, such division is impossible (for example because the person is dead), each defendant is entirely liable for the amount of damages. Of course, the injured person can only have one recovery. Nevertheless, where two or more persons act in concert to bring about a result, each is liable for the entire amount of damages.[79]

SPECIAL NEGLIGENCE DOCTRINES

Vicarious Liability

Master/servant or respondeat superior
Independent contractor vs. agent
Captain of the ship or borrowed servant
Ostensible agency

Presumptions

Res ipsa loquitor
Violation of statute or
Presumption of negligence or
Negligence per se

Special doctrines of negligence

Negligence law has developed certain doctrines that allow certain classes of persons to be liable for another's negligent conduct, ease the burden of proof with respect to causation, and allow inferences of negligence to be drawn under certain circumstances. These special rules, summarized in the box above, are examined next.

VICARIOUS LIABILITY

The law imputes negligence to certain persons who have not committed any negligent act because of their relationship with a negligently acting person. Under these circumstances, A is negligent and B is not, but because of some relationship between A and B, the law deems B liable for A's conduct. This is true even though B played no part in the negligent conduct, did nothing to encourage it, and may have done everything possible to prevent it.[80] This concept is sometimes called imputed negligence, captain of the ship, borrowed servant, or "respondeat superior." All of these doctrines are variations on vicarious liability.

The rationale for imposing vicarious liability is a rule of policy—a deliberate allocation of risk.[81] For example, the negligence of an employee is attributed to the employer as a cost of doing business. The so-called master-servant relationship historically compelled this equitable result. The traditional definition of a servant is one who is employed to perform services for another, whose physical conduct in the performance of his or her duties is controlled or is subject to a right of control by the master.[82] Factors considered by the courts in determining control or right to control include the extent to which the employer controls the details of work, whether work of this type is usually something supervised by an employer, whether the employer supplies the place and instrumentalities of work, and the method of payment, among others.[83]

Master-Servant Theory. Once it is determined that the worker is a servant, the master or employer becomes liable for the employee's negligence. On the other hand, if the worker is an independent contractor, the employer is not liable for the worker's negligence unless the employer was negligent in selecting the independent contractor or in some way ratified or authorized the negligent conduct.[84]

The employer's vicarious liability extends to all tortious conduct of the employee that is within the scope of the employment. The employee's conduct is within the scope of his or her employment if it is of the kind that he or she is employed to perform, occurs substantially within the authorized limits of time and space, and is actuated, at least in part, by a purpose to serve the employer.[85] Thus, hospitals are vicariously liable for their nurses' negligent acts committed during and in the scope of their employment.

Hooks, III v. Southern California Permanente Medical Group,[86] illustrates this principle. A child born to a woman who was murdered by an obstetrical nurse sued the nurse's employer, Kaiser Foundation Hospital, for negligence. Prior to the time when the obstetrical nurse began working for the hospital, she met the plaintiff child's mother, Ms. Viramontes, and they had a social relationship. After Ms. Viramontes became pregnant with the plaintiff, she asked the nurse's help in inducing labor.

Ms. Viramontes requested the nurse's help because of her experience with labor delivery and the fact that she knew the nurse worked for the hospital. Ms. Viramontes knew that the nurse would have access to the necessary instruments to induce labor, and she called the nurse at her home several times requesting her help. The nurse agreed to help her only because she could procure the necessary items.

The nurse, however, never represented to Ms. Viramontes that her services relating to inducing labor were related to her employment or were authorized by the hospital. Further, Ms. Viramontes was never a patient at the hospital.

During the inducement of labor, the nurse and Ms. Viramontes began arguing over Viramontes' relationship with the nurse's boyfriend. The nurse killed Ms. Viramontes by slashing her throat. She then delivered the baby, the plaintiff in the case, by cesarean section. The child later sued the nurse and the hospital for the wrongful death of his mother.

As a result of pretrial investigation, the plaintiff learned that while the nurse was employed with the hospital several months before the killing, the nurse delivered another woman's child, unassisted by anyone, substituted a dead fetus, and reported a stillbirth. Hospital records reflected that until the nurse came on duty and began assisting, the labor was proceeding normally with normal fetal heart rate, and it should have been a routine delivery. When the physician came to certify the death of the fetus, he noticed that the umbilical cord had been cut. This, under the hospital policy, was left for the attending physician to do. Nevertheless, no report and no investigation were undertaken. The nurse began raising the stolen child in her home.

The hospital argued to the court that the case should be directed in its favor because Ms. Viramontes was never a patient of the hospital and therefore it owed no duty of care to Ms. Viramontes. The plaintiff argued that because the hospital employed the nurse and the nurse was an employee whose dangerous conduct needed to be controlled, the hospital owed Ms. Viramontes and persons like her a duty of care.

The court rejected the argument because the hospital had no reason to know of the nurse's social relationship with Ms. Viramontes. She was never a patient, and the killing did not occur in the context of the nurse's authorized employment.

The court also refused to accept the plaintiff's argument that, had the hospital conducted an investigation into the earlier baby-snatching incident, as it should have, it would have learned of the nurse's bizarre characteristics and could have protected pregnant women like Ms. Viramontes. There was no evidence, however, that the results of an investigation—discovery of the baby-snatching incident—could have made the hospital aware that the nurse might later kill Ms. Viramontes over an argument about her boyfriend while inducing her labor at home. In other words, even if the hospital learned of the incident, that fact would not have made the later killing incident at Ms. Viramontes' home foreseeable.

Since there was no way that the plaintiff could establish a basis for imposing vicarious liability on the hospital for the nurse's actions, the hospital was not an appropriate defendant in the case.

Independent Contractor-Agency Theories. Several doctrines have been articulated by the courts concerning the hospital's liability for physicians who are not employed by the hospital but are on staff and treat patients at the hospital. As a general rule, such physicians are considered independent contractors and the hospital is not liable for their negligent conduct.[87] Similarly, the physician is not generally responsible for a nurse's negligence unless the physician had some control over the conduct or was negligent in ordering the nursing action.

Exceptions to these general rules have been created by the courts where the facts suggest that the physician "borrowed" the help of a nurse from the hospital or the physician was acting as the agent of the hospital. Where someone is acting as another's agent, vicarious liability for the agent's negligence should be imposed upon the principal, the person who hired the agent. This is especially true where the agent is acting with apparent authority of the principal. The common law has developed several doctrines that, for purposes of imposing liability, imply an agency relationship between a hospital and a physician or a surgeon and surgical nurses employed by the hospital. Examples of these doctrines, called the captain of the ship or the borrowed servant doctrine and the doctrine of ostensible agency, follow.

Captain of the Ship or Borrowed Servant. This doctrine is typically applied in surgery cases. The assisting physicians and nurses employed by the hospital become the temporary servants or agents of the surgeon, and the surgeon is deemed liable for their negligent acts on a respondent superior–captain of the ship theory.[88] The doctrine is founded on the physician's power and resulting duty to direct nurses under his or her supervision. Thus, a physician's reliance, "no matter how reasonable, on hospital nursing procedures does not extinguish [the doctor's] liability."[89] Under this doctrine, the physician is not relieved of liability because, for example, the nurses count the sponges.

In this context, the nurses are viewed by the law as the physician's temporary servants subject to the physician's control and direction. Thus, both the hospital and the surgeon will be held liable for the negligent acts of surgical nurses.[90] The surgeon will not, however, be found liable under this theory if the nursing errors are committed at a time when the surgeon is not present or not in control.[91]

Similarly, the doctrine does not apply where another specialist in the operating room, such as an anesthesiologist, is negligent. Because the anesthesiologist is a specialist and his or her authority in that field is supreme to that of the surgeon, the surgeon cannot exert control and supervision over the anesthesiologist. Consequently, the surgeon will not be deemed liable for the anesthesiologist's negligence under the captain of the ship or borrowed servant doctrine.

Ostensible Agency. The hospital may still be found liable for the acts of someone who is not an employee of the hospital but rather is an independent contractor who practices at the hospital, if the circumstances warrant implying a general representation to the public that the practitioner was an employee of the hospital and the patient relied on that fact in submitting to care. Unless there is evidence that the patient knew or should have known that the practitioner was *not* an employee when treatment was given, the law will imply an agency relationship between the hospital and the practitioner, and the hospital may also be found liable. This concept is known as ostensible agency.[92]

Because ostensible agency is implied by the law, the plaintiff does not have to prove a true agency relationship existed between the treating health care provider and the hospital. The plaintiff need not prove that there was any direct representation to him or her concerning the provider's status as an employee. Ostensible agency is applied most often by the courts in the emergency room context. There, even though a physician is not employed by the hospital, the court has found hospital liability based on ostensible agency because the physician was on the hospital staff and worked on an on-call basis.[93]

Although untested to date, by analogy it seems that this agency principle would be applicable to nurses hired as independent contractors, such as nurse midwives and nurse practitioners, and perhaps to those owners of nurse-managed centers who maintain the hospital's home health care on a contractual referral basis. Whether the court will imply an agency relationship and make the hospital liable is always determined on a case-by-case basis because it is the circumstances surrounding the treatment that may warrant implying a general representation to the public.

PRESUMPTIONS

Procedural rules have developed throughout the history of the common law, and particulary in the tort law area, concerning the proof or evidence to sustain a claim or a defense. In civil cases the plaintiff need only prove the claim beyond a preponderance of the evidence. This is called the burden of persuasion, and it remains with the plaintiff and does not shift to the defendant in a civil case.

The burden of persuasion is different from the burden of proof. Recall that the plaintiff must introduce proof of each element of the claim; in negligence cases, this includes duty, breach, proximate cause, and damages. If the plaintiff fails to introduce evidence on any of the elements, the court must direct a verdict for the defendant.

Once, however, the plaintiff has met the burden of introducing proof of the claim, the burden of introducing evidence to the contrary shifts to the defendant. If the defendant fails to contradict this proof or offer some affirmative defense justifying or excusing the action proven, the court must direct a verdict in favor of the plaintiff. When the defendant meets this burden, however, the only question is which side's proof is more likely than not true. That is generally a jury determination.

There are procedural rules of law called presumptions that affect the burden of introducing evidence. These presumptions require the other side to produce further evidence, or the court must direct a verdict against the other side. Once persuasive evidence is introduced, the presumption is not applied and the case is decided on whatever inferences can be drawn from the facts.[94]

Res Ipsa Loquitor. While it is true that there must be proof from which a reasonable person could determine that one version is more probable than not—that is, the proof cannot be speculative—this does not mean that every case requires eyewitnesses of the defendant's conduct. Negligence, like other cases, can be proved by circumstantial evidence. Circumstantial evidence is "evidence of one fact, or a set of facts, from which the existence of the fact to be determined [for example, someone's negligence] may reasonably be inferred."[95] For example, it may be reasonable to infer, from skid marks or other traces, that someone drove an automobile at an excessive speed.

Res ipsa loquitor is a kind of circumstantial evidence that gives rise to an inference or presumption of negligence. Literally, the phrase means "the thing speaks for itself."[96] Generally, when the three conditions for application of the principle are met, the law infers or presumes the fact that the defendant's negligence proximately caused the injury.

These three conditional facts are: (1) the injury must be of a kind that ordinarily does not occur in the absence of someone's negligence; (2) the injury must be caused by an agency or instrumentality within the exclusive control of the defendant; and (3) the event or injury must not be due to any voluntary action or contribution on the part of the plaintiff.[97] Some jurisdictions have imposed a fourth requirement: the evidence as to the truth of what really occurred must be more accessible to the defendant than the plaintiff.[98] The courts reason that the nature of the injury in these circumstances is within the jurors' common knowledge.

If the plaintiff establishes the basic facts of the *res ipsa loquitor* presumption and the defendant does not contest the existence of these basic facts but disputes existence of the presumed fact—that the defendant's negligence was the proximate cause of the plaintiff's injury—the defendant only has to introduce evidence sufficient to support a finding that the defendant was not negligent or that any negligence on the defendant's part was not the proximate cause of the injury. The defendant can also dispute the existence of the three foundational facts. For example, the defendant may introduce expert testimony to the fact that the injury occurs even when someone is not negligent.

This was the approach taken by a defendant surgeon in *Galloway v. Ioppolo*.[99] The plaintiff underwent surgery for anterior cervical decompression and fusion, and he suffered respiratory arrest and died. The autopsy reported that bleeding at the surgical site created pressure causing the trachea to collapse. Both the anesthesiologist and the surgeon testified that their procedures were uneventful. The surgeon claimed he did not cut any large vessels that needed ligation with sutures.

Two physicians who served on the hospital's panel to review the matter suggested that there was bleeding from a cut to a small artery over a prolonged period of time. Small cuts associated with electrocoagulation, they noted, had been reported in the literature as easily opening when the patient moves. Both physicians also testified that post-operative bleeding is a known possible complication of any surgery and not necessarily negligence. The court held that *res ipsa loquitor* would not apply since surgical bleeding, the cause of the injury, can occur in the absence of negligence.

The presumption also does not apply and is said to disappear if a defendant offers sufficient evidence of non-negligence or that the negligence did not proximately cause the injury. The plaintiff must prove by a preponderance of the evidence that the facts introduced establish that the injury was proximately caused by the defendant.[100]

Res ipsa loquitor has been applied where a patient suffered wrist-drop immediately after an injection performed by a nurse administered under physician's orders.[101] The doctrine is, however, most often invoked and applied in surgical cases. Perhaps one of the most famous applications of the doctrine is found in *Ybarra v. Spangard*.[102] There, the California Supreme Court held that where a plaintiff receives unusual injuries while unconscious and in the course of medical treatment, all those defendants who had any control over his or her body or control over any instrumentalities that might have caused the injuries may properly be called upon under the doctrine of *res ipsa loquitor* to meet the inference of negligence by giving an explanation of their conduct.

In *Ybarra*, the plaintiff underwent an appendectomy and awakened with a sharp pain halfway between his neck the point of his right shoulder. He complained about the pain and was given diathermy treatments. The pain increased and spread down to the lower part of his arm, and after he left the hospital, the pain grew worse. He was unable to rotate or lift his arm, and he developed paralysis and atrophy of the muscles around the shoulder. Two treating physicians testified that the injury was of a traumatic origin, caused by pressure or strain applied between his right shoulder and neck.

At the time of trial, none of the persons in the operating room at the time of the appendectomy offered any reason for the injury. Rather, they argued that because so many different persons cared for the patient in the operating room, the plaintiff could not prove the second requirement of the doctrine—that he was under any one person's exclusive control when the injury occurred.

In rejecting this argument and applying the doctrine, the court reasoned that without it, a patient who received permanent injuries of a serious character, obviously the result of someone's negligence, would be unable to recover damages unless the physicians and nurses voluntarily chose to disclose the identity of the negligent person and the facts establishing liability.

Chapter 12 provides additional examples of the doctrine applied in the operating room context and should be reviewed for further study of the *res ipsa loquitor* doctrine.

Violation of Statute. Under certain circumstances, the plaintiff may obtain a presumption of negligence when the defendant has violated a statute or regulation. Some jurisdictions refer to this presumption as negligence per se or negligence as a matter of law, while others characterize it as a rebuttable presumption.

Before the courts will apply the presumption where a defendant has violated a statute, three conditions must be met. First, the statute must be designed to protect a class of persons. For example, child abuse reporting statutes are designed to protect a class of persons, children.

Second, the plaintiff must be a member of that class of persons. So, for example, an abused child suing an emergency room nurse for injuries because the nurse failed to report the child abuse is clearly a member of the class of persons the child abuse reporting statute was designed to protect.

Third, the harm suffered by the plaintiff must be the kind that the statute is designed to prevent.[103] The child who is injured after returning home because of a failure to report abuse also satisfies this requirement. Injuries from child abuse are precisely the kind of injuries the child abuse statute is designed to prevent. Thus, if an emergency room nurse failed to report a child abuse injury and the child was later injured, the plaintiff child suing the nurse would be entitled to have the violation of statute presumption.[104]

Some courts may view the violation of statute as only some evidence of negligence[105] while others treat the violation as sufficient evidence of negligence to shift to the defendant the burden of producing evidence that will excuse the violation.[106] And, some view the violation as negligence itself, or negligence as a matter of law, requiring the plaintiff to show only that the violation was the proximate cause of the injury.[107]

Some cases suggest that the courts may apply the violation of statute presumption in instances where the state NPA has been violated. For example, in *Central Anesthesia Associates P.C. v. Worthy*[108] the Georgia Appellate Court held that a student nurse anesthetist and her employer may be found negligent per se for violating a statute that only allows certified and supervised nurse anesthetists to administer anesthesia.

The circumstances surrounding the case are as follows. The nurse anesthetist was a registered nurse and an employee of Central Anesthesia Associates P.C. (CAA). She was also a student at a training school for certified registered nurse anesthetists. CAA had an agreement with the hospital to provide anesthetic services and to operate the school. The student nurse anesthetist was supervised by another CAA employee who was a *physician's assistant*.

The Georgia statute, however, provided anesthesia could only be administered by a physician or a certified registered nurse anesthetist supervised by a physician. The court held that the violation of this statute was negligence per se and granted a pretrial motion of the plaintiff summarily judging the defendants negligent for the patient's injuries.

Washington state cases have also raised the violation of statute presumption in a case where a nurse midwife violated that state's statute defining the scope of nurse midwifery practice. In *Lustig v. The Birthplace*[109] there was a $725,000 settlement for the wrongful death of a mother and child caused by eclampsia during labor, and during negotiations, the plaintiff successfully argued that the violation of statute would apply.

A nurse midwife employed by the birthing clinic cared for the woman throughout her pregnancy and labor. In the last 3 months of pregnancy, the woman's blood pressure, reflexes, and edema increased, and she experienced more fatigue. When she presented at the clinic in labor, her blood pressure increased throughout the next 7 hours, culminating in seizures and unconsciousness. After being transported to the hospital, her blood pressure was 200/117 and she was still unconscious. Her son was stillborn, and she died 2 days later.

The midwife and the birthing clinic were sued for negligence per se because the nurse midwife violated a statute that established the duty of a midwife to consult with a physician whenever significant deviations from normal are found in either the mother or the fetus. Expert testimony established that the nurse midwife should have referred the woman to a physician. The violation of statute was established, and the defendants settled the case.

These two cases suggest that a nurse who violates the NPA may be subject to a violation of statute presumption for injuries sustained as a result of the violation. A strong argument, however, can be made, and has been successfully made, that the NPA does not meet the three requirements for the violation of statute presumption of negligence. In *Leahy v. Kenosha Memorial Hospital,*[110] the Wisconsin Appellate Court determined that the presumption should not apply to violations of the NPA because the act was primarily designed to regulate the nursing profession, not to protect the public.

A California case, however, suggests that a different result might be obtained in that jurisdiction. In *Cade v. Mid City Hospital,*[111] the court reviewed application of the presumption to a regulation that required that no medication or treatment be given except pursuant to an order by a person lawfully authorized to give such an order. The plaintiff contended that the presumption should apply because an unlicensed person failed to provide medication, causing injury.

The court first noted that the regulation was one of several that was intended to protect patients from harm resulting from care given by unqualified hospital personnel. The court reasoned that the regulation was designed to protect hospital patients from injury that might follow from an unauthorized medical procedure. Therefore, the court concluded, injury resulting from unauthorized acts was the type of injury intended to be prevented by the NPA. If the injury resulted from an unauthorized act, the presumption would have applied; however, the injury resulted from an omission of an authorized act. Under these circumstances, the presumption did not apply.

The violation of statute also must be the proximate cause of the injury. For example, in *McDonald v. Foster Memorial Hospital,*[112] the California Appellate Court held that any alleged violation of a hospital licensing regulation would be immaterial unless the plaintiff could show that the defendant's violation of the regulation had been the proximate cause of his or her injuries. The plaintiff was injured after falling from her hospital bed after being medicated with sedatives. At trial, she contended that the nurses who administered the medication to her were negligent per se because neither was licensed in the state as required by statute.[113]

The court rejected the argument, reasoning that even if the nurses were in technical violation of the statute, it did not follow that there would have been less likelihood of injury had the nurses been licensed in California. If the violation of statute has no direct bearing on the injury, proof of its violation becomes irrelevant to the lawsuit. There was no evidence that the actual administration of the medication was negligently performed or that such administration by a licensed nurse would have lead to a different result. Consequently, the plaintiff was not entitled to the presumption of negligence.

Although proximate cause must still be proven in a given situation, these cases suggest that nurses should examine their state practice acts to determine what duties of care are statutorily prescribed. Sound nursing practice requires that nurses meet the requirements of their state practice acts.

Defenses to negligence actions

There are a number of defenses, summarized in the box on p. 52, that may be raised to defeat a negligence action against a defendant nurse. In addition to proving that the nurse acted reasonably under the circumstances, the nurse may assert that one of the necessary elements of a negligence lawsuit—duty, breach of duty, proximate cause, or damages—has not been proved by the plaintiff. In addition, the defenses of assumption of the risk, contributory negligence or comparative negligence, the stat-

DEFENSES TO NEGLIGENCE ACTIONS

1. Failure to introduce proof on any of four elements necessary for negligence: duty, breach, proximate cause, and damages
2. Proof that the defendant acted reasonably under the circumstances
3. Assumption of the risk
4. Contibutory negligence or comparative negligence
5. Statute of limitations
6. Immunities

ute of limitations, and certain immunities may be applicable.

ASSUMPTION OF THE RISK

Where a plaintiff assumes the risk of injury, the plaintiff is really consenting to and relieving the defendant of liability from a course of treatment where there is a known risk of injury.[114] In other words, the plaintiff takes the chance, which relieves the defendant of a legal duty to protect against the chance. Under these circumstances, the defendant cannot be held negligent. The defense requires that the person know of the risk, that the risk is assumed voluntarily, and that there is no coercion.[115]

Parties may expressly agree in advance that the defendant will have no liability for the consequences of conduct that would otherwise be negligent.[116] The courts will not, however, uphold such an agreement if one party is at an obvious disadvantage in bargaining power such that he or she is at the mercy of the other.[117]

CONTRIBUTORY NEGLIGENCE

Contributory negligence is conduct by the plaintiff that contributes to the cause of his or her injury and that falls below the standard to which persons are expected to conform for their own protection.[118] The theory is that although the defendant has violated a duty of care to the plaintiff and would otherwise be liable, the plaintiff is barred from recovery because his or her own conduct contributed to the injury.[119] Although the law views both at fault, the unreasonable risk of harm created by the plaintiff bars his or her recovery against the defendant.

The plaintiff is required to conform to the broad standard of conduct of the reasonably prudent person. The same intelligence, attention, knowledge, and judgment are required of the actor for the protection of his or her own interests as is required for protection of other persons' interests.[120] Thus, if a particular course of treatment is recommended and the plaintiff does not follow through, contributory negligence may be a defense.

COMPARATIVE NEGLIGENCE

Some jurisdictions view contributory negligence as too harsh a result because it bars recovery against the defendant even if the defendant's negligence is far greater than that of the plaintiff. Thus, some jurisdictions have adopted comparative negligence. In general, this is a rule that apportions damages according to the degree of negligence. For example, if the defendant was 30% negligent and the plaintiff was 70% negligent, the monetary damage award will be reduced by 30%.[121]

STATUTE OF LIMITATIONS

The statute of limitations is simply a law or statute that limits the time within which a plaintiff may bring a lawsuit. The legislatures of many states have enacted statutes that shorten the limitations period for medical malpractice actions. Many provide that statute of limitations for such actions is 1 year. Patients are thus restricted, with certain exceptions, to filing their lawsuits within 1 year.

This statutory limit in which a claim must be filed thus serves as some protection to the practitioner. The time period, whether 1 or 4 years, varies from jurisdiction to jurisdiction and is largely a matter of state law. As a general rule, the limitations period does not begin in a negligence action until some damage has occurred.[122]

This general rule has led to the development of various exceptions in the health care context because often the time period runs before the plaintiff discovers the injury. To avoid a harsh result, some courts hold that the defendant's duty continues until the patient-practitioner relationship has ended. Other courts hold that the limitations period does not run until the plaintiff discovers or reasonably should have discovered the injury.[123]

If a practitioner fraudulently conceals the injury, the limitations period stops running during the time of the concealment or the fraud bars the statute of limitations defense. In *Sanders v. H. Nouri,*[124] for example, a physician failed to remove both fallopian tubes to achieve sterilization, and he allegedly concealed this fact from the patient. The patient became pregnant and sued for wrongful conception. The court held that the 2-year statute of limitations would not bar the lawsuit.

Sometimes, a plaintiff will try to get around the statute of limitations by characterizing the lawsuit as a breach of contract rather than a medical negligence case because contract actions generally have longer limitations periods. In *Murray v. University of Pennsylvania Hospital,*[125] the Pennsylvania Supreme Court held that if a patient and a practitioner contract that a specific course of treatment will produce a specific result and that result is not achieved, a claim of breach of contract is appropriate even though the practitioner used the highest degree of care. Thus, the longer contract limitations period applied.

The *Murray* decision involved a tubal ligation where the surgeon expressly warranted the surgery would prevent future pregnancies, but the plaintiff became pregnant and sued for breach of this warranty. Illinois, however, has held that the statute of limitations for negligence cases applies to actions for breach of contract for negligent sterilization cases.[126] These cases illustrate the courts' differing approaches to essentially the same factual injury.

This difference also appears with respect to the applicable limitations period in nursing malpractice cases. Some jurisdictions, such as Ohio, have been slow to accept the nurse as a professional in the medical malpractice context who is entitled to the malpractice statute of limitations.[127] Illinois also has recently adopted this view in *Penkana v. Kasbohm.*[128] In *Penkana,* the Illinois Appellate Court held that a 1983 lawsuit against a hospital and a physician over objects left in the patient during a 1975 hysterectomy was barred by the 4-year statute of limitations in Illinois. The court ruled, however, that the plaintiff could maintain a lawsuit against the registered nurse who assisted in the operating room since nurses are *not* covered by the malpractice statute of limitations.

These cases demonstrate that nurses must be familiar with the laws in their state. If the jurisdiction follows the Illinois approach, nurses need to work toward convincing the legislature to follow the example of other jurisdictions, such as California, which apply the malpractice limitations period to nurses.[129] Nurses also need to be aware of decisions by courts narrowly construing medical malpractice statutes of limitations to exclude nurses. Specific legislation overruling such decisions may be needed as, for example, in Illinois, if the Illinois Supreme Court upholds this decision.

IMMUNITIES

Under certain circumstances, governmental immunity from lawsuit will protect the nurse employee. Qualified or good faith immunity, which was developed from the common law, is discussed in Chapter 5. Some jurisdictions by statute also have provided additional immunities to their provider-employees.

For example, in New York, immunity exists for errors in professional judgments.[130] California similarly provides immunity to a public employee for any injury resulting from his or her act or omission where the act or omission was the result of the exercise of the discretion.[131] By judicial decision, this immunity extends only to policy decisions, not to administerial acts.[132]

Additional defenses to actions are discussed throughout the particular practice chapters. The nurse's best defense is to act within the limits of his or her professional knowledge and skill. Nurses who act according to a professional standard of care will minimize their exposure to liability.

Recommendations and trends

Nurses need to keep abreast of statutory changes and judicial modifications of negligence law; different jurisdictions may have developed different legal principles in the statutory and the common law of negligence. The autonomy of the nursing profession will be furthered by recognition of nursing malpractice as professional negligence. Efforts at the legislative level may be required. In every jurisdiction, nurses should insist that their standard of care be judged according to a professional standard of care, and that the legal system recognize nurses as the appropriate expert witnesses to testify to this standard in nursing malpractice cases.

Endnotes

1. W. PROSSER, LAW OF TORTS §30 at 143 (4th ed. 1971) (hereinafter cited as *Prosser*).
2. *See, e.g., Utter v. United Hospital Center,* 236 S.E.2d 213 (W.Va. 1977); *Norton v. Argonaut Insurance Co.,* 144 So.2d 249 (La. Ct. App. 1962).
3. Michigan and Ohio are two examples of jurisdictions holding nurses to an ordinary standard of care. *Kambas v. St. Joseph Hosp. of Detroit,* 205 N.W.2d 431 (Mich. 1973); *Richardson v. Doe,* 199 N.E.2d 878 (Ohio 1964). Since the *Kambas* decision, however, the Michigan Legislature has amended the statute of limitations statute to provide for a 2-year limitations period for malpractice actions. MICH. COMP. LAWS. ANN. Sec. 600.5805 (4) (West Supp. 1984). Section 5838 also provides that the statute of limitations for a malpractice action against a registered nurse, among other professionals, begins to run when the patient discontinues treatment with the registered nurse, or other designated professional, regardless of the time that the plaintiff discovers or knows of the potential claim.

   In *Adkins v. Annapolis Hospital,* 420 MICH. 87 (March 1984), the Michigan Supreme Court held that this statute altered the common law rule regarding the statute of limitations and subjected those health professionals listed to the 2-year statute of limitations. Thus, Michigan now provides that registered nurses are subject to a professional malpractice standard.

4. *See, e.g., Friajo v. Hartland Hospital,* 160 Cal. Rptr. 246 (Cal. App. 1979).
5. In certain states, such as California, CAL. BUS. & PROF. CODE §310 (West Supp. 1985), Good Samaritan statutes provide that the gratuitous rendering of services will not result in liability unless the professional is grossly negligent.
6. 160 Cal. Rptr. 246 (1979).
7. *Id.* at 251 n.7.
8. Some jurisdictions, such as Maryland and Mississippi, have adopted a national standard of care. *See, e.g., Shilkret v. Annapolis Emergency Hospital Assn.,* 349 A.2d 245 (Md. App. 1975); *Hall v. Hilbun,* 466 S.E.2d 856 (Miss. 1985). This approach is the modern trend. Under this standard, the nurse must exercise the care expected of reasonably competent practitioners in the same class to which the defendant nurse belongs. Whether an expert nurse witness practices in the same area as the defendant nurse does not matter; the standard of care for that class does not vary with location. Advances in the profession, availability of facilities, special services, and the proximity of specialists are all relevant inquiries.

   In other jurisdictions, there is a rule that the expert nurse witness practice in the same locality; thus the nurse is expected to practice as do the nurses in the same locality. Still others modify these two rules and require the expert to practice in a similar locality. PROSSER, *supra* note 1 at 164.
9. *Id.* at 252.
10. 211 Cal. Rptr. 368 (Cal. 1985).
11. CAL. BUS. & PROF. CODE, §2725 (West Supp. 1985) (the act was amended in 1975 and again in 1981 and explicitly recognizes the existence of overlapping functions between nurses and physicians and permits additional sharing of functions if done in organized health facilities and pursuant to standardized procedures. *See generally* Kelly & Garrick, *Nursing Negligence in Collaborative Practice: Legal Liability in California,* LAW, MEDICINE & HEALTH CARE 260 (December 1984).
12. *Fein v. Permanente Medical Group,* 211 Cal. Rptr. 368, 377 (Cal. 1985) (footnote omitted).
13. *See, e.g., Barber v. Reinking,* 411 P.2d 861 (Wash. 1966). There, a practical nurse giving an inoculation was held to the standard of registered nurse because she had assumed a registered nurse's duties.
14. 245 So.2d 571 (La. App. 1951).
15. *See, e.g., Fein v. Permanente Medical Group,* 211 Cal. Rptr. 368 (Cal. 1985) (examination and diagnosis of a patient cannot in all circumstances be said as a matter of law to be a function reserved to physicians; therefore trial court erred in instructing the jury that the standard of care of a nurse practitioner is that of a physician; the test is whether conduct measured up to that expected of a reasonably prudent nurse); *Whitney v. Day,* 300 N.W.2d 380 (Mich. App. 1980) (nurse administering anesthesia is held to the standard of care based on the skill and care normally expected of those with the same education and training, and nursing negligence is the failure to apply that degree of skill and learning in the treatment of a patient); *Webb v. Jorns,* 473 S.W.2d 328 (Tex. Civ. App. 1978) (nurse anesthetist's liability is measured by whether there was conformity on nurse's part to those standards of professional conduct justifiably expected of a nurse performing such duties), *rev'd on other grounds,* 488 S.W.2d 407; *Thompsom v. United States,* 368 F. Supp. 466 (W.D. La. 1973), *aff'd* 508 F.2d 840 (5th Cir. 1975) (court rejected plaintiff's argument that nurse practitioner should be held to a medical standard of care; actions by nurse should be measured against the standards of the nursing profession).
16. *Sermchief v. Gonzales,* 60 S.W.2d 683 (Mo. 1983) (en banc).
17. *Id.* at 690.
18. For example, in *Fein v. Permanente Medical Group,* 211 Cal. Rptr. 368 (Cal. 1985), the California Supreme Court found that even though a nurse is performing a function typically reserved to a physician, the jury should not be instructed that the nurse's standard of conduct is necessarily a physician standard of conduct. In other words, the question is still whether the nurse acted reasonably under the professional circumstances presented by the case; the particular function that resulted in injury may require a certain standard of care, and that standard does not change whether it is performed by a nurse or physician. Although performance of the function may require specialized training and knowledge and the nurse will be held accountable for this knowledge and skill, he or she is still judged by a professional nursing standard of care.
19. *Prosser, supra* note 1, at 209.
20. *See, e.g., Sanchez v. Bay General Hospital,* 172 Cal. Rptr. 342 (Cal. App. 1981); *see also Goff v. Doctors General Hospital of San Jose,* 333 P.2d 29 (Cal. App. 1958) (court explicitly approved of physician's testimony as establishing the duty and breach of duty of nurses employed by a hospital); *Chapman v. Pollock,* 317 S.E.2d 726 (N.C. App. 1984) (family practitioner can testify to the standard of care of an internist; evidence of what other qualified physicians do in treating same illness is relevant to internist standard of care because standard of care for diagnosis and treating appendectomy is the same for family practitioners and internal medicine practitioners); *but see Connelly v. Kortz,* 689 P.2d 728 (Colo. App. 1984) (specialist in internal medicine cannot testify to the standard of care of a surgeon; case involved the misdiagnosis of the patient's gastrointestinal disorder resulting in alleged unnecessary surgery); *Botchlo v. Bycura,* 320 S.E. 2d 59 (S.C. App. 1984) (orthopedic surgeon cannot testify to the standard of care of a podiatrist because procedure for performing metatarsal osteotomy is different than that of an orthopedic surgeon).
21. *See, e.g.,* ARIZ. REV. STAT. §12-563 (West Supp. 1976) (professional's standard of care should be measured against standards of his or her profession).
22. 262 S.E.2d 680 (N.C. App. 1980).
23. *Id.* at 684.
24. *Barnes v. St. Francis Hospital and School of Nursing, Inc.* 507 P.2d 288 (Kan. 1973).
25. *Prosser, supra* note 1, at 364.
26. *See, e.g., McCormick v. Lindberg,* 352 N.W.2d 30 (Minn. App. 1984) (thoracic cardiovascular surgeon is held to a national standard of care for specialists in that field).
27. *See, e.g., Shuffler v. Blue Ridge Radiology Associates, P.A.,* 326 S.E.2d 96 (N.C. App. 1985) (defendant's own testimony may establish the standard of care and the failure to meet it).
28. *See, e.g., Czubinsky v. Doctors Hospital,* 188 Cal. Rptr. 685, 687 (1983) (written hospital procedure).
29. *Id.*
30. *See, e.g., Prosser supra* note 1, at 191; *Cade v. Mid City Hospital Corporation,* 119 Cal. Rptr. 571 (1975); *but see Leahy v. Kenosha Memorial Hospital,* 348 N.W.2d 607 (Wisc. App. 1984) (hospital did not violate Wisconsin NPA and was not negligent per se even

though persons caring for plaintiff were not registered nurses within meaning of act; thrust of NPA is to regulate nursing profession, not to protect public).

31. *See, e.g., Landeros v. Flood,* 131 Cal. Rptr. 69 (Cal. 1976) (physician's failure to report child abuse resulted in application of the presumption of negligence).
32. 519 P.2d 981 (Wash. 1974).
33. 185 Cal. Rptr. 103 (Cal. App. 1982).
34. *See, e.g., Leonard v. Watonsville Community Hospital,* 291 P.2d 496 (Cal. App. 1956), *modified on other grounds,* 305 P.2d 36 (Cal. App. 1956).
35. 172 N.W.2d 427 (Wisc. 1969).
36. *See, e.g.,* 510 P.2d 190 (Kan. 1963).
37. *Graham v. St. Luke's Hospital,* 196 N.E.2d 355 (Ill. App. 1964).
38. *See, e.g., Jones v. Hawkes Hospital,* 196 N.E.2d 592 (Ohio 1964) (court rejected need for expert testimony where nurse left patient for 5 minutes and she broke her hip).
39. *Prosser, supra* note 1, at 151.
40. *Id.* at 146.
41. *Id.* at 146.
42. *Id.* at 146-149.
43. *Id.* at 162; *Fraijo v. Hartland Hospital,* 160 Cal. Rptr. 246 (1979); *see also Ouellette v. Subak,* 379 N.W.2d 125 (Minn. App. 1985) (physician not liable for an honest error in judgment in choosing between accepted methods of diagnosis or treatment).
44. *Id.*
45. *See, e.g., Czubinsky v. Doctors Hospital,* 188 Cal. Rptr. 685 (Cal. App. 1983).
46. 481 A.2d 750 (Conn. 1984).
47. *Leonard v. Watsonville Community Hospital,* 291 P.2d 496 (Cal. App. 1956), *modified on other grounds,* 305 P.2d 36 (Cal. App. 1956).
48. Resolution of The American Association of Nurse Attorneys.
49. *See, e.g., Shuffler v. Blue Ridge Radiology Associates, P.A.,* 326 S.E.2d 96 (N.C. App. 1985).
50. 325 S.E.2d 78 (S.C. App. 1985).
51. 471 N.E.2d 1315 (Mass. 1984).
52. 393 N.Y.S.2d 859 (N.Y. Sup. 1977).
53. 686 S.W.2d 87 (Tenn. App. 1984).
54. *Prosser, supra* note 1, at 236-237.
55. *Id.* at 239.
56. *Robertson v. Counselman,* 686 P.2d 149 (Kan. 1984) (Kansas Supreme Court adopts substantial factor in "lost chance of survival" cases; but for test would allow providers to be free of liability for even the grossest malpractice if patient only had a 50/50 chance of surviving disease or injury even with proper treatment, whereas substantial factor test allows a plaintiff recovery if he or she makes a showing that an appreciable chance of survival existed that was reduced or destroyed by the defendant).
57. *Id.* at 240.
58. *Id.* at 244.
59. *Id.* at 236.
60. 438 S.W.2d 408 (1982), *aff'd,* 455 S.W.2d 703.
61. 316 N.W.2d 1 (1982).
62. 393 N.Y.S.2d 859 (N.Y. 1977).
63. *Id.* at 865.
64. *Prosser,* supra note 1, at 143.
65. *Id.* at 144.
66. *Id.* at 144. Certain jurisdictions have altered this rule by statute. Some jurisdictions provide by statute or by judicial decision that the limitations period runs from the time that the patient discovers the negligence. *E.g., Malapanis v. Shirazi,* 487 N.E.2d 533 (Mass. App. 1986).
67. 103 Cal. Rptr. 856 (Cal. 1972) (en banc).
68. *Nelson v. Patrick,* 326 S.E.2d 45 (N.C. App. 1985).
69. *Dillon v. Legg,* 441 P.2d 912 (Cal. 1973), was the first case to recognize this kind of claim. The court required that those seeking recovery for witnessing a negligent injury to another must have a close relationship with that person, be in proximity to the scene of the injury, and have sensory and contemporaneous observation of the accident. The court has now abandoned this requirement of "sudden occurrence" but still requires observation of the injury by the third person. *E.g., Ochoa v. Superior Court for the County of Santa Clara,* No. 24637 (San Francisco, July 29, 1985).
70. *See, e.g., Accounts Adjustment Bureau v. Cooperman,* 204 Cal. Rptr. 881 (Cal. App. 1984).
71. *See, e.g., Bonbrest v. Kotz,* 65 F.Supp. 138 (D.D.C. 1946).
72. CAL. CIVIL CODE §29 (West 1964).
73. *Prosser, supra* note 1, at 89.
74. *Id.*
75. *See, e.g., id.* at 906.
76. *Prosser, supra* note 1, at 326.
77. *Summerfield v. Superior Court,* 698 P.2d 712 (Ariz. 1985); *Shirley v. Bacon,* 267 S.E.2d 809 (Ga. App. 1980).
78. *Prosser, supra* note 1, at 314.
79. *Id.* at 314-315. California altered this rule and apportions liability by fault.
80. *Id.* at 458.
81. *Id.* at 459.
82. *Id.* at 460.
83. *Id.* at 460.
84. *Id.*
85. *Id.* at 461; Restatement (second) of Agency §228-229.
86. 107 Cal. App. 3d 435 (Cal. App. 1980).
87. Unless, of course, the hospital was negligent in selecting or supervising the physician who is on staff. *See, e.g., Elam v. College Park Hospital,* 132 Cal. App. 3d 332 (1982).
88. *See, e.g., Ybarra v. Spangard,* 154 P.2d 687 (Cal. 1944); *Schultz v. Mutch,* 211 Cal. Rptr. 445 (Cal. App. 1985).
89. *Schultz v. Mutch,* 211 Cal. Rptr. 445, 49 (Cal. App. 1985).
90. *See, e.g., City of Somerset v. Hart,* 549 S.W.2d 814 (Kan. 1977) (surgical nurses acted as servants of both physicians and the hospital, and their negligence in failing to account for scalpel blades left in the patient was chargeable to hospital and physician).
91. *See, e.g., id.; see also Sherman v. Hartman,* 290 P.2d 894 (Cal. App. 1955) (postoperative negligence of nurses); *Hallinan v. Prindle,* 62 P.2d 1075 (Cal. App. 1936) (preoperative nursing negligence).
92. *Cf. Paintsville Hosp. Co. v. Rose,* 683 S.W.2d 255 (Ky. 1985) (doctrine applied in emergency room case to physician who was on staff and covered the emergency room on an on-call basis).
93. *Id.*
94. *Prosser, supra* note 1, at 209-211.
95. *Id.* at 212.
96. *Id.* at 213.
97. *Id.* at 214.
98. *Id.*

99. 464 So.2d 386 (La. App. 1985).
100. *Frantz v. San Luis Medical Clinic,* 146 Cal. Rptr. 146 (Cal. App. 1978).
101. *Bauer v. Otis,* 284 P.2d 133 (Cal. App. 1962).
102. 154 P.2d 687 (Cal. 1945).
103. *Prosser, supra* note 1, at 195.
104. *See, Landeros v. Flood,* 131 Cal. Rptr. 69 (Cal. 1976) (physician held liable for negligent failure to diagnose battered child syndrome resulting in child being returned to offending parents, who inflicted subsequent beatings); *see also* Kohlman, *Malpractice Liability for Failing To Report Child Abuse,* 49 STATE BAR JOURNAL 118 (1974).
105. *See, e.g., Neil v. Holyoke St. Ry.,* 109 N.E.2d 831 (Mass. 1952).
106. *See, e.g., Alarid v. Vanier,* 327 P.2d 897 (Cal. 1958).
107. *See, e.g.,* Green, *Duties, Risks, Causation Doctrines,* 41 TEXAS LAW REVIEW 215, 242 & n.105 (1962).
108. 325 S.E.2d 819 (Ga. App. 1984), *aff'd,* 333 S.E.2d 829 (Ga. 1985).
109. No. 83-2-07528-9 (Wash. King's Cty. Sup. Ct., decided Sept. 19, 1983) *reported in* 27 ATLA LAW REPORTER 87 (March 1984).
110. 348 N.W.2d 607 (Wisc. 1984).
111. 119 Cal. Rptr. 571 (Cal. App. 1975).
112. 338 P.2d 607 (Cal. App. 1959), *disapproved on other grounds* in *Siverson v. Weber,* 22 Cal. Rptr. 377 (Cal. 1962).
113. *Id.* at 610.
114. *Prosser, supra* note 1, at 440.
115. *Id.* at 447-452.
116. *Id.* at 442.
117. *Id.*
118. *Id.* at 416-417.
119. *Id.* at 417.
120. *Id.* at 419.
121. *Id.* at 436-437.
122. *Id.* at 144.
123. *Id.*
124. 688 S.W.2d 24 (Mo. App. 1985).
125. 490 A.2d 839 (Pa. 1985).
126. *Brown v. Mason,* 477 N.E. 2d 61 (Ill. App. 1985).
127. *Richardson v. Doe,* 199 N.E.2d 878 (Ohio 1964) (no reason for nurses to be given protection of 1 year through professional negligence statute of limitations because a nurse, although well trained and skilled, is not in the same category as a physician, who must exercise independent judgment on matters that may mean the difference between life and death).
128. 475 N.E.2d 975 (Ill. App. 1985).
129. CAL. CODE CIV. PRO. §72 (West Supp. 1985).
130. *See, e.g., O'Shea v. United States,* 623 F. Supp. 380 (D.C.N.Y. 1985).
131. CAL. GOV'T. CODE §820.2 (West 1976).
132. *E.g., Tarasoff v. Regents of the University of California,* 118 Cal. Rptr. 129 (Cal. 1974) (en banc).

Chapter 5

Intentional and quasi-intentional torts and civil rights

Mary E. Kelly

In contrast to negligence law, which remedies unintended harms, intentional torts remedy injuries to person or property that are intended by the actor. The quasi-intentional torts protect an individual's interests in reputation, privacy, and freedom from unfounded legal action. Civil rights actions redress violations of rights protected by the Constitution or federal law. The violation of state constitutional rights may also be remedied under state law. These theories of recovery have been asserted by and against health care providers with varying degrees of success.

This chapter provides an overview of selected intentional and quasi-intentional torts and civil rights actions. Each section also provides a review of cases applying these claims to the health care setting. A significant focus is the right to refuse treatment; judicial and legislative approaches to the incompetent or competent adult's right to refuse treatment are examined. Because reported federal civil rights actions are more prevalent in the health field, the civil rights section focuses on federal claims. Later chapters also analyze cases illustrating intentional and quasi-intentional torts and civil rights claims as applied to particular practice areas.

Intentional torts

Traditionally, the common law recognized five intentional torts: battery, assault, false imprisonment, trespass to land, and trespass to chattels (personal property). The latter two protect interests in property; the former three protect interests in one's person. While trespass to land and to property may occur in health settings, for example when angry demonstrators enter a clinic that performs abortions and damage its property, the most relevant intentional torts, from a provider's perspective, are the other three. Intentional infliction of emotional distress, a relatively new development in the common law, is currently being asserted against providers who refuse to terminate life-support systems.

ELEMENTS OF AN INTENTIONAL TORT: INTENT AND ACT

Each intentional tort requires that the defendant intended to act and did act in a way that interfered with the plaintiff's person or property. The intent at issue here is not necessarily a hostile intent or a desire to do any harm. Rather, the requisite intent is simply the intent to bring about a result which invades the legally recognized interests of another.[1] Consequently, even if the defendant (1) believes the conduct will not hurt another or (2) intends to play a practical joke, there may be liability if the conduct interferes with a personal or property interest that the law protects.

The defendant's act, however, must be a voluntary one. If the defendant is unconscious and hits another person's arm, the action would not be sufficient for an intentional tort, because it is not voluntary; the action is unintended.

The concept of intent extends further than the desire to bring about physical results. Intent also extends to consequences which the defendant believes (from an objective viewpoint) are substantially certain to follow from the act taken. Consequently, when someone throws a bomb into a crowded room, it is no defense that he or she did not intend to kill anyone.[2]

Negligence v. Intentional Tort. In contrast, mere knowledge and appreciation of a risk, short of substantial certainty, is not sufficient to meet the intent requirement. If a defendant acts with the belief or consciousness that he or she is causing an appreciable risk of harm to another, that act may be negligent, and if the risk is great that conduct may be characterized as wanton or reckless, but it is not an intentional tort.[3] The distinction between negligence and intentional torts is one of degree. "Apparently the line has been drawn by the courts at the point where the known danger ceases to be only a foreseeable risk which a reasonable [person] would avoid, and becomes a substantial certainty."[4]

The nature of recoverable damages also differs. Punitive damages, which are designed to punish or deter the defendant's intentional conduct, are recoverable in the intentional torts selected for review: battery, assault, false imprisonment, and intentional infliction of emotional distress. Punitive damages, as a general rule, are not recoverable in negligence actions precisely because the conduct is not intentional.

Another difference is that proof of damage or injury is not an element of intentional torts, as it is in negligence. The tort is complete when there is intentional interference with the plaintiff's person or property; nominal damages are awarded if no injury or damage results.[5] Further, no expert testimony is needed to prove any of the intentional tort claims against a health care provider. The professional standard of care is an issue only in professional negligence actions.

BATTERY

Battery, one of the five traditional intentional torts, protects the interest in freedom from unpermitted and intentional contacts with one's person.[6] The gist of the action is not the hostile intent of the defendant, but rather the absence of the plaintiff's consent to the defendant's contact. To be liable, the defendant must have done a positive and affirmative act which causes, and is intended to cause, an unpermitted contact. Unpermitted contacts which cause physical harm and contacts that are trivial, insulting, and offensive constitute battery.[7]

The protection against unpermitted contacts extends to any part of the body, or to anything which is attached to the body "and practically identified with it."[8] Examples include: contact with the plaintiff's clothing; cane; paper or other object in hand; or the car or the person against whom the plaintiff is leaning.[9]

Direct contact with the plaintiff is not necessary; there may be liability if the defendant merely sets in motion something which produces the result, such as contaminating the plaintiff's food or medication with poison.[10] The interest in personal integrity exists even though the plaintiff is asleep or under anesthetic, and therefore not aware of the unpermitted contact at the time the contact occurred.[11] Nominal damages are recoverable for the technical invasion of the plaintiff's integrity, as well as compensation for the mental disturbance inflicted, such as fright or humiliation.

The defendant is also liable for all harm resulting from the conduct, even unforseeable consequences. Since battery is considered the "worst kind of intentions" punitive damages are generally recoverable, unless the defendant has acted in good faith under a mistake of fact.[12]

ASSAULT

The cause of action for assault is frequently joined with a claim for battery. The action for assault protects the interest in freedom from *apprehension* of an immediate harmful or offensive contact, as opposed to the contact itself.[13] Unlike battery, actual contact is not an element of assault, and the plaintiff is protected against a purely mental disturbance of personal integrity.[14]

Assault covers any act which gives rise to an apprehension that a battery is about to be committed. Consequently, the plaintiff must be aware of the defendant's actions. There is no assault if there is no awareness.[15] Mere words, however violent, and threats to do something in the future do not give rise to a threat of immediate contact, and therefore do not constitute an assault.[16] The defendant must intend to arouse an apprehension of a battery in the plaintiff.[17]

Recoverable damages include those for mental disturbance including fright and humiliation, as well as any physical illness which may result thereby. Punitive damages may also be obtained.[18]

An interesting assault and battery claim by a registered nurse against a doctor was the underlying action in *Okehi v. St. Paul Fire & Marine Insurance Co.*[19] The issue was whether the physician's insurance policy covered his defense against the nurse's action for assault and battery. The court found that the insurance policy covered the doctor's defense against the underlying action for assault and battery. The assault and battery action stemmed from an argument between the physician and the nurse concerning a patient's consent to sterilization.

The physician's patient desired an elective sterilization immediately after delivery. After examining the patient, who was in active labor, the nurse informed the physician that the patient had not executed the proper consent form.

The physician questioned the nurse about the reason for the unsigned sterilization consent, and the nurse replied that the patient had refused the procedure. Words were exchanged; and as the nurse walked away, the physician reached out, put his hand on her shoulder, turned her around, and said he had not yet finished talking with her. Words were again exchanged, and others finally interceded. The nurse then filed suit against the doctor.

MEDICAL ASSAULT AND BATTERY

The classic case of medical battery exists where surgery is performed without a patient's consent.[20] In most jurisdictions, an action for battery exists where there is no consent to treatment; a negligence action for lack of informed consent applies where consent is given without knowledge of material risks attendant to the treatment.[21] Other jurisdictions, however, do not make this distinction, and an action for battery exists if the patient does not give informed consent to treatment.[22]

The crux of the issue is whether the patient consented to the particular treatment. *Mink v. University of Chicago*[23] illustrates this principle. There, mothers who had been given diethylstilbestrol (DES) while hospitalized at the Lying-In Hospital in 1953 brought a battery action against the University Hospital. These women had been unknowing members of a double-blind study, which ironically established the ineffectiveness of DES in the prevention of miscarriages. They were never told that they were ingesting DES; rather, they were told that the medication they were receiving consisted of vitamins.

The hospital attempted to defend its researcher's actions by arguing that the women consented to treatment when they admitted themselves to the University's Lying-In Hospital for prenatal care. The court, in refusing to summarily dismiss their action, reasoned that the *scope* of consent was an issue of fact for the jury to decide: the defendant hospital's privilege to treat is limited to acts substantially similar to those to which the patient consented. If the defendants went beyond the consent given, the court noted, and performed substantially different acts, they could be liable for battery. Because the women alleged sufficient lack of consent to the treatment involved, the court refused to dismiss their action for battery.

Consent. *Mink* illustrates the rule that even though consent to treatment is given, if the provider goes beyond the consent given and does something substantially different, the provider is liable for battery. Thus, consent to operate on the left ear is not consent to operate on the right ear[24]; and if a patient agrees to a blood test, this does not provide consent to a spinal puncture.

A general written consent, however, may cover the particular treatment at issue. For example, in *Danielson v. Roche,*[25] the California Court of Appeal held that a consent to all treatments deemed advisable to the surgeon authorized removal of sections of the patient's fallopian tubes.

The time, place, and circumstances surrounding the consent all affect the nature of the consent given.[26] If, for example, the patient consents with a mistaken understanding as to the nature and the character of the treatment, the provider may be liable if he or she is aware of the mistake or misrepresents the matter to the patient.[27]

Consent must be voluntarily given by a person competent to give it. Competence requires that the patient be able to understand the nature and consequences of the proposed treatment.[28] The careful practitioner, therefore, should document that recommendations were made to the patient without pressure and that the consent was uncoerced. Under certain conditions, a consent form that is required to be signed as a condition of admission may be deemed coercive.[29]

Minors, the mentally infirm, unconscious persons, and persons intoxicated or addicted to drugs all present competency to consent problems.[30] Generally, a minor's parent or guardian must consent to treatment of the minor.[31] With respect to the mentally infirm, competency to consent may depend on a given state's law. The fact that a person is involuntarily committed to a mental institution does not necessarily mean that he or she is incompetent to consent or refuse to consent to treatment.[32]

Where there exists a true emergency, and the patient is unconscious, incompetent, or a minor and therefore unable to consent, consent to treatment may be implied. The theory is that the patient, if conscious and able to understand the situation, would consent.[33]

The Right to Refuse Treatment. The right to refuse treatment is an issue that has generated quite a bit of litigation in recent years. The right to refuse treatment issue arises in cases both of competent and incompetent patients. Accordingly, the discussion of this issue that follows is organized around these two groups of patients.

Competent Adults. The obvious corollary to the principle that an adult competent patient has the right to control decisions about his or her health care is the principle that a competent adult patient has the legal right to refuse medical treatment.[34] Thus, in general, if an adult competent patient refuses a recommended treatment, the practitioner must respect the individual's decision. Otherwise treatment would leave the practitioner liable for assault and battery and civil rights claims.[35]

Whether the refusal must be respected when the patient's condition is life threatening or whether the provider should seek judicial confirmation of treatment or nontreatment depends on the provider's jurisdiction. The Kansas Supreme Court notes:

> Anglo-American law starts with the premise of thorough-going self-determination. It follows that each [person] is considered to be master of his own body, and he may, if he be of sound mind, expressly prohibit the performance of life-saving surgery, or other medical treatment.[36]

Courts become involved in treatment decisions when practitioners seek court orders to treat unwilling patients or to approve nontreatment of patients who so desire. In the past, when life was at stake, the courts recognized a variety of exceptions to the self-autonomy rule, sometimes without articulating the justification for the exception.[37]

The recent trend is to recognize the right to refuse treatment even where that refusal will clearly result in death. In *St. Mary's Hospital v. Ramsey,*[38] for example, a 27-year-old man suffering from kidney disease refused to accept a blood transfusion. The Florida Appellate Court ruled that no civil or criminal liability could be imposed on the hospital or the doctors for acceding to this refusal.

The Florida courts have also recognized that since a competent adult has the right to refuse treatment in the first instance, he or she has the right to discontinue treatment.[39] Other jurisdictions' courts respect the religious right of patients to prevent or discontinue treatment as they choose.[40]

The California Court of Appeal has considered the issue against a claim by the hospital and the physicians that the patient's ability to make a meaningful decision about terminating life-support systems was questionable because he vacillated about the decision.[41] The hospital and physicians also asserted that the patient's right to terminate treatment was outweighed by various state and personal interests, including the preservation of life, the need to protect innocent third parties, the prevention of suicide, and maintaining the ethics of the medical profession. The court held the right to refuse is paramount.

The plaintiff, Mr. Bartling, was a 70-year-old man who suffered from emphysema, chronic respiratory failure, arteriosclerosis, an abdominal aneurysm, and a malignant tumor of the lung. He also had a history of acute depression.

Mr. Bartling entered a hospital owned and operated by the Seventh-Day Adventist church for treatment of his depression. During a routine chest x-ray, a tumor in the lung was discovered. A subsequent needle biopsy caused the lung to collapse; a tracheotomy was required because the lung would not inflate as a result of emphysema. Mr. Bartling was placed on a respirator, and later efforts to wean him were unsuccessful.

Mr. Bartling was placed in soft restraints to prevent accidental or deliberate disconnection of the ventilator. In spite of requests from Mr. and Mrs. Bartling to remove the ventilator or the restraints, the hospital and treating physicians refused to do so.

Mr. Bartling filed an action seeking damages for battery for unconsented medical treatment, violation of federal and state constitutional rights, breach of fiduciary duty on the part of the treating physicians, intentional infliction of emotional distress, and conspiracy. He also sought an injunction restraining the defendants from administering any unconsented medical treatment, including the respirator. Mr. Bartling's family executed releases relieving the hospital and the treating physicians from any claim of civil liability if the physicians and hospital agreed to honor Mr. Bartling's wishes.

The hospital and treating physicians submitted to the lower court declarations asserting that because the hospital was a religious hospital devoted to the preservation of life, it would be unethical for them to disconnect the life-support systems from patients whom they viewed as having the potential for cognitive, sapient life. They also pointed to the fact that although Mr. Bartling had executed numerous documents evidencing his desires, he vacillated from time to time. During appellate proceedings, Mr. Bartling died.[42]

The court noted that Mr. Bartling's declarations reflected the knowlege that death would result if the ventilator were disconnected, but that he nevertheless preferred death to life sustained by mechanical means. Although he wanted to live, he preferred death to his intolerable living conditions on the ventilator. That he periodically wavered from this position because of severe depression did not mean that his capacity to make such a decision was impaired to the point of legal incompetency. The court relied on *Lane v. Candura,*[43] where the Massachusetts' court refused to find a patient legally incompetent to make a decision about amputating a gangrenous foot simply because she had earlier vacillated about the decision.

In rejecting the view that the interests of the state

and the medical profession outweighed those of Mr. Bartling, the court first reviewed a long line of cases recognizing a person's right to control his or her medical treatment. The court next noted that in enacting the Natural Death Act, which is discussed below, the California legislature had expressly recognized the person's right to control decisions about medical care. Last, but most important, the court stated that the right of a competent adult to refuse medical treatment has its origins in the right of privacy which is guaranteed by the California and United States Constitutions.

The court found that the interest of the hospital and the physicians in the preservation of life was sincere; nevertheless, it stated:

> If the right of the patient to self-determination as to his own medical treatment is to have any meaning at all, it must be paramount to the interest of the patient's hospital and doctors. The right of a competent adult patient to refuse medical treatment is a constitutionally guaranteed right which must not be abridged.[44]

The court also dismissed the physicians' claim that disconnecting the ventilator would have been aiding a suicide. Authority from other jurisdictions, the court noted, "placed this issue to rest."[45] Disconnecting the respirator would not have brought about Mr. Bartling's death by unnatural means, but rather would only have hastened his inevitable death by natural causes. Finally, the court summarily rejected the claim of potential criminal liability, noting that this issue had been substantially answered and rejected in *Barber v. Superior Court*,[46] discussed in the section entitled "Burdens and Benefits Approach" (right column).

Incompetent Patients. Where the treatment merely prolongs life, and the person is in a vegetative state, and therefore is not competent to make a decision as to treatment, different jurisdictions employ different tests to determine whether and when treatment may be terminated or not begun. In addition, statutes governing such situations have been enacted.

Judicial Remedies

Substituted Judgment Approach. Where the courts have confronted the issue of treating an incompetent or unconscious person in the past, they usually focused on the best interest of the patient to determine whether treatment should be given.[47] Recently, the courts and the legislatures have focused on a substituted judgment approach to decision making.

In the *Matter of Karen Quinlan*, the New Jersey Supreme Court broadly construed the right of privacy to encompass a patient's decision to decline medical treatment under certain circumstances.[48] The court held that treatment could be withdrawn without fear of civil or criminal liability if (1) the guardian of the patient and the attending physicians conclude there is no possibility of the patient ever emerging from a comatose state and (2) the hospital's ethics committee agrees there is no chance of emergence from the comatose state.

The Massachusetts Supreme Court in *Superintendent v. Saikewicz*[49] also adopted a substituted judgment approach to decision making in deciding whether a profoundly retarded sixty-seven year old man with acute leukemia should be subjected to prolonged and painful chemotherapy. The treatment would not cure him, but rather would merely prolong his life several months.

The court agreed with the *Quinlan* approach of allowing a guardian to substitute his or her judgment on behalf of the incompetent person. The substituted decision, ideally, is that which the incompetent person would have made if competent. The court, however, refused to grant a broad immunity from civil and criminal liability; rather, the court's involvement in the decision-making process would avoid the risk of liability.

Burdens and Benefits Approach. The California courts have adopted a different analysis of the issue that incorporates the substituted judgment approach.[50] In *Barber v. Superior Court,* the California Appellate Court observed that the difficult determinations in these cases are: the point at which further treatment will be of no reasonable benefit to the patient; who should have the power to make that decision; and who should have the authority to direct termination of treatment. The court declined to draw precise guidelines for resolving these questions because the determination of when or how these decisions should be made "is essentially a medical one to be made at a time and on the basis of facts which will be unique to each case."[51]

In an attempt to free practitioners to pursue their healing vocation,[52] the court formulated a rational approach to the problem which requires a determination of whether the proposed treatment is proportionate or disproportionate in terms of the benefits to be gained versus the burdens caused:

> Proportionate treatment is that which, in the view of the patient, has at least a reasonable chance of providing benefits to the patient, which benefits outweigh the burdens attendant to treatment. Thus, even if a proposed course of treatment might be extremely painful or intrusive, it would still be proportionate treatment if the prognosis was for complete cure or significant improvement in the patient's condition. On the other hand, a treatment course which is only minimally painful or intrusive may nonetheless be considered disproportionate to the potential

benefits if the prognosis is virtually hopeless for any significant improvement in condition.[53]

Determining whether the burdens of treatment are worth enduring for a particular patient depends on the facts unique to each case: namely, how long is the treatment likely to extend life and under what conditions. The patient's interests and desires are the key ingredients in the decision-making process. The focal point of the decision should be the prognosis for a reasonable possibility of return to cognitive life, as distinguished from the forced continuance of that biological vegetative existence. Prolongation of life does not merely mean a suspension of the act of dying, but rather, at the very least, contemplates a remission of symptoms enabling a return toward a normal functioning, integrated existence.[54]

When the patient is incapable of deciding, the family may substitute their judgment for that of the patient. Legal guardianship proceedings are not required. Any surrogate, court appointed or otherwise, should be guided in his or her decisions first by the knowledge of the patient's own desires and feelings, to the extent they were expressed before the patient became incompetent.

If, however, this is not possible to determine, the surrogate should be guided in the decision by the patient's best interests. Factors that may be considered include the relief of suffering; the preservation or restoration of functioning; and the quality, as well as the extent, of life. The impact of the decision on those closest to the patient may also be weighed.

Application of this analysis to the facts in *Barber* caused the court to conclude that the physicians had no duty to continue treatment. The evidence supported the reasonableness of the physicians' determination that the patient was in a persistent vegetative coma, with virtually no chance of recovering his cognitive or motor functions. The family requested the termination of all life-sustaining measures; the physicians, relying on the family's decision, did not institute guardianship proceedings prior to disconnecting the respirator and the intravenous tubes.

In an unusual twist, the state district attorney brought murder charges against the physicians for the discontinuation of treatment. The prosecution distinguished other jurisdictions' cases authorizing termination of life-support systems because these cases involved the use of a respirator rather than the use of a mechanical feeding apparatus. The prosecution claimed that this distinction warranted criminal sanctions in the *Barber* case. The court rejected the distinction because it was "based more on the emotional symbolism of providing food and water to those incapable of providing for themselves rather than on any rational difference . . ."[55]

The court reasoned that medical hydration and nutrition may not always provide net benefits to the patient. Since medical procedures to provide nutrition and hydration are more similar to other medical procedures than to typical human ways of providing hydration and nutrition, their "benefits and burdens ought to be evaluated in the same manner as any other medical procedure."[56]

The court rejected the analogy of a parent's murder conviction for failure to feed an infant. While the parent has a clear duty to feed an otherwise healthy child, the issue in *Barber* was whether the physicians were under a duty to continue to provide life-sustaining treatment. The court found no duty:

> The question presented by this modern technology is, once undertaken, at what point does it cease to perform its intended function and who should have the authority to decide any further prolongation of the dying process is of no benefit to either the patient or his family?
>
> A physician has no duty to continue treatment once it has proven ineffective. Although there may be a duty to provide life-sustaining machinery in the *immediate* aftermath of a cardio-respiratory arrest, there is no duty to continue its use once it has become futile in the opinion of qualified medical personnel.[57]

The *Barber* court concluded that Mr. Barber's wife was the proper surrogate to make the decision to terminate treatment. The court noted that there was no disagreement among the family members as to the proper course to take with respect to termination of treatment. Finally, the court concluded that in the absence of legislative directive, "there is no legal requirement that prior judicial approval is necessary before a decision to withdraw treatment can be made."[58] The court ordered that no further criminal proceedings take place.

Legislative Solutions. The legislatures of some states have attempted to resolve the question of the termination of life-support systems by enacting living will statutes and brain death statutes. California has enacted the Natural Death Act[59] and the Durable Power of Attorney For Health Care Act, which codify the concept of a living will.[60]

Natural Death Act. In enacting the Natural Death Act, the California Legislature determined that all adult persons have the fundamental right to control decisions relating to the rendering of their own medical care, including the decision to have life-sustaining procedures withheld or withdrawn.[61] Consequently, a "qualified patient,'' one who has been diagnosed and certified in writing by two physicians to be terminally ill,[62] may execute a directive for the withholding or the withdrawal of life-support procedures.[63]

The Act is intended for only a very limited number of persons. If the directive is executed by a person prior to being diagnosed terminally ill, it is not binding on the physician.[64] The procedural requirements, especially the requirement that the patient wait 14 days after the diagnosis of terminal illness, are so cumbersome that the California Court of Appeal views it as unlikely that any but a small number of highly educated and motivated patients will utilize the directive.[65]

Durable Power of Attorney for Health Care. The inadequacies presented by the Natural Death Act prompted the California legislature to enact the Durable Power of Attorney for Health Care.[66] Under this act, the patient may execute a durable power of attorney authorizing an ''attorney in fact'' to make health care decisions for the person executing the directive. An attorney in fact is simply the person designated to make health care decisions on behalf of the principal.

To be effective, the durable power of attorney must specifically authorize the attorney in fact to make health care decisions. In addition, it must be dated and witnessed by two persons who are not the attorney in fact and who are not related to the principal (the person executing the durable power of attorney). These witnesses must declare, under penalty of perjury, that they know the person signing the document is the principal, that the principal signed the document in their presence, and that he or she appeared to be of sound mind and not influenced by fraud or undue influence.[67]

One of the witnesses must also, under oath, assert that he or she is not related by blood, marriage or adoption and is not entitled to the estate of the principal. The witnesses may not be the health care provider or employees of the health care provider.[68] Thus, for example, nurses may not serve as witnesses.[69] A nurse may not serve as the attorney in fact if the principal becomes a patient at the health facility in which the nurse is employed.[70] This restriction also applies if the nurse is the treating health care provider.

If the principal is able to give informed consent with respect to a particular treatment, the attorney in fact may not make a decision for the principal. If the principal is unable to decide, then the attorney in fact may, subject to any limitation set forth in the durable power of attorney, make health care decisions for the principal, before and after the death of the principal, to the same extent as the principal could have. The attorney in fact has a duty to act in a manner consistent with the desires of the principal as expressed in the durable power of attorney or otherwise made known to the attorney in fact at any time. If the principal's desires are unknown, then the duty is to act in the best interests of the principal.[71]

The attorney in fact, however, many not consent to abortion, sterilization, psychosurgery, convulsive treatment, or commitment to a mental health facility.[72] The attorney in fact has the same right, unless qualified in the durable power of attorney, as the principal to receive information about the proposed health care, to review medical reports, and to consent to the disclosure of medical records.[73]

The durable power of attorney expires in seven years unless a shorter period is designated.[74] The principal is presumed competent to revoke it and may do so at any time.[75] Health care providers are immune from civil and criminal liability so long as the following conditions are met: (1) the decision is made by an attorney in fact whom the provider believes in good faith is authorized under the act to make the decision; and (2) the provider believes that the decision is not inconsistent with the desires of the principal as expressed in the durable power of attorney or as otherwise made known to the provider.

Immunity from liability for decisions to withhold or to withdraw health care necessary to keep the principal alive requires that the health care provider (1) make a good faith effort to determine the desires of the principal to the extent that the principal is able to convey these desires to the provider and (2) make the results of that effort a part of the principal's medical records.[76] No criminal, civil, or professional disciplinary liability results from the provider's failure to withdraw health care necessary to keep the principal alive.[77]

Altering the durable power document, withholding personal knowledge, or willfully concealing knowledge that the principal revoked the power, with the intent to cause withholding or withdrawal of life-sustaining health care, may result in liability for unlawful homicide if the principal dies as the result of the lack of care.[78] The act expressly does not authorize mercy killing, and it does not ''permit any affirmative or deliberate act or omission to end life other than withholding or withdrawal of health care pursuant to a durable power of attorney for health care so as to permit the natural process of dying.''[79]

Consent To Nursing Treatments. Nurses should obtain a patient's consent prior to instituting a particular nursing action. Recognition of the individual's autonomy in decision making requires that nurses respect the privacy and integrity of their patients. Increasing legal accountability has resulted in closer scrutiny of nurses' actions. To avoid battery claims by patients, nurses should document in the patient's chart that consent was obtained prior to performing the nursing action. The details of the discussion preceding the consent should also be included.

The nurse, as provider of care, is responsible for obtaining consent to nursing care prior to its administration. The principles discussed with reference to assault and battery are, by analogy, applicable to every provider of health care. Frequently, care given in a hospital or a home setting is a matter of routine, and the patient's consent is not obtained or recorded. The better practice, which respects the patient's autonomy, is to obtain consent prior to providing routine care.

Where, however, the patient is incapable of consenting, consult a family member for consent. If the treatment is emergency care, the law will imply consent. Where a do not resuscitate order is written in the chart, the nurse may follow the order, provided that he or she has no knowledge that the patient desires emergency measures. If the chart does not contain a do not resuscitate order, and the patient is incapable of consenting or refusing treatment, nurses should institute whatever measures the emergency requires to save the patient's life.[80]

FALSE IMPRISONMENT

False imprisonment protects the personal interest in freedom from restraint of movement.[81] The plaintiff must prove that there was some direct restraint imposed for some period of time which compelled him or her to go somewhere or stay somewhere against his or her will. The restraint is an apprehension of force resulting from a defendant's words, actions, or gestures. Thus, the plaintiff must be aware of the confinement.

Even a brief restraint, however, is sufficient, and there is no need that the plaintiff suffer damages from the confinement.[82] The plaintiff need only prove that the defendant intended to confine, not that the defendant intended to cause injury. Punitive damages are recoverable.[83]

To win a lawsuit charging false imprisonment, the plaintiff must prove that he or she was restrained physically or by intimidation, for example, that threats of force were used to intimidate the plaintiff into compliance. The restraint of movement must be against the plaintiff's will. If the plaintiff voluntarily agrees to the restraint, there is no imprisonment; consent is a complete defense.[84]

Generally, false imprisonment in the health care setting arises when a patient is hospitalized or moved for treatment against his or her will. Many states have codified the circumstances which authorize involuntary psychiatric hospitalizations. A person hospitalized in a mental hospital in violation of the state's statute may have a claim of false imprisonment against the hospital and its staff.[85] Treatment undertaken without the person's consent under such circumstances renders the staff potentially liable for assault and battery.[86]

False imprisonment may also be asserted if a patient is intentionally confined in a health care facility without the consent of the patient or an authorized person. Depending on the jurisdiction, there may be criminal liability as well. For example, in California, if the reason for confinement is solely for the nonpayment of a medical bill, the defendant may be guilty of a misdemeanor in addition to being liable for civil damages.[87]

INTENTIONAL INFLICTION OF EMOTIONAL DISTRESS

The tort of intentional infliction of emotional distress protects a person's interest in peace of mind.[88] Intentional infliction of mental disturbance by extreme and outrageous conduct constitutes the tort. The outrageous conduct need not be directed at the plaintiff; if a third person is present, and is known by the defendant to be present, and this person suffers mental disturbance as the result of observing the outrageous conduct directed toward another person, the person observing the conduct may recover.[89] This tort has been asserted by patients such as Mr. Bartling for refusal to terminate treatment.

Quasi-intentional torts

DEFAMATION

Defamation, an invasion of the interest in reputation and good name, is made up of the twin torts libel (written communication) and slander (oral communication).[90] A defamatory communication is one which holds the plaintiff up to hatred, contempt, or ridicule, or one which causes the plaintiff to be shunned or avoided by the community.[91] A defamatory communication injures a person's reputation by diminishing the esteem, respect, goodwill, or confidence in which the plaintiff is held or by inciting derogatory opinions or feelings about the plaintiff.

Any living person may be defamed; the defamation action is personal and cannot be maintained for the defamation of another unless the plaintiff and the third person are so close in relationship that the defamation of one necessarily implicates the other. Since the injury is to reputation, it follows that the defamatory communication must be published—expressed—to third persons. If the communication is not published, there is no defamation.

A publication which is defamatory on its face does not need additional proof of its defamatory meaning. Occasionally, the publication is not defamatory on its face, but carries a defamatory meaning which is only understood if the plaintiff explains it by evidence other than the mere communication itself. A publication may also be clearly defamatory to someone yet not make reference to the individual plaintiff. In these two circumstances, the plaintiff must plead and prove that the defamatory meaning is attached to him or her.[92]

The defendant may attempt to show that the words or communication were understood by others as a joke and therefore is not defamatory. Truth is another defense, and certain communications that are privileged are not defamatory.[93]

Slander. Because slander involves oral publications that injure reputation, the courts originally were reluctant to award damages for slander in the absence of actual damage.[94] Where, however, the defamatory communication qualifies as slander per se, actual damages need not be proved, and damage will be presumed. Slander per se is an oral defamatory communication which imputes to the plaintiff one of the following: (1) a crime; (2) a loathsome disease such as venereal disease; (3) something which affects or impugns a business, a profession, an office, or a calling; or (4) unchastity in a woman.[95] All other slanderous words, no matter how insulting or defamatory, are actionable only if the plaintiff proves special (economic) damage resulting from the defamation.

Barry v. Baugh,[96] in which a registered nurse sued a physician for slander, illustrates this last rule. The incident giving rise to the slander did not occur in her employment as a nurse. Rather, the physician made the allegedly slanderous comments while treating her husband.

The nurse went to the office of her husband's physician and requested an examination of her husband so that he could be certified for commitment to the state mental hospital. In response, the physician said in a voice, loud enough that patients in the next room could hear, that there was nothing wrong with her husband except that he was an old drunk who should be in jail instead of the hospital. The doctor indicated that, if she insisted, he would contact the proper personnel.

Thereafter, again in a loud voice, he stated to someone over the telephone that she, Mrs. Barry, was in his office and wanted her husband committed to the state hospital. The physician loudly stated that he would sign the papers if Mrs. Barry would also agree to be committed since they were both crazy.

Mrs. Barry alleged that these statements were heard or capable of being heard by patients in the waiting room. She further asserted the statements were false, willful, malicious, and intentional and caused her to suffer shock and fright because she feared what impact they would have on her job and her reputation. She claimed that the shock and fright caused her to be unable to sleep, and she sought $5,000 in damages.

The court, relying on Georgia law, rejected her claim because the complaint did not allege special damages (economic damages), and the slander did not fall within one of the per se categories. The plaintiff failed to allege that the words did in fact injure her professional reputation and that the words were spoken in reference to it.

The court reasoned further that the words were not calculated to injure her professional reputation because of the context in which they were said. Since nothing in the words stated alluded to the plaintiff in her capacity as a nurse, she could not recover for slander per se. The case represented oral abuse without any special or actual damages. In the absence of special damages, mere insult and contemptuous language alone do not state a cause of action for slander.[97]

Libel. The existence of damages is presumed where a written communication is defamatory on its face—that is, where the plaintiff need not introduce other evidence to show the defamatory sense of the communication or that it was directed at him or her. If, however, the plaintiff must introduce evidence to explain the defamatory nature of the communication or to show how it relates to him or her, the courts generally require proof of actual damages, unless the communication fits into one of the four slander per se categories outlined before. If the libelous communication fits one of the categories, damages are presumed.[98]

Intention and Malice. In either form of defamation, a defendant may be negligent or innocent in publishing a communication that is defamatory and is intended to injure a person's reputation. Unless the communication is privileged or involves some public figure, the fact that a defendant negligently defames someone is not a defense. The public figure who is defamed must prove that the defendant acted with malice.

Privilege. Privilege may be a defense to either form

of defamation. For example, defamatory communications made during judicial proceedings are absolutely privileged. Similarly, if the plaintiff consents to the defamatory communication, it is not actionable; one who invites or instigates defamatory words cannot complain of the resulting damage to his or her reputation.[99] Political broadcasts conducted according to the provisions of the Federal Communications Act requiring equal time to all political candidates also are absolutely privileged.[100]

Qualified privileges are defenses that may be lost if actual damages or malice is proved. For example, newsworthy stories and items about public figures are qualifiedly privileged, requiring that the plaintiff prove that the newspaper or writer acted with malice. A defamatory communication may also be privileged where it is necessary to protect another, so long as (1) the defendant has reason to believe that the publication is necessary for that purpose, and (2) the scope of the communication is limited to that necessary to achieve this purpose.[101]

Judge v. Rockford Memorial Hospital[102] illustrates privileged communications in an employment setting. There, a private-duty registered nurse brought an action for libel against a hospital where she had cared for a patient. The libelous communication was a letter written by the Director of Nursing which allegedly injured her reputation and prevented her from obtaining other employment. The plaintiff had intermittently been a private-duty nurse for various patients at the hospital for approximately a one year-period. She was a member of the Nurses Professional Registry in Rockford, Illinois.

The evidence at trial disclosed that the Director of Nursing at the hospital was charged with supervising all nursing care, including that given by private-duty nurses in the hospital. On three separate days, the Director received a report that a 30-ml vial of Demerol was missing. After the third loss, the Director spoke with the pharmacist and began checking the records of nurses who had been on duty on the floor where the losses occurred.

One of the nurses who reported the narcotic loss testified on behalf of the hospital. She stated that on the night she reported the loss, the plaintiff was working as a private-duty nurse on the same floor where the loss occurred. At 10:45 PM, all Demerol vials were present in the cabinet, but when she made her final check at the end of the shift, a vial was missing.

The Director also testified that she checked the records of the nurses who worked on the floor. In checking the plaintiff's records, she found 22 prior instances where the plaintiff had failed to properly record the administration of narcotics to patients which, as disclosed from the narcotics records, she had withdrawn from the supply on the floor. In addition, there were three prior instances where she had failed to properly record administering Demerol to a patient, although she had withdrawn Demerol from the narcotics cabinet.

The evidence also showed that there were 18 or 20 prior instances where the plaintiff had withdrawn codeine and had failed to record administering it. Further, the plaintiff had administered 6 ml of Demerol after a physician had discontinued it.

The plaintiff testified she had in fact administered the Demerol but had not recorded it on the patient's record or the nurse's record. She also asserted that she had administered the codeine.

The evidence further demonstrated that normal hospital operating procedures require the nurse to record on the narcotics record the withdrawal of any narcotic, and then to record on the individual patient's chart the fact that the medication was given. The court noted that the plaintiff offered no particular explanation as to the apparent record-keeping deficiencies except that she had administered it or wasted it, but had failed to communicate the same. The court also stated that "[a]ccurate records and a perpetual inventory of narcotics and the handling thereof are obviously necessary for many reasons, including the doctor's information, the patient's welfare, charging the patient, and inspection by the Federal Bureau of Narcotics. [The plaintiff] was an experienced nurse and knew the normal operating procedures."[103]

The court also stated that when the director called the plaintiff to her office and informed her of the losses and the plaintiff's prior record, the plaintiff said nothing. The director informed her that she could no longer take drugs from the cabinet unless another nurse was in attendance. The plaintiff responded that this would be all right. She did not offer any protestations or explanations as to her record keeping or the questioned narcotics.

When the nurse's care of the patient at the hospital concluded, the Director contacted the Rockford Nurses Professional Registry and asked that the plaintiff not be assigned as a private-duty nurse to the hospital in the future. The grievance committee then asked the Director to write a letter, which she did. In this letter, she explained the incidents and indicated that these did not in any way reflect on the care that was given to the patients but nevertheless she did not want the nurse working at the hospital.

Only committee members of the complaint or grievance committee of the Nurse's Registry had access to the letter. No copy of the letter was sent to any other person. The plaintiff shortly thereafter instructed the registry to take her off the on call list which indicates to the Registry that the nurse is immediately available for service. The plaintiff never requested that she be reinstated to the on call list at the Registry but she had never been taken off the list.

The evidence also showed that the Registry was the place to be contacted for private-duty work; hospitals did not hire private-duty nurses on an individual basis. Although patients themselves hired and paid the private-duty nurses, the purpose of the registry was to provide a centralized call service.

The court held that the letter was a privileged communication and therefore not defamatory. A privileged communication, the court explained, is one where circumstances exist, or are reasonably believed by the defendant to exist, from which he or she has an interest or duty, or in good faith believes he or she has in interest or duty, to make a certain communication to another person who has a corresponding duty.

Further, if the defendant makes the communication in good faith, under these circumstances, believing the communication to be true, even though it may not then be true, the communication is qualifiedly or conditionally privileged. Both the party making the statement and the party to whom the statement is made must have an interest or duty in respects of the matter to render it qualifiedly or conditionally privileged. If, however, actual malice is proved, the privilege is lost.

The privilege was applicable in the case because of several factors. First, the Director of Nurses was charged with supervising nurses, and her duty and interest extended to the patients as well as her employer—the hospital. Since the plaintiff was not an employee of the hospital, the Director could not discharge her. The hospital was under no obligation to keep the plaintiff working there. The Registry was necessarily interested in and had duties with respect to sending the plaintiff to other hospitals where private-duty nurses were needed. It was also interested in complaints against its members.

Moreover, the Director of Nurses did not volunteer to write the letter, but rather was requested to do so by the grievance committee. No other entity or person received a copy of the letter. There was no evidence of malice, and thus judgment for the defendant was proper, and no trial was required.

Buckley v. Litman[104] also demonstrates application of the qualified privilege. There, a physician published an allegedly defamatory letter concerning his former physician assistant to the appropriate authorities at the Physician Assistant's Licensing Board. The asserted defamation concerned missing confidential patient records about which the physician attempted to speak with the plaintiff but the plaintiff avoided his calls. A carbon of the letter was sent to the physician assistant's current employer.

The court held that both communications were entitled to the qualified privilege. The first communication was privileged as a communication addressed to an official body charged with responsibility for consideration and processing of complaints of professional misconduct on the part of the physician's assistants. It did not lose this quality because a carbon was sent to the plaintiff's current employer.

Rather, in the court's view, the carbon was also privileged. The plaintiff's current employer had been associated with the defendant doctor in a family practice. Thus, there was a common interest shared by plaintiff's new employer and the defendant which extended to matters of patient care and files, even though the communication was unsolicited by the new employer. The letter was reasonably calculated to serve their shared interest and thus the privilege applied.

Truth as a Defense. Truth is an absolute defense to a defamation action. Proving the truth of a statement may require a jury trial because the truth or falsity of a statement is usually disputed. Thus, truth as a defense rarely results in pretrial dismissals.

Malone v. Longo[105] illustrates the privilege and truth defenses in the context of a pretrial motion for summary judgment (dismissal). There, the defamatory communication stemmed from an incident that occurred while two nurses were working at the Veterans Administration Hospital. The claim asserted by one of the nurses included both slander and libel. The other nurse contended the statements were true. The lower court was asked to dismiss the action after considering various documents attached to motions for summary judgment.

The defendant nurse's slanderous statement informed various personnel at the hospital that the plaintiff had told her to give a medication for which she had no order. The libelous statement concerned a written report about the incident in which the defendant reported that the plaintiff had told her not to question the plaintiff's orders or those of the physicians.

The court acknowledged that the facts were not entirely clear. The plaintiff reportedly interpreted an order for medication and asked the defendant to give the medication. The plaintiff indicated that although the order did not state how often the patient was to receive the medication, they should give it once and then call the physician to determine how often the patient should receive the medication. The defendant allegedly stated that the order was not for the drug the plaintiff had described, and she refused to give the injection. Thereafter, the plaintiff determined that the order did not call for the drug she thought it did. She admitted the error and asked the defendant to give the proper medication.

The defendant, in the meantime, was discussing the correctness of the plaintiff's interpretation with another nurse. The plaintiff admonished her not to discuss their disagreements with others. An argument ensued, and another nurse intervened and suggested that a written report be made. The plaintiff asserted that the defendant thereafter told the defamatory words to other personnel at the hospital.

The defendant's version differed. She contended that the absence of an indication on the order as to how often the medication was to be given caused the plaintiff to check the medication with the head nurse and physician, who immediately corrected her erroneous interpretation of the order. In spite of their assurances, the plaintiff directed her to inject the wrong medication. After she refused to give the medication, the plaintiff again checked with the laboratory, the head nurse, and the physician.

The parties did not dispute that the following day the head nurse directed the defendant to make a written report of the events. This report contained the allegedly libelous statement. The plaintiff and the nurse on duty that night were also requested to report on the incident. A letter of admonishment was placed in the plaintiff's file.

The defendant sought to have the case dismissed because the truth of her statements barred the action. The defendant also argued that dismissal was required because the statements were absolutely privileged in that they were made in response to the direction of her superiors and were required by duty.

The court agreed that the written report was privileged and could not be the basis of a libel action. The court noted that federal officials have absolute immunity from common law suits for defamation for acts taken within the outer perimeter of their official duties. Statements made by federal officials in the course of disciplinary proceedings, evaluations, complaints, and related investigations in which the official is under a duty to complete a report are within the scope of the official's duty. Since the report was undertaken in this manner, it was privileged.

The court refused, however, to dismiss the action with respect to the oral statement because a factual dispute existed; consequently, the court could not find only one version of the facts that would entitle the defendant to a judgment as a matter of law (without a trial). The court reasoned the words were capable of more than one meaning and therefore precluded a conclusion that the words reflected the substantial truth.

The plaintiff conceded that she had mistakenly told the defendant to administer the wrong medication. Whether, as the defendant asserted, the plaintiff insisted defendant give the medication after being informed of the error was unclear. Thus while it was true that the plaintiff told defendant to give a medication for which she did not have an order, there was conflicting evidence as to when the plaintiff discovered her error and whether she insisted on the defendant giving an erroneous medication after the error was pointed out to her.

The statement, the court reasoned, could be interpreted to mean that the plaintiff had no order at all rather than to mean that she misinterpreted the order. The court concluded that the statement on its face could be taken as impugning the plaintiff's professional competence. Accordingly, the statement could be actionable. Since there was more than one plausible interpretation, the court refused to summarily decide the case.

MALICIOUS PROSECUTION

The action of malicious prosecution began as a remedy for unjustifiable criminal prosecutions, but American courts permit the action for civil proceedings.[106] In general, the plaintiff must prove that (1) the proceeding terminated in his or her favor, (2) the proceeding was initiated without probable cause, (3) the action was brought with malice, and (4) actual damages were sustained as a result of the action.[107]

In *Northwest Florida Home Health Agency v. Merrill*,[108] the Florida Appellate Court reversed a lower court's judgment in favor of a registered nurse who brought a malicious prosecution case against her supervisor and the employing agency. The nurse's action stemmed from a report of the circumstances surrounding her termination given to the Board of Nursing by the defendants.

Shortly after the nurse began working for the company, a nonprofit corporation that provided home nursing services, she was reprimanded for refusing to provide emergency nursing service to a patient who lived 2 miles from her home. Sometime after that, she received a favorable evaluation.

The nurse's supervisor agreed to take over the nurse's caseload of patients while she was on vacation. The supervisor discovered that the nurse had provided inadequate care, had inaccurately charted, and had falsified a mileage reimbursement claim. When the nurse returned, she was terminated.

The agency had received two letters from the Department of Regulation advising that Florida law required them to report any nurse who violated the Nurse Practice Act. Under Florida law,[109] unprofessional conduct is grounds for discipline. Unprofessional conduct includes inaccurate reporting, acts of negligence, failing to conform to accepted standards of nursing practice, and failing to report anyone whom the licensee knows is in violation of the rules of the Department of Regulation or the Board of Nursing.

The rules of the Board of Nursing make the Department of Regulation responsible for making a probable cause determination for purposes of filing an adminstrative complaint. There is immunity from civil liability for making a report so long as the person reporting maintains the confidentiality of the investigation. All proceedings and records during an investigation prior to a determination of probable cause to file an administrative complaint are confidential until the complaint is issued or until the person being investigated waives the confidential nature of the investigation.

The supervisor, with the agency's knowledge, contacted the department and cooperated in a confidential investigation of the nurse. She provided an affidavit identifying six areas of poor care by the nurse. Thereafter, the nurse was notified by the Department of Regulation as to the investigation. She told several of her friends and a prospective employer about the investigation. Ultimately, the investigation was dismissed because there was no probable cause to proceed with an administrative complaint.

The nurse's subsequent suit for malicious prosecution was based solely on her supervisor's conduct in reporting her termination. The appellate court rejected this basis as a valid ground for a malicious prosecution action.

The court first noted that the Board of Nursing had a policy of encouraging persons regulated by law to make confidential complaints where a registered nurse is disciplined for professional misconduct by reprimand, loss of privileges, or dismissal. The Board also discourages such persons from making their own independent determinations of probable cause.

An investigator testified at trial that 75% of the cases investigated result in a finding of no probable cause. He also testified that employers of registered nurses are expected to report all terminations of employment involving questionable nursing action. Another significant factor was that while the supervisor had maintained the confidentiality of the investigation, the nurse had waived her right to confidentiality by informing others of the investigation.

Several elements necessary to maintaining a claim for malicious prosecution were not substantiated by the nurse. First, there was no commencement of a civil or criminal proceeding. The confidential investigation process was not, as the nurse argued, a quasijudicial proceeding. The court reasoned that the statute expressly describes the investigation procedure, which occurs prior to a determination of probable cause, as a nonadversarial executive function.

The court also noted that an investigation can begin without a complaint being issued. The proceeding is not a quasijudicial one until the agency determination of probable cause is made because this is when the right to notice and a hearing come into play.

With respect to the element of probable cause, the court noted that the standard is whether the defendant has reasonable grounds of suspicion supported by circumstances sufficiently strong in themselves to warrant a person of caution to conclude that the Department should be informed. The truth or falsity of the charges is not the decisive material factor since the obligation to report possible violations is sufficient probable cause.

The plaintiff also failed to prove the element of malice. While ordinarily malice is inferred from a lack of probable cause and is an issue for the jury to decide, the statute which required the reporting at issue gives civil immunity to those who report unless the report is furnished in bad faith and with malice. Consequently, actual malice, similar to the actual malice that must be proved in defamation cases where a qualified privilege exists, must be proven. Inferred malice, such as that which arises from a lack of probable cause, was insufficient to overcome the privilege against civil liability.

The court rejected the nurse's argument that malice was demonstrated by the amount of time that elapsed between her termination and the supervisor's report. Equally meritless was the claim that the report was made without sufficient investigation. The investigator testified that the supervisor showed no malice in her cooperation with the investigation.

INTERFERENCE WITH OR INVASION OF THE RIGHT TO PRIVACY

Traditionally, interference with or invasion of the right to privacy[110] is comprised of four separate causes of action which protect a person's interest in and right to privacy: appropriation of name and likeness; intrusion upon solitude or seclusion; public disclosure of private facts; and false light in the public eye. Each of these is a personal right that does not extend to one's family members.[111]

Punitive damages may be recovered, except if the defendant acted innocently or with the belief that the plaintiff had consented.[112] Table 1 summarizes the similarities and differences in each that are discussed below. In addition, the breach of confidentiality, a related tort, is examined.

Appropriation of Name or Likeness. Appropriation of one's name or likeness is a cause of action that allows a plaintiff to recover damages when his or her name or picture or other likeness is used without consent for some business purpose such as to advertise a product or to accompany an article being sold. There is of course no exclusive right to a name; it is only when one's name is used to "pirate" the plaintiff's identity for some advantage of the defendant that a claim exists.[114] Where the plaintiff's character, occupation, and general outline of his or her career is used as the basis for a figure in a novel who is still clearly fictional, there is no liability.[115]

Intrusion upon Physical Solitude or Seclusion. This invasion of privacy claim includes protection of solitude or seclusion from physical intrusion, such as invasion of one's home, and provides a remedy for eavesdropping upon private conversations.[116] Thus, an unauthorized intrusion on childbirth may be actionable.[117] Similarly, taking the photograph of a patient confined to a hospital bed, even for educational use, has been held to be an invasion of privacy under this theory.[118]

Public Disclosure of Private Facts. The disclosure of private true facts is actionable as an invasion of privacy. Public disclosure of the x-rays of a woman's pelvic region has been held to be an invasion of privacy.[119] Similarly, public exhibition of the films of a cesarean section has been the successful subject of an invasion of privacy lawsuit.[120]

The disclosure of private facts must be public, not private. On the other hand, the facts disclosed must be private, not public. Matters of public record are not actionable. Thus, when a picture is taken in a private place without the plaintiff's consent, such as in a hospital, the appearance which is made public is still a private thing and actionable.[121] Similarly, where a physician discloses to an employer medical information about a patient without the patient's consent, an invasion of privacy action may be maintained.[122]

False Light In A Public Eye. Another invasion of privacy claim is publicity that places the plaintiff in a false light in the public eye. The false light must be something which would be objectionable to the ordinary prudent person under the circumstances.[123]

BREACH OF CONFIDENTIALITY

The breach of confidentiality cause of action has its roots in the concepts of trust and confidence, and thus may be properly asserted against the nurse. Although most cases involve physicians, the legal principles, by analogy, are applicable to nurses. Many states have statutorily created a physician-patient privilege protecting the physician from being compelled to testify to confidential communications of the patient. Legislation is needed to extend the privilege to nurses.

Because a physician is a confidante to the medical information of a patient, the courts have held that a patient should be entitled to freely disclose all symptoms to receive proper care without fear that those facts will be disclosed.[124] This premise applies by analogy to the nurse-patient relationship.

Where disclosure is necessary to preserve public welfare, there is no right to recover damages. Thus, in *Simonsen v. Swenson*,[125] a physician diagnosed a patient as having venereal disease and advised him to leave the hotel. When he refused, the physician disclosed the diagnosis to the hotel owner, and the patient was forced to leave. The court denied recovery because the disclosure of the contagious disease was necessary to preserve the public welfare.

In addition reporting statutes may require the disclo-

Table 1. Elements of the Tort: Interference with or Invasion of the Right to Privacy

	Something Secret or Private Invaded	Publicity	Falsity	Use for Advantage
Appropriation	No	No	No	Yes
Intrusion	Yes	No	No	No
Public disclosure	Yes	Yes	No	No
False light	No	Yes	Yes	No

sure of otherwise confidential information. Child abuse, violent injuries or gunshot wounds, contagious diseases, and occupational injuries are examples.[126] The psychiatric health care provider's duty to disclose a patient's violent threats to an intended victim is another exception in some jurisdictions.[127]

Where, however, there is no justification for the disclosure, the suit may be successful. For example, in *Humphers v. First Interstate Bank*,[128] the court held that a mother who had given up her child for adoption could sue a physician who delivered the child and revealed the mother's identity to him at a later time. The court distinguished the invasion of privacy claim, holding that the facts were insufficient for this tort.

Civil rights actions

Civil rights actions brought by and against health care providers involve Section 1983, a federal civil rights statute.[129] For this reason, an overview of Section 1983's elements and defenses and applicable case law follows. The chapter closes with an analysis of Section 1983 cases involving nurses as plaintiffs and other providers as defendants. Other civil rights cases are discussed in the practice chapters.

ELEMENTS OF A SECTION 1983 CIVIL RIGHTS ACTION

Section 1983[130] is one of several civil rights statutes adopted after the civil war.[131] It remedies violations of federal rights, so long as these violations are attributable to government action. Section 1983 actions must allege two essential elements: first, that some person has deprived the plaintiff of a federal right; and second, that this person acted under color of state law in depriving the plaintiff of his or her civil rights (state action).

Section 1983 Injuries. Section 1983 remedies the violation of all rights, privileges, or immunities secured by the federal Constitution and federal laws. Section 1983 does not itself establish any rights, it only provides a remedy—a claim for damages or equitable relief—when the plaintiff alleges a violation of federal constitutional, statutory, or regulatory rights.[132] Section 1983 does not remedy violations of rights protected by state laws.

Section 1983 reaches violations of any federal right; the Supreme Court has refused to distinguish personal liberties from property rights for purposes of the statute's coverage.[133] Thus, Section 1983 applies to the substantive, as well as procedural, deprivations of life, liberty, or property without due process of law.

Property and liberty interests are defined more broadly in this context than they are in state laws. Property interests under the Fourteenth Amendment include those entitlements, benefits, or expectations created by state law.[134] The plaintiff claiming a deprivation must have legitimate claim of entitlement to the benefit. Welfare recipients, for example, have a legitimate claim of entitlement to their welfare benefits. They have a property interest in their benefits that cannot be taken without due process of law.

A state employee whose job is created by state law also has a property interest in that job that cannot be deprived without a hearing.[135] People licensed by the state clearly have a property interest in their licenses that may not be deprived without due process of law.[136] Some commentators suggest that indigent patients potentially have a property interest in the Hill-Burton Act and regulations issued to implement the act that require the hospital to establish standards of eligibility for indigent patients.[137]

Liberty includes all of the Fourteenth Amendment substantive due process, privacy, and liberty interests recognized by the Court in the areas of family and sexual privacy, education, and reputation.[138] Violations of the First, Third, Fourth, Fifth, Sixth, Eighth, and Ninth Amendments, as well as the right to privacy, are actionable.[139] Any governmental action that denies equal protection of the law is a Section 1983 injury, so long as discriminatory intent is shown.[140] The discussion that follows demonstrates the liberty and privacy interests that are implicated in the health care context.

Actionable Conduct. Only those violations of federal law that are accomplished under color of state law are actionable. Proximate cause must also exist[141]: the violation must reasonably cause the injury, and the injury must not be too remote a consequence.[142]

State Action. In general, those who act under color of law include state officials, local officials, and private persons whose conduct is found to be "state action" within the meaning of the Fourteenth Amendment. In the health care context, the state action requirement is easily met when a state, federal, or public (county) hospital or a community or public health agency is involved.[143]

Private action, however, no matter how discriminatory or wrongful, is not actionable under Section 1983. Nevertheless, if that ostensibly private conduct can be fairly attributed to the government, the state action requirement may be satisfied.

There is no precise formula for determining when private conduct constitutes state action.[144] Nevertheless four tests, discussed below, have been formulated by the Supreme Court.[145]

*Symbiotic Relationship.*This test determines whether a *symbiotic relationship* exists between the private actor and the state. State action under this test has been found where a private restaurant refused to serve Blacks. The restaurant leased space from a municipal parking structure and received substantial tax benefits; the municipality earned profits from the restaurant.[146] The restaurant claimed its business would decrease if it served Blacks. The government, which profitted from this discrimination, was so far insinuated ''into a position of interdependence'' with the restaurant that it was deemed a joint participant in the challenged activity.[147]

Public Function. This test analyzes if the government has delegated a public function to a private person. Where historically traditional government tasks are carried out by a private person, there is state action.[148] Nursing home care has been held not to be a public function and thus cannot provide a state action Section 1983 civil rights suit.[149]

Nexus Test. This inquiry focuses on whether there is a sufficiently close nexus between the state and the challenged activity of the regulated entity so that the action of the latter can be fairly said to be that of the state itself.[150] State authorization of private conduct, standing alone, is not sufficient. Rather, the state must either order or significantly encourage the challenged activity.

Joint Participation. Where a private person acts jointly with the state or an official, there may be a finding of state action. Private persons engaged jointly with state officials in wrongful conduct are acting under color of law; to be liable, the defendant need not be a state official if he or she is a willing participant in joint action with the state or its agents.[151]

State action in recent years has been restricted. For example, the Supreme Court has refused to find state action in the termination of a person's employment from a privately owned school for maladjusted children, even though it received virtually all of its income from government funding and state agency contracts.[152] The Court's reasoning is that the acts of private contractors with the state do not become acts of the government by reason of their significant or even total engagement in performing public contracts. Likewise, education of maladjusted children is not a public function because it is not a function which has been traditionally the exclusive domain of the state.

State action arguments have also failed in the private hospital and nursing home context. In *Blum v. Yaretsky*,[153] the Supreme Court ruled that a nursing home's discharge and transfer of the plaintiff patients without a hearing did not constitute state action. Although the nursing home was extensively regulated, the state subsidized the cost of the facilities and paid the medical expenses of more than 90% of the patients, and state welfare officials responded to these decisions by terminating or reducing the transferred and discharged patients' Medicaid benefits, there was no state action.

In *Chrisman v. Sisters of St. Joseph of Peace*,[154] the Ninth Circuit determined that a private hospital's refusal to allow its facilities to be used for sterilization purposes was not actionable. The court rejected the argument that state action could rest on the following facts involving a private hospital: entitlement to a partial exemption from state taxes, being subject to state regulation, or receiving governmental funds either directly or as compensation for services rendered to patients under state and federal welfare Medicaid and Medicare programs.

Federal courts have rejected the argument that a private physician who provides medical services to an inmate of a state prison is acting under color of state law.[155] The rationale is that the private physician does not become a state actor simply because he or she is performing a private function traditionally filled by retained physicians. A physician employed by the prison is a state actor,[156] as is the employee prison nurse.

The fact that a nursing home exerts great control over its patients' lives has been deemed insufficient to make its conduct state action.[157] Similarly, the mere fact that a hospital receives state funds is insufficient to meet state action.[158] Courts have also rejected the view that receipt of federal Hill-Burton funds, standing alone, is state action.[159] Instead, there must be some connection between the claimed injury and the hospital's obligations under the Hill-Burton Act.

Thus, the courts, for example, have found state action where a hospital's utilization review committee makes a decision as to whether a Medicare patient's stay in the hospital is medically necessary. The rationale is that an adverse determination leads to termination of Medicare benefits.[160]

State action also has been found where a private social agency places wards of the state in foster homes pursuant to requirements of state law.[161] Similarly, the rule has been extended to private hospitals providing medical care, pursuant to a contract with the state, to involuntarily committed mental patients.[162] Similarly, if the private hospital acts jointly with the a state employee, such as a sheriff, to discharge an unruly patient, there may be state action.[163]

Another example of state action is *Downs v. Sawtelle*.[164] There, the court found state action in the defendants' alleged conspiracy to sterilize the plaintiff. The state was involved in many of the defendants' operations, and the defendants received 30% of their operating budget from Medicare. The court also noted that the hospital was subjected to significant governmental regulation. The profits earned were to be distributed to the town where the hospital was located. If the hospital dissolved all of its assets after payment of debts, any remaining profits reverted to the town where the hospital was located. Town officials also had authority to appoint the hospital's board of directors.

In *Tragerser v. Libbie Rehabilitation Center, Inc.*,[165] however, the court refused to find state action in a nurse's attempt to assert a Section 1983 claim for discrimination against her employer, a private corporation operating a nursing home for profit. The nurse's sight is impaired by a hereditary and progressive condition.

The nurse was hired in 1971, and in 1975, she was promoted to the Director of Nurses. In April of 1976, an officer from the department of health conducted a regular inspection of the nursing home. The inspector told the administrator that the plaintiff nurse's eyesight had deteriorated since the last inspection, and he asked what the home intended to do about it.

The administrator related these comments to the board of directors. At its meeting on June 7, 1976, the board resolved to dismiss the nurse. She resigned upon learning that decision, and thereafter filed a federal civil rights action which alleged discrimination against her for her handicap in violation of the equal protection clauses of the Fourteenth and Fifth Amendments.

The court rejected the nurse's section 1983 claim because there was no evidence that when the nursing home acted, it did so under color of either a state law or regulation or a state-enforced custom. The court also rejected the equal protection claim, noting that the plaintiff's reliance on the nursing home's receipt of public funds and the state inspector's role in the nursing home's decision to dismiss her was misplaced.

Significantly, the court noted that the nursing home did *not* participate in the Hill-Burton Construction Program, which subjects hospitals to an elaborate and intricate pattern of governmental regulations, both state and federal. The court also noted, relying on *Walker v. Pierce*,[166] that mere receipt of federal funds does not make an entity a state actor. The court also declined to ascribe state action to the nursing home's receipt of Medicare and veterans' benefits for the same reason.

The court further noted that although the inspector questioned the administrator and asked what the home intended to do about the plaintiff's sight, he did not include this observation about the nurse among the deficiencies that he found at the nursing home. Moreover, the nurse did not allege that the state would or could impose sanctions on the nursing home if it continued to employ her. Accordingly, the court concluded that the nursing home's subsequent decision to dismiss could not be considered the action of the state itself.

Vicarious Liability. Officials or private persons deemed to be acting under color of state law may be sued in their individual and their official capacities, or both. Generally, where an individual is sued in his or her official capacity, the plaintiff is seeking to hold some entity, like a municipality or state, responsible for the violation. This is known as vicarious liability. The courts have created tests to determine whether an entity should be vicariously liable for one of its officials or a private person who is deemed to be acting under color of law for the entity.

The first is where the deprivation of rights stems from an officially promulgated municipal policy or from a municipal "custom or usage." The second is where an official employed by the entity deprives another of a constitutional right and that may be fairly said to represent an official policy. Under these circumstances the entity is vicariously liable for the official's wrongdoings.[167]

An official who promulgates a policy that is enforced by subordinates may be liable under Section 1983 where enforcement of the policy violates rights.[168] Inaction by a supervisor or official may be viewed as tacit approval of the wrongful behavior. Where subordinate employees engage in conduct that violates rights, mere failure to discipline the employee is generally unduly sufficient to show that some policy has been adopted by the entity.[169] Gross negligence or deliberate indifference to the deprivation of the plaintiff's constitutional rights in failing to supervise or to train may be actionable.[170]

Section 1983 Damages. The purpose of Section 1983 damage awards is to compensate persons for injuries caused by the deprivation of constitutional rights.[171] With respect to violations of procedural due process, compensatory damages may be awarded only if the plaintiff proves actual injury resulting from the denial of due process.[172] The injury may be either emotional or mental distress that results from the violation of procedural rights or results from an unjustified deprivation of an interest protected by the due process clause. The appropriate test to measure damages stemming from other constitutional violations is found in tort law, provided that the interests protected by tort law closely parallel the interests protected by a particular constitutional right.[173]

Punitive damages may not be awarded against a municipal entity in a Section 1983 lawsuit.[174] They may be awarded, however, against a public official acting in his or her individual capacity whose conduct is shown to be motivated by evil motive or intent or to involve reckless or callous indifference to the federally protected rights of others.[175]

PROVIDER VIOLATIONS OF PATIENT'S LIBERTY AND PRIVACY RIGHTS

The Right To Freedom. *O'Connor v. Donaldson*,[176] a celebrated civil rights case in the mental health field, illustrates that a violation of a substantive due process liberty interest may be remedied by a Section 1983 action. The Supreme Court's opinion caused many states to alter their commitment statutes.

Mr. Donaldson, who had been civilly committed to confinement as a mental patient in a Florida State Hospital for 15 years, sued the hospital's superintendent, Dr. J.B. O'Connor, under Section 1983. He alleged that O'Connor and other members of the hospital staff named as defendants had intentionally and maliciously deprived him of his constitutional right to liberty.

Throughout his confinement, Donaldson repeatedly, but unsuccessfully, demanded his release. He argued that his confinement was improper because he was not dangerous to anyone, he was not mentally ill, and, in any event, the hospital was not providing treatment for his supposed illness. After a 4-day trial, the jury returned a verdict assessing both compensatory and punitive damages against O'Connor and a codefendant.[177]

The Supreme Court's review of the evidence leaves little doubt that Donaldson's commitment violated his right to liberty. The hospital staff had the power to release a patient, not dangerous to himself or to others, even if the patient remained mentally ill and had been lawfully committed. Yet the staff made no attempts while O'Connor was there; almost immediately after O'Connor retired as superintendent, Donaldson was released. For 15 years, O'Connor had refused to allow proceedings to be instituted for Donaldson's release.

O'Connor asserted that he had believed that Donaldson would have been unable to make a successful adjustment outside the institution, but he could not recall the basis for that conclusion. The trial testimony demonstrated, "without contradiction"[178] that Donaldson posed no danger to others during his long confinement or at any point during his life. O'Connor admitted that he had no personal knowledge or second-hand knowledge that Donaldson had ever committed a dangerous act. One of O'Connor's codefendants acknowledged that Donaldson could have earned a living outside the hospital.

Donaldson's most recent request for release was supported by responsible persons willing to provide him with any care that he might need upon his release. A representative from a half-way house had requested Donaldson's release to its facilities. O'Connor conceded the facility was a good one, but claimed that he rejected the offer because Donaldson could only be released to his parents—a rule invented by O'Connor. The Court pointed out that, at that time, Donaldson was 55 years old, which O'Connor knew, and his parents were too elderly and infirm to care for him.

On four separate occasions between 1964 and 1968, a long-time family friend requested Donaldson's release to his care. This friend, the evidence showed, was a serious and responsible person who was willing and able to assume responsibility for Donaldson's care.

The Court characterized this evidence as demonstrating that Donaldson's confinement was a simple regime of enforced custodial care, not a program designed to cure a supposed illness. Even one of O'Connor's codefendants admitted that Donaldson received nothing but custodial care while at the hospital. O'Connor described the treatment as milieu therapy, but other witnesses described this therapy as a euphemism for confinement in the milieu of a mental hospital.

Donaldson was kept in a large room with 60 other patients for substantial periods of time. His requests for occupational training, ground privileges, and opportunity to discuss his case with O'Connor or other staff members were repeatedly denied.

At trial and on appeal, O'Connor relied on the good faith immunity defense. He claimed that since he acted in good faith, he was immune from liability for money damages. His position was that state law, which he believed was valid, authorized indefinite custodial confinement of the "sick" even if the sick were not given treatment and their release could harm no one.

The jury found that Donaldson was neither dangerous to himself nor to others and that, if he was mentally ill, he had not received treatment. There simply was no basis for the confinement. The fact that the state law may have authorized confinement of the harmless mentally ill did not itself establish a constitutionally adequate purpose for the confinement.

A finding of mental illness alone cannot justify the state locking up a person against his or her will and keeping him or her indefinitely in simple custodial confinement. The Court concluded that even if mental illness could be given a reasonably precise content and the mentally ill could be identified with reasonable accuracy, "there is no constitutional basis for confining such persons involuntarily if they are dangerous to no one and can live safely in freedom."[179]

The state cannot confine persons to provide them with a better standard of living that they do not want—the "mere presence of mental illness does not disqualify a person from preferring his home to the comforts of an institution."[180] The state also may not "fence in the harmless mentally ill solely to save its citizens from exposure to those whose ways are different."[181]

> One might as well ask if the State, to avoid public unease could incarcerate all who are physically unattractive or socially eccentric. Mere public intolerance or animosity cannot constitutionally justify the deprivation of a person's physical liberty . . .
>
> In short, the State cannot constitutionally confine without more cause a nondangerous individual who is capable of surviving safely in freedom by himself or with the help of willing and responsible family members and friends.[182]

The Court concluded that since the jury found, upon ample evidence, that O'Connor, as an agent of the state, knowingly confined Donaldson, the jury properly concluded that O'Connor violated Donaldson's constitutional right to freedom.

The Right To Privacy. *Foster v. Tourtellotte*,[183] which is discussed in detail in Chapter 9, represents a trend in judicial decisions holding that the constitutional right to privacy encompasses the decision to terminate life-support systems. Other decisions so holding have been discussed earlier in this chapter in the right to refuse treatment section.

Courts have upheld civil rights cases against health providers for refusal to terminate life-support measures, based on a violation of the right to privacy.[184] While the success of federal civil rights actions against nurses employed by private hospitals is unlikely unless state action is found, state constitutions providing a right of privacy without state action limitations may be actionable.[185]

DEFENSES: GOVERNMENTAL IMMUNITY

Both the common law and statutes establish governmental immunity from Section 1983 lawsuits. The Eleventh Amendment affords the states immunity from *federal* court lawsuits, including civil rights actions, with some exceptions. Individual states that have established independent remedies for violations of federal rights (and remedies for violations of state rights) may by statute create immunity from suit under certain instances. Given the variation among states, the focus of this section is on federal Section 1983 immunity.

Eleventh Amendment. The Eleventh Amendment is a limitation on the judicial power of the federal courts; it does not apply to state judicial proceedings. The Eleventh Amendment bars federal court actions for monetary relief from the state to compensate for past injuries (retrospective relief) and thus protects the state treasury against a federal court award of monetary relief. The state may waive Eleventh Amendment immunity, however, by participating in a lawsuit. For example, a voluntary appearance by the state, intervening as a claimant in a federal court lawsuit, is a waiver.[186]

An exception to the state's immunity from federal suit exists where the plaintiff seeks federal court relief in the form of an injunction or a declaratory judgment that requires state officials to comply with the federal Constitution (prospective relief).[187] A federal court may require a state official to conform to the federal Constitution, but it cannot order the state to pay the plaintiff money for past conduct.

The prospective relief exception is only authorized against a state official and not against the state itself or its agency.[188] Consequently, the federal lawsuit must name the official in his or her individual and official capacity. The lawsuit must also seek prospective relief, such as an injunction, which prevents irreparable harm by restraining someone from continuing certain conduct or engaging in that conduct in the future. The fact that a state has an indemnification statute in which the state indemnifies the state official from a civil rights judgment does not give the official Eleventh Amendment immunity from federal court actions.[189]

The Eleventh Amendment ban on federal court relief applies only to the imposition of *state* liability.[190] It does not apply where the plaintiff seeks to recover damages against a public official sued in his or her *individual* capacity. The common law or state immunity statutes, however, may provide protection to individuals sued in their individual capacities.[191]

Thus, a federal court civil rights suit against a state

official to obtain money damages from the individual is proper; if, however, the suit seeks money from the state for the official's past conduct, the Eleventh Amendment bars the action.

Common Law Immunities. Common law immunity may protect an individual official from a Section 1983 action for monetary damages. Whether and to what extent a Section 1983 defendant is protected by a common law immunity are questions of federal law.[192] Thus, state law immunity defenses do not necessarily defeat a Section 1983 claim, even if the Section 1983 claim is asserted in state court.[193]

To determine whether a Section 1983 defendant is protected by a common law immunity, the court inquires into the immunity historically accorded the relevant officer at common law and the interests behind it.[194] If the immunity claimed by the defendant was well established at the time of enactment of Section 1983, and the rationale for the immunity is consistent with the purposes of the Civil Rights Act, Section 1983 is construed to incorporate that immunity.[195]

Certain public officials, such as judges, prosecutors, and legislators, are protected by absolute immunity from any lawsuit for money damages; however, they are not immune from suits seeking injunctions and equitable relief.[196] Witnesses who testify at trial are absolutely immune from Section 1983 liability from damages for their allegedly perjurious testimony.[197] Other officials, such as administrative and executive officials, are protected by a qualified immunity.[198] Private persons who act under color of law are entitled to qualified immunity according to the courts of appeals.[199] The Supreme Court has not resolved the issue.[200]

Qualified Immunity. The qualified immunity defense applies to virtually every public official who carries out administrative or executive tasks.[201] Unlike absolute immunity, it is an affirmative defense that must be raised by the defendant.[202] The defendant has the burden of proving the defense[203] by showing that the challenged action did not contravene clearly established statutory or constitutional rights of which a reasonable person in his or her position would have known.[204] This establishes the good faith of the defendant, which entitles him or her to qualified immunity.

The plaintiff can rebut the evidence of good faith. When the plaintiff's Section 1983 claim fails to state a violation of clearly established law, however, the qualified immunity defense entitles the defendant to dismissal of the action.[205]

Good faith, an essential ingredient of a successful qualified immunity defense, is tested by both subjective and objective factors.[206] In *Harlow v. Fitzgerald*,[207] the Supreme Court held that bare allegations of malice in a Section 1983 claim cannot establish a lack of good faith for qualified immunity. Rather, officials performing discretionary functions are protected from liability for civil damages "insofar as their conduct does not violate clearly established statutory or constitutional rights of which a reasonable person should have known."[208]

This objective test is now considered the heart of determining good faith.[209] The relevant inquiry is whether the official knew or reasonably should have known that his or her conduct violated the plaintiff's federally protected rights.[210] Consequently, if a federal right is not well established, an official who violates it cannot be characterized as acting in bad faith simply because the conduct violates state law. Violations of constitutional or federal statutory rights require the plaintiff to show that those rights were clearly established at the time of the challenged conduct.[211]

A different good faith test for professionals who act under color of state law was created by the Supreme Court in *Youngberg v. Romero*[212] to apply to administrators and professional staff of a state mental institution. The Court ruled that Section 1983 liability can only be imposed when the decision by the professional is such a substantial departure from accepted professional judgment, practice, or standards as to demonstrate that the person responsible actually did not base the decision on such judgment. The Court further held that when a professional is sued for money damages in an individual capacity, good faith immunity will bar the action if the professional can establish that he or she was unable to satisfy normal professional standards because of budgetary constraints.

Recommendations and trends

Nurses are providers of increasingly new and complex health care. Nursing care that is administered with respect for the privacy and liberty interests of patients is less likely to give rise to liability for intentional and quasi-intentional torts or for civil rights violations.

Nurses who work for governmental entities, such as the Veterans' Administration Hospital system, the Public Health Service, and state and county health facilities are more at risk for Section 1983 civil rights actions than are nurses who work in private hospitals. Nevertheless, the circumstances of the private entity's relationship with the state or federal government may meet the requirement of state action. The impact of the Diagnostic Related

Group (DRG) prospective payment system, early discharge, and limited access to health care for Medicaid patients makes compliance with federal statutes and proper discharge planning critical.

Endnotes

1. W. PROSSER, LAW OF TORTS §8 at 31 (4th ed. 1971) (hereinafter cited as *Prosser*).
2. *Id.* at 31-32.
3. *Id.*
4. *Id.* at 32.
5. T. CRISTOFFEL, HEALTH AND THE LAW 268 (1982) (hereinafter cited as *Cristoffel*).
6. *Id.* at 34.
7. *Id.* at 35, 36.
8. *Id.*
9. *Id.*
10. *See id.* at 34-35.
11. *Id.* at 35, citing *Mohr v. Williams,* 14 N.W. 12 (Minn. 1905); *Hively v. Higgs,* 253 P. 363 (Or. 1927).
12. *Id.*
13. *Prosser, supra* note 1, at 37.
14. *Id.* at 37-38.
15. *Id.* at 38-39.
16. *Id.* at 40.
17. *Id.* at 40-41.
18. *Id.* at 38.
19. 289 S.E.2d 810 (Ga. App. 1982).
20. *See, e.g., Mink v. University of Chicago,* 460 F. Supp. 713, 717 (D. Ill. 1978).
21. *Id.; see also, Skripek v. Bergamo,* 491 A.2d 1336 (N.J. 1985) (if some consent is received, the action is not one for battery but for lack of informed consent); *Cobbs v. Grant,* 502 P.2d 1 (Cal. 1972) (battery action reserved for those situations where there is no consent; when consent is given, but some undisclosed complication results, the practitioner may have violated the duty to disclose pertinent information which is a negligence action).
22. *E.g., Kohoutek v. Hafner,* 366 N.W. 2d 633 (Minn. App. 1985) *review granted,* (July 11, 1985). There, the court held that the administration of Pitocin to a patient in labor, who is cooperative and conscious, without that patient's informed consent, would give rise to a claim for battery.
23. 460 F. Supp. 713 (D. Ill. 1973).
24. *Moos v. United States,* 225 F.2d 705 (8th Cir. 1955) (wrong leg); *Hershey v. Peake,* 223 P. 1113 (Kan. 1924) (wrong tooth).
25. 241 P.2d 1028 (Cal. App. 1952).
26. *Mink v. University of Chicago,* 460 F. Supp 713, 718 (D. Ill. 1973).
27. *Wall v. Brim,* 138 F.2d 478 (5th Cir. 1943); *Paulsen v. Gunderson,* 260 N. W. 448 (Wisc. 1935).
28. *Cristoffel, supra* note 5, at 270.
29. *See, e.g., Wheeler v. St. Joseph Hospital,* 133 Cal. Rptr. 775 (Ca. App. 1976) (Hospital's "Conditions of Admission" form possessed all the characteristics of a contract of adhesion; and in view of testimony by plaintiff that he did not read the form before signing it, the lower court erred in finding an implied agreement to arbitrate, as contained in the form, existed).
30. *Cristoffel, supra* note 5, at 271, 272.
31. *See, e.g.,* B. WHITKIN, SUMMARY OF CALIFORNIA LAW §200 at 2486.
32. *See, e.g., Mills v. Rogers,* 457 U.S. 291 (1982).
33. *Prosser, supra* note 1, at 104.
34. *Barber v. Superior Court,* 195 Cal. Rptr. 484, 489 (Cal. App. 1983).
35. Even minors and incompetents have been afforded the right to refuse treatment where life is not at stake. In New York, for example, minors and incompetents have been allowed to refuse treatment where the medical situation is not life-threatening and if the treatment so refused could be postponed without critical consequences. *See, e.g., In the Matter of Martin Seferth,* 127 N.E.2d 820 (N.Y. 1955).
36. *Natanson v. Kline,* 350 P.2d 1093, 1104 (Kan. 1960).
37. *Cristoffel, supra* note 5, at 277.
38. 465 So.2d 666 (Fla. App. 1985). The case was certified to the state supreme court for a ruling on the issue.
39. *Saltz v. Perlmutter,* 362 So.2d 160, *aff'd,* 379 So.2d 359 (Fla. 1890).
40. *See, In re Osborne,* 294 A.2d 372 (D.C. App. 1972).
41. *Bartling v. Superior Court,* 209 Cal. Rptr. 220 (Cal. App. 1984).
42. The court decided the issue even though death technically made the issue moot; the issue came within the exception to the mootness doctrine (discussed in Chapter 1) because it was capable of being repeated yet evading review.
43. 376 N.E.2d 1232 (Mass. App. 1978).
44. *Bartling v. Superior Court,* 209 Cal. Rptr. 220, 225 (Cal. App. 1984).
45. *Id.* The court cited *In re Quinlan,* 355 A.2d 647 (N.J. 1976) and *Superintendent of Belchertown v. Saikewicz,* 370 N.E.2d 417 (Mass. 1977).
46. 195 Cal. Rptr. 484 (Cal. App. 1984).
47. *See, e.g., In re Quinlan,* 348 A.2d 810, 819 (N.J. Super.), *rev'd,* 355 A.2d 647 (N.J. 1976), *cert. denied,* 429 U.S. 922 (1976).
48. 355 A.2d 647 (N.J. 1976).
49. 370 N.E.2d 417 (Mass. 1977).
50. *Barber v. Superior Court,* 195 Cal. Rptr. 484 (Cal. App. 1983).
51. *Id.* at 491.
52. *Id.*
53. *Id.* at 491.
54. *Id.*, quoting *In re Quinlan,* 355 A.2d 647, 669 (N.J. 1976) and *In re Dinnerstein,* 380 N.E.2d 134, 138 Mass. App. (1978).
55. *Id.* at 490.
56. *Id.*
57. *Id.* at 490-491 (emphasis in original).
58. *Id.* at 493.
59. CAL. HEALTH & SAFETY CODE §7188 (West Supp. 1985).
60. CAL. CIV. CODE §2430 (West Supp. 1985).
61. CAL. HEALTH & SAFETY CODE §7186 (West Supp. 1985).
62. A terminal condition is an incurable condition caused by injury, disease, or illness which, regardless of the application of life-sustaining procedures, would within reasonable medical judgment, produce death and where the application of life-sustaining procedures only serve to postpone the death of the patient. CAL. HEALTH & SAFETY CODE §7187(f) (West Supp. 1985).
63. CAL. HEALTH & SAFETY CODE §7188 (West Supp. 1985).
64. *Id.* at §7191(C).
65. *See, e.g., Barber v. Superior Court,* 195 Cal. Rptr. 484 (Cal. App. 1983).
66. CAL. CIV. CODE §2410-2421, 2430-2451 (West Supp. 1986).

67. *Id.* at §2432(a) (3) (A).
68. *Id.*
69. *Id.* at §2432.
70. *Id.* at §2432(b) (1)-(2) (West. Supp. 1986).
71. *Id.* at 2434(a)-(b).
72. *Id.* at 2435.
73. *Id.* at 2436.
74. *Id.* at 2436.5.
75. *Id.* at §2437.
76. *Id.* at §2438.
77. *Id.* at §2438(c).
78. *Id.* at §2442.
79. *Id.*
80. *See, e.g., Barber v. Superior Court,* 195 Cal. Rptr. 484, 491 (Cal. App. 1983) (there may be a duty to provide life-sustaining machinery in the immediate aftermath of a cardiorespiratory arrest).
81. *Prosser, supra* note 1, at 42.
82. *Id.*
83. *Id.*
84. *Id.* at 44.
85. *See, e.g., Maben v. Rankin,* 10 Cal. Rptr. 353 (Cal. 1961).
86. *Id.* In *Maben,* the patient was admitted to a mental hospital in violation of the state statute and was forcibly anesthetized and later given shock treatment. The court found that a claim for false imprisonment, battery, and assault could go to the jury on these facts.
87. *See* CAL. HEALTH & SAFETY CODE §1285(c)-(d) (West Supp. 1985).
88. *Prosser, supra* note 1, at 49.
89. *Id.* at 60-61.
90. *Prosser, supra* note 1, at 737.
91. *Id.* at 739.
92. *Id.* at 749.
93. *See Judge v. Rockford Memorial Hospital,* 150 N.E.2d 202 (Ill. App. 1958). Ordinarily, the privilege attaches to statements and communications made in connection with the various activities of organizations such as lodges, societies, labor unions, and the like. A communication respecting the character of an employee is qualifiedly privileged if made in good faith by a person having an interest or a duty to another person with a similar interest or duty. The privilege may be lost if the communication goes beyond the defendant's interest or duty in the matter.
94. *Prosser, supra* note 1, at 754.
95. *Id.* at 754-759.
96. 143 S.E.2d 489 (Ga. App. 1965).
97. There were dissenting opinions. *Id.* at 493-495.
98. *Prosser, supra* note 1, at 762, 763.
99. *Id.* at 784.
100. *Farmers Educational and Coop Union of America v. WDAY, Inc.,* 360 U.S. 525 (1959).
101. *Prosser, supra* note 1, at 787.
102. 150 N.E.2d 202 (Ill. App. 1958).
103. *Id.* at 205.
104. 443 N.E.2d 469 (N.Y. App. 1982).
105. 463 F. Supp. 139 (E.D. N.Y. 1979).
106. *Prosser, supra* note 1, at 850-853.
107. *Id.* at 853-856.
108. 469 So.2d 893 (Fla. App. 1985).
109. FLA. STAT. CH. 464 §464.018(1) (1985).
110. The tort action for invasion or interference with the right of privacy is separate from a civil rights action based on a violation of the *Constitutional* right to privacy. The former is a right that existed at common law.
111. *Prosser, supra* note 1, at 814.
112. *Id.* at 815.
113. *Id.* at 805.
114. *Id.*
115. *Id.* at 806.
116. *Id.* at 807.
117. *DeMay v. Roberts,* 9 N.W. 146 (Mich. 1881).
118. *Barber v. Time, Inc.,* 159 S.W.2d 291 (Mo. 1942); *Clayman v. Bernstein* (1940), cited in *Prosser, supra* note 1, at 809 n. 71. In *Clayman,* a physician took a picture of a semiconscious patient. *But see Pearson v. Dodd,* 410 F.2d 701 (D.C. Cir. 1969) (without intrusion, publication of matters of public interest are privileged), *cert. denied,* 395 U.S. 947.
119. *Banks v. King Features Syndicate,* 30 F. Supp. 352 (S.D. N.Y. 1939).
120. *Feeney v. Young,* 181 N.Y.S. 481 (App. Div. 1920).
121. *Barber v. Time, Inc.,* 159 S.W.2d 291 (Mo. 1942).
122. *Horne v. Patton,* 287 So.2d 824 (Ala. 1973).
123. *Prosser, supra* note 1, at 813.
124. *Hague v. Williams,* 181 A.2d 345 (N.J. 1962); *Clark v. Geraci,* 208 N.Y.S.2d 564 (1960).
125. 177 N.W. 831 (Neb. 1920).
126. *See* NATIONAL COMMISSION OF CONFIDENTIALITY OF HEALTH RECORDS, HEALTH RECORDS CONFIDENTIALITY LAW IN THE STATES (1979).
127. *Tarasoff v. Regents of the University of California,* 551 P.2d 334 (Cal. 1976).
128. 696 P.2d 527 (Oregon 1985) (in Banc).
129. Other actions exist. For example, in *Bivens v. Six Unknown Named Agents of the Federal Bureau of Narcotics,* 396 U.S. 229 (1969), the Supreme Court authorized the remedy of damage suits against federal officials for violations of the Constitution. The action was brought against federal drug agents who had violated the plaintiff's Fourth Amendment rights during a search.
130. 42 U.S.C. §1983 (1984).
131. Section 1981, for example, prohibits racial discrimination in making or enforcing contracts, and it applies to private persons as well as the state and federal government. 42 U.S.C. §1981 (1984).
132. *Rodway v. United States Dept. of Agriculture,* 514 F.2d 809, 814 (D.C. Cir. 1975).
133. *Lynch v. Household Finance Corporation,* 405 U.S. 538 (1972).
134. *Board of Regents v. Roth,* 408 U.S. 564 (1972). Property interests are not created by the constitution but rather by rules and statutes.
135. G.C. PRATT, M. REAL, M. SCHWARTZ, SECTION 1983 CIVIL RIGHTS LITIGATION 1985, 351 (1985) (hereinafter cited as *Civil Rights*).
136. *Herz v. Degnan,* 648 F.2d 201 (3d Cir. 1981).
137. *Davis v. Ball Memorial Hospital,* 640 F.2d 30 (7th Cir. 1980).
138. *Roe v. Wade,* 410 U.S. 179 (1973); *Moore v. Cleveland,* 431 U.S. 494 (1977); *Pierce v. Society of Sisters,* 268 U.S. 510 (1925); *Board of Regents v. Roth,* 408 U.S. 564 (1972).
139. *Civil Rights, supra* note 135, at 389-392 & cases collected therein.
140. *Id.* at 390.
141. *Id.* at 46.

142. *Martinez v. California,* 444 U.S. 277 (1980). There, the Court held that the defendant parole board members could not be liable under Section 1983 for the death of the decendent plaintiff who was killed by a person whom the parole board released on parole. The Court reasoned that the parole board did not deprive the plaintiff of her life; the fact that the parolee had done so was too remote a consequence of the parole board's actions to hold them responsible.
143. *See, e.g., McCabe v. Nassau Cty. Medical Center,* 453 F.2d 698 (2d Cir. 1971); *Hathaway v. Worcester County Hosp.,* 341 F. Supp. 1385 (D. Md. 1969).
144. *Burton v. Wilmington Parking Authority,* 365 U.S. 715 (1961).
145. *Civil Rights, supra* note 135.
146. *Burton v. Wilmington Parking Authority,* 365 U.S. 715 (1961).
147. *Id.* at 725.
148. *Civil Rights, supra* note 135, at 74-79.
149. *Blum v. Yaretsky,* 102 S.Ct. 2777 (1982).
150. *Jackson v. Metropolitan Edison Co.,* 419 U.S. 345 (1974).
151. *Addickes v. S.H. Kress Co.,* 398 U.S. 144 (1970).
152. *Rendell-Baker v. Kohn,* 102 S.Ct. 2764 (1982).
153. 102 S.Ct. 2777 (1982).
154. 506 F.2d 308 (9th Cir. 1974).
155. *Calvert v. Sharp,* 78 F.2d 861 (4th Cir. 1984).
156. *Estelle v. Gamlile,* 429 U.S. 97 (1986).
157. *Hoyt v. St. Mary's Rehabilitation Center,* 711 F.2d 864 (8th Cir. 1983).
158. *Fike v. United Methodist Children's Home,* 547 F. Supp. 286 (E.D. Va. 1982).
159. *E.g., Modaber v. Culpepper,* 674 F.2d 1023 (4th Cir. 1982); *Madry v. Sorel,* 558 F.2d 303 (5th Cir. 1977), *cert. denied,* 434 U.S. 1086 (1978); *Schlein v. Milford Hospital,* 561 F.2d 427 (2d Cir. 1977).
160. *See, e.g., Kramer v. Heckler,* 737 F.2d 214 (2d Cir. 1984).
161. *Doe v. New York City Dept. of Social Services,* 709 F.2d 782 (2d Cir. 1983).
162. *See, e.g., Lombard v. Eunice Kennedy Shriver Center,* 556 F. Supp. 677 (D. Mass. 1983).
163. *Morrison v. Washington Cty.,* 700 F.2d 678 (11th Cir. 1983).
164. 574 F.2d (1st Cir. 1978).
165. 590 F. 2nd 87 (4th Cir. 1978).
166. 560 F. 2d 609 (4th Cir. 1977).
167. The Supreme Court recently held that a judgment obtained against a public servant in his or her official capacity is equal to imposing liability on the entity which the public servant represents, provided that the entity had notice of the suit and an opportunity to respond to it. *Brandon v. Holt,* 105 S.Ct. 873 (1985). The Court reasoned that when an official acts in his or her official capacity, the actions are the actions of the public entity itself.
168. *Wanger v. Bonner,* 621 F.2d 675 (2d Cir. 1980).
169. *Turpin v. Mailet,* 619 F.2d 196 (2d Cir. 1980).
170. *Owens v. Haas,* 601 F.2d 196 (2d Cir.), *cert. denied,* 444 U.S. 980 (1979).
171. *Carey v. Piphus,* 435 U.S. 247 (1978).
172. *Id.*
173. *Id.*
174. *City of Newport v. Fact Concerts,* 453 U.S. 247 (1981).
175. *Smith v. Wade,* 103 S.Ct. 1625 (1983).
176. 422 U.S. 563 (1975).
177. *Id.* The Fifth Circuit affirmed the judgment. The Supreme Court remanded the case to the Fifth Circuit to consider whether the district court's failure to instruct the jury with respect to the effect of O'Connor's claimed reliance on state law made the court's jury instructions erroneous with respect to damages.
178. *Id.* at 568.
179. *Id.* at 575.
180. *Id.*
181. *Id.*
182. *Id.* at 575-576 (citations omitted).
183. CV 81-5046-RMT (Mx) (November 16, 1981), *aff'd on other grounds,* 704 F.2d 1110 (9th Cir. 1983) *(per curiam).*
184. *See, e.g., Estate of Leach v. Shapiro,* 469 N.E.2d 10 (Ohio App. 1984).
185. *See, e.g., Bartling v. Superior Court,* 209 Cal. Rptr. 220 (Cal. App. 1984).
186. *See, Edelman v. Jordan,* 94 S.Ct. 1347 (1974).
187. *Ex Parte Young,* 209 U.S. 123 (1908).
188. *Civil Rights, supra* note 135.
189. *Id.* at 104.
190. *Id.* at 103-104.
191. *Id.*
192. *Martinez v. California,* 444 U.S. 277, 285 n. 11 (1980).
193. *Civil Rights, supra* note 135, at 120.
194. *Imbler v. Pachtman,* 424 U.S. 409 (1976).
195. *Owen v. City of Independence,* 445 U.S. 622 (1980).
196. *Civil Rights, supra* note 135, at 119.
197. *Briscoe v. LaHue,* 103 S.Ct. 1108 (1983).
198. *Id.*
199. *Id.* citing *Folsum Investment Co. v. Moore,* 681 F.2d 1032 (5th Cir. 1982).
200. *Lugar v. Edmundson Oil Co.,* 102 S.Ct. 2744, 2756 n.23 (1982).
201. *Civil Rights, supra* note 135, at 134.
202. *Gomez v. Toledo,* 446 U.S. 635 (1980).
203. *Civil Rights, supra* note 135, at 140-141.
204. *Id.*
205. *Mitchell v. Forsyth,* 105 S.Ct. 2806 (1985). The Court also ruled that the Attorney General of the United States is not entitled to absolute immunity from damage suits arising out of allegedly unconstitutional conduct in performing national security functions.
206. *Civil Rights, supra* note 135, at 135.
207. 102 S.Ct. 2727 (1982).
208. *Id.* at 2738.
209. *Civil Rights, supra* note 135, at 138.
210. *Davis v. Scherer,* 104 S.Ct. 3012 (1984).
211. *Civil Rights, supra* note 135, at 139.
212. 457 U.S. 307 (1982).

Chapter 6

Informed consent

Mary E. Kelly

Since the early 1900s, the courts have recognized the duty to obtain a patient's consent to treatment and have upheld liability in battery for the failure to do so.[1] The question of whether the patient truly understood the nature and effects of the proposed treatment, however, had no legal significance at that time.

The latter part of the century has experienced a dramatic increase in public consciousness concerning the patient's right to be actively involved in treatment decisions.[2] The theory of negligence has also gained acceptance, and the courts have applied its concepts of duty to a variety of new contexts. In developing negligence as a part of the common law, judges began applying negligence concepts to the consent to treatment process. The theory, known as the doctrine of informed consent, has now been adopted by judicial decision in many jurisdictions.

The rationale for imposing liability in negligence is that in addition to the duty to obtain consent, there is an analogous duty to ensure consent is voluntarily given. The concept of a voluntary consent necessarily implies that there has been full disclosure, and therefore full knowledge, of the consequences of the proposed treatment, as well as the decision to forgo the proposed treatment.

The purpose of this chapter is to provide an overview of the law of informed consent and the nurse's liability as a provider of services or as an active participant in the informed consent process between another health care provider and the nurse's patient. Although specific case examples involving the nurse's liability as a provider of services are scant, the law of informed consent is well established and its principles apply by analogy.

While nurses tend to view informed consent as a physician's responsibility, the trend is to view nurses as sharing this responsibility if the circumstances warrant. Whether nursing care is given pursuant to a valid order or the exercise of independent judgment, potential liability for lack of informed consent exists. The rationale for imposing liability is the breach of an independent duty that the health care provider owes to the patient. "The [principles] of existing law [relating to informed consent and physicians] . . . support the application of informed consent requirements to nonphysician practitioners who function as providers of health care."[3]

The issue of informed consent and nursing malpractice is largely undefined because of the early century's emphasis on physicians as providers of care.[4] Even the informed consent studies commissioned by the President's Commission for the Study of Ethical Problems in Medicine and Biomedical and Behavioral Research paid "very little attention . . . to nurses and other health professionals who interact with patients."[5]

The reality of today's health care setting, however, is that nurses are providers of health services. As providers of health services, nurses are accountable for the care they render, and they are responsible for obtaining informed consent from the patients for whom they provide health services.

Increased emphasis on independent practice has resulted in more nurses caring for patients outside the traditional hospital setting. Nurses practice in ambulatory settings, nursing homes, and the home. They perform physical examinations, maintain chronic disease follow-up, and, in some instances, manage acute disease. Nurses thus "order tests and initiate therapeutic interventions, sometimes with a physician's co-signature and other times independent of physicians."[6] Consequently, they are fully responsible "for informing patients about their conditions, treatments, and tests, for ensuring that the patient has understood the information, and for securing the consent."[7]

Nurses are increasingly involved in the direct application of complex technologies to patient care, even in the more traditional setting of the hospital. As the 1983 report of the President's Commission for the Study of Ethical Problems in Medicine and Biomedical and Behavioral Research noted[8]:

> Students of nursing learn to develop nursing care plans for patients that require skills in history-taking, physical examinations (which include diagnostic procedures) and . . . independent . . . nursing care procedures. . . . With the shift in disease patterns toward chronic illnesses, nursing education has increased its long established emphasis on the skills needed for educating patients, especially about self-care techniques and the long-term management of disease.[9]

Indeed, the nurse's participation in the informed consent process is often disguised under the rubric of patient education. Through patient education, the nurse provides information to the patient about his or her condition, treatment, alternatives, risks, and benefits.[10]

Frequently, hospital-employed nurses obtain the patient's signature on a consent form authorizing treatment by another provider. The patient may indicate a lack of understanding of the proposed treatment's risks, benefits, and alternatives. The nurse's duty to protect the patient from a dangerous condition may be breached if the nurse fails to take action.

Nurses may provide care to patients on an independent judgment as well as an interdependent basis. Where care is provided under the delegated authority of a physician's order, the nurse remains the provider of that care. Thus, when the nurse utilizes equipment ordered by a physician in the treatment of the patient, he or she must warn the patient of any obvious dangers arising from the equipment's operation.[11]

The doctrine of informed consent

The doctrine of informed consent developed from the common law of battery. As discussed in Chapter 5, an action for battery exists to remedy harmful or offensive nonconsensual touching.[12] The consent needed to avoid liability for battery is not very exacting. For example, consent may be given explicitly in words, it may be manifested by actions, or it may be implied from the circumstances.[13]

In considering liability for battery, the courts traditionally were not concerned with the patient's understanding of what was being consented to and the practitioner was merely expected to describe the procedure.[14] Nevertheless, fraud or deception could invalidate the patient's consent.[15]

In the latter half of the century, the courts began to recognize a new affirmative obligation of disclosure, or duty to warn, known as the doctrine of informed consent.[16] The highest courts of most states have considered the informed consent doctrine.[17]

THE PATIENT'S RIGHT TO SELF-DETERMINATION

The rationale surrounding the doctrine of informed consent is that adult competent patients have a right of self-determination. The California Supreme Court described the four premises underlying the rationale in *Cobbs v. Grant*[18]:

> [P]atients are generally persons unlearned in the medical sciences and therefore, except in rare cases, the courts may safely assume the knowledge of the patient and physician are not in parity. . . . [A] person of adult years and in sound mind has the right, in the exercise of control over his own body, to determine whether or not to submit to lawful medical treatment. . . . [T]he patient's consent to treatment, to be effective, must be an informed consent . . . [T]he patient, being unlearned in medical sciences, has an abject dependence upon and trust in his physician for the information upon which he relies during the decisional process, thus raising an obligation in the physician that transcends arm-length transactions.[19]

From these principles, the court found "a necessity, and a resultant requirement" of disclosure to the patient of "all information relevant to a meaningful decisional process."[20] The fact that the benefits of the proposed care seem evident to the provider does not end the inquiry; "it is the prerogative of the patient . . . to determine for himself the direction in which he believes his interests lie."[21] The court accordingly held that as an "integral part" of the "overall obligation to the patient, there is a duty of reasonable disclosure of the available choices with respect to proposed therapy and of the dangers inherently and potentially involved in each."[22]

Professional Nursing And Patients' Rights. Professional nursing traditionally has recognized, respected, and furthered the patient's right of self-determination. For example, the American Nurses' Association's CODE FOR NURSES WITH INTERPRETIVE STATEMENTS provides in part "whenever possible, clients should be fully involved in the planning and implementation of their own health. Each client has the moral right to determine what will be done with his/her person."[23]

The CODE FOR NURSES also sets forth that the nurse assumes responsibility and accountability for individual nursing judgments and actions. In addition, the CODE directs the nurse to participate in the profession's efforts to protect the public from misinformation and misrepresentation and to maintain the integrity of nursing.[24]

The President's Commission recognizes this tradition in professional nursing. The Commission notes that medical education is currently undergoing changes that are already an integral part of nursing education, "which traditionally has placed great emphasis on respect for patients' values, the therapeutic importance of patient participation in health care decision making, and teaching of good communication skills."[25]

NEGLIGENCE VS. BATTERY

Most states treat the lack of informed consent claim as a negligence claim.[26] In these jurisdictions, battery claims are reserved for cases where no consent to treatment is given by the patient. Where consent is given, but an undisclosed inherent complication occurs, there is no deviation from the consent, and the proper action is one for negligent failure to disclose or lack of informed consent.

A minority of jurisdictions[27] nevertheless continue to treat the failure to disclose as the intentional tort of battery. These jurisdictions reason that since the consent was not knowing, it could not have been voluntary and therefore was ineffective. Ineffective consent is viewed as tantamount to no consent and thus supports a claim of battery.

One of the advantages to a plaintiff in a jurisdiction that treats nondisclosure as battery is that punitive damages, which are not recoverable in negligence actions as a general rule, may be recovered. Another advantage of the battery claim is that the plaintiff need not introduce expert proof that the omitted disclosure was one that the medical community would require to be disclosed.

In spite of these advantages, the modern trend is to treat nondisclosure as a form of negligence. In these jurisdictions, the laws of negligence govern the action. Consequently, the following discussion focuses on the principles of negligence as they apply to the informed consent doctrine.

THE STANDARD OF CARE

Most of the litigation surrounding informed consent focuses on the provider's failure to disclose the material dangers associated with the treatment.[28] The jurisdictions are split as to the appropriate test to determine materiality.

In some jurisdictions, expert proof as to the medical community's view of the risk is required.[29] In these states, a provider may defend on the grounds that the disclosure he or she omitted to make is not reasonably required by the professional community to be disclosed. In other jurisdictions, such as California, expert proof is not required.[30]

The test used to determine whether breach of the duty to disclose exists differs according to the standard employed in each. Where the jurisdiction employs the professional standard, an expert witness must testify that, under the circumstances of the case, a reasonable practitioner would have disclosed the information that the defendant practitioner failed to disclose.[31]

In jurisdictions, such as California, that apply the reasonable patient standard, the breach of the provider's duty of disclosure is determined from the patient's point of view; that is, whether from the point of view of a reasonable patient the information should have been disclosed. Thus a patient, rather than a provider, viewpoint determines the materiality of the nondisclosure.[32] Under this standard, material dangers are those that a reasonable person under the same or similar circumstances would consider significant.

Some jurisdictions by statute have overturned court decisions establishing the reasonable patient standard. These statutes, adopted as part of the remedy to solve the malpractice crisis, require that the professional standard of materiality be applied to determine whether the nondisclosed risk is material.[33]

CAUSATION

In either type of jurisdiction, the plaintiff must prove the causal relationship between the failure to inform and the injury. The patient must establish that the failure to disclose caused him or her either to undergo or to forgo the treatment. The test is an objective one: would a reasonable person with knowledge of the undisclosed risks have nevertheless consented to the procedure?

Causation is not proven if a reasonable person would have gone forward with the treatment even knowing the risk. The plaintiff has no complaint for breach of disclosure or lack of informed consent if the patient would have submitted to treatment even if informed of the risk.[34] On the other hand, if a reasonable person would not have consented to the procedure knowing the risk, the plaintiff has sustained his or her burden of proving causation.

This objective standard reflects the courts' attempts to limit the impact of speculative and potentially self-serving testimony by the patient who in hindsight is unhappy with the results of the procedure.[35] The objective test—that is, the inquiry into what a reasonably prudent person in the patient's position would have decided if adequately informed of all the risks—is thought to solve this problem.[36]

In *Azzolino v. Dingfelder*,[37] the court upheld a directed verdict in favor of a family nurse practitioner (FNP) because the evidence failed to establish the element of causation. The plaintiff sued the FNP and the clinic where she received prenatal care. The gist of the suit was based on a conversation the plaintiff had with the FNP about amniocentesis. When the plaintiff indicated she wanted the procedure, the FNP allegedly asked her if she knew that the procedure was dangerous and could produce a miscarriage. The FNP then related that during her pregnancy, she was concerned about sickle cell trait and she wanted an abortion, but her husband advised her she should leave it in God's hands. The FNP did not advise her to discuss the matter with anyone else and did not provide her with information about anywhere else that she could go to get the procedure done.

Based on this failure to advise the mother to discuss amniocentesis with someone else and the failure to inform her of other facilities where she could go to get the procedure done, the plaintiff sued the nurse for the wrongful birth of her retarded child. At the trial, however, the mother testified that her conversation with the FNP did not affect her decision about amniocentesis, and she was still determined to have it even after the conversation. Under these circumstances, the court ruled that the FNP did not influence or cause the plaintiff to forgo amniocentesis, and the necessary causal link was missing. Consequently, the directed verdict was proper.

THE SCOPE OF THE DISCLOSURE

The courts have found that the scope of the required disclosure defies simple definition.[38] Judicial formulations of the scope of disclosure hold that the measure of the duty to reveal is the patient's right of self-decision. Since the right of self-determination can be exercised effectively only if the patient possesses adequate information to enable an intelligent choice, the scope of the communication "must be measured by the patient's need, and that need is whatever information is material to the decision."[39]

A minicourse in medical sciences is not required.[40] The President's commission notes that overly burdensome disclosure requirements may defeat the self-determination purpose of the doctrine of informed consent. The patient, badgered with a parade of horrible potentially attendant risks to the proposed care, is thereby overwhelmed and unable to distinguish truly significant information and to make sound decisions.[41]

Conversely, there is no duty to discuss "the relatively minor risks inherent in common procedures, when it is common knowledge that such risks inherent in the procedure are of low incidence."[42] Instead, the provider's focus should be on the concerns of the patient—the risk of harm or death and the problems of recuperation.

The courts have also recognized certain defenses to a claim of negligent failure to disclose material information. If the patient requests not to be informed of any risk, the provider has no duty to disclose. Nondisclosure is also not actionable if the procedure is simple and the danger is remote and commonly appreciated as remote. Hence there is no duty to warn a patient of the potential danger of infection and blood clots before taking a routine sample of blood.[43]

Another defense justifying nondisclosure is where the disclosure would "so seriously upset the patient" that the patient would not be able to dispassionately weigh the risks of refusing to undergo the care.[44] This is known as the therapeutic privilege. The provider must prove by a preponderance of the evidence that he or she relied on facts that would demonstrate to a reasonable person that the disclosure would in fact so upset the patient that a rational decision by him or her could not be made.

The patient's personal needs may expand the scope of the required disclosure. For example, in *Martin v. Brallian*,[45] a patient consulted a physician for a cut finger. The patient informed the physician of the nature of his employment and that he needed manual dexterity to perform his job. The physician, who recommended surgery, never disclosed the potential risk of paralysis from the surgery.

The patient sued after the surgery resulted in paralysis of his hand. The court held that the physician's duty to disclose was made greater by the fact that the patient informed the physician of the importance of hand dexterity to his job.

ELEMENTS NECESSARY TO INFORMED CONSENT

Legal, effective informed consent process requires that the patient have decision-making capacity. The law also requires that decisions be voluntary. Finally, there must be adequate information from which the patient can make a decision.[46]

Decision-Making Capacity. In order to effectively participate in the informational decision-making process, the patient must have the capacity to do so. The assessment of capacity necessarily must take place along a spectrum ranging from clear cases of incapacity, such as infants, young children, and comatose patients, to unclear cases.

The law generally presumes an adult to be competent unless an adjudication of incompetency has been made.[47] Consent given by a competent adult authorizes a practitioner to provide health care. On the other hand, consent given by an incompetent person is generally not legally sufficient to authorize professionals to proceed to provide care.[48]

Competent adults who refuse treatment have the right to do so and their decisions should be respected.[49] Conversely, the refusal of treatment by an incompetent person has no such legal effect, although it may be considered in determining how to proceed.[50]

In the President's commission view:

> . . . any determination of the capacity to decide one course of treatment must relate to the individual abilities of a patient, the requirements of the task at hand, and the consequences likely to flow from the decision. Decision making capacity requires, to greater, or lesser degree: (1) possession of a set of values and goals; (2) the ability to communicate and to understand information; (3) the ability to reason and to deliberate about one's choices.[51]

The commission also notes that questions about capacity in decision making "typically arise only when a patient chooses a course of conduct—often a refusal of treatment—other than the one the health professional finds most responsible."[52]

Voluntary Decision Making. The ultimate decision concerning care must be reached voluntarily by the patient. The law has long recognized that consent that is coerced by threats or induced by fraud or misrepresentation is legally viewed as no consent at all.[53] The commission notes that although nursing care in hospitals is not usually thought of as forced treatment, "a good deal of routine care in hospitals, nursing homes, and other health care settings is provided (usually by health professionals such as nurses) without explicit and voluntary consent by patients."[54]

There is an expectation on the part of professionals that patients, once in such a setting, will simply go along with routine care. Nevertheless, in the commission's studies of treatment refusals, it was the routine test that was most likely to be refused.[55] Professionals have an obligation to avoid coercion and manipulation of their patients.

Informational Process. Litigation is less likely if a strong pre-existing bond exists between the patient and the provider and the patient is prepared for the possibility of an adverse outcome.[56] In general, malpractice cases that are litigated involve interventions that were not successful.[57] Commentators suggest that, as a minimum, the patient should be informed of the following[58]:

1. The condition or problem
2. The nature and purpose of the proposed treatment
3. The risks and consequences of the proposed treatment
4. Any feasible alternatives to the treatment
5. The patient's prognosis if the proposed treatment is not given

The interaction should provide the patient with a basis for effective participation in sound decision making. Discussions between the professional and the patient ideally will bring the concerns, knowledge, and perspective of each to the process of seeking an agreement on a particular course of action.

The President's commission recommends that the health care professional invite the patient to participate in a dialogue in which the professional seeks to help the patient understand the situation and available courses of action and the patient expresses his or her concerns and wishes.[59]

The professional should be careful not to overwhelm the patient with detailed technical expositions of facts that are germane neither to the patient's understanding nor to the decision that must be made. Such practices can be destructive of the communication process, especially where the patient cannot understand the information being provided. Reciting all the facts in an insensitive manner can also destroy the communication process.

Generally, there will be a range of acceptable choices in any given health condition. In this situation, there are two components to the decision: whether to take some course of action and how to go about obtaining it. This discussion usually involves a comparison of several options and their attendant risks.

Patient education may be a shared responsibility with a physician, or it may be a delegated function. In either situation, nurses are responsible for bringing errors, omissions, and misunderstandings on the part of the patient to the attention of the physician. As the President's commission notes, although ultimate legal responsibility varies according to the context in which the care is delivered, the nature of the intervention, and the person treating the patient, nurses have a central role in the process of providing patients with information.[60]

Risks and Benefits. Today's consumers of health care, as well as the courts, believe that health care providers should discuss the nature, risks, and other consequences of the recommended treatment. Delivery of this information and proper documentation are the best protection against informed consent claims.

Liability for nondisclosure

The jury or the court in a lack of informed consent case is asked to determine whether required disclosures were in fact made. These cases almost inevitably lead to "testimonial contests" in which patients claim they were not warned of risks and providers claim the risks were disclosed.[61] Reliance on after-the-fact testimony by the patient may be deemed more reliable than that offered by the provider if the provider failed to adequately document the circumstances surrounding the disclosure.

Thus written documentation can provide useful evidence. This documentation should describe the informed disclosure process. The better practice is to utilize consent forms together with informational discussions that are documented.

Consent forms, used as a matter of course by most institutions to document a patient's informed consent, are considered evidence, which can be rebutted, that the patient's consent is based on an understanding of the information provided. As a matter of practice, the consent form is generally presented to the patient for signature sometime after the information has been disclosed, usually by someone other than the person who made the disclosure, that is, the nurse. In most instances, the nurse has not been a witness to the disclosure but is merely presenting the form for signature by the patient.

Consent forms may be attacked as unintelligible and written in abstruse and jargon-ridden language. Often, as part of the routine, the patient is asked to sign the form while drowsy from drugs or in a confused state. Quite frequently, consent forms are conclusively worded; the patient acknowledges that he or she has received adequate information about the risks, alternatives, and benefits, but the form does not actually recite this information. For this reason, merely obtaining a patient's signature on a consent form does not provide airtight insulation against liability.[62]

In *Ipock v. Gilmore*,[63] the North Carolina Appellate Court refused to dismiss a case on a pretrial motion simply because a consent form was signed. The court held that a fact issue warranting a jury trial existed because the procedure performed was more extensive than that specified in the consent form.

If, however, the informed consent process—disclosure, discussion, and consent—is documented, an attack on the consent form will most likely be unsuccessful.

In *Barth v. Rock*,[64] an informed consent issue was considered with respect to a nurse anesthetist. There, a 5-year-old girl broke her arm while riding a bicycle. Her father executed a standard consent form so that a closed reduction could be performed.

When the child's arm began to swell, the cast had to be split, which altered the alignment of the fracture. A second surgery to correct this was scheduled. Before surgery, the child's mother signed the consent form. A nurse anesthetist administered the anesthetics: sodium pentothal, succinylcholine drip, and nitrous oxide. Since general anesthesia was employed, an air bag was used to assist ventilation.

The surgery was uneventful until the child began to move and the anesthetist administered more sodium pentothal. Immediately, her blood pressure and pulse dropped. Atropine did nothing; epinephrine subsequently administered resulted in some response. Thereafter, the child was placed in intensive care, but she never regained consciousness.

Both the anesthetist and the surgeon admitted that they failed to inform the child's parents of the risks attendant to general anesthesia. Each of them thought that the other had done so. In the face of this evidence, the court held that the jury should have been instructed as a matter of law that there was no informed consent. The jury would have then been left with the question of whether the parents would have consented to the use of sodium pentothal in spite of the risks shown at trial.

LIABILITY FOR ANOTHER PROVIDER'S NONDISCLOSURE

The hospital setting presents the nurse with potential liability for another provider's failure to disclose material information. Lack of informed consent is minimized if the nurse independently inquires about and documents consent and takes steps to ensure that the consent given is informed.

These measures do not require that the nurse assume the legal responsibility to explain the treatment procedures to be performed by another practitioner. Legal responsibility for the actual informational content exists where (1) the nurse is providing the care that requires informed consent, (2) the nurse is collaborating with another practitioner in providing the care that requires informed consent, or (3) the nurse accepts the delegated duty to provide the requisite information material to the decision-making process.

Nevertheless, the nurse may be liable in negligence for another provider's failure to provide informed consent even where she is not involved in providing the care that is the subject of the consent and she has not accepted any delegation of duty to do so. To the extent that the nurse is aware that his or her patient is misinformed or uninformed about a procedure to be performed by another provider and does nothing to protect the patient, there may be a breach of the nurse's independent duty to protect the patient from dangerous conditions.

The nurse is required to take action to prevent any harm to his or her patient. Any uncertainty about the proposed treatment therefore should be reported to the provider of the treatment before the treatment is accomplished. If this does not alleviate the potentially dangerous condition, the administration should be notified.

Consider two case examples. In the first, the patient is admitted for an extremely experimental surgery that has serious and life-threatening risks. In the second the patient, a young woman, is admitted for a tubal ligation sterilization, which she refers to as Band-Aid surgery.

When the nurse presents the consent form, as is usually the custom in most hospitals, to the patient in the first case, the patient indicates her belief that the surgery is routine with little side effects and asks the nurse, "Isn't that right?" In the second case, the night before surgery, the patient shows the nurse a picture of her child and says, "I really want another child, but we just can't afford one right now. I'm so happy I can have this reversible Band-Aid surgery for birth control instead of taking the Pill. I figure I'll have my tubes untied in about 3 years. Then we'll be ready for another child."[65]

In either example, the circumstances clearly require action by the nurse even though he or she is not the person performing the surgery. The nurse has knowledge that the consent given is not informed. Obtaining the patient's signature on a consent form or simply refusing to obtain the signature on the form and taking no further action, in either example, is a breach of the nurse's independent duty to the patient.

Utter v. United Hospital Center Inc.[66] illustrates this principle. There, the plaintiff, injured on the job, was admitted to the hospital. His arm was placed in a cast below the knuckles of his right hand.

During the patient's 48-hour stay, his arm became progressively swollen and black. Later, the arm became more edematous, and the nurses noted a foul-smelling drainage from the cast. The patient developed a high temperature and was delirious. The attending physician was notified but did nothing. Unfortunately, the nurse failed to take further action, and the patient's arm ultimately had to be amputated in order to save his life. The hospital's liability was premised on the nurse's negligence in failing to take further action. On appeal the court agreed:

> Nurses are specialists in hospital care who, in the final analysis, hold the well-being, in fact in some instances the very lives, of patients in their hands. In the dim hours of the night, as well as in the light of the day, nurses are frequently charged with the duty to observe the condition of the ill and infirm in their care. If that patient, hopeless and wholly dependent, shows signs of worsening, the nurse is charged with the obligation of taking some positive action . . . better care will result and perhaps more patients will recover.[67]

The courts view the nurse-patient relationship as one of patient advocacy; they expect the nurse to protect the patient who is dependent on the health professional for good faith intervention when necessary to prevent injury. The *Utter* court's words vividly demonstrate this view.

The ANA's CODE FOR NURSES also provides support for intervention. Nurses are ethically obligated by the code to safeguard the client and the public when health care and safety are affected by incompetent, unethical, or illegal practice of any person.[68]

The ANA[69] and some courts generally view the physician independently responsible for informed consent.[70] Nevertheless, even in jurisdictions adopting this view, the nurse must be concerned with the patient's response or uncertainty. Any confusion or uncertainty must be communicated to the physician or, if necessary, ultimately to the hospital administration.[71] The nurse has both a legal and an ethical duty to protect the patient from danger.

Nurses, understandably and appropriately, are reluctant to assume responsibility for making disclosures to a patient about the material risks of treatment to be provided by another practitioner. Assuming this responsibility has potentially serious ramifications for the nurse, in the event the disclosure is inadequate. Of course, if the disclosure is adequate, there would be no liability.[72]

To take action, however, where the nurse knows that the patient is not informed does not require that the nurse assume responsibility for the disclosure. Rather, the situation is more analogous to those in which the nurse observes a dangerous condition but fails to report it to the physician. Under the principles of *Utter*, the nurse is liable for the omission.

Plaintiff's counsel may also be able to successfully argue that the nurse's failure to act under these circumstances is tantamount to carrying out an order that the nurse knows or should know is not in accordance with standard medical practice. In *Poor Sisters of St. Francis v. Catron*[73] the Indiana Appellate Court held that a hospital, as the nurse's employer, can be held liable if injury occurs to the patient from a physician's prescribed treatment that was not in accord with standard medical practice and was not questioned by the nurse.

The nurse must take action that is reasonably expected to eliminate the danger to the patient. Merely notifying a supervisor, if the nurse knows or should know that this will not eliminate the danger, is not enough. Nursing negligence may be based on the nurse's omission where the nurse's failure to report appropriately causes or contributes to the worsening of the patient's harm.[74] Thus proper action may require notification of a department head or the administration.

In support of liability, plaintiff's counsel may draw on the fact that nurses, both in the hospital setting and outside it, are responsible for much of the patient and family education regarding procedures and treatment as well as health status.[75] In general, nurses spend a greater amount of time with patients and their families than do physicians.[76]

One study documents that during the initial nursing assessment, medication rounds, and formal patient education sessions, nurses in a hospital setting provide substantial disclosure to patients.[77] Patient education, the study concluded, "was the most substantial single source of disclosure, with the possible exception of some of the informed consent disclosures by doctors prior to major diagnostic tests."[78] The study suggests, however, that nurses have not clearly defined their role as providing information necessary for patient decision making:

> It was not information for decision-making [which is what informed consent is about]. Nor did patients understand it that way. More important, it did not *necessarily* include the full information that the informed consent doctrine requires for patient decision-making. It emphasized heavily the nature of the procedure, but the purposes, risks (aside from some information about discomforts), benefits, and alternatives were completely ignored.[79]

The legal community recognizes that an important nursing function is the preparation of patients for surgery[80]:

> An important feature of this process is talking with a patient to assess the patient's understanding of the surgical procedure, answering questions about what to expect after surgery, and allaying anxiety by explaining in some detail the nursing procedures that will be rendered after surgery.[81]

This function strengthens the duty to act where the nurse knows, or reasonably should know, that the patient is uninformed about the treatment.

The fact that the nurse obtains the signature for consent to a particular treatment or surgery may also support a finding of liability. "In the atmosphere of urgency to treat, obtaining informed consent [by a physician] may often consist mostly of recommending a procedure and explaining its nature."[82] Consequently, the nurse must often answer questions that arise after the physician provides the patient with a risk-of-procedure explanation, and it is the nurse who must cope with a refusal to accept treatment or withdrawal of consent.

Little time exists in certain settings, such as emergency and critical care nursing, to have the physician return to deal with the situation. As a result, nurses must make judgments as to how best to proceed under the circumstances. This in turn may require the nurse to assume responsibility for making certain that the patient understands the consequences of refusal or assume the responsibility to reactivate a valid consent before proceeding with the treatment.

Moreover, the emphasis placed on patient teaching in the nursing profession may provide the plaintiff's counsel with a compelling argument that the nurse has an independent duty to ensure that consent is informed, even when he or she is not the provider of care.

The trend is to name hospitals as well as physicians in lawsuits concerning informed consent. Hospitals are tied into the informed consent claim by the fact that they generally require signed consent forms and the fact that these are presented to the patient by hospital-employed nurses. As a result of these activities, plaintiffs argue that hospitals owe the patient a duty to obtain informed consent independent of the physician's duty because they have assumed a duty to the patient.

The majority of courts have rejected this theory.[83] In *Magana v. Elie*, however, the Illinois Appellate Court held that the question of a hospital's responsibility for ensuring that a patient's informed consent was obtained is a factual one for the jury.[84]

In reaching this conclusion, the Illinois court noted that the hospital provides a myriad of services in connection with the surgical or medical treatment ordered by the physician. Services such as operating rooms, equipment, nursing assistance, radiology, pathology, anesthesia, laboratory tests, and *obtaining the signature of the patient on the informed consent form* were noted by the court.[85] Since a hospital is required to act reasonably to protect a patient in light of an apparent risk—a duty that continues even though the patient is under the care of a private physician—failure to act reasonably can subject the hospital to liability for damages.

The court determined that the jury must decide, after weighing the evidence, whether the hospital, in meeting its duty to act reasonably, should have required physicians with staff privileges to obtain informed consent. This evidence can include expert testimony, hospital bylaws, statutes, accreditation standards, customs, and community practice.

Magana relied on an oft-cited Illinois Supreme Court case, *Darling v. Charleston Community Memorial Hospital*.[86] In *Darling*, one of the issues was whether the hospital:

> failed to have a sufficient number of trained nurses for bedside care . . . capable of recognizing the progressive gangrenous condition of the plaintiff's right leg and bringing the same to the attention of the hospital medical staff and administration so that adequate consultation could have been secured and such conditions rectified.[87]

The court concluded that the nurses had the responsibility of recognizing that the patient was not receiving good and accepted medical care and taking action to rectify the situation.

Just as the nurse possesses the skill to recognize and to take action against substandard medical care, the nurse possesses the skill and knowledge to evaluate the adequacy of informed consent disclosures. Commentators have recognized the nurse's independent duty to protect the patient when the patient has not been adequately informed or did not understand the information provided.[88] Indeed, those courts holding that the hospital has no duty of informed consent independent of the physician's duty have distinguished the situation where the hospital had reason to suspect that the consent given was not informed.[89]

The nurse's failure to act reasonably to protect the patient under these circumstances could subject the hospital to liability for the employee nurse's negligence. In *Campbell v. Pitt County Memorial Hospital*,[90] a $6.5 million jury verdict was reached in a case brought against a hospital for its employee nurses' negligence in failing to ensure that the parents had given their informed consent to a vaginal delivery under circumstances that indicated the necessity for a cesarean delivery. The hospital was also sued for its own negligence in failing to establish a mechanism for ensuring that patients in labor have given informed consent to the method of delivery and for prompt reporting of anything that threatens the life of a patient.[91]

The plaintiff's mother was admitted to the hospital in active labor. Her vital signs and the fetal heart rate were normal. Pelvic x-ray examinations revealed that the fetus was in a double footing breech position. An external fetal monitor showed a 2-hour baseline of 170 to 180, with repetitive and progressively more severe variable decelerations. The nurses contacted the attending physician, but he elected not to perform a cesarean delivery, even though fetascope readings indicated worsening bradycardia.

Approximately 6 hours after admission, the infant was delivered vaginally by total breech extraction, with the umbilical cord wrapped tightly around her legs. Apgar scores were 1 at 1 minute and 2 at 5 minutes. The plaintiff, now 6 years old, suffers from cerebral palsy, mild retardation, and severe speech impairment. Gross and fine motor abilities are below those normal for a 1-year-old child.

The plaintiff contended at trial that since vaginal delivery presents a grave risk to an infant in the footing breech presentation, the parents should have been informed of the relative risks of vaginal vs. cesarean delivery. One and one-half hours after delivery, the nurse obtained the father's signature on a hospital consent form.

Recommendations and trends

The President's commission believes that because health care professionals are responsible for ensuring that patients can participate effectively in decision making regarding their care, educators have a responsibility to prepare nurses and physicians to carry out this obligation.[92] To that end, the commission suggests that "curricular innovations aimed at preparing health professionals for a process of mutual decision making with patients should be continued and strengthened."[93]

In addition, examinations and evaluations at the professional school and national levels should emphasize the importance of these issues, and "serious attention should be paid to preparing health professionals for team practice in order to enhance patient participation and well-being."[94]

As a practical matter, hospital policies, peer review, and other procedural mechanisms can impose the requirement that a patient's consent is informed and thus can provide incentives for physician compliance. These methods often address violations after the fact of their occurrence.

When the nurse acts to protect the patient, she or he not only fulfills a professional obligation to the patient but is also instrumental in aiding the hospital employer to fulfill its obligations.[95] "Only through its professional nurses, who are in constant contact with the patients and who have the expertise to evaluate, can the hospital intervene immediately if a physician fails to make the proper disclosures."[96] Hospital procedures therefore should specify the reporting mechanism and documentation requirements that the nurse should follow when reporting possible neglect of informed consent by a physician.

Endnotes

1. *Schloendorff v. Society of N.Y. Hospital,* 105 N.E. 92 (N.Y. 1914).
2. Overcast, Merrikin & Evans, *Malpractice Issues In Heart Transplantation,* 10 AMERICAN JOURNAL OF LAW AND MEDICINE 377 (No. 4 1985) (hereinafter cited as *Malpractice Issues*).
3. President's Commission for the Study of Ethical Problems in Medicine and Biomedical and Behavioral Research, MAKING HEALTH CARE DECISIONS, The Ethical and Legal Implications of Informed Consent in the Patient-Practitioner Relationship, Vol. I, 1 (1983) (hereinafter cited as *Making Health Care Decisions*).
4. *Id.* at 7 n.6.
5. *Id.*
6. *Id* at 148 (footnote omitted).
7. *Id.*
8. *Id.* at 147.
9. *Id.*
10. *Id.* at 145 (footnote omitted).
11. *Welsh v. Mercy Hospital,* 151 P.2d 17 (Cal. App. 1944).
12. W. PROSSER, HANDBOOK OF THE LAW OF TORTS 36, 165 (4th ed. 1971).
13. *Making Health Care Decisions, supra* note 3, at 19 & n.11.
14. *Id.* at n.12.
15. *See, e.g., Wall v. Brim,* 138 F.2d 478, 479 n.7 (5th Cir. 1943).
16. *Making Health Care Decisions, supra* note 3, at 20. The term informed consent was first used by the California Appellate Court in *Salgo v. Leland Stanford, Jr. University Board of Trustees,* 317 P.2d 170 (Cal. App. 1957).
17. As of 1982, 37 states had recognized a legal right of recovery for lack of informed consent. *See, e.g.,* Appendix L in Volume 3 of *Making Health Care Decisions, supra* note 3, for the states that have recognized the doctrine.
18. 104 Cal. Rptr. 505 (Cal. 1972) (en banc).
19. *Id.* at 513.
20. *Id.*
21. *Id.* at 514.
22. *Id.*
23. AMERICAN NURSE'S ASSOCIATION CODE FOR NURSES (1976) (hereinafter cited as *ANA Code for Nurses*).
24. *Id.* The code also requires the nurse to safeguard the client's right to privacy by judiciously protecting information of a confidential nature.
25. *Making Health Care Decisions, supra* note 3, at 145 (footnote omitted).
26. *Id.* at 21.
27. *See, e.g., Cobbs v. Grant* 104 Cal. Rptr. 505, 511-512 (Cal. 1972) (en banc) for an excellent review of this distinction.
28. *Malpractice Issues, supra* note 2, at 380.
29. *Cobbs v. Grant,* 104 Cal. Rptr. 505, 512 (Cal. 1972) (en banc).
30. *Id.*
31. *See, e.g., Karp v. Cooley,* 349 F. Supp. 827 (S.D. Tex. 1972), *aff'd,* 493 F.2d 408 (5th Cir. 1974).
32. *See Canterbury v. Spence,* 464 F.2d 772, 780-84 (D.C. Cir. 1972), *cert. denied,* 409 U.S. 1064 (1972).
33. *Making Health Care Decisions, supra* note 5, at 23 & n.31; *see also id.* Appendix L of Volume 3 for the states that enacted legislation relating to informed consent.
34. *Buzzell v. Libi,* 340 N.W.2d 36 (N.D. 1983) (physician performed surgery on left ear after discovering problem there; plaintiff had consented to surgery on the right, not the left ear).
35. *Making Health Care Decisions, supra* note 3, at 27.
36. Determining the materiality of information concerning risks is also done under an objective standard by most courts. *Making Health Care Decisions, supra* note 3.
37. 322 S.E.2d 567 (N.C. App. 1984), *rev'd in part on other grounds,* 337 S.E.2d. 528 (N.C. 1985).
38. *E.g., Cobbs v. Grant,* 104 Cal. Rptr. 505 (Cal. 1972) (in Banc).
39. *Id.* at 515.
40. *Id.*
41. *Making Health Care Decisions, supra* note 3, at 27-28.
42. *Id.*
43. *Cobbs v. Grant,* 104 Cal. Rptr. 505, 515 (Cal. 1972) (in Banc).
44. *Id.* at 516.
45. 540 P.2d (Cal. App. 1975).
46. *Making Health Care Decisions, supra* note 3, at 55.
47. *See, e.g., Lotman v. Security Mutual Life Insurance Co.,* 478 F.2d 868 (3d Cir. 1973).
48. *Making Health Care Decisions, supra* note 3, at 56.
49. *See, e.g., Bartling v. Superior Court* 209 Cal. Rptr. 220 (Cal. App. 1984); *In re Brooks' Estate,* 205 N.E.2d 435 (Ill. 1965).
50. *Making Health Care Decisions, supra* note 3, at 56.
51. *Id.* at 57.
52. *Id.* at 62 (footnote omitted).
53. *See, e.g.,* RESTATEMENT (SECOND) OF TORTS §892b (1979).

54. *Making Health Care Decisions, supra* note 3, at 64.
55. *Id.*
56. *Id.*
57. *Id.* at 25 & n.33.
58. A. ROSOFF, INFORMED CONSENT: A GUIDE FOR HEALTH CARE PROVIDERS (1981).
59. *Making Health Care Decisions, supra* note 3, at 38.
60. *Making Health Care Decisions, supra* note 3, at 147-48.
61. *See, e.g., Bloskas v. Murray* 618 P.2d 719, 720-721 (Colo. App. 1980); *accord, Beck v. Lovell* 361 So.2d 245, 248-49 (La. App. 1978).
62. *See, e.g., Demers v. Gerety,* 515 P.2d 645 (N.M. APP. 1973).
63. 326 S.E.2d 271 (N.C. 1985).
64. 674 P.2d 1265 (Wash. App. 1984).
65. *See generally* Kelly, *Sterilization Abuse: A Proposed Regulatory Scheme* 28 DePAUL LAW REVIEW 731 (1979).
66. 236 S.E.2d 213 (W. Va. App. 1977).
67. *Id.* at 216.
68. *ANA Code for Nurses, supra* note 23.
69. Fish, *The Role Of Consent,* AACN'S CLINICAL REFERENCE FOR CRITICAL CARE NURSING 1051, 1052-53 (hereinafter cited as *Fish*).
70. *See, e.g., Harnish v. Children's Hosp. Medical Center,* 439 N.E.2d 240 (Mass. 1982) (unsuccessful attempt to prove that physicians were employees of hospital and therefore hospital was liable for physician's failure to disclose inherent risk).
71. *Fish, supra* note 69, at 1052-53.
72. *Bulman v. Myers,* 467 A.2d 1353 (Pa. Super. 1983). The patient went to a dentist for treatment of impacted wisdom teeth, which were surgically removed. Following surgery, the patient suffered a marked loss of temperature, taste, and pain sensation in her tongue and a slurring of speech; the patient brought a suit against the dentist for performing the surgery without informed consent, contending that information disclosed by a nurse assistant was inadequate. The jury found disclosure was adequate and the appellate court upheld verdict.
73. 435 N.E.2d 305 (Ind. App. 1982).
74. Katz, *Reporting and Review of Patient Care: The Nurse's Responsibility,* 11 LAW MEDICINE & HEALTH CARE 76, 77 (April 1983).
75. Breu & Dracup, *Survey of Critical Care Nursing Practice. Part III. Responsibilities of Intensive Care Unit Staff,* 11 HEART & LUNG 157 (1982).
76. Careless, *Physicians and Nurses: Roles and Responsibilities in Caring for the Critically Ill Patient* 10 LAW, MEDICINE & HEALTH CARE 72 (April 1982).
77. Widtz, Meisel, Holden, Marx, & Munetz, *Informed Consent and The Structure Of Medical Care* Making Health Care Decisions *supra* note 3, at Vol. II 318, 368 (1983).
78. *Id.* at 373.
79. *Id.*
80. Comment, *Nurses' Legal Dilemma: When Hospital Staffing Compromises Professional Standards,* 18 UNIVERSITY OF SAN FRANCISCO LAW REVIEW 109, 120 (1983).
81. *Id.*
82. *Id.*
83. *See, e.g., Robertson v. Menorah Medical Center,* 588 S.W.2d 134 (Mo. 1979); *cf. Prooth v. Washington,* 432 N.Y.S.2d 663 (N.Y. Supreme Court 1980) (patient sued hospital, personal treating physician, chief surgeon, assistant surgeon and private consulting cardiologist for lack of informed consent; court held only parties charged with a duty to provide patient with information and obtain his knowing consent were treating physician and chief surgeon).
84. 439 N.E.2d 1319 (Ill. App. 1982).
85. *Id.* at 1322.
86. 211 N.E.2d 253 (Ill. 1965), *cert. denied,* 383 U.S. 946 (1966).
87. *Id.* at 258.
88. *See, e.g.,* Holder & Lewis, *Informed Consent and the Nurse,* 2 NURSING LAW & ETHICS 1 (Feb. 1981).
89. *Robertson v. Menorah Medical Center,* 588 S.W.2d 134 (Mo. 1979); *Cross v. Trapp,* 294 S.E.2d 446 (W.Va. 1982).
90. No. 83CVS336, N.C. Pitt County Superior Ct. (April 11 1985), *reported in,* 28 ATLA L. Rep. 419 (November 1985).
91. The obstetrician was also sued for failure to perform a cesarean delivery and failure to obtain informed consent to a vaginal delivery. Before trial, however, the obstetrician settled for $1.5 million.
92. *Making Health Care Decisions, supra* note 3.
93. *Id.*
94. *Id.* at 5.
95. *See* Greenlaw, *Should Hospitals Be Responsible For Informed Consent?* 11 LAW, MEDICINE & HEALTH CARE 173, 176 (Sept. 1983).
96. *Id.* at 176.

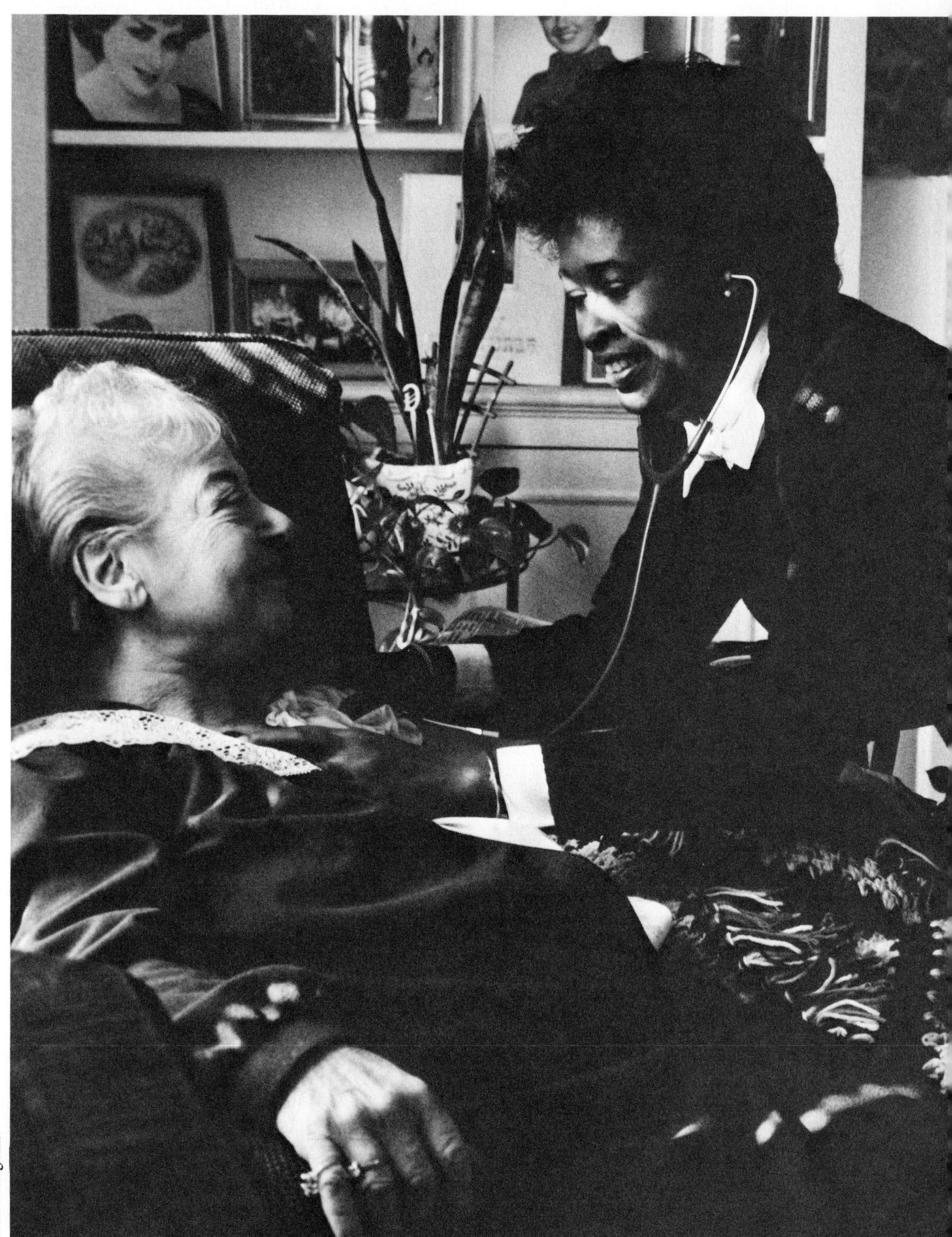

VNSNY/Bergman.

UNIT III

Particular Practice Areas

Chapter 7

Medical-surgical nursing

Mary E. Kelly

Many of the issues presented by reported case law have general application to all areas of hospital-based nursing practice. In a study of lawsuits involving nurses (including nurse's aides and practical nurses) during the 1967 to 1977 period, nurses were named codefendants or defendants in 11.8% of the 390 cases studied, while hospitals were defendants or codefendants in 72.6% of these cases.[1]

The nurse should be cognizant that with the rapidly changing economics of the health care marketplace, hospitals will be less willing to assume responsibility for the negligence of their employees. Nurses and hospitals who are codefendants may well have inconsistent or antagonistic defenses, such as shortage of staff. Nurses who rely on their hospital employers to defend them in a negligence act may risk a good defense, only to find themselves being sued by the hospital for indemnification.[2]

Legler v. Meriwether[3] illustrates a potential problem with respect to insurance coverage. The nurse's employer, a physician-partnership, advised her that she was covered by insurance, when actually there was no such coverage. When the nurse was sued, the physician's insurance company refused to defend the nurse. The nurse attempted to argue that she was an intended beneficiary of the insurance contract between the hospital and the insurance company because she was told that she was insured and relied on this information. The court rejected this argument, holding that the matter was one covered by contract, and since she was not covered, the insurance company had no obligation to defend her.

This chapter presents an overview of the negligence issues facing the nurse who practices in the general medical-surgical area of nursing and the recovery room. The range of nursing encompassed by this category is quite broad, as reflected by the American Nurse's Association's (ANA's) various standards of practice promulgated within the field of medical-surgical nursing.[4]

Nevertheless, the issues that arise—medication and intravenous (IV) therapy errors, equipment errors, failure to observe and to report the patient's condition, and failure to protect the patient from dangerous conditions—cut across practice lines. Many of these issues may confront the nurse in the home health care context as well as the hospital. Consequently, the principles discussed in this chapter may be applied in other practice areas and settings. Cases involving intentional torts and civil rights actions, discussed in other chapters, may also be applicable.

Standard of care

The ANA defines the practice of medical-surgical nursing "as the nursing care of individuals who have a known or a predicted physiological alteration."[5] Medical-surgical nursing is practiced in settings that deliver primary, acute, and long-term care.[6] The breadth of the scope of medical-surgical nursing is significant; it includes several specialized areas of practice such as cardiovascular and oncological nursing practice.[7] For this reason, in 1974, the ANA promulgated general standards with corresponding assessment factors that are broad in scope and provide the basis for subsequently promulgated specialty standards.[8] (See the box below.)

These standards provide a method with which to measure the quality of nursing practice given to a particular patient, "regardless of whether such services are provided solely by a professional nurse or by a professional nurse in conjunction with non-professional assistants."[9] This is because the professional nurse "is primarily accountable and responsible for the nursing process . . . ."[10]

The nursing process analyzes "the supportive and potentially disruptive influences on health status, and the related social and behavioral problems resulting from or affecting the patient's response and/or adjustments to the physiological alteration."[11] The box on p. 97 sets forth ANA's criteria for effective implementation of the nursing process.

In the ANA's SOCIAL POLICY STATEMENT,[12] nursing is defined as the diagnosis and treatment of human responses to actual or potential health problems. Janet Warren, a nursing expert, posits that one of the ways nurses can document their accountability in practice is with the nursing diagnosis.[13]

Warren defines nursing diagnosis as "the end result of the assessment phase of the nursing process [which] defines and communicates to others the specific problems a patient is experiencing which require nursing care."[14] Another definition states that nursing diagnosis is a clinical judgment about an individual, his or her family, or the community, which is derived through a deliberate systematic process of data collection and analysis.[15]

Breach of the standard of care

Nursing negligence can be broadly categorized into various types of errors or omissions. In addition to the duty to protect the patient from a dangerous condition, the nurse has a duty to follow hospital procedure, to record and report observations, and take necessary action.

FAILURE TO MONITOR AND TO REPORT PATIENT'S CONDITION AND TO TAKE APPROPRIATE ACTION

The nurse has a duty to observe the condition of the patient, report this condition to the physician, and take appropriate action. Several cases demonstrate the serious consequences when the nurse breaches this duty; many of these cases involve circulatory compromise.

A 1955 case, *Cooper v. National Motor Bearing Co.*,[16] is an early case illustrating the nurse's duty to observe the patient's condition. An occupational health nurse was individually sued, and the company employing her was also sued for the nurse's negligence in not reporting a dangerous condition and referring the patient to a physician. The nurse treated a puncture wound of one of the company's employees by merely swabbing it with antiseptic and applying a bandage. The patient testified the nurse never probed the wound or examined it.

After 2 months, the area began to swell and became

STANDARDS OF MEDICAL-SURGICAL NURSING PRACTICE

Standard I

The collection of data about the health status of the patient is systematic and continuous. These data are communicated to appropriate persons, recorded, and stored in a retrievable and accessible system.

Standard II

Nursing diagnosis is derived from health status data.

Standard III

Goals are nursing care for formulated.

Standard IV

The plan for nursing care prescribes nursing actions to achieve the goals; the plan for nursing care prescribes a systematic method to meet the goals.

Standard V

The plan for nursing care is implemented.

Standard VI

The plan for nursing care is evaluated.

Standard VII

Reassessment, reordering of priorities, new goal setting, and revision of the plan for nursing care are a continuous process.

Adapted from American Nurses' Association, Standards of Medical-Surgical Nursing Practice, 1974.

IMPLEMENTATION OF THE NURSING PROCESS

To implement the nursing process effectively, nurses who are engaged in the practice of medical-surgical nursing, according to ANA, should:

1. Base nursing practice on principles and theories of biophysical and behavioral sciences
2. Continuously update knowledge and skills, applying new knowledge generated by research, changes in health care delivery systems, and changes in social profiles
3. Determine the range of practice by considering the patient's needs, the nurse's competence, the setting for care, and the resource available
4. Ensure patient and family participation in health promotion, maintenance, and restoration

Adapted from American Nurses' Association, Standards of Medical-Surgical Nursing Practice, 1974.

red. Within 3 to 4 months, the area was puffy and raised. The employee pointed out to the nurse that the wound did not appear to be healing, and the nurse said that if it did not heal, she would have to do something about it. Several months later, a scab formed in the center. At the patient's request, the nurse referred him to a physician who excised the skin for a laboratory specimen. The results indicated basal cell carcinoma.

The court noted that the nurse worked under standing orders that were drawn up and signed by a physician. In the event the injury was beyond the scope of the nurse's practice, she was required to send employees to a physician who was on the company's panel.

Interestingly, the defendant nurse's testimony established her duty of care and that she had breached it. The nurse admitted it was her duty to refer to a physician for diagnosis any condition or injury if she was not familiar or not sure about it. She also acknowledged that the standard of good nursing care in the community required her to examine the wound for foreign bodies. If a wound failed to heal, proper nursing care would have required referral to a physician; the nurse admitted she was familiar with the seven warning signals of cancer, one of which is a sore that will not heal.

The trial court instructed the jury that "[t]he same degree of responsibility and the same duty of care is imposed upon a nurse in the making of diagnosis as is imposed upon her in prescribing and administering medication."[17] On appeal the defendant challenged the instruction, but the court upheld it:

> A nurse's diagnosis of a condition must meet the standard of learning, skill, and care to which nurses practicing in the community are held. A nurse, in order to administer first aid properly and effectively, must make a sufficient diagnosis to enable her to apply the appropriate remedy. . . . She should be able to diagnose . . . sufficiently to know whether it is a condition within her authority to treat . . . or whether it bears danger signs that should warn her to send the patient to a physician.[18]

Another early California case, *Goff v. Doctors General Hospital,*[19] held that nurses are negligent when they fail to notify their supervisors of a patient's critical condition that causes the patient serious injury. There, the nurses' failure to notify the supervisor of the patient's critical condition resulted in the patient's death.

Two nurses in *Goff* believed that a patient was hemorrhaging after childbirth because the physician had failed to suture her. At trial, the nurses testified that they were aware of the patient's dangerous condition and that her physician was not present in the hospital. The nurses also admitted they knew that the patient's condition would worsen without some intervention. Nevertheless, neither nurse contacted anyone except the physician, who failed to respond. Consequently, the hospital was held liable for the nurses' negligence.

Perhaps one of the most significant and clearly leading cases in this area is *Darling v. Charleston Community Hospital.*[20] A young football player broke his leg during a game. After being taken to the emergency room, he was admitted into the hospital. The emergency room physician applied traction and a plaster cast. Soon afterward, the man complained of severe pain in his toes. Later, his toes turned dark in color and became swollen, then they became cold and insensitive.

After 3 days, the physician split the cast, and in doing so, cut the patient's leg. The nurses observed blood and seepage oozing from the wound, and they smelled a foul odor. The nurses did not take any action to alleviate the condition, although they did document their findings. Two weeks after admission, the patient was transferred to another hospital. The patient's leg had become gangrenous and had to be amputated below the knee.

On appeal from the jury verdict against it, the defendant hospital argued that there was insufficient evidence to support the verdict. The court held that the nurses had a duty "to inform the attending physician of the patient's serious, worsening condition and, if [the physician] failed to act, to advise the hospital authorities so that appropriate action might be taken."[21]

Unreported circulatory compromise resulted in amputation of a patient's arm in *Sandhofer v. Abbot-Northwestern Hospital,*[22] and the nurses were deemed to have failed to follow the applicable standard of care. Complications from a cast placed on fractured wrist caused significant and observable circulatory changes, yet the nurses failed to notify the physician. Expert testimony at trial established that the standard of care in the community required that the nurses inform the physician of circulatory impairments and that the cast be split or removed when the extremities showed circulation problems.

Nurses who fail to record their observations will not later be very successful in attempting to convince the fact finder that the patient's condition was observed, particularly where the injury results in circulatory compromise. *Collins v. Westlake Community hospital* illustrates this principle.[23]

In *Collins,* a patient treated for a fractured leg developed ischemia within 3 days necessitating amputation. The physician had written an order for the nurses to watch the condition of the toes. Expert testimony at trial established that routine nursing care required monitoring the circulation of seriously injured patients as frequently as every 15 minutes, and at least every 2 hours, without a physician's order.

The court stressed the fact that the nurse's notes for the crucial 7-hour period when the patient's condition became critical failed to show that the nurse observed the patient's circulation at any time while she was on duty. In rejecting testimony that a nurse does not always record every observation of the patient, the court noted that absent a record, the jury could properly assume that no observations were made during the critical period. The court upheld the finding of negligence.

Some courts have held that this omission—failure to report the patient's critical condition—does not require expert proof to prove that it is a breach of the nurse's standard of care. For example, in *Karrington v. Nazareth Covenant Academy,*[24] a majority of the court held that expert testimony was not required to determine that nurses were negligent in failing to secure the attendance of a physician when a patient's condition became critical. The dissent argued that expert testimony was required to establish that the nurses breached their duty to the patient.

The patient, who was recovering uneventfully from gallbladder surgery, had a T tube drain removed by a physician the day before he was to be discharged. The site was left open. After the physician left, the patient began to complain of severe abdominal pain. A nurse attempted unsuccessfully to locate the physician, but reached his partner, another physician, who ordered Demerol.

At dinner, the patient received a full meal, including meat, which the nurse indicated was all right for the patient to eat. Thereafter, the patient began to vomit and there was blood observed in the emesis. The records did not reveal that the nurses made efforts to notify the physician of the patient's condition after the initial call. The records also failed to reflect that the nurses made efforts to obtain another medical practitioner for him. The physician arrived that night and diagnosed acute gastric dilation.

In *Sinks v. Methodist Medical Center,*[25] a settlement representing $580,000 was entered into between a hospital and a 49-year-old housewife who suffered brain damage due to electrolyte imbalance. This imbalance was caused, in part, by nursing negligence in failing to report the patient's condition.

The hospital's emergency room physician admitted the patient for gallbladder inflammation and scheduled elective cholecystectomy for 5 days later. On admission, serum electrolytes were within normal range.

During the next 4 days, the patient was treated with Aldactazide, and she received repeated radiographic procedures involving cathartics and enemas. Her fluid intake was restricted; she received, by IV, 3 L of 5% dextrose in water. When preoperative serum electrolytes taken on the fourth night revealed severe hypokalemia, hyponatremia, and hypochloremia, the laboratory notified the charge nurse.

Although the charge nurse unsuccessfully attempted to locate the attending family practitioner and surgeon, she failed to contact the hospital physician covering inhouse emergencies. One hour and 10 minutes later, the patient suffered a cardiac arrest. Semicomatose for almost 1 month, the patient was left with a moderate degree of cerebral atrophy, nonprogressive dementia, and visual field deficit. The cholecystectomy thus had to be postponed for 1 year. As a result, the patient suffered recurrent pancreatitis, necessitating a pancreatectomy. She became an insulin-dependent diabetic.

In *Jarvis v. St. Charles Medical Center,*[26] a patient with severe fracture of the left leg was admitted to the hospital. After the leg was placed in a cast, the patient developed circulatory compromise. Ultimately, two partial fasciotomies were performed to relieve pressure.

The patient's suit alleged failure to monitor the changes in the patient's condition and failure to notify the physician of observable changes due to decreased circulation. In addition, the hospital was charged with negligence in failing to provide sufficient staff to check the patient's condition every 30 minutes, as ordered by the physician. The jury awarded $350,000.

In *Paavola v. St. Joseph's Hospital,*[27] a $2.1 million settlement was reached in a case involving postoperative complications of pericardial effusion that went undetected. The patient had elective surgery for closure of an interatrial septal defect. Several days after surgery, the patient experienced cardiac tamponade secondary to pericardial effusion.

Plaintiff's condition went unrecognized, although she experienced nausea, increased size in the cardiac silhouette upon x-ray examination, pale skin color, and hypotension. The patient was left brain damaged. The lawsuit charged the hospital with negligence due to the failure of the nurse, interns, and residents to closely monitor the patient postoperatively and to timely diagnose pericardial effusion.

In *Duren v. Suburban Community Hospital,*[28] an overweight man, who had three previous attacks of pancreatitis and had been diagnosed a diabetic, was admitted to a hospital complaining of another onset of pancreatitis. The patient died from what his counsel characterized as complete indifference by the nursing staff to his condition. The medical records were also falsified. In a wrongful death action against the hospital and the attending physician, his family recovered $2.5 million against the hospital, $1.5 million for pain and suffering, and a couple of thousand dollars for funeral expenses. The physician was cleared of any negligence. The jury obviously blamed the nursing staff.

The patient's vital signs were recorded as normal upon his admission. The gastroenterologist ordered a number of tests on a stat basis. The calcium test, however, was not performed until 3 days later, and it revealed abnormally high levels. The physician also ordered fractional urine tests to be done at specified times, with administration of insulin in doses dependent upon the levels of sugar in the urine. The nurses obtained the level only once, and it was 5+, an obviously dangerous signal. Nevertheless, the medical record failed to document that any insulin was given.

At 10 PM, a practical nurse recorded that the patient's pulse was 144 beats per minute and his temperature was elevated. She failed to notify the physician or the registered nurse in charge. Thus, when the shift changed that night, the charge nurse was not alerted to the patient's deteriorating condition. The nurse's notes for the night shift indicated that the patient was in extreme pain, moaning, and thrashing in his bed. From midnight to 4 AM, the registered nurse failed to administer any medication, failed to perform any test, and failed to contact a physician. When the patient pulled out his IV, the house physician on call, who was one floor away, was contacted. He did not arrive until 2 hours later. The patient, at this time, had a fixed stare and could not be revived. At approximately 7 AM, the patient was pronounced dead.

The registered nurse on duty during the night shift testified that she was present the entire time; however, the records clearly were written in two different handwritings. The licensed practical nurse on duty later admitted that she had made the notations from midnight to 4 AM. An entry at 6 AM, 1 hour before the patient died, indicated that the patient's vital signs were normal; however, no one admitted making the entry.

Another $2+ million case was won against a hospital based on nursing negligence. The lawsuit alleged that the nurses failed to adequately assess the plaintiff's postoperative status and failed to maintain adequate oxygenation levels on at least three occasions, either by failing to respond to alarms, using malfunctioning equipment, or by refusing to provide supplemental oxygen when the respirator could not be properly reattached.[29]

Thomas v. Corso[30] illustrates the importance of attending to the patient who is transferred from another unit by establishing baseline vital signs and thereafter ensuring that a stable pattern exists, and if not, that further action is taken. A patient was admitted to the hospital directly from the emergency room. Due to an epidemic of influenza, no rooms were available; the patient was placed outside the nurses' station in the hall.

A staff nurse and an assistant supervisor checked the patient's vital signs: blood pressure, 70/50; pulse, 120 per minute; respirations, 140. The patient appeared rational and complained of pain. The nurse knew that the patient had been administered the maximum dose of Demerol and that this dose would depress blood pressure. The nurse also noticed that the patient's skin was cool and perspiring, his breathing deep but rapid. At 12:15 AM he was frequently asking for water. These are symptoms of shock[31] that require the reasonable medical-surgical nurse to take action.

Instead, the nurse here merely continued to record the vital signs and the quality of respirations. Later, the nurse found him in Cheyne-Stokes respiration with no detectable pulse. The nurse's defense for failing to take action in the face of symptoms of shock was that the patient had been drinking and he had been given Demerol.

She wanted to observe the patient to see if he improved before contacting the physician. The court called this a lame excuse as to why the physician was not contacted, and held that the jury was acting within its province in rejecting the argument.

FAILURE TO PROTECT THE PATIENT FROM A DANGEROUS CONDITION

Nurses have a professional duty to exercise reasonable care to see that no unnecessary harm comes to their patients.[32] In essence this duty encompasses all nursing negligence since medication errors, burns, equipment error, infection, and falls are all dangerous conditions.

Nurses must also question inappropriate medication orders, medication dosages, and other treatments that, in their judgement, would be harmful to the patient. If the physician refuses to alter the proposed plan, and the nurse is convinced that the plan will result in harm to the patient, further action must be taken at an administrative level. These efforts must be recorded and substantiated at the supervisory level.

Similar efforts must be taken if the patient has been abandoned by the nursing staff or a physician. There is a duty to take further action to replace the nurse or physician and report the abandonment to the administration. If nothing is done, the nurse must take additional steps to protect the patient, including obtaining other care. Again, a thorough written record of these events in the chart must be maintained.

Medication Errors. Negligence actions based on medication errors typically involve errors in the dosage, route of administration, and injection technique. Cases have also been brought for inadvertently administering the wrong drug and administering a drug that the nurse knows or should know is contraindicated or has been prescribed in the wrong dosage or with the wrong route of administration. In other words, a nurse is charged with a duty to have a basic understanding of the drugs he or she administers, including knowledge of their normal dosage, route, and side effects. One court noted in a case where a nurse administered to an infant a fatal intramuscular (IM) dose of medication that was to be an oral dose.

> A nurse who is unfamiliar with the fact that the drug in question is prepared in oral form for administration to infants by mouth is not properly and adequately trained for duty in a pediatric ward. As laudable as her intentions are conceded to have been on the occasion in question, her unfamiliarity with the drug was a contributing factor in the child's death. In this regard we are of the opinion that she was negligent in attempting to administer a drug with which she was not familiar.[33]

Hallinan v. Prindle[34] illustrates an action brought against the physician, the nurse, and the hospital for an injury resulting from the wrong anesthetic used during minor surgery. In accordance with local custom, the nurse set up the tray of sterile supplies, including anesthetic to be locally injected. Instead of pouring local anesthetic, the nurse poured formalin, a powerful germicide, into the medicine glass. This was drawn into a syringe and injected into the patient.

The nurse and the hospital were held liable. The physician was not found liable. On appeal, the court upheld the jury instruction that in the exercise of ordinary care, the physician would rely on the nurse's skill and judgment in preparation of the anesthetic.

Dessauer v. Memorial Hospital[35] demonstrates that medication errors have the potential for disaster when nurses are transferred to specialty areas with which they have no experience. An obstetrical specialty nurse, transferred to the emergency room, erroneously drew up a medication for injection from a vial containing a higher concentration of the same drug. The patient received about 50 times the amount ordered and suffered cardiopulmonary arrest and subsequently died.

The decedent's family sued the hospital and the nurse individually and won. Both the nurse and the hospital tried to bring the physician into the lawsuit by filing third-party complaints for indemnification. The trial court refused to find the physician vicariously liable and found the nurse directly liable.

In *Larrimore v. Homeopathic Hospital Association,*[36] the court ruled that a jury could find a nurse negligent in administering an overdose of ansolysen IM instead of a lesser dose orally administered. The nurse had previously administered the medication IM, but, during her days off, the physician had changed the route of administration to an oral dose. The medication order for the date the nurse returned to work and administered the drug was silent on the route of administration.

The nurse asked the physician if he intended to prescribe 30 mg, and the physician said yes. She questioned him again and he affirmatively answered. When the nurse approached the patient and told him that she had a needle for him, the patient and his wife explained that the physician had said he was not to get any more needles. The nurse reread the order sheet and explained that "he was going to get this needle"[37] and the patient again protested that he could not understand it since the physician had indicated he was to receive no more needles. He acquiesced upon the nurse's insistence.

When the nurse told him he was to receive another dose by injection the next day, he indicated he would refuse the medication. The nurse asserted she would call the physician, which she did. She then learned that the intended route was by mouth. The physician charted that the medication had been given in error, that "[n]o satisfactory explanation for this has been obtained."[38]

The court noted that the patient suffered no lasting ill effects from the drug. The physician ordered continuous nursing care, and the patient complained of violent headaches and temporary loss of vision. The patient, however, never experienced a drop in blood pressure.

At trial, both parties agreed that the medication error did not hasten the patient's death. The defense was lack of expert testimony. The appellate court noted that while expert testimony is generally required, the rule may be modified in cases where the subject matter of the evidence is within the understanding of the ordinary juror. The court thereafter characterized the nurse's conduct as breach of ordinary care. The order for route of administration of the drug could have been clarified by referring to orders for previous days.

The nurse attempted to defend on the ground that the patient had consented to the injection. The court held that consent could not be based on the patient's acquiescence. When the patient reluctantly permitted the injection, the court reasoned, he agreed only to proper administration of the drug, not to an overdose.

Defendant also appealed the $30,000 jury award of damages. The court ordered a new trial on the issue of damages, noting that the chief complaint was that the patient thereafter lost his optimism. The court characterized his damages as mental disturbance and temporary physical problems, and thus the verdict was grossly excessive.

Norton v. Argonaut Insurance Company[39] also represents serious consequences from the same kind of injury. A nurse who was unfamiliar with the fact that Lanoxin is prepared in elixir form for infants, and who did not check its recommended route of administration or consult with the prescribing physician, administered 3 ml of the drug to a 3-month-old infant by injection. The infant died, and the nurse was held responsible.

Nerve damage from improper injection of a drug is another injury often claimed as the result of a nurse's negligence. In *Holbrooks v. Duke University, Inc.*,[40] the court held that a jury could properly decide whether a nurse violated the standard of care and whether the patient's nerve damage to his thigh was proximately caused by injecting an IM dose of Demerol and Vistaril 3 to 4 inches above the knee.

In *Suburban Hospital Association v. Hadry,*[41] a patient underwent a liver biopsy with a needle that might have been unsterile and may have exposed the patient to infectious hepatitis. The cabinet from which the physician obtained the needle mixed sterile and unsterile needles; there was one shelf for each. The shelves, however, had no notation as to which shelf was sterile and which shelf was unsterile. Although the nurse offered to obtain the needle for the physician, he obtained it himself. The physician was not aware, and he was not warned, that the cabinet contained contaminated material.

The nurse subsequently discovered that the needle used by the physician might have been contaminated with hepatitis. Consequently, the patient had to be treated with massive gamma-globulin injections, which he alleged were painful. In addition, the patient had to suspend treatment for his psoriasis condition, which became worse.

Kalmus v. Cedars of Lebanon Hospital,[42] another unsterile needle, nursing negligence case, also demonstrates the use of physicians' testimony to support the element of proximate cause. The complaint charged that the nurse used an unsterile needle in administering an injection, and the hip became infected. The jury found against the hospital, based on the nurse's negligence.

On appeal, the hospital challenged the sufficiency of the evidence to support the jury's verdict. The appellate court affirmed the jury's verdict, noting that the physical examination conducted on admission revealed that there was no problem with the patient's hip; he had no previous blood disorders or abscesses.

The court also stated that the plaintiff testified the nurse did nothing to prepare the skin for injection; she came in the room, jabbed the needle in his hip, pulled it out, and put the needle right back in his hip. The standard of care, established by physician experts, required the instrument to be sterile and the skin to be scrubbed with an alcohol sponge.

The plaintiff testified the area began to sting and swell immediately after the injection. An abscess formed at the injection site; the plaintiff developed a fever, and a culture revealed there was a staphylococcal infection. A physician testified that only the injection could be the causative factor for the abscess. The treating physician testified that there was a connection between the two. Consequently, the court concluded there was direct expert evidence that use of the needle was the cause of the patient's injury.[43]

Pro re nata (PRN), which means "as needed," orders also raise liability issues for nurses. In *Fraijo v. Hartland Hospital,*[44] a nurse gave an injection of meperidine hydrochloride (Demerol) to relieve pain to an asthmatic patient in respiratory distress. Experts testified that Demerol should be used with caution in patients having an acute asthmatic attack, but that it was sometimes prescribed for asthma even though the drug depressed respirations.

The court upheld the use of an instruction to the jury that unsuccessful treatment is not necessarily negligent treatment. The court reasoned that the physician delegated to the nurse the responsibility for determining if the medication was necessary and that nurses often exercise independent judgment in the care of patients. Therefore, the nurse making a judgment is entitled to the same protection accorded a physician defending a malpractice action for an error in judgement.

Intravenous Therapy. One of the hazards of IV therapy is infiltration of the agent into the surrounding tissue. When the agent being introduced intravenously is caustic or potent, such as a cephalosporin or a chemotherapeutic agent, special care must be taken to protect against the danger of necrosis from infiltration. Negligence has been found where there is a failure to carefully monitor the IV line on a periodic basis to ensure that the line is firmly within the vein and that there is no infiltration of the surrounding tissues.

In *Ball v. Rolling Hill Hospital,*[45] a 66-year-old woman won a $647,041 jury verdict for the improper administration of IV chemotherapy that resulted in necrosis of the forearm. The patient was receiving IV chemotherapy at the defendant hospital to treat Hodgkin's disease. Intravenous infiltration of the forearm caused severe necrosis and the loss of several muscles and tendons.

Three subsequent surgical procedures were performed to remove the necrotic tissue, which left a disfiguring scar. Psychiatric care was also necessary to treat a reactive depression.

The inadvertent administration of drugs is a common error with respect to IV therapy. The accidental administration of potassium chloride in a concentrated bolus or otherwise is perhaps the most notable. What usually occurs is that the nurse picks up a bag of solution containing potassium chloride assuming that it is another drug (usually saline solution for irrigation of the IV tubing).[46] Such mistakes can result in tragic results.

In *Peltier v. Franklin Foundation Hospital,*[47] a $240,000 settlement was reached in a wrongful death action based on wrongful and incorrect administration of potassium chloride. The 76-year-old woman suffered tachycardia and ultimately died. The lawsuit charged that the nurses administered the drug even though it had not been ordered by any physician. Most likely, the error was the inadvertent administration of a bag of solution containing potassium.[48]

In *Sanchez v. Bay General Hospital,*[49] the medical-surgical[50] nurses failed to examine a patient's chart upon admission from the recovery room. While in the recovery room the patient had vomited. The patient had an atrial catheter that the nurses assumed was a peripheral line. The emergency physician also did not examine the records, and assuming the line was a peripheral IV, administered a cardiac stimulating drug. The patient died.

In *Beardsley v. Wyoming County Community Hospital,*[51] nurses failed to follow orders for replacement fluids in a patient who was postoperatively recovering from a splenectomy. The nurses overlooked the physician's orders to alternate an isotonic saline solution with dextrose and water solution. The patient suffered seizures, brain damage, and permanent physical disabilities in response to the increased brain pressure.

Infection. Occasionally, suits have been brought against nurses and hospitals for infections. In general these suits present causation problems. For example, in *Tripp v. Pate,*[52] a hospital was sued for alleged negligent care resulting in a postoperative infection of the patient's knee. The case was dismissed, however, because the plaintiff failed to present evidence that the hospitals' operating room lacked sterile conditions, thereby causing the infection.

In *DeFalco v. Long Island College Hospital,*[53] a similar result was reached where a plaintiff charged that his eye infection was caused by the nurse's negligence. The patient testified that the nurse dropped a sterile eye patch on the floor and then placed the eye patch on the patient's eye.

The court recognized that it was a matter of common knowledge that the act of placing a presumably soiled eye patch over the patient's eye was unsanitary and not in accordance with good nursing practice. The act, the court noted, by its very nature bespeaks of improper treatment and malpractice. Nevertheless, the plaintiff's claim failed because there was no expert evidence that the presumably soiled bandage was the cause of the infection.

Expert testimony, the court concluded, was needed to establish that the presumably unsterile eye patch carried the bacteria that caused the patient's eye infection. Although the organism that caused the infection was known, there was no testimony that the eye patch carried that organism from the floor to the plaintiff's eye, thereby causing the infection. Since the causal connection between the nurse's act and the patient's injury was not established by competent expert evidence, the claim of negligence against the nurse could not be upheld.

Equipment Errors. The nurse has been successfully charged with responsibility to check equipment and ensure that it is safe for its intended use. In *Florida Medical Center, Inc., v. Von Stetina*[54] a hospital's negligence was based on the nurse's failure to check products and equipment, particulary the proper functioning of a respirator. Operation of equipment that is nondefective nevertheless requires the nurse to warn the patient of obvious dangers attendant to the equipment's operation.[55] If the nurse fails to do so, and the patient is injured, the nurse may be deemed liable for the failure to provide a warning, even if the nurse operates equipment in the proper manner.[56]

Management of equipment is an important nursing responsibility; machines such as respirators, monitors, and cardiac paddles on crash carts need to be serviced to ensure that they are properly functioning. The date of last inspection and service tagged on the machines and some kind of reminder system for the next inspection will avoid unnecessary injury from equipment malfunction and failure. Obsolete machinery should not be used unless the delay in obtaining new machinery would cause greater harm.[57]

Sound equipment practice insulates the nurse from third-party liability. That is, the manufacturer of the equipment who is sued by the patient (these are the first and second parties) will not be able to defend and counterclaim against the nurse (thereby making her a third party to the lawsuit) for the alleged negligence of the nurse in failing to ensure proper maintenance of the equipment. Manufacturers may seek to defend[58] and to obtain indemnification against the nurse for failure to inspect and to examine their product.

Generally, a nondiscoverable defect in machinery will not result in nursing liability; the defect must be observable and discoverable.[59] In one case, a defective clamp on proctology equipment allowed hot water to flow unrestricted, severely burning the patient's bowel. The nurse was not in the room when this occurred. The court held the nurse could not be liable:

> [The nurse], although a trained professional, could reasonably rely upon the hospital's furnishing a proper clamp. We agree with defendant that if the article furnished was obviously unfit for the use for which it was furnished and intended, and the nurse used it in violation of the usual standards of due care of nursing practice, the defendant cannot be chargeable with any injurious effects therefrom. But the defect was not patent. The clamp was furnished apparently ready for use and it was not her duty to examine into its mechanical parts for the discovery of possible defects.[60]

The nurse thus is under a duty to use the equipment in its intended manner. If the equipment is misused by the nurse, the manufacturer will have a valid defense to a lawsuit by the patient and a good indemnification claim against the nurse.

Zach v. Centro Espano Hospital[61] illustrates a nurse's negligence for improperly using equipment that caused injury to a patient. The lawsuit charged a nurse with removing a Foley catheter with the cup inflated, thereby causing a fistula in the bladder. At trial, the nurse denied that she had removed the catheter with the cup inflated. A physician, however, testified that, in his opinion, the nurse must have removed it with the cup inflated, which caused the fistula. The jury found for the plaintiff. On appeal, the court held that this evidence was sufficient for the jury to find the nurse negligent.

In *Hall v. Bio-Medical Application, Inc.*,[62] a nurse was found liable for malpractice for disconnecting a patient from a dialysis machine and leaving the dialysis needles in his arm. The court rejected the nurse's defense that the patient was shouting obscenities at her and exhibiting provoking behavior.

Burns. The use of hot water bottles and other warming devices are frequently the subject of negligence claims for based equipment-related injuries. Placing a hot water bottle against a patient's body without checking its temperature has been characterized as the plainest sort of negligence where the scalding hot water has resulted in burns to the patient.[63] The courts have also defined as plain negligence a nurse's conduct in leaving an electric lamp under the patient's bed sheets, which burned the patient's foot.[64] Courts virtually uniformly hold that the nurse's neglect that results in such injuries to the patient constitutes negligence.[65]

In *Oldis v. La Societe Francaise De Bienfaisance Mutelle*,[66] the appellate court upheld a judgment against the hospital, the physicians, and the nurses in a case where a patient sustained third-degree burns on his abdomen after a major operation. The plaintiff was in a semiconscious condition under the influence of pain-relieving drugs and therefore he could not ascertain which of the defendants caused the burn. There was, however, some evidence that it might have resulted from the negligence of one of the nurses in applying hot water bottles that were too hot to the patient's abdomen.

Falls From Bed And Other Falls. The number of

claims concerning falls from bed filed each year ranks third among the 10 most common claims.[67] Walking-related falls and bathroom-related falls rank, respectively, ninth and tenth.[68] Documentation of the fact that the nurse has raised the bed rails on elderly or medicated patients, and thereafter has continued to check that the bed rails remain up, may lead to a defense verdict.

Where, however, a nurse leaves an elderly patient restrained in bed but unattended, the potential for liability exists. In *Moore v. Frankford Hospital,*[69] a $95,000 settlement was made because the patient suffered a fracture of the right distal femur under these circumstances. The patient had been admitted to the hospital and thereafter was taken to the eye clinic for a consultation. At the conclusion of the consultation, the consulting resident notified the nurses' station and requested them to take the patient back to her room.

The resident was called away and the plaintiff was left alone and restrained. She removed the restraints and fell, severely fracturing her leg.

Patients Requiring Assistance. In *Stevenson v. Alta Bates, Inc.,*[70] a 56-year-old woman who had previously suffered a stroke, fell while a nurse assisted her in learning to walk. The patient fractured her femur and brought a negligence action against the nurse and the hospital.

At the time of the injury, the patient was able to walk with assistance and a cane. Two nurses assisted her to a sunroom, each holding one of her arms. As one of the nurses released her hold on the patient to arrange a chair, the patient fell.

At trial, the evidence revealed that the nurse did not warn the patient, as she had done in the past, that she was about to loosen her hold on the patient's arm. The defense argued that the fall did not cause the fracture, but that the fracture had spontaneously occurred. The jury returned a verdict for the patient.

On appeal, the defendants argued that the trial court erred in failing to instruct the jury that proof of negligence requires expert testimony. The court rejected this argument, noting that expert testimony would be required if the events surrounding the incident required explanation by a jury; where, however, the facts are ascertainable by the senses of the jury or a layperson, no expert testimony is necessary.

FAILURE TO ATTEND TO PATIENT

In *Griffin v. Colusa County,*[71] an action was brought against two nurses, among others, for injuries a patient sustained through the alleged negligence of the nurses in leaving her unattended while she was unconscious and delirious. The patient's injuries were caused when she fell from bed. On appeal from an order dismissing the lawsuit against the nurses, the court held that the two nurses were properly named in the lawsuit and they should be compelled to answer and to defend.

In *Thompson v. United States,*[72] the Veterans Administration was sued for the negligence of a practical nurse in leaving a medicated patient unattended as he walked to the laboratory for tests during the day. The night before, the patient had experienced difficulty breathing and chest pain, and these facts were recorded in the nurse's notes. The nurse acknowledged that she had read the patient's record the following day.

When the nurse instructed the patient to walk to the laboratory, he protested that he could not ambulate. The nurse nevertheless told him to go to the laboratory. The defense expert nurse witnesses testified this was proper because the physician had not restricted his activities. The court rejected this view because the patient himself told the nurse he was unable to ambulate. The patient fainted as he walked to the laboratory. The injury he sustained necessitated a future amputation of his finger.

On appeal, the plaintiff contended that nurses should be held to the same standard of care as physicians. The court rejected this argument, holding that nurses are to be judged according to a professional nursing standard of care. Nevertheless, at trial, a physician testified for the plaintiff as to the standard of care and that the nurse breached the standard in allowing the patient to walk to the laboratory unassisted.

This case illustrates the potential danger posed by medicated patients who need to be transported. Nurses are charged with constructive knowledge of the contents of their patients' charts. Opportunity for review of the patient's condition during the shift report also provides notice of the patient's condition.

In *Hayden v. Cedars Medical Center, Inc.,*[73] a jury awarded an elderly plaintiff $70,000, which was reduced by 15% due to the plaintiff's negligence, because the nurses left her unattended, unrestrained, and unsupervised. The patient suffered a comminuted fracture of the shoulder when she fell from the hospital bed. The patient had been discovered once on the floor, uninjured but confused. The nurses placed her back in bed and left her unattended. Thirty minutes later, she was found on the floor.

In *Daniel v. St. Francis Cabrini Hospital of Alexandria,*[74] the patient was admitted to the defendant hospital, suffering from prostatic cancer with probable contiguous spread and metastatic disease, diabetes mellitus, and chronic organic dementia. He was 77 years old, had one arm missing, and was subject to spells of dizziness and weakness. On one occasion, he walked to the nurse's station, demanding an enema. The enema was administered, and he ordered the nurse to leave the room while he defecated. The nurse returned to the nurses' station. The patient became dizzy and fell, lacerating his penis.

In determining whether the evidence was sufficient to prove the nurse's negligence, the court noted the nurse had admitted that he had left the patient alone in the bathroom and returned to the station after administering the enema. The evidence also showed that he was taking a number of medications, including narcotics and tranquilizers, at the time of the accident. These drugs could have caused him to feel dizzy and weak. In addition, his left arm had been amputated. Except for the nurse's conduct in leaving the room and returning to the station, the patient probably would not have had the injury.

In considering the nurse's defense that the patient ordered him from the room, the court noted that "it would have been very simple for the nurse to remain in the hospital room just outside the bathroom. Had he done so, he would have been able to immediately respond to [patient's] call for help and to render assistance to him."[75]

The patient was awarded $3,300 and attempted to argue on appeal that an injury to his scrotum was due to the fall, but the court held that the 7-month delay between the accident and development of the problem meant causation problems for the patient. There was also evidence that cancer had caused the problem with the scrotum.

A verdict for the defense was upheld in *Stone v. Sisters of Charity of the House of Providence*.[76] The patient was left alone in a room after a nurse changed his corset-like binder. He began coughing, which opened his surgical wound. At trial, he contended that he was entitled to a *res ipsa loquitor* instruction on the nurse's negligence because had she been in the room, she could have prevented his coughing spell, and the coughing spell was caused by her negligent changing of the corset-like binder.

On appeal, the court upheld the verdict and rejected the plaintiff's argument. The court noted that there was no positive proof that the presence of the nurse in his room would have prevented the patient's coughing spell from opening the surgical incision or that the coughing was caused by the nurse's negligent changing of the binder. Consequently, the plaintiff was not entitled to a *res ipsa loquitor* instruction.

FAILURE TO EXERCISE INDEPENDENT JUDGMENT

This principle has been extended to inappropriate orders. Generally, if the physician prescribes a drug or course of treatment, the nurse, or hospital, will not be liable for any subsequent injury, unless the nurse is negligent in carrying out the order. Failing to carry out a valid order is considered malpractice,[77] assuming that the injury complained of is proximately caused by the nurse's failure to follow the valid order.[78]

Where, however, the nurse knows or reasonably should know that the order is not in accordance with accepted practice or is clearly inappropriate, the nurse has a duty to exercise independent judgment to protect the patient from danger. Under these circumstances, the nurse is justified in refusing to carry out the order. If the physician intends to go forward with the action, and there is a risk of danger to the patient, the administrator of the facility should be notified. All of the nurse's efforts should be documented in writing.

In *Poor Sisters of St. Francis v. Catron*,[79] the court applied this rule in a negligence action where the nurses had observed that an endotracheal tube was left in a patient too long, but they failed to report it to the physician. The court held "if a nurse or other hospital employee fails to report changes in a patient's condition and/or to question a doctor's orders when they are not in accord with standard medical practice and the omission results in injury to the patient, the hospital will be liable."[80] Thus, failure to recognize and report subnormal treatment is a breach of the nurse's duty of care.[81]

Consequently, the nurse has to bring substandard care to the attention of the physician, and if no further action is taken, to the administrator of the hospital. The nurse must take action that would reasonably be expected to eliminate the danger to the patient. Merely notifying one's immediate supervisor may not be enough if one knows no further action will be taken.

Utter v. United Hospital Center, Inc.,[82] illustrates this principle. The plaintiff was injured on the job, and his arm was placed in a cast below the knuckles of his right hand. After the first 48 hours, the patient was removed to the West Virginia University Hospital for treatment, which resulted in his arm being amputated.

During the patient's stay at the first hospital, his arm became progressively swollen and black. Later, the arm became more edematous, and the nurses noted a foul-smelling drainage was emitting from the cast. The patient developed a high temperature and became delirious. The attending physician was notified but did nothing. Unfortunately, the nurse failed to take further action, and the patient's arm ultimately had to be amputated in order to save his life. The hospital's liability was premised on the nurse's negligence in failing to take further action.

Where the nurse reports a patient's condition to the physician, and the physician fails to take any action, the nurse is required to take action either by obtaining the assistance of another physician or pursuing administrative channels. The following quote from *Utter* illustrates the courts' expectation that nurses should do whatever necessary to protect the patient.

> Nurses are specialists in hospital care who, in the final analysis, hold the well-being, in fact in some instances the very lives, of patients in their hands. In the dim hours of the night, as well as in the light of the day, nurses are frequently charged with the duty to observe the condition of the ill and infirm in their care. If that patient, hopeless and wholly dependent, shows signs of worsening, the nurse is charged with the obligation of taking some positive action. . . . [B]etter care will result and perhaps more patients will recover.[83]

The courts view the nurse-patient relationship as one of patient advocacy; they expect the nurse to protect the patient, who is dependent on the health professional for good faith intervention when necessary to prevent injury. The *Utter* court's words vividly demonstrate this notion. The rationale for this rule is that professional practice brings with it certain responsibilities.[84]

Mason v. Lodi Community Hospital[85] also demonstrates that mere requests of the physician to attend to the patient are insufficient to protect the nurse. In *Mason,* a 41-year-old nurse underwent surgery for vaginal hysterectomy and ''tummy tuck'' by a plastic surgeon. Postoperatively, the patient suffered from low blood pressure and was restless. A laparotomy revealed the patient had a ruptured spleen and extensive bleeding. The patient became comatose and eventually died.

The lawsuit charged poor postoperative care, failure of the physician to respond to registered nurses' requests to attend to the patient, and failure of the nurses to take further steps to aid the patient when they knew the physician failed to properly respond. The parties ultimately settled for $500,000.

In *Kleba v. Mount Sinai,*[86] a $400,000 settlement was reached in the wrongful death of a 30-year-old woman who died of postoperative complications from a hysterectomy. The hysterectomy followed a cesarean section that was complicated by placenta previa and placenta accreta.

Within 45 minutes of being returned to her room, the patient began vomiting, had an elevated temperature, and a decreased blood pressure of 90/60. Within the next fifteen minutes, she was cold and clammy.

Although these symptoms were recorded, the nurses did not call a physician until 20 minutes later when the patient's pulse was 150 beats per minute. A resident responded 10 minutes later and did not call the attending physician until 25 minutes later. The patient died within 3 hours of being returned to her room. The cause of death was hypovolemic shock caused by intra-abdominal hemorrhage.

FAILURE TO PROTECT PATIENT FROM ABANDONMENT

Nurses have a duty to act to protect a patient from danger, which includes the inadequate care of a physician. A physician who fails to provide adequate postoperative care to a patient by not appropriately instructing the nursing staff and not calling in to the unit to inquire about the patient's condition may be liable for an untoward result.[87] Nurses, however, simply cannot document this inadequate postoperative care, do nothing more, and expect not to be held accountable to the patient.

Nurses have an independent duty to the patient. This duty requires that they take further action to protect a patient from a condition they know, or should know, is dangerous to the well-being of the patient. Recall from the discussion in Chapter 4 that in determining whether the nurse breached this duty by failing to take further action, three factors are considered: the likelihood that the injury would have been foreseeable to a reasonably prudent nurse acting according to a professional standard of care; the severity of the injury; and the burden to the nurse of avoiding the injury.

The proximate cause analysis is similar: was the nurse's failure to act a cause in fact or substantial factor in bringing about the injury; and if it was, was the injury reasonably foreseeable? Invariably, the fact finder—courts and juries alike—and the appellate courts hold the nurse responsible.

Czubinsky v. Doctor's Hospital[88] illustrates this view. A patient experienced cardiac arrest as she was coming out of anesthesia, after a routine and uneventful surgical procedure to remove an ovarian cyst. She suffered a severe loss of oxygen to her brain resulting in permanent and total paralysis. The patient now exists in a semicomatose state. A unanimous jury awarded the 28-year-old woman damages in the amount of $982,000.

At the time of the postoperative complication, only the anesthesiologist and operating room (OR) technician were present in OR. The operating surgeon and the circulating nurse, at the surgeon's direction, had left the patient to prepare for another surgery. As a result of this situation, the OR was inadequately staffed at a most critical period following surgery. The appellate court characterized this evidence as sufficient for a finding of gross negligence. The court criticized the nurse particularly:

> The evidence is overwhelming that Czubinsky sustained catastrophic injuries as direct and proximate result of the hospital personnel's failure to properly monitor and render aid when needed. . . . [The surgeon testified] that monitoring is absolutely important, and all personnel in OR are required to observe the patient regardless of their job function. . . . [He] also said cardiopulmonary resuscitation (CPR), if administered properly, would provide adequate blood circulation and forestall permanent brain damage for as long as one-half hour; effective CPR required a joint effort by a number of people. Any significant change in cardiac activity necessitated prompt remedial measures. Any trained anesthesiologist, nurse or OR technician would have recognized this. [The surgeon] further testified that it would have *taken several minutes with observable warning signs* present for Czubinsky to reach a severe hypoxic [brain damaging] condition.[89]

The circulating nurse left the OR when the operating surgeon who testified and another surgeon "called her to come next door" where they had started another surgery. The nurse informed them she could not leave the patient because she had not completed her duties, yet she departed.[90] Her defense was that she was being yelled at by the physicians.

In rejecting this defense, the court noted the concession by the nurse that the patient was at a critical postoperative period because she was undergoing transition from anesthetized air to room air. The court also looked to the hospital's manual of procedures setting forth the specific duties of the circulating nurse in the OR. The manual provided that the circulating nurse should remain present during the entire procedure to assist the anesthesiologist.

The circulating nurse conceded her responsibility was to monitor the patient and to assist the anesthesiologist. She acknowledged she was familiar with OR procedures and rules and she was trained in CPR. The court noted that the "OR technician's presence in the room was not a substitute for . . . the registered nurse."[91]

Plaintiff's expert, a physician, testified that observing changes in a patient's condition is paramount. Short of an emergency, it was improper for a surgeon to request a circulating nurse to leave a patient while in the OR. There was no evidence of any emergency that would have justified the nurse's departure.

The anesthesiologist admitted that the postoperative period was one of the most dangerous in the anesthesia procedure. When he discovered the patient's problem, he needed assistance with CPR but had none. The court held the circulating nurse has a duty to remain with the patient until the patient is transferred to the recovery room. The jury could properly conclude leaving the unconscious patient's side was negligence.

The nurse's absence from the OR, the court continued, was a proximate cause of the patient's injuries. The nurse, in the court's view, was the second most skilled person present. "Her presence and skill should have led to a prompt observation of the preliminary warning signs of vital function failures."[92]

The court rejected the hospital's argument that expert testimony was needed. Due to the obvious "conceded abandonment—neglect in the purest sense—of a patient by nursing personnel at a life endangered time, no expert testimony is required either on the issue of neglect or causation. Want of care is so obvious as to render expert testimony unnecessary."[93] There was evidence of the standard of care, the approved practice, procedure, and duties of OR nurses and technicians. Defendants testified to their actions at the time. The jury, the court concluded, is capable of determining whether the actual actions of the OR staff met the standard of care presented.

In *Sanchez v. Bay General Hospital,*[94] a woman underwent an elective laminectomy. After being transferred to the recovery room, she vomited. For the 2½ hours the patient remained in the recovery room, she appeared to be satisfactorily recovering. Her vital signs, which were taken every 15 minutes, appeared normal. When she was transferred at 3:15 PM, to the postoperative ward, a series of complications arose.

An atrial catheter was left in place and apparently used and regarded by the nursing staff as a peripheral IV. No vital signs were taken at the time the patient was transferred from the recovery room, and none were taken when the patient arrived on the postoperative ward at 3:20 PM. The court also noted that no neurological examinations were conducted and no tests for responsiveness were performed. The medical record from the recovery room was not read, and none of the nurses on the ward was aware that the patient had an atrial catheter implant that had entered her heart.

The court further pointed out the following omissions of the nursing staff: no examination of the patient's pupils was done on her arrival in the ward; no suctioning equipment was ordered, "though her medical chart, had it been reviewed, reflected Sanchez was vomiting while in the recovery room"[95]; no comparison was made of the patient's vital signs in the recovery room and those taken at 3:30 PM, which showed a significant decrease; vital signs were not taken at an increased interval thereafter; no medication checks were undertaken; no neurological examination was done; no reflexes were tested; the nursing staff failed to realize the existence of the atrial catheter; no supervisory nurse or physician was notified of the deteriorating vital signs; requests by friends and family went ignored; and no report was made to the incoming shift about the patient's condition.

Although several family members reported that the patient was vomiting, they were told that everything had been taken care of and that they could give the patient water, in spite an order directing that no water be given. No physician or supervisor was contacted, and the patient's chart was never consulted.

At 3:45 PM the patient's vital signs decreased further, but no comparison was made with her former vital signs. She continued to vomit. The nurse caring for her reported this to her team. At 3:55 PM the patient had a cardiac arrest. Her friend saw her head jerk violently, her pupils dilate, and her skin become cyanotic. Her friend went to get assistance; when the nurse caring for her entered the room, she panicked.

The nurse ran out of the room without clearing the patient's airway, performing CPR, or checking her vital signs. She also did not signal the nursing staff. Another nurse overheard her scream and entered the room. She checked the pupils, pulse, and blood pressure and also panicked and did nothing to assist the patient.

A few moments later the emergency room physician attempted to treat the patient. He was not told that what appeared to be a peripheral IV was an atrial catheter. As a result of these oversights, all medications ordered by him were administered through the catheter directly into the heart. By 5:00 PM, the patient was brain dead, and she died 2 months later.

The patient was in a vegetative state until she died as the result of more nursing negligence. The nursing staff failed to properly inflate and care for the balloon cushion on the cuff of the tracheostomy tube. The nurses simply charted that none of them on the floor would "take responsibility for giving tube feeding due to inability to inflate the trach cuff completely and knowingly."[96]

As the result of this failure, the cuff of the tracheostomy tube gradually worked its way through the posterior of the trachea, eroded part of the left anterior aspect of the thoracic vertebrae, and eroded laterally on the right side of the innominate artery. When this artery eroded, the patient bled to death.

The trial court decided that liability was clear and directed a verdict in favor of the plaintiff on that issue. The appellate court agreed, noting that the failure to communicate, the failure to observe, the failures to take timely action, and the failure to have adequately trained staff caused the patient's brain death. Two months later, under circumstances that "could only be characterized as no less than gross neglect," the court noted, the patient bled to death.[97]

Another case that clearly could qualify for gross negligence on the part of the nursing staff, but was not so characterized by either the lawsuit or the court, is *Baylis v. Wilmington Medical Center, Inc.*[98] The nursing staff left a patient, who suffered from a skin condition that increased the portals of entry of bacteria, laying in her own feces and urine for long periods of time. In addition, they provided her with mouthwash, instead of water, with which to swallow a pill. She also was not given any padding to reduce skin irritation, although she was hospitalized for a number of weeks.

Perhaps the most horrifying fact of the case is that the nursing staff knew that the patient was incontinent of feces and urine and that she had a skin condition. Nevertheless, they failed to provide her with proper sanitary care.

In reversing a pretrial ruling that disposed of the case, the appellate court noted that the patient was bedridden for 3 weeks and suffered from a severe skin rash and exfoliation, yet no padding was utilized to reduce substantial skin breakdown. In addition, the increased porous quality of her skin demonstrated danger of bacterial infection, yet the nursing staff failed to remove feces from her bed. This raised a serious question as to egregious deviations from the standard of care. An expert in internal medicine provided his opinion that the nursing care was below the standard of care, and the appellate court remanded the case for trial.

Inadequate Staffing. The hazards created by shortages in staff, including the practice of "floating" nurses from different specialties, is discussed in detail in Chapter 10. Brief mention is made of the practice here as a potentially dangerous condition from which the patient should be protected. Accepting the responsibility to work with patients renders the nurse accountable for the subsequent care that is provided: "A nurse on an understaffed hospital unit will be held to a professional standard of judgment with respect to accepting responsibility and delegating nursing activities to others."[99]

> A nurse must consider a number of factors in arriving at a professional judgment regarding staffing on a hospital unit. These factors include an assessment of each patient's condition (including emotional factors) and the amount of direct nursing care necessary for that patient. The nurse must then evaluate the nursing care plan and note the longer-range nursing care needs—for example, teaching self-care procedures such as urine tests and insulin injections to a diabetic patient. Finally, the nurse must consider the number of staff members available for a particular shift, the level of experience and education of each . . . and the extent to which other professional staff is available.[100]

A nurse accepting an unreasonable assignment under protest should document in writing the protest and request for additional staff or a smaller assignment.[101] This gives the hospital notice of a dangerous condition and renders it liable under a theory of corporate liability or negligence. The California Nurse's Association (CNA) has a document available known as an "assignment despite objection."[102]

Some argue that from a professional perspective, the nurse should be responsible for accepting an unreasonable assignment.[103] This professional perspective assumes the nurse has some control over the numbers and make up of the unit. A nurse who has no control over the assignment, in that he or she must delegate nursing functions to whatever staff is provided on that unit for that shift, is carrying out tasks in a manner determined solely by the employer. Professional accountability in this instance is not warranted.[104]

RECOVERY ROOM

A 1978 study on malpractice claims conducted by the National Association of Insurance Commissioners rates the recovery room as having the highest percentage of injuries and claims out of all the hospital areas.[105] The Attorneys' Medical Advisory Letter reports that the recovery period following anesthesia is second only to the operating room as the most likely to be associated with anesthetic-related deaths.[106] The report also indicates that risk of postoperative anesthetic-related death diminishes when the patient is not transferred from one unit of a hospital to another until he or she is fully awake. Anesthetic risk is most likely inversely proportional to the ratio of recovery room nurses to occupant, and mortality rates probably rise during the evening and night during shift changes, when fewer nurses are present.[107]

The human factor associated with anesthetic risk is demonstrated in various cases. In *Torbert v. Befeler,*[108] the jury returned a $550,000 verdict against four recovery room nurses and a patient's cardiologist for death resulting from mismanagement of a patient's postoperative recovery room care. The patient, who was undergoing surgical closure of a colostomy, manifested multifocal, coupled premature ventricular contractions (PVCs) after anesthesia was administered. The consulting cardiologist, called by the surgeon, cleared the patient for the 2-hour surgery, after administering lidocaine to suppress her PVCs. Surgery went forward without any diagnosis of the underlying cause of the PVCs.

The patient continued to exhibit unifocal and multifocal PVCs while she was in the recovery room. Approximately 3 hours after the surgery, the patient experienced a cardiac arrest, causing hypoxic brain damage that led to her death 2 weeks later.

The patient's family brought suit against the nurses for failing to perform one-to-one monitoring of the patient. The evidence at trial established that the head nurse had interpreted the written protocols as requiring continual cardiac monitoring only until the patient was stabilized. The team leader administered 50 mg of Demerol about 45 minutes prior to the cardiac arrest. She failed to detect a clinically adverse reaction to the drug that resulted in cardiac arrest. The nurse who was providing one-to-one care of the patient was diverted from her task, and the cardiac arrest went undiagnosed and untreated for 5 to 10 minutes.

The jury divided the nurses' negligence as follows. The head nurse and the team leader were each 45% liable, and the nurse who was responsible for one-to-one monitoring of the patient was found 5% liable. The family also sued the cardiologist for negligently clearing the patient for major surgery and for failing to properly follow the postoperative recovery room course. The jury found him to be 5% negligent.

In *Slatkin v. Capitol Hill Hospital,*[109] a $2.75 million settlement was reached in a case where a 70-year-old woman suffered severe irreversible brain damage following plastic surgery. The patient suffered respiratory arrest in the recovery room and was not given immediate attention because the nurse had failed to turn on the alarm system on a heart monitoring machine when she left to attend to another patient.

Inexperienced Staff. In *Brown v. St. Vincent Infirmary,*[110] a wrongful death action, an inexperienced nurse working in the recovery room was charged with negligence for her inability to detect hypoxia in a patient. The patient had experienced complications from anesthesia, and therefore, the lawsuit charged, she required extra attention in the recovery room. The patient had a cardiac arrest in the recovery room, and CPR was performed. Nevertheless, the patient had severe brain damage and died.

The case settled after a deposition was taken and the plaintiff discovered that the original medical records were destroyed. The amount of the settlement was $310,000.

In *Jackson v. Sisters of St. Mary's Hospital,*[111] a $17.5 million jury verdict was reached in a case alleging negligence in the postsurgical care of a 59-year-old accountant. The plaintiff suffered cardiac arrest and brain damage after post-surgical venous bleeding caused a 30% to 35% blood volume loss. The cardiac arrest resulted in brain damage and a spastic paraplegia requiring 24-hour nursing care of the patient.

After prolonged endotracheal intubation necessitated by an auto accident, the plaintiff underwent elective tracheotomy. After transfer to the recovery room, four dressing changes were required in 2 hours and 20 minutes due to bleeding at the surgical site. He was transferred to the surgical intensive care unit (ICU), where the critical care nurses noted that his dressings were saturated every 10 to 15 minutes with blood. Blood loss was apparent from severe episodes of diarrhea and emesis.

Two hours after his admission to the surgical ICU, the attending physician ordered 2 units of blood, but the quantities of the patient's blood type were not available at the hospital. When the blood was obtained finally, he had sustained a 30% to 35% blood loss. The surgeon returned to the hospital to repair the bleeding. During surgery, the patient suffered a cardiac arrest, which resulted in severe brain damage.

The hospital was sued on three theories, two of which concerned nursing negligence. First, the recovery room nurses failed to record and measure blood loss. Second, the critical care nurses failed to take vital signs over a 2½-hour period. Finally, the blood bank failed to have the type and quantity required.

Recommendations and trends

The case law discussed throughout this chapter demonstrates that sound nursing practice requires nurses to use their nursing process skills to protect the patient from harm. Observation, reporting, and action are the key elements in preventing liability. The nurse is not protected by a physician's order where that order is not within accepted medical practice. The nurse has a duty to ensure that his or her patient is not harmed by the substandard care of others.

As the diagnosis-related group (DRG) system of payment encompasses the private sector, and patients are discharged to home care with complex machines and conditions, the nurse's role in discharge planning will be scrutinized. The duties described throughout this chapter will be argued by plaintiff's counsel to impose liability upon either the nurse individually or upon the hospital on a *respondeat superior* theory of liability for negligent discharge and negligent discharge planning.

To the extent that the patient is discharged without adequate teaching and planning, a dangerous condition exists. The nurse has a duty to protect the patient from dangerous conditions and thus must take action to accomplish this. The law holds nurses accountable as patient advocates. Consequently, nurses should participate in developing discharge planning policies and patient teaching programs.

Endnotes

1. Campazzi, *Nurses, Nursing and Malpractice Litigation: 1967-1977* 5 NURSING ADMINISTRATION QUARTERLY, 1-3 (1980) (hereinafter cited as *Nursing Litigation*). Nurses are being sued in their individual capacities. *See, e.g., Jones v. Harrisburg Polyclinic Hospital* 410 A.2d 303 (Pa. 1979) (nurse sued in individual capacity along with hospital and eventually settled case).
2. *See, e.g.,* Horsley *Legally Speaking Beware: Your Hospital Could Turn On You!* 43 RN, 65 (August 1980) (hypothetical case presented and analyzed). *See, also,* Chapter 27, Professional Liability Insurance.
3. 391 S.W.2d 599 (Mo. App. 1965). (Also discussed in Chapter 27).
4. *See, e.g.* AMERICAN NURSE'S ASSN., STANDARDS OFNEUROLOGICAL AND NEUROSURGICAL NURSING PRACTICE (1977); STANDARDS OF ORTHOPEDIC NURSING PRACTICE (1975); STANDARDS OF CARDIOVASCULAR NURSING (1982); STANDARDS OF REHABILITATION NURSING (1977); OUTCOME STANDARDS FOR CANCER NURSING PRACTICE (1979).
5. AMERICAN NURSE'S ASSN., STANDARDS OF MEDICAL-SURGICAL NURSING PRACTICE (1974) (hereinafter cited as *Medical-Surgical Standards*).

6. *Id.* The ANA has adopted the government's definition of primary, acute, and long-term care. *See, e.g., id.* citing DHEW SECRETARY'S COMMITTEE TO STUDY EXTENDED ROLES FOR NURSES, Extending the Scope of Nursing Practice 8, 10, 11 (1971). Thus, primary care has two dimensions: the first is the person's initial contact with the health care system in any given episode of illness that leads to a decision as to what should be done to resolve the problem; the second is the responsibility for maintenance of health, evaluation, and management of symptoms and for appropriate referrals.

   Acute care is those services that treat the acute phase of illness or disability and is intended to restore normal life processes and functions. Long-term care is those services that provide systematic treatment, maintenance, and rehabilitative services for patients of all age-groups in a variety of health care settings.
7. *Id.*
8. The ANA has promulgated several specialty standards within the field of medical-surgical nursing. *See supra* note 4.
9. *Medical-Surgical Standards, supra* note 5, at 1.
10. *Id.*
11. *Id.*
12. AMERICAN NURSE'S ASSN., A SOCIAL POLICY STATEMENT (1980).
13. Warren, *Accountability and Nursing Diagnosis* XIII, No. p. 10, THE JOURNAL OF NURSING ADMINISTRATION 34 (October 1983).
14. *Id.* (citation omitted).
15. *Id.* citing Shoemaker, *A Research Study on the Definition of Nursing Diagnosis* FIFTH CONFERENCE FOR CLASSIFICATION OF NURSING DIAGNOSIS (1982).
16. 288 P.2d 581 (Cal. App. 1955).
17. *Id.* at 587.
18. *Id.*
19. 333 P.2d 29 (Cal. App. 1958).
20. 211 N.E.2d 253 (Ill. 1965), *cert. denied* 383 U.S. 946 (1966).
21. *Id.* at 258.
22. 283 N.W. 2d 362 (Minn. 1979).
23. 312 N.E.2d 614 (Ill. 1974).
24. 510 P.2d 190 (Kan. 1973).
25. No. 82-L3868, Peoria County Cir. Ct. (Apr. 1, 1985), *reported in,* 28 ATLA L. REP. 466 (December 1985).
26. No. 33751, Or. Dechutes Cty. Cir. Ct. (Aug. 8, 1984), *reported in,* 28 ATLA L. REP. (March 1985).
27. No. 81-61143-NM, Genese Cty. Cir. Ct. (July 6, 1983).
28. No. 55142, Ohio, Cuyahoga Cty. Ct. of Common Pleas (Feb. 13, 1985), *reported in,* 28 ATLA L. REP. 168-169 (Apr. 1985).
29. *Lindsay v. Mueller,* No. 83-2-00271-6, Pierce County Superior Court (June 9, 1985), *reported in,* 28 ATLA L. REP. 276 (Aug. 1985).
30. 288 A.2d 379 (Md. App. 1972).
31. Chapter 9 describes additional cases concerning failure to detect shock.
32. *Stone v. Sisters of Charity of House of Providence,* 469 P.2d 229, 231 (Wash. App. 1970).
33. *Norton v. Argonaut Insurance Co.* 144 So.2d 249, 260 (La. App. 1962).
34. 62 P.2d 1075 (Cal. App. 1936).
35. 628 P.2d 337 (N.M. App. 1981).
36. 181 A.2d 573 (Del. Sup. 1962).
37. *Id.* at 365.
38. *Id.*
39. 144 So.2d 249 (La. App. 1962).
40. 305 S.E.2d 69 (N.C. App. 1983).
41. 322 A.2d 258 (Md. App. 1974).
42. 281 P.2d 872 (Cal. App. 1955).
43. Improper injection technique may be inferred from immediate injury to the patient. In *Bauer v. Otis,* 284 P.2d 133 (Cal. App. 1955), a plaintiff suffered wrist drop immediately after an injection was given by the nurse. The appellate court held that all the elements necessary for a *res ipsa loquitor* instruction were present.
44. 160 Cal. Rptr. 246 (Cal. App. 1979).
45. No. 341, 1983 Philadelphia County Ct. of Common Pleas (dec. April 16, 1985), *reported in,* 28 ATLA L. REP., 467-468 (December 1985).
46. *Death In The Recovery Room,* 1 ATTORNEY'S MEDICAL ADVISORY LETTER, 3 (November 1985) (hereinafter cited as *Recovery Room*).
47. No. 73-142-F (Jan. 19, 1985), 28 ATLA L. REP., 182 (May 1985).
48. Another problem area concerns insufficiently mixing the IV bag once the potassium chloride has been added to it. Some IV administration bags make mixing of the additives a problem because the additive port is situated at the bottom of the bag near the port that connects to the tubing. If the bag is not taken off the stand and thoroughly shaken, the fluid in the bottom of the bag may contain high concentrations of any additive, the most common of which is potassium. *Recovery Room supra* note 44, at 3.
49. 172 Cal. Rptr. 342 (Cal. App. 1981).
50. This is admittedly an assumption; the court refers, as the text here does, to the postoperative ward and its staff. In larger institutions, this will be a surgical unit; in small community hospitals, a postoperative ward would be a general medical-surgical combined unit.
51. 435 N.Y.S.2d 862 (1981).
52. 271 S.E.2d 407 (N.C. App. 1980).
53. 393 N.Y.S.2d 859 (N.Y. App. 1977).
54. 27 ATLA L. REP. 136 (April 1984).
55. *See, e.g., Welsh v. Mercy Hospital* 151 P.2d 17 (Cal. App. 1944).
56. *Id.*
57. *Payne v. Santa Barbara Cottage Hospital,* 37 P.2d 1061 (Cal. App. 1934).
58. *Nursing Litigation, supra* note 1, at 424.
59. *Butler v. Northwestern Hospital,* 278 N.W. 37 (Minn. 1938).
60. *Id.* at 39.
61. 319 So.2d 34 (Fla. App. 1975).
62. 671 F.2d 300 (8th Cir. 1982).
63. *Phillips v. Buffalo General Hospital,* 146 N.E. 199 (N.Y. 1924).
64. *Dillon v. Rockaway Beach Hospital,* 30 N.E.2d 373 (N.Y. 1940).
65. *See, e.g., Ware v. Culp,* 74 P.2d 283 (Cal. App. 1937); *Corey v. Beck* 72 P.2d 856 (Idaho 1937); *Ratcliffe v. Wesley Hospital & Nurses' Training School,* 10 P.2d 859 (Kan. 1932).
66. 279 P.2d 184 (Cal. App. 1955).
67. Top 10 Hospital Malpractice claims: St. Paul Insurance, MEDICAL LIABILITY ADVISORY SERVICE 2 (November 1985).
68. *Id.* For example, in *Hernandez v. Ara Living Centers,* No. C475796, Cal. La. Sup. Ct. (Aug. 12, 1984), *reported in* 28 ATLA L. REP. 137 (April 1985), a $75,000 settlement was

reached in a case where an 80-year-old woman suffered a fractured hip in a fall at the defendant's nursing home while she was assisted to the bathroom.

69. Pa. Phil. Cty Ct. of Common Pleas, No. 1231 (March 29, 1984), *reported in,* 27 ATLA L. REP. 424 (November 1984).
70. 66 P.2d 1265 (Cal. App. 1937).
71. 113 P.2d 270 (Cal. App. 1941).
72. 368 F. Supp. 466 (D. La. 1973).
73. No. 83-22558, Fla. Dade Cty. Cir. Ct. (June 20, 1984), *reported in,* 27 ATLA L. REP. 424 (November 1984).
74. 415 So.2d 586 (La. 1982).
75. *Id.* at 590.
76. 469 P.2d 229 (Wash. App. 1970).
77. *See, e.g., Bamert v. Central General Hospital* 430 N.Y.S.2d 336, *aff'd,* 438 N.Y.S.2d 999 (1981); *see also Chemnitz v. Livreri* 433 N.Y.S.2d 628 (1980) (failure to carry out physician's order to monitor vital signs every 4 hours and to perform a specified medical test was sufficient to present a colorable claim of malpractice).
78. *See, e.g., Lenger v. Physician's General Hospital,* 455 S.W.2d 703 (Tex. 1970) (where nurse fed postoperative patient solid food contrary to physician's orders; nurse nevertheless is not liable unless it is clearly shown that solid food caused the alleged injury).
79. 435 N.E.2d 305 (Ind. App. 1982).
80. *Id.*
81. Katz, *Reporting and Review of Patient Care: The Nurse's Responsibility,* 1 LAW, MEDICINE & HEALTH CARE, 76 (April 1973), citing *Poor Sisters of St. Francis v. Catron* 435 N.E.2d 305 (Ind. App. 1982).
82. 236 S.E.2d 213 (W. Va. 1977).
83. *Id.* at 216.
84. *Sermchief v. Gonzales,* 660 S.W.2d 683 (Mo. en banc 1983).
85. No. 165743, San Joquain Cty. Sup. Ct. (Aug. 24, 1983).
86. Wisc. Patients' Compensation Panel, No. Fl-1674 (Feb. 6, 1985), *reported in,* 28 ATLA L. REP. 227 (July 1985).
87. *Hail v. Hilburn,* 466 S.E.2d 856 (Miss. 1985).
88. 188 Cal. Rptr. 685 (Cal. App. 1983).
89. *Id.* at 686-687.
90. *Id.* at 687.
91. *Id.* at 687.
92. *Id.* at 688.
93. *Id.* at 688.
94. 172 Cal. Rptr. 342 (Cal App. 1981).
95. *Id.* at 345.
96. *Id.* at 346.
97. *Id.* at 352.
98. 477 A.2d 1051 (Del. Sup. 1984).
99. Comment, *Nurses' Legal Dilemma: When Hospital Staffing Compromises Professional Standards,* UNIVERSITY OF SAN FRANCISCO LAW REVIEW, 109, 123 (1983) (hereinafter cited as *Hospital Staffing*).
100. *Id.* at 116-117.
101. *Id.* at 128.
102. Copies of the form are to be given to the nursing supervisor, a second to the CNA office, and one is retained by the nurse. The form allows the nurse to document objections on the following grounds: not oriented to the unit; not trained or experienced in area assigned; not given adequate staff for acuity; unit is staffed excessively with registry personnel; unit is staffed with unqualified registry personnel; unit is staffed with an excessive number of unlicensed personnel; the unit is short staffed; there is no unit clerk; new patients have been admitted or transferred without adequate staff; or the nurse is given an assignment that poses a serious threat to health or safety. The nurse is to record a detailed staffing count, a patient census, and a statement of the problem. CALIFORNIA NURSES' ASSN., ASSIGNMENT DESPITE OBJECTION FORM.
103. *Hospital Staffing, supra* note 99, at 129.
104. *Id.*
105. 2 NATIONAL ASSN. OF INSURANCE COMMISSIONERS (December 1978).
106. *Recovery Room, supra* note 46, at 1.
107. *Id.* at 2. The report indicates blocking agents such as succinylcholine and curare and narcotic anesthetics such as fentanyl account for more anesthetic deaths than should be occurring. In addition, males, the very young, and the very old are more likely victims, and having more than one surgical procedure during the same hospitalization or in a short time span is more lethal. Risk also rises with concurrent disease, especially heart or lung problems. Recent myocardial infarction carries a high risk of fatal reinfarction following anesthesia.
108. No. L-17463-81, Union Cty. Sup. Ct. (April 25, 1985), *reported in,* 28 ATLA L. REP. 469 (December 1985).
109. No. 84-0443 (D.D.C. Oct. 18, 1984), *reported in,* MEDICAL LIABILITY REPORTER (compiled 1985).
110. No. 83-182, Ark., White Cty. Cir. Ct. (Nov. 30, 1984), *reported in,* 28 ATLA L. REP. 136 (May 1985).
111. No. CV8026747 Mo. Jackson Cty. Cir. Ct. (April 13, 1984), *reported in,* 27 ATLA L. REP. 375 (April 1985).

Additional Readings

Butler, *New Initiatives in Financing and Delivering Health Care for the Medically Indigent: Report on a Conference,* 13 LAW, MEDICINE & HEALTH CARE, 225 (Oct. 1985).

Kapp, *Legal and Ethical Implications of Health Care Reimbursement by Diagnosis-Related Groups,* 12 LAW, MEDICINE & HEALTH CARE 245 (Dec. 1984).

Kelly & Garrick, *Nursing Negligence in Collaborative Practice: Legal Liability in California,* 12 LAW, MEDICINE & HEALTH CARE 260 (Dec. 1984).

Northrop, *Status of Recent Nursing Litigation,* 2 NURSING ECONOMICS 423 (Nov.-Dec. 1984).

Note, *The Nurse and Malpractice: Legal Problems in the Nursing Profession,* 9 WESTERN STATE UNIVERSITY LAW REVIEW 227 (1982).

Chapter 8

Psychiatric nursing

Nancy J. Brent

Before the 1960s, the psychiatric patient had few if any legal protections. Today, however, the patient admitted to a psychiatric unit, or who seeks outpatient services, is afforded many legal rights. The nurse who practices psychiatric–mental health nursing needs to be aware of these rights, so that care is delivered to minimize intrusion on these rights.

This chapter presents an overview of admission procedures, client rights, and discharge procedures. Emphasis is placed on key court decisions, state and federal statutes, and constitutional protections that have formed the basis of the psychiatric patient's legal protections.

In addition, the role of the nurse in all of these areas will be highlighted. Many of these principles are applicable to practice in areas other than the hospital. Last, a look at recent trends and issues in the delivery of psychiatric and mental health nursing is presented.

The practitioner must ensure that the delivery of care meets the professional standard of care. The American Nurses' Association (ANA's) standards of psychiatric and mental health nursing are listed on p. 114 (box). These standards apply to any setting in which psychiatric and mental health nursing is practiced and to both generalists and specialists in psychiatric and mental health nursing.[1] This box also contains the standards that apply specifically to the specialist. All of the standards are written within the framework of the nursing process, which includes data collection, diagnosis, planning, treatment, and evaluation.[2]

Psychiatric and mental health nursing is practiced in a variety of settings including in-patient hospitals, outpatient clinics, and private offices. Nursing activities in this area of practice include therapeutic interventions, health teaching, activities of daily living, somatic therapies, provision of a therapeutic environment, and psychotherapy.[3] The nurse, as provider, is accountable "to the client, client rights, and client advocacy."[4]

Admission procedures for adults

How an individual is admitted to a psychiatric unit in a particular state is usually governed by state statute. Most often, this statute is called a mental health code, and it sets forth the responsibilities of the institution and the rights of the individual being admitted and treated in that institution. In California, for example, the applicable statute provides that a person against whom a petition is initiated does not forfeit any legal right or suffer legal disability.[5] California also has codified the rights guaranteed to persons with mental illness in California.[6]

All mental health codes define in some way what mental illness is for the purposes of any admission. The usual standard for voluntary admissions is that the individual is mentally ill and would benefit from treatment.

Although mental health codes vary from state to state, generally there are at least two types of admissions to a psychiatric in-patient setting—voluntary and involuntary. These are discussed below.

VOLUNTARY ADMISSION

Voluntary admission is, of course, the most desirable because it affords the individual the opportunity to make the decision to seek treatment himself or herself. By

STANDARDS OF PSYCHIATRIC AND MENTAL HEALTH NURSING PRACTICE

Professional Practice Standards

Standard I. Theory

The nurse applies appropriate theory that is scientifically sound as a basis for decisions regarding nursing practice.

Standard II. Data Collection

The nurse continuously collects data that are comprehensive, accurate, and systematic.

Standard III. Diagnosis

The nurse utilizes nursing diagnoses and/or standard classification of mental disorders to express conclusions supported by recorded assessment data and current scientific premises.

Standard IV. Planning

The nurse develops a nursing care plan with specific goals and interventions delineating nursing actions unique to each client's needs.

Standard V. Intervention

The nurse intervenes as guided by the nursing care plan to implement nursing actions that promote, maintain, or restore physical and mental health, prevent illness, and effect rehabilitation.

Standard V-A. Intervention: Psychotherapeutic Interventions

The nurse uses psychotherapeutic interventions to assist clients in regaining to improving their previous coping abilities and to prevent further disability.

Standard V-B. Intervention: Health Teaching

The nurse assists clients, families, and groups to achieve satisfying and productive patterns of living through health teaching.

Standard V-C. Intervention: Activities of Daily Living

The nurse uses the activities of daily living in a goal-directed way to foster adequate self-care and physical and mental well-being of clients.

Standard V-D. Intervention: Somatic Therapies

The nurse uses knowledge of somatic therapies and applies related clinical skills in working with clients.

Standard V-E. Intervention: Therapeutic Environment

The nurse provides, structures, and maintains a therapeutic environment in collaboration with the client and other health care providers.

Standard V-F. Intervention: Psychotherapy

The nurse utilizes advanced clinical expertise in individual, group, and family psychotherapy, child psychotherapy, and other treatment modalities to function as a psychotherapist, and recognizes professional accountability for nursing practice.

Standard VI. Evaluation

The nurse evaluates client responses to nursing actions in order to revise the data base, nursing diagnoses, and nursing care plan.

Professional Performance Standards

Standard VII. Peer Review

The nurse participates in peer review and other means of evaluation to assure quality of nursing care provider for clients.

Standard VIII. Continuing Education

The nurse assumes responsibility for continuing education and professional development and contributes to the professional growth of others.

Standard IX. Interdisciplinary Collaboration

The nurse collaborates with other health care providers in assessing, planning, implementing, and evaluating programs and other mental health activities.

Standard X. Utilization of Community Health Systems

The nurse participates with other members of the community in assessing, planning, implementing, and evaluating mental health services and community systems that include the promotion of the road continuum or primary, secondary, and tertiary prevention of mental illness.

Standard XI. Research

The nurse contributes to nursing and the mental health field through innovations in theory and practice and participation in research.

Standards of Specialists in Psychiatric and Mental Health Nursing Practice

Standard X. Utilization of community health systems

The nurse participates with other members of the community in assessing, planning, implementing, and evaluating mental health services and community systems that include the promotion of the road continuum or primary, secondary, and tertiary prevention of mental illness.

Standard V-F. Intervention: Psychotherapy

The nurse utilizes advanced clinical expertise in individual, group, and family psychotherapy, child psychotherapy, and other treatment modalities to function as a psychotherapist, and recognizes professional accountability for nursing practice.

Adapted from American Nurses' Association: Division on Psychiatric and Mental Health Nursing Practice, STANDARDS OF PSYCHIATRIC AND MENTAL HEALTH NURSING PRACTICE (1984).

signing oneself into the hospital, the individual is usually also given the right to make an application to sign out and must be discharged within a certain time period specified in the statute unless the institution initiates formal procedures to have the patient involuntarily committed.

For example, in Illinois, the ILLINOIS DÈPARTMENT OF MENTAL HEALTH AND DEVELOPMENTAL DISABILITIES MENTAL HEALTH CODE states that the voluntary patient shall be discharged at the earliest appropriate time, not to exceed 5 days, excluding Saturdays, Sundays, and holidays, after giving written notice of the desire to be discharged. Exceptions are where a petition and two certificates are filed with the court asserting that the individual is in need of involuntary admission or where the individual withdraws his or her notice.[7] Likewise, Florida provides that discharge must occur within 3 days of the delivery of a written request for discharge.[8]

INVOLUNTARY ADMISSION

In contrast to the voluntary admission, the involuntary admission is one that is usually initiated by someone other than the individual. Because this type of admission results in many restrictions on the individual, there are specific due process and equal protection rights guaranteed by the Fourteenth Amendment of the United States Constitution that must be afforded the individual subject to involuntary admission.[9]

As a result, the standard for involuntary admission to a psychiatric hospital is different than the one for voluntary admission. Illinois, for example, defines a person subject to involuntary admission as someone who is mentally ill and because of the mental illness is reasonably expected to inflict serious self-harm or harm to another in the near future. In addition, it includes someone who is mentally ill and because of the mental illness cannot provide for his or her basic needs in order to guard against serious harm.[10]

The state of Florida's standards include a refusal for voluntary admission, the presence of mental illness, the liability of the individual to determine if admission is necessary, and/or the inability to survive alone or with help and without treatment such that the person may suffer from neglect or harm himself or others.[11]

These definitions reflect the principles of the *O'Connor v. Donaldson* case,[12] which held that the existence of mental illness alone does not justify involuntary commitment. In *O'Connor,* a patient had been involuntarily committed for 15 years without any evidence that he was harmful to himself or others or was in need of treatment. The patient sued for violation of his constitutional right to liberty. In upholding the civil rights claim, the United States Supreme Court held that deprivation of liberty without any justification is actionable.

The procedure for the initiation of an involuntary admission is different than that for a voluntary one. Most state statutes provide several mechanisms for involuntary admission. One such mechanism is the emergency admission. When an individual is in immediate need of hospitalization, an emergency petition can be initiated by a police officer, a family member, or a mental health professional, who must specify, among other things, a detailed statement as to why involuntary admission is needed. Once the petition is initiated, the individual can then be immediately detained.

The state statutes mandate specific procedures that must be followed to ensure that no due process or equal protection violations occur. For example, in Illinois, the MENTAL HEALTH CODE requires that, if possible, the petition be accompanied by a certificate made out by a psychiatrist, psychologist, or other "qualified examiner" stating that the patient was examined by him or her not less than 72 hours before admission and needs immediate hospitalization; that the individual and his or her attorney be given a copy of the petition if the individual is hospitalized; that the individual be informed of any and all rights afforded him or her under the code; and specific time frames for the hearing that must take place to determine the continued need for hospitalization.[13]

If there is no emergent need for hospitalization, most state statutes provide a mechanism for a court-ordered admission where the individual who is alleged to be in need of hospitalization can remain at home before the court's determination. As with the emergency admission, however, a petition must be initiated and filed with the court[14]; a certificate of a physician, qualified examiner, or psychologist must accompany the petition. This certificate must substantiate the need for the involuntary hospitalization, and a hearing must be held within a specified time frame to determine if the involuntary admission is necessary.

The court hearings referred to in relation to involuntary admissions must meet the requirements delineated in *Lessard v. Schmidt.*[15] The rights afforded include the privilege against self-incrimination, the right to counsel, proof of mental illness beyond a reasonable doubt, and the right to the least restrictive alternative if confinement is needed. Since the decision, many states have provided rights in addition to those required in the decision.

For example, Illinois provides for the right of the individual to be present at the hearing concerning involuntary admission and the right to a jury trial on the question of whether or not he or she is subject to involuntary hospitalization.[16] Florida likewise provides for a right to counsel, the right to notice of any and all hearings concerning involuntary admission, and the ability to obtain a continuance on the hearing for involuntary admission should the individual request one.[17]

Some state statutes, such as the MENTAL HEALTH CODE of Illinois, allow for a third type of admission, namely, the informal admission. This type of admission allows the individual to be admitted by request without filling out admission papers. The individual also can be discharged at any time during the first day shift following admission when he or she requests discharge.[18] The nurse who works in psychiatric and mental health nursing must be familiar with the mental health code's provisions concerning admissions for adults in the state in which he or she practices.

Under some state statutes, such as that of Illinois, qualified examiners (those who can certify persons in need of involuntary admissions) include registered nurses meeting certain qualifications. For example, in Illinois, a qualified examiner may be a registered nurse with a master's degree or someone who has 3 years of postdegree clinical training and experience in treating and evaluating mental illness. In order to fulfill his or her duties, the nurse who is a qualified examiner must be certain that documentation is accurate and clear and conforms precisely to the code's requirements.

If the nurse is working on a psychiatric–mental health unit, he or she must be able to answer any questions the patient has concerning the admission, including what procedures are available for discharge. Discussion of these admission and discharge rights should be done as soon as possible after the patient is admitted to the unit. Once done, the fact that this information has been given to the patient must be documented in the nursing notes. In addition, clear, objective, and factual documentation concerning the patient's behavior while on the unit is vital, as the patient's record can be utilized at any hearings concerning the need for continued hospitalization or discharge.

Admission procedures for minors

In addition to knowledge concerning admission procedures and requirements for adults, the nurse practicing in psychiatric and mental health nursing must also be cognizant of the state's statutory provisions concerning the admission of minors to mental health facilities. The nurse must protect the minor's rights once he or she is admitted to the unit. For the most part, a minor may be admitted to an inpatient facility by his parent or guardian or a person *in loco parentis*. However, as with the adult, the minor must come within the definition of the need for hospitalization spelled out in the statute.[19] The determination is usually made by a psychiatrist before admission.

Although minors may be admitted to the unit by others, many states provide for minors of a certain age to admit themselves for inpatient treatment. In Illinois, if the minor is 16 years or older, he or she may self-admit.[20] Florida provides that a minor 14 years or older may apply for diagnosis or treatment.[21]

In addition to the above, most state statutes also contain provisions for emergency admissions of minors if there is an objection by the minor or the parent or if the minor is too young to consent to admission.

Like the adult admitted to a psychiatric unit, the minor has many legal protections afforded during the admission process and in relation to discharge from the facility. These due process protections include, but are not limited to, the right to notice of any hearings and the right to a hearing to determine the need for hospitalization. These rights were mandated by the U.S. Supreme Court in *Parham v. J.R.*,[22] decided in 1979.

Least restrictive alternative mandate

The important right of treating the adult or minor in a setting that results in the least restrictions on that individual's liberty and freedom has been underscored in several important court decisions. In *Wyatt v. Stickney*,[23] a federal district court and a federal appeals court decided and affirmed, respectively, that the least restrictive setting for treatment for the mentally ill is necessary. Likewise, in *Lake v. Cameron*,[24] a federal district court of appeals held that the state must prove that an alternative to involuntary commitment would not be suitable for a particular individual committed by the state. And, in *Lessard v. Schmidt*,[25] referred to earlier, a Wisconsin district court required that the least restrictive alternative treatment center be utilized if confinement was deemed necessary.

Although the least restrictive alternative treatment facility will vary from state to state and will also be based on the unique situation of each individual patient, many states now provide psychiatric help in settings other than inpatient facilities. Community mental health centers, outpatient programs, and home health programs are just a few of the many alternative treatment settings for the mentally ill patient. Most state statutes specifically contain provisions requiring the least restrictive alternative and provide for minors to consent to outpatient treatment, if feasible, if above a certain age.[26]

Because the psychiatric-mental health nurse may be involved in the decision to recommend hospitalization for a particular patient, it is vital that he or she be familiar with the state statute under which he or she practices. The nurse must also be aware of what community facilities are available in the community in order to be certain that the least restrictive alternative for treatment is being utilized.

Rights of patients while hospitalized

The rights of all patients admitted to mental health facilities of any kind have been enumerated in judicial opinions, Joint Commission on Accreditation of Hospitals (JCAH) standards, state and federal statutes, state constitutions, and the United States Constitution. The right to treatment, informed consent, right to refuse treatment, and confidentiality are all important.

RIGHT TO TREATMENT

The right to treatment was initially given its foundation in cases dealing for mentally ill individuals who committed a crime and were committed involuntarily to a mental institution. Cases such as *Rouse v. Cameron,*[27] *Robinson v. California,*[28] *Nason v. Bridgewater,*[29] *Wyatt v. Stickney,*[30] *O'Connor v. Donaldson,*[31] and *Youngberg v. Romeo*[32] all set forth the basic principle that involuntary commitment without treatment of the mentally ill individual is a deprivation of that individual's Eighth Amendment protection against cruel and unusual punishment and the Fourteenth Amendment's mandates of due process and equal protection.

Clearly, these constitutional underpinnings of the right to treatment have been helpful to the psychiatric patient. In addition, many state statutes provide for protection of these rights. For example, both Illinois[33] and Florida[34] mandate that the patient has a right to humane and adequate care and services.

Because it is the nurse who is with the patient most consistently, it is incumbent on him or her to document clearly and accurately any and all treatment given the patient in his or her medical record. Documentation of staffing or team meetings held concerning the patient and the decision for a plan of care must be carefully recorded. Nursing care plans must be kept current. Last, although not least, careful recording of the patient's response to treatment, including medications and psychotherapy, is vital in order to ensure that the right to treatment is being provided by the facility and the nurse.

Pisel v. Stanford Hospital[35] illustrates an egregious case of negligence where medical records were altered by the Director of Nursing to cover an incident where a psychiatric patient was locked in a seclusion room, was unattended for hours, and was left brain damaged from an injury. The hospital was found liable for a $3.6 million damage award; the treating physician who was sued was absolved from liability.

Before June of 1975, the patient was a normal, healthy 23-year-old woman. She contracted chorio-meningitis and a urinary infection that evolved into psychotic symptomatology. After a 6-week hospitalization, she returned to work and continued seeing her treating psychiatrist for about 2 months.

On January 14, 1976, her psychiatric problems recurred, and she was again admitted to the hospital. She was diagnosed as having schizophrenia. Because of her agitated state, her physician ordered her to be placed in the quiet room. All furniture, including a steel bed frame, was removed from the room. This was done for safety reasons.

On the fourth day, the steel bed was returned to the room. The hospital records contained no entry authorizing return of the steel frame bed, and the physician denied that he ordered it placed in the room. For a week, she continued to suffer from psychotic hallucinations. She was restrained and given electroconvulsive shock treatments. She had a grand mal seizure and after that became more agitated, hostile, and confused.

The physician ordered antipsychotic medication, but the nursing staff failed to record the order until the following day. At that time, it was discovered that the medicine was out of stock. Nevertheless, the staff failed to notify the physician or to seek a substitute drug. For the next 3 days, the patient received no medication and became increasingly agitated. On the evening of January 23, her condition became acute. The patient was agitated, disoriented, confused, and hallucinating.

Because of her condition, the staff maintained constant close observations. The patient told a staff member that she was hearing voices telling her to hurt herself. In response, the staff gave her a sedative and locked her alone in the seclusion room with the steel frame bed. One side rail was up and the other was down, even though the patient had a history of climbing over rails. No antipsychotic medication was given to alleviate her agitation or hallucinations, and the physician was not notified of her acute condition. From 6:15 AM to 10:00 AM no one entered her room to assess her condition. At 10:00 AM she was found with her head between the bed rails, with no pulse or respiration. The patient was left brain damaged.

A few days after the incident, the director of nursing ordered the entire staff who charted the patient's case to rewrite and change records pertaining to her care. The original record was removed, and a new revised one was substituted without knowlege of the hospital administration and in violation of explicit hospital policy.

The substituted record was demonstrably false and conflicted with other records and the statements of staff members as to actions observed. The court instructed the jury that they could consider the substitution of records as a circumstance indicating consciousness of negligence.

The evidence demonstrated that the staff failed to remove the steel frame bed from the seclusion room, failed to closely monitor the patient, failed to assess personally the patient's condition, and failed to break seclusion. They also failed to notify the hospital physician or the treating physician of significant changes in the patient.

In addition, the design and location of the seclusion room supported the verdict. The inside of the room was not clearly visible from the nurses' station. The hospital also failed to have written policies and procedures concerning seclusion and the need to break seclusion. These were all clear violations of the standard of care as testified to by the nursing and physician experts.

INFORMED CONSENT

A second right of the mentally ill patient is the right of informed consent for treatment. This is not specific to the mentally ill alone, for all patients, before receiving treatment, have the right to give their consent for that treatment. For minors, the consent usually comes from the parent, guardian, or person *in loco parentis* unless the mental health code or other state statutes provide for the minor to consent himself or herself.

In order to give consent, however, the individual must be aware of that to which he or she is consenting. In other words, the consent must be informed; that is, be based on a full disclosure of, for example, the type of treatment to be done, the risks, the hope for benefits, the alternatives to treatment, and what results will occur if the treatment is not undertaken.[36]

There are exceptions to the requirement of informed consent for treatment. Some of those exceptions include when an emergency exists and when a full disclosure, in the judgment of the physician, might adversely alarm the patient (the "therapeutic privilege" exception).

Generally, only the individual himself or herself, if an adult, can give consent for his or her treatment unless someone else designated by law is able to provide substituted consent for that person who is unable to do so. In many states, the probate act provides the legal mechanism for a guardian to be appointed who makes decisions for the disabled person (the ward) concerning his or her estate, his or her person, or both. In addition, some states have enacted statutes that allow others listed in the statute to consent for an individual without resort to the Probate Court when the individual is unable to consent. For example, some statutes allow for the next of kin or the spouse to consent for treatment if the patient is unconscious.

The mentally ill individual is presumed competent and therefore able to consent for treatment while hospitalized. Illinois' code contains specific provisions of a presumption of competence and mandates that when electroconvulsive therapy (ECT) or any unusual hazardous experimental services or psychosurgery is planned, the patient's written and informed consent must be obtained.[37] In addition, Illinois provides that care be provided in an emergency situation, for medical or dental services, where seeking the informed consent of the patient would endanger the life or health of the recipient of services. If treatment is done based on a "good faith determination" that such an emergency exists, immunity is provided the physician or dentist who treats the patient without his consent.[38] Florida assumes competency to consent for treatment unless the individual is declared incompetent by a hearing and also provides for care to be given a patient when consent cannot be obtained and an emergency exists.[39]

It is important for the psychiatric–mental health nurse to remember that it is the physician's responsibility to obtain the informed consent of his or her patient for the treatment or treatments to be done by him or her. However, the nurse may be asked to witness the patient's signature on the consent form.

In addition, the nurse should also record that the patient did or did not give consent for treatment in the nurse's notes. Complete recording of the patient's responses to treatment and daily progress on the unit is vital. If there is a question as to the ability of the patient to give consent, either in the past or in the future, the nurse's notes may be used to aid the court in determining if that consent was valid or if a guardian is necessary to consent for the patient if he or she is unable to do so. It is the responsibility of the nurse to notify the physician and supervisor, if the physician does not respond, of concerns about the patient's lack of understanding of the proposed care or treatment. Chapter 6 describes in detail the nurse's duty to obtain informed consent to nursing treatments.

If a patient does have a guardian appointed whose responsibilities include making decisions concerning treatment, the nurse should ask the guardian to see the order or the letters of administration appointing him or her guardian and should make a copy of it for the patient's chart. In addition, physicians and other health professionals involved in providing care to the patient should be notified of the guardianship. The notification should be included in the patient's chart to ensure that consent or refusal for treatment is obtained from the guardian.

The psychiatric–mental health nurse must keep in mind that for minors, the right to consent to treatment rests with the parents. It is possible, however, that in some instances the parents no longer have this right, and a guardian is appointed for the minor who has this responsibility. The nurse must be certain to determine that the guardian of the minor, if other than the natural parent, does have this right. In addition, if the minor's parents are divorced, it is important for the nurse to determine that the parent accompanying the child to the hospital does indeed have the right to consent for treatment. As with this determination with an adult, simply asking the parent or guardian if this is their responsibility, and recording this in the nurse's notes, can protect the nurse and his or her employer from possible allegations that consent was not properly obtained.

Some mental health codes provide minors of certain ages with the ability to consent for their own treatment, either alone or in conjunction with their parents' consent. The nurse must be aware of these provisions to ensure that the minor's right of consent is being protected.

RIGHT TO REFUSE TREATMENT

Concomitant with the right to give informed consent for treatment is the right to refuse treatment. At one time, this right was not afforded the mentally ill, because it was common practice that on admission to a mental health facility, the individual was presumed to be incompetent. As has been discussed, that is no longer the case, and the right to refuse treatment, including medications, has been codified in many states. Illinois' code contains provisions for the patient or guardian to refuse generally accepted mental health or developmental disabilities services, including medications,[40] as does Florida's statute.[41] This right is not absolute, however, and most statutes provide that medications and treatments can be given if they are needed to prevent serious harm from occurring to the individual or others.[42]

If a patient or guardian or, in the case of a minor, a parent refuses treatment, the refusal must be documented in the patient's record and the physician notified. No further treatment should be undertaken, so as not to expose the nurse and the employer to liability for battery. Any statutory requirements of the refusal, such as informing the parents or guardian of alternative services available, the consequences of such a refusal, and the risks of any alternative services should be undertaken and recorded by the appropriate person named in the statute.

If the nurse is working with a patient who refuses treatment but is someone who, in his or her judgment, needs the treatment to alleviate serious harm to self or others, then the nurse must document carefully, factually, and objectively the clinical signs and symptoms she has observed in order to support his or her judgment to give the treatment despite the patient's refusal. In addition, the patient's response to the treatment instituted should be recorded, and notification of other members of the health care team, such as the physician and nursing supervisor, should occur.

It may be that a patient, or guardian, or the parents of a minor may refuse services that are in conflict with his or her religious beliefs. Some state statutes, such as Illinois, provide that if the individual requests treatment in accordance with any well-recognized religious denomination that relies on spiritual means through prayer alone for healing, these services can be provided by a duly licensed practitioner thereof.[43]

PRIVACY AND CONFIDENTIALITY

Two other important rights that the psychiatric–mental health nurse must be aware of in relation to his or her patients are the rights of privacy and confidentiality. The right to be free from unreasonable interferences in one's personal affairs, or the right of privacy, has been a right afforded all individuals under the amendments to the United States Constitution, state constitutions, and case law. In addition, this right has been further extended to the mentally ill in the *Wyatt* decision discussed earlier in this chapter, and in standards set forth by the JCAH.[44] As a result, each mentally ill patient should be provided with storage space on the unit, a bed that is for the patient's use alone, and his or her own clothing while on the unit if not contraindicated. He or she should be allowed to send and receive mail and to use the telephone and to receive visitors (again unless contraindicated) without restriction, censorship, or monitoring, to use whatever personal property is feasible while on the unit, and to have the physical surroundings of the unit clean. In addition, no intrusion into the mentally ill individual's privacy while in the hospital, such as the taking of pictures or the use of video or audio tapes of the individual, can occur without his or her prior consent.[45]

The nurse can do much to afford privacy protections for patients. Orienting patients to the unit on admission and informing them of the privacy rights they have, along with the ways the rights may be restricted, are vital. Likewise, treating the patient with dignity and respect and interacting with him or her in a humane manner can help to make the recipient of mental health services realize that his or her privacy will be respected and maintained. Patients who share information with health professionals have an expectation that the information will not be shared with anyone who is not involved in their care. This expectation is even more important for individuals seeking mental health services because of the stigma that is still often associated with mental illness and the fact that the information shared is often highly personal. As a result, many states have confidentiality statutes that provide additional protections to mental health records and communications that protect them from disclosure unless the patient's written consent is given.

One such state, Illinois, mandates that the patient's consent must be obtained before disclosure of any information is released, including the fact that an individual is a patient.[46] Specific provisions are also included for minors of specific ages to give their written, informed consent before the release of any information in their records.[47] Florida provides protections for the confidentiality of mental health records as well.[48]

Duty To Report and To Warn. Like many other rights discussed in this chapter, the right of confidentiality is not an absolute one, and there are statutory exceptions to this basic principle. Although they vary from state to state, some of the more common exceptions include situations in which child abuse or neglect is suspected, when civil commitment procedures must be initiated by the mental health professional, when the disclosure is necessary to protect the individual or another from imminent, serious harm or death, or in investigations of homicide.[49] Obviously, in these situations, the consent of the patient is not needed to disclose the information, but often the statute requires a notation be made in the patient's record of disclosure made without his or her consent.

Despite these and other exceptions to the general principle that no disclosure can occur without the patient's consent, many of these exceptions also have additional restrictions. For example, Illinois's statute limits any disclosure to an administrative tribunal or court to those matters that are "relevant, probative, not unduly prejudicial or inflammatory."[50] In addition, any person to a proceeding can request an *in camera*[51] review of the record before disclosure in open court so that only information that is truly necessary to the issues at hand is released.[52]

Another important exception to the expectation of confidentiality that the psychiatric–mental health nurse must be aware of is what has been termed the duty to protect third parties from foreseeable harm by a patient. The landmark case in establishing this duty was *Tarasoff v. Regents of University of California*.[53] In that case, the court held that when a mental health professional determines that his or her patient may pose a serious danger to an identifiable victim, this mental health professional must exercise reasonable care to protect that potential victim. What the mental health professional must do to fulfill his or her responsibility will depend on the specific situation, and will be based on what another member of that profession would have done in the same or similar circumstance.[54]

In *Tarasoff*, a patient of a psychologist told the psychologist of his intent to kill a particular woman. The psychologist told the police this information, and the police briefly detained the patient but eventually let him go because they could not keep him without a reason and he did not appear irrational. No attempt was made to warn the young woman or her parents, nor was the patient involuntarily committed despite the psychologist's and two psychiatrists' recommendation that he be involuntarily committed. The patient then murdered his intended victim, and the parents sued based on the psychiatrists' failure to warn their daughter. The California Supreme Court reversed the lower court's dismissal of the case, holding that if proven, the facts alleged in the complaint could result in liability for failure to take steps to protect a person threatened by a patient.

Other exceptions to the expectation of confidentiality include nonmental health statutory mandates where the nurse is required to report information to state agencies. Some of those exceptions include child abuse and the presence of venereal disease.

The nurse working in psychiatry must be certain to protect the client's confidentiality rights, and to do so, he or she must know the statute concerning mental health records in the state in which he or she practices. When information is released, it must be done with the patient's consent, and any statutory requirements concerning the consent must be adhered to strictly.

If the nurse is given information by the patient concerning serious harm to another, he or she must assess the seriousness of the communication, and, at the very least, contact the physician and others on the unit. Warnings to the person who is the subject of the threats must be given in certain jurisdictions. Documenting the communication and any follow-up is also vital. The patient should also be told that the nurse has a legal responsibility to tell others of this information and to take whatever steps are necessary to ensure that no harm does occur to the potential victim.[55]

In addition to releasing information that might otherwise be protected by confidentiality provisions of the state's mental health code, the psychiatric nurse may be asked to testify in court concerning information about a particular patient. Although many states have "testimonial privileges" that allow certain professionals to assert a client-professional privilege (for example, attorney-client, physician-patient) not to testify, most states do not have this privilege for nurses. However, as has been stated earlier, this interest in confidentiality is one that has been in existence for some time, and for nurses, it is supported by the ANA's CODE FOR NURSES.[56] Item number 2 of the code states the following: "The nurse safeguards the client's right to privacy by judiciously protecting information of a confidential nature."[57] Under the interpretation of the item, the code states that the nurse must not disclose information in a court of law about a patient unless she or he has the patient's permission or is under legal compulsion to do so.[58]

In addition to the ANA's CODE, some mental health statutes do provide protections for the nurse who decides to assert a privilege not to testify in court. In Illinois, for example, any mental health professional, including nurses, can refuse to disclose and prevent disclosure of a patient's records or communications in a civil, criminal, administrative, or legislative proceeding, even when the patient consents to the disclosure.[59]

If asked or subpoenaed to testify in court concerning matters dealing with a patient, the psychiatric–mental health nurse should check the state statute for any specific guidelines. If no statutory guidelines exist, she or he may want to consult an attorney in order to be given specific advice about her or his responsibilities in the situation. At the very least, the nurse should let the patient know that he or she has been asked or subpoenaed to testify, and, if possible, obtain the patient's written permission to do so. If this is not possible, or the patient refuses to give permission, then it would be best for the nurse to respectfully refuse to testify in court and only do so if ordered by the judge or hearing officer.

RIGHT TO SAFE ENVIRONMENT

The mentally ill patient's protection against harm to himself or herself or to harm inflicted on others can be termed the right of safety. An individual's safety interest is an important one, particularly when admitted to a psychiatric facility, because often one's illness can affect this right in a marked way. The psychiatric–mental health nurse most often protects this right of patients by maintaining a safe environment and by utilizing restraints or seclusion when clinically necessary. To do so, he or she must be clear about the law's mandates when utilizing these modes of treatment.

When a patient is depressed or actively psychotic, the potential for suicide must be evaluated by the psychiatric–mental health nurse. Case law has clearly delineated the responsibility of the mental health professional, including nurses, to exercise reasonable care to prevent suicide by the patient. As a result, the nurse's actions in any particular situation in preventing suicide will be those of the ordinary, reasonable, and prudent professional in the same or similar circumstances in the same or similar community.

Likewise, many of the cases have discussed the institution's responsibility to prevent suicide in patients, and this duty exists as one of the institution's direct duties in addition to a vicarious responsibility through its employees. Therefore the nurse must carefully document and take action to ensure that suicide does not occur when a patient expresses suicidal thoughts, when a change in behavior occurs, or when the patient acts out against himself or herself in some way. Specific policies concerning suicidal patients and the care that is necessary for the potentially suicidal patient must be developed and followed closely. Care must also be taken to remove any objects that may be utilized to commit suicide from the patient's environment. If necessary, the patient may need to be placed in restraints or seclusion or both.

Restraints or seclusion or both are not used for the suicidal patient only. They may be clinically justified for other patients, especially those individuals whose illness results in potentially directing harm to others. However, it is important for the nurse in psychiatry to keep in mind the legal restrictions on their use. One such restriction has already been discussed, that of utilizing the least restrictive alternative treatment possible. In addition, restraints or seclusion cannot be used as a form of punishment or for staff convenience.[60]

Many cases have underscored this JCAH standard, and have held that the Fourteenth Amendment's mandate of liberty requires that a mentally ill individual be free from bodily restraints unless restraint is clinically necessary.[61] These case law decisions have been incorporated into many state mental health codes.

Illinois' statute, for example, contains specific guidelines concerning who can initiate seclusion or restraints, how long the initial order is valid, how often the individual in restraints or seclusion must be monitored, and documentation requirements.[62] Florida also has specific guidelines for the use of these treatment methods.[63]

One of the most important responsibilities of the psychiatric–mental health nurse is to inform the patient on admission of the possible utilization of restraints and seclusion when necessary in addition to the restrictions placed on their use. When restraints or seclusion is in use, the nurse must be careful to follow the specific statutory requirements, if any, concerning documentation and to do so on the institution's forms, if available. The existence of good, clear unit policies and procedures covering restraints and seclusion is also essential to ensure that the nurse is fulfilling his or her legal duties and, at the same time, is providing the patient with the external control he or she may need at the time to prevent harm to self or others.

Discharge procedures

As referred to earlier in this chapter, the patient who no longer needs to be hospitalized must be discharged pursuant to the statute in the state where he or she is hospitalized. If the patient is voluntarily admitted to a facility, ideally the physician and the patient can agree on when discharge is possible. If not, the patient can give written notice and request discharge. He or she must be discharged within a certain time period designated in the statute unless commitment procedures are instituted by the facility.

If the individual is involuntarily committed, discharge is somewhat more complicated. Although provisions usually exist for the patient to seek discharge himself or herself, court proceedings are usually necessary before discharge so that an objective evaluation of the need for continued hospitalization or the necessity of discharge can occur.

Whether the patient has been admitted to the facility voluntarily of involuntarily, if not discharged when he or she no longer needs hospitalization, there are several legal remedies the patient may pursue. One such remedy is to sue the hospital, psychiatrist, and any other mental health professionals for false imprisonment; that is, illegally restricting someone's freedom of movement.

Likewise, the individual could sue the hospital, if a governmental facility, for a violation of his or her right to freedom in violation of the Federal Civil Rights Act, Section 1983.[64] Last, but not least, the writ of *habeas corpus* (''let the body go'') provides a remedy for release of involuntarily committed patients by requiring the hospital to bring the patient to a court immediately for a determination as to the need for continued hospitalization. If the hospital cannot meet its burden of proving that continued hospitalization is needed, the patient must be immediately released.

The nurse's role in assisting with the appropriate release of a patient, or alternatively, with his or her continued hospitalization is an important one. An important measure is to keep accurate nursing notes as to the patient's response to treatment, his or her behavior while on the unit, and other matters that may impinge on the decision concerning discharge or continued hospitalization. Also, the nurse working in psychiatry must provide the patient with any information that he or she may need concerning the procedures for discharge including, but not limited to, any forms needed by the patient, the privacy to talk with his or her attorney, and supplying any information he or she may request or need clarified concerning discharge.

Recommendations and trends

In addition to protecting the patient's rights, the psychiatric–mental health nurse must also be aware of trends and issues that affect his or her practice. One such trend is, of course, the focus on the development of the psychiatric nurse as a consultant or liaison to other areas of the inpatient facility. The utilization of psychiatric nurses to help identify and offer solutions to psychological or psychiatric aspects of physical diseases experienced by patients has done much to foster the rapid growth of this specialty. In addition to providing input to improve the quality of care to patients, the psychiatric–mental health consultant or liaison has been utilized by his or her nurse colleagues to aid in the identification and the resolution of staff difficulties and to provide continuing education programs.

Perhaps the greatest growth for the nurse in psychiatry lies in the delivery of outpatient services. Specifically, more and more psychiatric–mental health nurses are developing their own private practices and providing crisis intervention and short- and long-term therapy to individuals, couples, families, and groups. The development of private practice for psychiatric–mental health nurses has been aided by the decision of some states to allow for third-party reimbursement for psychiatric services provided by the psychiatric–mental health nurse with the qualifications specified in the statute.

The development of the psychiatric–mental health nurse's role in the delivery of outpatient therapy and the ability of the client to receive reimbursement for those services has done much to help make high-quality, less expensive psychotherapy available to patients of all ages in an environment that is truly the least restrictive.

This chapter has presented an overview of the important legal concerns with which the nurse working in the area of psychiatric–mental health nursing should be familiar. Nurses who provide care with an understanding of these rights will further their patient's interests and minimize their liability.

Endnotes

1. AMERICAN NURSES' ASSOCIATION STANDARDS OF PSYCHIATRIC AND MENTAL HEALTH NURSING PRACTICE 1 (1984).
2. *Id.*
3. *Id.*
4. *Id.*
5. CAL. WELF. & INSTIT. CODE §5005 (West 1984).
6. CAL. WELF. & INSTIT. CODE §5325.1 (West 1984).
7. ILL. REV. STAT., Ch. 91 1/2, §3-4-3 (1979).
8. FLA. STAT. ANN., Ch. 394, §394.465 (1971).
9. The Fourteenth Amendment says, in pertinent part, ". . . No state may deprive any person of life, liberty, or property, without due process of law, nor deny to any person within its jurisdiction the equal protection of the laws." U.S. Const. Amend. XIV.
10. ILL. REV. STAT., Ch. 91 1/2, §1-119 (1979).
11. FLA. STAT. ANN., Ch. 394, §394,467 (1971).
12. *O'Connor v. Donaldson,* 422 U.S. 563 (1975).
13. ILL. REV. STAT., Ch. 91 1/2 §3-600-3-611 (1979).
14. *See, e.g.,* FLA. STAT. ANN., Ch. 394.467 (1971).
15. *Lessard v. Schmidt,* 349 F. Supp. 1078 (E.D. Wisc. 1972), *vacated* on procedural grounds, 414 U.S. 473 (1974), *vacated* on procedural grounds, 421 U.S. 957 (1975), *reinstated* 413 F. Supp. 1318 (E.D. Wisc. 1976).
16. ILL. REV. STAT., Ch. 91 1/2 §3-802, 3-806 (1979).
17. FLA. STAT. ANN., Ch. 394, §394.467 (4) (1971).
18. ILL. REV. STAT. Ch. 91 1/2 §3-300 (1979).
19. Illinois' standard is ". . . that the minor has a mental illness or emotional disturbance of such severity that hospitalization is necessary and that the minor is likely to benefit from in-patient treatment." ILL. REV. STAT. Ch. 91 1/2 §3-503 (1979).
20. ILL. REV. STAT., Ch. 91 1/2 §3-502 (1979).
21. FLA. STAT. ANN., Ch. 394, Section 394.465 (1) (b) (1971).
22. *Parham v. J.R.,* 442 U.S. 584 (1979).
23. *Wyatt v. Stickney,* 344 F. Supp. 373 (M.D. Ala. 1977). 344 F. Supp. 387 (M.D. Ala. 1971) *aff'd in part, Wyatt v. Aderholt,* 503 F. 2d 1305 (5th Circ. 1974).
24. *Lake v. Cameron,* 364 F. 2d 657 (D.C. Cir. 1966).
25. 349 F. Supp. 1078 (E.D. Wisc. 1972).
26. *See, e.g.,* ILL. REV. STAT., Ch. 91 1/2, §2-102 (a), 3-501 (1979); FLA. STAT. ANN., Ch. 394, §394.459 (1), (3) (a) (1971).
27. *Rouse v. Cameron,* 373 F. 2d 451 (D.C. Cir. 1966).
28. *Robinson v. California,* 370 U.S. 660 (1962).
29. *Nason v. Bridgewater,* 233 N.E. 2d 908 (1968).
30. 344 F. Supp. 373 (M.D. Ala. 1977).
31. 422 U.S. 563.
32. *Youngberg v. Romero,* 102 S. Ct. 2452 (1982).
33. ILL. REV. STAT, Ch. 91 1/2, §2-102 (a) (1979).
34. FLA. STAT. ANN., Ch. 394, §394.459 (1), (3). (a) (1971).
35. 430 A.2d 1 (Conn. 1980).
36. LIDZ, et al. INFORMED CONSENT: A STUDY OF DECISIONMAKING IN PSYCHIATRY 1984, 12; *Centerbury v. Spence,* 464 F. 2d (D.C. Cir.), *cert. denied* 409 U.S. 1064 (1972).
37. ILL. REV. STAT., Ch. 91 1/2 §2-101.2-102,2-110 (1979).
38. *Id.,* §2-111 (1979).
39. *See, e.g.,* Ch. 394, §394.467 (3) (1971); Ch. 743, Sec. 743.064 (1979).
40. ILL. REV. STAT., Ch. 91 1/2 §2-108 (1979).
41. FLA. STAT. ANN., Ch. 394, §394.459 (1), (3) (a) (1971).
42. See *Rennie v. Klien,* 720 F.2d 266 (3rd Circuit 1983); *Rogers v. Commissioner,* 458 N.E.2d 308 (1983); *In re Rose III,* 421 N.E.2d 40 (1981).
43. ILL. REV. STAT., Ch. 91 1/2, §2-102 (b) (1979). It should also be noted that the mentally ill individual's right to refuse treatment has also been supported by court decisions. In *Kamowirs v. Michigan Department of Mental Health,* No. 73-19434-AW (Cir. Ct. Wayne County Michigan) July 10, 1973, *Knecht v. Gillman,* 488 F.2d 1136 (8th Cir. 1973), and *Price v. Sheppard,* 239 N.W.2d 905 (1976), the courts upheld the mentally ill patient's refusal to consent for psychosurgery, aversive therapy with apomorphine, and electroconvulsive therapy, respectively.
44. JOINT COMMISSION ON ACCREDITATION OF HOSPITALS, *Consolidated Standards Manual for Child, Adolescent and Adult Psychiatric, Alcoholism and Drug Abuse Facilities,* Paragraph 14 -2-4. (1981) (hereinafter cited as *JCAH*).
45. *See, e.g., Anderson v. WROC-TV,* 441 N.Y.S. 2d 220 (1981); *Delan v. C.B.S., Inc.,* 445 N.Y.S.2d 898 (1981).
46. ILL. REV. STAT., Ch. 91 1/2, Sec. 802, 803 (a) (1979).
47. *Id.,* §805 (a), (1), (2) (1979).
48. FLA. STAT. ANN., Ch. 394, §394.459 (8) (a) (d) (1979).
49. ILL. REV. STAT., Ch. 91 1/2 §810 (a) (8),811 (1979).
50. ILL. REV. STAT., Ch. 91 1/2 §810 (a) (1) (1979).
51. This type of review generally takes place in the judge's chambers and the record is sealed.
52. ILL. REV. STAT., Ch. 91 1/2 §810 (b) (1979).
53. 131 Cal. Rptr. 14 (Cal. 1976).
54. E. BEIS, MENTAL HEALTH AND THE LAW 72 (1984). The *Tarasoff* decision has been controversial, to say the least. Sub-

sequent cases have refused to apply the *Tarasoff* decision because the victim(s) were not identifiable, *see, e.g., Cailr v. Minnesota,* 323 N.W.2d 30 (1982); or because the patient committed suicide rather than injuring or killing another, *see, e.g., Bellah v. Greenson,* 141 Cal. Rptr. 724 (Cal. App. 1980). Even so, the decision is being applied more and more in most states. Therefore, nurses working in psychiatry must seek out specific legal advice as to the appropriate course of action to take when confronted with a patient who is threatening harm to another.

55. For an excellent review of this issue, *see* Kjervik, *The Psychiatric Nurse's Duty to Warn Potential Victims of Homicidal Psychotherapy Outpatients,* 9 LAW, MEDICINE, & HEALTH CARE 11 (December 1981).
56. AMERICAN NURSE'S ASSOCIATION, CODE FOR NURSES WITH INTERPRETIVE STATEMENTS (1985).
57. *Id.,* 4-5.
58. *Id.*
59. ILL. REV. STAT., Ch. 91 1/2 §810 (a) (1979).
60. *JCAH, supra* note 44, at 19-21.
61. *Youngberg v. Romeo,* 102 S. Ct. 2452 (1982).
62. ILL. REV. STAT., Ch. 91 1/2, §2-108, 2-109 (1979).
63. FLA. STAT. ANN., Ch. 394, §394.459 (1), (3) (1971).
64. This section states in pertinent part ''. . . Every person who under color of any statue, ordinance, regulation, custom or usage, of any state or territory subjects or causes to be subjected, any citizen of the United States or other person within the jurisdiction thereof to the deprivation of any rights, privileges or immunities secured by the Constitution and laws, shall be liable to the party injured in an action at law, suit in equity, or other proper proceeding for redress.'' 42 U.S.C. §1983 (1982). See Chapter 5 for further information or civil rights claims.

Additional Readings

Books and Articles

Joint Commission on Accreditation of Hospitals. CONSOLIDATED STANDARDS MANUAL FOR CHILD, ADOLESCENT AND ADULT PSYCHIATRIC, ALCOHOLISM AND DRUG ABUSE FACILITIES. Chicago: Joint Commission on Accreditation of Hospitals, 1981.

Kjervik, *The Psychotherapist's Duty to Act Reasonably to Prevent Suicide: A Proposal to Allow Rational Suicide* 2 SPECIAL PERSPECTIVE 207 (No. 2 1984).

Lidz, et al. INFORMED CONSENT: A STUDY OF DECISION-MAKING IN PSYCHIATRY. New York: The Guilford Press, 1984.

Chapter 9

Critical care nursing

Mary E. Kelly

Approximately 4,900 hospitals have distinct critical care units.[1] Sixty-one percent of these hospitals have one critical care unit providing combined medical, surgical, and coronary care.[2] Larger hospitals often have more than one critical care unit, each of which has evolved along specialty or subspecialty lines. Examples include medical/surgical (most common), coronary, medical, surgical, neurological and neurosurgical, pediatric, neonatal, obstetrical, burn, cardiac surgery, respiratory, cardiovascular surgery, trauma, and combined burn/trauma.[3] Intensive care units (ICU) are characterized by a high concentration of nursing personnel. Today, both providers and consumers of health care expect intensive care units in all but the smallest community hospitals; the unit is evidence of technologically advanced, competent care.[4]

A patient admitted to a general or special critical care unit may have had severe trauma, major surgery, or life-threatening condition in any organ, such as myocardial infarction, stroke, or gastrointestinal hemorrhage.[5] Critical care admissions may also follow general surgery if there are other factors, such as age or coexisting disease, that increase the surgical risk. Special procedures, such as peritoneal dialysis, may also require admission to the critical unit.[6]

The length of stay varies according to the condition of the patient and the illness, but generally averages between 3 and 5 days.[7] Usually, patients with longterm illnesses, for example malignancies, are not admitted unless some benefit is expected.[8]

While the availability of physicians in ICUs varies with the size and type of hospital, all ICUs combine intensive nursing and constant patient monitoring. ICUs are characterized by a high concentration of nursing personnel. In general, ICUs employ specially trained registered nurses on a basis of one nurse to one to three patients.[9] "By definition, critical care nurses are those who provide high-level care for patients who require continuous and intensive care related to acute, life-threatening impairment."[10]

"Although intensive treatment of life-threatening ailments is acknowledged by society as a medical obligation, in critical care settings . . . the nurses . . . carry the primary responsibility for implementing and supporting the . . . lifesaving goal. . . ."[11] The philosophy of critical care nursing has been described as follows:

> Care of critically ill patients is based on the fact that, although there are thousands of pathologic conditions the mechanism of death is rather uniformly limited to a small number of physiologic events. Basically all health care practice is designed to observe and preserve the vital functions of respiration, circulation, assimilation, elimination, and integration of these functions. In some instances these vital processes may be amendable to control, at least on a temporary basis. Death can be prevented in many situations if time is gained to perform specific therapeutic measures and to allow the recuperative powers of the body to come into operation, so that the body can adjust its homeodynamic . . . state. Recovery, which would have been impossible otherwise, may then sometimes be achieved.[12]

Irrespective of specialty, the critical care nurse has

the responsibility to closely monitor patients in potentially life-threatening circumstances, and to render life-supporting treatment. Life-supporting treatment in a specialized open-heart surgery ICU, for example, may require the nurse to operate an intra-aortic balloon counterpulsation device which assists a failing heart to pump blood. In a general combined ICU, the nurse may be responsible for operating a ventilator/respirator, a defibrillator, as well as taking electrocardiograms (EKGs) and interpreting the results.[13]

Critical care nursing practice thus requires a thorough knowledge of physician-prescribed medical and surgical interventions, drug action and interaction, normal and abnormal biochemical laboratory values, and physical examination and assessment. In addition, proficiency in the use of a variety of technical skills is essential because critical care nursing requires the ability to make quick decisions in the face of a sudden emergency.

Given the nature of critical care nursing, the possibility of liability for negligence is a reality. In addition, critical care has perhaps a greater potential than other practice areas for battery actions and civil rights claims. These claims are generally premised upon a lack of consent to life-support systems or other "heroic" or "extraordinary" measures. Critical care nurses may be deemed responsible for informed consent in the critical care setting because they frequently implement treatment measures on an independent basis.

Scope of practice issues also cause many critical care nurses concern, even though to date there are no reported cases of challenges by medical associations. Similarly, while the potential exists for a critical care nurse's scope of practice to be an issue in a negligence action, there are no reported cases to date addressing this issue.

This chapter will first address the critical care nurse's standard of care and scope of practice. Next, a review of reported negligence actions against critical care nurses will be presented. A discussion of battery and civil rights claims will then follow.

Scope of practice

Until recent years, uncertainty existed as to the legal authority for the kind of practice which critical care nursing demands. Critical care nurses often undertook responsibilities for which there was no specific regulatory authority. Specifically, these nurses were, and still are, engaged in diagnostic assessment—a function traditionally thought to be medical in nature. In recent years, however, the nursing profession has given explicit and public recognition to the fact that nurses in every area of practice engage in diagnostic assessment necessary to implement nursing interventions.

Leaders in critical care nursing advocate the use of routine procedures, formulated by "a representative group of physicians, nurses and hospital administrators with final approval by the executive board of hospital," which authorize the nurse with special training to act in emergency situations.[14] Many critical care units require the admitting physician's authorization of use of emergency standing orders as a condition for patient admission.[15] In California, nurses implement treatment measures according to standardized procedures.[16]

Some authors suggest that to be valid, standing orders must be signed and accepted by all physicians in the specialty area.[17] There is no case authority for this view; the courts that have considered the validity of standing orders rely on the language of the particular state's nurse practice act (NPA) which does not contain such limitations.[18]

In any event, standing orders cannot substitute for consultation with the patient's attending physician; they merely permit the practitioner to respond to a particular situation when time is of utmost importance.[19] The better practice is to ensure that these orders are dated, reviewed, and updated.[20]

Contingency orders, which are instituted by the patient's physician, permit the critical care practitioner to act without notifying the physician.[21] Typically, these are used for diagnosis or therapeutic intervention. These orders provide that the practitioner may institute certain laboratory tests if the patient's condition changes. Based on the results of these tests, the practitioner decides whether to begin therapeutic intervention.

Standing orders that permit the treatment of cardiac dysrhythmias require a diagnosis before treatment can begin. Some suggest that the validity of such orders could be questioned because the nurse is making the diagnosis. Thus, to the extent that implementation of the order requires diagnosis and treatment, some question whether the critical care practitioner's actions violate the state's licensing provisions set forth in the practice act. The concern exists in jurisdictions where the practice of medicine is defined statutorily as diagnosis and treatment and the nurse practice act excludes authority to practice medicine.

There are no reported decisions specifically addressing the issue in the critical care context. Generally speaking, there would be no reason for the state to become involved in the issue unless some untoward result occurred to the patient. Even then, unless there was some culpable conduct, such as gross negligence, the state would be unlikely to prosecute for the illegal practice of medicine.

The scope of practice issue also arises in the context of civil lawsuits. Typically, these actions are brought by the state's medical society, and they challenge the nurses' authority to function in an expanded role.[22] To date, no medical society has sued to contest the validity of the practice of critical care nursing.

As the nurse's expanded role gains more legal acceptance, concern about being prosecuted for the illegal practice of medicine should diminish. Historically, nursing increasingly has assumed more tasks customarily thought to be medical in nature. For example, taking a person's blood pressure once was considered a medical, not a nursing, procedure. Today, the taking of vital signs is customarily viewed as a nursing function.

A scope of practice challenge could be successfully thwarted. At least two traditional legal theories could be successfully argued in support of the critical care nurse's expanded role. The first squarely confronts the activity and justifies it as nursing; the second is not concerned with the medical/nursing distinction but treats the action as a discretionary one delegated by the physician.

Under the former legal theory, the action which may be characterized as diagnosis and treatment is justified as nursing action. This may or may not be problematic under the state's nurse practice act. For example in *Sermchief v. Gonzales,*[23] the court upheld the use of standing orders and protocol because these practices were in effect when the legislature amended the state's NPA. Thus, although the statute did not address these practices, the fact that they existed when the legislature broadly amended the statute implied to the court that the practices were authorized. The *Sermchief* decision is reprinted in the appendix.

Missouri is not alone in amending its NPA to reflect the changing practice of nursing. Other states, such as Idaho, have amended their NPAs to recognize the diagnostic and treatment functions of nurses if authorized by joint resolution of state medical and nursing associations.[24] Some states have amended their NPAs without such limitations. California, for example, amended its NPA, expanding the authorized practice to include treatment under standardized procedures.[25] Still other jurisdictions, such as Delaware, continue to prohibit such practice by nurses.[26]

The second legal argument against a scope of practice challenge is less in keeping with the view of the nurse as an independent health care practitioner. This theory provides that a physician may properly delegate to a nurse the authority to implement a particular treatment if, in the nurse's discretion, the treatment is needed.[27] The classic example of this type of order is the P.R.N. order for medication. The rationale underlying the validity of the action is that a physician is entitled to delegate "medical functions" to competent registered nurses.[28]

The disparity in various NPAs suggests that the political arena is where nurses, through the efforts of nurse lobbyists, may have the most successful impact. Nurses, individually and through their representative associations, need to educate the legislatures and the public about the reality of critical care nursing practice: nurses diagnose and implement treatment.

Both the medical and nursing professions recognize this reality. The United States Department of Health, Education, and Welfare conducted a study based on specific tasks considered appropriate for nurses.[29] A majority of nurses and physicians agreed that it is appropriate for general duty nurses to elicit and record health histories; interpret selected laboratory findings; make diagnoses in certain situations; choose, initiate and, modify selected therapies in certain situations; provide emergency treatment; provide information to families about diagnoses or treatments; and make prospective decisions regarding treatment in collaboration with physicians.[30] Critical care nurses clearly perform all of these functions.

Standard of care

Given the state of malpractice litigation, nurses' increased responsibilities will likely result in more lawsuits brought against them. Specialty practice, such as critical care nursing, is now well established. The specialty nurse must ensure that he or she is competent to perform duties which require specialized care. Standing orders allow critical care nurses to initiate therapy, and this in turn requires them to assess competently many sophisticated parameters and to manage proficiently the devices that measure them.[31]

For example, critical care nurses are "depended upon to titrate a number of different drugs, with many cardiovascular effects and overall systemic interactions, in the management of a single patient. Those functions are subjects about which a reasonably prudent nurse outside the specialty area could not competently testify."[32]

The nationally based American Association of Critical Care Nurses (AACN) has defined the practice of critical care nursing as the "utilization of the nursing process in the prevention of and intervention in life-threatening situations."[33] The AACN's commitment to the standards of practice is demonstrated by its publishing of a journal of critical care, entitled *Heart & Lung,* co-edited by a nurse and a physician, with an emphasis on the collaborative practice of nursing and medicine and the skills and the knowledge required by both in the specialty practice of critical care.[34]

The existence of a specialty definition, in addition to the American Nurses Association definition of nursing practice,[35] may lead the courts to impose a higher standard of care upon the critical care nurse.[36] The AACN also encourages nurses to seek national certification as critical care registered nurses (CCRN) by completion of training and examination leading to such a credential.[37] This certification also lends support to the view that nurses holding such a credential should be held to a higher standard of care.

Although no cases exist with respect to the specific standard of care of a critical care nurse, the certified nurse anesthetist cases provide analogous precedent. In *Whitney v. Day*,[38] the court of appeals upheld the following jury instruction on the nurse anesthetist's standard of care: "[a] nurse administering an anesthetic is held to the standard of care based on the skill and care normally expected of those with the same education and training." The instruction correctly stated the law because the nurse involved was a specialist and possessed "responsibilities greater than those possessed by an ordinary nurse . . . in an area of expertise in which some physicians receive full residency training."[39]

This is not a suggestion that the nurse be held to a physician standard of care. That the nurse specialist has an expertise simply means that his or her conduct should be measured against the standard of care of other nurse specialists practicing under the same or similar circumstances. A 1985 California Supreme Court case, *Fein v. Permanente Medical Group*,[40] which is discussed in detail in Chapter 23, supports this view. There, the court held in part that the issue of the nurse practitioner's negligence was to be determined by whether he or she met the standard of care of a reasonably prudent nurse practitioner in conducting the examination and prescribing treatment in conjunction with her supervising physician. The trial court erroneously held that the nurse practitioner's conduct had to be measured by the standard of care of a physician.

The *Fein* case is an important decision for the autonomy of the standard of care for nursing. Nevertheless, a physician expert testified to the nurse practitioner's standard of care. Apparently, this was not an issue at the trial or the appellate level, but the physician expert's qualifications as to the practice of nurse practitioners

AACN STANDARDS FOR CRITICAL CARE NURSING

The practice of critical care nursing shall be based on:

A thorough knowledge of the interrelatedness of body systems and the dynamic nature of the life process

A recognition and appreciation of the individual's wholeness, uniqueness, and significant social and environmental relationships

An appreciation of the importance of the collaborative role of all members of the health team

Integral components of this practice are:

Individual professional accountability

The pursuit of knowledge and clinical expertise through continuing education

Adapted from AACN Standard Committee, STANDARDS FOR NURSING CARE OF THE CRITICALLY ILL (1981).

could have been challenged prior to trial. To maintain an autonomous professional standard of care, specialty nurses, nurse practitioners, and professional nurses must insist that the expert witnesses judging their conduct are their professional counterparts who act under the same or similar circumstances. An attorney who is not a nurse may not be sensitive to this issue.

Under the principles of *Fein*, the critical care nurse's conduct in a negligence action will be measured against the professional standards of critical care nursing. This can be established by reference to the standards of the critical care nurses' professional association. The professional standards adopted by the AACN are summarized above (see box). Standards of care may also be proved by reference to textbooks and learned treatises.

Textbooks in critical care nursing establish that the critical care nurse must be proficient in the use of a variety of technical skills and equipment. The critical care nurse is trained to be able to interpret EKG and other monitor readings and to assess quickly the appropriate nursing intervention in light of the patient's history and physical examination.[41]

In addition to requiring keenly focused time and attention on the more mechanical aspects of treatment, the practice of critical care nursing necessitates concurrent, continuous attention to the most subtle physical changes in a patient's condition. Detailed, simultaneous attention to multiple functions is required.[42] Organ system functions are highly interdependent, and any factor influencing one function will likely affect another function or several other functions.[43]

Sound critical care nursing practice includes frequent repetitions of the thorough and detailed history and physical examination of the patient conducted upon admission.[44] Follow-up questions to elicit information concerning the patient's history and repeated inspection, palpation, auscultation, and percussion[45] often lead to the detection of critical developments in the patient's condition.

The sophisticated care provided in the ICU requires highly skilled registered nurses. A critical care unit staffed by an adequate number of nurses who know the unit's setup, its protocols and procedures, and how to respond to the needs of the unit's patients provides a safe environment and enables the critical care nurse to fulfill his or her legal duty to protect the patient.

The nurse-patient ratio in critical care units is generally one nurse to two patients, and often a patient's condition will necessitate a one to one ratio or a two to one ratio.[46] Because changes in a critically ill patient's condition cannot always be anticipated, staffing shortages may occur. Adverse effects in the ICU have been particularly noted during periods of nursing shortages.[47]

The practice of "floating" nurses from other units to cover the shortage on a critical care unit may only increase both the nurse's and the hospital's exposure to liability. The inexperienced nurse who is unable to interpret an EKG reading and operate emergency and other equipment places the critically ill patient in grave jeopardy.

Professional nurses have the legal obligation to know the limits of their knowledge and capabilities and to act within those limitations.[48] When an inexperienced nurse is faced with a request to staff a specialty unit, such as a critical care unit, the better practice is to decline the assignment. To do otherwise exposes the nurse to independent malpractice liability. Every person is legally responsible for his or her own actions. The standard of care in the community of critical care practitioners recognizes that the "practitioner who accepts the responsibility for performing an act is responsible for the consequences of that act."[49] Some authors suggest that the two chief areas of liability for critical care practitioners are: (1) adequate training to make the crucial decisions inherent in any acute care unit; and (2) authority to perform the acts.[50] Authority to perform critical care nursing has been discussed in the scope of practice section; a discussion of adequate training follows.

ADEQUATE TRAINING

The nature and extent of training recommended by the experts in the critical care field include comprehensive orientation and continuing education programs by the employing institution.[51] Critical care practitioners must be prepared and competent. In most instances, critical care practitioners are performing tasks previously customary only if a physician was personally involved.[52]

The employing institution must provide adequate training to its practitioners. Joint Commission of Accreditation of Hospitals (JCAH) standards for nursing in a special care unit provide that all personnel "shall be prepared for their responsibilities in the special care unit through appropriate orientation, in-service training, and continuing education."[53]

The individual who knows the extent of his or her training and competence must be free from retaliation for refusing an assignment to a specialty unit like critical care. The issue here is not insubordination but rather patient safety. Given the critical nature of the patient's condition, a nursing error which in the medical-surgical setting may be harmless has the possibility for disaster in the critical care setting.

For example, the potential for medication errors is more likely in specialty areas such as critical care where multiple drugs are likely to be simultaneously administered. Intervention with complex technical instruments and machinery, often required on a routine, nonemergency basis, is dangerous in the hands of the inexperienced floating nurse. Misuse of the technology could lead to a life-threatening situation for the patient.

When the nursing administration is left with no other alternative but to staff the critical care unit with a nurse from another specialty unit, the critical care team should be made aware of the floating nurse's lack of experience in and knowledge of critical care nursing practice. This will allow patient care assignments to be made in light of the nurse's limitations in the critical care field.

Experienced members could assume responsibility for the technical tasks and treatments unfamiliar to the floating nurse. The team also is better able to develop a plan to cover emergencies that may arise in the care of patients assigned to the floating nurse. Clearly defined policies and procedures will assist new and temporary critical care team members.

The best plan, of course, is to respond to staffing needs by ensuring that adequate numbers of trained and properly oriented personnel are on duty in a specialty unit.[54] Professionally trained critical care nurses should staff the critical care unit at all times. A synchronized team approach to implementing the emergency plan is more easily accomplished when team members' roles are cohesive and clarified. Exposure to liability is also minimized. As one legal commentator notes:

> While there are few reported cases to date involv-

ing . . . specialty units, the potential for injury is great due to the utilization of sophisticated forms of technology. Adequate staffing, effective communication and efficient treatment procedures are acutely important to rendering safe care in such units. A basic factor underlying the existence and maintenance of such a safe environment, however, is the recognition that specialty nurses function in their area of expertise.[55]

A strong argument can be made by plaintiff's counsel that the hospital's duty to the patient and the nurse's independent duty to the patient encompass recognition of this principle. To prove the parameters of the duty to recognize one's professional limitations, plaintiff's counsel could rely on the standards set by the JCAH. As noted earlier, JCAH Standard Three directs that all personnel be prepared for their responsibilities in the special care unit through appropriate orientation, in-service training, and continuing education programs.[56]

Indiscriminate floating exposes both the nurse and the hospital to liability. A professional nurse is independently liable for negligently causing injury to a patient whose illness requires care unfamiliar to the practitioner. Thus, the nurse may be sued in an individual capacity, rather than or in addition to being sued as an employee of the hospital. As a protection against such liability, the inexperienced nurse who is ordered to staff the critical care unit should document in an incident report his or her objection and the reason.

In addition to the nurse's individual liability, the hospital may also be found liable for the nurse's negligence or for its own negligence. As the floating nurse's employer, the hospital remains vicariously liable for its employee's negligence. The hospital may also be found independently liable under the theory of corporate negligence. Administrative awareness of inadequate staffing could provide the basis for relief under this theory.

Leaders in the critical care field maintain that critical care units must be staffed by nurses who are selected cautiously for their superior skills and knowledge of the physiological and psychological aspects of critical care treatment, "because the quality of patient care and the outcome depend greatly on the persons providing that care."[57] Once selected, critical care nurses should participate in an indepth orientation and continuing education program.

The employing institution should develop comprehensive orientation and continuing education programs; nevertheless, the critical care nurse is responsible for maintaining current skills and knowledge of advances in critical care practice.[58] The critical care nurse is legally accountable for responsibilities that she or he assumes, and may be held liable if those services are performed in a negligent fashion. Consequently, "comprehensive training programs are essential."[59]

EQUIPMENT MANAGEMENT

The National Institutes of Health (NIH) Consensus Panel has identified the minimal technological capabilities an ICU should provide, regardless of the type of facility in which it is located. These include:

1. Cardiopulmonary resuscitation
2. Airway management, including endotracheal intubation and assisted ventilation
3. Oxygen delivery systems and qualified respiratory therapists or registered nurses to deliver oxygen therapy
4. Continual electrocardiographic monitoring
5. Emergency temporary cardiac pacing
6. Access to rapid and comprehensive, specified laboratory services
7. Nutritional support services
8. Titrated therapeutic interventions with fusion pumps
9. Additional specialized technological capability based on the particular ICU patient composition
10. Portable life-support equipment for use in patient transport[60]

The critical care nurse has taken over the responsibility for carrying out several procedures that have been performed in the past solely by physicians.[61] For example, critical care practitioners now initiate and carry out cardiopulmonary resuscitation, defibrillation, and endotracheal intubation.[62]

Respirators, pacemakers, pharmacological agents, transfusions, a multitude of monitors, and dialysis are a few of the interventions that may need to be implemented—often on an emergency basis. Critical care nurses use a variety of different types of machines to diagnose, monitor, and treat patients. In most settings, the critical care nurse has discretion to institute EKG monitoring or oxygen administration without order by the physician.[63] Not infrequently, the critical care nurse is called upon to use simultaneously several pieces of highly technological equipment on one patient.

The ICU environment produces "technology-oriented" treatment protocols which registered nurses utilize in implementing treatment.[64] These protocols presume a certain level of competency from the practitioner and a certain nurse to patient ratio during any given shift. While certain ICU monitoring and therapy protocols may work well under ideal circumstances, they may be particularly subject to human and mechanical error under less favorable circumstances.

In a study conducted at one teaching hospital, 145 reports of significant adverse occurrences in 4,720 ICU admissions during a 4-year period revealed that 92 of these were the result of human error, and 53 were due to equipment malfunctions.[65] Forty-three of the 92 incidents linked to human error involved equipment, mostly mechanical ventilators. Thus, about two thirds of the adverse events involved the technically complex equipment used in ICUs.[66]

Technology in the ICU has its attendant hazards of liability for the critical care nurse. The capability of monitoring the technology as well as the patient is clearly expected of the critical care nurse.

Thus, a reasonable expectation of the critical care nurse is mechanical aptitude. For example, the critical care nurse must know how to respond if a particular machine, such as a ventilator or IV infusion pump, malfunctions. This requires mechanical aptitude as well as ability to provide manual support. The critical care nurse has the duty to know the capabilities, limitations, and hazard and safety features of many instruments.[67]

The defense of machine malfunction will not protect the critical care nurse where the patient could have survived with adequate manual support. For example, in *Rose v. Hakim*,[68] the court addressed the defense in light of substandard nursing care of an infant in the intensive care unit.

The infant in *Rose* had suffered cardiac arrest during surgery and postoperatively was treated with a hypothermia machine. The continuous readout telethermometer was not functioning properly. Although known to be a common malfunction, the nurse did not check the machine's accuracy with a glass thermometer. The nurse also failed to exercise independent judgment and use any other body-cooling interventions, such as administration of aspirin, increased IV fluids, ice packs, or alcohol sponge baths.

The infant suffered a grand mal seizure and stopped breathing, requiring mechanical ventilation. The nurse noted poor air exchange but could not correct an obvious kink in the ventilator tubing. The nurse also failed to chart any neurological response of the infant and to notify the physician of the evening's events. The infant's permanent injury, the court held, was proximately caused by the negligent acts and omissions of the hospital's employees and the defective equipment used in the ICU.[69]

In addition to managing and maintaining equipment, the critical care nurse must manage other personnel's care. For example, other departments utilize technology on the critically ill patient. The nurse in these instances is the managing coordinator of care rather than the care giver and has a duty to properly coordinate the care. If coordination is not accomplished, continuity and quality of care may be compromised.[70]

The failure to do a simple act in the critical care context, such as turning on an alarm system on a heart monitoring machine, can be life threatening. In *Slatkin v. Capitol Hill Hospital*,[71] a 2.75 million dollar settlement was reached in a case where a 70-year-old woman suffered severe irreversible brain damage following plastic surgery. The patient suffered a respiratory arrest in the recovery room and was not given immediate attention because the nurse had failed to turn on an alarm system on a heart monitoring machine when she left to attend another patient.

EARLY DISCHARGE

With the advent of prospective payment systems such as diagnostic related groups (DRGs), administrators are encouraging physicians and nurses to be more fiscally minded in providing treatment to hospitalized patients. The DRG classification system appears to make it more difficult for hospitals to recover the cost per day, which is three times greater than the cost for a general hospital day, of caring for an ICU patient.[72] While currently DRGs are applicable to Medicare patients, insurance companies are considering adopting the DRG-based prospective payment system. The attendant fiscal impact may encourage early discharge from ICU or failure to admit to the ICU.

Patients discharged prematurely from the ICU may suffer adverse effects. One study found that 15% of patients electively discharged from the ICU and 23% of patients transferred out of the ICU because of lack of space suffered significant adverse effects including death; return to the ICU; or residence in a hospital a month after completion of the study.[73] Approximately one third of patients undergoing abdominal vascular surgery developed serious respiratory or circulatory complications, or both, after discharge from the ICU.[74]

To the extent that the decision to admit or discharge a patient from the ICU depends on a nursing assessment, the nurse may be implicated in liability for early discharge (abandonment) or failure to admit. Moderately sick ICU patients are discharged too soon or not admitted to the ICU at all usually because of a lack of bed space or recognition that the patients are at risk for serious complications. As a result, they suffer avoidable adverse health effects.[75]

The nurse, as part of nursing action, should consider proposing to the administration of the facility a transfer of the patient to another facility which has the actual capacity and the capability of treating the patient. This suggested proposal is based on the present facility's inability to provide ICU care because of a lack of capacity, capability, or both, *not* whether it is fiscally advantageous to "dump" the patient in a transfer to a tertiary facility, public and teaching hospital.

Tertiary care hospitals[76] and public and teaching hospitals receiving severely ill transferred patients will be likely to lose financially. Tertiary hospitals face the dilemma of either not accepting these patients in transfer or accepting them into a high-quality ICU at a financial loss. "At the extreme, tertiary care hospitals could, in effect, become large ICUs."[77] Public hospitals and teaching hospitals also may be unable to sustain the costs of ICU care and be forced to ration care even more strictly than they do now.[78]

Once care has been initiated, the primary responsibility of the provider is to meet the standard of care. The DRG system of payment encourages hospitals to avoid this responsibility by diverting and transferring patients in the first place, yet it provides no immunity from civil liability for abandonment.

ABANDONMENT

As in other practice areas, critical care nurses may be charged with providing inadequate care or abandoning their patients. *Wilson v. O'Connor Hospital*[79] illustrates this principle of negligence law. There, a 1.5 million dollar pretrial settlement was reached in a lawsuit involving a 19-year-old female who was brain damaged during recovery from gastroplasty.

The plaintiff received the surgery for treatment of obesity. The surgeon utilized surgical staples to reduce the capacity of the stomach. After surgery, the plaintiff experienced lower abdominal pain and increased pulse, respiration, temperature, and white cell count. A pulmonary specialist was consulted.

Thereafter, x-ray indicated that large amounts of air were present in the abdomen, and there were signs of infection. The patient was transferred to the ICU by the pulmonary specialist who then left the hospital. The patient was left unattended for a period of time in spite of the ICU charge nurse's order to closely observe the patient. During this time, the patient experienced respiratory arrest.

An exploratory laparoscopy revealed that the staples could not be found, and the abdominal cavity contained a large amount of purulent material, resulting in severe peritonitis. The patient suffered brain damage from the arrest and required 24-hour care. The negligence action against the hospital was based on inadequate ICU nursing care.

MEDICATION ERRORS

The potential for medication errors exists in any practice area. In the context of critical care, however, these errors may be devastating. The critical care nurse will not be able to defend successfully against a negligence action based on inappropriate medication by relying on a physician's order. The critical care nurse administering a medication—in fact, every nurse—is expected to know the indications for the drug, its dose, route of administration, any contraindications, its intended action, side effects, and potential interaction with other drugs.[80]

In *Brosseau v. Children's Mercy Hospital*,[81] a 375,000 dollar settlement was reached in a lawsuit charging the wrongful death of a 1-year-old who died as the result of digitalis overdose. The child was admitted for surgical repair of a congenital defect. After surgery, the child developed tachycardia. After consultation with a cardiologist, the surgeon ordered digitalis in amounts that caused profound bradycardia, and the child died.

The ICU nurse who administered the medication was charged with negligence in failing to prevent the overdose. The lawsuit charge that the ICU nurse should have correlated the child's body weight with the dose ordered prior to administering the medication. Had this been done, the ICU nurse would have realized that the dose ordered would be an overdose. Armed with this knowledge, the ICU nurse could have informed the physician of the improper dose, thereby preventing the child's death.[82]

FAILURE TO FOLLOW ESTABLISHED ICU POLICY OR PROTOCOL

The breach of a critical care nurse's standard of care may be established by proof that he or she failed to follow established protocol or policy. In *Kuchak v. Lancaster General Hospital*,[83] a 425,000 dollar jury verdict was reached in a wrongful death lawsuit involving such an allegation.

The plaintiff, a 15-year-old adolescent, developed a fat embolism which went undiagnosed after a surgical closed reduction to correct a comminuted fracture was accomplished. After the surgery, the plaintiff was admitted to the ICU with mildly abnormal vital signs. Throughout the first day of admission, the vital signs deteriorated, and the patient progressively became nonresponsive to stimuli. The critical care nurses failed to contact the patient's attending physician, and they failed to perform arterial blood gas studies. The patient was maintained on a respirator, but was restless and thrashing in bed.

A pulmonary specialist ordered valium, but the critical care nurse failed to administer it. Three hours later, the patient extubated himself, causing 60 seconds of hypoxia and bradycardia. Five days later, the patient died of a fat embolism.

The lawsuit charged the critical care nursing staff with failure to follow established policy for monitoring a patient's vital signs and failure to implement protocol for abnormal vital signs. The nurses were also alleged to be negligent for failure to notify the attending physician of increase in the patient's pulse rate and the patient's failure to respond to stimuli and for failure to give valium as ordered.

Informed consent

Critical care nurses are responsible for much of the patient and family education regarding procedures and treatment as well as health status.[84] In general, nurses spend a greater amount of time with patients and their families than do physicians.[85]

As in most hospital settings, the critical care nurse obtains the signature on the consent form. "In the atmosphere of urgency to treat, obtaining informed consent may often consist mostly of recommending a procedure and explaining its nature."[86] Consequently, the nurse must often answer questions that arise after the physician provides the patient with a risk of procedure explanation, and it is the nurse who must cope with a refusal to accept treatment or withdrawal of consent. Nurses are advised to document refusals of consent to treatment, including nursing procedures and patient teaching.

Little time exists in the critical care setting to have the physician return to deal with the situation. As a result, the critical care nurse must make judgments as to how best to proceed under the circumstances. This in turn may require the nurse to assume responsibility for making certain that the patient understands the consequences of refusal or assume the responsibility to reactivate a valid consent prior to proceeding with the treatment.

The ANA[87] and some courts generally view the physician as being independently responsible for informed consent.[88] Nevertheless, the nurse must be concerned with the patient's response or uncertainty and communicate any dissatisfaction to the physician or ultimately to the hospital administration.[89]

Moreover, particularly where, as in critical care nursing, the nurse is the care giver, the nurse is responsible for ensuring that voluntary and informed consent is obtained.[90] The concepts of voluntary and informed consent are discussed in Chapters 5 and 6. In addition to the case authority in these chapters, the emphasis placed upon patient teaching in critical care by academicians and practitioners in the field[91] may provide plaintiff's counsel with a compelling argument that the critical care nurse has an independent duty to provide informed consent.

For example, some experts in the field recommend a thorough discussion about short- and long-term goals, including, as the patient's condition improves, the following:

1. *Information about his [or her] condition.* If this is a recurring illness, include information that needs to be reinforced . . . [and] any relation to prior existing conditions.
2. *Symptoms* that need to be reported.
3. *Activity,* which may include adjustment to a change in . . . life style.
4. *Diet,* with inclusion of the family member who is responsible for meal preparation. . . .
5. *Medications* including expected effects, times, dosages, and major side effects that need to be reported.
6. *Other treatments* that need to be continued after discharge, and when . . . to recheck with [the] physician.
7. *Identification of [the] condition.* . . .
8. *Resources for additional help.* . . .
9. *Implications for family members.* [Advise of need for screening and] to be educated about [certain conditions like] diabetes.[92]

Given this extensive education responsibility, a strong argument exists that critical care nurses should obtain informed consent prior to administering care.

Consent forms, used as a matter of course by most institutions to document a patient's informed consent, are considered evidence, which can be rebutted, that the patient's consent is based on an understanding of the information provided. As a matter of practice, the consent form is generally presented to the patient for signature sometime after the information has been disclosed, usually by someone—the nurse—other than the person who made the disclosure. In most instances, the nurse has not been a witness to the disclosure, but is merely presenting the form for signature by the patient.

The trend is to name hospitals as well as physicians in lawsuits concerning informed consent. Hospitals are tied into the informed consent claim by the fact that they generally require signed consent forms and the fact that these are presented to the patient by a hospital-employed nurse. As a result of these activities, plaintiffs argue that hospitals owe the patient a duty to obtain informed consent independent of the physicians' duty. The majority of courts have rejected the theory[93]; however, the Illinois Appellate Court has held that the question of a hospital's responsibility for ensuring that a patient's informed consent was obtained is a factual one for the jury.[94] This case is analyzed in Chapter 6.

Intentional torts and civil rights actions

The ability to sustain a critically ill patient's life through technology has lead to a conflict between the practitioner's desire to save the patient's life and the patient's right to refuse treatment. This conflict has produced volumes of articles, including a treatise by the President's Commission for the Study of Ethical Problems in Medicine and Biomedical and Behavioral Research; legislation; and lawsuits charging battery and civil rights violations.[95]

Where the practitioners, the patient, and the patient's family or significant other agree on the appropriate course of action to be taken, the potential for an adversarial lawsuit is not great. Consequently, numerous institutions have attempted to formulate policies on "do not resuscitate" (DNR) orders; legislatures of various states have grappled with the issue by enacting statutes concerning living wills, natural death acts, and durable power of attorney in health care; and the courts have resolved challenges based on theories of battery, civil rights, and murder.[96]

THE PHILOSOPHICAL ISSUE

The technological imperative of the ICU—that ICU technology can dramatically and consistently sustain life for long periods of time—fosters the critical care practitioner's desire to do everything that he or she has been trained to do.[97] Where the ICU functions well, patients rarely die of respiratory failure or circulatory collapse because technology can delay these consequences.[98]

Consequently, some patients, particularly those with common ICU problems of cardiovascular, respiratory, and neurologic failure have their vital functions sustained by technology so as to forestall death, but their basic disease or diseases do not improve. Thus, for some disease processes, ICU care does not change the ultimate outcome, but rather results in a prolonged, yet inexorable course, with death occurring sometimes from complications of ICU care[99] or after a decision is finally made to terminate the special life support.

The Office of Technological Assessment[100] and others[101] have cautioned that measurements and monitoring are often viewed by ICU practitioners as ends in themselves, which can lead to depersonalized patient care. Sometimes the ICU staff, who treasure life so highly and go to any length to sustain it, ignore the qualities that render patients uniquely human.

"The technological imperative, which frequently results in more effective methods of managing very sick patients, can lead to the uncritical adoption of harmful therapies on the assumption that the most critically ill have little to lose from new approaches."[102] New ICU therapies, demonstrably efficacious in the hands of experts for specific problems, also have become widely adopted and routinely used where demonstration of their effectiveness is absent.[103] ICU physicians and nurses are generally believers in the technological intervention that they have mastered and often save lives that would have been lost under non-ICU conditions. Some are therapeutic activists, not prone to accepting the inevitability of a patient's deteriorating condition.[104]

> The highly technical nature of ICU care itself affects the way in which life and death decisions are made. The most critically ill patients have multiple organ systems failure and receive multiple interventions. The very exacting nature of this form of patient management results in standard protocols of treatment, perhaps at increased expense, and in concentration on the details of treatment.
>
> In such situations, the fundamental consideration of the long-term benefits to the patient receiving care is often overlooked among the seemingly endless technical decisions that are made throughout the course of an ICU stay. Yet, the most critically ill patients, who require the most concentrated focus on the details of day-to-day management are precisely those for whom fundamental likelihood and quality of survival questions are most appropriate.[105]

DO NOT RESUSCITATE (DNR) ORDERS

Do not resuscitate orders are commonplace in the ICU today. Where no order exists, it is usually the critical care nurse on the scene who makes the decision.[106] The nurse may well realize that if the emergency is called, the staff will so respond; and if given sufficient time to carry out resuscitative measures, the physician or team member may feel "obligated to start life saving procedures which no one will be brave enough to stop . . . There is a dilemma and we [nurses] share it tremendously with the physicians as we carry on."[107] An emergency code may result in a patient surviving on life support for an indeterminable amount of time.

"The nurse is in the crucial position to decide whether and when to call a physician, where needed to carry out resuscitative efforts. No call or one made too late may result in overall forfeiture of emergency efforts because sufficient time in which to resuscitate the patient is lacking."[108]

The patient's decision as to what, if any, resuscitation should be undertaken must be examined. The patient is more likely to discuss the matter with nursing staff than with medical staff.[109] Yet, writing DNR orders is still considered legally within the province of medical, not nursing, practice, although the *decision* not to receive life-sustaining measures remains with the patient.[110]

Carrying out the patient's wishes—effectuating a DNR order or disconnecting a respirator where no such order exists—places the nurse in a very precarious legal stance, as Chapter 24 clearly demonstrates. Consequently, critical care nurses at a minimum should insist that a policy governing DNR orders be adopted. Where no DNR order exists, the nurse is advised to institute all emergency measures appropriate to sustaining life in the immediate aftermath of a crisis.

Various professional associations considering the issue have suggested the following principles for a model DNR policy:

1. A statement that orders to resuscitate are a standing order in the institution and that this procedure should be initiated unless there is an order to the contrary
2. A statement regarding the patient's wishes
3. A statement of the medical conditions which should be present to justify an order not to resuscitate
4. A statement regarding the role of the family or close associates
5. A statement regarding entry of the DNR order in the patient's record
6. A statement about the scope of the DNR order
7. A statement regarding the obligation of various persons responsible for the care of the person[111]

The voluntary choice by a competent and informed patient should determine whether or not a life-sustaining therapy will be instituted or continued.[112] The ICU environment, however, is ill suited to guaranteeing patient competence and to providing the necessary flow of information to ensure informed consent.[113]

Because ICU patients may undergo acute psychological reactions due to sleep deprivation, sensory overstimulation, dependency, and nearness of death, these seriously ill persons do not always communicate in their own interests.[114] Other subtle metabolic disturbances may alter ICU patients' judgment. Patients on respirators may be reasonably competent to give informed consent yet be unable to satisfactorily communicate their intent.

The Patient Incapable Of Communicating Choice. When the patient is deemed to lack the capacity to provide informed consent, usually the family is recognized as having the authority to make a decision on the patient's behalf.[115] While this procedure in practice should work well, occasionally family members may have motivations which do not necessarily support the best interests of the patient, or they may disagree among themselves.[116] Because of moral and legal uncertainty, the team may adopt a policy of continuing intensive care until resolution of the dispute occurs.

This is understandable in light of the rise in malpractice lawsuits and the fear of criminal prosecution. Although all practitioners face the possibility of a malpractice suit and, to a lesser extent, criminal prosecution, concern is perhaps greatest among those who work with ICU patients. In the ICU setting, patients are critically ill; therefore, death is a common occurrence. Prosecutors may allege criminal conduct if they view actions such as "pulling the plug" and "overdosing" with pain medication as intentionally causing a person's death.

In *Barber v. Superior Court of the State of California*,[117] the California Appellate Court dismissed state homicide charges against two physicians for terminating certain treatments, including IV therapy and nasogastric feedings, given to a patient they diagnosed as hopelessly comatose. *Barber* makes clear that withdrawal of treatment where treatment is disproportionate to the benefits of treatment cannot constitute murder in California.

The case also adopted the benefits versus burdens approach to treatment decisions for patients incapable of communicating choice. This analysis defines proportionate treatment as that which, in the view of the patient, has at least a reasonable chance of providing benefits to the patient, and these benefits outweigh the burdens attendant to the treatment. For example, if a proposed course of treatment is extremely painful or intrusive, it is still proportionate treatment if the prognosis is complete cure or significant improvement in the patient's condition.[118]

Other courts adopted the extraordinary versus ordinary treatment approach to decision making which calls for a subjective analysis. For example, in *In re Conroy*,[119] the New Jersey Supreme Court reversed the appellate court's reversal of a lower court's decision that allowed removal of a feeding tube in an extremely ill, demented patient with no hope of recovery. The views of the lower court and the appellate court differed as to whether nasogastric feeding constituted ordinary or extraordinary treatment for this patient. The supreme court agreed with the lower court that removal was proper.

The President's Commission for the Study of Ethical Problems in Medicine and Biomedical and Behavioral Research has observed that fundamental moral and ethical distinctions are frequently made between actively causing death and allowing it to occur by declining to intervene, between withholding and withdrawing treatment, and between ordinary and extraordinary treatment.[120] Invocation of these moral distinctions has great importance in ICU decision making and yet may be so mechanical that it neither illuminates an actual case nor provides an ethically persuasive argument.[121]

Because many different individuals typically participate in ICU decisions, a range of moral attitudes exists. There may be a tendency to defer to the individual, whether physician, nurse, or family member, who firmly holds a traditional moral view.[122] ICU practitioners understandably are uncertain about the legal interpretation of these moral distinctions.

The moral distinction between withdrawal and withholding treatment may lead a provider to choose not to utilize life-sustaining treatment in the first instance out of concern that the treatment could not later be withdrawn. The President's Commission points out the fallacy in this view: if any distinction is to be drawn on a moral basis, greater justification ought to be required to withhold treatment rather than to withdraw it.[123]

The rationale is that whether a particular treatment will provide positive effects is often uncertain until it is actually tried.[124] If, once therapy is initiated, it becomes clear that the patient is not benefiting, then actual data exits, rather than conjecture, to support terminating treatment.[125]

The President's Commission recommends that each institution have clear policies and procedures for withdrawing and withholding life-sustaining treatment. Resorting to the court should be reserved for occasions when adjudication is clearly required by state law or when concerned parties have disagreements over matters of substantial importance that they cannot resolve. Preference is given to institutional ethics committees as capable of responding more rapidly and with more sensitivity than judicial review.[126]

The courts and various state legislatures have also grappled with review of decision making. Chapter 5 discusses the various approaches in some detail. In brief, institutional ethics committees,[127] judicial review,[128] and surrogate decision making[129] have been authorized by different jurisdictions. To the extent that these measures do not exist in a given jurisdiction, or a provider chooses not to utilize them when confronting the issue, civil remedies exist.

WRONGFUL TREATMENT: INVASION OF PRIVACY, FRAUD, AND INTENTIONAL INFLICTION OF EMOTIONAL DISTRESS

An Ohio Appellate Court has held that a cause of action exists for wrongfully placing and maintaining a patient on life-support systems against the express wishes of the patient and his family. In *Estate of Leach v. Shapiro*,[130] various medical personnel were sued for allegedly placing and maintaining a patient on life-support systems even though the patient had informed them that she did not wish to be kept alive by machines. The patient, who had been under care for a progressive, terminal disease, suffered a respiratory-cardiac arrest which left her in a chronic, vegetative state.

Without consulting the family, the defendants placed the patient on life-support systems in spite of the patient's wishes. The patient's husband instituted guardianship proceedings. As guardian, he obtained a court order directing that the patient's life-sustaining treatment be terminated. Three weeks after obtaining the order, the respirator was disconnected, and the patient died.

Thereafter, the patient's family sought to recover medical expenses and other damages incurred during the 5-month period that the patient was treated against her will. The trial court dismissed the lawsuit, holding that there was no legally recognizable claim for what had happened.

The appellate court reversed. The patient has the right to refuse medical treatment, the court reasoned, and therefore the defendants could be liable for failure to recognize that right.

If no emergency existed at the time when the life-support systems were initially introduced, the defendants had an obligation to obtain consent for these procedures from someone authorized to act on the patient's behalf. The presumption of implied consent to emergency treatment can be overcome by proving that the patient has expressed a specific desire—based on a full understanding of the nature of his or her condition and the specific treatment involved—to refuse such treatment.

Since the family alleged that the patient had expressly informed the defendants that she did not wish to be placed on life-support systems, the court ruled that the claim could not be dismissed. The family was entitled to prove their allegations at trial; and if they did, they could recover damages.

In discussing its conclusion, the court set forth a general rule that there is no liability for placing a patient on life-support systems if this measure is part of an attempt to treat a life-threatening emergency. The court further stated that once life-support systems have been introduced, these systems can be discontinued only by court order. Here, however, the patient had expressly informed the defendants that she did not want this form of treatment.

The court also ruled that the defendants could be liable for fraud for their alleged failure to inform the plaintiff of the irreversible nature of the patient's condition and for failing to obtain the plaintiff 's consent for various treatments and experimental drugs that were administered during the 5-month period at issue. The court reasoned that since an incompetent patient has the right to refuse treatment through a guardian or family member, the defendants had a duty to keep the plaintiff informed about the patient's condition; and a failure to do so would violate the defendant's fiduciary duty owed to the patient.

With respect to damages, the court held that the family members could recover for their own pain and suffering and emotional distress, as well as for that of the patient, but that no damages could be recovered for the defendants' alleged invasion of the patient's right to privacy because that right is personal in nature and thus lapses with death. In addition, the court held that punitive damages could be recovered if the defendants' conduct was proved to be particularly egregious.

WRONGFUL TREATMENT: BATTERY AND CIVIL RIGHTS ACTIONS

In addition to the family's causes of action, the patient has a claim for battery and violation of civil rights if state or governmental action is present. *Foster v. Tourtellotte*,[131] a case involving the Veteran's Administration Hospital, illustrates these claims.

The plaintiff brought the action to obtain a preliminary injunction against continued use of a respirator. The trial court found as fact that the plaintiff suffered from a progressive and irreversible neurological disease, "most likely amyotrophic lateral sclerosis."[132] From October 1980 through October 14, 1981, he remained fully aware of continuous pain and discomfort in his limbs and back, while paralyzed from the neck down.

On October 20, 1980, and August 27, 1981, the patient was found competent by Dr. Miriam Tasini, an attending psychiatrist on staff at the Veteran's Administration. Pursuant to court order, the plaintiff was examined by two independent psychiatrists on October 6, 1981, and October 12, 1981, who confirmed Dr. Tasini's finding of competency.

As of October 21, 1980, the plaintiff required the asssistance of a respirator attached through a tracheostomy. The patient, the court found, in all probability would die without the respirator. Nevertheless, there had been no improvement in the patient's condition since his admission, in spite of treatment. In fact, the court found, his neurological condition deteriorated, causing him "to feel extreme pain and loss of self-dignity with the continued application of the ventilator."[133]

Until October 14, 1981, the plaintiff was competent to decide questions of his future medical care, and he expressed a desire to discontinue the respirator and other life-sustaining treatment. All this time he had "full knowledge and appreciation of the consequnces . . . [that he would die] within a few minutes or hours, should such measures be discontinued."[134]

There was no evidence before the court to suggest that the plaintiff ever changed his mind about desiring to discontinue the treatment "so that he might be permitted to die naturally and as comfortably and peacefully as possible."[135] There was, however, evidence that the plaintiff and his wife, who intervened in the lawsuit to prevent withdrawal of life support, had a religious and philosophical disagreement.

In September 1981, the VA Hospital notified Mr. Foster that they refused to honor his request without a court order. The district counsel for the VA believed that California law on discontinuation of life-support systems was unclear. Plaintiff 's counsel notified the VA in writing that Mr. Foster withdrew his consent for further treatment effective September 28, 1981.

On October 14, 1981, plaintiff lapsed into a coma after suffering a cardiac arrest. At the time of the court's order discontinuing further treatment and providing medication for comfort, Mr. Foster had not emerged from the coma; but he was not brain dead. The court also found that there "is no competent medical evidence whatever that a person in deep coma completely ceases to experience sensations of pain or discomfort, or that indignity can no longer be appreciated, or that the need for privacy is diminished."[136]

Based on these facts, the court concluded that since the plaintiff withdrew his consent to the ventilator and further treatment, the continued treatment and application of the ventilator constituted an invasion of "the plaintiff's constitutional rights of self-dignity, privacy and liberty as guaranteed by the penumbra of specific guarantees of the Bill of Rights and more specifically the Fifth Amendment to the United States Constitution."[137] The court also determined that removal of the ventilator was not aiding and abetting a suicide or a form of euthanasia, and no criminal or civil liability would attach from following the court's order of removal.

The plaintiff's constitutional rights were deemed paramount to the desires of the family, and the court held they had no standing to object to the removal of the respirator. Consequently, the court isssued the preliminary injunction ordering the defendants to disengage the ventilator from the plaintiff and to administer medication to remove any suffering.

Although the plaintiff's counsel sought damages by amending the complaint after the plaintiff was comatose, the court refused to award any damages or attorneys fees. The court noted that the defendants acted in good faith, and therefore no attorneys fees could be awarded. With respect to the damages issue, plaintiff's counsel had failed to make the requisite allegations to support a damage award.

While faulty pleading prevented a damage award in *Foster*, proper pleading of a claim might well result in a damage award under similar circumstances. Battery only requires that an unconsented touching occur; federal civil rights violations require state governmental action. While federal civil rights actions may not be successsful against private hospitals unless state action is found, state constitutions providing a right of privacy without state action limitations may be actionable.[138] Battery actions also could be maintained for wrongful treatment. Once a competent person has declined treatment, continued treatment without consent is actionable battery.[139]

Recommendations and trends

The practice of critical care nursing presents challenges that require a thorough and scientific knowledge base, as well as a sensitivity to life and death issues in treatment. The professional knows the limits of his or her ability and acts accordingly; so long as he or she does so, the potential for liability is minimized.

Critical care nursing necessarily implicates important philosophical issues about life and death and life-sustaining treatment. Clear, written institutional policies on DNR orders will assist practitioners working in this field. Institutional ethics committees, although often only advisory, can assist providers in grappling with difficult choices. The critical care nurse's participation on these committees will help facilitate decision making and resolution of staff conflicts.

Endnotes

1. Office of Technology Assessment, HEALTH TECHNOLOGY CASE STUDY, INTENSIVE CARE UNITS (ICUs), CLINICAL OUTCOMES, COSTS, AND DECISIONMAKING (Nov. 1984) (hereinafter cited as *Regulation of Intensive Care Units*).
2. *Id.*
3. Kinney, *Survey of Critical Care Nursing Practice. Part II. Unit Characteristics,* 10 HEART & LUNG 1051 (1981); *Regulation of Intensive Care Units, supra* note 1, at 13; L.F. ABELS, MOSBY'S MANUAL OF CRITICAL CARE 3-4 (1979) (hereinafter cited as *Manual of Critical Care*).
4. Mulley, *The Allocation of Resources for Medical Intensive Care,* SECURING ACCESS TO HEALTH CARE, VOL. III 285 (Gov't Printing Office 1983) (hereinafter cited as *Mulley*).
5. L.O. BURRELL & Z.L. BURRELL, JR., CRITICAL CARE 4 (4TH ED. 1982) (hereinafter cited as *Burrell & Burrell*).
6. *Id.* at 4.
7. *Id.*
8. *Id.*
9. *Regulation of Intensive Care Units, supra* note 1, at 14.
10. Pyles & Stern, *Discovery of Nursing Gestalt in Critical Care Nursing: The Importance of the Gray Gorilla Syndrome,* XV IMAGE 51, 52 (No. 2 Spring 1983).
11. Quint-Benoliel, *Two Questions About Shared Responsibility,* AACN CLINICAL REFERENCE FOR CRITICAL CARE NURSING 1064 (M. Kinney ed. 1981).
12. *Burrell & Burrell, supra* note 5, at 3.
13. *See generally,* Breu & Dracup, *Survey of Critical Nursing Practice. Part III. Responsibilities of Intensive Care Unit Staff,* 11 HEART & LUNG 157 (1982).
14. *Burrell & Burrell, supra* note 5, at 15.
15. *Id.*
16. *See, e.g.,* CAL. BUS. & PROF. CODE 2725 (D) (West 1979). The California Nurses' Association and the California Emergency Department Nurses' Association Joint Task Force have developed a model for standardized procedures for the Mobile Intensive Care Nurse. *See, e.g.,* CALIFORNIA NURSES' ASSOCIATION AND CALIFORNIA EMERGENCY DEPARTMENT NURSES' ASSOCIATION JOINT TASK FORCE, MODEL STANDARDIZED PROCEDURE: MOBILE INTENSIVE CARE NURSING (1980).
17. *See, e.g., Manual of Critical Care, supra* note 3, at 14.
18. *See, e.g., Sermchief v. Gonzales,* 660 S.W.2d 683 (Mo. 1983)

(en banc); *Fein v. Permanente Group,* 211 Cal. Rptr. 368 (Cal. 1985); *Fraijo v. Hartland Hosp.,* 160 Cal. Rptr. 246 (Cal. App. 1979).

19. *See, e.g., Sermchief v. Gonzales,* 660 S.W.2d 683 (Mo. 1983) (en banc).
20. *Id.*
21. *Id.*
22. *See, e.g., id.*
23. *Id.*
24. IDAHO CODE §54-1402(d) (1979). It should be noted, however, that this provision is defined in the section concerning nurse practitioners without any further differentiation or clarification of that role.
25. CAL. BUS. & PROF. CODE §2725 (1975).
26. DEL. CODE ANN. tit. 24 §1902 (6) (1981) (practice of professional nursing reads in part that "[t]he foregoing shall not be deemed to include acts of diagnosis or prescription of therapeutic or corrective measures.").
27. *See, e.g., Frajio v. Hartland Hosp.,* 160 Cal. Rptr. 246 (Cal. App. 1979).
28. *Id.* Under certain circumstances, the physician may be deemed negligent for the delegation; for example, if the physician delegated the decision to institute emergency cardiac medications to a psychiatric nurse. The nurse performing the task, however, is liable for the negligent performance of the task, and lack of training will not be a defense where one voluntarily performs the task.
29. Reported in White, *The Expanded Role for Nurses,* 7 NURSING '77 90 (Oct. 1977).
30. *Id.*
31. Comment, CRITICAL CARE NURSES; A CASE FOR LEGAL RECOGNITION OF THE GROWING RESPONSIBILITIES AND ACCOUNTABILITY IN THE NURSING PROFESSION, 11 J. CONTEMPORARY LAW 239, 256 (1984) (hereinafter cited as *Critical Care Nurses*).
32. *Id.* at 256.
33. AACN STANDARDS COMMITTEE, STANDARDS FOR NURSING CARE OF THE CRITICALLY ILL 3-4 (1981).
34. *See* Thompson, *Critical care tomorrow: economics and challenges,* 10 CRITICAL CARE MED. 561 (1980).
35. *See generally* AMERICAN NURSES ASSN. THE NURSING PRACTICE ACT: SUGGESTED STATE LEGISLATION (1980).
36. *Critical Care Nurses, supra* note 31, at 258.
37. *Id.* at 258 n. 72.
38. 300 N.W.2d 380, 382 (Mich. App. 1980).
39. *Id.*
40. 211 Cal. Rptr. 368 (Cal. 1985).
41. *See, e.g., Manual of Critical Care, supra* note 3; *Burrell & Burrell, supra* note 5.
42. *Burrell & Burrell, supra* note 5, at 7.
43. *Id.*
44. *Id.* at 7-14.
45. *Id.* at 7.
46. *Critical Care Nurses, supra* note 31, at 274.
47. Abramson, Wald, Grenvik, et al., *Adverse Occurrences in Intensive Care Units,* 244 J.A.M.A. 1582 (No. 14 1982); Knaus & Thibalt, *Intensive Care Units Today,* CRITICAL ISSUES IN MEDICAL TECHNOLOGY (1982) (B.J. MCNEIL & E.G. CRAVALHO eds).
48. *Sermchief v. Gonzales,* 660 S.W.2d 683 (Mo. 1983) (en banc).
49. *Manual of Critical Care, supra* note 3, at 9.
50. *Id.* at 10.
51. *Id.* at 10, 12.
52. *Id.* at 12.
53. JCAH, ACCREDITATION MANUAL FOR HOSPITALS 183 (1983).
54. *Critical Care Nurses, supra* note 31, at 275.
55. *Id.* at 273 (footnote omitted).
56. JCAH, ACCREDITATION MANUAL FOR HOSPITALS 183 (1983).
57. *Manual of Critical Care, supra* note 3, at 6.
58. *Id.* at 7.
59. *Id.* at 10.
60. *Regulation of Intensive Care Units, supra* note 1, at 14, citing J.E. PARILLO & S.M. AYRES (eds.), MAJOR ISSUES IN CRITICAL CARE MEDICINE (1984).
61. *Id.* at 12.
62. *Id.*
63. *Burrell & Burrell, supra* note 5, at 15.
64. *Regulation of Intensive Care Units, supra* note 5 at 40.
65. *Regulation of Intensive Care Units, supra* note 1, at 40, citing Abramson, Wald, Grenvik, et al., *Adverse Occurrences in Intensive Care Units,* 244 J.A.M.A. 1582 (No. 14 1982).
66. *Id.*
67. *See, e.g.,* Laing, *The Impact of Technology on Nursing,* 16 MEDICAL INSTRUMENTATION 241 (1982).
68. 335 F. Supp. 1221 (D.D.C. 1971), *aff'd. in part, rev'd. in part,* 501 F.2d 806 (D.C. Cir. 1974).
69. *Id.* at 1223-1229.
70. *Critical Care Nurses, supra* note 31, at 265.
71. No. 84-0443 (D.D.C. Oct. 18, 1984), *reported in,* MEDICAL LIABILITY REPORTER (Compiled 1985).
72. *Regulation of Intensive Care Units, supra* note 1, at 49-50.
73. Schwartz & Cullen, *How Many Intensive Care Beds Does Your Hospital Need?"* 9 CRITICAL CARE MED. 625 (No. 9 1985).
74. *Id.*
75. *See, e.g., Regulation of Intensive Care Units, supra* note 1, at 39.
76. *Id.* at 50.
77. *Id.* citing Sanders, "Hospital Management Of Critical Care I," presentation at the National Institutes of Health Consensus Development Conference, Critical Care Medicine (Nov. 8, 1983).
78. *Id.*
79. No. 515680, Santa Clara Sup. Ct. (Feb. 24, 1980), *reprinted in,* 27 ATLA L. REP. 380 (Oct. 1984). Although this is not a decided case, and thus is not binding principle, the legal principle of abandonment is well established and has application to many factual contexts. The instant case merely illustrates its use in a case that settled, and thus technically did not create "law."
80. Case law clearly so holds. Chapter 7 reviews numerous cases involving medication errors.
81. No. CV-83-11343 Mo. Jackson Cty. Cir. Ct. (Aug. 3, 1984), *reported in,* 27 ATLA L. REP. 473 (Dec. 1984).
82. Additional cases on medication errors and equipment mismanagement are discussed in chapter 7. This chapter also contains cases concerning abandonment and failure to report and to protect a patient from a known danger.
83. No. 122, 1980 Pa. Lancaster Cty. Ct. of Common Pleas (Dec. 12, 1984), *reported in,* 28 ATLA L. REP. 136 (April 1985).
84. Breu & Dracup, *Survey of Critical Care Nursing Practice. Part*

III. Responsibilities of Intensive Care Unit Staff, 11 HEART & LUNG 157 (1982).

85. Coreless, *Physicians and Nurses: Roles and Responsibilities in Caring for the Critically Ill Patient,* 10 LAW, MEDICINE & HEALTH CARE 72 (April 1982).
86. *Critical Care Nurses, supra* note 31, at 263.
87. Fish, *The Role of Consent,* AACN CLINICAL REFERENCE FOR CRITICAL CARE NURSING 1051, 1052-1053 (M. Kinney ed. 1981).
88. *See, e.g., Harnish v. Children's Hosp. Medical Center,* 439 N.E.2d 240 (Mass. 1982) (unsuccessful attempt to prove that doctors were employees of hospital and therefore hospital was liable for physician's failure to disclose inherent risk).
89. Fish, *The Role of Consent,* AACN CLINICAL REFERENCE FOR CRITICAL CARE NURSING 1051, 1052-1053 (M. Kinney ed. 1981).
90. This is the position of the California Nurses' Association. CALIFORNIA NURSES' ASSOCIATION, POSITION PAPER ON INFORMED CONSENT 2 (1978). The American Nurses' Association Code for Nurses provides in part "[w]henever possible, clients should be fully involved in the planning and implementation of their own health. Each client has the moral right to determine what will be done with his/her person."
91. *See, e.g., Manual of Critical Care, supra* note 3, at 21-28; *Burrell & Burrell, Jr., supra* note 5, at 14.
92. *Burrell & Burrell, supra* note 5, at 14-15 (emphasis in original).
93. *See, e.g., Robertson v. Menorah Medical Center,* 588 S.W.2d 134 (Mo. 1979).
94. 439 N.E.2d 1319 (Ill. App. 1982).
95. *See* Chapter 5 for a discussion of legislation and cases concerning this issue.
96. These are addressed in Chapter 5.
97. *Regulation of Intensive Care Units, supra* note 1, at 55.
98. *Id.*
99. *Id.* at 55-56, citing Knauss, *Changing the Cause of Death,* 249 J.A.M.A. 1059 (No. 8 1983).
100. *Regulation of Intensive Care Units, supra* note 1, at 56.
101. Robin, *A Critical Look At Critical Care,* 11 CRITICAL CARE MED. 144 (No. 2 1983).
102. *Regulation of Intensive Care Units, supra* note 1, at 56.
103. *Id. See also* Tagge & Bryan-Brown, *Relationship of Therapy to Prognosis in Critically Ill Patients,* 2 CRITICAL CARE MED. 61 (No. 2 1974).
104. *Regulation of Intensive Care Units, supra* note 1, at 56.
105. *Id.*
106. Greenlaw, *Orders Not To Resuscitate: Dilemma for Acute Care as well as Long Term Care Facilities,* 10 LAW, MEDICINE & HEALTH CARE 29 (Feb. 1982).
107. Davis, *The Nurse's Dilemma,* in DILEMMAS OF EUTHANASIA (The Euthanasia Educational Council, Inc. 1971) cited in Comment, *CRITICAL CARE NURSES; A CASE FOR LEGAL RECOGNITION OF THE GROWING RESPONSIBILITIES AND ACCOUNTABILITY IN THE NURSING PROFESSION,* 11 JOURNAL OF CONTEMPORARY LAW 239, 266 & n.110 (1984).
108. *Critical Care Nurses, supra* note 31, at 266 (footnote omitted).
109. Yarling & McElmurry, *Rethinking The Nurse's Role In "Do Not Resuscitate" Orders: A Clinical Policy Proposal in Nursing Ethics,* ADVANCES NURSING SCI. 1, 4 (July 1983).
110. *Critical Care Nurses, supra* note 31, at 267 (footnote omitted).
111. President's Commission for the Study of Ethical Problems in Medicine and Biomedical and Behavioral Research, *Deciding to Forego Life-Sustaining Treatment,* A Report on the Ethical, Medical and Legal Issues in Treatment Decisions 494-497 (hereinafter cited as *President's Commission*) quoting NO CODE SUBCOMMITTEE, MEDICAL-LEGAL INTERPROFESSIONAL COMMITTEE, BAR ASSOCIATION OF SAN FRANCISCO MEDICAL SOCIETY.
112. *Id.; Regulation of Intensive Care Units, supra* note 1, at 59.
113. *Regulation of Intensive Care Units, supra* note 1, at 59.
114. Jackson & Yiybger, *"Patient Autonomy and 'Death With Dignity,'"* 301 N. ENGL. J. MED. 404 (No. 8 1979).
115. *See generally, President's Commission, supra* note 111.
116. *Regulation of Intensive Care Units, supra* note 1, at 60.
117. 195 Cal. Rptr. 484 (Cal. App. 1983).
118. *Id.* at 491.
119. 486 A.2d 1209 (N.J. 1985).
120. *President's Commission, supra* note 111.
121. *Id.; Regulation of Intensive Care Units, supra* note 1, at 58.
122. *Regulation of Intensive Care Units, supra* note 1, at 58.
123. *President's Commission, supra* note 111.
124. *Regulation of Intensive Care Units, supra* note 1, at 58 citing Cullen, "Results, Charges, and Benefits of Intensive Care for Critically Ill Patients," presentation at the National Institutes of Health Consensus Development Conference, Critical Care Medicine (March 7, 1983).
125. *President's Commission, supra* note 111; *Regulation of Intensive Care Units, supra* note 1, at 58.
126. *President's Commission, supra* note 111.
127. *In re Quinlan,* 355 A.2d 647, *cert. denied,* 429 U.S. 422 (1976).
128. *Superintendent of Belchertown State School v. Saikewicz,* 370 N.E.2d 417 (Mass. 1977).
129. *Barber v. Superior Court of the State of California,* 195 Cal. Rptr. 484 (Cal. App. 1983).
130. 469 N.E.2d 10 (Ohio App. 1984).
131. CV 81-5046-RMT (Mx) (November 16, 1981), *aff'd. on other grounds,* 704 F.2d 1109 (9th Cir. 1983) *(per curiam).*
132. *Id.* at 2.
133. *Id.* at 4.
134. *Id.*
135. *Id.*
136. *Id.* at 6.
137. *Id.* at 8.
138. *See, e.g., Bartling v. Superior Court,* 209 Cal. Rptr. 220 (Cal. App. 1984). This case is reviewed in Chapter 5.
139. *Id.*

Additional Readings

Laing, *The Impact of Technology on Nursing,* 16 MEDICAL INSTRUMENTATION 241 (1982).

Holder & Lewis, *Informed Consent and the Nurse,* 2 NURSING LAW & ETHICS 1 (Feb. 1981).

Greenlaw, *Should Hospitals Be Responsible for Informed Consent?"* 11 LAW, MEDICINE & HEALTH CARE 173, 176 (Sept. 1983).

Chapter 10

Emergency room nursing

Mary E. Kelly

Patient use of hospital emergency rooms (ERs) is rapidly increasing. Estimates are that from 1954 to 1958, ER visits doubled from 9 million to 18 million, and by 1968, the number doubled again to 36 million.[1] Approximately 310 people die daily from trauma, and 138,100 are injured or permanently impaired. The ER has become a specialty center yet also continues to be utilized for routine health problems, such as the flu or common cold. The ER thus doubles as a trauma center and as an occasional substitute or a replacement for a personal provider. Consequently, nurses practicing in the ER must be familiar with ambulatory care as well as emergency care.

The ER nurse is a specialty practitioner. The Emergency Department Nurses' Association administers an examination for certification in emergency nursing.[2] Nevertheless, to date, the department has not published standards of emergency practice.

More than 650,000 U.S. citizens die of myocardial infarction each year, and half of these die in the first 2 hours of the attack, often before reaching the hospital.[3] In response to this crisis event, prehospital cardiac care paramedic units came into being.

This, in turn, has lead to the development of subspecialty practice in ER nursing. For example, in California, mobile intensive care nurses (MICNs) have been functioning since 1973.[4] The MICN is a registered nurse who has successfully completed a training program including, but not limited to, advanced life support and field management of respiratory, cardiac, and medical emergencies.[5]

The MICN is expected to have a scientific understanding of the pathophysiology, signs and symptoms, and management relevant to the prehospital care of these conditions, as well as the ability to identify and to manage dysrhythmias and cardiopulmonary arrest.[6] The MICN provides advanced life support measures in the prehospital setting or issues instructions to prehospital medical personnel according to standardized procedures. Additional professional standards established by the California Nurses' Association and the California Chapter of the Emergency Department Nurses' Association Joint Task Force are contained in their publication on model standardized procedures for MICN.[7]

This chapter provides an overview of legal issues that arise in ER nursing practice. As in the other practice areas, liability may be based on theories of negligence, intentional torts, and civil rights violations. Unlike the other areas, however, the law with respect to negligence in certain ER settings has been altered in several states. By statute, some states provide immunity for members of mobile intensive care units or rescue teams and preclude civil damages for aid rendered gratuitously at the scene of an injury (Good Samaritan statutes).

The differences between immunity statutes and Good Samaritan statutes are first analyzed. Next, a discussion of traditional negligence liability in the ER setting and case illustrations are presented. Immunity and Good Samaritan statutes do not typically cover the traditional ER of a hospital. Consequently, the nurse practicing in this setting needs to be aware of traditional principles of professional negligence. Nurses practicing ER nursing in the hospital setting may also consult Chapters 7 and 9 for additional cases in analogous settings. Many of the issues discussed there, such as medication errors, equipment maintenance and ability to interpret technical readings, and abandonment, are equally applicable to the hospital ER setting.

The intentional tort of battery is also a potential claim because consent is often an issue in emergency treatment. Civil rights actions, which require state or governmental action, typically involve the hospital's refusal to render emergency care to a particular patient based on race or inability to pay. Arguments have been made, with inconsistent success, that the receipt of Hill-Burton funds supplies the requisite state action for civil rights actions. This is discussed more fully in Chapter 5.

Negligence

THE DUTY TO RENDER EMERGENCY SERVICES AND STATUTORY IMMUNITY

The Nurse's Duty. According to traditional common law, there is no duty to render assistance to someone who needs medical care, even in emergency situations, unless there is an established care relationship or the condition can be attributed to the provider's actions or previous actions.[8] Unless this rule has been altered by statute, nurses happening on the scene of an emergency are not *legally* obligated to act on behalf of the injured person, and if they do render care, they could be held liable for any negligent acts.

Good Samaritan Statutes. To encourage health professionals to render gratuitous emergency care without fear of liability, various states enacted Good Samaritan statutes providing immunity from civil liability for any act or omission of a person who in good faith, and not for compensation, provides emergency care at the scene of an emergency.[9] Thus these statutes usually apply where a person gratuitously renders emergency aid at the emergency scene.

Generally, the ER and other places where medical care is given in the hospital are excluded from the definition of "scene of an emergency."[10] The "not for compensation" language effectively excludes those who are paid to render emergency services. Finally, the acting or failing to act in good faith limitation still leaves the provider subject to liability for gross negligence or intentional misconduct.

Statutory Immunity for Rescue Teams. Because Good Samaritan statutes typically do not protect paid rescue personnel, the trend is to provide statutory immunity for emergency rescue teams, paramedics, and mobile units. For example, California has enacted legislation providing similar immunity to all members of a hospital's "Code Blue Team"[11] and to members of a mobile intensive care unit.[12] Physicians and nurses who in good faith give emergency instructions to any mobile intensive care unit paramedic at the scene of an emergency are also immune from civil liability.[13] Unless the action was taken in bad faith or in a grossly negligent manner, there is no civil liability.

This immunity extends to any good faith act or omission of a rescue team established by a licensed health facility or operated by a governmental agency, so long as the act performed or omitted is done while attempting to resuscitate any person who is in immediate danger of loss of life.[14] Health facilities, however, are not relieved of any duty otherwise imposed by law for designating and training members of a rescue team or for providing and maintaining equipment to be used by a rescue team.[15] Thus the good faith immunity defense would not apply to claims against a facility for failure to designate and train members of a rescue team or failure to provide and maintain adequate rescue equipment.

The Hospital's Duty. The common-law rule that there is no duty to come to another's aid once enabled a private health care facility to admit or refuse patients as it wished.[16] Public hospitals were treated differently, however, because they were established by statutes or charters that often set forth the requirements as to the types of patients they would treat.[17]

In recent years, this common-law principle has been eroded, particularly in the area of emergency admissions, by court decisions, state statutes, and regulations.[18] In most states, hospitals with emergency rooms have been held to offer service to the public and therefore must admit and treat patients in need of immediate or medically indicated emergency care.[19] The duty extends to public and private hospital patients, irrespective of their ability to pay.[20]

The ER nurse is typically an employee of the hospital or institution that has an ER. Frequently the nurse performs the initial assessment of the patient, and in some instances, the nurse's assessment determines whether the physician admits or refuses to admit the patient or sends the patient home or to another facility. In some instances, the nurse will make the determination to send the patient home.

The review of case law that follows demonstrates that liability may be imposed on the institution that improperly refuses to treat an emergency patient who is in imminent danger of loss of life or needs immediate medical care.[21] If the nurse employee is responsible and the institution is held liable to pay damages, the institution (employer) has the right to seek indemnification of damages from its nurse employee. For this reason, ER nurses must be aware of the duty to treat those whose emergencies pose an imminent threat to life or great bodily harm. Transfers or discharges based on race or creed are not valid justifications and may lead to civil rights liability.[22] Inability to pay also does not justify a transfer or refusal to admit and may lead to liability.

In *Garcia v. Valley Community Hospital*[23] a $1 million dollar jury verdict was obtained for wrongful death as a result of improper diagnosis and discharge from the hospital. The deceased was first treated at a medical center ER where he complained of severe abdominal pain. The ER physician diagnosed hepatitis and discharged the patient even though x-ray findings indicated a possibility of acute appendicitis.

The next morning, the patient was admitted to the defendant hospital and had an expedited laboratory work-up done. When the defendant hospital determined that he had no health insurance or funds to pay, he was transferred to another hospital and died. The medical center ER physician was charged with improper diagnosis, failure to perform a diagnostic work-up, and failure to admit. The second hospital was charged with failure to admit and negligent transfer.

Where the patient's condition is serious and dangerous and could create an imminent threat of loss of life if not treated but the condition does not presently pose such a threat, the courts have not been consistent in imposing a duty to treat. For example, in *Payton v. Weaver*[24] the California Appellate Court held that need for continuing treatment was not a condition that qualified for mandatory emergency services under the California statute. The court reached this conclusion, even though it recognized that the patient's condition, end-stage renal disease, is an extremely serious and dangerous condition that can cause imminent threat of loss of life if not treated.

If the hospital has undertaken to provide some care to a patient, however, liability may be imposed if a hospital discharges a patient even though there is no immediate need of emergency treatment. Once a hospital assumes the duty of treatment, it may be held liable for failure to continue that care.

In *La Juene Road Hospital, Inc. v. Watson*[25] a child suffering from appendicitis was admitted to the hospital, diagnosed, prepared for surgery, and then denied further care when the parent could not produce $200 as a cash deposit. The court upheld the award of damages for the additional pain and suffering caused to the child by the wrongful discharge, even though the patient was successfully treated at another hospital. The court reasoned that although the hospital may have a right to treat whom it pleases, once a hospital undertakes treatment, there is a duty to continue treatment.

The Arizona Supreme Court has held a private hospital liable for transferring a patient for financial reasons when emergency care was still medically indicated.[26] The patient must not be transferred, the court ruled, until after all medically indicated emergency care has been completed without consideration of the economic circumstances of the patient.

Today, many state statutes compel hospitals to maintain emergency services, or if such services are in existence, to provide them to patients requiring immediate attention. California's statute, for example, requires every licensed health facility that maintains an ER to provide emergency services to any person requesting such services for a condition in which the person is in danger of loss of life or serious injury or illness.[27]

California provides immunity from liability for refusal to provide emergency services if reasonable care is exercised in determining the condition of the person or in determining the appropriateness of the facility and the qualifications and availability of personnel to render emergency services.[28] This immunity applies to the nurse conducting triage.

Even if the facility does not maintain an ER, the nurses who are employees of the facility must exercise reasonable care to determine whether an emergency exists. If an emergency does exist, the statute requires the facility to direct and assist, in every way reasonable, including transportation, persons seeking emergency care to a nearby facility that can render the needed services.[29]

Illinois mandates that general medical-surgical hospitals provide emergency services and furnish those services to anyone suffering from injury or an acute medical condition capable of causing death, severe injury, and serious injury.[30] Other states prohibit hospitals from denying emergency services on the ability to pay, yet, at the same time, do not require them to provide ER services.[31]

New York has enacted a statute making it a misdemeanor for a hospital in a city with a population of 1 million or more to fail to provide emergency medical care and treatment to all persons in need of such care and treatment who arrive at the entrance of the hospital.[32] If the patient is denied emergency treatment, the ambulance attendants are required to report the denial of treatment to the state. Transfer to another facility is permitted only if the patient's condition is stabilized and transfer is in the patient's best interests, either because the hospital does not have the requisite services or because all of its beds are full.[33]

THE DUTY TO ASSESS AND TO REPORT

"Accurate initial assessment in the field or emergency department and precise reporting are the keys to effective emergency care."[34] Once the assessment of the patient had occurred and interventions for life-threatening conditions have been implemented, preparation of "a good report is essential."[35]

The Rescue Team or Mobile Unit Nurse. The nurse who has advanced training or functions as a member of a rescue team or mobile unit may be held to the higher standard of care required to perform a particular procedure or to assess a given condition.[36] Consequently, the measure of what constitutes gross negligence, the typical exemption to immunity, may be different than that for a labor and delivery nurse who renders gratuitous emergency services at the scene of an accident.

In the prehospital care setting (the field), all findings, both positive and negative, should be reported. To assure that errors of omission do not occur, the reasons why a certain parameter cannot be assessed should be reported.[37] If something is not recorded, both the team and the courts will most logically assume it was not observed. While immunity from civil liability exists if the MICN acts in good faith, grossly negligent conduct or bad faith actions are not immune from liability. Certain failures to observe and to report may be characterized as grossly negligent, particularly in view of specialized training.

The Emergency Room Nurse. The American Hospital Association (AHA) has promulgated guidelines for classifying ER patients according to the urgency of their need; these are set forth above (see box). The Joint Commission on Accreditation of Hospitals (JCAH) requires all accredited hospitals to have a well-defined plan for emergency care that includes a procedure to assess persons coming to the ER for care and to render appropriate services within the defined capability of the hospital.[38] This assessment must be done by qualified personnel and the patients must be either treated or referred to an appropriate facility.[39] The Arizona Supreme Court has interpreted these JCAH guidelines as prohibiting transfers based on economic considerations.[40]

The JCAH also requires the hospital to have written policies and procedures on the following[41]:

AMERICAN HOSPITAL ASSOCIATION'S EMERGENCY CRITERIA

Emergent: requires immediate medical attention. Delay is harmful to patient. Disorder is acute and potentially threatens life or function.

Urgent: requires medical attention within a few hours; patient is in danger if not attended. Disorder is acute but not necessarily severe.

Nonurgent: disorder is minor or acute and does not require emergency service.

Scheduled Procedure: procedure is planned in advance.

Adapted from M.R. Mancini & A.T. Gale, EMERGENCY CARE AND THE LAW 43,44 (1981) citing AMERICAN HOSPITAL ASSOCIATION, EMERGENCY SERVICES—THE HOSPITAL EMERGENCY DEPARTMENT IN AN EMERGENCY CARE SYSTEM (1972).

1. Providing care to an unemancipated minor not accompanied by parent or guardian, or providing care to an unconscious patient
2. Transfer and discharge of patients
3. Emergency medical records, including informed consent for treatment
4. Specification of treatment allowed, including which procedures may not be performed by medical staff in the ER service and the use of anesthesia
5. Identification of those persons, other than physicians, who may perform special procedures, under what circumstances, and under what degree of supervision
6. Use of standing orders
7. What circumstances require the patient to return to the ER for treatment
8. The handling of rape or suspected child abuse victims
9. Management of pediatric emergencies
10. Initial management of patients with acute problems such as burns, hand injuries, head injuries, fractures, poisoning, and gunshot and stab wounds

Most hospital ERs follow the JCAH requirements and the patient is seen by someone whose responsibility is to evaluate the urgency of medical treatment needed and to route the patient for appropriate further treatment (triage). Triage is often a nursing function carried out pursuant to protocols or standing orders. Depending on whether the physician is on site or on call, the nurse may exercise discretion in conferring with or summoning the on-call physician.[42]

Detailed nurse's notes should include a triage note stating the time the patient arrived, the condition he or she was in on arrival, an initial assessment of vital signs, and a statement of the chief complaint; a brief systems survey should also be conducted.

Once these data are collected and recorded, decisions must be made as to which of the various patients' conditions take priority over others and which of the patients' conditions are the most serious. Abnormalities in the assessments of patients must be communicated.

BREACH OF THE EMERGENCY ROOM NURSE'S STANDARD OF CARE

The reported case law that exists concerning the ER nurse's negligence centers around primarily three issues: failure to assess; failure to report; and failure to provide adequate instructions. The case law discussion that follows demonstrates that the ER nurse must assess the patient and report significant symptoms, whether discovered on physical examination or through a history, to the ER physician. If the patient is discharged or transferred, adequate instructions must be given.

Failure To Assess And To Report The Patient's Condition. Nurses responsible for evaluating patients in the ER usually conduct triage pursuant to protocols, standardized procedures, or standing orders.[43] Familiarity with the state nurse practice acts and administrative regulations that govern the nurse's practice is recommended. Although the hospital's policies may or may not allow the nurse to exercise discretion in calling the ER physician, these laws and regulations may impose on the nurse an independent duty to the patient to evaluate his or her status.

Lunsford v. Board of Nurse Examiners[44] illustrates this principle in the context of an administrative suspension of a nurse's license. In *Lunsford*, an ER nurse conducted the assessment of a patient who entered the ER complaining of severe chest pains. The nurse did not take the patient's vital signs even though she suspected cardiac involvement.

Instead, she relied on the instructions of a physician who had not examined the patient to send the patient to another hospital 24 miles away. The nurse informed the patient's friend that he should speed using his car emergency flashers and CB radio to summon assistance. The patient died a few minutes later while traveling to the other hospital.

The Texas Board of Nurse Examiners suspended the nurse's license for a 1-year period for unprofessional and dishonorable conduct likely to injure the public. In making its decision, the board relied on an administrative regulation that requires a registered nurse to evaluate the status of a patient and to institute appropriate nursing care to stabilize a patient's condition and to prevent complications.

On appeal, the nurse defended her actions on the ground that hospital policy required transfers of patients who did not have physicians on staff unless the patient's condition was a life-or-death situation. The reviewing court rejected the nurse's argument, noting that the patient was clearly in a life-or-death situation and therefore was not precluded treatment by the hospital's policy.

The nurse also contended that measuring vital signs and reporting them to the on-call physician would have been futile since the physician had already ordered the nurse to transfer the patient. In disagreeing, the court referred to the physician's testimony at the administrative hearing. There, the physician admitted he ordered the transfer but stated he had no idea of the patient's fatal instability since the only information he had was that the patient was having chest pains. The physician also testified that electrocardiogram (ECG) equipment and medications were available to the patient. In the court's view, the nurse failed to assess the patient's condition, failed to inform the attending physician of the life-or-death nature of the patient's condition, and failed to render appropriate measures to stabilize his condition and prevent his death.

Ms. Lunsford next argued that she had no legal duty to care for the patient because he was not her patient and he was not a patient of the hospital or the on-call physician. Moreover Texas law did not recognize a "nurse-patient" relationship.[45] The court flatly rejected the latter position, relying on numerous decisions, including one from Texas, that recognize a nurse-patient relationship and impose on nurses an independent duty to the patient.

With respect to the former position, the court held that the nurse's independent duty to the patient derives from the privilege of licensure, not from a third-party relationship such as that between the hospital and the patient or the physician and the patient. Consequently, even if the hospital had no policy permitting care of patients in a life-or-death situation, neither that fact nor the physician's order directing transfer could relieve the nurse of her duty to the patient.[46]

Rather, the duty owed to the patient requires the nurse to evaluate the medical status of an ailing person seeking his or her professional care and to institute appropriate nursing care to stabilize the patient's condition and prevent further complications. This duty would exist, the court reasoned, even without a specific regulation, since the duty stemmed from the privilege of licensure. The court construed the privilege of licensure as a covenant to serve the people of the state "with all her professional skills and powers."[47] The court deemed the nurse's actions a violation of her contractual duties to the people of the state to always act in a professional and honorable manner.

Inadequate Triage. *LeBlanc v. Northern Colfax County Hospital*[48] illustrates the nurse's duty to properly perform triage of a patient. The appellate court held that factual issues concerning the negligence of an ER physician and a "triage nurse"[49] employed by a hospital required a jury trial. The case illustrates a physician testifying to the nurse's standard of care as well as the ER nurse's potential liability for inadequate assessment during triage.

During the course of triage, an ER nurse examined and obtained the history of a patient who had been kicked in the stomach during a fight. He went to the hospital several hours after the injury and after taking a pain pill and some Maalox. The nurse contacted Dr. Floersheim, the physician on call, at home and related her findings and recommendations. She felt that the case did not present an emergency and that the patient could wait another 4 hours to be seen during regular office hours.

The physician agreed with this plan and prescribed pentazocine hydrochloride (Talwin) with instructions for the patient to see a physician in the morning if the pain continued. The physician, however, had treated the patient previously and knew that he was an alcoholic and a drug abuser.

Two days later, the patient went to the office of another physician who was too busy to see him and referred him back to the hospital. At the hospital, the ER nurses advised the patient to go to Dr. Floersheim's office because no physician was on duty at the hospital's ER. The patient arrived at the physician's office, but when he saw that the parking lot appeared full, he decided to go home.

Four days later, the patient was taken to Dr. Floersheim's office, and the physician had him immediately admitted to the hospital. The patient died the following day of bile peritonitis from traumatic laceration of the liver together with gastrointestinal hemorrhage from an ulcer. During the 6 days between the time the patient had left the hospital ER and the date of his admission to the hospital for observation, the patient had ingested two unprescribed propoxyphene hydrochloride (Darvon) pills every 4 hours and drank small amounts of liquid. The patient did not eat any food.

The trial court concluded that the plaintiff could not establish the requisite element of proximate cause because the patient had died 7 or 8 days after admission to the hospital's ER. The appellate court rejected this conclusion.

The appellate court relied on the pretrial testimony of the plaintiff's expert, a professor of ER medicine. This expert testified there were sufficient red flags to require further work-up and investigation given the patient's history of being kicked in the abdomen, an elevated pulse, low blood pressure, and increased respirations, coupled with abdominal tenderness and pain.

The physician expert also described the nurse's standard of care. He testified that the nurse's failure to recognize the potential dangers fell below "the standard of care expected in even a community hospital."[50] Even with this inadequate assessment, the expert stated, there was enough indication of abnormality for Dr. Floersheim to be on notice to conduct further evaluation of the patient.

Dr. Floersheim, however, testified that the patient's vital signs were normal and that no emergency existed at the time the patient came to the ER. He described as adequate his instruction to see a physician in the morning if the pain continued. The hospital had a policy of providing more detailed information to the patient only in cases involving head injuries or the need for a cast. Dr. Florsheim further asserted that, had the patient returned within 3 days of the injury, he most likely would have survived.

Dr. Floersheim also testified to the standard of care of the ER nurse. He stated that even with hindsight, his actions and those of the ER nurse would not have been different. The patient's condition at the time of the ER evaluation had not yet reached a point where a diagnosis could have been made.

Based on the conflicting pretrial testimony, the appellate court held that a fact question had been presented as to the negligence of the defendants and consequently justified a trial on the merits. With respect to the issue of proximate cause, the court noted that the plaintiff had conceded that the patient's own negligence in failing to obtain medical attention after his condition worsened was a proximate cause of his death and that a jury would probably apportion most of the fault to him. The plaintiff argued, however, that the defendants' negligence constituted a concurrent cause of death and that therefore, to some extent, they were also liable. The appellate court agreed that a disputed issue of fact existed as to proximate cause, and where reasonable minds could disagree, the matter is a question of fact for the jury rather than one of law for the court.

Failure to Communicate Assessment. *Baker v. Werner*,[51] a wrongful death action brought against a physician and a hospital for negligent ER treatment, illustrates the potential liability for a nurse's failure to assess and to communicate the patient's condition. Although the jury found in favor of the defendants and the defense jury verdict was upheld on appeal by a majority of the court, both the dissenting and the majority opinions demonstrate that the result could be different in another jurisdiction or with another jury.

The plaintiff's husband, who was the patient at the defendant hospital's ER, ultimately died of the combined effects of alcohol and propoxyphene napsylate (Darvocet). The claim against the hospital was based on the negligence of its ER nurse employee.

The ER at the defendant hospital, a small 24-bed entity, provided care at all times. The physician covering the ER had an on-call arrangement that did not require him to be present in the hospital at all times. If a patient sought treatment when the physician was not present in the hospital, an attending nurse would call him; based on this call, the physician would then determine if an emergency existed that required immediate medical attention.

At approximately 5:30 AM, Mrs. Baker brought her husband to the hospital's ER. Earlier that morning, Mrs. Baker had contacted the hospital by telephone after her husband informed her that he had ingested 30 propoxyphene napsylate pills. She expressed in general terms to the nurse answering the phone that she was concerned that her husband had taken an excessive amount of medication. The nurse advised her to bring him to the hospital for observation. Mr. Baker had a history of poor health for several years and regular use of pain medication containing propoxyphene hydrochloride (Darvon).

On the way to the hospital, Mr. Baker told his wife that he had consumed 20 propoxyphene napsylate pills. Mrs. Baker testified that she did not detect any symptoms of intoxication at this time.

The attending nurse, "an experienced RN"[52] testified that while Mr. Baker's speech was somewhat slow and slurred, he was able to comprehend and answer her questions. The patient told her he had consumed 10 pills. Although the patient's wife was present at the interview, she did not tell the nurse that her husband had earlier told her he had consumed substantially more pills. The patient's vital signs were within the lower normal boundaries for a man of his size. The nurse did not check medical records available at the hospital, and she did not pursue any procedures to test sensorium.

When the nurse contacted the physician, she informed him that the patient had taken 10 Darvocet pills over a period of time to relieve severe pain in his right side. She also described his ability to answer questions and conveyed his vital signs. The patient's wife interrupted the conversation to tell the nurse that her husband may have consumed half of a bottle. The nurse testified that she repeated this statement to the physician; the physician asserted she did not make this statement but rather indicated that the patient may have taken a few more pills. The physician concluded no emergency existed that required immediate attention. He instructed the nurse to advise the patient to return home.

Mr. Baker returned home and died the next day. An autopsy revealed high levels of propoxyphene napsylate and alcohol in the patient's blood. The experts at trial agreed that 10 propoxyphene napsylate pills over a 6 hour period would not be life threatening. There also was testimony that propoxyphene napsylate is generally prescribed in 20 pills per bottle.

Mrs. Baker argued to the jury that proper observation of her husband's sensorium impairment would have disclosed that the harmful effects of the drug were increasing during the visit to the hospital. The defendants presented testimony that they acted reasonably given the information known to them and alternatively that the patient may have consumed more alcohol and propoxyphene hydrochloride when he returned home.

The jury returned a verdict for the defendants. On appeal, a majority of the court upheld the verdict. The majority noted that the evidence on each side was inconsistent with that of the other and there were conflicts in the testimony. The majority pointed out, however, that issues of a witness' credibility and resolution of conflicts in testimony are for the fact finder—here, the jury—to resolve. Since these issues were resolved in favor of the defendants, there was no reason to reverse the case for a new trial.

The dissent viewed the jury's verdict as inconsistent with the evidence and would have granted a new trial. The dissent argued that since the patient's wife told the nurse the patient may have taken half of a bottle, and the nurse may have relayed this information to the physician, the physician had a duty to take further action. If, on the other hand, the nurse did not communicate this critical statement to the physician, she plainly was negligent for failing to do so.

The dissent criticized the majority's opinion because the evidence was to the effect that the physician had a duty to take further action if he had information that half of a bottle of pills had been ingested. The dissent also was critical of the majority's view that the nurse's possible omission was reasonable. The dissent concluded that all of the testimony relating to the standard of care of a nurse in this situation was that the nurse had the obligation to pass on the information relating to the consumption of half of a bottle of pills.

Failure to Consider Patient's Complaints. ER experts caution that ER practitioners should treat the inebriated patient seriously and not as a drunk to be sobered up and sent home. Alcohol is a dominant factor in claims, and the person who is drunk is a risk.[53] *Thomas v. Corso*[54] illustrates this principle.

In *Thomas*, the patient, who had sustained injuries during an automobile accident, was brought to a hospital ER. The nurse on duty checked and recorded the patient's blood pressure, pulse, and respiration and also recorded his complaint of numbness in his right anterior thigh. She also noted that the patient could move the leg and that it did not appear deformed. After administering meperidine hydrochloride (Demerol), the patient's blood pressure dropped to 90/60 and the nurse contacted the physician. The physician instructed her to admit the patient to the hospital, which she did.

The patient was transferred to another unit. No rooms, however, were available because of an influenza epidemic. The patient was placed in the hall outside the nurse's station. About 20 minutes after the transfer, the patient's blood pressure dropped to 70/50, his respirations increased to 40, and his pulse increased to 120. The patient complained of pain but appeared to the nurse on duty to be rational. The patient's skin was cool and perspiring, and his breathing was deep and rapid. He repeatedly asked for water.

About 30 minutes later, the patient's skin was warmer and he seemed more comfortable, although he complained of pain and thirst. The nurse caring for him noticed a strong odor of alcohol. Fifteen minutes later, the nurse recorded a blood pressure of 89/100; 30 minutes later it was 94/70, his pulse was 100, and his respirations were 28. An hour later, the nurse found the patient breathing in Cheyne-Stokes respirations with no pulse. Attempts at cardiopulmonary (CPR) were unsuccessful.

The assistant nurse supervisor saw the patient in the hall; she testified that he had complained of pain in his leg and thirst. She refused to give him water because he had been drinking. She recalled that the general duty nurse was concerned about his blood pressure of 70/50 but the supervisor was not because he had been drinking and had been given meperidine hydrochloride. The next time the nurse saw the patient, he was being given CPR by the general duty nurse.

An autopsy revealed a lacerated liver and a badly comminuted fracture of the femur with hemorrhage; the cause of death was traumatic shock, fractured femur, and fractured pelvis. The plaintiff's expert testified that the vital signs of the patient indicated a life-threatening situation demanding immediate treatment and the measurement of vital signs at least every 15 minutes. The nurses who cared for the patient after he had been transferred admitted that they should have contacted the physician when the blood pressure reading was 70/50 and the pulse was 120 because this indicated shock. The nurses, however, paid little attention to the symptom of thirst, although they knew this was a classic indicator of shock, because the patient had been drinking.

In upholding the verdict against the hospital, the appellate court criticized the nurses for exercising little, if any, judgment:

> [T]he jury may well have rejected the rather lame excuses made by the nurses that they did not call Dr. Thomas because [the patient] had been given Demerol and had prior to admission to the hospital consumed alcohol and they were waiting to see if he improved before calling the doctor. The jury may well have thought that in view of the admittedly low blood pressure, the administration of the maximum dose of Demerol with the presence of some alcohol in the patient's bloodstream—both depressants—these factors were *added* reasons to call the physician when the signs of shock were clearly present.[55]

In *Silberg v. St. Anthony Hospital*,[56] a delayed diagnosis of circulatory compromise resulted in a $47,500 jury verdict. The plaintiff, who had been admitted to the defendant hospital's psychiatric unit in the past, came to the ER screaming of intense leg pain and paralysis. The ER staff could find no physical basis for the complaints, and because of his past psychiatric admissions, the patient was placed in a special room, restrained, and given psychotropic drugs for 32 hours.

Thereafter, the staff discovered that a blood clot had lodged at the aortic bifurcation, causing circulatory compromise to the legs. The plaintiff had to have one half of his right foot amputated and he also suffered severe nerve damage to the legs, necessitating the use of crutches for his permanent disability.

In *Vassey v. Burch*,[57] the North Carolina Supreme Court determined that a plaintiff had sufficient proof of nursing negligence to take the case to the jury. The appellate court had ruled for the hospital, which had defended on the grounds that the nurse was not an employee. The hospital denied any responsibility for negligence.[58]

The plaintiff had visited his physician's office complaining of nausea and abdominal pain. After an examination, the physician gave him a shot of penicillin and a prescription and informed him that he was suffering from intestinal flu. After returning home, the plaintiff's abdominal pain intensified and he began vomiting violently. Together with his parents, he went to the ER. Although the plaintiff's mother suggested to the ER nurses that her son might have appendicitis, the nurses denied that this was a possibility and did not report this suggestion to the plaintiff's physician when they contacted him by telephone. They told the physician that the plaintiff had no signs and symptoms of appendicitis. The physician ordered medication and told the nurses to send the patient home if he was better in 30 minutes.

The plaintiff was sent home, and his condition worsened. He returned to his physician's office the next day and was hospitalized immediately for an appendectomy. By the time of surgery, he had a ruptured appendix and peritonitis.

The plaintiff criticized the nurses' conduct because they made their conclusion without benefit of any examination or blood tests. In upholding the plaintiff's right to go forward with a trial, the court noted that one of the plaintiff's experts, a physician, asserted that the nurses were negligent.

The nurses, the court noted, could obviously see that the patient was in intense discomfort and pain and that he had vomited. Based on these symptoms, they should have immediately recognized the true nature of the plaintiff's condition and reported it to the physician. The statement to the physician that there were no symptoms of appendicitis was made without any basis in fact and without the benefit of blood tests. This negligence delayed proper care.

Failure to Recognize an Obstetrical Emergency. In *Midler v. Harris Hospital-Methodist, Inc.*,[59] another failure to assess case, a settlement was reached for the wrongful death of a 30-year-old bank teller who was discharged from a hospital ER in active labor. The woman came to the ER in her last month of pregnancy, complaining of severe abdominal pain, weakness, dizziness, and disorientation. A nurse examined the patient and contacted her obstetrician. Although the obstetrician knew of a prior cesarean delivery, he ordered sleeping pills and discharged her from the hospital. Later that night, the woman died from a ruptured uterus.

Liability against the hospital was based on the failure of the nurse to recognize the symptoms of active labor in a patient in her last month of pregnancy. The obstetrician also was sued for negligent discharge.

Valdez v. Lyman-Roberts Hospital, Inc.[60] illustrates both of these bases of liability. There, a Hispanic pregnant woman's family brought her to an ER because she had been vomiting. She thought she might be in labor, but her midwife had informed her that she was seriously ill and had to be taken to the nearest hospital.

At the first hospital she went to, she was taken to the labor and delivery room in a wheelchair. The nurse contacted a physician by telephone. The nurse testified at the trial that the physician told her to tell the patient that the hospital had limited facilities and if she was seriously ill she should go to another hospital to get the best care possible. The nurse so informed the family, and they left. The patient had been at this hospital about 20 minutes.

At the second hospital (another 25 minutes for travel time had elapsed), the nurse on duty in the ER told the family that she would have to be taken to yet another hospital because the woman was not a patient of any physician on staff. They left but returned immediately, informing the nurse that the woman was in even greater pain. They requested an ambulance.

The nurse went out to the car and saw that the woman had vomited and appeared lethargic. Her skin was pale and moist, but she was not perspiring freely and she was not hyperventilating. The nurse told the family she did not see any signs of premature labor. The family requested the nurse to call a specialist, but the nurse informed them that the quickest help would be available at another hospital. When the family arrived at this hospital, the woman died within 10 minutes of a ruptured uterus.

Both hospitals that had turned away the pregnant woman admitted negligence in a wrongful death action brought by the family. They contended, however, that this negligence had not caused the woman's death.

The court rejected this argument. A private hospital, the court noted, may be liable for refusing to serve a patient in the case of an unmistakable emergency if the patient relies on the custom of the hospital to render aid. The evidence showed that both hospitals had such a reputation.

Moreoever, the plaintiff's experts supported a finding of proximate cause. One physician testified that although ruptured uterus is a rare finding, the symptoms exhibited by the patient were similar to abruptio placentae, which is not uncommon. Thus the nurses should have recognized that the patient needed to be examined and to have her vital signs checked. The nurse employed at the second hospital, in his view, negligently assessed the patient's condition. Had a proper assessment been done, the patient could have lived. A second expert testified that an attending physician should have been notified.[61]

Failure to Recognize a Pediatric Emergency. Pediatric emergencies present special difficulties in assessment because practitioners frequently must rely on the parents for a history. In some instances, the parents' failure to properly present the history will lead to a defense verdict. Where, however, the nurse fails to communicate to the physician all of the information provided to her by the parents, liability may be imposed.

In *Johnson v. St. Paul Mercury Insurance Co.*[62] parents brought a 2½-year-old child to the defendant hospital's ER. The physician misdiagnosed the child's condition based on the information relayed by the parents. The trial court found in favor of the defendant on the basis that the hospital physician had a right to rely on the parent's recitation of facts since the child could not speak.

A different result was reached in *Reynolds v. Swigert*,[63] a failure to assess properly symptoms of meningitis. Meningitis cases are fairly frequent and are usually filed after a patient's complaints have been repeatedly ignored during several hospital visits to the ER.[64]

In *Reynolds*, a 16-month-old child was diagnosed with bronchopneumonia but was not admitted to the hospital. The child was discharged from the ER with medication, but after 5 days, she had not improved. After returning to the ER, the child was diagnosed with spinal meningitis and admitted to the hospital. She died 4 days later.

The pretrial issue concerned the ER nurse's negligence in failing to take the child's vital signs and an adequate history and report the findings to the treating physician. The court held that a question of fact existed as to whether these alleged omissions of the nurse proximately contributed to the child's death. Consequently, the plaintiff was entitled to have the case presented to a jury.

Similarly, in *Ramsey v. Physician's Memorial Hospital*[65] an ER nurse was found negligent in failing to report information to the attending physician. A mother brought two of her children to the ER complaining that they had symptoms of rash and high fever. The mother told the nurse that she had removed two ticks from one of the boys. This testimony was not contradicted by the ER nurse.

The ER nurse never informed the physician of this fact. The physician diagnosed the children with measles. Later, the mother brought the children back to the ER, and she was told not to come back. One of the children died. On autopsy, the child was found to have died of Rocky Mountain spotted fever.

Failure to Recognize a Psychiatric Emergency. A large percentage of ER patients today are seeking help for psychiatric conditions, most notably depression.[66] As a result, ER nurses must be able to assess the depressed patient's suicide potential.[67] In addition, if the patient threatens harm to a third person who is reasonably identifiable to the nurse, the nurse, depending on the jurisdiction, may have a duty to take action to protect that third person.[68] This duty to use reasonable care to protect the intended victim may call for warning the intended victim, notifying the police, or instituting other reasonable steps,[69] such as admitting the patient.

Failure To Adequately Instruct The Patient. *Thomas v. Corso*,[70] discussed above, illustrates the importance of adequate instructions. Although the patient had been involved in an automobile accident and the nurse told the patient to see a physician the following morning if the pain continued, the nurse did not explain *why* this return visit would be required.

In analyzing the ''quality of the instruction'' given the patient to see a physician in the morning if his pain continued, the court noted that the nurse did not warn the patient as to any of the potential dangers or the consequences of failing to obtain medical attention. The nurse admitted in her deposition that if she had thought a patient had sustained an internal injury, she would not send him or her home. Since in this case she saw no evidence of internal injury or the need to investigate further, she saw no need to advise the patient as to why he should see a physician if the pain continued. The court stated that when medical providers fail to recognize a problem or the danger signs indicating a need for further investigation, the law will not impose a higher duty on the patient.

The court also noted that the plaintiff's expert testified that the best course of treatment would have been not to release the patient from the hospital. Nevertheless, the expert continued, if the patient had returned within 24 hours and his condition had been diagnosed and treated, the deficient ER examination would not have mattered because the patient would have survived. Both the expert and the defendant physician agreed that the patient could have survived if he had received treatment within 3 days of the ER visit.

Based on this evidence, the court reasoned, the trial court erred in ruling that the patient's failure to return to the hospital was the sole proximate cause of his death. The court held that the fact finder could determine that the patient was lulled into thinking that the pain would go away based on the nurse's assessment of a nonemergency benign situation. While the patient might have known that he should have taken action because his condition was worsening, even though there had been a failure earlier to determine the seriousness of his injury, that fact alone did not end his case.

Proximate cause, the court reasoned, requires only that the negligent act actually aid in producing the result as a direct cause; it need not be the sole cause. A finding of proximate cause may rest on the negligent act being a concurrent cause of the injury.

Thus, because the failure of the nurse and the physician to detect a potentially life-threatening injury and the failure to give instructions that would apprise the patient of the seriousness of his condition may have concurred in producing the death of the patient, the court held that the case could proceed to a trial on the merits. The court concluded that the case was a close one but that had the physician or nurse given instructions that would have alerted a reasonable person to the dangers of not obtaining medical attention, the result might have been different.

The importance of policies concerning instructions to patients who are sent home cannot be overemphasized. Written instructions provide more protection than oral instructions. Where patients are alone and are to be sent home with instructions, the better practice is to have a family member come to the hospital to transport the patient and receive whatever instructions are necessary. This practice should be recorded.

Crawford v. Earl Long Memorial Hospital[71] illustrates this principle. There, the plaintiff's son suffered injuries in an altercation. He had been hit in the head with a baseball bat, and he had been stabbed. He was treated at an ER.

When he was to be discharged from the ER, the nurse called his mother and told her to pick him up. The mother asked that he be placed in a cab and sent home, but the nurse insisted that she come to the hospital.

After the mother picked up the patient and brought him home, he went to sleep. The next day, he was found dead. The mother sued.

The court determined that objective symptoms of head injury were not present, and thus it was proper to release the patient to his home under supervision of family members or friends. The home treatment program required that the injured person be awakened at regular intervals to be questioned to determine whether the person's comprehension was adequate and to examine the pupils of the eyes to see if they are the same size.

At the time of the suit, in 1975, the community practice was to give oral instructions to the patient or to persons responsible for the patient's home care. The plaintiff claimed she never received any instruction. The nurse recalled that she gave instructions to the plaintiff, but she could not recall if she did so in writing.

The trial court found both witnesses credible, but the deciding factor in favor of the nurse was her insistence that the plaintiff come to the hospital rather than send the patient home in a cab as the mother had requested. The court also relied on the long-standing custom of the ER to provide instruction to relatives of patients who had suffered head trauma. The court also found it difficult to believe that an experienced nurse would not communicate instructions.

The appellate court also found persuasive the fact that the nurse insisted that the plaintiff come to the hospital. In the court's view, this fact was consistent with the nurse's contention that the sole reason to have her come to the hospital was to give her home care instruction.

EXPERT TESTIMONY

Several of the cases discussed above demonstrate that physicians often testify as experts on the standard of care of the ER nurse. The better practice is to have specialty nurses testify as to the specialty nurse's standard of care. To allow physicians to testify as to the nurse's standard of care may encourage courts to hold nurses to a physician standard of care rather than a professional nursing standard of care.

Fein v. Permanente Medical Group,[72] a California Supreme Court decision reviewed in detail in Chapter 23, supports the legal principle that specialty nurses are entitled to be held to the standard of care of their nursing specialty rather than a physician specialty standard of care. Yet, in *Fein,* a physician expert testified to the standard of care of a nurse practitioner. Thus, in spite of encouraging precedent, nurses must ensure that their accountability to the professional nursing standard of care is judged by experts who are professional nurses. The first step is for professional associations that represent specialty nurses to adopt standards for specialty practice.

In addition, specialty nurses must become familiar with the legislative process and utilize lobbying efforts to accomplish their goals. For example, professional nursing associations in California promulgated standardized procedures for MICNs, a laudable effort, but not all emergency care statutes providing protection to the ER physician have been extended to the ER nurse in California.

One such statute restricts who may testify as an expert in a negligence case against a physician that arises out of emergency services provided in an acute care ER.[73] The statute, which applies only to physicians, directs the trier of fact to consider all relevant factors constituting the emergency, "and the degree of care and skill ordinarily exercised by reputable members of the physician and surgeon's profession in the same or similar locality, in like cases, and under similar emergency conditions."[74]

The statute then defines emergency medical services and emergency medical care as those medical services required for the immediate diagnosis and treatment of medical conditions, which if not immediately diagnosed and treated, could lead to serious physical or mental disability or both. Only physicians who have "substantial professional experience within the last five years while assigned to provide emergency care in a general acute care hospital emergency department" are authorized to testify as experts in a negligence action against a physician.[75]

Substantial professional experience is determined by "custom and practice of the manner in which emergency medical coverage is provided in general acute care hospital emergency departments in the same or similar localities where the alleged negligence occurred."[76] This, in effect, operates as a locality rule standard of care, which allows the physician's conduct to be measured by the standards in the community and not by national standards such as those of a board-certified specialty.

ER nurses could clearly benefit from this kind of restrictive law, yet the statute explicitly is limited to physicians. Thus nurses may not testify to the physician's standard of care, but nothing prohibits the physician from testifying as to the ER nurse's standard of care. Nurses need to know about the existence of such statutes and take measures to amend them so that they too receive the benefits of having their professional conduct judged by experienced ER specialty nurses.

Intentional torts

As in other practice areas, liability may be imposed for failure to obtain consent to treatment. Actions for intentional torts, such as battery, false imprisonment, and invasion of privacy could be maintained in such circumstances. In the context of an emergency, however, where the patient is unable to consent because of age or lack of consciousness, an exception to the consent rule exists.

IMPLIED CONSENT

In life-threatening emergencies, the courts will imply consent to lifesaving treatment on the part of the patient. The circumstances surrounding the injury and treatment dictate whether a court will acknowledge an emergency to exist. In general, an emergency exists if a patient is threatened with death or serious bodily injury[77] unless immediate care is not rendered.[78] Chapter 5 discusses the various exceptions in more detail. Where an emergency exists, liability based on a lack of consent—intentional torts—will not be successful.

Failure to report certain crimes

Nurses practicing in the ER are required in most states to report certain kinds of injuries to a particular state or county agency. Child abuse, knife or stab or gun wounds, and rape are a few examples of injuries treated in the ER that generally must be reported to officials. Some states provide for criminal misdemeanor penalties for failure to report child abuse and gun or knife wounds.[79]

Failure to report child abuse leaves the nurse open to civil damages as well.[80] If the nurse should have suspected child abuse given the injuries sustained by the child, she or he may be deemed negligent for failing to do so. The plaintiff in this instance may rely on expert testimony to establish the breach of the standard of care or may choose to proceed under a violation of statute theory. In either instance, the jury would be most likely sympathetic to the plight of the child given the statutory duty to report and the horror of the abuse.

Although rape must generally be reported, the victim does not have to speak with the police once they are contacted. The role of determining whether a rape in fact occurred is neither a medical nor a nursing function. The role of the ER staff is to assure physical well-being, to collect specimens, and to provide for psychological well-being.

Policies and procedures concerning the handling of evidence in suspected child abuse cases or other mandatory reporting cases should be developed for the ER.

There should be a written record of the date, time, and disposition of any evidence obtained pursuant to a statutory duty.

POLICE REQUESTS TO OBTAIN EVIDENCE

The ER nurse may be requested by the police to obtain samples of blood or urine for evidence. The nurse's potential liability to the patient depends on the law in the jurisdiction. For example, state law may require that certain tests be done to save evidence when a rape victim is treated.

The rise in laws implying consent to alcohol testing as a condition of obtaining and maintaining a driver's license has led to increased police requests of ER personnel to perform blood alcohol level tests in persons suspected of driving under the influence of alcohol. The nurse's liability for doing so depends on the laws of the particular jurisdiction.

By statute in California, for example, registered nurses *may* (but are not required to) withdraw blood for purposes of determining blood alcohol if requested by a police officer.[81] If a nurse does so, she or he is provided immunity from civil or criminal liability so long as the test is done in a reasonable manner in a hospital, medical laboratory, or medical clinic environment, according to accepted medical practices, and without violence. The police officer must request the test in writing.[82] The statute also authorizes the Department of Motor Vehicles and the Department of Health Services to adopt uniform standards for the withdrawal, handling, and preservation of blood samples before analysis.[83]

Where the jurisdiction does not provide immunity, the nurse may be liable for battery if the patient refuses to consent and the nurse nevertheless administers the test at the insistence of the police. The nurse is under no legal obligation to obtain evidence for the police, unless a statute so directs or the nurse is employed in a facility that is under contract with the police to conduct such testing on behalf of the police.

Similarly, absent a statute so directing, the nurse is under no legal obligation to take evidence from a patient and preserve it for the police. Doing so may leave the nurse exposed to liability for invasion of privacy, unless the nurse is acting under authority of a statute or under compulsion of a mandatory reporting statute.

Well-written, clear-cut, up-to-date policies and procedures within the employing institution clearly enhance the nurse's exercise of judgment. These policies should be regularly reviewed, and measures should be taken to ensure that personnel are familiar with them.[84]

Recommendations and trends

Urgent care centers that are not associated with hospitals are becoming more prevalent. The liability principles discussed in this chapter are equally applicable to these ''freestanding'' clinics. Any development of professional standards for nurses practicing the specialty of emergency nursing should also incorporate nurses practicing in these centers.

ER nurses must develop and publish professional standards of practice. This is the first step toward obtaining legal recognition of a professional standard of nursing practice. Accountability to this standard is furthered by continuing education and frequent in-service trainings. At the legislative level, state statutes should be monitored to ensure that ER nurses are afforded comparable legal protections as other ER practitioners in the delivery of emergency care services.

Endnotes

1. Tuttle, *Hospital Emergency Rooms—Application of Good Samaritan Laws,* MEDICAL TRIAL TECHNIQUE QUARTERLY 145-146 (1981).
2. Greenlaw, *Nursing Negligence in the Hospital Emergency Department,* LAW, MEDICINE, & HEALTH CARE 118 (June 1984) (hereinafter cited as *Greenlaw*).
3. AMERICAN HEART ASSOCIATION, STANDARD AND GUIDELINES FOR CARDIOPULMONARY RESUSCITATION (CPR) AND EMERGENCY CARDIAC CARE (ECC), J.A.M.A. 244 (SUPPL):485 (1980).
4. CALIFORNIA NURSES' ASSOCIATION AND CALIFORNIA EMERGENCY DEPARTMENT NURSES' ASSOCIATION JOINT TASK FORCE, MODEL STANDARDIZED PROCEDURE: MOBILE INTENSIVE CARE NURSING vi (1980) (hereinafter cited as *Joint Task Force*).
5. *Id.* at 2.
6. *Id.* at 8.
7. *Id.* at 1.
8. K. WING, THE LAW AND THE PUBLIC'S HEALTH 202 (1985).
9. *See, e.g.,* CAL. HEALTH & SAFETY CODE §1799.102 (West Supp. 1985).
10. *Id. See also* ARIZONA REV. STAT. ANN. §32-1471 (1985).
11. CAL. HEALTH & SAFETY CODE §1317 (West 1979).
12. CAL. HEALTH & SAFETY CODE §1769 (West Supp. 1986).
13. CAL. HEALTH & SAFETY CODE §1799.104 (West Supp. 1985).
14. *Id.*
15. *Id.*
16. *Hill v. Ohio County,* 468 S.W.2d 306 (Ky. Ct. App. 1970), *cert. denied,* 404 U.S. 1041 (1972).
17. M.G. MACDONALD, K.C. MEYER, & B. ESSIG, HEATH CARE LAW §20.01[1] (1985).
18. *Id.* at §20.01[2] [a].
19. *Williams v. Hosp. Authority of Hall County,* 168 S.E.2d 336 (Ga.

App. 1969); *Wilmington Gen. Hosp. v. Manlove,* 174 A.2d 135 (Del. Supr. 1961).

20. *Manlove v. Wilmington Gen. Hosp.,* 169 A.2d 18 (Del. Super. 1961), *aff'd,* 174 A.2d 135 (Del. Supr. 1961); *Mercy Medical Center of Oshkosh v. Winnebago County,* 206 N.W.2d 198 (Wisc. 1973); *Thompson v. Sun City Community Hospital Inc.,* 688 P.2d 605 (Ariz. 1984).
21. The first major care imposing a duty to render emergency case is *Wilmington General Hospital v. Manlove,* 174 A.2d 135 (Del. 1961). There, an infant died of bronchial pneumonia shortly after being denied admission to a private Delaware hospital. The hospital staff sent the child home without examination, after the child's private physician could not be reached. While the state supreme court acknowledged that a private hospital had no legal obligation to establish an emergency room, once it had done so, and a seriously hurt person relied on the established custom of the hospital to render aid by seeking emergency assistance, the hospital could not reject that person without some valid justification.

    A valid justification would be inadequate facilities to treat the patient's emergency injury. A hospital is not required to admit a patient when it is not adequately equipped to provide necessary continuing treatment. The hospital in this case has a positive duty to transfer or refer the patient to a facility where appropriate care can be rendered. *Carrasco v. Bankoff,* 33 Cal. Rptr. 673 (Cal. App. 1963).
22. Kucera, *Narrow Definitions of "Emergency" Can Spell "Litigation,"* 7 HOSPITAL MEDICAL STAFF 21, 23 (September 1978).
23. No. 81-2078-C (Texas), *reported in,* 27 ATLA L. REP. 423 (APRIL 1984).
24. 182 Cal. Rptr. 225 (Cal. App. 1982).
25. 171 So.2d 202 (Fla. App. 1965).
26. *Thompson v. Sun City Community Hospital Inc.,* 688 P.2d 605 (Ariz. 1984) (teenager was taken to private hospital after accident which severed femoral artery and doctors determined that he needed surgical repair; he was transferred without surgery to a public hospital because his insurance did not satisfy the hospital's financial requirements for admission).
27. CAL. HEALTH & SAFETY CODE §1317 (West 1979).
28. *Id.*
29. *Id.*
30. ILL. ANN. STAT. ch. 111 1/2 §86 (Smith-Hurd 1977).
31. *See, e.g.,* FLA. STAT. ANN. §401.45 (West 1982); KY. REV. STAT. §216 B. 400 (1982); IDAHO CODE §39-139lb (1977).
32. N.Y. PUB. HEALTH LAW §2805b (McKinney 1984).
33. *Id.* Facilities which have received federal loans or grants under the Hill-Burton program are subject to Hill-Burton regulations which prohibit a facility from denying emergency services to persons who reside in a facility's service area on the ground that the person is unable to pay. 42 C.F.R. §124.603(b)0 (1984). When medical personnel have determined that discharge or transfer will not subject the person to substantial risk of deterioration of their medical condition, discharge or transfer of a person who has received emergency services is authorized. *Id.*
34. S.A. BUDASSI & J. BARBER, MOSBY'S MANUAL OF EMERGENCY CARE 11 (1984).
35. *Id.*
36. *See Fein v. Permanente Medical Group,* 211 Cal. Rptr. 368 (Cal. 1985); Kelly & Garrick, *Nursing Negligence in Collaborative Practice: Legal Liability in California,* LAW, MEDICINE, & HEALTH CARE 10 (December 1984) (hereinafter cited as *Kelly & Garrick*).
37. *Kelly & Garrick, supra* note 36, at 13.
38. JCAH ACCREDITATION MANUAL FOR HOSPITALS 23 (1983) (hereinafter cited as *JCAH Manual).*
39. *Id.*
40. *Thompson v. Sun City Community Hospital Inc.,* 688 P.2d 605 (Ariz. 1984) (en banc).
41. *JCAH Manual, supra* note 38, at 29-30.
42. *Greenlaw, supra* note 2.
43. *Id.*
44. 648 S.W.2d 391 (Tex. App. 1983).
45. *Id.* at 394.
46. The court relied on *Childs v. Greenville Hospital Authority,* 479 S.W.2d 399 (Tex. Civ. App. 1972) in reaching this conclusion. There, a nurse refused a woman's entrance to the hospital when the woman was in active labor, because the emergency room admitting physician ordered the woman to seek help from her personal physician. The nurse had examined the pregnant woman and had explained to the doctor by phone the woman's medical condition.

    The issue concerned the accuracy of the nurse's communication of the physician's instructions. The *Childs'* court, in reversing the dismissal of the lawsuit by the trial court, expressly found that a nurse-patient relationship existed. The court based the relationship upon the defendant nurse's employment as a nurse for the hospital and her position to the expectant mother who came to the hospital seeking her medical assistance.
47. *Id.* at 395.
48. 672 P.2d 667 (N.M. 1983).
49. *Id.*
50. *Id.* at 668 (citation omitted).
51. 654 P.2d 263 (Alaska 1982).
52. *Id.* at 264.
53. *How To Minimize Malpractice Exposure in The Hospital Emergency Room,* 10 MEDICAL ADVISORY SERVICES (May, 1985) (hereinafter cited as *Malpractice Exposure*).
54. 288 A.2d 379 (Md. 1972).
55. *Id* at 391 (emphasis in original).
56. No. C-79-2935, Oklahoma Cty Dist. Ct., (December 10, 1984), *reported in* 28 ATLA L.REP. 135 (April 1985).
57. 269 S.E.2d 137 (N.C. 1980).
58. This case illustrates that the potential conflict of interest between the nurse and the hospital is a reality whenever the hospital is sued for the negligence of its empolyee nurses. Nurses are cautioned that reliance on the hospital for a defense may not be in their best interests.
59. No. 67-66169 Texas Tarrant County, 67th Jud. Dist. Ct. (1984).
60. 638 S.W.2d 111 (Tex. 1982).
61. *Id.*
62. 219 So.2d 524 (La. App. 1969).
63. 697 P.2d 504 (N.M. App. 1984).
64. *Malpractice Exposure, supra* note 53, at 2.
65. 373 A.2d 26 (Md. App. 1977).
66. Jones, Jones, & Yoder, *How "Urgent" is the Psychiatric Patient in the Emergency Room?* 4 JOURNAL OF PSYCHIATRIC TREATMENT AND EVALUATION 243 (1982); Jones, Jones, & Meisner, *Identification of Patients in Need of Psychiatric Intervention in the ER,* 16 MEDICAL CARE 372 (1978).
67. Jones & Pelikan, *Nursing Management of the Depressed Patient*

in the Emergency Room PSYCHIATRIC NURSING FORUM (case study reprint). For an excellent review of cases imposing liability for suicide, please see Kjervik, *The Psychotherapist's Duty to Act Reasonably to Prevent Suicide: A Proposal to Allow Rational Suicide,* 2 SPECIAL PERSPECTIVE 207 (No.2 1984).

68. *See, e.g., Tarasoff v. Regents of University of California,* 131 Cal. Rptr. 14 (Cal. 1976).
69. *Id.* at 31.
70. 288 A.2d 379 (Md. 1972).
71. 431 So.2d 40 (La. 1983)
72. *Fein v. Permanente Medical Group,* 211 Cal. Rptr. 368 (Cal. 1985).
73. CAL. BUS. & PROF. CODE §1799.110 (West Supp. 1986).
74. *Id.* at (a).
75. *Id.*
76. *Id.* at (c).
77. W. PROSSER, HANDBOOK OF THE LAW OF TORTS 103 (4TH ED. 1971).
78. *Tabor v. Scobee,* 254 S.W.2d 474 (Ky. 1951).
79. *See, e.g.,* CAL. HEALTH & SAFETY CODE.
80. *See, e.g., O'Keefe v. Dr. Osorio & Osorio Med. Center,* No. 70 L 14884, Cir. Ct. Cook Cty, (July 24, 1984), *reported in,* 27 ATLA L. REP. 392 (February 1984).
81. CAL. VEHICLE CODE §23158 (West Supp. 1986).
82. *Id.* at (d).
83. *Id.* at (f).
84. *Greenlaw, supra* note 2, at 121.

Additional Readings

L.F. ABELS, MOSBY'S MANUAL OF CRITICAL CARE (1979).

M.R. MANCINI & A.T. GALE, EMERGENCY CARE AND THE LAW (1981).

K. WING, THE LAW AND THE PUBLIC'S HEALTH 202 (1985).

Chapter 11

Maternal and child health nursing

Mary E. Kelly

The practice of nursing in the field of maternal and child health covers a broad spectrum and extended period of care for both the mother and the newborn. Maternal and child health nursing is practiced in ambulatory and institutional settings. Ambulatory settings include schools, the home, day-are agencies, physicians' offices, and clinics. Institutional settings include general and specialty hospitals.[1]

This chapter analyzes various theories of legal liability that may be asserted against the nurse in the field of maternal and child health nursing. Because this field encompasses such a broad spectrum of care, the discussion of legal issues is organized around specific periods of the childbearing continuum. The reader should bear in mind, however, that the legal issue involved may have application to another period in the childbearing continuum. In other words, the legal principle may be applicable to a totally different factual setting.

Negligence is the most frequent theory of liability in this field; nevertheless, certain conduct or conditions also make the practitioner liable for intentional torts and civil rights violations. The most common intentional tort is battery, although claims for intentional infliction of emotional distress and invasion of privacy are potential hazards in the labor and delivery area.

The potential for civil rights actions is greater in the field of maternal and child health nursing than other fields of nursing practice, with the exception of public health nursing.[2] The typical civil rights action in this area affects some aspect of reproduction and thus generally implicates the constitutional right to privacy.

Although technically standard of care is not an issue in lawsuits charging civil rights violations and intentional torts actions, common sense compels the conclusion that if the nurse's practice complies with professional standards, it is unlikely that he or she would commit a battery, invade another's privacy, or violate someone's constitutional right to privacy or personal autonomy.[3]

Thus a strong argument can be made that compliance with professional standards has a "real life" impact on lawsuits other than those charging negligence. As a rule of thumb, if the nurse acts according to a professional standard of care, exposure to liability across the board is minimized. Consequently, the professional standard of care is first addressed, and thereafter liability along the childbearing continuum is analyzed.

The professional standard of care

The American Nurses' Association (ANA) has defined maternal and child health nursing as "a specialized area of nursing focused on (1) health needs of women, their partners, and their families throughout their reproductive and childbearing years, and (2) children through adolescence."[4] The standards of practice and essential knowledge and skills promulgated by the ANA in the maternal and child health nursing field are listed on p. 158 (see box). These standards provide nurses practicing in this field with a framework within which to minimize their potential liability.

The ANA defines two categories of nurse providers within the practice of maternal and child health nursing: the nursing generalist who practices within the field of

MATERNAL AND CHILD NURSING PRACTICE STANDARDS AND ESSENTIAL KNOWLEDGE AND SKILLS

Standards of practice*

The nurse helps children and parents attain and maintain optimum health.

The nurse assists families to achieve and maintain a balance between the personal growth needs of individual family members and optimum family functioning.

The nurse intervenes with vulnerable clients and families at risk to prevent potential developmental and health problems.

The nurse promotes an environment free of hazards to reproduction, growth and development, wellness and recovery from illness.

The nurse detects changes in health status and deviations from optimum development.

The nurse carries out appropriate interventions and treatment to facilitate survival and recovery from illness.

The nurse assists clients and families to understand and cope with developmental and traumatic situations during illness, childbearing, child rearing, and childhood.

The nurse actively pursues strategies to enhance access to and utilization of adequate health care services.

The nurse improves maternal and child health nursing practice through evaluation of practice, education, and research.

Essential knowledge and skills†

Nursing process as it applies to maternal and child health

The relationship of genetics and embryology to the outcome of childbearing

Growth and development

Anatomy and physiology and related pathophysiology

The impact of the environment, including socioeconomic conditions and culture, on childbearing and child rearing

Human sexuality

Developmental stages of families

Interviewing-counseling theory

Teaching learning theory

Childbearing process and child-rearing process

Affiliative processes, such as attachment

Crisis theory and intervention

Health assessment of childbearing women and of children, including developmental assessments

Interdisciplinary team skills

*Adapted from AMERICAN NURSES' ASSOCIATION DIVISION ON MATERNAL & CHILD HEALTH NURSING PRACTICE, STANDARDS OF MATERNAL & CHILD NURSING PRACTICE (1983).

†Adapted from AMERICAN NURSES' ASSOCIATION, A STATEMENT ON THE SCOPE OF MATERNAL AND CHILD HEALTH NURSING PRACTICE 5 (1980).

maternal and child health nursing; and the maternal and child health nurse specialist.[5] Nurse generalists have had a generic nursing preparation with additional in-service or continuing education in specialized areas of maternal and child health nursing, such as labor and delivery, neonatal, postpartum, and prenatal nursing; ambulatory care of children; care of hospitalized children; women's health; family planning; care of children with developmental disabilities; oncological care of children; and well-child care.[6]

The maternal and child nursing specialist has educational preparation at the master's level; the specialist's practice is characterized by expertise in the nursing care of children, prenatal nursing, and women's health care. According to the ANA, "The nursing specialist explores and tests scientific theories on which the practice of maternal and child health nursing is based, and uses investigative skills to systematically study and solve complex problems in their specialty area."[7]

A major concept of maternal and child health nursing is a differentiation of resources into primary, secondary (intermediate), and tertiary levels of care.[8] Who provides the care and where the care should be given are functions of the complexity of the patient's needs.

Primary care, practiced in ambulatory and in all institutional settings, involves a commitment to prevention of illness and to maintenance of optimal health.[9] The areas of concern and the nursing activities in primary care maternal and child health nursing are listed on p. 159, upper left (see box).

Secondary or intermediate care includes "primary care and maintenance of mothers and children requiring treatment of common complications for which necessary resources are present."[10] In general, the skills required incorporate more technology than those required for primary care situations; intermediate care most often occurs in the hospital setting.[11] The areas of concern and nursing activities associated with secondary care are listed on p. 159, bottom (see box).

Tertiary care involves women and children with com-

PRIMARY CARE IN MATERNAL AND CHILD HEALTH NURSING

Areas of concern to practitioners

Prevention of risk factors such as (1) abuse and neglect of parents and children and (2) malnutrition and disease, both environmental and familial.

Treatment of low-risk mothers and infants during the perinatal period.

Nursing activities associated with primary care

Health assessment
Case finding
Anticipatory guidance
Counseling
Parent teaching
Immunizations
Nutrition programs
Family planning services
Surrogate care of infants
Women's health care, from reproductive assessment and counseling to assessment and guidance during menopause and postmenopause

Adapted from AMERICAN NURSES' ASSOCIATION, A STATEMENT ON THE SCOPE OF MATERNAL AND CHILD HEALTH NURSING PRACTICE 4 (1980).

plex diseases and disabilities.[12] This kind of care requires "a greater degree of interdisciplinary collaboration among health care providers and dependence on scientific technology and machinery."[13] Moreover, this level of care is highly specific and directed toward reducing mortality and morbidity. Examples include ambulatory and inpatient settings providing high-risk pregnancy and prenatal care that are regionalized within communities of high population density.[14] In addition, intensive care units of obstetrical and pediatric hospitals provide such highly specialized care.

Maternal and child nursing activities are differentiated according to the level of care being provided in a specific setting.[15] Within this broad spectrum of specialized nursing practice is the subspecialty of high-risk prenatal nursing. High-risk prenatal nursing is defined by the ANA as "a specialized area of maternal and child health nursing providing prenatal care to childbearing families at risk."[16] "Perinatal care" is the "care of the health needs of families during the child bearing continuum, through the fourth trimester."[17]

"High risk perinatal care" refers to the care of the health needs of childbearing families who are at risk for increased maternal-fetal neonatal morbidity and mortality."[18] This care focuses on "acute and chronic psychosocial and physiological illness, with the goal of maintaining and restoring optimal levels of health attainable by the childbearing family."[19] The nurse's role in providing this care is "determined by [the nurse's] specific knowledge, skills, and ability to make clinical judgments."[20]

The ANA defines two categories of nurses within the high-risk perinatal area: nurses practicing in high-risk perinatal settings and high-risk perinatal clinical specialists.[21] Nurses practicing high-risk perinatal nursing who are not clinical specialists[22] have in-service or short-term continuing education preparation in the areas of the childbearing continuum and high-risk practice that is additional to their generic training.[23] According to the ANA, nurses practicing in high-risk perinatal settings have a comprehensive knowledge base of the childbearing continuum, with current, in-depth knowledge and specialized skills in maternal-fetal or maternal-neonatal care.[24] Additional professional responsibilities are listed in the box on p. 160.

SECONDARY CARE IN MATERNAL AND CHILD HEALTH NURSING

Areas of concern

1. Treatment of women experiencing a limited degree of hypertension or diabetes
2. Treatment of neonates needing short-term assisted ventilation or needing electronic monitoring
3. Treatment of mildly premature infants
4. Treatment of children having congenital anomalies requiring corrective surgery
5. Treatment of children having contagious and infectious diseases
6. Women with complications arising during childbirth and other experiences related to reproduction

Activities associated with secondary or intermediate care

Provide environmental conditions that enhance the individual's physical and social well-being and enhance development

Adapted from AMERICAN NURSES' ASSOCIATION, A STATEMENT ON THE SCOPE OF MATERNAL AND CHILD HEALTH NURSING PRACTICE 5 (1980).

PROFESSIONAL RESPONSIBILITIES OF NURSES PRACTICING IN THE HIGH-RISK PERINATAL AREA

In addition to the standards, knowledge, and skills prescribed for maternal and child health nursing practice that are set forth in the box on p. 158, nurses practicing in the high-risk perinatal area are professionally obligated to:

- Maintain their knowledge and skills in order to practice according to the standards established by the ANA in general and in maternal and child health nursing
- Establish and maintain current practice through evaluation, education, and research
- Assume accountability and responsibility for the high-risk perinatal family
- Initiate and participate in interdisciplinary collaboration
- Identify those factors that interfere with the effective practice of nursing and implement strategies for change
- Participate in the recognition of professional achievement in high-risk perinatal nursing
- Promote awareness of and participation in the initiation of necessary legislative changes at local, state, and national levels that affect the high-risk population
- Serve professional and consumer groups as a resource for high-risk perinatal nursing

Adapted from AMERICAN NURSES' ASSOCIATION, A STATEMENT ON THE SCOPE OF HIGH-RISK PERINATAL NURSING PRACTICE 5 (1983).

Nurses who are high-risk perinatal clinical specialists have advanced educational training at the master's or doctoral level. The box above sets forth the standards of practice for the high-risk perinatal specialist. Although legal issues concerning the clinical specialist are addressed elsewhere in this book, the principles discussed in this chapter may be applicable to the maternal and child health specialist and the high-risk perinatal specialist.

Presumably, the ANA does not view nurses practicing maternal and child health nursing as adequately prepared to care for high-risk perinatal patients. In many hospital settings, however, this distinction is not made; labor and delivery units are not divided into high-risk and normal deliveries and there may not be a pediatric intensive care unit. Nevertheless, case law makes clear that nurses who work within labor and delivery settings are expected to recognize and to act on behalf of the high-risk mother or neonate.

If the hospital is not equipped to care for the high-risk perinatal patient, the appropriate action may require a transfer to a regional perinatal center. Such centers generally serve a defined geographical region, accepting from other hospitals referrals of patients with complicated conditions. These centers are briefly discussed.

In addition to the ANA's standards of practice, general standards of care or rules of conduct can be gleaned from case law and other sources to increase awareness of the areas that leave practitioners prone to liability for negligence. Many of the issues addressed in this chapter, such as inadequate staffing and abandonment, apply to all areas within the maternal and child health nursing field; other legal issues, such as inadequate fetal monitoring and inaccurate birth control counseling, relate to a specific stage along the childbearing continuum.

The nurse's standard of care in the field of maternal and child health nursing, or its subspecialties, is established in the same manner as other professional standards of care: expert testimony; textbooks; journals; statutes; administrative regulations; institutional policies and procedures; and standards established by the profession. The nurse's conduct will be judged by or measured against the conduct espoused by others in the profession.

In addition to knowing and acting in accordance with the employing institution's policies and procedures (unless of course they are professionally inappropriate) and the standards set by professional associations, the nurse needs to be cognizant of advancements and developments discussed in textbooks and journals.

Both maternal and child health nursing and the subspecialty of high-risk perinatal care demand updated knowledge and skill, as well as sensitivity. Nurses practicing within the field of maternal and child health nursing are responsible to have an understanding of the reproductive process, its possible complications, the care of the mother and her child in health and illness, an appreciation of the role of the family, and a knowledge of community resources.[25] Nurses practicing in the high-risk perinatal setting are responsible for "maintain[ing] a comprehensive knowledge base of the childbearing continuum, with current, in-depth knowledge and specialized nursing skills in at least one of the interdependent high-risk perinatal areas, i.e. maternal-fetal or maternal-neonatal care."[26]

Sound nursing practice in the maternal and child health care field necessitates the ability to recognize the signs and symptoms of the leading causes of maternal and infant death. Failure to keep abreast of developments in the detection, prevention, and treatment of these causes may leave the practitioner vulnerable to liability.

Preconception period

Liability for care during the preconception period usually involves some aspect of birth control, sterilization, or Rh sensitization. Sterilizations performed without consent may be remedied either under a battery theory (intentional tort) or a civil rights theory (assuming that there is some government action). These actions are discussed in the labor and delivery section. A discussion of the nurse's liability for negligence follows.

LIABILITY FOR NEGLIGENCE

Rh Incompatibility. The courts recognize that a legal duty is owed to those persons not yet in existence; consequently, a child not yet conceived but forseeably harmed by a breach of the duty owed to the mother can recover for damages.[27] The nurse who participates in the negligent transfusion of incompatible blood thus may be held liable for prenatal injuries resulting from the later incompatibility.

In *Renslow v. Mennonite Hospital*,[28] a child born to a woman negligently transfused with incompatible blood sued a hospital and its director of laboratories. When the unborn child's mother was 13 years old, the defendants negligently transfused the mother, on two occasions, with 500 ml of Rh-positive blood. The mother's Rh-negative blood was incompatible with, and was sensitized by, the Rh-positive blood. The mother had no knowledge of an adverse reaction from the transfusions, and she did not know that she had been improperly transfused or that her blood had been sensitized. In 1973, she became pregnant, and a routine screening test ordered during her prenatal care disclosed the sensitivity.

Although defendants discovered before 1973 that they had administered incompatible blood to the mother when she was a young girl, they did not notify her or her family. The resulting desensitization of her blood allegedly caused prenatal damage to her child's hematologic processes. This damage put the child's life in jeopardy and necessitated an induced premature birth. At birth, the child was jaundiced, suffering from hyperbilirubinemia. Although two complete exchange transfusions of the child's blood were immediately accomplished, she sustained permanent damage to various organs, including her brain and nervous system.

The defendants argued that there could be no liability because the plaintiff child had not yet been conceived and thus was not in existence at the time of the negligent acts. The court rejected this defense, reasoning that although the child was not in existence at the time of the negligent activity, her ultimate existence or potential existence was reasonably forseeable. Consequently, the defendants were held liable for the child's injuries.

Kyte v. McMillion[29] illustrates another suit brought against a nurse for irreversible sensitization. There, a patient underwent a blood transfusion following an automobile accident. By the time that the nurse realized that the transfusing blood was the wrong Rh factor, 0.25 ml of Rh-positive blood had been absorbed. Although the patient suffered a burning rash that lasted only 1 hour, a blood test performed several weeks later revealed antibody formation. The hospital eventually settled the case.

Failure to Warn about Contraceptive Failure and Amniocentesis. The advent of sterilization procedures and amniocentesis and resulting births has led to the common-law development of claims known as "wrongful birth" and "wrongful life." Presently, three jurisdictions, California,[30] Washington,[31] and New Jersey,[32] recognize the wrongful life cause of action.

In general, wrongful birth is the term given to the type of lawsuit that is brought by the parents of an unwanted child. The typical case is brought against a practitioner for negligent performance of sterilization procedures or failure to advise of genetic hazards and the availability of amniocentesis and abortion.

The theory of failed sterilization or wrongful birth cases is that if the sterilization had been properly performed, or the parents had been warned that it was not fully effective so that other measures to prevent conception could have been taken, the child would not have been born.[33] In the genetic defect case, the theory is that if amniocentesis had been performed the genetic defect would have been discovered and the child would have been aborted.

The first courts faced with a claim by parents for wrongful birth denied all damages as a matter of public policy.[34] The reasoning the courts utilized is that the intangible benefits of a child to the parents outweigh the economic loss in rearing and educating a normal and healthy child. Other courts have determined that damages may be recovered by balancing the damages from the anxiety and economic costs of an unwanted pregnancy against the benefits of a child.[35]

Wrongful life is the term given to the claim brought against the practitioner by the child who has some genetic or other defect. In essence, the child is asking the court to award damages because he or she has been born defective because of the health care provider's failure to inform the infant's parents of the availability of amniocentesis, thereby precluding them from aborting the fetus based on test results.

A number of courts have rejected this claim outright, reasoning that it is impossible to know whether existence in an impaired state is worse than never having existed at all.[36] California, however, has allowed the child to recover damages for treating the impairment that could have been discovered before birth and would have led the parents to abort the child.[37]

Wrongful life and birth claims thus may also stem from the failure to provide adequate genetic counseling and prenatal testing in light of a mother's positive family history of Down's syndrome.[38] The availability of amniocentesis, ultrasound, and phenylketonuria (PKU) testing makes these claims more viable. Some courts allow the parents to recover for medical expenses, costs of raising the child, and emotional damages.[39]

In *Phillips v. United States*,[40] a navy medical center was held liable for the failure of its staff to provide adequate genetic counseling and prenatal testing in light of the mother's positive family history of Down's syndrome. Liability was also premised on the fact that the staff failed to refer the child to a pediatric cardiologist at the first sign of congestive heart failure.

Failure to Warn of Risks of Refusing Diagnostic Tests. Women patients must be taught about the necessity of routine physical gynecological examinations and yearly Papanicolaou (Pap) smears. Where a patient refuses a particular screening test, such as a Pap smear, extra care must be taken to instruct the patient about the reason for the screening test and the potential consequences of refusing the test. The patient-teaching session should be recorded, and the patient should be asked to sign a waiver that acknowledges the relevant hazards from nontreatment. In *Truman v. Thomas*,[41] the court held that a physician's duty of disclosure included warning a patient of the consequences of refusing a Pap smear. The legal principle would extend to nurses as well.

Prenatal period

Originally, an action for injuries could not be maintained for the wrongful death of a child who did not survive premature birth[42]; however, currently,[43] a wrongful death action may be maintained on behalf of a viable child wrongfully injured in utero. The recent trend is to allow the parents of a stillborn child to recover for the child's wrongful death.[44]

Plaintiffs' attorneys scrutinize the prenatal records of pregnant women suffering from preeclampsia to determine whether prenatal care was appropriate and if pregnancy was appropriately terminated at the optimal time for maternal and neonatal well-being.[45] Early detection and management of mild preeclampsia may well prevent both a late progression to more serious stages and a lawsuit based on negligence.

When preeclampsia progresses to eclampsia, this suggests to plaintiffs' attorneys "questionable care somewhere along the line" because better prenatal care will prevent eclampsia.[46]

Labor and delivery

LIABILITY FOR NEGLIGENCE

Liability for negligence in the labor and delivery period generally centers around the failure to attend to the patient or to monitor the progress of the fetus during labor. Measures should be taken to relieve the discomfort and fear of the woman in labor. Proper monitoring requires periodic observations that should be recorded. Maternal blood pressure and fetal heart tones should be recorded every 15 minutes in the first stage of labor and more frequently in the second stage.[47] The length, duration, and intensity of uterine contractions should be monitored.

Nurses should be familiar with the signs and symptoms indicating a high-risk delivery. A thorough understanding of the risks and indications for agents used to induce labor (primarily oxytocin [Pitocin]) is essential. The American College of Obstetrics and Gynecologists recommends the continuous use of electronic fetal monitoring when labor is induced by intravenous oxytocin.[48]

Where labor is induced by amniotomy, delivery should occur within 24 hours to avoid infection. Nurses should also be observant for the signs and symptoms of prolapse of the cord, another risk from amniotomy.[49]

The following cases, organized around specific allegations of negligence, demonstrate that labor and delivery is an area of practice that is the subject of frequent lawsuits. These allegations have either resulted in settlements or jury verdicts.

Failure to Recognize Symptoms of Labor. The nurse's failure to recognize the signs of labor so that adequate care may be provided may support a charge of negligence. In *Midler v. Harris Hospital-Methodist, Inc.*,[50] a case discussed in Chapter 10, a hospital settled a negligence case because its employee nurse failed to recognize that a woman in her last month of pregnancy, complaining of severe abdominal pain, weakness, dizziness, and disorientation, was in active labor. The woman died from a ruptured uterus.

In *Hogan v. Almond*,[51] the hospital was charged with the negligence of its employee nurse who failed to recognize evidence of labor. The patient, a primipara, was admitted to the hospital with abnormally heavy vaginal bleeding, increased uterine tonus, and fetal bradycardia. She was diagnosed with placental separation.

Throughout the night, the single attending nurse observed the patient to be crying. The nurse examined the patient but did not recognize evidence of labor. At 6:30 AM, the patient, unattended, spontaneously delivered a 7 pound, 5 ounce baby. The diagnosis of partial placental separation was confirmed by examination of the placenta and the lacerations suffered by the patient.

Within 4 or 5 hours, the baby began experiencing severe respiratory distress, and a thick bloody mucus was suctioned from his lungs. The baby died within 29 hours of his birth. At trial, the plaintiff introduced evidence that the baby died from pneumonia caused by the unsterile conditions at birth.[52]

Failure to Monitor Contractions and Fetal Heart Rate. In *Herrup v. South Miami Hospital Foundation, Inc.*,[53] labor and delivery room nurses were charged with negligence in failing to monitor a patient's contractions and fetal heart rate every 30 minutes as required by obstetrical nursing standards and the hospital's written policies. The claim of negligence was also based on the nurses' failure to attach an external monitor, although one was available at all times.

The patient was admitted in early labor. Her obstetrician found a normal fetal heart rate but nevertheless ordered that the patient be attached to an electronic monitoring device. The monitor was never attached, and at the next examination 1½ hours later, the fetal heart tones indicated distress.

In the operating room where an emergency cesarean delivery was to be performed, the fetal heart tones stopped. The mother delivered vaginally; the fetus was stillborn. The mother sued for her own pain and suffering, and a $200,000 settlement was reached.

Improper Management of High-Risk Labor. Attorneys evaluating cases involving fetal distress are advised by expert plaintiffs' attorneys to evaluate utilization of fetal heart monitoring, lateral positioning of the mother, oxytocic stimulation of labor, and scalp pH assessment.[54] If signs of fetal distress are present, and prompt action to effect delivery is not taken, then the likelihood of a lawsuit is great.

The greatest number of reported lawsuits in the high-risk category appear to stem from oxytocin-induced labor. Plaintiffs' attorneys now equate the failure to use electronic fetal heart rate monitoring with negligence.[55] When the electronic recordings are ambiguous or are obscured by something, or a hypotoxic event is suspected but not verifiable through electronic readings, they argue that the scalp pH testing, an absolute indicator of hypoxia, "should be performed whenever the appropriate resources are available."[56]

Plaintiffs' attorneys also argue that sonograms should be utilized to determine if oxytocin use is contraindicated, for example, to detect cephalopelvic disproportion, fetal distress, or fetal malposition and when major bleeding occurs from abruptio placentae or placenta previa.[57] The use of sonograms leaves "no excuse" for a fetus experiencing intrauterine growth retardation.[58] This is because sonograms allow detection, and thus successful treatment (eliminating the specific complicating condition, bed rest for the mother, and a timely delivery that avoids asphyxiation) can occur.

The sonogram also allows diagnosis of the postmature fetus. By repeated sonograms, appropriate measurements denoting gestational time can be made. Consequently, "[given the sonogram's ready availability today, there should be no excuse for an obstetrician's failure to take these measurements, no matter how certain a mother may be of her last menstrual period . . . again the issue is these easily completed diagnostic tests should be performed routinely."[59]

One critique of this position is that the long-term effects of sonograms and other "easily completed diagnostic tests" on the infant are unknown at this time. How persuasive this critique would be as a defense is hard to assess, especially if the plaintiff infant has sustained a serious injury that could have been detected by some existing diagnostic test.

Plaintiffs' attorneys also argue that whenever a potentially compromised birth is detected, the mother and child must be assured complete hospital care, including the presence of a pediatrician at birth. Transfer from a primary or secondary facility to a tertiary facility is "red flag to the lawyer that some error indicative of malpractice has occurred."[60]

In addition, whenever a high-risk mother delivers, preparation for resuscitation of the infant by a pediatrician or neonatologist must be made in advance.[61] Some argue that a "reasonably responsible standard of medical malpractice should not permit a nurse to perform a job, in a predictable emergency situation, that should properly be performed by a specializing physician."[62]

This attitude reflects a misunderstanding of the nurse who practices as a perinatal nurse specialist. The perinatal nurse specialist has advanced educational preparation in perinatal nursing at the master's or doctoral level and is prepared to perform cardiopulmonary resuscitation.[63] The potential liability of this practice area is discussed elsewhere; however, the standards of practice are set forth below (see box).

Stack v. Wapner[64] illustrates the importance of recording observations, fetal heart tones, and maternal vital signs where labor is induced by oxytocin. IV administration of oxytocin began at approximately 2:45 AM. The hospital chart failed to include a notation that the administration of oxytocin was monitored. Entries were made at 5:15 AM and again at 7:05 AM. At 8:00 AM, a notation indicated that the delivery was being attended by the patient's obstetrician. The patient suffered a ruptured uterus after delivery, necessitating an emergency hysterectomy.

The patient sued the physician and the hospital alleging a negligent failure to monitor the administration of oxytocin. The court affirmed the jury verdict, noting that expert testimony established that the woman's injury was caused by the negligent failure to monitor the administration of oxytocin and this was a breach of the standard of care. The court further reasoned that the jury could infer from the absence of entries in the hospital chart that the administration of oxytocin was not monitored.

Nurses were also found negligent in failing to monitor the administration of oxytocin in *Long v. Johnson*.[65] There, the patient was admitted to the hospital for delivery of her thirteenth child. At 4:45 AM, she was admitted to the labor room. At 5:05 AM, the physician performed amniotomy. He instructed the nurse to monitor the contractions and fetal heart tones.

At 7:05 AM, the nurse observed meconium staining and contacted the physician. The physician returned and examined the woman, noting nothing unusual except the meconium staining. He again examined her at 8:05 AM. At 8:20 AM, the nurse began administration of IV drip oxytocin to accelerate labor.

STANDARDS OF THE PERINATAL NURSE SPECIALIST

1. Data collection
   The nurse assesses the childbearing family to identify risk factors, educational needs, care needs, referral needs, and transport needs.
2. Diagnosis
   The nurse uses nursing diagnosis and accepted perinatal classification system diagnoses to express conclusions supported by recorded assessment data and current scientific premises.
3. Planning
   The nurse establishes a plan of care for the childbearing family based on nursing diagnosis that includes specific goals and interventions delineating nursing actions unique to that family's needs.
4. Intervention
   The nurse implements interventions based on the developed plan of nursing care.
   - 4a. Intervention: physiological and interpersonal intervention
     The nurse implements specific physiological and interpersonal therapeutic interventions that promote optimal perinatal health care.
   - 4b. Intervention: patient education and support
     The nurse develops and participates in educational programs to assist clients and families in achieving optimal family development.
   - 4c. Intervention: perinatal transport
     The nurse participates in the organization and implementation of perinatal (maternal and neonatal) transport programs.
5. Evaluation
   The nurse evaluates client and family responses to nursing interventions and evaluates specific programs in order to provide for the revision of the data base, nursing diagnoses, nursing care plans, and program development.
6. Collaboration
   The nurse collaborates with nurses and other professionals in providing care to perinatal families.
7. Education
   The nurse contributes to the educational and professional development of colleagues.
8. Community service
   The nurse promotes standards for perinatal care in the community.
9. Research
   The nurse improves the quality of perinatal nursing through scientific inquiry.
10. Professional development
    The nurse assumes responsibility for personal professional growth.

Adapted from THE AMERICAN NURSES' ASSOCIATION, STANDARDS OF PRACTICE FOR THE PERINATAL NURSE SPECIALIST (1985).

The plaintiff established at trial that the hospital nurses were charged with the duty of monitoring the effects of oxytocin unless the attending physician was present and personally monitoring the patient. Although hospital regulations required the prescribing physician to be in the hospital during administration of oxytocin, there was no requirement that the physician be with the patient.

The patient testified that no one continuously monitored her contractions between 8:20 AM and 10:20 AM at which time the infant was born. The hospital record contained no notation of monitoring. The patient was transferred to the labor room at 9:00 AM, and she was given a saddle block anesthetic.

The physician arrived at 9:40 AM. At this time, the patient began experiencing abdominal pain and developed Bandl's ring. A cesarean delivery was not performed until 10:15 AM. The patient's uterus had already ruptured, and the infant was expelled into the woman's abdomen. The infant suffered hypoxia and developed cerebral palsy.

The jury found in favor of the physician but not the hospital. The trial court nevertheless entered judgment in favor of the hospital. On appeal, the court reinstated the jury's verdict against the hospital and affirmed the jury's verdict in favor of the physician. The court reasoned that the jury reasonably could have concluded the physician was not negligent in administering oxytocin.

The court further determined that the jury could have reasonably concluded that the nurses were negligent in failing to monitor the contractions. The hospital admitted that its nurses were responsible for monitoring unless the physician was present and personally monitoring the patient. Since the physician did little, if any, monitoring, the duty fell to the nurses.

The failure to monitor and to attend a high-risk pregnancy led to a $1.5 million jury verdict for an infant who sustained brain damage during delivery. The parents were awarded $350,000 for the staff's failure to recognize and treat symptoms of prenatal separation of the placenta.[66] The case illustrates the importance of nursing action in the management of high-risk labor.

The patient was admitted to the hospital at 11:30 AM in premature labor. She also complained of severe pain and vaginal bleeding and she had a history of prior cesarean delivery and premature labor. Nevertheless, the patient was in labor 8 hours before being transferred to a labor and delivery unit. From 12:30 PM to 8:00 PM her vital signs were never recorded.

At 8:15 PM, when vital signs were taken manually, the fetal heart tones were found to be within normal range. Morphine for pain caused by moderate vaginal bleeding was administered, but the nurses did not notify any physician of this fact. At 9:00 PM, a fetal monitor was attached that indicated a heart rate of 80. In spite of this reading, the infant was delivered vaginally at 9:27 PM. The infant sustained brain damage.

Another case illustrating inadequate labor nursing care, as well as neonatal nursing care, is *Schager v. Davoli*.[67] There, a $2.2 million settlement was reached for an infant who sustained unexplained brain damage during labor.

In *Schager*, oxytocin was administered during labor and a fetal monitor was attached to the patient. Late decelerations appeared and continued over 5 hours. The hospital records did not contain nurses' notes or physician notes concerning the last 30 minutes of labor. After delivery, the neonate sustained a cardiac arrest and had uncontrolled seizures for 2 hours before being intubated. The suit alleged that the nurses had negligently failed to observe the mother in labor and to chart developing symptoms. The nurses also were charged with negligence in failing to intubate and to properly manage the infant's airway.

A $268,036 jury verdict was obtained for the wrongful death of a fetus before delivery in *Patel v. South Fulton Hospital*.[68] In *Patel*, the mother came to the hospital as a high-risk patient with ruptured membranes. Five and one-half hours passed before the hospital staff checked the fetal heart tones and discovered they were absent. The nurses were charged with negligence in failing to continuously monitor a high-risk patient.

In New York, a $10.9 million jury verdict was awarded to an infant who sustained anoxic brain injury during delivery. The case, *Capaccio v. Newman*,[69] charged violations of a hospital rule requiring discontinuation of oxytocin administration in the absence of the obstetrician in charge of monitoring labor. The unmonitored oxytocin administration, the suit alleged, caused an unusually rapid dilation and labor resulting in strong, long, and frequent contractions, poor uterine-placental blood flow, and fetal hypoxia.

The mother was admitted to the hospital 2 weeks after her due date. The obstetrician ordered IV drip oxytocin and it was continued without the presence of a physician. Although external fetal monitoring tracings were obtained, the nurses never notified the obstetrician of readings showing fetal tachycardia. The monitor was discontinued about 1½ hours before delivery.

In the labor room, the mother passed meconium, but the nurses failed to advise the physician of this fact, and the oxytocin was not discontinued. The nurses failed to record the rapid progression of labor or to notify the physician of this fact. The nurses also failed to discontinue the oxytocin, in violation of the hospital policy, because the obstetrician was absent. This fact was aggravated by the presence of meconium staining, which the nurses should have known indicated fetal distress.

In *Trevino v. United States*,[70] a $6.33 million bench verdict was awarded to an infant who sustained brain damage during a high-risk delivery. The mother was admitted to the Madigan Army Medical Center in labor and bleeding. After several hours of walking at the staff's instructions, she was diagnosed with marginal separation of the placenta. The mother was instructed to continue walking.

One and one-half hours later, while still bleeding profusely, the labor room nurse administered an enema to speed the expulsion of water. For the next hour, the nurses failed to continuously monitor the fetal heart rate and the physician failed to order bed rest.

When the patient was in the delivery room, a fetal reading was obtained electronically that revealed bradycardia. Although the mother was not fully dilated, a vacuum extraction delivery was unsuccessfully attempted. Thereafter a forceps delivery was performed from the mid-station. The infant suffered cerebral palsy, motor, speech, and developmental delays, a convulsive disorder, and mental retardation.

The lawsuit charged, among other things, failure to recognize and diagnose abruptio placentae, negligence in instructing the mother to walk for hours in spite of vaginal bleeding, and failure to monitor fetal heart rate. In addition, the negligence claim was based on the vacuum extraction and the forceps delivery.

Inability to Read Fetal Monitor. In *Dobrzeniecki v. University Hospital of Cleveland*,[71] a $2.2 million settlement was reached in a case charging failure to respond to fetal distress. There, a high-risk obstetrical patient with prior admission for preeclampsia went into labor at 36 weeks and was admitted to the defendant hospital. Two hours later, a monitor indicated fetal distress, but this was unrecognized by the labor room nurse and never reported to the obstetrician. Four hours later, the child was delivered by cesarean delivery in an asphyxiated state, necessitating intensive resuscitation efforts. The child was profoundly retarded and totally blinded and needed custodial care.

In *Olsen v. Humana, Inc.*,[72] a Kansas jury awarded $15 million, including $8.8 million in punitive damages, against a hospital corporation and an obstetrician following the birth of an infant who sustained severe brain damage as a result of the defendants' failure to respond adequately to fetal distress. The bulk of the punitive damages award was allocated against the hospital's parent corporation, which failed to hire a competent and well-trained nursing staff.

In *Olsen*, the nurse who attended the mother during labor was not trained to read the electronic fetal heart monitoring system. Consequently, she failed to detect the infant's distressed fetal heart rate. The physician who delivered the infant failed to properly resuscitate the infant because he lacked adequate training in resuscitation of neonates.

Nevertheless, the physician was found only 20% negligent. The hospital corporation employing the nurse was found 70% negligent. The plaintiff argued to the jury that the hospital was liable for the nurse's negligence under the theory of respondeat superior, and for its own flagrant misconduct in failing to provide adequately trained staff.

While the plaintiff's counsel did not seek damages independently from the nurse in this case, nurses should be aware that independent liability for negligence exists and that the employer hospital has the right to seek indemnification from its employee nurses even though the nurse has not been individually served and named in the underlying lawsuit. Consequently, the fact that the plaintiff's counsel has looked to the hospital as the "deep pocket" for damages does not render the nurse immune from liability for his or her own negligence.

Abandonment. Abandonment has been defined as the unilateral severance of the professional relationship with the patient without adequate notice and while the necessity for attentions still exists.[73] Failure to attend to the patient in labor is a form of abandonment. In *Hiatt v. Groce*[74] the nurse's failure to notify a physician that delivery was imminent caused the patient's delivery to be unattended by a physician. The woman sustained lacerations that resulted in a loss of sensation in the vagina and labia.

The mother and father of the patient testified that they repeatedly called the nurse and reported their observations of pain and severe contractions. The patient's husband testified that he told the nurse of the patient's complaints of increased pain. He also told the nurses that during the patient's first labor, delivery progressed rapidly after the patient was dilated 8 cm. The nurse told him not to worry and kept reading a magazine. Shortly thereafter, the nurse checked on the patient and told her she was 8 cm dilated. The husband repeatedly requested that the nurse notify the physician, but she refused to do so.

The obstetrician testified that he expected the nurse to take into consideration various factors and to exercise independent judgment as to notifying him about the impending delivery. Expert witness testimony by an obstetrical nursing instructor established that the nurse's care fell below the standard of care of the nursing profession in the nurse's community. The evidence also showed that the hospital records had been altered to show that the physician delivered the patient's baby when in fact the nurse did so.

In *Samii v. Baystate Medical Center, Inc.*, labor and delivery room nurses were found negligent in allowing a patient to remain unattended without an examination by a physician. The patient, already in labor, had entered the hospital, and a normal delivery was anticipated. The head of the fetus, however, was not engaged at this time.

After almost 7 hours of labor, the patient's dilation had not progressed, and her contractions intensified in severity and duration. She was in great discomfort and was vomiting. The fetal heart beat was difficult to detect, and it was fluctuating.

A fetal monitor was available, but the labor room nurse was not educated in its use. The resident on duty, however, did know how to use the monitor. When the nurses could not detect a fetal heart beat they called the resident. Thereafter, the resident examined the patient and found indications of fetal distress and possible asphyxiation. He performed an emergency cesarean delivery before the administered anesthetic took effect on the patient, but the baby was born stillborn.

A very disturbing fact pattern is presented by *Daniels v. Brown*, which illustrates the potential liability for nursing abandonment and following improper orders.[75] There, a $250,000 settlement was reached where a newborn was left abandoned and died. The drug-impaired obstetrician first told the newborn's parents that their child was dead; subsequently he told them the newborn was alive, and finally he told them the child was dead.

The neonate was born premature, weighing 1 pound, 4 ounces. The defendant obstetrician concluded the child could be abandoned without care and told the parents the child had died. The chief obstetrical registered nurse placed the infant in the labor room, and then in an office armchair, and called the Director of Nursing. The Director of Nursing contacted the Chief of Staff who gave no instructions.

Thereafter, the Director of Nursing received permission from the defendant obstetrician to move the child to the nursery. The child was there 10 hours but received no fluids or oxygen administration. No vital signs were recorded. When the Director of Nursing learned that the child lived through this period, she contacted the neonatal unit, but there were no available beds. Fourteen hours after birth, the neonate died.

The professional corporation who employed the physician was sued for allowing the obstetrician to practice although he was drug impaired. The hospital was sued for the acts of the Chief of Obstetrical Nursing, the Director of Nursing, and the Chief of Staff in failing to secure help for the infant. The hospital was also charged with the negligence of the labor and delivery room and the nursery room nurses who followed improper orders.

May v. William Beaumont Hospital,[76] also illustrates a disturbing fact pattern. There, a $10.5 million jury verdict was obtained for a mother and an infant who were virtually left unattended.

The mother, a non-English-speaking immigrant, was admitted to the hospital complaining, through an interpreter, of great pain. The nurses and attending physician did not believe the pains were labor pains; they planned to induce the labor with oxytocin. They did not place her in a bed and virtually ignored her throughout her labor. The nurses failed to implement orders for fetal monitoring and IV therapy.

The mother delivered her infant while standing next to a bed. The infant fell headfirst and slid across the floor, sustaining a depressed right parietal skull fracture and trauma. The child was left mentally retarded.

Failure to Exercise Independent Judgment. Recently, nurses are being sued for failure to exercise independent judgment in carrying out orders that they know or should know are inappropriate. For example, in *James v. Kennebec Valley Medical Center of Maine*,[77] a $700,000 structured settlement was reached in a lawsuit charging the nurses with negligence in carrying out orders that they should have known were inappropriate. The neonate suffered hypoxic brain damage during an oxytocin-induced labor.

An external fetal monitor was placed on the patient when the oxytocin was first administered. Data from the monitor, however, were unreadable. The plaintiff's obstetrician continued the induction of labor with oxytocin, monitoring the fetal heart rate by stethescope every 15 minutes. Five and one-half hours after inducement, the infant spontaneously delivered, covered with a thick meconium. The neonate suffered meconium aspiration and seizures secondary to perinatal hypoxia. The subsequent diagnosis was cerebral palsy, mental retardation, and microcephaly.

The lawsuit charged that the obstetrician negligently induced labor by IV oxytocin without use of an infusion pump. The complaint also alleged that the physician allowed the administration of oxytocin to begin without adequate continuing electronic monitoring and that he failed to institute internal monitoring when external tracings were uninterpretable. The labor and delivery nurses were charged with negligence in carrying out orders that they should have known were inappropriate.

The report of the settlement does not make clear whether an internal monitoring system was available on the labor and delivery room unit. The fact that the hospital did not have such equipment could provide the nurses with a basis on which to counterclaim against the hospital. Conversely, if the nurses were sued in their capacity as employees of the hospital under the respondeat superior theory of liability—that is, if the hospital rather than the nurse is the entity from whom damages are sought—lack of equipment could be a defense to a later indemnification suit by the hospital.

The possibility of a successful counterclaim for indemnification against the hospital, however, should not lure the nurse into a false sense of security. Nursing texts in maternal and child health nursing note that the nurse "must be familiar with . . . techniques of intermittent evaluation [other than electronic fetal heart monitoring]."[78] Consequently, the mere fact that electronic monitoring equipment is not available to the nurse may not establish the hospital's primary negligence.

Inadequate Suctioning of Neonate. In *Sanders v. Sisters of Mercy*[79] a $247,500 settlement was reached for the wrongful death of a 4-day-old infant. During birth, the infant suffered fetal distress resulting in perinatal aspiration of meconium. Nasopharyngeal suctioning was initially performed by the obstetrician. The infant was subsequently transferred to the labor and delivery room nurse for further suctioning. The nurse, however, failed to remove all of the meconium from the lower airway; no deep suctioning was ever done.

One hour after delivery, a neonatologist was contacted who ordered tests but gave no instructions. Tests results were never obtained, and treatment was not initiated. Twelve hours later, the infant was transferred to a neonatal intensive care unit at another hospital where he died.

LIABILITY FOR LACK OF INFORMED CONSENT

In *Cambell v. Pitt County Memorial Hospital*,[80] a $6.5 million jury verdict was reached in a case brought against a hospital for its employee nurses' negligence in failing to ensure that the parents had given their informed consent to a vaginal delivery under circumstances that indicated the necessity for a cesarean delivery. The hospital was also sued for its own negligence in failing to establish a mechanism for ensuring that patients in labor have given informed consent to the method of delivery and for ensuring prompt reporting of anything that threatens the life of a patient.[81]

The plaintiff's mother was admitted to the hospital in active labor. Her vital signs and the fetal heart rate were normal. Pelvic x-ray films revealed that the fetus was in a double footing breech position. An external fetal monitor showed a 2-hour baseline of 170 to 180, with repetitive and progressively more severe variable decelerations. The nurses contacted the attending physician, but he elected not to perform a cesarean delivery, even though fetascope readings indicated worsening bradycardia.

Approximately 6 hours after admission, the infant delivered vaginally by total breech extraction, with the umbilical cord wrapped tightly around her legs. Apgar scores were 1 at 1 minute and 2 at 5 minutes. The plaintiff, now 6 years old, suffers from cerebral palsy, mild retardation, and severe speech impairment. Gross and fine motor abilities are below those normal for a 1-year-old child.

At trial, it was successfully argued that since vaginal delivery presents a grave risk to an infant in the footling breech presentation, the parents should have been informed of the relative risks of vaginal vs. cesarean delivery. What actually happened is that 1½ hours after delivery, the nurse obtained the father's signature on a hospital consent form.

LIABILITY FOR INTENTIONAL TORTS

In the labor and delivery setting, as well as the postpartum setting discussed below, the typical intentional torts claimed are assault and battery. The battery actions generally involve a lack of consent to some procedure or medication such as hysterectomy or tubal ligation, physical examination, or the administration of drugs used to induce labor or to prevent miscarriage.

Battery

Failure to Obtain Consent to a Procedure. In *Davidson v. Shirley*,[82] a registered nurse was admitted for a caesarean delivery of her second child. Before her admission, she had discussed and requested a tubal ligation for the purpose of rendering her sterile.

On admission, the plaintiff signed a consent form authorizing the cesarean delivery, tubal ligation, and other operations or procedures deemed therapeutically necessary on the basis of findings during the course of the operation. At a deposition, the plaintiff testified she read and understood this language.

Following the surgery and birth of a healthy but large child, the plaintiff's uterus contracted at a slower than normal rate and she was losing blood. Nevertheless, her condition was stable, and the physicians removed a tumor the size of a grapefruit. This necessitated the severance of additional blood vessels, which caused more blood loss. IV oxytocin was unsuccessful, and the physicians, fearing a loss of life, removed her uterus.

The issue, as the appellate court viewed it, was whether the hysterectomy was therapeutically necessary since the plaintiff consented to any procedure deemed therapeutically necessary. The plaintiff admitted in her deposition that the removal of the tumor was therapeutically necessary and that she would have consented to the procedure because it was a hazard to her health. The plaintiff's expert also agreed that a hysterectomy was necessary to halt the flow of blood. Under these circumstances, the court ruled that there was no issue of fact for the jury to decide; the procedure was therapeutically necessary and the plaintiff consented to any therapeutically necessary procedure.

Failure to Obtain Consent to a Physical Examination. Nurses working in the postpartum and labor and delivery room areas are advised to obtain a patient's consent before conducting any physical examination. While the following case may present a factually extreme application of the principle, patients have a legal right to be free from unconsented touchings and this right is protected by the remedy of battery.

In *Inderbitzen v. Lane Hospital*,[83] the California Appellate Court held that a woman could proceed with a lawsuit charging assault and battery where, on admission for delivery of a child, she was repeatedly examined several times each day by at least 10 to 12 men who rolled her around in her bed and poked her over her protest. The patient testified that whenever she protested, the men would laugh and tell her to shut up.

The evidence showed that when the plaintiff was admitted for delivery of her child, she was examined by someone she presumed to be a medical student. She demanded to be examined by a physician. Thereafter, an older man entered the examining room and subjected her to vaginal and rectal examination without washing his hands. The younger man whom she believed to be a student again examined her without washing his hands.

The plaintiff was then brought to the delivery room, "where she was examined intimately two or three times by at least ten or twelve young men whom she took to be students."[84] When she screamed and protested, these men merely laughed. They repeatedly poked and prodded her. A physician who treated her several months later testified that the patient's uterus had a tear that was infected and profusely discharging.

In upholding the plaintiff's judgment, the court noted that the hospital could be liable "to a patient who had paid it for medical attention if it permitted unlicensed students to experiment upon her and treat her without her consent."[85] The hospital asked the court to rule that the treatment was necessary and proper because their plaintiff failed to prove it was improper by way of medical testimony.

The court refused to so hold, noting that "common sense will tell any reasonable person that such treatment at the hands of so many is unnecessary and improper" and that scientific evidence is not essential to prove an obvious fact.[86] The physician or medical student, the court further held, "has no more right to needlessly and rudely lay hands upon a patient against her will than has a layman."[87]

Failure to Obtain Consent to Administration of Drugs. In *Kohoutek v. Hafner*,[88] the court determined that the failure to obtain consent to induction of labor by drugs could constitute a battery. The court rejected the hospital's argument that injection of a hormone to induce or to augment labor could not be a battery because vaginal delivery is the natural outcome of pregnancy.

The plaintiff, expecting her first child, was advised that she should be admitted to the hospital for induction of labor with oxytocin because her baby was large. She did so, but the attempt was unsuccessful, and she was sent home.

About 5 days later, her physician advised her that she should return 2 days later to the hospital for a cesarean delivery by another physician. The plaintiff agreed and signed a consent form for the procedure. The physician who was to perform the surgery was notified.

On admission, the admitting nurse notified another physician for a second opinion about the cesarean delivery. Hospital policy required this procedure with respect to first-time mothers. This physician thought that rupture of the membrane had occurred and that therefore induction of labor by oxytocin was warranted. Because the attending physician could not be reached, another physician from the attending's clinic was contacted and agreed with the induction.

The physician who administered the oxytocin admitted she never discussed the specific risks of vaginal delivery with the patient. Three witnesses—the physician, the patient, and the admitting nurse—testified the patient did not want to have a vaginal delivery. The nurse and the physician, however, asserted this was because the patient's insurance covered cesarean delivery.

The admitting nurse's notes acknowledged that the patient was confused about being induced. The hospital consent form did not specifically cover the oxytocin injection.

The patient objected to the administration of the drug, but she did not refuse it. The patient's attending physician admitted he was displeased when he arrived at the hospital and found that the induction was occurring, but he did not change the treatment course. The administration continued to the following morning. Due to shoulder dystocia, the delivery was difficult. Upon delivery, the baby was blue and the Apgar score was 0 at 14 minutes. Attempts at resuscitation did not prevent brain damage.

With respect to the issue of consent to the administration of oxytocin, the court noted that the three witnesses present when the drug was administered testified that the patient objected, or at least was confused about, the change in treatment from cesarean delivery to induced natural delivery, and that she objected to the injection of oxytocin. Consequently, the plaintiff was entitled to have her case heard by a jury to resolve the factual issue dispute, and the trial court erred in refusing to submit the issue to the jury.

The hospital, however, was absolved from liability because the nurses acted under orders of physicians who were not employees of the hospital. The court noted that although hospitals may be liable for the intentional torts of nurses committed within the scope of their employment, where a physician takes over the direction and control of a nurse's work, the physician becomes liable under the borrowed servant doctrine. Because the nurses administered the injection under the physician's orders, the hospital was relieved from liability.

LIABILITY FOR CIVIL RIGHTS ACTIONS

Sterilization is perhaps the most frequent subject of civil rights actions in the maternal and child health care area. Sterilizations have been performed following deliveries that raise questions about adequate and informed consent[89]; however, questionable practices have also been implicated during other periods of the childbearing continuum.

The issue involved is generally whether the now sterilized person consented to the procedure. If he or she did, additional issues of voluntariness and informed consent may be implicated.[90] Sterilizations of "incompetents" or mentally retarded persons also raise these concerns.[91]

The U.S. Supreme Court has recognized that procreation is fundamental among the basic civil rights and thus protected by the Constitution.[92] The right to be free from governmental intrusion in the childbearing decision-making process was recognized in *Roe v. Wade*,[93] where the court held that the fundamental right to privacy encompassed the decision to seek an abortion in the first trimester.[94]

In *Walker v. Pierce*,[95] the Fourth Circuit Court of Appeals considered and rejected a civil rights claim filed against an obstetrician who required consent to sterilization as a condition of providing obstetrical services to women receiving federal or state aid who were pregnant with their third, fourth, or fifth child. The plaintiffs were two black women, and they alleged that Dr. Pierce sterilized them, or threatened to do so, solely on account of their race and number of children.

One of the plaintiffs refused sterilization after delivery of her third child. On notice of the refusal, the physician discharged the woman from the hospital. The other plaintiff, while pregnant with her fourth child, was threatened by the physician with termination of welfare assistance and medical care if she did not consent to sterilization. One witness who had sought medical service from the physician testified that she was introduced to him as follows:

> He came in and he hadn't examined me or anything. I was laying on the table. And, he said, "Listen here young lady." He said, "This is my tax money paying for something like this." He said, "I am tired of people going around here having babies and my tax money paying for it." He said, "So if you don't want this done [i.e., the sterilization], go and find yourself another doctor."[96]

Unfortunately, as one commentator pointed out, Dr. Pierce was the only obstetrician in the county.[97]

Nevertheless, the court of appeals rejected the civil rights claim, reasoning that the physician was not acting under color of state or governmental law. The court stated:

> We perceive no reason why Dr. Pierce could not establish and pursue the policy. . . . Nor are we cited to judicial precedent or statute inhibiting this personal economic philosophy. Particularly is this so when all persons coming to him as patients are reasonably made aware of his *professional* attitude toward the increase in offspring and his determination to see it prevail. At no time is he shown to have forced his view upon any mother.[98]

The majority of the court found there was no state action, and therefore no valid civil rights claim, even though during a 1½-year period, the physician had been reimbursed $60,000 by the federal government for sterilizations and at least 16 of these were performed on black women. The dissenting justice, however, viewed the physician's policy of sterilization for economic reasons as establishing the requisite state action.

The dissenting justice reasoned that the physician's activity consisted of granting or denying medicaid benefits for fiscal reasons unrelated to health. Since under the medicaid program the state is responsible for determining who is entitled to federal benefits, the physician assumed a state function because the state allowed physicians to accept or reject any medicaid patient seeking their services. Consequently, the state delegated its function of determining eligibility to the medicaid program to its physicians who informed the state of eligibility when a bill was presented.

Under this view, the physician's role as a physician was isolated from his role as a participant in the administrative and fiscal aspects of the medicaid program. The dissent concluded that the physician assumed a state administrative function by conditioning medical benefits on requirements not related to health while publicly representing himself as a qualified medicaid practitioner. The dissent also noted that the physician was free not to treat any medicaid patients at all but chose to do so and was paid by the federal government.[99]

Postpartum period

The first 2 hours of the postpartum period require nurses to pay special attention to the mother to observe for signs and symptoms of shock and excessive bleeding. Thereafter, the nurse's observations center on the appearance of the perineum, the nature of the vaginal discharge, and the consistency and location of the fundus.

LIABILITY FOR NEGLIGENCE

Failure To Attend/Abandonment. In the postpartum setting, liability may be premised on injuries to sedated patients who are not properly attended by nurses. For example, in *Vick v. Methodist Evangelical Hospital, Inc.*,[100] the court held that a jury had to resolve the question of whether the hospital was negligent for failing to properly attend to a sedated postpartum patient. The court noted that the sedatives that had been administered to the patient were of sufficient amount to support a finding that the patient was not alert and oriented and therefore required greater assistance than she was in fact given.

Failure to Recognize Retained Placenta, Infection, and Hemorrhage. *Rizzo v. Nassau Community Medical Center*[101] illustrates the potential for liability in the postpartum setting. Although the case concerns the liability of a hospital for the negligence of a physician in allowing a portion of the placenta to remain in the uterus following delivery, the principles of negligence—failure to recognize infection and hemorrhage—would be equally applicable to nurses working in the postpartum setting.

Following the birth of her child, the plaintiff remained in the hospital for 5 days because of complaints of nausea, weakness, fever, and excessive vaginal bleeding. The physician never instituted treatment or performed a vaginal examination. The patient was discharged with very low hematocrit and hemoglobin levels.

A few hours later, the plaintiff returned to the hospital in a worsened condition, requiring a transfusion of 3 pints of blood. She was discharged 3 days later but was again readmitted with the same complaints and a 104° F fever. Four days later, the plaintiff was admitted to another hospital with complaints of severe hemorrhaging, fever, weakness, and uterine tenderness. A dilation and curettage was performed. No further treatment was undertaken for 1 month, when she began to hemorrhage large clots of blood. Treatment required a total abdominal hysterectomy.

Neonatal period

Nurses practicing in the newborn nursery must be alert to admissions from high-risk deliveries. Plaintiffs' attorneys view continuous nursing care as critical for the newborn who has undergone fetal distress or whose mother had been evaluated as a high perinatal risk because seizures frequently occur after a successful delivery.[102]

Nurses should be alert for signs of transient episodes such as a minor tremor of the extremities, eye rolling, or staring, which indicate seizures. Continued seizures may cause or exacerbate brain damage, particularly if the neonate has already suffered from an anoxic event. Transfer to a neonatal intensive care unit may be warranted.

Plaintiffs' attorneys "as a matter of course" investigate all records to determine the degree and quality of postnatal nursing care accorded if a high-risk infant who has been delivered successfully nonetheless suffers from hypoxia-related damage.[103] This is because "[i]t is not unusual for a nurse to record symptomatology that defines infant seizure, *yet fail to take corresponding action be-*

cause specific instructions pertaining to such symptoms had not been noted on the newborn's chart.''[104]

This is a sad commentary on nursing practice that reflects the exception rather than the rule. Nevertheless, the moral must be heeded: nurses need to be aware that they have a duty to act, even in the absence of a specific order; the courts will not recognize the lack of a physician's order as a defense to negligence where nursing action could have prevented the harm.

LIABILITY FOR NEGLIGENCE

Failure to Observe Increased Head Circumference and Signs of Intracranial Bleeding. In *Harris v. Skrocki*,[105] a hospital reached a $1.86 million settlement in a lawsuit brought for the negligence of its nurses and residents which resulted in brain damage to an infant as the result of a contraindicated forceps delivery. The plaintiff's mother had previously delivered a child who suffered from hemophilia. In spite of this family history, forceps were used during delivery.

Although an initial physical examination of the infant revealed a bulging fontanelle indicative of intracranial hemorrhage, no treatment was undertaken until 3 days later when the infant was discovered convulsing. After a spinal tap, the infant was diagnosed with perinatal intracranial hemorrhage. He was left mentally retarded, partially blind, deaf in the right ear, and suffering from intermittent seizures.

The nurses, residents, and pediatrician were charged with negligence in failing to observe the increased head circumference and failing to recognize and treat the signs and symptoms of intracranial bleeding. The obstetrician was charged with negligence in performing a forceps delivery.

Failure to Monitor Equipment. Failure to monitor the equipment utilized in labor and delivery and the newborn nursery frequently leads to injury and liability. *Register v. A & A Ambulance Service, Inc.*,[106] a case involving ambulance attendants, has application to the newborn nursery.

In *Register*, a thriving premature infant was transferred out of the neonatal intensive care unit at the University of Alabama after significant progress and was transported to his hometown. The Isolette in which he was transported overheated, and he sustained hyperthermic injuries to his colon. Readmittance to the neonatal intensive care unit at the University of Alabama was necessary. Ultimately, the infant recovered, but only after prolonged treatment, including a colostomy and reclosure. The plaintiff successfully claimed that the ambulance attendants were negligent in their failure to monitor the child properly and that the Isolette was not thermostatically controlled.[107]

Jones v. Samaritan Health Service[108] illustrates nursing negligence failing to monitor an infusion pump. There, a $4 million settlement was reached for a neonate who suffered fluid overload and respiratory arrest, resulting in severe brain damage.[109]

The delivery was induced and the infant was delivered with an Apgar score of 8 at 1 minute and 9 at 5 minutes. The infant was resuscitated and transferred to the newborn nursery where she received dextrose and water by a volumetric infusion pump. Because of fluid overload, the infant again suffered a respiratory arrest. The suit alleged alternate theories of liability, including malfunction of the pump (manufacturer's negligence), a nurse's mishandling of the pump, and/or incorrect concentrations prescribed by the pediatrician.

Failure to Provide Intensive Care Services. In *Clark v. University of Washington*,[110] a $125,000 settlement was reached for the wrongful death of a premature infant. The neonate delivered at 30 weeks and suffered respiratory difficulties, including major spells of apnea after the first 4 days of life that went largely untreated. The neonate was left brain damaged and eventually died.

The hospital was sued for the negligence of its nurses in failing to switch on the respirator and failing to provide intensive care services to the neonate. The lawsuit also charged that the nurses were improperly trained and supervised and that they failed to medically manage the neonate or respond to his periods of apnea. The hospital admitted the nursing negligence but claimed as a defense that the preexisting brain lesion caused the death.

Failure to Monitor Oxygen Levels. In *Willis v. El Camino Hospital*,[111] a settlement with a $4.35 million value was reached in a lawsuit charging nurses with negligence in the administration of oxygen to twins born 9 weeks premature. The twins sustained total blindness because of retrolental fibroplasia and suffered developmental and educational delays as a result of the blindness.

The lawsuit charged the pediatrician with failure to monitor blood gases during the last 9 days of oxygen administration and failure to respond appropriately to abnormally high blood gases as reflected in the levels obtained during the first 7 days of oxygen administration.

The hospital was sued for the negligence of its employee nurses in failing to adhere to protocols for monitoring oxygen levels, failing to advise the pediatrician that excessive levels of oxygen were being administered, and failing to independently reduce the amount of oxygen administered.

In *Williams v. St. Joseph's Hospital*,[112] a $2.5 million jury verdict was awarded to an infant plaintiff who suffered retrolental fibroplasia because of continuous oxygen therapy. The mother had a difficult pregnancy and, at delivery, a diagnosis of placenta previa was made. The infant delivered prematurely at 29 weeks and was transferred to the newborn nursery. There, he received oxygen therapy for 38 days, followed by 10 additional nights of further therapy. *No blood gases were drawn to determine oxygen blood levels.*

At 5 months, the infant developed retrolental fibroplasia. On reaching 5 years, glaucoma in his right eye caused continuous pain, necessitating its removal. The vision in the child's remaining eye was also impaired.

The physician was charged with negligence in failing to reduce the percentage of oxygen content to wean the plaintiff from therapy to determine oxygen levels in the blood. The hospital newborn nursery staff caring for the infant was claimed to be negligent in continuing oxygen administration without any clinical signs or symptoms justifying its use.

Failure to Recognize and to Report Jaundice. In *Butts v. Cummings*,[113] nurses were charged with negligence in failing to recognize and to report signs and symptoms of jaundice to the treating pediatrician. Five days after a normal birth, the infant was found to have bilirubin levels of over 34 mg/100 ml. Hyperbilirubinemia is considered to be pathological if the serum bilirubin exceeds 12 mg/100 ml or if obvious jaundice appears in the first 24 hours.[114]

At trial, the plaintiff's evidence showed that jaundice is clinically observable at levels in excess of 10 mg/100 ml. The evidence also established that it would take a number of hours for bilirubin levels to increase from 10 mg/100 ml to 34 mg/100 ml and that the probability of brain damage markedly increases as bilirubin levels increase. The case settled for $2.3 million.

Pediatric period

LIABILITY FOR NEGLIGENCE

Negligence in hospital-based pediatric nursing practice raises issues common to other areas of hospital-based nursing practice: abandonment; medication errors; and failure to monitor and to maintain equipment. The potential for disaster from these and other seemingly less significant errors is greater in the pediatric setting than in the adult setting.

In some instances, the same nursing error that would not result in any damage to an adult will be life threatening to an infant or child. Consequently, the nurses working in this field must have a thorough understanding of the ramifications of their action, or inaction, on the pediatric patient.

Errors in Medication. In *Norton v. Argonaut Insurance Co.*,[115] a nurse was deemed negligent in failing to determine with absolute certainty the intended dose and route of administration of prescribed pediatric medication. As a result of the medication error, the 3-month-old infant sustained an overdose of digitalis and died.

The infant had been admitted to the pediatric unit for evaluation and treatment before surgery for a congenital defect. The pediatrician's order prescribed a 2.5 ml pediatric elixir of digoxin (Lanoxin) (0.125 mg) every 6 hours for three doses and thereafter a single dose daily of 0.251 mg. The infant weighed 11 pounds. The physician instructed the infant's primary nurse in the use of the elixir, and the medication was administered as prescribed. The child was discharged to await surgery on readmission.

On readmission, the physician's order prescribed a single dose of 3.0 ml digoxin for only that day. A nursing supervisor who had not previously taken care of the child administered the *injectable* form of the drug. Unfortunately, the nurse was not aware that digoxin was prepared in an elixir form for pediatric patients. The nursing supervisor did contact two other physicians to question them about the order; however, they both told her that she should administer whatever the prescribing physician ordered.

At trial, the supervising nurse defended against the charge of negligence on the grounds that nothing in the chart indicated that the drug should have been orally administered. The prescribing physician, who was also named as a defendant, claimed that the supervising nurse was grossly negligent in carrying out the order and that this negligence was an independent and intervening cause of the infant's death. Consequently, he argued, the nurse's negligence superseded any negligence on his part in prescribing the medication and she, rather than he, should be liable for the infant's death.

The court rejected this argument, reasoning that the nurse's action was a forseeable result of the physician's unclear order and therefore would not absolve the physician from liability. In resolving the issue of the nurse's negligence, the court concluded that the nurse should contact the attending physician whenever there is doubt as to the correctness of a medication order. A nurse expert witness had testified at trial that if a nurse is in doubt as to the appropriateness of an order, the nurse should contact the attending physician.[116]

Failure to Detect Signs and Symptoms of Dehydration and Electrolyte Imbalance. In *Doerr v. Hurley*,[117] a hospital was sued for the negligence of its residents and nurses in administering an enema to a 7-month-old infant. The wrongful death lawsuit alleged a failure to recognize the signs and symptoms of dehydration and electrolyte imbalance.

The child was admitted to the hospital to determine the etiology and treatment for failure to thrive and chronic constipation. X-ray examination indicated that the child suffered from megacolon, and the child vomited on several occasions.

On the day of discharge, a Fleet's enema was ordered and administered for constipation. For 4 hours thereafter, the child exhibited signs and symptoms of dehydration and electrolyte imbalance—lethargy, paleness, flaccidity of extremities, loss of muscle tone, and sunken eyes. The child subsequently died of respiratory arrest.

At trial, the plaintiff presented evidence that the *Physician's Desk Reference* indicated that Fleet's enema is contraindicated in cases of megacolon with vomiting. Moreover, there was no dosage schedule provided for children under 2 years. Consequently, the nurses erred in administering the enema and the jury awarded $500,000.

Failure to Protect from Burns. *Kozemczak v. St. Louis Children's Hospital*[118] illustrates the caution that nurses practicing in the pediatric field must take in utilizing equipment—even a simple feeding apparatus. There, a $140,000 settlement was reached in a case involving a 3-month-old infant who sustained burns from an overheated bottle.

The infant had been admitted to the hospital for treatment of cystic fibrosis. The defendant nurse placed the infant's bottle into a microwave oven and set the heating control at maximum intensity for 1 minute. The nurse removed the bottle and without testing the contents, placed the bottle into the infant's mouth for 15 minutes while the infant screamed. The infant suffered second-degree burns to the cheek, which left a scar approximately 2 cm × 0.5 cm, and first-degree burns to the tongue and hard palate, which healed.

The hospital was sued for negligent failure to supervise its employees, failure to enforce internal safety regulations, taped to the front of the microwave oven, that prohibited the warming of infant bottles in microwave ovens, failure to require its employees to test the contents of heated bottles, and failure to treat the infant's burns. The nurse was sued independently for negligently heating the bottle in violation of hospital policy and for failure to test the bottle's contents before feeding the infant. Evidence at trial revealed that the nurse was being treated with imipramine hydrochloride (Tofranil) for depression at the time of this incident.

Premature infant transfers in Isolettes from neonatal intensive care units to community hospitals have also resulted in liability for burns.[119]

Abandonment. In *Crowe v. Provost*,[120] an office nurse left a 22-month-old infant baby positioned on her back on an examining table. While the nurse was eating lunch, the child, still positioned on her back, vomited and died.

The court upheld the jury's determination that the nurse's negligence was the cause of the child's death. The court held that the jury could reasonably conclude the nurse was negligent in leaving the child unattended and this negligence caused the infant's death, even though there was testimony that the child died of an overwhelming virus infection.

Improper Restraints. In *Moore v. Halifax Hospital District*,[121] a 6-year-old child was hospitalized for surgery to his eyes. Following surgery, both eyes were patched. To prevent him from touching the dressings, his arms were restrained on boards covered with cloth taped to each arm. Thereafter, the restraints were replaced with smaller boards and more tape.

The nurse testified that she checked the child's circulation in both arms and he had no complaints or difficulties on the evening shift. During the night shift, he began to struggle and to complain about his arm. There was no evidence that the circulation in his arm was checked. The mother, who was present with the child in the room while the child was complaining, asked the nurse to check the restraints. The nurse told her the restraints were not too tight.

After the restraints were removed, a raised, red area in the elbow was visible that was also hot to touch and swollen. A physician expert testified that this injury was caused by the restraints being too tightly secured or by the child's struggle against the restraints. The court determined that an issue of fact existed for the jury to decide as to whether the nurse acted within the proper standard of care to be exercised when dealing with a sedated child.

Failure To Report Child Abuse. Failure to report child abuse on the part of a nurse may lead to criminal and civil liability. Most states, such as California,[122] by statute require health professionals, among others, to report to state agencies instances of *suspected* child abuse. Failure to do so is a misdemeanor and may lead to imprisonment or imposition of a fine.

For example, in California, the Penal Code contains a comprehensive Child Abuse Reporting Statute.[123] The law prohibits sexual exploitation of children,[124] and its reporting requirements carry criminal misdemeanor sanctions for noncompliance. The statute also provides that the person making the report of known or suspected child abuse is immune from civil or criminal liability, unless the person knowingly makes a false report.[125]

Landeros v. Flood,[126] a case concerning a physician's failure to report child abuse that resulted in the application of the presumption of negligence, illustrates the potential civil liability for nurses who fail to report child abuse. There, a minor child sued a physician for failing to report the fact that his parent was abusing him.

The child was severely beaten by her mother and the latter's common-law husband on several occasions. The mother brought the child to a hospital for treatment of a comminuted spiral fracture of the right tibia and fibula, which gave the appearance of being caused by a twisting force. The mother had no explanation for the injury.

The child also had bruises over her entire back and superficial abrasions on other parts of her body. In addition, a healing nondepressed linear fracture of the skull was discovered. The child appeared apprehensive when approached.

Although the child exhibited classic symptoms of the battered child syndrome, the physician never ordered x-ray films, and he never reported the injuries to law enforcement or any social agency. Consequently, the child was released and returned to the custody of her mother who resumed physically abusing her until she sustained traumatic blows to her right eye and back, severe bite wounds, second- and third-degree burns, and puncture wounds over her leg and back. The mother thereafter brought the child to another hospital where the child was diagnosed and removed from the custody of her mother.

The court determined that liability for negligently failing to report the abuse could be remedied by a civil damage award. The court reasoned that the statute created a duty that had been violated and thus a negligence action could be maintained, assuming that the child's injuries were proven to be proximately caused by the failure to comply with the statute. The child's additional injuries at the hands of her abusive mother were reasonably forseeable.

INTENTIONAL TORTS AND CIVIL RIGHTS

Battery and Minor Consent. Generally, a minor cannot give consent to treatment; consent must be obtained by the minor's parent or legal guardian.[127] Failure to obtain consent to a given treatment, except under certain circumstances, leaves the practitioner vulnerable to liability for battery. Consequently, consent is a concern to the nurse practicing pediatric nursing.

There are four generally recognized exceptions to the parental consent requirement. The first exception is a minor who needs emergency treatment. This generally requires that there is a danger to the minor's life necessitating immediate attention.[128]

The second is an emancipated minor, one who is under the age of majority yet is no longer under the care or custody of his or her parent or guardian.[129] Another exception exists where the parents are so far away it would be impracticable to obtain consent.[130] Finally, if the child is close to maturity and knowingly gives informed consent, some courts have held that the mature unemancipated minor can provide effective consent.[131]

Parental consent to first-trimester abortions performed on females under 18 years of age, mandated by state law, has been deemed unconstitutional by the U.S. Supreme Court.[132] The court, however, has upheld statutes that require parental notification before providing contraceptive or abortion services.[133]

Handicapped Newborns. The issue of life-sustaining treatment for severely handicapped infants frequently arises in the context of the neonatal intensive care unit. This issue has received a great deal of attention recently, culminating in administrative regulations issued by the U.S. Department of Health and Human Services (HHS), known as the "Baby Doe" regulations,[134] and a federal child abuse statute.[135]

The Baby Doe regulations were the result of the Reagan administration's interpretation of section 504, Congress' amendment to the Rehabilitation Act of 1973,[136] which prohibits discrimination against the handicapped. The Reagan administration, through the HHS, interpreted this amendment as prohibiting the withholding of medical treatment from children, no matter how imminent the death of the infant. Thus, extremes were reached; infants with a 2- to 12-day life expectancy were aggressively treated and transported by air to special intensive care units even though death was certain to occur.[137]

Two cases began the department's crusade. Baby Doe was born in Bloomington, Indiana in April of 1982 with Down's syndrome and an intestinal blockage that precluded normal feeding. His parents refused to consent to corrective surgery and asked that food and water be withheld.[138] The hospital sought court intervention, but the state court refused on the grounds that the parents had made a reasonable decision. Baby Doe died after 6 days, and the U.S. Supreme Court refused to hear the case.[139]

Baby Jane Doe was born in October of 1983 in a

New York hospital. She suffered from multiple birth defects including spina bifida, microcephaly, and hydrocephalus. Although surgery would prolong her life, nothing could be done about many of her handicaps. Her parents decided to forgo risky surgery and chose a conservative course of treatment that included antibiotics, good nutrition, and dressing changes of the exposed spinal sac.

A Vermont lawyer, who was not a relative, instituted a lawsuit seeking to become the baby's guardian. The New York Supreme Court Trial Division ordered the University Hospital to conduct the surgery, but the following day the Appellate Division of the same court reversed the trial court.[140]

The following day, HHS demanded Baby Jane Doe's hospital records to investigate an anonymous report that the baby was being denied proper medical treatment. Following the hospital's refusal, HHS sued and lost.

On appeal to the Second Circuit Federal Court of Appeals, a majority of the court[141] rejected the Reagan administration's view of section 504 and its authority to conduct this kind of investigation. The court reasoned that Congress did not intend to address this particular problem through the Rehabilitation Act. In the absence of clear congressional directive, the court noted, Congress rather than an executive agency must weigh the competing interests at stake, and until Congress has spoken, the court cannot approve the investigation.

The HHS' belief that it was authorized to investigate the matter stemmed from regulations it had promulgated in 1983 under authority of section 504. Three days after Baby Doe died, President Reagan instructed the Secretary of HHS to ensure that hospitals complied with section 504 of the Rehabilitation Act of 1973. HHS promulgated regulations that required health facilities to post notices warning against discrimination toward the handicapped and providing a toll-free number to report suspected violations to the federal government.[142] Violations would then result in a loss of federal funds to the hospital.

These initial regulations were held to be arbitrary and capricious under the federal Administrative Procedure Act because HHS had failed to consider important factors and had waived public comment before issuing the regulations.[143] HHS then issued new regulations, similar to the old regulations, after receiving public comment.

Once again, these regulations were successfully challenged.[144] The Second Circuit Federal Court of Appeals affirmed the district court's ruling. The Supreme Court agreed to hear the case and ruled that the federal government has no authority to regulate and investigate the care given to severely handicapped children.[145]

The Supreme Court noted that although the basis for federal intervention was a perceived discrimination against handicapped infants in violation of section 504, there was no evidence that discrimination had occurred.[146] The administrative record thus did not support federal intervention into a historically state-administered decisional process that appeared, for lack of evidence to the contrary, to be functioning in full compliance with section 504.

The Secretary of HHS, however, can require state agencies to document their own compliance with section 504. Nevertheless, the court reasoned, nothing in this section authorizes him to "commandeer state agencies to enforce compliance by *other* recipients of federal funds such as hospitals."[147] "State child protective services agencies are not field offices of the HHS bureaucracy" and they may not be forced "against their will as the foot soldiers in a federal crusade."[148]

The American Medical Association filed a brief in the case outlining for the court the reality of the regulations: HHS sent "Baby Doe squads" to hospitals during the day and the night after receiving anonymous telephone tips. They demanded to see confidential patient records, interrogated nurses and physicians, and in some instances, asserted the right to examine the physical condition of the newborn infant.[149] Many have found the Reagan administration's crusade untenable in view of the fact that the administration does not provide financial support to the parents who must care for the handicapped child.[150]

While the issue was being litigated in the lower courts, Congress passed the Child Abuse Amendments of 1984, noted above. These amendments direct the states, as a condition of receiving federal child abuse funds, to consider withholding of medically indicated treatment from handicapped children as medical neglect subject to state prosecution. Congress specifically did not address the Rehabilitation Act in these amendments.

A variety of recommendations have been made as to how to approach the problematic cases. Various states have considered, and in some instances passed, amendments to child abuse laws concerning treatment of handicapped infants.[151] These are comparable to the federal law.

Some suggest that parents may have personal interests in mind when they request a physician or nurse to withhold life sustaining treatment.[152] Thus institutional ethics committees are suggested as a way to avoid decision making by interested persons.[153]

To determine the potential liability for nontreatment of severely handicapped children under state child abuse abuse laws, nurses should consult their individual state statutes. The ethical implications of nontreatment are discussed generally in Chapter. The issue is not one that is easily resolved for parents or nurses who must care for these severely handicapped infants.[154]

Recommendations and trends

The field of maternal and child health nursing covers a broad expanse of care along the childbearing continuum. Nurses practicing in particular areas or subspecialties within the field must keep current their skills and knowledge base. As the discussion in this chapter illustrates, the field is particularly fertile for liability, and damage awards tend to be quite large. If the nurse is unfamiliar with a procedure or the requisite care required to attend to the patient, that care should not be undertaken by him or her.

The Supreme Court's recent ruling will end the Baby Doe squads, but nurses working in pediatrics and neonatal nurseries need to be aware of state child abuse laws that may influence nontreatment of severely handicapped infants. Nurses practicing in these areas may want to become involved by establishing and participating in institutional ethics committees. This forum may provide a vehicle to resolve difficult treatment issues.

Endnotes

1. AMERICAN NURSES' ASSOCIATION, A STATEMENT ON THE SCOPE OF MATERNAL AND CHILD HEALTH NURSING PRACTICE 4 (1980) (hereinafter cited as *ANA Statement on Maternal and Child Practice*).
2. This is because civil rights actions require state or federal governmental involvement in the challenged activity. See Chapters 2 and 5 for a thorough discussion of the legal theory in civil rights actions.

   Consequently, although maternal and child health nursing practice is a fertile area for civil rights actions, such actions will not be successful, as a general rule, unless the nurse is employed by the state or federal government, or the court decides that the state or federal government is sufficiently involved by virtue of its receipt of federal funds or other activity.

   Of course, sound nursing practice in the maternal and child health field, as in other fields, dictates that nurses be cognizant of, and act according to, the appropriate standard of care in their particular field, irrespective of the probable success or failure of a lawsuit.
3. If the profession's standards explicitly tolerated such conduct, the court would deem the standards inadequate as a matter of law for purposes of negligence. Recall that the professional standard of care is not an issue in civil rights cases or intentional torts and thus the adequacy or inadequacy of the standard would have no bearing on lawsuits charging either of these two theories.
4. *Id.; accord* AMERICAN NURSES' ASSOCIATION, A STATEMENT ON THE SCOPE OF HIGH-RISK PERINATAL NURSING PRACTICE 1 (1980) (footnote omitted) (hereinafter cited as *ANA Statement on High-Risk Practice*).
5. *ANA Statement on Maternal and Child Health Practice, supra* note 1, at 11.
6. *Id.*
7. *Id.*
8. *Id.* at 4.
9. *Id.*
10. *Id.*
11. *Id.* at 4-5.
12. *Id.*
13. *Id.*
14. *Id.*
15. *Id.*
16. *Id.*
17. *Id.* (footnote omitted). The fourth trimester is defined as the first three months following birth for both mother and infant.
18. *Id.*
19. *Id.*
20. *Id.*
21. Legal issues affecting clinical specialists are addressed elsewhere in this book.
22. Clinical specialists in the area are nurses with master's preparation. *ANA Statement on High Risk Practice, supra* note 4.
23. *Id.* at 4.
24. *Id.* at 4.
25. A.J. INGALLS & M.C. SALERNO, MATERNAL AND CHILD HEALTH NURSING 10 (1983) (hereinafter cited as *Ingalls & Salerno*).
26. *ANA Statement on High Risk Practice, supra* note 24, at 4.
27. *Renslow v. Mennonite Hosp,* 367 N.E.2d 1250 (Ill. 1977).
28. *Id.*
29. 259 A.2d 101 (Md. App. 1969).
30. *Turpin v. Sortini,* 643 P.2d 954 (Cal. 1982).
31. *Harbeson v. Parke-Davis,* 656 P.2d 483 (Wash. 1983).
32. *Procanik v. Cillo,* 478 A.2d 755 (N.J. 1984).
33. *See, e.g., Blaser v. Gibson,* 325 S.E.2d 607 (Ga. App. 1984) (lawsuit brought for negligent sterilization procedure which resulted in the birth of a healthy baby; court determined damages for delivery costs, lost wages and loss of consortium were proper but older children were not entitled to damages for having to share family income with new sibling).
34. *See e.g., Terrel v. Garcia,* 496 S.W.2d 124 (Tex. Civ. App. 1973), *cert. denied,* 415 U.S. 927 (1974).
35. *See, e.g., Troppi v. Scarf,* 187 N.W.2d 511 (Mich. App. 1971); *Stills v. Gratton,* 127 Cal. Rptr. 652 (Cal. App. 1976); *Coleman v. Garrison,* 327 A.2d 757 (Del. Super. 1974), *aff'd,* 349 A.2d 8 (Del. Supr. 1975).
36. *See, e.g., Berman v. Allan,* 404 A.2d 8 (N.J. 1979) (child born with Down's syndrome); *Park v. Chessin,* 387 N.Y.S.2d 204 (Sup. Ct. 1976) (failure to warn of polycystic kidney disease).
37. *See, e.g., Turpin v. Sortini,* 643 P.2d 954 (Cal. 1982).
38. *See e.g., Phillips v. United States District Court,* 566 F. Supp. 1 (D. S.C. 1981).
39. *See e.g., Blake v. Cruz,* 698 P.2d 315 (Idaho 1984).

40. 566 F. Supp. 1 (D. S.C. 1983).
41. 611 P.2d 902 (Cal. App. 1980).
42. *See Chrisafogeoris v. Brandenberg,* 304 N.E.2d 88 (Ill. 1973) (Illinois court originally refused to recognize cause of action for wrongful death of fetus who had attained viability).
43. *Green v. Smith,* 377 N.E.2d 37 (Ill. 1978) (cause of action exists for wrongful death of infant if at time of occurrence, the fetus had attained viability; question of fact existed for jury to determine whether the fetus at age 14 to 18 weeks was viable).
44. *Id; Summerfield v. Superior Court,* 698 P.2d 712 (Ariz. 1985).
45. Olender, *Obstetric Negligence, An Introduction To a High-Risk Specialty,* TRIAL 53, 56 (May 1984) (hereinafter cited as *Olender*).
46. *Id.*
47. I. PRITCHARD & P. MACDONALD, WILLIAMS OBSTETRICS 329 (15th ed. 1976).
48. AMERICA COLLEGE OF OBSTETRICIANS AND GYNECOLOGISTS, STANDARDS FOR OBSTETRIC/GYNECOLOGIC SERVICES 29 (5th ed. 1982). In *Rice v. Rizk,* 453 S.W.2d 732 (Ky. App. 1970), a court upheld a jury's finding that the defendant obstetrician was liable for the death of a viable fetus caused by infection following amniotomy with unsterile gloves. Nurses could be found negligent for similar reasons or failing to report signs and symptoms of infection.
49. R. WILSON & E. CARRINGTON, OBSTETRICS AND GYNECOLOGY 387 (6th ed. 1979).
50. No. 67-66169 Texas Tarrant County, 67th Jud. Dist. Ct. (1984).
51. 205 S.E.2d 440 (Ga. App. 1974).
52. The issue on appeal concerned the defendant doctor and whether the trial court properly directed a verdict for the doctor before the jury's decision. The appellate court held that an issue of fact as to the doctor's negligence existed for the jury to decide, and remanded the case for a jury trial against the doctor.
53. No. 83-37139, Fla. Dade Cty Cir. Ct. (October 24, 1984), *reported in,* 28 ATLA L. REP. 88 (March 1985).
54. *Olender, supra* note 45.
55. Weitz, *The Need To Keep Up-To-Date,* THE NATIONAL LAW JOURNAL 15 at col. 1 (March 4, 1985) (hereinafter cited as *Weitz*).
56. *Id.*
57. *Id.* at 18.
58. *Id.*
59. *Id.* (footnotes omitted).
60. *Id.*
61. *Id.*
62. *Id.*
63. AMERICAN NURSES' ASSOCIATION, STANDARDS OF PRACTICE FOR THE PERINATAL SPECIALIST 8 (1985).
64. 368 A.2d 895 (Pa. App. 1976).
65. 381 N.E.2d 93 (Ind. App. 1978).
66. *Taylor v. Richmond Memorial Hospital,* No. LG-915 Va. Richmond Cir. Ct. (December 7, 1984), *reported in,* 28 ATLA L. REP. 136 (April 1985).
67. No. 16486/82 N.Y. Bronx Cty. Sup. Ct. (November 20, 1984), *reported in,* 28 ATLA L. REP. 138 (April 1985).
68. No-C-65704, Fulton Cty. Superior Ct. Georgia (October 5, 1984), *reported in,* 28 ATLA REP. 42 (February 1985).
69. No. 21831/81, New York Superior Court (October 26, 1984), *reported in,* 28 ATLA L. REP. 89 (March 1985).
70. No. V84-179T, (W.D. Wash.), *reported in,* 28 ATLA L. REP. 465 (December 1985).
71. No. 17, 843 Cyahoga Cty. Ct. of Common Pleas (May 22, 1984), *reported in,* 27 ATLA REP. 425 (November 1984).
72. No. 107480, Johnson County Dist. Ct. (Kan. November 7, 1984).
73. *Norton v. Hamilton,* 89 S.E.2d 809 (Ga. App. 1955).
74. 523 P.2d 320 (Kan. 1974).
75. No. GC-G-82-2746, Fla., Polk Cty. Cir. Ct. (September 2, 1983), *reported in,* 27 ATLA L. REP. 137 (April 1984).
76. No. 81-230-540-NO, Mich. Oakland County Cir. Ct. (April 23, 1985), *reported in,* 28 ATLA L. REP. 419 (November 1985).
77. No. 80-CV649 Kennebec Cty. Superior Ct. (August 2, 1983), *reported in,* 27 ATLA L. REP. 89 (March 1984).
78. *Ingalls & Salerno, supra* note 25, at 103.
79. No. 83-264633 Oakland Cty. Cir. Ct., (February 4, 1985), *reported in,* 28 ATLA L. REP 183 (May 1985).
80. No. 83CVS336, N.C. Pitt County Superior Ct., (April 11, 1985), *reported in,* 28 ATLA L. REP. 419 (November 1985).
81. The obstetrician was also sued for failure to perform a cesarean section and failure to obtain informed consent to a vaginal delivery. Prior to trial, however, the obstetrician settled for 1.5 million dollars.
82. 616 F.2d 224 (5th Cir. 1980).
83. 12 P.2d 744 (Cal. App. 1932), *aff'd,* 13 P.2d 905 (Cal. 1932).
84. 12 P.2d at 746.
85. *Id.* at 747.
86. *Id.*
87. *Id.*
88. 366 N.W.2d 633 (Minn. App. 1985), *review granted,* July 11, 1985.
89. *See generally,* Kelly, *Sterilization Abuse: A Proposed Regulatory Scheme,* 28 DePAUL L. REV. 731 (1979).
90. *Id.*
91. In a famous case, *Buck v. Bell,* 274 U.S. 200 (1927), the Supreme Court upheld a state law which authorized sterilization of mental patients under certain circumstances. Citing *Jacobsen v. Massachusetts,* 197 U.S. 11, the Court noted that the principle that authorizes compulsory vaccinations is broad enough to encompass the fallopian tubes. The Court reasoned in an oft-quoted statement, that three generations of imbecile are enough.

    Although the Supreme Court has never overruled this decision, modern courts have severely narrowed the reach of this power. Today, the courts reject eugenics theory as valid justification for the government to sterilize mental patients. *See, e.g., In re Grady,* 426 A.2d 467 (N.J. 1981).

    Other cases reflecting the modern view of statutes that authorize involuntary sterilization are *Stump v. Sparkman,* 435 U.S. 439 (1978); *North Carolina Ass'n for Retarded Children v. North Carolina,* 420 F. Supp. 451 (D.N.C 1976); and *In re A.W.,* 637 P.2d 366 (Colo. 1981).
92. *Skinner v. Oklahoma,* 316 U.S. 369 (1967).
93. 410 U.S. (1973).
94. *See also Eisenstadt v. Baird,* 405 U.S. 438, 453 (1972) (right to privacy includes the right of an individual to be free from governmental intrusion in the fundamental decision as to ''bear or beget a child.'').
95. 560 F.2d 609 (4th Cir. 1977), *cert. denied,* 434 U.S. 1075 (1978).
96. *Id.* at 614 (Butzner, J. dissenting).
97. T. LITTLEWOOD, THE POLITICS OF POPULATION CONTROL 109 (1977).

98. *Walker v. Pierce,* 560 F.2d 609, 613 (4th Cir. 1977), *cert. denied,* 434 U.S. 1075 (1978) (emphasis added).
99. *Id.* at 614-15 (Butzner, J. dissenting).
100. 408 S.W.2d 428 (Ky. 1966).
101. No. 32-82, N.Y. Nassau County Supreme Ct. (May 29, 1985), *reported in,* 28 ATLA L. REP. 467 (December 1985).
102. *Weitz, supra* note 55, at 18.
103. *Id.* at 19.
104. *Id.* (emphasis added).
105. No. 84-2430-NM, Mich. Macomb County Cir. Ct. (May 30, 1985), *reported in,* 28 ATLA L. REP. 420 (November 1985).
106. Jefferson County Circuit Court, *reported in,* MEDICAL MALPRACTICE VERDICTS, SETTLEMENTS & EXPERTS 14 (Nov. 1985).
107. *See also Cornell v. United States Fidelity & Guaranty Co.,* 8 So.2d 364 (La. App. 1942) (hospital liable for negligence of student nurse in failure to test and to insulate hot water bottle placed in infant's incubator, which caused burns).
108. No. C 487995, Maricopa County Superior Court (April 5, 1985), *reported in,* 28 ATLA L. REP. 421 (November 1985).
109. Of this, the hospital contributed almost half, with the obstetrician, manufacturer of the pump, and the pediatrician contributing the remainder of the settlement. *Id.*
110. No. 81-215756-4, Kings County Superior Ct. (June 13, 1983), *reported in,* 27 ATLA L. REP. 42 (February 1984).
111. No. 468929, Santa Clara Sup. Ct. Cal., *reported in,* 28 ATLA L. REP. 227 (June 1985).
112. No. 800 L 30605, Cir. Ct. Cook County (June 24, 1985), *reported in,* 27 ATLA L. REP. 42 (February 1984).
113. No. 234, 350, La. Cadd Parish First Judicial Dist., 28 ATLA REP. 182 (May 1985).
114. *Ingalls & Salerno, supra* note 25, at 292.
115. 144 So.2d 249 (La. App. 1962).
116. The physician expert also testified at trial that, in his opinion, the supervising nurse was untrained for pediatric nursing because she was unaware that Lanoxin is manufactured in elixir form.
117. No. 82-67439-NM, Genese Cty. Cir. Ct. (July 5, 1984), *reported in,* 28 ATLA L. REP. 42 (February 1985).
118. No. 822-06798, Mo. St. Louis Cir. Ct. (April 29, 1985), *reported in,* 28 ATLA L. REP. 418 (November 1985).
119. *Register v. A & A Ambulance Service, Inc., reported in,* MEDICAL MALPRACTICE VERDICTS, SETTLEMENTS & EXPERTS 15 (November, 1985).
120. 374 S.W.2d 645 (Tenn. App. 1963).
121. 202 So.2d 568 (Fla. App. 1967).
122. *See, e.g.,* CAL. PENAL CODE §11160 -11162 (West Supp. 1985).
123. CAL. PENAL CODE §11165.1-11174.5 (West Supp. 1986).
124. *Id.* at §11165 (a) (2).
125. *Id.* at §11172 (a).
126. 131 Cal. Rptr. 69 (Cal. App. 1976).
127. *Darrah v. Kite,* 301 N.Y.S.2d 286 (N.Y. A.D. 3 Dept. 1969).
128. Pipel, *Minor's Right to Medical Care,* 36 ALA. L. REV. 462, 467 (1972).
129. K. FIEBERG, J.D. PETERS, J.R. WILSON, & D. KROLL, OBSTETRICS-GYNECOLOGY AND THE LAW 38 (1984).
130. *Id.*
131. *Younts v. St. Francis Hosp. & School of Nursing, Inc.,* 469 P.2d 330 (Kan. 1970).
132. *Planned Parenthood v. Danforth,* 428 U.S. 52 (1976); *Bellotti v. Baird,* 428 U.S. 132 (1976). In *City of Akron v. Akron Center for Reproductive Health,* 462 U.S. 416 (1983), the Supreme Court invalidated a law requiring parental consent to abortion for all minors under 15 years of age. The Court reasoned that the statute failed to provide a procedure whereby a pregnant minor could demonstrate to a judge that she is sufficiently mature to make the abortion decision herself, or that, despite her immaturity, an abortion would be in her best interest. The Court held that a law cannot make a blanket determination that all minors under the age of 15 are too immature to make the abortion decision or that an abortion can never be in the minor's best interest without parental approval.
133. *H.L. v. Matheson,* 450 U.S.398 (1981).
134. *See, e.g.,* Nondiscrimination on the Basis of Handicap; Procedure and Guidelines Relating to Health Care for Handicapped Infants, 49 Fed. Reg. 1,622 (1983); H.R. B. 1904 (1983) (to amend 42 U.S.C. §5105-107); *Weber v. Stony Brook Hospital,* 456 N.E.2d 1186 N.Y. 1983), *cert. denied,* 464 U.S. 1026 (1983); *United States v. University Hospital,* No. CV83-4818 (E.D.N.Y. November 17, 1983).
135. Child Abuse Amendments of 984, Pub. L. No. 98-457, 98 Stat. 1749-55 (1984) (to be codified at 42 U.S.C. §5105-05).
136. Rehabilitation Act of 1973, Pub. L. No. 93-112, 7 Stat. 355 (codified as amended at 29 U.S.C. §701-794 (1984)). Section 504 provides that no otherwise qualified handicapped individual shall be subject to discrimination under any program or activity receiving federal aid solely on the basis of a handicap.
137. *See generally,* Kelly, *The Right To Die,* 6 WHITTIER L. REV. 819 (1983) (hereinafter cited as *Kelly*).
138. Hoving, *The Baby Doe Cases,* ABA JOURNAL 50 (April 1, 1986) (hereinafter cited as *Hoving*).
139. *Doe v. Bloomington Hospital,* 464 U.S. 961 (1983).
140. *Hoving, supra* note 138, at 51.
141. *United States v. University Hospital,* 729 F.2d 144 (2d Cir. 1984).
142. 48 Fed. Reg. 9630 (1983) (to be codified at 45 C.F.R. pt 84) (proposed Mar. 7, 1983).
143. *American Academy of Pediatrics v. Heckler,* 561 F. Supp. 395 (D.D.C. 1983).
144. *American Hospital Association v. Heckler,* 585 F. Supp. 541 (S.D.N.Y. 1984).
145. *Bowen v. American Hospital Association,* 106 S.Ct. 2101 (1985).
146. *Id.* at 2116-2117.
147. *Id.* at 2120.
148. *Id.*
149. *Hoving, supra* note 138, at 51.
150. *Id.* at 53 quoting Commissioner Mary Frances Berry of the United States Commission on Civil Rights.
151. For a review of the various state laws, *see generally,* Feldman & Murray, *State Legislation and the Handicapped Newborn: A Moral and Political Dilemma,* 12 LAW, MEDICINE & HEALTH CARE 156 (September 1984).
152. *See,* Lund, *Infanticide, Physicians, and the Law: The Baby Doe Amendments to the Child Abuse and Treatment Act,* 11 AMERICAN J. LAW & MED. 1 (No. 11985).
153. *Hoving, supra* note 138, at 53.
154. *See Kelly, supra* note 137 for a discussion of Baby Doe regulations and the impact on nurses caring for such infants.

Additional Readings

Child Abuse Prevention and Treatment and Adoption Reform Act Amendments of 1983: Hearings Before the Subcomm. on Family and Human Services of the Senate Committee on Labor and Human Resources, 98th Cong., 1st Sess. 6, (1983).

Ellis, *Letting Defective Babies Die: Who Decides?* 7 AMERICAN JOURNAL OF LAW & MEDICINE 393 (1982).

Kelly, *Sterilization Abuse: A Proposed Regulatory Scheme,* 28 DePAUL L. REV. 731 (1979).

Note, *Life or Death in the Intensive Care Nursery: Who Should Decide?* 11 WM. MITCHELL L. REV. 127 (1985).

Saltz, *Better Off Never Born?* ABA JOURNAL 46 (April 1, 1986).

Wing & Silton, *Constitutional Authority for Extending Federal Control over the Delivery of Health Care,* 57 N.C.L. Rev. 1423 (1979).

Chapter 12

Operating room and perioperative nursing

Ellen K. Murphy

The legal duty of operating room nurses to their patients undergoing surgery is the same duty as that of all nurses: deliver reasonable and prudent care so as not to cause injury to the client. There are several factors unique to the operating room (OR) setting, however, that are cause for particular vigilance to the possible legal ramifications of the activities of the OR nurse.

Overview of the practice area

Roles of nurses in the OR and in perioperative nursing are many, and the focus of practice is on the individual experiencing surgical intervention.[1] The standards of perioperative nursing are listed on p. 182 (see box). The dimensions of this practice area include preoperative assessment and planning in the home or clinic, on the care unit, holding area of the operating room suite, to intraoperative intervention, postoperative evaluation and documentation in the operating room and post-anesthesia area.[2] Although material presented in this chapter applies to the Certified Registered Nurse Anesthetist (CRNA) as well, Chapter 23 includes more information specifically pertaining to the CRNA role.

Operating room patients are more vulnerable to injury than other patients for two reasons: (1) the patient's anesthetized or sedated condition and (2) the intrusive procedures. For the most part, patients in the operating room are totally unable to protect themselves. The same anesthetics that allow the surgical team to perform otherwise prohibitively painful procedures compromise all of the protection otherwise afforded by the pain response.

Unlike the unsedated, conscious patient, the usual operating room patient cannot detect pain or take action to prevent its further infliction. For example, the conscious patient will feel the beginning of a chemical or electrical injury and withdraw from the source of the burn before additional damage can take place; the anesthetized patient will not. The anesthetized patient lacks these protective responses. The anesthetized patient is unable to sense a beginning injury, take any action to prevent the continued infliction of the injury, or even verbalize that something hurts so that the nurse can intervene to protect the patient from further injury. The nurse's exposure to potential liability is increased as the patient's potential for injury is increased.

The operating room setting compounds this vulnerable patient's already heightened potential for injury with the provision of highly intrusive procedures and sophisticated technology. The inherent danger and sophisticated nature of the equipment and the procedures serve to further increase the potential for patient injury.

As a result, operating room nurses and operating room nursing standards rightly place much emphasis on patient safety. This emphasis on patient safety provides the operating room nurse with the best "legal protection": avoiding the injury prevents the filing of a negligence suit.

This chapter begins with a presentation of two legal

STANDARDS OF PERIOPERATIVE NURSING PRACTICE

STANDARD I: The collection of data about the health status of the individual is systematic and continuous. The data are retrievable and are communicated to appropriate persons.

The fundamental step of the nursing process is initiated by the operating room nurse after the individual consents to have surgical intervention.

STANDARD II: Nursing diagnoses are derived from health status data.

The nursing diagnoses are judgments the operating room nurse makes based on the analysis and interpretations of data about the individual's problems and needs and health status.

STANDARD III: The plan of nursing care includes goals derived from the nursing diagnoses.

Goals for care are derived from the nursing diagnoses and are mutually formulated with the individual, significant others, and other health personnel.

STANDARD IV: The plan for nursing care prescribes nursing actions to achieve the goals.

Priorities for the provision of nursing care are established by the operating room nurse in collaboration with the individual, significant others, and members of the health care team.

STANDARD V: The plan for nursing care is implemented.

The nursing actions performed are consistent with the plan and provide continuity of nursing care in the preoperative, intraoperative, and postoperative periods.

STANDARD VI: The plan for nursing care is evaluated.

Evaluation is a process the operating room nurse uses to determine the degree of goal attainment.

STANDARD VII: Reassessment of the individual, reconsideration of nursing diagnoses, resetting of goals, and modification and implementation of the nursing care plan are a continuous process.

Reassessment allows the operating room nurse to critically examine the total process from which the planned and delivered nursing interventions are derived.

Adapted from AMERICAN NURSES' ASSOCIATION AND ASSOCIATION OF OPERATING ROOM NURSES, STANDARDS OF PERIOPERATIVE NURSING PRACTICE (1981).

concepts unique to the operating room setting, the captain of the ship doctrine, including a discussion of the borrowed servant doctrine, and the *res ipsa loquitur* doctrine. The chapter continues with a discussion of legal implications of practice issues of particular concern to nurses in the operating room. These concerns include retained foreign bodies, burns, paralysis and injuries more likely to occur in the operating room, informed consent, and the registered nurse as first assistant to the surgeon. The chapter concludes with legal implications of practice in the perioperative setting with emphasis on the emerging trend of ambulatory surgery and its implications for patient teaching.

Unique legal doctrines

Because the operating room is a unique setting within a hospital, the operating room nurse should be aware of two particularly applied doctrines that are more relevant to their practice in that setting than to nursing practice in other settings. These doctrines are the "captain of the ship" and "borrowed servant" doctrines, and the doctrine of *res ipsa loquitur*. Each will be discussed and defined, including case examples involving the operating room nurse.

CAPTAIN OF THE SHIP DOCTRINE AND BORROWED SERVANT DOCTRINES

The operating room is unique from other patient care settings in the applicability of the "captain of the ship" rule. The phrase "captain of the ship" was first used in a medical malpractice case by a Pennsylvania court in 1949.[3] In that case, the phrase was used as an analogy of the responsibility of the surgeon to the responsibility of a navy captain. In some states, the use of the phrase evolved into a separate doctrine that, as matter of law, the surgeon, like a ship's captain, is in total command and is charged with full responsibility for the care and efficiency of the ship (operating room) and the welfare of all hands (all persons present). Simply stated, the surgeon had complete authority in the operating room, and the surgeon was responsible to the patient for all acts performed by everyone there.

This concept was actually very unfair to surgeons. Under the captain of the ship doctrine, a surgeon's mere presence in the OR made him or her liable for any and every negligent act that might occur there, no matter who committed the act, even if there was no way for the surgeon to know of the possibility of such act or to control its occurrence.

In 1971, the Pennsylvania Supreme Court clarified that the use of the phrase "captain of the ship" in *McConnell* was not intended as a separate doctrine but rather as an adaptation of the long established legal principle of the "borrowed servant" which generally applies in the law of agency.[4] They explained that the captain of the ship concept imposes liability on the surgeon in charge of an operation for the negligence of assistants during the period *when these assistants are under the surgeon's control*, even though the assistants are also employees of the hospital.[5]

The real issue, under this clarification of the captain of the ship concept by the state court that first used the phrase, is the right to control. Thus, when deciding the liability of a surgeon or the negligent acts of an operating room nurse, the question is whether or not the surgeon had a right to control the actions of the nurse, not whether the surgeon was in charge of the operation. In most cases, it will be up to the jury to decide if the surgeon had the right to control the actions of the nurse based on the evidence before them.

In 1977, the Texas Supreme Court had occasion to clarify that the usual rules of the law of agency, including the borrowed servant principle, and not some special rule called captain of the ship applied to operating surgeons and operating room nurses.[6] In *Sparger* the plaintiff sued the hospital and the surgeon for injuries resulting from the failure to remove a sponge from the plaintiff's abdominal cavity after an operation.

The jury found that the operating room nurses failed to make a correct sponge count, and this failure was the proximate cause of the plaintiff's injury. The jury refused to find that the surgeon had failed to exercise care by looking for the sponge before closing the incision in the plaintiff's abdomen. The jury also refused to find that in watching after the sponges, the nurses were the borrowed servants of the surgeon. "Borrowed servant" as defined to the jury, meant "one, who, while in the general employment of the hospital, is subject to the right of the physician to direct or control the details of the particular work inquired about, and is not merely cooperating with suggestions of said physician."[7] The jury had exonerated the surgeon from every act of negligence for which he was charged and found instead that the nurses were negligent.

On appeal, the jury's finding was reversed. The Texas Court of Civil Appeals held, as a matter of law, that the surgeon was liable under the captain of the ship doctrine even though the jury found him not liable and that the defendants, surgeon, and hospital (as employer of the nurses) were jointly and severally liable. Therefore, the surgeon and the nurses were all liable.

It is important to note that even when a court is willing to apply the captain of the ship doctrine, the finding of surgeon liability does *not* exonerate the nurses from liability. The nurses remain liable for their own negligent acts even though their employer may be liable under *respondeat superior,* and even when the surgeon is also liable under the captain of the ship doctrine.

The Texas Supreme Court reversed the judgment of the Texas Court of Civil Appeals. In its decision, the supreme court specifically rejected the assertion that the surgeon's mere presence in the operating room makes him or her liable for the negligence of other persons as a matter of law. They held that the captain of the ship doctrine is a "false special rule" of agency, and that surgeons and hospitals are subject to the same rules of agency, including the borrowed servant principle that applies to the general population.

The Texas Supreme Court then turned to the question of whether the facts showed the nurses were borrowed servants of the surgeon. The following facts were relevant to this question:

1. The nurses were hired and assigned by the hospital.
2. The surgeon did not participate in their selection.
3. The duties of the scrub and circulating nurses were detailed in the hospital's policy and procedure manual.
4. The procedures for the sponge count were intended for use regardless of the surgeon who performed the operation.
5. The nurses counted sponges before the surgery began.
6. The scrub nurse testified that the surgeon did not direct her and the circulating nurse to take the count.

In light of these facts, the Texas Supreme Court upheld the initial jury verdict that the nurses were not borrowed servants of the surgeon, and the surgeon was not liable for their negligence in conducting the sponge count. On motion for rehearing the court did remand the case to the court of civil appeals to rule on the question of whether the jury's finding was against the great weight of the evidence. This remand does not alter the rule of law rejecting the captain of the ship doctrine.

Most states now apply the borrowed servant principle rather than the captain of the ship doctrine to the question of operating room nurse liability. However, a 1982 decision has come close to having the practical effect of resurrecting the captain of the ship doctrine. That court held that if a surgeon has the right to control the actions of a nurse anesthetist, the surgeon can be liable for the nurse anesthetist's negligent acts even if the surgeon does not exercise the right to control.

In this case, the surgeon was found liable for the injuries incurred when the nurse anesthetist moved the patient even though he did not direct her activities at the time of the move.[8] The Ohio Supreme Court disclaimed that its ruling breathes new life into the now prostrate doctrine (of captain of the ship) and that it sought only to ensure that where, as in the OR, a surgeon does control or realistically possesses the right to control events and procedures, he or she does so with a high degree of care.

If other states choose to follow this line of reasoning, surgeons could again be liable for all negligent acts in the OR. This could be possible if surgeons are willing to testify that they are in complete charge of the operation, that they have the right to tell everyone what to do, and that everyone is supposed to do what the surgeon directs and if the jury accepts this testimony as fact.

A more recent California appellate case, *Schultz v. Mutch*,[9] reflects continuing confusion between the captain of the ship doctrine and the borrowed servant principle. The facts of this case involved physician liability for the negligence of obstetrical nurses in the care of a patient in labor. The plaintiff infant's mother had been admitted to an obstetrical unit for delivery of an infant which by all prenatal indications was expected to be born normal and healthy. After a series of events involving questionable assessment of the plaintiff's labor progress and monitoring of the infant's fetal heart tones, the child was born quadriplegic and mentally retarded.

The legal issue before the court was the propriety of the plaintiff's jury instruction that read: ". . . if . . . the nurse is under the direction of a certain physician in charge, so as to be his temporary servant or agent, any negligence on the part of any such assisting person, occurring while the latter is under the physician's direction, is deemed in law to be the negligence of such physician."[10] While this instruction appears to restate the borrowed servant principle, the court chose to uphold its validity after a discussion of the captain of the ship doctrine.

The court distinguished previous cases that had scaled back the captain of the ship doctrine in California as cases where the errors had been those of anesthesiologists, over whom surgeons have no control or power of supervision, or where the errors had been those of nurses where the defendant physician was neither present nor in control. Having distinguished cases that had not followed the captain of the ship doctrine, the court stated it was constrained to continue to follow the captain of the ship doctrine. A closer reading of the case suggests an alternative interpretation: that the court was really reaffirming the borrowed servant principle of agency and deciding that this principle can be applicable to settings outside the operating room (for example, labor and delivery) or that the defendant physician (who was present in the suite, but occupied with a cesarean section on another patient) was liable for his own negligence in failing to assess and monitor this patient and for knowingly occupying the skills of all available nurses as assistants to the cesarean section without making inquiry as to the status of his other patient.

RES IPSA LOQUITUR

Meaning, literally, the thing speaks for itself, *res ipsa loquitur* is a legal doctrine that changes the plaintiff's burden of proof in a negligence or malpractice case. This doctrine is another legal concept that is applied to the operating room nurse's practice with much more frequency than to any other area of nursing practice. Usually, the plaintiff must prove the standard of care, breach of the standard, causation, and injury (see Chapter 4). However, if the plaintiff can show that this doctrine applies, the burden of proof will change or shift. The defendant will have to show that the standard was not breached, rather than the usual requirement that the plaintiff show that the standard was breached.

To successfully invoke the *res ipsa loquitur* doctrine the plaintiff must establish the following:

1. That the injury does not ordinarily occur in the absence of negligence.
2. That the instrumentality that caused the injury was within the exclusive control of the defendant(s).
3. That the plaintiff did not contribute to the injury in any way.

In most personal injury cases, it is very difficult for the plaintiff to establish these elements and convince the judge that *res ipsa* should apply. It is easier to establish these elements when injury occurs in the operating room than in other areas of nursing care. First of all the anesthetized patient could not have contributed to his or her own injury. Secondly, it is also relatively easy to convince a judge that injuries such as burns and paralysis away from the operative site would not occur in the absence of negligence. And thirdly, the equipment that caused the burn or paralysis is clearly controlled by the defendant(s)—nurse, physician, and hospital.

An incident that occurred in the OR provided the context for the landmark case of *Ybarra v. Spangard.* This case applied the *res ipsa loquitur* doctrine to health care malpractice cases even where the plaintiff does not show that the act of any particular defendant, nor any particular instrumentality caused the injury.[11]

In *Ybarra* the plaintiff had undergone an appendectomy. Prior to the operation he had never had any pain in or injury to his right arm or shoulder. He testified that he remembered being pulled to the head of the operating room table and felt two hard objects at the top of his shoulders about an inch below his neck. He then lost consciousness. When he awakened he felt a sharp pain between his neck and right shoulder.

Despite diathermy treatments, the pain did not cease, and ultimately he developed paralysis and atrophy of the muscles around his shoulder. The plaintiff's physicians testified that the paralysis was not pathological or systemic, but rather was due to trauma by pressure applied between his neck and right shoulder. The plaintiff argued that this evidence presented a proper case for the application of the doctrine of *res ipsa loquitur.*

The defendant surgeons, nurses, and anesthesiologist argued that there was no showing that any particular defendant nor any particular instrumentality was the cause of the plaintiff's paralysis. They argued that the *res ipsa loquitur* doctrine cannot apply where there are several defendants and a division of responsibility in the use of an instrumentality causing the injury; where the injury might have resulted from the separate act of one or more persons; and where there are several instrumentalities, and no showing was made as to which caused the injury.

The California Supreme Court rejected the defendants' arguments by asserting that the plaintiff's case had satisfied the conditions required for application of the doctrine. The court explained that it was unreasonable to limit the doctrine in the manner the defendants urged (that the plaintiff must identify any one of them as the person who did the negligence or identify any one instrumentality as the cause of injury). The court stated that the plaintiff was rendered unconscious and that it is manifestly unreasonable to insist he identify any one person or instrumentality involved. The court held that "where a plaintiff receives unusual injuries while unconscious and in the course of medical treatment, all those defendants who had any control over his body or the instrumentalities which might have caused the injuries may properly be called upon to meet the inference of negligence by giving an explanation of their conduct."[12] The importance of documentation to assist the nurse in "giving an explanation of their conduct" to "meet the inference of negligence" is discussed below.

Common sense suggests that patients that go to the OR without ulnar nerve paralysis or skin burns would not emerge with those injuries unless some person or persons failed to take reasonable care to prevent them. The *res ipsa loquitur* instruction to a jury frequently, but not always, is given for these types of injuries. The burns tend to be caused by iodine or other pooled solutions, electrocautery, or improperly aerated equipment sterilized with ethylene oxide. Ulnar or peroneal nerve injuries are the most frequently seen types of injuries due to positioning. OR nurses will recognize these as potential injuries that they routinely take actions to prevent.

Informed consent

The nurse constantly encounters the issue of informed consent in daily practice in the operating room. Informed consent is discussed in detail in Chapter 6. This chapter should be reviewed in detail to provide a proper context to the following discussion of specific implications of informed consent for the operating room nurse.

As discussed in Chapter 6, the responsibility to inform the patient of the risks, benefits, and alternatives of a surgical procedure and obtain consent clearly lies with the person performing the procedure, that is the surgeon. The operating room nurses' role is confined to assuring that informed consent has been obtained and documented in the health record in accordance with the policy of the institution. The OR nurse's role does not include undertaking to inform the patient of procedures, risks, benefits or alternatives nor ascertaining the extent of the patient's understanding of the procedure.

Courts have consistently refused to require that hospitals or hospital employee nurses or technicians assume the surgeon's duty to inform the patient or to obtain the patient's consent. In 1967, a New York court held that a hospital had no obligation to make certain that the patient had given informed consent to an unusual and dangerous "spinal jack" operation performed by a privately retained surgeon, unless the patient could show that the hospital knew or should have known that the patient's informed consent was lacking or that the operation was not permissible under existing standards.[13]

Appellate courts in Missouri have held on two separate occasions that the hospital is under no duty to inform patients of surgical risks or alternative treatments and does not assume that duty by giving a patient a consent form.[14] This is true even though the hospital's employee nurse presented a consent form to the patient and clarified the meaning of the term "vaginal hysterectomy" with her.[15]

While cases are clear that the hospital and its employee nurses do not have and should not have a duty to educate the patient about the procedure and obtain the patient's consent, the hospital may have a duty to ascertain whether informed consent has been obtained. Some courts recognize *in dicta* that in some circumstances the hospital, presumably through its employee nurses, might have some responsibility for preventing contraindicated surgery, such as illegal or fraudulent treatment or other operations not permissible under existing standards[16] or a dilation and curettage (D & C) without first ascertaining if the patient was pregnant, as required by hospital policy.[17]

But this limited responsibility falls far short of placing upon the hospital the onus of explaining risks of surgery and availability of alternatives.[18] The hospital does not share and should not share in the responsibility to advise patients of the nature and risks of the procedure.[19]

A New Mexico court followed the *Fiorentino* line of reasoning as it refused to find that a defendant hospital had a duty to obtain the patient's informed consent to bilateral cataract extraction.[20] In this case, the patient had requested that both cataracts be removed during one hospital stay. The patient had signed a consent form for the first operation although it did not state what the operation was to be. She did not sign a second consent form for the second operation, on her left eye. Subsequent to the second operation she became blind.

The majority of the court held that the hospital liability should not be extended in the area of informed consent and that to do so would interfere in the physician-patient relationship. In a strongly worded dissent, one of the judges urged that while the hospital may not have a duty to obtain the educated consent of a patient prior to surgery, the hospital does have a duty to exercise reasonable care to ascertain whether the physician has obtained consent. Since the first consent form was defective and the second nonexistent, the hospital knew or should have known that consent had not been obtained, and the hospital should be held liable.[21]

A Louisiana court specifically discussed the role of the operating room nurse in a 1978 case that involved the issue of informed consent.[22] In that case, the plaintiff entered the defendant hospital for caesarean delivery of her third child. Her blood type was Rh negative, and her husband's was Rh positive. On numerous prenatal visits she had discussed a tubal ligation with her obstetrician. The plaintiff maintained that she never expressly or impliedly consented to ligation, but in every instance told the obstetrician she would think about it and let him know.

Conversely, the obstetrician contended that these discussions led him to believe that the plaintiff desired to have her tubes ligated following delivery. Based upon this belief, he wrote "C-section, T.L." on the face of his office record.

Upon admission to the hospital, the plaintiff signed a consent form provided by the hospital at the request of the admitting nurse. The form contained the following provision, "I am aware that sterility may result from this operation, I know that a sterile person is incapable of becoming a parent." At the plaintiff's insistence, this provision was stricken from the form. The record does not show whether the plaintiff herself or the admitting nurse marked out the provision.

As thus altered, the consent form accompanied the patient and the patient's chart to the operating room. After the C-section delivery the obstetrician and his assistant discussed the tubal ligation and the question of consent. The surgeon's attention was directed to the lack of a signed consent form for the tubal ligation. The surgeon directed the OR nurse to take the form to the patient's husband for signature. The OR nurse did so and returned the form to the operating room, and the ligation ensued.

The court refused to find the OR nurse negligent. The court noted that the surgeon's attention had been directed to the fact that no tubal ligation consent form had been signed, and that once this was done, the OR nurse acted pursuant to the physician's orders. This result suggests that this OR nurse met her legal duty by directing the surgeon's attention to the fact that the data available to the nurse indicated a lack of consent.

Note that even in those cases that suggest there may be a duty to ascertain whether consent to surgery had been obtained (in addition to the surgeon's duty to obtain consent), that duty to ascertain whether consent has been obtained rests with the hospital, not with the nurse. This is not an instance where the hospital is liable for the negligence of its employee nurses. In this case, the hospital is corporately liable for its independent duty to the patient.

Operating room nurses should demand that their hospitals develop an official written policy to follow when a patient arrives in the operating room with defective or absent documentation that consent has been obtained by the surgeon. At present, the OR nurse's legal duty to the patient appears to be met as long as the nurse ascertains that consent has been obtained and documented according to the policies and procedures of the institution, provided they adequately safeguard the patient.

Retained foreign bodies

The most prevalent injury that results in litigation for the operating room nurse is that of retained foreign bodies. Many states regard leaving a sponge, needle, or instrument in the patient as negligence per se. That is, the fact that a foreign body was left, in and of itself, proves negligence. Other states routinely apply the *res ipsa loquitur* doctrine discussed previously.

Under either doctrine, the burden of proof shifts from the plaintiff to the defendant(s) to show they were not negligent. This has proved to be nearly impossible for the defendant to do. As a result, in foreign body cases, the legal questions tend to involve the extent of damages rather than whether someone was negligent.

Dicta in some cases suggest that the presence of an emergency situation is a possible defense to negligence for retained foreign bodies.[23] No other factual defense has been successfully raised in identified reported cases. In the past, the running of the statute of limitations has occasionally barred recovery in retained foreign body cases. However, by judicial or legislative action, most states have now adopted some form of the discovery rule. This rule provides that the statute of limitations begins to run when the patient discovers his or her injury (learns he or she has a retained foreign body), rather than from the time the action occurred (the date the foreign body is left).[24]

Retained foreign bodies are the quintessential examples of situations where the best legal protection for the nurse is making an effort to prevent the injury from occurring in the first place. Clear and consistent count policies will assist in the prevention of retained foreign bodies.

Once the foreign body is left, however, there is almost no defense. If a count was taken, the nurses were obviously negligent in counting. If a count was not taken, the nurses were negligent in not adhering to the policy. If there was no policy or the policy did not require a count, the hospital could be negligent for failure to devise an effective accounting mechanism.[25]

Abandonment

The nurse-patient relationship continues until it is terminated, generally by mutual consent of both parties. Withdrawal from the relationship by the professional without notice to the patient and while the patient has a continued need for services of the professional can result in a claim of abandonment. There is confusion about whether abandonment is properly classified as a breach of contract, an intentional tort, or negligence.[26]

Traditionally, abandonment cases have been brought against physicians rather than nurses and have involved situations such as failure to continue to render care without arranging for follow-up care or without telling the patient that the physician is withdrawing or telling the patient the physician is withdrawing but without giving the patient adequate time to locate another physician. While theoretically a potential abandonment action could apply to all areas of nursing practice, it was not until 1983 that a state appellate court addressed nursing abandonment. This case was a negligence case and involved a circulating nurse.[27]

The plaintiff in this case was a 28-year-old woman who suffered cerebral hypoxia during cardiac arrest. The arrest occurred in the operating room as she emerged from anesthesia after an otherwise uneventful ovarian cystectomy. Severe loss of oxygen to her brain resulted in permanent and total paralysis. At the time the plaintiff arrested, only the anesthesiologist and the scrub technician were present. The operating surgeon had left the room to prepare for another surgery. The circulating nurse had also left the room in response to a request from the surgeon. When the arrest was detected, the scrub technician left to get help, leaving the anesthesiologist alone to attempt to resuscitate the patient.

In its decision, the California court noted the circulator's testimony that she had told the surgeon she could not leave the patient because she had not completed her duties and that she knew the patient was at a critical postoperative period. The nurse nonetheless did leave the patient and defended her leaving because she was "being yelled at."[28] The court also noted that the hospital's procedure manual, which set forth duties of the circulating nurse, provided, in pertinent part, "He/She is also the member of the team who will be on hand to assist the anesthesiologist during the entire procedure."[29] A physician testified as an expert witness that cardiac arrest should be anticipated at any time in the OR and that appropriate modalities be ready to cope with it; that vigilance in observing change in a patient's condition is paramount; and that short of an emergency, it would be inappropriate for a surgeon to request a circulator to leave a patient while in the operating room.[30]

The court held that from this evidence, the jury could properly conclude that it was a breach of duty, negligence, for the nurse to leave the unconscious patient's side. Having accepted the jury's decision on the elements of standard of care and breach, the court then turned to the element of causation. The court found that:

> . . . the nurse's absence from the OR was patent, proximate, efficient cause of [the patient's] injuries. She was the second most skilled person present. Her presence and skill should have led to a prompt observation of the preliminary warning signs of vital function failures. Had [she] been present, she could have assisted the anesthesiologist with CPR . . . This neglecting, abandoning and ignoring the patient was a prime reason why effective CPR was unavailable and therefore an immediate, direct and effective cause of [the patient's] brain damage.[30]

Having found breach of the standard and causation, the court upheld the jury award of damages against the hospital in the sum of $982,000. (The anesthesiologist had previously settled his lawsuit with the patient for $500,000).

This case reinforces that the nurse's legal duty is to the patient, to provide reasonable and prudent care to the patient. Circulators must take care to confine their absences from the room to a minimum and then only as necessary for safe care.

The operating room nurse as first assistant

Many operating room nurses have assumed the role of first assistant to the surgeon during operative procedures. This practice has initiated a continuing discussion as to whether functioning as the surgeon's first assistant falls within the scope of professional nursing practice as defined by state nurse practice statutes and the standard of care applicable to the first assistant. There are no cases applying any standards to the first assistant, nor is the question of RN first assistants addressed in any state statute. Federal regulations, conditions of participation which must be met by hospitals in order to receive federal funding for services, establish standards for the department of surgery.[31] These are listed in the box, opposite, including one which mentions first assistants. In addition some state boards of nursing still have yet to adopt official positions regarding this practice.

Of those state boards that have ruled on the issue, many have determined that the RN first assistant is permissible either as an expanded role or as an acceptable delegated medical act. However, some boards have ruled the practice of first assistant as outside the practice of nursing. Therefore, nurses functioning as or contemplating assuming the first assistant role should contact the board of nursing in the states where they practice to ascertain whether the role has been determined to be within the scope of nursing practice and what rules or regulations apply or limit the role.

FIRST ASSISTANT'S STANDARD OF CARE

There is not as yet a reported case that deals with the RN first assistant. However, the courts' discussions in two other cases provide some guidance as to how a court might regard a negligence case against an RN first assistant. These will be discussed below.

If an action by an RN first assistant causes a patient injury, the court would compare the nurse's action to the relevant standard of care. Even though the usual rule is that one who undertakes the activities of another profession is held to the standard of that profession, a recent California case suggests that an RN first assistant could be held to an RN standard rather than a physician standard of first assisting. In the case of *Fien v. Permanente*[32] (discussed in detail in Chapter 23) the California Supreme Court held that a standard of care for nurse practitioners rather than a physician standard applies to nurse practitioners engaging in traditional areas of medical practice, such as diagnosis, as long as these acts are also within the scope of the nurse practitioner's practice.

VIEW 1: WITHIN THE SCOPE OF NURSING PRACTICE

Presumably, if the activities of the RN first assistant have been determined to be within the scope of nursing practice in the relevant state, the reasonableness of the activities under scrutiny would be compared to a reasonable RN first assistant rather than a physician first assistant. The Association of Operating Room Nurses' official statement on RN first assistants could also serve as evidence of the standard of care for registered nurses functioning as first assistants.[33]

If the negligent action of an RN first assistant causes a patient injury, the surgeon could also be liable to the patient. As discussed above, the surgeon could be liable under the theory of *respondeat superior,* if the surgeon were the employer of the nurse, or under the borrowed servant principle of agency law, since the surgeon clearly has the right to control the actions of the RN first assistant.

A Michigan case suggests that the surgeon would be liable for the acts of an RN first assistant because the surgeon has a nondelegable duty to the patient to see that the operation is performed with due care.[34] The Michigan Supreme Court allowed a jury to find the surgeon liable

FEDERAL STANDARDS: HOSPITAL DEPARTMENTS OF SURGERY AND ANESTHESIA

The Department of Surgery has effective policies and procedures regarding surgical privileges, maintenance of the operating rooms, administration of anesthetics, maintenance of strict safety controls, and evaluation of the surgical patient. The factors explaining the standards are as follows:

1. Surgical privileges are delineated for all physicians doing surgery in accordance with the competencies of each physician. A roster of physicians, specifying the surgical privileges of each, is kept in the confidential files of the operating room supervisor and in the files of the hospital administrator.
2. In any procedure with unusual hazard to life, there is present and scrubbed as first assistant a physician designated by the credentials committee as being qualified to assist in major surgery.
3. Second and third assistants at major operations and first assistants at lesser operations may be nurses, aides, or technicians if designated by the hospital authorities as having sufficient training to properly and adequately assist in such procedures.
4. The operating room register is complete and up-to-date.
5. There is a complete history and physical work-up in the chart of every patient prior to surgery. If such has been transcribed, but not yet recorded in the patient's chart, there is a statement in the chart to that effect and an admission note by the physician.
6. A properly executed consent form for operation is in the patient's chart prior to surgery.
7. There are adequate provisions for immediate post-operative care.
8. An operative report describing techniques and findings is written or dictated immediately following surgery and is signed by the surgeon.
9. All infections of clean surgical areas are recorded and reported to the administration. A procedure exists for the investigation of such cases.
10. The operating rooms are supervised by an experienced registered professional nurse.
11. The following equipment is available in the operating suites: call-in system, cardiac monitor, resuscitator, defibrillator, aspirator, thoracotomy set, and tracheotomy set.
12. The operating room suite and accessory services are so located that traffic is controlled and there is no through traffic.
13. Precautions are taken to eliminate hazards of explosions, including use of shoes with conductive soles and prohibition of nylon garments.
14. Rules and regulations and/or policies related to the operating room are available and posted.
15. The following are required for every patient:
    a. Preanesthetic physical examination by a physician, with findings recorded within 48 hours of surgery
    b. Anesthetic record on a special form
    c. Postanesthetic follow-up, with findings recorded by an anesthesiologist or nurse anesthetist
16. The department of anesthesia is responsible for all anesthetics administered in the hospital; in hospitals where there is no department, the department of surgery assumes responsibility for establishing general policies and supervising the administration of anesthetics.
17. The director of anesthesia preferably is also the director of inhalation therapy.
18. If anesthetics are not administered by a qualified anesthesiologist, they are administered by a physician anesthetist or a registered nurse anesthetist under the supervision of the operating physician. The hospital staff designates those persons qualified to administer anesthetics and delineates what the person is qualified to do.
19. The postanesthetic follow-up note is written 3 to 24 hours after the operation, notes any postoperative abnormalities or complications, and states the blood pressure, the pulse, the presence or absence of the swallowing reflex and cyanosis, and the general condition of the patient.
20. Safety precautions include: shockproof and sparkproof equipment; humidity control; proper electrical grounding; posted safety regulations; storage of flammable anesthetic and oxidizing gases that meets the standards of the National Fire Protection Association Code.

Adapted from 42 C.F.R. Section 405.1031(a) (1985) (Surgery); and 42 C.F.R. Section 405.1031(b) (1985) (Anesthesia).

to the patient for an injury allegedly caused when the regionally anesthetized patient heard one of the physicians say, "Oops, I cut in the wrong place." The trial judge had found this testimony by the patient insufficient evidence of negligence because the patient could not tell which physician, the surgeon or his assistant, made the statement.

This court held that even assuming the assisting physician made the statement, the surgeon would not be relieved of the responsibility since he had a "nondelegable duty to see that the operation was performed with due care."[35] If the court was unwilling to allow the patient's surgeon to delegate this duty to a physician first assistant, it is unlikely a surgeon could delegate this duty to an RN first assistant.

VIEW 2: OUTSIDE THE SCOPE OF NURSING PRACTICE

The nurse who functions as first assistant in states where first assisting is not within the scope of nursing practice incurs many risks. These include disciplinary action, criminal charges, and difficulty with insurance coverage and standard of care in a negligence case. The nurse could face disciplinary action, including revocation or suspension of the nurse's license to practice, for practicing beyond the scope of nursing. The nurse could face criminal charges for the unauthorized practice of medicine.

Should the nurse be sued for negligence, the nurse's actions as first assistant would probably not be covered by malpractice insurance, since most malpractice policies specifically exclude coverage for acts outside the scope of nursing practice. Additionally, if the RN first assistant is sued for negligence, it is uncertain to which standard of care the nurse would be held. Probably it would be the standard of care for physicians functioning as first assistants, since it is the general rule that a person who undertakes to perform the activities of another profession will be held to the standard of care for that profession.

New modes of delivering surgical procedures

Increases in the numbers of surgical procedures done on an ambulatory or same-day admission basis is a trend with specific legal implications for perioperative nursing practice. These implications involve differences in preoperative preparation and supervision of the patient which have implications for the surgical episode itself and postoperative implications that involve assessment of the patient's readiness for discharge and assessment of patient or caregiver knowledge levels to carry out safe postoperative home care.

Perioperative nurses will need to be extra vigilant in their immediate preoperative assessments for ambulatory or same-day surgery patients. They will be less able to rely upon their nursing colleagues on the units for pertinent data such as history, allergies, mobility deficits, sensory impairments or for assurance that the patient has been NPO (had nothing to eat, nothing by mouth). Perioperative nurses will also need to become more actively involved in discharge teaching so as to assure that the patient or the caregiver has a sufficient knowledge base to care for the patient safely after discharge.

A 1975 Missouri case serves to illustrate the importance of discharge planning and discharge teaching in perioperative nursing practice.[36] This case involved a 48-year-old woman who had undergone a tonsillectomy as an outpatient in a physician's office. The surgery took place about 10 AM, and the patient remained in an observation area of the office. During that time she was given constant attention by an attendant, not a nurse, who noted blood on the patient's fingers. A friend arrived about 4 PM to drive the patient home, but not planning to stay with the patient, arranged for a neighbor to stay with her. The patient was placed in bed on her back and was making loud snoring sounds. When the snoring sounds stopped, the neighbor assumed the patient had fallen asleep.

When the husband returned home about 6:30 PM, he found his wife cold and lifeless. The cause of death was asphyxia due to blood in the bronchial tree and edema of the glottis. The friend testified that she had not received instructions about positioning the patient, although the physician did tell her to place an ice pack on the patient's throat and indicated he had ordered some prescriptions that would be delivered later.

The court held that the surgeon's duty to the patient does not end with the conclusion of an operative procedure. Rather, the surgeon had a continuing duty to the patient to either provide care himself or to turn her over to some person who could safely do so.

Discharge planning must begin in the surgeon's office or clinic, before admission, to enable the patient to make the arrangements that will be needed for a safe postoperative course. These arrangements must be reviewed for appropriateness prior to discharge. Patients and their caregivers should receive express, preferably written, instructions on assessments and interventions necessary to care for the patient at home.

Patients must have sufficient knowledge not only to care for themselves safely but also to prevent them from endangering others. In one of the first cases to recognize that a health care professional could be liable to third parties, the court held that a physician could be liable for the injuries received when a bus driver lost consciousness after the use of a drug the physician had prescribed.[37]

The plaintiff was a passenger on a bus when the driver lost consciousness due to the side effects of a drug (pyribenzamine) which had been prescribed for him by the defendant physician. Evidence at trial showed that the standard of care in prescribing this drug included warning the patient of possible side effects. The bus driver testified that the physician gave him no warning concerning possible side effects of the drug and that he had taken the first dose of the drug prior to the accident. The court instructed the jury that if they determined that no warning had been given to the bus driver, the verdict should go against the prescribing physician.

A Texas court similarly found that a physician can owe a duty to use reasonable care to protect the driving public.[38] That court found that the plaintiff's injuries from being struck by a car driven by the patient were the reasonably foreseeable consequence of the physician's negligence in failing to warn his patient not to drive while under the influence of a prescribed drug (quaalude).

A California court also found that a physician could be liable for failing to warn the patient against driving while in an uncontrolled diabetic condition, but that the physician's duty did not extend so far as to require that the physician control the conduct of the patient so as to prevent her from driving.[39]

These cases suggest that with respect to an ambulatory surgery unit, physicians and nurses could be liable to the driving public should a patient attempt to drive home while still under the influence of an anesthetic or sedative. Standards of the Joint Commission on Accreditation of Hospitals[40] and federal regulations require that all patients be discharged in the company of a responsible adult.[41] At a minimum, patients must be instructed as to the danger incurred should they attempt to drive. Reasonable attempts should be made to provide the patient with alternatives. The nurse should always apprise the treating physician and the administrator of the situation prior to the patient's departure. This is yet another example of a situation with possible legal ramifications that is best dealt with by prevention. The patient should know and understand the importance of the accompanied home policy before he or she arrives in the unit so that plans can be made accordingly.

Federal regulation of ambulatory surgical services is relatively new.[42] The conditions for coverage (Medicare payment) dealing with nursing state that the nursing services must be directed and staffed to assure that the nursing needs of all patients are met.[43] Patient care responsibilities must be delineated for all nursing personnel. Nursing service must be provided in accordance with recognized standards of practice, and there must be a registered nurse available for emergency treatment whenever there is a patient in the ambulatory surgical center.[44]

Standards of care

Written policies and procedures and documentation in this area of nursing practice is extremely important. Both determine how, under what conditions, and if an operating room nurse, including the perioperative nurse, has met a standard owed a patient. Both of these areas will be discussed below.

WRITTEN POLICIES AND PROCEDURES

While written policies and procedures are important in any nursing care setting, the increased potential for injury to OR patients and the prospect of a *res ipsa loquitur* instruction to a jury make them even more important in the OR. Written policies serve to protect the OR nurse from successful suits for negligence in at least two distinct ways:

1. Consistent adherence to uniform policy and procedure provides safer patient care, decreasing the likelihood that patient injury will occur.
2. If injury does, nonetheless, occur and suit is filed, it will be easier to show that the nurse complied with the standard of care if the nurse followed the policy and procedure of the institution.

Preventing injury to patients can be accomplished through many techniques, including, for example, developing a sponge count procedure. Proving that a nurse followed OR procedures and policies will assist in proving that the nurse was not negligent in the case of a *res ipsa loquitur* situation.

Cynics will sometimes argue that it is "legally safer" not to have written policies and procedures because, if not followed, they can be used to show the nurse failed to comply with the standard. While this is theoretically true, the cynics do not explain why they expect nurses to disregard policy. Furthermore, if a particular patient situation makes adherence to policy a threat to patient safety, the nurse's professional judgment will also be considered when adjudicating the reasonableness of the decision not to follow policy.

Far from insulating the nurse or hospital from negligence suits, the failure to have policies may *in itself* be negligence. That was the holding in a 1982 California case, stating that a hospital had a legal duty to devise adequate sponge accounting procedures.[45]

OPERATING ROOM DOCUMENTATION

Because of the greater possibility that *res ipsa loquitur* doctrine will apply in cases involving injury in the OR, documentation of OR nursing care is particularly important. The defendant OR nurses will be better able to meet the burden of proof that they were not negligent if the OR record reflects that the standard of care was met. Given this particular importance of documentation in the operating room, it is unfortunate that some OR nurses have not felt confident in their ability to document care in the patient's health care record.

One strategy to prevent potential injuries in the OR and hence prevent possible suits for negligence is to brainstorm all possible injuries that predictably can occur in the operating room. Then identify all the measures OR nurses routinely take to prevent these injuries. Use these lists in developing the OR record form. The use of such a checklist serves at least two functions:

1. Prevention of injury by serving as a reminder to the circulating nurse of indicated safety measures
2. Documentation for purposes of the record that the safety measures were taken

The record's use in legal proceedings is merely a subset of the record's primary purpose of documenting the health status, interventions, and responses of the patient. Hence, what and how to chart are questions most properly addressed to the health care professions, not the legal profession.

Perioperative documentation should meet the Association of Operating Room Nurses' recommended practices for documentation.[46] These are guidelines for documentation in specific settings. Additional information on documentation is given in Chapter 28.

Recommendations and trends

Several recommendations for the practice of operating room and perioperative nursing have already been made in this chapter. The most important recommendation is to pay special attention and vigilance to patient care, thereby preventing injury to OR patients. Because of these patients' vulnerability to injury, OR nurses need to be especially involved in the development, implementation, and evaluation of safety procedures and precautions. Documentation and written policies should be designed which address the special care needs of OR patients and OR nurses. Thorough and complete documentation will provide OR nurses with the best resource for explaining their actions if questioned later, especially under a *res ipsa loquitur* situation.

While the OR nurse is not responsible for obtaining the informed consent (surgeon responsibility), there may be a duty to see that hospital policy has been carried out; that is, the informed consent has been documented in the patient's record. Specific informed consent policies should exist in each institution.

First assisting may present unique legal questions for the OR nurse who functions in this role. Prior to assuming this role, the nurse should know and review the AORN statements and the position of the state board of nursing.

Given the trend toward new, one-day ways of doing surgical procedures, OR nurses need to be aware of new legal implications for their practice, including the responsibility for more complete assessment prior to a procedure and for proper and appropriate discharge from the unit with instructions for postoperative care by the patient or other caregiver.

Endnotes

1. AMERICAN NURSE'S ASSOCIATION AND ASSOCIATION OF OPERATING ROOM NURSES, STANDARDS OF PERIOPERATIVE NURSING PRACTICE 3 (1981).
2. *Id.*
3. *McConnell v. Williams,* 65 A.2d 243 (Pa. 1949).
4. *Thomas v. Hutchinson,* 275 A.2d 23 (Pa. 1971).
5. *Id.* at 27 (emphasis added).
6. *Sparger v. Worley Hospital, Inc.,* 547 S.W.2d 582 (Tex. 1977).
7. *Id.* at 583.
8. *Baird v. Sickler,* 433 N.E.2d 593 (Ohio 1982).
9. 211 Cal. Rptr. 445 (Cal. App. 1985).
10. *Id.* at 450. (Footnote 8 gives plaintiff's special instruction no. 3.)
11. *Ybarra v. Spangard,* 157 P.2d 687 (Cal. 1944).
12. *Id.* at 691.
13. *Fiorentino v. Wenger,* 227 N.E.2d 296 (N.Y. 1967).
14. *Roberson v. Menorah,* 588 S.W.2d 134 (Mo. App. 1979); *Ackerman v. Lerwick,* 676 S.W.2d 318 (Mo. App. 1984).
15. *Roberson v. Menorah,* 588 S.W.2d 134, 138 (Mo. App. 1979).
16. *Fiorentino v. Wenger,* 227 N.E.2d 296, 300 (N.Y. 1967).
17. *Gridley v. Johnson,* 476 S.W.2d 475, 483-485 (Mo. 1972).
18. *Roberson v. Menorah,* 588 S.W.2d 134, 138 (Mo. App. 1979).
19. *Fiorentino v. Wenger,* 227 N.E.2d 296, 301 (N.Y. 1967).

20. *Cooper v. Curry,* 589 P.2d 201 (N.M. App. 1979).
21. *Id.* at 207 (dissenting opinion).
22. *Beck v. Lovell,* 361 So.2d 245 (La. App. 1978).
23. *Peihl v. The Dalles,* 571 P.2d 149 (Or. 1977); *Harrison v. Wilkerson,* 405 S.W.2d 649 (Tenn. App. 1966).
24. *Ruth v. Dight,* 453 P.2d 631 (Wash. 1969), *overruling, Lindquist v. Mullen,* 277 P.2d 724 (Wash. 1954).
25. *Truhitte v. French Hospital,* 180 Cal. Rptr. 152 (Cal. App. 1982).
26. A. SOUTHWICK, THE LAW OF HOSPITAL AND HEALTH CARE ADMINISTRATION 98 (1978).
27. *Czubinsky v. Doctor's Hospital,* 188 Cal. Rptr. 685 (1983).
28. *Id.* at 687.
29. *Id.*
30. *Id.*
31. *Id.* at 688.
32. 42 C.F.R. §405.1031(a) (1985).
33. 695 P.2d 665 (Cal. 1985). (Note: U.S. appeal pending.)
34. Association of Operating Room Nurses, *Official Statement: RN First Assistant.* 40 A.O.R.N. J., 441 (September 1984).
35. *Orozco v. Henry Ford Hospital,* 290 N.W.2d 363 (Mich. 1980).
36. *Id.* at 365.
37. *Bateman v. Rosenberg,* 525 S.W.2d 753 (Mo. App. 1975).
38. *Kaiser v. Suburban Transportation System,* 398 P.2d 14 (Wash. 1965), *modified,* 401 P.2d 350 (Wash. 1965), to state that the jury finds he [the physician] failed to give warning of the side effects of the drug.
39. *Gooden v. Tips,* 651 S.W.2d 364 (Tex. App. 1983).
40. *Myers v. Quesenberry,* 193 Cal. Rptr. 733 (Cal. App. 1983).
41. JOINT COMMISSION ON ACCREDITATION OF HOSPITALS, ACCREDITATION MANUAL (1985).
42. 42 C.F.R. §416.42(c) (1985).
43. 42 C.F.R. §416.1 *et seq* (1985).
44. 42 C.F.R. §416.46 (1985).
45. 42 C.F.R. §416.46(a) (1985).
46. *Truhitte v. French Hospital,* 180 Cal. Rptr. 152 (Cal. App. 1982).
47. Association of Operating Room Nurses, *AORN Recommended Practices for Documentation,* 35 A.O.R.N. J. 744 (March 1982).

Additional Readings

Creighton, *Captain of the Ship Doctrine* 8 SUP. NURS., 66 (1977).

Greenlaw, *Liability for Nursing Negligence in the Operating Room* 10 LAW, MED. & HEALTH CARE, 222 (October 1982).

Murphy, *Informed Consent: Role of the Operating Room Nurse* 5 TODAY'S OR NURS., 51 (March 1983).

Murphy, *Documenting OR Nursing Care* 5 TODAY'S OR NURS., 47 (May 1983).

Murphy, *Sponge Counts* 5 TODAY'S OR NURS., 30 (July 1983).

Murphy, *Judgment: Abandonment . . . a Circulating Nurse Has a Legal Duty to Remain With Her Patient* 5 TODAY'S OR NURS., 40 (November 1983).

Murphy, *When is the RN First Assistant Practicing Within the Scope of Nursing* 40 A.O.R.N. J., 256 (August 1984).

Murphy, *When is the RN First Assistant Protected by Institutional Policy* 40 A.O.R.N. J., 436 (September 1984).

Murphy, *Legal Aspects of Perioperative Care Extend to Ambulatory Surgery Settings* 40 A.O.R.N. J., 699 (November 1984).

Murphy, *Can the RN First Assistant be Liable for Patient Injury?* 41 A.O.R.N. J., 1006 (June 1985).

Rosen, *The Right to Refuse—Can an OR Nurse Refuse to Participate* 6 TODAY'S OR NURS., 29 (December 1984).

Chapter 13

Community and public health nursing

Cynthia E. Northrop

A review of case law involving community and public health nurses shows that most often the community health nurse (CHN) is involved in child abuse or parental rights termination cases. Public health nurses (PHNs) are also unique within the nursing profession in that their practice more than any other area of nursing practice involves the enforcement of public health laws and regulations at the federal, state, and local levels. This chapter will discuss the multidimensional role of the CHN and its legal issues.

Definition of practice

Several nursing groups are involved in defining and setting standards for the community and public health nurse. They include the American Nurses' Association (ANA), the American Public Health Association, Public Health Nursing Section (APHA), the Association of State and Territorial Directors of Nursing, the Association of Graduate Faculty in Community and Public Health Nursing, and the National League for Nursing (NLN), formerly the National Organization for Public Health Nursing. A thorough discussion of community or public health nursing practice is the subject of many other texts.[1]

The ANA defines community health nursing as a synthesis of nursing practice and public health practice applied to promoting and preserving the health of populations. The nature of this practice is general and comprehensive. It is not limited to a particular age or diagnostic group and is continuing, not episodic. The primary responsibility is to the population as a whole, while including activities directed to individuals, families, or groups. CHNs are involved in health promotion, health maintenance, and prevention of disease.[2] The ANA Standards of Community Health Nursing Practice are listed in the box on p. 196.

The APHA, PHN section, also defines public health nursing. It synthesizes the body of knowledge from the public health sciences and professional nursing theories for the purpose of improving the health of the entire community. This goal includes primary prevention and health promotion and is the foundation for public health nursing practice. The PHN section states that success in reducing the risks and in improving the health of the community depends on the involvement of consumers, especially groups experiencing health risks, and others in the community, in health planning, and in self-help activities.[3]

While there is a difference, conceptually or otherwise, between community health nursing and public health nursing,[4] for the purposes of this chapter they are used interchangeably. Within case law the term public health nurse or nursing is used overwhelmingly more often than community health nurse or nursing.

STANDARDS OF COMMUNITY HEALTH NURSING PRACTICE

Standard I Theory

The nurse applies theoretical concepts as a basis for decisions in practice.

Standard II Data Collection

The nurse continuously collects data that are comprehensive, accurate, and systematic.

Standard III Diagnosis

The nurse uses data collected about the community, family, and individual to determine a diagnosis.

Standard IV Planning

The nurse develops plans at each level of prevention which delineates nursing actions unique to client needs.

Standard V Intervention

The nurse, guided by the care plan, intervenes to promote, maintain, or restore health, prevent illness, and effect rehabilitation.

Standard VI Evaluation

The nurse evaluates responses of the community, family, and individuals to interventions in order to revise the data base, diagnosis, and plan to determine progress toward goals.

Standard VII Professional Development

The nurse assumes responsibility for professional development and contribution to the professional growth of others. The nurse participates in peer review and other means of evaluation to assure quality of nursing practice.

Standard VIII Interdisciplinary Collaboration

The nurse collaborates with other health care providers, other professionals, and community leaders in assessing, planning, implementing, and evaluating programs for community health.

Standard IX Research

The nurse contributes through research to theory and practice in community health nursing.

Adapted from AMERICAN NURSES' ASSOCIATION, STANDARDS OF COMMUNITY HEALTH NURSING PRACTICE (1986).

Variety of roles

PHNs are employed in the private and public sectors. The primary public sector employers of PHNs are local and state governments. PHNs working for the federal government should review Chapter 18. PHNs employed by the local or state government are usually in health departments, although they also work in state education and labor departments. The government-employed PHN may be a generalist, responsible for a caseload of families within a particular geographic area or a census track, and provide nursing services in homes, clinics, schools, and workplaces within that geographic region. In at least two legal disputes the PHN and public health nursing service were identified as essential components of the health department and as important community services.[5]

Government-employed PHNs may also be specialists. These PHNs may be assigned to work solely in schools, as a school nurse, or in clinics. Chapter 14 discusses the subject of school nurses. Other government-employed PHNs include nurses employed in the department of corrections or by individual jails or prisons. These nurses are the subject of Chapter 16. Sometimes government-employed, but usually employed by the private sector, are occupational health nurses. Occupational health nursing is the subject of Chapter 15. Nursing care of the elderly, Chapter 17, is relevant to private and public sector PHNs.

Some CHNs work in private and public hospitals, however, in at least two areas: discharge planning and infection control. Still others function solely in home care, hospices, health maintenance organizations, outpatient services, private physician offices, nurse-managed centers and other community settings. Legal issues of these CHNs will be addressed in this chapter.

The employment status, private or governmental, of the PHN is relevant to determinations of liability and responsibility. As will be discussed, a government-employed PHN may be required by law to enforce the law, whereas the privately employed PHN is usually not legally designated as an agent of the state.

Enforcement of public health laws

Protecting the public's health is primarily a state government's responsibility. There are a few federal powers related to the nation's health as well. The state, however, may take steps through legislation and regulation to protect its citizens based upon its broad police power.

While the range and amount of public health legislation varies among states, the government-employed

PHN's job description, policy and procedure manuals, and other descriptions of responsibilities will rely heavily upon the particular jurisdiction's legislation and regulation. Private sector PHNs must also know these laws and follow them (for example, report child abuse), but their practice may not be as affected by them because their agencies are not legally responsible for enforcing public health laws.

Presented below (see box) is a sample listing of a state legislature's laws and regulations in public health. The box on p. 198 lists sample federal legislation. The PHN works with a number of other public health officials, such as community nutritionists, social workers, investigators, health educators, sanitation engineers, and many others, in carrying out public health laws, both federal and state.

Given the breadth of statutes available to discuss, only three areas which consume large portions of the usual PHN role will be discussed. It is these areas in which PHN case law was found.

COMMUNICABLE DISEASES

At the turn of the century the first PHNs' practice was comprised of measures to protect the public from epidemics and spread of contagious diseases within the community. By 1920 all states and most large cities had health departments, with the majority staffed by CHNs. Disease prevention is still a major focus of the CHN's role.

Federal Legislation. Congress created the Public Health Service (PHS) and, specifically, the Centers for Disease Control (CDC) for the purpose of surveillance, data collection, and analysis.[6] This legislation requires that all states and U.S. territories report on a weekly, monthly, and annual basis the occurrence of certain diseases. In addition, states may voluntarily report other conditions. Mandatorily notifiable diseases include acquired immune deficiency syndrome (AIDS), gonorrhea, chickenpox, syphilis, hepatitis, salmonellosis, tuberculosis, shigellosis, measles (Rubeola), mumps, and aseptic meningitis.

AIDS has been named the number one priority of the U.S. Public Health Service.[7] Legal issues pertaining to AIDS include concerns about confidentiality, mandated screening, and transmission of the disease. Guidelines issued by the Centers for Disease Control stress the importance of maintaining confidentiality while reporting the existence of the disease. CDC has developed guide-

SELECTED STATE PUBLIC HEALTH LEGISLATION

- Department of health, county boards of health, health officers
- Statistics and records: birth, death, fetal death certificates; marriage, divorce, annulment records; personal medical records; disclosure
- Death: determination and definition of death, postmortem examiners, medical examiners, autopsies, organ donation, anatomy board, unclaimed bodies
- Juvenile services, mental retardation and developmental disabilities law
- Misuse of alcohol and drugs, programs and facilities
- Mental hygiene law: rights of mentally ill institutionalized individuals, incompetency and insanity in criminal cases
- Other health care programs: hereditary disorder programs, high blood pressure programs, kidney disease programs, physical fitness
- General day care: children, elderly, and medically handicapped adults
- Indigent and medically indigent
- Preventive services and home care
- Medical assistance program
- Family support services program
- Programs for crippled children, educational programs for handicapped children
- Reimbursements and collections: court ordered examinations
- Laboratories: public health and clinical laboratories, medical laboratories, tissue banks, medical test units
- Disease prevention: reports on diseases; control of infectious and contagious diseases; cancer; diethylstilbestrol; diseases of pregnancy and infancy; syphilis; gonococcal ophthalmia neonatorum; therapeutic nutrition for pregnant women, infants, and children; rabies; tuberculosis; pertussis; drugs and vaccines; liabilities and warranties for blood; religious exceptions
- Health care facilities: comprehensive health planning, health services cost review commission, hospitals and related institutions, home health agencies, chronic disease centers, health maintenance organizations, hospices
- Consent provisions: minors, disabled individuals, action without consent, abortions, artificial insemination, sterilization
- School health: mandated examinations, vision and hearing screening, early detection programs, required immunizations

SELECTED FEDERAL PUBLIC HEALTH LEGISLATION

Food and Drug Act
Vocational Education Act
Nurse Training Act
Mental Health System Act
Social Security Act and Medicare and Medicaid Amendments
Health Planning and Resources Development Act
Medicare End-Stage Renal Disease Amendments
Medical Devices Act
Public Health and Community Mental Health Amendments
Sudden Infant Death Syndrome Act
Consumer Product Safety Act
Emergency Medical Services Systems Act
Rehabilitation Act
National Sickle Cell Anemia Control Act
Communicable Disease Control Act and Amendments
Comprehensive Drug Abuse Prevention and Control Act
Occupational Safety and Health Act
Family Planning Services and Population Research Act
Comprehensive Alcohol Abuse and Alcoholism Prevention, Treatment, and Rehabilitation Act
Federal Coal Mine Health and Safety Act
Lead-based Paint Poisoning Prevention Act
Heart Disease, Cancer, and Stroke Amendments
Health Services for Agricultural Migratory Workers
National Health Survey Act
Environmental Protection Acts

lines and recommendations for preventing transmission of AIDS.[8] These guidelines are examples of standards which could be used in malpractice and other litigation.

State Legislation. While state requirements do vary, most states require certain communicable disease reporting. The usual list of diseases includes: gonorrhea, hepatitis (viral, types A and B), meningitis (haemophilus, meningococcal, streptococcus types A and B, viral), meningococcemia, yellow fever, typhus fever, leprosy, smallpox, diphtheria, typhoid fever, scarlet fever, chancroid, typhoid or nontyphoid salmonellosis, syphilis, and tuberculosis.[9]

The state health department is responsible for obtaining accurate and complete reports on communicable diseases, determining the prevalence of each and devising a means to control the communicable disease.[10] Most states promulgate additional regulations regarding reporting and communicable diseases.[11]

States have specific powers in relation to communicable diseases. These usually include the right to investigate the disease, to inspect the person and enter premises, to order physical examinations such as a chest x-ray, and to confine and quarantine individuals and disinfect property.[12]

In most states the physician, hospitals, and laboratories are required to report to the state.[13] However, the PHNs often are the initial identifier of the disease and have a responsibility to inform the public health physician and PHN supervisor of assessment and findings. In addition, the PHN is often the implementor of the corrective and protective measures instituted to prevent the spread of disease and provide a cure for the individual affected by the disease. This responsibility places additional legal obligations upon the nurse to fulfill the requirements of the laws and regulations and to act reasonably under the circumstances.

Because reporting is required, state legislatures have provided for an acceptable breach of confidentiality for the good of the entire society. But the information which is reported—usually name, address, age, race, sex, and identity of the disease or suspected disease—is still to remain confidential. A legislature may provide prohibitions against the maintenance of lists of names of those with certain diseases or, if rosters exist, may require that such information remain confidential within the health department and not be open for public scrutiny.[14]

Because of the importance to society in having the data about communicable diseases and other conditions, many states grant civil immunity from suit for good faith reporting.[15] No cases were found which involved an allegation against a PHN for breach of confidentiality or for failure to report a communicable disease. However, most legislation provides for penalties in the form of misdemeanors which carry fines.[16]

Other penalties may apply to PHNs and others who willfully disobey an order or obstruct the carrying out of an order of a health officer to move an individual whom a physician has certified as having an infectious disease that endangers the public.[17] In addition, legislation and regulations may exist that prohibit individuals with infectious diseases from exposing others and that prohibit another person from willfully taking an individual who has an infectious disease and endangering the public by exposing another to that person.[18]

In some states government-employed PHNs are granted immunity from personal liability for giving immunizations for the prevention of communicable diseases. In one state the law provides that a person who lawfully administers a drug or vaccine is not liable for any adverse effect that arises from the use of the drug or vaccine if the drug or vaccine (1) is administered to immunize a person against a disease or (2) is approved by the U.S. Food and Drug Administration for the purpose for which the drug or vaccine is administered.[19]

In some states in immunization projects that are found by the state secretary of health to conform to good medical and public health practice and where written approval for the project to be administered in the state is given, a physician, nurse, or other person participating in the project is not liable for any adverse effect that arises from the use of a drug or vaccine in the project.[20] The law usually does not exempt a person from liability for gross negligence, exempt a drug manufacturer from the duty to use ordinary care in preparing and handling a drug or vaccine or exempt a person from liability that arises out of the improper or illegal administration of a drug or vaccine.[21]

The state's power of requiring immunizations in order to prevent communicable diseases is not an unchecked governmental power. The primary exception to required immunization is if the individual or a child's parent objects to the immunization because it conflicts with the individual's bona fide religious beliefs and practices.[22] All exceptions, however, may be denied should an emergency or disease epidemic be declared by the state official.[23]

In the last few years the vaccine for pertussis has caused major adverse reactions. Public reaction to these stirred legislative action in many states. For example, one legislature passed laws designed to collect information about the adverse reaction in order to develop guidelines for circumstances under which pertussis vaccine should not be administered or should be delayed, any categories of potential recipients who are significantly more vulnerable to major adverse reactions than the general population, consent procedures, and procedures to notify all physicians of the content of the guidelines.[24]

This is one example of how the PHN's role is shaped by legislation. The CHN is included in the definition of health care provider and, hence, through this new legislation has gained new legal responsibilities. These include specific duties to inform parents, to elicit information regarding any possible exceptions for giving the child the pertussis vaccine, and to report adverse reactions. Record-keeping duties are specifically addressed by the legislation, including what information about the vaccine is to be kept in the child's health record (date, manufacturer, lot number, identifying information on the vaccine used, and name and title of the health care provider) and information about any adverse reactions.[25]

Case Law. PHNs have been involved in some lawsuits dealing with tuberculosis, venereal disease, and polio, either as defendants, witnesses, or the ones who gave the medication, immunization, and/or treatment that brought the cases to trial. These cases involved the issues of negligence, product liability, and informed consent for state mandated treatments. The cases involving the latter two issues will be discussed below; the other case will be discussed on p. 201.

There have been situations where children or parents have contracted polio from the child's ingestion of the polio vaccine. In one case the key issue was the adequacy of the warning to parents given by the manufacturer of the vaccine.[26] The unique manner in which immunization programs are administered across the nation was discussed as a key factor in the court's decision. The court held that the manufacturers should have known how the vaccine was administered (for example, without a physician's consideration of individual needs and circumstances, a "learned intermediary," and on a mass scale) and therefore was liable for failure to adequately inform the ultimate consumer of the risk associated with ingestion of the vaccine.

The PHN who administered the immunizations was not viewed as a "learned intermediary," one who is seen as responsible for informing the parents of the risks associated with the immunizations, even though in one of the cases it was shown that the PHN read about and knew what the risks were but had not passed them on to the parent.

However, courts are divided on this issue. One court found a county health department and the manufacturer not liable for the death of a father who contracted polio from his daughter, who received the immunization, administered by a licensed practical nurse in a well baby clinic, upon the order of a pediatric nurse practitioner.[27] In this case the evidence showed that exercise of due care by a parent would have been to allow the vaccine to be administered knowing the ravaging effects of polio upon children, even if the plaintiff knew the slight risk (1 in 5 million) of contracting polio. The court also noted that there was no other vaccine readily available.

The court pointed to the fact that millions of Americans have the vaccine given to their children and that it was the vaccine recommended and approved by the federal government and the National Academy of Pediatricians. The plaintiff in this case was unable to say at trial that she would not have, under any circumstances, permitted her child to receive the vaccine.

In a case involving the issue of whether a physician and health department were negligent in prescribing the drug INH to the plaintiff without warning her of the risks, a Louisiana court held that a reasonable person would have consented to the INH treatment even with the knowledge of the risk of hepatitis.[28] The court said weighing the risk of hepatitis against the possibility of tuberculosis, a prudent individual would have submitted to the treatment.

PHNs are involved in enforcing laws related to many other communicable diseases. One situation involved a PHN's follow-up of a report of infectious intestinal parasites and worms.[29] A PHN's client's neighbor wrote a letter complaining about the manner in which the PHN went about collecting the specimens. Apparently, the PHN approached the client in a public place, embarrassing her and her family.

The neighbor's letter went to the health department, which investigated the situation and determined that the nurse was carrying out the usual functions of a PHN (checking into the possible spread of an infectious ailment in the family per request of a family physician). The PHN sued the neighbor for defamation (libel) but was unsuccessful. The court held that the communication was not defamatory, that it was criticism which did not amount to a communication which harmed the PHN's reputation. In addition the court held that a private citizen, interested in the proper administration of the local health department, was qualifiedly privileged to express a concern regarding the alleged improper conduct of an employee of the county health department. Chapter 5 has further discussion of defamation.

HEREDITARY DISEASES AND OTHER CONDITIONS

Another important area of enforcing public health laws is that of reporting conditions and rendering treatments and services connected with occupations, toxic substances, cancer, pregnancy, infancy, rabies, and the prevention of mental retardation and birth defects. Defined within state laws, these conditions are to be reported to the state health department, usually by physicians and hospitals. The state may adopt procedures for obtaining information about diseases which are related to these substances and conditions.[30]

PHNs, again, are often the ones who gather information, monitor their assigned communities, and render services and information to those in need. In a case involving issues of physician malpractice, a PHN's referral letter, sent with the parent's permission, was admitted as evidence to demonstrate the pediatrician's failure to diagnose hypothyroidism, the subject of the PHN's letter to the medical center.[31] In addition, hospital nurses or laboratory technicians are required to do testing for phenylketonuria (PKU) and other conditions and will be held liable, for example, for failure to conduct the proper test.[32]

Most states have services for crippled children which locate children who have organic diseases, defects, or conditions which may hinder normal growth and development. In order to participate in state-funded projects, children must meet eligibility requirements, such as age, medical, and financial. In some states nurses are mandated to report physical defects observed in children. For example, in one state a licensed nurse who has professional knowledge that any child under 5 years of age has a physical defect shall, within 48 hours from the time of acquiring such knowledge, mail a report to the department of health services.[33]

ENVIRONMENT, SANITATION, AND HOUSING

PHNs participate in the enforcement of laws regarding physical condition and environment of property and goods, including food and drugs. Most health departments have a wide variety of professionals involved in this area, including sanitation engineers, chemists, biologists, environmental specialists, and industrial hygienists.

Federal Legislation. The federal legislation in the area of food and drugs is the Food, Drug, and Cosmetic Act.[34] The Food and Drug Administration (FDA) has authority over most processed foods; drugs, including serums and vaccines, both prescription and over-the-counter; cosmetics; and medical devices. The federal powers in this area involve establishing mandatory standards for the products, including that new drugs be shown safe and effective prior to marketing; regulating food additives and artificial colorings; packaging and labeling of foods, drugs, devices, and cosmetics; regulating animal drug safety; and regulating vaccines, blood, and other biological products.[35]

Federal laws which have as their aim the prevention and elimination of health hazards in the environment include the National Enviromental Policy Act (NEPA),[36] the Clean Air Act,[37] the Clean Water Act,[38] the Resource Conservation and Recovery Act,[39] and the Consumer Product Safety Act.[40] The Occupational Safety and Health Act and the Toxic Substances Control Act will be discussed in Chapter 15 on occupational health nursing.

The NEPA requires the federal government to produce environmental impact statements for its proposed actions. This act also established a mechanism for information to be gathered on the state of the nation's environment. The Clean Air Act provides for federal air quality standards and requires that states enforce such standards. Preventing water pollution is the primary goal of the Clean Water Act. Its goals are accomplished through nationwide standards, use of the best available technology, and regulation of all pollutants discharged into navigable waters. The Resource Conservation and Recovery Act deals with solid wastes and hazardous and toxic wastes. Minimum criteria have been established for the transportation, storage, and dumping of wastes.

The Consumer Product Safety Commission, an independent regulatory commission, has authority to administer several federal safety laws addressing hazardous substances, poison prevention and flammable fabrics. The commission collects and disseminates data on product hazards and resulting injuries, establishes and enforces product safety standards, gathers injury information from participating hospital emergency rooms, conducts its own tests, and receives information directly from consumers.

Enforcement of these federal laws ranges from voluntary actions to court-ordered actions. For example, the Consumer Product Safety Commission may require manufacturers to notify consumers of a danger and to repair, replace, or refund the purchase price; or it may initiate a court-ordered ban of a product.

PHNs are often involved in data collection and prevention programs which exist based on federal legislation, including child restraint programs, seat belt programs, and laws relating to the prevention of accidents caused by drunk driving. In addition, as important community resources, CHNs often refer clients for services provided by federal legislation.

State Legislation. State legislation parallels federal laws and is often required by federal legislation. For example, states have their own environmental protection legislation, consumer product safety laws, highway safety protections, and other regulations. PHNs often work within divisions of the state health department, state labor department, and state highway department as nurses, collecting data and conducting surveys and epidemiological studies of the health of aggregates affected by certain environmental conditions.

In at least one case a PHN has been involved as the agent of the state and the inspector of premises.[41] In this case the PHN's inspection report led to a court order to clean up the property which contained old cars, parts, and other junk. The state's action was deemed proper because the property condition harbored and bred rodents and was dangerous and hazardous to children in the area.

CONFIDENTIALITY, PRIVACY, AND INFORMED CONSENT

Because of the state's police power to protect the health, welfare, and safety of its citizens, individual freedoms which exist in other contexts may be altered or in some situations denied because of the state's necessity of action in order to protect all citizens. Ordered treatment of individuals and seizure of property or person may violate individual rights. Requiring or mandating immunizations, for example, does away with the voluntariness with which informed consent must exist in other contexts (for example, consent to surgical treatment). Readers should review Chapter 5, which describes situations that give rise to violations of civil rights, and Chapter 6, which thoroughly discusses informed consent.

Despite the state's power to act, however, PHNs must conduct their practice in a manner which allows for as much privacy, confidentiality, and informed consent as possible. To the fullest extent possible these rights still must be protected and given full consideration prior to the state's action. The key question for public health officials and PHNs is how the entire public's health can be protected while still affording individuals their rights. Only in extreme cases, such as epidemics, might individual rights give way totally to the right of the state to take measures for the good of the entire public.

Negligence in public health nursing practice

There have been very few negligence cases involving PHNs in public or private employment. However, two cases of negligence—both in the context of nursing services to tuberculosis (TB) patients, one in the clinic and one in the home—will be discussed.[42] In these two cases the court scrutinized several important areas applicable to PHN practice:

1. Clinic assessment procedures and documentation of signs and symptoms of adverse reactions to prescribed treatments
2. Assessment of health status in the home
3. Coordination of care between health department services and those of private physicians

CASE EXAMPLES

In the first case, a PHN received a telephone call from a private medical doctor (PMD) requesting TB services for a patient. Two different versions of what the conversation was came out at trial. The PMD said he discussed the patient's condition with the PHN and told the PHN that the patient had a positive sputum culture and that he had not treated anyone with TB for several years, so was unfamiliar with the drugs. He testified that he asked the nurse to put the patient on the health department's protocol and treat her and that he informed the patient that she was now under the care of the health department for the TB. The PMD denied prescribing any drugs for the patient.

The PHN, on the other hand, relayed to the court that she and the PMD discussed available treatment of TB; that the PMD ordered a standard combination of ethambutol, isoniazid, and vitamin B-6 for the patient; and that the PMD asked her to deliver the drugs to the patient on the following Monday.

In order to facilitate the patient beginning the treatment as soon as possible, the PHN went to her supervisor, a part-time health department physician, for his signature on the prescriptions. She marked the prescriptions per telephone order of PMD, noting the PMD's name. The health department physician signed the forms, and the PHN made the home visit later that day.

During the home visit the PHN testified she warned the patient that the drugs could affect her kidneys and that the patient should watch her urine for a red coloring. The PHN learned during the home visit that the patient had cataracts. The remainder of the conversation with the patient was disputed. The PHN testified that she checked the patient's vision with a 10-foot eye chart and recorded the readings as 10/100 in the right eye; 10/50 in the left eye.

The patient, supported by testimony from her sister who was present during the initial home visit, stated that the PHN told her she had forgotten the eye chart and to check the patient's vision she asked the patient to identify certain objects in the room. The patient testified that the PHN told her to watch the whites of her eyes and to notify her physician if they turned yellow. Interestingly, the eye chart the PHN said she used did not have a 10/100 line. The PHN further testified that she told the patient to watch for any decreased visual acuity.

The patient took the medications prescribed for one month. At the end of that month another PHN made a home visit, delivering another month's supply of drugs. The PHN testified she checked the patient's vision. It was undisputed that during home visits made in the following 2 months the patient's vision was not checked. The patient suffered rapid loss of vision during these 4 months. Uncontradicted expert testimony was presented at trial stating that if vision checks had been performed, the patient's loss of vision could have been detected, the ethambutol would have been stopped, and vision loss possibly could have been reversed.

In the fifth month of taking the drugs the patient saw the PMD for a regular checkup. She informed the PMD of her vision problems; however, it was disputed by the PMD to what extent the patient had informed him about the extent of the loss. Another month went by until the patient went to see the ophthalmologist, who immediately referred her to a neurologist who admitted her to the hospital, saw the ethambutol, and immediately concluded that it was the cause of her vision loss.

On procedural grounds the court remanded this case for a new trial. However, the court made several points which the trial court was to follow. The court determined that there was evidence in the record from which a jury could find, in pertinent part, that the:

1. PHN was negligent in failing to properly inform the patient of side effects of the drugs and to check the vision
2. PMD was negligent in failing to assess the patient's condition; that the PMD was still the patient's physician, not the health department
3. Health department was negligent for the PHN's negligent conduct; that the health department physician who was her supervisor may be liable but only for his own failure to properly supervise the PHN

In the second case, the court also examined PHN practice, but in the clinic setting. In this case a man who spoke broken English, an immigrant with the equivalent of fourth or fifth grade education, died following several months of taking INH. The patient, as part of a pre-employment physical, received a tuberculin skin test at a local health department clinic. It was positive, so a chest x-ray was done, which proved to be clear.

Since the patient was at risk for developing TB, he was placed, by a health department physician who reviewed his health department record, on INH for a year. The patient was enrolled in a U.S. Public Health Service study protocol examining the relationship of INH to hepatitis. The court noted that despite the fact that INH was a prescription drug, no physician ever saw the patient and despite the fact that the program was a special surveillance program, no informed consent form to utilize the drug was ever signed by the patient.

This case has quite a legal history consisting of several trials and appeals. During each trial and on each appeal the court and jury found the health department physicians negligent (neither of the PHNs were sued, although their actions were in question, nor was the health department because in this state it had sovereign immunity). However, the jury also found the patient to be contributorily negligent. In this jurisdiction a finding of contributory negligence prevents any remedy and is a complete bar to the suit.

In essence the court held that the question of contributory negligence was properly for the jury. The jury (and the court supported its finding) was convinced that the documentation used in the clinic, which was computer cards, and testimony of PHN supervisors provided a clear basis for an inference that the patient was questioned about symptoms each time he visited the clinic, that the importance of reporting adverse reactions was emphasized, and that the patient failed to heed these instructions and denied any symptoms. Thus, he was contributorily negligent.

SCOPE OF EMPLOYMENT

Because CHN services are rendered in a wide variety of settings, the CHN's scope of employment is very broad. The case law discussing this issue for CHNs deals with the question of whether the CHN's scope of employment includes travel to and from a patient's home. The cases arise most often in situations where a CHN has been injured in an automobile accident or has injured another through negligent driving.[43] The implication of whether a CHN is inside or outside the scope of employment is that if a PHN is deemed outside the scope of employment during travel and an accident occurs, the employer as *respondeat superior* may not be liable, only the CHN.

Therefore, if the nurse is under the control, direction, and guidance of the employer when going to a patient's home, the employer may be liable along with the CHN for any negligence. However, if the nurse is in transit to the place of employment at the beginning of the day, is on the way home, or is shopping during lunch hour or on other personal business, the employer will not usually be liable for the nurse's negligent actions.

Insurance on both private and government-owned vehicles which are used in the PHN's practice should be reviewed. The terms of these policies may determine the answer to this issue.

SOVEREIGN IMMUNITY AND OTHER DEFENSES

Sovereign immunity may prevent an injured patient from suing a governmental entity, such as the health department. Immunities and defenses in general are discussed in Chapters 4 and 5. Sovereign immunity does not mean the PHN, individually, cannot be sued. Government agencies may not carry any insurance, and this is something the PHN should assess. On the other hand state legislatures may provide malpractice insurance for their employees.

In one case, public health physicians attempted to say they were immune because they were public officials.[44] The court held that the physicians failed to establish that they were public officials rather than public employees. In this jurisdiction governmental immunity extended to public officials when performing discretionary, rather than ministerial, acts in furtherance of their official duties. No cases were found where the issue of whether a PHN is a public official or public employee was discussed or decided. Given the physician's experience, the PHN's classification would probably be considered one of a public employee rather than a public official.

Payment for services

Payment and eligibility for health services varies, depending on the type of service and who is providing it. The sources of funding are public and private sources. Each carries its own rules and regulations. The principal federal and state funding for health care is through government insurance and payment programs, including Medicare, the federal health insurance plan for the elderly and disabled, and Medicaid (the jointly financed state and federal, but state-administered program for the poor and disabled).

The government-provided funding creates entitlement rights in those eligible. Each payment source may carry its own eligibility requirements. These may involve state or local rules and regulations. Failure to screen patients for their eligibility may give rise to allegations of fraud and misuse of public funds.

Overall, the PHN may be an integral part of the financial contract for services which is formed between the client and agency. Promises, reliance, and other considerations given by the nurse during the negotiating of the fees and services become part of the legal contract. Witnessing signatures of those accepting financial responsibility for the services creates a responsibility upon the nurse should legal questions arise later. The nurse's legal status in relation to the client is that of an agent for the employer.

In addition, questions of whether governmental insurance and other insurance programs will pay for nursing services in, for example, home or hospice programs can depend upon how well the CHN knows the federal regulations, conditions for participation in Medicare,[45] rules of the fiscal intermediaries, and state regulations.

For example, Medicare regulations will not allow for reimbursement of nursing services rendered to an individual who is not homebound. Therefore, when documenting that the nurse attempted patient contact and the telephone call went unanswered, the nurse should not document that no one was home, but rather the factual, objective comment that no one answered the telephone. Other principles of documentation, outlined in Chapter 28, will be helpful to CHNs.

Discharging indigent clients, those whose financial resources have been exhausted, or refusing to accept into the program those who are unable to pay have raised additional legal and ethical questions for CHNs and agencies. Agency policy will determine when a contractual relationship begins between the agency and the patient. Often, the contract begins after the CHN has made an initial home visit. Governmental agencies cannot discriminate; private agencies may or may not be prohibited from discriminating on the basis of ability to pay.

Reasonable and proper steps should be taken to assure that other resources are made available to the client who is not accepted into the service. For example, information about other agencies who may accept the client should be provided. Any necessary follow-up with the client's physician should be completed, especially notifying the physician that the agency is not accepting the client.

Another frequently arising situation is one in which the client cannot pay after nursing services have begun. Depending on the agency's policies, bylaws, and articles of incorporation and government or private status, an agency may withdraw services from the client upon reasonable notice and follow-up. Usually, agency policies provide that even where the client's ability to pay may not be the issue, services may be terminated where reasonable measures are taken. The client may also terminate the services.

Case law in this area is nonexistent. However, by anology to other cases of negligence, an agency and the CHN would be judged by whether its own policies were followed in terminating services. To avoid allegations of abandonment, the CHN and agency should be sufficiently satisfied that the client understands clearly that the service is being terminated and that all reasonable steps were taken under the circumstances.[46]

High risk clients

Care and treatment of certain high risk clients, including abused and neglected children, the elderly, infants who are not thriving, and migrant workers, raise legal issues for CHNs. Other high risk clients of CHNs exist, such as immigrants, the homeless, and runaways. Several governmental documents have defined high risk groups.[47] Many of these groups have been addressed in federal or state public health laws. The PHN should have copies of these laws for each group to whom care is given.

CHILD AND ADULT PROTECTIVE SERVICES

Both federal and state laws exist which focus on children who have been abused and neglected. Abuse of the elderly is also addressed in some state statutes but, nationally, has been addressed to a much lesser extent. The Child Abuse Prevention and Treatment Act[48] provides funds to states for identification, treatment, and prevention programs for child abuse. To be eligible for funds a state must meet many requirements, including having a child abuse and neglect law that provides legal immunity for persons who report and provides for an investigation promptly if child abuse is found. Immediate steps must be taken to protect the health and safety of the abused or neglected child.

In response to this federal initiative most states updated their laws regarding child abuse and neglect.[49] In all states every nurse, including the PHN, must report suspected child abuse. The definitions of child abuse vary among the states. Some define abuse to mean the sustaining of physical injury by a child as a result of cruel or inhumane treatment or as a result of a malicious act by any parent or other person who has permanent or temporary care, custody, or responsibility for supervison of a child under circumstances that indicate that the child's health or welfare is harmed or threatened thereby; or sexual abuse of a child, whether physical injuries are sustained or not.[50]

Other states define child abuse and neglect as physical

injury or injuries inflicted upon a child other than by accidental means; injuries which are at variance with the history given of them; a condition which is the result of maltreatment such as, but not limited to, malnutrition, sexual abuse, sexual exploitation, deprivation of necessities, emotional maltreatment, or cruel punishment; or neglect.[51]

Most state statutes also require that a nurse report to either the police or department of aging or social services suspected cases of abuse, neglect, exploitation, and abandonment of the elderly.[52] Chapter 17 discusses legal issues in nursing services to the elderly. In addition, PHNs may be involved in detection and services for victims of spouse abuse.

Legal questions of CHNs in reporting child and/or adult abuse include issues of liability in fulfilling the obligation to report, failure to report, and investigating reports. Each of these concerns is usually answered in the statutes and case law of the PHN's jurisdiction. Reporting statutes usually provide for fines and misdemeanor charges which would apply to a nurse if a report is not made and should have been.

No cases could be found in which a nurse was sued for reporting but in a case involving a physician who made a good faith but erroneous report, a court held that recovery of damages was precluded because the report was filed in good faith.[53] If the report had been made in bad faith, the court indicated this would be the situation in which an injured party might successfully sue the reporter.

Failure to respond to a report of child abuse raises another possible liability area. Again, no cases were found which involved a PHN. But in one case a social worker was convicted by a lower court for failing to properly respond to a report of suspected child abuse. The court reinforced that, at least in this jurisdiction, a public servant commits second degree official misconduct if he or she knowingly, arbitrarily, and capriciously refrains from performing a duty imposed by law.[54] However, the caseworker's legal duty in this case can be distinguished from a PHN's usual duty. Depending on the facts of a particular situation and the state laws, generally, the social worker is legally charged with responding to a child abuse report, not a PHN.

Discussing a physician's failure to diagnose and report child abuse, a court has found liability.[55] By analogy, the PHN could also be held civilly liable for failing to report child abuse. In another situation a county government and its youth services agency was successfully sued for negligently returning a child to her mother without adequately investigating the possibility of further abuse by the mother and her boyfriend. The court held that the county could be liable under Section 1983 (see Chapter 5 for further information) for the child's subsequent death from abuse by the boyfriend and mother in violation of the child's constitutional rights.[56]

There have been many examples of cases where the nurse reported child abuse promptly and properly.[57] PHNs who are members of child or elder abuse investigation teams may have special liability questions in carrying out such investigations. Being part of the team which exists based upon state laws, a PHN must fulfill the policies and procedures of the official duty. Investigations must be carried out properly, according to state laws and constitutional rights, such as those related to search and seizure, privacy, and confidentiality.

In a defamation case where the coordinator for a state department of health and rehabilitative services sued a trade association of licensed adult group residences for allegations made to the press about a visit made to an adult home to investigate charges of elder abuse and neglect, a CHN was part of the investigation team whose "physical assessments" of the elderly residents was the subject of the dispute.[58] These, the trade association reported to the press, humiliated the elderly and were unauthorized. The state coordinator was unsuccessful in the defamation case because he was deemed a public official, and he could not prove the required element of malice—that the trade association involved the press with a malice intent.

The issue of whether the nurse's physical assessments were unauthorized was not the subject of the litigation. However, the investigation team was acting upon a report of negligent treatment of the elderly residents. They entered the home and carried out legally assigned responsibilities. Licensing laws and abuse statutes provided the framework for these actions and responsibilities. The court noted that the nurse's assessment was observation of the outward behavior and physical appearance of a patient and was not a complete medical examination.

In a case involving the care of two elderly, bedridden women in their home, a PHN's actions were viewed as proper, under the circumstances.[59] The caretaker refused to provide badly needed medical care for the women. The PHN contacted the welfare department and, together with the social worker, arranged for an emergency order to hospitalize the women. While the issue in the case was who was responsible for paying for this emergency care, the propriety of the PHN's actions were not questioned.

FAILURE TO THRIVE

Clients in cases of failure to thrive, usually infants and their parents, represent another high risk group which PHNs serve. Unless there are state statutes which mandate referrals for follow-up by the state, permission for referral and involvment of the health department or home health agency must be obtained from the parent.

The failure to thrive diagnosis and condition may lead to a legal action for neglect or, where other statutes for protecting children exist, an action for children in need of assistance. Mandated reporting may still be necessary. Privacy, confidentiality, and consent should still be important considerations in the design of all programs for failure to thrive children.

MIGRANT WORKERS AND THEIR FAMILIES

Another high risk group which is the subject of federal and state laws is migrant workers. Because of the highly transient nature of this population, CHNs may serve such groups in their assigned communities on a seasonal basis. These agricultural workers and their families are not recognized as industrial workers, hence, are not covered by the Occupational Safety and Health Act, discussed in Chapter 15.

Since this group is poorly organized and economically disadvantaged and has major health problems, such as the results of pesticide exposure and exposure to farm equipment, the federal government has enacted legislation which provides health, social, and legal services.[60] In at least one case a PHN's involvement in visiting migrant workers and their families on a farm has caused some legal disputes and concerns.[61] In this case it was decided that before lawyers, nurses, or social workers could visit migrant workers they must give reasonable notice, except in emergency situations.

Teaching and advice in community health nursing practice

Of special concern to CHNs are the legal issues of giving advice regarding over-the-counter medications, being involved in health fairs, and public health screening activities, and dispensing prescription drugs within certain health department programs, such as drug abuse or family planning programs.

It is of particular importance to the practice of community health nursing that a state nurse practice act's definitions of the scope of nursing practice be broad. For example, teaching is specifically mentioned in Maryland's Nurse Practice Act.[62]

PHNs may be asked for any type of advice, as in the case of a woman who asked advice about whether to change her will.[63] In this case it was not clear how the PHN responded, except that she later testified in the will dispute that the client asked her advice. Certainly, in non–health related situations the PHN may decline to give advice. Even with health advice, the CHN at times may defer giving the advice until such time as he or she is certain of the reliabilty and accuracy of the information.

CHN standards of care (see p. 196) indicate that nursing actions provide for consumer participation in health promotion, maintenance, and restoration. Further, the standard specifies that the consumer is provided with the data needed to make informed decisions about promoting, maintaining, and restoring health; seeking and using appropriate health care services; and maintaining and using health care resources.

Evaluation of liability if a client is injured because of reliance upon any CHN advice would be based upon whether the CHN breached the legal standard of care owed the patient under the circumstances. The standards, for example, would provide evidence of whether the PHN breached a duty. No cases exist where a patient has sued a CHN for advice given. Such suits are possible, however.

Screening programs available to the public in which CHNs participate as part of their employment or as a volunteer may create special legal concerns. In both instances, the CHN would want to assess the need for having individual malpractice insurance. The volunteer, especially, would want to know what provisions have been made by the program planners for insurance.

Before participating in any mass screening programs the CHN should have a clear understanding of the protocols for what health assessment findings are to be referred to a physician. In one case, a PHN referred a man who had a high blood pressure reading to his family physician.[64] While the legal issue in the case did not involve the PHN's action, the court did not criticize it either. Further, what documentation will be kept should be reviewed for its adequacy in being evidence at a later time, should a question arise of whether the nurse referred the patient or not or whether a referral should have been made.

Generally, because the encounter with the member of the public is brief and for a single, limited purpose and because the client is essentially a well adult, the legal liability which attaches to the relationship is narrow and involves only the reasonable fulfillment of the responsibilities outlined in screening protocols.

The question of whether the CHN is "dispensing" drugs in violation of state pharmacy acts has been raised in the context of when a CHN is employed in certain clinic settings. Most state nurse practice acts indicate that a nurse may administer medications ordered by a physician licensed to practice medicine in the jurisdiction.[65] Standing orders and protocols used within certain health department or home health agency programs are an acceptable means of delivering care and are physician orders. Certainly, the *Sermchief* case clarified for nurse practitioners that the use of standing orders is an appropriate nursing activity in one jurisdiction.[66]

But, when a CHN distributes medication to patients, giving more than one dose at a time, she or he may be practicing pharmacy without a license. This issue should be clarified through the boards of nursing, medicine, and pharmacy within each state. For example, in one state the Pharmacy Act provides that "dispensing" can be done by pharmacists and "authorized prescribers."[67] A CHN may not specifically be mentioned in the legislation defining authorized prescribers. However, because the nurse functions under physician orders in administering medications, it can be argued that the nurse is the physician's agent in dispensing the medication and, thereby, the law intended to include nurses.

Because this may vary among jurisdictions, the state board of nursing should be contacted to clarify the exact position of the CHN within that jurisdiction. Nursing regulations may exist that clarify the situation. In addition, the state board and/or the attorney general of the particular state may have rendered an opinion on this topic.

Coordinating care: administering medications and treatments in the home and clinic

Medical orders pertaining to medications, diet and equipment in the home can take several forms: written or verbal (often via telephone). As diagnostic related groups (DRGs) determine shorter lengths of stay in the hospital for patients, home care services will be caring for more acutely ill individuals in the home. A major sign of this is the more advanced and complicated equipment and drugs being ordered for use and supervision in the home.

The usual analysis of liability will be applied to this changing area of care. Procedures and other agency documentation, orientation, and preparation of personnel will often answer the question of whether there has been a breach of nursing standards. As with any case, before the CHN accepts it, he or she must be certain and comfortable with the assignment, evaluating its complexity and care requirements in light of the CHN's preparation to carry out the assignment. Any lack of knowledge or skill should be identified immediately, and corrective steps should be taken.

It is common practice, in order to facilitate early assessment and care of patients leaving the hospital and entering home care services, that CHNs function on verbal orders for a period of time. It is also common practice that the CHN may be functioning on verbal orders recorded by an intake nurse who is part of the home care service. Given these conditions, the CHN is responsible, as would be any nurse, for evaluating the medical orders completely before relying upon them. As soon as possible, written orders should be signed by the client's physician and be made part of the patient's record.

Medicare regulations specify further requirements which have to be met. These regulations are also discussed in the section on record keeping, but regulations pertaining to medications require that:

1. Drugs and treatments be administered by agency staff only as ordered by the physician
2. The nurse immediately record and sign oral orders and obtain the physician's countersignature
3. Agency staff check all medicines a patient may be taking to identify possibly ineffective drug therapy or adverse reactions, significant side effects, drug allergies, and contraindications and promptly report any problems to the physician[68]

Communicating to the physician changes in signs and symptoms and the patient's condition needs to be done as soon as possible. Often reaching the physician may be a concern for the CHN. Careful documentation of attempts to reach, including date, time, whether the answering service was reached, if another physician responded, and all the details of the communication should be documented.

When it becomes unsafe for the patient to be at home, for example, the patient's condition worsens severely, or the patient becomes medically incompetent to make decisions, several options should be outlined in agency policies. For example, when is legal counsel to be involved in questions of patient care, perhaps regarding instituting guardianship proceedings for the patient who is incompetent? Or, when is a multidisciplinary conference to be called, including a representative of the patient, in order to handle the very complex health, medical, and social care of a client and family? The reasonableness of the agency and CHN's actions in management of each case will be evaluated based upon legal standards and the agency's policies.

The use of standing orders, sometimes referred to as medical directives or protocols, is another area of concern for the CHN. The box below outlines suggested questions for evaluating the use of standing orders. Among the most important documents to use in evaluating these orders is the state nurse practice act and regulations and the standards of CHN.

Infection control: nosocomial infections

Another CHN role, often termed a nurse epidemiologist or infection control nurse (ICN), involves the surveillance, prevention, and control of nosocomial infections, those infections acquired from being in an institution.[69] Legal standards, specific actions required for the prevention of such infections, apply to hospitals. These must be met in order for the hospital to be licensed and in order to participate in federal financing programs.[70] These federal regulations require the hospital to provide a sanitary environment to avoid sources and transmission of infections. The factors which are part of the federal standard include:

1. An infection committee, composed of members of the medical and nursing staffs and administration, responsible for investigating, controlling, and preventing infections in the hospital. The committee is to establish:
   a. Written infection control measures
   b. Techniques and systems for discovering and reporting infections in the hospital

SUGGESTED GUIDELINES FOR STANDING ORDERS IN COMMUNITY HEALTH NURSING PRACTICE

1. *Is the content, the specific orders, appropriate to be standing?*
   a. What are the unique needs of the clients, e.g. special groups, children, workers, which makes "standing" necessary?
   b. Is the standing order required or necessary because of the nature of the group's health needs, for emergencies, or for first aid?
   c. Is the act called for by the standing order within the scope of practice of the nurse?
   d. Have the state nursing, medical, and pharmacy practice acts been reviewed?
   e. Does the standing order exceed the limits of professional nursing practice?
   f. Is the order one which requires specialized education, judgment, and skill based on knowledge and application of principles derived from biological, physical, social, and nursing sciences? Is it nursing within the meaning of the state practice act's definition?
   g. Are nursing peers carrying out similar standing orders? What has been their experience with the orders?
   h. Is the act called for by the standing order a currently identified customary practice of a community health nurse? Does the order provide for care for accidental injuries; safeguards for reactions to medicines or other substances; care for common health problems; care of previously medically diagnosed high risk groups?
   i. What is the preparation of the nurse, level of training, degree of skill? Does this level match what the order requires?
   j. Are situations when referral to a physician is necessary, when following the standing order would be unreasonable nursing practice, known by the nurse responsible for implementing the "standing order"?
2. *How is the standing order written or documented?*
   a. Is the wording specific; are orders exact? What is the format?
   b. Is it signed by the physician? Is the signature dated?
   c. When an order is used, how and where is it documented?
   d. How and where do nurses who use the standing orders indicate their agreement or disagreement with them?
3. *What is the procedure for reviewing and updating the orders?*
   a. How often is this done? Is it part of the nurse's job description? Who is responsible for the review? Is it part of the physician's contract?
   b. How often are orders actually used? Have any problems resulted? How are these dealt with?
   c. Are periodic reports on the use of the standing orders indicated?
   d. What resources are available on the unit for update, refresher, and more information in order to properly execute "standing orders"?
   e. Is there on-going in-service or continuing education on the topics of specific standing orders?

2. Written procedures governing the use of aseptic techniques and procedures in all areas of the hospital
3. Keeping infections at a minimum, regularly reviewing procedures and techniques, particularly those concerning food handling, laundry practices, disposal of wastes, traffic control and visiting rules in high risk areas, air pollution, and routine culturing of autoclaves and sterilizers
4. Method of control used in relation to the sterilization of supplies and water and written policy requiring sterile supplies to be reprocessed at specified time periods
5. Formal provisions to educate and orient all appropriate personnel in the practice of aseptic techniques, such as handwashing, scrubbing practices, proper grooming, masking and dressing routines, disinfecting and sterilizing techniques, handling and storage of patient care equipment and supplies
6. Measures which control the indiscriminate use of preventive antibiotics in the absence of infection and the use of antibiotics in the presence of infection based upon necessary cultures and sensitivity tests
7. Continuing education to all hospital personnel on the cause, effect, transmission, prevention, and elimination of infections
8. Inspection and reporting of any hospital employee with an infection who may be in contact with patients, their food, or laundry[71]

A patient who gets an infection during hospitalization must prove that the infection was acquired from the hospital, that the hospital was negligent in allowing the patient to contract the infection, and that this negligence was the cause of not only the infection but any injury that stemmed from it. Later chapters on risk management (see Chapter 26) and quality assurance (see Chapter 28) elaborate on risk prevention.

Discharge planning: hospital to home

The discharge planning nurse or community liaison nurse, is responsible for providing hospital patients with a link to services in the community that their unique needs might require, for example, home health care. "It is the discharge planner's responsibility to be knowledgeable regarding the quality and quantity of available community agencies and to share this knowledge with physicians, hospital staff, patients and families."[72]

Discharge planning, if done properly, diminishes the hospital's liability for abandonment and allegations of negligent discharge and improves the health status of patients. In one particular case the nurses and social workers made a recommendation for placement of the patient in a nursing home, in conflict with the physician who wanted the patient cared for at home.[73] The Commissioner of the New York State Department of Social Services upheld the department's decision to terminate the patient's home care services and to place him in a nursing home.

In this case home care was being provided to the patient under Medicaid. The regulations regarding home care stated that it would be provided if the patient's health and safety in the home could be adequately assured. The Medicaid agency conducted an extensive evaluation at the hospital where the patient had been admitted for recurring urinary problems and determined that the level of care needed for the patient could not be provided in the home. The agency notified the patient that he must accept the first nursing home bed available or lose the financial assistance. The physician was of the opinion that adequate care could be maintained in the home. The local medical director reviewed the situation and agreed with the opinion of the nurses and social workers that safe care could not be provided in the home. This decision was upheld by the court.

Another legal issue confronting the discharge planner is the exclusivity of referrals that are made. While no case law exists on this topic and given the amount and degree of competition among home health agencies, profit and nonprofit, the discharge planner should be aware of the potential for violations of antitrust laws[74] and the Medicare and Medicaid antifraud and antikickback laws.[75] Fraud and restraint of trade questions in the context of discharge planning programs are new questions for health care agencies.[76] Chapter 22 discusses the antifraud laws further; antitrust is also the subject of other chapters on nursing businesses and advanced nursing practice.

The discharge planner, physician, and others involved in making community arrangements for continuity of care for the patient should be aware of state mandated referrals to health departments, such as those mentioned before related to child abuse and other reporting statutes. Consent should always be obtained before referrals are made. If consent is not given where it is a mandated referral, the nurse must still report. But for all referrals confidentiality is still to be maintained and protected.

A PHN discharge planner in a veteran's hospital was scrutinized for whether she properly transferred a patient between VA facilities.[77] Without physician advice, because he could not to be located, and in order to prevent delay in arranging the transportation, the PHN discussed with the transportation clerk the alternatives for transporting the patient. The PHN decided on a two-person ambulette (a vehicle which contains none of the usual medical equipment in a regular ambulance). The PHN specifically decided to order a two-person vehicle because the patient was "confused." At trial the physician testified in support of the PHN's decision.

The liability for the injuries sustained by the patient were borne by the ambulance company, based upon a contract the government had with them to provide transportation services. The contract contained an indemnification clause under which the company indemnified the government from any negligence caused by the company unless the government was the sole, competent, and producing cause of such liability.

When the ambulette driver who had transported patients before between these facilities arrived for the patient, the PHN handed him a large envelope marked in large print with the name of the destination institution and place within that institution that the patient was to be taken. The PHN asked the driver if another person was with him in the vehicle. The driver told the PHN there was another person. This turned out to be false; in addition the driver took the patient to the VA but did not take him to the admitting department, as indicated on the envelope. Instead he left the patient unattended in an old part of a building in the main lobby area. From there the patient wandered away, eventually onto a highway where he was struck by a car and killed.

The court found that the government was not liable with regard to the transfer of this patient from one VA hospital to another since the VA employees, including the PHN, did all that they could to ensure proper transfer. The ambulance company, through its employee-driver, distinctly and overwhelmingly breached its duty of care to the patient by leaving him unattended. This act was the proximate cause of the patient's death.

Another issue for discharge planning involves discharge instructions. A physician has been found liable in one case for failing to give discharge instructions regarding side effects of a prescribed drug.[78] Also, failure to give discharge instructions where a hospital had a policy requiring it has been found by at least one court to be negligence.[79] However, the plaintiff must prove that harm resulted from not receiving the instructions. If the instruction sheet indicates that the patient is to contact the hospital emergency room from which the sheet was received if the patient experiences a sudden or unusual change in condition, and the hospital fails to respond properly, liability can be found.[80]

In addition hospitals have been found liable for discharging patients inappropriately. In a recent case a court held that before a patient is discharged the hospital has a duty to warn a patient of adverse effects of drugs that were administered by it, if the hospital knows or should know that the drugs will impair the patient's mental or physical abilities or will be potentially dangerous in combination with particular foods, beverages, or other drugs.[81] On the other hand discharges have been found adequate and proper by courts.[82]

Hospice and home health care

Many states have licensure laws not only for home health agencies but also for hospice programs.[83] Federal law and legislation also exist for home health and hospice care.[84] These laws and the regulations establish standards of care which must be met. Violations of such statutes may lead to liability.

A home health agency is defined in federal regulations as a public agency or private organization which is primarily engaged in providing skilled nursing services and other therapeutic services; has policies established by a group of professional personnel, including one or more physicians and one or more registered professional nurses, to govern the services which it provides and provides for supervision of such services by a physician or registered professional nurse; maintains clinical records on every patient; has in effect an overall plan and budget; and meets applicable state and local laws.[85]

A legal definition of a hospice is a facility that provides a hospice care program; is separate from any other facility; and admits at least two but not more than eight individuals who are unrelated, have no reasonable prospect of a cure, and are expected to die within 6 months.[86] Hospice care program means a coordinated, interdisciplinary program for meeting the special physical, psychological, spiritual, and social needs of dying individuals and their families by providing palliative and supportive medical, nursing, and other health services through home or inpatient care during the illness and bereavement.[87]

In addition to licensing which establishes standards and gives the state or federal government the power to inspect the agency and revoke its ability to provide services if the standards are not met, there are many private organizations which have standards. These include the National League for Nursing, National Association for

Home Care, and the National Hospice Organization. These are professional associations whose focus is home care. Their publications are an important part of practice and can be used in court as evidence of the standard of care.[88]

In recent years the issue of pronouncement of death and the nurse's responsibility has been the topic of much discussion. In New Jersey a state law was adopted which allows registered professional nurses (in addition to physicians and county medical examiners) to attend the patient at the time of death, make the actual determination and pronouncement of death, and attest to this by signing the death certificate.[89] The law applies only to a death which "occurs in the home or place of residence of the deceased, in a hospice or in a long-term care facility or nursing home."[90]

The nurse pronounces the patient dead by checking the patient for absence of respiration and heartbeat. The attending physician is informed, and the funeral director contacted. The nurse is under a legal duty to sign the death certificate and furnish "death and last sickness particulars."[91] Within 24 hours the funeral director must then contact the physician who must execute and sign the death certificate.

In case of any death occurring without medical attendance, the funeral director must notify the medical examiner or local registrar.[92] However, under this new law, the attending registered professional nurse, under circumstances described above, is considered "medical attendance."

Managed care programs

As has been stated, CHNs may be employed in a variety of health care service delivery systems. The alternative systems, such as managed care programs, present new legal issues for nurses. These programs include health maintenance organizations (HMOs), preferred provider organizations, nurse managed centers, individual practice associations, and competitive medical plans. In addition, combinations of all of these may exist within a network of providers who contractually agree to join services for particular patient groups. No published standards of nursing care exist for these programs.

A health maintenance organization is an organization that provides, directly or through contracts with others, a specified range of health services to a voluntarily enrolled population for prepaid per capita payments. HMOs are both insurers and providers of health care. Federal and state laws regulate HMOs.[93] For example, New York law defines an HMO as "a person or corporation or any group of persons who enter into an arrangement, agreement or plan which proposes to provide a comprehensive health service plan."[94]

A plan involves enrollment and receiving comprehensive health services in consideration for a basic advance or periodic charge. The services provided include all health services which an enrolled population might require in order to be maintained in good health. The New York legislation does not specifically list nursing services as one of these services.[95] However, other state legislation does specifically list nursing care and services.[96]

Under new federal regulations those eligible for Medicare may now choose to enroll in an HMO.[97] This is also discussed in Chapter 17. Nurses who are employed or who share in the ownership of the HMO or other entity must be familiar with the federal and state laws and regulations mentioned above. Additionally, issues of contract and insurance law will be important to litigation involving how and to what extent an HMO delivered services and met its obligations to its members.

Two characteristics of the managed system raise legal concerns: (1) the goal of the managed health care system to avoid unneccesary hospitalization and other health care and (2) the fact that enrolled members are "locked-in"; that is, their choice of health care provider is limited to those in the managed system. Health care decisions in managed systems, however, will be evaluated in terms using traditional legal means. For example, was the decision reasonable under the circumstances? Was necessary care withheld?

Record keeping

Home health agency and health department policies on records and record keeping set standards which, unless met, may raise questions of liability for the CHN. It is important, therefore, that the CHN have input into the formation and periodic revision of these. In addition the federal regulations outlining the conditions for participation in the Medicare program cover certain aspects of clinical record keeping in the home health agency.

The home health clinical record is required to contain pertinent past and current findings in accordance with accepted professional standards.[98] Every patient receiving services is to have a record. The record should include a plan of treatment; appropriate identifying information; name of physician; drug, dietary, treatment, and activity orders; signed and dated clinical and progress notes; copies of summary reports sent to the physician; and a discharge summary.

Clinical records are to be retained for 5 years after the month the cost report to which the records apply is filed with the intermediary unless state law stipulates a longer period of time.[99] The home health agency is required to safeguard the clinical records against loss or unauthorized use. Written procedures govern use and removal of records and conditions for release of information. A patient's written consent is required for release of information not authorized by law.[100]

The home health agency clinical note is a dated written notation by a member of the health team of a contact with a patient containing a description of signs and symptons, treatment and/or drugs given, the patient's reaction, and any changes in physical or emotional condition.[101] Federal regulations require that home health agency clinical notes be written the day service is rendered and incorporated no less often than weekly.[102]

The plan of treatment is also described in the federal regulations.[103] Developed in consultation with the agency staff, the plan covers all pertinent diagnoses, including mental status, types of services and equipment required, frequency of visits, prognosis, rehabilitation potential, functional limitations, activities permitted, nutritional requirements, medications and treatments, any safety measures to protect against injury, instructions for timely discharge or referral, and any other appropriate items. The total plan of treatment is reviewed by the attending physician and home health agency personnel as often as the severity of the patient's condition requires, but at least once every 60 days.[104]

Parental rights termination and child abuse cases

Most often the PHN has been involved in legal actions involving parental rights and child abuse. PHN's have provided testimony in child custody disputes between parents, in child abuse and neglect proceedings, in children in need of assistance and/or termination of parental rights cases. This testimony was provided either from an initial nursing assessment that a child was in need of state intervention or from observations gained through rendering services to a family because of a referral from the court or social service department. Often PHN services have been ordered by courts as a condition for return or maintaining custody of children. In these situations the PHN must often deal with angry and resentful parents. This only adds to the PHN's difficult responsibility in maintaining objectivity and fairness in assessing and evaluating the progress of the family.

PHN observations and opinions as to the fitness of the parents, the safety of the home, and the health of the children and family have been provided to civil, juvenile, family, and criminal courts through testimony and through documentation in health department records. This information helps courts decide when and under what conditions a child will be removed, temporarily or permanently, from the custody and control of the parent.

STATE'S STANDARD AND BURDEN OF PROOF

Certain conditions must be met before the state can justify its action. These standards and burden of proof are usually provided by state statutes. It improves the quality of PHN testimony if the PHN reviews the state statute and knows the standard which the state must prove. Understanding how the PHN's observations and opinions support or refute the termination of a parent's right to control his or her children is an important part of participating in the legal process in this area. In addition a continuing education program on family law in general within the PHN's jurisdiction would be helpful. PHNs are often asked questions by clients whose answers lie within family law.[105]

The state must mount clear and convincing proof of parental neglect, abuse, disregard, and/or abandonment.[106] These cases usually involve the most extreme circumstances, often including continuous, repeated failure to protect and provide for the children. Often the family's lack of involvement or response to public health nursing services themselves is evidence of need to terminate their rights to their children.[107]

EFFECT OF A NURSE-PATIENT PRIVILEGE

In the states which have a legislatively provided nurse-patient privilege, the courts have reviewed the issue of whether this privilege prevents the PHN from testifying about child abuse or parental termination of rights. In one case, a court determined that the privilege did not apply because the nature of child abuse and the need to protect the child far outweighed the need to protect the parent's right to the privilege.[108] In another state a court decided the PHN's testimony was properly admitted because the nurse-patient privilege applied only to information acquired in caring for the patient, which was necessary to enable the nurse to care for the patient.[109] The court held that the nurse was not engaged in furnishing nursing care to the mother, but was acting in a protective function.

Safety in community health nursing practice

The nature of CHN practice may involve personal risks to the CHN when he or she visits homes or community resources in high crime areas. Because there have been cases where the PHN has been the victim of rape, robbery, and other criminal activity, special attention should be paid by the nurse and the employer to the need for protective strategies.[110] These may include learning to be streetwise, knowing the area extremely well, knowing how to protect and physically defend oneself, developing a buddy-system, knowing when not to go into the community, and providing other necessary security measures at clinics and offices of the health agency.

Standards of community health nursing practice

Many standards exist to judge the efficiency, effectiveness, and reasonableness of CHN practice. In this chapter several have been highlighted, including those from several associations, such as the American Nurse's Association, American Public Health Association, National League for Nursing, National Association for Home Care, and National Hospice Association. As noted before these and other professional associations provide standards of accreditation and certification for individual practitioners and for health agencies.

Licensing standards have also been mentioned throughout the chapter. These are legally enforceable standards for individual health care practitioners and for the agencies themselves, health departments, hospitals, home health agencies, and hospices. Federal statutes also provide standards of CHN practice applicable in specific situations, such as communicable diseases, infection control, discharge planning, and payment for services, such as Medicare.

Recommendations and trends

Given the fast changing health care system, health departments and home health agencies, discharge planning and infection control will only be increasing their legal responsibilities. As health care technology advances and as society's health needs shift and change, it is anticipated that new types of reporting requirements for communicable disease and other public health concerns will change.

While there have been few lawsuits against PHNs for negligence, it is expected that these will increase. Advanced equipment and more complicated health needs to be serviced in the home will present new liability situations for CHNs. Other areas of more liability include abandonment and antitrust, for these areas represent new and untested legal ground for CHNs.

More CHNs will be designing their own businesses, for example, in the home care and hospice area, as part of the changing health care scene. Such independent practice will raise new legal concerns for nurses, such as business and tax law, insurance, incorporation, third-party reimbursement, and scope of practice debates. Chapter 33 gives further information on nursing businesses.

Lastly, the PHN will continue to promote the best interests of children, parents, and families through their involvement in the prevention, treatment, and early detection of disease and other conditions, such as child abuse. This important social and legal responsibility cannot be underestimated.

Active involvement in community health nursing associations which develop and set standards should be stressed. Proper, safe, and reasonable CHN practice depends upon knowing the standards which assess it. Continuing education and staff development are essential components of CHN practice.

Endnotes

1. M. STANHOPE AND J. LANCASTER, COMMUNITY HEALTH NURSING, PROCESS AND PRACTICE FOR PROMOTING HEALTH (1984); R. FREEMAN AND J. HEINRICH, COMMUNITY HEALTH NURSING (1983); DIVISION OF NURSING, BUREAU OF HEALTH PROFESSIONS, HEALTH RESOURCES AND SERVICES ADMINISTRATION, PUBLIC HEALTH SERVICE, U.S. DEPT. OF HEALTH AND HUMAN SERVICES, CONSENSUS CONFERENCE ON THE ESSENTIALS OF PUBLIC HEALTH NURSING PRACTICE AND EDUCATION (August 1985).
2. AMERICAN NURSE'S ASSOCIATION, STANDARDS OF COMMUNITY HEALTH NURSING PRACTICE 1 (1973, 1986); AMERICAN NURSE'S ASSOCIATION, DIVISION OF COMMUNITY HEALTH NURSING, A CONCEPTUAL MODEL OF COMMUNITY HEALTH NURSING 2 (1975); AMERICAN NURSE'S ASSOCIATION, DIVISION OF COMMUNITY HEALTH NURSING PRACTICE, CONCEPTS OF COMMUNITY HEALTH NURSING PRACTICE 1 (1975).
3. AMERICAN PUBLIC HEALTH ASSOCIATION, PUBLIC HEALTH NURSING SECTION, THE DEFINITION AND ROLE OF PUBLIC HEALTH NURSING IN THE DELIVERY OF HEALTH CARE 4 (1981).
4. Williams, *Community Health Nursing—What Is It?* 25 N.O. 250 (April 1977); Archer, *Synthesis of Public Health Science and Nursing Science* 30 N.O. 442 (September-October 1982).
5. *See, e.g., Ball v. Branch,* 16 So.2d 524 (Fla. 1944).
6. 42 U.S.C. §236, 289c-4, 247d, 4362a (1982) (Center for Disease Control).
7. PUBLIC HEALTH SERVICE, U.S. DEPT. OF HEALTH AND

HUMAN SERVICES, FACTS ABOUT AIDS (August 1985); PHS AIDS Hotline is 1-800-447-AIDS.

8. CENTER FOR DISEASE CONTROL: *Recommendations for Preventing Transmission of Infection with Human T*-Lymphotropic Virus Type III/Lymphadenopathy-Associated Virus in the Workplace 34 MORBIDITY AND MORTALITY WEEKLY REPORT (MMWR) (November 15, 1985); *Revision of the Case Definition of Acquired Immunodeficiency Syndrome for National Reporting—United States* 34 MMWR, 373 (1985); *AIDS: Precautions for Health-care Workers and Allied Professionals* 32 MMWR 450 (1983).
9. MD. HEALTH-GEN. CODE ANN. §18-205 (1982); CONN. GEN. STAT. ANN. §19a-215 (West Supp. 1985).
10. MD. HEALTH-GEN. CODE ANN. §18-103 (1982).
11. *See, e.g.,* MD. ADMIN. CODE tit. 10. Maryland's Secretary of the Department of Health and Mental Hygiene has promulgated additional requirements regarding communicable diseases.
12. MD. HEALTH-GEN. CODE ANN. §18-102 (2) (b) (1982) (right of entry), 18-205(g) (inspection of laboratory records), 18-208 (general duties), 18-210 (disinfecting), 18-211 (moving infected individuals), 18-308 (a) (order use of prophylactic), 18-324 (a) (order examination of individual suspected of having tuberculosis in a communicable stage and in a public place, exposing others), 18-324 (b) (removal for treatment TB), 18-325 (a) (an individual may not refuse to enter a health facility TB), 18-503 (prohibit common cups and towels).
13. MD. HEALTH-GEN. CODE ANN. §18-201 (1982) (physicians), 18-202 (institutions), 18-205 (laboratory).
14. MD. HEALTH-GEN. CODE ANN. §18-205 (e), (f), and (h) and §18-322(b) (1982) (confidential tuberculosis registry).
15. *See, e.g.,* ILL. ANN. STAT., Ch. 126, §21 (Smith-Hurd Supp 1985) provides that any medical practitioner or other person making a required communicable disease report in good faith shall be immune from suit for slander or libel based upon any statements contained in such reports.
16. MD. HEALTH-GEN. CODE ANN. §18-215 (1982).
17. MD. HEALTH-GEN. CODE ANN. §18-211, 18-216 (1982).
18. MD. HEALTH-GEN. CODE ANN. §18-501, 502 (1982).
19. MD. HEALTH-GEN. CODE ANN. §18-401 (1982).
20. MD. HEALTH-GEN. CODE ANN. §18-401 (b) (1982).
21. MD. HEALTH-GEN. CODE ANN. §18-401 (c) (1982).
22. *Id.*
23. MD. HEALTH-GEN. CODE ANN. §18-401 (a) (Supp. 1985).
24. MD. HEALTH-GEN. CODE ANN. §18-332 (Supp. 1985).
25. MD. HEALTH-GEN. CODE ANN. §18-330 (Supp. 1985).
26. *Reyes v. Wyeth Laboratories, Inc.*, 498 F.2d 1264 (5th Cir. 1974). *cert. denied,* 419 U.S. 1096. *See also Davis v. Wyeth Laboratories, Inc.*, 399 F.2d 121 (9th Cir. 1968); *Williams v. Lederle Laboratories,* 591 F. Supp. 381 (W.D. Ohio 1984); *Givens v. Lederle,* 556 F.2d 1341 (5th Cir. 1977).
27. *Sheehan v. Pima County and Lederle,* 660 P.2d 486 (Ariz. 1983).
28. *Jackson v. State of Louisiana,* 428 So.2d 1073 (La. App. Cir. 1983).
29. *Nuyen v. Slater,* 127 N.W.2d 369 (Mich. 1964).
30. MD. HEALTH-GEN. CODE ANN. §18-104 (1982) (cancer), 18-105 (1982) (toxic substances), 18-106 (1982) (occupational diseases), 18-107 (1982) (infant mortality, pregnancy, childbirth, infancy, early childhood), 18-206 (Supp. 1985) (sentinel birth defects), 18-302 (1982) (amygdalin), 18-303 (Supp. 1985) (diethylstilbestrol), 18-307 (1982) (syphilis-pregnancy), 18-308 (1982) (gonococcal ophthalmia neonatorum), 18-316 (Supp. 1985) (reports of possible rabies cases), 13-101 (1982) (hereditary disorder program).
31. *Hansen v. Bussman,* 549 P.2d 1265 (Or. 1976).
32. *See, e.g., Jacobs v. Magma Cooper Co.,* Ariz. Pima County Superior Ct., No. 206219, March 21, 1985, 29 ATLA L. REP. 83 (March 1986), where hospital personnel performed a urine test to screen for PKU on a 3-day-old infant. The evidence showed that the blood test for PKU (Guthrie) should have been used. The hospital was held liable for failure to diagnose PKU.
33. CONN. GEN. STAT. ANN. §19a-53 (West Supp. 1985) (Reports of physical defects).
34. 21 U.S.C. §301-392 (1982).
35. J. MICHAEL, WORKING ON THE SYSTEM: A COMPREHENSIVE MANUAL FOR CITIZEN ACCESS TO FEDERAL AGENCIES 637 (1974).
36. 42 U.S.C. §4331 (1982).
37. 42 U.S.C. §1857 (1982).
38. 33 U.S.C. §1251 (1982).
39. 42 U.S.C. §6901 (1982).
40. 15 U.S.C. §2051 (1982).
41. *Peters v. Township of Hopewell,* 534 F. Supp. 1324 (D. N.J. 1982), *aff'd.,* 729 F.2d 1448 (1984).
42. *Bass v. Barksdale, et al,* 671 S.W.2d 476 (Tenn. App. 1984); *Santoni v. Schaerf, et al,* 428 A.2d 94 (Md. App. 1981); *Santoni v. Moodie,* 452 A.2d 1223 (Md. App. 1982) (second appeal of the same case), *rev'd.,* 441 A.2d 323 (Md. 1982).
43. *City of Dallas v. Bradford,* 646 S.W.2d 302 (Tex. App. 5 Dist. 1983).
44. *Santoni v. Schaerf,* 428 A.2d 94, 106 (Md. App. 1981).
45. Home health agencies: 42 U.S.C. §255, 300u-2, 1395x, 1395y, 1395gg, 1395hh (1982) and regulations at 42 C.F.R. §405.1201 (1985); Hospice: 42 U.S.C. §1302, 1395c-1395f, 1395x-1395cc, 1395hh (1982) and regulations at 42 C.F.R. §418.1 (1985).
46. *Becker v. Janinski,* 15 N.Y.S. 675 (1891). Physician abandonment case where the court outlined a general rule to follow in terminating a physician-patient relationship: consent of patient, give the patient time and notice so that another physician can be employed, or if the physician's judgment is that no further care is necessary, the physician may end his (or her) services to the patient.
47. U.S. DEPARTMENT OF HEALTH AND HUMAN SERVICES, PROMOTING HEALTH, PREVENTING DISEASE, OBJECTIVES FOR THE NATION (1980); A CLASSIFICATION SCHEME FOR CLIENT PROBLEMS IN COMMUNITY HEALTH NURSING (1980).
48. 42 U.S.C. §5103 (b)(2) (1982) and regulations at 45 C.F.R. §1340.3-3 (1985); Child Abuse Prevention and Treatment Act, 42 U.S.C. §5101 *et seq* (1982). *See also* Juvenile Justice and Delinquency Prevention Act, 42 U.S.C. §5601 (1982).
49. See the Appendix for state citations.
50. MD. FAMILY LAW CODE ANN. §5-901(b) (1984); *See also* MD. FAMILY LAW CODE ANN. §5-701(g) (1984) (defining neglected child).
51. CONN. GEN. STAT. ANN. §17-38a (b) (West Supp. 1985).
52. CONN. GEN. STAT. ANN. §46a-14 (1984).
53. *Awkerman by Awkerman v. Tri-County Orthopedic Group, PC,* 373 N.W.2d 204 (Mich. App. 1985).
54. *People of the State of Colorado v. Beruman,* 638 P.2d 789 (Colo. 1982).

55. *Landeros v. Flood,* 551 P.2d 389 (Cal. 1976); *See also O'Keefe v. Osorio,* Ill, 27 ATLA L. REP. 391 (November 1984) where a jury awarded a child $186,851 for physician's negligent breach of child abuse reporting statute.
56. *Estate of Bailey v. County of York,* 768 F.2d 503 (3rd Cir. 1985). Section 1983 of the Civil Rights Act of 1871. *See also Monell v. Dept. of Social Services,* 436 U.S. 658 (1978) where municipalities or similar public entities may be sued under Section 1983, not on the basis of respondeat superior, but on the ground that customs, practices, or policies, such as inadequate training of officers, were substantially responsible for the victim's harm in violation of his or her constitutional rights.
57. *Ilee M. v. State of Oklahoma,* 577 P.2d 908 (Okla. 1978).
58. *Wilkerson v. Florida Adult Care Association,* 450 S.2d 1168 (Fla. 1984).
59. *Reitz v. Christensen,* 431 P.2d 33 (Colo. 1967).
60. 42 U.S.C. §254b (1982) Migrant health centers.
61. *Long v. Bonnes* 651 F.2d 214 (4th Cir. 1981) and *Kenly v. Young,* 641 F.2d 192, *cert. denied,* 455 U.S. 961 (1982).
62. MD. HEALTH OCC. CODE ANN. §7-101(f)(2) (1986) ("For these purposes, 'practice registered nursing' includes: (i) administration; (ii) teaching; (iii) counseling; (iv) supervision, delegation and evaluation of nursing practice; (v) execution of therapeutic regimen, including the administration of medication and treatment; (vi) independent nursing functions and delegated medical functions; and (vii) performance of additional acts authorized by the Board.")
63. *King v. Young,* 150 S.E.2d 631 (Ga. 1966).
64. *Jacobson v. Kansas City Life Insurance Co.,* 652 P.2d 909 (Utah 1982).
65. *See e.g.,* N.Y. EDUC. LAW §6902 (McKinney 1986).
66. *Sermchief v. Gonzales,* 660 S.W.2d 683 (Mo. Banc. 1983).
67. MD. HEALTH OCC. CODE ANN. §12-101(b), 12-102(a), (b) (1986).
68. 42 C.F.R. §405.1223(c) (1985).
69. Chavigny & Helm, *Ethical Dilemmas and the Practice of Infection Control,* 10 LAW, MED. & HEALTH CARE 168 (September 1982).
70. 42 C.F.R. §405.1022(c) (1985).
71. *Id.*
72. Runner-Heidt, *Where Does the Hospital Discharge Planner Go From Here?* 2 HOME HEALTHCARE NURSE 30 (July-August 1984).
73. *Bentley v. Perales* 103 A.D.2d 1005 (N.Y. 4th 1984).
74. 15 U.S.C. §1 (1982).
75. 42 U.S.C. §1395nn(b), 1396h(b) (1982). These sections deal with illegal remunerations, false statements and representations, illegal patient admittance and retention practices, and violation of assignment terms.
76. O'Neil, *Exclusive Referral Agreements for Home Care* 2 NURS. ECON. 326 (September-October 1984).
77. *McCluskey v. United States,* 583 F.Supp. 740 (S.D. N. Y. 1984).
78. *Goodman v. Tips,* 651 S.W.2d 364 (Tex. App. 1984).
79. *Niles v. City of San Rafael,* 116 Cal. Rptr. 733 (Cal. App. 1974).
80. *Adamski v. Tacoma General Hospital,* 559 P.2d 970 (Wash. 1978).
81. *Kirk v. Michael Reese Hospital & Medical Center,* 483 N.E.2d 906 (Ill. App. 1985).
82. *See e.g., Willis v. Western Hospital Association,* 182 P.2d 950 (Idaho 1947) where a hospital properly transferred a patient to a psychiatric hospital, even though it was later determined that the transfer hastened the patient's death. In addition, hospitals have been found liable for not discharging a patient to a more appropriate facility; *see also, Carroasco v. Bankoff,* 33 Cal. Rptr. 673 (Cal. App. 1963) where a burn patient was retained for 53 days even though the hospital was not equipped to treat serious burns.
83. *E.g.* MD. HEALTH-GEN. CODE ANN. §19-401 19-409 (1982 and Supp. 1985) Home health agencies; §19-901 19-913 (1982 and Supp. 1985) (hospices).
84. 42 C.F.R. §418.1 (1985).
85. 42 C.F.R. §405.1201(a) (1985).
86. MD. HEALTH-GEN. CODE ANN. §19-901(b) (Supp. 1985).
87. MD. HEALTH-GEN. CODE ANN. §19-901(c) (Supp. 1985).
88. *See, e.g.* NATIONAL ASSOCIATION FOR HOME CARE, CODE OF ETHICS (1982) and TOWARD A NATIONAL HOME CARE POLICY, BLUEPRINT FOR ACTION (January 1985). Contact: National Association for Home Care, 519 C Street, N.E., Washington, D.C. 20002. One membership benefit is "free legal advice short of litigation" and "access to a lawyer referral service to help sort out complicated legal questions."
89. N.J. STAT. ANN. §26:6-8.1 (West Supp. 1985).
90. *Id.*
91. N.J. STAT. ANN. §26:6-8 (West Supp. 1985).
92. N.J. STAT. ANN. §26:6-9 (West Supp. 1985).
93. Federal law: 42 U.S.C. §300e, 1395mm (1982); 42 C.F.R. §417 110 (1985); State laws: *see, e.g.,* MD. HEALTH-GEN. CODE ANN. §19-701 *et seq* (1982 and Supp. 1986); N.Y. PUB. HEALTH LAW §4400 (McKinney 1985).
94. N.Y. PUB. HEALTH LAW §4401.1 (McKinney 1985).
95. N.Y. PUB. HEALTH LAW §4401.4 (McKinney 1985), includes "in-patient and out-patient services . . . emergency and preventive health services."
96. *See* MD. HEALTH-GEN. CODE ANN. §19-701(d)(2) (1982).
97. 42 C.F.R. §417 (1985).
98. 42 C.F.R. §405.1228 (1985).
99. 42 C.F.R. §405.1228(a) (1985).
100. 42 C.F.R. §405.1228(b) (1985).
101. 42 C.F.R. §405.1202(d) (1985).
102. 42 C.F.R. §405.1228 (1985).
103. 42 C.F.R. §405.1223(a) (1985).
104. 42 C.F.R. §405.1223(b) (1985).
105. *See, e.g., Williams v. Estate of J.D. Long,* 338 So.2d 563 (Fla. 1976) where a PHN testified that she was asked advice by a client about changing names on birth certificates and the rights of illegitimate children.
106. *Santosky v. Kramer,* 455 U.S. 745 (1982).
106. *See, e.g., Jones v. Jackson County Department of Public Welfare,* 436 N.E.2d 849 (Ind. 1982), where a PHN was seen as part of "sufficient and reasonable services" offered the parents for rehabilitation; *In re Kelley,* 262 N.W.2d 781 (Iowa 1978) where the PHN worked with the mother "to no avail."
108. *In re D.K.,* 245 N.W.2d 644 (S.D. 1976).
109. *State v. Banker,* 615 P.2d 1168 (Or. 1980).
110. *Deming v. State,* 387 S.W.2d 394 (Tex. 1965).

Additional Readings

Anthony, *Developing a Network Strategy, Involvement with Managed Care Programs* 5 CARING, 57 (May 1986).

T. CHRISTOFFEL, HEALTH AND THE LAW (1982).

D. CRITTENDEN, DISCHARGE PLANNING FOR HEALTH CARE FACILITIES (1983).

Deakers, *Continuity of Family-Centered Nursing Care Between the Hospital and the Home* 7 NURS. CLIN. N. AM., 83 (March 1972).

Harvey, *Your Patient's Discharge Plan* 9 NURSING '81, 48 (July 1981).

HEALTH CARE: LEGAL RESPONSE TO NEW ECONOMIC FORCES (R.M. McNair, ed. 1985)

Wald, *The Hospice Movement as a Health Care Reform* 33 N. O., 173 (March 1980).

K. WING, THE LAW AND THE PUBLIC'S HEALTH (2d ed. 1985).

Chapter 14

School nursing

Cynthia E. Northrop

This chapter reviews selected state and federal school health legislation and case law, including material that focuses on the role of the school nurse in enforcing public health laws and on legal issues relevant to the school nurse such as administration of medications in the school setting, managing emergencies and accidents, health teaching, advice and referral, child abuse, and school health records. Legal issues surrounding the care of children with special health and education needs, such as handicapped children, nutritionally deprived children, and children with behavior problems, is also discussed.

The school nurse has been involved in child abuse and neglect cases and termination of parental rights actions. A few negligence cases have been brought against school nurses. In addition, school nursing practice has been the subject of parents' lawsuits that have sought to enforce their children's education rights.

School nurses have been involved in many other types of litigation involving issues of collective bargaining, arbitration, choice of union, unfair labor practices, certification requirements, and seniority rights. Employment disputes, contract issues, tenure, termination of positions, sex discrimination, and salary disputes have been legal issues for the school nurse. School nurses have also been involved in worker's compensation cases, their own, and those of other school employees. The law in these cases is described in Chapters 30 and 31.

Definition of school nursing practice

The traditional school health program is generally described as having three functions: provision of a safe and healthful school environment, implementation of an ongoing and effective health education curriculum, and delivery of health services to students and staff.[1] State legislation describes required school health program components. For example, one state's school health program is to provide adequate school health services, instruction in health education, and a healthful school environment.[2]

State licensing laws apply to school nurses, and state certification may be required of school nurses. In a recent survey of state laws regarding school nurse practitioners, Frels found that 32 states required some form of school nurse certification.[3]

Standards for school nursing practice, summarized on p. 218, were developed jointly by school nurses in the American Nurses' Association, National School Nurses' Association, National Association of State School Nurse Consultants, American School Health Association, National Association of Pediatric Nurse Associates and Practitioners, and Public Health Nursing Section of the American Public Health Association.[4] The standards state that the purpose of school nursing is to enhance the educational process by modifying or removing health-related barriers to learning and through promotion of optimal level of wellness.[5]

The many possible roles of the school nurse are often determined by the content and responsibility, the work

STANDARDS OF SCHOOL NURSING PRACTICE

Standard I: Theory

The school nurse applies appropriate theory as a basis for decision making in nursing practice.

Standard II: Program Management

The school nurse establishes and maintains a comprehensive school health program.

Standard III: Nursing Process

The nursing process includes individualized health plans that are developed by the school nurse.

A. Collection of Data
The school nurse collects information about the health and developmental status of the student in a systematic and continuous manner.

B. Nursing Diagnosis
The nurse uses data collected about the health and educational status of the student to determine a nursing diagnosis.

C. Planning
The nurse develops a nursing care plan with specific goals and interventions delineating school nursing actions unique to student needs.

D. Intervention
The nurse intervenes as guided by the nursing care plan to implement nursing actions that promote, maintain, or restore health, prevent illness, and effect rehabilitation.

E. Evaluation
The nurse assesses student responses to nursing actions in order to revise the data base, nursing diagnoses, and nursing care plan and to determine progress made toward goal achievement.

Standard IV: Interdisciplinary Collaboration

The school nurse collaborates with other professionals in assessing, planning, implementing, and evaluating programs and other school health activities.

Standard V: Health Education

The nurse assists students, families, and groups to achieve optimal levels of wellness through health education.

Standard VI: Professional Development

The school nurse participates in peer review and other means of evaluation to assure quality of nursing care provided for students. The nurse assumes responsibility for continuing education and professional development and contributes to the professional growth of others.

Standard VII: Community Health Systems

The school nurse participates with other key members of the community responsible for assessing, planning, implementing, and evaluating school health services and community services that include the broad continuum of promotion of primary, secondary, and tertiary prevention.

Standard VIII: Research

The school nurse contributes to nursing and school health through innovations in theory and practice and participation in research.

Adapted from AMERICAN NURSES' ASSOCIATION, STANDARDS FOR SCHOOL NURSING PRACTICE, 1983.

setting, and employer of the nurse. Public health nurses may be school nurses, employed by a health department, and either responsible for the school within a particular geographic area or assigned to only one or more schools as part of a team of school nurses.

School nurses are also employed by state or local boards of education to provide services to one or more schools. In some states school nurse teachers combine health and education responsibilities through employment with a board of education and/or specific school. These individuals usually are responsible for a classroom as well as a health room.

School nurse practitioners also function in school health programs. They have expanded nursing skills and usually carry more responsibilities in the area of diagnosis, treatment, and primary care of the students. Readers who are nurse practitioners will want to review other chapters in this book relating specifically to expanded practice.

The school nursing role involves emergency care, counseling, primary care, health teaching and education, prevention, and maintenance of health. The role includes that of manager of health care within the school health program; deliverer of health services; advocate for health rights of children; counselor for health concerns of children, families, and staff; and educator for school/community health concerns.[6]

Wold identified six basic responsibilities of the school health program and school nurse:

1. Identify and exclude from school those students

and staff with communicable diseases and initiate appropriate follow-up to ensure their prompt readmission.
2. Prevent the outbreak and spread of communicable diseases through consistent enforcement of existing laws and school policies regarding immunizations for students and school personnel.
3. Limit disability through early diagnosis and prompt treatment for such potentially chronic problems as hearing loss, impaired vision, and scoliosis.
4. Maintain a safe and healthful school environment so that conditions that might interfere with the teaching and learning climate are minimized.
5. Develop a practical and appropriate system for providing first aid and emergency care for students and staff who become injured or ill at school.
6. Develop, implement, and evaluate a comprehensive health education curriculum to prepare students to assume responsibility for their own health.[7]

Work settings vary greatly, including private and public schools, and involve many levels of education, from day care, through elementary, junior, or middle school, to high school and college. The school nurse's clients are the students and their parents, the school and its employees, and the general community.

The school nurse must not only be familiar with the health care system but also the educational system. Both systems vary as to their standards and requirements. This is because of several factors, including (1) school boards are elected bodies, (2) schools may individualize their programs above and beyond the state mandates, and (3) wide, local discretion applies to the design of school curriculum and policies.

Enforcing public health laws

School health legislation exists mostly at the state and local level, although some federal legislation provides funding for health-related projects in schools and is administered through the states. The constitutionality of school health services in private schools relates to the enforcement of state school health laws in these settings.

FEDERAL SCHOOL HEALTH LAWS

Many federal laws fund projects related to school health, including those on child abuse, nutrition, handicapped and disabled children, and the school environment. The first and last areas were discussed in more detail in Chapter 13. Under the section in this chapter on children with special needs, the other federal legislation will be addressed.

Medicaid programs, joint federal and state responsibilities, pay for medical services for everyone who qualifies either on income criteria or disability or age. Known as Title XIX, this program provides aid for dependent children (AFDC)[8] and ensures that preventive health services be given to Medicaid children. This program is called the Early and Periodic Screening, Diagnosis and Treatment (EPSDT) program.[9] School nursing practice has been involved in implementing all of these federal programs.

STATE SCHOOL HEALTH LEGISLATION

Some state laws are broad and general; others are specific and detailed on the topic of school health. The state departments of health and/or education have regulatory power based upon the school health legislation. Each school nurse should obtain copies of all regulations and legislation that pertain to school health matters. Both legislation and regulations on school health services are enforced by the school nurse. The mandated activities basically fall into three categories:

1. Immunizations and physical health requirements, health assessment, and screening
2. Required health topics in curriculum
3. Other areas, such as school environment, personnel, nutrition programs, transportation, records, and safety

Physical Requirements. The box on p. 220 lists sample titles of school health legislation in two states.[10] Physical health requirements usually include submission of proof of a satisfactory physical examination by a physician and substantiation that certain immunization requirements have been met. In most states immunizations must be complete upon admission to the school.[11] The health assessments may require a physical, including assessment of hematocrit, hemoglobin, height, weight, blood pressure, vision, hearing, speech, and teeth. A health history and developmental history is also required. Other assessments may be required, including tests for tuberculosis, sickle cell anemia, and lead paint poisoning.

Physical health assessments are required not only upon admission to school but at certain times during the student's program. For example, vision and hearing screening must occur three times in Maryland: when one enters a school system; in the fourth, fifth, or sixth grade; and in the ninth grade.[12] In Connecticut vision screening is required annually in kindergarten, grades 1 through 6,

SAMPLE STATE SCHOOL HEALTH LEGISLATION

Sanitation	School Lunch Program
Vaccination	School Breakfast Program
Required Immunizations	Tuberculosis Screening
School Medical Advisers	School Employees
Health Assessments	Protective Eye Devices
Health Records	Fire Drills
Referral and Follow-up	Physical Education Programs
Free Health Assessments	Safety Education Programs
Free and Reduced Price Meals	Drug Education Programs
Physical Restrictions	Alcohol Abuse Program
School Nurse and Nurse Practitioner	Driver Education Program
Administration of Medications	School Health Pilot Program
Dental Hygienists	Pediatric School Nurse Practitioner
Vision Screening	State Free Feeding Program
Hearing/Audiometric Screening	Transportation
Scoliosis/Postural Screening	Professional Communications
Compliance Reports	Effect of Drugs, Alcohol, Nicotine, or Tobacco
Child Nutrition Programs	Annual Report

and grade 9; hearing screening is to be provided annually in kindergarten to grade 3, grade 5 and grade 8.[13] Scoliosis screening or postural screening is required in the fifth and eighth grades in Connecticut and at least once in grades 6 through 8 in Maryland.[14]

In addition, new diseases have created new school nursing roles and responsibilities, not only in relation to student's physical requirements but in other areas. An example of this has been the recent controversy over school attendence of children with acquired immune deficiency syndrome (AIDS). The reaction of parents has included activities such as picketing and protesting, boycotting, staging sick-ins, taking steps to inform themselves of the issues, and arranging for the school nurse and others to monitor these children while attending school.

State and local school board decisions regarding the exclusion and inclusion of children with AIDS from school have varied. Some have totally excluded the child from school, making provisions for education through home teaching, closed-circuit television, or other technological means. Other boards have allowed the children to attend, subject to the right of the school personnel, often the school nurse, to inspect the condition of the child.

Fullest confidentiality protections should be afforded these children and their families. Chapter 13 also discusses legal issues surrounding AIDS. The approach to the question of school attendance is on a case-by-case basis, allowing for the fullest consideration to be given to the individual and unique characteristics of the child's situation. The needs of the child under the circumstances are weighed against the need to protect other children and the school community.

The screening and monitoring activities of the school health nurse has also involved the assessment of other employees' health status, including screening for physical requirements. In this role the school nurse is acting as the occupational health nurse for the school as a workplace. The only case in which a school nurse's screening activity was mentioned involved the issue of discriminatory discharge of an employee based on the results of a hearing test conducted by the school nurse.[15] No question was raised about how the school nurse took the measurements, except the discharged employee tried to convince the court that the school nurse had no special preparation or training to do the test. The court did not address this, concluding that a physical impairment such as hearing was related to the employment as a bus driver and that there was no discriminatory dismissal. Chapter 30 discusses employment claims further.

Health Curriculum. Most states have legislated health education curriculum, including requiring content in the curriculum about drugs, alcohol, tobacco, driving, safety, and physical education. For example, in Maryland each public school, under the direction of teachers trained in the field of drug education, must start a drug education program before the sixth grade.[16] In Connecticut the effect of alcohol, nicotine or tobacco, and drugs on health, character, citizenship, and personality development is taught every academic year to pupils in all grades in the public schools.[17] Connecticut's legislation also provides for trained teachers.

Content of health curriculum is particularly affected by local customs and characteristics, as is the extent to which the school nurse may initiate and disseminate information to students about sex, contraceptives, abortion, drugs, and alcohol. Some state regulations may prevent the school nurse from any role in this area; in other states making referrals and giving information is expected and rarely questioned.

The standards of school nursing practice specifically focus upon health education. The standards indicate that a school nurse should identify needs of students for health education, employ principles of learning and appropriate teaching methods, teach basic principles of health, teach decision-making skills, counsel students and families, serve as a member of the curriculum committee, act as a resource person, and promote preventive self-care strategies.[18]

Other Areas. State legislation also addresses other school health program components, such as environment and administration of the program. For example, Connecticut specifically identifies the role of the school medical advisor, school nurse, and school nurse practitioner.[19] The school medical advisor has responsibilities to students and employees, including school nurses, for building safety and cleanliness, and for prevention and elimination of communicable diseases. The school nurse and nurse practitioners are appointed by each local or regional board of education. According to Connecticut laws, school nurses may also act as visiting nurses, may visit homes of pupils in the public schools and assist in executing the orders of the school medical advisor.

Alterations in the student's environment may also be provided for in state laws. For example, in both Maryland and Connecticut protective eye devices are required for students in classes with laboratories and workshops.[20] The Maryland statute is very specific in identifying hazardous exposures that require the use of protective eye devices, such as in chemical or combined chemical-physical laboratories, vocational or industrial art shops, or laboratories that use hot molten metal; milling, sawing, turning, shaping, cutting, or stamping of solid materials; heat treatment, tempering, or kiln firing; gas or electric welding; repair or servicing of any vehicle; or any other caustic or explosive material.

Thus far, the discussion has addressed primarily the elementary and secondary levels of education. Schooling before and after these levels may also be under state regulation. Specific health regulations exist for day care alone. College health services are not generally mandated as other school health services are. Because the school nurse's client in a college health service is often an adult (over age 18 or of legal age), this school nurse may not be that involved with the student's parent.

That the state's department of education is the community system ultimately responsible for school health services has raised some interesting legal questions. Can an education system employ health providers? The question of whether a board of education could employ a school nurse was addressed by a Georgia attorney general.[21] In deciding that the board could properly employ a school nurse, the attorney general pointed to the fact that the board is the entity mandated by state law to provide school health services. Even though this question has not been litigated, the opinion indicates how a court might answer the question.

In another situation school nurses have had to litigate the issue of whether they were professional staff members of the school that employs them. Several cases have held that the school nurse is a professional employee.[22]

PRIVATE SCHOOLS: CONSTITUTIONALITY OF SCHOOL NURSING SERVICES

There are private nonsectarian and private religious schools that must also meet the state's school health requirements. The state can make minimal demands upon private schools, including those that are religiously affiliated. The state can provide school health services in private schools without violating the first amendment rights to freedom of religion as long as it maintains the separation of church and state and does not become excessively entangled with the private school. A couple of cases have determined that school nurse services is not "entanglement" with religion.[23]

However, careful analysis of how nursing services are delivered in private schools, according to state legislation, reveals that the state is much less involved with private, religious schools. The distinction of what can be essentially required of the private school should be evaluated periodically. This legal issue for school nurses may change from time to time and is worth watching carefully. Certainly, the controversy over prayer in school, use of silent meditation, and use of public school teachers in parochial schools for their handicapped and disadvantaged students has raised similar types of constitutional questions.[24]

Consent, privacy, confidentiality, and the school health program

Enforcement of public health laws related to schools and school children by no means diminishes the nurse's responsibilities to obtain consent for nursing procedures and maintain privacy and confidentiality of the nurse-client relationship. While immunizations and screening are mandated, consent is still an important part of school health care delivery and treatment.

In addition, exceptions do exist for these mandates. For example, the parent who objects on the grounds that the requirement violates religious principles may not be required to fulfill the mandate. Chapter 13 discusses other exceptions.

For example, in one state where health assessments are to be conducted by a physician or the school medical advisor or designee, the parent or guardian is first given written notice and reasonable opportunity to get the health assessment completed. If the parent does not, the medical advisor may examine the child, but only after the parent has had an opportunity to be present; if not present, the advisor must have another school employee present during the assessment.[25] Records of medical examinations, including psychological examinations, are not open to the public.[26]

Questions of consent and working with persons under age or minors are often raised by school nurses. Varying state laws have carved out several possible legal concepts, including mature minor and emancipated minor. Generally, these terms refer to persons who are under the age of 18, 19, 20, or 21 (depending on where the particular state draws the line) and who are "mature" or "emancipated" from their parents. Defined by state consent statutes for minors, emancipated or mature generally includes one who has married or one who is a parent or one who lives independently from any parent or guardian.[27]

The implication for school nurses is that if a person is classified as mature or emancipated, the person may consent to any medical or health care treatment just as an adult may. Adult, defined by statutes as well, refers to one who had reached the age of majority (18 to 21 years, depending on the state).[28]

As was discussed in Chapter 5, in emergency situations the health care provider may treat a minor without any consent from the minor or parents. An emergency situation demands taking the life-saving measures without wasting valuable time to locate a parent. The courts that have reviewed emergency situations have implied the consent of the parent, given society's and the state's interest in preservation of life.

For selected, statutorily defined health care treatments, minors may consent as adults for treatments, without their parents' permission. For example, in one state, a minor has the same capacity as an adult to consent to:

1. Treatment for or advice about drug abuse, alcoholism, venereal disease, pregnancy, and contraception (except sterilization)
2. Physical examination and treatment of injuries from an alleged rape or sexual offense
3. Physical examination to obtain evidence of an alleged rape or sexual offense[29]

Services, referral, and information about abortions is also an area of concern for the school nurse. Again, state statute and case law will be the determining factor, along with local custom, of the school nurse's role in this area. For example, in one state a physician must first give notice to an unmarried minor's parent before performing an abortion. The physician may perform an abortion without notice to a parent if the physician's opinion is that notice may lead to physical or emotional abuse of the minor; or the physician may perform an abortion without notice if the minor does not live with a parent and a reasonable effort to notify the parent is unsuccessful.[30] However, this may not be the practice in other states.

State statutes will also govern the question of whether the school nurse must disclose to a parent information about their minor's care and treatment. For example, in one state a physician or member of the medical staff of a hospital or public clinic may, but need not, give a parent information about treatment needed by the minor or provided to the minor (except information about an abortion, as discussed).[31] Under this statute it is not clear whether a school nurse would be included, unless he or she was part of a medical staff in a hospital or public clinic.

Just as adults seek health care advice and may not be forced to accept it, one court determined that a minor who may consent to medical treatment may not be forced, more than an adult, to accept treatment for advice concerning pregnancy.[32] Chapter 5 should be consulted for more information about informed consent.

Administration of medications and treatments in the school

Questions arise in school nursing practice regarding the student's use of prescription and nonprescription drugs in schools and the school nurse's role in administering and dispensing them. A related issue is the use of nonprofessional assistants in school health. At least two sources of law are relevant to the discussion of these issues: the state nurse practice act, medical and pharmacy acts, and other school health legislation and case law. Since no case law exists dealing with a school nurse and medication in the schools or the school nurse's responsibility for the assistant, the legislation, state regulations, and standards of practice formed by school policy and procedures and professional associations must be examined.

A medications policy for any school should require permission from parents and a physician's order. Both of these should be written and exist prior to the administration of any medication. The school nurse is responsible for knowing the side effects and contraindications of any medications to be administered.

Prescription and nonprescription drugs should be treated the same. State statutes are beginning to address the issue of administration of medications in the schools. For example, the law in Connecticut on administration of medicines by school personnel states that a school nurse, the principal, or any teacher of a school may administer medicinal preparations, including controlled drugs which the commissioner of health services, by regulation, designates. This law requires the written order of a physician licensed to practice medicine or a dentist licensed to practice dental medicine in Connecticut or another state and the written authorization of a parent or guardian.[33]

In addition, the statute requires that, when controlled drugs are administered, the school must keep records the same as those that are required of hospitals and that storage of the drugs must follow regulations provided by the commissioner of health.[34]

The law also provides immunity from civil damages for any personal injury that may result from acts or omissions of the school nurse, principal, or teacher in administering medications, amounting to ordinary negligence. Immunity is not available if the school nurse's act or omission constitutes gross, willful, or wanton negligence.[35] Chapter 2 distinguishes these two types of negligence.

In the area of medication administration, each school nurse must first know what state legislation exists and if none does, pursue getting a state law on the topic of administration of medications in schools. For issues related to the school nurse's responsibilities in giving immunizations, please refer to that section in Chapter 13. Some school nurses base their actions on standing orders. These were also dealt with in Chapter 13, including a set of guidelines for reviewing standing orders.

Supervision of nonprofessional assistants in schools may be a school nurse's responsibility. For example, school nurses may work centrally in a school district and supervise and arrange for hearing and vision technicians to conduct the necessary screening of students. This position places upon the school nurse additional responsibilities: proper supervision, training, and evaluation of the nonprofessional staff. Negligence on the part of a technician will only include the school nurse's negligence if the school nurse did not evaluate, place, assign, or supervise the person properly. Technicians are responsible for their own actions, and only if the school nurse should have known of the technician's inabilities will the school nurse be implicated.

Another area of concern for the school nurse is the breadth of responsibility, including the number and distance between geographic locations for which the school nurse may be responsible. Careful evaluation and attention should be paid by the school nurse when he or she has responsibility for places and people when not physically present in the same building. The school nurse is responsible for making proper and reasonable delegation decisions. It has become customary school nursing practice that other school personnel, such as health aides, teachers, secretaries, and administrators, are responsible for implementing emergency treatments or other health care practices when the school nurse is not present. Some schools may have only part-time school nurses and utilize volunteer parents during other times. The relationship between the school nurse and these other persons should be clarified from the outset of employment because the nurse, depending on what her or his responsibility to the other person is, may be legally responsible for evaluating the person and orienting them to the policies and procedures or other activities.

Managing accidents and first aid

The school nurse's responsibilities in accidents and first aid are many. Responding to an emergency requires careful yet efficient assessment of the situation and appropriate treatment decisions and use of professional judgment. After the accident has occurred, the nurse is often responsible for administrative responsibilities such as filing an accident report form. Not only has this role been examined by the courts, but it is in this area that the school nurse has been sued for negligence.

The school nurse has also been involved in litigation because of care given a fellow employee who was injured at school. In addition, the standards of school nursing indicate that the nurse has responsibility for arranging in-service programs for school personnel for first aid and emergency care procedures as well as in-service programs on current health issues.[36] While there have been no cases discussing negligence in delivering these programs, the school nurse is responsible for the accuracy of the content given during these sessions and for proper evaluation of the in-service participants. If a certificate is awarded at the end of the program and the participant is expected to perform a new function, then the school nurse is responsible for making a proper judgment regarding the level of proficiency obtained at the conclusion of the in-service program.

In a case reviewing the role of the school nurse in filing an insurance form, the parents of a 9-year-old boy sought recovery from the school board for injuries sustained by their son in an after-school fight.[37] Immediately following the incident, he was assisted by the school nurse and school principal. As required for all school accidents, the next day both the principal and the nurse completed a form that contained the names of the students involved; the time, date, and location of the event; how the injury had occurred; and the name and address of the injured child's parents. The form was filed with the school district's director of finance.

At the time of this case in Minnesota there was a notice-of-claim statute that required notice of a claim so that the board of education could have ample opportunity to investigate an incident. The child's family filed suit for injuries 6 days after the 30-day time limit. The court decided that the effect of the nurse filing the form gave the requisite notice of a claim and that the board of education had knowledge of the injuries and the manner in which they occurred.

In a case involving allegations of nursing negligence, a school nurse was sued individually for failure to obtain emergency care for a child injured at school.[38] The case was dismissed because the plaintiff failed to state a claim. The plaintiff presented no facts to establish what happened. However, the court discussed whether there was immunity for the nurse's actions. Even though some immunity exists for school personnel actions, known as discretionary immunity, it is never available for negligent acts. School nurses' employers, depending on the jurisdiction, may also have sovereign immunity, and therefore individual school nurses alone could be sued for their negligence.

Knowing when to refer an accident victim for further medical attention is a responsibility of the school nurse. In one case, where the facts were better established by the plaintiff than in the previous case, a board of education was sued for failing to provide adequate instruction and supervision during class and for unreasonable delay in obtaining proper medical attention for an injured student.[39] The situation involved a student who, during gym class, was accidentally kicked in the right temple by another student. He fell to the mat but stood up within seconds and in response to questioning by the gym teacher, said he had not lost consciousness.

The teacher told another student to take the injured student to the locker room and run cold water over his forehead. When they returned from the locker room, the teacher asked how he felt. When he said he did not feel well, the teacher told the other student to stay with him while he dressed and then take him to the school nurse.

The student arrived at the nurse's office 22 minutes after the accident. He complained to the school nurse of a pain in the right temple and a tingling sensation in the jaw. The school nurse observed some redness in the temple area but no swelling or ecchymosis. The student gave no indication of the severity of the injury by moaning, crying, or making special complaints. The school nurse's assessment included the fact that the student's pupils were normal and that there was no vomiting and no complaints of nausea.

The school nurse applied an ice water compress to the right temple and had the student lie down while she telephoned the parent. The first call was ineffective; there was no answer. The second call was made 6 to 7 minutes later, at which time the parent was reached and told of the student's injury. The nurse told the parent that the student should be seen by the family physician. The parent had no transportation, but the student had an automobile at school. The parent told the nurse it would be quicker if the student drove himself to the physician. This is what he did, accompanied by a friend.

The family physician examined the student about 30 minutes later and admitted him to the hospital within the hour. At the hospital the student became comatose. A neurosurgeon immediately performed an emergency craniectomy, finding both a blood clot, which he removed, and a skull fracture. The student remained in a coma and died 13 days later.

The lower court dismissed the complaint that alleged negligent instruction and supervision in the classroom, but allowed the question of whether there was unreasonable delay in obtaining medical treatment to go to the jury. They found in favor of the plaintiff. On appeal, however, the court held that there was no proof to support the allegation of unreasonable delay, reversed the jury's decision, and dismissed the case. Under this set of facts the school nurse was not negligent in the manner in which she managed the school injury. The assessment, contact with the parent, and decision on how and what type of follow-up to provide this student did not involve unreasonable delay. The parents had no proof that the nurse unreasonably delayed in getting medical assistance.

There are two aspects of this case that deserve further attention. The first aspect has to do with authorizing a student to use their own transportation; the second is a related issue, that of accompanying students to the emergency room. What liabilities may be present in both areas depends on school policies and the facts of each situation. The school nurse in the above situation did not authorize the student to drive. The parent gave the authorization. Yet, the parent's authorization was clearly based upon the school nurse's assessment. If the student had not been safe to drive and the school nurse knew this and did not tell the parent or take steps to stop the student, then the school nurse may have incurred liability for faulty judgment.

Acompanying students to the community emergency room may be part of the school nurse's responsibility. The school nurse's liabilities will depend on what he or she is required to do. If a rescue squad or ambulance crew should be called, they become responsible for the care and treatment of the student during transport. If it is the nurse's responsibility to see that the student is transported to the hospital, then he or she is to fulfill this responsibility in a reasonable manner.

Giving first aid to other employees may also be of concern to the school nurse. For example, in one case a school nurse removed an object from the eye of the school's chief engineer.[40] The school nurse's action was not questioned but was simply included as part of the engineer's worker's compensation case. However, in each first aid situation the school nurse is expected to meet the requisite standard of care under the circumstances.

In some states legislation provides specific immunity from civil liability for school nurses when managing school accidents or injuries. For example, in one state a teacher or other school personnel on the school grounds or in the school building or at a school function who has completed a course in first aid and renders emergency first aid to a person in need shall not be liable to such person in rendering the emergency first aid, which may constitute ordinary negligence.[41] However, the immunity does not apply to acts or omissions constituting gross, willful, or wanton negligence.[42]

This same state's legislature further addresses a teacher or other school personnel who has completed both a course in first aid and a course given by the medical adviser of the school or by a licensed physician in the administration of medications by injection. When rendering emergency care by administration of medication by injection to someone in need, this person shall not be liable to that person for civil damages for any injuries that result from acts or omissions by the person rendering the emergency care that may constitute ordinary negligence.[43] Again, the immunity does not apply to acts or omissions constituting gross, willful, or wanton negligence.[44]

Other states may have similar statutes. These should be part of a school nurse's policy and procedure manuals and kept up to date as changes occur. If none exists in a particular state, a school nurse may wish to consider becoming involved in establishing such laws. The standards for school nursing state that the nurse consults with school administration to establish, review, and revise policy and procedure for a comprehensive school health program, including emergency procedures, medication administration protocols, safety measures and programs, student/personnel health services, and health education.[45] The standards further state that the nurse determines training of paraprofessionals, extent of orientation, and amount and type of supervision that will be needed to comply with state nurse practice acts and other legal considerations.[46] Lastly, according to the standards, the school nurse promotes the routine practice and evaluation of periodic emergency drills such as bus evacuation and fire drills.[47]

Health teaching, advice, and referrals for services

As already mentioned, these are very important components of the school health program and the school nurse's responsibilities. In general, nurses are involved with teachers and others in designing educational and health plans for students. Individual needs of students are addressed by the school nurse. It is expected that the nurse will refer and inform students about community resources to meet their needs, including where to obtain health services for venereal diseases, mental health, contraception and abortion, and drug and alcohol abuse.

As mentioned earlier, state legislatures have specified required curriculum, including courses on the topics of drug abuse, alcohol abuse, driving, sex, and family education. Examples of this can be found in most state legislatures. In Maryland a drug education program and an alcohol abuse program provided in public schools is required.[48] Connecticut, on the other hand, requires courses on the topics of alcohol, nicotine or tobacco, and drugs.[49]

Drug and alcohol abuse advice and counseling may involve other issues. This is particularly true of drugs since their possession and use is an illegal act.[50] Schools, principals, and school boards handle drug abuse in different ways. Under some conditions, a search of student's possessions and lockers is done.[51] Under other conditions the police may be involved and a search warrant, based upon probable cause, is required before inspecting the student's belongings.

State statutes have attempted to provide protection for students in the form of privileged communication statutes. Usually statutes also address turning over evidence without giving a student's name and provide the school personnel with immunity from civil and criminal liability.

The Maryland statute provides that if a student seeks information to overcome any form of drug abuse from a teacher, counselor, principal, or other professional educator employed by an educational institution, whether oral or written, an observation or conclusion made by the student and derived from the statement is not admissible against the student in any proceeding.[52]

The Connecticut law provides that any such professional employee (the law specifically includes the school nurse) shall not be required to disclose any information acquired through a professional communication with a student, when such information concerns alcohol or drug abuse or any alcoholic or drug problem of such student.[53]

Both states provide that no disclosure is required. Connecticut's statute goes further in that it requires that any physical evidence obtained from the student indicating that a criminal activity is involved be turned over to school authorities within 2 days.In doing so, however, the employee is never to be asked to disclose the name of the student. Civil immunity and immunity from prosecution for possession of such evidence is also provided in the statute.[54]

School discipline, expulsion, and suspension may be involved in the area of drug and alcohol abuse. School board policies and procedures must be followed prior to the disciplining act. Readers might review Chapter 19 on nursing students for more information on the principles of due process and student rights. Parental involvement in such situations is expected.

Child abuse and neglect

School nurses have been involved in the legal process relating to child abuse and parental termination of rights cases. Chapter 13 gives further information about this area. A few case examples involving school nurses will be mentioned here.

In one situation a court criticized the school nurse for not reporting physical abuse and malnutrition.[55] In another case the school nurse conducted a physical examination of a child, a victim of sexual abuse, in the school health room.[56] In yet another case a school nurse testified in a sex offense criminal case about the school program on sex education for adolescent girls.[57] In none of these cases was the school nurse directly charged with anything, rather the school nurse participated through varying roles in the legal process.

In a last example, the school nurse was shown to be part of an efficient school child abuse team, using an approach that involved collaboration and cooperation on the part of the principal, nurse, teachers, counselors, and social services personnel.[58]

School health records

Given the unique arrangements in the delivery of school health services, school nurses may be subject to at least two sets of policies and procedures regarding records, those of a health department and those of a school board. School nurses maintain not only the individual student health records, which are permanent records of the student and, for example, transferred with the student to a new school, but also health center or health room attendance records and daily logs of student complaints.

The ideal in record keeping, however, is that information in logs is also in the permanent record. Not only would this improve the continuity of care and quality of care but it would also enhance the school nurse's ability to defend a lawsuit. The brevity of the log also increases the inability of the nurse to later reconstruct assessment factors and intervention steps taken should questions of negligence later arise.

The school nurse also may be responsible for insurance forms and claims forms. In addition, school nurses may maintain other official records for the health department, for example, a narrative and health department records, and unofficially maintain other records such as personal memorandum, notes, and calendars.

These documents have been included in litigation.[59] In the case discussed earlier where the nurse testified as to her actions in obtaining medical treatment for an injured student, the careful and detailed documentation supported the conclusion of the court of no proof of negligence. Since the allegation in that case was delay in treatment, the court carefully examined the time when care was given. Documentation reflected the exact time the student arrived in the health room, when phone calls were made, when decisions were made, and when the student left the school for the physician's office.

All records must be kept in a confidential manner. The business records of the agencies (schools or health departments) may be subject to student and parent review. States may have statutes on this topic. In one state a law provides that upon written request and within reasonable time, a parent or legal guardian is entitled to knowledge of and access to all educational, medical, or similar records maintained in such student's cumulative record (except communications that are privileged, described previously under drug and alcohol abuse programs.)[60] There are also federal laws that apply, known as the Buckley Amendment, which allow parents' access to student records.[61]

Collection of information about students is also the subject of the nursing practice standards. The school nurse is to establish a recording system that provides for continuity and accountability of the program.[62] The outcome criteria for this data collection standard are that the student's cumulative school health record is initiated upon enrollment and becomes a part of the permanent record; that the data base is synthesized and recorded in a standardized format; and that the records demonstrate periodic updating of student health status information.[63]

The standard lists the health status data that the nurse should collect, including growth and developmental history, health history, screening results, physical assessment, emotional status, performance level of activities of daily living, interactional patterns, nutritional status, immunization status, student's perception of health status, student's health goals, and cultural variance.[64]

Children with special health needs

Children with special needs are provided school health and school nursing services. These children include those who are handicapped or disabled, chronically or terminally ill children, children with special nutritional needs, and children with behavior problems. The standards of school nursing practice state that the nurse engages in appropriate and necessary nursing care to ensure optimal educational opportunity for the:

1. Handicapped: set goals to habilitate/rehabilitate to highest potential for specific disability.
2. Chronically ill: educate client, family, and school personnel regarding the specific condition; monitor treatment regime and ensure continuity of care.
3. Terminally ill: arrange for physical care, medication, and treatments; offer anticipatory guidance to student, family, school personnel, and peers in preparation for death.[65]

The outcome criterion for this standard is that handicapped and chronically and terminally ill students show evidence of participation in educational activities to the fullest extent possibble in relation to the individual's health status.[66]

HANDICAPPED OR DISABLED CHILDREN

In 1980 several professional associations accepted a policy statement regarding school nurses and handicapped children.[67] This statement established a standard of care by identifying some of the health care needs of handicapped children and what the role of the school nurse should include. In response to the federal law, Education of All Handicapped Children Act of 1975, the statement outlined several aspects of the nursing role:

1. School health services to handicapped students should be provided by school nurses. The ratio of nurse to student should be based on the handicapping condition. Trained health aides, supervised by the school nurse, should be employed to assist the nurse.
2. School nurses should assume responsibility for obtaining information about the handicapped student, including initial evaluation, comprehensive history, health and developmental history, and physical examination. The school nurse provides the health information and makes specific recommendations related to managing health problems in the construction of the individual education plan called for by the federal legislation.

3. Nursing care plans should be recorded, identifying problems and continued evaluation.
4. School nurses, in collaboration with others, should determine the safety program necessary for the handicapped student.
5. Members of the school health team, including children, parents, teachers, and school nurses, should work together as a team in providing assistance to students with handicaps.
6. A nationwide program of continuing education for school nurses should be initiated to expand and update rehabilitation knowledge and skills.[68]

Federal Laws and Supreme Court Decisions. Federal legislation and federal case law have both addressed the special education and health needs in the schools for handicapped and disabled children. Children needing special education in the community subjected to mandated schooling are no longer isolated, kept separate, institutionalized, or placed in special schools. Where possible children with handicapping conditions are to be taught in the routine, usual manner. This has resulted in an even closer relationship between health and education systems. Sharing resources and expertise, the school nurse has had an impact upon the mainstreaming trend. The school nurse must incorporate treatment needs, medications, and communication with other school and health personnel to more complicated case management and coordination of care.

Two laws, primarily, relate to the issue of school health services for the handicapped or disabled child. They are P.L. 94-142, Education of All Handicapped Children Act (EAHCA)[69] and the Rehabilitation Act of 1973.[70] The EAHCA requires the development of an individual education program (IEP) for handicapped children. The IEP is to be jointly developed by the school officials, teachers, parents, and when appropriate, the child. It is to be an educational blueprint that specifies how the child is to be taught, sets goals, and determines how progress is to be measured. EAHCA defines special education as specially designed instruction, at no cost to parents or guardians, to meet the unique needs of a handicapped child, including classroom instruction, instruction in physical education, home instruction, and instruction in hospitals and institutions.[71]

Standards of school nursing practice discuss the role of the school nurse and interdisciplinary collaboration. Specifically, the care plan developed by the school nurse and the IEP should reflect collaboration and team functioning. The professionals are to work together to formulate a shared outline of a problem statement and goals, an integrated plan with a common focus, and shared responsibility for implementation and evaluation.[72]

The concept of mainstreaming is outlined in the EAHCA.[73] It requires that, to the maximum extent appropriate, handicapped children will be educated with nonhandicapped children and that removal of handicapped children from regular classes will occur only when their handicaps cannot be accommodated by supplementary aids and services.

In the first case in which the Supreme Court considered the EAHCA, it reviewed the goal of the act.[74] That goal is to provide a basic floor of opportunity for students, consisting of personalized instruction and related services designed to enable handicapped children to benefit from education. The court also reviewed the state's choice of educational means or method, stating that the state is accorded wide discretion to choose education means and need not maximize each child's potential.

The court outlined certain standards that the required instruction and related services must meet:

1. Instruction and services must be provided at public expense.
2. They must meet state educational standards.
3. They must approximate the grade levels used in the state's regular education.
4. They must comport to the child's individual education plan.

A case specifically involving school nurse services was brought by the parents of a handicapped child.[75] The parents alleged that the school district was required by federal laws to provide their child with special services, including clean, intermittent catheterization during the time the child would be in school classes. The parents also argued that the school board's refusal to provide the catheterization violated Section 504 of the Rehabilitation Act of 1973.

As a result of a birth defect (spina bifida), their child had speech and orthopedic impediments and a neurogenic bladder, a condition that requires several daily catheterizations to maintain health. The parents asked the local school district to provide special education. In a series of meetings an individual education program (required by EAHCA) was developed that provided for the child's placement in the school's early childhood development classes and other services, including physical and occupational therapy. The plan did not provide for a clean, intermittent catheterization (CIC).

The school maintained that it was not legally obligated to provide the catheterizations. The school's reasons included:

1. That the catheterization may not be performed by a nurse or other qualified person unless a physician is physically present to control and supervise the procedure
2. That the catheterization was not a related service within EAHCA for this child because it is not required to assist her to benefit from special education

In dealing with the school's first argument, the court reviewed evidence proffered by the Texas Medical Association and the Dallas County Medical Society,[76] the Texas Medical Practice Act, and the Texas Nursing Practice Act. In Texas, as in many other states, a physician may prescribe treatment and delegate its administration to others. The Texas Nursing Practice Act defines administration of treatments prescribed by a licensed physician as a professional nursing act. Hence, the court reasoned, that the CIC would not be an unlawful practice of medicine.

The court further relied upon Attorney General Opinions of Texas, which defined physician's supervision as not requiring the constant, physical presence of a physician. The court held that a catheterization could be performed by a nurse without the physical presence of a physician.

The court then turned to the school district's second argument, that the catheterization was not a related service and not required to assist this child to benefit from special education. In deciding that the catheterization was a related service, the court examined and relied upon the individual education plan (IEP), which had determined that the child should attend early development classes.

The IEP included a justification for the choice of these classes over other educational means, stating that it was the most appropriate and least restrictive means and that testing indicated the need for this type of placement. In order to attend day classes, the child needed the catheterizations every 3 hours.

The court, holding that the school district must provide the catheterization, indicated that the district is entitled to require a detailed prescription and instructions tailored to the particular needs of each individual child for whom it is asked to provide health-related services under EAHCA. So that the school would not be in the position of having to exercise medical discretion, the court outlined several items that the school could require:

1. A prescription that clearly indicates that the child is under the continuing care of a prescribing physician, who will monitor the child's continuing need for the services and modify the prescription accordingly
2. A prescription that identifies the circumstances in which the school district personnel should seek further guidance from the physician
3. Written parental permission (The court noted that in addition to a physician's prescription, the parents had given their written consent.)

Because of this case, the school and school nurse can make similar requirements when providing related health services in order to educate other similarly handicapped children. In addition, state laws govern education services for disadvantaged, gifted, deaf, blind, and handicapped children.[77]

CHILDREN WITH SPECIAL NUTRITIONAL NEEDS

Several state and federal nutrition programs are available for children who are eligible according to criteria of income. School nurses may initiate these programs for school children and may be involved in administering and evaluating them. The federal programs have diminished in size, as have the state programs. However, certain school meals, breakfasts, and lunches can be provided either free to certain children and/or subsidized to other and all children. Each state has wide discretion as to the amount of resources it places in the nutritional programs.

The federal programs include the Special Supplemental Food program for women, infants, and children (WIC program administered by the U.S. Department of Agriculture); Title I of the Elementary and Secondary Education Act of 1965[78] (School Health and Nutrition Services for Children from Low Income Families); and the Child Nutrition Act.[79]

State laws usually provide that schools may establish lunch or breakfast programs under the federal laws and may establish other child feeding programs as necessary.[80] In other states a statewide program may be established, with funds controlled and distributed centrally according to state-developed standards by the department of education.[81]

In addition, states may develop policies for administration of these nutritional programs, which school nurses need to be aware of. For example, in Maryland the legislation provides that the identity of the children who participate in free or subsidized feeding programs should remain anonymous, and positive procedures should be adopted to accomplish this. Applications for participants in the program should be brief and simple, based on a statement of present income and family size or of participation in a social services or welfare program.[82]

CHILDREN WITH BEHAVIOR PROBLEMS

Legislation exists in all states that requires school attendance beginning and continuing until a certain age. The legislation usually identifies the duties of parents and those of the school board. For example, in Connecticut a parent having control of a child between ages of 7 and 16 shall ensure that the child attends a public day school regularly.[83] Duties of the school board are to furnish school accommodations so that each child over age 5 and under 21 (who has not graduated from high school or vocational school) may attend.[84]

In addition state law requires that the schools have truant officers or attendance officers whose responsibility it is to:

1. Investigate absence or irregular attendance.
2. Ensure attendance regularly.
3. Present cases requiring prosecution for violation of school laws to prosecuting officers.[85]

Behavior problems are handled differently in schools. Depending on the severity and nature of the problems, the resources available to the school, and the philosophy of those involved, children who are aggressive, do not comply with school rules, do not attend regularly, or get involved in fights are of special concern to school nurses.

Most schools have personnel besides the attendance officer and school nurse, for example, the counselor, psychologist, social worker and special teachers, who investigate and evaluate children with behavior problems. The school nurse is an integral part of the investigation, often responsible for an evaluation of the child's physical health but also for an evaluation of the home setting and family.

The only litigation involving school nurses in this area of concern has involved the school nurse giving support to attendance officers and their duties. In one case a school nurse was charged with assault and battery for her role in management of school discipline. In this case the court indicated that the school principal's and school nurse's actions would be within a discretionary function immunity available in that state.[86] The court defined this immunity as one involving functions of school personnel that must be handled in a discretionary manner, and the manner in which school discipline is managed must be left to discretion, depending on the actions that require disciplining. Of course, certain school policies must be followed, but not all disciplinary problems are addressed by these policies. When one of these situations arises, discretion of the principal or other disciplinary authority in the school must be allowed.

This type of immunity from a lawsuit may be available in other states, and the school nurse's disciplinary actions may be provided for within the state statute or case law. However, an immunity for discretionary functions does not apply to health care functions carried out in a negligent manner. Standards of school health services and school nursing services exist that are not discretionary. For example, emergencies and referrals for health care are items of a school nurse's role that do not involve discretion.

School nurses have been involved in other cases dealing with students with behavior or attendance problems. In one the school nurse followed-up with an attendance enforcement agreement that a student had made with the school. Based upon the school nurse's visit to the home on one day of the student's absence, it was determined that the truant violated the agreement. No one answered when the nurse visited and this is what she testified.[87]

In another lawsuit the school nurse went with the attendance officer to visit a child in her home.[88] In yet another suit the school nurse and truant officer made a home visit and took a child and her sister whom she was babysitting to school. The parents sued, alleging false imprisonment, unlawful entering of their home, and compelling the children to leave home against the parents' directions to children.[89] The court remanded the case, after reviewing the powers and duties of the school attendance officer, stating that a jury would have to decide whether the attendance officer and nurse had authority under state laws.

State laws relating to the role of the school nurse in this area of enforcing attendance should be known in order to evaluate what the statute provides in regard to a nurse carrying out such functions.

Standards of care in school nursing

The standards for school nursing practice were highlighted in several places throughout this chapter. In addition one of the American School Health Association's major contributions to the field of school health has been the *Journal of School Health*. Through this journal many school nursing studies, standards, and policies of individual school and health systems are reported. For example, guidance can be found on the issue of medications in the school.[90] These documents could be used as evidence in court to establish an indication of the professional standard.

In addition, the American Academy of Pediatrics, a physician organization also is involved in defining standards of practice for school health.[91] Other physician groups are also involved in shaping the nature of school health services.

Recommendations and trends

The school nurse has many legal responsibilities specified not only in case law but in state and federal legislation. Keeping up to date with changes in school health legislation and regulation and participating in the improvement of school health services through legislation and funding are important nursing responsibilities.

The school nurse role has evolved from one in which only first aid was rendered to one that encompasses a wide range of functions and responsibilities. With the rapid changes in health care in general, school health will naturally be affected. School nurses will be expected to manage more complicated cases and will be involved not only with developing policies on the use of medications in the schools but with using advanced medical technology in the schools.

It is also projected that school health may develop into a more centralized health service for children and that the service will assume more primary care functions for children. This will raise new legal concerns for school nurses.

Endnotes

1. S. WOLD, SCHOOL NURSING, A FRAMEWORK FOR PRACTICE, 21 (1981) (hereinafter cited as *Wold*).
2. MD. EDUC. CODE ANN. §7-401(a), (b) (1985) which provides for development of public standards and guidelines.
3. Frels, *National Survey of School Nurse Certification Re-visited,* 52 JOURNAL OF SCHOOL HEALTH 446 (September 1983).
4. AMERICAN NURSES' ASSN., STANDARDS FOR SCHOOL NURSING PRACTICE (1983) (hereinafter cited as *ANA Standards*).
5. *Id.* at 1.
6. WOLD, *supra* note 1, at 22.
7. *Id.*
8. 42 U.S.C. §601-676 (1982).
9. 42 U.S.C. §701-709 (1982) (Maternal and Child Health Services Block Grant).
10. MD. EDUC. CODE ANN. §7-401 7-417 (1985) (health and safety of students), 7-501-7-505 (1985) (subsidized and free feeding programs), 7-5A-01-7-5A-03 (1985) (Breakfast Program); §7-601 to 7-606 (1985) (Transportation); CONN. GEN. STAT. ANN. §10-203-10-217b (West 1977 & Supp. 1985) (school health and sanitation), §10-19 (West Supp. 1985) (curriculum), §10-154a (West Supp. 1985) (professional communications), §10-184 to 10-200 (West Supp. 1985) (school attendance). Each state has school health legislation that is generally found in the state's education code, e.g., New York's laws are found at N.Y. EDUC. LAW §901-914 (McKinney 1984 & Supp. 1985), or code portions dealing with schools and education.
11. MD. EDUC. CODE ANN. §7-402(a) (1985); CONN. GEN. STAT. ANN. §10-204a (West Supp. 1985).
12. MD. EDUC. CODE ANN. §7-403(b)(1) (1985).
13. CONN. GEN. STAT. ANN. §10-214 (West Supp. 1985).
14. CONN. GEN. STAT. ANN. §10-214(c) (West Supp. 1985); MD. EDUC. CODE ANN. §7-403.1(b) (1985).
15. *State Division of Human Rights v. Averill Park Central School District,* 388 N.E.2d 729 (N.Y. 1979).
16. MD. EDUC. CODE ANN. §7-409(b)(1) (1985).
17. CONN. GEN. STAT. ANN. §10-19 (West Supp. 1985).
18. *ANA Standards, supra* note 4, at 13.
19. CONN. GEN. STAT. ANN. §10-205, 10-207, 10-212 (West Supp. 1985) (the last section deals with appointment of school nurses and nurse practitioners).
20. MD. EDUC. CODE ANN. §7-405 (1985); CONN. GEN. STAT. ANN. §10-214a (West Supp. 1985).
21. Opinion 77-52, 1977 Op. Atty. Gen. 88, July 12, 1977.
22. *The Town of Wallingford v. The Board of Education of the Town of Wallingford,* 152 Conn. 568 (1965); *Spiewak v. Board of Education of Rutherford,* 90 N.J. 63 (1982); *Scott v. Philadelphia Parking Authority,* 402 Pa. 151 (1960), which quotes the school system definition of professional employee, including the school nurse.
23. *Meek v. Pittenger,* 421 U.S. 349 (1975) *Opinion of the Justices,* 345 A.2d 412 (N.H. 1975); *People and Klinnger v. Howlett,* 56 Ill.2d 1 (1973).
24. N.Y. Times, at 1, col. 1, High Court Bars Public Teachers in Church Schools, July 2, 1985.
25. CONN. GEN. STAT. ANN. §10-206 (West Supp. 1985).
26. CONN. GEN. STAT. ANN. §10-209 (West Supp. 1985).
27. *See, e.g.,* N.Y. PUB. HEALTH LAW §2504 (McKinley 1985) where any person who is 18 or older, is the parent of a child, or has married may give effective consent for medical, dental, health and hospital services for himself or herself and for his or her child.
28. *Id.*
29. MD. HEALTH-GEN. CODE ANN. §20-102(c) (1982).
30. MD. HEALTH-GEN. CODE ANN. §20-103 (1982 and Supp. 1985).
31. MD. HEALTH-GEN. CODE ANN. §20-102(e) (1982).
32. *In re Smith,* 295 A.2d 238 (Md. App. 1972).
33. CONN. GEN. STAT. ANN. §10-212a(a) (West Supp. 1985).
34. CONN. GEN. STAT. ANN. §10-212a(b) (West Supp. 1985).
35. CONN. GEN. STAT. ANN. §10-212a(a) (West Supp. 1985).
36. *ANA Standards, supra* note 4, at 5.
37. *Jenkins v. Board of Education,* 228 N.W.2d 265 (Minn. 1975).
38. *Kersey v. Harbin,* 531 S.W.2d 76 (Mo. 1975) and same case 591 S.W.2d 745 (Mo. 1979).
39. *Peck v. Board of Education of the City of Mount Vernon,* 283 N.E.2d 618 (N.Y. 1972).
40. *Odell v. Unified School District et al.,* 481 P.2d 974 (Kan. 1971).
41. CONN. GEN. STAT. ANN. §52-557b(b) (West Supp. 1985).
42. *Id.*
43. CONN. GEN. STAT. ANN. §52-557b(c) (West Supp. 1985).

44. *Id.*
45. *ANA Standards, supra* note 4, at 4.
46. *ANA Standards, supra* note 4, at 5.
47. *Id.*
48. MD. EDUC. CODE ANN. §7-409, 7-411 (1985).
49. CONN. GEN. STAT. ANN. §10-19 (West Supp. 1985).
50. *See, e.g.,* MD. EDUC. CODE ANN. §26-103 (1985), which prohibits drinking or possession of alcohol on school grounds.
51. *See, e.g.,* MD. EDUC. CODE ANN. §7-307 (1985), which allows searches of students and the school premises if there is a reasonable belief that there is criminal possession. Searches are to be conducted in the presence of a third party and announced previously that the school authorities may conduct such searches.
52. MD. EDUC. CODE ANN. §7-410(a) (1985).
53. CONN. GEN. STAT. ANN. §10-154a (West Supp. 1985).
54. *Id.*
55. *Crawford v. State,* 251 S.E.2d 602 (Ga. App. 1978).
56. *People v. Rodrequez,* 137 Cal. Rptr. 594 (Cal. App. 1977).
57. *State v. Spreigl,* 139 N.W.2d 167 (Minn. 1965).
58. *Griffin v. Pate,* 644 P.2d 51 (Colo. 1982).
59. *Snyder v. Beers,* 405 P.2d 288 (Ariz. 1965).
60. CONN. GEN. STAT. ANN. §10-15b (West Supp. 1985).
61. Family Educational and Privacy Act of 1974, 20 U.S.C. §1232g (1982).
62. *ANA Standards, supra* note 4, at 5.
63. *ANA Standards, supra* note 4, at 6.
64. *Id.*
65. *ANA Standards, supra* note 4, at 10.
66. *Id.*
67. AMERICAN NURSES' ASSN., SCHOOL NURSES WORKING WITH HANDICAPPED CHILDREN (1980), in collaboration with the American School Health Association, the National Association of School Nurses, and endorsed by the National Association of State School Nurse Consultants.
68. *Id.* at 4, 5.
69. 20 U.S.C. §1400 (1982 & Supp. I 1983).
70. 29 U.S.C. §794 (1982); discussed in detail in Chapters 30 and 33, this federal act prohibits discrimination against handicapped persons in federally funded programs.
71. 20 U.S.C. §1412(1)-(6) (1982).
72. *ANA Standards, supra* note 4, at 12.
73. 20 U.S.C. §1412(5) (1982).
74. *Board of Education v. Rowley,* 458 U.S. 176 (1982).
75. *Tatro v. State of Texas,* 703 F.2d 823 (5th Cir. 1983), *aff'd in part, rev'd in part, sub. nom. Irving Independent School District v. Tatro,* 104 S.Ct. 3371 (1984).
76. *Tatro v. State of Texas,* 516 F. Supp. 968 (N.D. Tex. 1981). *See Amicus Curiae of the Texas Medical Association* at 987.
77. *See e.g.,* MD. EDUC. CODE ANN. §8-101-417.6 (1985).
78. *See generally,* 20 U.S.C. §1 (1982).
79. 42 U.S.C. §1771 (1982).
80. CONN. GEN. STAT. ANN. §10-215 (West Supp. 1985).
81. MD. EDUC. CODE ANN. §7-501-7-505 (1985).
82. MD. EDUC. CODE ANN. §7-505(a)(2) and (3) (1985).
83. CONN. GEN. STAT. ANN. §10-184 (West Supp. 1985).
84. CONN. GEN. STAT. ANN. §10-186 (West Supp. 1985).
85. CONN. GEN. STAT. ANN. §10-199 (West Supp. 1985).
86. *Cady v. Plymouth-Carver Regional School District,* 457 N.E.2d 294 (Mass. 1983).
87. *In re* 683 P.2d 931 (Mont. 1984).
88. *In re Sherol A.S., v. Department of Institutions,* 581 P.2d 884 (Okla. 1978).
89. *Holmes v. Nester,* 306 P.2d 290 (Ariz. 1957).
90. *See, e.g.,* Gadow, *Administration of Medications by School Personnel,* 53 JOURNAL OF SCHOOL HEALTH 178 (March 1983); Courtnage, *The Use of Prescribed Medication in the Schools: A Status Report on the State Policies and Guidelines,* 52 JOURNAL OF SCHOOL HEALTH 543 (November 1982); Ross, *An Analysis of Policies Regulating Medication in Ohio Public Schools,* 53 JOURNAL OF SCHOOL HEALTH 589 (December 1983); Kinne, *Accidents,* 52 JOURNAL OF SCHOOL HEALTH 564 (November 1982); Carey, *Sports Trauma Management and the High School Nurse,* 52 JOURNAL OF SCHOOL HEALTH 156 (March 1982).
91. *See, e.g.,* Committee on School Health, *Medical Emergencies and Administration of Medication in School,* 61 PEDIATRICS 115 (January 1978).

Additional Readings

AMERICAN SCHOOL HEALTH ASSN., GUIDELINES FOR THE SCHOOL NURSE IN THE SCHOOL HEALTH PROGRAM (1974).

C. ANDERSON AND W. CRESWELL, SCHOOL HEALTH PRACTICE (7th ed. 1980).

Cohn, *Legal Issues in School Nursing Practice*, 12 LAW, MEDICINE & HEALTH CARE 219 (October 1984).

CROMWELL, THE NURSE IN THE SCHOOL HEALTH PROGRAM (1963).

Joint Statement of the ANA, DSN/NEA and ASHA, Guidelines on Educational Preparation and Competencies of the School Nurse Practitioner, 48 JOURNAL OF SCHOOL HEALTH 265 (May 1978).

JONES, *P.L. 94-142 and the Role of School Nurses in Caring for Handicapped Children*, 49 JOURNAL OF SCHOOL HEALTH 147 (March 1979).

P. NADER, OPTIONS FOR SCHOOL HEALTH, MEETING COMMUNITY NEEDS (1978).

Chapter 15

Occupational health nursing

Cynthia E. Northrop

The workplace plays a significant role in the health status of many Americans. Improvements in working conditions have been achieved since the turn of this century. States first enacted industrial safety legislation in the late 1800s. Most states had worker's compensation legislation by 1921. The federal government first became involved in the regulation of occupational health and safety in 1936. In that year Congress enacted the Walsh-Healey Act, which imposed some occupational safety and health requirements on federal goverment contractors.[1]

Much voluntary and private efforts to improve working conditions have been undertaken by labor, public interest groups, industry, and the general community. Much of the focus on occupational safety parallels the concerns of environmentalists and environmental protection. Today, this effort continues and has been joined by government enforcement of state and federal occupational safety and health laws and regulations, state worker compensation statutes, and common laws.

The relationship of the environment and the workplace to illness is becoming more evident. There are 4.6 million workplaces and about 100 million workers in the United States. A recent report issued by the Office of Technology Assessment (OTA), U.S. Congress, indicates that there are about 6000 working injury deaths per year, or about 25 deaths each working day.[2] Estimates indicate that 106,000 illnesses result from workplace conditions.[3] The OTA report states that there are an estimated 5.6 million occupationally related injuries. The report also shows that there has been a drop in injury rates (from 9 out of 100 in 1979 to 7.6 out of 100 workers in 1983), resulting more from the economic downturn than governmental regulation and enforcement practices. The economic downturn has involved fewer new employees, fewer young employees, and fewer new pieces of equipment and therefore less danger. The report does indicate, however, that government regulation of vinyl chloride, cotton dust, and lead has clearly reduced workplace exposure.[4]

Description of occupational health nursing practice

The occupational health nurse (OHN) has contributed significantly to the improvements in working conditions. Sometimes referred to as an employee health service nurse, a corporate nurse, a company or industrial nurse, the OHN may be delivering health care and nursing services to a variety of workers and within many types of industries. According to the professional association of OHNs, the American Association of Occupational Health Nurses (AAOHN), the practice of the OHN is the application of nursing principles in conserving the health of workers and maintaining a safe and healthful environment in occupational settings. The OHN is primarily concerned with the preventive approach to health care, which includes early disease detection, health teaching, and counseling. The knowledge base is a synthesis of principles from several disciplines in the health sciences, including nursing, medicine, safety, industrial hygiene, and toxicology.[5] The standards of practice, authored by the AAOHN, are listed in the box below.

There are over 20,000 OHNs providing health services at the workplace. Many of these nurses work alone in single-nurse-managed health units. It is estimated that 75% of the worksites with a health service have an OHN as their sole provider.[6] The majority work in manufacturing industries and workplaces with more than 500 employees. The larger the company, the more likely the nurse is not the only health care provider and works with others, including physicians.[7] In most instances OHNs are considered "managerial" employees; however, in a recent case four OHNs were granted the right to form a collective bargaining unit. In making its decision, the National Labor Relations Board noted that the OHNs were not "managerial" employees and were covered by the National Labor Relations Act.[8] See Chapter 31 for more information on collective bargaining.

Generally, the nurse is a full-time employee, although there are OHNs employed on a part-time basis. The OHN who works alone is provided medical backup either on a part-time basis or on a retainer basis. A part-time occupational health physician (OHP) usually collaborates with the OHN on standing orders and sees workers on a limited basis; the retainer OHP usually only provides medical directives or standing orders for the OHN. This collaboration has been an ongoing area of discussion between physicians and nurses in the field.[9]

Physician involvement in one-nurse units was studied by McKechnie, who found that 29.2% of the one-nurse units had no physician employed in the industry; in 25% the physician was employed but spent no time in the unit; and in 37.5% the physician spent 1 to 10 hours per week in the unit.[10]

The particular arrangement of health services has a great deal to do with sorting out liabilities and legal responsibilities when questions arise. Besides directly hiring health care providers to staff and manage the occupational health program, some industries have gone the route of contracting out health services to medical group practices. Nurses, under the latter situation, are not the employee of the industry but of the medical or other group. OHNs are among those that have independently contracted with industries to provide nursing services. In this instance the OHN is an independent contractor, not an employee.

Given this backdrop, the OHN's practice has many unique legal aspects. The OHN's practice was greatly affected by the passage of the Occupational Safety and Health Act (OSHA) in 1970.[11] This act legally mandated certain OHN functions in the area of health screening, documentation, and recordkeeping. The OHN also has a unique relationship to the state worker's compensation

STANDARDS OF PRACTICE: OCCUPATIONAL HEALTH NURSING

Standard I: Policy

A defined philosophy, goals, and specific objectives are established for the health and safety program. They provide direction for the health services that are implemented in relation to real and potential health hazards in the work environment and to the health needs and status of employees.

Standard II: Staff

The occupational health nursing (OHN) service is administered by a professionally qualified nurse. Sufficient staff with adequate time and authority to design and implement the nursing service, as set forth in policy, is necessary to ensure a quality service.

Standard III: Resources

Management provides adequate resources to facilitate the implementation of an occupational health program.

Standard IV: Nursing Practice

The practice of OHN promotes a safe and healthful work environment. The nurse uses the nursing process in providing health care directed toward prevention, health maintenance, and rehabilitation. Protocols developed in collaboration with the physician describe the scope of nursing practice. These plans or guides facilitate the nurse's ability to assess, manage, and follow a problem that may be work-related or an emergency.

Standard V: Evaluation

A systematic evaluation of the nursing component of the occupational health program is conducted on a periodic basis to determine goal achievement.

Adapted from AMERICAN ASSOCIATION OF OCCUPATIONAL HEALTH NURSES, STANDARDS OF PRACTICE (1985).

acts. In some states the OHN is defined as a fellow employee of the injured worker, and therefore that worker's only recourse for compensation is what is available under the Worker's Compensation Act, regardless of a nurse's negligence. In other states the OHN's status is not that of fellow employee but of independent contractor making it possible for a worker to sue the OHN directly for negligence. Examples of state statutes are given below.

In addition to these legal issues, the OHN may have concerns over the issues of using standing orders, managing emergencies, reporting the employer who violates OSHA requirements, having access to medical records, and ensuring confidentiality. The OHN also is involved in the issue of the worker's right to know. Each of these issues will be discussed in this chapter.

Enforcing public health laws

As mentioned in other chapters, nurses play an important role in the enforcement of public health laws. In the case of the occupational health nurse, one major piece of federal legislation and the related state legislation regarding occupational safety and health impact the practice greatly.

Among the major federal laws that are partly enforced by the OHN's practice are the:

1. Occupational Safety and Health Act (OSHA)[12]
2. Toxic Substances Control Act (TOSCA)[13]
3. Walsh-Healey Act[14]
4. Federal Coal Mine Health and Safety Act of 1969, Title IV, as amended (MSHA)[15]

Since OSHA is of prime importance to the OHN's practice it will be described in some detail.

OCCUPATIONAL SAFETY AND HEALTH ACT

OSHA was approved on Dec. 29, 1970, and became effective on April 28, 1971. It has long been heralded as the most significant piece of public health legislation ever passed. The U.S. Congress indicated in the act that its goal was "to assure as far as possible every working man and woman in the Nation safe and healthful working conditions and to preserve our human resources."[16] The intent of this legislation is to prevent injury and illness, differing from state worker's compensation laws, whose effect has been rehabilitative and compensatory after the fact of injury. OSHA's primary rationale is to decrease the incidence of occupational illnesses.

The act established an elaborate structure to implement its enforcement and educational activities. The Occupational Safety and Health Administration, headed by an assistant secretary, was established in the U.S. Department of Labor (DOL). Its responsibility is to develop and enforce occupational safety and health standards. Not only is it OSHA's responsibility to promulgate standards, but they must ensure compliance through an inspection program. OSHA is entitled to assess penalties for violations. Since OSHA's enactment, the Bureau of Labor Statistics has been designated to implement a program of collection, compilation, and analysis of occupational safety and health statistics.

The act also established The National Institute for Occupational Safety and Health (NIOSH) within the U.S. Department of Health and Human Services (HHS). NIOSH is responsible for research and training in the area of occupational safety and health. NIOSH is authorized to conduct research in the workplaces covered by OSHA. Included in this ability to conduct research is the right of NIOSH to inspect and question employers and employees and to require employers to measure, record, and make reports on the exposures of employees to substances that may be dangerous to health. NIOSH may establish programs of medical examinations and tests, as may be necessary for determining the incidence of occupational illnesses and the susceptibility of employees to such illnesses. In addition, NIOSH has provided funds for training and education of occupational health nurses and other health care, safety, and industrial personnel who work in this area.

NIOSH develops and periodically revises recommendations for limits of exposure to potentially hazardous substances or conditions in the workplace. It also recommends appropriate preventive measures designed to reduce or eliminate adverse health effects of these hazards. To formulate these recommendations, NIOSH evaluates all known and available medical, biological, engineering, chemical, trade, and other information relevant to the potential hazard. These recommendations, published as criteria documents, are then transmitted to OSHA in the Department of Labor for use in promulgating legal standards.[17]

A third component of the occupational safety and health legislation established the adjudicatory arm of the process. The Occupational Safety and Health Review Commission (OSHRC), three members appointed by the president, adjudicates the enforcement actions.[18] OSHRC is an entirely separate entity from DOL or HHS. The members review contested enforcement actions. This review takes the form of a hearing by an administrative judge, whose report to the commission stands as the final order of the federal government, subject only to appeal to the U.S. Court of Appeals, unless one of the three commissioners asks for full review by the entire commission.

Within OSHA there is another component, advisory committees. The National Advisory Committee on Occupational Safety and Health (NACOSH) consists of 12 representatives of management, labor, professions, and the public. In addition, other advisory committees can be appointed to assist in setting standards. Their role consists of advice, consultation, and recommendation. The first NACOSH members included an occupational health nurse.[19] Additional occupational health nurses have been appointed to advisory committees.[20]

OSHA itself is very pervasive. The only employees in the U.S. workforce not covered by the act are federal, state, or local government employees; those employees already covered by federal statutes; employees in domestic service in a residence, in agriculture on a family-owned-and-operated farm, or in a religious service; and those self-employed. Federal employees are now covered by OSHA by order of the president.[21] State and local government employees were ordered by the act to be covered by the state's occupational safety and health plan. Thus, the majority of workers are covered by OSHA.

Even though the coverage of OSHA is wide, the promulgation of standards operates under many constraints. The term *occupational safety and health standard* means a standard that requires conditions, or the adoption or use of one or more practices, means, methods, operations, or processes, reasonably necessary or appropriate to provide safe or healthful employment and places of employment.[22] Standards must be technologically feasible and clearly attainable by the employer. The Supreme Court refused to accept the cotton industry's argument that in addition to reasonable necessity, appropriateness, and feasibility, the standard must be significant in light of the costs of attaining that reduction.[23] The court rejected this cost-benefit aspect of a standard, noting that Congress, by enacting OSHA, had placed the benefit of worker health above all other considerations, except those making attainment of this benefit unachievable.

The resources available to carry out OSHA and its many component's activities greatly influences the degree and extent to which it can fulfill its legal responsibility. The effect of the Reagan Administration on OSHA has been identified by many as leaving OSHA as an ''empty shell.''[24]

RIGHTS AND RESPONSIBILITIES OF EMPLOYEES AND EMPLOYERS UNDER OSHA

OSHA created certain legal responsibilities for employers and employees. A general duty of the employer to employees was delineated. A place of employment must be provided by the employer that is free of recognized hazards causing or likely to cause death or serious physical harm. The employer must comply with safety and health standards developed by OSHA.[25] Certain records, inspections, and reports must be made by the employer. The employer is obligated to keep a record regarding activities relating to the act and post informational notices for employees.

In addition, the employer must keep records and periodically report work-related deaths, injuries, and illnesses other than minor injuries requiring only first-aid treatment and not involving medical treatment, loss of consciousness, restriction of work or motion, or transfer to another job.[26] The employer is also prohibited from taking retaliatory action against an employee who reports to OSHA a violation or participates in any activity protected under the act.

OSHA regulations specifically address medical services and first aid.[27] The employer must ensure that medical personnel are readily available for advice and consultation on matters of health. In the absence of an infirmary, clinic, or hospital close to the workplace that is used for the treatment of all injured employees, a person or persons shall be adequately trained to render first aid. First-aid supplies approved by the consulting physician are to be readily available. If the eyes or body of any person may be exposed to injurious corrosive materials, suitable facilities for quick drenching or flushing of the eyes or body are to be provided within the work area for immediate emergency use.

In addition, OSHA regulations specify certain medical services dealing with specific hazards.[28] The employer, for example, must provide pulmonary function tests and chest x-ray films for all workers who are exposed to asbestos.[29] Other medical requirements of OSHA health standards regulating toxic substances are listed in the box, opposite.

Employees have certain rights under OSHA, including the right to file a complaint with OSHA, accompany OSHA inspectors during their inspections, and ask the federal district court to compel the secretary of DOL to take action in case of imminent danger. OSHA not only creates standards by administrative process, involving

SELECTED MEDICAL PROCEDURES REQUIRED BY OSHA TOXIC SUBSTANCES STANDARDS

Acrylonitrile: complete medical history and examination, with attention to peripheral and central nervous system, gastrointestinal system, skin, and thyroid gland; chest x-ray studies; fecal occult blood screening for all workers over age 40 years

Asbestos: pulmonary function tests, chest x-ray examination

Carcinogens: complete medical history, including genetic and environmental factors; consideration of reduced immunological competence of employees, especially those undergoing treatment with steroids or cytotoxic agents, pregnant women, and cigarette smokers

Coke oven emissions: complete history, chest x-ray examination, pulmonary function tests, sputum cytology, urine cytology

Cotton dust: complete medical history, standardized respiratory questionnaire, pulmonary function tests

1,2-Dibromo-3-chloropropane: complete medical and reproductive history, examination of genitourinary tract, serum specimen for radioimmunoassay

Inorganic arsenic: complete medical history and examination, chest x-ray studies, sputum cytology

Inorganic lead: complete medical history and examination, detailed blood studies

Vinyl chloride: complete physical examination, liver studies

Data from 29 C.F.R. §1001, 1003-1018, 1025, 1029, 1043-1045 (1985).

study, comment, and publication of proposed rules, but also has the power to issue emergency temporary standards to deal with grave dangers and exposures of workers.[30] There have been four emergency temporary standards issued for asbestos, the 14 carcinogens, pesticides, and vinyl chloride.[31]

In addition, if a violation of an OSHA standard is discovered, workers have the right to be notified immediately. They also have the right to challenge the length of time their employer is given to correct the violation. Employers, under the act, may ask for additional time to correct violations; for variances, which may allow the industry to continue under current conditions until a specified time; or for exemption from coverage by the standard.

Under OSHA the employer is entitled to consultative assistance from OHSA. The employer may also take disciplinary action against an employee who refuses to comply with safety and health standards, including the medical requirements, physical examinations, and other medical screening requirements. An overview of OSHA regulations is provided in the box on p. 238.

STATE OSHA PROGRAMS

The federal Occupational Safety and Health Act sets forth the framework for state participation in the OSHA program.[32] The federal act basically preempts state control and jurisdiction over occupational safety and health and requires that each state submit a plan for approval by OSHA. The plan is to contain standards and methods of their enforcement that are at least as effective as the federal standards and enforcement. Certain qualifications are required of state personnel who carry out the enforcement of standards.

At times the jurisdiction over occupational safety and health programs has been concurrently federal and state jurisdiction. The federal program is authorized to pay up to 50% of the cost of an approved state plan and is required to monitor the effectiveness of the state plan. As of 1984 there were 24 states and jurisdictions with approved plans.[33] The federal OSHA evaluates the state program through case-file reviews, spot-check visits by federal monitors and accompanied visits by federal monitors of actual state inspections, or consultation visits. Results of the federal evaluation are transmitted to the state with recommendations for change.

In states with approved plans for occupational safety and health programs, the federal and state administrations try to work together. The state OSHA is usually located in the state department of labor, with collaboration established with other state administrative offices, such as the state department of health.

An important part of state laws are the statutes called "worker's right to know" legislation. These and other state laws are discussed later in this chapter.

WORKER'S COMPENSATION LAWS

An OHN's practice includes a good understanding of the state worker's compensation program and legislation in the jurisdiction in which he or she is employed.[34] In

OCCUPATIONAL SAFETY AND HEALTH STANDARDS

1. General adoption and extension of established standards
2. Access to employee exposure and medical records
3. Walking and working surfaces
4. Means of egress
5. Powered platforms, lifts, and vehicle-mounted work platforms
6. Occupational health and environmental control
7. Hazardous materials: compressed gas, acetylene, hydrogen, oxygen, nitrous oxide, flammable or combustible liquids, spray finishing, dip tanks, explosives or blasting agents, liquified petroleum gases, anhydrous ammonia
8. Personal protective equipment: general, eye, face, respiratory, head, foot, and electrical protective devices
9. General environmental controls: sanitation, temporary labor camps, nonwater carriage disposal system, safety color code for marking physical hazards, accident prevention signs and tags
10. Medical and first aid
11. Fire protection
12. Compressed gas and compressed air equipment
13. Materials handling and storage
14. Machinery and machine guarding
15. Hand-powered and portable powered tools and other hand-held equipment
16. Welding, cutting, and brazing
17. Special industries: pulp, paper, textiles, bakery, laundry, sawmills, pulpwood logging, agriculture, telecommunications
18. Electrical
19. Commercial diving operations
20. Toxic and hazardous substances: air contaminants, asbestos, coal tar pitch volatiles, 4-nitrobiphenyl, alpha-naphthylamine, methylchloromethyl ether, 3.3′-dichlorobenzidine, bis-chloromethyl ether, beta-naphthylamine, benzidine, 4-aminodiphenyl, ethylenediamine, beta-propiolactone, 2-acetylaminofluorene, 4-dimethylaminoazobenzene, *N*-nitrosodimethylamine, vinyl chloride, inorganic arsenic, lead, coke oven emissions, cotton dust, 1,2-dibromo-3-chloropropane, acrylonitrile, ethylene oxide
21. Hazard communication

Adapted from general headings of 29 C.F.R. §1910 (1985).

addition, there are several federal worker's compensation laws in which an OHN may be involved.[35] The OHN interacts with the worker's compensation system in many ways. Whether the worker is compensated for injuries while at work may depend on how the OHN recorded the contacts the worker had with the first-aid station or company health services.[36] The extent of a worker's injuries is often determined from evidence provided by the OHN, either in the worker's health record or through testimony, where the OHN may offer material and expert testimony about the worker's injuries, disabilities, and rehabilitation needs. An OHN may be authorized by the company to approve worker's requests to see and be treated by a family physician.[37]

Prior to worker's compensation, employees who were injured on the job or developed job-related illnesses had a common law right to sue their employer. Employers had many defenses available to such suits, such as contributory negligence and assumption of the risk. If the employer could prove that the employee assumed the risk of the job or contributed in any way to the outcome there was no recovery for the employee.

State statutes establishing worker's compensation changed the common law greatly. These statutes are a form of strict liability where the employer is charged with the injuries of an employee arising out of the job, without regard to fault. Refer to earlier chapters in the book that discuss torts and negligence in general for further information. There are several basic objectives of the worker's compensation system. They include:

1. Provide sure, prompt, and reasonable income and medical benefits to injured workers or income benefits to their dependents, regardless of fault.
2. Provide a single remedy and reduce court delays, costs, and workloads arising out of personal injury litigation.
3. Relieve public and private charities of financial drains involving uncompensated industrial accidents.
4. Eliminate payment of fees to lawyers and witnesses, as well as the expense of time-consuming trials and appeals.
5. Encourage maximal employer interest in safety and rehabilitation through an appropriate experience-rating mechanism.
6. Promote frank study of the causes of accidents to prevent future accidents.[38]

Under the worker's compensation statutes the employee is ensured of medical expenses and income maintenance; employers are protected against personal injury judgments and are ensured of relatively fixed production costs that can be passed along to consumers. The statutes are the exclusive and only remedy available to the employee with respect to the employer, if the employee is injured on the job.

To successfully be awarded compensation under the various state laws depends on several items. An injured worker must give proper notice of an injury or accident within a statutory period of time. Although it is relatively easy to prove an injury's relationship to the workplace and to be compensated for it, occupational diseases can present problems of proof. The worker must demonstrate the causation of the disease and that it is a result of the job and workplace exposure not an ordinary disease of life.

There are many problems and criticisms voiced about the worker's compensation system. One concern is the variation among state systems. Benefits are inconsistent among jurisdictions. Some states require that a worker be exposed to a health hazard for a specified period of time in order to be eligible for compensation.

Medical screening becomes very important to an employer who wishes to avoid high worker's compensation insurance payments. Workers may have to litigate the issues of whether they are entitled to unemployment insurance and whether nonoccupational factors such as diet, smoking, and drinking should influence the compensation. Sometimes workers with prior occupational exposures have problems being compensated through the current employer. There are at least three different general rules that states have developed: (1) the current employer is fully responsible, (2) compensation will be apportioned among employers, and (3) the present employer is liable for that portion of the disability attributable to the present employment.[39] Workers may also claim cumulative injuries.

There are many exceptions to the coverage of the compensation system. The most prevalent exceptions include the employer's failure to take out adequate insurance or be a qualified self-insurer; the employee's job classification is not covered by the state worker's compensation law (such as domestic servants, agricultural workers); the injury complained of was caused by an intentional act; and a malpractice action of one in a second capacity or an independent contractor. Of most importance to the OHN is the last area, which will be discussed in a separate section.

In general the state worker's compensation acts are the exclusive remedy for a worker who is injured due to the job, but it does not cover injuries resulting from intentional acts. Therefore, if an OHN commits an intentional tort upon a worker he or she may be sued directly for such an act. Intentional torts are a major exception to the worker's compensation exclusive remedy clause. While not involving an OHN, there have been cases involving defamation, intentional infliction of emotional distress, and interference with expectancy of employment.[40] Chapter 5 discusses intentional torts further. Some state laws provide that a worker may sue directly the one who commits a willful physical assault or fraudulent concealment.[41]

Rothstein cites a trend of expanding employer liability for willful and intentional torts.[42] Employers have been held liable for willful, wanton, or reckless misconduct (such as removing a safety guard and ordering a worker to work, resulting in injuries); for fraudulent concealment (failing to disclose an employee's state of impaired health); and assault and battery and other acts where there was a deliberate attempt to injure the employee.

In addition, employees may bring suits against third parties who are not their employer. Employees have sued, primarily on the theories of contract and products liability, general contractors, property owners, and manufacturers. Again, state statutes also may provide that an employee may sue directly one who produces a defective product.[43]

At least one state's case law indicates specifically that employees may pursue their common law remedies against co-employees.[44] Yet another specifically indicates that a worker has no right against a fellow employee except when willful or malicious acts are involved.[45]

Besides failure to warn of the dangers of materials with which the employee works, such as asbestos, employees have sued manufacturers and employers for defective safety and medical equipment used to prevent exposure, such as respirators and filter apparatus.

Nurse-patient relationship in occupational health practice

One of the primary legal questions for the occupational health nurse is whether a nurse-patient relationship exists between the OHN and the worker. Conflicts of interest exist for the OHN as for the physician. Who is the nurse's employer? The industry that hires the nurse is the employer, not the patient. This is the same for the hospital nurse, whose employer is the hospital and not the patient. The occupational safety and health services are provided for the worker by the employer. They are not selected by the worker, nor obtained by the worker as a patient but as a requirement to continue employment. However, it is interesting to note that OHN case law more than other nursing case law discusses the issue of the nurse-patient relationship.

The traditional legal view is that no physician-patient/worker relationship exists between employee and employer-provided physician.[46] By analogy the same would be true for the OHN. However, the current status of this issue is unclear. OHN case law is divided depending on the jurisdiction. A nurse-patient/worker relationship has been found in one instance, as discussed later. In other situations, however, courts have held that no nurse-patient/worker relationship existed. In these cases, the worker/patient's only recourse for any injuries, including those that resulted from nursing negligence, is through the state worker's compensation act.

In a malpractice claim the employment status and relationship of the nurse to the worker while rendering services in a negligent manner will determine whether a suit is barred or may continue on to the question of whether there was a negligent act and if it caused the worker's injuries. Some courts have held that the state worker's compensation act provides the worker's exclusive remedy, and therefore an OHN or other health care provider cannot be sued. As mentioned earlier, the worker's compensation act has certain provisions indicating that a worker injured on the job has an exclusive remedy through the provisions of the act. Another provision relevant to this discussion is the "fellow employee" or "co-employee" clause, which operates to bar lawsuits between fellow employees. Specific case examples are discussed below.

Depending on the state case law, there are at least three possible scenarios involving the question of whether a worker can sue the OHN for malpractice. If the OHN is considered a co-employee, then the worker's suit would be dismissed. If the OHN is considered to have dual capacity or be an independent contractor, the worker may sue successfully if the negligence occurred while the OHN was in the nonemployee relationship to the worker. Dual capacity means that at the same time the OHN is an employee just like the worker and a nurse who exercises independent judgment separate from the employment toward the worker. The case examples clarify this concept further.

Examples of court cases analyzing the question of the OHN's relationship to the worker have held that, depending on the jurisdiction, the OHN may be a fellow employee or an independent contractor. For example, in one situation a nurse, along with the company and an orderly, was sued for the wrongful death of a worker by his wife and children.[47] In yet another example, the OHN was an independent contractor.[48]

In the first case the family claimed that the worker had gone to the plant's aid station shortly after arriving at work. He was returned to work almost immediately, but soon after a fellow worker called the medical facility and asked that the worker be taken back as he was in obvious distress. The nurse examined the worker and told him to lie down to rest. Approximately 30 minutes later he died. Shortly after that the physician of the facility arrived and an ambulance was called. Interpreting the California labor code and its sections on worker's compensation, the court held that the worker's family's exclusive remedy was the compensation act. The suit against the company, nurse, and orderly was dismissed because the court held that the worker's injury was work-related.

Other courts have held that the same ruling is applicable in their states.[49] In one case the court denied a nursing negligence case because the worker made no indication that the nurse's actions aggravated a preexisting condition. This is yet another argument offered to establish nursing negligence in relation to worker's injuries and nursing treatment of them.[50]

In another case a Pennsylvania court decided that the results of an OHN's negligence was defined as an accident and was covered by the state worker's compensation statute.[51] The employee, who became ill at work, went to the employer's first-aid room and the employer's nurse failed to call a physician, although the employee had severe chest pains, was vomiting, had chills, and was perspiring; the employee died about 2 hours later while being taken home by fellow employee. The court ruled this was an "accident" within the worker's compensation act.

A Wisconsin case has held similarly that the OHN cannot be sued for malpractice because the exclusivity of the remedy of worker's compensation bars a third-party tort action for contribution for negligence of the employer in the course of providing medical attention to an injured employee.[52] In this case a worker was injured as a result of a prank of a fellow worker and taken to the medical facility, where he claimed to have been negligently treated. Quoting earlier law, the court indicated that any medical injury resulting from treatment of a work-related injury relates back to the original compensable event and the consequences of medical treatment, whether the result of negligence or not, and is the liability of the employer under the act (worker's compensation). The Wisconsin court refused to accept the dual-capacity arguments and held that the sole remedy for these injuries was through the state worker's compensation act.

The dual-capacity view of health professionals in occupational health was discussed in a leading California case involving a nurse, but as the injured worker.[53] The nurse's employer was a chiropractor. She was injured in the course of her employment and then was negligently treated by the chiropractor-employer. The court allowed a cause of action against the employer because the negligence occurred when the employer was acting in a second capacity as a chiropractor. It is interesting to note, however, that in 1982 the California legislature amended the worker's compensation act to preclude actions based on dual capacity.[54]

There is a wide divergence of judicial opinions about the dual-capacity rule. In Alabama the rule was held not to apply to the provision of emergency medical services rendered after an accident.[55] But in Colorado the court has held that a company-employed physician and worker relationship was identical to the private physician-patient relationship.[56] In this case the physician held dual capacity of co-employee and physician. The physician, a full-time employee of a brewing company, had examined and treated the worker for back injuries suffered in an on-the-job accident. The worker missed almost a month of work recovering from the accident. The worker's claim for compensation was settled. Several days after he returned to the job, he reinjured his back. The worker brought a malpractice action against the physician, alleging that he had misdiagnosed his injury and advised him to return to work before he was fully recovered.

The physician claimed that the worker's compensation act provided the worker his only remedy and that the physician was immune from suit because of his status as a co-employee. The court held that the physician was liable for negligence committed as a physician (not in the capacity of co-employee, but in the second or dual capacity of physician). The court stated there was no logical reason to treat a company physician differently than a private physician. One of the court's primary points was that the employer, under the state's compensation act, had voluntarily provided medical services. The court also noted that medical malpractice was not an inherent risk of the brewing business and that the company could not practice medicine and had hired a physician to do so. The physician had entered a physician-patient relationship, not an employee-employee relationship, and therefore owed the same duty owed by any physician to a patient.

Meanwhile, in Indiana, an OHN was determined to be an independent contractor and thus could be sued by a worker for negligence.[57] A worker became ill and went to the infirmary for treatment by the physician and nurse. After the physician examined the worker, he prescribed an injection of medication and directed the OHN to give it. Testimony at trial indicated that the injection was given near the elbow, not in the deltoid muscle as the nurse had testified. The worker presented evidence that immediately after the injection he experienced unusual physical reactions and sustained damage to the left ulnar nerve.

The worker sued the physician and the nurse. The worker claimed that not only was the nurse liable for negligence but that the physician was also liable because the nurse was his agent. The evidence presented indicated that the physician did not instruct the nurse as to the location of the injection or otherwise supervise her actions. The court rejected the agency theory, noting that an agent is subject to the principal's control with respect to work details and this was not the factual situation in this case. The evidence at trial revealed that the physician and nurse were individually employed by the company, that the physician's sole direction to the nurse was to administer the injection to the worker, and that the nurse administered it outside the presence of the physician and independent of his direction or supervision. The court noted that the nurse was the employee of the company, not the physician.

The second issue in the case was whether the nurse's action was precluded by the "fellow employee" rule of the state's worker's compensation statute. A previous Indiana case involving a company physician had held that the "fellow employee" immunity provision did not protect that physician from a claim of medical malpractice brought by an employee of the same company. The worker urged the court to accept the view that the nurse, similarly to a physician, acts not as a fellow employee but as a professional nurse in relation to the worker. The court decided that the OHN was an independent contractor for the following reasons:

1. The licensed registered nurse was engaged in an independent profession.
2. Although she met all the requirements for being a salaried employee of the company, the company did not control the OHN's placement of the injection.

3. The nurse's training, experience, and skill as a professional, licensed registered nurse determined the placement of the injection.
4. Although the OHN may take instructions and directions from a licensed medical practitioner, the OHN must reject any instruction from the company as to the manner and location of administering the injection.
5. The OHN's liability arises from the nurse-patient relationship with the worker and not from the employer-employee relationship that the worker's compensation act was designed to regulate.

The court held that for these reasons the OHN was an independent contractor and that the worker's suit was not precluded by the worker's compensation statute. A new trial was ordered to decide the question of the OHN's negligence.

Knowing which capacity the courts have applied in the jurisdiction in which the OHN practices is of primary importance. There is general divergence of opinion among OHNs themselves about within which capacity they should belong. The AAOHN has no official policy, analysis, or guidance on the subject of whether the OHN is a fellow employee, able to hold dual capacity, or an independent contractor. However, in relation to this issue the AAOHN Code of Ethics provides some guidance, that OHNs should "1. provide nursing service in the work environment with respect for the human dignity, unrestricted by consideration of nationality, race, religion or sex; 2. safeguard the employee's right to privacy by protecting confidential information and releasing information only as required by law or upon written consent of the employee; 3. maintain individual competence in OHN practice, recognizing and accepting responsibility for individual actions and judgment; 4. act to safeguard the health and safety of the employee in the work environment."[58]

While this statement does not specifically indicate that the OHN owes an overall legal duty directly to the worker, it does support the idea that the OHN does have some legal responsibilities to the worker distinct from the obligations of the OHN to the employer.

Another related issue in the relationship of the nurse and client involves the OHN who may deliver emergency or other nursing services to nonworkers, visitors, customers, or guests. For example, OHNs who work for large department stores may provide emergency resuscitation to heart attack victims who are customers of the store. The customer is not a store employee and hence not the traditional "worker" for whom the OHN is hired to provide health services. State Good Samaritan laws may not apply to the OHN's situation if services to the nonworker are part of the job expectations. Employer policy should state clearly what responsibilities the OHN owes the nonworker, guest, or visitor to the workplace. It may in fact be the function of the store OHN to provide emergency services to a customer. These responsibilities must be delivered by the OHN in a reasonable and prudent manner. The OHN would be liable to the nonworker if these responsibilities were not fulfilled adequately.

Other legal issues in occupational nursing practice

The OHN's relationship to OSHA and to state worker's compensation programs are major areas of legal responsibility. In addition, the OHN may be involved in related issues that present legal concerns. Those issues include the worker's right to know, health screening and examinations, reporting OSHA violations, administering medications and emergency treatments, ensuring confidentiality, and access to worker's health records.

WORKER'S RIGHT TO KNOW

When an employee first enters into employment and at least yearly after that time, every employer must inform employees exposed to toxic substances or harmful physical agents of the location and availability of health, exposure, and analyses records; the person in charge of such records; and the employee's right to access records.[59] Having such an orientation to the workplace is a first step in knowing the health and safety implications of a job. Gaining access to records is a second important way in which the worker learns of the exposures and implications.

In 1983 OSHA finalized its hazard communication rule.[60] The OSHA standard covers an estimated 14 million employees and 300,000 manufacturing establishments. Chemical manufacturers and importers are required to assess the hazards of chemicals that they produce or import and inform the employees about the hazardous chemicals by means of a hazard communication program. That program includes labeling, material safety data sheets, training, and access to certain records. The standards took effect in late 1985 and early 1986.

One of the effects of the standard will be to preempt the "right-to-know" laws currently enacted in 16 states.[61] Whether state or federal law, the intent of the right-to-know legislation is primary prevention and recognizes individual worker autonomy and responsibility to act upon the knowledge imparted. In no other area of nursing practice is it legally mandated to educate the patient. The OHN certainly has a unique advantage. The relationship of the OHN to the worker's right to know has been discussed in a recent article.[62]

One role of the OHN in this area of law is that of collaborating with others in writing and developing the material safety data sheet (MSDS). OSHA has guidelines for MSDS.[63] In some instances the OHN may be responsible for the update and currentness of the material sheets. Emergency telephone numbers accessing the OHN or other person to the manufacturer on a 24-hour basis is important data to include.

If the chemical information involves a trade secret, on an emergency basis an OHN may have access to that information.[64] In some instances, manufacturers may require a written statement of need and a confidentiality agreement, but they must issue the information regardless of whether they have the statement or agreement if an emergency has been called.

However, the information is also available in nonemergency situations to a "health professional providing medical or other occupational health services to exposed employees."[65] Regulations specify how the health care provider asks for the information, the protections, confidentiality, use of the information, and release of the trade secret information.

As the regulation currently stands, it is not clear whether the OHN is included in the meaning of "health professional" for nonemergency access to trade secrets because the regulation states: "(i.e., physician, industrial hygienist, toxicologist, or epidemiologist)." AAOHN has asked for clarification and that the OHN be included.[66]

The OHN's roles may increase in relation to the hazard communication rule and the worker's right-to-know laws. Besides directly informing the employee, giving screening and emergency care to workers who work with toxic substances and other hazards, and developing the material necessary to have on hand to deal with emergency treatment or health screening activities, the OHN may also be involved in worker orientation and mass-scale education and training programs. It will mean developing a strong chemical knowledge base. Guidelines for right-to-know training programs do exist.[67]

There are still many questions in dealing with this issue. If the OHN writes the MSDS, what is the responsibility being assumed? Could the OHN be held liable for errors and misinformation? The answer is probably yes. At this time, since the standard is relatively new, no cases exist that help clarify this question. Any health teaching, education, or information given by a nurse is expected to be accurate and reliable. What information is taught should be documented and lists of chemicals kept up-to-date.

HEALTH SCREENING AND EXAMINATIONS

Health screening and examinations involve a process by which a workforce is selected and maintained by application of medical criteria.[68] The OHN is a key person in this process in terms of evaluating the worker's health status. Screening and examinations are provided at the employer's expense. Prior to OSHA there was no common law obligation of the employer to conduct medical tests of job applicants or employees. Only where modified by OSHA has this changed. Other than OSHA medical requirements, the employer is under no legal obligation to provide more. However, many industries do voluntarily provide more. In addition to OSHA medical requirements, however, collective bargaining agreements may increase the employer's obligations regarding certain health screening activities. The OHN can be in a position of recommending more health care programs and services for workers.

The initial health screening may result in hiring or eliminating an individual's opportunity for a job. Physicians have been held liable for wrong diagnosis that resulted in denial of employment.[69] In one case a court held that if the physician had negligently performed the examination and as a result gave an inaccurate report of the state of the applicant's health, and the applicant was injured as a proximate result of the inaccuracy, actionable negligence would be shown. While no cases exist alleging that an OHN acted negligently during the health screening process of an applicant or employee, the OHN may in the same manner as a physician be held legally accountable to the job applicant or employee if there is failure to evaluate properly, failure to screen properly, or if the screening is done in an inaccurate and discriminatory manner. In bringing such suits, the applicant or employee must first prove that there is a nurse-applicant/employee relationship from which the nurse owed the person a legal duty. As noted in the discussion of the OHN's duty, state legislation and case law may have differing views of this issue.

Failure to inform the applicant or employee of findings of the screening, in particular those negative indicators of health status, may also lead to liability. An employer can require a preemployment or preplacement physical examination, including laboratory work, and periodic screening of an employee. The occupational health program is also involved with episodic or sick care and sometimes provides rehabilitation services to employees deemed disabled or impaired because of their work.

State laws may require physicians to report occupational diseases, especially those resulting from lead, phosphorus, arsenic, brass, wood alcohol or mercury, anthrax, compressed-air illness, or any other disease from employment.[70]

The OSHA health standards specify the particulars of the occupational health program or medical surveillance program. OSHA's mandate applies only to certain medical procedures in the areas in which it regulates. In general OSHA requires that employers conduct preplacement physical examinations on all employees. The physician must furnish employers with a copy of the physician's statement of suitability for employment in the regulated area. Periodic examinations upon termination of employment may also be required. Failure to conduct these health examinations and screening can lead to citation by OSHA.

If an employee is found unfit by the findings of the health screening and examination, he or she may be discharged. If the employee refuses examinations, discharge may also result. Some exceptions are allowed in the regulations involving religious objections. Other exceptions are found in the reproductive health area. For example, requiring sterilization as a condition of employment is prohibited in Connecticut.[71] Chapter 22, which focuses on the nurse administrator's legal reponsibilities, contains further information on this topic.

Even if the screening and evaluation are for research purposes, it is viewed as a condition of employment. However, the employer (and NIOSH, if applicable) cannot treat the worker as a guinea pig.

OSHA regulations also attempt to control the effects of the medical screening on employment by providing for medical removal protection (MRP) and rate retention (RR). When a screening indicates that a worker has adverse symptoms of exposure to a substance, the employee is to be removed from further exposure to a job that carries the same rate and benefits. MRP and RR is not available for all toxic substances and has stimulated much litigation dealing with many complex issues.[72]

There are some limits on the scope of the employer's inquiries about their employees. Medical questionnaires and history forms have been held to violate a worker's privacy. For example, it has been held that school teachers need not disclose organizations to which they belong[73]; an inquiry into a police officer's private sexual activities violated his right to privacy[74]; and federal employees need not disclose associations to which themselves and members of their families belong.[75] If an employee can demonstrate discrimination in the practice of collecting health information (one woman was able to show that similar questions were not asked of male employees), an employee may successfully show an invasion of privacy.[76]

In some cases, however, invasion of privacy allegations were not successful. For example, it has been held that a utility's requirment that employee sign a form consenting to an investigation to screen out security risks did not constitute an invasion of privacy.[77] In another case, a court held that the employer was justified in asking an applicant if he had ever filed an industrial accident claim.[78] An employee's discharge was upheld by an Arizona court when he refused to sign a consent form that was required before employees could take the mandatory "psychological stress evaluation test."[79]

Most employees complete any questionnaire given to them. The only way an invasion of privacy issue arises is if the employee refuses to complete the information, is discharged or not hired or promoted, and then sues the employer. It is highly unlikely that an OHN would be sued individually or directly for the content of the health forms: however, the unlikely is always possible.

Some states have taken steps to curtail by legislation the questions an employer may ask of an employee. For example, the Maryland legislation provides: "an employer may not require an applicant to answer any questions, written or oral, pertaining to any physical, psychological, or psychiatric illness, disability, handicap or treatment which does not bear a direct, material, and timely relationship to the applicant's fitness or capacity to properly perform the activities or responsibilities of the desired position."[80] The law does indicate that it does not prohibit medical evaluation by a physician for the purpose of assessing an applicant's ability to perform a job.

REPORTING OSHA VIOLATIONS

One of the ways in which OHNs have handled information gained about the health status of workers is to identify and report employer's errors or exposures of workers not being identified by the employer. For example, any OHN may report a violation of standards to OSHA or the state occupational safety and health program. As noted under the discussion of OSHA, any employee has the right to report. The OSHA law provides that the employer may not retaliate against the employee for making a report. Further, some state laws protect employees from discrimination, discharge, or other penalty or retaliation for disclosing employer's illegal activities or for exercising constitutional rights.[81]

In one case an OHN became aware of hematological abnormalities in plant employees.[82] The OHN served 1200 employees. A complaint was filed with OSHA from which the employer was issued a citation. The OHN was dismissed from her job. She brought a lawsuit in federal court alleging that she had been wrongfully discharged and otherwise discriminated against in retaliation for her involvement in OSHA. Under the theory that this discharge was wrongful based upon public policy, the OHN proceeded into court. Unfortunately, the court did not decide this case on the merits of this question because, as is true of all cases, before a court will hear the merits of the case, it must first have appropriate jurisdiction over the case. For procedural reasons, the federal court ruled that the case belonged in a state court.

ADMINISTERING MEDICATIONS AND EMERGENCY TREATMENTS

At least two concerns of OHNs exist when it comes to giving medications and rendering emergency first aid, cardiopulmonary resuscitation (CPR), or other emergency treatments. Those concerns include the use of standing orders and the legal scope of nursing practice. Accidents and injuries in the workplace are expected, more so in industries where risks to health and safety are greater. As discussed under the description of their practice, many OHNs work alone or in very small health units. To satisfy state laws relating to nursing, medicine, and pharmacy, *standing orders* for certain treatments and for administration of medications are required.

Sometimes called *medical directives, protocols,* or *health directives,* standing orders have made it possible for nurses to provide treatments that are not usually (without the orders) within the meaning and legal definition of nursing practice. While many states have indicated that a nurse may diagnoses, it is not a medical diagnosis that is contemplated by the legislation but a nursing diagnosis.[83]

Napholtz gives enlightened discussion about standing orders and their use in occupational health.[84] The usual definition of directives is written procedures approved and signed by the physician. Napholtz argues for nursing input into these directives and describes a framework in which an OHN's activities are divided among those that are independent nursing responsibilities, those that are shared responsibilities with medicine, and those that are delegated by medicine to nursing. Nursing policies and procedures contain the first two types of activities; standing orders are the last category. State nurse practice acts often use the division to which Napholtz refers. For example, in Maryland the definition of nursing practice includes "independent nursing functions and delegated medical functions."[85]

The OHN must have the level of knowledge, skill, and experience required by the directive in order to perform safe practice. A recent case analyzing the use of protocols jointly developed by physicians and nurse practitioners identified the characteristics of adequate standing orders:

1. Signed by the physician
2. Directed to specifically named nurses
3. Approved by the physician
4. Implemented by nurses whose level of training and degree of skill matched the content of the orders[86]

This court noted that the hallmark of the professional is knowing the limits of one's professional knowledge. Therefore, knowing which standing order to use, knowing the scope of legal practice, how to implement orders, and when to refer to the physician or obtain additional assistance are important legal obligations surrounding standing orders. Chapter 13 contains a discussion of standing orders, including a set of guidelines for evaluating them. These guidelines are applicable to occupational health practice.

There have been lawsuits against OHNs that have focused upon the appropriate use of standing orders. In one case a worker was injured when another worker let a piece of metal slip from his hand.[87] The worker received a puncture wound on the left side of his forehead. He went directly to the company nurse in the first-aid room. The OHN swabbed the wound with antiseptic solution and put a bandage on it. The OHN testified that she did not examine or probe the wound.

For 3 days the worker visited the first-aid room. The wound appeared to be closed but left a red area. After about 3 months the redness spread. The area became puffy and raised in about another month. During visits to the dispensary in this time period, the worker pointed out to the nurse the wound's condition. Finally the worker asked the nurse to send him to a physician. Tissue from the wound was excised and found to contain a basal cell carcinoma.

The worker based his case against the nurse on the theory that a foreign body was left in the wound by the negligence of the nurse and that the foreign body, acting as an irritant, caused the cancer. The nurse testified that it was her duty to refer any condition or injury she was not familiar with or not sure about to a physician for diagnosis. The standard of care required the nurse to examine the wound for foreign bodies. If a wound persisted and did not heal, proper nursing care would require that the worker be sent to the physician.

Even though the nurse testified that she was familiar with the danger signals of cancer, she continued to treat the wound for 10 months before sending the worker to the physician. The court indicated that a nurse's diagnosis of a condition must meet the standard of learning, skill, and care to which nurses practicing that profession in the community are held. In order to administer first aid properly and effectively, a nurse must make sufficient diagnosis to enable the application of the appropriate remedy. The nurse had testified in the case that it was the practice of a nurse in this type of industry to probe wounds for foreign objects, know the signs that one exists, and be aware of the possibility of foreign objects in such wounds.

At least one state attorney general's opinion and the opinion of the state boards of nursing, medicine, or pharmacy have discussed the use of standing orders and scope of practice of occupational health nurses and other nurses. For example, one Ohio attorney general's opinion indicates that an OHN, not certified as an emergency medical technician (EMT), could perform tasks that EMTs are authorized to perform as long as the nurse possessed the necessary skills to perform them. In addition, by use of standing orders, physicians may authorize registered nurses to perform any emergency medical task that EMTs perform provided the nurse has the necessary skills.[88]

Another concern is that the OHN often is the person who teaches and prepares other workers to render first aid or emergency procedures. If the OHN is responsible for teaching first aid, the legal obligation assumed is that the teaching is accurate, meets current standards of teaching, and provides evaluation of the in-service participant's performance and ability to deliver emergency care properly after the program.

ENSURING CONFIDENTIALITY; ACCESS WORKER'S HEALTH RECORDS

This legal issue for the OHN can be quite an underestimated problem. Not only do questions arise about when the worker can access his or her own record, but questions can arise about when management and even OSHA can access the worker's record. Confidentiality of health records is an important legal and ethical responsibility of an OHN. AAOHN has developed a statement dealing with privileged communications and in their code of ethics, OHNs are advised to "safeguard the employee's right to privacy by protecting confidential information and releasing information only as required by law or upon written consent of the employee."[89] AAOHN also developed a statement and guidelines regarding OSHA standard on employee's access to records.[90]

In 1980 OSHA promulgated regulations in the area of employee's access to their medical records.[91] Regulations also define other records to which the employee may gain access. Those include substance exposure records and records of analyses in the workplace. In addition, regulations exist that control the practice and procedure OSHA personnel must use in order to access worker's records.[92] A collective bargaining agreement may increase the information available to the employee, as may company policies.

OSHA defines the employee health record as a record concerning the health status of an employee that is made or maintained by a physician, nurse, technician, or other health care personnel, including: questionnaires, histories, results of examinations (preemployment, preassignment, periodic, and episodic), laboratory test results, medical opinions, diagnoses, progress notes, recommendations, descriptions of treatments and prescriptions, and employee's medical complaints.[93]

Questions may arise about access to records of the employee's participation in alcohol or drug abuse programs. If maintained separately, the regulations specify that the medical record does not include records concerning voluntary employee assistance programs (alcohol, drug abuse, or counseling programs).[94]

The consent for release of information must be written, containing the name and signature of the employee authorizing the release, the date of the authorization, the name of the individual or organization authorized to release the medical information, the name of the designated representative authorized to receive the released information, a general description of the medical information to be released, description of the purpose for the release, and a date or condition upon which the written authorization will expire.[95] Releases are good only up to a year. Employers must keep employee medical records for the duration of the employment plus 30 years.[96]

The regulation specifies that when an employee requests access to a record (health, exposure, or analyses records), the employer must grant that access within a reasonable time, place, and manner, but the request must be granted 15 days after the request is made.[97] Employees may copy their records.

The regulation provides that when access to employee medical records is requested, a physician representing the employer may recommend that the employee consult with the physcian, accept a summary of the record, or accept release of the record to a physician.[98] If a physician (representing the employer) believes that direct employee access to information contained in the records regarding a specific diagnosis of a terminal illness or a psychiatric condition could be detrimental to the employee's health, the employer may inform the employee that access will only be provided to a designated representative of the employee with that employee's written consent. The employer, only under these circumstances, may deny the employee's request for access to this information only. If an employee chooses to use a representative, the employer must give access even when it is known that the designated representative will give the information to the employee.[99]

A nurse may delete from requested medical records the identity of a family member, personal friend, or fellow employee who has provided confidential information concerning an employee's health status.[100] Employers may delete trade secret information from requested records. In some instances, the employer may have to provide alternative information. The employer may make a condition of access to trade secret information the agreement in writing not to use the information for purpose of commercial gain or misuse.[101]

The conditions under which an employer accesses medical records of an employee has also raised legal and ethical issues for the OHN. There are no legal restrictions on the intracompany dissemination of employee medical records.[102] As mentioned, the OHN's code of ethics indicates that confidentiality is to be protected unless required by law or upon written consent of the employee. The code of ethics of occupational health physicians provides, in part, that "employers are entitled to counsel about the medical fitness of individuals in relation to work, but are not entitled to diagnoses or details of a specific nature."[103]

The common practice has evolved that employers are provided all medical information necessary in relation to a worker's job assignment. The primary legal remedy for the employee would be to sue for breach of confidentiality. But as discussed, some courts determine that there is no nurse-patient/worker or physician-patient relationship where both are provided by the employer.

Workers, in order to receive benefits, are often asked to give blanket consent for access to health records by insurance companies and, if applicable, the worker's compensation system. In addition, OSHA may access the employee's records without the worker's consent.[104] However, OSHA must produce a written access order containing the purpose of the access, description of the kind of employee medical information that will be examined, and why there is a need to examine personally identifiable information, how long and where the record examination will occur, what will be copied and removed from the workplace, and the name, address and phone number of the OSHA Investigator and others who will be reviewing the records. Without identifying individual workers, the employer must post a copy of the order so that employees are aware of OSHA's activity. Sometimes, OSHA gains access to employee's health records when the employee designates a named OSHA investigator on the written consent form or through an OSHA physician acting as a consultant with the industry's physician.

To summarize, Reif offers the following statement: "the worker must be assured that access to health records will be limited to health care providers within the company" with the following exceptions:

1. Life-threatening emergencies
2. Authorized release to personal physician
3. Worker's compensation cases (as mandated by law)
4. Compliance with government regulations[105]

Standards of care

The AAOHN's standards of practice and code of ethics are two sources of standards available to OHNs and others. Also, a certification process managed by the American Board for Occupational Health Nurses provides an important resource for defining excellence in OHN practice. AAOHN has other publications that establish standards.[106] In addition, the legal scope of nursing practice has been the topic of several articles.[107]

In the areas of OHN practice that overlap with medicine, documents of the American Occupational Medical Association and American Academy of Physician Assistants also contains evidence of the standard of care.[108]

Other consumer, industrial, governmental, environmental, and professional organizations have studied and shaped this area of practice. The Intersociety Forum is a coalition of professional societies in occupational health and safety. The American Conference of Governmental

Industrial Hygienists has greatly shaped the standards applied in the field. There is also an Occupational Health Section of the American Public Health Association.

Sources of literature available to the OHN also discuss current issues, knowledge, research, and status of the field.[109] Lastly, NIOSH and OSHA publications serve as important sources of standards of care.[110]

Recommendations and trends

Occupational health nursing practice is an exciting field highly influenced not only by federal and state occupational safety and health laws but by worker's compensation statutes as well. Workers are devising litigation strategies to avoid and circumvent or demonstrate the inadequacy of OSHA programs and resources and worker's compensation plans; for example, by showing the applicability of intentional tort theories or the liabilities of third parties. Companies and managment are attempting to maintain their current legal protections and may argue the negative economic impact of worker safety and health standards. Given these trends, the OHN should expect an increased involvement in litigation and lobbying efforts.

One of the most pressing issues is the unsettled law relating to the relationship of an OHN to the worker who is being cared for and treated in the health facility. Appropriate nursing professional organizations need to address this issue together with knowledgeable legal counsel.

The OHN will continue to be an advocate for the worker's right to know. OHNs may experience an increased awareness of the conflict of interest between the goals of the employer and the goals of providing health services. OHNs may find themselves torn between labor and industry on many issues. One example of another form of advocacy demonstrated by an OHN and described in this chapter is that of reporting violations of law and standards to OSHA. OHNs take these steps knowing of their rights to be protected from retaliation by the employer. The OHN's judgment must be as accurate as possible when involved in this form of advocacy.

The OHN is constantly updating and reviewing the necessity for standing orders for medications and emergencies. These orders are evaluated against several items, including the state nurse practice act of the jurisdiction. Case law, state board of nursing regulations, or advisory statements and legislation should become part of this process of continual review.

The trend in access and confidentiality of worker records since OSHA was passed in 1970 has been slowly in favor of more and broader access for the employee to information about screening results, physical assessments, treatments, exposure rates, and the environment of the workplace. Additional lawsuits regarding the OHN's use and protection of worker medical records are anticipated.

The importance of keeping up-to-date with state and federal (OSHA) law and particularly the regulations cannot be overly stressed. State laws vary and must be checked after each legislative session. The OHN's network should include association with at least one organization that serves to inform its members of proposed new rules and changes in regulations that affect OHN practice. Regularly reviewing the *Federal Register* can assist in keeping up-to-date.[111]

Endnotes

1. 41 U.S.C. §35-45 (1982).
2. OFFICE OF TECHNOLOGY ASSESSMENT, U.S. CONGRESS, PREVENTING ILLNESS AND INJURY IN THE WORKPLACE 4 (1985).
3. *Id.* at 5. *See also* The Nation's Health, May/June 1985, at 1, col. 5, where the estimated number of work-related illnesses may be higher and where caveats exist regarding the available data on this issue.
4. *Id.* at 33, 34, 35.
5. AMERICAN ASSN. OF OCCUPATIONAL HEALTH NURSES, STANDARDS OF OHN PRACTICE (1985); *See, e.g.,* Hannigan, *OHN Practice: A State of the Art,* 32 O.H.N. 17 (January 1984).
6. Babbitz, *Occupational Health Nursing in the United States,* 29 O.H.N. 18 (May 1981).
7. ASHFORD, CRISIS IN THE WORKPLACE: OCCUPATIONAL DISEASE AND INJURY (1976).
8. *Noranda Aluminum, Inc. v. National Labor Relations Board,* 751 F.2d 268 (8th Cir. 1984).
9. *See, e.g., Council on Industrial Health, The Legal Scope of Industrial Nursing Practice,* 169 JOURNAL OF THE AMERICAN MEDICAL ASSOCIATION 1072 (March 7, 1959); *Medicolegal Aspects of Industrial Nursing Practice,* 38 CUR. MED. 29 (Spring 1959); Gallagher, *Occupational Health Nursing: Autonomy and Interdependence,* 81 OCCUPATIONAL HEALTH AND SAFETY 43 (February 1981).
10. McKechnie, *A Descriptive Study of the Scope of Practice of OHNs in One-Nurse Units,* 31 O.H.N. 18 (March 1983).
11. Occupational Safety and Health Act of 1970, P.L. 91-596, 29 U.S.C. 651-678 (1982).
12. *Id.*
13. 15 U.S.C. §2601-2629 (1982 & Supp. I 1983) (federal law regulating public health and environmental effects of toxic substances).
14. 41 U.S.C. §35-45 (1982) (federal law requiring government contractors to provide their employees with safe and healthful workplaces).
15. 30 U.S.C. §901-945 (1982). Federal law provides benefits for

victims of "black lung"; 30 U.S.C. §801-878 (1982) (Mine Safety and Health Standards).

16. 29 U.S.C. §651(b) (1982). NIOSH was authorized by 29 U.S.C. §671 (1982).
17. *See, e.g., NIOSH Recommendations for Occupational Safety and Health Standards,* 34 MORBIDITY AND MORTALITY WEEKLY REPORT (MMWR) Supplement, July 19, 1985, which identifies potential hazards, the date NIOSH transmitted its recommendation to OSHA, the OSHA standard, NIOSH recommended exposure limit, and health effects and gives additional comments about each potential hazard.
18. 29 U.S.C. §661 (1982), Occupational Safety & Health Review Commission and regulations found at 29 C.F.R. §2200 (1985).
19. ASHFORD, CRISIS IN THE WORKPLACE 288 (1976); The National Advisory committee on Occupational Safety & Health and advisory committees is authorized by 29 U.S.C. §656 (1982).
20. AAOHN NEWS, January 1985, at 1, col. 2. *Former AAOHN Treasurer and board member appointed to term on NACOSH;* AAOHN NEWS, December 1985, at 3, col. 1. *Second nurse named to NACOSH.*
21. Exec. Order No. 12196, 45 FEDERAL REGISTER, 12,769 (Feb. 26, 1980). It was ordered that it is "the responsibility of the head of each federal agency to establish and maintain an effective and comprehensive occupational safety and health program which is consistent with the (OSHA) standards." *See* 29 U.S.C. §668 (1982) (programs of federal agencies).
22. 29 U.S.C. §652(8) (1982).
23. *American Textile Manufacturers Institute v. Donovan,* 101 S. Ct. 2478 (1981).
24. CHRISTOFFEL, HEALTH AND THE LAW 182 (1982); MINTZ, OSHA: HISTORY, LAW, AND POLICY (1984); ROTHSTEIN, OCCUPATIONAL SAFETY AND HEALTH LAW (2nd ed. 1983 & Supp. 1985).
25. 29 U.S.C. §654(a) (1982).
26. 29 U.S.C. §657 (1982).
27. 29 C.F.R. §1910.151 (1985).
28. 29 C.F.R. §1900-1990 (1985).
29. 29 C.F.R. §1910.1001 (1985).
30. 29 U.S.C. §655(c) (1982).
31. ASHFORD, CRISIS IN THE WORKPLACE, 251 (1976).
32. 29 U.S.C. §667 (1982) (state jurisdiction and plans). *See also* 29 U.S.C. §672 (1982) (grants to states).
33. MINTZ, OSHA: HISTORY, LAW, AND POLICY 618 (1984); *See also* selected state OSH acts, MD. ANN. CODE art. 89, §28-49D (1985); CONN. GEN. STAT. ANN. §31-367-31-385 (West 1972 & Supp. 1985).
34. *See, e.g.,* selected state worker's compensation acts, CONN. GEN. STAT. ANN. §31-275-31-355 (West 1972 & Supp. 1985); MD. ANN. CODE art. 101 (1985).
35. Federal Employee's Compensation Act, 5 U.S.C. §8101-8193 (1982) (for federal civilian employees); Federal Employer's Liability Act, 45 U.S.C. §51-60 (1982) (railroad workers); Jones Act, 46 U.S.C. §688 (1982 & Supp. I 1983) (seamen); Longshoremen's and Harbor Workers' Compensation Act, 33 U.S.C. §901-950 (1982 & Supp. I 1983) (maritime employees).
36. *B.F. Goodrich v. Martin,* 253 So.2d 37, 39 (Ala. App. 19-71) (a company nurse documented allergic reaction of worker to "something on his job and that it could be the cement he was placing on the rubber."); *Mouts v. Bechtel Corp.* 507 S.W.2d 99 (Ark. 1974) (nursing testimony contradicted worker's claims, nurse's testimony supported by log and medical card on worker); *Abell v. Goetze,* 226 A.2d 253 (Md. 1966) (nurse's testimony and records used to determine applicability of the worker's compensation provisions).
37. *Marion Homes of Bear Creek v. Dulaney,* 441 So.2d 955 (Ala. Civ. App. 1983).
38. U.S. CHAMBER OF COMMERCE, ANALYSIS OF WORKER'S COMPENSATION LAWS (1983).
39. ROTHSTEIN, MEDICAL SCREENING OF WORKERS 172 173 (1984).
40. Goerth, *Top Eastern Executives Face Intentional Tort Claims of Ulane,* 53 OCCUPATIONAL HEALTH AND SAFETY 23 (June 1984).
41. *See, e.g.,* CAL. LAB. CODE §3602(a) (West 1985).
42. ROTHSTEIN, MEDICAL SCREENING OF WORKERS 101 (1984).
43. CAL. LAB. CODE §3602(a) (West 1985).
44. *Connor v. Hauch,* 437 A.2d 661 (Md. Ap. 1981), *aff'd,* 453 A.2d 1207 (Md. 1983). *See also* MD. ANN. CODE art. 101, §58 (1985).
45. CONN. GEN. STAT. ANN. §31-293a (West Supp. 1985).
46. 10 A.L.R. 3d 1071 (1966).
47. *Dixon v. Ford Motor Co.,* 125 Cal. Rptr. 872 (1975).
48. *McDaniel v. Sage,* 419 N.E.2d 1322 (Ind. 1981).
49. *See, e.g., Warwick v. Hudson Pulp & Paper Co.,* 303 So.2d 701 (Fla. App. 1974); *Collier v. Wagner Castings Co.,* 408 N.E.2d 198 (Ill. 1980), where the employee was precluded from suing for civil damages since his injuries were compensable under the worker's compensation act and he had already collected.
50. *Akins v. Hudson Pulp & Paper Co.,* 330 So.2d 757 (Fla. App. 1976). This case is interesting also because of the court's review of the different documentation kept on work-related and non-work-related injuries. The nurse dispensed Mentrax and kept no record of it because it was the practice to document only work-related complaints and treatments. This practice is not an acceptable one in terms of defending a nurse and proving what action was taken.
51. *Baur v. Mesta Machine Company,* 176 A.2d 684 (Pa. 1962).
52. *Jenkins v. Sabourin,* 311 N.W.2d 600 (Wisc. 1981).
53. *Duprey v. Shane,* 249 P.2d 8 (Cal. 1952).
54. CAL. LAB. CODE §3602(a) (West 1985).
55. *Therrel v. Scott Paper Co.,* 428 So.2d 33 (Ala. 1983).
56. *Wright v. District Court,* 661 P.2d 1167 (Colo. 1983).
57. *Ross v. Schubert,* 388 N.E.2d 623 (Ind. App. 1979).
58. AMERICAN ASSN. OF OCCUPATIONAL HEALTH NURSES, CODE OF ETHICS (1985).
59. 29 C.F.R. §1910.20(g) (1985).
60. 29 C.F.R. §1910.1200 (1985).
61. McElveen, *Despite Pre-emption Threat Local Right to Know Laws Increase,* 54 OCCUPATIONAL HEALTH AND SAFETY, 20. (January 1985).

    See selected state laws, MD. ANN. CODE art. 89, §33A (1985); CONN. GEN. STAT. ANN. §31-40k (West Supp. 1985); N.Y. PUB. HEALTH §4800-4808 (McKinney 1985).
62. Van Den Eeden, *The Right to Know and the OHN,* 33 O.H.N. 281 (June 1985).
63. OSHA, GUIDELINES FOR MATERIAL SAFETY DATA SHEETS (1977).
64. 29 C.F.R. §1910.1200(i)(2) (1985): "where a treating physician or nurse determines that a medical emergency exists and the

specific chemical identity of a hazardous chemical is necessary for emergency or first-aid treatment, . . . shall immediately disclose. . . .''

65. 29 C.F.R. §1910.1200(i)(3) (1985).
66. *Federal Hazard Communication Rule Criticized by AAOHN,* 13 OSH RPTR. 877, 921, 955 (December-May, 1983-84); AAOHN NEWS, December 1985, at 1, col 2. *AAOHN calls for nurses to be included in proposed federal legislation (High Risk Occupational Disease Notification and Prevention Act of 1985, H.R. 1309).*
67. *Ensuring Compliance with right-to-know laws,* 53 OCCUPATIONAL HEALTH AND SAFETY 36 (August 1984); Samways, *Informing those with a need to know,* 24 JOURNAL OF OCCUPATIONAL MEDICINE 387 (1982); Santodonato, *Design and implementation of a worker's right to know program,* 42 AMERICAN INDUSTRIAL HYGIENE ASSOCIATION JOURNAL 666 (1981).
68. ROTHSTEIN, MEDICAL SCREENING OF WORKERS 8 (1984).
69. *Armstrong v. Morgan,* 545 S.W.2d 45 (Tex. Civ. App. 1977).
70. CONN. GEN. STAT. ANN. §31-40a (West Supp. 1985).
71. CONN. GEN. STAT. ANN. §31-40h (West Supp. 1985).
72. *See, e.g., United Steelworkers of America v. Marshall,* 647 F.2d 1189 (D.C. Cir. 1980), *cert. denied sub nom., Lead Indus. Ass'n, Inc. v. Donovan,* 453 U.S.913 (1981).
73. *Shelton v. Tucker,* 364 U.S. 479 (1960).
74. *Shuman v. Philadelphia,* 470 F. Supp. 449, 461 (E.D. Pa. 1979).
75. *Government Employees AFCE, Local 421 v. Schlesinger,* 443 F. Supp. 431 (D.D.C. 1978).
76. *Wroblewski v. Lexington Gardens, Inc.,* 448 A.2d 801 (Conn. 1982).
77. *Spencer v. General Telephone Co.,* 551 F. Supp. 896 (M.D. Pa. 1982).
78. *Ohio Brass Co.,* 261 N.L.R.B. 137 (1982).
79. *Larson v. Motor Supply Co.,* 573 P.2d 907 (Ariz. App. 1977).
80. MD. ANN. CODE art. 100, §95A (1985).
81. CONN. GEN. STAT. ANN. §31-379, 51m, 51q (West Supp. 1985).
82. *McLaughlin v. ARCO Polymerrs, Inc.,* 721 F.2d 426 (3rd Cir. 1983).
83. *See, e.g.,* N.Y. EDUC. LAW §6901 (McKinney, 1985), which states ''1. Diagnosing in the context of nursing practice means that identification of and discrimination between physical and psychological signs and symptoms essential to effective execution and management of the nursing regimen. Such diagnostic privilege is distinct from a medical diagnosis.''
84. Napholtz, *Nursing Directives for Nursing,* 30 O.H.N. 29 (July 1982).
85. MD. HEALTH OCC. ANN. CODE §7-101(f)(2)(vi) (Supp. 1985).
86. *Sermchief v. Gonzales,* 660 S.W.2d 683 (Mo. banc 1983).
87. *Cooper v. National Bearing Co.,* 288 P.2d 581 (Cal. App. 1955).
88. 80 Op. Att'y Gen. 80-023 (Ohio 1980).
89. AAOHN, CODE OF ETHICS (1985); AAOHN, PRINCIPLES OF PRIVILEGED COMMUNICATION (1983).
90. AAOHN *Statement and Guidelines—OSHA Standard 29 C.F.R. 1910.20, Access to Employee Exposure and Medical Records,* 29 O.H.N., 32 (April 1981).
91. 29 C.F.R. §1910.20 (1985).
92. 29 C.F.R. §1913 (1985).
93. 29 C.F.R. §1910.20(c)(6)(i) (1985).
94. 29 C.F.R. §1910.20(c)(6)(ii)(C) (1985).
95. 29 C.F.R. §1910.20(10)(i) (1985).
96. 29 C.F.R. §1910.20(d)(1)(i) (1985) (except where an OSHA standard specifies differently).
97. 29 C.F.R. §1910.20(e)(1)(i) (1985).
98. 29 C.F.R. §1910.20(e)(2)(ii)(C) (1985).
99. 29 C.F.R. §1910.20(e)(2)(ii)(D) (1985).
100. 29 C.F.R. §1910.20(e)(2)(ii)(E) (1985).
101. 29 C.F.R. §1910.20(f) (1985).
102. ROTHSTEIN, MEDICAL SCREENING OF WORKERS 91 (1984).
103. AMERICAN OCCUPATIONAL MEDICAL ASSN., CODE OF ETHICAL CONDUCT, Principle 7 (1976).
104. 29 C.F.R. §1913.10 (1985).
105. Reif, *Access to Employee Medical Records,* 31 O.H.N. 38 (May 1983).
106. *See, e.g.,* A GUIDE FOR THE EVALUATION OF AN OCCUPATIONAL HEALTH NURSING SERVICE, GUIDE TO INTERVIEWING AND COUNSELING FOR THE OHN, A GUIDE FOR ESTABLISHING AN OCCUPATIONAL HEALTH NURSING SERVICE, GUIDE FOR SETTING UP A RECORD SYSTEM, A GUIDE FOR THE PREPARATION OF A MANUAL OF POLICIES AND PROCEDURES FOR THE OCCUPATIONAL HEALTH SERVICE, GUIDELINES FOR DEVELOPING JOB DESCRIPTIONS, and GUIDELINES FOR IMPLEMENTION OF A RESPIRATORY SURVEILLANCE PROGRAM. AAOHN is located at 3500 Piedmont Rd., NE, Suite 400, Atlanta, GA 30305.
107. Bowyer, *The Liability of the Occupational Health Nurse,* 11 LAW, MEDICINE AND HEALTH CARE 224 (October 1983); Mancini, *The Law and the Occupational Health Nurse,* 79 AMERICAN JOURNAL OF NURSING 1628 (September 1979).
108. *See, e.g.,* American Occupational Medical Association, *Guidelines for Employee Health Services in Hospitals, Clinics and Medical Research Institutions,* 25 JOURNAL OF OCCUPATIONAL MEDICINE 771 (1983).
109. *See, e.g.,* EMPLOYMENT SAFETY AND HEALTH GUIDE (Commerce Clearing House [CCH]); OCCUPATIONAL HEALTH NURSING, OCCUPATIONAL HEALTH & SAFETY, OCCUPATIONAL SAFETY AND HEALTH CASES (Bureau of National Affairs [BNA]); OCCUPATIONAL SAFETY AND HEALTH DECISIONS (CCH); OCCUPATIONAL SAFETY AND HEALTH REPORTER (BNA).
110. *See, e.g.,* the following NIOSH and OSHA Publications: POCKET GUIDE TO CHEMICAL HAZARDS (NO. 78-210); THE INDUSTRIAL ENVIRONMENT—ITS EVALUATION AND CONTROL (NO. 74-117); CRITERIA FOR A RECOMMENDED STANDARD: OCCUPATIONAL EXPOSURE TO. . . . ; SPECIAL HAZARD REVIEWS; OCCUPATIONAL HAZARD ASSESSMENTS; REGISTRY OF TOXIC EFFECTS OF CHEMICAL SUBSTANCES (NO. 80-102. AND QUARTERLY UPDATES; MORBIDITY AND MORTALITY WEEKLY REPORT (published by Centers for Disease Control); OCCUPATIONAL CHARACTERISTICS OF DISABLED WORKERS.
111. *See, e.g.,* N.Y. Times, Dec. 2, 1985, at A1, Col. 4, an article entitled *U.S. to Propose New Rules on Workplace Health.* The article notes that after years of consideration OSHA will propose new workplace health standards soon on the use of three common substances (benzene, formaldehyde, and cotton dust) that

are suspected of causing cancer or other illnesses in human beings.

Additional Readings

P. BARTH & H. HUNT, WORKERS' COMPENSATION AND WORK-RELATED ILLNESSES AND DISEASES (1980).

D. BERMAN, DEATH ON THE JOB, OCCUPATIONAL HEALTH AND SAFETY STRUGGLES IN THE UNITED STATES (1978).

M. BROWN, OCCUPATIONAL HEALTH NURSING: PRINCIPLES AND PRACTICE (1981).

Cerran, *Negligent OSHA Inspections: Liability for Employee Injuries*, 68 AM. J. PUB. HEALTH 601 (1978).

T. DENEBERG & R. DENEBERG, ALCOHOL AND DRUGS: ISSUES IN THE WORKPLACE (1983).

J. LADOU, OCCUPATIONAL HEALTH LAW (1981).

A. LARSON, WORKMAN'S COMPENSATION FOR OCCUPATIONAL INJURIES AND DEATH (current ed. 1985).

NATIONAL TOXICOLOGY PROGRAM, ANNUAL REPORT ON CARCINOGENS (latest ed. 1985).

D. NELKIN & M. BROWN, WORKERS AT RISK, VOICES FROM THE WORKPLACE (1984).

Richter, *The worker's right-to-know: obstacles, ambiguities and loopholes*, 6 J. HEALTH, POLIT., POL. & LAW 339 (1981).

Schute and Ringen, *Notification of workers at high risk: An emerging public health problem*, 74 AM. J. PUB. HEALTH 485 (May 1984).

F. WALLICK, THE AMERICAN WORKER: AN ENDANGERED SPECIES (1972).

J. WORREL & D. APPEL, WORKERS' COMPENSATION BENEFITS: ADEQUACY, EQUITY, EFFICIENCY (1985).

Chapter 16

Nursing practice in correctional facilities

Cynthia E. Northrop

The health problems of incarcerated individuals are complex and varied. For example, one study described inmates in New York as 91% male and 9% female; three fourths of the population was under the age of 30; 57% were Black, 24% Hispanic, and 17% White. Inmates suffer many of the same health problems of others, but especially the following health problems: drug abuse, alcoholism, psychiatric disorders and suicide, trauma, seizure disorders, asthma, venereal disease, tuberculosis, dental problems, and hypertension.[1]

The number of prisoners in state and federal prisons is staggering. In the latest statistical report produced by the U.S. Department of Justice, Bureau of Justice Statistics, federal and state prisons housed 490,000 inmates.[2] Uniform Crime Reports (UCR) and the National Crime Survey (NCS) are the main sources of national crime statistics.[3] Generally, these statistics show that:

1. Property crimes outnumber violent crimes by 9 to 1.
2. Most crimes are committed by men, especially men under age 20.
3. Offenders are predominately male and disproportionately young, Black, and unmarried, as compared to the general population.
4. Violent offenders, like victims of violent crime, are typically low-income youths with a high likelihood of unemployment.
5. Many offenders have backgrounds that include a turbulent home life, lack of family ties, and poor education.
6. More than 1% of the U.S. population is under some form of correctional sanction.[4]

Medical and health services for prisoners present many complex legal and constitutional issues. Although many individuals are in custody in the United States, there is no coherent body of law establishing their rights and setting forth the obligations of and limitations on the institutions where they are confined.[5]

Definition and scope of practice

In 1985 the American Nurses' Association (ANA) established standards for the practice of nursing in correctional facilities.[6] While many standards which will be highlighted in this chapter discuss not only health care in corrections but all aspects of prison life have existed since the 1960s, these were the first national nursing standards developed.[7] The nursing profession has defined nursing practice in corrections as follows:

> The major thrust of nursing care in correctional settings is the provision of primary care services for the population from the time of entry into the system, through transfers to other institutions, to final release from custody. Primary health services in this field include the use of all aspects of the nursing process in carrying out screening activities, providing direct health care services, analyzing individual health behaviors, teaching, counseling, and assisting individuals in assuming responsibility for their own health to the best of their ability, knowledge, and circumstances.[8]

The standards of nursing care in the correctional setting are listed in the opposite box. These standards incorporate the ANA CODE FOR NURSES[9] and are an excellent guide to practice in correctional facilities. In the future they will certainly be used in the courtroom since they are a national professional statement of the desired and expected nursing practice in this setting. Not only will the nurse working in corrections be held to the legal definition of nursing practice in the state nurse practice act but also the nurse can be held to this ANA statement.

The many and varied needs of inmates call for different types of nursing backgounds and skills. Not only must the nurse working in corrections be a skilled community heath nurse, medical-surgical nurse, psychiatric nurse, and emergency room nurse, but also, as described in the ANA standards, must fulfill different roles of nurses in corrections: staff nurses, nurse practitioners, and nurse specialists. Nurses play a valuable and essential role in identification and management of health problems of inmates.[10]

Correctional facilities and security

Administration of correctional facilities is a governmental responsibility. State and federal governments through state departments of corrections and the Federal Bureau of Prisons, U.S. Department of Justice, respectively, administer most of the prisons in the country. Local correctional facilities are administered by county, city, or local sheriff's departments. Whether administered directly by the government or contracted out to others (for example, the trend toward for-profit prison systems administered by private corporations and the trend toward health services being contracted out to private groups), the nurse employed in the system carries unique legal responsibilities.[11] The type of employer affects the legal relationships of the nurse toward others.

Chapter 25 on criminal law complements the issues discussed in this chapter. In addition those nurses employed in the federal prison system will want to refer to Chapter 18 for a review of legal aspects of the federal government employee.

There are several settings available to nurses practicing in correctional facilities. The prisons are large, state or federally administered facilities; jails are usually small, locally run institutions. There are also training schools, work farms, and community detention centers characterized, usually, by less security.

Individuals are classified within the criminal justice system according to their relationship to the system. For example, before someone is tried and sentenced he or she is a pretrial detainee or arrestee. Once sentenced, the conviction carries a penalty which classifies the prisoner according to length of stay in an institution. The state department of corrections or Federal Bureau of Prisons, depending on which system it is, determines placement within a maximum, medium, or minimum security institution. The levels and amounts of security deemed necessary are an administrative decision of the system.

The response to crime comes in the form of the criminal justice system, including prosecution, adjudication, sentencing or disposition, and corrections. Community supervision and confinement are the two options of correctional sanction. Confinement is in jails, prisons (federal and state), and community-based facilities. State prisons are generally old and large. The levels of prison security include:

1. Maximum or close custody prisons—typically surrounded by a double fence or wall (usually 18 to 25 feet high) with armed guards in observation towers. Such facilities usually have large interior cell blocks for inmate housing areas.
2. Medium custody prisons—typically have double fences topped with barbed wire to enclose the facility. Housing architecture is quite varied, consisting of outside cell blocks in units of 150 cells or less, dormitories, and cubicles.
3. Minimum custody prisons—typically do not have armed posts and may or may not have fences to enclose the institution. Housing consists of open dormitories.[12]

Prisoners or inmates can be adults or juveniles (under 18 years, usually), men or women, with special health care needs. As mentioned before, most are under the age of 20. Most are from poor and urban areas. The women prisoners, usually housed in completely separate institutions, sometimes have unique needs, especially in the area of pregnancy, family planning, and child care.

Special concerns of correctional health nurses

It is the responsibility of the prison administrators to maintian internal order and discipline, secure the institution against unauthorized access or escape, and provide rehabilitation (given human nature and resources). Nurses in this system are serving a health care function, not any of the security functions. They actually have no independent way in and out of the facility. They are never in possession of keys or other security measures.

The nurse's judgment is constantly surrounded by the

NURSING PRACTICE IN CORRECTIONAL FACILITIES: STANDARDS OF CARE

Standard I. Organization of Nursing Services

Nursing services provided in correctional settings will be planned, organized, and administered by a professional registered nurse who has education and experience commensurate with responsibilities.

Standard II. Data Collection

The nurse in the correctional setting accurately collects data pertinent to the health of the inmate in an organized and systematic manner.

Standard III. Diagnosis

The nurse in the correctional setting uses nursing diagnoses to express conclusions supported by health assessment data.

Standard IV. Planning

The nurse in the correctional setting develops a nursing plan with specific goals and interventions delineating nursing actions that contribute to the health and well-being of the inmate.

Standard V. Intervention

The nurse in the correctional setting intervenes as guided by the nursing care plan to implement nursing actions that promote, maintain, or restore health; prevent illness; and effect rehabilitation.

Standard V-A. Intervention: Health Education

The nurse in the correctional setting promotes individual and group well-being through health education activities, including health counseling, health teaching, and formal programs in health education.

Standard V-B. Intervention: Suicide Prevention

The nurse in the correctional setting uses current mental health concepts in the assessment of suicide risk and in the planning and coordination of interventions that prevent suicidal behavior in the correctional setting.

Standard V-C. Intervention: Communicable Disease Control

The nurse in the correctional setting uses current principles of community health nursing to promote a healthful environment and reduce the incidence of communicable diseases within the correctional setting.

Standard V-D. Intervention: Alcohol and Drug Rehabilitation

The nurse in the correctional setting participates with other members of the health care team in the treatment of inmates who have substance abuse problems.

Standard V-E. Intervention: Somatic Therapy

Administration of medications within the correctional setting shall be under the supervision of a registered nurse. The nurse shall supervise the administration of medications in accordance with state regulations and national standards for the practice of nursing and pharmacy.

Standard V-F. Intervention: Psychosocial Counseling

The nurse in the correctional setting uses clinical skills to provide inmates with crisis intervention and episodic and ongoing psychosocial counseling.

Standard V-G. Intervention: Emergency Care

The nurse in the correctional setting initiates emergency care as needed according to community standards of care.

Standard V-H. Intervention: Environmental Health

The nurse in the correctional setting regularly monitors the environment for conditions that would have a negative impact on health and safety within the facility and reports significant findings to the institution's management.

Standard VI. Evaluation

The nurse in the correctional setting periodically evaluates outcome of nursing actions and revises as necessary plan of care, data base, and nursing interventions.

Standard VII. Collaboration

The nurse in the correctional setting collaborates with other health care providers and colleagues in the facility in assessing, planning, implementing, evaluating, and coordinating health care services consistent with the needs of the institution's population.

Standard VIII. Continuing Education

The nurse in the correctional setting shall increase knowledge and skills in nursing practice through participation in continuing education and professional development activities that include an understanding of the uniqueness of the correctional setting.

Standard IX. Professional Conduct

The nurse working in the correctional setting must maintain a professional identity and consistently promote health and be an advocate in health promotion.

Standard X. Ethics

The nurse in the correctional setting shall use the code for nurses as established by the American Nurse's Association as a basis for practice.

Adapted from AMERICAN NURSES' ASSOCIATION: STANDARDS OF NURSING PRACTICE IN CORRECTIONAL FACILITIES (1985).

balancing of the need for security and the need to deliver adequate health services and care. Given that nurses are socialized into a caring and helping role and that corrections is a coercive, punitive environment, it is easy to understand how some of the legal and ethical issues arise.

As one nurse put it, "Corrections personnel have concentrated on control, containment and isolation. Their orientation is to dangerous inmates, not sick ones. In contrast, health care providers tend to minimize the dangerous aspect of their patients in an effort to treat each prisoner as an individual. It is no consolation to prison officials that the majority of prison escapes have been from hospital institutions."[13]

The ANA standards identify that it is inappropriate that nurses be involved in the security functions of their employment setting. Registered nurses would not participate in procedures performed solely for correctional purposes; for example, conducting body cavity or strip searches to detect contraband. It is inappropriate for nurses to participate in disciplinary decisions or committees. Likewise, it is inappropriate for nurses to particpte directly or indirectly in executions by lethal injection.[14]

Further, nurses often must vigilantly watch for the inmate who tries to con him or her into doing something unprofessional, unethical, or illegal. Detecting the feigned illness can be a challenge to nursing practice in this area. To be prepared for extreme situations, while the nurse must not be cast into a security role, he or she must have a thorough understanding and knowledge of the security system. Even being taken hostage is a possibility to actively know how to avoid.

Support for the need to keep separate as much as possible the security and health care functions can be found in the American Bar Association (ABA) standards for the criminal justice system. These standards provide that correctional personnel should not be authorized or allowed to inhibit an inmate's access to medical personnel or to interfere in medical treatment, including medications, diets, after care, or work assignments.[15]

Prisoner's rights

In general, inmates have certain rights, including rights to visitation, association, use of the mail, religion, legal services, access to the courts, rehabilitation programs, medical aid, access to a law library, paper and pencils, and access to publications. The prison officials have a limited use of isolated confinement ("the hole"), force and punishment, and prison discipline.[16]

Prisoners have the rights to be confined in conditions that are not cruel and unusual and to be nourished, housed, clothed, and medically provided for in reasonable ways. Prisoners cannot be abused, have a limited right to privacy and confidentiality, and basically have no protection from searches and seizure.[17]

Inmates and detainees have the right to sue the government or a prison authority or employee, including nurses and other health care providers. Several of the cases brought by prisoners will be discussed later in relation to nursing and health care services. The bases of these suits may be three: constitutional, statutory, or common law. Violations of the First, Fifth, Eighth, and Fourteenth Amendments to the U.S. Constitution may be alleged by an inmate depending on the circumstances. A state or federal prisoner may have rights under the federal or related state tort claims acts; or the prisoner may sue for negligence, malpractice, lack of informed consent, or under other state common laws. Earlier chapters also discussed some of these concepts, particularly Chapter 2.

A court can look at the totality of circumstances in resolving allegations of inadequacy against an entire prison health care system without attributing fault to an individual administrator.[18] In addition, the doctrine of *respondeat superior* is unavailable in prison litigation, so that a prison administrator would only be liable for a nurse's action if it is demonstrated that the administrator directed or participated in the neglect of the health care needs of prisoners.[19]

Although the prisoner has a right to sue, the reality is that legal aid that is provided to the indigent prisoner has varying rules about bringing private tort actions for negligence on behalf of prisoners. In order to bring malpractice actions prisoners may need to hire their own attorneys since the government is only required to provide legal representation for an adequate defense against the charges. Legal assistance organizations sometimes bring civil rights violation suits to challenge health care services, including nursing services. These are attacked more often on constitutional or federal statutory grounds.

History of law, corrections, and health care for inmates

As has been mentioned most criminal law in this country is dealt with at the state government level. The criminal justice system and its administration are largely functions of state and local agencies. The Bureau of

Prisons, established in 1930, administers the federal prisons and the federal correctional system.[20]

Until the 1970s court involvement in review of medical and health care in prisons was minimal. Taking a "hands off" approach, the Supreme Court advised:

> The problems of prisons in America are complex and intractable, and, more to the point, they are not readily susceptible of resolution by decree. Most require expertise, comprehensive planning, and the committment of resources, all of which are peculiarly within the province of the legislative and executive branches of government. For all these reasons, courts are ill equipped to deal with the increasingly urgent problems of prison administration and reform. Judicial recognition of that fact reflects no more than a healthy sense of realism.[21]

The 1970s brought a flood of litigation which attacked the constitutionality of all aspects of prison life, including medical services. In 1976 the Supreme Court established a new standard for assessing the alleged civil rights violations of prison authorities and employees against inmates. This standard will be described below. As the prison reform movement increased, the courts became more and more involved in review of conditions and prison systems.

The purpose of the corrections system has been reviewed over decades of thought and study. The age-old debate centers on whether an individual is placed in a jail or prison for punitive or rehabilitative purposes. The prison reform movement has stirred much discussion in this area. At least one author has succinctly offered, in addition to rehabilitation, three theoretical justifications for prison: retribution, deterrence, and isolation.[22]

The challenges facing physicians and nurses employed in corrections are great, and courts which have reviewed allegations of inadequate health care systems available to inmates recognize these challenges. In *Collins* a grand jury report was reviewed in which it noted slip-shod medical staff, which often left nurses forced to prescribe medicines, and conditions under which health care providers had to cope with inmates who fabricated medical complaints and subjected nurses and others to extreme verbal abuse and threats. Noting the fear that pervades all, workers and inmates alike, in the corrections system, the court stated that "the problems faced by doctors—even more so by nurses—and by other staff must not be overlooked or lightly dismissed."[23]

General health care rights of inmates

Inmates' health care rights include the rights to access care, refuse care, confidentiality, informed consent, and privacy. The prisoner's right to health care is the right to access minimum and decent health care services. Once an individual is incarcerated the government is obligated to provide health care. Generally, medical and health services must be provided which are at least comparable to those available to the general population.[24]

Based upon case law, the right to health care is outlined in the ABA standards as follows:

> (a) Prisoners should receive routine and emergency medical care, which includes the diagnosis and treatment of physical, dental, and mental health problems. A prisoner who requires care not available in the correctional institution should be transferred to a hospital or other appropriate place for care.
> (b) Personnel providing medical care in the correctional institution should have qualifications equivalent to medical care personnel performing similar functions in the community.
> (c) If an institution operates a hospital, it should meet the standards for a licensed general hospital in the community with respect to services it offers.[25]

The right to access health care includes initial health screening and periodic examiniations, as well as sick care and emergency care. Upon admission to a correctional facility a detainee should receive an examination by a person trained to ascertain visible or common symptoms of communicable disease and conditions requiring immediate medical attention by a physician.[26] The ABA standards suggest that a sentenced prisoner should receive a physical (including mental and dental examinations) within 2 weeks of admission and not less than every 2 years thereafter and upon release. The detainee (one who is not sentenced) should be given a physical upon request when the person is confined for more than 2 weeks.[27]

The ABA standards also address the special needs of women prisoners. Those standards indicate "that accommodations for all necessary prenatal and postnatal care and treatment are available for women prisoners."[28] Every attempt is to be made for pregnant women inmates to deliver their children in a hospital outside the correctional institution. The ABA standards specifically advise that the fact that a child was born in a correctional institution should not be mentioned in the birth certificate. It is also recommended that women prisoners keep their young children with them for a reasonable time, preferably on extended furlough or in an appropriate community facility, or, if that is not feasible, that alternative care be arranged promptly. Where young children stay with their mothers in a correctional institution, a nursery staffed by qualified persons should be provided. There is limited authority on the issue of whether women prisoners can be forced to give up their children. The issue depends upon interpretation of state statutes, but the cases suggest that women prisoners cannot be forced to give up their children without valid supporting reasons.[29]

The converse of the right to access health care is the right to refuse treatment. The ABA standards and the standards of the American Corrections Association (ACA) deem informed consent an essential component of the prison health care system.[30] Every prisoner may refuse examination and treatment[31] with three exceptions which are provided for in the ABA standards:

1. When required by order of a court
2. When reasonably believed by the responsible physician to be necessary to detect or treat communicable disease or otherwise to protect the health of other persons
3. When reasonably believed to be necessary in an emergency to save the life of the person or to prevent permanent and serious damage to the person's health

In some cases prison administrators have compelled kidney dialysis treatment to preserve the life of a prisoner whose refusal to undergo treatment was a protest to gain a transfer to a minimum security institution. The courts found that the administrators could properly do this.[32] The courts have also held that constitutional rights of healthy inmates are impaired if reasonable safeguards are not taken to isolate infected inmates.[33] However, prison authorities cannot force treatment for alcoholism during jail incarceration.[34] There are some unsettled areas of the law where prisoners refuse treatment. For example, the issue of forced feeding and involuntary medical treatment of a prisoner on a hunger strike when the prisoner is not mentally ill is unsettled.[35]

In the case of juvenile inmates, regarding parental consent, consent and refusal of treatment provided within state laws apply. The law regarding juveniles varies greatly among jurisdictions. Some states allow juveniles to consent to treatment without parental consent as long as they are mature enough to comprehend the consequences of their decisions; others require parental consent until the age of majority, which also may vary among states. The law of the state in which the correctional facility is located is the law upon which facility policy should be formulated.[36]

Because correctional facilities are nontraditional settings for health care, it is thought that, as an institution isolated from the community, in general state and federal laws which apply in other health care settings do not apply in the correctional facility. This is not the case. Many laws that apply to nurses in traditional health care settings still apply to correctional health nurses. For example, physical and sexual abuse statutes apply to nurses working in correctional facilities. Every nurse is required by law to report incidents of child abuse.

Involvement of prisoners in human experimentation is discussed in standards relating to prison life. Chapter 21 also discusses the federal regulations which apply to the use of prisoners in research.[37] Prohibitions exist for nontherapeutic experimentation, including aversive behavior modification, psychosurgery, drug testing, electrical stimulation of the brain, and psychopharmacology. However, prisoners are allowed to participate in therapeutic medical programs deemed beneficial to them, provided that the program is judged medically sound and in conformance with medical standards and the prisoners have given full, voluntary, and informed written consent. If the program involves psychosurgery, electrical stimulation of the brain, and aversive conditioning, approval must be given by an appropriate court after a hearing to determine that the program is sound and that the prisoner has given informed consent.[38]

The ANA standards specify that the nurse "advocates for the inmate in the areas of confidentiality and informed consent" and "employs appropriate protective guidelines when conducting or participating in research on inmates."[39] These rights could be bases of lawsuits involving nursing services which violate prisoners' rights.

Confidentiality of health records is another important right of prisoners. ACA standards provide that the health record is maintained separately from the confinement record, that access to the health record is controlled by the health authority, and that the health authority shares with the facility administration information regarding a prisoner's medical management, security, and ability to participate in programs.[40] In addition, ANA standards require that health records be maintained in a manner that protects against unauthorized access to health information.[41] The ABA recommends that medical records be retained for at least 5 years after the prisoner's release.[42]

The prisoner's right to privacy was discussed in *Robbins,* a case involving a male inmate who claimed that a female staff nurse violated his right to privacy when she dispensed medications in the cell block.[43] The court held that this practice did not infringe on his privacy because a prisoner does not enjoy the same right of privacy as do ordinary citizens in their homes and offices.[44] The court noted that the prisoner's reduced privacy right must be balanced with the female staff nurse's right of equal job opportunity regardless of sex, as set forth in the Civil Rights Act of 1964. The court held that the intrusion was minor and consistent with limited privacy rights retained by a state prisoner. The court pointed out, however, that there was no evidence that the prisoner was under constant or even frequent surveillance by the female staff nurse, suggesting that this fact may have made a difference in the court's holding.

Cruel and unusual punishment: deliberate indifference in health care

Estelle v. Gamble changed the applicable standard of medical services to prisoners greatly.[45] In *Estelle* an inmate suffered a work-related injury when a bale of cotton fell on him while unloading a truck. A prison hospital medical assistant checked him in his cell. After 2 hours of pain he was brought to the prison hospital, given pain pills by an inmate nurse and examined by a physician who ordered pain killers, rest, and placement in a lower bunk. The prison authorities failed to comply with the orders, and the prescriptions were lost and not filled for 4 days. The medical assistant testified before the prison disciplinary committee, which reviewed the inmate's refusal to work, that the inmate was in first class medical condition. On several occasions guards refused the inmate's requests to see the physician.

The Supreme Court began its analysis of the situation by reviewing the history and intent of the the prohibition against cruel and unusual punishment. The Eighth Amendment to the United States Constitution states: "Excessive bail shall not be required, nor excessive fines imposed, nor cruel and unusual punishments inflicted."[46] This legal concept was first applied in a case to proscribe physically barbarous punishments.[47] In discussing this further the Court stated that:

> The elementary principles [of the amendment] establish government's obligation to provide medical care for those whom it is punishing by incarceration. An inmate must rely on prison authorities to treat his medical needs; if the authorities fail to do so, those needs will not be met. In the worst cases, such a failure may actually produce physical "torture or a lingering death," the evils of most immediate concern to the drafters of the Amendment. In less serious cases, denial of medical care may result in pain and suffering which no one suggests would serve any penological purpose. Infliction of unnecessary suffering is inconsistent with contemporary standards of decency as manifested in modern legislation codifying the common view that it is but just that the public be required to care for the prisoner, who cannot, by reason of deprivation of his liberty, care for himself.[48]

Estelle's rule is that deliberate indifference to serious medical needs of prisoners constitutes the unnecessary and wanton infliction of pain proscribed by the Eighth Amendment. States and the federal government are to furnish inmates with reasonably adequate food, clothing, shelter, sanitation, medical care, and personal safety.

Under federal law "every person who under color of any statute, of any state territory, subjects, or causes to be subjected, any citizen of the United States, or other person within the jurisdiction thereof to the deprivation of any rights, privileges, or immunities, secured by the Constitution and laws, shall be liable to the party injured in an action at law, suit in equity, or other proper proceeding for redress."[49] Therefore, one of the possible claims of an injured prisoner may be a violation of his or her constitutional rights, the Eighth Amendment prohibition of cruel and unusual punishment, and the violation of this federal statute.

Inmates have demonstrated that the health care provided them was deliberately indifferent by showing that:

1. The medical care involved a series of incidents closely related in time which may disclose a pattern of conduct amounting to deliberate indifference to the medical needs of the prisoners.
2. The medical facilities were so wholly inadequate for the prison population's needs that suffering would be inevitable.[50]

Inmates, regardless of whether they are state or federal prisoners, whose constitutional rights have been violated may bring their legal action in federal court.

Prison health care: malpractice claims

Inmates, as mentioned earlier, do have the right and can bring an action for negligence or malpractice in a state court. The inmate must establish a duty of care, establish that it was breached by a nurse's action and that the breach was the cause of the injury and demonstrate how the inmate was injured. The usual compensatory damages—including loss of wages, future wages, and income; pain and suffering; and medical expenses—are often difficult for the prisoner to establish since he or she is not employed and does not have substantial wages and the medical expenses are paid by the state or federal government.

From this author's review of the case law which inmates have brought they have been more successful with private suits based on state tort law where the injuries were most severe. Their cases have also more frequently succeeded where the prison authority or employee has acted with malice or ill intent. Case examples are provided below. The type of damages often pursued by an inmate under these circumstances is punitive damages.

In any case the extent of the nurse's liability would be as it is in other practice settings, to deliver reasonable care under the circumstances.

The nurse who is employed in the correctional facility to provide health care services may be sued individually. However, there are certain state and federal statutes which provide qualified governmental immunities as a defense to an individual nurse being sued. Essentially these qualified immunities hold that defendants (corrections officials or employees) are immune from suit if they can show that they acted in good faith.[51] This type of immunity/defense varies among jurisdictions. Other forms of governmental immunity, such as sovereign immunity, also may be available to a nurse defendant as a defense. However, if a jurisdiction has waived sovereign immunity by judicial decision or through legislation, tort liability can be asserted against an appropriate governmental unit based on negligence, as it can against prison employees and agents directly.[52]

To summarize, in *Hampton* the distinction was drawn clearly between the types of actions an inmate may bring against a nurse or other health care provider. The federal civil rights action, discussed previously and known as a Section 1983 action, requires a showing that a constitutional right has been violated. For example, a 1983 action involves the indifference manifested by prison physicians or nurses in their response to the prisoner's needs or by prison guards in intentionally denying or delaying access to medical care or intentionally interfering with treatment once prescribed.[53]

Using the *Estelle* standard, a prisoner presents a case which alleges that there was deliberate indifference to serious medical needs of prisoners which constituted unnecessary and wanton infliction of punishment. Lastly, the state tort action involves a claim by the prisoner that the health care provider has been negligent in diagnosis or treatment of a medical condition of an inmate.

Specific legal issues and nursing practice

Cases are rare in which a correctional health nurse has been sued individually for negligence, malpractice, or violation of prisoners' constitutional rights. However, most cases brought by inmates alleging inadequate medical care and services have involved an examination and critique of nursing services. Here are examples of cases in which nursing practice was found to be cruel and unusual punishment and ordered by the courts to be changed:

1. Forcible treatment (against the inmate's consent) through use of intramuscular injections of major tranquilizers without nursing assessment of inmate's condition[54]
2. Improper execution of standing orders[55]
3. Juvenile inmate injected with promazine (Sparine) in retaliation for behavior[56]
4. Prescribing and administering of controlled medications without authorization from or consulting with physician[57]
5. No quality assurance measures[58]
6. Lack of training in CPR and emergency care and lack of inservice[59]
7. Chaotic recording, inaccurate records, unprofessionally maintained[60]
8. No written policies or procedures for nursing care[61]
9. Use of nurse inmate in sick call and other aspects of care[62]
10. Lack of response to inmates in need of care for drug abuse[63]
11. Decisions that patient's complaints are imaginary and administration of placebos[64]
12. Antitherapeutic, punitive use of isolation, restraints, and Thorazine and other tranquilizing drugs[65]
13. Inadequate observation of and communication with inmate patients in hospital sick wing[66]
14. Denial of access to a physician, failure to screen properly[67]

The amount and frequency of nursing services have also been discussed in a case where an inmate alleged that there was a constitutional right to registered nurses on a 24-hour basis. The court held that there was no constitutional requirement that RNs be available on such a basis.[68]

The use of incarcerated nurses (inmate nurses) within the prison health care system has been evaluated by the courts as well. As mentioned before and in another case, one of the issues the court reviewed was the use of inmates to fill medical staff positions.[69] It held that prisons should refrain from this practice but be encouraged to use trained and competent inmate personnel only to supplement the medical staff. ANA standards state that inmates shall not provide nursing care or control access to care.[70]

In addition to these cases and the issues they represent, standards which are based on case law have dealt with and reviewed several specific areas of health care for the inmate. These areas include medications, emergency care, the physical environment of the prison or jail, the use of isolation and segregation, sick call, coordination of care, and referrals. Particular standards exist for inmate health problems, including alcohol and drug abuse, suicide, and health teaching. Each of these areas will be discussed.

ADMINISTRATION OF MEDICATIONS

Some of the legal problems of nurses employed in correctional facilities stem from dispensing, administering, and securing medications in the facility. The guidelines for use of standing orders outlined in Chapter 13 are equally applicable to the evaluation of such orders in correctional facilities. The ANA standards, noting the prevalence of substance abuse behaviors in inmates, point out that control and security of drugs in the prison hospital or health unit can be problematical. The standards suggest that "the nurse administers prescription medications only on the order of licensed physicians, dentists, or others legally authorized to prescribe medications."[71] Controlled substances need special handling and security within the prison system.

If correctional personnel, other than health care personnel, are involved with administering medications, the ANA standards recommend that personnel be credentialed and trained in accordance with community standards.[72] However, the ABA standards state that:

> All drugs should be under the control and supervision of the physician in charge of the institution's medical care program. Normally, only medical care personnel should administer prescription drugs. In an emergency, correctional officials may administer such drugs at the direction of medical care personnel. In no instance should prisoners administer drugs.[73]

Several lawsuits have successfully been brought dealing with the misuse of medications by prison health care personnel. In *Jackson*, the court held that drugs should not be prescribed for the convenience of the institution, only as indicated by the individual treatment plan of the inmate and his or her personal welfare. Medication, especially psychogenic drugs, should not be administered except on the prescription of a physician who has examined the prisoner personally.[74]

In addition, members of the legal profession who work in the area of prison litigation may quickly act to prevent the misuse of drugs upon their clients. One author states that "a lawyer who becomes aware of the misuse of drugs on his [or her] institutionalized client has the responsibility of demanding a protective order and perhaps bringing a class action [lawsuit]."[75]

EMERGENCY CARE, SICK CALL, AND REFERRALS

Health care for inmates can involve emergency treatment for injuries or illnesses and nonemergency care which involves care of routine ailments and prevention programs. Standards designed to improve and adequately care for incarcerated individuals provide that the correctional facility have policies and procedures which include 24-hour provision of emergency treatment, use of emergency rooms in nearby hospitals, use of emergency vehicles, and training of correctional personnel in first aid and CPR.[76]

Not every inmate who brings a case is successful in convincing the court that the nursing or health care services provided are unconstitutional or violate the inmate's rights. This was true in a case involving the review of a jail's emergency, sick call, and referral system. In *Hutchings* an inmate complained of a rash and claimed that the nurse was indifferent.[77] An expert presented testimony at trial about the jail health care system, stating that:

1. Medical records were awful, consisting of notes by the nurse which paraphrased lab reports and physician's instructions, with no physical assessment or diagnosis noted, and were kept outside the jail.
2. There was a lack of preventive medicine.
3. There was no follow-up or continuity of care.
4. Medical screening was miniscule.
5. The nurse was underutilized.

The expert did acknowledge that the standards for medical care are different when inmates are confined for very short periods of time, as was the case here.

The court found that no evidence was presented showing that the health care system was deliberately indifferent. There was no evidence that the nurse failed to possess sufficient professional qualifications. The custody staff was trained in CPR, first aid, and medical screening. The inmate testified that he had had no adverse consequences from the lack of care. The medical records needed improvement, but the court believed that the record system presented no threat to the inmate's health. The court also found that there were time delays between admission to the facility and health screening (for tuberculosis, blood tests, and completion of the history form), which needed improvement, but that the inmate was free to be seen by the nurse; and there was a policy at the facility that, if a nurse was not available, the inmate would be transferred to the emergency room of a nearby hospital.

Nurses have a special responsibility to refer inmates needing immediate medical attention to the facility's physician or, if applicable, to the hospital emergency room. The ANA standards specify six policy areas for the treatment and referral of inmates. According to these standards, institutional policies should provide the nurse with criteria for making judgments about referral of inmates for immediate treatment and intervention, ambulatory care services (sick call), onsite inpatient infirmary or hospital, transfer to a community hospital, referral for mental health care, and observation and referral to other specialty consultants.[78]

In *Miller*, pretrial detainees brought a legal action charging inadequate medical treatment, including an inadequate communication system between inmates and correctional officers and their failure to communicate with the medical staff.[79] Their claim also pointed out that no medical staff coverage existed between 11 PM and 7 AM during the week and between 4 PM and 7 AM on the weekends. In addition none of the following services were available to the detainees: x-rays, clinical laboratories, convalescent or holding beds, special diets, physical therapy, immunizations, special cells for the mentally ill, physical examinations, preventive medical care, psychiatrist or psychologist. The prison facility had no formal arrangement with a hospital for emergency services. The court ordered that the facility hire additional personnel, including nurses, and that a formal contractual agreement be made with a nearby hospital for emergency services.

ENVIRONMENT AND PHYSICAL PLANT

Most prisons were built in the late 1800s. Outdated equipment, inadequate space, lighting, heating and air conditioning systems, and other environmental conditions plague correctional institutions. The ANA standards define a role for the nurse in this area. The nurse is to monitor basic sanitation; food processing and handling; safety; waste disposal; quality of air, water, and food; and other environmental factors that influence the spread of communicable disease within the facility.[80] The nurse works with others in performing inspections of the facility. Specific licensing regulations exist within each jurisdiction which are used as minimal standards to be met in this area.

Often a prison facility may try to defend its situation by claiming that the services and facilities are in their current state because of the legislature's lack of support and shortage of funds. In *Gates*, the shortage of funds argument was not successful. The court held that shortage of funds is not a justification for continuing to deny citizens their constitutional rights.[81] In another case the court held that humane considerations and constitutional requirements are not to be measured or limited by dollar considerations.[82]

USE OF RESTRAINTS, ISOLATION, AND SEGREGATION

Retraints, isolation, and segregation are methods employed by corrections officers and administrators for disciplinary purposes. Care and observation of inmates housed in segregation cells is an area where the nurse may find it necessary to vigorously distinguish between health and security functions. The ANA standards offer the advice that the nurse assume responsibility for reporting harmful or inappropriate behavior on the part of others.[83]

While no cases specifically address a nurse's liability in the use of these disciplinary procedures, many cases have been brought by inmates for inhumane conditions during punishment. For example, in *Davis,* a pretrial detainee was placed in a punishment cell three times for a total of 16 days.[84] It was a bare, concrete cell with more than six prisoners in it. It was 6 by 10 feet in size, with no mattresses, blankets, pillows, or heat; with a hole in the floor with an outside flush for a toilet, no personal hygiene items, and no wash basin or running water. The court defined this as cruel and unusual punishment, stating that ''abuses, degradation and denials of basic amenities of life cannot be tolerated within any lawful confinement.''[85]

SUICIDE AND SUBSTANCE ABUSE

Recognizing that suicide and substance abuse are an overwhelming concern to health care providers working in correctional institutions, the ANA's standards place an obligation upon the nurse to work toward prevention of suicide and rehabilitation of substance abusers. The nurse is to initiate casefinding techniques to identify those at risk for suicide and for those in need of detoxification and treatment of drug or alcohol abuse.[86]

Under some situations the nurse may be liable, as are psychiatric nurses, for failure to prevent suicide, failure to recognize signs and symptoms of it, and failure to institute emergency psychiatric care and crisis intervention. Nurses' legal accountability would be similar to those presented in Chapter 8 on psychiatric nursing practice.

HEALTH COUNSELING AND TEACHING

Preventive health care services, especially health teaching, is urged in the ANA standards. The standards specify that the correctional facility shall have a health education plan consistent with the needs of the population.[87] As in other areas of nursing practice, the correctional health nurse would be responsible for imparting appropriate and accurate information and recognizing situations in which the information may cause harm or inflict emotional distress. As in every area of practice, collaborating with others and maintaining current and up-to-date information is an important responsibility.

Standards of care

This chapter has referred most often to the ANA and ABA standards for correctional facilities. The ANA standards provide an excellent focus on the expectations and legal responsibilities of the nurse working in a correctional facility. The ABA standards focus on the rights of the inmate and the responsibilities of the correctional facility and its administration, including health care providers.

The many other standards available to the practitioner of health care in prisons or jails as guidelines and requirements to assess their prison health system are listed in the box on p. 264. There is also the American Association of Correctional Health which offers publications and conferences in the specialty practice area. In addition journals in this area include:

1. CAPITOL UNIVERSITY LAW REVIEW, a journal of corrections and institutional control
2. JOURNAL OF PRISON HEALTH, MEDICINE, LAW, CORRECTIONS AND ETHICS
3. NEW ENGLAND JOURNAL ON CRIMINAL AND CIVIL CONFINEMENT, formerly the NEW ENGLAND JOURNAL ON PRISON LAW

Not yet finalized is the draft of the ABA's criminal justice mental health standards. Part X of the standards discusses mentally ill and mentally retarded prisoners. They deal both with voluntary and involuntary transfers of prisoners from correctional to mental health or mental retardation facilities and their return from such facilities to correctional institutions. The general rights of transferred or committed prisoners, as well as the rights of prisoners to refuse treatment, are addressed. The standards provide that prisoners committed to mental health or mental retardation centers must be released when the sentence of incarceration expires unless such prisoners may then be committed under the jurisdiction's general civil commitment statutes.

State corrections laws also establish standards.[88] The state department of corrections is responsible for establishing rules for administrative practice and custodial and rehabilitation methods in accordance with recognized corrections standards, some of which have been discussed at some length in this chapter. There are state laws and regulations relating to discharge, diagnosis, classification of inmates, treatment, vocational and academic education, research and statistics, training, and development of services and programs.[89]

In Maryland, however, funds may not be expended for implementation of standards except as provided for in the state's budget.[90] This is true in other states. Approved state regulations in Maryland include standards on personnel, training, administration, management, planning and coordination, research and evaluation, physical plant, management of inmates, rules and discipline, mail and visiting, reception and orientation, property control, work programs, education and vocational training, library, religious services and observation, recreation, counseling, release preparation, and volunteers.[91]

Recommendations and trends

The cases discussed and the standards outlined in this chapter have described the legal aspects of a nurse's practice in a correctional facility. It is a complicated area of practice, surrounded by many nontraditional influences and considerations. Recognizing a basic conflict between the mission, philosophy, and roles of health providers and the mission, philosophy, and roles of personnel in corrections, the ANA has carefully guided the nurse practicing in this area to be nonjudgmental and nondiscriminatory.[92] It is in this same standard that the ANA has indicated that the nurse is responsible for reporting harmful or inappropriate behavior on the part of others. Further, even though the practice environment is frequently negative, the nurse is advised to avoid pressures to compromise ethical commitments to the inmate and to the profession of nursing and to resist assuming custody functions that compromise the nurse's role in providing effective health care to the inmate.[93]

Community interest and support can make a tremendous difference in the type and amount of health care available to the incarcerated. Not much attention is paid to the health care needs of the incarcerated. The nursing community has generally overlooked this area of prac-

SELECTED STANDARDS OF CARE APPLICABLE TO CORRECTIONAL FACILITIES

From the American Bar Association

STANDARDS OF CRIMINAL JUSTICE (1983)
DRAFT CRIMINAL JUSTICE MENTAL HEALTH STANDARDS (1983)

From the American Correctional Association

STANDARDS FOR ADULT CORRECTIONAL INSTITUTIONS (2d ed. 1981)
ADULT COMMUNITY RESIDENTIAL SERVICES (2d ed. 1981)
ADULT LOCAL DETENTION FACILITIES (2d ed. 1981)
ADULT PAROLE AUTHORITIES (2d ed. 1981)
ADULT PROBATION AND PAROLE FIELD SERVICES (2d ed. 1981)
THE ADMINISTRATION OF CORRECTIONAL AGENCIES (2d ed. 1981)
JUVENILE COMMUNITY RESIDENTIAL FACILITIES (2d ed. 1983)
JUVENILE DETENTION FACILITIES (2d ed. 1983)
JUVENILE PROBATION AND AFTERCARE SERVICES (2d ed. 1983)
JUVENILE TRAINING SCHOOLS (2d ed. 1983)

From the American Law Institute

MODEL PENAL CODE—PART III ON TREATMENT AND CORRECTION (1962)

From the American Medical Association

STANDARDS FOR HEALTH SERVICES IN JAILS (1976)
STANDARDS FOR HEALTH SERVICES IN PRISONS (1979)

From the American Nurses' Association

STANDARDS FOR NURSING PRACTICE IN CORRECTIONAL FACILITIES (1985)
CODE FOR NURSES WITH INTERPRETIVE STATEMENTS (1976, 1985)

From the American Public Health Association

STANDARDS FOR HEALTH SERVICES IN CORRECTIONAL INSTITUTIONS (1976, 1986)

From the International Council of Nurses

ROLE OF THE NURSE IN THE CARE OF DETAINEES AND PRISONERS (1975)

From the Federal Government

FEDERAL STANDARDS FOR PRISONS AND JAILS (1979)

From the National Advisory Commission on Criminal Justice Standards and Goals

REPORT ON CORRECTIONS (1973)

From the National Institute of Corrections

ACCREDITATION FOR CORRECTIONS (current ed.)

From the National Sheriffs Association

STANDARDS FOR INMATES' LEGAL RIGHTS (1974)
JAIL ADMINISTRATION (current ed.)
JAIL PROGRAMS (current ed.)
JAIL SECURITY, CLASSIFICATION, AND DISCIPLINE (current ed.)

From the New York State Nurses' Association

STANDARDS FOR NURSING SERVICES IN THE PRISON HEALTH SYSTEM, CORRECTIONAL FACILITIES, AND JAILS (1980)

From the United Nations

STANDARD MINIMUM RULES FOR THE TREATMENT OF PRISONERS AND RELATED RECOMMENDATIONS (1958)

tice. Because of the conditions of prisons in this country, nurses are obligated to learn more about nursing services to prisoners, provide student experiences, and encourage and upgrade the nursing skills and tools available to those who work in the corrections system.

The future of prison health care litigation remains in question, however. Political, economic, and societal trends probably will mean a decrease in successful litigation. There are some legal issues though that may be brought in the future. For example, a prisoner's right to access medical care outside the prison at the inmate's own expense is an issue likely to be litigated more in the future. Other issues may involve the rights of infants born in prison and issues of foster care, abortion, adoption, and placement of women prisoner's children.

While many would argue that there is still a long way to go, the prison reform movement has made significant inroads into improvements in health care for prisoners. Little nursing research has focused on the nurse's participation in and/or contribution to the bad or good in the system. However, lawsuits have acted as change agents and have forced changes in nursing practice in correctional facilities.

Endnotes

1. L. NOVICK AND M. AL-IBRAHIM, HEALTH PROBLEMS IN THE PRISON SETTING (1977).
2. N.Y. Times, September 16, 1985, at B8, col. 1.
3. BUREAU OF JUSTICE STATISTICS, U.S. DEPT. OF JUSTICE, REPORT TO THE NATION ON CRIME AND JUSTICE: THE DATA (1983) (hereinafter cited as *Report*).
4. *Id.*
5. Forer, *Enforcement of standards is necessary to protect the welfare of incarcerated individuals* 68 A.B.A.J. 563 (May 1982).
6. AMERICAN NURSES' ASSOCIATION, STANDARDS OF NURSING PRACTICE IN CORRECTIONAL FACILITIES (1985) (hereinafter cited as *ANA Standards*).
7. *But see,* NEW YORK STATE NURSES' ASSOCIATION, STANDARDS FOR NURSING SERVICES IN THE PRISON HEALTH SYSTEM (CORRECTIONAL FACILITIES AND JAILS) (1980) developed 5 years earlier than national standards.
8. *ANA Standards, supra* note 6, at 3.
9. AMERICAN NURSES' ASSOCIATION, CODE FOR NURSES WITH INTERPRETIVE STATEMENTS (1985).
10. Rodo-Edwards, and Alexander-Rodriguez, *Nursing Assessment in Prison: One Case Study,* 1 J. PRIS. HEALTH 130 (Fall-Winter 1981).
11. *See, e.g.,* N.Y. Times, September 17, 1985, at A17, col 1, an article entitled, *Experts Foresee Adverse Effects from Private Control of Prisons.*
12. *Report, supra* note 3, at 79.
13. Chaisson, *Correctional Health Care—Beyond the Barriers* 82 A.J.N. 737 (April 1982).
14. *ANA Standards, supra* note 6, at 3.
15. AMERICAN BAR ASSOCIATION, STANDARDS OF CRIMINAL JUSTICE, Standard 23-5.2 (1983) (hereinafter cited as *ABA Standards*).
16. J. PALMER, CONSTITUTIONAL RIGHTS OF PRISONERS (3rd ed. 1985).
17. van den Haag, *Rights and Obligations of Prisoners* 11 N. Eng. J. Crim. & Civ. Confin. 1 (Winter 1985).
18. *Ramos v. Lamm,* 693 F.2d 559 (10th Cir. 1980), *cert. denied,* 450 U.S. 1041 (1981).
19. *Layne v. Vizant,* 657 F.2d 468, 471 (1st Cir. 1981); *Speed v. Adams,* 502 F. Supp. 426 (E.D. Ark. 1980); *May v. Enomoto,* 633 F.2d 164 (9th Cir. 1980).
20. J. HUMPHREY, THE ADMINISTRATION OF JUSTICE, LAW ENFORCEMENT, COURTS AND CORRECTIONS 145, 156 (1981).
21. *Procunier v. Marinez,* 416 U.S. 396, 404, 405 (1974).
22. D. KELLY, CRIMINAL BEHAVIOR 479 (1980).
23. *Collins v. Schoonfield,* 344 F. Supp. 257, 278 (D. Md. 1972).
24. J. PALMER, CONSTITUTIONAL RIGHTS OF PRISONERS (3rd ed. 1985).
25. *ABA Standards, supra* note 15, at Standard 23-5.1.
26. *ABA Standards, supra* note 15, at Standard 23-5.3 (a).
27. *ABA Standards, supra* note 15, at Standard 23-5.3 (b) and (c).
28. *ABA Standards, supra* note 15, at Standard 23-5.7.
29. *Apgar v. Beauter,* 347 N.Y.S.2d 872 (1973) (interpretation of state statute). *But see, Wainwright v. Moore,* 374 So. 2d 586 (Fla. App. 1979) (where state statute does not grant to incarcerated mother sole and exclusive prerogative to retain newborn child during first 18 months of child's life.) *See also* state statutes, CONN. GEN. STAT. ANN. §18-69, 69a (West Supp. 1985) (infants of inmates are not to be maintained at institution beyond planning for placement 60 days); MD. ANN. CODE art. 27, §699 (1982).
30. *ABA Standards, supra* note 15 at Standard 23-5.5; *See also,* the AMERICAN CORRECTIONS ASSOCIATION, STANDARDS FOR ADULT CORRECTIONAL INSTITUTIONS 2-4313 (2d ed. 1981); ACA, STANDARDS FOR ADULT LOCAL DETENTION FACILITIES 2-5284 (2d ed. 1981); AMERICAN PUBLIC HEALTH ASSOCIATION, STANDARDS FOR HEALTH SERVICES IN CORRECTIONAL INSTITUTIONS (1976).
31. *Runnels v. Rosendale,* 499 F.2d 733 (9th Cir. 1974) (nonconsensual surgery would violate federal constitutional rights).
32. *Commissioner of Correction v. Myers,* 399 N.E.2d 452 (Mass. 1979).
33. *Lareau v. Manson,* 651 F.2d 96, 109 (2nd Cir. 1981); *Hines v. Anderson,* 439 F. Supp. 12, 23 (D. Minn. 1977).
34. *Lang v. City of Des Moines,* 294 N.W.2d 557 (Iowa 1980).
35. *Zant v. Prevatte,* 286 S.E.2d 715 (Ga. 1982) (forced feeding not to be ordered); *White v. Narick,* 292 S.E.2d 54 (W. Va. 1982) (forced feeding proper).
36. AMERICAN CORRECTIONS ASSOCIATION, STANDARDS OF JUVENILE DETENTION FACILITIES 2-8287 (2d ed. 1983).
37. 45 C.F.R. §46.306 (1985).
38. *ABA Standards, supra* note 15, at Standard 23-5.8.
39. *ANA Standards, supra* note 6, at 22. Standard X. Ethics, Process Criteria 6 and 7.
40. ACA, STANDARDS FOR JUVENILE DETENTION FACILITIES 2-8384 (2d ed. 1983).
41. *ANA Standards, supra* note 6, at 7. Standard II, Structure Criteria 3.
42. *ABA Standards, supra* note 15, at Standard 23-5.4 (c).
43. *Robbins v. South, et al.,* 595 F. Supp. 785 (D. Mont. 1984).
44. *See U.S. v. Dawson,* 516 F.2d 796, 805 (9th Cir. 1975).
45. 429 U.S. 97 (1976).
46. U.S. CONST. Amendment VIII.
47. *Weems v. U.S.,* 217 U.S. 349 (1910).
48. 429 U.S. 97, 103, 104 (1976). *See also Spicer v. Williamson,* 132 S.E. 291, 293 (1926).
49. 42 U.S.C. §1983 (1982).
50. *Hutchings v. Corum,* 501 F. Supp. 1276 (U.S. Dist. Ct. W.D. Mo. 1980) quoting *Burks v. Teasdale,* 492 F. Supp. 650 (W.D. Mo. 1980), *Bishop v. Stoneman,* 508 F.2d 1224, 1226 (2d Cir. 1974) citing to *Todaro v. Ward,* 565 F.2d 48, 52 (2d Cir. 1977).
51. *Procunier v. Navarette,* 98 S. Ct. 855 (1978).
52. *Estelle v. Gamble,* 429 U.S. 97, 107 (1976) text accompanying n.15. *Plummer v. U.S.,* 508 F.2d 72 (3rd Cir. 1978) invoked the Federal Tort Claims Act in an instance of negligent exposure to tuberculosis.
53. *Hampton v. Holmesburg Prison Officials,* 546 F.2d 1077 (3rd Cir. 1976).
54. *Knecht v. Gillman,* 488 F.2d 1136 (8th Cir. 1973).
55. *Knecht v. Gillman,* 488 F.2d 1136 (8th Cir. 1973); *Nelson v. Heyne,* 491 F.2d 352 (7th Cir. 1974); *Lightfoot v. Walker,* 486 F. Supp. 504 (D. Ill. 1980); *Palmigiano v. Garrahy,* 443 F. Supp. 956 (D. R.I. 1977), *aff'd,* 616 F.2d 598; *Inmates v. Pierce,* 442

F. Supp. 1368 (W.D. Pa. 1978); *Grubbs v. Bradley,* 552 F. Supp. 1052 (M.D. Tenn. 1982); *Pena v. New York State Div. for Youth,* 419 F. Supp. 203 (S.D. N.Y. 1976).
56. *Nelson v. Heyne,* 491 F.2d 352 (7th Cir. 1974).
57. *Id. Knecht v. Gillman,* 488 F.2d 1136 (8th Cir. 1973); *Lightfoot v. Walker,* 486 F. Supp. 504 (S.D. Ill. 1980).
58. *Lightfoot v. Walker,* 486 F. Supp. 504 (S.D. Ill. 1980).
59. *Id. Palmigiano v. Garrahy,* 443 F. Supp. 956 (D. R.I. 1977).
60. *Burks v. Teasdale,* 492 F. Supp. 650 (W.D. Mo. 1980).
61. *Lightfoot v. Walker,* 486 F. Supp. 504 (S.D. Ill. 1980).
62. *Id. But see, Burks v. Teasdale,* 492 F. Supp. 650 (W.D. Mo. 1980) (nurse inmates were used appropriately to monitor patients in an intensive care unit).
63. *Palmigiano v. Garrahy,* 443 F. Supp. 956 (D. R.I. 1977).
64. *Id.*
65. *Knecht v. Gillman,* 488 F.2d 1136 (8th Cir. 1973); *Nelson v. Heyne,* 491 F.2d 352 (7th Cir. 1974); *Inmates v. Pierce,* 442 F. Supp. 1368 (W.D. Pa. 1078); *Pena v. New York State Div. for Youth,* 419 F. Supp. 203 (S.D. N.Y. 1976).
66. *Todaro v. Ward,* 431 F. Supp. 1129 (S.D. N.Y. 1977).
67. *Id.*
68. *Bennett v. Reed,* 534 F. Supp. 83, 87 (E.D. N.C. 1981), *affd.,* 676 F.2d 690; *Burks v. Teasdale,* 492 F. Supp. 650 (W.D. Mo. 1980).
69. *Gates v. Collier,* 501 F.2d 1291 (5th Cir. 1974).
70. *ANA Standards, supra* note 6, at 7. Standard I., Structure Criteria 11.
71. *ANA Standards, supra* note 6, at 14. Standard V-E, Process Criteria 1.
72. *ANA Standards, supra* note 6, at 14. Standard V-E, Structure Criteria 2.
73. *ABA Standards, supra* note 15, at Standard 23-55.6.
74. *Jackson v. Hendrick,* 321 A.2d 603 (Pa. 1974).
75. Forer, *Enforcement of standards is necessary to protect the welfare of incarcerated individuals,* 68 A.B.A. J. 563 (May 1982).
76. *ANA Standards, supra* note 6, at Standard V-G; *ABA Standards, supra* note 15, at Standard 23-5.2.
77. *Hutchings v. Corum,* 501 F. Supp. 1276 (W.D. Mo. 1980).
78. *ANA Standards, supra* note 6, at 9. Standard IV., Structure Criteria 2.
79. *Miller v. Carson,* 401 F. Supp. 835 (M.D. Fla. 1975), *affd.,* 563 F.2d 741.
80. *ANA Standards, supra* note 6, at 17. Standard V-H.
81. *Gates v. Collier,* 501 F.2d 1291, 1319, 1320 (5th Cir. 1974).
82. *Rozecki v. Gaughan,* 459 F.2d 6, 8 (1st Cir. 1972).
83. *ANA Standards, supra* note 6, at 21. Standard IX. Process Criteria 5.
84. *Davis v. Smith, et al.,* 638 F.2d 66 (8th Cir. 1981).
85. *Id.*
86. *ANA Standards, supra* note 6, at Standard V-B, V-D, V-F.
87. *ANA Standards, supra* note 6, at 11. Standard V-A.
88. *See, e.g.,* MD. ANN. CODE art. 41 and 27 (1982 & Supp. 1985); CONN. GEN. STAT. ANN. §18 (1975 & Supp. 1985)
89. CONN. GEN. STAT. ANN. §18-81 (1975).
90. MD. ANN. CODE art. 27, §704 (1982).
91. MD. ANN. CODE art. 41, §70C(b)(8) (1982).
92. *ANA Standards, supra* note 6, at 21. Standard IX, Rationale and Outcome Criteria 1.
93. *ANA Standards, supra* note 6, at 22. Standard X, Rationale, Process Criteria 4.

Additional Readings

E. BECKMAN, CRIMINAL JUSTICE DICTIONARY (2d ed. 1983).

E. BRECHER and P.D. PENNA, HEALTH CARE IN CORRECTIONAL INSTITUTIONS (1975).

R. CLARK, CRIME IN AMERICA (1971).

F. ELLISTON AND N. BOWIE, ETHICS, PUBLIC POLICY AND CRIMINAL JUSTICE (1982).

D. GLASER, HANDBOOK OF CRIMINOLOGY (1974).

S. GOLDSMITH, PRISON HEALTH: TRAVESTY OF JUSTICE (1975).

Holly, *Jail Matron* 72 A.J.N., 1621 (September 1972).

J. HUMPHREY, THE ADMINISTRATION OF JUSTICE: LAW ENFORCEMENT, COURTS AND CORRECTIONS (1981).

Kennedy, *Health Care in Prison: A View from Inside* 75 A.J.N., 417 (March 1975).

S. KRANTZ, THE LAW OF CORRECTIONS AND PRISONERS' RIGHTS IN A NUTSHELL (2nd ed. 1983).

McDowell, *Health Care in Prison: Change in One City's System. Leadership at the Cell Block Level* 75 A.J.N., 423 (March 1975).

McLaren and Tappen, *The Community Nurse Goes to Jail* 22 N. O., 35 (January 1974).

McNiff, *Nursing in a Psychiatric Prison Service* 73 A.J.N., 1586 (September 1973).

Murtha, *Health Care in Prison: Change in One City's System. It Started with a Director of Nursing* 75 A.J.N., 421 (March 1975).

M. WEISZ, MODEL CORRECTIONAL RULES AND REGULATIONS (1977).

Chapter 17

Nursing care of the elderly

Cynthia E. Northrop

Rapid demographic, social, and technological changes in American society are major forces which impact nursing and health care of the elderly. While there have been significant gains in life expectancy, both at birth and at older ages, and major improvements in health status, declining fertility rates have "aged" the U.S. population.[1] Today there are more persons over age 65 than there are teenagers. Recognizing the universally accepted definition for "elderly," this chapter uses the term to mean all persons 65 years of age and over.

Probably the most significant concern is the change in physical and mental functioning of the older person. Most people do not fear growing old as much as they fear becoming chronically ill or frail. The ability of older people to remain functionally independent or to be minimally dependent on various types of assistance is the fundamental characteristic that determines the older person's quality of life. Nurses and the nursing profession are the largest group of caretakers which care for the elderly in a variety of settings. The type and quality of nursing care will decide the quality of life for the older person.

The major chronic conditions affecting the elderly include dementia, urinary incontinence, hearing and visual impairment, osteoporosis, and osteoarthritis, in addition to heart disease, stroke, cancer, and diabetes.[2] Dementia, including Alzheimer's disease and other dementing illnesses, is becoming the overwhelming health problem of the elderly. All of these conditions may lead the nurse and older person to questions of clinical, legal, ethical, and social importance. It is the goal of this chapter to focus upon the unique legal concerns of nurses who work with the elderly. In doing this, laws which relate to older persons in general will also be addressed.

Following a description of nursing practice and the elderly, several issues will serve to organize this chapter. Those issues include decision making and the elderly, protective services and elder abuse, rights of the institutionalized elderly, and governmental financing. Each will be discussed, highlighting nursing's legal responsibilities as defined by statutes and case law.

Definition of nursing care

The American Nurses' Association has defined gerontological nursing as an area of practice which "is concerned with assessment of the health needs of older adults, planning and implementing health care to meet these needs and evaluating the effectiveness of such care."[3] Seven standards are set out in the document defining nursing practice, as well as a listing of the primary factors which are specific to nursing care of older persons. Both are listed in the box on p. 268.

Prepared in many ways, including advanced levels, nurses may be generalists or may be gerontological nurse practitioners and clinical nurse specialists. Nursing care of the elderly happens in a variety of settings. The majority of the population aged 65 and over lives in the general community; only 5% lives in any kind of institution.[4] Settings in which nurses deliver care to the elderly vary by level of care required for the older person.

STANDARDS OF GERONTOLOGICAL NURSING PRACTICE AND PRIMARY FACTORS SPECIFIC TO NURSING OF OLDER PERSONS*

Standard I

Data are systematically and continuously collected about the health status of the older adult. The data are accessible, communicated and recorded.

Standard II

Nursing Diagnoses are derived from the identified normal responses of the individual to aging and the data collected about the health status of the older adult.

Standard III

A plan of nursing care is developed in conjunction with the older adult and/or significant others that includes goals derived from the nursing diagnosis.

Standard IV

The plan of nursing care includes priorities and prescribed nursing approaches and measures to achieve the goals derived from the nursing diagnosis.

Standard V

The plan of care is implemented, using appropriate nursing actions.

Standard VI

The older adult and/or significant other(s) participate in determining the progress attained in the achievement of established goals.

Standard VII

The older adult and/or significant other(s) participate in the ongoing process of assessment, the setting of new goals, the reordering of priorities, the revision of plans for nursing care, and the initiation of new nursing actions.

Primary Factors

1. Ramifications of the aging process
2. Different rates at which people age
3. Multiplicity and collectiveness of an older person's losses
4. Grief work necessary in accepting losses
5. Interrelationship between the social, economic, psychological and biological factors
6. Frequently atypical response of the aged to disease and to the treatment of disease
7. Accumulated disabling effects of multiple chronic illnesses and/or degenerative processes
8. Cultural values associated with aging and social attitudes toward the older adult

*Adapted from AMERICAN NURSES' ASSOCIATION, STANDARDS OF GERONTOLOGICAL NURSING PRACTICE (1976).

For example, types of settings are often categorized by skilled nursing facility (SNF), intermediate care facility (ICF), health related facility (HRF), and home health programs.

Extended care is defined as care which involves 24-hour-a-day skilled nursing services and rehabilitative care, with an emphasis on medical supervision and therapy. Care in these settings is most often delivered to those who are more critically ill, terminally ill, or in need of convalescence. Comprehensive care facilities provide services to persons who need regular nursing assistance and help with daily living activities, but who can take some care of themselves and do not need continuous 24-hour nursing care.

Nurses deliver health services to many elderly persons in their homes or upon hospitalization in general or psychiatric hospitals. For the elderly who remain in their communities a wide variety of services may exist, including housekeeping services, day care, respite care, companionship programs, sheltered housing, transportation services, and meal assistance programs. Nurses, therefore, provide services to the elderly through employment in nonprofit, voluntary, and for profit organizations; nursing homes; and associations. Nurses also own and manage businesses and provide services through independently owned gerontological nursing businesses.

Unfortunately, the history of care of the elderly, especially the institutionalized elderly in nursing homes and psychiatric facilities, is replete with instances of patient abuse, criminal and civil investigations, and lawsuits revealing tremendous problems in the care and safety of the elderly. Nursing care in particular has come under scrutiny and has been cited as responsible for the sorry conditions.[5]

Decision making and the elderly

As discussed in Chapter 5 all competent adults have the right to make their own health care decisions, including those decisions which involve consent to or refusal of or removal of life-sustaining treatments, including life-prolonging and life-saving measures. In general, state law defines competent adult as one who has reached a chronological age, such as 18 or 21 years old, depending on the state. Questions of competence to make health care decisions are frequently raised in the care of the elderly. Individuals over age 18, however, are generally presumed competent. Those under that age are presumed incompetent.

State legislatures have declared minors (those under the age of majority, usually 18 to 21 years) competent to have the capacity to consent as if an adult for certain types of health care. For example, a person can consent at age 17 to give a blood transfusion and may consent for certain services, such as pregnancy, mental health, venereal disease, drug abuse, or alcohol abuse.[6] Regardless of age, upon marriage or parenthood, the state usually deems an individual competent.

COMPETENCY

First and foremost, the elderly person, unless adjudicated legally incompetent by a court, is deemed competent to make his or her own decisions. When questions of competence arise, other decision makers, such as family members, physicians, nurses, administrators, lawyers, and courts, may become involved. As discussed below some state legislatures have passed laws indicating who may participate in the decision making for questionably incompetent individuals. It is anticipated that as a result of the rapid increase in the prevalence of dementia, particularly Alzheimer's disease, many elderly may become clinically and/or legally incompetent.

Competence to make decisions is a highly protected element of American life. A proceeding to declare a person incompetent is a very serious matter. The consequences of being declared incompetent include the most severe restraints on personal freedom and self-determination. For this reason many state legislatures have made the burden of proof in such cases a clear and convincing evidence standard, a higher standard than that required in other types of legal disputes.[7]

Because competency can be a changing and fluctuating condition and because our society views the determination of incompetency as a severe intrusion into personal autonomy and privacy rights, many health care providers have devoted extensive time and energy into assessing how competency judgments should be made. Most states have specially designated courts which handle determinations of competency. While this may create a situation in which a judge may have a good understanding of the issues presented, the judge still relies heavily on the opinion of the health care providers in arriving at a decision.

ADVANCED DIRECTIVES BY THE ELDERLY

While competent, an elderly person can indicate in advance his or her wishes regarding health care treatment. There are several ways in which a competent elderly person can make "advanced directives." They may include verbal indications through discussions with health care providers and family members about what they would want done to them under certain conditions; and indications of their wishes in written form, depending on state law, through a living will or power of attorney (general and/or durable). These are discussed in Chapter 5.

Legal implications for nurses who know of the elderly person's treatment wishes include the obligation to document and record in the patient's chart the advance directive information and to inform the physician and institution of that information. Knowledge gained in verbal discussions with the elderly patient and his or her family is also to be documented in the patient's chart, as well as discussed with the treatment team. Under some situations the nurse may educate the patient about advanced directives and link the patient to legal counsel if the patient wishes to exercise or issue an advanced directive.

If the elderly person has granted a power of attorney to someone or if the court has appointed a guardian or conservator for the elderly person, the extent of the grant of appointment should be determined. For example, often a court may appoint a guardian only for limited purposes, such as management of property. Under this example, health care decisions are not considered part of the guardian's responsibilities. An appointment of guardianship over the person indicates that the guardian may make health care decisions.

Written advanced directives should be placed in the patient's chart and reviewed by the nurse. Just as is true of any part of the patient's chart, the nurse is responsible for knowing the content and implications of the elderly patient's advanced directive. Prior to a crisis the process of how the advanced directive will be implemented and observed should be clarified among all concerned, including, of course, the elderly person and legal counsel.

Where the competency of an elderly person is questioned health care decisions can be made through a shared decision-making process. The elderly patient should participate in decision making to the fullest extent possible. Family, significant others, and the health care team should work with the elderly person. When the elderly person's competence diminishes to the point that he or she can no longer participate or indicate treatment wishes, guardianship proceedings or committment proceedings may be instituted by any of the parties, particularly where disagreements exist between the elderly person, health care team, institution or agency, and family and where substituted consent may not be available, according to some state statutes. For further information about involuntary committment and the mentally ill person the reader should review Chapter 8.

In guardianship proceedings many nurses have been involved in the determination of the judgment that should be substituted for the elderly person and what care is in the best interest of the elderly person. Health care providers, especially nurses because they most often care for the elderly, are an important source for identifying older individuals who lack functional capacity to handle their own affairs and are in need of guardians. Formal guardianship proceedings will often involve presentation to the court of the nurse's assessment of the elderly person and nursing testimony as to condition, care, and safety of the elderly person. Nurses experienced in care of the elderly, including gerontological nurse specialists or practitioners may be called as expert witnesses in such proceedings.

In any guardianship proceeding the court is bound by the state legislation which indicates the grounds and burden of proof necessary before a person is declared incompetent and a guardian can be appointed. Often the court must determine from clear and convincing evidence that a person lacks sufficient understanding or capacity to make or communicate responsible decisions concerning his or her person, including provisions for health care, food, clothing, or shelter, because of any mental disability, senility, disease, or alcohol or drug addiction. The court may be required to review and conclude that less restrictive forms of intervention are not available prior to determining the question of competence.[8]

SUBSTITUTED CONSENT FOR DISABLED ELDERLY

Many state legislatures have acted recently, not only in the area of advanced directives which were discussed above but also in the area of identifying disabled persons who lack sufficient understanding or capacity to make or communicate responsible decisions on health care and proper ways of handling situations. For example, in Maryland statutes indicate that treatment without consent is permissible if it is an emergency. Substituted consent may be used in the absence of a durable power of attorney or in the absence of a judicially appointed guardian. Those identified in the statute as ones who may provide substituted consent in an order of priority include a spouse, an adult child, a parent, an adult sibling, a grandparent, and an adult grandchild.

The substituted consent may only be given if two physicians, after attempting to consult with the disabled individual, certify in writing that clear and convincing evidence exists that the disabled individual is incapable of making a responsible decision regarding the proposed health care.

According to one state law, substituted consent may not be used in four situations:

1. If the proposed health care is for an abortion; sterilization; or observation, diagnosis, treatment, or hospitalization for a mental disorder
2. If the health care provider is aware that the person for whom the health care is proposed has expressed disagreement with the decision to provide health care (including if the health care provider knows that the treatment is against the religious belief of the disabled person)
3. If the health care provider knows that the individual giving substituted consent is not acting in a reasonable and prudent manner
4. If the health care provider has been informed in writing that one or more of the persons who may give substituted consent is opposed to the performance of the treatment.[9]

The definition of health care provider includes registered nurses and licensed practical nurses, making nurses legally responsible for their part in the decision making and care issues for the disabled elderly. If any of the four above situations occur, then court intervention is often indicated.

THE *CONROY* CASE

A recent case, *In the Matter of Claire C. Conroy*, involved the issue of circumstances under which life-sustaining treament may be withdrawn or withheld from an incompetent, institutionalized, elderly nursing home patient with severe and permanent mental and physical impairments and a limited life expectancy.[10] The case dealt with the request of a guardian to remove artificial feeding, specifically a nasogastric feeding tube (NG tube), the primary mode for nutrients, from his aunt Claire Conroy. Aged 84, Conroy was a bedridden woman who was unable to move from a semifetal position and suffered from organic brain syndrome, arteriosclerotic heart disease, diabetes, and hypertension. She was not brain dead, comatose, or in a chronic vegetative state. She was, however, severely demented, unable to respond to verbal stimuli, confused, and unaware and had been adjudicated incompetent.

Conroy was under the care of a physician and registered nurse (who was also the nursing home administrator). She was admitted to a 30-bed nursing home by her nephew, who was her guardian. During a hospitalization for elevated temperature and dehydration, her eating became inadequate, and an NG tube was inserted. She was discharged from the hospital back to the nursing home with the NG tube in place. Attempts were made to feed her through the mouth, but these failed to supply adequate amounts of food because she had extreme difficulty swallowing.

During hospitalization, the diagnostic evaluation showed that Conroy had necrotic gangrenous ulcers of the left foot. While the surgeon recommended that the leg be amputated to save her life, Conroy's guardian refused to consent to the surgery because he said he was confident that she would not have wanted it.

The trial court granted the guardian permission to remove the tube. The guardian *ad litem* (appointed for litigation who opposed the guardian's petition) appealed the case to the higher court, which reversed the lower court's decision. The Supreme Court of New Jersey reviewed all trial testimony and evidence, including that of the physician, nurse, and expert medical witness. Both Conroy's physician and nurse testified that the tube should not be removed. The nurse further testified that in her view the NG tube was not an extraordinary treatment.[11] Later in its opinion the court rejected the classification of treatments as ordinary (common and usual) or extraordinary (optional, elaborate, or heroic) measures because the terms "assume too many conflicting meanings to remain useful"[12] and because a person may refuse any treatment, regardless of type or classification.

The court's analysis included a review of the unique facts of this patient's life. She had lived a cloistered life, was a Roman Catholic, had never married, and had few friends and only one surviving blood relative, her nephew and guardian. This relationship was examined, and only good intentions and no real conflicts of interest existed between them. The guardian testified that his aunt avoided physicians, had rarely seen one, and had relied upon the nephew's wife, a registered nurse, for health care needs. One time, he testified, his wife took his aunt to the emergency room where Conroy refused to sign in and indicated, if admitted, she would immediately sign herself out.

The law which the court applied to these facts included the constitutional right to privacy, right to informed consent, and right to refuse treatment, even life-sustaining treatment. Noting that the right to refuse treatment is not absolute, the court explored each of the state's interests—preserving life, preventing suicide, safeguarding the medical profession's integrity, and protecting innocent third parties—where it found a person's right to refuse treatment would not be recognized.

The court concluded that Conroy, if competent to make the decision and if resolute in her determination, could have chosen to have the NG tube withdrawn.[13] The court also urged the state legislature to formulate clear standards. In light of the rights and concerns the court had reviewed, it outlined three standards or tests to apply in similar patient care situations. Each of these will be discussed.

Subjective Test. Life-sustaining treatment may be withheld or withdrawn from an incompetent patient when it is clear that the particular patient would have refused treatment under the circumstances.[14]

Under this test the question is what the particular patient would have done if able to choose for himself or herself. The wishes of the patient may have been expressed through an oral directive, a living will, a durable power of attorney, or appointment of proxy. It might also take the form of reactions that the patient voiced regarding medication, treatment, or administration of treatment to others or through religious beliefs and tenets. The court urged that the matter be dealt with in advance in a thoughtful and explicit manner.

The court held that medical evidence including the patient's condition, treatment, and prognosis in addition to the evidence of the patient's wishes, is an essential prerequisite to decision making under this standard.[15] The court specifically limited the application of this standard to like situations where the patient "fits the Conroy pattern."[16] That pattern includes elderly, incompetent nursing home resident with physical and mental impairments and a life expectancy of a year or less. Information suggested by the court to be included was:

1. Present level of physical, sensory, emotional, and cognitive functioning
2. Degree of physical pain resulting from the condition

Best Interest Tests. The court stated that life-sustaining treatment may also be withheld or withdrawn from a patient in Conroy's situation if either of two "best interests" tests were met. The court called these two tests "limited-objective" or "pure-objective" tests.

Limited-Objective Test. Under this test the court stated that life-sustaining treatment may be withdrawn or withheld when there is some trustworthy evidence that the patient would have refused the treatment and where the decision maker is satisfied from the medical evidence that it is clear that the burdens (pain and suffering) of the patient's continued life with treatment outweigh the benefits of that life for him or her.[17]

Pure-Objective Test. This test provides that life-sustaining treatment may be withdrawn from a formerly competent person like Conroy when the net burdens of the patient's life with treatment clearly and markedly outweigh the benefits that the patient derives from life and when the recurring, unavoidable, and severe pain of the patient's life with treatment are such that the effect of administering life-sustaining treatment would be inhumane.[18]

Court's Focus on Nursing. The court indicated that evidence concerning the nursing home patient's wishes, advanced directives, and condition should be furnished by the attending physician *and nurses*.[19] In many ways this is the first time such judicial recognition has been given to nursing. The court recognized that nursing was a component in decisions regarding care for the elderly nursing home patient. In addition, it is important to note that testimony from the nurse involved in the patient's care was important to the court.

Nursing care was reviewed by the court when it examined the trial transcript. Noting that no exploration of the discomfort and risks that attend nasogastric feedings was done,[20] the court commented that there was a casual mention by the nurse/administrator of the need to restrain the patient to prevent the removal of the tube but that this was not followed by an assessment of the detrimental impact, if any, of those restraints.

The court further commented that alternative modalities, including gastrostomies, intravenous feeding, subcutaneous or intramuscular hydration, or some combination, were not investigated. The court indicated that were Conroy still alive, the guardian would have been required to explore these issues prior to reaching any decision.

Therefore, the role for nurses in similar cases would include assessment of the patient's wishes and condition, documentation and court testimony, if applicable, and participation in the decision-making process.

GUIDELINES FOR PARTICULAR NURSING CARE ISSUES

Care decisions most frequently cited as problematical by nurses working with the institutionalized elderly or sometimes with elderly in their homes include the following:

1. Do not resuscitate orders (DNR) or other orders relating to respiratory assistance
2. Do not hospitalize orders
3. Orders to remove food and fluids
4. Supportive care only orders, including orders dealing with catheters, dialysis, transfusions, and laboratory and x-ray tests
5. Do not medicate orders, including antibiotics, analgesics, laxatives, and narcotics.

Given the general legal rule that competent adults may consent to or refuse health care and given case law and state legislation which outline patient rights, advanced directives, guardianship, and conservatorship proceedings and which indicate appropriate uses of substituted consent, it is appropriate nursing practice to accept such orders if the following conditions are met:

1. Orders are made by the attending physician of that patient based upon thorough collaboration and discussion among the health care team, elderly, and family.
2. There is agreement among all parties.
3. The orders are indicated by the diagnosis, prognosis, and treatment plan of that patient.
4. Such medical orders are consistent with agency policy and federal and state legislation, including the nurse practice act.

Some medical societies have issued guidelines on no-code orders.[21] These guidelines indicate that when disagreement exists among patient, family, and physician a DNR order should not be written.

Case law does exist which indicates that a no-code order is an appropriate medical order.[22] In addition nurses' failure to institute a "Dr. Quickstep" (emergency cardiopulmonary resuscitation procedure) was reviewed in a case which concluded that the nurses had acted appropriately and were not negligent.[23] Although this case did not involve a situation where a physician had written a no-code order and it occurred in an acute care setting, the court reviewed written hospital policy and the actions of the nurses and was convinced that there was no need to call a code under the circumstances. This case points to one way in which the nursing standard of care is measured, through agency policy and procedure manuals.

Adult protective services and elder abuse statutes

Domestic violence can involve anyone, including a spouse, child, or elderly person. Generally, elder abuse is defined as the frequent victimization of older persons within the community, in their own or someone else's home, by members of their family or surrogate family.[24] The form of abuse includes mistreatment, battering, physical violence, psychological abuse, denial of basic human needs, violation of civil rights, medical neglect, financial exploitation, misuse and abuse of drugs, unsanitary environment, and destruction of personal property or pets.[25]

The abuse of the elderly demands a multidisciplinary approach. Nurses are involved in the entire spectrum of the issue, from identifying members of the community who are victims of abuse, being educated about signs and symptoms of elder abuse, giving care to victims and abusers, and becoming involved in designing and implementing community solutions, including state legislation for the problem.

States have taken different approaches to the problem of elder abuse. Some have statutes specific to elder abuse, with an age requirement and mandated reporting by health professionals. The first states to pass such elder abuse statutes were Connecticut, Florida, Missouri, Oklahoma, and Vermont.[26]

A second approach by states is to pass a general adult abuse statute which is not limited by an age requirement.[27] A third possibility is that a state might have an adult protective service statute.[28] These may or may not have mandated reporting by health professionals.

Each of these types of statutes may be available for the protection of the elderly in their state. For example, the Connecticut elder abuse reporting statute requires a registered nurse or licensed practical nurse to report the name and address of the elderly person; information about the abuse, neglect, exploitation, or abandonment; and any other helpful information. The nurse's decision to report must be based upon reasonable cause to suspect or believe that the elderly person has been abused. The report must be made within 5 days to the commissioner on aging in the state.[29]

These laws address the abuse of the elderly in the community, not the elderly in institutions. Separate state statutes cover abused patients in nursing homes and are discussed below. Private duty and office nurses in all clinical areas, including gerontology, psychiatry, community health, home care, and out-patient or ambulatory care, can be instrumental in the recognition, care, and treatment of abused elderly, including reporting to authorities and giving testimony in court.

Rights of the elderly in long-term care facilities

Most states have statutes which provide a listing of rights for the nursing home resident. Under federal law, specifically the Medicare regulations, patient rights are outlined and are enforceable.[30] Generally, state and federal laws deal with consent, refusing treatment, withholding and withdrawing treatment, respect and dignity, privacy, and the right to be free from abuse. Nursing home federal regulations are also discussed in Chapter 22. The rights of nursing home residents required by federal regulations are listed on p. 274.

In addition to specific state statutes which indicate nursing home patients' rights, specific statutes also prohibit abuse of nursing home patients. Under state law abuse is defined, reporting mandated, an investigation required, usually by the State Office on Aging, the ombudsman program, involving law enforcement and state licensing personnel. One who reports in good faith is not civilly liable for making the report; participating in the investigation or judicial proceeding; or participating in the transfer, suspension, or termination of the employment of any individual who is believed to have abused or aided in abusing a resident.[31]

Abuse in a nursing home facility cannot be tolerated. Any nontherapeutic infliction of physical pain or injury or any persistent course of conduct intended to produce or resulting in mental or emotional distress should be reported.[32] In some instances not only may the injured elderly person bring civil suit for violation of civil rights and statutorily provided rights and actions based upon breach of contract and negligence, but also criminal prosecution may ensue. For example, in a recent case in Texas criminal (murder) charges were filed against a nursing home as a corporation and its top management, including the director of nursing and a nursing consultant, for neglecting a resident of the home.[33] Lack of nursing care was the basis of the prosecutor's charge of murder.

Case law in the area of patient abuse in nursing homes

PATIENTS' RIGHTS*

Each patient admitted to the nursing home:

1. Is fully informed, as evidenced by the patient's written acknowledgment, before or at the time of admission and during stay, of these rights and of all rules and regulations governing patient conduct and responsibilities
2. Is fully informed, before or at the time of admission and during stay, of services available in the facility, and of related charges including any charges for services not covered under Titles XVIII or XIX of the Social Security Act, or not covered by the facility's basic per diem rate
3. Is fully informed, by a physician, of medical conditions unless medically contraindicated,* and is afforded the opportunity to participate in the planning of medical treatment and to refuse to participate in experimental research
4. Is transferred or discharged only for medical reasons, or for welfare of that of other patients, or for nonpayment of stay (except as prohibited by Titles XVIII and XIX of the Social Security Act), and is given reasonable advance notice to ensure orderly transfer or discharge, and such actions are documented in the medical record
5. Is encouraged and assisted, throughout the period of stay, to exercise rights as a patient and as a citizen, and to this end may voice grievances and recommend changes in policies and services to facility staff and/or outside representatives of choice, free from restraint, interference, coercion, discrimination, or reprisal
6. May manage personal financial affairs, may designate another person to manage them, or may authorize the facility, in writing, to hold, safeguard, and account for personal funds in accordance with 42 C.F.R. 1121(m) and related provisions
7. Is free from mental and physical abuse and free from chemical and (except in emergencies) physical restraints except as authorized in writing by a physician for a specified and limited period of time, or when necessary to protect the patient from injury to self or others
8. Is assured confidential treatment of personal and medical records, and may approve or refuse their release to any individual outside the facility, except, in case of transfer to another health care institution, or as required by law or third-party payment contract
9. Is treated with consideration, respect, and full recognition of dignity and individuality, including privacy in treatment and in care for personal needs
10. Is not required to perform services for the facility that are not included for therapeutic purposes in the plan of care
11. May associate and communicate privately with persons of choice, and send and receive personal mail unopened, unless medically contraindicated*
12. May meet with, and participate in activities of, social, religious, and community groups with discretion, unless medically contraindicated*
13. May retain and use personal clothing and possessions as space permits, unless to do so would infringe upon rights of other patients, and unless medically contraindicated*
14. If married, is assured privacy for visits by the spouse; if both are residents in the facility, they are permitted to share a room, unless medically contraindicated*

Adapted from 42 C.F.R. §405.1121(k) (1984).
*As documented by the physician in the medical record.

has provided less guidance than the state and federal regulations and statutes on the topic. The elderly resident may sue a facility, nurse, or physician for malpractice in the delivery of health care.[34] In addition, disciplinary actions by a state board of nursing may be brought for abuse of patients, for failure to report abuse, or for malpractice in the care of the elderly. See Chapter 25 on licensure revocation for further information.

PROTECTIVE DEVICES AND RESTRAINTS

As indicated by an individual treatment plan, safe and proper nursing care may include the use of protective devices and restraints. These measures include the use of physical as well as chemical agents. However, these measures are only indicated under limited and circumscribed situations where:

1. The patient's treatment plan indicates it is necessary as an integral part of that plan (not for the convenience of the staff or facility but for the safety of the patient or others).
2. There is an authorizing physician's order based upon personal observation and assessment of the patient which is consistent with state regulations and institutional policy.
3. The least restrictive measures have been, in good

faith, attempted, prior to applying the more severe and restrictive restraint.

In emergency situations and only for the safety of the nursing home resident are physical restraints applied for a very limited time until personal physician evaluation determines the next steps in care.

Reasonable and safe nursing practice in the use of restraints also includes the close monitoring, assessment, and care of one subjected to them. Common practice may be to check restrained patients every 30 minutes and that 10 minutes out of every 2 hours of restraint be time of motion and exercise free of restraint. Patients who have received chemical restraint demand the most careful monitoring and surveillance. Given the large number of drugs which are prescribed for the elderly, the overall need for careful assessment and monitoring is heightened in order to provide for the safety of the elderly.

Removal of the restraints should be done as soon as is feasible. Applying restraints is done only after careful evaluation and only for a limited period of time. It has become unacceptable nursing practice to apply restraints when needed (PRN). The blank order to restrain is unacceptable. Usually, restraints are applied to prevent falls and other injuries to the resident.[35]

TRANSFER TRAUMA

There have been some cases involving the issue of transfer from a nursing home. Labeled transfer trauma, it has been experienced by many elderly without due process or just cause. Courts, however, have been hesitant to recognize it.[36] Generally, a nursing home may decide to transfer a resident based upon breach of contract (between the facility and the resident), the resident's medical or psychiatric condition, the resident's welfare or that of another resident, or upon nonpayment.[37]

State statutes have attempted to outline proper and improper situations involving questions of transfer. For example, one state specifies that a resident of a nursing home may not be transferred as a result of a change in status from self-paying to Medicare or Medicaid.[38] Legislation may require that no transfer or discharge be made unless a discharge plan has been developed. The plan must include an evaluation of the effects of the transfer and a statement of actions taken to minimize those effects. The plan is to be made available to all concerned, resident and physician, 30 days prior to the transfer or discharge.[39]

Often nurses may be members of the utilization review committees which monitor levels of care and may decide that a nursing home resident should be transferred to another level of care. The nurse's responsibility includes being fully informed about all aspects of the elder's care, including the implications of involuntary transfer. If the resident requests a hearing on the decision, the utilization review nurse may be involved in giving testimony at the hearing about the decision to transfer and its rationale.

ENFORCING NURSING HOME STATUTES

A nursing home's license may be revoked if state and federal laws, including those specifically designed to protect residents, are not followed. Revocation of a nursing home license may result if standards for care, staffing, and structural safety developed by the state administrative agency are violated.

Sanctions in state statutes include receivership, civil penalties, disclosure of inspection records to the public, monitors, suspension of admissions, and creation of statutory private rights for nursing home residents.[40] These remedies and penalties for violations of nursing home statutes will be discussed below.

Receivership state statutes provide a system for coping with nursing homes that have been decertified or delicensed or under some state statutes an enforcement mechanism for the facility's violation of state regulations, for example, patient right's violations.[41] The purpose of the receivership is to protect the residents of the nursing home and to provide for a smooth transition.

Usually the state agency may petition for a receivership, but in some states anyone may petition for one.[42] The grounds for receivership must be either that the facility was decertified by federal or state agencies or its license was denied or revoked by the state or to rehabilitate the facility.[43]

The court appoints a receiver who acts to preserve and prevent injury to the residents. The powers of the receiver are provided within the statute and are supervised by the court. For example, the use of money by the receiver may require court approval.[44]

The goal of levying civil penalties against nursing homes that violate the law is to correct their deficiencies. This system of civil penalties usually allows the nursing home, upon citation by the state, an opportunity to correct the problems. If the problems are not corrected within a reasonable time period or in a timely manner, the court may order collection of the penalty. The amount of the monetary penalties may be a fixed amount or may be established through the use of a formula. For repeaters additional penalties may be ordered. Special penalties exist in some states for staffing violations.[45] Whistleblowing statutes to prevent retaliation against employees for reporting nursing home facility violations exist in some states as well.[46]

Another means of enforcing state laws and better nursing-home care is through public or consumer involvement. For example, in Florida nursing homes are rated superior or conditional by the responsible state agency.[47] The goal of rating systems is to inform the public. In addition, in some states nursing homes are required to post or make available the inspection results and any deficiencies; in other states the inspection results are public information and are available from the state agency.[48] Yet another strategy used in some states is public monitors. These may take the form of state advisors on compliance, community advisory groups, and citizen observers.[49]

While the preceding enforcement mechanisms are usually initiated by the state government, there are some nursing home statutes which create the right of a private person to enforce the statutes. These statutes create private rights of action against nursing home facilities by the residents or other interested parties.[50] Usually, a violation of the statutorily provided patient bill of rights is the basis of the private litigation.

Lastly, the creation of state offices on aging and in particular the state ombudsman programs, mandated by the Older Americans Acts,[51] provide trained advocates for nursing home residents.[52] Not only does the ombudsman have a responsibility to investigate complaints and abuses in the care of the elderly in institutions, but also, as in the recent case of *In the Matter of Claire C. Conroy* discussed earlier, the New Jersey court identified a role for the state ombudsman in health care decision making.[53]

The court held that, "a person who believes that withholding or withdrawing life-sustaining treatment would effectuate an incompetent patient's wishes or would be in his [or her] best interests should notify the Office of the Ombudsman of the contemplated action."[54] The court further stated, however, that "any person who believes the contrary, that is, who has reasonable cause to suspect that withholding or withdrawing the life-sustaining treatment would be an abuse of that patient, should also report such information to the ombudsman."[55]

The court indicated that the ombudsman should treat every notification that life-sustaining treatment will be withdrawn or withheld from an institutionalized, elderly patient as a possible abuse. As discussed above within the section on abuse of nursing home patients, the ombudsman, under state statutes, is responsible for investigating all reports of abuse.

Financing and entitlement rights of the elderly

Approximately four out of five elderly persons have not only Medicare but also some kind of insurance coverage. About 67% of the aged Medicare population are estimated to have private insurance in addition to Medicare; approximately 13% had Medicaid.[56] With respect to expenditures, it is estimated that noninstitutionalized aged Medicare beneficiaries incurred total medical expenses of $41.7 billion in 1980. Of this amount, Medicare paid 56%, patients and their families paid 18%, private insurance plans paid 15%, and Medicaid paid 7%. The estimated per capita total expenditure for each noninstitutionalized person was $1,791. Aged beneficiaries with both Medicare and Medicaid had the greatest estimated per capita total expenditure ($3,133) followed by those with Medicare and private supplemental insurance ($1,818), and those with Medicare only ($1,087).[57]

All indications are that many elderly persons will become impoverished by the experience of paying for care in an institution, a nursing home, or extended home health care.[58] One study in Massachusetts found that two thirds of those single and one third of those married elderly would face poverty after just 13 weeks of long-term care.[59] Nationwide, nursing homes cost about $25,000 annually, but in some states, such as New York, the cost can go as high as $60,000 a year.[60]

Private health insurance paid only 0.8% of the cost of nursing home care in 1983; Medicare covered 1.7%. Personal, family contributions and Medicaid paid most of the costs.[61] Most private insurance policies do not cover long-term custodial care, but will supplement some gaps left by Medicare. Major insurance carriers are studying ways to change this. For example, in several states the American Association of Retired Persons (AARP) is piloting policies which would pay $40 a day toward nursing home care, even custodial care or personal care service.[62]

Medicare, the federal health insurance program for the elderly provides no benefits for custodial care. It only provides payment if the patient is hospitalized first and then transferred to a skilled care facility for treatment.

Medicare will only pay 100% of allowable costs, which are not necessarily the actual costs to the patient. This payment is only for the first 20 days. For the following 80 days the patient pays a deductible of $50 per day. After 100 days the coverage ends.

Medicaid, the program designed to provide medical benefits for the poor (regardless of age), on the other hand, covers nursing home costs, but only if the elderly qualifies financially. This means that the elderly person's assets must be spent first. Financed by taxes, state Medicaid programs control the reimbursement of nursing home facilities for chronic or long-term care. For example, in one state Medicaid will only pay for nursing home care if the elderly person qualifies financially, if the long-term care is the only alternative for the elderly person, and if the nursing facility has a transfer agreement with a general hospital.[63]

Each state has its own unique regulations for the Medicaid program. In addition, health care financing is a rapidly changing area and one which requires continual tie-ins to legal resources to keep current.[64]

While Medicaid is the largest government purchaser of long-term care in the United States, private family members still assume major financial responsibility. The concept of a legally enforceable family responsibility for long-term care is being explored by many state Medicaid programs. The federal Medicaid law authorizes state governments to require that adult children of Medicaid recipients pay for part of the care provided to their parents by nursing homes.[65] At present Idaho and Virginia have mandatory family responsibility statutes.[66] Legal and ethical principles behind these statutes are heavily debated.[67]

Another important consideration in financing of health care for the elderly is the method in which the elderly person gains access to the services. A physician's order is required for admission to a skilled nursing facility[68] and for access to hospice programs, acute and general psychiatric hospitals, and home health agencies. Intermediate care facilities may or may not require medical orders for admission. The physician and others are sometimes called upon to substantiate the elderly person's need for health services in order for payment.

The prospective payment system, diagnostic related groups (DRGs), applying to Medicare coverage also involves the substantiation of need for care to stay in the hospital for longer periods of time than indicated by the time specified by diagnosis in the Medicare regulations. Premature discharge from a hospital can result. New Medicare regulations will allow elderly people to challenge a hospital's decision to discharge them.[69] As soon as these patients learn of the discharge plan, they may challenge the decision if they believe the discharge is medically inappropriate.

It is anticipated that changes in third party reimbursement laws and insurance systems will increasingly provide that gerontological nurse specialists and other nurse practitioners also be identified as appropriate professionals to admit patients to these health services.[70] With the enactment of the Tax Equity and Fiscal Responsibility Act of 1982, a new prospective reimbursement system for Medicare services by health maintenance organizations (HMOs) and competitive medical plans (CMPs), was initiated.[71] In 1985 the Health Care Financing Administration (HCFA), responsible for the administration of Medicare, enacted regulations for HMOs and CMPs which specify requirements that an organization must meet in order to be eligible to enter into a contract with HCFA as an HMO under the health insurance program for the aged and to be reimbursed through capitation payments for covered items or services the HMO furnishes to enrolled elderly.[72] Under these regulations, HMOs must conform with the conditions for participation for each service which it renders to its members.[73] The HMO's health delivery system must provide for supervison by a physician. In the case of services furnished by the HMO's clinics, the HMO must demonstrate that services by other health care providers are under the direct supervision of a physician, that a physician is present to perform medical rather than administrative services at all times that the HMO's clinics are open, and that each patient is under the care of an HMO physician.[74]

Lastly, substitute or representative payees may be involved in the care of the elderly. By statute the Social Security Administration (SSA) may appoint a person to manage an individual's finances.[75] That person becomes the representative, charged with the fiduciary duty of managing the person's funds for the person's benefit. A representative payee is selected by the SSA when it believes that the interest of the beneficiary will be served and has determined that the beneficiary is not able to manage benefit payments in his or her own interest. Due to a mental or physical condition or the condition of youth, the SSA investigates, gives advance notice to the beneficiary, and appoints a payee representative according to an order of preference. That preference for individuals over the age of 18 years begins with the beneficiary's legal guardian, spouse, or other relative with custody or who demonstrates strong concern for the personal welfare of the beneficiary.[76] If objections are raised following the advance notice of appointment, a request for reconsideration can be made.[77]

Standards of care

There are several sources of standards of care in nursing of the elderly population. The American Nurses' Association standards for gerontological nursing are included in this chapter in the box on p. 268 and discussed earlier in this chapter. Other professional associations have also provided material on standards of care which may be relevant to nursing practice.[78]

The American Bar Association (ABA) and its Committee on Legal Problems of the Elderly has many publications which monitor legal problems of the elderly.[79] The ABA has also developed model acts which, if adopted by a state legislature, establish standards of care. For example, the Model Act For Regulating Board and Care Homes addresses boarding homes, which are not nursing homes but homes which provide living arrangements, usually not involving the delivery of medical or health care.[80] While this is an area which is beyond the scope of this chapter, nurses may wish to explore these living arrangements for clients. The ABA has also made recommendations regarding enforcement of nursing home legislation.[81]

State and local bar associations have reduced fee lawyer referral services for the elderly. Legal Aid services are also actively involved in providing legal services for the elderly. Many senior centers offer comprehensive community services, including social and legal services to which nurses may refer their elderly clients. In addition, there may be other legal resources, in particular in communities which support the elderly.[82]

The American Health Care Association (AHCA), a national association which includes state affiliates whose members are nursing home owners and other long-term care facility owners and practitioners, is also active in the standard-setting arena. For example, their Facilities Standards Committee has developed a self-appraisal guide.[83] The guide uses a survey method similar to the inspection method used by federal and state nursing home inspectors. AHCA encourages quality assurance programs and standard setting by individual long-term facilities.

The nursing service standards and desired outcomes recommended by AHCA include:

1. The nursing department is properly administered.
2. Patient problems are identified early and properly addressed.
3. Patient health status is maintained at the highest level possible.
4. Patient health is promoted through health education, encouragement of good nutrition, opportunity for physical and mental exercise, and general good health practice.
5. Nursing and other clinical research findings are incorporated into practice.
6. Patients care for themselves as much as possible.

Several associations distribute guidelines for selecting a nursing home. These documents are also statements on standards of care. They cover assessment of whether the nursing home is licensed, requires physician orders and examinations, staffs physicians, requires periodic reports to the patient's physician, has a 24-hour nursing staff and assessment of the nursing home's level of preparation and supervision, safety precautions, standards of food service, and provision of a safe and conducive environment.[84]

The Joint Commission on Accreditation of Hospitals accredits two types of nursing homes: long-term health care facilities and residential care facilities.[85] In addition, the National League for Nursing has developed criteria for nursing services in long-term care.[86]

Lastly, state and federal regulations and laws, many of which have been discussed in this chapter, establish standards of care. Licensure, certification, conditions for participation and payment, and fraud provisions of state and federal laws specify the levels, types, and requirements for delivery of care to the elderly in nursing homes, hospitals, health maintenance organizations, home health and hospice programs, and other programs. These standards are often enforced through decertification. If a facility is decertified by the Medicaid or Medicare program, payment may be withheld until the facility is recertified or until violations of the standards are eliminated.[87]

Recommendations and trends

State laws vary; what is case law or legislation in one state may not be the law in another. For example, the *Conroy* case is current law in New Jersey; courts in other states may consider New Jersey's decision but are not bound to follow that decision.

There is great need to assure the adequacy of and to improve nursing care for the elderly client. Several recommendations, noting trends, can be made. Nurses' involvement in decision-making process regarding care of elderly persons, especially for the more vulnerable elderly, needs to be increased. The nursing profession should articulate the nurse's role in educating older adults about retirement to assist in preparing them for health care decision making which may lie ahead.

Nursing can affirmatively establish a responsibility to encourage the use of advanced directives by patients. This would greatly aid in the care of the elderly. Policies for decision making, especially protocols for competency evaluations, should be reviewed and clarified.

Nurses are becoming more involved in institutional ethics committees or other activities of a similar nature. Developing these agency ethics committees[88] and adhering to established guidelines for nurses' involvement is important.[89]

The number of qualified nurses to care for the elderly needs to be increased. Working to alter the current emphasis in health care on critical care, shifting the focus to chronic care, would aid in the obtainment of this recommendation. So, too, would increasing nursing education and preparation to participate in decision-making processes, especially guardianship, committment, and other legal proceedings and improving, overall, nurses' preparation for care of elderly persons and their health needs, including increased focus on nursing research.[90]

Lastly, nurses who serve the elderly and their families and communities should be comfortable in participating in activities which link elderly clients to community services, including legal services which will aid in the satisfactory resolution of the elderly person's legal problems.

Endnotes

1. OFFICE OF TECHNOLOGY ASSESSMENT, CONGRESS OF THE UNITED STATES, TECHNOLOGY AND AGING IN AMERICA (1984).
2. HEALTH CARE FINANCING ADMINISTRATION, U.S. DEPT. OF HEALTH AND HUMAN SERVICES, THE 1979 NATIONAL CENTER FOR HEALTH STATISTICS SURVEY (1981).
3. AMERICAN NURSES' ASSOCIATION, STANDARDS OF GERONTOLOGICAL NURSING PRACTICE 3 (1976).
4. M. KAPP, A. BIGOT, GERIATRICS AND THE LAW 6 (1985) (hereinafter cited as *Geriatrics and the Law*).
5. *See, e.g.,* SUBCOMMITTEE ON LONG TERM CARE, SPECIAL COMMITTEE ON AGING, SENATE, U.S. CONGRESS, NURSES IN NURSING HOMES: THE HEAVY BURDEN (THE RELIANCE ON UNTRAINED AND UNLICENSED PERSONNEL) (1975); FRAUD AND ABUSE AMONG PRACTITIONERS PARTICIPATING IN MEDICAID PROGRAM (1976). The level of physician involvement in continuing care of nursing home residents has also been scrutinized and criticized. *See, e.g.,* SENATE COMMITTEE ON AGING, NURSING HOME CARE IN THE U.S.: FAILURE IN PUBLIC POLICY, includes a paper titled *Doctors in Nursing Homes: The Shuned Responsibility* (1975).
6. MD. HEALTH-GEN. CODE ANN. §20-101, 20-102, 20-104 (1982).
7. *See, e.g.* MD. EST. & TRUSTS CODE ANN. §13-705 (b) (Supp. 1985), which states, "A guardian of the person shall be appointed if the court determines from *clear and convincing evidence* [emphasis added] that a person lacks sufficient understanding or capacity to make or communicate responsible decisions concerning his person, including provisions for health care . . . because of any mental disability, senility, other mental weakness, disease, habitual drunkenness, or addiction to drugs, and that no less restrictive form of intervention is available which is consistent with the person's welfare and safety."
8. *Id.*
9. MD. HEALTH-GEN. CODE ANN. §20-107 (Supp. 1985).
10. 486 A.2d 1209, 1216 (N.J. 1985). This is the law at this time in New Jersey; each state may set its own precedent.
11. *Id.* at 1217.
12. *Id.* at 1234-35.
13. *Id.* at 1226.
14. *Id.* at 1229.
15. *Id.* at 1231.
16. *Id.*
17. *Id.*
18. *Id.*
19. *Id.* at 1242.
20. *Id.* at 1243.
21. *See, e.g.,* MEDICAL SOCIETY OF THE STATE OF NEW YORK, GUIDELINES FOR HOSPITALS AND PHYSICIANS ON "DO NOT RESUSCITATE" ORDERS (1982).
22. *In re Shirley Dinnerstein,* 380 N.E.2d 134 (Mass. App. 1978).
23. *Battles v. Aderhold,* 430 So.2d 307 (La. 1983).
24. Beck and Phillips, *Abuse of the Elderly* 9 J. GERON. NURS. 97 (1983).
25. *Geriatrics and the Law, supra* note 4, 79 (1985).
26. *Id.* at 82. *See also,* Faulkner, *Mandating the Reporting of Suspected Cases of Elder Abuse: An Inappropriate, Ineffective and Ageist Response to the Abuse of Older Adults,* 16 FAM. L. Q., 69 (1982). Cites to state elder/adult abuse statutes are located in the appendix.
27. *Id.* See Appendix for citations.
28. *Id.* See Appendix for citations.
29. CONN. GEN. STAT. ANN. §46a-15 (West Supp. 1985) (Protection of the Elderly); CONN. GEN. STAT. ANN. §17-135h (West Supp. 1985) (Department of Aging).
30. 42 C.F.R. §405.1121(k), 442.311(c) (1985); 42 U.S.C. §1395-1396 (1982).
31. *See, e.g.,* MD. HEALTH-GEN. CODE ANN. §19-347 (Supp. 1985).
32. *Id.*
33. Reinhold, *Trial Opens in Death at Texas Nursing Home,* N.Y. Times, October 1, 1985, at A17, col. 1.
34. *See, e.g., Campbell v. Payton Health Care Facilities,* Fla., Polk County Cir. Ct., No. GCG-84-1170, Jan. 28, 1985, where a jury awarded $2.2 million, including $1.7 million in punitive damages, for the wrongful death of a 69-year-old man whose decubitus ulcers were not properly treated. Other cases involving malpractice allegations included failure to assist and attend residents, falls, lack of siderails, and confused patients leaving nursing home premises. *See also,* S. JOHNSON, N. TERRY, AND M. WOLFF, NURSING HOMES AND THE LAW: STATE REGULATION AND PRIVATE LITIGATION 68 (1985); Butler, *Nursing Home Quality of Care Enforcement: Part I—Litigation by Private Parties* 14 CLEARINGHOUSE REV., 622 (special issue 1980) which iden-

tified 35 reported cases in private nursing homes from 1950 to 1978. The cases involved burns, falls, attacks, harm from wandering, amputations, false imprisonment, mental anguish, death from apparent drowning, death from a fight with another patient, and harassment in connection with taking a deposition; Nemore, *Protecting Nursing Home Residents, Torts Actions Are One Way* 21 TRIAL 54 (December 1985); and Jost, *Enforcement of Quality Nursing Home Care in the Legal System* 13 LAW, MED. & HEALTH CARE 160 (September 1985).

35. *See, e.g.,* Lund and Sheafor, *Is Your Patient About to Fall?* 11 J. GERON. NURS. 37 (April 1985).
36. *See, e.g., O'Bannon v. Town Court Nursing Center, Inc.*, 586 F. 2nd 280 (3rd Cir. 1978), *rev'd.*, 447 U.S. 773 (1980). The Supreme Court held that the nursing home residents had no constitutional right to a hearing before a state or federal agency which revoked the home's authority to provide them nursing care at government expense. *See also Yaretsky v. Blum,* 447 U.S. 787 (1982). In *Blum,* the Supreme Court ruled that a nursing home's decision to discharge or transfer a resident (Medicaid), based on utilization review committee judgment, to a lower level of care without prior notice did not violate due process rights of residents. Robert, *Relocation of Nursing Home Residents and Transfer Trauma* 24 ST. LOUIS. U. L. J. 758 (1981).
37. 42 C.F.R. §1121(k) (1985); *See also* JOINT COMMISSION ON ACCREDITATION OF HOSPITALS LONG-TERM CARE STANDARDS (1980).
38. CONN. GEN. STAT. ANN. §19a-535 (West Supp. 1985).
39. *Id.*
40. S. JOHNSON, N. TERRY, AND M. WOLFF, NURSING HOMES AND THE LAW: STATE REGULATION AND PRIVATE LITIGATION (1985); *See also* Johnson, *State Regulation of Long-term Care: A Decade of Experience with Intermediate Sanctions* 13 LAW, MED. & HEALTH CARE 173 (September 1985).
41. Johnson, *Nursing Home Receiverships: Design and Implementation* 24 ST. LOUIS U. L. J. 681 (1981).
42. *See, e.g.,* MD. HEALTH-GEN. CODE ANN. §19-334 (1982) provides that the Secretary of the Department of Health and Mental Hygiene may file a petition for appointment of a receiver for a nursing home if, after investigation . . . or after investigation at the request of the Director on Aging.
43. *See, e.g.,* MD. HEALTH-GEN. CODE ANN. §19-334(a)(1)-(a)(4) (1982), providing that the petition for receivership is filed when the secretary reasonably believes that: (1) a person is operating the nursing home without a license for it; (2) the nursing home will be closed within 30 days, and arrangements to relocate its residents have not been approved . . .; (3) the nursing home or its residents have been abandoned; or (4) a situation, physical condition, practice, or method of operation presents an imminent danger of death or serious mental or physical harm to the residents of the nursing home.
44. *See, e.g.,* MD. HEALTH-GEN. CODE ANN. §19-337 (1982) includes the following powers of the receiver: correct each condition on which the appointment of the receiver was based, ensure adequate care for each resident of the nursing home, and preserve the property of the owner of the nursing home. This section also provides that the receiver of a nursing home may use any private or third party reimbursements to the nursing home, including any Medicaid and Medicare payments and, with approval of the court, money from a special revolving fund.
45. ILL. ANN. STAT. Ch. 111½ §4153-305(7) (Smith Hurd Supp. 1985).
46. CAL. HEALTH & SAFETY CODE §1432(a) (West Supp. 1985).
47. FLA. STAT. ANN. §400.23(3) (West 1985).
48. *See, e.g.,* ILL. ANN. STAT. Ch 111½, §3152-205 and 4153-702(b) (Smith-Hurd Supp.); MO. ANN. STAT. §198.026 (Vernon Supp. 1986).
49. *See, e.g.,* OKLA. STAT. ANN. tit. 63, §1-1931, 1-1911(B), and 1-1911(C) (West 1984); IOWA CODE ANN. §135C.25 (West Supp. 1985); N.C. GEN. STAT. §128 (Supp. 1985).
50. *See, e.g.,* CAL. HEALTH & SAFETY CODE §1439 (West 1979); CONN. GEN. STAT. ANN. §19a-550(b) (West. Supp. 1985); ILL. ANN. STAT. Ch. 111½, §4153-601 (Smith-Hurd Supp. 1985); MASS. ANN. LAWS Ch. 111, §70E (Michie/Law. Co-op. 1985); MO. ANN. STAT. §198.093 (Vernon 1983); N.J. STAT. ANN. §30:13-8 (West 1981); N.Y. PUB. HEALTH LAW §2801(d) (McKinney 1985); N.C. GEN. STAT. §131E-115-128 (Supp. 1985); OKLA. STAT. ANN. tit. 63, §1-1918F (West 1984); W. VA CODE §16-5C-15(c) (1985).
51. Older Americans Act, 42 U.S.C. 3001 (1982).
52. *See, e.g.,* Wolff, House, and Erickson, *Long-Term Care Ombudsmen: Training, Role and Responsibility,* in LONG-TERM CARE AND THE LAW 191 (S. Johnson ed. 1983).
53. 486 A.2d 1209, 1241, 1242 (N.J. 1985).
54. *Id.* at 1241.
55. *Id.* at 1242.
56. OFFICE OF RESEARCH AND DEMONSTRATIONS, HEALTH CARE FINANCING ADMINISTRATION, U.S. DEPT. OF HEALTH AND HUMAN SERVICES, NATIONAL MEDICAL UTILIZATION AND EXPENDITURE SURVEY 1 (1985). In addition, see federal statutes on financing services for the elderly: 42 U.S.C. §1395-1395xx (1982), (health insurance for aged and disabled); 42 U.S.C. §1396-1396p (1982), (medical assistance); 42 U.S.C. §1397-1397f (1982), (social services); 42 U.S.C. §1201-1206 (1982), (grants for the blind); 42 U.S.C. §301-306 (1982), (granted to states for old age assistance); 42 U.S.C. §401-433 (1982), (federal old age, survivors and disability insurance benefits); 42 U.S.C. §501-504 (1982), (grants to states for unemployment compensation administration); 42 U.S.C. §1381-1383c (1982), (supplementary security income for aged, blind and disabled); 42 U.S.C. § 1395mm (182), (payments to health maintenance organizations and competitive medical plans).
57. *Id.*
58. Schwartz, *Some Moves Made toward Nursing Home Coverage,* The Nation's Health, September, 1985 at 26, col. 1.
59. *Id.*
60. Rankin, *Coping with the Cost of a Nursing Home,* N.Y. Times, August 25, 1985 at F9, col. 1.
61. Schwartz, *Some Moves Made toward Nursing Home Coverage,* The Nation's Health, September, 1985 at 26, col. 1.
62. Rankin, *Coping with the Cost of a Nursing Home,* N.Y. Times, August 25, 1985 at F9, col. 1.
63. MD. HEALTH-GEN. CODE ANN. §15-115 (Supp. 1985).
64. R. BUCHANAN AND J. MINOR, LEGAL ASPECTS OF HEALTH CARE REIMBURSEMENT (1985).
65. HEALTH CARE FINANCING ADMINISTRATION, STATE MEDICAID MANUAL PART 3, §3812 (1983).
66. IDAHO CODE §32-1002. §32-1008A (1983), and §56-203B (Supp. 1985); VA. CODE §20.88 (Supp. 1985).

67. *See, e.g.*, Daniels, *Family Responsibility Initiatives and Justice Between Age Groups* 13 LAW, MED. & HEALTH CARE 153 (September 1985).
68. 42 C.F.R. §405.1123 (1984).
69. Pear, *Medicare Extends Patients' Rights,* N.Y. Times, January 9, 1986, at A13, col. 1.
70. AMERICAN NURSES' ASSOCIATION, OBTAINING THIRD PARTY REIMBURSEMENT: A NURSE'S GUIDE TO METHODS AND STRATEGIES (1984).
71. P.L. 97-248, 96 Stat. 324; 42 U.S.C. §300e 1395mm (1982).
72. 42 C.F.R. §417.201 (1985).
73. 42 C.F.R. §417.207(a) (1985).
74. 42 C.F.R. §417.207(b)(1) (1985).
75. 42 U.S.C. §405, 1302 (1982) and regulations at 20 C.F.R. §404.2001 (1985).
76. 20 C.F.R. §2021(a)(1) (1985).
77. 20 C.F.R. §2030(a) (1985).
78. *See, e.g.*, publications and activities of the American Academy of Medical Directors, the American Association of Nursing Home Administrators, the Alzheimer's Disease and Related Disorders Association, Concern for Dying, National Hospice Organization, National Citizens' Coalition for Nursing Home Reform, American Society on Aging, National Council on Aging, Gerontological Society of America, American Association of Retired Persons, American Geriatrics Society.
79. *See, e.g.*, BIFOCAL, newsletter published by the Committee on Legal Problems of the Elderly, American Bar Association.
80. COMMISSION ON LEGAL PROBLEMS OF THE ELDERLY AND COMMISSION ON THE MENTALLY DISABLED, AMERICAN BAR ASSOCIATION, A MODEL ACT REGULATING BOARD AND CARE HOMES: GUIDELINES FOR STATES (1984).
81. AMERICAN BAR ASSOCIATION, MODEL RECOMMENDATIONS: INTERMEDIATE SANCTIONS FOR ENFORCEMENT OF QUALITY CARE IN NURSING HOMES (1981).
82. *See, e.g.*, Legal Counsel for the Elderly, Washington, D.C.; National Senior Citizens' Law Center, Los Angeles; Senior Adults Legal Assistance, Palo Alto, California.
83. AMERICAN HEALTH CARE ASSOCIATION, QUEST FOR QUALITY: A SELF-APPRAISAL GUIDE FOR LONG-TERM CARE FACILITIES (1982).
84. COMMITTEE ON NURSING HOMES AND LONG-TERM CARE, UNITED HOSPITAL FUND, FACILITIES FOR THE AGING: A GUIDE TO CHOOSE A NURSING HOME (1983); AMERICAN MEDICAL ASSOCIATION, WHAT TO LOOK FOR IN A NURSING HOME (1971); AND OFFICE OF NURSING HOME AFFAIRS, PUBLIC HEALTH SERVICE, U.S.H.E.W., HOW TO SELECT A NURSING HOME (1977).
85. JOINT COMMISSION ON ACCREDITATION OF HOSPITALS, MANUAL FOR ACCREDITATION OF LONG TERM CARE FACILITIES (current ed.).
86. NATIONAL LEAGUE FOR NURSING, CRITERIA FOR DEPARTMENTS OF NURSING IN LONG-TERM CARE SETTINGS (1980).
87. 42 C.F.R. §489.50 489.57, and 431.151 431.154 (1985).
88. *See,* R. CRANFORD AND E. DOUDERA, INSTITUTIONAL ETHICS COMMITTEES & HEALTH CARE DECISION MAKING (1984).
89. *See,* AMERICAN NURSES' ASSOCIATION, GUIDELINES FOR NURSE'S PARTICIPATION IN INSTITUTIONAL ETHICS COMMITTEES (1985).
90. *See,* NATIONAL INSTITUTE ON AGING, PUBLIC HEALTH SERVICE, DEPT. OF HEALTH AND HUMAN SERVICES, REPORT ON EDUCATION AND TRAINING IN GERIATRICS AND GERONTOLOGY (1984).

Additional Readings

J. BEYER, J. BULKLEY, AND P. HOPKINS, A MODEL ACT REGULATING BOARD AND CARE HOMES: GUIDELINES FOR STATES (1984).

R. BROWN, THE RIGHTS OF OLDER PERSONS: THE BASIC ACLU GUIDE TO AN OLDER PERSON'S RIGHTS (1979).

B. CLOSE, M. GREENBERG, AND B. MORGENSTERN, NURSING HOME PATIENT ABUSE: REALITIES AND REMEDIES (1981).

Cushing, *Wronged Rights in Nursing Homes* 84 A.J.N. 1213 (October 1984).

A. DAVIS AND M. AROSKAR, ETHICAL DILEMMAS AND NURSING PRACTICE (2nd ed. 1984).

Furrow, *Caring for the Elderly: Striking a Balance* 12 LAW, MED. & HEALTH CARE 96 (1984).

Hasko, Holoch and Yound, *Gerontology and the Law: A Selected Bibliography* 56 S. CAL. L. REV. 289 (1982).

Nolan, *Functional Evaluation of the Elderly in Guardianship Proceedings* 12 LAW, MED. & HEALTH CARE 210 (1984).

PRESIDENT'S COMMISSION FOR THE STUDY OF ETHICAL PROBLEMS IN MEDICINE AND BIOMEDICAL AND BEHAVIORAL RESEARCH, DECIDING TO FOREGO LIFE-SUSTAINING TREATMENT, ETHICAL, MEDICAL, AND LEGAL ISSUES IN TREATMENT DECISIONS (1983); DEFINING DEATH, MEDICAL, LEGAL AND ETHICAL ISSUES IN THE DETERMINATION OF DEATH (1981); MAKING HEALTH CARE DECISIONS, 4 Vols. (1982); SECURING ACCESS TO HEALTH CARE, 3 Vols. (1983).

Chapter 18

Nursing in federal employment

Diane Trace Warlick

Nurses employed by the federal government occupy a unique position. The professional actions of both military and civilian nurses are governed by a combination of federal and state laws. The discussion in this chapter focuses primarily on the potential professional liability of both civilian and military nurses and on the applicable federal statutes as interpreted by the courts. Nursing in this context as in others is measured by standards of nursing practice.[1] The box on p. 284 lists several federal statutes that affect federally employed nurses.

This chapter also focuses on the federally employed nurse as defendant and concludes with a review of the Uniformed Code of Military Justice and a discussion of confidentiality, privacy, and informed consent issues as they are applied in military, veterans', and other parts of federal health care system.

Professional liability

Several aspects of the professional liability of federal government nurses are unique to that practice. Federal statutes define limits and applicability of legal principles to this area of practice. Many laws that apply to nurses working with or for the federal government are discussed in this section.

CIVILIAN EMPLOYEES OF THE FEDERAL GOVERNMENT

Nurses are employed by a number of different agencies of the federal government. The most prominent of these include the Veterans Administration (VA), Department of Defense (DOD), Public Health Service (PHS), National Health Corps (NHC), National Space Program (NSP), and the Peace Corps.

The U.S. Congress has protected the employees of these and other federal agencies from personal liability to third parties arising from the employees' actions in the performance of their jobs. The Federal Tort Claims Act (F.T.C.A.),[2] which authorizes suits against the U.S. government based on the negligence of its employees, also provides that the remedies against the United States "shall be exclusive."[3] Federally employed nurses are one of the few groups of nurses who enjoy this personal immunity.

The protection afforded by F.T.C.A., however, only extends to cases that are within the scope of the statutes' coverage. Nurses employed by the federal government must be aware that there are cases arising from the provision of health care services that have been held to be outside the scope of the statute. These cases will be discussed later in the chapter. In this situation, the F.T.C.A. exclusive remedy provision would not preclude a lawsuit against the individual nurse-employee.

EXCLUSIVE REMEDY STATUTES

Potential gaps in the personal immunity of some federally employed nurses and other health care personnel have been filled by Congress by the enactment of exclusive remedy statutes specifically precluding malpractice

MAJOR LEGISLATION APPLICABLE TO NURSES EMPLOYED BY THE FEDERAL GOVERNMENT

Federal Tort Claims Act:
28 U.S.C. §2671-2680, all federal employees
Exclusive Remedy Statutes:
38 U.S.C. §4116, nurses, physicians, and other health care providers employed by the Veterans Administration
42 U.S.C. §233, medical, dental, surgical, and related personnel employed by the Public Health Service
42 U.S.C. §2458, physicians, dentists, nurses, and other supporting personnel employed by the National Aeronautics and Space Administration
10 U.S.C. §1089, physicians, dentists, nurses, and supporting personnel who are members of the armed forces or employed by the Department of Defense, Central Intelligence Agency, or U.S. Soldiers' and Airmen's Home
5 U.S.C. §8101 *et seq.*, federal employees, including military and civilian nurses
Federal Employees Compensation Act and other related acts:
42 U.S.C. §2000e-16, Title VII of Civil Rights Act (federal application)
5 U.S.C. §5596, Back Pay Act
5 U.S.C. §7101, labor-management relations
5 U.S.C. §7201, antidiscrimination, right to petition Congress
5 U.S.C. §7311-7313, strike and civil disorder
5 U.S.C. §7321-7327, political activities (Hatch Act)
5 U.S.C. §1201-1209, Merit Systems Protection Board and special counsel
5 U.S.C. §1501-1508, political activity of certain state and local employees
5 U.S.C. §2101-2305, merit system principles
5 U.S.C. §4301-4315, performance appraisal, general and senior executive service
29 U.S.C. §204(f), Fair Labor Standards Act (FLSA) (federal application)
29 U.S.C. §206(d), Equal Pay Act Amendments (under FLSA)
29 U.S.C. §791, Rehabilitation Act
29 U.S.C. §621-634, Age Discrimination in Employment Act
42 U.S.C. §4561, alcohol abuse and alcoholism prevention, treatment, and rehabilitation for federal civil employees
Uniform Code of Military Justice:
10 U.S.C. §801 *et seq.;* all active duty military personnel, members of military reserves on active duty, and retired military personnel
Veterans Administration:
38 U.S.C. §4131, patients' rights
38 U.S.C. §4132, confidentiality

actions against the individual employee of the VA, PHS, and NSP, including National Aeronautics and Space Administration (NASA).[4] The first one, the statute that applies to employees of the Department of Medicine and Surgery of the VA, expressly applies to nurses, physicians, and paramedical and other supporting personnel. The statute provides that:

> (T)he remedy against the United States . . . for damages for personal injury including death, allegedly arising from malpractice or negligence . . . in furnishing medical care or treatment while in the exercise of such persons duties in or for the Department of Medicine and Surgery shall hereafter be exclusive of any other civil action or proceeding by reason of the same subject matter. . . .

The same immunity is provided to nurses employed by NASA. Although the statutory language is different than the language of the VA statute, it also expressly applies to nurses and precludes malpractice lawsuits against the individual health care employee.[5] This statute also includes an element not found in the VA law, which provides that the F.T.C.A. exclusion of actions for assault and battery does not apply to "actions arising out of a negligent or wrongful act (or) omission in the performance of medical, dental or related health care functions. . . ."[6] The deletion of this exclusion is significant because actions based upon certain categories of wrongful conduct in the health care setting have been held to constitute assault and/or battery. This exclusion and its significance will be discussed in detail later in the chapter.

The exclusive remedy provision applicable to the PHS employees similarly provides that the assault and battery exclusion included in the F.T.C.A. does not apply to actions based upon the performance of health care services.[7] The PHS statute also provides personal immunity for individual health care employees, but it differs from the previous two statutes in a very important respect. Its terms do not specifically include nurses within its coverage. This statute applies instead to actions for "damages . . . resulting from the performance of medical, surgical, dental or related functions. . . ."[8] At least one court has held that this statute precludes a malpractice suit against a nurse practitioner.

In *Flickinger v. United States*,[9] the court held without

specifically deciding, that 42 U.S.C. §233 (a) applies to nurse practitioners under the facts of the case. In *Flickinger*, the plaintiff stepped on a thumbtack and suffered a puncture wound to the ball of her foot. She was initially treated on the day of the injury in a local hospital emergency room. Subsequently, her foot became infected and developed symptoms of gangrene. On the third day following the injury, the plaintiff's daughter allegedly telephoned a local health clinic and spoke to a nurse practitioner, expressing concern about her mother's condition. The daughter described her mother's condition in the following manner: the toes on her right foot were turning purple, there was redness around the purple area, and the flesh around the base of the toes was very white. The nurse practitioner merely reassured the woman that her mother's condition did not require any attention and took no further action. Four days later the plaintiff was admitted to the hospital, where she underwent amputation of two toes and surgical debridement of gangrenous tissue from the rest of her foot.

The plaintiff instituted a lawsuit against the nurse practitioner and the clinic in state court. Under the provisions of the F.T.C.A. and 42 U.S.C. Sec. 233 (b),[10] the attorney general certified that at the time of the incident at issue, the nurse practitioner was an employee of the PHS and was acting within the scope of her employment.

The question, whether as a nurse practitioner, the defendant's work-related actions fell within the definition of a "medical, surgical . . . or related function" was not raised by the parties. The court implicitly presumed the exclusive remedy statute was applicable and dismissed the action against the nurse practitioner. The case was transferred to the federal district court and the United States was substituted as the proper defendant.

Although it may seem obvious to nurses and even to some courts that nursing services fall within the coverage of the PHS exclusive remedy statute, this cannot be assumed. Where a statute is not specific, its applicability is left open to interpretation by the courts in specific cases. Whereas the attorney general is empowered to determine whether the individual is an employee acting within the scope of employment, statutory interpretation is a matter for the courts. The issue, whether nurses and nursing practice are categorically covered by 42 U.S.C. §233 (a), has not yet been decided by any federal court. Thus, the nurse may find it necessary to establish that her or his professional services are a function related to the performance of medical, surgical, or dental care.

EFFECT OF PERSONAL IMMUNITY

The personal immunity of nurses under the F.T.C.A. and exclusive remedy statutes protects the nurse and his or her personal assets from prospective malpractice plaintiffs, but it does not mean that the nurse's professional conduct can or will not be the subject of litigation. The liability of the United States in actions based upon negligent provision of health care services must necessarily stem from the conduct of its employees, including nurses. At the present time, only a small percentage of the reported cases involve allegations of negligent nursing care, with most suits involving the propriety of medical or dental services.

The nurse whose acts or omissions in the performance of duties are alleged to constitute malpractice will be required to actively participate in the defense of the lawsuit. The nurse will be involved in discovery proceedings and trial to the same degree as if the suit was brought against her or him directly. Although, if the case is lost, the government, not the nurse, will be required to pay the judgment, the emotional and physical strains may be just as great as when the nurse is the named defendant.

FEDERAL TORT CLAIMS ACT

Prior to the enactment of the F.T.C.A., the federal government could not be sued for the torts of its employees unless Congress passed a special bill permitting lawsuits on a case-by-case basis. To alleviate the harsh impact and lack of remedy available to persons injured by the negligence of federal employees, Congress enacted the Federal Tort Claims Act in 1946.[11] With the passage of the F.T.C.A., Congress waived the immunity of the government and gave its consent to suits against the government based upon allegations of negligence on the part of its employees. The present test of allowable claims is codified at 28 U.S.C. §2674. It provides that the United States shall be liable for tort claims in the same manner and to the same extent as a private individual under like circumstances. Since the F.T.C.A. is the primary law that impacts federal nursing practice, the scope of this consent to be sued, the exceptions, limitations, and procedural requirements as they apply to actions based upon the provision of health care services by federal employees are discussed in the following sections.

Applicability of the Federal Tort Claims Act. The scope of the government's consent to suit is determined by reference to the definition sections of the F.T.C.A.,[12] its express exclusions,[13] and the grant of jurisdiction to the federal district courts in actions where the United States is a defendant.[14] The district courts are vested with exclusive jurisdiction of:

> . . . civil actions on claims against the United States for money damages . . . for injury or loss of property or personal injury or death caused by the wrongful act or omission of any employee of the Government while acting within the scope of his office or employment, under circumstances where the United States, if a private person, would be liable to the claimant in accordance with the law of the place where the act or omission occurred.

This provision raises two key issues for nurses with respect to coverage under the statute: (1) who is an employee? and (2) was the employee acting within the scope of employment at the time of the incident? Each of these will be discussed.

Employee or Independent Contractor. Employees covered by the F.T.C.A. are defined in §2671 and include officers or employees of any federal agency, active duty members of the armed forces, and members of the National Guard while engaged in training or duty. The statute expressly excludes independent contractors from coverage under the F.T.C.A. It states that the term federal agency does not include any contractor with the United States.

Supreme Court decisions of the early 1970s held that the distinction between an employee and an independent contractor rests on whether the federal government has the power to control the detailed physical performance of the agency or its personnel.[15] Recent court cases discuss this test of employee status in lawsuits based upon alleged acts of medical malpractice. *Wood v. Standard Products Co., Inc.,* involved a suit against a physician under contract to the PHS to furnish outpatient medical care to eligible PHS beneficiaries.[16] An injured commercial fisherman sued the United States for medical malpractice under F.T.C.A., claiming that the physician was an employee of the federal government. The United States denied that the physician was an employee, arguing the he was an independent contractor excluded from coverage under F.T.C.A., and the court agreed. The following factors were found by the court to support its finding that the physician was an independent contractor rather than a government employee: designation in the contract as a "contract physician," absence of contract provision prescribing the manner in which medical services were performed, absence of control over drugs and medical supplies that might be used in treatment, absence of mandated office hours, no requirement that specific persons be accepted as patients, and a requirement that the physician furnish all secretarial and nursing services, supplies, equipment, and office space. The obligations of the physician to maintain accurate medical records, complete specific paperwork, and familiarize himself with PHS eligibility requirements did not make the physician a federal employee.

Federal courts have reached the same conclusion in suits based upon medical services provided at a military hospital and a VA hospital.[17] In the first case the court held that a board-certified urologist who was a civilian consultant at an Air Force hospital was an independent contractor, not a federal employee. The decision was based in part upon the findings by the court that the physician billed the hospital for his time, handled his own Social Security and income tax payments, and had no limitations placed on his authority to select and employ physician assistants or residents to assist him. The court specifically concluded that the government had primarily contracted for urological services but that the manner and method in which these services were delivered were controlled exclusively by the physician. The only control or supervision exercised by the hospital in this case was related to the location of the surgery and the requirement that the physician use hospital facilities and personnel where practical. These factors were not sufficient to make the physician a government employee.

In the second case, the court held that a neurosurgeon affiliated with a university and performing neurosurgical services at a VA hospital under the university's contract with the VA was not a government employee. The court specifically stated that federal law determines whether an agency is an independent contractor and therefore excluded from coverage under the F.T.C.A.[18] The court held that the critical element in distinguishing a government agency from an independent contractor is the power to control the detailed physical performance of the contractor. The court found that the VA hospital did "not control the manner in which the medical treatment was provided; therefore, the physician was an independent contractor."[19]

Although no cases have been found to date where a nurse's status as a government employee was challenged, these cases can be anticipated in the future. As nurses become more entrepreneurial and move away from traditional employment relationships, they may cross the line into independent contractor status.

Scope of Employment. The second key limit on the scope of coverage of the F.T.C.A. is the requirement that the government employee be acting within the scope of employment at the time of the incident in question.[20] The law of the state where the act or omission occurred must be applied to resolve this issue. Under the *Restatement of Agency (Second)*,[21] the doctrine of *respondeat superior,* is stated as a general rule that a "master is subject to liability for torts of his servants committed while acting in the scope of their employment."[22]

The general criteria for determining whether conduct is within the scope of employment include the following: (1) whether the conduct is of the kind the employee is hired to perform; (2) whether it occurs substantially within the authorized time and space limits; (3) whether it is actuated at least in part by a purpose to serve the master; and (4) if force is intentionally used by the servant against another, whether the use of force is not unexpected by the master.

An affirmative answer to each of these questions indicates that the conduct was in the scope of the servant's employment. When the conduct at issue was not authorized by the employer, it may still be deemed within the scope of employment if the conduct is substantially similar to or incidental to authorized conduct.

The definition section of the F.T.C.A. states that in the case of a member of the armed forces, "acting within the scope of employment" means "acting in the line of duty."[23] Subsequent judicial interpretations have held, however, that the meaning of "line of duty" is coextensive with the *respondeat superior* doctrine under applicable state law.[24] By this circuitous legislative-judicial route, essentially the same test applies in determining whether a military or civilian employee of the federal government is acting within the scope of employment.

Exclusions of F.T.C.A. Coverage. The scope of the federal government's consent to be sued for the alleged wrongful acts of its employees is strictly governed by the terms of the statutes. Section 2680 lists 13 circumstances and cases that are expressly excluded from the F.T.C.A. coverage. The exceptions with potential applicability to nurses and nursing practice include claims based upon assault, battery, libel, slander, misrepresentation, and deceit. Other intentional torts included in the statutes are false imprisonment, false arrest, malicious prosecution, abuse of process, and interference with contract rights.

The F.T.C.A. also expressly excludes claims against employees exercising due care in the performance of a statute or regulation or a discretionary function, claims for damages caused by the imposition of a quarantine, and claims arising during combat or in a foreign country. The Supreme Court stated as recently as 1984 that when faced with determining whether a particular case is subject to the F.T.C.A. or excluded from it, the court must look at the ordinary meaning of the statutory language in light of the general purposes of the tort claims act and the legislative reasoning behind the exclusions.[25] Thus, federal law determines whether, under the facts of a particular case, the case falls within one of the 13 statutory exclusions.

The impact of the statutory exclusions on professional liability issues is most confusing and potentially hazardous to the unwary nurse when the assault and battery, misrepresentation, and false imprisonment theories are implicated in a malpractice action. The applicability of these theories to professional malpractice cases is unsettled and varies from state to state. Thus, whether a suit is within or without the F.T.C.A. coverage may depend upon the state in which the alleged wrongdoing occurred. The following cases demonstrate some of the problems and legal issues that may be raised in litigation based upon the actions of a federally employed nurse or other health care provider.

Assault and battery are most frequently seen in the context of malpractice cases where the plaintiff claims that an invasive procedure was performed without legally sufficient consent. As discussed in Chapter 5, where no consent is given, the invasive procedure is generally held to constitute a battery; thus, any action against the United States would presumably be precluded by 28 U.S.C. §2680. However, this question is not well settled. If consent was given but was allegedly uninformed, there is a divergence of opinion. Many states deem informed consent actions to be based upon a battery, whereas other states hold that they are based upon professional negligence, not battery.[26]

The significance of the two viewpoints is pointed out in *Hernandez v. United States*.[27] In *Hernandez*, the plaintiff alleged that physicians at a VA hospital surgically removed a small mass from his left breast without his consent. In response to the government's motion for summary judgment and in an effort to avoid dismissal of the suit, the plaintiff attempted to bring his claim within the informed consent doctrine, which under Kansas law is professional negligence rather than battery. The court found, however, that Hernandez was actually claiming that he gave no consent at all, which constituted battery, and held that the United States was immune under the F.T.C.A. exceptions. The lawsuit against the United States was dismissed. However, in a state such as Pennsylvania, where lack of informed consent is classified as an assault, a plaintiff will not be able to avoid dismissal of his suit by claiming the consent was uninformed rather than absent altogether.[28] These factors may influence the manner in which a plaintiff phrases the claim.

The efforts of government attorneys to have malpractice actions dismissed have recently involved attempts to bring cases within the misrepresentation and deceit exclusions of the F.T.C.A. In *Ramirez v. United States*, a suit was initiated against the United States alleging that a government physician was negligent in failing to warn his patient of the risk of granuloma in connection with a stapedectomy.[29] The district court dismissed the action on grounds that failure to warn constituted a misrepresentation within the meaning of the F.T.C.A. exclusion. The Ninth Circuit Court of Appeals reversed and reinstated the suit, holding that the failure to warn of risks attendant to surgery did not constitute a misrepresentation. The court found that "the creation of strained distinctions to encompass aspects of ordinary medical malpractice within the misrepresentation exception" was not justified by the language, purpose, or legislative history of the statute.[30]

The same conclusion had been reached earlier by a federal district court. In *Wright v. Doe*, the plaintiff alleged that the defendant physician misrepresented the characteristics of a medication that he prescribed and deceived the plaintiff regarding its effects.[31] The plaintiff specifically worded his complaint to bring it within the F.T.C.A. misrepresentation exclusion, on the assumption that he would be permitted to pursue the claim in state court against the physician personally. The court found that this result might have been inescapable under the F.T.C.A.; however, Congress precluded the action against the individual physician by enacting the exclusive remedy statute for the protection of health care providers employed by the VA.[32] The personal immunity of the individual health care providers may have influenced both courts in concluding that the malpractice lawsuits did not fall within the misrepresentation exclusion. This decision permitted the suits to proceed in federal court against the United States.

The misrepresentation exception was also implicated in *Blanton v. United States*, where the plaintiff claimed that she was mislead and deceived by medical personnel who advised her that Hyp-Rho-D was as effective as Rho-Gam in suppressing the autoimmune response of a Rh-positive infant.[33] Although the court found that it was not necessary to decide whether the case fell within the F.T.C.A. exclusions, it expressed the opinion that "the clear violation . . . of the duty of accurate description may be a misrepresentation or battery and therefore not actionable" under the F.T.C.A.[34]

Few courts have addressed these issues and those doing so have often reached different conclusions. For example, in the case of *Lojuk v. Quandt*,[35] the court came to the completely opposite conclusion than the court in the previously above mentioned *Wright* case on the interrelationship of the F.T.C.A., and exclusive remedy statutes applicable to VA medical personnel.[36]

In *Lojuk*, a psychiatric patient alleged that a VA psychiatrist subjected him to electroconvulsive therapy without his consent. The court found that the plaintiff was bringing suit for battery, that the United States was immune from suits for battery, but that the exclusive remedy statute that protected VA health care providers from "malpractice" suits did *not* immunize the individual health care provider from suit for intentional torts. The court in *Wright* had previously held that the word "malpractice" included claims based upon any action arising from the performance of professional duties, regardless of how the claim is phrased. Thus, in *Wright*, the lawsuit proceeded against the United States because the physician was immune. On the other hand, in *Lojuk*, the lawsuit was allowed to proceed against the individual physician while the United States was held to be immune.

Lojuk points out a critical distinction between the exclusive remedy statutes, mentioned earlier in the chapter, which may be significant in future judicial decisions regarding the F.T.C.A. intentional tort exclusions. The exclusive remedy statutes applicable to PHS and NASA employees specifically provide that the F.T.C.A. exclusion for assault and battery does not apply to assault and battery arising out of the performance of medical, dental, or related functions.[37] These provisions bring consent cases under the F.T.C.A. where the suit is based on the conduct of a PHS or NASA employee in providing health care. The exclusive remedy statute applicable to VA personnel does *not* include a similar provision. Obviously, employees of other federal agencies who are not covered by a specific exclusive remedy statute in addition to the F.T.C.A. do not have this assurance that they cannot be held personally liable for "medical battery" or assaults.

It is significant to note that the PHS statute applies only to assault and battery, whereas the NASA statute applies to all the intentional torts excluded by the F.T.C.A.[38] This distinction may be critical in cases alleging false imprisonment. False imprisonment may be implicated by patients complaining of improper restraint or seclusion. It is not possible to predict how a given court will rule on these emerging issues.

Although the intentional tort exclusions are precipitating much uncertainty, other F.T.C.A. exclusions potentially applicable to federally employed nurses are more clearly defined. The foreign country exclusion was intended to prevent potential problems with applying and interpreting foreign law, which would be applicable as the law of the state where the wrongdoing occurred. This exception would preclude malpractice actions against the United States based upon health care provided in its overseas military medical facilities and embassies.[39]

The discretionary function exception has been held to bar actions based upon the refusal to admit a nonmilitary patient to a military hospital.[40] This rule stems from a federal statute and regulations that authorize military medical officers to provide medical services to dependents of military personnel whenever practicable. It is generally accepted that claims arising from the provision of health care services once a patient has been admitted are not barred by the discretionary function exception.[41]

A judicially created circumvention of the exclusive remedy provision under the F.T.C.A. was fashioned by the U.S. Supreme Court to allow redress of constitutional violations of federal employees. In *Bivens v. Six Unknown Federal Narcotics Agents*, the Supreme Court held that victims of a constitutional violation by a federal agent have the right to recover damages against the official in federal court despite the absence of any statute conferring that right.[42] Known as the "Bivens remedy," the Court has held that it allows suit against the individual federal employee even though a remedy was also available through an action against the United States under the F.T.C.A. The parameters of the Bivens remedy are complicated, and its applicability to health care providers has not been fully explored by the courts. Chapter 5 discusses civil rights claims further. The implication for nurses is that potential personal liability exists where the plaintiff claims that constitutional rights have been violated. One example might involve the nurse employed by the federal corrections system. See Chapter 16 for more on this topic.

Procedural Effects and Requirements of the F.T.C.A. Once it has been determined that the F.T.C.A. governs the claim, specific statutory procedural requirements and limitations are triggered. The F.T.C.A. contains a mandatory prelitigation filing requirement that precludes suit unless the claimant (plaintiff) first presents the claim to the appropriate federal agency.[43] The agency must deny the claim either in writing or by failing to make a final disposition of the claim within 6 months. The purpose of the administrative procedure is to allow the government the opportunity to review, compromise, and settle meritorious cases, if possible, and discourage frivolous litigation.[44] The claim must be presented to the agency in writing within 2 years after the claim accrues and suit must be initiated in court within 6 months of the agency's written denial.[45]

Until a 1979 Supreme Court decision, the rule for determining when a claim accrues in a malpractice action under the F.T.C.A. was unsettled. *Kubrick v. United States*, a suit arising from allegedly negligent medical treatment in a VA hospital, brought this issue to the Supreme Court.[46] This case involved a claim by a veteran treated for an infection of the right femur. The infected area was irrigated with neomycin and eventually resolved. He subsequently developed ringing in the ears and hearing loss, which was diagnosed as bilateral nerve deafness. Although a physician informed Kubrick in 1969 that the hearing loss was possibly related to the neomycin, he did not seek legal advice until 1972, after another physician stated that the neomycin caused the injury and should not have been given.

The Supreme Court held that the claim accrues when the plaintiff knows both the existence and the cause of his injury, and *not* at a later time when he knows that the acts inflicting the injury may constitute medical malpractice. The court stated that a claimant in possession of the critical facts that he has been hurt and who has inflicted the injury has an affirmative duty to seek advice in the legal and medical community to determine whether he has been wronged. The court carefully distinguished a plaintiff's ignorance of his legal rights from ignorance of the fact of injury and its cause. The *Kubrick* majority concluded that the accrual of a claim is not delayed until the plaintiff is aware that the injury was negligently inflicted.

The contours of this rule and possible exceptions are now the subject of considerable litigation. One federal district court recently held that "blameless ignorance" tolled the statute of limitations where it was a result of the claimant's incompetence.[47] Another court has held that while the relevant medical data remained lost in inaccessible medical files, the limitations period did not begin to run. The date on which a claim accrues is dependent on the specific facts presented by each case. Because there is no strong consensus on many issues involved, a review of the current case law in the appropriate jurisdiction is necessary before an opinion could be given with any degree of reliability.[48]

Other procedural effects and limitations in F.T.C.A. proceedings provided by statute are better established. An action against the United States under the F.T.C.A. must be filed in the district court (U.S.) for the judicial district where the plaintiff resides or the act or omission complained of occurred.[49] The lawsuit must be defended by the attorney general,[50] and no jury is allowed.[51] The suit may not seek damages in excess of the amount of the claim presented to the federal agency unless the additional amount claimed is based upon intervening facts or newly discovered evidence.[52] No punitive damages or prejudgment interest can be recovered, but in other respects, the United States is subject to the same liability as a private person under similar circumstances.[53]

Liability issues are governed by the law of the state where the alleged wrong occurred.[54] This means that the applicable standard of nursing care is determined by reference to state law, including the nurse practice act of that state. In the U.S. Virgin Islands, health care professionals, including nurses, are required to exercise "the skill and knowledge normally possessed by members of the profession in good standing" who are practicing in the same field and in the same or similar community.[55]

State law also determines whether any remedy exists for the alleged wrong. This is highly significant in cases involving newly emerging legal theories, such as wrongful birth and wrongful life claims. One court has found that a remedy did exist under state law for a wrongful birth claim brought against the United States by the parents of a child born with Down's syndrome.[56] The court acknowledged, however, that a cause of action for wrongful birth is not recognized in all jurisdictions. In these and other situations where state laws differ, whether a particular claim will be allowed will depend upon where the plaintiff happened to be when the wrongful act occurred.

The foregoing discussion of the F.T.C.A. and its application to malpractice actions against civilian employees of the federal government is an overview. This discussion alerts nurses to potential issues in their practice. The issues are complex and can only be addressed through thorough analysis of the facts in each case.

ACTIONS BY AND AGAINST MEMBERS OF THE ARMED FORCES

"Members of the military or naval forces of the United States" are specifically included within the F.T.C.A. definition of "employee of the government."[57] In 1976 Congress made an action against the United States under the F.T.C.A., the exclusive remedy for malpractice by health care providers, including nurses, in the armed forces, Department of Defense (DOD), and the Central Intelligence Agency (CIA).[58] Accordingly, the F.T.C.A, applies to all malpractice actions based upon the conduct of nurses and others who are members of or employed by the armed forces unless the action is barred by statutory or judicially created exceptions.

Actions by Members of the Armed Forces. The largest and by far the most notable exception to government liability for the actions of its military nurses and other health care providers is the judicially created *Feres* doctrine. This doctrine developed from three cases that were heard by the Supreme Court in 1950 and decided in one opinion.[59] The issue in all three cases was whether the government could be held liable under the F.T.C.A. for injuries to members of the military where the injuries arose out of or were in the course of activity incident to service. The Supreme Court concluded that Congress did not intend to create a civil remedy for service connected injuries under the F.T.C.A.; thus the government could not be held liable.

The *Feres* decision was subsequently discussed by the Supreme Court in *United States v. Brown* and the line between allowable and barred claims was explained.[60] The court adhered to the line drawn in *Feres* between injuries that did and injuries that did not arise out of or in the course of military duty. Injuries to active duty service personnel as a result of health care provided in military hospitals have consistently been held to be "incident to service" and barred by the *Feres* doctrine. Brown's action for aggravation of a service-connected injury by negligent medical care at a VA hospital following his discharge from active duty was allowed.

Another court extended the *Feres* reasoning to prohibit an action by an enlisted person in the armed services against an army surgeon personally for alleged negligence in the performance of an operation at an army hospital.[61] The court pointed out that compensation is available to the injured member of the armed forces and reasoned that considerations of the military command structure and discipline that underlie the *Feres* group of decisions were equally applicable when the physician was sued personally.[62] This same court also expanded the immunity of military surgeons to include suits for alleged malpractice in the course of their duties where the injured plaintiff is a retired army enlisted person no longer on active duty.[63]

The limitations of the *Feres* doctrine barring suits for injuries to active duty personnel are being actively explored in contemporary litigation. Recovery was recently denied for injuries to a third party, allegedly derivative of a service-connected injury to a member of the armed forces.[64] In this case the court, relying on the *Feres* doctrine, decided that the daughter of a former member of the service could not recover for birth defects resulting from genetic changes in her father that occurred as a result of exposure to radiation while on active duty.

Another court has held that the *Feres* doctrine bars a F.T.C.A. suit by an infant born with congenital rubella syndrome as a result of her mother's exposure while on active duty in the Air Force.[65] In yet another case, the court followed the lead of several lower courts and held that the *Feres* doctrine precluded government liability for failure to warn active duty military personnel of hazards from exposure to radiation while on active duty.[66] The court recognized, however, that if the duty to warn arose from an independent negligent act by the government after the person was discharged from active duty, an action could be maintained. The court suggested that failure to warn and failure to monitor an ex-service person's condition would be an independent postdischarge negligent act if the government did not learn of the potential hazard until after the person left active duty.

The applicability of the *Feres* doctrine and the intentional tort exclusion of the F.T.C.A. to an action based upon the murder of one off-duty service person by another has been considered by the Supreme Court.[67] The mother of an army private, who was killed by a fellow serviceman while off duty, brought an action against the United States under the FTCA, claiming that the army's alleged negligence caused her son's death. The Supreme Court held that the *Feres* doctrine barred recovery notwithstanding that the incident occurred off base and off duty or that the mother characterized the claim as a challenge to a straightforward personnel decision, because the matter involved a decision of command.

The rule is now well accepted, however, that malpractice to an active duty soldier in a military hospital is, by its very nature, considered activity incident to service and therefore a lawsuit is barred under *Feres*.

Claims of Military Dependents and Other Non-active Duty Military Patients. In 1976 Congress severely restricted potential malpractice actions against active duty military personnel by enacting an exclusive remedy statute similar to those previously discussed. Prior to the effective date of this provision (Oct. 8, 1976) military nurses and others were essentially unprotected against malpractice lawsuits that were outside the scope of the F.T.C.A. coverage and the *Feres* doctrine.[68] As discussed previously, the gaps could be significant in the cases of alleged malpractice causing injury to military dependents and other nonmilitary patients in military hospitals. The exclusive remedy statute enacted to fill this gap applies to actions based upon the negligent or wrongful acts or omissions of physicians, dentists, nurses, pharmacists, and paramedical and other supporting personnel in the armed forces, or employed with the DOD, CIA, and the U.S. Soldiers' and Airmen's Home. The statute provides that the F.T.C.A. remedy for injuries resulting from the performance of medical, dental, or related functions is exclusive of all other civil actions. The statute also expressly provides that the intentional tort exclusions, as already discussed, under F.T.C.A. do not apply to actions based upon the performance of medical, dental, or related health care functions, including clinical studies. Although the courts that have addressed the issue have held that the purpose of the statute is to provide complete immunity for individual military medical personnel and to eliminate the need for personal malpractice insurance, small areas of potential vulnerability may remain.[69] For example, claims arising in foreign countries are excluded from the F.T.C.A.[70]

The *New York Times* has reported that the quality of care provided by military medical facilities is under increasing attack and criticism from the individuals they serve.[71] According to this account, a 1984 survey of more than 19,000 patients revealed that most families were dissatisfied with military care, ranking it below civilian care in all respects. The author reports that malpractice claims filed against the government for military medical care jumped 24% from 1982 to 1984, with the total amount paid in settlement of claims rising 41% in the same period. The Pentagon asserts that the rate of malpractice suits based upon military medical care is below the rate of claims against civilian health care professionals and facilities, with 854 claims filed in 1984.[72]

Despite new quality assurance procedures being developed and implemented by the Pentagon, claims will certainly continue to be filed. Even though the military nurse has personal immunity, this is no guarantee that he or she cannot become involved in a malpractice lawsuit or that the quality of care delivered cannot be called into question.

Other statutes affecting nursing practice in the federal government

Although the Federal Tort Claims Act and its several exclusive remedy statutes are an important part of nursing practice in the federal government, many other statutes are also of importance to the practice of a federally employed nurse. These include the Uniform Code of Military Justice, the Federal Employees Compensation Act, and statutes on particular topics such as confidentiality, patient rights, and medical records in the federal government facilities.

UNIFORM CODE OF MILITARY JUSTICE

Nurses who are in military service or whose employment is in any way connected with the U.S. Armed Forces are governed by the provisions of the Uniform Code of Military Justice (UCMJ).[73] This code establishes a military criminal justice system that includes offenses and penalties unique to the military service and a completely separate judicial system. Article 2 lists those persons who are subject to the UCMJ. Its application is not limited to active duty members of the armed services and includes students at military academies, members of the military reserves while on duty under written orders, and military retirees entitled to pay. In addition, the UCMJ applies by its terms to members of the National Oceanic and Atmospheric Administration, the PHS, and other organizations when serving with the armed forces; persons serving with, employed by, or accompanying armed forces outside the United States, Panama Canal Zone, Guam, or Virgin Islands; and persons within areas leased by or reserved for the use of the United States or its territories. The last categories would include civilian nurses working in military hospitals both in and outside the United States, nurses working in embassies, and those who work in any area under the control of the U.S. government or its territories.

When the question was first raised in 1866, the U.S. Supreme Court upheld the applicability of the UCMJ to civilians, holding that individuals connected with military and naval services surrender their rights to be tried by civilian courts.[74] That rule has been severely, if not completely, eroded, however, by subsequent decisions. In *Reid v. Covert*, the court held that the U.S. Constitution rendered inapplicable the provision of clause 10 U.S.C. §802 (11) to a trial of civilian dependents of members of the armed forces overseas for capital offenses when no hostilities were underway.[75] Three years later, the Supreme Court held that an overseas civilian employee of the U.S. armed services was not subject to court-martial jurisdiction for capital or noncapital offenses.[76] Whether any areas of UCMJ are applicable to nonmilitary personnel in peacetime is uncertain. Civilian nurses employed or associated with the military or U.S. government overseas can check with the installation legal office for additional information on the UCMJ.

Persons who are subject to UCMJ are governed by its provisions in all places.[77] The military authorities are authorized to deliver a member of the armed forces accused of an offense against civil authority to that authority for trial.[78] A commanding officer is authorized to impose nonjudicial punishment upon officers or other personnel for minor offenses without court-martial.[79] Other punishable offenses require trial by court-martial and conviction before any punishment can be imposed. Articles 18 to 20 establish the jurisdiction of general, special, and summary court-martial proceedings. The box on p. 293 outlines courts-martial jurisdiction composition, and limits on punishment. Articles 77 to 134 establish offenses and maximum punishment that would be imposed.

Many offenses that would not be punishable in a nonmilitary situation *are* punishable under the UCMJ. These include, for example, absence without leave, which includes failing to report for duty; behaving with disrespect toward a superior commissioned officer; willfully disobeying a lawful order; being derelict in the performance of duties; intentionally self-inflicting injury; and feigning illness, physical disablement, mental lapse, or derangement. The box on p. 294 contains a partial list of offenses and punishments under the UCMJ.

The procedural requirements for courts-martial are set forth in Articles 22 to 54. Under constitutional authority, the UCMJ provides that persons subject to the UCMJ waive the right to grand jury indictment and the right to trial in civilian courts.[80] Although not all constitutional safeguards applicable to nonmilitary criminal defendants are constitutionally required with respect to military offenders, the UCMJ does incorporate most of the constitutional protections. The military defendant in court-martial proceedings is entitled to representation by appointed counsel and to confront witnesses.[81] The box on p. 295, upper left, lists additional protections afforded the accused in courts-martial proceedings. The military nurse can seek further information about court-martial proceedings from the legal officer at the military installation.

MILITARY HEALTH RECORDS

The military nurse and civilian nurse treating military patients are subject to the provisions of the UCMJ regarding maintaining military health records. Intentional self-inflicted injuries and malingering are punishable offenses and can subject the military member to a dishonorable discharge and confinement at hard labor. Breaking medical quarantine can be punished by forfeiture of pay and/or imprisonment. Because of these laws, nursing documentation should be carefully constructed. Concluding statements regarding malingering and self-inflicted injuries in medical rec-

COURTS-MARTIAL PROCEEDINGS

General Courts-Martial

Composition: military judge and not less than five members (unless waived)

Jurisdiction: may try persons subject to UCMJ for any offense punishable under UMCJ

Limits on punishment: may impose any punishment authorized by UCMJ

Who may convene: president of the United States, secretary of branch concerned (Army, Navy, Air Force), or designated commanding officer

Special Courts-Martial

Composition: not less than three members; may also include military judge (Defendant may waive all but the judge.)

Jurisdiction: may try any person subject to UCMJ for any non–capital offense

Limits on punishment: may impose any punishment except death, dishonorable discharge, dismissal, confinement at hard labor for more than 6 months, hard labor without confinement more than 3 months, or forfeiture of pay more than 3 months

Who may convene: any person who may convene general courts-martial; designated commanding officer

Summary Courts-Martial

Composition: one commissioned officer

Jurisdiction: no person may be tried by summary proceedings if he or she objects; officers and students at military academies may not be tried

Limits on punishment: may impose any punishment except death, dismissal, dishonorable or bad conduct discharge, confinement more than 1 month, or hard labor without confinement more than 45 days

Who may convene: any person who may convene a general or special courts-martial; designated commanding officers

Adapted from Uniform Code of Military Justice, Arts. 18-20.

ords should be avoided. Since a member of the armed forces can be involuntarily separated from the military for health reasons, military medical records can have a substantial impact upon a military career. This does not mean, however, that recordkeeping is not complete and contain all pertinent facts and observations. Article 107 of the UCMJ makes it a punishable offense to sign any false record, return, regulation, order, or other official document.

Unlike its civilian counterpart, in the military health care system, medical records must accompany the military member when transferred to a new duty station. Before leaving one base for a new assignment, the individual is required to *clear base*. This procedure requires the member of the service to pick up outpatient medical records and obtain the signature of the medical records custodian that this has been done.

CONFIDENTIALITY AND INFORMED CONSENT

Congress has enacted two statutes that expressly recognize the rights of patients in VA hospitals and provide for their protection. An informed consent statute requires the VA to ensure that medical and prosthetic research is carried out only with the full and informed consent of the patient.[82] The statute also requires informed consent be obtained for all patient care but only to the maximum extent practicable. Neither the statute nor subsequently adopted regulations clarify the meaning or limits of "practicality" with respect to obtaining consent. The regulations explain the requirements for informed consent and place responsibility for providing the information and obtaining consent upon "the practitioner who has primary responsibility for the patient or who will perform the particular procedure or providing the treatment."[83] The box on p. 295, bottom, lists 16 patient rights in VA facilities.

The impact of the statutory recognition of patient's rights, uniquely applicable to VA facilities and patients, has not been explored by the courts. A nurse may violate any of these rights, however, if nursing practice is not evaluated on the basis of these regulations. A court could hold that proof of the violation of a patient's right is sufficient by itself to prove malpractice. The patient's rights statute could also play a part in a Bivens remedy situation, as mentioned earlier in the chapter.

The VA nurse must be familiar with the patient's rights statutes and regulations and affirmatively plan for their protection. Two provisions of the current regulations are particularly significant in modern, expanded nursing practice. These regulations mandate that a patient may be restrained, placed in seclusion, or administered medication *only* on the written orders of a physician. Although telephone orders are permitted, an order for restraint or seclusion must be signed by the physician

SELECTED OFFENSES AND PUNISHMENTS UNDER THE UCMJ

Absence without leave, failing to go to or going from authorized place of duty

For more than 3 days: confinement at hard labor, not to exceed 1 month; forfeiture of two-thirds pay, not to exceed 1 month

For more than 3 days but less than 30 days: confinement at hard labor, not to exceed 6 months; forfeiture of two-thirds pay, not to exceed 6 months

For more than 30 days: dishonorable discharge, forfeiture of all pay and allowances; confinement at hard labor, not to exceed 1 year

Behaving with disrespect toward superior commissioned officer: bad conduct discharge, forfeiture of all pay and allowances; confinement at hard labor, not to exceed 6 months

Willfully disobeying a lawful order of a superior commissioned officer: dishonorable discharge, forfeiture of all pay and allowances; confinement at hard labor, not to exceed 5 years

Violating or failing to obey any lawful general order or regulation: dishonorable discharge, forfeiture of all pay and allowances; confinement at hard labor, not to exceed 2 years

Being derelict in the performance of duties: confinement at hard labor, not to exceed 3 months; forfeiture of two-thirds pay per month, not to exceed 3 months

Signing any false record, return, regulation, order, or other official document: dishonorable discharge, forfeiture of all pay and allowances; confinement at hard labor not to exceed 1 year

Found drunk on duty: bad conduct discharge, forfeiture of all pay and allowances; confinement at hard labor not to exceed 9 months

Feigning illness, physical disability, mental lapse, or derangement: dishonorable discharge, forfeiture of all pay and allowances; confinement at hard labor not to exceed 1 year

Intentional self-inflicted injury: dishonorable discharge, forfeiture of all pay and allowances; confinement at hard labor not to exceed 7 years

Drugs, habit forming—wrongful possession, sale, transfer, use, or introduction into a military unit: dishonorable discharge, forfeiture of all pay and allowances; confinement at hard labor not to exceed 10 years

Drugs, marijuana—wrongful possession, sale, transfer, use, or introduction into a military unit: dishonorable discharge, forfeiture of all pay and allowances; confinement at hard labor not to exceed 5 years

Breaking medical quarantine: confinement at hard labor not to exceed 6 months; forfeiture of two-thirds pay per month, not to exceed 6 months

Unclean accoutrement, arms, clothing, equipment, or other military property: confinement at hard labor, not to exceed 1 month; forfeiture of two-thirds pay, not to exceed 1 month

Uniform—unclean, appearing in or not in prescribed uniform, or in uniform worn in other than manner prescribed: confinement at hard labor not to exceed 1 month; forfeiture of two-thirds pay, not to exceed 1 month

Wearing unauthorized insignia, medal, decoration, or badge: confinement at hard labor not to exceed 6 months; forfeiture of two-thirds pay, not to exceed 6 months

Adapted from Uniform Code of Military Justice, Arts 83-134.

within 12 hours and medication orders countersigned within 24 hours. A copy of the statement of patient's rights must be given to each patient upon admission and to each staff member who works directly with patients and must be posted at each nurse's station.

A second statute applicable solely to the VA establishes the confidentiality of certain medical records.[84] This law mandates that records disclosing the identity, diagnosis, prognosis, or treatment of any patient in any VA drug abuse, alcoholism or alcohol abuse, or sickle cell anemia program shall be confidential. The law prescribes the circumstances under which the content of the records may be disclosed, which include prior written consent of the patient, disclosure to medical personnel to the extent necessary to meet a bona fide medical emergency, and where authorized by court order. The records referred to in the statute may not be used to initiate or substantiate any criminal charges or conduct any investigation of the patient except when authorized by court order.[85] The court must find good cause for disclosure that outweighs the potential injury to the patient, the physician-patient relationship, and the treatment services.

The rule of strict confidentiality is not applicable to the release of medical records within the military system. The statute specifically authorizes the interchange of records within the VA health care system and between the VA and the armed services. There are policy and procedures, including Army and other armed forces regulations, which govern confidentiality.

SELECTED RIGHTS OF MILITARY PERSONNEL UNDER UCMJ

Charges and specifications must be in writing, signed, and served on an accused person.
Compulsory self-incrimination is prohibited.
Accused person has right to be represented by military counsel of own selection or by civilian if provided by accused.
No person may be tried a second time for the same offense without consent (prohibition against double jeopardy).
All parties to courts-martial have equal opportunity to obtain witnesses and other evidence, the right to compel witnesses to appear and testify, and the right to compel production of evidence.

Adapted from Uniform Code of Military Justice, Arts. 27, 30-31, 35, 38, 44, 46.

Recommendations and trends

This chapter has familiarized the reader with the basic statutes and judicially created doctrines uniquely affecting the federally employed nurse as defendant. The rights of patients to seek compensation for the professional negligence of nurses employed by the federal government are largely controlled by federal legislation. The judiciary has defined and carved out exceptions to this legislation as it has deemed necessary. Certain statutes mentioned in this chapter need some legislative action to clarify that they include the federally employed nurse.

Changes in military health care are underway. For example, Defense Secretary Weinberger has ordered the armed services to make wartime medical readiness rather than peacetime health care their first priority.[86] In addition, legislation is being considered that would allow military personnel the right to sue the government in medical malpractice cases.[87] Meanwhile, the Veterans Administration, the United States' largest health care system, is also coming under scrutiny.[88] Improved and increased quality assurance measures are needed.

Endnotes

1. *See, e.g.*, DEPT. OF ARMY, ARMY MEDICAL DEPT. STANDARDS OF NURSING PRACTICE (1981); STANDARDS OF SPECIALTY NURSING PRACTICE, COMMUNITY HEALTH NURSING (1983); OCCUPATIONAL HEALTH NURSING (1986). Those apply to both army nurses and civilian nurses who are employed by the army. Other nursing standards discussed in this book should also be reviewed.
2. 28 U.S.C. §2671-2680 (1982). These provisions apply to all federal employees, not only to nurses and other health care personnel.
3. 28 U.S.C. §2674 (1982) provides that the claims that are cognizable under 28 U.S.C. §1346(b) and the remedies provided by the Federal Torts Claims Act (F.T.C.A.) for those claims "shall be exclusive." 28 U.S.C. §1346(b) applies to "claims against the U.S., for money damages, accruing on and after January 1, 1945, for injury or loss of property, or personal injury or death caused by the negligent or wrongful act or omission of any employee of the Government while acting within the scope of his office or

PATIENTS' RIGHTS IN VETERANS ADMINISTRATION FACILITIES

1. Informed consent: practitioner performing procedure must inform patient of (a) nature of proposed procedure or treatment; (b) expected benefits; (c) reasonable foreseeable risks, complications, or side effects; (d) reasonable and available alternatives; and (e) anticipated results if nothing done.
2. Treatment with dignity in a humane, safe environment
3. Privacy with regard to personal needs
4. Prompt and appropriate treatment for physical or emotional disability
5. Least restrictive conditions necessary to achieve treatment purposes
6. Right to exercise legal rights, such as manage property, enter contractual relationships, execute legal instruments, register to vote, marry and divorce, and hold professional occupational or vehicle operator's licenses
7. Opportunity to communicate freely with persons outside the facility and to receive visitors
8. Right to wear own clothing and keep and use personal possessions to extent consistent with safety regulations and rights of other patients
9. Regular physical exercise, indoors and outdoors
10. Right to keep and use personal possessions and money
11. Opportunity for religious worship
12. Opportunity to interact with others
13. Freedom from physical restraint or seclusion, except when substantial risk of imminent self-injury or harm to others exists
14. Freedom from unnecessary or excessive medication
15. Confidentiality of all information obtained from the patient in the course of treatment
16. Right to present grievances with respect to infringement of rights

Adapted from 38 C.F.R. §17.34, 17.34a (1985).

employment, under circumstances where the U.S., if a private person, would be liable to the claimant in accordance with the law of the place where the act or omission occurred."

4. 38 U.S.C. §4116 (1982) (Veterans); 42 U.S.C. §233 (1982) (PHS); 42 U.S.C. §2458 a. (1982) (NSP and NASA).
5. 42 U.S.C. Sec. 2458 a. (1982) provides: "(a) The remedy against the U.S. . . . for damages for personal injury, including death, caused by the negligent or wrongful act or omission of any physician, dentist, *nurse* (emphasis added), pharmacist or paramedical or other supporting personnel (including medical and dental technicians, nursing assistants and therapists) of the Administration in the performance of medical, dental, or related health care functions (including clinical studies and investigations) while acting within the scope of his duties or employment therein or therefore shall hereafter be exclusive of any other civil action or proceeding by reason of the same subject matter against such physician, dentist, nurse, pharmacist or paramedical or other supporting personnel (or the estate of such persons) whose act or omission gave rise to such action or proceeding."
6. 42 U.S.C. §2458 a. (c) (1982).
7. 42 U.S.C. §233 (e) (1982) states: "Assault or battery. For purposes of this section, the provisions of section 2680 (h) of title 28 shall not apply to assault or battery arising out of negligence in the performance of medical, surgical, dental or related functions, including the conduct of clinical studies or investigations."
8. 42 U.S.C. §233 (a) (1982) provides: "Exclusiveness of remedy. The remedy against the U.S. provided by §1346 (b) and 2672 of Title 28 or by alternative benefits provided by the U.S. where the availability of such benefits precludes a remedy under §1346 (b) of title 28, for damages for personal injury, including death, resulting from the performance of medical, surgical, dental, or related functions, including the conduct of clinical studies or investigations, by any commissioned officer or employee of the PHS while acting within the scope of his office or employment, shall be exclusive of any other civil action or proceeding by reason of the same subject matter against the officer or employee (or his estate) whose act or omission gave rise to the claim."
9. 523 F. Supp. 1372 (W.D. Pa. 1981).
10. 42 U.S.C. §233 (b) (1982) provides that the attorney general of the United States shall defend all actions against any person covered by §233 (a). It requires employees who are sued directly to deliver all documents relating to the suit (or certified copies) to his or her immediate superior, who must then forward the documents to the U.S. attorney for the district where suit is brought.
11. *See, e.g., Feres v. United States,* 340 U.S. 135, 138-40 (1950) for discussion of the history and purpose of the F.T.C.A. The statute as originally enacted, Aug. 2, 1946, is found at 60 Stat. 843.
12. 28 U.S.C. §2671 (1982).
13. 28 U.S.C. §2680 (1982).
14. 38 U.S.C. §1346 (b) (1982).
15. *United States v. Orleans,* 425 U.S. 807 (1971); *Logue v. United States,* 412 U.S. 521 (1973).
16. 671 F.2d 825 (4th Cir. 1982); The plaintiff also sued his employer, Standard Products, claiming the physician was an agent of the employer and that the employer was responsible for the physician's negligence.
17. Air Force Hospital: *Walker v. United States,* 549 F. Supp. 973 (W.D. Okla. 1982); VA Hospital: *Lurch v. United States,* 719 F.2d 333 (10th Cir. 1983), *cert. denied,* 104 S. Ct. 1710 (1984).
18. Other circuits have held that the issue of employment status is determined by state law. *E.g., Fries v. United States,* 170 F.2d 726 (6th Cir. 1948), *cert. denied,* 336 U.S. 954; *Buchanan v. United States,* 305 F.2d 738 (8th Cir. 1962).
19. *Lurch v. United States,* 719 F.2d 333, 337 (10th Cir. 1983), *cert. denied,* 104 S.Ct. 1710 (1984).
20. 28 U.S.C. §2671, (1982) and 28 U.S.C. §1346 (b) (1982).
21. The *Restatements* are compilations of the prevailing rules of common law published by the American Law Institute. They are the applicable rules of law in the U.S. Virgin Islands in the absence of contrary local law. V.I. CODE ANN. tit. 1, §4 (1967).
22. *Restatement of Agency (Second),* §219-237. Section 220 defines a "servant" and lists factors for determining whether "one acting for another is a servant or an independent contractor." *See* box.
23. 28 U.S.C. §1271 (1982).
24. *See, e.g., Williams v. United States.* 350 U.S. 857 (1955); *Mandelbaum v. United States,* 251 F.2d 748 (2nd Cir. 1958); *Witt v. United States,* 319 F.2d 704 (9th Cir. 1973); *Mider v. United States,* 322 F.2d 193 (6th Cir. 1963); *Merritt v. United States,* 332 F.2d 397 (1st Cir. 1964).
25. *Kosak v. United States,* 104 S. Ct. 1519 (1984). The court recognized that the general purposes behind the congressionally created exceptions to the F.T.C.A. were to ensure that "certain governmental activities" not be disrupted by the threat of damage suits, to avoid exposure of the United States to liability for excessive or fraudulent claims, and not to extend coverage of the act to suits for which adequate remedies were already available. *Id.* at 1524-1527.
26. *See generally, Note, The Evolution of the Doctrine of Informed Consent,* 12 GEORGIA LAW REVIEW, 581 (1978).
27. 465 F. Supp. 1071 (D. Kan. 1979).
28. *Marino v. Ballestras,* 749 F.2d 162, 167 (3rd Cir. 1984).
29. 567 F.2d 854 (9th Cir. 1977).
30. *Id.* at 857.
31. 347 F. Supp. 833 (D. Fla. 1972).
32. 38 U.S.C. §4115 (1982).
33. 428 F. Supp. 360 (D. D.C. 1977).
34. *Id.* at 362.
35. 706 F.2d 1456 (7th Cir. 1983).
36. 38 U.S.C. §4116 (a) (1982).
37. 42 U.S.C. §233 (c) (1982) (PHS); 42 U.S.C. §2458 a. (e) (1982) (NASA).
38. 28 U.S.C. §2680 (h).
39. 28 U.S.C. §2680; 38 U.S.C. §1346 (b).
40. *See Denny v. United States,* 171 F.2d 365 (5th Cir. 1948), *cert. denied,* 337 U.S. 919 (1949), where the court held that suit seeking damages for the stillbirth of a child allegedly caused by the military hospital's failure to promptly dispatch an ambulance was barred by the discretionary function exception.
41. *See, e.g., Grigalauskas v. United States,* 103 F. Supp. 543 (D. Mass. 1951), *affd,* 195 F.2d 494 (1st Cir. 1952); *Costley v. United States,* 181 F.2d 723 (5th Cir. 1950). *But see Blitz v. Boog,* 328 F.2d 596 (2nd Cir.), *cert. denied,* 379 U.S. 855 (1964).
42. 403 U.S. 388 (1971).
43. 28 U.S.C. §2674 (1982).
44. 28 U.S.C. §2672 (1982) authorizes the heads of federal agencies to settle claims prior to suit.
45. 28 U.S.C. §2401 (1982).
46. 444 U.S. 111 (1979).
47. *Pardy v. United States,* 575 F. Supp. 1078 (S.D. Ill. 1983), which

involved a comatose patient. The court held that during this period the plaintiff could not have known the existence and cause of his injury.

48. *See Annotation, Statute of Limitations,* 29 A.L.R. FED. 482 (1976).
49. 28 U.S.C. §1346 (b), §1402 (b) (1982). Forum shopping can occur as the plaintiff can change the venue of a potential suit by changing residence prior to filing.
50. 28 U.S.C. §2679 (c) (1982).
51. 28 U.S.C. §2402 (1982).
52. 28 U.S.C. §2675 (b) (1982).
53. 28 U.S.C. §2674 (1982).
54. 28 U.S.C. §1346 (b) (1982).
55. RESTATEMENT (SECOND) OF TORTS, §299 A (1965).
56. *Phillips v. United States,* 508 F. Supp. 522 (D. S.C. 1981).
57. 28 U.S.C. §2671 (1982).
58. 10 U.S.C. §1089 (1982 & Supp. I 1983).
59. *Feres, Executrix v. United States,* 340 U.S. 135, 136-37 (1950). The companion *Griggs* and *Jefferson* cases were both medical malpractice actions.
60. 348 U.S. 110 (1954).
61. *Bailey v. DeQuevedo,* 375 F.2d 72 (3rd Cir.), *cert. denied,* 389 U.S. 923, (1967). This suit occurred before the enactment of the exclusive remedy statute prohibiting suits against military physicians and nurses.
62. 38 U.S.C. §301-1008 (1982 & Supp. I 1983) provides "no-fault" compensation as a substitute for tort liability for service-related injuries.
63. *Martinez v. Schrock,* 537 F.2d 765 (3rd Cir. 1976), *cert. denied,* 430 U.S. 920 (1977).
64. *Monaco v. United States,* 661 F.2d 129 (9th Cir. 1981), *cert. denied,* 456 U.S. 989 (1982).
65. *Scales v. United States,* 685 F.2d 970 (5th Cir. 1982)., *cert. denied,* 460 U.S. 1082 (1983). The mother claimed that the rubella resulted from an immunization that was administered to her without determining whether she was pregnant.
66. *Broudy v. United States,* 661 F.2d 125 (9th Cir. 1981).
67. *Shearer v. United States,* 723 F.2d 1102 (3rd Cir. 1984), *rev'd* 105 S. Ct. 3039, *on remand,* to 772 F.2d 896 (3rd Cir. 1985).
68. 10 U.S.C. §1089 (1982 & Supp. I 1983).
69. *Howell v. United States,* 489 F. Supp. 147 (D. Tenn. 1980); *Hall v. United States,* 528 F. Supp. 963 (D. N.J. 1981), *affd,* 688 F.2d 821.
70. *See, e.g., Pelphrey v. United States,* 674 F.2d 243 (4th Cir. 1982).
71. Boffey, *Pentagon Adopts Steps to Improve Quality of Military Medical Care,* New York Times, June 10, 1985, at A1, col. 1.
72. *Id.* at D-10.
73. 10 U.S.C. §801 (1982 & Supp. I 1983).
74. *Ex parte Milligan,* 71 U.S. 2 (1866).
75. 354 U.S. 1 (1957).
76. *Grisham v. Hagan,* 361 U.S. 278 (1960) (capital offenses); *McElroy v. U.S. ex rel. Guagliardo,* 361 U.S. 281 (1960) (non-capital offenses).
77. 10 U.S.C. §805 (1982).
78. 10 U.S.C. §814 (1982).
79. 10 U.S.C. §15 (1982).
80. U.S.C.A. Const. Amdt. 5 (1983 & Supp. 1985).
81. 10 U.S.C. Sections 827, 838, and 846 (1982 & Supp. I 1983).
82. 38 U.S.C. §4131 (1982).
83. 38 C.F.R. §17.34 (1984).
84. 38 U.S.C. §4132 (1982).
85. 38 U.S.C. §4132 (b) (2) (c) (1982).
86. N.Y. Times, Sept. 17, 1985 at A23, col. 1.
87. N.Y. Times, Oct. 7, 1985 at A15, col. 1. The House passed the bill 317 to 90 and sent it to the Senate. The measure's primary sponsor, Rep. Barney Frank, said the measure was a compromise that was carefully drawn to restrict claims to medical treatment rendered at permanent domestic medical facilities.
88. N.Y. Times, Oct. 13, 1985, §1, at 1 and 42, col. 1.

Additional Readings

BUREAU OF NATIONAL AFFAIRS, GOVERNMENT EMPLOYEES RELATIONS REPORT (current ed.)

E. BUSSEY, FEDERAL CIVIL SERVICE LAW & PROCEDURES (1984).

E. BYRNE, MILITARY LAW (3d ed. 1981).

CONGRESSIONAL BUDGET OFFICE, CONGRESS OF THE U.S., OPTIONS FOR CHANGE IN MILITARY MEDICAL CARE (1984).

C. GOODMAN, HANDBOOK ON PUBLIC PERSONNEL LAW (1978).

P. INGRAHAM & C. BAN, LEGISLATING BUREAUCRATIC CHANGE: THE CIVIL SERVICE ACT OF 1978 (1984).

Note, *Reservist Employment Rights,* 22 AIR FORCE LAW REVIEW 374 (1980-81).

R. O'NEIL, THE RIGHTS OF GOVERNMENT EMPLOYEES: THE BASIC ACLU GUIDE TO GOVERNMENT EMPLOYEE'S RIGHTS (1978).

D. SCHLUETER, MILITARY CRIMINAL JUSTICE, PRACTICE & PROCEDURE (1982).

Section D Nursing Education and Research

Chapter 19

Nursing students

Cynthia E. Northrop

Legal issues exist for nursing students, too. Their role in the educational system and nursing programs carries with it legal rights and responsibilities. The nursing student may be involved in legal actions as a defendant or as a plaintiff. Issues confronting the nursing student will be organized in this chapter according to admission into a nursing program, progression through the program, and graduation from the program. Negligence while learning to practice nursing will be discussed in the progression section of the chapter. Issues for the graduate nurse, one who has graduated from a nursing program and is not yet licensed, will also be included.

This chapter focuses on nursing students; Chapter 20 focuses on nursing faculty and their legal responsibilities. Consequently, there are overlaps between these chapters; they should be read together for an overall description of the legal aspects of the student and faculty relationship. When students are accused of negligence, they may be named as defendants, and the faculty may be as well. When students promote a right as a plaintiff, the faculty and school are often involved, but as defendants.

The faculty-student relationship carries many rights and responsibilities. These are defined from several sources, including statements of beliefs and practices of institutions and associations and legal decisions. Many of these sources for determining reasonable and proper faculty-student relationships are discussed throughout the two chapters.

Relationship of education and courts

In disputes between students and faculty regarding grades or discipline, courts have traditionally maintained a hands-off approach. However, in cases involving allegations of a student's negligence while the student is in the clinical setting, courts will treat these cases just like other negligence cases.

The hands-off approach by courts is explained in their view of the role of faculty and the education system. Courts hesitate to interfere in faculty and college decisions out of respect for education, willing instead to defer to the best judgment of the faculty. Courts readily acknowledge education's contribution to society and contribution to the ideals of justice.

Courts, generally, support the missions of education because those missions support the purposes of government and the betterment of a civilized society. Courts have supported the general rule that an educational institution may establish any standards reasonably relevant to the lawful missions, processes, and functions of the institution.[1]

To summarize, as a general rule, courts have intervened on behalf of students if the situation involves allegations of:

1. A violation of due process
2. Bad faith, arbitrary, or capricious decision by faculty

3. Criminal activity
4. A breach of contract

As mentioned in Chapter 2 the U.S. Constitution sets out explicit powers of the federal government and describes the rights of individuals. The portions of the U.S. Constitution of particular significance to faculty and students include:

1. The First Amendment, which states: "Congress shall make no law respecting an establishment of religion or prohibiting the free exercise thereof; or abridging the freedom of speech, or of the press, or the right of the people peacably to assemble and to petition the government for a redress of grievances"[2]
2. The Fourth Amendment, which provides protection against "unreasonable searches and seizures"[3] (This amendment particularly affects housing of students and policies surrounding the school and administration's ability to search those facilities.)
3. The Fourteenth Amendment, which provides for equal protection under the law and requires due process of law for the denial of "life, liberty, or property"[4]
4. The Tenth Amendment, which makes applicable to state action the above listed protections[5] and the Fourteenth Amendment, which applies to states as well

These four amendments provide much of the basis for protection of individual rights in the collegiate setting. In addition, powers which are not in the federal Constitution are left to the states. These are known as police powers, general and broad powers, based on the state's desire to protect the public's, its citizens', health, safety, and welfare. These powers also are often involved in student and faculty disputes.

There are two primary legal concepts which are involved in all student-faculty disputes. They are due process and state action. Each will be described below.

STATE ACTION

Issues of constitutional law and individual rights are most often heard by federal courts, since the federal Constitution provides for the above listed protections, including due process, for nursing students. Some state constitutions may give due process rights that are applicable to private sector schools. In order for federal courts to intervene on behalf of nursing students, the courts must first decide whether there has been state action. This concept is defined in Chapter 5.

If the educational program in which the nursing student is enrolled is a tax-supported, state educational institution (e.g., community colleges or state universities), federal courts have jurisdiction to hear cases involving allegations of due process violations because, as mentioned before, the Fourteenth Amendment to the U.S. Constitution, prohibits the states from making such violations.

Thus the reach of federal courts into private institutions, including religious schools, is limited by the Constitution to first finding the presence of state action. The court determines its jurisdiction by whether there is any type of state action. Examples of state action, even though the school of nursing is a private institution, include the acceptance of federal funds, licensure, and state accreditation. Tax-supported institutions, of course, are public and are supported by the government, which gives courts jurisdiction to review what goes on inside them. The federal government and the state are under a legal obligation to operate without discrimination and in accordance with all federal laws and regulations.

The U.S. Constitution prohibits the government from unreasonably restricting rights, therefore private schools may not always be reached by federal courts, and due process requirements may not necessarily be enforceable in these schools. Hence, what has developed is a dichotomy about what amount, if any, of due process is owed students, depending on whether the school is a private or a public institution.

Generally, accepting federal funds obligates the school, private or public, to abide by all federal laws and regulations. However, in a recent case the U.S. Supreme Court decided that being a recipient of federal funds required only the particular program within the school receiving the funding to abide by the federal laws and regulations.[6] The Court held that the entire school was not subject to federal requirements that came with the federal funding, only that portion of the school which actually received the funds was so subject.

Clearly, state-run schools of nursing are subject to constitutional review. Private facilities, however, usually are not subject to review unless something about the school involves state action, such as the acceptance of federal monies. Even this indication of state action has been limited by the recent Supreme Court case. As noted before, in this case the Court stated that only the specific program within the school that accepted federal funds was subject to constitutional and other federal requirements.

Without a finding of state action, courts will not have

jurisdiction over cases brought by nursing students for violations of constitutional rights. One of the first things a student's legal counsel will do is review the facts of the student's situation and, where possible, present facts to the court establishing jurisdiction. Courts will not review the allegations of due process violation without first determining that they have jurisdiction to hear the case.

DUE PROCESS

The major constitutional law principle which impacts nursing education is due process. This principle, contained in the Fourteenth Amendment of the U.S. Constitution, is defined as a guarantee that certain procedural steps will be taken prior to denying an individual liberties and rights.

For many years, the school and its faculty and administrators were viewed as acting in the place of the parents. This common law doctrine of *in loco parentis* allowed the school to enforce any rule concerning the students which parents would make and without heed to due process.

The civil rights movement of the 1960s brought a change in the use of this common law doctrine. Constitutional law indicated that students must be afforded rights just as any other citizen. In 1969 the Supreme Court of the United States stated that students do not "shed their constitutional rights at the schoolhouse gate."[7]

Prior to this, a landmark decision established the right of students at a state institution to notice and a hearing in disciplinary proceedings in which suspension or expulsion was a possibility.[8] The court offered guidelines about what constituted the due process owed students, including notice, an outline of specific charges, a fair and impartial hearing, names of witnesses, content of witnesses' statements, and the opportunity to speak in their own defense. The court further indicated that the results and conclusions from the hearing are to be presented to the student.

In 1965 the court made a distinction about the amount, if any, of due process owed a student, when an academic dismissal is contemplated.[9] *Connelly* established the principle that a student is not owed the same due process rights when the question is academic dismissal. Instead of due process violations, the student must demonstrate that arbitrariness, capriciousness, or bad faith was involved in the academic decision before a court will interfere. Case examples that follow this section help clarify these concepts.

The rationale the court has used in making a distinction between academic and disciplinary decisions is that academic decisions are subjective and evaluative and disciplinary decisions are based on factual evidence. In addition, the courts see academic decisions as those which involve expert evaluation, based on cumulative information, not readily adaptable to judicial review.

In disciplinary hearings, however, courts have elaborated upon the specifications for the fairness or due process owed to the student.[10] Specifications for disciplinary actions identified in case law are listed above (see box). Later, additional standards of due process will be discussed.

However, in academic dismissal cases courts have held that in order to satisfy due process prior to termination or suspension of a student for deficiencies in meeting academic performance, the faculty or school need only to advise the student with regard to such deficiencies in any form. All that is required is that the student be made aware prior to termination of the failure or impending failure to meet these standards.[11] Consensus seems to be that students have been treated fairly when academic decisions are made, and they have received what is listed on p. 302 (see box).

The dichotomy of disciplinary versus academic may be difficult to apply. The court seems to say that significantly less due process is required when academic eval-

DUE PROCESS AND DISCIPLINARY DECISIONS

Generally, students are entitled to:

1. Written charges, available 10 days before the hearing
2. A hearing before those with power to suspend or expel
3. An opportunity to review in advance the information to be submitted at the hearing
4. The right to bring counsel to furnish advice but not to question witnesses
5. The right to present a version of the facts through personal and written statements, including statements of witnesses
6. An opportunity to hear all information presented against him or her and to question adverse witnesses personally
7. A determination of the facts of the case based solely on what is presented at the hearing by the authority that holds the hearing
8. A written statement of the findings of fact
9. The right to make a record of the hearing at his or her own expense

DUE PROCESS IN ACADEMIC DECISIONS

Generally, students are entitled to:

1. Understand as precisely as possible what is required
2. Receive an explanation as soon as possible why they are not meeting these requirements
3. Know what steps might be taken to correct their noncompliance
4. Be aware, beforehand, of the possible outcomes of their actions or nonactions pertaining to academic matters

Adapted from LaMorte and Meadows, *Educational Sound Due Process in Academic Affairs,* 8 J. LAW & EDUC., 197 (1979).

uative judgments, such as grading or determinations of students' suitability for a profession, are involved than in a discipline case, when fact-finding seeks to establish whether a student violated a rule of behavior. In academic decisions careful and deliberate faculty decision making is required as opposed to arbitrary, capricious decisions.

Given that due process owed a student differs between academic or disciplinary decisions, it's important also to realize that the due process in the learning or academic context also differs from the due process owed an accused criminal. In the criminal context the purpose of due process protections is to ensure that no punishment will be given until there has been proof beyond a reasonable doubt that a crime has been committed. In a criminal proceeding the accused is entitled to:

1. Preliminary hearing/refuse to testify
2. Right to counsel
3. Right to confront accusers
4. Right to object/introduce evidence
5. Right to present witnesses/cross-examination
6. Right to a record and to appeal

Due Process. One of the leading cases discussing the type and amount of due process owed students involved a medical student. Upon reviewing the case, the U.S. Supreme Court reconfirmed the long-standing tradition of the American court system to stay out of the academic arena.[12] In this case the university had dismissed a student who was close to graduation and who had received excellent grades on written examinations. The student was dismissed because of deficiencies in clinical performance, peer and patient relations, and personal hygiene. In addition some faculty members had repeatedly expressed dissatisfaction with the student's work.

On evaluation, the university counsel recommended that the student not be allowed to graduate on time and that, absent radical improvement in the remainder of the year, the student be dropped from the program. The student was allowed to take a special set of oral and practical examinations administered by practicing physicians. Although several letters of recommendation were written in favor of the student, the faculty and school decided to dismiss the student from the program.

The Supreme Court stated that academic due process does not require an adversarial hearing. All rights of the student in an academic dismissal are met when the institution informs the student of the inadequacies of the student's performance and of their consequences on the student's academic standing.

This case is a good example of how and why the courts have developed a distinction between due process in disciplinary and academic decision making. The medical school faculty had formed an academic opinion. Such a judgment is by its nature more subjective and evaluative than the typical factual questions presented in the average disciplinary decision. Like the decision of an individual professor as to the proper grade for a student in a course, the determination whether to dismiss a student for academic reasons requires an expert evaluation of cumulative information and is not readily adapted to the procedural tools of judicial or administrative decision making.

As mentioned before, the distinction between academic and disciplinary may be hard to apply. The issue of which type of decision was made can be raised in the litigation. For example, in a nursing student dismissal case the issue was whether the dismissal was the result of an academic judgment or one involving disciplinary misconduct.[13] In this case the nursing student was asked to withdraw from the program because of an alleged failure to submit a physical examination report (required prior to admission), failure to report prior attendance at a hospital school of nursing and to submit a transcript of records, and failure to attend class regularly.

In order to decide whether the student was entitled to the injunction being sought, the court first had to determine whether these acts were violations of academic standards or disciplinary misconduct in order to decide what should be the student's due process rights. If the student had been asked to withdraw or dismissed because of disciplinary misconduct, the student was entitled to a hearing (due process); if the student was dismissed because of failure to meet academic standards, no hearing was required.

The court reiterated its hands-off position, stating that it will not intrude into the domain of academic standards where the school officials, not the judicial system, are those properly qualified to execute their judgment. However, it noted that courts are not totally precluded from examining dismissals if the student was actually expelled for reasons other than the quality of the work or if the student was failed because of bad faith or arbitrary and capricious action by a faculty member.

In this case the nursing student's grades were B, C, and Incomplete (which was later made up). The evidence before the court revealed that the faculty had never rendered an opinion concerning the nursing student's suitability for nursing. The allegation regarding the physical examination report involved disputed facts. The nursing student said it was submitted on August 24. It was due July 5. The school secretary could not find it. The student discussed the matter with a school administrator, explaining that there was no money to get another until the first week of the second semester, at which time the student did have another examination. The physician confirmed that a physical was given to the student in August and again in March.

The allegation regarding attendance at a hospital school of nursing also involved disputed facts. The student interpreted the application instructions as referring only to prior college or university enrollment. After being informed that a transcript must be submitted, one was submitted.

The last allegation involved class attendance. The student admitted missing three classes each in nursing, biology, and psychology. The only attendance record available was from the biology professor, which indicated that the student was absent three times. Evidence revealed that the college did not normally retain class attendance records, nor did it have any firm policy as to the number of permitted absences.

The court held that these alleged failures were more like disciplinary misconduct. The court determined that they each involved a factual question: did or didn't the student comply with the school rules? Scholastic standards were not involved but rather disputed facts. Therefore, the court ordered an injunction and reinstatement conditioned on a reasonable, prior opportunity to hold a hearing.

In another nursing case, the court held that a due process hearing was not required in a challenge by a nursing student of an academic decision.[14] Therefore, where the decision involves grading and evaluation of nursing students' course performance, different due process requirements as listed on p. 302 must exist. However, in disciplinary decision making, such as cheating or other improper conduct that is factual in nature, due process as outlined on p. 301 is required. No criminal or full-blown adversarial proceeding is required; simply a fair and ample opportunity for both sides to present facts.

Additionally, the exercise of due process should be evenly distributed. Academic decisions can be challenged by students only if they are found to be made in bad faith or capriciously or arbitrarily. This is discussed further beginning on p. 305. These requirements set out by case law and legislation are a minimum. Institutions of learning, of course, may provide more due process.

Nursing students and admission requirements

Courts have for the most part determined that schools of nursing may place reasonable entrance requirements on potential nursing students. These requirements are judged by their relevance to the missions of the school and the philosophy of the nursing school.

If a potential nursing student wishes to enroll in a nursing program, the catalog and application process outlined must be followed. Often community colleges have a stated purpose which is different from university or college schools of nursing. This difference can determine what type and amount of admission requirements the programs can make. For example, some nursing programs have what is called an open door admissions policy. This policy means that a minimum of requirements can be made, such as an age limit, a high school diploma, and residency.

Some schools have re-admission policies. Should a student withdraw or be dismissed for any reason, these policies usually allow a former student to be considered for re-admission. However, most program catalogs provide that a re-admission candidate can be denied admission if it would be considered detrimental to the best interest of the college and program.

Re-admission provisions of the school's catalog may provide that the student's progression will be governed by the policies in the catalog of the student's initial admission. This was the issue in the *Babb* case where a nursing student was advised prior to the end of a term that she was failing a 12-hour course and that she should withdraw from the program, send a letter asking for readmission, and re-enter the school.[15] This the nursing student did and, upon readmission, successfully made up for the previous withdraw failing grade but received two D grades.

Under the catalog in effect when she was re-admitted, there was a provision that a student with more than two D's in the program would be required to withdraw. This provision was not in the catalog in effect during the first admission.

This re-admitted nursing student was notified of termination from the program because the school policy required it. Evidence before the court revealed that the student tried to talk with the dean about the expulsion, but was repeatedly denied an interview.

One of the issues before the court was whether it was a breach of contract to apply policies in a different catalog to this student. While recognizing the school's right to change its catalog, the court said that an express promise, a contract, existed between the school and this student. That contract was the school catalog.

In this case the student entered under the 1978-1979 catalog and had a right to rely on its terms. This catalog permitted a student to complete the degree requirements under its terms, within 6 years, regardless of the school's later amendments to the catalog. The catalog did not permit the school to dismiss a student based on the number of bad grades; it only required a student to maintain a 2.0 grade point average (GPA). Therefore the student could not be terminated from the program.

State laws also govern admissions.[16] For example, admission standards are established for public institutions by state legislatures.[17] A State Board of Higher Education administers these and other standards.[18] Students have representation on these state boards.[19] State laws have also created special training programs and scholarships for nurses.[20] Major curriculum decisions and revisions and assuring the widest possible educational opportunities for students in the state are a few of the responsibilities of the board.[21]

Issues in the admissions process for potential nursing students may also involve questions of discrimination and requirements about the physical health of the applicant. Should a potential nursing student wish to explore possible violations of rights involved in the process of admissions, the key evidence the court will examine is the school catalog and other evidence describing the admissions process in general and for the particular applicant. The court will examine whether the school of nursing followed its own rules during the admissions process.

DISCRIMINATION

Schools of nursing across the nation must not discriminate through their admissions policies, or during any part of the program, on the basis of sex, race, or national origin. There has been one case of interest involving a potential nursing student as plaintiff in pursuing the right to enter a nursing program.

The case involved a male applicant who was denied admission to an all female, state-supported school of nursing in Mississippi. The Supreme Court of the United States concluded that the school denied admission based on the sex of the applicant.[22] The Court said this was a violation of the U.S. Constitution, sex discrimination, and a violation of the equal protection clause. The only acceptable justification for gender discrimination, the Court stated, is when it exists to intentionally, directly assist that gender, one which has been disproportionately burdened. This is known as the compensatory purpose.

No evidence was presented which showed that women lacked training in the field of nursing or that women nurses were unable to attain positions of leadership in the nursing field. In fact the evidence reviewed by the Court revealed that 98.6% of the nursing degrees earned in the United States were earned by women (94% in Mississippi).

State laws may exist which prohibit state schools from expelling or refusing admission to students because the student cannot attend classes or take examinations because of tenets of his or her religion. It is the responsibility of the faculty and administration to make available opportunities for makeup work.[23] In another state discrimination is prohibited on account of the applicants' refusal to receive, perform, or recommend any forms of medical care contrary to their conscious.[24] Each state may have different and other examples of state laws dealing with discrimination issues.

PHYSICAL HEALTH REQUIREMENTS

Schools of nursing may place reasonable physical health requirements upon applicants. This was discussed in another U.S. Supreme Court case. In the *Davis* case a hearing-impaired applicant was denied admission into a state school of nursing.[25] The Court supported the school and faculty decision to exclude applicants who could not hear sufficiently in their judgment to function as a safe nursing practitioner.

The Court said a nursing school may require reasonable physical qualifications for admission to clinical training programs. This was not a violation of the federal

Rehabilitation Act of 1973, which prohibits discrimination of an "otherwise qualified handicapped person."[26] A physical requirement needed to function safely in giving patient care is within the term and meaning of "otherwise qualified"—this student couldn't "otherwise qualify" for admission into the nursing program.

Progression through nursing programs

Several possible legal issues for nursing students may arise during the learning process. Academic decisions involving the methods of teaching, evaluation of student progress, grading criteria, and other requirements of specific courses may involve legal questions. Nursing students in addition may have questions about disciplinary action taken by a faculty or school. It is during clinical courses in particular that questions of potential negligence and liability are present for the nursing student. Academic decisions, disciplinary misconduct, crimimal cases, requirements for clinical courses, and negligence in the clinical setting will be discussed below.

ACADEMIC DECISIONS: GRADING, EVALUATION, AND TEACHING METHODS

The general rules which govern when a court will review academic decisions made about nursing students have been discussed earlier in the chapter. Courts have made it fairly clear that the college has the power to govern itself and maintain proper academic standards. The failure of a nursing student to maintain scholastic requirements is justifiable cause for dismissal.

Courts will not interfere in the methods of determining whether a student has failed to meet academic requirements unless school authorities (such as, nursing faculty):

1. Acted in bad faith
2. Exercised their discretion arbitrarily and capriciously

BLACK'S LAW DICTIONARY and WEBSTER'S DICTIONARY both provide some basic understanding of the terms arbitrary and capricious.

BLACK's states that arbitrary means in an arbitrary manner, as fixed or done capriciously or at pleasure; without any adequate determining principle; not founded in the nature of things; nonrational; not done or acting according to reason or judgment; depending on the will alone; tyrannical and despotic.[27]

WEBSTER's, on the other hand, adds the following thoughts to the term's meaning: a sudden, impulsive, and seemingly unmotivated change of mind; an arbitrary and typically fanciful or impracticable notion; caprice emphasizes lack of evident motivation and suggests willfulness.[28]

Case law also provides definition and examples of arbitrary and capricious and bad faith. In one case a second-year medical school student had failed an examination which the student claimed was given in an arbitrary and capricious manner.[29] During a final examination session, a few of the students received the wrong examination. Realizing the error only a few minutes into the examination, the faculty member interrupted the session, collected the wrong ones, and distributed the right ones.

The plaintiff in this case was one of the affected students. The student asked for additional time since others in the room had received the correct examination and had been working on it since the examination began. No additional time was given, and the student failed the examination by only a few points. Subsequently, the student was dismissed for academic failure. The trial court was presented with evidence that showed that there were irregularities and that the school failed to investigate. The court decided the grading was unfair and arbitrary and ordered a hearing on the academic dismissal order.

In another case a law student's examination was singled out by the professor as the examination of a probationary student. The court determined that this was evidence of bad faith and that it was unfair, unjust, arbitrary, and capricious.[30]

While in these examples the courts found arbitrary and capricious actions, in other cases involving nursing students where the students made allegations of arbitrary and capricious faculty decisions, courts have found no arbitrariness or capriciousness. For example, a nursing student in a state university sought and was denied admission to candidacy for a doctorate in nursing.[31] The student claimed that the grading techniques and evaluation procedures were faulty (arbitrary and capricious). The student made the following specific allegations:

1. The assistant dean failed to supervise the procedure for evaluation of the exam.
2. The faculty were personally prejudiced against the student.
3. The faculty were aware of and revealed the identity of the student when grading.

The court reviewed the evaluation of student progress procedure. That procedure included:

1. The rule that each student successfully complete a written examination

2. That questions be selected from a pool of questions
3. That there be three parts to the examination, all of which the student must pass

This student passed one question and failed two. The failed portion of the examination was rewritten, and the student passed one question, failing the other. The faculty offered a third time to rewrite, and the student declined the offer and was terminated from the program. The court found no arbitrary, capricious acts or ill will or bad faith in this academic procedure.

In another nursing case a nursing student challenged a grade and inability to receive a degree.[32] In the second enrollment in a course entitled NURS 410 the student received a grade of 69.713 (the passing grade was 70). One multiple choice question determined passing and graduating. The school's policy was that a student failing that course twice would not be awarded a degree. The court found no arbitrary, capricious acts. No policy of rounding off existed within the program. The court supported the power of educational institutions to set standards and to maintain them.

In yet another nursing case a nursing student challenged a change in grading policy.[33] Students were given notice of the policy change through the catalog prior to course registration. The court determined there was no arbitrary and capricious act and that proper notice had been given to the nursing students. The faculty had changed the grade the students must obtain in order to register for sequential courses from a D to C grade. The nursing student tried to say it was a change in curriculum but was unconvincing.

In a case involving a graduate nursing student, the allegation was that the school had unfairly denied the right to continue in the program for a master's degree in nursing.[34] The student needed three courses to graduate. In the first course in a sequence, the student had submitted two papers. The student received a grade of A on the first and F on the second. A failing grade for the course was given. The nursing student presented a complaint in court, asking for a grade of C, an injunction enjoining the university from preventing continued study, and a temporary restraining order permitting participation in the next course during the time an administrative review of the grade was conducted within the university. The university agreed to the last request.

The university faculty senate held a hearing and determined that C was the proper grade for the student's work in the first course. Following this decision the student voluntarily dismissed the court claim. Later, in the second course, the student received a D (all other students received A's and B's). The issue discussed by the court was whether the student could raise the lawsuit again, and it said that it could be raised again.

In another case a nursing student challenged the college's conduct during a grade appeal process, not on the basis that it was arbitrary or capricious but on the basis that it amounted to a breach of contract.[35] This student was a senior nursing student who had received A's and B's in nearly all courses and had served as president of the class.

The student missed three classes and two clinical experiences because she accompanied an ill friend to a hospital. The student consulted with the faculty person who assured her that the only result of the absence would be that a grade of "Incomplete" for the course would be given. The faculty person claimed that no such assurances were given. In any case, the student continued to attend classes, submitted papers and took the final examination (even though the student's option could have been to withdraw from the course without incurring a grade of F had it been done before the last day of class).

When the grades came out, the student had been given an F. The student formally appealed the grade. According to the College Academic Information and Registration Materials for 1975 the appeal was to be initiated by the student as follows:

1. Meet with the faculty person and resolve matter, if possible
2. Request a grade appeal committee by contacting the dean of students; the grade appeal committee is selected as follows:
   a. The student chooses a faculty member to serve
   b. The faculty chooses a member to serve
   c. A third committee member is selected by mutual decision
3. Committee hears both sides of the case and recommends to dean

The appeal committee decided two in favor of the student and one in favor of the faculty. The dean of students overruled the committee decision. The issue which the student took to court was whether the dean could overrule the committee's decision.

The lower court reviewed the school catalog, hearing committee procedures, and memorandum between the dean and the nursing student. It applied contract law and determined that the catalog was a contract between the student and school and made the inference that from all documents that had been prepared by the dean to assist in the process, that the grade appeals committee was the final decision maker, not the dean.

The school appealed the decision, and the higher court determined that the lower court had inappropriately applied, and in too strict a manner, principles of contract law. The court held that some elements of the law of contracts are to be used in the analysis of the relationship between student and school but that this does not mean that contract law must be rigidly applied in all its aspects. The court indicated that the student-university relationship was unique and that reasonable meaning and normal, everyday meaning of the grade appeals system established by the school should be applied. The court stated that nothing in the student manual suggested that a recommendation by the committee could reasonably be thought to be anything more than an expression of the committee's opinion as to the preferred course of conduct to be followed by the dean in resolving the issue between the teacher and the student. Therefore, the dean's ability to be the final decision maker was upheld by the court. However, the court did indicate that the catalog and other materials could be viewed as evidence of a contract between the student and the institution.

REQUIREMENTS FOR CLINICAL COURSES

While there are no cases on point, a logical extension of the *Davis* case, mentioned above, is that should physical health status change during the student's progression, faculty can require the student to delay clinical practice until the student's physical health status meets standards of safe and reasonable clinical practice. This would include temporary and permanent changes in health status, such as injuries involving wearing of a cast or a progressive hearing or sight disability which will mean inability to accurately assess patient vital signs.

Faculty may also remove students from clinical practice when they exhibit unsafe behavior. Expectations and criteria for clinical assignments should be clearly known and stated prior to accepting responsibility for patient care. Usually, written expectations and objectives are distributed to students prior to their clinical assignments. It is the student's legal responsibility to know what is expected behavior and to abide by the rules for safe practice.

However, part of the learning process is testing the ability of a student to practice safely. Therefore, removal from clinical and/or academic evaluation or disciplinary action based upon the student's behavior should occur only when the behavior is habitual or gross, thus justifying removal. One mistake is not enough, unless the result of the mistake is extreme and the mistake was the result of recklessness or gross disregard for a patient's well-being.

Students who attend class and/or clinical under the influence of alcohol or drugs represent a hazard to patients, others, and themselves. Faculty have the responsibility to protect patients assigned to students. Any student who cannot deliver care safely and reasonably must be removed from the situation where another person may be harmed. Schools of nursing may have policies on clinically impaired nursing students which identify behaviors which interfere with the course of study or threaten the welfare of patients. These policies identify behaviors which are cause for disciplinary action by the faculty. The policies usually also identify what action will be taken, such as removal of the student from the clinical area, confrontation of the student with the unacceptable behavior, referral of the student to counseling, and requiring the student to complete a rehabilitation program as a condition for continuing the nursing program.

DISCIPLINARY MISCONDUCT

As noted earlier in the chapter, due process requirements must be afforded the nursing student when disciplinary action is contemplated. They are, as discussed before in more detail (see p. 301), generally, notice, hearing, and appeal.

Several nursing students have brought court actions in the area of disciplinary misconduct, alleging that the faculty and school did not afford the student adequate due process. In one such case a second-year nursing student was suspended following 30 incidents, ranging from refusal to sign in and out of the residence, unwillingness to abide by the rules, receiving administrative warnings regarding personal and professional responsibilities, failing the operating room course, repeated lateness and absences, and failure to appear for clinical.[36] A school committee gave the student one more chance. After the student failed to attend again, an indefinite suspension was given.

The student attempted to say that the seriousness of the warnings was minimally stated in the handbook, that inadequate notice of the gravity of excessive tardiness was given, and that the penalties were disproportionate. The court reviewed the facts and determined that adequate notice of the problem had been given, and a hearing had been received. The court went on to say that punctuality is an absolute requisite in the proper functioning of a nursing staff.

In the case of another nursing student, however, a court granted an injunction to reinstate until the question of alleged cheating was reviewed.[37] The student allegedly cheated on a final examination by getting answers to two questions and changing the paper. Five days later the student was informed by the dean of the accused cheating and was offered an F or a hearing. The student selected a hearing. The student was found guilty of cheating.

The student appealed to the next level, which determined that irregularities existed and ordered another hearing in which it was found that the student was not guilty of cheating. The university counsel objected, and the vice-chancellor reviewed the situation and found the student guilty, recommended an F grade and probation, and canceled course registration.

Because of the irreparable damage and injury to the student not to be able to continue the program while the issue was resolved, the court ordered that the nursing student be reinstated in the nursing program.

In another case a licensed practical nursing student was discharged from a nursing program because of certain violations of ethics and discipline, including:

1. Abruptly leaving classes prior to their conclusion in a manner disruptive to the morale of the faculty and operation of the classes
2. During clinical, avoiding having to handle patients by having other personnel take hourly urinary output and vital signs
3. During clinical, failing to follow through with the care of patients
4. Loudly complaining and displaying a defensive attitude about hospital personnel
5. Discussing and questioning with another student the care and treatment provided by a physician—in violation of both instructions given by the instructor and standards established for the nursing profession of which the student was cognizant
6. Discussing, outside of the classroom, a patient's case and condition with another student not assigned to that particular patient[38]

The student sought damages for breach of contract and negligence for wrongful discharge. The lower court entered a judgment for the student; appeal was taken. The court of appeals reversed the decision, holding that the trial court lacked subject matter jurisdiction. (See Chapter 2 for a discussion of this concept). The student appealed and the Louisiana Supreme Court reversed and remanded the case. On remand the court held that (1) there was no enforceable contract between the nursing student and technical school and (2) the doctrine of detrimental reliance did not imply an enforceable contract.

The student attempted to argue that she and the school had entered an implied contract wherein the school agreed to educate her as a practical nurse in exchange for her agreement to meet the academic and disciplinary requirements of the nursing program. This argument was not successful; no contract was found because the student was neither required to pay fees to attend the program, nor was the student under any civil obligation to maintain the prescribed level of academic achievement or observe the school disciplinary requirements. In addition the court determined that there was no reciprocity of obligation. For example, the school had no legal cause of action against the student who breached school rules or didn't make the grades. The student could leave the program at any time; the school evaluated the student and rendered a grade. Because of this the court dismissed the student's case.

CRIMINAL CASES

Students of nursing may have legal recourse against faculty and schools of nursing based on the school's or faculty's negligence in maintaining the campus and in assigning students to clinical practicums. Two such cases drive the point home.

In recent times the courts have extended liability for criminal acts which occur on school and educational campuses and in their facilities. In a recent California case, the court found San Francisco City College had a duty to warn students of known dangers posed by criminals on campus and to take affirmative steps (such as trimming bushes) to prevent criminal activity on campus.[39] The facts of this case were that criminal activity had occurred in the same spot on several occasions prior to this student being attacked. The court said that students who pay fees to use the facilities where they spend a significant portion of their time and may even live can reasonably expect to be free from conditions that increase the risk of crime.[38]

In addition faculty who assign students to clinical agencies in crime-ridden areas must be especially vigilant, even to the point of not sending students for clinical practicums. In a highly publicized criminal case a nursing student making home visits as part of her public health nursing clinical practicum was brutally raped and murdered. While the school and faculty were not sued, the court sharply questioned and criticized the state university's program that prompted the student's unescorted visit to the housing project.[40]

NURSING STUDENTS AND NEGLIGENCE LITIGATION

The common causes of nursing malpractice include errors in administration of treatments, communications, supervision of patients, administration of medications, foreign objects left in patients, postoperative injuries or infections, anesthesia given by nurse anesthetists, and assisting patients with ambulation.[41] In this study of nursing malpractice, one case was found involving the negligence of a nursing student. The case involved an award of $150,000 to a 16-year-old girl who had been admitted to the hospital with an injured knee. A nursing student with 3 month's experience helped the patient to the bathroom, and the patient fell, injuring the sacrum.[42]

In other cases nursing students have burned a patient with a hot water bag, given an injection injuring the right sciatic nerve, and incorrectly prepared oral medications.[43] In these cases the plaintiff was unable to prove anything about the students and/or the students were immune from suit because of state laws, hence the students and the hospitals were found not liable.

In a more recent case, two nursing students brought a portable x-ray machine into a patient's room, got the wheels tangled in a cord, and caused the machine to fall on the patient.[44] The hospital was sued for damages allegedly resulting from personal injuries caused by hospital employees (presumably the nursing students). Although there was no mention of faculty or school responsibility and whether the accident occurred during the students' clinical assignment or during employment with the hospital, the jury award of $17,500 was upheld by the appeals court which found that there was sufficient evidence to show proximate cause and that the hospital was negligent.

In yet another recent case involving a registered professional nurse who was a nurse anesthetist student in a hospital school of anesthesia for nurses, the student negligently administered anesthesia to a patient having a tubal ligation.[45] As a result the patient suffered cardiac arrest and severe brain damage. The student was sued individually, along with the hospital and corporation which ran the school, by the patient's husband and guardian.

In Georgia a statute prohibits anyone except those licensed and certified to do so from administering anesthesia. The student (who was not certified to give anesthesia) had been assigned the task by a supervising physician assistant. The court said:

> Certainly the . . . [nurse anesthetist student] had a duty not to practice medicine beyond what the law allowed. Her duty to comply with the law as a student did not end at the point where she was assigned by her supervisors to attend this patient as part of her schooling.[46]

The court held the nursing student liable, along with the hospital and school for negligence per se, for violation of a state statute. This case presents a situation where a state statute prohibits a student from giving anesthesia without direct supervision of an anesthesiologist.

The court also held that a board of nursing rule providing an exception to the statutory certification requirement of R.N. anesthetists, where a registered professional nurse is duly enrolled as a bona fide student and is under the direct supervision of an anesthesiologist or a certified registered nurse anesthetist (CRNA), did not apply to relieve medical defendants of liability for allowing the nurse, who was a student and not a CRNA, to give anesthesia to a patient, as the nurse was under no such "direct supervision" of an anesthesiologist or CRNA.[47] This case is also discussed in Chapter 20, further highlighting the school and faculty responsibilities.

Generally, state nurse practice acts have a provision which exempts nursing students from application of the act.[48] Allegations of practicing nursing without a license cannot be brought against nursing students because the state statute allows them to practice nursing while learning to become nurses. Therefore, nursing students, generally, will not violate state statutes while learning to be nurses and not yet licensed. However, nursing programs should inform students of any state statutes which may apply to any areas which students are learning.

In all cases, however, involving allegations of student negligence, courts must determine the standard of care under which a student will be evaluated. Usually, a court would examine:

1. The practice of the clinical agency and school to allow a student at a certain point in studies to give the particular treatment to a patient by asking if this student was appropriately allowed to carry out this activity (It is important to the court that this practice be approved and similar to the practice of nursing students in other clinical agencies with students.)
2. The knowledge of the student by asking whether

there had been proper instruction in all related subjects in school and whether adequate knowledge and sufficient ability as a student nurse had been demonstrated to be entrusted with such tasks

A nursing student's insurance company has also been held liable for a student's negligent driving to a clinical practicum.[49] Even though the school of nursing owned and provided the van, the nursing student driver was sued for the injuries which occurred. While the school could have been sued as well, it was not; therefore, the school's liability was not at issue. As will be seen in the next chapter, a school of nursing may also be liable for the negligence of a student who drives others to clinical placements.[50]

Nursing students are accountable and personally liable for their actions. Their actions in the classroom and in the clinical setting will be judged by their experience and the amount of their education. A nursing student must know the limits of his or her experience and education; and when questions arise about how to carry out an activity or if the student is not sure how to proceed, the nursing faculty must be contacted. If the topic has been covered in class, and even if the student was absent for the class material, it is assumed that the student has sufficiently mastered the content to put it into practice. This is especially true when the faculty has evaluated the student on clinical performance and the student has passed the established criteria.

In addition, nursing student and faculty responsibilities to the clinical agency will be governed by the contract which exists between the agency and the school. Details about this contract arrangement are discussed in Chapter 20.

However, two important items usually dealt with in a contract are that nursing students are not employees of the agency and that nursing students must carry their own liability insurance. The relevance of the first item is that if a student is injured while on the premises of the clinical agency, no worker's compensation will be available. Schools of nursing usually require that students carry liability insurance and other insurance coverage. The importance of the second contractual item is that a student's insurance carrier may be liable for the student's action and will then provide the compensation should an award be made against the nursing student.

Graduation

A school may deny graduation if the nursing student does not meet the standards of the educational institution. In one case, a nursing student was not permitted to graduate, pursuant to the written policy that students must obtain at least a grade of C for every required nursing course.[51] The student had received a grade of D in one course and in the next required course she received an F. The student argued that the constitutional rights to substantive and procedural due process were violated. The court reiterated that no due process need be afforded students where academic decisions are made. The school of nursing followed its published rules and procedures regarding the result of not maintaining a C in each required nursing course and had applied them to all students.

The court went on to note that the consequences to the nursing student attendant upon the grades awarded were not a result of arbitrariness or capriciousness. The court also noted that the student was given a re-examination in one course and several additional opportunities to demonstrate clinical proficiency in the other course before the final grades were determined.

After graduation, the student and faculty part. The educational institution's accountability for the graduate's performance has been established. Graduation means that the graduate has successfully completed a nursing program and has passed, at the least, minimal standards developed by the nursing faculty. The nursing program has placed a stamp of approval on this person and deemed him or her to be able to practice according to the school's standards.

The standards for the program have been developed and adopted by the faculty and have incorporated other sets of standards, such as the state board of nursing accreditation requirements, other state accreditation requirements, and the National League for Nursing accreditation criteria. Having the program meet the requirements of these bodies supports the credibility of the program, and assures that students have been provided with an acceptable program.

The judgment of the faculty represents cumulative information gathered during the student's progression through the curriculum. Graduates have personal liability for their own actions. No cases were found where a graduate successfully sued a school of nursing for negligent teaching and inability to pass a licensure examination. The future may hold such suits, however.

Students may succeed in allegations of negligent teaching where they can show that the curriculum, faculty preparation, institutional support, and other aspects of the nursing program failed to meet the standards of nursing education. The defense to allegations of negligent teaching is to show the extensive preparation, approval by other groups, success of other students, and activities undertaken to continue and support the standards of the nursing program.

Licensure laws in all states provide that a nursing graduate may practice under the supervision of a registered nurse until the results of the licensure examination are known.[52] Successful completion of the licensure tests is an additional measure of minimum ability to practice nursing. In some states unsuccessful attempts at the registered or licensed practical nurse examination require that the graduate nurse not practice any further until successful in passing the examination. Situations are often reviewed by the state board on an individual basis. Nursing students should make it a point to be well versed in the nurse practice act that applies to them.

In addition, employers also have responsibilities for evaluating the abilities of new employees. They can assume that the school of nursing has prepared the graduates sufficiently but the employers must act independently upon their own evaluation of graduates as new employees.

Standards of care

Printed policies and common, unwritten practices of educational institutions often contain legal rights and responsibilities of students and faculty. In addition, schools of nursing usually have adopted statements outlining rights and responsibilities of both students and faculty. Publications of the National Student Nurses' Association (NSNA)[53] and the American Association of University Professors (AAUP) provide useful documents for examining legal rights of both students and faculty.[54] The box on p. 312 contains excerpts from the AAUP statement that represent standards of care. The NSNA statement substantially parallels the AAUP excerpts.

When questions arise, these documents and the specific educational program's policies and procedures are seen as guideposts for settling disputes between students and faculty. Often the standard of care is established by answering the question, did the school follow its own rules and regulations? Students are obligated to first pursue their challenges and seek remedies within the educational structure. Following exhaustion of the steps provided within the school, students may then take their challenges outside the school and into the court system.

The standard of care applied in cases of student negligence during clinical practicums are similar to other negligence standards of care. As discussed before the student will be held accountable for the amount and level of education and experience obtained at the point at which the alleged negligence occurred. Sources which describe this standard include course materials, objectives, test scores, and other evaluations of performance.

Schools of nursing are to establish and follow policies which reflect fundamental fairness and elements of fair play, including the elements of due process outlined in this chapter. Standards of the American Nurses' Association and the National League for Nursing are discussed in the next chapter.

Recommendations and trends

Courts will be continuing their cautious approach to reviewing faculty and school of nursing decisions regarding students. From the review of case law involving nursing students, it appears that more often students sue their teachers and schools based on allegations of arbitrary and capricious actions than on disciplinary misconduct. Students have the right to challenge and will continue to challenge both types of decisions. The student, as the plaintiff, has the burden of proving that faculty acted in violation of student rights.

Whether a catalog is viewed as a contract or whether the student-school relationship is a contractual one varies among jurisdictions. As cases discussed in this chapter have revealed, some states consider the catalog evidence of a contract, and some do not; some states view the school-student relationship as a contractual one, and some do not. Each state is bound only by federal law and its own laws, looking to other states only for information on how they have dealt with similar issues.

Cases brought by nursing students are really very few considering the number of nursing programs and the volume of nursing students graduated each year. Given this perspective and continuing faculty attention to student concerns, an unusual rise in the number of suits by nursing student is not anticipated.

Student participation in university policy setting is crucial to the continued cooperative relationship between students and faculty. On-going review of policies and academic standards is essential to this effort. After all, it is within the educational context that students learn and experience the democratic process and principles of American justice.

Endnotes

1. *General Order on Judicial Standards of Procedure and Substance in Review of Student Discipline in Tax Supported Institutions of Higher Education,* 45 F.R.D. 133 (W.D. Mo. 1968).
2. U.S. CONST. amend. I.
3. U.S. CONST. amend. IV.

RIGHTS AND FREEDOMS OF STUDENTS

I. FREEDOM OF ACCESS TO HIGHER EDUCATION: The admissions policies of each college and university are a matter of institutional choice provided that each college and university makes clear the characteristics and expectations of students which it considers relevant to success in the institution's program.

II. IN THE CLASSROOM: Student performance should be evaluated solely on an academic basis, not on opinions or conduct in matters unrelated to academic standards.

A. Protection of Freedom of Expression: Students should be free to take reasoned exception to the data or views offered in any course of study and to reserve judgment about matters of opinion, but they are responsible for learning the content of any course of study for which they are enrolled.

B. Protection against Improper Academic Evaluation: Students should have protection through orderly procedures against prejudiced or capricious academic evaluation.

C. Protection against Improper Disclosure: Information about student views, beliefs, and political associations which professors acquire in the course of their work as instructors, advisers, counselors should be considered confidential.

III. STUDENT RECORDS: To minimize the risk of improper disclosure, academic and disciplinary records should be separate, and the conditions of access to each should be set forth in an explicit policy statement. Administrative staff and faculty members should respect confidential information about students which they acquire in the course of their work.

IV. STUDENT AFFAIRS

A. Freedom of Association: Students should be free to organize and join associations to promote their common interests.

B. Freedom of Inquiry and Expression: Students and student organizations should be free to examine and discuss all questions of interest to them, and to express opinions publicly and privately. Students should be allowed to invite and to hear any person of their own choosing.

C. Student Participation in Institutional Government: As constituents of the academic community, students should be free, individually and collectively, to express their views on issues of institutional policy and on matters of general interest to the student body.

D. Student Publications: The student press should be free of censorship and advance approval of copy, and its editors and managers should be free to develop their own editorial policies and news coverage.

V. OFF-CAMPUS FREEDOM OF STUDENTS

A. Exercise of Rights of Citizenship: College and university students are both citizens and members of the academic community. As citizens, students should enjoy the same freedom of speech, peaceful assembly, and right of petition that other citizens enjoy and, as members of the academic community, they are subject to the obligations which accrue to them by virtue of this membership.

B. Institutional Authority and Cival Penalties: Activities of students may upon occasion result in violation of law. In such cases, institutional officials should be prepared to appraise students of sources of legal counsel and may offer other assistance.

VI. PROCEDURAL STANDARDS IN DISCIPLINARY PROCEEDINGS: The administration of discipline should guarantee procedural fairness to an accused student. Practices in disciplinary cases may vary in formality with the gravity of the offense and the sanctions which may be applied.

Adapted from Excerpts from AMERICAN ASSOCIATION OF UNIVERSITY PROFESSORS, JOINT STATEMENT ON RIGHTS AND FREEDOMS OF STUDENTS (1967). Endorsed by U.S. National Student Association, Association of American Colleges, National Association of Student Personnel Administrators, and National Association of Women Deans and Counselors.

4. U.S. CONST. amend. XIV.
5. U.S. CONST. amend. X.
6. *Grove City College v. Bell,* 104 S. Ct. 1211 (1984).
7. *Tinker v. Des Moines Independent School District,* 393 U.S. 503 (1969).
8. *Dixon v. Alabama State Board of Education,* 294 F.2d 150 (5th Cir. 1961).
9. *Connelly v. University of Vermont,* 244 F. Supp. 156 (D. Vt. 1965).
10. *See, e.g., Esteban v. Central Missouri State College,* 415 F.2d 1077 (8th Cir. 1969), *cert. denied,* 398 U.S. 965.
11. *Gaspar v. Bruton,* 513 F.2d 843 (10th Cir. 1975).
12. *Board of Curators of the University of Missouri v. Horowitz,* 435 U.S. 78 (1978).
13. *Brookins v. Bonnell,* 362 F. Supp. 379 (E.D. Pa. 1973).
14. *Ayton v. Bean,* 436 N.Y.S.2d 781 (N.Y. 1981), *rev'd. on other grounds,* 469 N.Y.S.2d 672 (N.Y. 1983).
15. *The University of Texas Health Science Center at Houston, School of Nursing v. Babb,* 646 S.W.2d 502 (Tex. 1982).
16. *See, e.g.,* CONN. GEN. STAT. ANN. §10a (West Supp. 1985); MD. EDUC. CODE ANN. §11, 12, 16, 18 (1985).

17. *See, e.g.,* MD. EDUC. CODE ANN. §11-101 (1985) which requires high school graduation.
18. *See, e.g.,* MD. EDUC. CODE ANN. §12-102 (1985); CONN. GEN. STAT. ANN. §10a-6(a) and (b) (West Supp. 1985).
19. *See, e.g.,* MD. EDUC. CODE ANN. §13-102 (1985); CONN. GEN. STAT. ANN. § 10a-81 (West Supp. 1985).
20. *See, e.g.,* MD. EDUC. CODE ANN. §18-804 (1985) which established nurse practitioner training program funding ($1500 for each nurse practitioner who completes a program); MD. EDUC. CODE ANN. §18-805 (1985) which provides for post-baccalaureate nursing student scholarships, i.e. in gerontological nursing; ILL. ANN. STAT. ch. 144, §1902, which includes assistance for nursing programs in geriatrics. State legislatures have also made available (through legislation) loans to nurses in order to obtain a bachelor's degree in nursing. *See, e.g.,* ILL. ANN. STAT. ch. 144, §1401 (Smith-Hurd Supp. 1985), Baccalaureate Assistance Law for R.N.s, administered by the Dept. of Public Health, loans available at a low interest rate to a maximum of $4500 per year.
21. *See, e.g.,* MD. EDUC. CODE ANN. §16-104(h) and (i) (1985); CONN. GEN. STAT. ANN. §10a-6(a)(8) and (b) (West Supp. 1985).
22. *Mississippi University for Women v. Hogan,* 102 S. Ct. 3331 (1982).
23. *See, e.g.,* CONN. GEN. STAT. ANN. §10a-50 (West Supp. 1985).
24. *See, e.g.,* ILL. ANN. STAT. ch. 111½, §5307 (Smith-Hurd Supp. 1985).
25. *Southeastern Community College v. Davis,* 442 U.S. 397 (1979).
26. 29 U.S.C. §793 (1982 & Supp. I 1983).
27. BLACK'S LAW DICTIONARY 134 (4th ed. 1968).
28. WEBSTER'S NEW COLLEGIATE DICTIONARY 165 (1976).
29. *Connelly v. University of Vermont,* 244 F. Supp. 156 (D. Vt. 1965).
30. *Abbariao v. Hamline University School of Law,* 258 N.W.2d 108 (Minn. 1977).
31. *Nuttleman v. Case Western Reserve University,* 560 F. Supp. 1 (N.D. Ohio, 1981), *aff'd.* 708 F.2d 726.
32. *In re McIntosh v. Borough of Manhattan Community College,* 55 N.Y.2d 913 (N.Y. 1982).
33. *Atkinson v. Traetta,* 359 N.Y.S.2d 120 (N.Y. 1974).
34. *Prendergast v. Rush-Presbyterian-St. Luke's Medical Center,* 397 N.E.2d 432 (Ill. App. 1979).
35. *Lyons v. Salve Revina College,* 422 F. Supp. 1354 (D. R.I. 1976); *rev'd.* 565 F.2d 200 (1st Cir. 1977), *cert. denied,* 435 U.S. 971.
36. *Bonwitt v. Albany Medical Center School of Nursing,* 353 N.Y.S.2d 82 (N.Y. 1973).
37. *Jones v. Board of Governors of the University of North Carolina,* 704 F.2d 713 (4th Cir. 1983).
38. *Simmons v. Sowela Technical Institute,* 458 So.2d 565 (La. App. 3rd Cir. 1984), *rev'd. and remanded,* 462 So.2d 1255 (La. 1985), *rev'd. and dismissed,* 470 So.2d 913 (La. 1985).
39. N.Y. Times, September 30, 1984, at 50, col. 4.
40. *Times-Picayune Publishing Corp.,* 95 S. Ct. 1 (1974).
41. Campazzi, *Nurses, Nursing and Malpractice Litigation* 5 NURS. ADMIN. Q., 1 (1981).
42. *Webber v. State,* 305 So.2d 235 (Fla. App. 1973).
43. *Howe v. Medical Arts Center Hospital,* 261 App. Div. 1088 (N.Y. 1941); *Bryant v. Presbyterian Hospital in the City of New York,* 110 N.E.2d 391 (N.Y. 1953); *Habuda v. Trustees of Rex Hospital,* 3 N.C. App. 11 (1968).
44. *Carter v. Anderson Memorial Hospital,* 325 S.E.2d 78 (S.C. App. 1985).
45. *Central Anesthesia Associates v. Worthy,* 325 S.E.2d 819 (Ga. App. 1984), *affd.,* 333 S.E.2d 829 (Ga. 1985).
46. *Id.* at 823, 824.
47. *Id.* at 829.
48. *See, e.g.,* MD. HEALTH-OCC. CODE ANN. §7-301(c) (1981), which states: "This section (referring to the nurse practice act) does not apply to: . . . (2) a student enrolled in an approved education program while practicing registered nursing or licensed practical nursing in that program."
49. *Central Security Mutual Insurance Company v. DePinto,* 673 P.2d 122 (Kan. App. 1983), *affd.* 681 P.2d 15 (Kan. 1983).
50. *Whittington v. Sowela Technical Institute,* 438 So.2d 236 (La. 1983). (See Chapter 20 for further discussion.)
51. *Hubbard v. John Tyler Community College,* 455 F. Supp. 753 (E.D. Va. 1978).
52. Appendix IV cites all nursing practice acts.
53. NATIONAL STUDENT NURSE'S ASSOCIATION, THE BILL OF RIGHTS AND RESPONSIBILITIES FOR STUDENTS OF NURSING (1978).
54. AMERICAN ASSOCIATION OF UNIVERSITY PROFESSORS, JOINT STATEMENT OF RIGHTS AND FREEDOMS OF STUDENTS (1967). (See excerpts in box, p. 312.)

Additional Readings

E. BERNZWEIG, THE NURSE'S LIABILITY FOR MALPRACTICE (4th ed. 1986).

Chickadonz, *Breaking Barriers: Educating a Deaf Nursing Student* 4 NURS. & HEALTH CARE 327 (1983).

Greenlaw, *Mississippi University for Women v. Hogan: The Supreme Court Rules on Female-Only Nursing School* 10 LAW, MED. & HEALTH CARE 267 (1982).

Niedringhaus and Driscoll, *Staying Within the Law—Academic Probation and Dismissal* 31 N. O. 156 (1983).

Northrop, *Faculty and Students: Academic and Disciplinary Decisions* 6 DEAN'S NOTES, 1 (1984).

Northrop, *Student Nurses and Legal Accountabilities* 32 IMPRINT 16 (November 1985).

Chapter 20

Nursing schools and faculty

Cynthia E. Northrop

The legal issues surrounding the role of the nursing faculty and the school of nursing within a hospital, community college, or university nursing education department include not only those issues discussed in the previous chapter but issues of faculty and school liability for student actions during clinical practicums, issues of documentation, and relationships between clinical agencies and nursing education programs.

Appointment, promotion, and tenure are also of prime importance to nursing faculty and programs. Neither faculty nor educational programs are immune to salary disputes, charges of discrimination, contract disputes, and issues related to curriculum and academic freedom. These issues will be addressed in this chapter.

However, this chapter should be read in conjunction with the other parts of the book, particularly Chapters 19 and 21, since both of those chapters contain content essential to the faculty and school role.

There are many types of educational programs in nursing. These programs vary based on the length of program, the degree and/or diploma awarded, the academic setting of the program, and whether the program might be considered "innovative" (e.g., the external degree program, classroom without walls, or outreach programs). Entry into practice legislation, for example, recently enacted in Maine and North Dakota, may set a trend toward only two levels of basic nursing education, requiring either an associate degree or a baccalaureate degree.[1] Continuing education programs are also part of nursing education.

The school of nursing program and faculty fill three important societal functions: teaching, service, and research. With high expectations often, schools and faculty balance all three functions. The criteria for how much time and effort is to be spent in each of the three areas may be written or unwritten. Above all, how the faculty role and school mission are to be carried out should be clearly known to all who participate. Students and community need to be among those who participate.

Legal issues for nursing faculty and programs will be presented according to two of the three primary functions and missions: teaching and service. The legal issues around publication and committee work will be discussed within the service mission. Legal issues for the nurse researcher and faculty and the institution which sponsors nursing research is the topic of Chapter 21.

Teaching

Teaching—important task of the faculty and educational programs—should not be underestimated. Nursing curricula are made and designed to meet the health care delivery needs of society. Rules and regulations of schools are developed to provide a conducive learning environment and to assure that students are evaluated properly. As mentioned in the previous chapter, faculty and educational institutions may govern their functioning. Courts have historically refrained from interfering in faculty decisions. The only basis upon which the courts will intervene is when the school and faculty do not follow their own rules or act in an arbitrary and capricious manner (see Chapter 19).

Public and private institutions are directly influenced by state law. The power and authority for governance of the institution derives directly from state law, for example, through incorporation or chartering and licensure or coordination bodies. All states incorporate or charter public and private postsecondary educational institutions.

Schools of nursing are subject to regulations of state agencies, for example, the state board of nursing which may mandate its approval of a nursing program prior to its functioning.[2] Educational facilities must also abide by state laws pertaining to employment, such as labor laws, unemployment compensation, and worker's compensation, which will be discussed later.

Legal issues unique to the teaching function of the faculty and university that were not discussed earlier include, liability for faculty and school malpractice, the relationship of faculty and school liability to the liability of student activities, documentation, and issues pertaining to the contract for placement of students. Each of these will be discussed.

LIABILITIES

Faculty and institutions may be liable not only for their own direct actions but for failing to prevent the actions of unprepared students. These questions are particularly relevant when students are in the clinical area rather than the classroom. However, practice or skills laboratories may also be sites where liability may arise, since often faculty require students to practice techniques and skills upon one another before practicing in the clinical area.

While there were no cases found by this author in which a nursing faculty was sued individually for malpractice, there were cases involving nursing schools which had been sued for malpractice and negligence. In one particular case a nursing student driving a van with students and faculty in it to clinical lost control of the van, and it overturned.[3] The husband of one of the nursing students who was killed in the accident brought a negligence action against the school. The court held that the school had negligently selected the driver, that students in the van had complained about the driver, and that the faculty in the van took no corrective steps.

The court found that the student nurse who was driving the van was an agent of the school, even though she had rented the van for the trip and it was not owned by the school. The school of nursing argued that the students were on a joint venture and that the releases they had signed were contracts within which the students agreed to waive personal rights allowed by Louisiana law.

The court, however, noted that an essential element of a contract is consent and that consent must be a free and deliberate exercise of the contracting party's will. The court found that, although the students had signed the documents, the context surrounding the execution of the releases negated consent.

Students and schools of nursing, the court said, are not parties which can deal at arms length. The school dictated the terms of the purported release of any and all liabilities in an attempt to release the school from a reasonably foreseeable danger. The school trip for the senior nursing students occurred annually. Twelve credit hours (double the normal hours earned per day) were earned for participating. The school did not offer alternative classes for any student who chose not to participate. In view of these facts the court said the students could not give free and deliberate consent. The court's summary comment was that, "Public policy forbids the release whereby an attempt was made to *prospectively* absolve the school of nursing of liability for injuries negligently caused through instrumentalities in the exclusive control of the school" (emphasis added).[4]

The court went on to define the *independent* negligence of the school of nursing as follows:

1. The school of nursing owed a duty to its students to provide transportation under safe conditions. The trip was a school function.
2. A greater degree of care must be exercised if students are required to engage in an activity where it is reasonably foreseeable that an accident or injury may occur.
3. The school of nursing made the trip a part of its curriculum but failed to have a uniform policy for the transportation of its students. The school knowingly approved of an overcrowded condition in the van by allowing 18 persons to travel in a van designed to carry 15 passengers.
4. The two nursing instructors were on duty just as though they were in the classroom. They failed to take any corrective measures to protect the students, despite the complaints and comments made about the student's ability to drive safely.
5. The school of nursing failed to ensure that a trained, competent driver would be used to transport students.

Many principles from this case can be applied to other nursing faculty and school liability questions. In the clinical setting, classroom setting, and skills laboratory, nursing faculty and school administrators have a duty to their students. That duty is to teach in a safe and reasonable manner under the circumstances and to abide by its contract with students, avoiding the formation of illegal and ineffective contracts.

TORT LIABILITIES OF INSTITUTIONS OF HIGHER EDUCATION

Institutions May be Liable For:

Accidents associated with transportation
Accidents associated with chemical exposures, such as shop work, manual and vocational training
Accidents due to conditions of buildings, equipment, or outside premises
Injuries caused by other students
Accidents associated with physical education classes
Accidents in the use of premises and equipment for other than school purposes
Injuries due to conditions of grounds, walks, or playgrounds
Injuries resulting from lack of or insufficient supervision
Failure to protect students from crime
Educational malpractice (although such suits are usually not allowed because courts have held that they violate public policy)

The school of nursing has a duty to the students to provide safe and competent nursing faculty. If students are harmed or injured, faculty and schools will be liable for failure to be reasonable and act in a safe manner, including preventing foreseeable harm to students.

As in the case discussed, a greater degree of care is expected where it is reasonably foreseeable that injury will occur. Therefore, in any educational activity, be it practicing giving injections, changing beds, or interviewing patients, that activity must be thought of in terms of reasonableness and prevention of harm to the students.

Listed in the box above are some common tort liabilities of institutions of higher education. For example, school personnel have been found to be negligent in permitting students to use a known-defective burner in the science laboratory[5]; and faculty members have the responsibility to know what the limits of safety are for any equipment to be used by students.[6]

Questions often asked to assess proper supervision of students include:

1. Whether the faculty's immmediate presence could have prevented the student's injury
2. Whether the faculty adequately instructed subordinate or substituted employees
3. Whether the faculty made and enforced adequate safety rules
4. Whether the number of supervisory personnel were adequate for the circumstances

Courts are increasingly viewing the student-school relationship as a contractual one. Students have challenged faculty and school decisions based on constitutional deprivation, misrepresentation, fraud, and breach of contract. In virtually every case, the written or oral representations of the institution, such as those contained in catalogs, syllabi, student handbooks, written rules and regulations, and verbal promises, have provided the bases for the claims.

In addition, faculty are responsible for their decisions regarding clinical assignments of students. Schools are vicariously responsible for those decisions as well under the doctrine of *respondeat superior*. The school employs and controls the assignment of its faculty to teach in certain areas. Judgments regarding faculty assignments can be the basis of a lawsuit against the school of nursing.

Therefore, when a nursing instructor assigns a student to a particular patient and clinical agency, the instructor in essence has said that the student is prepared properly and sufficiently to carry out the assignment. This usually means that the instructor has personally evaluated the student and the student's capabilities. If a student begins the assignment and has any questions about the activities that must be done for which the student has previously been ''checked-out'' by the instructor, the student must return to the instructor immediately for assistance. In general, if the faculty made a reasonable assignment and the student is unsure and goes ahead and does something which injures a patient, only the student and the clinical agency may be liable.

As is discussed on p. 319, the question of who is liable may often be influenced by the contract between the clinical agency and school of nursing. If the instructor has made an unreasonable evaluation, or perhaps no evaluation, of the student and assigns him or her to a situation which calls for more skills than the student possesses or has had an opportunity to learn, then both the student and the nursing instructor and school will be liable if patient injury occurs. The clinical agency liability will be discussed later.

In a recent case a corporation which ran a school of anesthesia for nurses was held liable for improper assignment of the faculty supervisor and for the faculty's resulting student assignment.[7] The case involved a nurse anesthetist student who gave anesthesia as instructed by the faculty person which harmed a patient. Only those licensed and certified to give anesthesia, according to a state law, may give anesthesia. The student was not certified to give anesthesia.

The court held the student, clinical agency, and school liable for violating the state statute, which is negligence per se. The court stated that the duty of the school was to properly assign students and in the case of anesthesia, the duty was not to assign students to administer anesthesia and not to assign a nonphysician to supervise the students (a physician assistant was the nursing student's instructor).[8]

The duty of the clinical agency was established by the contract between the hospital and school. It contemplated the use of student nurse anesthetists. The hospital's duty was to uphold all laws and not to permit the violation of the law. The hospital was also liable under its duty to ensure that an adequate, competent staff served the patients.[9]

This case was also discussed in Chapter 19 in terms of the student's negligence. Also discussed was that most state nurse practice acts provide an exemption for nursing students under the act itself, meaning that nursing students are not violating the nurse practice act because they are not licensed to practice nursing when learning nursing.

Of special and recent, more pressing concern to nursing faculty and program administrators is the issue of chemical dependence in nursing students. While neither the school of nursing nor nursing faculty were in any way implicated, there has been at least one reported criminal case involving a nursing student who was found guilty of dealing drugs.[10] The nursing instructor's most important function is to provide an opportunity for students to learn the skills of a nurse who will provide safe and competent care. When a student's behaviors indicate that the student is under the influence of alcohol or drugs while in the classroom or clinical setting, faculty must take preventive actions for the safety of the student, the patients, and others.

Possible steps, depending on the severity of the student's behavior, may involve close, one-to-one supervision or immediate removal of the student from the clinical or classroom setting. The situation mandates that the faculty be well versed, knowledgeable, and aware of the signs and symptoms of chemical dependence and the approaches to individuals in that condition. Schools of nursing may wish to consider developing resource information for faculty who in turn can advise students of school or community resources for counseling and help. Every opportunity must be afforded the student within the context of school rules and regulations. Faculty must balance the ability to provide a safe learning environment with the student's ability to continue in the program. This issue was also discussed in Chapter 19.

DOCUMENTATION

No other item is as helpful and as credible to clarifying legal disputes than the records, notes, and documents kept in conjunction with any activity. As mentioned in the previous chapter, attendance records, school catalogs, grading appeals procedures, course outlines, and clinical evaluations are just a few of the records which nursing faculty and school administrators maintain. Anecdotal notes, examinations, student papers, references, committee minutes, school bylaws, handbooks (faculty and student), and policy and procedures manuals also provide important data that schools of nursing and faculty keep in the course of their usual business. All of these documents may be used as evidence to demonstrate that standards were met or that they were not met.

Individual student records are also important. Most state laws and the federal law, the Family Educational and Privacy Act of 1974 (known as the Buckley Amendment), provide that students may read and copy most documents of which they are the subject of discussion.[11] Generally, school policies that have been developed following this law permit students to inspect their education records, limit disclosure to others of personally identifiable information from education records without students' prior written consent, and provide students the opportunity to seek correction of their education records where appropriate.

Examples of documents not accessible to students are records maintained by the security section of the school or their parents' confidential financial statements. All student records are confidential, with the students holding the right to give permission that they be shared with others whom they must specify.

State laws may also govern student records. For example, in one state all publicly supported institutions of higher education must hold confidential, except with the express consent of the individual student, all academic records of students.[12]

Wanting to respect the students' right to confidentiality and protect students from breaches of it and violations of their privacy, schools of nursing have placed increased emphasis upon with whom and methods by which grades and evaluations are shared. For example, some schools of nursing do not post grades nor do they give out grades over the telephone. Conferences are conducted in private between faculty and students. At times faculty may involve other persons, but with the permission of the students. And at times, students may wish to involve additional persons, perhaps parents, in a conference, again with the permission of the faculty.

Schools have also developed policies and forms for release of references upon permission of the students. Given that there is proper permission for release of a reference, faculty often raise concerns about the content of the reference, especially in light of the law of defamation. Explained in depth in Chapter 5, this quasi-intentional tort can be avoided by faculty if the reference is truthful, objective, accurate, and factual. Statements made in references should be able to be substantiated by factual data, including referring to some of the documentation mentioned before which is kept as part of the usual faculty activity.

Documentation within the school of nursing should follow similar principles as for documentation within the clinical area. These are discussed in Chapter 28 on quality assurance and documentation. Regular, periodic written evaluations of students provide factual and important data to trace the students' progress. Students being well-informed about their progress is also important to emphasize. It is common practice for the written evaluations to be signed by both faculty and students. Space is provided for student responses to evaluations.

Balanced data, noting positive achievements and unsuccessful attempts, should be kept about students. Data which reflect progress toward stated course criteria, objectives, and expected behaviors should be collected about each student.

RELATIONSHIPS WITH CLINICAL AGENCIES

Nursing education depends heavily upon clinical agencies for the availability of clinical practice for students. Being able to test the skills of students in an active learning environment is essential to preparing safe and competent nurses. Agencies also benefit greatly from associating with students and faculty. School of nursing and clinical agency relationships aid recruiting efforts, improve morale of staff, and provide for the future needs for qualified health care practitioners. From clinical–school associations have come innovations in the delivery of nursing education and service, including the development of joint nursing faculty–clinical appointments and the increased role and use of nursing research.

The relationship between education and service should be formalized into a contract.[13] Faculty, staff, and administrators should be involved in the development of this mutual agreement. There are many possible clinical arrangements. Each arrangement should be individually evaluated to determine whether a specific written contract is desirable. However, whether written or verbal, if arrangements are made to accept students into a particular facility, a contract has usually been formed.

How complex the written agreement is often depends on the number of students to be placed, what they will be doing, how supervision will be handled, and how frequently the agency will be used. If one student wishes to observe a public health nurse in a well-baby clinic for a day during a semester, a letter exchanged between the clinic administrator and the nursing instructor will specify the few parameters of the arrangement: one student, observation, no direct patient care, 1 day. If, however, several students will need a clinical arrangement throughout their program 2 or 3 days per week, a written contract should be developed.

A formal agreement should contain the main points of the arrangement, and an implementation plan should be developed which may change from time to time depending on school schedule, number of students, supervising faculty, learning objectives, and evaluation methods. The contract should be reviewed by counsel, and often school and agency lawyers will want to be involved in the entire contract negotiating process and perhaps even meet together.

Suggested content of the formal contract between school and clinical agency is shown on p. 320 (see box). In creating a contract, the negotiations must be done by those authorized to contract within their respective institutions. This usually is the dean or administrator in the school of nursing and the director of nursing or administrator in the clinical agency. The rules of the particular facility determine who the authorized party is.

However, it is common practice to involve the staff and the instructors who will be operating within the contract in the negotiation of the contract. Other guidelines may exist within the facilities which must be reviewed in preparing the contract. In addition standards, accreditation criteria, and state board of nursing regulations for approval of nursing programs often make requirements regarding clinical agencies. For example, in Maryland the State Board of Examiners of Nurses Regulations provides that faculty shall determine, select, and evaluate the facilities to be used; that the facilities to be used be approved by the appropriate authorities; that the board be notified in writing of agencies selected by faculty; and that the board may survey the facility at its discretion.[14]

Problem areas experienced by faculty and staff of schools and clinical agencies can be resolved through a

CONTRACTUAL RELATIONSHIPS BETWEEN SCHOOLS OF NURSING AND CLINICAL AGENCIES: SUGGESTED CONTENT FOR FORMAL CONTRACTS

CONTRACTUAL PARTY: *Health Care Facility*

Agency is responsible for patient care.

School is to provide competent supervision and registered staff.

Students are to conform to policy and follow directives of staff.

Agency retains the right to require students or faculty to leave.

Students and faculty are covered by own malpractice insurance; amounts may be specified.

Students and faculty are held to confidentiality regarding patient and staff information.

Services available to students are identified.

Students are not employees while engaged in an educational program.

School is to advise facility of changes in curriculum and school.

Termination procedures and time frames are specified.

CONTRACTUAL PARTY: *School of Nursing*

Educational program is under the control and responsibility of the school.

Information gained by the staff is confidential.

Any resources available to students is delineated.

School may publish that there is an affiliation with the facility.

Terms of termination, notice, and time element of when contract is to expire or to be renewed are set.

Any benefits accrued by the agency will be identified, e.g. tuition vouchers.

Students and faculty are covered by own malpractice insurance.

School conforms to legal requirements of state and local governments with regard to students and faculty.

written contract. Faculty are concerned that they and their students will be used to supplement staffing in the facility. Staff are concerned that faculty provide inadequate supervision. Staff often assume that the student and faculty substitute for their responsibility for patient care. Students' eligibility for worker's compensation should they be injured while at the clinical agency is often left uncertain. Questions of who is liable for student and faculty negligence are also of concern.

Specific contract clauses can provide answers to these problem areas. Here are some sample contract clauses that help to clarify these areas:

1. The hospital shall at all times be in charge and responsible for the nursing care of patients through the employment of professional personnel who will cooperate with faculty responsible for the planning and supervision of student assignments.
2. The hospital retains ultimate responsibility for the quality and safety of the patient care.
3. Students participating in the clinical experience at the hospital shall be deemed to be students of the college and shall not be deemed servants, agents, or employees of the hospital.
4. While participating in the clinical experience at the hospital, the college shall assume any and all obligations to the extent they may be imposed by law for any employment relationship or employer responsibilities that may arise out of a student's participation in the clinical experience while at the hospital, including but not limited to the state worker's compensation law.
5. The university and hospital shall maintain ongoing communication to coordinate the scheduling of academic and clinical field work experiences, including reciprocal on-site visits and participation in faculty and staff meetings.
6. The school shall advise students of their responsibility to conduct themselves in accordance with the hospital's rules and regulations, and the students will be responsible for this information. The hospital reserves the right to dismiss from the hospital at any time any student whose condition or conduct jeopardizes the well-being of the patients or employees of the hospital. Unless unusual circumstances occur, such dismissal shall not occur without prior consultation with the school.
7. Except in the case of negligence on the part of the hospital, the hospital shall not be liable for any injuries sustained by any students or faculty participating in the clinical educational program. The sole recourse for the student or faculty in such situations shall be to pursue whatever insurance

benefits that may be available pursuant to the group medical insurance policy offered by the university, if any.

8. It shall be the responsibility of the students and faculty members to maintain professional liability insurance coverage in amounts acceptable to the hospital. The university agrees to maintain general liability coverage. In addition the university agrees to name the hospital as an additional insured on its general liability policy with respect to those activities of the university students and faculty in the program which are not under the supervision and control of the hospital.
9. The school agrees to hold harmless and indemnify the hospital, its trustees, officers, employees, and agents from and against all expenses, including but not limited to claims, liabilities, penalties, losses, fines, attorney's fees, and judgments arising out of injury or disability to any person of any nature, including death, or any damage or loss of property of any nature arising out of the wrongful or negligent activities of any student or faculty member of the school under this agreement.

These are sample contract clauses, not to be used without advice of counsel, assuring that they apply to the unique situation, needs, and wishes of each school and clinical agency. As competition for clinical placements increases, in some instances hospitals or other clinical agencies have been successful in requiring schools of nursing to agree to a "hold harmless clause," as outlined in number 9 above. As supply and demand of clinical agencies and student populations ebb and flow, so to do the contract terms, depending on how badly the school needs the clinical arrangement or how important the teaching is to the clinical agency mission.

Once developed, the meaning and content of the contract should be communicated to faculty and staff. Faculty should review the content of the contract with students at orientation and periodically. These contracts represent the best efforts of nursing service and education working together to mutually benefit each other and the profession.

Community service and faculty practice

The community service and faculty practice functions of a nursing faculty involves the respresentation of the school of nursing within the community and the faculty's own clinical practice. Participating in school committee work and publishing are also forms of this representation. Legal issues in this area of faculty practice are probably least thought about. Faculty in most schools of nursing are expected to devote a percentage of their time to participating in activities for the betterment of the community and profession and to maintaining their clinical skills.

Faculty are encouraged to belong to professional associations and community groups and are required to publish and do committee work of the school. When they do so as part of their job and faculty role, they are responsible for their own actions, and the school of nursing is vicariously responsible for the faculty's actions based on the earlier mentioned doctrine of *respondeat superior.*

COMMUNITY SERVICE

While this author could find no cases involving nursing faculty or school negligence or other torts or possible breaches of contract in the area of community service or faculty practice, potential liabilities should at be least identified. Particularly in the situation where the school pays or officially sends the faculty as a representative or spokesperson to a selected organization or community group, special duties and relationships have been created. In this capacity, the school would, along with the faculty, be liable for the results of negligent acts which the faculty caused.

Faculty should be aware of "facility use policies" if they are planning to hold meetings at the school. Especially publicly funded, tax-supported schools have legal constraints on who may use their facilities. This becomes especially apparent when religious groups wish to use public facilities for their meetings.

Faculty advisors to student organizations must understand that the students are permitted to conduct safe, unfettered extracurricular activities on campus. The institution is responsible for faculty advisors implementing policies on student organizations. Therefore it is important to know the extent of the authority as a faculty advisor and the personal liability in the decisions made as part of that role. It may help if the faculty advisor and the administrator know what the institution's litigation response policy is when dealing with student groups.

In the role of spokesperson or college representative for the school of nursing, faculty members should have a clear understanding with the person appointing them as to the expectations in terms of what must be checked by the administration prior to release by the faculty, for example, at a community meeting. The internal rules and regulations of the school must be followed, including those unpublished common practices and usual customs of faculty representatives.

FACULTY PRACTICE

Faculty practice is a growing area and carries with it unique legal concerns. It can take several forms, including joint appointments or independent clinical practice. In the former form the faculty's liabilities are sorted out according to the joint appointment contract between the faculty, school, and clinical agency. This assumes that a contract exists. One is highly recommended and should state the expected functions of the faculty and obligations and duties of all parties involved in the appointment.

In the latter form of practice, there may be no formal arrangement between the school and faculty person, but the practice is done independently, outside the faculty employment and contract. Chapter 33 focuses more on independent nursing practice. Faculty also can review the clinical chapter with which their practice is affiliated.

Faculty may also need to retain accounting as well as legal advice regarding these types of arrangements. The question of payment for clinical services by the patient to the nurse faculty, to the clinical agency, or even portions to the school must be clarified.

PUBLICATION

"Publish or perish" is often the motto of academic life. Laws which have an impact on the process of publication involve contract law and federal legislation, such as the Copyright Act.[15] This federal statute provides a mechanism through which faculty can protect their creative works. The law states that no person may duplicate or use these works, once registered, without the author or the holder of the copyright's permission. Copyright is a form of protection provided to authors of literary, dramatic, musical, artistic, and certain other intellectual works.[16]

When a publisher and faculty member negotiate the publication of material developed by the faculty member, their conclusions will be a contract. Principles of state contract law then will apply should disputes arise. Depending on the type of creative work, other federal statutes may apply, such as the Trademarks and Patents Act.[17] Often faculty are subject to internal policies and procedures of education institutions regarding publication. Faculty should be knowledgeable about what rules do exist and must consult these.

Disputes can arise among faculty about the rights to publish. This can happen particularly when research or other similar projects are undertaken by faculty jointly. These disputes can be avoided if, at the outset of the project, the faculty discuss and agree about who has the right to access the data and study results and publish them. This agreement is a contract among the project participants.

Other aspects of publications and legal implications involve the use of printed, video, audio, and computer software in the classroom or clinical setting. Faculty may reproduce copyrighted material for classroom use provided that reproduction of copyrighted material is for "criticism, comment, news reporting, teaching (including multiple copies for classroom use), scholarship, or research."[18]

Determining whether material can be copied and not infringe on the copyright, and thus be a "fair use," involves an assessment of:

1. The purpose and character of the use
2. The nature of the copyrighted work
3. The amount and substantiality of the portion used
4. The effect of the use upon the potential market for or value of the copyrighted work

Distribution of materials to students must be within fair use. In a recent case a teacher had used approximately 50% of a booklet on cake decorating in preparing a learning activity package, and this amounted to virtually all the substance of the author's work.[19] The teacher's use was held to amount to substantial, quantitative, and qualitative copying of the copyright owner's booklet. Thus, the court determined that it was not a fair use.

Guidelines have been developed regarding photocopying material for classroom use.[20] These guidelines suggest that teachers may make single copies for their own use and multiple copies for classroom use using the following considerations:

1. Meets tests of brevity, spontaneity (defined below)
2. Meets the cumulative effect test (defined below)
3. Includes in each copy a notice of copyright

Tests for brevity means that either a complete article, story, essay, or illustration of less than 2500 words may be used or an excerpt from any prose work of not more than 1000 words or 10% of the work, whichever is less. Spontaneity means that the copying is done at the inspiration of the individual teacher for maximum teaching effectiveness.

Cumulative effect refers to the amount of copying of any one article or reference. The guidelines suggest that:

1. Copying be done for only one course in the school
2. Not more than one article may be copied from the

same author, nor more than three from the same collective work or periodical volume during one class term

3. Not more than nine instances of such multiple copying for one course occur during one class term

The guidelines make exceptions for newspapers or news periodicals.

The guidelines indicate that copying shall *not*:

1. Be used to create or to replace or substitute for compilations or collective works
2. Be intended to be consumable
3. Substitute for the purchase of books
4. Be repeated with respect to the same item by the same teacher from term to term
5. Carry a charge to the student beyond the actual cost of the photocopying

These are not legal guidelines but guidelines from private individuals who have studied the concerns of both faculty and authors.

Faculty may also be involved in videotaping television broadcasts or in the preparation or use of videotapes with students. The copyright law allows nonprofit institutions to videotape certain noncommercial educational television broadcasts for use in face-to-face teaching activities but only if used within 7 days of broadcast and then erased.[21] Permission and consent from students or other individuals who are videotaped are mandated and are the legal responsibility of the producer–faculty member to obtain. If students are not the age of majority in the jurisdiction, their parents' permission must be obtained. Prior permission is required of all who participate.

The growing use of computer programs and programming in schools of nursing is proving to be an exciting and effective part of teaching and research. The use of software is governed by the copyright law. For example, the purchaser of computer software programs may make a copy where it is an essential step in the utilization of the computer program in conjunction with a machine or where it is for archival purposes only and will be destroyed when rightful use of the computer program ceases.[22] The software manufacturer holds the copyright, and allows others to use their product by not selling but granting a license for its use, not the right to copy it. The faculty become the end-user and must agree to the terms of the software owner. Violations of the agreement may lead not only to civil penalties but also, under some circumstances, to criminal prosecution.

Copy protection devices, such as programming codes, are properly used by owners in an attempt to protect their products from unlawful duplication. Again, software is licensed, not sold. Terms of the licensing generally grant that a nonexclusive license be extended to use the software product on one computer; that the owner of software retains title and ownership; that software may not be modified without the consent of the owner; and that duplication of the software product for any purpose other than back-up protection, including duplication for any commercial purpose, is a violation of the copyright laws.

COMMITTEE RESPONSIBILITIES

Committee work is also an expected part of a faculty member's role. Rules and laws also govern this area. The bylaws developed by the school and its faculty will govern the function and structure of committees and should include the authority of the committee and to whom it reports and is responsible. Usually faculty committees, such as the Appointments, Promotion, and Tenure Committee, are composed of faculty members and report to the faculty through a faculty assembly or faculty council. Often nursing faculty must participate in committees of the whole university. These are also governed by bylaws of the institution. The chief reference for orderly meeting conduct and proceedings is ROBERT'S RULES OF ORDER.[23] There is no other more widely accepted and authoritative statement of parliamentary law. Thorough understanding of it greatly aids the faculty member in successful meeting management.

Appointment, promotion, and tenure

The principal means for protecting faculty members from unjustified dismissals is tenure. The most widely accepted statement of academic tenure, formulated by the Association of American Colleges and the American Association of University Professors, provides: "After the expiration of a probationary period, teachers . . . should have permanent or continuous tenure, and their services should be terminated only for adequate cause, except in the case of retirement for age or, under extraordinary circumstances, because of financial exigencies."[24]

The essential characteristic of tenure is continuity of service in that institution in which the teacher serves, where that institution has in some manner relinquished the freedom or power it otherwise would possess to terminate the teacher's services.

Closely related to the legal concepts of contracts, due process and principles of academic freedom, the issues of denial of appointment, breach of contract for nonrenewal of appointment, denial of promotion and tenure, termination of tenured faculty, and disputes regarding salary and other benefits, including worker's compensation, have been the subject of litigation involving nursing faculty and schools of nursing. Chapter 30 on employment claims provides further information related to what will be discussed here. In the discussion below the nursing faculty is plaintiff, and the school of nursing is defendant.

Generally, courts have upheld the right of faculty to select their own colleagues, to determine the curricular and research missions of their departments, and to evaluate their peers within and outside their institutions. On the other hand, courts have generally also upheld the right of the school or university to curtail or eliminate academic programs, lay off tenured faculty and establish standards for faculty conduct and performance.

ACADEMIC FREEDOM

Based on the First Amendment to the U.S. Constitution,[25] academic freedom signifies intellectual autonomy of members of the academic community, including the freedom of faculty to research and teach, the freedom of students to learn, and the freedom of both from *imposed* conceptions of truth.[26] Academic freedom represents the ability of the faculty to seek and ascertain truth. It is a freedom to inquire, to investigate, to interpret data, and to arrive at and announce conclusions without controls in or out of the classroom and without fear of sanction.[27]

Therefore, in disputes involving denial of promotion and tenure and academic freedom, faculty are entitled to due process. As described in the preceding chapter, due process involves notice and a hearing, an opportunity to state both sides of the claim. It also involves assurances that the school must follow its own rules and regulations pertaining to tenure and promotion. These rules should be well known to faculty and administrators and should be readily available in faculty handbooks.

However, the amount and type of due process varies according to whether the faculty is tenured or not. Courts have held that absent evidence of any violation of constitutional rights (such as academic freedom) by the school, the untenured faculty member is not entitled to a hearing or a statement of reasons for the decision not to rehire.[28] Untenured faculty have no legitimate expectation for continued employment, beyond their present contract. Yet, courts have overturned dismissals of nontenured faculty where it has found that the school violated the faculty member's right of free speech.[29] These issues will be discussed further.

DENIAL OF APPOINTMENT, NONRENEWAL OF CONTRACT

The primary questions in the area of denial or nonrenewal of contract are when is a contract established and under what circumstances is nonrenewal proper? As discussed in Chapter 30, contract formation is based on a mutual understanding of and agreement to terms, including a specific time within which performance is to occur. Most nursing faculty have contracts.

In a Massachusetts case, a nursing instructor who had been employed under term contracts for 3 academic years was advised to report to work the following fall on a specific date.[30] She did not appear until 10 days after the specified date. She also did not inform the university about her absence or her whereabouts. The school tried to locate her by mail, telephone and a visit to her last known address, but she had moved without notifying the university. On the ninth day of absence the dean of the nursing school sent her a written notice that her contract was at an end because of her failure to appear.

The court held that the nursing instructor's behavior indicated a serious and substantial breach of the employment contract, that it had been abandoned, and that the university was justified in terminating it before service began. The court held that the grievance procedures set forth in the faculty manual constituting part of the employment contract were inapplicable.

In a Maryland case, also involving breach of contract, a nursing instructor sought to recover monetary damages.[31] Following a 30-day leave of absence for surgery in April and May of 1973, the nursing instructor returned to work and received a letter indicating that the school did not want her back the following year. The contract was modeled on a state board of education tenure agreement. The dispute boiled down to the interpretation and understanding of two of the contract clauses:

1. "It is further agreed that either of the parties to this contract may terminate it at the end of the school year by giving notice in writing to the other not later than May 1 of such school year"
2. "This contract shall continue for the duration of 1 year subject to the aforegoing conditions."[32]

A principle of contract law is that the clear and unambiguous language of an agreement will be the contract intended by the parties. The court held that this contract was plain and unambiguous, there was no room for other construction or meaning, and it must be presumed that the parties meant what they expressed in the contract. In addition, the trial court found as a fact that there was no question as to the nursing instructor's competency as a nurse or that the performance evaluation was less than required. The court could find no evidence that an effort was made to terminate the nursing instructor according to the contract provisions. The letter to the nursing instructor was sent 18 days after the time of notice required by the contract. The case was remanded for a determination of the amount of damages and a question of the instructor's obligation to mitigate them.

DENIAL OF TENURE AND/OR PROMOTION

Nursing faculty and schools of nursing have litigated the issues of denied tenure and promotion many times. Questions of proper due process in the decision-making process, including review of the internal appeals and grievance procedures used, are most often the focus of the litigation. One example, a case involving the denial of tenure of a co-ordinator of nursing education in a high school licensed practical nursing (LPN) program, demonstrates the importance of following published procedures.[33]

Following service to the school for 3 probationary years, the instructor was notified by a letter from the school that she would not be recommended for tenure and that her employment would be terminated. The letter stated that she was knowledgeable and able to perform satisfactorily the normal professional obligations required in the teaching of an LPN program. The letter also stated that her ability to lead and inspire those who work in the program was less than acceptable. The nursing instructor wrote a letter requesting that the superintendent formally detail the reasons for the proposed recommendation. With no further communication, the board terminated her employment, and tenure was denied.

In this lawsuit the nursing instructor alleged that the discharge was not a result of dissatisfaction with her qualifications, which were bona fide reasons, but as a retaliatory measure because she had objected to the initiation of an educational program for the training of practical nurses and nurses' aides which she claimed was being done in a manner violating the guidelines and curriculum issued by the state department of education. She argued that she had been ordered to act in a manner which violated the "code of ethics" and that she was refused tenure for exercising constitutional rights in expressing her views. She asked the court for a hearing to determine whether she was discharged for improper reasons.

The court found that tenure should not be denied because the nursing instructor made requests that the school adhere to the lawful curriculum, as she understood it to be, established by the state board of education and adhere to what she deemed to be the lawful procedures established for the evaluation and supervision of nursing teachers and students. The court said that notification to supervisors of her views concerning the proper procedures to be followed in order to conform with the law is a practice which should not be curtailed by the denial of tenure. However, the court specifically said that such activity does not provide a shelter for a teacher whom the board decides not to retain for bona fide, legitimate reasons.

Bona fide, legitimate reasons for nonrenewal of contracts of tenured nursing faculty were outlined in *Kelly*.[34] In this case the court found substantial evidence to support the complaints of conduct detrimental to the nursing program and inability to cooperate with and maintain harmony among the staff as legitimate reasons for denial of tenure rights.

In this case two nursing instructors had participated in activities such as "constant sniping" in faculty meetings; they were uncooperative with other faculty and refused to provide information and test materials to other members of the nursing department. One faculty member had canceled class without approval. The other was reported to have disrupted patients in a clinical setting. Many other examples of this type existed for more than 2 years.

During a state board of nursing site visit for accreditation, one of the board representatives, after she had met with these two faculty, among others, to assess the program, told the director of the nursing department that she must get the faculty problem solved or plan on closing the school doors. The director met with the college dean and president, and all recommended nonrenewal of these two faculties' contracts. The board of trustees approved this recommendation, and letters were sent to the two instructors.

Upon the instructors' request a due process hearing was held. A hearing committee was formed; the hearing was held; and the committee made its report, finding that the board had not sustained its burden of proof. It recommended by a two to one vote that the two teachers be renewed for the next school year. A minority report was also filed.

After considering the reports and hearing oral argument the school's board of trustees rejected the hearing panel's recommendation and voted to terminate the teacher's contracts. The nursing instructors then brought the issue before the court. The court began its review of the school's action by stating that the court cannot substitute its judgment for the decision of an administrative hearing (in this case the internal faculty appeals procedure) unless the decision makers acted fraudulently, arbitrarily or capriciously, unless the decision was not substantially supported by evidence, or unless the decision was outside the scope of the decision makers authority.

Having found substantial evidence to support the complaints, the court then examined the issues of whether the decision was without authority or was arbitrary. During the lower court proceeding, the parties agreed to explore and the judge allowed the instructors to review the mental processes of the decision makers. Stating that this was not to be allowed, unless the parties stipulate (agree), the court then reviewed the due process to which *tenured* faculty are entitled. To summarize, it is:

1. Notice
2. A hearing, full and complete, including the ability to cross-examine and present rebuttal evidence—a fair method of decision making
3. An appeal mechanism—a forum where written and oral argument can again be offered

However, as noted before in the AAUP definition of tenure, tenured faculty may be terminated for cause and for reasons of financial exigency. The latter reason for termination will be discussed in the salary and benefits section. Courts have generally required only that the procedures used to terminate the individual be fair, including an impartial hearing where the faculty member is permitted to question witnesses.[35]

Tenure grants a property right in a job. Termination can only be for cause. Tenure means that a faculty member is legitimately entitled to remain in that position absent unusual circumstances, and, furthermore, that the faculty member's employment may not be terminated without notice and a hearing. Cause is defined as incompetence, neglect of duty, or moral turpitude, although specific institutional policy statements may define cause more specifically. Courts have indicated that "the administration of the internal affairs of a college and especially the determination of professional competency is a matter of peculiarity within the discretion of a college administrator."[36]

Tenure is an unintegrated, unilateral, lifetime employment contract.[37] Unintegrated means that not everything is spelled out in the contract document, but other documents are also part of the contract, such as faculty handbooks. Unilateral refers to the fact that in granting tenure the university offers lifetime employment without defining specific tasks to be performed by faculty members, leaving them great freedom in fulfilling their responsibilities for teaching and research.

When a school denies tenure or promotion, courts will examine the fairness of procedures and whether similarly situated candidates for promotion or tenure were treated equitably.

SALARY AND BENEFIT DISPUTES

Many times faculty must present to a court, following administrative review within the school, arguments that certain rights to benefits have been denied, sometimes asking the court to decide the merits of salary disputes. For example, the issue in an Indiana case was the nursing faculty's eligibility for retirement benefits.[38] The state statute provided that teachers employed less than 600 hours per year were not eligible for these benefits. The court determined that the normal hours required to qualify for benefits include those specified in the employment contract and may also include other conduct which may be required in performance of the job.

The nursing instructor's employment contract stated 12 hours (4 hours teaching and 8 hours laboratory/clinical instruction). In addition, however, the evidence indicated that the nursing instructor was required to attend staff meeting (3 hours); do student counseling (2 hours) and travel (2 hours). These figures, the court noted, did not include the amount of time spent in preparing for class and processing the paperwork for the laboratory/clinical portion of the class. The court decided that even if the nursing instructor was not given credit for travel time, she still worked 17 hours per week, for a total of 612 hours per year. She, therefore, was entitled to the retirement benefit.

In another case a nursing faculty member at a community college was injured while supervising students in a clinical experience, when she bent down and hit her left eye on the edge of a table.[39] She sustained a 100% vision loss to the left eye. The board of higher education tried to say that she was not eligible for worker's compensation since she was a teacher and not engaged in hazardous employment as enumerated in the compensation law. The worker's compensation board found that the nursing instructor was an employee within the meaning of the worker's compensation law, noting that a nurse employed in a hospital was included in the hazardous employment section definition.

The court reviewed the facts that the nursing instructor spent approximately 15 hours per week teaching nursing students, two thirds of which was spent in a hospital engaged in nursing activities. The evidence revealed that the nursing instructor spent the bulk of the teaching demonstrating or actually doing nursing work in a hospital. The court held that substantial evidence existed to determine that the decision of the worker's compensation board that the nursing instructor was covered by the law should not be disturbed.

Salary—how it is established, how raises are given, and criteria used to make salary offers and decisions—is also a possible area of dispute between faculty and schools. In a case involving the calculation of salary, a court stated that unless the faculty member knew of a mistake, the school of nursing would be obligated to pay what it had offered to the faculty member in an appointment letter.[40]

Federal laws applicable to situations of alleged discrimination in salary and benefits, including discrimination during promotion and tenure decisions in higher education include:

1. Title VII of the Civil Rights Act[41] and the Equal Pay Act of 1963[42] as amended by the Education Amendments of 1972[43] which made applicable to higher education both of these civil rights laws
2. Title IX of the Education Amendments of 1972 which states that no person in the United States shall, on the basis of sex, be excluded from participation in, be denied the benefits of, or be subjected to discrimination under any educational program or activitiy receiving federal financial assistance[44]
3. The Age Discrimination in Employment Act[45]

Institutions of higher education facing reduced budgets may rely on "financial exigencies" as a reason to reduce staff. Courts have certified that financial exigencies is a valid rationale for removing not only untenured but also tenured faculty. The institution, however, may be challenged and has the burden of proving that the financial exigency exists and that the school acted reasonably. When tenured faculty are to be layed off due to financial exigencies their due process rights must include:

1. Reasonably adequate written statement of the basis for the initial decision to lay off
2. Reasonably adequate description of the manner in which the initial decision was reached
3. Reasonably adequate disclosure to the faculty of information and data upon which decision makers had relied
4. Providing each faculty the opportunity to respond[46]

For all concerned, generally, courts have required only that colleges show that their declaration of financial exigency was made in good faith.[47]

Despite the courts' willingness to review peer evaluations in cases where faculty have alleged discrimination by a college, courts have rarely ruled against faculty peer determinations; when they have done so, the plaintiffs have built strong cases of the evaluators' misconduct.[48]

In several situations nursing faculty have sued their universities alleging violations of the Equal Pay Act, Section 1983 of the Civil Rights Act, and sex-based wage discrimination within Title VII of the Civil Rights Act of 1964.[49] In none of these cases have their allegations successfully been proved. Chapter 30 on employment claims discusses these issues further.

Financing nursing education

Private and public funding supports nursing education. Created by law, public federal funding of nursing education is governed under Title VII and VIII of the Public Health Service Act.[50] Congress recently authorized \$54.1 million for fiscal year (FY) 1986; \$55.35 million for FY 1987; and \$56.6 million for FY 1988. In addition the Health Professions Training Assistance Act of 1985 includes several amendments to promote geriatric and gerontological training under the Title VIII nurse education programs.[51]

Funding is provided for:

1. Special projects (e.g. geriatric training)
2. Advanced nursing education (master's and doctoral programs only, training of nurse researchers, priority to geriatric and gerontological nursing)
3. Nurse practitioner programs
4. Professional nurse traineeships (for nurse midwifery students, students in master's and doctoral programs, and includes grants for postbaccalaureate fellowships for faculty in schools of nursing)
5. Nurse anesthetist traineeships
6. Nursing student loans (Borrowers after June 30, 1986 must be "of exceptional financial need"; the school's delinquency rate is still calculated, and, further, the law authorizes the Secretary of Health and Human Services to obtain from tax records and release to schools the addresses of

individuals who have defaulted on loans under the nursing student loan.)[52]

The Division of Nursing of the Bureau of Health Professions in the Department of Health and Human Services currently administers the federal nursing education programs. As discussed in the following chapter, there is a newly created Center for Nursing Research in the National Institutes of Health, which may be given the authority over the financing of nursing research. It is not yet clear whether the nursing education funding will also be under the authority of the new center.

The Division of Nursing has two branches which focus upon nursing education, the advanced nurse training resources branch and the nursing education branch.[53] The purposes of these legally created branches are to:

1. Assess national resources for graduate nurse training for adequacy and for changing needs of the population
2. Administer grant support for programs preparing nurses in specialties and as nurse practitioners
3. Administer student support for nurses pursuing programs of advanced nurse training or research
4. Support and conduct programs related to development, adequacy, and use of educational resources to improve nurse education and training
5. Conduct a national special project grants program that enables nursing schools and other entities to foster new and improved nursing education and practice.[54]

Standards of care

No matter the setting or type of nursing program, faculty and schools of nursing share similar legal issues and must meet established standards for nursing education. Program administrators, deans, and faculty have to deal with similar issues of liability and responsibility. Important sources which describe the standards of care and practice of nursing faculty and schools should be part and parcel of faculty and school materials. Two such sources are the AMERICAN NURSES' ASSOCIATION STANDARDS OF PROFESSIONAL NURSING EDUCATION[55] and the National League for Nursing accreditation criteria for nursing programs.[56] The ANA standards are listed opposite (see box).

The accreditation process is a voluntary, institutional evaluation by an objective organization which establishes standards to be met. Faculty and administrators are encouraged to participate in the accreditation process not only to assure that their own courses and performance meet standards but also, through participating in the accrediting organization, to be developers of the standards and evaluators of other schools' and faculties' performance.

Routinely, the National League for Nursing (NLN) conducts site visits to schools of nursing across the country. The accreditation process is an important measure of self-evaluation and of self-regulation. Decisions are made to grant or deny accreditation status or to provisionally approve a school of nursing. Schools may legally challenge an NLN decision after exhausting the internal appeal process provided within the accreditaion procedures. NLN accreditation status is a valuable credential to a school, potentially having an impact on, for example, financial status or access of graduates to advanced education and, hence, the ability to attract a student body.

Legally mandated accreditation is required by state departments of education[57] and the state board of nursing, as well as other state governmental agencies. They have the right to approve or disapprove nursing education programs. Their criteria for approval are also examples of standards which define nursing education, liabilities, and responsibilities.

Other important standard-setting documents are authored by the American Association of University Professors.[58] The activities of the American Association of Colleges of Nursing is also an important resource for monitoring standards of care in nursing education.[59] Lastly, the literature provides an important resource for following the development and definition of standards which apply to nursing schools and faculty.[60]

Recommendations and trends

Law is only one source of accountability for faculty in meeting their responsibilities for preparing students and developing and contributing to the nursing profession and society. Careful and frequent consideration by the faculty and school administration should be given to:

1. Recognizing student and faculty rights, especially activities which enhance and provide for due process
2. Having fair and adequate admission policies and appointment, promotion, and tenure practices
3. Providing safe and reasonable clinical instruction, minimizing hazards to patients which may be presented by student practice
4. Having clear understanding with clinical agencies about the role and function of nursing education in their facility
5. Establishing progressions and grade appeal pro-

STANDARDS FOR PROFESSIONAL NURSING EDUCATION

Standard I

The educational unit in nursing is located in an institution of higher education that grants degrees in several disciplines.

Standard II

The philosophy of the educational unit in nursing reflects the mission of the parent institution and is expressed throughout the curriculum.

Standard III

The education unit in nursing is consistent with the administrative structure of the parent institution and clearly delineated organizational relationships, responsibilities, and communication pathways.

Standard IV

The human, financial, and material resources of the educational unit in nursing are sufficient in quality and quantity to facilitate the educational process.

Standard V

The policies of the educational unit in nursing governing the recruitment, selection, and progression of students reflect the philosophy and standards of the institution.

Standard VI

The environment of the educational unit in nursing fosters scholarly productivity, professional involvement, and leadership development of faculty and students.

Standard VII

The objectives and curriculum designs of professional nursing education programs reflect the philosophy of the educational unit in nursing and provide for the development of attitudes and competencies specific to the roles for which students are being prepared.

Standard VIII

The educational unit in nursing engages in systematic internal and external program evaluation.

Standard IX

Graduates of professional education programs in nursing assume professional responsibilities commensurate with their level of educational preparation.

Adapted from AMERICAN NURSES' ASSOCIATION, STANDARDS FOR PROFESSIONAL NURSING EDUCATION (1984). See also, AMERICAN NURSES' ASSOCIATION, STANDARDS FOR CONTINUING EDUCATION IN NURSING (1984).

cesses which are designed to enhance justice and fair decisions

6. Developing, consistently, within the school of nursing means of documenting student achievement and progress
7. Devoting time to review of policies (written or otherwise) giving recognition to this project as an important ongoing part of the faculty, student, and school relationship

Significant aspects of administering fair student discipline should include:

1. Specifying rules and regulations, avoiding vague terms
2. Specifying composition of hearing boards
3. Specifying how off-campus incidents will be dealt with on-campus
4. Providing for interim or emergency suspension
5. In dealing with mandatory psychiatric withdrawal, having a specifically drafted disciplinary code which indicates what observable behaviors constitute prohibited behavior.[61]

In addition colleges should reach employment decisions through clear data and careful documentation. While peer review criteria may vary among disciplines, the procedures for review must be consistent and applied evenly across disciplines. Academic employment decisions are more defensible if faculty are included. The result will be better-made decisions, enhanced faculty-school relations, and less susceptibility to reversal by the courts.

Faculty should be fully informed from the time of hiring about what criteria will be used in tenure decisions and how the criteria will be weighted. Annual evaluations are essential.[62] Salary determinations and increases should be based upon documentation. School administrators should review salaries using regression analysis; develop a set of written guidelines for setting initial salaries for new faculty; and decide regular salary increases, upgrading salaries to keep pace with new entry salary levels and determining merit increases (collective bargaining or individual contracts may already fix the salary scale). Criteria for deciding salaries should be made clear to the faculty, including what documentation will be needed and how it will be collected.

The process for selection of faculty should be free of discrimination. Schools should analyze their fringe benefits policies to ascertain whether differences exist based strictly upon actuarial considerations and not on the basis of gender or age.

Endnotes

1. *See e.g.,* ME.REV.ANN. tit. 2, 2101, 2251 (Supp. 1986); *Maine Law is first to call for two education levels,* THE AMER. NURSE, p. 1, 18 at col. 3 (May 1986); *North Dakota Hospitals file suit to stop implementation of BSN,* THE AMER. NURSE, p. 3, 6 at col. 3 (May 1986); *Court Upholds North Dakota Education Rules,* THE AMER. NURSE, p. 1 at col. 2 (February 1987).
2. Citations to all state nursing practice acts are in Appendix IV.
3. *Whittington v. Sowela Technical Institute,* 438 So.2d 236 (La. App. 1983), *but, see, Central Security Mutual Ins. Co. v. Depinto,* 681 P.2d 15 (Kan. 1984) which held that the use of college van by nursing student to drive herself and others to clinical programs at hospitals and towns around college was not a "regular use" for purposes of exclusionary provision of auto liability policy.
4. *Whittington v. Sowela Technical Institute,* 438 So.2d.
5. *Station v. Travelers, Ins. Co.,* 292 So.2d 289 (La. App. 1974).
6. *Miller v. Macalaster College,* 115 N.W.2d 666 (Minn. 1962).
7. *Central Anesthesia Associates v. Worthy,* 325 S.E.2d 819 (Ga. App. 1984), *affd.* 333 S.E.2d 829 (Ga. 1985).
8. *Central Anesthesia Associates v. Worthy* 325 S.E.2d. 819, 824 (Ga. App. 1984).
9. *Id.*
10. *Matje v. Leis,* 571 F. Supp. 918 (S.D. Ohio 1983).
11. Family Educational and Privacy Act of 1974, 20 U.S.C. §1232g (1982).
12. *See, e.g.,* KY. REV. STAT. ANN. §164.283 (Baldwin 1985).
13. Kelly, *Hospital-college education contracts ensure mutual protection* HOSPITALS 95 (January 16, 1981).
14. MD. ADMIN. CODE tit. 10, §27.03.06 (1981) (Department of Health and Mental Hygiene, Board of Examiners of Nurses, Minimum Requirements for Approved Nursing Education Programs Leading to Eligibility for Registered Nurse Licensure, Resources, Facilities and Services)
15. 17 U.S.C. §101 (1982 & Supp. I 1983) (original works, literary, musical, dramatic, pantomines, pictorial, graphic, sculptural, motion pictures, audio, visual, sound recordings); *See, also,* W. PATTON, AN AUTHOR'S GUIDE TO COPYRIGHT LAW (1980).
16. 17 U.S.C. §102(a) (1982).
17. 15 U.S.C. §1051-1127 (1982).
18. 17 U.S.C. §107 (1982).
19. *Marcus v. Rowley,* 695 F.2d 1171 (9th Cir. 1983).
20. *See, e.g.,* Agreement on Guidelines for Classroom Copying in Not-for-Profit Educational Institutions with Respect to Books and Periodicals, found in, Mawdsley and Permuth, *Multiple Photocopying in Educational Institutions* 10 NOLPE SCHOOL LAW J., 18, 27-29 (1981); *See also* COPYRIGHT OFFICE, LIBRARY OF CONGRESS, COPYRIGHT AND THE LIBRARIAN 3 (1977).
21. 17 U.S.C. §118(d)(3) (1982).
22. 17 U.S.C. §101, 117 (1982).
23. ROBERT'S RULES OF ORDER (rev. ed. 1970).
24. *1940 Statement of Principles on Academic Freedom and Tenure,* 44 AM. ASS'N. OF UNIVERSITY PROFESSORS BULL. 290, 291, 292 (1958) and *1970 Interpretive Comments,* A.A.U.P. POLICY DOCUMENTS AND REPORTS 2 (1973). *See also* W. METZGER, THE CONSTITUTIONAL STATUS OF ACADEMIC TENURE (1977).
25. U.S. CONST. amend. I.
26. Gregory, *Secrecy in University and College Tenure Deliberations: Placing Appropriate Limits on Academic Freedom* 16 U.C.D. LAW REV. 1023 (Summer 1983).
27. DeBardeleben, *The University's External Constituency,* DIMENSIONS OF ACADEMIC FREEDOM (Metzger, ed. 1969).
28. *Board of Regents v. Roth,* 408 U.S. 564 (1972).
29. *See, e.g. Endress v. Brookdale Community College,* 364 A.2d 1080 (N.J. Super. 1976).
30. *Mendez v. Trustees of Boston University,* 285 N.E.2d 446 (Mass. 1972).
31. *Billmyre v. Sacred Heart Hospital of the Sisters of Charity, Inc.,* 273 Md. 638 (1975).
32. *Id.* at 638.
33. *Brown v. Board of Education, City School District of the City of New Rochelle,* 76 Misc. Rptr. 923 (N.Y. 1974).
34. *Kelly v. Kansas City, Kansas Community College,* 648 P.2d 225 (Kan. 1982).
35. *Poterma v. Ping,* 462 F.Supp. 328 (S.D. Ohio 1978).
36. *Chung v. Park,* 514 F.2d 382 (3rd Cir. 1975), *cert. denied,* 423 U.S. 948.
37. R. HENDRICKSON & B. LEE, ACADEMIC EMPLOYMENT AND RETRENCHMENT: JUDICIAL REVIEW AND ADMINISTRATIVE ACTION 82 (1983).
38. *Board of Trustees of Public Employees Retirement Fund of the State of Indiana v. Baughman,* 450 N.E.2d 95 (Ind. App. 3 1983).
39. *In re Kessler v. Board of Higher Education of the City of New York, Workers' Compensation Board,* 86 A.D.2d 908 (N.Y. 1982).
40. *Commonwealth of Pennsylvania, Department of Education, Millersville State College v. Miller,* 466 A.2d 791 (Pa. Cmwlth. 1983).
41. 42 U.S.C. §2000c (1982).
42. 29 U.S.C. §206 (1982).
43. 20 U.S.C. 1001 (1982) (Higher Education Resources and Student Assistance).
44. 20 U.S.C. §1681(a) (1982); *See, also,* 34 C.F.R. §106 (1984), entitled "Nondiscrimination on the basis of sex in activities receiving or benefiting from federal financial assistance."
45. 29 U.S.C. §621-634 (1982).
46. *Johnson v. Board of Regents of the University of Wisconsin System,* 377 F.Supp. 227 (W.D. Wisc. 1974), *aff'd.,* 510 F.2d 975 (7th Cir. 1975).
47. *AAUP v. Bloomfield College,* 346 A.2d 615 (N.J. 1975).
48. R. HENDRICKSON AND B. LEE, ACADEMIC EMPLOYMENT AND RETRENCHMENT: JUDICIAL REVIEW AND ADMINISTRATIVE ACTION (1983).
49. *Spaulding v. University of Washington,* 740 F.2d 686 (9th Cir. 1984), *cert. denied,* 105 S.Ct. 511 (1984); *Equal Employment*

Opportunity Commission v. University of Pittsburgh, 643 F.2d 983 (3rd Cir. 1981), *cert. denied,* 454 U.S. 880; *Coser v. Moore,* 587 F.Supp. 572 (E.D.N.Y. 1983) (State University of New York, Stonybrook), *aff'd.,* 793 F.2d 746 (2nd Cir. 1984).

50. Nurse Education Amendments of 1985 (P.L. 99-92, August 16, 1985); 42 U.S.C. §296, 296d, 296e, 296k to 296m, 297 to 297c, 297e, 297j (1982).
51. P.L. 99-129, October 22, 1985.
52. BUREAU OF HEALTH PROFESSIONS, U.S. DEPT. OF HEALTH AND HUMAN SERVICES, HIGHLIGHTS OF 1985 NURSE EDUCATION AMENDMENTS (November 1, 1985).
53. DIVISION OF NURSING, BUREAU OF HEALTH PROFESSIONS, HEALTH RESOURCES AND SERVICES ADMINISTRATION, PUBLIC HEALTH SERVICE, U.S. DEPT. OF HEALTH AND HUMAN SERVICES, DIVISION OF NURSING (1985).
54. *Id.*
55. AMERICAN NURSES' ASSOCIATION, STANDARDS OF PROFESSIONAL NURSING EDUCATION (1984); *See, also,* AMERICAN NURSES' ASSOCIATION, STANDARDS FOR CONTINUING EDUCATION IN NURSING (1984) and the AMERICAN NURSES' ASSOCIATION, STANDARDS FOR ASSOCIATE DEGREE EDUCATION (forthcoming from ANA).
56. NATIONAL LEAGUE FOR NURSING, POLICIES AND PROCEDURES OF ACCREDITATION FOR PROGRAMS IN NURSING EDUCATION (4th ed. 1982); NLN, CRITERIA FOR THE EVALUATION OF BACCALAUREATE AND HIGHER DEGREE PROGRAMS IN NURSING (5th ed. 1983); NLN, CRITERIA FOR THE EVALUATION OF DIPLOMA PROGRAMS IN NURSING (6th ed. 1982); NLN, CRITERIA FOR EVALUATION OF ASSOCIATE DEGREE PROGRAMS IN NURSING (6th ed., rev. 1982); NLN, CRITERIA FOR THE EVALUATION OF EDUCATION PROGRAMS IN PRACTICAL NURSING (4th ed. 1981). *See, also,* NLN, COMPETENCIES OF GRADUATES OF EDUCATIONAL PROGRAMS IN PRACTICAL NURSING (1977); NLN, COMPETENCIES OF GRADUATES OF NURSING PROGRAMS (1982); NLN, COMPETENCIES OF THE ASSOCIATE DEGREE NURSE ON ENTRY INTO PRACTICE (1978); NLN, ROLE AND COMPETENCIES OF GRADUATES OF DIPLOMA PROGRAMS IN NURSING (1978).
57. In some states public colleges and universities are governed by a board of trustees and the legislature controls the state system of higher education. *See, e.g.,* CONN. GEN. STAT. ANN. §10a-1 and 10a-20 (West Supp. 1985); MD. EDUC. CODE ANN. §12, 13, 16 (1985).
58. *See, e.g.,* AMERICAN ASSOCIATION OF UNIVERSITY PROFESSORS, STATEMENT ON PROCEDURAL STANDARDS IN THE RENEWAL OR NONRENEWAL OF FACULTY APPOINTMENTS (1971); and POLICY DOCUMENTS AND REPORTS (1969) which contains standards in faculty dismissal proceedings, for notice of nonreappointment, statement on professional ethics, on recruitment and resignation of faculty members, role of faculty in acrediting colleges and universities, principles of academic retirement and insurance plans, leaves of absences.
59. AMERICAN ASSOCIATION OF COLLEGES OF NURSING, ESSENTIALS OF COLLEGE AND UNIVERSITY EDUCATION FOR PROFESSIONAL NURSING: FINAL REPORT (1986).
60. *See, e.g.,* JOURNAL OF PROFESSIONAL NURSING and AACN NEWSLETTER, (published by the American Association of Colleges of Nursing, One Dupont Circle, Suite 530, Washington, D.C. 20036); CHRONICLE OF HIGHER EDUCATION (weekly publication of The Chronicle of Higher Education, Inc., 1333 New Hampshire Ave. N.W., Washington, D.C.); JOURNAL OF LAW AND EDUCATION (a quarterly publication by the Jefferson Law Book Company, 646 Main Street, Cincinnati, OH 45201); JOURNAL OF COLLEGE AND UNIVERSITY LAW (published by the National Association of College and University Attorneys, Suite 510, One Dupont Circle, Washington, D.C. 20036); THE YEARBOOK OF HIGHER EDUCATION LAW (an annual publication of the National Organization on Legal Problems of Education, 5401 S.W. 7th Avenue, Topeka, KS 66606); NURSING OUTLOOK (published by the American Journal of Nursing Co.); NURSING AND HEALTHCARE (publication of the National League for Nursing); JOURNAL OF NURSING EDUCATION; THE COLLEGE STUDENT AND THE COURTS (a volume, updated quarterly, containing cases and commentary about students); HIGHER EDUCATION AND NATIONAL AFFAIRS (a weekly publication of the American Council on Education, focusing primarily on federal law and regulation impacting education); DEAN'S NOTES (published by Janetti Publications for the National Student Nurse's Association for all deans of schools of nursing).
61. Ardaiolo, *What Process Is Due?* STUDENT AFFAIRS AND THE LAW 22, 23, 24 (M. Barr, ed. 1983).
62. *See, e.g.,* Cudney, *Reaping the Professional Rewards of Faculty Evaluation* 16 NURS. & HEALTHCARE 451 (October 1985).

Additional Readings

K. ALEXANDER AND E. SOLOMON, COLLEGE AND UNIVERSITY LAW (1972).

T. BLACKWELL, COLLEGE LAW MANUAL (current ed.).

COMMITTEE ON NURSING AND NURSING EDUCATION, INSTITUTE OF MEDICINE, NURSING AND NURSING EDUCATION: PUBLIC POLICIES AND PRIVATE ACTIONS (1983).

H. EDWARDS & V. NORDIN, HIGHER EDUCATION AND THE LAW (1979).

P. HOLLANDER, A LEGAL HANDBOOK FOR EDUCATORS (1978).

W. KAPLIN, THE LAW OF HIGHER EDUCATION (1980).

W. KAPLIN, THE LAW OF HIGHER EDUCATION: LEGAL IMPLICATIONS OF ADMINISTRATIVE DECISION MAKING (1978).

STUDENT AFFAIRS AND THE LAW (M. Barr, ed. 1983).

Chapter 21

Nursing research

Cynthia E. Northrop

Research always begins with a problem, and research in nursing practice begins with problems in nursing practice.[1] Historically, nursing research has its roots in the very beginnings of the nursing profession. Florence Nightingale examined issues of nursing care through a systematic approach. Nursing research is pursued to advance the level of knowledge and the application of that knowledge to nursing practice in order to improve patient care. It is an activity that seeks to discover or confirm the facts that relate to a specific problem or problems in the field of nursing or patient care.[2]

Early nursing research focused on curriculum studies or studies of nurses. However, practice-focused research is receiving increased attention. As evidenced in nursing research journals, NURSING RESEARCH, RESEARCH IN NURSING AND HEALTH, and the WESTERN JOURNAL OF NURSING RESEARCH, topics of nursing research can be quite diverse and enriching.[3] Nursing research, no matter the topic, can present unique legal issues. Ethical dimensions of nursing research are also important to consider.

Nurses participate in research in a variety of ways. Not only are more nurses the researcher or primary investigator of a study, but nurses may be employed in research institutions to provide care and carry out other's scientific protocols. Nurses may be data collectors on studies, their patients may be subjects in other studies, and they may be subjects of studies as well. Particularly of concern to nurses may be the questions that arise when they are called upon to administer experimental drugs and treatments within or as part of others' research protocols.

The legal issues surrounding research and human experimentation have been organized in this chapter to include the rights of nurse researchers, the rights of human subjects, and governmental review processes over research activities. Following a brief overview of the historical development of these issues and standards of care, the role of the nurse researcher will be highlighted. Legal issues of nurse researchers and nurses working with research projects involving special groups, including pregnant women, children, and prisoners, will be described. Chapter 6 contains important supporting material to the understanding of this chapter.

Historical background: standards of care

Since World War II much has been written about human experimentation, especially covering the topic of rights of the human subjects, abuses, and infringements on human rights. The first written principles dealing with human experimentation came from the famous Nuremberg trials. The Nuremberg Code comes from the case, *United States v. Karl Brandt,* which involved Nazi war criminals (including scientists and physicians) who committed gruesome atrocities in the name of science on human beings without the slightest hesitation or thought to their individual rights.[4] The Declaration of Helsinki, which set forth principles of ethical conduct of research, was authored by the World Medical Association, also following World War II.[5] American physicians endorsed these principles in their American Medical Association's STATEMENT OF ETHICAL CONDUCT OF RESEARCH.[6]

It was not until 1968 that the American Nurses' Association (ANA) approved guidelines on ethical values for the nurse in research.[7] Standards of nursing research are provided not only in this early document but later publications dealing with nursing and research, including ANA's CODE FOR NURSES WITH INTERPRETIVE STATEMENT and ANA's HUMAN RIGHTS GUIDELINES FOR NURSES IN CLINICAL AND OTHER RESEARCH.[8]

ANA's CODE, Item 7, specifically addresses nursing and research: "The nurse participates in activities that contribute to the ongoing development of the profession's body of knowledge."[9] ANA revised the interpretive statements of the CODE in 1985. General guidelines for participating in research are offered in the interpretive statements of this code item. The current CODE interpretive statement says that the nurse has an obligation to:

1. Ascertain that the study protocol is approved by the appropriate bodies, such as institutional review boards.
2. Obtain information about the intent and the nature of the research.[10]

The earlier CODE interpretive statement also listed that a nurse was obligated to:

1. Determine whether the research is consistent with professional goals.
2. Be fully informed about both nurse and client rights and responsibilities.
3. Determine whether the research is conducted by only scientifically qualified persons or under such supervision.
4. Maintain vigilance in protecting the life, health, and privacy of human subjects from unanticipated as well as anticipated risks.
5. Understand in advance how the research can be expected to affect treatment and their own moral and legal responsibilities to clients.[11]

The current CODE also states that it is the duty of the nurse functioning in any research role to maintain vigilance in protecting the life, health, and privacy of human subjects from both anticipated and unanticipated risks and in assuring informed consent.[12] The interpretive statement further indicates that if the subjects are unable to protect themselves because of incapacity or because they are in a dependent relationship to the research investigator, the nurse must especially safeguard their integrity, privacy, and other rights.[13] If the continuation of the research or investigation might be harmful to the subject, it should be discontinued.[14]

The current CODE also supports the earlier statements by noting that research should be conducted and directed by qualified persons; the nurse who participates in research in any capacity should be fully informed about both the nurse's and the client's rights and obligations.[15]

In addition, however, the earlier CODE states that a nurse has the right not to participate or to withdraw from participating in any research endeavor (as a subject or in any relationship to research of others).[16] The nurse who is a subject in a research study has the same rights as any other subject; he or she may refuse to participate and withdraw at any time. The nurse who is a participant in another way in research of others should make the objection known in advance and in time for other appropriate arrangements to be made for the client's nursing care. The nurse withdraws only when assured that alternative sources of nursing care are available to the client.[17]

ANA's GUIDELINES address ethical principles, mechanisms for protection of rights, and the personal responsibility of the nurse involved in the research process.[18] The ANA Cabinet on Nursing Research revised the GUIDELINES in 1985. This current version focuses on nursing activities and ethical issues, protection of human rights, subjects, and society's obligation and the public good.[19] Three mechanisms for protection of human subjects in research are stressed in the GUIDELINES: assurance of informed consent, assurance that institutions and agencies develop procedures to safeguard human rights, and assurance that the profession publicly support the inclusion of nurses in research activities, including as regular members of institutional review boards.[20]

In the 1960s three prominent abuses led to congressional hearings to explore research and human experimentation. Congress was especially interested in that, increasingly, most research was federally funded. Revealed during the hearings were situations that called for legislation and regulation. Among those situations were the following:

1. One involving a physician researcher who had injected live cancer cells into elderly hospital patients without consent[21]
2. One involving rural black men who were subjects of a longitudinal study of syphilis when a cure was discovered and researchers made a decision not to treat the men and complete the study[22]
3. One in which Mexican-American women were given placebo birth control pills to study the psy-

chological side effects of oral contraception and the subjects were not informed of the placebos[23]

These abuses involved vulnerable groups and questionable research methodology, for example, lack of consent, use of deception, placebos, or strict adherence to the research protocol at the risk of death or injury to the subjects. In response, the U.S. Congress passed the National Research Act of 1974, which established laws on the protection of human subjects, and a National Commission for the Protection of Human Subjects of Biomedical and Behavioral Research.[24] This law and the regulations that were developed as an outgrowth of the commission's authority are discussed in the section entitled "Protection of Human Subjects."

Rights and duties of nurse researchers

A right to research has been identified within the first amendment to the U.S. Constitution: "Congress shall make no law . . . abridging the freedom of speech or of the press."[25] The Fourteenth Amendment makes applicable to states the proscription against such laws.[26] At least one legal scholar has analyzed the definition of research as a concept with a set of specific behaviors that are *expressions* within the meaning of the First Amendment.[27] Davidson reviewed judicial opinions that described the freedom of speech as one that involves being able to converse freely, communicate, access, acquire, and convey information. These behaviors are essentially research. When scientists communicate findings of studies to the public through publication or lecture, they are engaged in protected expression. Therefore, Davidson argues that the right to communicate would be destroyed if the ability to do research is significantly impaired.

The nurse as a scientist engaged in development and testing of hypotheses regarding the nursing profession and areas of practice has a right to conduct such research. Although no case law exists involving a nurse researcher, one case was found where expert witness testimony of a nurse could appropriately be based upon nursing research.[28]

As with other individual rights, none is absolute. The right to free speech, encompassing the right to do research, can be subject to reasonable regulation by the government. As discussed and defined in Chapter 1, this is a key principle of constitutional law. Several considerations go into developing the criteria for determining reasonable regulation by the government of an individual's right to research. The government must demonstrate a compelling state interest for prohibiting or restricting research.

Davidson reviewed arguments for minimal or less regulation and arguments for more or increased regulation. These are presented in the above box. Recognizing that freedom of speech and thought does not encompass the freedom to cause injury to others, governmental regulation is often based upon the desirability to protect others from intrusions. As can be seen from the box, this is just one basis upon which the government may regulate research.

For those nurse researchers who are also faculty in universities and colleges, their right to research is also based upon the principles of academic freedom. As defined in the previous chapter, these principles of freedom of thought in the faculty role support the ability of a nurse to define research problems and develop methodologies to investigate those problems.

Duties of nurse researchers include not only meeting the standards of nursing research discussed in the above

THE RIGHT TO CONDUCT NURSING RESEARCH: EXTENT OF GOVERNMENTAL REGULATION

Arguments for Less Regulation

1. Nursing research is a protected expression under the First Amendment.
2. Nursing research affords the opportunity for individuals to realize self-fulfillment, to contribute knowledge, and to fulfill a role as citizen who participates in policy formulation.
3. Nursing research exists for the betterment of society and is essential for progress. Free inquiry ensures that best possible information will be available for the well-being of society. Research facilitates social reform, alleviation of pain, and eradication of disease and directs the development of mankind.
4. In academic setings, freedom judicially recognizes protection of the faculty research and education function.

Arguments for Increased Regulation

1. Others' rights and interests are affected to a greater degree.
2. The research methodology becomes more invasive and intrusive.
3. The proposed activity deviates further from usual and acceptable nursing practice.
4. The subject is exposed to more potential danger as the risk of death becomes greater.

Adapted from Davidson, *First Amendment Protection for Biomedical Research*, 19 ARIZONA LAW REVIEW 893 (1977).

section, but generally include the duty of full disclosure, informed consent, documentation of informed consent, guarantee of privacy, and confidentiality, including anonymity where indicated. Abiding by agency policies and state and federal laws and regulations is an important duty of the nurse researcher. The nurse researcher must also prepare and follow an accurate and complete proposal, including significance of the research, study design, subject selection, exclusion criteria, review of identified risks, and handling of emergencies and adverse reactions.

Failure to meet the obligations of nursing research may lead to liabilities discussed in the next section. However, the nurse's right to reseach may also be infringed upon, for example, by others restricting the access to research subjects. Should obtaining subjects and funding become problems, possible arguments of discrimination and violation of constitutional rights may be available to nurse researchers to enforce their right to do research.

Liabilities of nurse researchers

Given the nurse's right to do research, the law requires that this right be carried out in a reasonable manner. Not only are nurse researchers responsible for reasonable and safe conduct of research under the circumstances, the malpractice or negligence tort liability standard, but they are also responsible for adhering to state and federal laws regarding the research process and avoiding the tort of battery. Generally, intentional torts, including battery, are discussed in Chapter 5. As defined in this section, research usually involves doing an activity that is not accepted reasonable practice or care. Therefore, nurse researchers must give careful attention to their activities and gauge the extent of the research activity's deviation from standard, acceptable nursing practice.

Nurses who are employed to do others' research should know fully the extent of their involvement, and whether data collection is part of the expected function and a condition for the position, prior to accepting the job. For example, if giving out the ordinary doses of experimental drugs is part of the job expectation, this should be known prior to accepting the position. Given the research and experimental nature of the tasks, the legal parameters of the position should be explored and an understanding reached during the job interview.

There have been no cases involving allegations of malpractice in nursing research or malpractice by a nurse who was implementing another's research protocol. However, physician researchers and universities have been involved in cases where they were shown to have committed battery and failed to adequately inform research subjects. One such case involved a double-blind study of women and diethylstilbestrol (DES). The women were never informed about the DES.[29]

Receiving prior peer approval for all nursing research would be deemed an important step in assuring that the nurse researcher is acting in a reasonable manner. Even where the nurse researcher's activity may not require review under the federal law, which is discussed below, a peer review process is highly recommended for the previous reason.

In addition, participating in the institutional review board process is also another professional assurance of peer acceptability for the nursing research. These and other federal laws outlining the requirements for institutional review boards and informed consent for human subjects are discussed later in this chapter.

Nurse researchers may also be involved with other torts, such as battery, invasion of privacy, and breach of confidentiality. These torts were defined and discussed earlier in Chapter 5. Battery was the primary tort used as a basis for unconsenting touching. Therefore, if the nurse researcher touches subjects without their consent, he or she has committed battery. Negligence is the basis for the action involving allegations of lack of informed consent. Federal regulation requirements for informed consent are presented below. These are particularly helpful in answering the question of how much information makes one informed. Nurse researchers must meet these and may provide information in addition to these legal requirements.

Nurse researchers also have responsibilities regarding the funding and proper administration of their grants and contracts. Depending on the situation, the nurse researcher may be involved in allegations of breach of contract, fraud, embezzlement, or mishandling and misuse of funds. If proved, these types of wrongs often carry severe monetary damages and criminal penalties. Other aspects of financing nursing research are discussed later.

Since most research is sponsored by an institution, that entity would also be responsible for the reasonable and safe conduct of nursing research. If the nurse researcher is an employee of an institution, that institution, as the *respondeat superior* of the nurse researcher, would be vicariously liable for the negligence of the nurse researcher. If the nurse researcher is an independent contractor with the institution solely for the purpose of conducting the research, the institution still would have corporate liability for results of misconduct or negligence by the independent contractor.

Any other personnel, such as research assistants or data collectors, employed to carry out the study would also have as their *respondeat superior* the institution sponsoring the research. Nurse researchers would be responsible for proper hiring and supervision of any assistants that are part of the delivery of the research. Chapter 22 discusses administrative nursing responsibilities and their legal implications.

An additional consideration for nurse researchers is to review their own malpractice insurance policy to see that research activities are covered by the policy. Often, because research may be testing new or innovative means of practice, it may not be covered by a policy specifying that usual and customary nursing practice only is covered. Discussion with the insurance agent and confirmed in writing (such as drafting a new clause for the insurance policy to specifically cover nursing research) should clarify the question for both the insurance company and the nurse researcher.

In recognition of these responsibilities and in compliance with federal and state laws, institutions have established institutional review boards (IRBs) that provide *prior* review of research protocols. Institutions receiving federal funding for research must provide for this review and must provide "assurances" to the federal government that they will conduct research according to the federal law and regulations.[30] Therefore, these regulations are of prime importance for nurse researchers.

Protection of human subjects

The autonomous right to be free, to self-determine a course in life, is an essential and tremendously important right provided citizens of the United States. This legal and ethical principle has formed the basis for the regulations on research with human subjects. Further study and reading are suggested in the area of ethical conduct of research. The additional readings list provides information in this area.

After reviewing the legal definition of research and discussing what research must be reviewed by the institutional review board, this section discusses the membership, functions, and operation of the IRB. Requirements for informed consent for human subjects are then identified. Special requirements for children, pregnant women, fetuses, human in vitro fertilization, and prisoners are also included.

LEGAL DEFINITION OF RESEARCH

In the federal regulations research is defined as follows: "Research means a systematic investigation designed to develop or contribute to generalizable knowledge. Activities which meet this definition constitute 'research' for purpose of these regulations, whether or not they are supported or funded under a program which is considered research for other purposes."[31]

The regulations elaborate through a definition of human subject: a living individual about whom an investigator (whether professional or student) conducting research obtains (1) data through intervention or interaction with the individual or (2) identifiable private information.[32] "Intervention" includes both physical procedures by which data are gathered (for example, venipuncture) and manipulations of the subject or the subject's environment that are performed for research purposes.[33]

"Interaction" includes communication or interpersonal contact between investigator and subject.[34] "Private information" includes information about behavior that occurs in a context in which an individual can reasonably expect that no observation or recording is taking place and information that has been provided for specific purposes by an individual and that the individual can reasonably expect will not be made public (for example, a medical record).[35] Private information must be individually identifiable (that is, the identity of the subject is or may be readily ascertained by the investigator or associated with the information) in order for obtaining the information to constitute research involving human subjects.[36]

The ANA CODE states that if the nurse wishes to use a client's treatment record for research or nonclinical purposes where anonymity cannot be guaranteed, the client's consent must be obtained first.[37] The CODE notes that this step ensures that the client's right to privacy is protected and that the nurse does not invade a client's privacy unlawfully.

Other definitions of research exist. For example, as discussed by one author, research is the use of experimental remedies, not accepted remedies.[38] Fried further clarifies that in justification of the greater need for informed consent, as the therapy moves away from the standard and the accepted toward the experimental, explicit consent, fuller disclosure of risks, and alternatives become necessary.

Therapeutic and nontherapeutic experimentation are also important to distinguish: experimentation is nontherapeutic when it is carried out on a person solely to obtain information of use to others and in no way to treat some illness that the subject might have. Therapeutic experimentation is when a therapy is tried with the sole view of determining the best way of treating that subject-patient. Much has been written about the randomized clinical trial, where the research result might be mixed therapeutic and nontherapeutic for a subject-patient. As will be seen, the subject must be informed about the methodology of the study. The benefits of the research to the subject are an important consideration in the regulations and requirements dealing with informed consent.

THE INSTITUTIONAL REVIEW BOARD

The development of the IRB system is said to be a unique blend of public incentive, private initiative, public oversight, and peer control.[39] The purpose is to promote complete and adequate review of research activities conducted by the institution. This includes ongoing review of approved proposals as the research is in progress and to its conclusion. The group must be professionally competent to review specific research activities and to ascertain the acceptability of the proposed research in terms of institutional commitments and regulations, applicable law, and standards of professional conduct and practice.[40]

According to federal regulations, IRBs must have at least five members, with varying backgrounds.[41] Membership is to be diverse, not all men and not all women and not all members of the same profession, with consideration given to racial and cultural backgrounds, as well as professional expertise and community attitudinal issues. There must be one member whose primary concerns are in nonscientific areas, for example, lawyers, ethicists, or clergy. One member must also be one who is not otherwise affiliated with the institution. Members of the IRB cannot participate in review of proposals in which they have a conflicting interest. Nonvoting members may be invited to participate where complex issues may arise needing further expertise.

Increasingly, IRBs have appointed nurse members. As nursing research becomes more of a force in health care delivery and since nursing participation is often critical to others' research success, it is almost undefensible and unjustifiable that an IRB would not have a nurse member. The regulations indicate that nurses certainly could be contributing members and leaders in the research review process.

Early federal regulations required that every research protocol be reviewed, from the most invasive, biological, experimental research to the least invasive, sociological, descriptive study. In 1981 the federal regulations regarding the IRBs carved out exempted research activities and expedited review procedures. The box (p. 339, top) lists the exempted research. Expedited review may be conducted by the IRB on studies involving no more than minimal risk, which is defined as: "the risks of harm anticipated in the proposed research are not greater, considering probability and magnitude, than those ordinarily encountered in daily life or during the performance of routine physical or psychological examinations or tests."[42]

Many IRBs may still require that nurse researchers conducting activities in the exempted area file their proposals with the IRB, indicating under which exemption the proposal falls. The nurse researchers, then, are responsible for that decision and judgment.

Not only must the IRB follow its written procedures and review proposed research at convened meetings, with a majority of its members present, but it must approve research by a majority vote of those present. The IRB must report serious or continuing noncompliance by investigators to appropriate officials. The IRB has the authority to approve, require modifications, and disapprove all research activities. Specifically, the IRB may require the researcher to, in addition to meeting all other regulation requirements:

1. Provide subjects with certain information about the study (even information not required by regulations).
2. Document informed consent (although the IRB may also waive this requirement under certain circumstances).
3. Suspend or terminate research that is not being conducted in accordance with its requirements.[43]

IRBs must communicate to researchers in writing their decision. When a proposal is disapproved, the IRB must include in its written notification a statement of the reasons for its decision and give the nurse researcher an opportunity to respond in person or in writing.[44] Further review may be done of research by officials of the institution, but they may not approve research unless it has been approved by an IRB.[45] A further appeal procedure is not specified in the regulations. However, should a nurse researcher wish to appeal an IRB's decision, he or she could do this through common law methods and under state or federal laws.

One possible basis for external appeal would be where the IRB's reasons for nonapproval are not within the criteria for review of proposals (p. 339, bottom). For example, an arbitrary decision that a nurse researcher cannot do research because a physician does not want his or her patients asked to be in the study is arguably an improper reason to restrict the nurse researcher's access to subjects. No cases exist where a nurse researcher

CATEGORIES OF EXEMPTED RESEARCH

1. Research conducted in established or commonly accepted educational settings, involving normal educational practices
2. Research involving the use of educational tests, if information taken from these sources is recorded in such a manner that subjects cannot be identified, directly or through identifiers linked to the subjects
3. Research involving survey or interview procedures, except where:
   a. Responses are recorded in such a manner that the subjects can be identified, directly or through identifiers linked to the subjects.
   b. Responses, if they become known outside the research, could reasonably place the subject at risk of criminal or civil liability or be damaging to the subject's financial standing or employability.
   c. The research deals with sensitive aspects of subject's own behavior, such as illegal conduct, drug use, sexual behavior, or use of alcohol.
4. Research involving the observation of public behavior (including observation by participants, except if subjects are children), except where all the following exist:
   a. Observations are recorded in such a manner that the subjects can be identified, directly or through identifiers linked to the subjects.
   b. Observations recorded about the subject, if known outside the research, could reasonably place the subject at risk of criminal or civil liability or be damaging to the subject's financial standing or employability.
   c. The research deals with sensitive aspects of the subject's own behavior, such as illegal conduct, drug use, sexual behavior, or use of alcohol.
5. Research involving the collection or study of existing data, documents, records, pathological specimens, or diagnostic specimens, if:
   a. These sources are publicly available.
   b. The information is recorded by the investigator in such a manner that subjects cannot be identified, directly or through identifiers linked to the subjects.
6. Certain research and demonstration projects conducted to study, evaluate, or examine programs under the Social Security Act or other benefits or service programs

Data from 45 C.F.R. §46.101(b) (1985).

CRITERIA FOR INSTITUTION REVIEW BOARD (IRB) APPROVAL OF RESEARCH

1. Risks to subjects are minimized:
   a. By using procedures that are consistent with sound research design and that do not necessarily expose subjects to risk
   b. Whenever appropriate, by using procedures already being performed on the subjects for diagnostic or treatment purposes
2. Risks to subjects are reasonable in relation to anticipated benefits, if any, to subjects and the importance of the knowledge that may reasonably be expected to result. In evaluating risks and benefits, the IRB should consider only those risks and benefits that may result from the research. The IRB should not consider possible long-range effects of applying knowledge gained in the research as among those research risks that fall within the purview of its responsibility.
3. Selection of subjects is equitable, taking into account the research purposes and the setting in which the research will be conducted.
4. Informed conset is sought from each prospective subject or the subject's legally authorized representative.
5. Informed consent is appropriately documented.
6. Where appropriate, the research plan makes adequate provision for monitoring the data collected to ensure the safety of the subjects.
7. Where appropriate, there are adequate provisions to protect the privacy of subjects and to maintain the confidentiality of data.
8. Appropriate additional safeguards are included in a study when some or all subjects are likely to be vulnerable to coercion or undue influence, such as persons with acute or severe physical or mental illness or those who are economically or educationally disadvantaged.

Data from 45 C.F.R. §46.111 (1985).

has brought such a lawsuit. However, suits for negligent review of research may be brought by researchers as well as subjects.[46]

The IRB has mandated criteria that it must use in order to approve research, as listed in the box. Where cooperative research involving more than one institution is being reviewed, one IRB may review the study or a joint review may be done.[47]

Certain recordkeeping responsibilities belong to the IRBs. They must maintain copies, for at least 3 years, of all procedures, proposals, approved sample consent forms, progress reports, reports of any injuries to subjects, minutes of meetings (showing attendance, actions taken, votes on the actions), basis for requiring changes in proposals and for disapproving proposals, and a summary of discussion of issues and their resolution. In addition, the IRB must maintain a list of its members, noting name, degrees, representative capacity, experience, expertise brought to the IRB, and any employment or other relationship to the institution. Statements of significant new findings provided to subjects must also be kept.[48]

INFORMED CONSENT

As discussed in Chapter 6, the elements of informed consent are that it be voluntary, competent, and informed. Much of the law of informed consent has evolved from case law involving informed consent to medical and surgical procedures. Informed consent in the research setting carries added requirements, focus, and importance. All research, except that exempted within the federal regulations, must meet general and basic elements of informed consent.

General elements include that the nurse researcher must obtain the legally effective informed consent of the subject or the subject's legally authorized representative. The circumstances under which this consent is obtained should be such that the subject has sufficient opportunity to consider whether to participate. No coercion or undue influence is allowed.

The information about the study, its effects, and its implications is to be given in language understandable to the subject. No informed consent may include any exculpatory language. Such language is an attempt to have the subject waive his or her legal rights. This includes language that appears to release the investigator, sponsor, institution, or others from its liability for negligence.

The basic elements of informed consent to participate in research are listed in the box on p. 341. This list contains the information that must be included. Additional elements of informed consent, when appropriate, may also be provided to each subject. They include:

1. A statement that the risks involved with the particular treatment or procedure may be unforeseeable
2. Circumstances under which the investigator may terminate the subject's participation
3. Any additional costs that may result from participation and consequences of subject's decision to withdraw from the study
4. A statement that significant new findings developed during the course of the research that may relate to the subject's willingness to continue participation will be provided to the subject
5. The approximate number of subjects in the study[49]

The IRB may waive an informed consent procedure in studies that involve approval by state or local governmental officials or examine Social Security programs. When the research involves no more than minimal risk, when the waiver or alteration will not adversely affect the rights of the subjects, when the research could not be carried out without the waiver or alteration, and whenever appropriate, the subject will be provided with additional pertinent information after participation.[50]

Written consent forms are required by the federal regulations, although under certain circumstances the IRB may waive this requirement. The consent form itself must be approved by the IRB, and each subject must sign one. Each subject must receive a copy of the form. The consent form may take two shapes:

1. A written consent document that embodies the required elements of informed consent
2. A "short form" written consent document stating that the required elements of informed consent have been presented orally to the subject

When the second type is used, there must be a witness to the oral presentation. The IRB must approve a written summary of what is to be said to the subject. The witness signs both the short form, which the subject signs, and the copy of the summary. The subject receives a copy of the summary. The person obtaining the consent also signs the summary.[51]

As mentioned, a written consent form requirement may be waived by the IRB. This is usually done when the only record linking the subject to the research would

BASIC ELEMENTS OF INFORMED CONSENT

1. A statement that the study involves research, an explanation of the research purposes, the expected duration of the subject's participation, a description of the procedures to be followed, and identification of any experimental procedures
2. A description of any reasonably foreseeable risks or discomforts to the subject
3. A description of any benefits to the subject or to others that may reasonably be expected from the research
4. A disclosure of appropriate alternative procedures or courses of treatment, if any, that might be advantageous to the subject
5. A statement describing the extent to which confidentiality of records identifying the subject will be maintained
6. For research involving more than minimal risk, an explanation as to whether any compensation and/or medical treatments are available if injury occurs and, if so, what they consist of or where further information may be obtained
7. An explanation of whom to contact for answers to pertinent questions about the research, subjects' rights, and in the event of a research-related injury to the subject
8. A statement that participation is voluntary, that refusal to participate will involve no penalty or loss of benefits to which the subject is otherwise entitled, and that the subject may discontinue participation at any time without penalty or loss of benefits to which the subject is otherwise entitled

Data from 45 C.F.R §46.116(a) (1985).

be the consent document and the principal risk would be potential harm resulting from a breach of confidentiality. If this is the situation, each subject should be asked whether he or she wants the documentation. The subject's wishes will govern. Written consent may also be waived by the IRB if the research presents no more than minimal risk of harm to subjects and involves no procedures for which written consent is normally required outside of the research context.[52]

Fetuses, Pregnant Women, and Human in Vitro Fertilization. Additional protections have been afforded certain groups within the law. Ethical advisory boards have been established by the secretary of the Department of Health and Human Services (HHS) to deal with medical, legal, social, ethical, and related issues having to do with experimentation with pregnant women, fetuses (viable, nonviable, and dead), and in vitro fertilization. Nurses and nurse researchers can be members of these boards. Their purposes are to render advice to the secretary of HHS and establish classes of research proposals that require HHS review, with the exception of research involving in vitro fertilization, which must be reviewed by the board.[53]

Additional responsibilities of the IRB for approval of studies with these subjects involve determining that adequate consideration has been given to the manner in which potential subjects will be selected and that adequate provision has been made by the researcher for monitoring the actual informed consent.[54]

For these groups of subjects, certain general limitations apply. No activity may be undertaken unless:

1. Appropriate animal studies and studies on nonpregnant individuals have been completed.
2. Except where the purpose of the activity is to meet the health needs of the mother or the particular fetus, the risk to the fetus is minimal and, in all cases, is the least possible risk for achieving the objective of the research.
3. Individuals engaged in the activity will have no part in (a) any decisions as to the timing, method, and procedures used to terminate the pregnancy and (b) determining the viability of the fetus at the termination of the pregnancy.
4. No procedural changes that may cause greater than minimal risk to the fetus or the pregnant woman will be introduced into the procedure for terminating the pregnancy solely in the interest of the activity.[55]

In addition, no inducements, monetary or otherwise, may be offered to terminate pregnancy for purposes of the research.[56]

Consent requirements also differ for research involving pregnant women and fetuses. Both mother and father must be legally competent and have given their informed consent after having been fully informed regarding the possible impact on the fetus. The father's informed consent need not be secured if (1) the purpose of the activity is to meet the health needs of the mother; (2) his identity or whereabouts cannot reasonably be ascertained; (3) he is not reasonably available; or (4) the pregnancy resulted from rape.[57]

Fetuses in utero may not be involved in a study as subjects unless the purpose of the activity is to meet the health needs of the particular fetus, who will be placed at risk only to the minimal extent necessary to meet such needs. Research may be conducted also where the risk to the fetus imposed by the research is minimal and the purpose of the activity is the development of important biomedical knowledge that cannot be obtained by other means. Consent must also be obtained, as specified previously, from the parents.[58]

Fetuses outside the uterus, when it has not been ascertained whether the fetus is viable, are not to be involved in research unless there is no added risk to the fetus, the purpose of the activity is the development of important knowledge that cannot be obtained by other means, or the purpose of the research is to enhance the possibility of survival of the fetus to the viability point. Parental consent must also be obtained.

Fetuses who are not viable may not be involved in research unless vital functions of the fetus will not be artificially maintained, unless experimental activities that would terminate the heartbeat or respirations of the fetus will not be employed, and unless the purpose of the research is the development of important knowledge that cannot be obtained by other means. Parental consent is a requirement.

Prisoners. Regulation of research involving prisoners stems from the fact that they may be under constraints because of their incarceration. The fact that one is in prison could affect his or her ability to give a voluntary and uncoerced decision to participate in research as a subject. Additional safeguards are necessary because of this unique situation.[59] Chapter 16 discusses nursing care in correctional facilities in general.

In addition to satisfying regulations already discussed regarding the composition of the IRB, if an IRB reviews research proposals where prisoners are contemplated subjects, the IRB must have at least one member who is a prisoner or prisoner representative. A majority of the IRB members are to have no association with the prison involved.[60]

Those approaching prisoners to be subjects must take into account several considerations. The advantages coming to the prisoner who will participate must not be of such a magnitude that his or her ability to evaluate the risks of the research against the value of the advantages in the limited-choice environment of the prison is impaired. The risks involved in the research have to be commensurate with risks that would be acceptable by nonprisoner volunteers. Procedures for selecting prisoner-subjects must be fair and available to all prisoners. In some instances random selection is required. Assurances must also exist that parole boards will not take into consideration the prisoner's participation in a research study. Prisoners must be clearly informed of this and in advance of their decision to participate in a study.[61]

The regulations involving prisoners also outline permitted areas of study. Those areas include the study of:

1. Causes, effects, and processes of incarceration
2. Prisons as institutional structures or prisoners as incarcerated persons
3. Conditions particularly affecting prisoners as a class (for example, diseases that are prevalent in prison populations)
4. Practices that have the intent and reasonable probability of improving the health and well-being of the subject.

Studies in areas 1 and 2 can be conducted provided that the study presents no more than minimal risk and no more than inconvenience to the subjects. Studies in areas 3 and 4 require the secretary of HHS to consult with experts and publish notice of intent to approve such research prior to the approval of the research.[62]

Children. The legal definition of children is anyone under the age of majority defined by state laws. The federal regulations define children as persons who have not attained the legal age for consent to treatments or procedures involved in research, under the applicable law of the jurisdiction in which the research will be conducted.[63]

Research with children as subjects must include the child's assent where appropriate and parental permission. The IRB may require the child's assent where it considers the child capable according to his or her age, maturity, and psychological state. Assent means a child's affirmative agreement to participate in research.[64] Mere failure to object should not, without affirmative agreement, be construed as assent. The IRB may waive the requirement of getting the child's assent, especially if the child's capacity is so limited. Permission, on the other hand, means the agreement of parent(s) or guardian to the participation of their child or ward in research.[65] Parental or guardian consent is always required.

Certain research is not exempted (see the box on p. 339) when children are the potential subjects. Where research entails observation of public behavior and the researcher does not participate, this category of research remains exempt. The exemption of research involving survey or interview procedures does not apply to research involving children.[66]

The federal regulations specify four different classifications of research involving children:

1. Research not involving greater than minimal risk[67]
2. Research involving greater than minimal risk but presenting the prospect of direct benefit to the individual subjects[68]
3. Research involving greater than minimal risk and no prospect of direct benefit to individual subjects, but likely to yield generalizable knowledge about the subject's disorder or condition[69]
4. Research not otherwise approvable that presents an opportunity to understand, prevent, or alleviate a serious problem affecting the health or welfare of children[70]

Research in these categories is approved if the IRB finds that adequate provisions are made for obtaining the child's assent and the parent's permission. Additional requirements are necessary as the risks increase and the benefits to the individual child decrease. For example, category 2 research requires that the risk is justified by the anticipated benefits to the subject and that the relationship of the anticipated benefit to the risk is at least as favorable to the subjects as that presented by available alternative approaches.[71]

In category 3 the IRB must consider that the risk represents a minor increase over minimal risk; that the intervention or procedure presents experiences to subjects that are reasonably commensurate with those inherent in their actual or expected medical, dental, psychological, social, or educational situations; and that the intervention or procedure is likely to yield generalizable knowledge about the subjects' disorder or condition, which is of vital importance for the understanding of the subject's disorder or condition.[72]

Parental permission also may vary among these categories of research with children. Permission of one parent may be sufficient in the first two categories; both parents must give their permission in the other two categories, unless one parent is deceased, unknown, incompetent, or not reasonably available or when only one parent has legal responsibility for the care and custody of the child.[73]

Financing nursing research

Public and private funding exists for nursing research. Legally created funding for nursing research emanates from federal and state governments. Two federal sources specifically identified as nursing research funding exist in the Department of Health and Human Services: the Division of Nursing, located in the Bureau of Professions, Public Health Service, Health Resources and Services Administration; and the National Center for Nursing Research, located in the National Institutes of Health (NIH).[74] Nursing research is not only publicly funded through these mechanisms; nurse researchers also may apply for government research grants through many other government departments concerned with health, family, and community.

The Center for Nursing Research is new. Leadership and specific projects are yet to be determined. The purpose of the center is the conduct, support, and dissemination of information regarding basic and clinical nursing research, training, and other programs in patient care research.[75] This center has been placed within the NIH where other scientific research programs are located. It will have a director appointed by the secretary of Health and Human Services who will report to the director of NIH.

The Division of Nursing, on the other hand, has had a long-standing federal focus on nursing education, practice, and research. Specifically, the nursing reseach and analysis branch of the division administers grant support for research to improve nursing education and practice, expand the knowledge base, and stimulate research to meet the nation's health needs. It also is responsible for designing, conducting, and supporting studies and evaluations of nursing personnel supply, requirements, and distribution.[76]

The Division of Nursing administers two national research service awards and one nursing research grant. The service awards include a nurse fellowship and institutional grants. The nurse fellowships are provided to individual registered nurses with active licenses, for predoctoral or postdoctoral research training in specified areas of nursing, and in the biomedical and behavioral fields important to nursing.[77]

Nonprofit, private, or nonfederal public institutions are eligible for the institutional grants, which are meant to develop or enhance postdoctoral research training opportunities for individuals who are selected by the institutions and are interested in careers in nursing research and related behavioral and biomedical research.[78]

The nursing research grants are available to any individual, corporation, institution, agency, or other legal entity. Research grant support is to enlarge the body of scientific knowledge that underlies nursing practice, nursing education, and nursing services administration. Six types of support are available:

1. For individual projects
2. For clusters of at least three studies focused on a single theme
3. For studies that emphasize the special health needs of the United States and enhance the research efforts and resources of faculty in schools of nursing offering doctoral programs
4. For small studies of high quality carried out by new investigators
5. For projects to bridge the gap between different generations of knowledge through research and utilization of such knowledge in nursing practice, nursing education, and nursing services administration
6. To encourage small businesses in the private sector to participate in nursing research activities[79]

Funding levels vary from year to year, according to the authorization by Congress. In fiscal year 1985 nursing research grants were appropriated totaling $9.4 million.[80]

State laws

Although most legal regulation of research is federally controlled, some states have laws on the protection of human subjects. For example, the state of New York's law applies to research not subject to federal regulations.[81] The law states that no one except a researcher shall conduct human research in New York.[82] Each agency conducting research must have a human research review committee that requires the agency to develop a policy regarding the rights and welfare of human subjects, reviews research projects to determine necessity, and ensures that (1) rights of subjects are adequately protected, (2) risks are outweighed by potential benefits, (3) voluntary informed consent is obtained by adequate and appropriate methods, and (4) the persons conducting the research are competent and qualified.[83] This state law requires that the subject's informed consent be subscribed to in writing and declares the use of language that involves the waiver or appearance of waiver of any of the subject's rights prohibited.[84]

Recommendations and trends

Although the Department of Health and Human Services' regulations regarding the protection of human subjects have remained essentially unchanged since the early 1980s, it is always necessary to monitor the *Federal Register* for any proposed changes and accepted changes. Nurse researchers should participate in public comment concerning proposals and change their practices based on new regulations.

Nursing research is a very exciting area within the nursing profession. As nursing research expands into areas of appliances, medical devices, and experimental drugs, other regulations must be consulted.[85] Federal and state laws may impact nursing research. Each state may differ in the laws that apply to nursing research.

Nurses participating in others' research have the right to be thoroughly informed, to ask questions, and to make an independent decision whether or not to participate by carrying out someone else's protocol on subjects. Especially with experimental drugs and the more intrusive and invasive experimental procedures given as medical orders, the nurse should understand the IRB process, and the risks and benefits to the subject, science, and technological advancement. Additionally, before participating in an experimental practice, nurses should seek opinion as to the impact on their liability for malpractice, including a review of their malpractice insurance policy coverage.

Nursing representation on IRBs should be a requirement. If nursing research is exempted from federally required IRB review, nursing groups should consider developing a peer review mechanism, a self-regulatory system, to provide assurances to the profession and the public that careful, prior thought and analysis is given to nursing research proposals.

The ANA's Council on Nursing Research should be part of each nurse researcher's network. Nurses employed in research facilities who carry out others' research would find this council helpful as well. Being part of a nursing research network may prove beneficial should legal questions arise as to reasonable practices of nurse researchers. Should the need arise, this peer group or its members could provide consultation and expert testimony. Since to date there has been no litigation against or by nurse researchers, and given the continued advancement of nursing research, taking preventive steps to protect both subject and researcher can never hurt.

Endnotes

1. D. DIERS, RESEARCH IN NURSING PRACTICE 10 (1979).
2. McNemar and Simmons, *Ethical Concerns in the Research Review Process,* ETHICAL DIMENSIONS OF NURSING RESEARCH 66 (University of Maryland, 1980).
3. *See also* ANNUAL REVIEW OF NURSING RESEARCH VOL. 3 (H. Eerly and J. Fitzpatrick, eds., 1985); and publications of Sigma Theta Tau, International Honor Society of Nurses, IMAGE, and of the American Nurses' Assn. (ANA) Foundation and the ANA Council of Nurse Researchers.

4. 2 TRIALS OF WAR CRIMINALS BEFORE THE NUREMBERG MILITARY TRIBUNALS UNDER CONTROL COUNCIL LAW NO. 10 181, 182 (1949).
5. WORLD MEDICAL ASSN., DECLARATION OF HELSINKI (1964, rev'd 1975).
6. AMERICAN MEDICAL ASSN., STATEMENT OF ETHICAL CONDUCT OF RESEARCH (1967); *see also* AMERICAN PSYCHOLOGICAL ASSN., ETHICAL PRINCIPLES IN THE CONDUCT OF RESEARCH WITH HUMAN PARTICIPANTS (1973).
7. Committee on Research and Studies, ANA, *The Nurse in Research: ANA Guidelines on Ethical Values,* 17 NURSING RESEARCH 104 (March-April, 1968).
8. AMERICAN NURSES' ASSN., CODE FOR NURSES WITH INTERPRETIVE STATEMENTS (1976, 1985) (hereinafter cited *ANA Code 1976* or *ANA Code 1985*); AMERICAN NURSES' ASSN., HUMAN RIGHTS GUIDELINES FOR NURSES IN CLINICAL AND OTHER RESEARCH (1975, 1985) (hereinafter cited *ANA GUIDELINES 1975* or *ANA GUIDELINES 1985*); *see also* AMERICAN NURSES' ASSN., GUIDELINES FOR THE INVESTIGATIVE FUNCTION OF NURSES (1981); Yeaworth, *The ANA Code: A Comparative Perspective,* 17 IMAGE 94 (Summer 1985).
9. *ANA Code 1976, supra* note 8, at 14; and *ANA Code 1985, supra* note 8, at 12.
10. *ANA Code 1985, supra* note 8, at 13.
11. *ANA Code 1975, supra* note 8, at 14, 15.
12. *ANA Code 1985, supra* note 8, at 12.
13. *Id.*
14. *ANA Code 1985, supra* note 8, at 13.
15. *Id.*
16. *ANA Code 1976, supra* note 8, at 5, 15.
17. *ANA Code 1976, supra* note 8, at 5.
18. *ANA Guidelines 1975, supra* note 8.
19. *ANA Guidelines 1985, supra* note 8.
20. *ANA Guidelines 1985, supra* note 8, at 12, 13, 14, 15.
21. *Hyman v. Jewish Chronic Disease Hospital,* 206 N.E.2d 338 (N.Y. 1965).
22. PUBLIC HEALTH SERVICE, TUSKEGEE SYPHILIS STUDY AD HOC ADVISORY PANEL: FINAL REPORT (1973); J. JONES, BAD BLOOD: THE TUSKEGEE SYPHILIS EXPERIMENT (1981).
23. Veatch, *The Ethical Complexities of Experimentation with Oral Contraceptives,* 1 HASTINGS CENTER REPORT 2 (JUNE 1971).
24. P.L. 93-348, 88 Stat. 342, 42 U.S.C. §2891-2893 (1982) (created Institutional Review Boards, ethics guidance program); The Commission for the Protection of Human Subjects of Biomedical and Behavioral Research was repealed by P.L. 95-622, Nov. 9, 1978, 92 Stat 3442.
25. U.S. CONST. amend. I.
26. U.S. CONST. amend. XIV.
27. Davidson, *First Amendment Protection for Biomedical Research,* 19 ARIZONA LAW REVIEW 893 (1977).
28. *Rodriquez v. Jackson,* 574 P.2d 481 (Ariz. App. 1978).
29. *Mink v. University of Chicago,* 460 F.Supp. 713 (N.D. Ill. 1978).
30. 45 C.F.R. §46 (1985).
31. 45 C.F.R. §46.102(e) (1985).
32. 45 C.F.R. §46.102(f) (1985).
33. *Id.*
34. *Id.*
35. *Id.*
36. *Id.*
37. *ANA Code 1985. supra* note 8, at 5.
38. C. FRIED, MEDICAL EXPERIMENTATION: PERSONAL INTEGRITY AND SOCIAL POLICY (1974).
39. Robertson, *The Law of Institutional Review Boards,* 26 UCLA LAW REVIEW, 484 (1979).
40. 45 C.F.R. §46.107(a) (1985).
41. 45 C.F.R. §46.107(b)(c)(d)(e)(f) (1985).
42. 45 C.F.R. §46.102(g) (1985).
43. 45 C.F.R. §46.108, 46.109(a)(b)(c), and 46.113 (1985).
44. 45 C.F.R. §46.109(d) (1985).
45. 45 C.F.R. §46.112 (1985).
46. Robertson, *The Law of Institutional Review Boards,* 26 UCLA LAW REVIEW, 484, 536 (1979).
47. 45 C.F.R. §46.114 (1985).
48. 45 C.F.R. §46.115 (1985).
49. 45 C.F.R. §46.116(b) (1985).
50. 45 C.F.R. §46.116(c), (d) (1985).
51. 45 C.F.R. §46.117(b) (1985).
52. 45 C.F.R. §46.117(c) (1985).
53. 45 C.F.R. §46.204 (1985).
54. 45 C.F.R. §46.205 (1985).
55. 45 C.F.R. §46.207(a) (1985).
56. 45 C.F.R. §46.206(b) (1985).
57. 45 C.F.R. §46.207(b) (1985).
58. 45 C.F.R. §46.208 (1985).
59. 45 C.F.R. §46.302 (1985).
60. 45 C.F.R. §46.304 (1985).
61. 45 C.F.R. §46.305 (1985).
62. 45 C.F.R. §46.306 (1985).
63. 45 C.F.R. §46.402(a) (1985).
64. 45 C.F.R. §46.402(b) (1985).
65. 45 C.F.R. §46.402(c) (1985).
66. 45 C.F.R. §46.401(b) (1985).
67. 45 C.F.R. §46.404 (1985).
68. 45 C.F.R. §46.405 (1985).
69. 45 C.F.R. §46.406 (1985).
70. 45 C.F.R. §46.407 (1985).
71. 45 C.F.R. §46.405 (1985).
72. 45 C.F.R. §46.406 (1985).
73. 45 C.F.R. §46.408(b) (1985).
74. 42 U.S.C. §295h-6 (health and allied health professions and personnel, advanced training); 42 U.S.C. §295h (grants for graduate programs in health administration); 42 U.S.C. §295h, 296, 297, 298, 2891 (1982) (Division of Nursing). Health and Allied Health Professions and Personnel, Advanced Training 42 U.S.C. §295h-6; Grants for Graduate Programs in Health Administration, 42 U.S.C. §295h; Traineeships for Students in Other Graduate Programs, 42 U.S.C. §295h-1a; Traineeships for Students in Schools of Public Health, 42 U.S.C. §295h-1b; Project Grants and Contracts with Eligible Entities, 42 U.S.C. §295h-5; Nurse Training, 42 U.S.C. §296; Assistance to Nursing Students, 42 U.S.C. §297; National Advisory Council on Nurse Training, 42 U.S.C. §298.
75. *The American Nurse,* November/December 1985, at 2, col. 1.
76. BUREAU OF HEALTH PROFESSIONS, HEALTH RESOURCES AND SERVICES ADMINISTRATION, PUBLIC HEALTH SERVICE, U.S. DEPT. OF HEALTH AND HUMAN SERVICES, FACT SHEET: DIVISION OF NURSING (1985).
77. BUREAU OF HEALTH PROFESSIONS, FACT SHEETS ON

GRANT PROGRAMS ADMINISTERED BY DIVISION OF NURSING (March 1985).

78. *Id.*

79. *Id.*

80. P.L. 98-619; BUREAU OF HEALTH PROFESSIONS, HEALTH RESOURCES AND SERVICES ADMINISTRATION, PUBLIC HEALTH SERVICE, U.S. DEPT. OF HEALTH AND HUMAN SERVICES, FACT SHEETS ON PROGRAM ADMINISTERED BY BUREAU OF HEALTH PROFESSIONS 20 (March 1985).

81. N.Y. PUBLIC HEALTH LAW §2445 (McKinney 1985).

82. *Id.* at §2443.

83. *Id.* at §2444.

84. *Id.* at §2442.

85. *See, e.g.*, Research on the Handicapped, 34 C.F.R. §350 (1985); Consumer Product Safety Commission Research, 16 C.F.R. §1029 (1985); Defense Project Research, 32 C.F.R. §219 (1985); Energy Department Research, 10 C.F.R. §745 (1985); Food and Drug Administration Research, 21 C.F.R. §50, 56 (1985); Additional Research in Prisons, 28 C.F.R. §512 (1985).

Additional Readings

AMERICAN NURSES' ASSN., ETHICS IN NURSING: REFERENCES AND RESOURCES (1979).

A. DAVIS and M. AROSKAR, ETHICAL DILEMMAS AND NURSING PRACTICE (2d ed. 1983).

B. GRAY, HUMAN SUBJECTS IN MEDICAL EXPERIMENTATION (1975).

A. JAMETON, NURSING PRACTICE, THE ETHICAL ISSUES (1984).

NATIONAL COMMISSION FOR THE PROTECTION OF HUMAN SUBJECTS OF BIOMEDICAL AND BEHAVIORAL RESEARCH: THE BELMONT REPORT, ETHICAL PRINCIPLES AND GUIDELINES FOR THE PROTECTION OF HUMAN SUBJECTS OF RESEARCH (1978); REPORT AND RECOMMENDATIONS: RESEARCH INVOLVING CHILDREN (1977); REPORT AND RECOMMENDATIONS: RESEARCH INVOLVING PRISONERS (1976); REPORT AND RECOMMENDATIONS: RESEARCH ON FETUSES, PREGNANT WOMEN (1978); REPORT AND RECOMMENDATIONS: INSTITUTIONAL REVIEW BOARDS (1978); REPORT AND RECOMMENDATIONS: ETHICAL GUIDELINES FOR THE DELIVERY OF HEALTH SERVICE (1978); RESEARCH INVOLVING THOSE INSTITUTIONALIZED AS MENTALLY INFIRM (1978).

NATIONAL INSTITUTE ON AGING, PROTECTION OF ELDERLY RESEARCH SUBJECTS (1979).

PRESIDENT'S COMMISSION FOR THE STUDY OF ETHICAL PROBLEMS IN MEDICINE AND BIOMEDICAL AND BEHAVIORAL RESEARCH, FINAL REPORT ON STUDIES OF THE ETHICAL AND LEGAL PROBLEMS IN MEDICINE AND BEHAVIORAL RESEARCH (1983).

Scott, *Ethical Issues in Nursing Research: Access to Human Subjects*, 4 TOPICS IN CLINICAL NURSING 74 (April 1982).

Section E Advanced Nursing Practice

Chapter 22

Nurse executives and administrators

Cynthia E. Northrop

The management process has been defined as including four steps: planning, organizing, leading, and evaluating.[1] These steps will provide a framework for arranging the discussion in this chapter of the legal issues involved in the nurse executive and administrator position. In a recent study the nurse executive's role was found to be expanding with more financial and community responsibility.[2]

Overview of nurse executives and administrators

The American Nurses' Association (ANA) describes nursing services as "all those health care services performed by a registered professional nurse within the scope of professional nursing practice as defined by state law."[3] The nurse executive is the top ranking administrative nurse appointed by the governing body or chief executive officer to administer a division of nursing.[4] The division of nursing is the management unit within a health care organization which is organized to deliver nursing services. In recognition of the nursing administration role as an expanding and specialized role the American Nurses' Association offers certification to individual nurse administrators.

Nurse administrators are individuals who are part of the management team of the nursing department. The titles of nurse administrators vary according to the type and size of health care institution or facility. These titles may include director of nursing, vice president for patient care, nurse manager, executive director, nursing supervisor, head nurse, charge nurse, nursing coordinator, assistant director, associate director, administrative nursing supervisor, chief nurse, and first line manager.

The standards for nursing administrators developed by the ANA are listed on p. 348 (see box). These standards are for use in organized departments of nursing which may exist in many settings, including hospitals, community health agencies, long-term care facilities, industry, schools, ambulatory services, and other health care organizations. The ANA Commission on Nursing Services includes in the standards document a self-assessment checklist of characteristics of a nursing department which follows the ANA standards.[5]

Weighty demands are part of the usual nurse executive and administrator position and responsibilities. Today's nurse executives are required to effectively combine clinical practice and research knowledge with managerial and leadership skills.[6] The functions of the nursing supervisors, executives, and administrators involve: budget development, staff development, long-range planning, recruitment, staffing, direct patient care, indirect patient care, quality assurance, policy and standards, bargaining and union-related activities, wage and salary determination and supervision.[7]

STANDARDS FOR ORGANIZED NURSING SERVICE

Standard I

The Division of Nursing has a philosophy and structure that ensure the delivery of high-quality nursing care and provide means for resolving nursing practice issues throughout the health care organization.

Standard II

The Division of Nursing is administered by a qualified nurse executive who is a member of corporate administration.

Standard III

Policies and practices of the Division of Nursing provide for equality and continuity of nursing services.

Standard IV

The Division of Nursing ensures that the nursing process is used to design and provide nursing care to meet the individual needs of patients and clients in the context of their families.

Standard V

The Division of Nursing provides an environment that ensures the effectiveness of nursing practice.

Standard VI

The Division of Nursing ensures the development of educational programs to support the delivery of high-quality nursing care.

Standard VII

The Division of Nursing initiates, uses, and participates in research studies or projects for the improvement of patient care.

Adapted from AMERICAN NURSES' ASSOCIATION, STANDARDS FOR ORGANIZED NURSING SERVICES (1982).

Federal regulations for skilled nursing facilities list responsibilities of the Director of Nursing, as follows:

1. Developing and maintaining nursing service objectives
2. Setting and enforcing standards of nursing practice
3. Establishing nursing policy and procedures
4. Writing job descriptions
5. Scheduling daily rounds to see all patients
6. Coordinating services
7. Recommending number and levels of staff members to be employed
8. Planning staff development, orientation, ongoing educational programs, inservice (specified topics to be included: prevention and control of infections, fire prevention and safety, accident prevention, confidentiality of patient information, preservation of patient dignity, protection of privacy, personal and property rights)
9. Maintaining records.[8]

The most pressing issues for nurse executives are those involving changes in fiscal responsibilities and fiscal systems within the health care system. Health care management literature abounds with information about health status, health resources, and financial concerns.[9]

The latest data available indicates that health care expenditures in the United States totaled $355.4 billion, an average of $1,459 per person, and comprised 10.8 percent of the gross national product.[10] Hospital care expenditures continue to claim the largest share of the health care dollar, accounting for 41% of health care expenditures in 1983. Physician services, dentist services, and nursing home care accounted for 19%, 6%, and 8%, respectively.[11]

Since the advent of Medicare and Medicaid programs in the mid-1960s, the federal government's share of personal health care expenditures has increased from 10.1% in 1965 to 29.7% in 1983.[12] Between 1970 and 1982 the number of registered nurses per 100,000 population increased by 59 percent, from 369 to 586, compared with a 35 percent increase in the physician-population ratio during the same period. Substantial regional variation in the nursing supply persisted in 1982, with the greatest supply found in the Northeast (764 nurses per 100,000 population) and the smallest supply in the South (466).[13] The number of people employed in the health care industry grew by nearly 90% between 1970 and 1983, from 4.2 million to 7.9 million.

In 1982 the average length of stay in short-stay hospitals in the United States was 7.6 days, with wide variation among the states. The longest average stays were in New York (9.7), Minnesota (9.4), and Massachusetts

(8.9); the shortest average stays were in Utah (5.4), Wyoming (5.5), and Washington (5.7).[14] Diseases of the heart and malignant neoplasms are the two leading causes of death in the United States.[15]

In this fiscal and management environment certain legal issues become apparent. These will be presented according to the steps of the management process.

Planning nursing services

The legal issues in the planning stage of nursing services involve establishing policy and procedure, recruiting and hiring appropriate staff, and making proper assignments. Setting up nursing services involves not only concurrence with professional standards but with legal standards, such as those within governmental regulations and laws pertaining to the delivery of nursing services. The chief example of these are the conditions for participation outlined in federal regulations which must be met in order for payment to be received from Medicare and Medicaid.

Depending on the setting (hospital,[16] skilled nursing facility,[17] health maintenance organization,[18] hospice care,[19] home health agency[20] or renal dialysis[21]), conditions for participation (federal regulations) require that nursing services be provided through a "well-organized departmental plan of administrative authority with delineation of responsibilities and duties of each category of nursing personnel."[22]

The best prepared nurse executive has reviewed the requirements of state laws, too. For example, the state labor code, worker's compensation code, and unemployment code are three important areas with which to be familiar. In planning nursing services of a particular specialty the chapter relevant to that specialty will also enhance the nurse executive's perspective on unique legal issues. For example, CHN administrators will want to refer to chapters in Section B on nursing in the community. In addition Chapter 15 (Occupational Health Nursing) and Chapter 30 (Employment Claims) should be reviewed since they also discuss employee and employer rights and responsibilities.

POLICY AND PROCEDURE

The planning of nursing services begins with the development of a goal and mission statement and purpose of the nursing department or division. Policies and procedures are developed from that statement. The purpose of policy and procedure manuals is to standardize care, set standards, and make evaluation easier. They should be well defined, clearly presented, and based on current and accurate knowledge and research.

Qualifications for employment are an important part of the agency policies. Generally, these requirements must not require a particular gender, religion (except for religious organizations), residency, citizenship, language, age, or handicaps. Exceptions to this are discussed below.

Nepotism is still a generally accepted restriction. If any pre-employment testing is to be done, it should be certain that the test measures the qualifications and is nondiscriminatory. State laws must be reviewed. For example, Connecticut and Maryland prohibit polygraphs as a condition for employment.[23] In addition tests that operate to exclude minorities and other protected classes and are not job related are illegal.[24]

Qualifications for nursing positions are also specified in federal regulations and are legally required by the agency if it wishes to participate in federal payment for services. For example, hospital nursing staff are qualified by education, experience, and demonstrated ability for the positions to which they are appointed.[25] Federal law indicates that the director of nursing makes decisions relative to the selection and promotion of nursing personnel based on their qualifications and capabilities and recommends the termination of employment when this is necessary.[26]

Hiring foreign nurses may be of concern to the nurse executive. As long as they have met the state licensing requirements and are indeed licensed, they can be hired. However, most states prohibit an employer from hiring an alien, one who is not entitled to lawful residence in the United States.[27] Therefore, the foreign nurse must have fulfilled all immigration laws and legally be present and approved to work in the United States.

Job performance expectations and all policies are presented to employees upon being hired and during orientation to the facility. The employee and administrator are responsible for knowing the content of the policies and how they affect job fulfillment. Reviewing and updating the content of policies is an important administrative responsibility. Hospitals and other health care agencies are liable for failure to use care in the selection of its employees.[28]

Disciplinary procedures are an important part of nursing administration and the policy and procedure manuals. Clarity and specificity in all policy areas greatly enhance the nurse administrator's ability to defend decisions and actions taken to assure safe patient care and staff competency. An employee's best challenge to disciplinary action by an employee is often the administrator's failure to follow the institution's rules on disciplining employees.

RECRUITING AND HIRING

Whether the nurse administrator does his or her own hiring or whether the agency uses a nurse recruiter, the administrator is responsible for the recruitment and hiring process and resulting decisions. Careful screening, use of effective personnel policies, determining salary, negotiating the employment agreement, checking references, and adherence to licensing requirements are all important parts of the process.[29]

Federal regulations require that health care agencies have written personnel policies. For example, home health agencies must have current, appropriate, written personnel records which include the job description, qualifications, licensure, performance evaluation, and health examination of each employee.[30] The skilled nursing facility must have written personnel policies and current personnel records.[31] Personnel records are to be available to the employee. Employees must be examined for communicable diseases; those with skin lesions are not permitted to work.[32] The skilled nursing facility is to keep records of incidents and accidents to patients and personnel and review them to identify health and safety hazards.[33] Hospitals are required to have on file personnel files which include application forms and verification of credentials.[34]

In hospital outpatient departments which participate in federal reimbursement mechanisms, regulations require that they have effective policies and procedures relating to the staff, functions of the service, and outpatient medical records and adequate facilities in order to assure the health and safety of the patients.[35] Federal regulations specify that in the outpatient department a registered professional nurse be responsible for the nursing services of the department.[36]

Hospitals participating in federal funding mechanisms must have at least a procedure for taking care of the occasional emergency case it might be called upon to handle.[37] Written policies control emergency room procedures; they are supervised by a qualified member of the medical staff, and nursing fuctions are the responsibility of a registered professional nurse.[38]

Nursing services in the psychiatric hospital are also part of the federal regulations for participation in federal funding mechanisms. The legal requirements include that the nursing services be under the direct supervision of a registered professional nurse who is qualified by education and experience for the position; and the number of registered professional nurses, licensed practical nurses, and other nursing personnel is adequate to formulate and carry out the nursing components of the individual treatment plan for each patient.[39] Federal law mandates that the registered professional nurse supervising the nursing program have a master's degree in psychiatric or mental health nursing or its equivalent from a school of nursing accredited by the National League for Nursing or is qualified by education, experience in the care of the mentally ill, and demonstrated competence to participate in interdisciplinary formulation of individual treatment plans; to give skilled nursing care and therapy; and to direct, supervise, and train others who assist in implementing and carrying out the nursing components of each patient's treatment plan.[40]

Most state nurse practice acts require that employers report to the state board that an employee holds a job as a licensed nurse.[41] As part of the hiring process, the nurse employee must produce his or her license and give the employer a copy. The administrator may verify the currentness of the license and that no questions about the license exist with the state board of nursing. Federal law requires that hospitals have a procedure to ensure that nursing personnel for whom licensure is required have valid and current licenses.[42]

During the application process, the potential employee indicates and grants permission to contact references. The applicant's permission alleviates allegations of breaches in confidentiality or invasion of privacy when the prospective employer contacts references and asks for information about the nurse's job performance and work habits. All previous jobs may be verified and checked by the nurse administrator.

The application form should be designed to avoid collection of information which is discriminatory in nature. Generally, the application may not solicit information about race, color, sex and marital status, age, religion, and national origin. If a prospective employee can show evidence of unlawful discrimination (did not get a job and is within a protected class), he or she may be successful in a lawsuit.[43]

The interview provides an opportunity for the employer and potential employee to review qualifications for the job and whether the applicant is suitable for employment. The employer may pose a wide spectrum of questions and situations to the applicant. However, as with the application form, the interviewer is prohibited from asking certain questions. Chapter 30 on employment claims provides detailed information about these areas. Generally, questions about child care, childbearing, marriage and sexual orientation, pregnancy, religion, race, gender, ethnic background, national origin, handicaps, physical or mental disability, arrest record, political affiliation, age, and retirement are areas to be avoided. However, under some circumstances, the job requires a qualification which might fall in these categories. These are permissible if the employer can show business necessity or that the qualification, for example, gender, is a bona fide occupational qualification (BFOQ). An example might be a job modeling women's clothes which would require the female gender and exclude males. As stated above, however, qualifications must be related to the job itself. Chapter 30 discusses nursing examples of BFOQs.

The nurse executive as recruiter and hirer of personnel for the department is an agent of the facility or health care program. The nurse executive is not the hired person's employer but is that employer's agent. The nurse administrator is not the *respondeat superior* of the employee. The agency, business or corporate entity itself is the vicarious liable *(respondeat superior)* party for any negligent actions of its employees, including the nursing executives.

Conditions and terms agreed upon during the interview and the entire hiring process by the nurse executive and the applicant may become part of the employment agreement. The executive is responsible for knowing to what extent the employer can deliver on what is promised the employee. The law of agency applies in the nurse executive and nurse employee relationship. Questions can be raised by the employee at a later time about what was said in an employment interview and the obligations of the employer that were created in that interview by the agent, the nurse administrator.

Generally speaking, however, most nurses do not have an employment contract. Nursing faculty are a general exception to this. All the elements of a contract, including a specified length of time for the employment (this is usually the element missing in nursing employment arrangements), must be certain. Some nurses are subject to collective bargaining agreements. If applicable, this would be the employee's contract. Otherwise, the nurse without a contract is terminable at will. Chapter 30 discusses this concept further.

All employee files, documentation, and records created and established during the hiring process (and throughout the employment period) are confidential. Employee privacy must be protected to the fullest, especially reports from any required medical examination.

WAGES AND SALARIES

Salaries differ according to geographic area, size, and type of health care agency. A recent study found that nursing executives, supervisors, and head nurse salaries ranged from $23,000 to over $60,000, general duty or staff nurse salaries vary from $19,200 to $27,100, a clinical nurse specialist's salary ranged from $23,000 to $38,000, an occupational health nurse's salary varied from $20,000 to $26,000, and a nurse anesthetist's salary ranged from $23,000 to $40,000.[44]

All states have wage and hour laws. Most states have adopted the federal laws regarding wages, including the minimum wage.[45] While adopting the federal minimum wage, other states have established a formula for state wage calculation based on the federal.[46] Wage and salary discrimination on the basis of sex is prohibited.[47]

There may also be specific state laws on hospital employees or other types of employees. For example, Connecticut requires that there be an agreement between the hospital and the employee before performance of work that 14 consecutive days in lieu of 7 consecutive days will be used to determine overtime compensation.[48] If an employee works more than 8 hours per day and more than 80 hours in 14 days the employee, by law, is to receive 1½ times the regular pay rate for that portion of overtime worked.[49]

In establishing salary and wage scales the nurse executive must be certain not to participate in any antitrust activities. For example, if nurse executives from several different health agencies discuss and agree upon nursing salaries to apply in their individual hiring processes, this would impede competition and be a potential antitrust violation. The Federal Trade Commission enforces the Federal Trade Commission Act[50] part of which states that unfair methods of competition in or affecting commerce and unfair or deceptive acts or practices in or affecting commerce are declared unlawful.[51] The commission has challenged concerted activities by health care providers and professional groups that have attempted to unlawfully influence (1) reimbursement policies, (2) hiring decisions of hospitals, (3) the establishment of professional practices on other than a fee-for-service basis, and (4) the dissemination of truthful information to the public.[52]

ASSIGNMENTS AND STAFFING

Minimum staffing requirements are determined legally for hospitals, skilled nursing facilities, and other health care agencies who choose to participate in federal funding for health services. Through federal regulations, known as conditions for participation, a hospital, for example, must have an organized nursing department, a licensed registered professional nurse on duty at all times, and professional nursing services available for all patients at all times.[53] Further, the regulations state that "there is an adequate number of licensed registered nurses to meet the following minimum staff requirements:

1. Director of the department
2. Assistant to the director for evening and night services
3. Supervisory and staff personnel for each department or nursing unit to insure the immediate availability of a registered professional nurse for bedside care of any patient when needed
4. Registered nurse on duty at all times and available for all patients on a 24-hour basis"[54]

The ratio of registered professional nurses to patients, together with the ratio of registered professional nurses to other nursing personnel, is to be adequate in order to provide proper supervision of patient care and staff performance, taking into consideration the characteristics of the patient load.[55]

Patient care assignments are to be made by registered professional nurses to other nursing personnel in accordance with the patient's needs and the preparation and competence of the nursing staff available.[56]

Governmental regulations for the skilled nursing facility require different staffing specifications. The nursing home must provide 24-hour service by licensed nurses, including the services of a registered nurse at least during the day tour on duty 7 days a week.[57] The 24-hour nursing service must be sufficient to meet total nursing needs and be in accordance with patient care policies developed by the facility.

Nursing personnel, including at least one registered nurse on the day tour of duty 7 days a week, licensed practical (vocational) nurses, nurse aides, orderlies, and ward clerks, are to be assigned duties consistent with their education and experience and based on the characteristics of the patient load. The regulations require that weekly time schedules be maintained which indicate the number and classifications of nursing personnel, including relief personnel, who worked each unit for each tour of duty.[58]

Regulations also require the skilled nursing facility to furnish the state surveying agency information from payroll records which set forth the average numbers and types of personnel (in full-time equivalents) on each tour of duty during at least 1 week of each quarter. The week is selected by the survey agency.[59]

Legal standards established through regulations (conditions for participation) for home health agencies also deal with assignments and staffing issues. In home health, staff are often under hourly or per visit contracts. An agency which uses such personnel is required to have a written contract with them. The regulations specify that the contract contain the following terms:

1. That patients are accepted for care only by the primary home health agency
2. The services to be provided
3. The necessity to conform to all applicable agency policies including personnel qualifications
4. The responsibility for participating in developing plans of treatment
5. The manner in which services will be controlled, coordinated, and evaluated by the primary agency
6. The procedures for submitting clinical and progress notes, scheduling visits, periodic patient evaluation
7. The procedures for determining charges and reimbursement[60]

Services provided by the home health agency (part-time or intermittent skilled nursing services and at least one of the following: physical, speech, occupational therapy, medical social services, or home health aide services) under arrangements must also be conducted through written contracts conforming to the above list of terms.[61]

The staffing pattern in psychiatric hospitals which participate in federal funding is to be such that ensures the availability of a registered professional nurse 24 hours each day for direct care, for supervising care performed by other nursing personnel, and for assigning nursing care activities not requiring the service of a professional nurse to other nursing service personnel according to each patient's needs and the preparation and competence of the nursing staff available.[62] The regulations further require that the number of registered nurses, including nurse consultants, be adequate to formulate in writing and assure that a nursing care plan for each patient is carried out.[63] State regulations based on state laws regulating health facilities may also mandate staff-patient ratios. For example, in Connecticut regulations governing hospital licensing specify that the ratio of patients to RNs on duty throughout the hospital will at no time exceed 25 patients to 1 RN.[64] Further, for all nursing personnel these regulations indicate that hospitals must have a 7 (patients) to 1 (nursing personnel) ratio from 7 AM to 7 PM and a 15 to 1 ratio from 7 PM to 7 AM.[65] A special staffing ratio is established for labor and delivery: the number of nursing personnel on duty each shift will be one half the average number of deliveries per day, based on the previous fiscal year.[66] Similar licensing regulations on staffing exist for other health facilities, such as nursing homes and mental retardation facilities.[67] Nursing administrators should be familiar with all state licensing regulations for their particular facilities.

Professionally, it has been recommended that staffing concerns be addressed using a system of assignment by patient acuity, alternative staffing resources such as matrix staffing, and use of per diem staff, either the facility's own pool or an outside supplemental staffing agency.[68]

Understaffing and dealing with staff who object to staffing decisions is an important area of concern for the nurse administrator. Generally, hospital and skilled nursing home nursing staffs have no employment contract, or if they do, the contract is a general one under which administration has the freedom to assign staff throughout the facility where they are needed. A staff nurse who considers an assignment unsafe and is incapable of meeting the needs of patients is legally and morally obligated to notify the supervisor of the unsafe situation.

Where staff nurses have collective contracts the nurse may be required to indicate to the administration and to the union that he or she has accepted an unsafe assignment despite the objection to it.[69] Regardless of the type of employment arrangement (contract or no contract), many staff nurses will document, either in memoranda to their own files or directly to the administration, the circumstances of assignments which they believe to be unsafe. Nursing administration must carefully evaluate understaffing and short staff situations and communicate their conclusions to higher agency administration. The corporate entity is ultimately responsible for all staffing decisions. In-between, however, nursing administrators must make reasonable assignments and are accountable for patient injuries if such occur as a result of negligent assignment decisions.

Use of temporary staff or supplemental staff from outside or from agency established pools of personnel can also raise special legal considerations. The arrangement with the outside agency is a contract. Written contracts should specify the terms of the agreement and indicate where legal responsibility lies for the supplemental staff person's negligence.

Organizing nursing services

The most important part of organizing nursing departments is having appropriate organizational, financial, and human resources. Designing programs and services to match the needs of the community is important. The health care facility's goals and mission determine the nursing department's goal and mission. Organizational issues such as the legal basis of the facility, bylaws, lines of authority, staff organizations, committee structure, and privileges are all important to defining legal responsibilities.

FINANCIAL RESOURCES

Federal regulations for funding through Medicare and federal and state regulations for funding through Medicaid have a large impact upon the financial resources of health care facilities and programs. The conditions for participation legally require that hospitals, skilled nursing facilities, home health agencies, and others have an annual operating budget and capital expenditure plan.[70] All anticipated income and expenses related to items which, under generally accepted accounting principles, would be considered income and expense items are to be included in the annual budget. The regulations indicate, however, that an item-by-item identification of the components of each type of income or expense is not required.[71]

Budgets are to be reviewed yearly and updated by the governing body of the health care agency or program.[72] Capital expenditures are deemed those which exceed $100,000. If the anticipated source of financing a capital expenditure is, in any part, the anticipated reimbursement from Title V (Maternal and Child Health and Crippled Children's Services) or Title XVIII (Health Insurance for the Aged and Disabled—Medicare) or Title XIX (Grants to States for Medical Assistance Programs) of the Social Security Act, the capital expenditure plan must state whether the expenditure is required to conform to legal requirements, whether it has been submitted to the designated planning agency for approval, and whether the planning agency has approved or disapproved the proposed expenditure.[73]

According to federal regulation, the overall financial plan and budget of an agency is to be prepared under the direction of the governing body of the facility or program by a committee consisting of representatives of the governing body, the administrative staff, and the medical staff.[74]

The financial and tax status of the health care agency determines how profits are handled. The governmental (federal, state, and local) agencies, those which are tax supported, and other nonprofit agencies must return all profits to the services and agency. Proprietary or for-profit, private agencies and programs distribute their profits to the shareholders or owner-investors of the corporation.

Agencies and facilities which accept Medicare and Medicaid funding are subject to antifraud and abuse laws.[75] These laws and regulations do the following:

1. Prohibit false statements and representations
2. Make it illegal to solicit or receive remuneration for referring an individual for a service
3. Make it illegal to solicit or receive remuneration for purchasing, leasing, ordering, or arranging for or recommending purchasing, leasing, ordering any goods, facility, service, or item for which payment may be made in whole or part from Medicare or Medicaid funds
4. Prohibit false statements or representations with respect to institutions in order that the institution may qualify (certification)
5. Prohibit violation of assignment terms, if any

In addition, those eligible for reimbursement (e.g., hospitals, home health agencies, skilled nursing facilities, and individual health care providers) will be excluded from participation in Medicare or Medicaid reimbursement programs for the following reasons:

1. Making a false statement in request for payment
2. Providing services substantially in excess of the beneficiary's needs or providing services which do not meet professionally recognized standards
3. Submitting bills for payment substantially in excess of customary charges or costs[76]

Civil and criminal penalties may be levied against one found in violation of these antifraud and abuse statutes and regulations. Nurse administrators will want to avoid participation in fraud, misrepresentation, and overcharging.

PROGRAMS AND SERVICES

Organizational issues, such as the legal status of the organization, the administrative structure, bylaws, and staff organization, also lead to some legal questions and concerns for the nurse executive. The organization determines the role, mission, and objectives of the nursing department.

Most health care agencies, hospitals, nursing homes, home health agencies, and health departments are organized under state corporation laws. Their formation must follow state corporation statutes and state and federal tax laws.

Generally, a board of directors or trustees is the governing body of the agency, although some facilities may not have an organized governing body. The conditions for participation, the federal financing regulations, establish that hospitals have an effective governing body legally responsible for the conduct of the hospital as an institution. The regulations indicate that if a hospital does not have an organized governing body, the persons legally responsible for the conduct of the hospital carry out the functions of the governing body cited in the regulations.[77]

The governing body of a hospital adopts bylaws, appoints members of the medical staff, appoints a qualified hospital administrator or other chief executive officer who acts as the executive officer of the governing body, is responsible for the management of the hospital, and provides liaison among the governing body, medical staff, nursing staff, and others. The governing body is responsible for establishing a policy which requires that every patient be under the care of a physician, providing a physical plant equipped and staffed to maintain the needed facilities and services for patients, and preparing an overall plan and budget.[78]

Similarly, home health agencies and skilled nursing facilities are required to have governing bodies which effectively function with full legal authority and responsibility for the agency. Nursing homes and home health agencies, according to federal regulations, must disclose their ownership.[79] The regulations specify that the home health agency governing body appoints a qualified administrator, arranges for professional advice, adopts and periodically reviews written bylaws or an acceptable equivalent, and oversees the management and fiscal affairs of the agency.[80]

The skilled nursing facility is required to have a governing body which adopts and enforces rules and regulations relative to health care and safety of patients, to the protection of patients' personal and property rights, and to the general operation of the facility. This governing body is also required to adopt effective patient care policies and administrative policies and bylaws governing the operation of the facility.

Further, the governing body of the skilled nursing facility must establish written policies regarding the rights and responsibilities of patients and, through the administrator, is responsible for development of, and adherence to, procedures implementing such policies. Chapter 17 describes in more detail the patient rights of nursing home residents.

Bylaws of hospitals typically do the following:

1. Stipulate the basis upon which members are selected, their terms of office, and their duties and requirements
2. Specify to whom responsibilities for operation and maintenance of the hospital, including evaluation of hospital practices, may be delegated and the methods established by the governing body for holding such individuals responsible
3. Provide for the designation of necessary officers, their terms of office, and their duties and for the organization of the governing body into essential committees
4. Specify the frequency of meetings
5. Provide for the appointment of members of the medical staff
6. Provide mechanisms for the formal approval of the organization, bylaws, rules, and regulations of the medical staff and its departments in the hospital[81]

Federal regulations require that the hospital medical staff organization be formed under bylaws approved by the governing body and be responsible to the governing body of the hospital for the quality of all medical care provided patients and for the ethical and professional practices of its members.[82]

Regulations refer to the hospital nursing department without mentioning nursing staff bylaws. Medicine and nursing within the hospital are organized very differently. However, as mentioned in Chapters 23, 29, and 33, chapters on advanced nursing practice and nursing businesses, nurses are applying for medical staff privileges within hospitals. The nurse executive in a hospital should be well versed in the staff privileges available within the facility. In addition, the nurse executive may want to organize the nursing department as a nursing staff under its own staff bylaws, similar to the medical staff.

The medical staff bylaws are the mechanism through which the medical staff is self-governing and self-regulating. Federal regulations require that medical staff bylaws, rules, and regulations include the following:

1. A descriptive outline of the medical staff organization
2. A statement of the necessary qualifications which physicians must possess to be privileged to work in the hospital and of the duties and privileges of each category of medical staff
3. A procedure for granting and withdrawing privileges to physicians
4. A mechanism for appeal of decisions regarding medical staff membership and privileges
5. A definite and specific statement forbidding the practice of the division of fees under any guise whatsoever
6. Provision for regular meetings of the medical staff
7. Provision for keeping accurate and complete clinical records
8. A statement to the effect that the physician in charge of the patient is responsible for seeing that all tissue removed at operation is delivered to the hospital pathologist and that a routine examination and report is made of such tissue
9. Provision for routine examination of all patients upon admission and recording of preoperative diagnosis prior to surgery
10. A ruling permitting a surgical operation only on consent of the patient or the patient's legal representative, except in emergencies
11. A statement providing that, except in emergency, consultation is required as outlined above
12. A regulation requiring that physicians' orders be recorded and signed
13. If dentists and oral surgeons are to be admitted to staff membership, the necessary qualifications, status, privileges, and rights of this group[83]

Several organizational aspects of the hospital nursing department which are federal law have been discussed earlier in this chapter. In addition, federal regulation mandates that there be a well-established working relationship between nursing and other services of the hospital, both administrative and professional. The regulations indicate that this requirement is based upon the following:

1. That registered professional nurses confer with physicians relative to patient care
2. That interdepartment policies affecting nursing services and nursing care to patients be made jointly with the director of nursing
3. That there be established procedures for scheduling laboratory and x-ray examinations; for ordering, securing, and maintaining supplies and equipment needed for patient care; and for ordering diets[84]

Nursing departments are to have staff meetings at

least monthly to discuss patient care, nursing service problems, and administrative policies.[85] Minutes of all meetings are kept and are to be available to staff members.

Leading the nursing department

Providing direction and programs that assure the development and productive performance of the nursing department personnel is an important responsibility of the nurse executive.[86] Leading encompasses supervising and managing nursing care and the personnel who carry out that care. Nurse executives are personally responsible for the reasonable exercise of their own supervision activities. While leading the department, the nurse executive is privy to evaluative information about the staff. Acting upon that information in a reasonable manner is part of the nurse executive's legal responsibility.

SUPERVISION

A legal definition of supervision is provided in the federal conditions for participation. The regulations define supervision as the authoritative procedural guidance by a qualified person for the accomplishment of a function or activity with initial direction and periodic inspection of the actual act of accomplishing the function or activity.[87]

Responsibilities for others through supervision of direct and indirect patient care can involve allegations of negligence and malpractice. While filling in during a short staffing situation, a nursing supervisor was found negligent for a medication error.[88] This case is an example of a supervisor's responsibility when providing direct patient care.

Another nursing supervisor was found negligent for delay in notifying a physician of the change in a patient's signs and symptoms,[89] another situation where the supervisor assumed direct patient care responsibilities. When involved in direct patient care, the supervisor will be reviewed similarly to any other nurse who provides direct care.

A supervisor's assignment of staff nurses has been the subject of litigation. In one case the nursing supervisor's assignment of two nurses to the operating room was questioned. The supervisor's knowledge about the staff, including their competence to fulfill the assigned tasks, was reviewed.[90] The court found that there was no evidence to support the allegation of negligent assignment.

In a case involving a physician who was chairperson of the hospital medical department, a member of whom treated a patient, the court held that the physician could be sued for failing to provide proper supervision of members of the department and for failure to develop and implement appropriate rules and regulations governing quality of staff available to care for and provide good and prudent care to patients.[91]

By analogy, this case indicates that nurse executives also could be sued for their negligence if they fail to provide proper supervision for members of their departments, and for failure to establish and implement policies which govern the quality of such staff and the care they deliver.

In a rather startling $3.6 million judgment for malpractice against a physician and a psychiatric hospital, the Director of Nursing ordered the entire staff who charted the plaintiff's care to rewrite and change hospital records pertaining to the care in question.[92] The original record was surreptitiously removed, and a ''revised'' record was substituted without the knowledge of the hospital administration and in violation of an explicit hospital policy. Substitution of the records was known to the jury, and the higher court held that the court properly instructed the jury that they could consider the substitution a circumstance indicating the defendant's consciousness of negligence.[93]

These cases involved the negligence of executives and supervisors for their own independent responsibilities. Where staff, not the supervisor, are liable for negligent acts, it is not the supervisor who is the *respondeat superior,* or the vicariously liable party, but the entity or corporation itself. The executive's or supervisor's employer, the corporate entity or association, would also be vicariously responsible for the supervisor's negligence. The nursing supervisor is a co-employee of the staff nurse.

An important condition for participation regulation for hospitals that are involved in Medicare reimbursement pertains to physician availability to the nursing staff. The regulation states that a physician should be on duty or on call at all times and available within 15 to 20 minutes.[94]

The corporate entity has its own independent responsibilities and liabilities. For example, a hospital has a duty to enforce its policies[95] and a duty to monitor the treatment of its patients and to intervene if there is obvious negligence.[96]

The ability of an employee to sue his or her supervisor is the subject of state legislation. In Maryland, a supervisor (who is the co-employee of the employee) is subject to liability, but only for negligently breaching a duty of care personally owed the employee.[97] Depending on the facts the employee may also sue the employer and third parties, if applicable.

MANAGING CONTRACTS

Nurse executives and administrators are involved in negotiating and managing many contracts with individuals, such as employees, consultants, and independent contractors, and with collective entities, such as nursing unions. Chapter 31 provides the nurse executive an important review of legal issues involved with collective bargaining and union activities, including unfair labor practices to be avoided. Chapter 20 features content about contracts between clinical agencies and schools for student placement, nursing research activities, joint practice, and other service and education relationships.

Evaluating nursing services and personnel

Assessing whether department goals, services and needs of the community are met is another important step in the management process. Legal concerns in this area pertain to risk management, quality assurance, and legal requirements for utilization review; to recommendations about nursing personnel; and to termination of employees.

Generally, state laws may prohibit certain methods of evaluation. For example, the use of electronic surveillance devices for the purpose of monitoring activities of employees, intentionally overhearing, or recording conversations pertaining to employment contract negotiations is prohibited in Connecticut.[98]

RISK MANAGEMENT AND QUALITY ASSURANCE

Chapters 26 and 28 in this book are devoted to the topics of risk management and quality assurance. Information is provided about audits, incident reports, and staff development, to name a few of the topics. Evaluating nursing services and care as part of the overall evaluation of the agency is required by federal conditions of participation in Medicare. Many such conditions were highlighted earlier in the chapter. Nurse administrators are responsible for overseeing these activities as they pertain to the nursing department.

Just as activities related to establishing salaries may involve antitrust laws, so, too, may standard setting and quality assurance activities. General opinion seems to be that most quality assurance activity can pass antitrust scrutiny, since, if they are not overbroad, they may serve to improve the market and thereby enhance competition.[99]

RECOMMENDATIONS

Giving and obtaining recommendations is an essential part of the hiring and evaluation process. The handling of personnel files as confidential documents is imperative to successful management. With the employee's permission a reference or recommendation can be provided, in either a verbal or written form. Concerns over possible invasion of privacy and defamation can be dealt with when proper steps are taken. The concern usually arises when negative references are given.

Statements made about employee performance, based upon factual, objective, well-documented, and substantiated data are appropriate. Employee evaluation data should come as no surprise to the employee, if the employee is kept well informed and is evaluated at regular intervals during the employment.

State laws govern personnel files and recommendations. For example, in Connecticut employees have access to personnel files. Employers are required to keep files until a year after employment termination.[100] Employees may remove or correct information in personnel files.[101] The removal may be by agreement, or the employee may submit a written statement to accompany any transmittal or disclosure to third parties. Additionally, no individually identifiable information contained in personnel files of any employee shall be disclosed without written authorization of that employee.[102]

However, exceptions do exist. Information may be released where it is limited to the verification of dates of employment and the employee's title, position, and wage or salary or where the disclosure is required by law (e.g., search warrant or subpeona), by a law enforcement agency (limited to the employee's home address and date of attendance at work), in response to a medical emergency, or to comply with laws and regulations. In Connecticut, by statute, employees have a right to obtain copies of all or part of their personnel files.[103]

State laws may place fines on employers for blacklisting or may prohibit intentionally inaccurate employment references. However, these laws do not apply to truthful statements of facts concerning the employee.[104] Only laws of two states were presented here. The best practice is for the nurse executive to discuss his or her own state labor code with legal counsel for the employer.

TERMINATING EMPLOYMENT

Acting upon negative personnel evaluations can be problematical, but without action, the administrator and the facility may be acting unreasonably. As noted before, the agency is responsible for employees' actions. Hence, the importance of knowing the competency and skills of employees and how they match the assigned tasks is for the employer's benefit and should assure safe patient care.

Termination of employment is generally justified when an employee refuses work assignments; the termination is based upon below standard work performance or involves falsification of an application; or there are business reasons, for example, the employer's economic problems. Unjust firings are those involving sex discrimination, pregnancy, medical conditions, age, political beliefs, or union activity. Employers must make reasonable accommodations for religious practices of employees unless the employer can show that it creates an undue hardship to the efficient running of the business.[105]

Wrongful termination, however, should be avoided. Following the established, written personnel policies of a facility is the cornerstone of permissible termination. Employment claims are the subject of Chapter 30 and should be reviewed by the nurse administrator. Hospitals have been held liable to former employees for failure to properly investigate charges against the employee prior to termination.[106]

Nursing supervisors have been among those being discharged for reasons other than bona fide causes or business reasons. In an action by a 62-year-old day-shift nurse supervisor against a hospital for age discrimination, the following evidence sufficiently established that the supervisor was terminated with discriminatory intent of the hospital administrator, that he:

1. Expressed surprise at the longevity of the hospital staff
2. Indicated that the hospital needed "new blood"
3. Intended to recruit younger physicians and nurses
4. Stated that the nursing supervisor's "advanced age" caused stress during employment
5. Failed to interview and investigate complaints
6. Approved the appointment of two people 15 years younger than the supervisor to take the supervisor's place[107]

As mentioned before and discussed in Chapter 30, most nursing personnel, including supervisors, are "at will" employees, meaning that the employee may be terminated at the will of the employer, without cause. However, several exceptions exist within the law. These are discussed at length in Chapter 30.

Drugs and alcohol in the workplace are growing concerns to managers. The incidence of nurse chemical dependency is 50% higher than in the general population.[108] One in seven nurses is at risk.[109] Managers responsible for employee job performance must be aware of warning signs and develop policies on the steps to deal with the problem and ensure patient safety. There are many options other than terminating employment available to employers, such as developing employee assistance programs or participating in peer assistance programs through nursing associations.

Employment policies that mandate screening for drugs and alcohol, AIDS, and other communicable diseases raise special legal and ethical concerns. This highly volatile issue has multiple dimensions. The primary reasons offered by businesses, including hospital and health care agencies, for drug screening is that it will reduce drug abuse in the workplace, improve the health of workers, protect the public and other employees, and preserve and improve the quality of products and services. At the present time there is no federal or state constitutional provision that directly prohibits the use of substance abuse detection programs. However, the violation of the employee's privacy is a primary concern. But employers have a duty to ensure that employees perform their jobs competently. So, if alcohol use or illegal drug use reduces job performance and endangers co-workers, the employer has adequate legal grounds for tests or screening.[110]

Generally, the handicap and disability discrimination laws prohibit inquiries as to whether a job applicant suffers from AIDS.[111] However, for health care employers physical examinations can be required; having AIDS cannot be a basis for job termination or refusal *unless* the condition is job related and substantially interferes with the person's ability to do the job.[112]

It is law in many states that nursing administrators report actions or conditions of employee nurses that might be grounds for action within the state nursing practice act by the state board of nursing.[113] These statutes proved that an individual who acts without malice is not civilly liable for making a report.

A recent Florida case elaborates on these nursing administration duties and responsibilities. In this case a home health agency nursing supervisor terminated a staff nurse's employment for providing inadequate treatment and inaccurate charting and for falsifying mileage claims.[114] Two months later at a seminar on the legal aspects of nursing the nursing supervisor learned of the law in Florida obligating a nurse to report potential violations of the nursing practice act. After discussing the matter with the home health agency head, the nursing supervisor notified the board of nursing of the staff nurse's termination.

During the investigation, confidentiality was maintained. The staff nurse was notified of the investigation. At the conclusion, the staff nurse was advised by the board that there was no probable cause and that the case would be closed. Shortly thereafter, the staff nurse instituted this case against the nursing supervisor and home health agency for malicious prosecution.

Malicious prosecution is an action which requires proof of six elements: (1) commencement or continuation of an original criminal or civil proceeding, (2) its legal causation by the present defendant against the plaintiff who was defendant in the original proceeding, (3) its bona fide termination in favor of the present plaintiff, (4) absence of probable cause for the proceeding, (5) presence of malice, and (6) damages.

The court held that (1) a confidential investigation conducted by the board of nursing was a quasijudicial proceeding; (2) evidence did not establish lack of probable cause, so that such determination presented question of law for the court; and (3) evidence was insufficient to establish that either the nursing supervisor or home health agency was motivated more by desire to harm the nurse than by obligation to report circumstances of a staff nurse's termination, so that requisite malice was not established.

The state investigator for the board of nursing testified that it is expected that employers of nurses will report all terminations of employment involving questionable nursing activity, as well as the reasons. The Florida Board of Nursing filed an *amicus curiae* brief (friend of the court) which not only pointed out that a significant amount of disciplinary cases are filed as a result of complaints made by directors of nursing or other employers, but also that the reporting requirement was intended to protect the public and that civil immunity was granted to the reporter as an encouragement to report, which in turns improves nursing services.

Stressed in the above case, confidentiality was maintained. Confidentiality is also important when working with an impaired nurse. Mandating treatment as condition for employment is an option. What the manager can know about the nurse's treatment while in a rehabilitation program is protected by confidentiality. Yet, the manager may know that the worker is enrolled, attending, and progressing through the program. Chapter 25 discusses licensure revocation, including the issues of drug and alcohol abuse, the criminal activity of stealing drugs, and the reporting of such activity to state boards of nursing by nurse administrators.

Standards of care

The standards of organized nursing services developed by the American Nurses' Association are presented in the box (p. 348). In addition the ANA has nursing administration certification programs which are available to nursing administrators, consultants, and educators engaged in nursing service administration at the middle managment or executive level on a full-time or part-time basis. The program includes two levels of certification, nursing administration and nursing administration, advanced.[115]

The Joint Commission on Accreditation of Hospitals has established standards for nursing services, as followed:

1. Nursing department assignments in the provision of nursing care shall be commensurate with the qualifications of nursing personnel and shall be designed to meet the nursing care needs of patients.
2. Individualized, goal-directed nursing care shall be provided to patients through the use of the nursing process.
3. Written policies and procedures that reflect optimal standards of nursing practice shall guide the provision of nursing care.[116]

The state nursing practice act and the scope of nursing it defines apply to the practice of nursing administration. Many state boards of nursing have the power to establish regulations which define the practice of expanded roles within nursing, including nursing administration. For example, the Maryland State Board of Nurse Examiners accepted in 1984 standards of practice for nurse administrators.[117]

Recommendations and trends

Because of these and other factors, nurse administrators face immense challenges. One nurse executive recently suggested strategies for maintaining quality of care while recognizing the need to economize. These strategies included costing nursing services according to diagnostic related groups (DRGs), the prospective payment system adopted by Medicare and some insurance companies for most hospitals; developing generic care plans; hiring an all registered nurse staff; computerizing patient management information systems to streamline documentation; and using group teaching and group discharge instruction and developing videotape packages of nursing programs and information.[118]

This author also suggested that innovative ways of delivering nursing services must be developed. Strategies to consider include developing levels of nursing care within the facility where the patient may select to stay on a self-help unit, collaborative family-care unit, hotel unit, or the regular patient-care unit. Other strategies included increasing the use of ambulatory services and expanding hospital services into home care, hospices, health maintenance organizations, long-term care, respite and day-care services. Marketing and community outreach and assessment are now identified as important nurse executive responsibilities.

These innovations represent new legal issues and considerations. Questions of liability and responsibility among health care providers and patients in new health care arrangements will be settled using principles discussed throughout this book. New laws and legal principles will emerge, as well, to address these changes. Nurse managers should have conferences with agency legal counsel on a regular basis.

Endnotes

1. P. DRUCKER, MANAGING IN TURBULENT TIMES (1980).
2. Poulin, *The Nurse Executive Role: A Structural and Functional Analysis* 14 J. NURS. ADMIN. 9 (1984).
3. AMERICAN NURSES' ASSOCIATION, STANDARDS FOR ORGANIZED NURSING SERVICES 10 (1982). (hereinafter cited as *ANA Standards*)
4. *Id.*
5. *ANA Standards, supra* note 3, at 8.
6. Simms, Price, Pfoutz, *Nurse Executives: Functions and Priorities,* 3 NURS. ECON. 238 (July/August 1985); *see also* AMERICAN NURSES' ASSOCIATION, ROLES, RESPONSIBILITIES, AND QUALIFICATIONS FOR NURSE ADMINISTRATORS (1978), which lists similar responsibilities.
7. *Id.* at 240.
8. 42 C.F.R. §405.1124(a) and 405.1121(h) (1985).
9. *See, e.g.,* recent issues of journals for nurse administrators: JOURNAL OF NURSING ADMINISTRATION, NURSING ADMINISTRATION QUARTERLY, NURSING MANAGEMENT (formerly, SUPERVISOR NURSE), and NURSING ECONOMICS.
10. NATIONAL CENTER FOR HEALTH STATISTICS, DEPARTMENT OF HEALTH AND HUMAN RESOURCES, HEALTH, UNITED STATES 3 (1984).
11. *Id.*
12. *Id.*
13. *Id.*
14. *Id.*
15. *Id.* at 59.
16. 42 C.F.R. §405.1011 (1985); Authority: 42 U.S.C. §1302, 1320c-3(a)(10), 1395x(e), (f), (g), (k), 1395hh, 1395ww (1982).
17. 42 C.F.R. §405.1101 (1985); Authority: 42 U.S.C. §1302, 1395f, 1395k, 1395l, 1395x, 1395z, 1395bb, 1395cc, 1395hh (1982).
18. 42 C.F.R. §110 and 417 (1985); Authority: 42 U.S.C. 300e, 1302, 1395l(a)(1)(A), 1395hh, 1395kk, 1395mm (1982).
19. 42 C.F.R. §418.1 (1985); Authority: 42 U.S.C. 1302, 1395c-1395f, 1395x-1395cc, 1395hh (1982).
20. 42 C.F.R. §405.1201 (1985); Authority: 42 U.S.C. §1302, 1395u, 1395x, 1395y, 1395gg, 1395hh (1982).
21. 42 C.F.R. §405.2100 (1985).
22. 42 C.F.R. §405.1024(a) (1985).
23. CONN. GEN. STAT. ANN. §31-51g (West Supp. 1985); MD. ANN. CODE art. 100, §95 (1985).
24. *Griggs v. Duke Power Co.,* 401 U.S. 424 (1971).
25. 42 C.F.R. §405.1024(e) (1985).
26. *Id.*
27. *See, e.g.,* CONN. GEN. STAT. ANN. §31-51k (West Supp. 1985).
28. *See, e.g., Howe v. Medical Arts Central Hospital,* 261 A.D. 1088 (N.Y. 1941).
29. *See,* EQUAL EMPLOYMENT OPPORTUNITY COMMISSION, UNIFORM GUIDELINES ON EMPLOYEE SELECTION PROCEDURES (1978); 29 C.F.R. §1607 (1985); EEOC, GUIDE TO PRE-EMPLOYMENT INQUIRIES, 8 F.E.P. MANUAL (BNA); OHIO CIVIL RIGHTS COMMITTEE'S GUIDE FOR APPLICATION FORMS AND INTERVIEWS, 8A F.E.P. MANUAL (BNA); C. ROBERSON, STAYING OUT OF COURT: A MANAGER'S GUIDE TO EMPLOYMENT LAW (1985).
30. 42 C.F.R. §405.1221(e) (1985).
31. 42 C.F.R. §405.1121(g) (1985).
32. *Id.*
33. *Id.*
34. 42 C.F.R. §405.1024(e)(5) (1985).
35. 42 C.F.R. §405.1032 (1985).
36. 42 C.F.R. §405.1032(b)(2) (1985).
37. 42 C.F.R. §405.1033 (1985).
38. 42 C.F.R. §405.1033(a)(1) and (3) (1985).
39. 42 C.F.R. §405.1038(d) (1985).
40. *Id.*
41. *See, e.g.,* MD. HEALTH OCC. CODE ANN. §7-505 (1986) where each employer shall report periodically to the Board (of Nursing) the name and license number of each licensee employed or placed to practice registered nursing or licensed practical nursing. *See, also,* discussion below on *Northwest Home Health Agency v. Merrill,* 469 So.2d 893 (Fla. App. 1st Dist. 1985).
42. 42 C.F.R. §405.1024(e)(4) (1985).
43. *See, e.g., Albermarle Paper Co. v. Moody,* 422 U.S. 405 (1975). Chapter 30 gives further information on this topic.
44. ROTH YOUNG WAGE AND SALARY REVIEW (1985) cited in *New Hats for Nurses,* The New York Times Advertising Supp., Health and Medicine Employment Outlook 14 (Nov. 3, 1985).
45. *See, e.g.,* MD. ANN. CODE art. 100, §81-93A and §83 (1985).
46. *See, e.g.,* CONN. GEN. STAT. ANN. §31-58(j) which requires that the Connecticut minimum wage be 1½% higher than the federal minimum wage.
47. Not only by federal law, as discussed in Chapter 30, Employment Claims, but also by state law. *See, e.g.,* MD. ANN. CODE art

100, §55A (1985); CONN. GEN. STAT. ANN. §31-75 (West 1972).
48. CONN. GEN. STAT. ANN. 31-76h (West Supp. 1985).
49. For further discussion of this, *see,* Mech, Mills, Arnold, *Wage and Hour Laws: Their Impact on 12-Hour Scheduling* 14 J. NURS. ADMIN. 24 (March 1984).
50. 15 U.S.C. §41 *et seq.* (1982).
51. 15 U.S.C. §45(a)(1).
52. Pollard and Schultheiss, *FTC and the Professions: Continuing Controversy* 1 NURS. ECON. 158, 159 (November-December 1983).
53. 42 C.F.R. §405.1024 (1985).
54. 42 C.F.R. §405.1024(b) (1985).
55. 42 C.F.R. §405.1024(b)(3) (1985).
56. 42 C.F.R. §405.1024(b)(4) (1985).
57. 42 C.F.R. §405.1124 (1985).
58. 42 C.F.R. §405.1124(c) (1985).
59. 42 C.F.R. §405.1121(b) (1985).
60. 42 C.F.R. §405.1221(f) (1985).
61. 42 C.F.R. §405.1221(h) (1985).
62. 42 C.F.R. §405.1038(d)(2) (1985).
63. 42 C.F.R. §405.1038(d)(3) (1985).
64. CONN. AGENCIES REGS. §19-13-D3(e)(2) (1985).
65. *Id.*
66. *Id.* at §19-13-D3(e)(5).
67. *Id.* at §19-13-D8t, §19a-467-14.
68. Sovie, *Managing Nursing Resources in a Constrained Economic Environment* 3 NURS. ECON. 85 (March-April 1985).
69. *See, e.g.,* California Nurses' Association, Assignment Despite Objection Form, which provides the nurse the opportunity to document objections to the assignment, such as, not oriented to unit, not trained or experienced in assigned area, not given adequate staff for acuity, transferred or admitted new patient to unit without adequate staff, given an assignment which posed a serious threat to my health or safety. The form provides space for the staffing count, patient census, and a statement of the problem. Copies go to the nursing supervisor and the CNA office, and one is retained by the staff nurse. Other state nurse's associations provide similar mechanisms under collective bargaining agreements.
70. 42 C.F.R. §405.1121(f) (1985) (Skilled Nursing Facilities); 42 C.F.R. §405.1221(i) (1985) (Home Health Agencies); 42 C.F.R. §405.1021(j) (1985) (Hospitals). *See also* Health Maintenance Organizations and Competitive Medical Plans, 42 C.F.R. §417 (1985), discussing contract requirements, cost-basis and risk-basis, principles of reimbursement.
71. *Id.*
72. *Id.*
73. *Id.* The regulation states that the capital expenditure plan must be submitted to the planning agency pursuant to 42 U.S.C. 1320a-1 (1982).
74. *Id.*
75. 42 U.S.C. §1302, 1320a-7, 1395y(d), 1395y(e), 1395cc(b)(2)(D), (E) and (F), 1935hh, 1396a(a)(39), 1396b(i)(2) (1982); and regulations 42 C.F.R. §420 (1985).
76. 42 C.F.R. §420.101 (1985).
77. 42 C.F.R. §405.1021 (1985).
78. 42 C.F.R. §405.1021 (a)—(j) (1985); *See also* case law such as *Sibley v. Board of Supervisors of Louisiana State Univ.,* 477 S.2d 1094 (La. 1985), holding that a hospital's governing board may be held independently liable for failure to (1) furnish reasonably adequate equipment, supplies, appliances, and facilities; (2) provide adequate procedures for maintenance of safety and sanitation; and (3) select employees with reasonable care.
79. 42 C.F.R. §405.1121(a) and 42 C.F.R. §420.206 (1985) (Nursing Homes); 42 C.F.R. §405.1221(b) (1985) (Home Health Agencies—the name and address of each officer, director, and owner are disclosed).
80. 42 C.F.R. §405.1221(b) (1985).
81. 42 C.F.R. §405.1021(a) (1985).
82. 42 C.F.R. §405.1023 (1985).
83. 42 C.F.R. §405.1023(i) (1985).
84. 42 C.F.R. §405.1024(f) (1985).
85. 42 C.F.R. §405.1024(h) (1985).
86. AMERICAN NURSES' ASSOCIATION, ROLES, RESPONSIBILITIES, AND QUALIFICATIONS FOR NURSE ADMINISTRATORS (1978).
87. 42 C.F.R. §405.1101(u) (1985) (Skilled Nursing Facilities); 42 C.F.R. §405.1202(y) (1985) (Home Health Agencies). *See also* 42 C.F.R. §417.207 (1985) where health maintenance organizations for services provided must meet conditions for participation of that service, e.g. hospital, skilled nursing facility, home health agency and a standard exists which states that an HMO's health delivery system must provide for supervision by a physician. The HMO must demonstrate that services provided by it through other health care professionals are provided under the direct supervision of a physician, that the physician is present to perform medical rather than administrative services at all times that the HMO clinics are open, and that each patient is under the care of a physician.
88. *Norton v. Argonaut Insurance Co.,* 144 So.2d 249 (La. 1962).
89. *Lewis v. Davis,* 410 N.E.2d 1363 (Ind. App. 1980); *Valentin v. La Societe Francaise de Bien Faisance Muteulle de Los Angeles* 172 P.2d 359 (Cal. App. 1946).
90. *Bowers v. Olch,* 260 P.2d 997 (Cal. App. 1953).
91. *Maxwell v. Cole,* 482 N.Y.S.2d 1000 (N.Y. 1984).
92. *Pisel v. Stamford Hospital,* 430 A.2d 1 (Conn. 1980).
93. *Id.* at 6.
94. 42 C.F.R. §405.1021(h)(2) (1985).
95. *Williams v. St. Claire Medical Center,* 657 S.W.2d 590 (Ky. App. 1983); *See also* case mentioned in note 74, *supra.*
96. *Schoening v. Grays Harbor Community Hospital,* 698 P.2d 593 (Wash. App. 1985).
97. MD. ANN. CODE art. 100, §58 (1985); *But, see, Athas v. Hill,* 476 A.2d 710 (Md. 1984) which held that §58 does not authorize the employee to sue the supervisor for negligently discharging the employer's duty to provide a safe workplace.
98. CONN. GEN. STAT. ANN. §31-48b (West Supp. 1985).
99. OFFICE OF POLICY PLANNING, FEDERAL TRADE COMMISSION, ANTITRUST AND THE HEALTH PROFESSIONS 67, 69 (July 1981).
100. CONN. GEN. STAT. ANN. §31-128a (West Supp. 1985).
101. *Id.* at §31-128e.
102. *Id.* at §31-128f.
103. *Id.* at §31-128g.
104. CONN. GEN. STAT. ANN. §31-51 (West Supp. 1985); CAL. LAB. CODE §1050, 1053, 1054 (West 1985).
105. 42 U.S.C. §2000e(j) (1982).
106. *Crenshaw v. Bozeman Deaconess Hospital,* 693 P.2d 487 (Mont. 1984).

107. *Buckley v. Hospital Corporation of America, Inc.*, 758 F.2d 1525 (11th Cir. 1985).
108. Kapp, *Chemical Dependency, Helping Your Staff* 14 J. NURS. ADMIN. 18 (November 1984).
109. Beck and Buckley, *Taking Drugs on the Job: Nurses with Bad Habits* NEWSWEEK 54 (August 1983).
110. L. DOGOLOFF, R. ANGAROLA, & S. PRICE, URINE TESTING IN THE WORKPLACE (AMER. COUNCIL DRUG. ED. 1985); Chineson, Mandatory Drug Testing: *An Invasion of Privacy?* TRIAL 91 (Sept. 1986)
111. 29 U.S.C. §791 (1982) prohibits recipients of federal financial assistance (e.g., Medicare funds) from discriminating in employment on the basis of a handicap. See *Arline v. School Board of Nassau County,* 772 F.2d 759 (11th Cir. 1985), *cert. granted,* 54 L.W. 3687 (1986), holding that a teacher suffering from tuberculosis (a contagious disease), enjoys the protections of this statute)
112. On Aug. 5, 1986, the Office of Civil Rights completed its investigation of a complaint filed by a nurse in North Carolina, complaining that he had been placed on involuntary leave of absence, without pay, for a handicap for which the employer (hospital) failed to provide the nurse with reasonable accommodations (Complaint No. 04-84-3096, OFFICE FOR CIVIL RIGHTS, Dept. of Health & Human Services). In May, 1984, the nurse was concerned about sight loss, fatigue, and a recent needle stick he had suffered while giving an injection to a patient who had been exposed to the AIDS virus. He requested an examination and the physician determined that the nurse suffered from symptoms of AIDS. The hospital removed him from his position and would not assign him to any other job. The Office of Civil Rights charged the hospital with illegal discrimination for their decision not to reevaluate the nurse's employment status.)
113. *See, e.g.,* MD. HEALTH OCC. CODE ANN. §7-506 (1986); FLA. STAT. ANN. §464.018(1)(i) and 455.225(10) (West Supp. 1985).
114. *Northwest Florida Home Health Agency v. Merrill,* 469 So.2d 893 (Fla. App. 1985).
115. AMERICAN NURSES' ASSOCIATION, CERTIFICATION CATALOG (1986).
116. JOINT COMMISSION ON ACCREDITATION OF HOSPITALS, JOINT COMMISSION ON ACCREDITATION OF HOSPITALS MANUAL FOR 1985 (1984). *See, also,* AMERICAN HOSPITAL ASSOCIATION, THE ROLE OF THE NURSING SERVICE ADMINISTRATION IN HEALTH CARE INSTITUTIONS (1977) and publications of the AMERICAN ORGANIZATION OF NURSE EXECUTIVES.
117. MARYLAND STATE BOARD OF EXAMINERS OF NURSES, STANDARDS OF PRACTICE FOR NURSE ADMINISTRATORS (1984).
118. Sovie, *Managing Nursing Resources in a Constrained Economic Environment* 3 NURS. ECON. 85 (March-April 1985).

Additional Readings

R. BUCHANAN & J. MINOR, LEGAL ASPECTS OF HEALTH CARE REIMBURSEMENT (1985).

T. DENENBERG & R. DENENBERG, ALCOHOL AND DRUGS: ISSUES IN THE WORKPLACE (1984).

R. GORDON, ISSUES IN HEALTH CARE REGULATION (1980).

HOSPICE HANDBOOK: A GUIDE FOR MANAGERS AND PLANNERS (L. Paradis, ed. 1985).

R. MILLER, PROBLEMS IN HOSPITAL LAW (4th ed. 1983).

R. ROEMER & G. MCKRAY, LEGAL ASPECTS OF HEALTH POLICY: ISSUES AND TRENDS (1980).

L. SIMMS, S. PRICE, & N. ERVIN, THE PROFESSIONAL PRACTICE OF NURSING ADMINISTRATION (1985).

A. SOUTHWICK, THE LAW OF HOSPITAL AND HEALTH CARE ADMINISTRATION (1978).

B. STEVENS, THE NURSE AS EXECUTIVE (3rd ed. 1985).

Chapter 23

Nurses employed as practitioners, anesthetists, midwives, clinical specialists

Jo Ann Smith and Mary E. Kelly

The practice of registered nursing is regulated by the state's nursing practice act (NPA), and the NPA is a reference for determining scope of practice. Judicial decisions also have defined the nurse's scope of practice, both with and without reference to statutory authority. Nevertheless, determining the parameters of scope of practice is often an elusive process. In recent years attention to the invisible line separating the permissible from the nonpermissible has focused on the distinction between the practice of medicine and the practice of registered nursing.

This concern has developed as nursing has evolved and has taken on more activities that have traditionally been considered exclusively the practice of medicine. The majority of legal activity in this respect has involved nurse practitioners who function within an overlapping area between nursing and medicine but do so in an ambulatory setting: nurse midwives, nurse practitioners, and clinical nurse specialists.

The nurse anesthetist, another nurse practitioner, early on faced challenges to scope of practice, at a time when this practice was not mentioned or addressed in state NPAs. Court decisions considering illegal practice of medicine challenges noted that the practice of medicince and nursing overlapped in certain areas and upheld the nurse anesthetist's legal authority to practice anesthesia under the direction and supervision of a physician.[1]

This chapter first examines, from an historical perspective, the recognition of overlapping areas of practice and the development of legal authority for advanced practice. Next a discussion of the various sources for determining the nurse practitioner's scope of practice is presented. Finally, the nurse practitioner's potential liability to the patient for advanced practice is analyzed. Particular emphasis is given to the standard of care applicable to the nurse practitioner.

Recognition of overlapping practice

Judicial recognition of the need and ability of registered nurses to perform functions overlapping with medicine sometimes preceded corresponding statutory changes. The nurse anesthetist's authority to practice, as noted already, is one example. More recently, broad amendments to NPAs that recognize overlapping functions have been cited by the courts, which considered and rejected the claim that the exercise of independent judgment by nurses allows them to exercise medical discretion.[2]

The recognition of overlapping practice led to the establishment of a National Joint Practice Commission in 1971 by the American Medical Association and the American Nurses' Association (ANA). One of the commission's tasks was to promote communication between medicine and nursing about areas of overlapping practice.[3] The commission defined joint practice as "nurses and physicians collaborating together as colleagues to provide patient care,"[4] a clear recognition of the more independent nature of nursing practice and the more equal position of nurses and physicians as members of the health care team.

Another impetus for change in 1971 stemmed from a federal report calling for an expansion of the scope of practice for registered nurses.[5] The report noted, among other things, the increased educational standards for nurses, shortage of primary care physicians, and the need for less expensive health care.

During the 1970s and the 1980s, various states amended statutes and regulations governing the nurse's legal scope of practice to more closely reflect the reality of nursing practice. Statutory and regulatory recognition of overlapping practice areas clearly reflect the trend toward redefinition of the line between medicine and nursing.

Counterbalancing this movement have been political forces at work that hold in check the scope of practice of the expanded-role nurse. The countervailing pressure comes primarily from organized medicine, which is reluctant to relinquish the singular control over health professional practice that it has gained.[6]

Several recent cases exemplify the tug and pull between nurse practitioners and physicians. These cases, discussed in Chapter 29, challenge advanced nursing practice as the illegal practice of medicine. Significantly, the medical profession has centered its challenges against nurses who practice advanced nursing in ambulatory settings; specialty nurses, such as critical care nurses, apparently are not seen as an economic threat. As health care delivery continues to move out of the hospital and into the ambulatory and the home settings, competition among providers will increase.

Compounding the pressures for both professions is a prediction of an oversupply of physicians by 1990, although it is unclear whether this will increase the numbers of primary care physicians.[7] Requirements for physician linkage, restrictions on prescription of medication, diagnostic limitations, barriers to third-party reimbursement, uncertain liability, and lack of hospital admitting or attending privileges all plague nurse practitioners in various degrees.

Although these requirements and restrictions, or the lack of them, may impact on a nurse practitioner's liability, they will not provide a defense to liability. As one author notes[8]:

> Nurses are independently licensed to practice. As such, they do not require the supervision of a physician. They are accountable to their patients for their clinical decisions, regardless of whether or not the physician is immediately available for consultation.[8]

Scope of practice

Scope of practice refers to that area of practice legally considered to fall within the expertise of the registered nurse. For nurse practitioners, the legal scope of practice may be the same as or different from that accorded all registered nurses. Nurses may look to several sources of law to determine the scope of their practice. These are the state NPAs, regulations and rules, and case law. Attorney general opinions may be utilized to persuade a court as to a particular view; these opinions, however, do not bind the courts.

Not all NPAs define the scope of a nurse practitioner's practice. In the early 1970s, nurse practitioner advocates favored expanding the basic definition of a registered nurse.[9] Under this approach, all registered nurses function under the same basic NPA, and the nursing profession credentials specialty nurses.

In other states, role redefinition has been accomplished through additional specific language in legislation authorizing advanced nursing practice by specially qualified nurses. Several examples of this are provided in Chapter 29.

Another approach is to include an additional acts clause within the state NPA. Under this approach, the NPA authorizes additional acts requiring appropriate education and training that are recognized as properly performed by a registered nurse.

Some states define the advanced practice nurse and in so doing, specify a permissible scope of practice, often in combination with an additional acts clause. For example, the New Hampshire Practice Act states, "A registered nurse who presents certifying credentials from a program acceptable to the board of nursing, as indicative of having had specialized preparation, as determined by the board, shall be identified on the license issued as an advanced registered nurse practitioner or A.R.N.P. The nurse certified as such shall be qualified to function in collaborative relationships with physicians as well as in private practice."[10]

A few states have enacted a specific law authorizing a specific scope of practice for a particular nurse practitioner. California takes this approach by referring to the nurse midwife in a practice act separate from the basic definition of nursing practice.[11]

Administrative rules and regulations of state nursing boards may also impact on the nurse's scope of practice. Chapter 29 provides examples of states that rely on administrative rules and regulations to authorize advanced nursing practice. All state nursing practice acts citations are listed in Appendix IV.

Case law may also establish scope of practice. The most noteworthy case, *Sermchief v. Gonzales*,[12] which is reprinted in the appendix, held that the broadly worded Missouri NPA authorized the activities of nurse practitioners performed under written standing orders and protocols signed by the physicians in the employing agency. The activities at issue were breast and pelvic examinations, pregnancy testing, Pap smears, gonorrhea cultures, blood serologies, administration of contraceptive methods, and counseling.

The trial court held that the nurses were, in fact, engaged in the unlawful practice of medicine, but this ruling was reversed by the Missouri Supreme Court. The Missouri Supreme Court interpreted the Missouri NPA to permit nursing practice to advance without statutory constraint:

> The legislature substantially revised the law affecting the nursing profession with enactment of the Nursing Practice Act of 1975. Perhaps the most significant feature of the Act was the redefinition of the term "professional nursing,". . . . Even a facile reading of that section reveals a manifest legislative desire to expand the scope of authorized nursing practice. . . . Equally significant is the legislature's formulation of an open-ended definition of professional nursing. The earlier statute limited nursing practice to "services . . . in the care of the sick, in the prevention of disease or in the conservation of health." . . . The 1975 Act not only describes a much broader spectrum of nursing functions, it qualifies this description with the phrase "including, but not limited to." We believe this phrase evidences an intent to avoid statutory constraints on the evolution of new functions for nurses delivering health services.[13]

The court's reasoning is important for registered nurses practicing in advanced roles in states with broadly worded NPAs that do not specifically cover nurse practitioners or clinical nurse specialists. Practitioners in such states must rely on the wording of the basic NPA and any judicial interpretations that address their practice.[14]

Scope of practice issues concerning nurse midwives and nurse anesthetists appear to be less frequently litigated. This may be because of their longer history and a more easily defined scope of practice.

Nurse midwifery practice is defined by the American College of Nurse-Midwives as the "independent management of care of essentially normal newborns and women antepartally, intrapartally, postpartally and/or gynecologically. . . ."[15] Questions concerning scope of practice tend to focus on what falls within "normal."[16]

Nurse anesthetists were recognized early in the twentieth century, but as subordinates to the physician.[17] Issues involving the nurse anesthetist's scope of practice concern the necessary extent of physician supervision.[18] Different state courts have reached opposite conclusions about the requirement of physician supervision.[19]

Standard of care

In proving that the nurse practitioner's act or omission is actionable negligence, the plaintiff must establish the standard of care against which the practitioner's action, or lack of action, is to be measured. As discussed in Chapter 4, the professional is required to exercise that degree of care that other reasonably prudent professionals would exercise under similar circumstances.[20] This standard applies to professional nurses, physicians, and nurse practitioners.

Nurses who practice in specialty areas are expected to render the same level of care as would be rendered by the reasonable specialty nurse practicing in the same specialty area of nursing.[21] The existence of a specialty definition, in addition to the ANA definition of nursing practice,[22] may lead the courts to impose a higher standard of care upon the nurse practitioner than would be imposed upon a registered nurse without advanced training.

ANA standards for clinical nurse specialists' areas generally require master's degree preparation and certification.[23] Certified nurse midwives and certified nurse anesthetists also have advanced educational training and certification. Advanced educational preparation and certification lend support to the view that nurses with such credentials should be held to a higher standard of care.

The issue concerning many nurse practitioners is whether they will be held to a physician's standard of care for performing acts traditionally thought of as medical functions, or whether they will be held accountable to their own professional standard of care. Early cases suggest that the function performed dictates the standard.

For example, in *Barber v. Reinking*, a practical nurse who exceeded her scope of practice was held to the standard of care of a registered nurse since she had assumed the duties of a registered nurse.[24] In *Thompson v. Brent*,[25] the court ruled that a negligently performed medical function resulting in injury, performed by someone other than a physician, is governed by the same rules that apply to physicians. Consequently, it was appropriate to consider the degree of care that would have been expected of the physician if he or she were performing the function.

Applying a physician standard of care to the nurse practitioner raises a concern that stems from the dual legal duty imposed upon a professional. The law requires that the professional have both the degree of learning and skill possessed by reputable members of that profession and that they use the care and skill ordinarily exercised by reputable members of their profession.[26] If a physician standard of care is applied to the nurse practitioner, the learning requirement would be prejudicial.[27]

Recent cases involving nurse practitioners suggest a trend toward holding the nurse practitioner to the standard of care applicable to that practitioner's profession. In *Whitney v. Day*, the court of appeals upheld the following jury instruction on the nurse anesthetist's standard of care: "[a] nurse administering an anesthetic is held to the standard of care based on the skill and care normally expected of those with the same education and training."[28] The instruction correctly stated the law because the nurse involved was a specialist and possessed "responsibilities greater than those possessed by an ordinary nurse . . . in an area of expertise in which some physicians receive full residency training."[29]

That the nurse specialist has an expertise thus means that his or her conduct should be measured against the standard of care of other nurse specialists practicing under the same or similar circumstances.[30] *Fein v. Permanente Medical Group*,[31] which involves the standard of care of a nurse practitioner, also illustrates this principle.

In *Fein*, the plaintiff, a 34-year-old attorney, sued the Kaiser Permanente group for negligently failing to diagnose his impending heart attack and failing to treat his condition so as to prevent his heart attack or to lessen its residual effects. The plaintiff first noticed a brief chest pain, lasting a minute or two, as he rode his bicycle to work. He noticed a similar pain the following day as he was jogging. Three days later, he experienced another episode while walking after lunch, and the chest pain again returned that evening as he was working.

The following morning, he contacted his regular physician who was employed by an affiliate of the Kaiser Health Foundation. His physician had no available appointments, and he was advised to call the central appointment desk for a short appointment. The plaintiff did not feel the problem was so severe as to warrant an emergency room visit, and he worked until his appointment that afternoon.

When the plaintiff arrived for his appointment, he was examined by a nurse practitioner who was working under the supervision of a physician-consultant. The court noted that the plaintiff knew he was being seen by a nurse practitioner and he did not ask to see a physician. After the examination, the nurse practitioner consulted with the supervising physician and advised the plaintiff that they both believed the pain was caused by muscle spasm. The physician prescribed Valium, which the plaintiff took that night.

In the early morning hours, the plaintiff awoke with severe chest pains. At the Kaiser emergency room, a physician examined him and ordered a chest x-ray film. Based on these, the physician also concluded the plaintiff was experiencing muscle spasms. The plaintiff was given an injection of Demerol and a prescription for codeine.

The plaintiff continued to experience intermittent chest pain at home. When the pain became more severe, about noon that same day, the plaintiff returned to the Kaiser emergency room. He was seen by a different physician, who also believed the pain was caused by muscle spasm. After administering pain medication, however, he ordered an electrocardiogram (EKG). The EKG revealed that the plaintiff was suffering from an acute myocardial infarction, and he was transferred to the cardiac care unit.

At trial, plaintiff's expert, the head of cardiology at a major medical center, testified that chest pain that is not relieved by rest or pain medication is an important signal indicating a heart attack may be imminent. If properly diagnosed, the expert continued, Inderal can be given to stabilize the condition, and additional medication or surgery may relieve the condition.

The expert also asserted that any patient who appears with chest pain should be given an EKG to rule out the worst possibility—a heart problem. He further asserted that the nurse practitioner should have ordered an EKG based on the symptoms presented to her. The emergency room physician also should have ordered an EKG when the plaintiff arrived with chest pain unrelieved by pain medication. Had an EKG been ordered at those times, the plaintiff's imminent heart attack would have been revealed, and treatment could have been administered that would have prevented or minimized the attack.

Although defense experts contradicted this evidence, the jury found in plaintiff's favor. On appeal, the Kaiser-Permanente group challenged, among other things, an instruction given to the jury on the nurse practitioner's standard of care. The trial court had instructed the jury that the standard of care required of a nurse practitioner is that of a physician and surgeon when the nurse practitioner is examining a patient or making a diagnosis.

The California Appellate Court ruled that the trial court erroneously instructed the jury that the standard of care required of a nurse practitioner is that of a physician.[32] The court reasoned that when the legislature amended the state NPA, expressly intending to recognize the overlapping functions of physicians and nurses, it did not expand the role to include the practice of medicine or surgery.

Nevertheless, the court, in dicta, noted that the challenged instruction was not erroneous insofar as it informed the jury that the when the plaintiff went to the health facility for treatment, ''he was entitled to the standard of care of a physician. Whether Defendant chose to provide that care through the services of a physician or through the services of a nurse practitioner whom the facts show worked under the supervision and direction of a physician, the standard of care to which the Plaintiff was entitled was the same.''[33]

This ruling caused the California Coalition of Nurse Practitioners concern, and they intervened on appeal to the California Supreme Court.[34] They believed these dicta were the death knell of nurse practitioners because it suggested that the standard of care was to be determined by the function performed rather than the professional group performing it.[35]

The California Supreme Court[36] clarified that this was not the legal rule. The court reasoned that the erroneous instruction was inconsistent with the state's NPA, which explicitly recognizes the existence of overlapping functions of physicians and registered nurses. The court stated that, based on the NPA, examination and diagnosis of a patient ''could not, in all circumstances, be said—as a matter of law—to be a function reserved to physicians, rather than registered nurses or nurse practitioners.''[37]

The court noted that the plaintiff was entitled to have the jury decide whether the medical center was negligent in permitting a nurse practitioner to see a patient who exhibited plaintiff's symptoms and whether the nurse practitioner met the standard of care of a reasonably prudent nurse practitioner in conducting the examination and prescribing treatment in conjunction with her supervising physician. The jury, however, should not have been instructed that the nurse practitioner's conduct had to be measured by the standard of care of a physician.

The *Fein* case is an important decision for the autonomy of nursing. Although the case does not preclude proof that the nurse practitioner, as a factual matter, has the same duty of care as a physician in performing a particular function, the nurse practitioner's conduct will be measured against that of other nurse practitioners acting under similar circumstances. The case recognizes that the professional standard of care is essentially a factual issue that must proved.

A crucial issue not challenged in *Fein* concerns *how* the nurse practitioner's standard of care is proved at trial. In *Fein*, that standard was proved by testimony from a *physician* expert. If, however, the standard of care of nurse practitioners is to be independent of the physicians' standard, then the evidence of the nurse practitioner's standard of care must come from nurse practitioner experts. Nurse practitioners must insist that nurse practitioner experts, not physician experts, testify to the standard of care. Otherwise, the *Fein* holding is rendered meaningless as a practical matter.[38]

Reliance on expert testimony allows a profession to establish its own standards and encourages the exercise of independent judgment. It is considered a unique concession to professional groups.[39] In *Sermchief*, the court explicitly recognized the right of the nursing profession to establish its own standards. The ability of nurse practitioners to provide expert testimony on their standard of care is a crucial element in assuring that the courts understand the nurse practitioner's role.

Sermchief relied on the state's broad mandate for nursing practice, which is similar to the mandate in the California NPA upon which the *Fein* court relied in considering the applicable standard.[40] The issue in *Sermchief* was whether or not the functions in question were the practice of nursing. The court held that the amendments to the NPA repealing strict prohibitions against the practice of medicine by nurses and requirements for physician supervision of nursing practice were broad enough to encompass the nurse practitioner's actions. *Fein* and *Sermchief*, read together, provide a foundation for measuring acts performed by nurses against a nursing standard of care.[41]

As explained in Chapter 4, standard of care can be established with documentary evidence and with reference to statutes and to administrative regulations. The use of written protocols may also be used to assist the court in determining the expected responsibility and actions of the nurse practitioner. Protocols should always be developed with the awareness that they may be used as a measuring stick for the nurse's actions. The use of hospital policy and procedure[42] and professional standards of care may also be used to establish a standard of care.

The ANA standards for nursing detail the levels of performance the nurse must meet. Many of these standards are discussed throughout this book. These standards cover both generic and specialty nursing, and they include assessment factors for determining whether the applicable standard has been met. Nurses should insist that attorneys review these standards and use nurse experts to testify on the application of the standards to the act in question. Chapter 32 discusses expert nurse witnesses further.

If the plaintiff attempts to prove the nurse practitioner's standard of care with the testimony of a physician, defense counsel should be urged to challenge the physician's qualifications as an expert. The physician expert in *Fein*, the head of cardiology at a medical center, apparently qualified as an expert on the standard of care of the defendant nurse practitioner without objection from the defense.[43]

Nurse anesthetist as defendant

The greatest number of reported nurse practitioner negligence cases involve the nurse anesthetist, perhaps because this group of nurse practitioners has a longer history of practice. Liability for negligence may occur in the selection, administration, and management of anesthesia. Lack of informed consent may also be an issue.

These areas of liability are illustrated by *Brown v. Dahl*,[44] where a nurse anesthetist, the anesthesiologists' employing group, and the anesthesiologists were sued. The plaintiffs, Mrs. and Mr. Brown, met with Dr. Dahl, an anesthesiologist, prior to Mr. Brown's surgery. Dahl asked them to complete a preanesthetic evaluation checklist and afterward told them that he recommended a general anesthetic procedure (sodium pentothal). Dahl also allegedly assured them he would personally perform the proposed procedure. Although he asked if they had any questions about the procedure, he did not disclose any of the risks associated with anesthesia.

The nurse anesthetist testified that the following morning she met with Mr. Brown when he was transported to surgery. At this time, she explained that she was going to perform the general anesthetic procedure. Mr. Brown voiced no complaints about her performing the procedure in the absence of Dr. Dahl.

After completing the standard preanesthetic preparations and selection of agents, the nurse anesthetist began to administer general anesthetic. As the anesthetic began to take effect, Mr. Brown's airway became partially blocked and he experienced difficulties in breathing. The nurse anesthetist unsuccessfully attempted to correct the blockage and asked for help.

The elapsed time between discovery of the breathing problem and the first call for help was a hotly contested issue at trial. Within moments after her call for help, several physicians appeared, including Dr. Dahl. After several attempts, an airway was established. Thereafter, however, Mr. Brown sustained a cardiac arrest and suffered mental and physical impairment.

At trial, the plaintiffs contended that Dahl's preanesthetic evaluation was negligent. They also claimed that he was negligent in allowing the nurse anesthetist to perform the anesthetic procedure without his presence in view of his representation that he would personally perform it. The suit charged the nurse anesthetist with negligence in administering the anesthetic, in attempting corrective measures, and in delaying requests for help.

The court held there was enough evidence of the nurse anesthetist's negligence to allow the jury to decide the issue; however, the jury returned a defense verdict. On appeal, the court reversed and remanded the case for a new trial because, among other reasons, the trial court had incorrectly instructed the jury and overemphasized the defense case. The trial court also failed to give a *res ipsa loquitor* instruction.[45]

Wentling v. Medical Anesthesia Services,[46] a wrongful death action, also illustrates a malpractice case based on improper administration of anesthesia. The plaintiff's wife, who had experienced an uneventful pregnancy, was given an epidural block of 0.25% Marcaine when she went into labor. A cesarean section was necessary the next day.

A nurse anesthetist administered a spinal anesthetic of 0.75% Marcaine without the presence of a physician and without a physician's order. The anesthetic caused the patient to begin vomiting, which resulted in immediate seizures, cardiac arrest, and loss of consciousness. After calling a code blue, the child was delivered. The mother remained in a coma and was pronounced dead thereafter.

At trial, the defendants admitted liability. The only issue for the jury to decide was the amount of damages. The jury awarded $786,166.00.

FAILURE TO MONITOR

Failure to monitor for aspiration of gastric contents and negligent overdosing with anesthesia are claims that may bring about large settlements when severe injury occurs. In one case, these allegations resulted in a $1.5 million settlement for a 19-year-old patient who was left brain damaged.[47] The claim was that the nurse anesthetist administered an excessive amount of ethane and failed to properly monitor the patient.

Ipock v. Gilmore,[48] where the jury found a nurse

anesthetist negligent, also illustrates the nurse anesthetist's liability for failure to monitor. The lawsuit charged that the nurse anesthetist and anesthesiologist failed during surgery to properly maintain a patient's open airway, respirations, and cardiac output. The plaintiff also alleged that, following the plaintiff's cardiac arrest in the operating room, they failed to properly resuscitate, treat, and monitor her hypoxic and posthypoxic conditions.

Additional charges of negligence centered on the defendants' failure to perform a proper preanesthetic evaluation of the plaintiff, and in particular, their failure to insist that electrolytes and a complete blood count be obtained prior to administration of anesthesia. The plaintiff further maintained that the defendants administered improper preoperative, operative, and postoperative medications.

The patient underwent surgery for an elective sterilization via laparoscopy. The surgeon expanded the procedure to include a total hysterectomy and a bilateral salpingo-oophorectomy. Postoperatively, the plaintiff was diagnosed as suffering from hypoxic brain damage caused by a lack of oxygen to the brain either during or immediately after surgery.

Allegations of administration of excessive anesthesia and failure to monitor resulted in a $1 million jury verdict in *Theolphelis v. Lansing General Hospital*.[49] A 7-year-old child underwent a tonsillectomy and a bilateral tympanotomy. The anesthesia was performed by a certified registered nurse anesthetist and an anesthesiologist, both of whom were employed by a professional corporation.

During surgery, the child suffered a cardiac arrest. After extensive resuscitative efforts, his heartbeat and breathing returned. Once in the intensive care unit, however, the child experienced a second cardiac arrest. The respirator was removed when an electroencephalogram (EEG) revealed he had no brainwaves. The pathologist diagnosed anesthetic death.

The child's parents instituted a wrongful death action against the hospital and the personnel involved. Specifically, they charged that the nurse anesthetist and anesthesiologist overdosed the child with anesthetic, inadequately monitored the child, and failed to have an anesthesiologist in the operating room at all times. The suit also charged that they failed to use a precordial stethoscope and to employ certain standard resuscitative techniques.

The hospital was charged with the failure to establish and to enforce adequate standards for the administration of anesthesia in the operating rooms. In addition, the hospital was charged with negligence in failing to advise the parents that a nurse anesthetist rather than an anesthesiologist would be present throughout the surgery. Ultimately the nurse anesthetist and anesthesiologist settled the case. The jury found against the hospital.

A nurse anesthetist's failure to properly ventilate a patient was the basis of a negligence action brought against an anesthesiologist in *Morgan v. Children's Hospital*.[50] The plaintiff underwent surgery for removal of his thymus as treatment for myasthenia gravis. The surgery necessitated the opening of the plaintiff's chest and splitting the sternum to reach the gland.

The anesthesia was administered by an anesthesiologist and his agent, a certified registered nurse anesthetist (CRNA). The administration commenced at 12:30 PM, and his vital signs remained normal until 1:45 PM, when respirations increased from 20/minute to 40/minute. The nurse anesthetist administered succinylcholine to paralyze the plaintiff's muscle and Demerol to minimize the pain. The drugs were administered because the increase in respiration rate showed that pain was penetrating the anesthetized level of the patient.

These drugs prevented the plaintiff from breathing on his own. As a result, the nurse anesthetist thereafter assisted the plaintiff's respiration via a bag.

At 2:40 PM, when the surgeon was closing the patient's chest, a slowing of the heart rate occurred. The record, the court noted, contained conflicting testimony between the surgeon and the CRNA as to when exactly the bradycardia was noticed. Nevertheless, when it was noticed, the surgeon performed closed cardiac massage, followed by open cardiac massage. One of the anesthesiologist's associates and the CRNA administered drugs to speed the heart rate and stabilize the heart muscle.

At 3:20 PM, the plaintiff was taken to the intensive care unit, where he suffered grand mal seizures. As a result, the plaintiff entered a vegetative state.

At trial, the experts agreed that he had suffered global brain damage as the result of oxygen deprivation. Plaintiff's expert said the deprivation resulted from the CRNA's failure to adequately ventilate the plaintiff, while the defendant's experts said the damage was caused by an air emboli that blocked the vessels to the brain.

The trial court refused the plaintiff's request for a *res ipsa loquitor* instruction, and the jury returned a verdict for the defense. On appeal, a majority of the court determined that the instruction should have been given. The defense verdict was reversed, and the matter was remanded for a new trial. The court reasoned that even though the plaintiff offered evidence of specific acts of negligence, other circumstantial evidence justified giving the instruction. Specifically, the court noted that expert testimony established that the injury was such that it would not have occurred in the absence of negligence.

In *Lupton v. Torbey*,[51] a malpractice action was brought for improper monitoring against an anesthesiological team, which included a CRNA and others. The patient sustained brain injury, and the anesthesiological team settled after paying $75,000.00.

At trial, the plaintiff introduced evidence that she had been hospitalized to verify a diagnosis as to the nature of her long history of stomach pain and difficulties with digestion, which had required several hospitalizations. Her physician diagnosed the problem as one arising from a constriction of arterial blood supply to the stomach. The plaintiff was admitted to the hospital for a celiac axis study to be performed by a radiologist.

The patient requested general anesthesia, and her physician arranged to have an anesthesiologist administer the anesthesia. During the procedure, the anesthesiologist supervised the administration of anesthesia by his nurse anesthetist employee. A student nurse anesthetist was also present. There was testimony that the drug solution was prepared in a much stronger dosage than that recommended by the manufacturer.

The anesthesiologist left the operating room, and the CRNA continued to observe the patient, although he failed to monitor her breathing or her pulse. The radiologist entered the operating room suite, checked the patient's pulse, determined it was normal, and left to scrub, dress, and arrange his instruments.

During the next 5 to 10 minutes, the nurse anesthetist became concerned about the "rapidity at which [the patient] had gone under."[52] He left the patient to talk with the anesthesiologist, leaving the student to manage the anesthesia. Neither the student nor the nurse anesthetist informed the radiologist of their alarm, "having been instructed not to disturb the surgeons about their anesthesiological problems."[53]

When the radiologist commenced the diagnostic procedure, he became alarmed because the patient's pulse could no longer be felt. The student began emergency procedures, administering oxygen and a drug to increase blood pressure. The evidence was unclear as to whether these measures were performed in response to orders from the radiologist or upon the student's own initiative. The radiologist, however, did not take any other emergency measures and he did not examine the patient.

FAILURE TO FOLLOW PHYSICIAN ORDERS OR ADVISE OF DISAGREEMENT

In *Carlsen v. Javurek, M.D.*,[54] a CRNA was charged with negligence in the selection and administration of a general halogenated anesthetic against the orders of a surgeon. The patient developed a liver dysfunction that eventually caused her death.

The patient entered the hospital to have a cholecystectomy, under the care of her family physician. The family physician called in a surgeon to perform the surgery. The admitting hospital history indicated that the patient had suffered from hepatitis during childhood. The surgeon testified that the day before surgery, he had informed the patient of the risks of general anesthesia, including death. He also asserted that he had explained to her that due to her history of hepatitis, there were anesthetics he would not use.

The surgeon further asserted that he decided not to use Penthrane, a halogenated anesthetic, because some believed it was contraindicated in a patient with a history of hepatitis. He also claimed that he told the nurse anesthetist not to use a halogenated anesthetic. He further testified that although it was customary for the nurse anesthetist to choose the anesthetic, it was also customary at this particular hospital that the nurse anesthetist would follow any direct order of a surgeon.

The nurse anesthetist admitted she was obligated to follow any direct order of a physician, but she denied that the surgeon had any conversation with her concerning the prohibition against using a halogenated anesthetic during surgery. She claimed that prior to administering the anesthetic, she had informed the patient's family physician of her choice of a halogenated anesthetic, and he had merely raised his eyebrows and shrugged his shoulders. The family physician denied that this exchange occurred. His role was to assist in the surgery, but he denied that he had any role in the selection of anesthesia.

Since the family physician did not exert any control over the surgeon or participate in the selection of anesthetic, the appellate court held that the case was properly dismissed against him. The fact that the nurse anesthetist informed him of her selection did not mean that he had participated in the selection.

In reviewing the nurse anesthetist's potential liability, the court noted that a nurse anesthetist is obligated to follow a surgeon's order, or at a minimum, to advise the surgeon of any disagreement. The defense expert, a physician, acknowledged that a discussion between the surgeon and the nurse anesthetist was necessary, and without agreement, the surgery should have been cancelled. The appellate court ordered a new trial against the nurse anesthetist, her employer, and the surgeon.

Nurse midwife as defendant

Perhaps the most significant potential area of liability for nurse midwives concerns the duty to refer complicated pregnancies. Violations of state statutes prescribing the nurse midwife's scope of practice may be used in negligence actions to obtain a presumption of negligence.[55] *Lustig v. The Birthplace*[56] illustrates the application of this doctrine in a negligence action brought against a nurse midwife. A $725,000.00 settlement was reached for the wrongful death of a mother and child caused by eclampsia during labor. During settlement negotiations, the plaintiff successfully argued that the violation of statute doctrine would apply.

A nurse midwife employed by the birthing clinic cared for the woman throughout her pregnancy and labor. In the last 3 months of pregnancy, the woman's blood pressure, reflexes, and edema increased, and she experienced more fatigue. When she arrived at the clinic in labor, her blood pressure increased throughout the next 7 hours, culminating in seizures and unconsciousness. After being transported to the hospital, her blood pressure was 200/117 and she was still unconscious. Her son was stillborn, and she died 2 days later.

The midwife and the birthing clinic were sued for negligence per se because the nurse midwife violated a statute that established the duty of a midwife to consult with a physician whenever significant deviations from normal are found in either the mother or the fetus. Expert testimony established that the nurse midwife should have referred the woman to a physician. The violation of statute was established, and the defendants settled the case.

A legal magazine reported that the mother never was seen by an obstetrician, but rather was informed by nurse midwives who staffed the center that she was at low risk and that delivery at their facility was safe.[57] "This assurance continued despite the fact that as [the mother] entered the final trimester, her blood pressure continued to rise and she had increased reflexes, edema, and fatigue. When she came to labor, her pressure continued to rise for seven hours, until she experienced seizures and became unconscious. Only then was she taken to a hospital where her son was delivered stillborn and she died two days later."[58]

The plaintiff's attorney characterized the problem as one of no physician backup regularly checking the charts. In his estimation, had the nurse midwives had such backing, then "in all probability" the subtle preeclampsia would have been recognized and treated; "the nurse midwives, due to their inexperience and frank ignorance, were unable to see the problem."[59] Although the nurse midwives advised the mother to stop working when she was 29 weeks pregnant, "they did not provide the follow-up and careful monitoring that good medical care would have required."[60]

Nurse practitioners and clinical specialists as defendants

As nurse practitioners and clinical specialists take on additional methods of practice, such as prescribing drugs, the potential for liability increases. To date, only a few reported cases concern the alleged negligence of nurse practitioners, and none involves clinical specialists. Nevertheless, the legal principles addressed throughout this book are clearly applicable to these practitioners. The *Fein* case, discussed earlier, suggests that negligent history taking and physical examination or negligent failure to order diagnostic tests may be the basis of negligence actions. Failure to properly diagnose and to refer may also be actionable negligence.

Principles from cases involving other health care practitioners, such as physicians, also provide a framework within which to analyze the potential liability of nurse practitioners and clinical specialists. As prescribers of medications, for example, nurse practitioners and clinical specialists have legal duties to the patient that are similar to those of the physician.

Informed consent and capacity to consent, discussed in Chapters 5 and 6, are issues particularly relevant to nurse practitioners and clinical specialists. Failure to inform of the risks of drugs, such as birth control pills, or other birth control methods, such as intrauterine devices (IUDs), may support a claim of negligence. Failure to obtain consent in the first instance may subject the nurse practitioner or clinical specialist to liability for the intentional tort of battery.

Nurse practitioners and clinical specialists should also consult the chapters relevant to their particular practice areas. Psychiatric and mental health clinical specialists, for example, are potentially liable for failure to warn foreseeable victims of their clients' expressed intentions to cause the victim harm[61] and for failure to recognize the suicidal potential of their clients.[62]

Clinical specialists in other fields may be deemed negligent for failure to act in accordance with professional standards applicable to their specialty. Those involved in collaborative practice with physicians who undertake treatment decisions must be certain that they have the necessary skill and training to do so. The *Sermchief* decision makes clear that nurses are professionally responsible for the practice they undertake. Moreover, this is an established principle of tort law: the jury is generally instructed that the practitioner must have the skill and learning commonly possessed by members of the profession in good standing or else he or she is liable if harm results because they are lacking.[63]

Nurse practitioners and clinical specialists in entrepreneurial practice are potentially liable as business owners as well as practitioners. Chapter 33 addresses areas of potential liability from the business owner's perspective.

Issues of informed consent, the duty to assess, and the duty to refer are also relevant. Documentation of discussions and educational teaching sessions is, as in other practice areas, essential to substantiate the fact that they occurred.

FAILURE TO INFORM OF KNOWN RISKS AND IMPROPER MANAGEMENT

Gugino v. Harvard Community Health Plan[64] illustrates the importance of informing patients of the risks associated with certain treatments and conducting a proper history and physical examination. The plaintiff sued to recover personal injuries as a result of the alleged malpractice of several defendants, including a nurse practitioner.

In 1972, the plaintiff had an IUD device, the Dalkon Shield, implanted to prevent pregnancy. In June of 1974, the plaintiff became a member of the defendant health plan who employed the nurse practitioner. The plaintiff read an article about the risks of an IUD and consulted the physician to whom she was assigned in the group. She asked him about the potential risks of pregnancy and infection and informed him that she was experiencing dysfunctional bleeding. The physician told her he knew of no pregnancy or infection problems associated with the device and reassured her to continue using it.

In mid-April of 1975, the plaintiff began to experience a foul vaginal odor like that of dead fish. She called the plan for an appointment and informed the nurse practitioner of the problem. The nurse practitioner told her to douche with yogurt. A little over a week later, the plaintiff developed intense pain and again called the plan. She said, "I'm having a baby, only I'm not pregnant. Do you know what I mean?"[65] The defendant nurse practitioner said she probably had a lower gastrointestinal flu and should call back if she developed a fever.

On April 30, 1975, when she kept a scheduled appointment at the plan, she could hardly walk. The IUD was removed, and the plaintiff was given an antibiotic and pain medication. The plaintiff was told to return to the clinic on May 2, 1975. When she did so, multiple abscesses were diagnosed. On May 5, 1975, she underwent a total hysterectomy.

The plaintiff's expert, a primary care internist who had considerable experience in working with and supervising nurse practitioners, testified as to the standard of care of the nurse practitioner. The expert asserted that, based on a review of the records, the defendant nurse practitioner and the physician were under a continuing obligation to inform the plaintiff of the risks known to be associated with the Dalkon Shield. Failure to so inform the patient was negligence. Omission of this disclosure in June of 1974 probably determined the plaintiff's retention of the device and contributed to the infection.

The expert also noted that the nurse practitioner's management of the case months later was clearly negligent. The yogurt douche, a substandard lay remedy, was inappropriate for symptoms described, particularly the odor of dead fish. Moreover, delay of more than 48 hours in scheduling diagnosis and treatment was substandard care. The time factor was critical, and each day of delay increased the likelihood of surgery; this critical delay was the factor that caused the need for a total hysterectomy.

In addition to this expert testimony, the court cited the plaintiff's articles about the hazards of IUDs. As of 1973, there were reports published that IUD users were complaining of a persistent vaginal odor like that of rotting fish, which was resistant to all forms of local therapy. These reports concluded that patients should be advised of the potential serious hazards of the IUD and instructed to notify their physician immediately upon the appearance of abnormal bleeding, foul-smelling leukorrhea, or persistent pelvic pain. In 1973 and 1974, *New York Times* articles also warned of the risks of infection with the IUD.

The court further noted that plaintiff's expert also criticized the very sketchy nature of the plan's records. In the court's view, these records were unintelligible. Significantly, no records of any telephone calls were made. The appellate court held this proof was sufficient evidence of negligence to allow the case to go to the jury.

Negligent Diagnosis. The act of diagnosing has been viewed by the medical profession as so tightly associated with the practice of medicine that diagnosis by nurses in the ambulatory setting is treated as an encroachment on medical practice.[66] The ANA Standards of Practice refer to nursing diagnosis, and state NPAs such as Missouri use this terminology. Other NPAs, such as California, describe diagnosis without using the specific term.[67]

Because diagnosis is both a product and a process, nurses often diagnose without identifying it as such. Certain court decisions have followed this phenomenon. For example, in *Cooper v. National Motor Bearing Co.*,[68] the California Appellate Court held an occupational health nurse accountable for negligent diagnosis, even though the NPA did not explicitly refer to diagnosis as a nursing function. The court described the nurse's duty to diagnose as the reasonable opportunity for examination and treatment; if the nature of the injury or the ailment is discoverable by such examination and treatment, the nurse is answerable for failure to make such a discovery.

Statutory differentiation of nursing diagnosis from medical diagnosis has been criticized as confusing.[69] Those who believe that statutory delineations of practice will avoid legal challenges by the medical profession are mistaken, as the cases discussed in Chapter 29 clearly demonstrate.[70] The *Sermchief* challenge to the activities of nurse practitioners under the Missouri NPA, which refers to nursing diagnosis, also proves this point.

The *Sermchief* court broadly interpreted the NPA's reference to nursing diagnosis as including the use of findings derived from pelvic examinations performed by nurse practitioners to diagnose the existence or nonexistence of contraindications to the use of oral contraceptives, IUDs, and vaginal medications, as described in standing orders and protocols. Because nurses acted under standing orders and protocols when the legislature amended the NPA to grant nurses the right to make assessments and nursing diagnoses, the court reasoned, this activity came within the NPA.

Consequently, the court concluded, a nurse undertakes only a nursing diagnosis, as opposed to a medical diagnosis, when she or he finds or fails to find symptoms described by physicians in standing orders and protocols for the purpose of administering courses of treatment prescribed by the physician in such orders and protocols.

Although the court recognizes a difference between nursing diagnosis and medical diagnosis, its reasoning sheds little light on how to make the distinction between the two when the nurse is not acting pursuant to protocol or standing order. The statute's reference to nursing diagnosis as opposed to the term *diagnosis* alone compels the court to find something that distinguishes it from medical diagnosis.

The solution reached by the *Sermchief* court is to define nursing diagnosis as that process the nurse undertakes when he or she acts pursuant to a standing order or protocol in diagnosing a condition and prescribing a treatment. The analysis thus begs the question; it is somewhat similar to the delegated discretion doctrine adopted by some courts to uphold the nurse's authority to decide whether and when to administer PRN medication.[7]

This type of reasoning may ultimately be a limitation similar to the direct physician and control restrictions in some advanced practice statutes.[72] Colorado's NPA, which defines diagnosis without the nursing modifier, seems to avoid the potential for such limitations. The Colorado NPA defines professional nursing as the performance of both independent nursing functions and delegated medical functions, "including the initiation and performance of nursing care through prevention, diagnosis, and treatment of human disease. . . ."[73]

Improper Treatment. Negligent diagnosis, as distinct from unauthorized diagnosis, has as its counterpart improper treatment. There are "minimum requirements of skill and knowledge as to both diagnosis and treatment, particularly in light of modern licensing statutes."[74] The practitioner must exercise reasonable care in ascertaining the operational facts upon which a diagnosis is based. Failure to do so will result in liability if harm results.[75]

Unless the practitioner contracts to accomplish a particular result, he or she will not be liable in most jurisdictions for an honest mistake of judgment where the proper course of treatment is open to reasonable doubt.[76] Where there are different schools of thought, the practitioner is entitled to be judged according to the tenets of the school that he or she follows, as long as the school of thought is a recognized one and a line of thought of a respectable minority of the profession.[77] The minimum professional standards must be met, no matter what the practitioner's personal views on treatment.

Failure to Refer. As nurses take on more responsibility in diagnosing and treating patients, the responsibility to refer patients whose illness requires referral to physicians or other health professionals becomes increasingly important. The duty to refer has been applied to all health professionals, and the courts have long recognized a duty on the part of nurses to refer and report.[78]

The *Sermchief* decision also noted that "[t]he nurse,

either upon reaching the limit of her or his knowledge or upon reaching the limits prescribed for the nurse by the physician's standing orders or protocols should refer the patient to the physician.''[79] As nurses assume more responsibilities thought traditionally to be medical in nature, that body of case law concerning physicians will be analogized to nurses. The courts have held that jury instructions concerning a physician's duty to refer to a specialist could be used to explain the similar duty of a nurse to seek assistance from more highly skilled medical personnel.[80]

The general rule that has been applied to physicians is that the patient must be advised of the need for other treatment if the professional discovers or should have discovered that the patient's ailment is beyond his or her knowledge or technical skill to treat. The patient has a right to expect information from the practitioner as to who is properly qualified to assist in his treatment. The practitioner may be negligent if he or she is not qualified to treat and the patient suffers injury as a result of the failure to refer.[81]

Marchese v. Monaco[82] makes it clear that the duty to refer goes beyond mere consultation and must constitute adequate consultation. The court declared that the less the practitioner knows, the more he or she must inquire of the consultants. A consultation is not adequate unless the practitioner makes sure the specialist knows all the essential facts and obtains answers to all questions he or she should reasonably ask. Further, the practitioner may be held liable for negligence where the consultant was negligently selected,[83] or the practitioner should have known of the consultant's negligence.[84]

LIABILITY FOR NEGLIGENT PRESCRIPTION PRACTICES

Authority for Prescribing. Prescriptive authority and its attendant liability for nurses has been clouded by limited and uncertain coverage in various state statutes. Most medical practice acts specifically mention the act of prescribing as being an integral part of the practice of medicine, thereby potentially subjecting others to charges of practicing medicine without a license. This is discussed in Chapter 29.

The function of prescribing is a legally defined act. In California, for example, prescribing is defined as ''an oral order given individually for the person or persons for whom prescribed, directly from the prescriber to the furnisher, or indirectly by means of a written order, signed by the prescriber. . . .''[85] In contrast, ''administer'' is described as the ''supplying or giving of a drug to a patient for immediate use,''[86] while ''dispense'' means the ''furnishing of drugs upon a prescription.''[87]

Of these three functions, only administration is clearly recognized in all states as an integral part of the registered nurse's scope of practice. These distinctions are important since nurses have been given some flexibility in managing drugs, albeit tacitly in many cases, and some of the current functions nurses carry out may appear to be, but are not, prescribing.

For example, standing orders are commonly used and in most states are a legal and convenient way for drugs and treatment to be given on a physician's order but within the discretion of the nurse. Likewise, PRN orders are a common tool for assuring the patient receives medication in the physician's absence and within the nurse's discretion. The significant difference between those techniques and prescribing, however, is in their relative patient specificity. A California attorney general's opinion seized on this distinction in declaring that standardized procedures (protocols) authorized by the NPA do not encompass prescribing by registered nurses but do include an *individualized* protocol for the registered nurse to carry out. As explained below, this distinction is not sound.

Nurse practitioners and clinical specialists seeking to determine the extent of legal coverage for prescribing activities generally look to the NPA. If the NPA has addressed this function, it will often set forth specific conditions under which the nurse must operate. Other statutes may provide authority for prescriptive actions. In Vermont, the authority is found in the Pharmacy Act.[88] In other states, such as California, the Pharmacy Act omits reference to nurses issuing a prescription.[89] In Utah, the prescriptive authority for nurses is contained in a statute separate from both the nursing and the medical practice acts.[90]

In those states with specific legal authority for nurses to prescribe, there are fewer problems of interpretation. In states with broadly worded practice acts, the question of whether prescriptive activity is covered may be resolved by the courts, as in *Sermchief*. In other states, such as California, only advisory attorney general opinions exist interpreting the NPA in a restrictive manner.[91]

The attorney general reasoned that the Medical Practice Act made it a misdemeanor for a person who, among other things, ''prescribes for any ailment . . . without being authorized to perform such act pursuant to a certificate obtained in accordance with some other provision of law.''[92] Since the NPA did not specifically authorize prescribing, but rather addressed the ability to administer medications when ordered by a physician, the attorney general concluded there was a legislative intent that a ''physician's judgment is needed in each individual case and that the treatment be only as ordered by the physician.''[93]

This reasoning obviously cannot be reconciled with the delegation of discretion doctrine, which authorizes nurses to administer medication on a PRN basis without the physician's judgment—a doctrine recognized in California. Moreover, the California NPA expressly permits additional sharing of functions between collaborating physicians and registered nurses and authorizes implementation of standardized procedures based on observed abnormalities. Thus, the NPA is another act that authorizes prescribing, and since the misdemeanor penalties of the Medical Practice Act disclaim coverage for other professionals who are authorized by their own practice acts to carry out certain medical functions, nurses should be able to avoid violation of the statute.[94]

The Pharmacy Act may also limit those from whom a pharmacist may accept a prescription, and this may result in restricting the nurse's ability to prescribe. There is, however, a growing trend toward identifying the prescriber as a ''person lawfully authorized to prescribe,'' and this language is recommended by the National Association of Boards of Pharmacy.[95] This avoids any restriction on professionals authorized by their own practice acts to prescribe.

The impact of other statutes is especially important when relying on a broadly worded NPA to uphold prescriptive authority. If the medical practice act and pharmacy act do not prohibit prescribing by those otherwise lawfully authorized to prescribe, then a broadly worded NPA, read together with these statutes, can be the basis of such authority. A general rule of statutory construction is that statutes must be construed to be in harmony with one another. The separation of the various statutes into codes is for convenience only, and the codes are to be read together.

Negligent Prescribing. In general, for prescription drugs the drug manufacturer has a duty to warn the prescribing physician of the harmful risks associated with the drug; the duty does not extend to the ultimate consumer.[96] The physician who prescribes the drug then has an independent duty to assess the dangers of medication and transmit relevant warnings to his or her patients. The rationale for the rule is twofold: first, the information is technical and not easily grasped by the layperson, hence a learned intermediary, the prescriber, is necessary; second, it is virtually impossible for the manufacturer to deliver a direct warning to the consumer.

Certain exceptions to this rule exist in the area of vaccines and birth control pills. These depend on the manner of dispensing. Although a prescription may be necessary for such drugs, they may not be dispensed in this manner. That is, the vaccine is dispensed at a mass community clinic without the normal individualized balancing of risks involved.[97] Birth control pills, on the other hand, contain patient inserts warning of the most common and serious side effects.

When the manufacturer warns of a risk associated with a drug, the prescriber may be liable for failure to warn the patient if the risk was material to the patient's decision to take it.[98] *Gugino*, discussed earlier, makes clear that the practitioner must keep abreast of literature concerning risks of treatment and he or she is charged with constructive knowledge of these risks. Although virtually no negligent prescription cases have been brought against nurse practitioners or clinical specialists to date, *Gugino* makes clear that these principles would apply to the nurse prescriber.

Sheenan v. Pima County[99] illustrates a wrongful death action brought against a county for the asserted failure of a pediatrician nurse practitioner to warn of the dangers of polio vaccine. Both the county and the drug manufacturer were sued. Daniel Sheenan died after contracting polio from his daughter, who had been given a dosage of the Sabin oral polio vaccine. The suit alleged a failure to warn of the danger of contact polio.[100] The jury returned defense verdicts, and the plaintiff appealed.

The mother of the child brought her to the well-baby clinic to be vaccinated. The order for the vaccine was given by a pediatric nurse practitioner. The drug was administered by a licensed practical nurse. There was a physician present at the clinic, but he did not examine the child. The well-baby clinic was operated by the county health department and provided free preventative services to children up to 6 years of age.

There was no dispute that the deceased died from a case of contact polio due to the vaccine administered to his daughter; the Sabin oral polio vaccine contains a live attenuated virus. The evidence disclosed that Mrs. Sheenan was never warned of the risk of getting contact polio from her child, which occurs in approximately one in 5 million cases. The appellate court upheld defense verdict.

Recommendations and trends

Although nurse practitioners they have faced adversities and uncertainties in their struggle to practice, their pioneering spirits have been an inspiration for the entire profession. Advanced practice, however, is not without drawbacks: it exposes the nurse practitioner to greater liability. The courts most likely will apply legal principles that have evolved in physician malpractice cases to decide new areas of nursing malpractice, such as negligent prescribing. The best defense against liability is to know the limitations of one's abilities and to refer the patient when these limits are reached.

The applicable standard of care is an important protection for the nurse practitioner faced with potential liability for advanced practice. Nurse practitioners must act to ensure that the standard to which they are held is provided by members and standards of their particular practice. Legislative efforts may be necessary to establish and to protect the nurse practitioner's autonomous standard of care.

Endnotes

1. *See, e.g., Chalmers-Francis v. Nelson,* 57 P.2d 1312 (Cal. 1936); *Magit v. Bd. of Medical Examiners,* 366 P.2d 816 (Cal. 1961).
2. *See, e.g., Fraijo v. Hartland Hosp.,* 160 Cal. Rptr. 246 (Cal. App. 1979).
3. NATIONAL JOINT PRACTICE COMMISSION, DEFINITION OF JOINT OR COLLABORATIVE PRACTICE IN HOSPITALS (1977).
4. NATIONAL JOINT PRACTICE COMMISSION, GUIDELINES FOR ESTABLISHING JOINT OR COLLABORATIVE PRACTICE IN HOSPITALS (1981).
5. U.S. PUBLIC HEALTH SERVICE, DEPARTMENT OF HEALTH, EDUCATION AND WELFARE, EXTENDING THE SCOPE OF NURSING PRACTICE: A REPORT OF THE SECRETARY'S COMMITTEE TO STUDY EXTENDED ROLES FOR NURSES 4-6 (1971).
6. Bullough, *Licensure And The Medical Monopoly,* THE LAW AND THE EXPANDING NURSING ROLE 22 (1975).
7. GRADUATE MEDICAL EDUCATION NATIONAL ADVISORY COMMITTEE, REPORT OF THE GRADUATE MEDICAL EDUCATION NATIONAL ADVISORY COMMITTEE TO THE SECRETARY, DEPARTMENT OF HEALTH AND HUMAN SERVICES 52-53 (1980).
8. Baker, *Entrepreneurial Practice for Nurses: A Response To Hershey,* 11 LAW, MEDICINE AND HEALTH CARE, 257, 258 (December 1983).
9. Bullough, *The Current Phase in the Development of Nurse Practice Acts,* 28 ST. LOUIS UNIV. LAW JOURNAL 376, 383 (1984) (hereinafter cited as *Bullough*).
10. N.H. REV. STAT. ANN. §326-B:10 (Supp. 1981).
11. CAL. BUS. & PROF. CODE §2746.5 (West Supp. 1984).
12. *Sermchief v. Gonzales,* 660 S.W.2d 683 (Mo. 1983) (en banc).
13. *Id.* at 689.
14. *See, e.g.,* Greenlaw, *Sermchief v. Gonzales and the Debate Over Advanced Nursing Practice,* 12 LAW, MEDICINE, AND HEALTH CARE 30 (February 1984).
15. AMERICAN COLLEGE OF NURSE-MIDWIVES, WHAT IS A NURSE-MIDWIFE? (June 1979).
16. *Bullough, supra* note 9, at 376.
17. *Frank v. South,* 194 S.W. 375 (Ky. 1934); *Chalmers-Francis v. Nelson,* 6 Cal. 2d 402 (1936); *Magit v. Bd. of Medical Examiners,* 57 Cal. 2d 74 (1961).
18. *Chalmers-Francis v. Nelson,* 6 Cal.2d 402 (1936).
19. *Compare Arkansas State Department of Health v. Drs. Thibault & Council,* 664 S.W.2d 445 (Ark. 1984) (presence of licensed physician or dentist required when any nurse administers anesthesia) *with Brown v. Allen Sanitarium,* 364 So.2d 661 (La. App. 1978) (hospital was not negligent merely because it did not require a physician to supervise the nurse anesthetist in either the selection or the method of anesthetizing the patient; legislature did not intend to require such degree of supervision over a person with the skill and training of a registered nurse anesthetist). The Louisiana Court of Appeals has upheld, however, the dismissal of a certified registered nurse anesthetist (CRNA) who failed to report blood pressure accurately and failed to administer fluids according to a surgeon's orders. *Young v. Dep't. of Health and Human Resources,* 405 So.2d 1209 (La. App. 1981).
20. *Ybarra v. Spangard,* 25 Cal.2d 486 (1944).
21. *See, e.g.,* W. PROSSER, LAW OF TORTS 161 (1971) (hereinafter cited as *Prosser*).
22. *See generally* AMERICAN NURSES' ASSN., THE NURSING PRACTICE ACT: SUGGESTED STATE LEGISLATION (1980). All state nursing practice act citations are listed in Appendix IV.
23. The standards for clinical specialists in maternal and child health nursing and psychiatric and mental health nursing are described, respectively, in Chapters 11 and 8.
24. 411 P.2d 861 (Wash. 1966).
25. 205 So.2d 751 (La. App. 1971).
26. BAJI JURY INSTRUCTION NO. 6.00 (1977 rev.).
27. Amicus Brief at 5, California Coalition of Nurse Practitioners, *Fein v. Permanente Medical Group,* Civ. No. 18349 (filed 1983).
28. 300 N.W.2d 380, 382 (Mich. App. 1980).
29. *Id.*
30. *See Webb v. Jorns,* 473 S.W.2d 328 (Tex. Civ. App. 1980), *rev'd on other grounds,* 488 S.W.2d 407 (nurse anesthetist's liability is measured by whether there was conformity on his or her part to those standards of professional conduct justifiably expected of a nurse performing such duties); *Mohr v. Jenkins* 393 So.2d 245 (La. App. 1981) (holding).
31. 211 Cal. Rptr. 368 (Cal. 1985).
32. *Fein v. Permanente Medical Group,* 175 Cal. Rptr. 177 (Cal. App. 1981).
33. *Id.* at 192.
34. Amicus Brief, California Coalition of Nurse Practitioners, *Fein v. Permanente Medical Group,* Civ. No. 18349 (filed 1983).
35. *Id.* at 5.
36. 211 Cal. Rptr. 368 (Cal. 1985).
37. *Id.* at 377 (footnote omitted). The court specifically relied on the fact that the California's NPA recognizes as nursing practice a variety of functions, including the observation of signs and symptoms of illness, reactions to treatment, general behavior, or general physical condition, as well as the determination of whether such signs, symptoms, reactions, behavior, or general appearance

exhibit abnormal characteristics. *Id.*, citing CAL. BUS. & PROF. CODE §2725 (West 1979).

38. The cases discussed throughout this book demonstrate numerous instances in which physicians have testified to the standard of care of a nurse in a nursing malpractice case. The instances of nurses testifying to a physician's standard of care are virtually nonexistent. *See, e.g., Rudy v. Mashorer,* 706 P.2d 1234 (Ariz. App. 1985) (testimony of psychiatric nurse cannot establish standard of care of psychiatrist in a failure to recognized suicide potential of a patient and to order appropriate preventive action); *but see Maloney v. Wake Hospital Systems, Inc.*, 262 S.E.2d 680, 684 (N.C. App. 1980) (court accepted a nurse's testimony regarding intravenous therapy in a malpractice case, stating that "The role of the nurse is critical in providing a high standard of health care in modern medicine. Her expertise is different from, but no less exalted than, that of the physician"). See Chapter 32 on expert nurse witnesses.
39. *Prosser, supra* note 21, at 164.
40. *Compare* MO. REV. STATE. §335.016(8) (Supp. 1982) *with* CAL. BUS. & PROF. CODE §2725 (West Supp. 1984).
41. Kelly and Garrick, *Nursing Negligence in Collaborative Practice: Legal Liability in California,* 12 LAW, MEDICINE, AND HEALTH CARE 260 (December 1984).
42. *Czubinsky v. Doctors Hospital,* 188 Cal. Rptr. 685 (Cal. App. 1983).
43. The opinion does not state that he testified over defense objection.
44. 705 P.2d 781 (Wash. App. 1985).
45. *Res ipsa loquitor* is explained in Chapter 4.
46. 710 P.2d 939 (Kan. 1985).
47. *Savarese v. East Jefferson General Hospital,* No. 255-867 C/W 261-062, *reported in,* 27 ATLA LAW REPORTER 232 (June 1984).
48. 326 S.E.2d 271 (N.C. App. 1985).
49. 366 N.W.2d 249 (Mich. App. 1985).
50. 480 N.E.2d 464 (Ohio 1985).
51. 548 F.2d 316 (10th Cir. 1977).
52. *Id.* at 318.
53. *Id.*
54. 526 F.2d 202 (8th Cir. 1975).
55. This concept is explained in Chapter 4.
56. No. 83-2-07528-9 (Wash. King's Cty. Sup. Ct., decided Sept. 19, 1983), *reported in,* 27 ATLA LAW REPORTER 87 (March 1984).
57. *Alternative Procedures: There Is More to Birth Than Scissors, String, and Boiling Water,* TRIAL 8 (May 1984).
58. *Id.*
59. *Id.*
60. *Id.*
61. *See, e.g., United States v. Jablonski,* 712 F.2d 392 (9th Cir. 1983), where the court upheld a judgment against the government based on psychiatrists' failure to adequately warn an identifiable victim of their patient's potential violence against her, even though the patient made no specific threat against the victim. Court based its ruling on the patient's past history of violence contained in old medical charts and because the patient threatened violence against the victim's mother. The court based its holding on *Tarasoff v. Regents of the University of California,* 131 Cal. Rptr. 14 (Cal. 1976), which is discussed in Chapter 8.

    The California Supreme Court has extended its ruling in *Tarasoff* to psychologists. In *Hedlund v. Superior Court of Orange County,* 194 Cal. Rptr. 805 (Cal. 1983), the court's reasoning makes it clear that the ruling would extend to clinical nurse specialists in this field. The court noted that therapists have a duty to warn an identifiable potential victim that a patient has threatened violence. The therapist also has a duty to persons in close relationship to the object of a patient's threat, "for the therapist must consider the existence of such persons both in evaluating the seriousness of the danger of the patient and in determining the appropriate steps to be taken to protect the named victim." *Id.* at 811. Thus, in *Hedlund,* a claim was proper against psychologists who were providing counseling and psychotherapy to a woman and her friend and who had been told of the friend's intent to do serious injury to the woman. The psychologists failed to warn her of his intent, and she was seriously injured by the man. Her child who was present at the shooting could also assert a negligence claim.

    For an excellent review of the psychiatric nurse's standard of care in this area, *see* Kjervik, *The Psychiatric Nurse's Duty to Warn Potential Victims of Homicidal Psychotherapy Outpatients,* LAW, MEDICINE, AND HEALTH CARE 9 (December 1981).
62. Kjervik, *The Psychotherapist's Duty to Act Reasonably to Prevent Suicide: A Proposal to Allow Rational Suicide,* 2 SPECIAL PERSPECTIVE, 207 (No. 2 1984). See Chapter 8 for further information.
63. *Prosser, supra* note 21, at 162.
64. 403 N.E.2d 1166 (Mass. 1980).
65. *Id.* at 1167.
66. The claim that diagnosis is a medical act, and hence nurses who perform it are illegally practicing medicine, has never been raised in a lawsuit challenging critical care nursing practice. Rather, the challenges chiefly concern nurse practitioners whose practice is an economic threat in the ambulatory care setting.
67. *E.g.*, CAL. BUS. & PROF. CODE §2725 (West Supp. 1986) (nursing practice includes the "observation of signs and symptoms of illness, reactions to treatment, general behavior, or general physical condition, and (1) determination of whether such signs, symptoms, reactions, behavior, or general appearance exhibit abnormal characteristics; and (2) implementation, based on observed abnormalities, or appropriate reporting, or referral, or standardized procedures, or changes in treatment regimen in accordance with standardized procedures, or the initiation of emergency procedures . . .").
68. 288 P.2d 581 (Cal. App. 1955).
69. *Bullough, supra* note 9.
70. The nurse practitioner or clinical specialist will not become discouraged. Remember that the measurement of blood pressure was once thought to be a medical act, and California's Medical Practice Act *continues to define it as a medical function. See, e.g.*, CAL. BUS. & PROF. CODE §2038 (West Supp. 1984).
71. *E.g., Fraijo v. Hartland Hospital,* 160 Cal. Rptr. 246 (Cal. App. 1980).
72. These are reviewed in Chapter 29.
73. COLO. REV. STAT. §12-38-103(10) (Supp. 1982).
74. *Prosser, supra* note 21, at 162.
75. *Id.* at 163.
76. *Id.*
77. *Id.*
78. *See, e.g., Cooper v. National Motor Bearing Co.*, 288 P.2d 581 (Cal. App. 1955); *Goff v. Doctor's General Hospital of San Jose,* 333 P.2d 29 (Cal. App. 1958); *Samaii v. Baystate Medical Center,*

Inc., 395 N.E.2d 455 (Mass. App. 1979); *Utter v. United Hospital Center,* 236 S.E.2d 213 (W. Va. 1977).

79. *Sermchief v. Gonzales,* 660 S.W.2d 683, 690 (Mo. 1983) (en banc).
80. *E.g., Fraijo v. Hartland Hospital,* 160 Cal. Rptr. 246 (Cal. App. 1979).
81. *Prosser, supra* note 21, at 145.
82. 145 A.2d 809 (N.J. App. 1958).
83. *Id.*
84. *See id.; see also Sing v. Owens,* 205 p.2d. 3 (Cal. 1949) (failure to recognize inadequacy of treatment is strong evidence of a breach of the standard of care); *Prosser, supra* note 21, at 469.
85. CAL. BUS. & PROF. CODE §4306 (West Supp. 1984).
86. *Id.* at §4213.
87. *Id.* at §4049.
88. VT. STAT. ANN. tit. 26, §1571-1584 (1983).
89. CAL. BUS. & PROF. CODE §4036 (West Supp. 1984).
90. UTAH CODE ANN. §58-31A-16 (Supp. 1983).
91. 64 Ops. Cal. Att'y Gen. 240 (March 1981).
92. CAL. BUS. & PROF. CODE §2052 (West Supp. 1984).
93. 64 Ops. Cal. Att'y Gen. 240, 251 (March 1981).
94. *See, e.g.,* CAL. BUS. & PROF. CODE §2052 (West Supp. 1984).
95. National Association of Boards of Pharmacy, THE MODEL STATE PHARMACY ACT (1977).
96. *See, e.g., Hoffman v. Sterling Drug Co., Inc.,* 485 F.2d 1132 (3d Cir. 1973); Rheingold, *Products Liability—The Ethical Drug Manufacturer's Liability,* 18 RUTGERS LAW REVIEW, 947 (1964).
97. *Davis v. Wyeth Laboratories, Inc.*, 399 F.2d 121 (9th Cir. 1968).
98. *Cobbs v. Grant,* 109 Cal. Rptr. 505 (Cal. 1972).
99. 660 P.2d 486 (Ariz. App. 1983). This case is also discussed in Chapter 13; issues are elaborated on there also.
100. The theory was that the product was unavoidably unsafe and therefore was a defective product because no one warned of the dangers. This is known as strict liability in tort, which is discussed in Chapters 2 and 33.

Additional Readings

Eskreis, *The Legal Implications In Utilizing The Nurse Anesthetist In Place Of The Anesthesiologist,* 7 WHITTIER LAW REVIEW 855 (1985).

Kelly and Garrick, *Nursing Negligence in Collaborative Practice: Legal Liability in California,* LAW, MEDICINE, AND HEALTH CARE, 260 (December 1984).

Wolff, *Court Upholds Expanded Practice Roles For Nurses,* LAW, MEDICINE, AND HEALTH CARE 28 (February 1984).

Note, *The Legal Implications of Utilizing the Nurse Anesthetist in Place of the Anesthesiologist,* 7 WHITTIER LAW REV. 855 (1985).

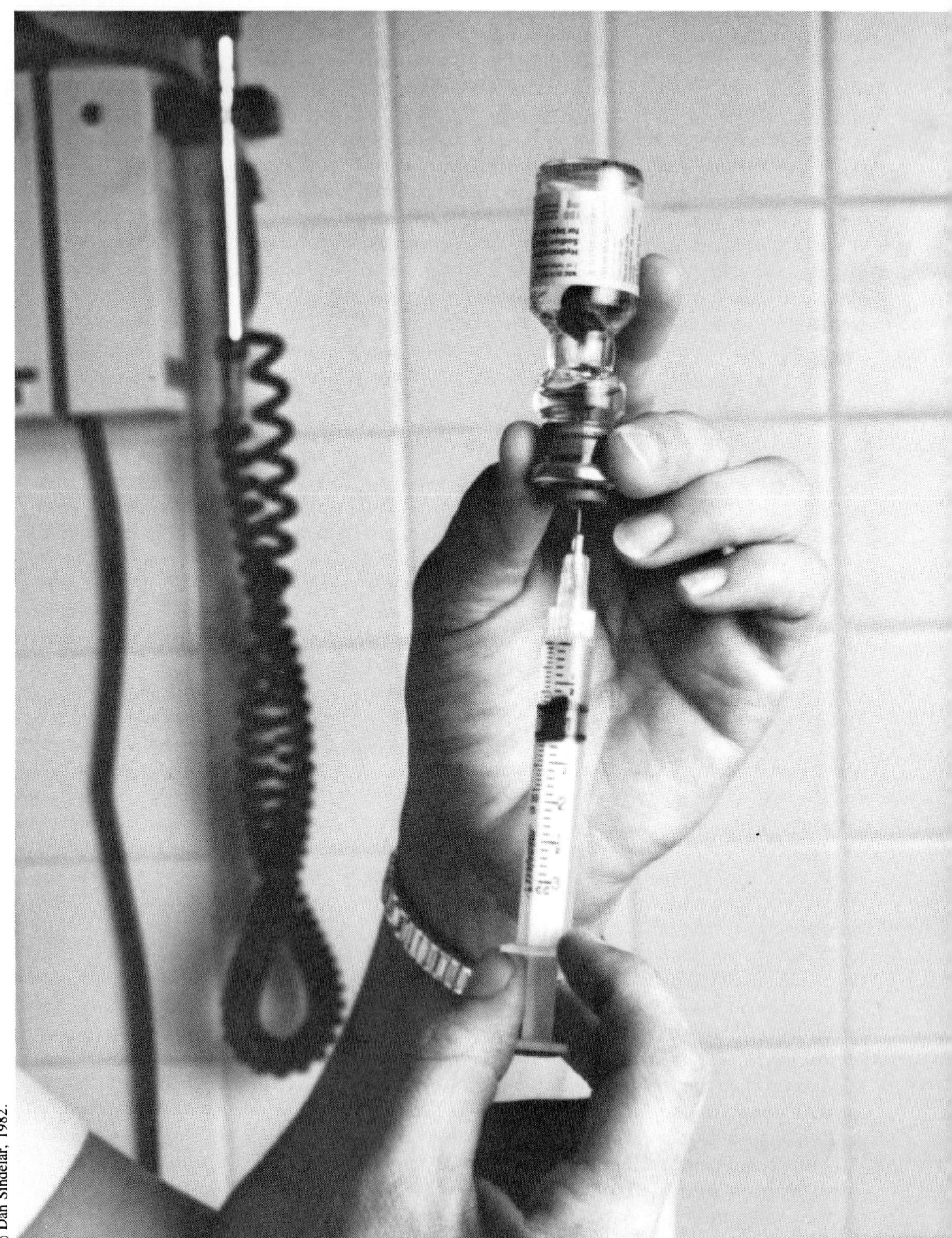

UNIT IV

Criminal and Administrative Law

Chapter 24

Criminal law overview

Mary E. Kelly

The number of criminal prosecutions brought against health care providers has increased in the last 2 decades. Nurses who enter the criminal justice system get a lot of publicity—some say more than nurses who accomplish great achievements.[1] The celebrated cases generally involve the death of the terminally ill or the intensive care unit (ICU) patient, and the nurse is portrayed as either the angel of mercy or the angel of death depending on the press' perception of the nurse's intent and role.

The nurse's criminal liability in the health care setting may be based on misdemeanor or felony charges. Misdemeanor crimes include, for example, the illegal practice of medicine, the failure to report child or elder abuse, or the falsification of medical records. Felony crimes are more serious; examples include murder, manslaughter, or unlawful possession of narcotics.

Certain business practices in independent nursing practice also have the potential for criminal liability. Any kind of inducement or compensation for patient referrals is prohibited by federal law with respect to Medicare patients; many states prohibit such practices with respect to all patients. Fraudulent business practices are also proscribed by federal and many states' laws.

This chapter provides an overview of the criminal justice system and an analysis of the nurse's potential criminal liability in various health care settings. Although the chapter's focus is on crimes occurring in the health care context, the principles apply equally to nurses charged with crimes arising outside the health care area.[2] The chapter is organized around the two components of the criminal justice system: the substantive law—the substance or definition of crimes and criminal law; and the procedural law—the rights or protections that apply throughout the criminal process.

Substantive criminal law

The broad aim of the criminal law is to prevent harm to society[3] by declaring what conduct is criminal and prescribing the punishment for such conduct.[4] Consequently, crimes are often classified according to the various interests of society that are protected from harm.

These interests include protection of people from physical harm,[5] and of property from loss, destruction, or damage.[6] Other recognized interests are protection of government from injury or destruction[7]; protection against interference with the administration of justice[8]; protection of the public health,[9] the public peace, and order[10]; safeguards against sexual immorality[11]; and protection of interests that are continually evolving.[12]

Crimes are generally categorized as felonies or misdemeanors. Some jurisdictions distinguish between felonies and misdemeanors by defining a felony as any crime punishable by imprisonment in the state penitentiary or prison or by death and defining a misdemeanor as anything punishable by fine or imprisonment in a local jail or both of these.[13] Others define the two in terms of the length of imprisonment. In these jurisdictions, any crime punishable by death or imprisonment for more than

1 year is a felony; any other crime (those punishable by under a year in a prison or a fine or both) is a misdemeanor.[14]

LIMITATIONS ON SUBSTANTIVE CRIMINAL LAW

Each of the three branches of government has a role in the criminal justice system. The legislative branch of both the federal and the various state governments defines crime. The executive branch prosecutes crime.

The judicial branch oversees the trial, and in some cases, it may act as the fact finder instead of the jury. This is known as a "bench trial," where the defendant waives his or her right to a jury trial[15] and the judge decides guilt. If a guilty verdict is reached in either a bench or a jury trial, the judge determines the sentence of a convicted defendant (certain death penalty statutes, however, allow the jury to impose death or life sentences).

The judicial branch also reviews appeal and postconviction claims of the defendant. These claims usually challenge the trial court's pretrial and/or trial rulings or the sufficiency of the evidence.

Federal vs. State Jurisdiction Over Substantive Crimes. Federal substantive criminal law is created by statute; state law, on the other hand, is the creation of common law and statutory law. In many states, common-law crimes have been codified by the legislatures.

Whether the state or the federal government has jurisdiction to prosecute the crime depends on the nature of the crime. Generally there are four kinds of powers: those that belong exclusively to the states; those that belong exclusively to the federal government; those that may be exercised concurrently and independently by both; and those that may be exercised by the states but only until Congress begins to act on the subject.[16]

The United States Constitution specifically authorizes Congress to legislate on certain matters, such as commerce among the states.[17] The Supreme Court has overturned some state criminal statutes that operate as regulations of interstate commerce.[18]

State and federal statutes may prohibit the same conduct; an example is possession of a controlled substance with intent to sell it. If Congress did not intend to make its jurisdiction exclusive over the crime and the state statute does not conflict with federal law, the state's concurrent jurisdiction over the crime will usually be upheld.[19] Certain state offenses committed on federally owned property may also be the subject of federal jurisdiction.[20]

In certain other circumstances, Congress has enacted criminal statutes where the states individually have been unable to prosecute crimes because, for example, the accused has fled the state's jurisdiction with stolen property. The basis of Congress' authority to outlaw interstate transportation of stolen property is Congress' broad power over interstate commerce, which authorizes federal prosecution of crimes that impact on interstate commerce.

The federal system generally prosecutes crimes committed on federal lands or property, such as those occurring on the grounds of Veterans' Administration facilities and reservations. Federal law also prohibits transporting stolen goods across state lines, narcotics trafficking and importing, and certain fraudulent business practices that involve the government or government property, impact on interstate commerce, or involve the mails as a means to accomplish the scheme.

State laws generally define crime and delegate authority to various agencies to prosecute them. Crimes that existed as common law such as breaking and entering, forgery, larceny, robbery, murder, rape, and theft are typically state crimes.

Constitutional Limitations. The federal constitution imposes limitations on the substantive exercise of federal and state legislative power. First, the definition of a crime is strictly construed and it must not be so vague that it fails to provide the individual adequate notice of what conduct is prohibited. Second, the definition of the crime must not unduly restrict or impede the individual's exercise of constitutional rights.

The courts strictly construe criminal statutes to make sure that they meet the historical notions of fundamental fairness because in the criminal context, liberty, a fundamental right, is at issue. A basic premise is that there must be some advance warning to the public as to what conduct is criminal and how it is punishable.[21] This ensures that the crime with which the accused is charged is the crime that the law prohibits. Otherwise, the statute is unconstitutional.

The courts also may invalidate a statute defining a crime if it unreasonably restricts or "chills" the exercise of a constitutional right and the government does not have a compelling interest for outlawing the activity. Statutes imposing restrictions on speech, assembly, religion, privacy, and the like are the most vulnerable to successful constitutional attack.[22] For example, legislation making the use of contraceptives illegal has been overturned by the Supreme Court because the crime as defined invades the right to privacy.[23]

On the other hand, a challenge to the legality of a criminal statute based on the failure of the statute to achieve its objective is generally rejected. The courts will virtually always defer to the legislature and uphold the statute if the statute bears a rational relationship to injury to the public.[24] Under this principle, crimes that relate generally to social and economic welfare and that do not unreasonably impede the exercise of the right to privacy or other constitutional right have been upheld where any rational relationship to social and economic welfare can be offered.

THE SUBSTANCE OR ELEMENTS OF CRIMES

In general, crimes are defined in terms of (1) prohibited conduct or results and (2) any attendant circumstances. Attendant circumstances may be the requirement of previous marriage (bigamy) or an under-age girl (statutory rape). The prohibited results, conduct, or attendant circumstances are generally known as the elements of a crime, and the prosecution must prove each one beyond a reasonable doubt. The statute defining the crime sets forth the penalty for the crime.[25]

A basic premise underlying Anglo-American law is that there can be no punishment for bad thoughts alone. Generally, the law requires two elements: (1) an act, or nonaction where there is a duty to act,[26] called *actus reus;* and (2) criminal intent or a guilty mind, known as *mens rea*. Both *actus reus* and *mens rea* must be present.[27]

The Defendant's Mental State. The Model Penal Code establishes four basic types of crimes that require fault.[28] The first category requires that the defendant intentionally or purposefully did an act, or failed to act, or intentionally caused a specific forbidden result by virtue of the act or omission. The next concerns crimes that have as a necessary element knowledge of the nature of the act, of the failure to act, or of the result that will follow from the attendant circumstances. The third category requires recklessness in doing the act or omission or in causing the result (actor should have known risk that conduct involves). The final category concerns negligence in doing the act, causing the result, or failing to act (subjective fault or realization of the risk is not required). In addition to these categories, there exists a class of crimes that imposes strict liability and does not require any mental state.[29]

Examples of the differences in crimes that focus on conduct as opposed to results include (1) reckless and careless driving crimes, which do not refer to any bad result of such conduct, (2) crimes such as involuntary manslaughter and battery, which may be committed by reckless conduct that causes death or bodily injury (battery) to another human being, and (3) reckless conduct causing injury or destruction of another's property.[30]

Fewer crimes are defined in terms of negligence as compared to recklessness.[31] Nevertheless, in some states negligent conduct in driving an automobile that causes death constitutes a crime, and there are other special statutory crimes based on bad results negligently caused.[32]

Criminal negligence clearly requires greater fault or awareness of the risk than that required in civil negligence. Just how much more—whether greater risk, subjective awareness of the risk, or both—is not always clear from the statute or court decisions, and different jurisdictions may reach different conclusions on the three variations.[33]

Many jurisdictions have strict liability crimes. These crimes typically do not contain any mental state element; they impose liability in the absence of fault. For example, any person present in the United States illegally, an "illegal alien," who possesses a firearm is guilty of a felony. The law is not concerned with whether or if the alien knows the law prohibits possession of the gun.[34]

Causation. Criminal law, like civil law, requires causation. Where the definition of a crime requires that certain conduct produce a certain result (in murder the conduct must produce death; in arson the conduct must produce a tangible item to burn), the prosecutor must prove that the conduct caused the result.[35]

Sometimes a person acts with intent to kill another but succeeds in inflicting a wound that, in a healthy person, would not be a fatal wound. Perhaps the victim is in a weakened condition or would have died eventually from disease. If the defendant's action causes death to occur sooner than anticipated, the defendant is guilty of murdering the victim.[36]

Prohibited Conduct. Criminal penalties extend not only to the perpetrator of the crime, the principal, but also to someone who assists the perpetrator or principal commit a crime. This is known as accomplice liability.

In the life support system context, practitioners have been concerned that their compliance with a terminally ill patient's request to terminate treatment might be viewed as aiding and abetting a suicide or as murder. A California Court of Appeals recently held, however, that a competent patient may refuse treatment, even if that refusal will lead to death, and those respecting the patient's wishes cannot be subjected to criminal liability.[37]

Nurses and physicians who fail to act after observing

a practitioner steal narcotic medication or provide care while in a drug- or alcohol-impaired state are potentially subjecting themselves to criminal prosecution under an aiding and abetting theory of criminal liability. Because nurses and physicians have a duty to act to protect the patient from known or forseeable danger, failure to act may be characterized by a zealous prosecutor as assisting, abetting, or covering up the criminal conduct of another.

Criminal liability for failure to act is a potential reality where deliberate or reckless indifference to protecting the patient can be shown. Where the provider knew or should have known of another provider's criminal conduct that endangered the patient and yet failed to act, an argument may be made that the practitioner should, at the very least, be found liable as an accomplice of the other person[38] or even be found guilty as a principal for criminally or recklessly negligent conduct.

Criminal assistance may occur either before or during the crime (accessory before the fact, aider, and abetter) or after the crime has been committed (accessory after the fact). Obstructing justice and harboring a fugitive are additional crimes that may be used to punish someone who assists a criminal at a more remote time than immediately before, during, or after the commission of the crime.

Those who agree to do something illegal may be found guilty of a crime even though the crime was never actually carried out or was unsuccessful. This is the crime of conspiracy; and the gist of the offense is the agreement to do something illegal.

In some jurisdictions, the law requires the prosecution to prove that an overt act in furtherance of the conspiracy was done. The act need not be criminal in itself; innocent activity is sufficient so long as the act is done to further the object of the conspiracy.[39]

A person may be convicted of both conspiring to do an illegal act and the substantive offense proscribing the illegal act. For example, a person may be convicted both of conspiring or agreeing to possess narcotics and of possessing these narcotics.

Elements of Selected Crimes

Murder. Murder is a crime that existed at common law and is frequently defined as the unlawful killing of another with malice aforethought.[40] In some jurisdictions, murder has been divided into degrees for the purpose of awarding a more severe penalty for some murders than other murders.[41] If by force or duress, one causes another to commit suicide, that person will be guilty of murder.[42]

A Los Angeles coronary care nurse was found guilty of murdering 12 elderly patients at two Riverside County hospitals by giving them lethal doses of a heart medication.[43] The case was tried before a judge without a jury, and the trial lasted 5 months. In addition to convicting the defendant of 12 counts of first-degree murder, the court made the finding of special circumstances under California's multiple murder rule, making the defendant eligible for the death penalty.

The nurse, who worked as a temporary nurse on the night shift at a community hospital, had been in prison since his arrest in 1981. His arrest stemmed from an incident where patients he cared for at the hospital began mysteriously dying in the late night hours. After months of investigation, including exhumation of several victims, the investigators determined the deaths were homicides. Ten times the normal dose of lidocaine was found in each victim on autopsy. Each of the patients was under the care of the defendant nurse, according to the prosecutors.

At trial, evidence established that three of the syringes used on three of the patients who ultimately died had been analyzed and found to have contained 1000 mg of lidocaine. The normal dose is 50 to 100 mg. The defense maintained that there was no evidence that the drug was used purposely to kill the patients and that the high level of lidocaine found in the patients' bodies was the result of buildup of similar doses given over a long period of time.[44]

Another murder conviction was obtained against a vocational licensed nurse, Geneve Jones, for murdering small children hospitalized or treated in institutions for which she worked. She was first convicted in early 1984 of the murder of a 15-month-old girl she had cared for in the spring of 1982 in Kerrville, Texas. She received a 99-year prison sentence.[45] She had been charged with seven other counts of causing injury to a child as a result of seizures suffered by children after she gave them injections at the office of a local pediatrician who employed her as a nurse.

In San Antonio, Jones was the subject of a year-long investigation into the unexplained deaths of 10 infants and an undisclosed number of seizures that her patients sustained on her night shift from 1980 to early 1982.[46] The investigation had produced an indictment against the nurse on a charge of causing injury to a 1-month-old boy who suffered massive hemorrhaging after the nurse allegedly injected him with an anticoagulant drug, heparin. The nurse was employed in the pediatric intensive care unit.

The year-long investigation into additional charges

had been hampered by the fact that the hospital shredded a number of documents concerning pharmaceutical records from 1974 to 1981. The hospital alleged that these records were unrelated to the ICU or the nurse; the shredding was a matter of routine. Nevertheless, this action came at the same time that Dr. Corum, the hospital's executive director, had resigned at the request of the hospital's board of directors. The grand jury was considering whether any hospital administrator or staff intentionally impeded the inquiry.[47]

The prosecution's theory was that the nurse murdered the baby as part of a scheme to end up "a heroine and the head of a pediatric intensive care unit by injecting children with a powerful drug and then saving them."[48] The prosecutor claimed that the child's death and injuries to six other children who survived allegedly similar injections by defendant Jones were part of a scheme by the nurse to show a need for a pediatric ICU in the small hospital.

Nevertheless, the defendant nurse was only convicted of one count of murder. Witnesses testified that the infant went limp, stopped breathing, and appeared to suffer a seizure shortly after Jones injected the child with what she had said were routine immunizations at the clinic. The child died about 2 hours later of cardiac and respiratory arrest.

Manslaughter. Manslaughter, a common-law crime that exists in virtually every jurisdiction,[49] "is an intermediate crime which lies half-way between the more serious crime of murder, at the one extreme, and at the other extreme, justifiable or excusable homicide, which is not criminal at all."[50] Manslaughter is generally divided into voluntary and involuntary.

Voluntary manslaughter is often termed the heat of passion crime.[51] Extenuating circumstances exist in that the defendant, at the time of killing, was in a state of passion as a result of some provocation on the part of the victim. Voluntary manslaughter also is extended in some jurisdictions to intentional homicides where the defendant raises imperfect self-defense, defense of others, or defense of crime prevention.[52]

In *State of New Jersey v. Winter*,[53] a nurse was convicted of manslaughter in the death of a patient. The death resulted from a transfusion of incompatible blood, causing a transfusion reaction in the patient.

The nurse concealed her conduct, disposing of the remainder of the blood. The nurse also altered the records. Although the case was reversed on appeal because of prejudicial error, the nurse's concealment behavior supported an inference of criminal intent. In some jurisdictions, alterations of a medical record or creation of a false medical record is a misdemeanor crime in itself.[54]

Involuntary Manslaughter/Criminal Negligence. Involuntary manslaughter may be separated into either criminal negligence manslaughter or unlawful act manslaughter. Criminal negligence involuntary manslaughter has been imposed for failing to act where there is a duty to act, for example, where a parent refuses to provide medical care for his or her sick child.[55] Unlawful act involuntary manslaughter usually involves death-causing conduct in the commission of an unlawful act (generally a misdemeanor).

In *Commonwealth v. Pierce*,[56] the defendant, who was not a physician, was charged with involuntary manslaughter for wrapping a sick woman in rags soaked with kerosene. The rags caused burns that ultimately caused the woman's death. The defendant requested that the court instruct the jury that, however much risk of death to the victim his conduct created, he could not be found guilty if he honestly believed his treatment would cure her.

The trial court instead instructed the jury that the defendant could be guilty if his conduct created a great risk whether he realized it or not. On appeal, the conviction was affirmed. The appellate court noted that the defendant's conduct had to be riskier than that required for civil negligence and that an objective standard rather than a subjective standard should be the measure.

Other courts have held that no greater risk of harm is required for criminal negligence but apply a subjective standard: the defendant must realize the risk.[57] For example, in a case charging manslaughter where the physician prescribed a fatal treatment or medicine for his sick patients, the court held that the defendant could not be convicted of manslaughter if he honestly believed that his treatment or medicine would cure.[58]

Some courts require both greater risk and subjective realization of that risk. For example, in one case, the court held both were present because the defendant's action caused another's death when he lost consciousness while driving and the defendant had been warned by a physician not to drive alone because of a past history of suffering blackouts.[59]

In *People v. Weiner*,[60] a physician was convicted of 12 counts of involuntary manslaughter because of the deaths of 12 of his patients from hepatitis after receiving intravenous (IV) injections. The defendant physician was a neuropsychiatrist whose treatments included IV injections of certain drugs and also the IV infusion of saline solution and sodium thiamylal (Surital) solution. The state's theory was that death was caused by serum hepatitis transmitted into the bloodstream by these injections.

The appellate court, in considering a challenge to the sufficiency of the evidence, characterized the case as unusual in that the physician was charged with crimes in pursuing procedures he intended to aid the patient. The court also noted that the state failed to prove causation—the precise failure or misconduct that transmitted the fatal disease. The court found particularly disturbing the fact that the specific type of hepatitis (serum or infectious) could not be cultured and that identification of the virus was accomplished by a process of inference.

The court noted that the incidence of viral hepatitis among the defendant's patients as compared to that generally occurring in the locality convincingly pointed to the defendant's office as the place where the infection was transmitted. Although serum hepatitis was transmitted in the defendant's practice, the state had failed to establish that all of the patients had in fact died from serum hepatitis. The court also cited the possibility that one of the defendant's employee nurses was careless.

The court noted that if the case had been one seeking civil relief, *respondeat superior* would make the physician liable for the negligence of the nurse. In a criminal context, negligence must be reckless and wanton and of such character as shows an utter disregard for the safety of others under circumstances likely to cause death. One cannot be criminally convicted on the basis of *respondeat superior* alone. The matter was remanded for a new trial.

Assault and Battery. These are misdemeanor crimes that exist in virtually every jurisdiction.[61] Battery requires physical contact of some sort: bodily injury or offensive touching. Assault places someone in apprehension of a battery, but no physical touching occurs.

Occasionally, assault or battery is classified as a felony where there exists special circumstances such as intent to do great bodily harm or intent to murder. Nurses who work in the home health care setting as private duty nurses may be especially vulnerable to angry family members' accusations. These may range anywhere from simple criminal assault or battery to felony assault or battery.

Commonwealth v. Knowlton[62] illustrates one private duty nurse's nightmare. The family of a critically ill patient cared for in the home by a private duty nurse convinced the prosecutor to bring charges of assault with attempt to murder. The nurse was accused of turning off the respirator attached to a critically ill and severely disabled patient. The alleged victim, 59-year-old William Cronin, who suffers from amyotrophic lateral sclerosis, a degenerative nerve disease, used nods of the head and a lap computer to communicate with the jury.

In videotaped testimony, Cronin told the jury how he watched the nurse pull the life-sustaining machine out of his reach and allegedly tell him, "You're going to die."[63] Cronin had barely been able to move or to speak for the past 2 years because of his affliction.

The prosecution attempted to sway the jury from believing this was an euthanasia or mercy killing case while the defense suggested that Cronin himself might have purposefully pulled the switch. As the trial progressed, neither side could understand the motives or means surrounding Cronin's brush with death.

The trial, which ultimately ended in a defense verdict, took 9 days of the nurse's life. The family portrayed Cronin as a man with a strong will to live. Yet Cronin "appeared only as a slight shadowy figure on the court's television monitors."[64]

In January of 1984, the family hired Knowlton to care for Cronin, who was confined to the home on a respirator. The prosecutor characterized her as a troubled, unsteady woman, beset by professional problems and given to periods of heavy drinking.

On February 16, the family took Cronin to the hospital after he had collapsed. Later that night, after he was revived, he told police that he had been watching television with Knowlton when suddenly, and without explanation, she turned off his machine. At that time Cronin could communicate by drawing letters in the air, which he could not do at the time of trial. Cronin told police that as he gasped for air, Knowlton went into the kitchen and smoked a cigarette. The nurse eventually woke family members.

Family members testified that as they worked to revive Cronin, the nurse stood holding her hands to her head wailing that the patient was dead. Thereafter, the family noticed the machine was off and they turned it back on.

Police officers said *when they questioned Knowlton later that night she seemed drunk and they smelled alcohol; she seemed "spaced out."*[65] Although this occurred after the event occurred and could have been done in response to the event, the nurse's willingness to be questioned and her general behavior were used against her.

This case thus illustrates the importance of obtaining the advice of defense counsel before talking with the police, a procedural right discussed more fully below in the section on procedural criminal law. This evidence, innocently provided with the hope that it would protect her from prosecution, allowed the prosecutor to bootstrap a quasimotive for the alleged murder—that Knowlton was a different person when she drank that she had been drinking that night and therefore was not thinking clearly.

The testimony of Cronin was videotaped the day before it was presented to the jury, because he was too ill to appear in person. Cronin used a computer to give his answers. His testimony was interrupted twice when he became too weary to answer the questions. When asked if he wanted to die, wanted the machine turned off, he said no. On cross-examination, he denied that he had been despondent a few days earlier.

Knowlton testified that she had spent the night watching television with Cronin until around midnight when she went to adjust his bed. She found him slumped over and gray. She acknowledged that she ran over to the patient and said something to the effect that he was dead. Thereafter, the nurse said, she roused the patient's family and urged them to move him to the floor to revive him. She started to cry when the family blamed her for turning off the machine and they would not let her help.

During 3 hours of cross-examination, the prosecutor pressed her about drinking and her claim that she was sober. She admitted she had been fired from or resigned from four hospitals or nursing homes in the past several years because of her drinking problem or questions about her competence. That included her resignation from a hospital 5 months before the Cronin incident after being charged with improperly responding to a man who had suffered a heart attack.

During the closing argument to the jury, defense counsel stressed that the state's case rested on the testimony of a very sick and confused man. The defense attorney suggested that in the chaos, it was possible that one of the family members had turned off the respirator. The prosecution, he noted, never proved a motive.

The prosecutor responded, correctly, that there is no obligation to prove a motive in a criminal case. After the jury returned a not guilty verdict, one anonymous juror said that they did not find the nurse entirely convincing but that they had just as much difficulty with Cronin.[66]

Reporting Statutes. Misdemeanor penalties are often provided for by statute for the failure to report certain injuries. As discussed elsewhere in this book, mandatory child abuse laws punish a nurse's failure to report suspected child abuse. As discussed in Chapter 17, adult protective statutes have begun to include mandatory reporting of elder abuse by health professionals.

Willful Failure to Provide Emergency Services. In some jurisdictions, such as New York, the willful failure to provide emergency services is a misdemeanor crime. There has been at least one hospital that has been convicted of the misdemeanor charge of willfully refusing to provide emergency care and services.[67] A nursing home patient had been transported by private ambulance to a general hospital for emergency treatment of congestive heart failure. When the ambulance arrived, its attendants were advised by a nurse on duty in the emergency room to transport the patient to another hospital for treatment because according to the nurse there were no beds available. The attendants transported the patient to another hospital where she died within hours.

Based on the treating physician's affidavit that his patient's condition presented a medical emergency that the defendant hospital could have managed, the hospital was charged with violating the Public Heath Law. The hospital pleaded guilty and was sentenced to the maximum fine of $2000.00.

The trial court refused the hospital's motion to withdraw its guilty plea to the misdemeanor charge. The court viewed the defense of lack of beds as insufficient to meet the strict liability imposed by the statute. If a hospital refuses emergency treatment for any reason, the court noted, it is liable under the statute provided that the patient is in need of emergency treatment.

Crimes Relating to Property. In addition to laws aimed at punishing conduct that causes physical injury to the public, laws punish thefts of property and trespass to property. Nurses who steal from the facility in which they are working are subject to prosecution. If the theft is done to obtain narcotics, felony possession of narcotics may also be charged.

Criminal trespass to property in recent years has been used to prosecute nuclear war protestors who break into nuclear power plants and antiabortion protestors who break into abortion clinics and cause damage to property. The same laws could be used to prosecute nurses on strike at a hospital who trespass on the hospital's property.

In *People v. Clark*,[68] a licensed practical nurse was charged with assault, criminal trespass, and menacing. The charges stemmed from an incident in which the defendant nurse refused to show her identification card to a hospital security officer.

An argument ensued, and the prosecution contended that the nursing supervisor relieved her of her duties and ordered her to leave the hospital. She allegedly refused to leave, shouted obscenities, threw a telephone at a security officer, and kicked him in the leg. The nurse contended she was beaten and taken unconscious to the emergency room at the hospital and remained in the hospital 3 days for treatment.

The prosecution eventually moved to dismiss the case. Two months later, the prosecutor attempted to restore the case to the calendar on the grounds that the nurse had instituted a civil action against the hospital. The defendant nurse argued that the prosecution was aware of a potential civil action and did not condition the dismissal of the case on abandoning the civil relief.

The court recognized the principle that the prosecutor has the sole authority in determining who should be prosecuted, and the courts should not interfere with the exercise of this authority. Implicit in the court's statement is the view that the separation of powers principle discussed in Chapter 1 deserves deference.

Nevertheless, the court refused to allow the prosecutor to condition dismissal on the defendant's giving up of her civil remedy. Although such a plea bargain is permissible, it must be scrutinized carefully to determine that the consent was freely and voluntarily given. The court noted that several other courts had found agreements to dismiss charges in exchange for dismissal of civil actions to be fundamentally coercive. One court, the California Supreme Court, however, had approved of the practice. Rather than resolve the conflict, which was not necessary to the court's ultimate resolution of the case, the court decided the matter on a much narrower ground.

Fraudulent Business Activities. Laws also exist making criminal both fraudulent business activities and schemes to defraud others of their property. For example, use of the mails to carry out a fraudulent scheme is a federal felony.[69] Occasionally, these types of crime overlap with theft and theft-related crimes. Forgery, embezzlement, and obtaining property are related theft crimes generally prosecuted as state crimes.

In *Adams v. United States*,[70] the owner and operator of a school for practical nurses was charged with the felony federal offense of mail fraud and conspiracy to violate the mail fraud statute. On appeal, the conviction was affirmed.

According to the government's proof, the defendant fraudulently held out that graduates of his school's course would be highly trained and well-qualified practitioners with unlimited employment opportunities at a greater pay rate than a nurse's aide. In fact, the correspondence school offered only limited training with no practical experience, producing nurses who were not qualified for licensure. These graduates could not work in most hospitals.

There was conflicting expert testimony as to the value of the course. Some registered nurses and physicians testified that it provided the practical nurse all that was needed to be known. Others said a graduate of such a program would not be given any more consideration by a prospective employer than would someone who had not taken the course.

The court focused on the fact that the practical nurse had no statutorily defined meaning or recognition in Texas at that time. The state only recognized registered nurses and licensed vocational nurses. A practical nurse, the court noted, is more akin to a nurse's aide.

The court also reasoned that since most hospitals do not hire unlicensed nurses, then graduates of the defendant's program could obtain jobs as nurses' aides, but there was no proof that the diploma or training had any effect in making it easier to do.

There was evidence that some of the sales personnel represented that there would be a license issued; however, the printed material did not mention a license. The defendant's usual reply to license inquiries was that the applicant did not have to be licensed in Texas. The court noted that although this was true, the types of nurses who get jobs as nurses are registered nurses and licensed vocational nurses who do have to have a license.

Nurses who practice in an independent role should be wary of providing or accepting compensation or any other inducement for patient referrals. Some jurisdictions provide misdemeanor penalties for such practices.[71]

Fraudulent reimbursement practices are also the subject of criminal prosecution under federal and state law.[72] These practices may also lead to charges of grand theft. In addition, the defense against such charges may not be covered by the nurse's malpractice policy.

In *Jaffe v. Cranford Insurance Company*,[73] child psychiatrist Jaffe requested his malpractice carrier to provide a criminal defense to his prosecution for Medi-Cal fraud and theft. Generally, most liability policies do not cover criminal conduct. A jury found Jaffe innocent of all charges and the Superior Court of California made a finding that Jaffe's alleged criminal conduct was the result of mistakes and/or errors in submitted billings.

After the trial, Jaffe made a demand for reimbursement of expenses including attorney fees incurred in his criminal defense. When the insurance company denied the request, he instituted a lawsuit for tortious breach of contract.

The court held that there was no potential policy coverage arising from the criminal action against Jaffe, and therefore the insurance company had no duty to defend. The policy, labeled a malpractice liability policy, specifically excluded coverage for damages awarded in several categories of lawsuits, including suits arising out of the performance of criminal acts. The policy covered awards of damages from suits based solely on malpractice, error, or mistake. Jaffe argued that his conduct came within this definition of coverage.

The court disagreed. While an insurer's duty to defend is not coextensive with its duty to pay a damages award, an insured may be entitled to legal defense against a lawsuit even though the insurer is ultimately prohibited from paying the losses therefrom. Where there is no potential that the insurance company will have to assume coverage, there is no duty to defend the insured. In Jaffe's case, the outcome could not have resulted in the insurance company paying the damages under the policy since neither imprisonment nor a fine constitute damages for insurance purposes. The court also looked to the fact that criminal conduct was specifically excluded under the policy. (See also Chapter 27.)

Crimes Relating to Property and Person. Misdemeanor crimes such as the illegal practice of medicine and health or safety code violations may affect property and injure persons. On occasion, a practitioner has been charged with aiding another in the illegal practice of medicine. A conviction for illegal practice may lead to license revocation in some jurisdictions.[74]

In California, practicing midwives must have a certificate to attend cases of normal childbirth.[75] Registered nurses who lack midwifery certification but nevertheless hold themselves out as midwives have been convicted of the illegal practice of medicine, and these convictions have been upheld on appeal.[76] Those who hold proper certification under the healing arts act or who practice in a manner authorized by statute are specifically exempted from the "illegal" practice of medicine and the statute's misdemeanor penalties.[77] Those who do not may be subjected to misdemeanor liability for illegally practicing medicine. California's statute states:

> Any person, who practices or attempts to practice, or who advertises or holds himself out as practicing any system or mode of treating the sick or afflicted in this state, or who diagnoses, treats, operates for, or prescribes for any ailment, blemish, deformity, disease, disfigurement, disorder, injury or other mental or physical condition of any person, without having at the time of so doing a valid, unrevoked certificate as provided in this chapter, or without being authorized to perform such act pursuant to a certificate obtained in accordance with some other provision of law, is guilty of a misdemeanor.[78]

In *Bowland v. Municipal Court for Santa Cruz County*,[79] the California Supreme Court held that this section proscribes two kinds of medically related activities. First, an unlicensed person is prohibited from practicing or holding himself or herself out as practicing any system or mode of treating the sick or afflicted. Second, unlicensed persons are prohibited from making any actual diagnosis, treatment, surgery, or prescription for a mental or physical condition, even if these do not equal a system or mode of treating the sick or afflicted.

In considering whether the section was constitutional as applied to the unlicensed practice of midwifery, the California Supreme Court noted that pregnancy was not a sickness or affliction. Nevertheless, the court noted that the prohibition was against unlicensed persons treating, diagnosing, operating on, or prescribing for a woman undergoing normal pregnancy or childbirth. The court determined the statute was constitutional, not void or overbroad.

The court also held the statute did not interfere with the mother's right to privacy since that right does not protect "a woman's choice of the manner and circumstances in which her baby is born."[80] The court further stated:

> It is true that the Legislature has never attempted to require women to give birth in attendance, just as it has not generally sought to compel adults to obtain medical treatment. But the state has a recognized interest in the life and well being of an unborn child. . . . Its interest in regulating the qualifications of those who hold themselves out as childbirth attenders is . . . equally strong, for many women must necessarily rely on those with qualifications which they cannot personally verify. Nor is the State's interest in requiring a license diminished by the fact that childbirth with assistance, even the assistance of an unlicensed person, may be safer than self-delivery. The state need not prohibit the most unlikely of circumstances—childbirth without assistance—in order to justify regulating the much more common event—assistance of the mother at childbirth. In the area of public welfare, the Legislature need not attack every social problem at once. Plaintiffs' further arguments as to the safety of home deliveries are more properly addressed to the Legislature than to the courts, particularly since the Legislature by its recent enactments to midwifery (e.g., §2350-2359), has shown continuing interest in the area.[81]

Several principles outlined by the court in this quotation are known as principles of statutory construction.

These are principles that a court applies to a civil or criminal statute to analyze the statute's constitutionality. In *Bowland*, application of these principles to the statute's prohibition against unlicensed persons treating a physical condition led the court to conclude that the statute was intended to encompass the practice of midwifery without proper certification.[82] Thus the court ordered that the trial commence on the misdemeanor complaint.

Bowland need not give nurses practicing in an independent role great cause for concern so long as they are acting within their statutory authority. A significant fact in *Bowland* is the fact that the state required separate certification for the practice of midwifery and the registered nurse failed to comply with this requirement. Had the nurse obtained the necessary certification, there would have been no basis for the prosecution.

Nurse practitioners acting properly under authority of state nursing practice acts (NPAs) or specific nurse practitioner statutes have had to defend themselves against criminal charges of illegal practice of medicine that are instituted by states at the behest of state medical boards and state medical associations. For example, in 1977, criminal charges were filed against Joy Adler by the New Jersey Attorney General at the request of the Board of Medical Examiners. Physicians and the institution that employed the nurse were charged with aiding and abetting the illegal practice of medicine. The State Board of Nursing reviewed the charges and determined them to be unfounded and stated that Adler had simply been practicing within the scope of existing nursing practice.[83]

As discussed in Chapter 23, a Missouri Supreme Court case[84] and cases from other jurisdictions[85] support the view that NPAs are to be broadly construed against challenges to authorized nursing practice. The Missouri court dismissed a declaratory judgment action brought by the medical association charging various nurse practitioners with the illegal practice of medicine. The court held that nurse practitioners acting pursuant to a recently amended NPA were authorized to diagnose and to prescribe certain medicines according to protocol and were not practicing medicine without a license.

In a somewhat unusual application of the misdemeanor crime, a registered nurse who was involved in a respirator-related death pleaded guilty to charges of practicing medicine without a license.[86] Thomas Engel worked in a Milwaukee hospital and had provided care to the respirator-dependent patient for 18 days—since the date of the patient's stroke and the resulting severe damage to the brain stem.

Engel had watched the "motionless man's condition worsen by the day, despite all the machines, wires, and tubes that were feeding him and monitoring him, and draining him and even breathing for him."[87] Engel had also watched the distraught family visit every day and learn that there was less and less hope. Engel admitted disconnecting the comatose patient's respirator. He received 20 months' probation for his conviction of practicing medicine without a license.

Perhaps the relatively minor charge brought against Engel as compared to the grave felony with which Knowlton was charged represents a regional difference in attitude. Perhaps the difference between the victims (one whose mind did not function because of brain stem involvement and one whose mind still functioned and whose family still cared for him at home) accounts for the disparate difference in the crimes with which they were charged. Perhaps the difference supports the view of the Michigan Nurses' Association that gender is a factor.

While each of these is plausible and most likely has some bearing, what seems the most compelling difference is family support: the nurse in *Knowlton* lacked the family's support, while Engel had the family's support in taking affirmative action.

Several days before the fatal incident in *Engel*, the patient's physician had informed the family that the patient had suffered irreversible brain damage and would die soon. The family asked the physician to disconnect the life support system, but he refused, although he acknowledged that death was imminent even with life support systems. Consequently under hospital-developed guidelines, the attending physician could have disconnected life support systems if the patient so desired.

Engel admitted that he turned off the alarm systems on the patient's heart monitor and on the respirator. He disconnected the patient's oxygen supply. After waiting 6 to 8 minutes until there was no heartbeat, he reconnected the ventilator and summoned a physician who pronounced the patient dead. Engel notified the family that the patient had died peacefully and without pain.

Engel talked about what he had done with several of his colleagues including a nurse who was married to a police officer. Eight months later, Engel was charged in a criminal complaint with practicing medicine without a license. The district attorney's position was that although the respirator could have been properly disconnected, it could have been accomplished only by a physician. Engel, according to the prosecutor, intentionally and willfully arrogated to himself and acted out of a role the law has reserved to the physician.[88] Is this role really one reserved in law to the physician or merely one that as a matter of custom and hospital practice has fallen to the physician?

ELEMENTS OF SELECTED DEFENSES

Several defenses developed from the common law either justify criminal conduct or excuse it. These defenses are discussed below. Several of these that depend on the intent or belief of the defendant, such as self-defense and defense of others, would have no application to strict liability crimes.

Insanity. The insanity defense is unlike other defenses in that if it is successful, the defendant does not win an outright acquittal but a special verdict or finding is made of not guilty by reason of insanity.[89] Thereafter the defendant is usually committed to a mental institution. The debate over the propriety of the insanity defense has become more vocal since the attempted assassination of President Reagan and the subsequent jury verdict of not guilty by reason of insanity.

If a defendant is found to be incompetent, that is, suffering from a mental disease or defect that renders him or her unable to understand the criminal proceedings or to assist in his or her defense, the defendant cannot be tried, convicted, or sentenced so long as that condition persists. The defendant is generally committed to a mental institution until he or she recovers.[90]

Intoxication. Voluntary or involuntary intoxication, whether brought about by drugs or alcohol, is a defense to a crime when it negates an element of the crime.[91] The most common example is where intoxication negates some mental state element, such as intent or knowledge, which is required by the statute.[92]

Ignorance or Mistake. Ignorance or mistake as to a matter of fact or law is a defense if it negates a mental state required to establish a material element of the crime. The rule does not apply where a defendant would have been guilty of a different crime had the situation been as he or she believed it to be.

An example of an honest mistake of fact (where that mistake may defeat a mental state element in a crime) is the crime of receiving stolen property. If the defendant by a mistake of fact did not know the goods were stolen, the defense might apply.

Generally, the mistake of law defense is not valid where the mistake of law is that the defendant believes his or her conduct is not prohibited by the law.[93] A modern view is that such a belief may be a defense when (1) the defendant does not know that the statute has been enacted and it has not been reasonably made available, or (2) the defendant has reasonably relied on an official statement of the law subsequently determined to be incorrect or invalid. These circumstances may exist in situations where charges of the illegal practice of medicine have been made.

Entrapment. Entrapment may be raised as a defense where a government agent or a private person acting as a government agent, for example, an informer, originates the idea for crime and then induces another person to engage in conduct constituting the crime. The defense also requires that the defendant (the person induced to commit the crime) must not have a preexisting disposition to commit the crime.[94]

The defense may have application in certain ''sting'' operations. For example, it may be asserted where government agents pose as patients and encourage providers to prescribe narcotic drugs under questionable circumstances. Fraudulent medicaid practices may also be the subject of an entrapment defense if government agents posing as patients originate the idea and induce the provider to commit the crime.

A related defense is outrageous government conduct. This is generally raised before trial, and the defendant seeks dismissal of the charges because the government conduct in obtaining the evidence or the indictment is so outrageous that the due process clause is violated.[95] Often it is raised in imperfect entrapment defenses where the defendant clearly had the predisposition to commit the crime but government conduct pushed the defendant to commit the crime.

The entrapment defense will not be successful simply because the government prosecution is the result of a sting operation. In investigating crime, the government may provide the opportunity for crime and if a person who is predisposed to commit crime takes the opportunity, the defense is not valid. The government is free to conduct undercover investigations that provide tools for defendants to use in committing crimes while at the same time collecting evidence of those crimes.

Duress. Duress is a common-law defense that applies in appropriate cases even if no statute authorizes it. The defense requires that there be an unlawful threat made to the defendant by another person that causes the defendant to believe reasonably that the only way to avoid imminent death or serious bodily injury to himself or herself or to another is to engage in conduct that violates the literal terms of the law. This belief must cause the defendant to engage in the illegal conduct. The defense does not apply to the intentional killing of an innocent third person or to a crime committed by an employee who claims that he or she was only carrying out orders.[96]

Necessity. Necessity, another common-law crime that applies even though no statute authorizes it,[97] generally requires some emergency that forces the defendant to choose between the lesser of two evils: either violate the law and produce a harmful result or comply with the law and produce greater or equal harm. For example, the defense could be successfully asserted by a mobile intensive care nurse who breaks the law by speeding over 55 mph to get to the scene of an emergency about which he or she has just been notified. The law views the nurse's conduct under these circumstances as justified because greater harm would result if the nurse did not drive over the speed limit in order to provide necessary emergency care.

Self-defense. Self-defense may apply where the defendant, who is not the aggressor in an encounter, is justified in using a reasonable amount of force against the adversary. The defendant is justified in using a reasonable amount of force if the defendant believes (1) he or she is in immediate danger of unlawful bodily harm from adversary and (2) the use of such force is necessary to avoid the danger.[98] The circumstances may make it reasonable to use deadly force against the adversary's deadly attack that threatens death or serious bodily harm.[99]

This defense may be utilized by nurses in the home health care context who confront violent patients and use force against them. Nurses in private duty may find themselves charged with criminal negligence for abandonment of the patient or criminal assault and battery. The nurse who encounters a physically abusive patient should attempt to call for assistance or leave the premises. The police and the nurse's supervisor should be contacted and detailed charting about the incident should be done.

Making a record is the nurse's best protection against any kind of criminal charge. In the event that charges are brought, documentation of the circumstances surrounding the incident may support the validity of the defense.

Defense of Others. Reasonable force may also be justified in defense of another person, even a stranger, when the defender reasonably believes that the person is in immediate danger of unlawful bodily harm from the adversary. The defender must also reasonably believe that force is necessary to avoid the danger. Deadly force is reasonable when the attack of the adversary on the other person reasonably appears to the defender to be a deadly attack.[100]

Defense of others may be applicable where a nurse uses force against a patient who attacks another patient. The defense also may be invoked by a nurse who uses force against a patient who is attacking a colleague.

The criminal procedural system

The procedural rules that govern the criminal process are created by the constitutions of the federal government and the state in which the crime is being prosecuted. Procedural rules are also created by statute, court rule, or court decision.

The federal and state systems have independent rules governing the procedural aspects of criminal proceedings, as well as variations in the nature and definitions of crime. While the state may provide greater procedural protections than those set forth in the federal constitution, it cannot restrict federal constitutional rights.

CONSTITUTIONAL PROTECTIONS

The Fourteenth Amendment contains a prohibition against state governmental deprivations of life, liberty, and property as does the Fifth Amendment, which applies to the federal government. By Supreme Court decision, various provisions of the Bill of Rights to the United States Constitution have been incorporated to the states through the Fourteenth Amendment. These rights apply in both state and federal proceedings.

A unanimous Supreme Court in 1897 held that the Fifth Amendment right to compensation for property taken by the government was incorporated to the states by virtue of the due process clause of the Fourteenth Amendment.[101] Since then, the Fourteenth Amendment has been held to incorporate to the states the following rights: (1) the speech, press, and religion rights of the First Amendment; (2) the unreasonable searches and seizures provisions of the Fourth Amendment and the right to have illegally seized evidence excluded from a criminal trial; (3) the privilege against self-incrimination guaranteed by the Fifth Amendment; (4) the criminal trial rights to counsel, to a speedy trial and public jury trial, to confrontation of opposing witnesses, and to compulsory process for obtaining witnesses guaranteed by the Sixth Amendment[102]; (5) the Fifth Amendment right prohibiting a defendant from being placed in jeopardy twice for the same offense[103]; and (6) the prohibition against the imposition of cruel and unusual punishment.[104]

With respect to jury trials in criminal cases, the Supreme Court has held that the right to a jury trial exists in all cases that do not involve "petty offenses,"[105] offenses where the potential punishment is greater than 6 months' imprisonment.[106] A jury in a criminal case may be composed of fewer than 12 people,[107] and a unanimous verdict is not required by the Constitution for a conviction.[108]

These constitutional rights mean that certain steps need to be taken in both systems of criminal justice. If these steps are not taken, remedies exist such as the exclusion of evidence at the criminal trial and civil rights actions against the police.[109] On occasion, convictions are reversed if the defendant's constitutional rights have been violated. Reversal generally requires some showing of prejudice to the defendant. Some constitutional rights, such as the denial of the right to counsel, require automatic reversal without a showing of prejudice; prejudice is presumed from the lack of counsel.

The Due Process Clause. The necessity of greater procedural protections in the criminal and quasicriminal setting than those available in the civil context is due to the nature of what is at stake in each of these. In criminal proceedings, life and liberty are usually at stake. In civil proceedings, generally money is the core issue. The criminal trial provides the accused with a process that includes full notice of the charges, the right to compel witnesses on the accused's behalf at the trial, and the right to confront the witnesses against him or her.

Criminal defendants have occasionally been able to successfully argue that the due process clause of the Fourteenth Amendment requires the reviewing court to examine the whole course of the trial proceedings resulting in conviction to determine if the proceedings offend the canons of decency and fairness and express notions of justice.[110] The court will not often overturn a conviction on this ground, and the facts surrounding the case must be so compelling as to "shock" the conscience of the court.

In the case where the rule was applied, police officers illegally broke into the accused's home because of some information they had that the accused was selling narcotics. They observed him swallow two capsules and forcibly, but unsuccessfully, attempted to remove them from his mouth. Thereafter, they transported him against his will to a hospital, where they directed a physician to force an emetic solution into his system by gastric gavage. The stomach pumping produced two capsules of morphine, which the state later introduced as evidence against the accused.

The Supreme Court ruled that the evidence was inadmissible, analogizing the activity to the rack and screw. Coerced confessions, the Court noted, are inadmissible evidence because they offend the community's sense of fair play and decency. The Court reasoned that it would be incongruous to hold that in order to convict a person, the police cannot extract what is in the person's mind but can extract what is in the person's stomach.

ENTRY INTO THE CRIMINAL SYSTEM

The executive branch of government is responsible for prosecuting crimes. In the federal system, the United States Attorney's office is responsible for prosecution of federal crimes; in the various state systems, a similar component of the executive branch, known as the district attorney's or state's attorney's office, conducts the prosecution. The various criminal agencies under both state and federal governments are branches of their executive branches.

Generally, the criminal justice system responds to crime when it is reported or discovered. Once a law enforcement agency has determined that a crime has been committed, a suspect must be identified and apprehended for the case to proceed through the system. Sometimes a suspect is apprehended at the scene, but usually, suspect identification requires investigation.

INVESTIGATION/INTERROGATION

The police will usually approach various suspects and question them about the crime. Depending on whether this questioning can be defined as custodial interrogation, they must provide certain warnings to the suspect before he or she is questioned. The basis for this rests in part on the right against self-incrimination and the due process clause.

In *Miranda v. Arizona*,[111] the Supreme Court held that an accused who is undergoing custodial interrogation must be advised before questioning that he or she has a right to remain silent, that any statement made may be used as evidence against him or her, that he or she has the right to have an attorney present, and that one will be appointed if the person has no money. Custodial interrogation is any police questioning of a person who has been taken into custody or deprived of his or her freedom of action in any significant way.[112] The Fifth Amendment right to remain silent is testimonial in nature, meaning that it only protects speech, not the physical evidence such as hair samples and fingerprints.

The nurse who is questioned about any conduct that indicates in any way suspicion of a crime should request a consultation with an attorney before answering questions. Before being interviewed or answering questions about any incident that has criminal liability overtones, the nurse should consult an attorney with experience in criminal law, with emphasis on scope of practice issues. A nurse attorney may well be the most qualified to assess the accused nurse's culpability vìs-a-vìs the health care setting.

In any event, the nurse is cautioned against granting interviews with law enforcement or the press without the advice and presence of counsel. Caution is never undue in the criminal context. The nurse must always bear in mind when providing statements to hospital or other employer investigators that these statements may and probably will be used as evidence. Not infrequently, the practice setting pits the interests of the nurse against those of the hospital. Depending on the circumstances, either may wish to blame the other for the conduct that is the subject of criminal proceeding. Thus the importance of independent counsel cannot be overemphasized.

With respect to the protections of the Bill of Rights, nurses should keep in mind that these provide protection against certain conduct of the government. Consequently, if a private person violates constitutional rights, there is no remedy in the sense of a civil rights action or in excluding evidence at a criminal trial.

For example, the rights under the *Miranda* decision apply only where an agent of the government is doing the custodial interrogation. Consequently, information given to a supervisor may be turned over to the police and used against the nurse unless an argument can be made that the supervisor was acting on behalf of the police. Even then, it is unlikely that the court would view such questioning as custodial interrogation because the nurse's freedom was not being restrained.

On the other hand, if a nurse is confronted by police on the premises of a hospital or agency and it is clear that he or she is not free to leave the encounter, there is custodial interrogation, which means that the *Miranda* warnings must be given. The question is: how does the nurse know if he or she is free to leave the encounter? If the police have asked the nurse for identification, the nurse is free to leave the encounter, unless, of course, the police indicate that the nurse will be detained or arrested if he or she leaves.

The Supreme Court has held that a person is free to leave any encounter with the police unless and until the police give some objective indication that the person is being detained or arrested.[113] An arrest must be based on probable cause to believe that the nurse committed a crime. A detention, which is supposed to be a brief encounter to dispel the officer's reasonable suspicion that the person committed a crime, requires that the suspicion be based on articulable facts.[114] This means that although a person may be detained for questioning during a brief investigation, the official detaining must have reason to believe that person is involved in some activity connected with a crime that has occurred, is occurring, or is about to occur.

To find out whether the officer intends to detain, the nurse should merely politely inform the officer that he or she does not wish to be interviewed at this time. The officer will either allow the nurse to leave, detain the nurse, or even arrest the nurse. The nurse has the right to have counsel and should assert this right if the nurse is not free to terminate the encounter with law enforcement voluntarily or otherwise.

Of course, the nurse should not resist an arrest or detention if informed that either an arrest or a detention is taking place. Resisting arrest may constitute a separate crime in many jurisdictions. Nevertheless, insistence on the presence and advice of counsel is always appropriate and should be repeatedly asserted by the nurse who is either detained or arrested.

An arrest or a search may be authorized by warrant. A warrant is a piece of paper that is issued by a magistrate or a trial court that authorizes a police officer to arrest an individual (arrest warrant) or search someone or some place (search warrant). These warrants must be based on probable cause or reasonable cause to believe that the person committed a crime or that specific evidence of criminality will more likely than not be found at a particular location.

If the officer requests to search the contents of the nurse's belongings and the officer does not have a search warrant, the nurse may refuse the search. If the officer nevertheless conducts the search, any evidence found as a result of the search may be excluded from a later prosecution, which might then require dismissal of the charges for lack of evidence. This is known as the exclusionary rule.

Where, however, the nurse consents to the search, or some exigent circumstance justifying the search exists, the evidence may not be suppressed under the exclusionary rule because the search is then reasonable.[115] For example, if the nurse were destroying the evidence or the police were in hot pursuit of the nurse after witnessing his or her crime, no warrant would be required, and the evidence obtained would be admissible at a later trial.[116]

If the nurse consents to the search, then the Fourth Amendment right against unreasonable searches and seizures has been waived. When the right is waived, there is no basis to exclude evidence seized as a result of the search, even though probable cause for the search was lacking, unless the consent can be attacked as coerced.[117]

Without consent or some other limited exception such as exigent circumstances,[118] the officers must have a warrant to search or to arrest the nurse in his or her home.[119] Search warrants are different from arrest warrants although both must be based on probable cause. With respect to the arrest warrant, probable cause to believe the person arrested committed a crime must be found by a judge or magistrate before the police officer may arrest. A search warrant requires probable cause to believe that a crime has been committed and that the place to be searched will probably (more likely than not) contain contraband. The search warrant also is required to describe with particularity the thing to be seized at the location.

If the nurse refuses to consent to search in the absence of a warrant and the circumstances fail to provide any emergency that would make obtaining a warrant impracticable (the exigent circumstance exception), a warrantless seizure and/or search in the home is illegal. A court will very likely suppress any evidence obtained in this manner, assuming the nurse is prosecuted.

If the police are in a place where they have the right to be (the nurse has consented to the search, or an emergency justifying the warrantless search exists, or the arrest or search is done with a warrant), anything the police see in plain view (plain sight) that might be incriminating may be seized and used against the defendant at trial. Where an arrest occurs in the home and the police have a warrant, the police may conduct a limited search of the area of the house in which the defendant is arrested. If the officer believes suspects may be present, a more detailed search may occur.

The nurse has the right to examine the warrant to determine that the officers have the right to search a particular place or arrest a person. If a court later determines that the warrant is defective because probable cause is lacking and the supporting allegations in the officer's affidavit do not demonstrate good faith in asserting probable cause, the evidence obtained thereby may be suppressed. If, on the other hand, a reviewing court determines that probable cause to issue the warrant was lacking but the police acted in good faith by presenting the warrant to a magistrate or trial court, who then issued the warrant to the officers, the evidence obtained thereby is admissible.[120]

If the officers come to the nurse's home without a warrant to conduct a routine felony arrest or a search, the nurse does not have to allow or consent to the search. In practical terms, refusal may be fruitless or impossible, but the nurse should nevertheless assert that she refuses consent and demand to see a warrant, as well as request counsel.[121]

Nurses are advised that the rights against self-incrimination and unreasonable searches are extremely important; the nurse cannot be forced to answer questions, and this silence cannot be used at a trial to establish guilt. The nurse also cannot be forced to submit to a search of his or her home or possessions without a warrant or some exception to the warrant requirement. If the nurse waives this right and answers questions, or allows a search, whatever information is disclosed and whatever evidence is discovered *will* be used against him or her. The better practice is to request to speak with an attorney.

If the nurse's duty requires the care of a dying patient. any care given should be meticulously documented. In the event that some suspicion as to the patient's death places the nurse in the suspect category, the nurse must keep in mind that his or her interests are distinct from the hospital's or other health agency's and seek independent legal counsel. This is illustrated by a Baltimore nurse's first-degree murder trial that eventually ended in a hung jury.[122]

Mary Robaczynski was working in the ICU on the night shift. One of her patients, who had cancer and was ventilator dependent, died after a 26-hour coma. A few staff nurses informed the director of nursing that they suspected their colleague had performed a mercy killing by shutting off the ventilator temporarily and then reconnecting the ventilator to avoid detection. The hospital "quietly investigated the suspicion without uncovering any evidence."[123] The nurse neither confirmed the suspicion nor denied it. She merely resigned.

The hospital thereafter called in the district attorney, and after a year-long investigation, the nurse was indicted on several counts of murder. During the trial on the first count, the nurse admitted on the witness stand that she had disconnected the ventilator but insisted that the patient was dead when she did so. After the judge told the jury to disregard the conclusion of death by the nurse, she explained that the patient had no pulse and had no blood pressure. When asked by the prosecutor if she was aware that she was "not to disconnect equipment" she replied that she acted in the best interests of the patient.[124]

Because of the state's definition of murder, the prosecution had to prove that the patient lost spontaneous brain function after the nurse had disconnected the ventilator. Experts argued about the definition of spontaneous death, and the jury ultimately could not agree.[125]

This is not to suggest that the nurse should hide information.[126] The legal process, once instituted, however, is a formidable one and the nurse's statements may be interpreted in a manner not intended by the nurse. In addition, defense counsel may be able to negotiate a reduced charge in exchange for information and will be able to do so in a manner that will not impair the nurse's right against self-incrimination. Moreover, if evidence is obtained through an illegal search or seizure and it is suppressed, very often the prosecution's case is weakened, and the nurse stands a greater chance of a defense verdict.

United States v. Narciso[127] illustrates how naivete in the criminal justice system can work against the nurse. This widely publicized case involved two nurses employed by the Veterans' Administration who were indicted for murder. One reporter writing for a nursing journal notes that the Michigan Nurses' Association supported the accused nurses, and it appears that the nurses were unjustly and rashly accused of the crimes.[128] The reporter's warning is clear: "a nurse's proximity to a suspicious death makes her a likely 'first choice' when the interrogations begin."[129]

What happened during the investigation of the Ann Arbor Veterans' Administration case illustrates the importance of knowing and exercising one's constitutional rights. Both of the defendant nurses, who worked in the 11-bed ICU, were Philippine citizens in the United States on work visas, and they had met only 2 months earlier.

During the months of July and August of 1975, 34 patients at the Ann Arbor Veterans' Administration Hospital suffered a total of 51 cardiopulmonary arrests.[130] Eleven patients died. An anesthesiologist was convinced that someone caused the 34 arrests by administering a muscle relaxant to the patients.[131] Hospital officials contacted the Federal Bureau of Investigation (FBI).

Some have charged that the FBI's investigation was done with "such zeal" in an effort to restore its image after being unable to solve several other major crimes.[132] The FBI very quickly determined that most of the respiratory arrest victims had been ICU patients and most of the arrests occurred on the 3 PM to 11 PM shift. Thereafter the "net began to close around 3 PM to 11 PM nurses Perez and Narciso,"[133] who worked in the 11-bed ICU.

> In the first month of the investigation, agents interrogated [the Philippino nurses], other VA staff members, and patients and their families. Some staff members, Perez and Narciso among them, claim the agents harassed and intimidated them during interrogations lasting four or more hours.
>
> • • •
>
> Cooperative, full of faith in American justice, concerned that a false step might threaten their work visas, Perez and Narciso endured many interrogations during the winter of 1975 and the spring of 1976. They didn't seek a lawyer's advice until late in the investigation because as they later told reporters, in the Philippines, only the guilty have lawyers.[134]

Reports also indicate that the FBI's investigation sought to find a nurse to blame:

> Outsiders claim that the agents also used selectivity—with sexist bias. A statement by the Michigan Nurses' Association (MNA) claimed, "[A] witness testified in court that she was told by the FBI that there were five nursing suspects and that it was going to be a nurse on the afternoon shift. She asked, 'Why does it have to be a nurse? Why can't it be a doctor?' The FBI agent allegedly replied that the hospital chief of staff didn't want the doctors harassed."
>
> An article on the trial in the Dec. 3, 1977 issue of *The Nation* reported, "The FBI claims that it did question many men, but there can be no doubt that men were questioned differently: as witnesses not as suspects."[135]

The investigation uncovered "irrefutable evidence," as one reporter described it,[136] that the patients had been murdered and poisoned with a curarelike muscle relaxant, pancuronium bromide (Pavulon). Perez and Narciso were near many of the victims before and after their respiratory arrest. Yet the evidence also disclosed that a male psychiatric patient was near at least one of the victims close to the time of his death, and a man in a green suit was seen near at least one other patient. There was no direct evidence linking a particular killer to the crime.

After the investigation, a federal grand jury returned an indictment charging the two nurses with five counts of murder, ten counts of unlawfully mingling a poison in the food and medicine of certain patients, and conspiring to commit those offenses. The nurses, if convicted, faced life imprisonment. Fortunately they were able to make bail so that they could be released from the jail where, handcuffed, they had been brought after their arrest. Bail also allowed them to remain at liberty during the 2-year period between indictment and trial.

Of the 89 witnesses for the government, 17 were experts. There was no evidence that the defendants were more familiar with the drug than other staff members or that they had more access to the patients than other staff members. There also was no direct evidence that the nurses had injected the drugs into the patients. No witness attacked the character of either nurse. The government's theory was that the murders were done for shock value to protest the nursing shortage in the Veterans' Administration.

Nevertheless, after 13 days of deliberation, Perez was

found guilty of conspiracy and poisoning three patients. Narciso was found guilty of poisoning three patients and of murdering one. The Michigan Nurses' Association publicly criticized the verdict, pointing out that the government merely placed the nurses at their patients' sides at the time of the respiratory arrest, and that for the nurses to be anywhere else would have been below the standard of care of sound nursing practice: "[i]f a nurse is now under suspicion because she (or he) is in the proper place, fulfilling a basic responsibility for nursing practice, what does that do for nursing care and the role of all nurses?"[137] Nurses at the Veterans' Administration hospitals began refusing to provide medication to their patients unless witnesses were available.

Posttrial motions on the part of the defense team, however, convinced the trial court to grant the nurses a new trial because of serious errors that occurred during the first trial.[138] The court questioned the strength and reliability of certain nontraditional kinds of evidence, such as hypnotically induced interviews.

Another problem with the case was the number of interviews conducted by the FBI and the manner in which they were conducted. The defense's requests to examine the interviews with persons the government chose not to call as witnesses had been repeatedly denied.

After the trial court ordered a new trial, the government prosecutors dismissed the indictment rather than pursue another trial against the nurses.[139] Although the nurses ultimately were free, they remain in a kind of fugue state of never having been found not guilty.

COMMENCEMENT OF PROSECUTION

Law enforcement agencies present the results of their efforts to prosecutors who in turn decide whether there is sufficient evidence to prosecute a crime. This may occur before or after the suspect is arrested. The charging document, which is a written statement of the charge, called an information, indictment, or complaint, is then issued.

If the crime is federal and a felony, a grand jury is usually convened. The grand jury has the power to issue subpoenas and compel witnesses to testify. Usually, the prosecutor, an Assistant United States Attorney, presents evidence; this evidence may be in the form of hearsay. Based on this evidence, the grand jury decides whether there is "probable cause" to believe a crime has been committed.

In the state system, a police officer usually presents an affidavit to the prosecutor outlining the basis of evidence of crime. A complaint or information is then issued. Some states utilize the grand jury system.

If the person has already been arrested before the indictment, complaint, or information is issued, he or she is brought before a judge or a magistrate to have bail set and to be arraigned. Of course, if no charging document is issued, the person must be released. Depending on whether the person can meet the requirements of bail, he or she is released on the promise of returning for a particular court date. If the person cannot make bail, or the judge refuses to set bail because the person is a danger to the community or a flight risk, he or she is taken into custody.

If the person has not been arrested before the charging document has issued, then a warrant for the person's arrest usually issues. This allows the police or marshall to find the person and take the person into custody. Thereafter, the person is arraigned and bail is set or not set.

The arraignment is the first formal court appearance. During this proceeding, the court informs the defendant of the nature of the charges and his or her constitutional rights. The defendant informs the court that he or she is either pleading guilty or pleading not guilty.

As a matter of practice, defendants usually plead not guilty at this stage if the crime is a serious one. There may be defenses or the prosecution may not be able to prove its case beyond a reasonable doubt. Consequently, pleading guilty at this stage, unless some reduced charge has been negotiated, would seriously impair the defendant's due process rights.

In some jurisdictions, where a grand jury system is not used, the court may also review whether there is sufficient evidence for the crime to be charged. In other states, this kind of review is done at a preliminary hearing. The focus is to determine whether there is probable cause to believe that the accused committed a known crime within the jurisdiction of the court.

If the court determines there is no probable cause to so believe, the case must be dismissed. If the judge finds probable cause or the accused waives a preliminary hearing, the case may go forward.

The accused has a constitutional right to a jury trial in federal felony cases, but this right may be waived, and the case may be heard by a judge or the accused may waive the right to trial and plead guilty.

If the accused pleads guilty, the judge is constitutionally required to make an inquiry into the factual basis for the plea and determine that the accused is pleading guilty voluntarily. A guilty plea waives all of the due process rights guaranteed by the Constitution and the right to appeal, but if the accused later wants to challenge the guilty plea, he or she may do so by a writ of habeas corpus.

DISCOVERY, PRETRIAL MOTIONS, AND NEGOTIATION

If the defendant pleads not guilty, generally there is a discovery phase where evidence is turned over to the defense. The prosecutor is required by the U.S. Constitution to turn over to an accused evidence material to guilt or innocence or evidence of the defendant's statements to a police officer.[140] The prosecutor violates due process of law if he or she withholds evidence material to guilt or punishment, irrespective of the good faith or bad faith of the prosecution.[141]

By statute in many jurisdictions, and in the federal system, there is a requirement that the defendant give pretrial notice of certain defenses such as an alibi or insanity defense. If that notice is not given to the prosecutor, the court may exclude evidence of the defense.

Once the defense attorney has reviewed the evidence, he or she will generally make certain pretrial motions to exclude evidence, such as statements by the defendant or other evidence seized by police, because the statements or evidence were illegally obtained. Statements obtained from a defendant that were not voluntarily given are excluded from evidence because they are not trustworthy.[142]

A defendant's statement may also be suppressed and not allowed into the prosecution's case if it was obtained in violation of the rules established by the Supreme Court in *Miranda v. Arizona* for custodial interrogation or if the statements were not voluntarily given.[143] If the defendant waived the *Miranda* rights and provided statements to the police, the question then is simply whether the waiver was voluntary. If so, the statements are admissible.

Motions to exclude evidence may also be based on the Fourth Amendment. Evidence obtained in violation of the right to be free from unreasonable searches and seizures is excluded.[144] There are numerous other motions that are available to the defense. Occasionally, if these are successful, the defense is in a better negotiating stance with the prosecution. Prosecutors in general have a great deal of discretion to either go forward with a case or dismiss it.

In addition to the Fifth and Fourth Amendments, the Sixth Amendment right to counsel may also provide a basis for exclusion of evidence if that evidence is obtained by violating the interests protected by the Sixth Amendment. This right to counsel applies to every critical stage of the prosecution. Consequently, the right to counsel does not materialize or "attach" until the prosecution commences, generally when a complaint is filed.

Additional motions may be made attacking the criminal statute under which the defendant is charged. If the statute is fatally defective, an accused may obviate prosecution under the statute altogether by a determination that the statute is unconstitutional.

The basis for the challenge may be made on due process grounds—that the statute is vague and fails to provide notice of the conduct that is prohibited. Criminal responsibility should not attach where one could not reasonably understand that contemplated conduct is proscribed.[145]

If the court finds a statute unconstitutionally vague, the statute is void, and a criminal conviction based on the statute is reversed. In the area of health and safety, statutes are generally deemed constitutional so long as an accused can reasonably be held to understand by the terms of the statute that his conduct is prohibited.

Where the statute impinges on speech, assembly, or association the First Amendment is implicated and greater precision in the charging language of a statute is required to give notice and defeat a vagueness attack.[146] The statute may also be deemed overbroad if it prohibits constitutionally protected conduct, such as speech. Enforcement of such statute may be a denial of due process.[147]

Occasionally, cases are dismissed for severe violations of the right to a fair trial or because of prosecutorial misconduct. Of course, prosecutors have the discretion to dismiss cases that their investigation reveals are without merit or that present significant evidentiary problems. The box on p. 401 lists other persons in the criminal justice system who have the power to exercise discretion. At almost every level, from investigation to sentencing to the parole board hearings, a lawyer can negotiate a better result for his or her client.

THE TRIAL

The United States Constitution provides that every defendant in a criminal case shall have the right to a speedy trial judged by a jury of one's peers. At the trial, the defendant has the Sixth Amendment right to confront his or her accusers, cross-examine them, and compel other witnesses to testify. The judge presiding over the trial makes the decisions concerning legal matters such

THOSE WHO EXERCISE DISCRETION IN THE CRIMINAL JUSTICE SYSTEM

Police	Enforce specific laws
	Investigate specific crimes
	Search people, buildings, vicinities
	Arrest or detain people
Prosecutors	File charges or petitions
	Seek indictments
	Dismiss charges or indictments
	Reduce charges
Judges	Set bail or conditions for release
	Accept pleas
	Dismiss charges
	Impose sentence
	Revoke probation
Correctional officials	Assign to type of correctional facility
	Award privileges
	Punish for disciplinary infractions
Paroling authority	Determine date and conditions of parole
	Revoke parole

as objections to evidence and the like; the jury, unless waived by the defendant, decides the accused's guilt or innocence.

The government must prove beyond a reasonable doubt that the defendant committed the crime that is charged. The defendant does not have to present any evidence or testify, but the right against self-incrimination may be waived and the defendant may choose to testify.

Although at first glance it may seem that the state's burden of proof is unfair, one must bear in mind that the government has all the powers of investigation (the FBI, the Drug Enforcement Administration [DEA]) and generally a considerable budget. A person's life or liberty is at stake, and thus the law requires a greater degree of proof than is the case when money is at stake.

Evidence at trial is presented through the testimony of witnesses, the admission of documents, and other tangible evidence. Direct evidence directly proves a particular proposition. Circumstantial evidence allows an inference that the particular proposition is true. Certain restrictions apply in criminal proceedings that may not apply in civil cases, but generally, the rules of evidence are the same as in civil cases.

POSTTRIAL PROCEEDINGS

If a defendant is acquitted of the charges, the matter is over; the government cannot retry the case. If the defendant is convicted, the judge imposes sentence, unless, for example, as in a murder case, some jurisdictions allow the jury's input. The judge usually hears all the aggravating factors and mitigating circumstances before reaching a final decision. Judges have broad discretion in sentencing matters, and they frequently rely on presentence reports of probation agencies.

There are four objectives in punishment: rehabilitation; deterrence; incapacitation; and retribution. The kinds of sentences that are given are the death penalty, incarceration, probation, split sentences of 6 months' incarceration and the remainder of the sentence suspended while probation is completed, restitution, community service, and fines.

The convicted person, if sent to prison, is eligible for parole after a certain period of time, depending on the nature of the crime and any past record. Parole decisions are made by parole boards throughout the country.

The defendant may also appeal a court's ruling or the conviction, contending that the evidence is insufficient or some procedural error caused prejudicial error. In some instances, a new trial is required. In other situations, the appellate court recognizes the error, but weighs it against all the evidence and concludes that given the overwhelming evidence, the defendant's right to a fair trial was not prejudiced by the error.

Once the appeal process is finished, the defendant may seek review of his case by way of a writ of habeas corpus. Few of these petitions are ever successful.

Recommendations and trends

The concern about criminal prosecution is ever present in the treatment of a patient who insists he or she does not want a simple life-preserving treatment, blood transfusion, or life support system. Termination of life support has generated a lot of speculation and controversy as to which acts are criminal. The modern trend, however, is to view good faith treatment decisions in the care of the persistently comatose patient—whether to institute treatment in the first instance or to terminate it—as outside the reach of criminal law.[148]

In *St. Mary Hospital v. Ramsey*,[149] the court held that a physician and a hospital are not criminally liable for agreeing to the refusals of a competent adult to take a blood transfusion. The patient, the court reasoned, should be given the right to refuse treatment even though the patient may die because of the decision. The patient was a 27-year-old man.

California courts have reached similar results in the

case of a competent adult who wanted a respirator disconnected[150] and in the case of a persistently vegetative comatose patient whose family wanted IV therapy discontinued.[151] In the case of the competent adult, the right to refuse medical treatment is constitutionally protected by the right to privacy.[152] In the case of a patient who is incompetent to make that decision, the decision should be made by a surrogate such as a family member.

Perhaps the most significant trend seen is the nurse charged with practicing illegal medicine rather than murder in a terminally ill treatment setting. Nevertheless, the disparity in the number of nurses as criminal defendants in this context and the number of physicians[153] similarly charged suggests that nurses, at a minimum, must carefully document their actions in the care of the terminally ill. Clear policies concerning do not resuscitate orders are essential. (See Chapters 5, 6, and 17, which thoroughly discuss the issues of treatment refusal.)

Special care should also be given when dealing with controlled narcotics. Careful attention to the surroundings and to recording is imperative. Drug-impaired employees pose a dangerous condition to patients, and the nurse who witnesses an employee consuming drugs while working has a duty to bring this fact to the attention of the administration. Failure to act where there is a duty to act may subject the nurse to criminal liability. The drug-impaired nurse who injures or kills a patient may be charged with criminal negligence or a more serious crime.

The nurse who is employed in home health care should also scrupulously document actions taken and any problems encountered with the family. If anyone becomes abusive and the nurse becomes concerned for personal safety, arrangements must be made immediately for substitute care.

In any treatment setting, caution is required. Careful documentation and clear policies will help against potential criminal liability. Nurses should be familiar with their nursing practice acts and their constitutional rights. When potential criminal liability becomes a distinct probability, the exercise of these constitutional rights may be the nurse's best protection from false accusation.

Endnotes

1. Wiley, *Liability For Death: Nine Nurses' Ordeals,* NURSING 81 34 (September 1981) (hereinafter cited as *Wiley*).
2. For example, the discussion of the nurse's constitutional rights throughout the criminal process is applicable in general to all persons irrespective of the crime charged or the occupation of the person accused of the crime. In other words, these basic rights apply irrespective of the nature of the crime—whether theft or criminal negligence.
3. W.R. LaFAVE & A.W. SCOTT, CRIMINAL LAW 9 (1972) (hereinafter cited as *LaFave*).
4. *Id.* at 5.
5. *Id.* at 21 & n.2 (citing the crimes of murder, manslaughter, assault, battery, mayhem, and kidnapping; rape should also be included here).
6. *Id.* & n.3 (citing the examples of larceny, embezzlement, false pretenses, burglary, robbery, bad checks, blackmail, extortion, forgery, receiving stolen property, arson, forgery, malicious destruction of property).
7. *Id.* & n.6 (citing treason, sedition, sabotage, and bribery of government officials).
8. *Id.* & n.7 (citing perjury, bribery of witnesses, judges, and jurors).
9. *Id.* & n.8 (citing pollution laws, food and drug laws, narcotic and liquor laws).
10. *Id.* & n.9 (citing public drunkenness and disorderly conduct).
11. *Id.* & n.5 (citing bigamy, adultery, fornication, sodomy, incest, and obscenity).
12. *Id.* & n.10 (citing crimes of gambling, cruelty to animals, bribery of athletes).
13. *Id.* at 26.
14. *Id.*
15. This is known as a court trial as opposed to a jury trial.
16. *Ex parte McNiel,* 80 U.S. (13 Wall.) 236 (1872).
17. U.S. CONST. art. I, §10.
18. *See, e.g., Dean Milk Co. v. City of Madison,* 340 U.S. 349 (1951) (municipal health ordinance making it unlawful to sell milk not pasteurized at a plant within five miles of municipality and defendant was an out-of-state milk company); *Edwards v. California,* 314 U.S. 160 (1941) (criminal prosecution for violating state depression-born statute forbidding importation of nonresident indigent into state).
19. *LaFave, supra* note 3, at 171.
20. *See, e.g., United States v. Sharpnack,* 355 U.S. 286 (1958).
21. *LaFave, supra* note 3, at 7.
22. *See, e.g., Weems v. United States,* 217 U.S. 349 (1910).
23. *See, e.g., Griswold v. Connecticut,* 381 U.S. 479 (1965).
24. *LaFave supra* note 3, at 7.
25. *Id.* at 7-8.
26. *Id.*
27. *Id.*
28. *Id.* at 194.
29. *Id.*
30. *Id.* at 208.
31. *Id.*
32. *Id.*
33. *Id.* at 211.
34. *See, e.g.,* 18 U.S.C. App. §1202 (1984).
35. *LaFave, supra* note 3.
36. *See, e.g., People v. Brown,* 216 P. 411 (Cal. App. 1923).
37. *See, e.g., Bartling v. Superior Court,* 209 Cal. Rptr. 220 (Cal. App. 1984); *accord Barber v. Superior Court,* 195 Cal. Rptr. 484 (Cal. App. 1983).
38. In the federal system, one who aids or abets another in a crime is guilty as the principal and may be punished as if he or she committed the crime and did not merely assist another to commit it. 18 U.S.C. §2 (1984).

39. *LaFave, supra* note 3, at 471-81.
40. *Id.* at 528.
41. *Id.* at 562.
42. *Id.* at 570.
43. N.Y. Times, March 3, 1984.
44. *Id.*
45. N.Y. Times, Apr. 11, 1984 at 1, col. 1.
46. *Id.*
47. *Id.* at col. 2.
48. *Jones v. State,* 716 S.W.2d 142 (Tx. 1986).
49. *LaFave, supra* note 3, at 571.
50. *Id.*
51. *Id.* at 572.
52. *Id.* at 583.
53. No. A-35 (decided July 2, 1984, New Jersey Superior Court).
54. *See, e.g.,* CAL. PENAL CODE §471.5 (West Supp. 1986).
55. *See, e.g., Craig v. State,* 155 A.2d 684 (Md. 1954); Treacher & O'Neill, *Medical Care for Dependent Children: Manslaughter Liability of the Christian Scientist,* 109 U. PA. L. REV. 203 (1960).
56. 138 Mass. 165 (1884).
57. *LaFave, supra* note 3, at 213.
58. *See, e.g., State v. Schultz,* 8 N.W. 469 (1881).
59. *State v. Gooze,* 81 A.2d 811 (N.J. Super. 1951).
60. 194 A.2d 467 (1963).
61. *LaFave, supra* note 3, at 602.
62. No. 84-7322 (Mass. 1984), *reported in,* The National Law Journal, Oct. 29, 1984, at 13.
63. *Id.*
64. *Id.*
65. *Id.* (emphasis added).
66. *Id.*
67. *People v. Flushing Hospital & Medical Center,* 471 N.Y.S.2d 745 (N.Y. Crim Ct. 1985).
68. 474 N.Y.S.2d 409 (N.Y. City Crim. Ct. 1984).
69. *See, e.g.,* 18 U.S.C. §1341 (1984) (making it a felony to use the mails to carry out a scheme to defraud a victim of his or her money or other property).
70. 347 F.2d 665 (5th Cir. 1965).
71. *See, e.g.,* CAL. BUS. & PROF. CODE §650 (West Supp. 1986).
72. *See, e.g.,* CAL. PENAL CODE §72 (West Supp. 1986); CAL. WELF. & INST. CODE §14107 (West Supp. 1986).
73. 4 Civ. No. 508454 (decided May 30, 1985) *reported in* 85 DAILY JOURNAL D.A.R. 1871 (Monday, June 10, 1985).
74. *See, e.g.,* CAL. BUS. & PROF. CODE §2761(a)(2) (West 1985). Chapter 25 discusses this in detail.
75. CAL. BUS. & PROF. CODE §2140 (West Supp. 1985).
76. *See, e.g., Bowland v. Municipal Court for the Santa Cruz County Judicial District of Santa Cruz County,* 134 Cal. Rptr. 1082 (Cal. 1977) (en banc).
77. CAL. BUS. & PROF. CODE §2140 (West Supp. 1986).
78. *Id.* at §2141; current version CAL. BUS. & PROF. CODE §2052 (West Supp. 1986).
79. 556 P.2d 1061 (Cal. 1977) (en banc).
80. *Bowland v. Municipal Court for Santa Cruz Cty.,* 556 P.2d 1081, 1089 (Cal. 1977) (en banc).
81. *Id.* at 1089 (citations omitted).
82. The court reasoned that the definition of midwifery excludes the practice of medicine and surgery as defined by the same section of the code. In 1949, the statute was amended to exclude midwifery from that group of practices for which new certificates would issue. While new certificates did not issue, the statute's prohibition against practicing midwifery without a license continued. In 1975, the statute was amended to provide for certification of midwifery. These provisions, the court reasoned, would be meaningless unless the practice of midwifery without a valid certificate would be considered a violation of section 2141.
83. Adler, "You are charged with . . . ," NURSE PRACTITIONER 6 (January-February 1979).
84. *Sermchief v. Gonzales,* 660 S.W.2d 683 (Mo. 1983) (en banc).
85. *See, e.g., Fraijo v. Hartland,* 160 Cal. Rptr. 246 (Cal. App. 1979).
86. Reported in the N.Y. Times, Sept. 23, 1984, at 1, col. 1.
87. *Id.*
88. *Id.* at 56, col. 2.
89. *LaFave, supra* note 3, at 268.
90. *Id.* at 295.
91. *Id.* at 343 & n.8.
92. *Id.*
93. *Id.* at 356.
94. *Id.* at 369.
95. *United States v. Twigg,* 588 F.2d 373 (3d Cir. 1978).
96. *LaFave, supra* note 3, at 374-81.
97. *Id.* at 374.
98. *Id.* at 391.
99. *Id.*
100. *Id.* at 397.
101. *Chicago, Burlington and Quincy R.R. v. Chicago,* 166 U.S. 226 (1897).
102. *Duncan v. Lousiana,* 391 U.S. 145 (1968).
103. *Benton v. Maryland,* 395 U.S. 784 (1969).
104. *See, e.g., Robinson v. California,* 370 U.S. 660 (1962).
105. *Baldwin v. New York,* 399 U.S. 66 (1970).
106. *Id.*
107. *Williams v. Florida,* 399 U.S. 78 (1970).
108. *Apodaca v. Oregon,* 406 U.S. 404 (1972) (convictions of two men by votes of 11 to 1 and 10 to 2 were upheld).
109. The prosecutor and the judge are absolutely immune from liability for their decisions in the case.
110. *Rochin v. California,* 342 U.S. 165 (1952).
111. 384 U.S. 436 (1966).
112. *Id.* at 444.
113. *See, e.g., Forida v. Royer,* 104 U.S. 491 (1983).
114. *Id.*
115. The exclusionary rule only applies to criminal proceedings, not civil proceedings such as deportation proceedings or even quasicriminal proceedings such as license revocation.
116. This is known as the exigent circumstances doctrine. *See, e.g., United States v. Manfredi,* 722 F.2d 519 (9th Cir. 1983).
117. *See, e.g., United States v. Jabara,* 618 F.2d 1319 (9th Cir. 1980).
118. Exigent circumstances are emergency or urgency situations such as when the defendant realizes the police are present and begins destroying evidence. Automobile searches are generally subject to a variation on this exception because of the automobile's mobility, *e.g., United States v. Chadwick,* 433 U.S. 1 (1977).
119. *Payton v. New York,* 445 U.S. 573 (1980).
120. *United States v. Leon,* 82 LEd 2d 677 (1984).
121. Certain locations, it should be noted, do implicate greater privacy rights and thus warrant greater Fourth Amendment protection against unreasonable government searches and seizures than do

other locations. For example, a home is generally considered more sacred than an automobile in terms of the kinds of intrusions the government can make in its crime detection procedures at either location. Thus police are generally required to obtain a warrant before searching or arresting someone in the home but not in the automobile.

122. *Wiley, supra* note 1, at 34.
123. *Id.*
124. *Id.* at 37.
125. *Id.*
126. Indeed, the hospital may use the lack of cooperation as evidence that it reasonably suspected the nurse. *Wiley, supra* note 1, at 38. Linda Kurle, a nurse from the Chicago suburbs, was so accused by Good Samaritan Hospital when one of the patients assigned to her during the night shift died of an overdose of exogenous insulin. The patient was not a diabetic. All of the staff who had any proximity to the patient took and passed lie-detector tests except Linda Kurle. Because of this refusal, the hospital fired her. The hospital also turned its evidence over to the local police.
127. 446 F. Supp. 252 (E. D. Mich. 1977).
128. *Wiley, supra* note 1, at 34.
129. *Id.* at 37.
130. *Id.*
131. *Id.* at 34.
132. *Id.* at 36.
133. *Id.*
134. *Id.* at 36. The investigation also apparently uncovered poor morale, poor documentation, and lax security at the Veterans' Administration Hospital.
135. *Id.*
136. *Id.*
137. *Id.* at 37.
138. *United States v. Narciso,* 446 F.Supp. 252 (E. D. Mich. 1977).
139. *Wiley, supra* note 1, at 37.
140. *Clewis v. Texas,* 386 U.S. 707, 712 n.8 (1967).
141. *Brady v. Maryland,* 373 U.S. 83 (1963).
142. *Brown v. Mississippi,* 297 U.S. 278 (1936).
143. 384 U.S. 436 (1966).
144. *United States v. Chadwick,* 433 U.S. 1 (1977).
145. *United States v. National Dairy Corp.,* 372 U.S. 29 (1963).
146. *See Smith v. Goguen,* 415 U.S. 566 (1970).
147. *Godding v. Wilson,* 405 U.S. 518 (1972).
148. *See, e.g., Bartling v. Superior Court,* 209 Cal. Rptr. 220 (Cal. App. 1984); *Barber v. Superior Court,* 195 Cal. Rptr. 484 (Cal. App. 1983).
149. 465 So.2d 666 (Fla. App. 1985).
150. *See, e.g., Bartling v. Superior Court,* 209 Cal. Rptr. 220 (Cal. App. 1984).
151. *Barber v. Superior Court,* 195 Cal. Rptr. 484 (Cal. App. 1983).
152. *See, e.g., Bartling v. Superior Court,* 209 Cal. Rptr. 220, 225 (Cal. App. 1984).
153. For example, in *Barber v. Superior Court,* 195 Cal. Rptr. 484 (Cal. App. 1983), one of the few reported criminal cases involving physicians in the right to refuse life-sustaining treatment area, the California Appellate Court overturned a decision of the lower court holding that two physicians could be prosecuted for murder and conspiracy to commit murder. Acting on the family's written request, the physicians had ordered termination of a comatose patient's treatment by respirator and IV hydration. The court rejected the view that the criminal convictions could go forward merely because the physicians acted intentionally and knew that the patient would die.

Chapter 25

Licensure revocation

Cynthia E. Northrop

The legal basis for licensure is the state's police power, the state government's ability to act to protect the public's health, safety, and welfare. There are many examples of the state's exercise of this power within the health care delivery system. For example, communicable diseases must be reported, thus violating individual confidentiality but protecting the public from an epidemic. Another example is school immunization laws, which also exist because of the state's responsibility for the entire public's health. Licensure that is based on the state's police power is exhibited in legislative acts to protect the public from unqualified, unsafe practitioners and health care institutions. These laws exist in most states and require licensure of both individuals and institutions.

The state legislature's authority and power to regulate are well documented. So also is the right of a person, including nurses, to select and practice a profession. This right to practice is an important property right but is not an absolute or unqualified right. It is subject to minimal and reasonable regulation by the state under and within its legitimate police power. The responsibility of the licensed nurse is to practice in a reasonable, safe, and competent manner. The state's responsibility is to protect the public from those who would harm them through incompetent care.

Purposes of licensure

Licensure sets standards for entry into practice, defines a scope of practice, and allows for disciplinary action. The nursing practice act in most states as provided in state legislation meets all of these purposes. Examinations conducted by the state boards of nursing of individuals wanting to be licensed to practice nursing in their jurisdiction include and exclude individuals on the basis of the standards set by the testing process. Most nursing practice acts define what the practice of nursing is and thereby may discipline unauthorized practice or practice that exceeds the scope of practice. Nursing educational programs are also regulated by the state boards; these programs admit or deny individuals who then may or may not make it to the examination.

Once nurses are in practice by virtue of passing the examination the licensing boards may take disciplinary action against them. The board of nursing has the power to discipline incompetent, unscrupulous, and unqualified nurses by removing them, permanently or temporarily, improving them, or requiring rehabilitation—because they may harm the public.

Even though licensing exists as a means to control practice and prevent incompetent practice, in recent years challenges have been raised about licensing. Licensing not only works for the public but also many times may work against the public. One author has identified four ways in which licensing may operate against the public's health and welfare[1]:

1. Licensing schemes have kept information from the public.
2. It has artificially inflated prices, insulating professionals from influences of consumer preferences.

3. It has unfairly barred competent practitioners.
4. It may prevent individuals from taking on new responsibilities as they gain expertise to do so.

Types of nursing practice acts

Shimberg[2] defines licensing as the process by which an agency of a state government grants permission to an individual to engage in a given occupation upon a finding that the applicant has attained the minimal degree of competency necessary to ensure that the public health, safety, and welfare will be reasonably protected. Nursing licensing is carried out in two ways: (1) title regulation and (2) regulation of the scope of practice.

In the first type of practice act only the use of the title registered nurse or licensed practical nurse or licensed vocational nurse is regulated. In the second type the practice of a particular profession is defined and set out in the legislation itself. In this type of act more than the title is regulated. Anyone who functions within the definition of practice can be restricted and required to meet licensing requirements in order to continue to practice.

The history of nursing licensure began in the early 1900s with laws that regulated only the title or simply required registration. Very few states today have the first type of licensing; most have practice acts that define and regulate the scope of nursing practice.[3]

State boards of nursing

Each state legislature establishes an administrative governmental agency, called a state board of nursing or board of nurse examiners, to enforce the nursing practice act that they have made law. This administrative body is usually part of the state's executive branch of government. Chapter 1 has more detailed information about state governments. The fundamental principles governing the exercise of authority by an administrative agency such as a board of nursing are that it is of limited jurisdiction and has only those powers that are expressly conferred by statute (nursing practice act) or that may be reasonably implied to carry out express authority.[4]

The boards' powers usually include rule-making authority and power to adjudicate. They are organized in several models across the country ranging from fully autonomous boards to boards that exist only in advisory capacities.[5] Members of the boards are usually members of the profession that is being regulated and consumers. Nursing boards are made up of registered and licensed practical nurses and consumer members.[6] Appendix IV contains the citations to all state nursing practice acts. A state board of nursing has many powers, including the power to examine and license; regulate and define nursing practice; approve nursing educational programs; and investigate and discipline nurses, through either revocation, suspension, reprimand, or denial of a license. Chapters 23 and 29 discuss in further detail the powers and activities of the board over the practice of nurse midwives, nurse anesthetists, nurse practitioners, and clinical nurse specialists, raising the scope of practice issues. Chapter 20 highlights the entry into practice issues, affecting levels of nursing education.

Grounds for discipline

The power to discipline has been upheld by higher courts, including the power of the legislature to identify which acts will be considered a ground or a basis for discipline. The legislature sets out general statements as reasons for disciplining in the act and also usually empowers the board to define these grounds further through the rule-making or regulation power. When courts analyze cases they weigh and assess every word selected by the legislature. Legislative history is also important when the court needs to evaluate the intent of the legislature.

The boxes on pp. 407 and 408 list the grounds for revocation of a nurse's license in Maryland and Connecticut. These two states' grounds differ in that Maryland's are more specific and detailed, especially with regards to fraud and records. Both cover substance abuse, negligence, incompetency, and criminal activity. Connecticut, on the other hand, specifically addresses physical illness, including the aging process as a basis for disciplining a nurse.

As in any state these grounds may be further defined by board of nursing regulations. In Maryland 3 years of study by the board has culminated in regulations specific to the nursing profession. These regulations are based on the American Nurses' Association's (ANA) *Standards of Nursing Practice*[7] and make it law that nursing practice involves collection of health status data, use of the nursing process in documentation, use of nursing diagnosis, and development of a plan of care, including goal setting and evaluation. Standards also exist for the nurse's relationship to the nursing profession, including responsibilities for knowing the law, practicing within legal boundaries, accountability for judgments, maintaining competency, and knowing policies and procedures. In

GROUNDS FOR DENIALS, REPRIMANDS, SUSPENSIONS, REVOCATIONS IN MARYLAND

1. Fraudulently or deceptively obtains or attempts to obtain a license for the applicant or for another;
2. Fraudulently or deceptively uses a license;
3. Is disciplined by a licensing or disciplinary authority of any other state or country or convicted or disciplined by a court of any state or country for an act that would be grounds for disciplinary action under the Board's disciplinary statutes;
4. Is convicted of or pleads guilty or nolo contendere to a felony or to a crime involving moral turpitude, whether or not any appeal or other proceeding is pending to have the conviction or plea set aside;
5. Willfully and knowingly:
   a. Files a false report or record of an individual under the licensee's care;
   b. Gives any false or misleading information about a material matter in an employment application;
   c. Fails to file or record any health record that is required by law;
   d. Obstructs the filing or recording of any health record as required by law;
   e. Induces another person to fail to file or record any health record required by law;
6. Knowingly does any act that has been determined by the board in its rules and regulations to exceed the scope of practice authorized to the individual under this title;
7. Provides professional services while:
   a. Under the influence of alcohol; or
   b. Using any narcotic or controlled dangerous substance, as defined in Article 27 of the Code,* or other drug that is in excess of therapeutic amount or without valid medical indications;
8. Does an act that is inconsistent with generally accepted professional standards in the practice of registered nursing or licensed practical nursing;
9. Is grossly negligent in the practice of registered nursing or licensed practical nursing;
10. Has violated any provision of this title;
11. Submits a false statement to collect a fee; or
12. Is professionally, physically or mentally incompetent.

Data from MD. HEALTH OCC. CODE ANN. §7-313(a) (1986).
*This refers to the state criminal laws.

addition, the Maryland State Board of Examiners of Nurses has developed standards in regulation form for nurse administrators.[8]

Table 2 compares the grounds for revocation of licenses offered in three model practice acts. Authors of the model nursing practice acts are the ANA[9] and the National Council of State Boards of Nursing.[10] The result of a federal government study, the Model Health Profession's Practice Act, provides another interesting comparison.[11]

In general eight categories of grounds can be found in most nursing practice acts. They include fraud and deceit; criminal acts; unfitness, incompetence, negligence, and malpractice; substance abuse; mental incompetence; unprofessional conduct; revocation in another jurisdiction; and violations of the act. In many states these grounds are found listed not only within the nursing practice act but also in general provisions of the law that apply to all occupations and professions.

FRAUD AND DECEIT

A nurse may lose a license or be disciplined if fraud was committed in the licensing procedure, in employment, in practice, or in financial matters. State boards of nursing until the last 10 years were most active in enforcing this ground over all others. Most case law until the last 10 years discussed the board's power to take action against those who used a fraudulent diploma in order to obtain a license. Today, state boards are still enforcing this ground but have been more involved with the ground on drugs and alcohol abuse discussed below.

CRIMINAL ACTS

States vary widely on the type of crime that would constitute a ground for losing a license or being disciplined. The types of crimes in the grounds range from any crime to only felonies, misdemeanors, or specific crimes, such as possession of narcotics.[12] The point at which a state board may discipline a nurse accused of a crime may also vary among states. In some states a licensee must be convicted or found guilty of the crime before disciplining.[13] Some state boards may make independent decisions as to whether a nurse has been sufficiently rehabilitated and may decide that no discipline is necessary.[14] In some instances a state may discipline a licensee only for crimes that were committed during a

IMPROPER PROFESSIONAL CONDUCT IN CONNECTICUT

Conduct which fails to conform to the accepted standards of the nursing profession includes, but is not limited to, the following:

1. Fraud or material deception in procuring or attempting to procure a license to practice nursing;
2. Illegal conduct, incompetence or negligence in carrying out usual nursing functions;
3. Physical illness or loss of motor skill, including but not limited to deterioration through the aging process;
4. Emotional disorder or mental illness;
5. Abuse or excessive use of drugs, including alcohol, narcotics, or chemicals;
6. Fraud or material deception in the course of professional services or activities;
7. Willful falsification of entries in any hospital, patient or other record pertaining to drugs, the results of which are detrimental to the health of a patient; and
8. Conviction of the violation of any of the provisions of this chapter or by any court of criminal jurisdiction.

Data from CONN. GEN. STAT. ANN. §20-99(b) (West 1985).

certain time period.[15] Most states require that the criminal act must relate to nursing practice before one can be disciplined. The wording of the state nursing practice act may vary but usually includes words such as "the criminal act must bear directly, substantially relate to qualifications to practice nursing, or be reasonably related to nursing practice."[16]

UNFITNESS, INCOMPETENCE, NEGLIGENCE, AND MALPRACTICE

A licensee may be disciplined if the practice is unfit or incompetent because of personal habits or physical or mental disabilities. Usually a state board cannot discipline on this basis unless the particular unfitness or condition inhibits the nurse's ability to provide reasonable and safe care.[17]

SUBSTANCE ABUSE

State boards of nursing are increasingly and more actively disciplining nurses on the basis of this ground. Nursing legislation often lists a variety of drugs that may be involved in a disciplinary proceeding: narcotics, controlled drugs, chemicals, barbiturates, and others. Some state laws include the use or abuse of *any* drug as grounds for discipline.[18] Many states allow disciplining only if the drug or alcohol was used while rendering care, without reasonable skill or endangered patient safety, or while practicing.[19] A few state boards have been empowered by their legislatures with an automatic suspension power that includes the ability to order a licensee (nurse) to be medically and/or mentally examined.[20] In some states refusal to be examined as ordered by the board may constitute an admission of guilt.[21]

MENTAL INCOMPETENCE

The ground of mental incompetence usually includes reference to mental illness, insanity, being mentally unfit, or having an emotional disorder. Some states require adjudication of mental illness before the state board may take disciplinary action.[22] A few states have the ability to require examination and may order immediate suspension of a license when adjudicated or hospitalized for mental illness.[23]

UNPROFESSIONAL CONDUCT

Unprofessional conduct has been defined in different ways in many states. Words used with this ground have included unethical conduct, misconduct, or practicing contrary to standards of practice. The ANA's *Code for Nurses with Interpretive Statements,*[24] the nurse's code of ethics, was referred to in past Delaware nursing legislation but was removed in a subsequent legislative session.[25] Delaware was the only state to incorporate this document, which defines unprofessional conduct.

Specific acts of unprofessional conduct have been defined by some states to include unnecessary treatment, sexual misconduct, dividing fees, misrepresentation, and refusing to provide professional service to a person because of such person's race, creed, color, or national origin.[26]

REVOCATION IN ANOTHER JURISDICTION

Almost all state nursing practice acts have revocation in another jurisdiction as a ground for discipline. This ground allows one state to discipline a licensee based on another state's disciplinary action.[27] Since reciprocity is easily obtained by nurses there is a network of information that is exchanged between states.[28] It is standard procedure that applicants for licensure through reciprocity grant permission for an investigation of their other licenses.

VIOLATIONS OF THE ACT

Most states also have the ground of violations of the act, which includes aiding and abetting others to violate

Table 2. Comparison of Grounds for Revocation of Licenses in Model Practice Acts

Category	American Nurses' Association Model*	National Council of State Boards of Nursing Model†	Model Health Profession's Practice Act‡
Fraud and deceit	Has committed fraud or deceit in securing or attempting to secure such license Has falsified or in a repeatedly negligent manner made incorrect entries or failed to make essential entries on essential patient records	Has practiced fraud or deceit in procuring or attempting to procure a license to practice nursing in filing any reports or completing patient records, signing any report or record in the nurse's capacity as a registered nurse or as a licensed practical nurse; in representing his or her authority to practice nursing; or in submitting any information on record to the board	Fraud or misrepresentation in any phase of procuring a license or in renewing a license Advertising designed to mislead the public Advertising of prices charged for services§ Advertising or representing that certain procedures can be done painlessly or with greater authority or expertise Advertising in application other than that approved by the board Fraud or misrepresentation in treatment procedures or statements regarding the ability to treat
Criminal acts	Has been convicted of a felony or a crime involving moral turpitude or has had accepted by a court a plea of *nolo contendere* to a felony or a crime involving moral turpitude (a certified copy of the judgment of the court of competent jurisdiction of such conviction or pleas shall be *prima facie* evidence of such conviction; in considering the possible disciplinary action, the board shall be governed by determination that such licensee is incompetent or unsafe to continue the practice of nursing or the practice of practical nursing.) Has engaged in any other conduct, whether of the same or of a different character from that specified in this section, that would constitute a crime as defined in general criminal statutes and that relates to such a person's employment as a registered nurse or licensed practical nurse (in conjunction with any disciplinary proceedings pertaining to this section, the board shall be governed by the provisions of ________(Cite applicable state laws.)	Has been found guilty by a court or another board of nursing or has entered a plea of *nolo contendere* to a crime in any jurisdiction that relates adversely to the practice of nursing or to the ability to practice nursing	Conviction of any crime involving moral turpitude Conviction for violation of any state or federal drug law Conviction of any felony

Adapted from AMERICAN NURSES' ASSOCIATION: THE NURSING PRACTICE ACT: SUGGESTED STATE LEGISLATION (1981).
Adapted from NATIONAL COUNCIL OF STATE BOARDS OF NURSING: THE MODEL NURSING PRACTICE ACT (1982).
Adapted from U.S. DEPARTMENT OF JUSTICE, DRUG ENFORCEMENT ADMINISTRATION, OFFICE OF COMPLIANCE AND REGULATORY AFFAIRS: A MODEL HEALTH PROFESSIONS PRACTICE ACT AND STATE REGULATORY POLICY (1977).
§This is no longer considered a valid ground since recent case law has allowed professions to advertise prices of services. (See, e.g., *Bates v. State Bar of Arizona*, 433 U.S. 350 [1977]).

Table 2. Comparison of Grounds for Revocation of Licenses in Model Practice Acts—cont'd

Category	American Nurses' Association Model*	National Council of State Boards of Nursing Model†	Model Health Profession's Practice Act‡
Unfitness and incompetence; mental incompetency; unprofessional conduct	Has a physical or mental disability that renders him or her unable to perform nursing services or duties with reasonable skill and safety to the patient and that endangers the health or safety of a person under his or her care Engages in unprofessional conduct of a character likely to deceive, defraud, or harm the public Engages in any other unprofessional conduct as identified by the board in its rules Has negligently or willfully practiced nursing in a manner that fails to meet generally accepted standards of such nursing practice Has negligently or willfully acted in a manner inconsistent with the health or safety of the persons under his or her care	Is unfit or incompetent to practice nursing by reason of negligence, habits, or other causes, including but not limited to: 1. Being unable to practice nursing with reasonable skill and safety to patients by reason of physical or mental disability, or use of drugs, narcotics, chemicals, or any other type of material 2. Performance of unsafe or unacceptable and prevailing nursing practice, in which case actual injury need not be established 3. Failure to supervise adequately the performance of acts by any person working under the nurse's supervision 4. Abandoning a client without properly notifying appropriate personnel Has engaged in any act inconsistent with the standards of nursing practice as defined by the board rules and regulations	Rendering services while will with disease in the communicable stage Unprofessional conduct or conduct likely to impair the general reputation of the profession Fee splitting or kickback of any kind, except where services are provided jointly Solicitation of patients in any way Failure to maintain acceptable sanitation standards Adjudication of mental incompetence Malpractice, gross negligence, or wanton disregard of acceptable professional standards Lack of fitness to practice by reason of mental of physical health, or otherwise
Drug and alcohol abuse	Is addicted to or dependent on alcohol or other habit-forming drugs or is a habitual user of narcotics, barbiturates, amphetamines, hallucinogens, or other drugs having similar effect	Has diverted or attempted to divert drugs or controlled substances for unauthorized use See above category also	Addiction to narcotics or dependence on drugs not taken in the ordinary course of treatment Chronic alcoholism Rendering services while under the influence of drugs not taken in the ordinary course of treatment Conviction for violation of any state or federal drug law
Revocation in another jurisdiction	Has had a license to practice as a registered nurse or licensed practical nurse suspended or revoked in any jurisdiction (a copy of the order of suspension or revocation shall be *prima facie* evidence of such suspension or revocation.)	Has had a license to practice nursing or to practice in another health care discipline in another state denied, revoked, suspended, or otherwise restricted, other than by reason of failure to renew or to meet continuing education requirements	None
Violations of the act or scope of practice	Has violated any provision of this act; has negligently or willfully violated any order, rule, or regulation of the board pertaining to nursing practice or licensure	Has engaged knowingly in any act that before it was committed had been determined to be beyond the scope of the individual's nursing practice	None

Table 2. Comparison of Grounds for Revocation of Licenses in Model Practice Acts—cont'd

Category	American Nurses' Association Model*	National Council of State Boards of Nursing Model†	Model Health Profession's Practice Act‡
		Has practiced nursing within this state without a valid current license or as otherwise permitted under this act Has failed to report to the board any violation of the act or of board administrative rules and regulations Has been found by the board to have violated any of the provisions of this act or of board administrative rules and regulations	

the act, failure to report violations of the act, violation of the board rules and regulations, exceeding the scope of practice, the unlawful invasion of another field, or unauthorized practice (see boxes, pp. 407-408).

Since grounds and regulations vary and potentially could change at each state legislative session, it is imperative to keep an up-to-date copy of the relevant nursing practice act and regulations.

Procedure and due process rights

If a state board of nursing has received a complaint about a licensee, they must investigate and decide whether to discipline. Notice must be given to the nurse, stating the charges and time and place of a hearing. At least 30 days is the usual notice. The procedures followed before and during a hearing are defined in the state's administrative procedure act or other state code provisions. Nurses and their attorneys may hold informal conferences with state boards and their counsel before going to a formal hearing. At a minimum, a nurse is entitled to due process throughout the investigation, conferences, hearing, and disciplinary action, if any. The box summarizes the basic due process requirements in an administrative hearing.

GENERAL DUE PROCESS REQUIREMENTS

Unless waived, the nurse charged is at least entitled to:

1. Notice of a time and place of hearing
2. A hearing before a properly authorized group
3. A reasonable, definite statement of the charge or charges
4. The right to cross-examine the witnesses who testify against the nurse
5. The right to produce witnesses on the nurse's behalf
6. A full consideration and a fair determination according to the evidence of the controversy by the group before whom the hearing is held
7. The right to appear with counsel
8. The right to a record of the proceeding
9. Some form of judicial review

Defenses

As with other types of legal actions, there are no magical defenses to disciplinary proceedings. The most important thing to do is to get a knowledgeable attorney who knows the applicable law. One should not rely on oneself to defend oneself when one's livelihood is at stake. Legal counsel that may have been provided through a nursing malpractice insurance policy will not be available for this administrative, quasicriminal proceeding. A nurse must obtain counsel *early* and will be independently responsible for paying counsel's fees.

For a disciplinary proceeding before a board one should be thoroughly prepared. Allow plenty of time to prepare a defense. Do not wait until the day before the hearing to locate an attorney. The most important defense is strong preparation and, if applicable, the ability to dispute the facts of the situation. Pleading innocence, if that is the case, will depend on persuading and convincing the board of nursing of one's point of view. Producing credible and convincing character witnesses is an important part of the defense.

Under some circumstances a nurse may voluntarily surrender the license to practice or accept voluntary suspension of the license. The time for reapplication or reinstatement of the license can sometimes be negotiated during the licensure review process.

Other defenses that may apply include pardon, entrapment, illegal search and seizure, lack of jurisdiction, statute of limitations, and violations of due process. The latter two defenses are often the most fruitful. A statute of limitation may exist that would prevent the state board from bringing an action against a nurse if it does not bring the action within the time provided by the legislature. However, the statute of limitation may also prevent a nurse from seeking a change in a state board's action.[29]

Violations of the nurse's due process rights may provide viable arguments that if accepted may diminish the board's action. As mentioned above and in the box on p. 411, if a nurse is not provided with due process then there may be a defense to the board's further action.[30]

Lack of jurisdiction and due process violations were recently argued by a nurse charged with unauthorized practice of midwifery constituting gross misconduct in the practice of nursing.[31] The facts in the case were that a registered nurse, practicing as a midwife without board of nursing authorization to practice as a nurse in the expanded role of nurse midwife, was determined to be within the board's jurisdiction even though lay midwives may practice without meeting board of nursing requirements. In Massachusetts, professional midwives are prohibited through board regulation from assisting in home births. Lay midwives may do so, however. The unsuccessful argument was that the nurse was practicing as a lay midwife, not a nurse midwife. The court held that there was no distinction between lay midwifery and nurse midwifery with regard to registered nurses. A nurse, engaged in the practice of midwifery, must be certified by the board of nursing and meet all of its requirements.

Evidence and burden of proof

Any board of nursing decision must be supported by facts reflected in a record taken of the hearing held before the decision. The form of disciplinary hearings varies widely. In Maryland members of the board of nursing are the judge and jury. But other jurisdictions have a non-nurse hearing officer or non-nurse panel which decides the case. Regardless of who decides, that decision must be based on facts disclosed at the hearing.

In administrative hearings such as disciplinary hearings the legal rules of evidence are not as restrictive as those in civil and criminal cases. Therefore hearing officers or a board of nursing will usually admit most or all of the evidence offered. Often expert testimony may be used. That the rules of evidence are not usually applicable can have a damaging effect on the nurse defendant's case; on the other hand, it may mean that the nurse can present evidence not usually admissible in other legal forums.

The amount of proof necessary before a board of nursing can make a decision varies. In *Arkansas State Board of Nursing v. Long*, the "substantial evidence" test was defined as "evidence which is valid, legal and persuasive and such relevant evidence as a reasonable mind might accept as adequate to support a conclusion."[32] In other states other tests may be used, including a preponderance test, a clear preponderance test, a clear and satisfactory proof test, and a clear and convincing proof test. The vast majority of jurisdictions employ the substantial evidence test defined above.[33]

Actions available to the board

Generally, a state board may apply sanctions appropriate to the offense and the situation. For example, when disciplining a licensee who has abused drugs or alcohol while rendering nursing services, most boards recognize that they are dealing with an illness. When choosing among possible actions the board will consider the deterring effect on future violators or offenders. Most boards try to select actions that encourage the professional to seek help. However, the board's final responsibility is to weigh preventing harm to patients and desire to keep professionals in practice.

A wide variety of actions is available to most nursing boards. The most extreme sanction is denial or revocation of a license. This action is usually reserved for the most extreme situations. A board may suspend a license, placing specific conditions on the application for reinstatement, or a license may be suspended without conditions. The latter should be avoided. The licensee should have a clear understanding of what conditions exist in order to know how to regain his or her ability to practice nursing. For example, a board may limit the licensee's practice to a particular area or place, require supervision, forbid involvement in particular activities, such as prescribing or administration of medications (for example, controlled substances), or require education or retraining. A board may also reprimand a licensee through a letter. This is a mild form of discipline. Money penalties, uncompensated service, and ordered examinations or rehabilitation, such as blood or urine testing or required attendance in a drug rehabilitation program, may also be actions of a board.

Many state nurses' associations and the ANA have developed impaired nurse programs. These usually include services such as a hotline and referral center for help. Many of the state nurses' associations work closely with state boards to develop mechanisms for rehabilitating the professional while being disciplined.[34] The Florida legislature recently created a liaison position within the board of nursing to coordinate the rehabilitation programs of those persons the board disciplines for drug and alcohol abuse.[35] This novel approach has much potential for decreasing the prevalence of substance abuse among practicing nurses.

If a nurse's license is suspended, revoked, or otherwise disciplined, and the requisite conditions and time requirements are met, the action for reinstatement follows. This step involves similar procedural actions and often the same people. Nurses need legal representation at this stage of the case just as much as before the initial proceedings. The nurse's case is presented showing the rehabilitation, the change, the progress, and the reasons why the board should reinstate the license.

Once the nurse is disciplined, the action taken by the board remains on the nurse's record virtually forever. This alone should stress the overwhelming importance of a thorough understanding of the laws governing nursing and the need to obtain *early* legal advice.

Judicial interpretation

Compared to the experience of judicial review of statutes dealing with medicine and dentistry, nursing statutes have come under minimal judicial review. The reason for this probably relates to the extent to which the act has been invoked, the amount of active enforcement, frequency of appeal, and the ability of the nursing profession to maintain minimal standards. A review of cases that were appealed by disciplined nurses shows that state boards of nursing' decisions are upheld, meaning the court agreed with the state board's decision, slightly more often than not upheld. Examples of cases are presented below.

A court that reviews a case of nursing disciplinary action can only disagree with the state board's decision if it was not warranted because it did not relate to the basis or ground used or because there were questions of a procedural nature, adequacy of the record, or amount and type of evidence proffered and where the state board is required to prescribe in advance by regulation what constitutes misconduct. Courts must uphold a board's decision unless there has been an error of law, there has been a violation of constitutional rights, or the decision is not supported by substantial evidence.[36] A court may overturn a board's decision also if it is found that the board acted outside its scope of statutory authority or its action was arbitrary, capricious, unreasonable, or characterized by abuse of discretion.[37]

UPHELD CASES

Situations where denial, revocation, suspension, or reprimand decisions of the board of nursing have been upheld include cases where the nurse:

1. Removed drugs from the hospital without authorization or for an unauthorized use[38]
2. Acted in a manner derogatory to the morals or standards of the profession by interfering in treatment which caused friction between the physician and patients[39]
3. Permitted and instructed her daughter to perform and serve as a registered nurse[40]
4. Diverted controlled substances and was shown to be addicted to drugs and alcohol[41]
5. Acted in a manner that was improper professional conduct by obtaining and converting to her own use a controlled drug[42]
6. Obtained large quantities of controlled drugs through the improper and unauthorized use of her father's drug registration number and injected these drugs in patients as part of a weight reduction program without orders from a licensed physician and without maintaining records of these treatments[43]
7. Altered records, spoiled or returned unused tubes of meperidine (Demerol), substituting water[44]
8. Restarted infiltrated intraveneous fluids against hospital policy and forged physician's name to obtain penicillin[45]
9. Was arrested at place of employment on charges of fraudulently obtaining from hospital controlled substances by listing names of nonexistent patients[46]
10. Had practiced unsafely, had an unsatisfactory work attendance, and failed to utilize satisfactory judgment in administering nursing practices[47]
11. Was reprimanded for violating a board regulation requiring administration of anesthesia under the direction and in the presence of a licensed physician or dentist[48]
12. Substituted a quantity of unknown pills for acetaminophen (Tylenol no. 3)[49]

13. Diverted for her own use 50 mg meperidine[50]
14. Failed to assess patient's condition, failed to inform physician of life-death situation, and failed to take appropriate measures to stabilize condition and prevent demise and complications[51]
15. Acquired and administered certain controlled substances without written physician's orders and failed to properly record such activity[52]
16. Was intoxicated twice while on duty in the emergency room[53]
17. Self-administered a narcotic while on duty, which constituted unprofessional conduct[54]
18. Failed to administer medications in a reasonable manner deemed to be unprofessional conduct (the nurse appropriated, without authorization, the drug meperidine, signed out diazepam [Valium] and oxycodone hydrochloride [Percodan] without a physician's order)[55]
19. Failed to fulfill the statutory requirement that each person applying for a license to practice a profession certify under oath compliance with tax laws[56]

OVERTURNED CASES

Cases where the board's decision was not upheld include the following:

1. Nursing home administrator who was a registered nurse was charged with negligence and unprofessional conduct but the court found that the board lacked substantial evidence to support their decision.[57]
2. A registered nurse's license was reinstated in Tennessee when the court decided the practice of lay midwifery was not within the nursing board's jurisdiction[58] (this is opposite the decision made recently in Massachusetts, discussed above).
3. A nurse was charged with fraud and making false statements in hospital narcotics record book but in fact made correct entries and gave less medicine than ordered to the patient, giving herself the remainder.[59]
4. A nurse was charged with unprofessional conduct because she failed to call an obstetrical patient's physician, used improper and profane language, and treated the patient discourteously, but the court found no testimony to support the charge and in fact found that the patient had been given customary treatment and that the nurse's failures had no serious results.[60]
5. A nurse was guilty of a misdemeanor but the court held that this fact did not in itself warrant a revocation of the license but did allow a 2-year suspension.[61]
6. A nurse was charged with addiction to drugs, and evidence supported a finding of occasional use that was not addiction.[62]
7. A nurse was charged for alleged "lack of candor" in a matter in which she could not respond, and the court found an abuse of discretion.[63]
8. A nurse was charged with slapping a patient and hence violating a board regulation on nursing standards, but there was sufficient evidence to show that the nurse had tried less severe methods of getting the patient to release his hold on her, that the patient was in danger of falling, and that the nurse's action was not willful but justifiably excusable.[64]
9. A nurse was denied reinstatement because of vague regulations and lack of a hearing.[65]
10. A nurse failed to renew her license; consequently, she was charged with unprofessional conduct and the court refused to include this act in the meaning of unprofessional conduct.[66]
11. A nurse was charged with distribution of drugs when she removed drugs to her home, but the court determined that this act was not distribution.[67]
12. A nurse challenged the adequacy of the record.[68]
13. A nurse anesthetist was charged with misappropriation of narcotics (converting the narcotics to her own use), but in fact she was unable to reasonably account for wasted narcotics, which did not amount to a showing of misappropriation.[69]
14. A licensed practical nurse challenged the amount of time the office of professional discipline had investigated her license; the court found there was a delay of 5 years in commencing a hearing and this substantially prejudiced the nurse's due process rights.[70]

CASES OF SPECIAL INTEREST

There have been several cases of special interest in the licensure revocation area affecting nurses. These cases are from Idaho, Pennsylvania, and Wisconsin and discuss the issues of unprofessional conduct and deal with critical care and "no code" issues. Each will be discussed below.

There is precedent in Idaho that indicates that nursing boards should prescribe by regulation what acts constitute unprofessional conduct or misconduct. This is contrary to regulatory trends in other disciplines where boards are not required to prescribe by regulation what acts are considered misconduct.[71] In addition, it has been held that if the statute specifically enumerates grounds, the board has been held powerless to further define "unprofessional conduct" according to its opinion of what the term should encompass or according to commonly accepted standards of the profession in the area.[72] The Idaho case specifically alters this trend and, in fact, as will be discussed below, state boards of nursing across the country have promulgated specific rules and regulations further elaborating the legislatively defined grounds for discipline.

In the Idaho case, Tuma, a clinical instructor of nursing, was accused of interfering with the patient-physician relationship by informing a patient about alternatives to chemotherapy treatment.[73] Tuma's duties included performing nursing services while supervising nursing students at a community hospital. She was interested in the special needs of dying patients and asked to be assigned to a patient who had been informed by her attending physician that she was dying of malignant myelogenous leukemia.

Tuma discussed the patient's condition and background with the patient. The patient had fought leukemia for 12 years and attributed her success to her belief in God and to her faithful practice of her religion.[74] They discussed the work done by the Latter Day Saints Hospital in Salt Lake City using chaparral and laetrile, as well as the side effects of the drugs used in chemotherapy. The patient pleaded with Tuma to return that evening to discuss an alternative treatment using natural products with the patient's family. Tuma consented to the meeting.

Tuma and a nursing student then commenced the patient's chemotherapy. Testimony given at the licensure hearing included that Tuma told the patient that discussing these matters "wasn't exactly ethical" and that Tuma told the nursing student to forget what she had heard because it wasn't "exactly legal."[75] The patient called her family and asked them to come to the hospital that evening to meet Tuma and discuss the alternative treatment. The patient asked her family not to inform the physician because "this could cause trouble for Tuma."[76] However, the family called the physician and told him of the pending discussion with Tuma. The physician did nothing to stop the meeting. However, he ordered the chemotherapy stopped.

That evening Tuma met with the patient and her family. They discussed the prescribed treatment, its side effects, and alternatives provided by natural foods and herbs, as well as the fact the patient would have difficulty getting treatment if she left the hospital. Laetrile was discussed. The patient's son testified at the licensure hearing that Tuma said her discussion with them was "somewhat unethical."[77]

After the discussion, the patient and her family decided she should remain in the hospital and continue chemotherapy. The treatment resumed that evening. The patient died 2 weeks later. There was no contention or evidence that the nurse's actions in any way contributed to the death of the patient.

The court record indicates that hospital personnel telephoned the board of nursing, complaining that Tuma had interfered with the physician-patient relationship. The board's investigation included writing to individuals familiar with the situation and asking them to submit their complaints in writing. Hospital personnel, but not the patient's family, responded.

Following the hearing, the hearing officer found the following as facts:

1. Tuma did not tell the patient that chemotherapy would kill her.
2. Tuma did not say that the patient should discharge herself from the hospital.
3. Tuma did discuss natural products as an alternative treatment but did not say that the alternative treatment would cure the patient.
4. Tuma said that care of a "reflexologist" would be arranged if the patient decided to accept the alternative form of treatment and circumstantial evidence indicates that Tuma would make the arrangements.
5. The physician stopped the treatment for a brief time after hearing of the conversation.
6. Tuma's actions interfered with the physician-patient relationship.[78]

The hearing officer, who was not a nurse, concluded that Tuma had violated the nursing practice act by interfering with the physician-patient relationship and thereby constituting unprofessional conduct.[79]

The board of nursing approved the findings of the hearing officer and suspended Tuma's license for 6 months. On appeal, the trial court entered a judgment affirming the hearing officer's decision and the board's ordered suspension. Tuma appealed to the Supreme Court of Idaho, asking the court to determine whether her due process rights were satisfied by a statute that authorized the suspension of her license to practice nursing on the grounds of unprofessional conduct in the absence of regulations specifically defining unprofessional conduct.

The Idaho Supreme Court ruled that in order for the nursing board to interpret this act (informing a patient of treatment alternatives) as unprofessional it must have first provided definitions of unprofessional conduct in its rules and regulations that would give notice to nurses in Idaho as to what acts constitute unprofessional conduct. The court ordered Tuma's license reinstated.

The Idaho court recognized that the right to practice one's profession was a valuable property right and that a state cannot exclude a person from the practice of his or her profession without having provided the safeguards of due process. Further, the court recognized that a "teaching position was a property interest and a teacher could not be deprived of this interest without notice and an opportunity to be heard."[80]

Tuma's primary argument was that she could not be punished for acts the doing of which at the time done had not been proscribed by the legislative definition or by any definition of standards by the board.[81] The board argued that unprofessional conduct need not be further defined, that such "is that which is recognized to be unsafe or improper by the profession itself."[82] The court, however, noted that the "profession itself" through the state board of nursing had not availed itself of its legislatively given opportunity to expand on the definition of unprofessional conduct. The board had not declared standards of professional conduct, nor had it defined or declared those acts that are either forbidden or required on penalty of being held guilty of unsafe or improper practices. Further, the court noted that the hearing officer, who was not a nurse, had no guidelines on which to make a decision about nursing conduct.

While Tuma argued that the nursing statute was unconstitutional, the court did not agree to go that far. Rather, the court held that the nursing statute lacked further definition. Further, the court found nothing in the statute that could be said to have adequately warned Tuma of the possibility that her license would be suspended if she engaged in discussions with a patient regarding alternative procedures. Therefore the court held that the statute, without board rules and regulations, did not prohibit the conduct with which Tuma was charged.[83]

The current grounds for disciplinary action in Idaho do not include the phrase "unprofessional conduct" but refer to "standards of conduct and practice as may be adopted by the board."[84] At some time before Tuma's hearing (but after the incident in question) the board of nursing had issued in pamphlet form, "Minimum Standards, Rules and Regulations for the Practice of Nursing." The court reviewed these and noted, interestingly, that they seemed to support Tuma's decision to discuss with a patient the alternatives to chemotherapy. This further emphasized the court's point that given no written guidelines as to what conduct might result in discipline for unprofessionalism, a nurse could not know what acts constitute the grounds for discipline.

Another case of special interest involved a nurse working in a neurosurgical intensive care unit.[85] While bathing a patient, Rafferty disconnected the respirator to check for spontaneous respirations. The patient did not respond and the nurse reconnected the patient to the respirator. The patient subsequently suffered a cardiac arrest and died.

The ground that the Pennsylvania Board of Nursing employed to discipline Rafferty was that: "the licensee has willfully or repeatedly violated any of the provisions of the act (nursing act) or of the regulations of the Board."[86] The nursing board regulations involved were as follows:

1. From Regulation 21.11(a)(1) and (4):
   The RN assesses human responses and plans, implements and evaluates nursing care for individuals and families for whom the nurse is responsible. In carrying out this responsibility, the nurse performs all of the following functions:
   (1) Collects complete and ongoing data to determine nursing care needs and
   (2) Carries out nursing care actions which promote, maintain and restore the well-being of individuals.[87]
2. From Regulation 21.13:
   External cardiac resuscitation and artificial respiration, mouth-to-mouth, are procedures regulated by this section, and such functions shall not be performed unless both of the following provisions are met:
   (1) External cardiac resuscitation and artificial respiration, mouth-to-mouth, shall only be performed by a nurse on an individual when respiration or pulse, or both cease unexpectedly.
   (2) A nurse shall not perform external cardiac resuscitation and artificial respiration, mouth-to-mouth, unless the nurse has had instruction and supervised practice in performing the procedures.[88]

The Commonwealth Court focused their analysis on the words, "repeatedly" and "willfully." The first word was defined as more than once and the latter word, relying on *Leukhardt*,[89] was defined as an intentional, designed act and one without justifiable excuse. The Commonwealth Court reversed the board's revocation of the nurse's license because they held that "a mere intentional act which results in a violation is not a designed act unless, by motivation, the act was intended to violate the regulation."[90] The court reasoned that the board found no deliberate or knowing violation but only acts that deviated from accepted nursing practice. They based their finding on the facts that this nurse had an unblemished 7-year record and showed no intent and that this act was not a designed, deliberate, and knowing act. The court stated that the nurse was certainly subject to criticism in her errors of judgment but that the evidence presented did not raise her conduct to the level of willfulness. There was no evidence that Rafferty had caused the patient's death.

The Commonwealth of Pennsylvania, State Board of Nurse Examiners (board) appealed this court's decision. The issue on appeal was one of first impression in the state of Pennsylvania: "whether the burden of proving a willful violation requires a showing of a specific intent to violate the statute or regulation."[91] The board's findings were again reviewed.

Rafferty was employed in the neurosurgical intensive care unit during an 11 PM to 7 AM shift during which she was assigned to care for a patient who had developed serious complications following surgery. The patient was comatose and in respiratory distress, pupils were fixed and dilated, and he was unresponsive to deep pain stimuli. He was on a Bennett MA-I Respirator. The patient's blood pressure was maintained by a dopamine infusion.

The patient was presumed to be brain dead, but this status had not been conclusively established during the nurse's shift. Two electroencephalograms had been done, but the results were not attached to the chart. The patient did not have a "no code" order in his chart. It was the hospital's policy that in case of respiratory or cardiac failure that all efforts for resuscitation were to be attempted unless a "no code" order was documented.[92]

The evidence established that the nurse had reviewed the patient's progress notes before undertaking the care. Rafferty decided to give the patient a bath, but before that she checked and recorded the patient's vital signs, disconnected the ventilator from the endotracheal tube, suctioned secretions present, and reconnected the ventilator. During the suctioning procedure, there were no signs that indicated the patient was assisting ventilation.

The nurse noted premature ventricular contractions (PVCs) 15 minutes later. She determined that they were not life threatening after viewing the monitor and proceeded with the bath. After bathing the head and neck region, the nurse tested the patient for spontaneous respiration. She performed the test by adjusting the ventilation so that the patient was given two or three deep breaths of 100% oxygen and then removing the ventilator tubing from the endotracheal tube. She laid the tubing across his chest and observed the patient for any signs of movement. The patient, during this test, was deprived of oxygen in excess of 30 seconds although room air was available. Following this, Rafferty reconnected the ventilator tubing, restoring the oxygen, and continued the bath.

At this point the evidence showed that the nurse noted a significant change in the vital signs and the PVCs increased drastically. However, the cardiac monitor strips documenting the PVCs were never incorporated into the chart. Rafferty sought out another registered nurse regarding the status change. The other nurse told her to call the code team. Instead, Rafferty called a third registered nurse who, once again, told her to call the code team. She left the room, called the neurosurgical resident, and then called the code team. The code team arrived while the other two nurses were attempting to resuscitate the patient. The resuscitation was unsuccessful, and the patient was pronounced dead.

The board of nursing concluded that Rafferty had violated the above mentioned provisions of board regulations by:

1. Allowing the patient in his condition to remain disconnected from his respirator
2. Leaving the patient on noting that his cardiac monitor displayed asystole
3. Failing to immediately call for the code blue team while the other two registered nurses were engaged in resuscitation procedures
4. Failing to attach the cardiac monitor strip displaying the patient's PVCs to the chart
5. Failing to perform external cardiac resuscitation and artificial respiration, even though she was qualified to render this necessary treatment

The Supreme Court of Pennsylvania held that the Commonwealth Court had erred in holding that the board must prove a specific intent to violate the nursing act or its regulations in order to establish a willful violation.[93] The court indicated that such a holding disregards the very purpose of the board of nursing to ensure safe nursing services for the citizens of Pennsylvania. The court noted that the preeminent interest of the board is for patient care. An interpretation of the term "willful" that incorporates an element of the nurse's motivation would subordinate the interest in patient care to that of policing a nurse's conduct.[94] The court stated it would then become irrelevant whether the nurse's action exposed a patient to unsafe nursing practice as long as the unacceptable action was not intended to violate the nursing act or regulations. The court held that not only would this be an unintended result of the statutory language, it is contrary to the unambiguous statement of the board's purpose.

The court then turned to the question of whether the board's decision was supported by substantial evidence, the only remaining basis for overturning the board's decision. A registered nurse employed at the same hospital, qualified as an expert in the field of critical care, testified that there were limited instances in which a nurse could properly remove a patient from a respirator; namely:

1. To transport a patient
2. During a suctioning procedure

This nursing expert testified that Rafferty's actions in taking a patient in a comatose condition off the respirator was not one of those limited instances and was a deviation from accepted nursing standards.[95]

The nursing expert had also testified that spontaneous repirations should not be evaluated by a nurse and that it was not a nursing function to do so at this hospital.[96] Her opinion that removing a comatose patient from a respirator was inappropriate was reiterated by Rafferty's own expert witness, a nursing supervisor at the same hospital. He testified that the appropriate time for a nurse to check for spontaneous respiration was when a patient showed signs of becoming conscious. He stated, however, that such a test was improper when a comatose patient did not display signs of activity.

The board had based its decision on the above testimony and that the acceptable method to check for spontaneous respiration is to use the assist button on the respirator to determine whether a patient's own efforts are triggering respiration. The court concluded that the Board's decision that Rafferty's conduct was a willful violation of Section 21.11(a)(4) (No. 1) (see p. 414) was amply supported by the record.[97]

However, the court decided that the board's finding of Rafferty's failure to perform external cardiac resuscitation was not supported by the record. This regulation's intent was as a limitation on the individuals who may perform resuscitation; Rafferty's failure to undertake such efforts, although she was qualified, was a violation of Section 21.11(a)(4) but was not a willful violation of Section 21.13 (No. 2) (see p.414).

The court, however, held that the board's conclusions that Rafferty had willfully violated Section 21.11(a)(4) (No. 1) (see p. 414) by leaving the patient, by failing to call the code team, and by failing to attach the cardiac monitor strip to the patient's chart were supported by substantial evidence. At the hearing, testimony by Rafferty indicated that she knew the importance of charting abnormal PVC patterns, but that the strip had been thrown out. She testified that she had been ordered to do this. However, this testimony was refuted by other testimony and by the fact that the hospital policy was that whenever a change occurs the strip is to be saved. The board believed the other testimony rather than Rafferty.

The testimony of the other two registered nurses established that Rafferty had left the patient to seek an opinion, that she failed to call a code until commanded to do so a second time. Expert testimony indicated that the nurse under these circumstances should have checked the patient for a carotid pulse, ensured that the leads and monitor's "inop" signal were connected, summoned another nurse to call a code, and begun resuscitation. Expert opinion also indicated that the nurse is capable of recognizing the elementary arrhythmia and that she did not need another opinion to take the necessary steps.

Rafferty testified that she understood the relationship between the heart and lungs; that she knew a hypoxic state may be indicated by PVCs on the cardiac monitor. Nevertheless, she abandoned the patient when the PVCs were shown on the monitor. Her response was improper since she should not have left the patient. The other nurses undertook the necessary resuscitation efforts and emergency measures that Rafferty failed to do.

Given all of this evidence, the Supreme Court of Pennsylvania held that in order to revoke a nurse's license for willful violation of the professional nursing law or regulations, the Board of Nurse Examiners need not prove a specific intent to violate the act or regulations. The court reversed the lower court's decision on this issue, upholding the board's order revoking Rafferty's license to practice nursing. However, on her appeal to the Commonwealth Court, Rafferty had also raised the issues of constitutionality of the regulations, presence of the hospital's attorneys at the hearing, and the board's failure to reopen the record for additional testimony.[98] Because of the Commonwealth Court's resolution of the issue of intent to violate the act they did not address these remaining issues. Therefore the Supreme Court of Pennsylvania remanded the case (returned it to the Commonwealth Court) on the remaining issues.[99]

Also, in 1985 the Wisconsin Board of Nursing revoked the license of a registered nurse who disconnected the life support equipment of an elderly stroke victim in an act of mercy.[100] The board concluded that what the nurse did was outside the scope of the nursing profession. The board revoked the license for 1 year and provided that the nurse may be licensed again after 1 year if the nurse completed a course in nursing ethics and met routine conditions. The board will require a 2 year probationary period to follow reinstatement. This case is currently being appealed on the issue that the nurse has already not practiced for 413 days and that this time should count toward the revocation period.

Recommendations and trends

Occupational licensing in general has been described in the literature as having persisted for a long period of time and as having grown significantly in recent decades.[101] There is a steeply ingrained belief that licensing benefits society and protects consumers, while establishing minimal restraints on the freedom to practice an occupation. Licensing of health occupations, in particular, represents an example of successful consumer protection. However, challenges on the extent of licensing schemes must continue to be raised in order to maintain a healthy balance between state powers and individual rights.

Any disciplinary action, especially licensure revocation actions, has serious implications. Yet, just as important is the nurse's responsibility to practice safely, reasonably, and competently. Nurses are required in most states to report violations of the nursing practice act to the state board of nursing.[102] Additionally, each nurse has a moral obligation to not only report violations but participate in and support efforts to reasonably regulate the practice of nursing.[103] In many states the mandatory reporting requirement carries penalties if one fails to report and immunity from civil liability for making a report without malice.[104]

One must stay informed of changes in legislation and regulation that affect one's practice. Actively participating in lobbying efforts and administrative hearings is an important step to being well informed.

Given that drug and alcohol abuse among nurses is a major reason for licensure revocation, nurses should carefully monitor drug and medication policies in their agencies, especially the narcotic wasting policies. Full support needs to be given to the efforts of those who have established hotlines, halfway houses, and rehabilitation programs for the impaired nurse. In order to protect patients and promote the integrity of the profession one should actively be aware of signs and symptoms of drug and alcohol addiction.

In response to the growing drug and alcohol problem many legislatures have created a mechanism for temporary surrendering of one's license. For example, in New York a nurse may temporarily surrender his or her license during treatment for drug or alcohol abuse.[105] In summary, this statute provides that the license of a person who may be temporarily incapacitated as a result of a problem of drug or alcohol abuse *that has not resulted in harm to a patient or client* may voluntarily surrender the license. The voluntary surrender is not deemed an admission of disability or of professional misconduct, unless the licensee practices while the license is surrendered.

A surrendered license can be restored on showing to the satisfaction of the licensing agency that the licensee is not incapacitated for the active practice of the profession. However, the licensing agency may impose reasonable conditions on the licensee if it determines that because of the nature and extent of the former incapacity, such conditions are necessary to protect the health, safety, and welfare of the public.

The New York statute also establishes a committee on drug and alcohol abuse that advises on matters relating to practice by professional licensees with drug or alcohol abuse problems and that administers the temporary surrendering law. The application to temporarily surrender one's license is submitted to this committee who will identify a rehabilitation program. The licensee must consent to the release of all information concerning his or her treatment to the committee who must keep the information confidential.

Another legislative approach to the problem is to specify when reporting a nurse to the board is not required. For example, in Maryland if a registered nurse has reason to know that a licensee has committed an action or has a condition that might be grounds for discipline because the licensee is alcohol or drug impaired, the registered nurse is not required to report the licensee to the board under the following conditions[106]:

1. The registered nurse knows that the licensee is in an alcohol or drug treatment program that is accredited by the Joint Commission on the Accreditation of Hospitals, is certified by the state department, or is under the care of a health care practitioner who is competent and capable of dealing with alcoholism and drug abuse.
2. The action or condition of the licensee has not caused injury to any person while the licensee is practicing registered nursing.

The ANA's *Code for Nurses Interpretive Statements* provides guidance to nurses in dealing with incompetent colleagues.[107] Begin with the person carrying out the questionable practice. If the patient's welfare is threatened, discuss and report the observations to the supervisor so that agency administration can take appropriate steps. For example, many employers provide drug and alcohol programs for their employees. The ANA's code further suggests that the nurse report unsafe practice and incompetence to the state board.[108] As mentioned above, depending on the jurisdiction a nurse may be mandated by law (nursing practice act) to report.

ANA expects nurses to participate in self-disciplinary activities. State nurses' associations have the power to discipline their members through censure or expulsion for violation of the *Code for Nurses* or the association bylaws.[109] State nurses' association ethics committees have the authority to investigate and hold hearings on receipt of complaints and to censure members. Some states censure nonmembers for violations of the *Code for Nurses*.[110]

Obtaining legal counsel *early* when the question of discipline arises is essential to a good defense. State boards of nursing should also stay in close contact with their assigned counsel and, in addition, consider hiring outside counsel for consultation, not on individual cases, but on the status of case law and legal procedure in disciplinary actions.

Endnotes

1. Baron, *Licensure of Health Care Professionals: The Consumer's Case for Abolition,* 9 AM. J. LAW & MED. 335 (Fall 1983).
2. S. SHIMBERG, OCCUPATIONAL LICENSURE: A PUBLIC PERSPECTIVE (1982).
3. *See, e.g.,* D.C. CODE ANN. §2-1701.1 and 2-1702.1 (1981), which is an example of a nursing practice act that does not contain a definition of nursing practice. The appendix contains all nursing practice act citations. As a general reference *see,* B. BULLOUGH AND V. BULLOUGH, THE LAW AND THE EXPANDING NURSING ROLE (2nd ed. 1980).
4. *See, e.g.,* California Opinion No. CV 74-62, 58 Op. Cal. Att'y Gen. 388 (June 10, 1975) citing *Kerr's Catering Service v. Dept. of Industrial Relations,* 57 Cal. 2d 319, 330 (1962); 55 Ops. Cal. Atty. Gen. 303 (1972); 35 Ops. Cal. Atty. Gen. 85, 86 (1960).
5. *See, e.g.,* American Nurses' Association publications entitled: STATUTORY REQUIREMENTS FOR LICENSURE OF NURSES (1985); THE REGULATION OF ADVANCED NURSING PRACTICE AS PROVIDED FOR IN NURSING PRACTICE ACTS AND ADMINISTRATIVE RULES (1983); PRESCRIBING PRIVILEGES FOR NURSES: A REVIEW OF CURRENT LAW (1984); STATUTORY DEFINITIONS OF NURSING PRACTICE AND THEIR CONFORMITY TO CERTAIN ANA PRINCIPLES (1983); THE NURSING PRACTICE ACT: SUGGESTED STATE LEGISLATION (1981); NURSING: A SOCIAL POLICY STATEMENT (1980); and ISSUES IN PROFESSIONAL NURSING PRACTICE (1985).
6. *See, e.g.,* S.C. CODE ANN. §40-33-210 (Law. Co-op. Supp. 1984) includes lay members; and S.D. CODIFIED LAWS ANN. §36-9-5 (Supp. 1984) includes two public members.
7. AMERICAN NURSES' ASSOCIATION, STANDARDS OF PRACTICE (1973). (See also the many standards mentioned in this book.)
8. MARYLAND STATE BOARD OF EXAMINERS OF NURSES, STANDARDS OF PRACTICE FOR NURSE ADMINISTRATORS (December 18, 1984) and MARYLAND STATE BOARD OF EXAMINERS OF NURSES, PROPOSED R.N. STANDARDS OF PRACTICE (1984).
9. AMERICAN NURSES' ASSOCIATION, THE NURSING PRACTICE ACT: SUGGESTED STATE LEGISLATION (1981).
10. NATIONAL COUNCIL OF STATE BOARDS OF NURSING, THE MODEL NURSING PRACTICE ACT (1982).
11. DEPARTMENT OF JUSTICE, DRUG ENFORCEMENT ADMINISTRATION. OFFICE OF COMPLIANCE AND REGULATORY AFFAIRS. A MODEL HEALTH PROFESSION'S PRACTICE ACT AND STATE REGULATORY POLICY (1977).
12. *See, e.g.,* S.C. CODE ANN. §40-33-93(a) and (c) (Law. Co-op. Supp. 1984) where a nurse may be disciplined for a felony and/or violation of drug laws; MASS. ANN. LAWS ch. 112, §74 and 74a (Michie/Law Co-op. 1985) where a nurse may be disciplined if found guilty of a felony; and TEX. REV. CIV. STAT. art. 4525(a)(3) (Vernon Supp. 1986) "felony or crime of lesser grade which involves moral turpitude."
13. *See, e.g.,* N.C. GEN. STAT. §90-171.37(2) (1985), which states "has been convicted of . . . any crime which indicates the nurse is unfit or incompetent. . . ."
14. *See, e.g.,* N.D. CENT. CODE §43-12.1-14 (1978 & Supp. 1985), which provides, "3. to have been convicted of an offense determined by the board to have a direct bearing upon a person's ability to serve the public as a nurse, or when the board determines, following conviction of any offense, that a person is not sufficiently rehabilitated . . ."; and *see,* S.C. CODE ANN. §40-33-935 (Law. Co-op. Supp. 1984) "(a) independent conclusion as to the commission of a felony."
15. *See, e.g.,* S.D. CODIFIED LAWS ANN. §36-9-49(2) (Supp. 1984) providing, "been convicted during the past 5 years of a felony."
16. *See, e.g.,* N.D. CENT. CODE § 43-12.1-14 (1978 and Supp. 1985) stating, "direct bearing."
17. *See, e.g.,* DEL. CODE ANN. tit. 24, §1922(a)(7) (Supp. 1985) which states, "physical condition is such that performance of nursing services is injurious or prejudicial to patients or public."
18. *See, e.g.,* N.C. GEN. STAT. §90-171.37(3) (1985), which states, "uses any drug to a degree that interferes with fitness to practice nursing."
19. *See, e.g.,* TEX. REV. CIV. STAT. art. 4525(a)(8) (Vernon Supp. 1986) "intemperate use includes practicing nursing, being on duty or call while under the influence of alcohol or drugs."
20. *See, e.g.,* R.I. GEN. LAWS §5-34-26 (Supp. 1985) which allows automatic suspension while hospitalized for mental illness or for substance abuse; PA. STAT. ANN. tit. 63 §224(2) (Purdon Supp. 1985), which states, "compel, upon probable cause, submission to mental or physican examination"; S.D. CODIFIED LAWS ANN. §36-9-49.1 (Supp. 1984) where majority of the board may demand an examination (refusal to submit constitutes immediate grounds for suspension).
21. *See, e.g.,* PA. STAT. ANN. tit. 63, §224(2) (Purdon Supp. 1985) where failure to submit to an examination constitutes an admission of the allegation.

22. *See, e.g.,* TEX. REV. CIV. STAT. ART. 4525(A)(10) (VERNON SUPP. 1986), requires "adjudication of mental incompetency."
23. *See, e.g.,* R.I. GEN. LAWS §5-34-26 (Supp. 1985), stating "hospitalization for mental illness or for substance abuse."
24. AMERICAN NURSES' ASSOCIATION, CODE FOR NURSES WITH INTERPRETIVE STATEMENTS (1985); *see also* AMERICAN NURSES' ASSOCIATION, GUIDELINES FOR IMPLEMENTING THE CODE FOR NURSES (1980).
25. DEL. CODE ANN. tit. 24, §1921(a)(7), included any violation of the code of ethics adopted by the American Nurses' Association. *But see* the current law at DEL. CODE ANN. tit. 24, §1922(a)(9) (Supp. 1984) which states "is guilty of unprofessional conduct as shall be determined by the Board or the willful neglect of a patient."
26. *See, e.g.,* N.Y. EDUC. LAW §6509 and 6509-a (McKinney 1985).
27. *See, e.g., Shoenhair v. Com. Dept. of State, Bureau of Prof. & Occ. Affairs,* 459 A.2d 877 (Pa. Comwlth. 1983), holding that the Board did not err or violate nurse's due process rights when it considered another state's revocation of nurse's license.
28. *See, e.g.,* D.C. CODE ANN. §2-1702.12 (1981) which authorizes the Mayor to furnish a list of names and addresses of persons to whom licenses, or renewal of licenses, have been denied, revoked or suspended . . . to the board of examination of a state, territory or possession of the U.S., Puerto Rico, or a foreign country, upon written request of such board.
29. *Jackson v. University of the State of New York, the State Education Department,* 484 N.Y.S.2d 153 (1984).
30. R. REAVES, THE LAW OF PROFESSIONAL LICENSING AND CERTIFICATION (1984 AND Supp. 1986) (hereinafter cited as *Reaves*).
31. *Leigh v. Board of Registration in Nursing,* 481 N.E.2d 1347 (Mass. 1985). This case was remanded to determine whether the board based its decision on a violation of regulations applicable to nurses alone or for the mere practice of midwifery. *See also* N.Y. Times, August 18, 1985, at 45, col. 1, entitled, *Massachusetts Nurse Loses Midwifery Case.*
32. *Arkansas State Board of Nursing v. Long,* 651 S.W.2d 109 (Ark. 1983).
33. *Reaves, supra* note 30, at 196.
34. Jefferson and Ensor, *Help for the Helper: Confronting a chemically-impaired colleague,* 82 A. J. N. 574 (1982); Mereness, *Protect Your Patients from Nurse Addicts,* 3 NURS. LIFE 71 (July-August, 1981).
35. FLA. STAT. ANN. §458.3315 and 464.0185 (West Supp. 1984). *See also* N.Y. EDUC. LAW §6510-b (McKinney 1985 & Supp. 1986) which allows under certain circumstances, temporary surrender of licenses during treatment for drug or alcohol abuse. This will be discussed further below.
36. *Rafferty v. Commonwealth,* 471 A.2d 1339 (Pa. 1984), *rev'd in part, remanded in part,* 499 A.2d 289 (Pa. 1985), *on remand* 505 A.2d 357 (Pa. Comm. 1986). This case is discussed in detail in a later section on cases of special interest.
37. *Scott v. State of Nebraska ex re. Board of Nursing.* 244 N.W.2d 683 (Neb. 1976); *Lunsford v. Board of Nurse Examiners for the State of Texas,* 648 S.W.2d 391 (Tex. 1984).
38. *Pierce v. Board of Nursing Education and Nurse Registration.* 63 Cal. Rptr. 107 (Cal. 1967).
39. *Stefanik v. Nursing Education Committee,* 37 A.2d 661 (R.I. 1944).
40. *Ward v. Oregon State Board of Nursing,* 510 P.2d 554 (Or. 1973).
41. *Davin v. New York State Board of Regents,* 393 N.Y.S.2d 832 (1977).
42. *Leib v. Board of Examiners for Nursing,* 411 A.2d 42 (Conn. 1979).
43. *Livingston v. Nyguist,* 388 N.Y.S.2d 42 (1976).
44. *Tighe v. Commonwealth, State Board of Nurse Examiners,* 397 A.2d 1261 (Pa. 1979); *Conlon v. Commonwealth, State Board of Nurse Examiners,* 449 A.2d 108 (Pa. 1982).
45. *Ullo v. Commonwealth, State Board of Nurse Examiners,* 398 A.2d 764 (Pa. 1979).
46. *Derrick v. Commonwealth, Department of State, Bureau of Professional & Occupational Affairs,* 432 A.2d 282 (Pa. 1981).
47. *Scott v. State of Nebraska ex rel. Board of Nursing,* 244 N.W.2d 683 (Neb. 1976).
48. *McCarl v. Commonwealth, State Board of Nurse Examiners,* 396 A.2d 866 (Pa. 1979).
49. *Smith v. State of Alabama Board of Nursing,* 435 So.2d 108 (Ala. 1983).
50. *Arthur v. District of Columbia Nurses' Examining Board,* 459 A.2d 141 (D.C. 1984).
51. *Lunsford v. Board of Nurse Examiners for the State of Texas,* 648 S.W.2d 391 (Tex. 1984).
52. *Ledo v. University of the State of New York, State Education Department,* 478 N.Y.S.2d 108 (1984).
53. *Alabama Board of Nursing v. Herrick,* 454 So.2d 1041 (Ala. 1984).
54. *Stevens v. Blake, Alabama Board of Nursing,* 456 So.2d 795 (Ala. App. 1984).
55. *Hassell v. The Board of Nurse Examiners,* 695 S.W.2d 284 (Tex. App. 1985). However, it should be noted that the court could not make a proper decision because the appellant-nurse who had the duty to present the court with a complete administrative record, failed to bring it before the reviewing court. Arguments challenging the weight and substantial characteristics of the evidence could not be evaluated by the court.
56. *Walden v. Board of Registration in Nursing,* 479 N.E.2d 665 (Mass. 1985). In this case the nurse raised constitutional challenges to the right of the state to require certification of compliance with tax laws. The court held that that nurse was not entitled to a hearing, that the certification requirement rationally furthered legitimate government goals, and that the nurse did not show that she had been denied her right against self-incrimination.
57. *Arkansas State Board of Nursing v. Long,* 651 S.W.2d 109 (Ark. 1983).
58. *Leggett v. State Board of Nursing,* 612 S.W.2d 476 (Tenn. App. 1980).
59. *Application of Sutton,* 207 N.Y.S.2d 550 (1960).
60. *Colorado State Board of Nurse Examiners v. Hohu,* 268 P.2d 401 (Colo. 1954).
61. *Hoyte v. Board of Regents,* 304 N.Y.S.2d 693 (1969).
62. *Carruthers v. Allen,* 239 N.Y.S.2d 756 (1963).
63. *Ahsaf v. Nyquist,* 371 N.Y.S.2d 705 (1975).
64. *Leukhardt v. Commonwealth, State Board of Nurse Examiners,* 403 A.2d 645 (Pa. 1979).
65. *Woods v. District of Columbia Nurses' Examining Board,* 436 A.2d 369 (D.C. 1981).

66. *Kansas State Board of Nursing v. Burkman,* 531 P.2d 122 (Kan. 1975).
67. *Garrison v. Washington State Nursing Board,* 550 P.2d 7 (Wash. 1976).
68. *Appeal of Jean F. Doherty,* 464 A.2d 1113 (N.H. 1983).
69. *Hogan v. Mississippi Board of Nursing,* 457 So.2d 931 (Miss. 1984).
70. *Wildman v. Axelrod,* 475 N.Y.S.2d 743 (Sup. 1984).
71. *Bell v. Board of Regents of University of State of New York,* 65 N.L.2d 184 (N.Y. 1946); *Dubin v. Board of Regents of State of New York,* 141 N.Y.S.2d 54 (1955); *In Re Mintz,* 378 P.2d 945 (Or. 1963).
72. *Leib v. Board of Examiners for Nursing,* 411 A.2d 42 (Conn. 1979).
73. *Tuma v. Board of Nursing,* 593 P.2d 711 (Idaho 1979).
74. *Id.* at 712.
75. *Id.* at 713.
76. *Id.*
77. *Id.*
78. *Id.*
79. *Id.* at 714, referring to IDAHO CODE §54-1422(a) (7).
80. *Id.*, citing *Ferguson v. Bd. of Trustees of Bonner Cty Sch. Dist. No. 82,* 564 P.2d 971, 976 (Idaho 1977).
81. *Id.* at 715.
82. *Id.*
83. *Id.* at 717.
84. IDAHO CODE §54-1412(7) (1979 & Supp. 1985).
85. *Rafferty v. Commonwealth, State Board of Nurse Examiners,* 471 A.2d 1339 (Pa. Comm. 1984), *rev'd. in part, remanded in part,* 499 A.2d 889 (Pa. 1985), *on remand* 505 A.2d 357 (Pa. Comm. 1986).
86. PA. STAT. ANN. tit. 63, §224(3) (Purdon 1978).
87. 49 PA. ADMIN. CODE §21.11(a) (1) and (4) (Shepard's 1978).
88. 49 PA. ADMIN. CODE §21.13 (Shepard's 1978).
89. *Leukhardt v. St. Bd. of Nurse Examiners,* 403 A.2d 645, 648 (Pa. 1979), citing *Commonwealth ex re. Wright v. Hendrick,* 312 A.2d 402 (Pa. 1973).
90. *Rafferty v. Commonwealth, State Board of Nursing,* 471 A.2d 1339, 1341 (Pa. Comm. 1984).
91. *Rafferty v. Commonwealth, State Board of Nursing,* 499 A.2d 289, 292.
92. *Id.* at 290.
93. *Id.* at 292.
94. *Id.*
95. *Id.*
96. *Id.* at 293.
97. *Id.*
98. *Id.* at 292.
99. *Id.* at 294.
100. N.Y. Times, March 9, 1985, at 1, col. 1.
101. Gellhorn, *The Abuse of Occupational Licensing,* 44 U. CHI. L. REV. 6, 10 (1976).
102. *See, e.g.,* MD. HEALTH OCC. CODE ANN. §7-506 (1986), which states, in part, if a . . . registered nurse . . . knows of an action or condition that might be grounds for (discipline) . . . the . . . registered nurse . . . shall report the action or condition to the Board. *See also* N.J. ADMIN CODE 13:37-1,4 (1986) (Every nurse licensee shall report in a timely manner any and all incidents or series of incidents, which upon objective evaluation leads to the good faith belief that the conduct violates the Nurse Practice Act or Regulations.) The N.J. Board of Nursing has issued GUIDELINES FOR REPORTING UNLAWFUL ACTIVITIES BY LICENSED NURSES (1986).
103. ANA, CODE FOR NURSES WITH INTERPRETIVE STATEMENTS (1985).
104. *Id.* But see N.J. CODE ANN §2A:47A-1 (West Supp. 1986), which provides for liability for damages for false complaints of unprofessional conduct by allowing a malicious prosecution action for a false, malicious, and without probable cause complaint. However, refer to Chapter 22 for a discussion of a Florida case involving a nursing administrator who reported a staff nurse to that State Board.
105. N.Y. EDUC. LAW §6510-b (McKinney 1985) (effective January 24, 1986).
106. MD. HEALTH OCC. CODE ANN. §7-506(b), (c) (1986). The statute further provides that a person is not required under this section to make a report that would be in violation of any federal or state law, rule, or regulation concerning the confidentiality of alcohol and drug abuse patient records.
107. AMERICAN NURSES' ASSOCIATION, CODE FOR NURSE WITH INTERPRETIVE STATEMENTS 6 (1985). Interpretive statement 3.2 Acting on Questionable Practice.
108. *Id.*
109. AMERICAN NURSES' ASSOCIATION, GUIDELINES FOR IMPLEMENTING THE CODE FOR NURSES (1980).
110. *Id.* at 24. Mechanism of the Tennessee Nurses' Association for Processing Complaints and Charges of Violation of the Code for Nurses or of Bylaws.

Additional Readings

Beck and Buckley, *Taking drugs on the job: Nurses with Bad Habits*, NEWSWEEK 54 (August 1983).

Bissell, *The Alcoholic Nurse*, 29 N. O. 96 (February 1981).

Bullough, *The Current Phase in the Development of Nurse Practice Acts*, 28 ST. LOUIS U. L. J. 365 (1984).

Cohn, *Revocation of Nurse's License: How Does it Happen?* 11 LAW, MED. & HEALTH CARE 22 (February 1983).

Daniel, *Impaired Professionals: Responsibilities and Roles* 2 NURS. ECON. 190 (May-June 1984).

Greenlaw, *Definition and Regulation of Nursing Practice: An Historical Survey*, 13 LAW, MED. & HEALTH CARE 117 (June 1985).

Slater, REGULATION OF HEALTH PROFESSIONALS (1975).

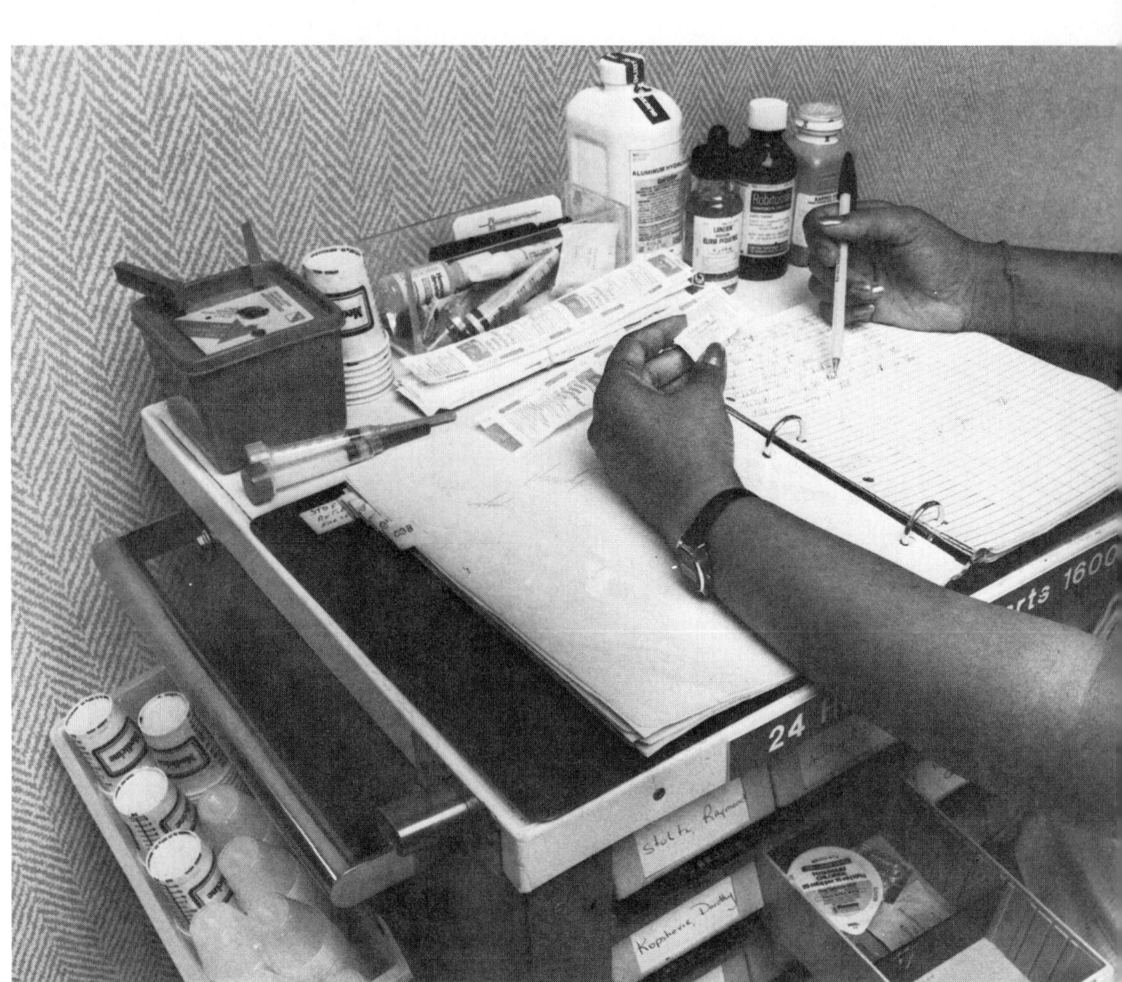

UNIT V

Risk Prevention and Management

Chapter 26

Risk management

Elizabeth A. Bowyer

Health care risk management is a relatively new concept. ''Risk management,'' an insurance term first used in the 1960s, refers primarily to minimizing or financing, through insurance mechanisms, predictable losses in business and industry.[1] The health care industry, in response to the malpractice crisis of the mid-1970s, sought to develop new approaches to examine the causes of malpractice liability and reduce loss exposure. The resulting movement in health care risk management has evolved into a responsibility which includes prediction of patient injury, avoidance of exposure to risks, and minimization of malpractice losses.[2]

While risk financing is an important feature of risk management, the focus in health care settings is loss prevention and loss control as it relates to patient, staff, and visitor safety, as well as effective claims management when a loss does occur. While most of the risk management literature and activity has to date occurred in the hospital setting, the principles apply to all health care settings.

This chapter will define risk management as it is used in health care, provide an overview of the risk management process in hospitals, and describe specific tools used to achieve the goals of risk management. Finally, recent legislative mandates in risk management will be explored, as well as the role of the risk manager and the need for nursing participation in an effective risk-management program.

Two related concepts, insurance and quality assurance, are discussed in detail in Chapters 27 and 28. This chapter will maintain a focus on risk management, noting that a strong relationship exists between all three concepts—risk management, quality assurance, and liability insurance.

Risk management

Risk management (RM) is defined as the science for identification, evaluation, and treatment of the risk of financial loss.[3] Health care risk management has been defined more specifically as:

> [T]he identification, analysis, evaluation, and elimination or reduction to the extent [possible, of] risks to hospital patients, visitors, or employees. A risk management program should be a totally integrated program involving hospital and medical staff quality assurance activities, hospital safety and security activities, a patient relations (feedback) program, and a mechanism for handling incidents, claims, and other insurance and litigation related tasks.[4]

Risk management activities concern loss prevention (attempts to prevent incidents which result in losses) and loss control (attempts to minimize the losses flowing from an incident which has occurred). Until recently, risk managers were primarily concerned with loss control, not becoming involved until after an event occurred. However, today, the major emphasis in risk management is identification of potential risk areas and intervention to enhance patient safety and prevent losses or manage those which cannot be prevented.

Risk management may encompass all of a hospital's

(or other health care service's) liability exposures, including worker's compensation, general liability, and professional liability concerns. The risk manager generally coordinates event reporting and investigation, participates in claims management, and may be responsible for risk financing.

Risk management objectives

Hospital risk management has several objectives. They include:

1. Loss prevention: to improve the quality of patient care, thereby preventing or reducing the frequency of preventable adverse occurrences that lead to malpractice liability (The risk management of hospital property, visitor and employee safety is important, but patient safety should be the primary goal of a hospital risk management program)
2. Loss control: to develop systems to promptly identify, follow-up and resolve patient, visitor, and employee safety problems in an effort to minimize the financial, human, and intangible costs of risks
3. Risk financing: to seek the most economical method for financing the institution's potential losses from among alternatives in the insurance market or self-insurance programs.[5]

Similar objectives would exist for risk management in any health care setting or service.

Risk management functions

The functions of RM include:

1. Protect the financial assets of the hospital (or other facility or service)
2. Protect human and intangible resources
3. Prevent injury to patients, visitors, employees, and property
4. Reduce loss, focusing on *individual* loss or single incidents
5. Prevent loss by improving the quality of care through continuing and ongoing monitoring
6. Review each incident and the patterns of incidents through an RM system (outlined below).[6]

Quality assurance (QA) and RM are related functions within an institution. As defined in Chapter 28 on quality assurance, they differ in the following ways:

1. The motivation and focus of each function is different.
2. RM is concerned with acceptable care from a legal perspective, while QA is concerned with optimal care.
3. RM addresses all hospital exposures, while QA is solely concerned with patient care.
4. RM is concerned with legal, insurance, and other distinct loss prevention activities.
5. QA facilitates improved care through coordination of various activities, while RM specializes in more focused loss prevention activities.

Between the two efforts, there are many areas of common concern, including identification and prevention of adverse patient occurrences; emphasis on monitoring of trends to identify patterns of risk; correction of risks by education, changes in policies and procedures, and disciplinary actions. Both RM and QA emphasize complete and correct documentation (discussed in Chapter 28), and both require cooperation from the medical and nursing staff and hospital administration to effect the needed changes.[7] Finally, many of the tools used to identify risks are equally effective in both efforts. Therefore, there should be a formal integrated relationship between the QA and RM departments to maximize the use of problem identification data.

Risk management process

The RM process is a four-step approach used to identify, confront, and prevent risks and to accomplish the goals of a risk management program. The components are:

1. Risk identification
2. Risk analysis
3. Risk treatment
4. Risk evaluation

Prompt identification of risk is a key element in an RM program. Early problem identification permits the risk manager to initiate appropriate follow-up procedures in a timely manner. This also promotes better management of any resulting claims and prompt implementation of loss control and loss prevention activity. Each of these steps will be discussed.

RISK IDENTIFICATION

The first step of the RM process is risk identification. The events that a risk manager is concerned with may be identified by a variety of terms. An "adverse patient outcome" is defined as "any untoward patient event which, under optimal conditions, is not a natural consequence of the patient's disease or procedure."[8] A "potentially compensable event" refers to any occurrence which could result in liability exposure. Other terms used frequently in risk identification systems include: "mal-occurrence,'' ''mishap,'' ''patient safety problem,'' and ''incident.''

In risk identification the risk manager relies on many data sources, ranging from incident reports, verbal communication, and committee reports to sophisticated occurrence screening systems.[9] Ideally, all patient liability exposure and patient safety problems are reported to the risk manager as soon as an event has occurred. This is not as easy as it sounds. In many cases a potential claim can be recognized immediately. For example, when a nurse administers the wrong drug to a patient who suffers a severe reaction necessitating extended hospitalization or resulting in a permanent injury, there is clear potential liability.

Other potential liability situations may be less obvious. For example, the risk manager may learn from the infection control nurse that patients on a particular nursing unit have an unusually high rate of subclavian line infections, which are apparently related to poor aseptic technique by one of the nurses who routinely changes subclavian dressings. It is uncertain which of the affected patients, if any, presents potential liability exposure.

When a particular event is recognized, whether it is an isolated occurrence or a pattern which indicates a recurring problem, there must be a formal mechanism for reporting such events to the risk manager. Several common event reporting tools and other important risk identification data sources are discussed below.

Incident Reports. Incident reporting systems are a familiar mechanism for identifying risks in the hospital setting. The traditional incident report is a useful tool for identifying falls, burns, medication errors, and other clearly identifiable incidents. A sample incident form from the Risk Management Foundation is found in Fig. 1. However, incident reports are not effective for identifying the type of clinical occurrences that typically result in large loss exposure. Incident reporting can be a valuable tool if designed and implemented properly. Attributes of an effective incident reporting program include[10]:

1. Clear definition of the term ''incident,'' such as: ''an accident, discovery of a hazardous condition, or any occurrence which is not consistent with routine operation of the institution or routine care of a patient.''[11]
2. Clear reporting forms which are easy to complete and analyze. Reports should use checklists and short, objective answers rather than encourage open-ended narrative responses.
3. Clear procedures. All occurrences should be reported, even if no injury results. Completed forms should be routed immediately to the risk manager.
4. Prompt response. Reports should reach the RM office within 24 hours, and appropriate follow-up should begin immediately.
5. Trending. Incident report data should be trended and reviewed with the QA and RM committees and with individual departments.
6. Feedback. Results of trending analysis should be shared with staff, including examples of patient safety problems which were resolved because of incident reporting. Prompt investigation of reported incidents shows providers that their reports initiate follow-up action.
7. Education. Inservice programs on incident reporting should emphasize that the intended use of reports is identification of risk exposure, *not* as a basis for staff disciplinary actions. Programs should also include specific instructions for completing reports and a review of the laws affecting discoverability and admissibility of incident reports in the jurisdiction.[12]
8. Top level commitment. Administration and medical and nursing staff leaders must express commitment to the incident reporting system clearly and often.

In fact, hospitals are being urged to consider expanding present incident reporting systems into occurrence reporting programs.[13] The change would result in increased reports of potentially compensable events and enhanced staff awareness of potential liability situations. This will be discussed further.

Inspections and Assessments. Many insurance companies and RM consultants provide inspection surveys and questionnaires for health care providers to use to identify potential risk areas.[14] In addition, the Joint Commission on Accreditation of Hospitals (JCAH)[15] and medical and nursing professional organization assessment tools can aid in risk identification. Many institutions have developed their own surveys as well.

Quality Assurance Feedback. QA data is an important source of RM input. Anything that affects patient care quality becomes a risk management concern. Similarly, identification of potential liability exposure raises quality of care issues. As mentioned before, the relationship between RM and QA departments must be collaborative, and there should be formal, integrated channels of communication.[16]

REPORT OF INCIDENT OR UNUSUAL OCCURRENCE
CONFIDENTIAL – NOT PART OF MEDICAL RECORD

INSTITUTION

ALWAYS complete this report in the event of an accident, discovery of a hazardous condition; or any occurrence which is not consistent with routine operation of the institution or routine care of a patient.

ATTENDING PHYSICIAN

1 NAME ______

ADDRESS ______

AGE ______ SEX ______

2

EXACT LOCATION OF INCIDENT	BUILDING	FLOOR	ROOM NO.	DATE	TIME ☐ AM ☐ PM
DISCOVERY	DATE	TIME ☐ AM ☐ PM	DISCOVERED BY	TITLE	

3 INCIDENT
☐ Slip/Fall
☐ IV or Med.
☐ Burn
☐ Equipment
☐ Procedure
☐ Other ______

CONCISE DESCRIPTION OF OCCURRENCE (State significant facts in chronological order)
______
(Use back of this copy for additional information)

4 WITNESSES

NAME (Position if employee)	ADDRESS	TELEPHONE NO.
NAME	ADDRESS	TELEPHONE NO.

5 BACKGROUND
☐ Inpatient
☐ Outpatient

PATIENT'S DIAGNOSIS | ADMISSION DATE

SURGICAL PROCEDURE/OUTPATIENT TREATMENT

MEDICATION WITHIN PAST 6 HOURS ☐ YES ☐ NO | NAME OF MEDICATION | ☐ SEDATIVE ☐ LAXATIVE ☐ DIURETIC ☐ OTHER

ORDERED ACTIVITY LEVEL AT TIME OF OCCURRENCE
☐ RESTRAINTS TYPE: ______ | PATIENT ORIENTED ☐ YES ☐ NO | ☐ BEDREST ☐ UP WITH ASSISTANCE | ☐ UP WITHOUT ASSISTANCE

BED POSITION ☐ LOCKED ☐ FIXED ☐ HIGH ☐ LOW | BED RAILS ☐ UP ☐ DOWN | LAST SEEN BY | TIME ☐ AM ☐ PM

6
☐ Visitor
☐ Employee
☐ Other

REASON FOR BEING AT HOSPITAL

DEPARTMENT | TITLE | ON DUTY ☐ YES ☐ NO

DISPOSITION OF CASE ☐ RETURNED TO WORK ☐ SENT HOME ☐ HOSPITALIZED | ESTIMATED DATE OF RETURN TO WORK

7 TREATMENT

WAS THERE AN INJURY? ☐ YES ☐ NO PATIENT/FAMILY AWARE OF INCIDENT? ☐ YES ☐ NO WAS EXAMINATION OR TREATMENT REFUSED? ☐ YES ☐ NO

ATTENDING PHYSICIAN NOTIFIED? ☐ YES ☐ NO – IF YES, DATE ______ TIME ______ ☐ AM ☐ PM

X-RAY ORDERED ☐ YES ☐ NO RESULTS (If known) ______

CLINICAL FINDINGS: ______

______ SIGNATURE ______ M.D.

8 FOLLOW-UP

REPORTED TO: (Supervisor, Administrator, Security, Safety)

PERSON(S) RESPONSIBLE FOR FOLLOW-UP

COPY TO:

SIGNATURE OF PERSON PREPARING THIS REPORT	TITLE	DATE

RMF 1 (5-79)

THIS REPORT IS FOR DATA ANALYSIS AND LOSS CONTROL PURPOSES ONLY. IT IS NOT TO BE CONSTRUED AS NOTIFICATION TO THE INSURANCE COMPANY OF A POSSIBLE CLAIM.

Fig. 1. Example of report of incident or unusual occurrence form. (Reprinted with permission from Risk Management Foundation, Cambridge, Mass. ©1979.)

Patient Relations. The patient relations department, ombudsman, or patient advocate is often a source of risk identification information. Patient complaints about a particular provider, dissatisfaction with care, a refusal to pay hospital bills, or angry letters and phone calls often provide the first indication of a potential problem. Some patient representative departments use occurrence screening systems for patient complaints which parallel the hospital occurrence screening systems for QA and RM.[17] Any potential claims identified through this mechanism are referred immediately to the risk manager.

Claims Data. Analysis of closed claims data from insurance companies or captive insurance programs can provide useful information about risks. A claim can take several forms, including:

1. A suit for damages
2. Actual damages for compensating a patient or family member
3. A statement by a patient or family member charging the insured with malpractice and making a demand for compensation
4. A letter of representation from an attorney stating an intent to seek compensation on behalf of the patient

When a claim is made, a file is opened in which all information pertaining to the claim is kept. A closed claim is any file that has been resolved and is no longer active.

Whether the closed claims are from a particular employing institution or another area of the country, evaluation of data from actual closed claims can reveal problems with particular policies and procedures and forewarn nurses of situations with high liability potential. For example, a recent study by the St. Paul Companies found that patient falls resulted in almost as many lawsuits as all other forms of questionable medical care combined.[18] Further, the study showed that most patient falls are from or near the bed.[19]

In another closed claim analysis, the Risk Management Foundation reviewed 22 closed anesthesia related claims.[20] The Harvard Anesthesia Department Risk Management Committee also reviewed the claims and found that many of the incidents that led to claims might not have occurred had there been improved patient monitoring. As a result, the anesthesia department promulgated minimal monitoring standards for anesthesia administration.[21]

A disadvantage of closed claims review is the long delay between occurrence of an adverse incident and the review. However, there is much valuable risk management information found in actual claims.

Occurrence Screening and Reporting. Occurrence screening and occurrence reporting mechanisms are systems for identifying adverse patient events. An occurrence screening system, such as Craddick's MEDICAL MANAGEMENT ANALYSIS,[22] is based on a concurrent or retrospective criteria-based review of all patient records.

The occurrence screening identifies ''adverse patient occurrences [or] untoward patient events which, under optimal conditions, are not a natural consequence of the patient's disease or treatment . . . [T]hey are events which health professionals agree are not desirable outcomes of optimal medical management.''[23]

Ideally, every medical record is reviewed by a screener, and any variation from the objective screening criteria is reported and triggers an assessment of the record. Identification of a deviation from the objective criteria does not indicate that there was inappropriate care; it merely identifies a variance from the criterion. Judgments regarding the patient care are made by a peer review process in the assessment phase of occurrence screening. Because occurrence screening relies on record review, the tool will not capture potential liability situations that are not reflected in the medical record.

Occurrence reporting systems rely on individual reports of deviation from objective generic criteria. Many generic screening programs focus on high-risk areas, such as emergency room or labor and delivery. In such systems reporting is done by individual providers rather than special screeners. Therefore, additional staff is not required. Occurrence reporting criteria can be designed to capture many clinical adverse patient occurrences, as well as falls and burns which are traditionally reported in incident reports. However, because occurrence reporting is event related, medical occurrences such as misdiagnosis are not as likely to be reported. Chart-based screening programs would capture these problems much more consistently.[24]

Sample audit criteria and occurrence reporting criteria are presented in the box on p. 432 and Fig. 2. No single system can be expected to procure all of the quality assurance and risk management data that an organization requires. Every organization should implement a system which integrates several risk identification mechanisms to provide the information needed for an effective risk management program.

AUDIT CRITERIA SHEET FOR RETROSPECTIVE AND CONCURRENT AUDIT TO IDENTIFY UNTOWARD OCCURRENCES NEEDING INVESTIGATION

Directions

When anyone perceives an untoward occurrence:
—Circle appropriate criteria
—Imprint the patient's name in upper right hand corner
—Forward to risk manager, copy to unit supervisor and medical records department

Emergency Unit

Criteria	*Exception*
1. Patient discharged from hospital or seen within the past 10 days.	Condition on previous encounter with instructions to return at a specified interval or for specific reasons.
2. Patient discharged from or admitted to hospital without being seen by physician.	None.
3. Patient arrives dead (DOA) and has either been discharged from hospital or seen in emergency unit within the past 10 days.	None.
4. Patient dies in emergency unit.	None.
5. Patient refuses treatment, hospitalization or leaves without signing against medical advice form.	None.
6. Final x-ray report differs substantially from emergency diagnosis and/or x-ray interpretation in emergency unit (especially fractures, foreign bodies, and abnormal air).	Unimportant incidental findings related to aging or normal anatomical variance.
7. Unexpected abnormal diagnostic test results returned to emergency unit after patient discharged.	None.
8. Patient or visitor falls and is injured.	None.
9. Medication error.	None.
10. Transfusion error.	None.
11. Treatment/procedure errors (e.g., laboratory, x-ray wrong patient, wrong treatment).	None.
12. No written consent or improper consent for nonemergent procedure or treatment.	None.

Used with permission. From D.-M. Boulay, R.N., J.D. Health-Law Consultants.

RISK ANALYSIS

Once an area of potential risk is identified, the next step is to analyze the cause and scope of the problem. This involves determining the frequency of the particular occurrence and the severity of the risk identified. For example, questions such as these might be asked:

1. Was the event an isolated occurrence or evidence of a trend?
2. Is the loss potential minimal or serious?

One approach to risk analysis is statistical or mathematical. The risk is assessed in terms of: probable frequency of occurrence of the loss; probable or possible severity of the loss; and the effect that the loss will have on the organization, both clinically and financially.[25] By qualifying the extent of the problem, the risk manager can prioritize the needed interventions and allocate resources appropriately.

Besides statistical analysis, risk analysis may also be performed by a multidisciplinary risk management committee. The committee may look at an individual incident to identify trends and patterns in potential loss areas.

As an example, Fig. 3 and Table 3 illustrate the results of a risk analysis from the Risk Management Foundation of the Harvard Medical Institutions.[26] The Foundation reviewed all of the claims filed against gynecologists and found that the most frequent and costly claims were related to diagnostic problems, including failure to diagnose, misdiagnosis, delay in diagnosis, and improper performance of diagnostic tests. The risk manager or department chief uses this information to plan inservice

MATERNAL AND INFANT RELATED OCCURRENCES TO BE REPORTED CONCURRENTLY TO THE HOSPITAL'S RISK MANAGEMENT REPRESENTATIVE

1. Maternal or infant death ☐
2. Apgar: Less than 6 at 1 minute and less than 8 at 5 minutes. (Review all charts exhibiting these apgars to assess cause of low apgar. Note presence or absence of electronic fetal monitoring.) ☐
3. Infant injury (e.g., skull fracture, brachial palsy, paralysis) ☐
4. High forceps delivery ☐
5. Admittance to newborn ICU or transfer to another hospital's newborn ICU for complications ☐
6. Newborn resuscitation ☐
7. Prolapsed cord ☐
8. Delivery unattended by physician with Ob privileges ☐
9. Maternal blood loss resulting in transfusion or Hgb drop greater than 2.5 gm ☐
10. Mother in recovery room more than 2 hours postdelivery or transferred to ICU for medical complications ☐
11. Mother's unplanned return to the delivery room or surgery. ☐
12. Maternal injury or complications, i.e., laceration requiring extensive repair, temperature greater than 35°C retained placenta, etc. ☐
13. Any second stage of labor longer than 2 hours ☐

Comments: ______________________________

____

____

Fig. 2. Sample occurrence screening tool. (Reprinted with permission from Chicago Hospital Risk Pooling Program.)

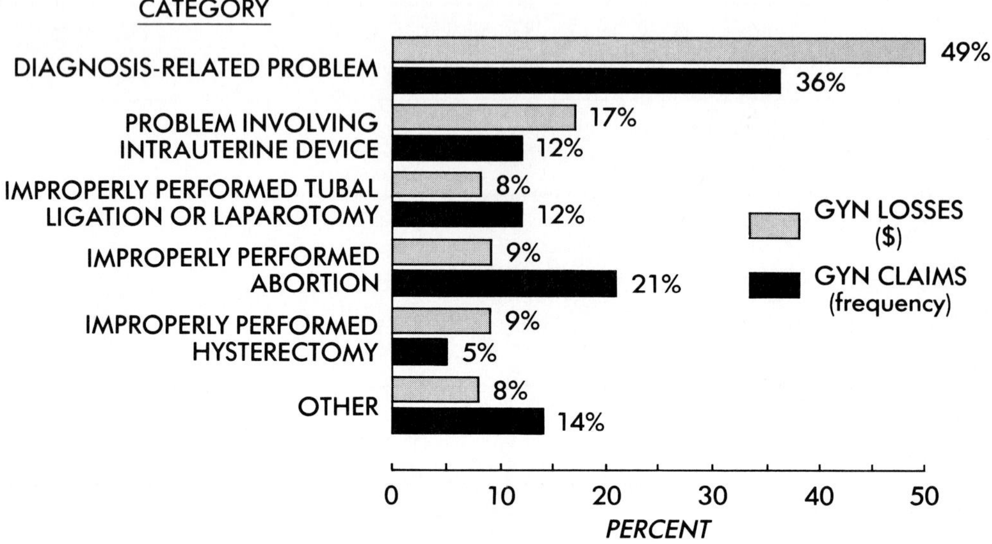

Fig. 3. Sample claims file analysis. (From *Diagnostic Errors Most Frequent and Costly Allegations in GYN Claims,* 5 RISK MANAGEMENT FOUNDATION FORUM 1 [Spring 1984]. Reprinted with permission.)

programs, peer review, or review of policies relating to specific procedures.

RISK TREATMENT AND INTERVENTION

The third phase of the risk management process is risk treatment and intervention. Once risks have been identified and assessed, the risk manager must determine how to deal with the problem. There are three basic mechanisms to control risks: eliminate the risk, reduce the impact or loss related to the risk, or transfer responsibility for the risk.

Elimination of Risk. There are some activities or procedures which present such great loss potential that the institution or provider may simply choose to limit or eliminate that activity. For example, many hospitals grant limited privileges to providers to ensure that certain providers perform only specific procedures. Likewise, a manufacturer may decide to remove certain medications or products from the market because the risk to users creates high potential liability for the manufacturer.

Reduction of Risk. Risk reduction involves loss prevention and loss control mechanisms. Loss prevention activity focuses on reducing recurrence of loss-producing events.[27] Patient, staff, and visitor education programs; revision and updating of policies and procedures; strict credentialing requirements; safety assessments; and improved documentation of informed consent are examples of loss prevention interventions which might be used to address a particular risk.

Loss control focuses on minimizing the impact of a particular loss.[28] The risk manager should be advised of an adverse patient occurrence as soon as possible, and the risk manager should take immediate action to avoid further injury to the patient and decrease the potential loss exposure of the hospital and staff. Claims management follow-up of an incident varies among institutions. In some programs the risk manager plays a major role in claims investigations and management. In others, insurance company claims representatives and attorneys provide this service with the risk manager's assistance.

The Maryland Hospital Education Institute[29] describes a four-step incident follow-up approach:

1. Immediate response: Check that the patient is receiving appropriate medical care, review the

Table 3. Gynecology Claims Analysis: Gynecology Data by Major Treatment/Procedures

Procedure/Treatment	Major Allegations	Resulting Injuries or Complications	Range of Losses
Abortion	Improper performance Procedure not properly completed Unnecessary procedure	Continued pregnancy/birth Need for further treatment Perforation/organ damage Infection	$ 7,400–$ 90,000
Tubal ligation and laparotomy	Improper performance Improper choice of treatment/procedure	Pregnancy/birth Further surgery Perforation/organ damage Infection	$ 1,900–$112,500
Treatment with IUD	Improper choice of treatment Improper performance/placement Delay in diagnosing complication Failure to instruct in use Failure to follow up known product hazards of device	Pregnancy Abortion Infection Need for further treatment Inability to conceive	$30,000–$290,000
Diagnostic examination	Failure to diagnose Delay in diagnosis Misdiagnosis Improper performance of diagnostic procedure	Cancer (cervical, ovarian, breast) Pregnancy (including ectopic) Death Worsened condition Inability to conceive Further treatment/surgery Pain/emotional distress	$1,300–$327,000

From *Diagnostic Errors Most Frequent and Costly Allegation in GYN Claims,* 5 RISK MANAGEMENT FOUNDATION FORUM 2 (Spring 1984).

chart, notify the patient and family, preserve any equipment or other evidence, notify administration and the insurance carrier, instruct billing department to hold bills until investigation is complete.

2. Further investigation: Gather all the facts about the incident including a description of the scene, parties involved, events leading up to the incident, and the damages resulting; assess the degree of hospital responsibility and provider responsibility; keep in contact with the patient and family.
3. Loss control and prevention:
   a. Loss control: continue communication with the family; if appropriate, have facility pay bills; open a file with complete documentation of the incident and follow-up.
   b. Loss prevention: enter the incident into the data collection system; determine through the quality assurance and risk management committee whether policy or procedure changes, inservice programs, or other intervention is needed.
4. Elimination of defensibility prior to settlement or litigation: Determine whether the incident would be defensible in court; evaluate the standard of care provided; assess sufficiency of medical record to defend the case; estimate cost of possible jury award and legal expenses; if appropriate, initiate settlement discussions.

Transfer of Risk. Risks which cannot be prevented or sufficiently minimized must be transferred. The usual mechanism of risk transfer is purchase of insurance to pay for losses which may occur. Professional liability insurance is discussed in the following chapter.

Another method of transferring risk is by contract, agreement of certain parties (for example, hospitals and their employees, hospitals and service organizations). Through this mechanism the parties agree that one or both will assume responsibility for any losses flowing from the contract. However, attempts to contract or gain the agreement of patients to waive their right to litigate or agree to assume responsibility for any negligence are illegal or unconscionable contracts of adhesion. These types of contracts are unenforceable and against public policy.[30]

RISK MONITORING AND EVALUATION

The final element of the RM process is continual monitoring and evaluation of the RM program itself. As with any program, evaluation occurs on several levels. First, the RM program is reviewed to assure that it is functioning in accordance with its stated objectives and that it is in compliance with applicable laws (discussed below). Second, it is determined whether all adverse outcomes are actually identified by the reporting system in place. A high "surprise rate" (unanticipated appearance of claims which should have been detected by the reporting system) may indicate inadequacy of the screening mechanism itself or poor compliance with reporting procedures.

Third, the RM process is audited to assure that each identified risk received appropriate follow-up and intervention. Finally, new reports are monitored to see whether preventable mishaps are re-ocurring; pre- and post-intervention data are compared to evaluate the success of educational programs, tightened credentialing requirements, improved policies, and other risk management interventions. The RM program should be modified as needed.

Legislative mandates for risk management

Many states have risk management statutes,[31] but to date only four states,[32] Alaska, Florida, New York, and Maryland, have enacted risk management statutes specifically applicable to hospitals and other health care organizations.

The general risk management statutes typically authorize a risk manager to establish standardized specifications for procurement of insurance coverage for state agencies, departments, institutions, or property.[33] The risk manager is also charged with the responsibility for instituting programs to control losses and encourage safety and to establish systems for reporting insured and uninsured losses.[34]

The four hospital risk management statutes essentially require establishment and maintenance of internal hospital risk management programs and generally contain provisions requiring investigation, reporting, and prevention of incidents which may cause harm to patients. The four statutes are described in greater detail below.

ALASKA

The Alaska RM statute requires that each hospital have an internal RM program as a prerequisite to licensure. The RM program shall (1) investigate the frequency and causes of incidents which result in injury to patients, (2) develop and implement measures to minimize the risk of injury to patients, and (3) analyze patient grievances related to patient care.[35]

FLORIDA

The Florida statute also requires establishment of an internal RM program as a prerequisite for licensure. In addition Florida mandates development and implementation of an incident reporting system and at least annual risk management and risk prevention education programs for all personnel.

Under this statute RM is the responsibility of the governing board of the health care facility, and all licensed facilities must hire a certified risk manager who is responsible for implementation and oversight of the program.[36] The statute encourages innovative approaches intended to reduce the frequency and severity of medical malpractice and patient injury claims. Such innovative approaches include extension of risk management activities to providers' offices.[37]

The statute also requires that incident reports filed with the risk manager be reviewed to identify problem areas and that those problem areas be addressed and corrected. The facility must file an annual report which describes adverse incidents causing patient injury, including specific categorization of types of incidents reported, the names of individuals involved in the incidents, a description of all malpractice claims against the facility, and a listing of staff disciplinary actions pertaining to patient care. In addition, the report must contain the name of the risk manager and copies of policies and procedures which are in place to reduce the risk of injury and adverse incidents.[38]

Another provision requires prompt (within 3 days) reporting of incidents which result in death, brain damage, or spinal damage to a patient.[39] Other sections of this statute provide the risk manager access to medical records[40] and limit the uses of incident reports[41] and annual reports filed by each institution.

Finally, the statute states that information regarding trends and preventive data derived from risk management activities will be disseminated to facilities to be utilized for RM purposes.[42] The requirement of a certified risk manager for every licensed facility is unique to Florida. This requirement will be discussed below.

NEW YORK

The New York risk management statute requires that every hospital maintain a coordinated program for the identification and prevention of medical and dental malpractice.[43] The program must establish a quality assurance committee to review all services rendered in the hospital in order to improve patient care and reduce malpractice. The committee also coordinates a malpractice prevention program.

The statute requires the hospital to develop a privileges procedure for physician staff and all hospital employees which includes periodic review of credentials, physical and mental capacity, and competence in delivering health care services.[44] The program must include a patient grievance procedure and maintenance and collection of information about negative health care outcomes and incidents, patient grievances, professional liability premiums, settlements, awards, and costs incurred by the hospital injury prevention program.[45]

In addition, hospitals must provide risk management education programs on subjects such as patient safety, injury prevention, staff responsibility to report professional misconduct, legal aspects of patient care, improved communication with patients, and causes of malpractice claims.[46] Finally, medical and dental staff members are further required to participate in continuing education programs in their area of specialty.[47]

MARYLAND

The Maryland law requires that hospitals, as a condition of licensure, develop a risk management program that includes a credentialing process, a formal written appointment process, probation for new physician staff members, and mandatory review of each physician every 2 years.[48] The law provides that a consumer member be appointed to the Commission on Medical Discipline (CMD). The CMD must notify hospitals of certain disciplinary actions and complaints filed against physicians on the hospital's staff.

In Maryland a hospital RM program must include a policy statement indicating the commitment to RM and have one person assigned responsibility for coordinating the program. An internal staff committee must conduct ongoing review and evaluation of risk management activities. The hospital must have a formal patient complaint system and a facility-wide risk reporting system, as well as ongoing education in RM for all staff. Finally, the RM and QA programs are to share relevant information.

This RM law was one portion of a major tort reform package passed by the Maryland General Assembly in April 1986. As other states consider broad changes in their tort liability laws, it is likely that more attention will be given to prevention programs such as RM as an essential element in the control of patient injuries.

Role of the risk manager

Nationwide there is no formal preparation or degree required for a risk manager. The role and background of the hospital risk manager vary widely among institutions. Early risk managers with only business and industry experience often found health care risk management difficult because of unfamiliarity with the heath care setting. Today, many risk managers from backgrounds such as nursing, administration, law, insurance, safety, engineering, and medicine are prepared to deal with the complex issues facing a hospital risk manager.

WHAT RISK MANAGERS DO

A 1983 survey by the American Society for Hospital Risk Management[49] (ASHRM) reported that many hospitals have a designated "risk management coordinator or director," while others place risk management responsibility in a senior executive. Many have staff investigators and patient advocates as well. The ASHRM survey showed the following functions commonly reported by the individual responsible for risk management[50]:

Responsibility	Percent
Risk identification/evaluation	94.3
Loss prevention	87.8
Safety administration	73.7
Patient complaints	65.9
Property/casualty claims	65.5
Product liability claims	52.9
Security	51.2
Workers' compensation claims	45.2
Patient satisfaction surveys	40.6
Other employee benefits design/administration	31.2
Premium forecasting and budgeting	30.2
Group insurance plan design/administration	29.2
Group insurance benefit claims	28.6
Insurance accounting	27.0
Department personnel management	25.6
Pension/retirement income payments	21.8
Family counseling	20.3

While there appears to be no "average" risk manager role, there are many functions common to risk management. The state of Florida is the first to establish minimum requirements for a health care risk manager.[51] Florida law, which went into effect in June 1986, created a health care risk manager advisory council consisting of two health care risk managers, a hospital administrator, an employee of a medical malpractice insurer, and a health care consumer.[52] The law requires certification of all health care risk managers who are responsible for implementing and maintaining an effective risk management program. Risk managers must demonstrate competence in the following areas[53]:

1. Standards of health care risk management
2. Federal, state, and local health and safety laws and rules
3. General risk management administration
4. Patient care
5. Medical care
6. Personal and social care
7. Accident prevention
8. Departmental organization and management
9. Community interrelationships
10. Medical terminology

Further, the statute requires completion of a 2-year state-approved health care risk management program, or 1-year of practical experience in health care risk management.

The Florida legislature found that an essential method of controlling medical injuries is a comprehensive program of risk management, and the key is a competent and qualified risk manager.[54] Other states may follow this lead and establish minimum requirements for the health care risk manager and further define the role of this profession.

NURSING AND RISK MANAGEMENT

It is difficult to envision an effective health care risk management program which does not involve significant input from the nursing providers. In hospitals, as well as other health care facilities and businesses, nurses as a professional group have the greatest contact with patients, families, and visitors. Nurses are in a most advantageous position to observe, identify, and report loss control issues and for many years have been the primary source of adverse patient occurrence reports, usually in the form of incident reports.

Nurses are also essential in the analysis, intervention, and evaluation phases of the risk management process.[55] Nursing preparation in quality assurance and risk management activities will increase awareness of those areas of practice which may be sources of liability for the individual nurse and for the health care facility.

Some of the identified high-risk areas for nurses include:

1. Failure to assess and take histories
2. Failure to perform a procedure properly
3. Failure to follow a physician's order promptly and correctly
4. Failure to report deviations from accepted practice
5. Failure to supervise patients, resulting in injuries such as falls and intravenous line monitoring failures
6. Failure to summon medical attention[56]

A review of occurrences or actual claims within a facility can indicate whether these or other issues are frequent problems for the nursing staff and trigger appropriate intervention. Knowledge of the particular risks to watch for and prevent and of practical risk reduction mechanisms will enhance the quality of patient care and in turn prevent lawsuits.

Recommendations and trends

Risk management is a growing profession and an important movement in health care. Hackenburg, president of the Risk and Insurance Management Society, predicted that risk managers will become more powerful and effective and that insurance will be a less important treatment mechanism—risk will be controlled not transferred.[57] Holzer, president of the American Society for Hospital Risk Management, anticipates more consumer awareness and participation in health care risk management.[58] He also predicts that consumers will look for providers who demonstrate a high level of commitment to quality of care and self-assessment evidenced by aggressive risk management programs.

At one time RM programs were initiated only at the insistence of an insurer or, more recently, in response to legislative mandates. More and more programs are starting because providers and administrators recognize the need to control liability exposure, keep insurance premiums down, and minimize the exposure of self-insurance programs. In addition, all recognize that RM can have only a positive influence on the health care provider. It is likely that future tort reform legislation will include risk management requirements. All providers can expect to hear more about risk management and actively participate in loss control and loss prevention efforts. Several publications are available on a regular basis to keep up with the trends in risk management.[59]

Although this chapter focused on traditional hospital risk management, the tools and process discussed are applicable to any practice setting, including health maintenance organizations, home health agencies, hospices, nursing homes, and independent practice.[60] The nurse entrepreneur will need to consider using risk management approaches in the regular management of a practice.

Finally, the field of risk management can provide a unique professional opportunity for nurses. Nurses with an interest and preparation in the fields of insurance, finance, or law may be particularly suited to use their expertise to improve health care and reduce liability exposure.

Endnotes

1. J.E. ORLIKOFF, W.R. FIFER, H.P. GREELEY, MALPRACTICE PREVENTION AND LIABILITY CONTROL FOR HOSPITALS 28, 29 (1981) (hereinafter cited as *Orlikoff*).
2. *Id.* at 29.
3. Dankmyer and Groves, *Taking Steps for Safety's Sake* 51 HOSPITALS 60 (1977).
4. *Orlikoff, supra* note 1, at 32, 33.
5. AMERICAN COLLEGE OF SURGEONS, PATIENT SAFETY MANUAL 101 (2nd ed. 1985) (hereinafter cited as *Amer. Col. Surg.*).
6. Orlikoff and Lanham, *Why Risk Management and Quality Assurance Should be Integrated* 55 HOSPITALS 54 (1981).
7. J.W. CRADDICK, 1 MEDICAL MANAGEMENT ANALYSIS: A SYSTEMATIC APPROACH TO QUALITY ASSURANCE AND RISK MANAGEMENT 21, 22 (1983) (hereinafter cited as *Craddick*). (Developer of the Medical Management Analysis Program.)
8. *Id.* at 7.
9. *Id.*
10. *Adapted from Amer. Col. Surg., supra* note 5, at 71, 72.
11. *Id.*
12. *See, e.g.,* Cushing, *Incident Reports: For Your Eyes Only?* 85 A.J.N. 873 (1985).
13. *See, e.g., Amer. Col. Surg., supra* note 5, at 72.
14. *E.g.,* ECRI, SELF ASSESSMENT QUESTIONNAIRE (1984).
15. JOINT COMMISSION ON ACCREDITATION OF HOSPITALS MANUAL (1986).
16. Culp, Goemaere, and Miller, *Risk Management: An Integral Part of Qualilty Assurance, in* QUALITY ASSURANCE: A COMPLETE GUIDE TO EFFECTIVE PROGRAMS 169 (C.G. Meisenheimer ed. 1985).
17. *Amer. Col. Surg., supra* note 5, at 77.
18. Top 10 Hospital Malpractice Claims: St. Paul Insurance, MEDICAL LIABILITY ADVISORY SERVICE 2 (November 1985).
19. *Id.*
20. Bowyer, *Anesthesia Claims Study Identifies Recurring Areas of Loss,* 6 RISK MANAGEMENT FOUNDATION FORUM 3 (March-April 1985).
21. Department of Anesthesia, *Harvard Medical School Standards of Practice,* 7 RISK MANAGEMENT FOUNDATION FORUM 13 (March-June 1986).
22. Craddick, *supra* note 7, at 24-31.
23. *Id.* at 23.
24. *Amer. Col. Surg., supra* note 5, at 62-4.
25. G.T. TROYER AND S.L. SALMAN, HANDBOOK OF HEALTH CARE RISK MANAGEMENT 165 (1986) (hereinafter cited as *Troyer and Salman*).
26. *Diagnostic Errors Most Frequent and Costly Allegations in GYN Claims* 5 RISK MANAGEMENT FOUNDATION FORUM, 1 (Spring 1984). (Data from claims managed by the Foundation.)
27. *Troyer and Salman, supra* note 27, at 174-5.
28. *Id.* at 175.
29. AMERICAN COLLEGE OF SURGEONS, PATIENT SAFETY MANUAL 103-5 (2nd ed. 1985), *citing* MARYLAND HOSPITAL EDUCATION INSTITUTE, *Incident Follow-up: A Four Step Approach* 2 QA/RM BULLETIN 2 (1982).
30. *See, generally,* J. MURRAY, MURRAY ON CONTRACTS, §334 (2d ed. 1974).
31. General risk management statutes: *See, e.g.,* ARIZ. REV. STAT. ANN. §15-382, 20-289, 41-622 (1984 and Supp. 1985); ARK. STAT. ANN. §66-5701-5713 (Supp. 1985); CONN. GEN. STAT. ANN. §7-479(a) (West. Supp. 1986); IDAHO CODE §67-5773 (1980); IOWA CODE ANN. §18.160 (West. Supp. 1986); KAN. STAT. ANN. §12-2615 (1982); LA. REV. STAT. ANN. §39-1527 (West. Supp. 1986); ME. REV. STAT. ANN. tit. 5, §1725-A (Supp. 1985); MINN. STAT. ANN. §62A-046 (West. Supp. 1986); NEV. REV. STAT. §331.182-188 (1985); PA. STAT. ANN. tit. 42, §8564 P(Purdon 1982); UTAH CODE ANN. §63-1-45 to 50 (Supp. 1985); WASH. REV. CODE ANN. §48. 62.030 (Supp. 1986).
32. ALASKA STAT. §18.20.075 (1981); FLA. STAT. ANN. §395.041 (West Supp. 1986); N.Y. PUB. HEALTH LAW §2805-j (McKinney Supp. 1986); MD. HEALTH-GEN. CODE ANN. §19-319(g) (Supp. 1986).
33. *See, e.g.,* ARK STAT. ANN. §66-5701-5713 (Supp. 1985).
34. *Id.*
35. ALASKA STAT. §18.20.075 (1981).
36. FLA. STAT. ANN. §395.041 (West Supp. 1986).
37. FLA. STAT. ANN. §395.041 (3) (West Supp. 1986).
38. FLA. STAT. ANN. §395.041 (5) (a), (b) (West Supp. 1986).
39. FLA. STAT. ANN. §395.041 (6) (West Supp. 1986).
40. FLA. STAT. ANN. §395.041 (4) (West Supp. 1986).
41. *Id.*
42. FLA. STAT. ANN. §395.041 (9) (West Supp. 1986).
43. N.Y. PUB. HEALTH LAW §2805-j (1) (a) (McKinney Supp. 1986).
44. N.Y. PUB. HEALTH LAW §2805-j (1) (b), (c) (McKinney Supp. 1986).
45. N.Y. PUB. HEALTH LAW §2805-j (1) (d), (e) (McKinney Supp. 1986).
46. N.Y. PUB. HEALTH LAW §2805-j (1) (g) (McKinney Supp. 1986).
47. N.Y. PUB. HEALTH LAW §2805-j (1) (h) (McKinney Supp. 1986).
48. MD. HEALTH-GEN. CODE ANN. §19-319(g) (Supp. 1986); MD. HEALTH OCC. CODE ANN. §14-402 and §14-512 (Supp. 1986).
49. AMERICAN SOCIETY FOR HOSPITAL RISK MANAGEMENT, SUMMARY REPORT OF HOSPITAL RISK MANAGEMENT ACTIVITIES—1983 (1984), *cited in* ACS MANUAL 102-3.
50. *Id.* at 103.
51. FLA. STAT. ANN. §626.941-945 (West Supp. 1986).

52. *Id.* at Section §626.942.
53. FLA. STAT. ANN. §626.944 (1) (West Supp. 1986).
54. FLA. STAT. ANN. §626.941 (West Supp. 1986).
55. *See, e.g.*, Ryan, *The Role of Nursing in Risk Management* 3 RISK MANAGEMENT FOUNDATION FORUM 2 (July-August 1982) and Ryan, *The Role of Nursing in Risk Management—Part II* 3 RISK MANAGEMENT FOUNDATION FORUM 6 (September-October 1985).
56. *Build Risk Management Rapport with Nurses to Reduce Claims* 8 HOSPITAL RISK MANAGEMENT 1, 2 (January 1986), *citing* J. Napiewocki, RN, JD. *See also* Campazzi, *Nurses, Nursing and Malpractice Litigation* 5 NURS. ADMIN. Q. 1 (Winter 1981); Northrop, *Current Status of Nursing Litigation* 3 NURS. ECON. 423 (November-December 1984); and Northrop, *Nursing Actions in Litigation, in* RISK MANAGEMENT AND QUALITY ASSURANCE: ISSUES AND INTERACTIONS (1986), special publication of QUALITY REVIEW BULLETIN, JOINT COMMISSION ON ACCREDITATION OF HOSPITALS.
57. *Future Holds Less Risk Transfer, More Risk Control: RIMS Officer,* 7 HOSP. RISK MANAGEMENT 165 (December 1985).
58. Personal communication (January 1986).
59. *See, e.g.*, FORUM (publication of the Risk Management Foundation, Harvard Medical Institutions, Cambridge, Mass.); HOSPITAL RISK MANAGEMENT (monthly publication, American Health Consultants, Atlanta); OCCURRENCE (quarterly publication, Chicago Hospital Risk Pooling Program, Chicago); PERSPECTIVES IN HOSPITAL RISK MANAGEMENT (newsletter, American Society for Hospital Risk Management, American Hospital Association, Chicago); RESOURCE (monthly audiocassette program, Risk Management Foundation, Harvard Medical Institutions); RISK MANAGEMENT (publication, Risk and Insurance Management Society); and TACTICS (monthly publication, Chicago Hospital Risk Pooling Program).
60. *See, e.g.*, Harris, *Legal Currents: Fine Tuning Risk Management* 11 AM. HEALTH CARE ASSOC. J. 51 (1985). Discusses risk management in long-term health care facilities.

Additional Readings

Berns, *Uncovering Malpractice Before it Happens* 14 THE BRIEF, 16 (Winter 1985).

B.L. BROWN, RISK MANAGEMENT FOR HOSPITALS: A PRACTICAL APPROACH (1979).

Crane and Reckard, *Hospital Liability, Risk Management, and the Medical Record* 2 TOPICS IN HEALTH RECORD MANAGEMENT: LEGAL ISSUES PART II 49 (September 1981).

Innes and Turman, *Risk Management: Evaluation of Patient Falls* 9 QUAL. REV. BULL. 30 (February 1983).

INTERQUAL, CLINICAL RISK MANAGEMENT—A PRACTICAL APPROACH (1985).

LaCava, *The Roles of Legal Counsel in Hospital Risk Management* 11 QUAL. REV. BULL. 20 (January 1985).

M. MACDONALD, K. MEYER, & B. ESSIG, HEALTH CARE LAW: A PRACTICAL GUIDE (1986).

J.F. MONAGLE RISK MANAGEMENT, A GUIDE FOR HEALTH CARE PROFESSIONALS (1985).

Oulton, *Use of Incident Report Data in a System-wide Quality Assurance/Risk Management Program* 7 QUAL. REV. BULL. 2 (June 1981).

E.P. RICHARDS AND K.C. RATHBUN, MEDICAL RISK MANAGEMENT: PREVENTIVE LEGAL STRATEGIES FOR HEALTH CARE PROVIDERS (1983).

J. SMITH, HOSPITAL LIABILITY (1986).

Chapter 27

Professional liability insurance

Sheryl A. Feutz

An important way of managing one's risks is to shift those risks to another source. Insurance is an arrangement for transferring and distributing risk. It is an agreement under which one (called an *insurer*) contracts to do something that is of value to another (usually called an *insured,* but sometimes called a *beneficiary*) on the occurrence of a specified harmful contingency.[1]

The uninsured or underinsured nurse has decided that the risk of being sued is not worth the premium price of the insurance and has decided to assume any risks personally. A judgment against an uninsured nurse is satisfied out of the nurse's personal assets. Under some circumstances liens may be placed on property owned by the nurse, or wages may be garnished and future inheritances taken. The underinsured nurse also satisfies the balance of a judgment from personal assets.

Legislative proposals for tort reform in the malpractice area have established not only arbitration panels and prelitigation mechanisms, but changes in the statute of limitation, alterations in the standards of care and liability, controls on the insurance industry by the states' insurance commissions, and limits on jury awards—either for economic loss or damages and/or for pain and suffering (noneconomic damages)—among other areas of reform.[2] Given the depth of emotion and the breadth of ecomonic impact that malpractice insurance premiums and jury awards have, tort reforms such as these will be continuing issues.[3]

This chapter defines and discusses the basic terminology and principles pertinent to professional liability insurance policies. The duties and conditions required under the policy, any limitations imposed, and rights and obligations of both the insurer and the insured are discussed.

Types of liability policies

There are at least three types of insurance policies relevant to nurses. They are individual professional liability insurance policies, institutional liability policies, and commercial liability policies. Each of these is defined and described in the following sections.

INDIVIDUAL PROFESSIONAL LIABILITY

The first type of policy covers individual health care providers, such as nurses. This policy is issued in the name of the insured (the nurse) and provides coverage for specifically defined professional activities undertaken by the insured at any time and any place. The general language in the contract provides that the insurer (the insurance company) will pay on behalf of the insured all sums that the insured shall become legally obligated to pay as damages because of injury arising out of malpractice, error, or mistake in rendering or failing to render professional services. A list of key points to review in a professional liability insurance policy is shown in the box on p. 442.

INSTITUTIONAL LIABILITY

Another type of insurance policy, the institutional policy, is available to hospitals and related institutions,

IMPORTANT ASPECTS OF PROFESSIONAL LIABILITY INSURANCE POLICIES

1. Named insured
2. Defense provided for others than named insured
3. Occurrence or claims-made policy
4. Coverage period
5. Scope of professional acts covered
6. Policy limits
7. Punitive damages specifically excluded
8. Authority to select attorney
9. Instructions as to how claim is to be brought to notice of
10. Authority to settle claim, with or without consent of insured

including home health agencies, nursing homes, and psychiatric facilities. The standard institutional insuring agreement provides the following:

The insurer will pay on behalf of the insured all sums that the insured shall become legally obligated to pay as damages because of injury to a person arising out of rendering or failure to render the following professional services:

1. Medical, surgical, dental, or nursing treatment to such person or persons inflicting injury
2. Furnishing or dispensing drugs or medical, surgical, or dental supplies or appliances if injury occurs after named insured has relinquished possession thereof to others
3. Handling of or performing postmortem examinations on human bodies
4. Services by any person as member of any formal accreditation or similar professional board or committee of the named insured, or as person charged with duty of executing directives of any such board or committee.

This type of policy provides coverage for nurse-employees acting within the scope of their employment, as in *(1)*, which specifically includes nursing, or as defined in *(4)*.

COMMERCIAL LIABILITY

The third type of insurance policy available in health care settings covers partnerships, corporations, professional service corporations, and other business entities. This is the type of policy that extends coverage to nurses who are shareholders, partners, directors, officers, agents, or employees of commercial enterprises. Depending on the language of the contract and the position of the nurse, both individual and commercial liability policies may be necessary.

State laws regulate the operation, and define the liability, of business entities. For more information on aspects of law and business for nurse entrepreneurs, refer to Chapter 33.

Basic structure of an insurance policy

The rights and duties contained in the insurance policy are contractual in nature and are defined by the terms and conditions of the policy.[4] The risk is the legal liability; it is the possibility that the insured may become legally liable, which requires the insurer to pay money damages to another. The risk assumed by the insurer is the possibility of a loss.

A professional liability insurance policy is composed of three parts: the insuring agreement, the conditions, and the exclusionary clauses. Each is defined in the following sections.

INSURING AGREEMENT

The insuring agreement is the promise of the insurer to provide legal counsel to defend lawsuits and to pay damages up to specified policy limits in exchange for the insured's promise to pay a premium. The damages include costs of defense and any judgment awarded against the insured as a result of injury to any person arising out of the insured's asserted malpractice, or mistake. The term *injury* is broad enough to include both physical, nonphysical, and economic injuries.

Whether a nurse was included in an insuring agreement has been litigated. In *National Union Fire Insurance Co. of Pittsburgh*[5] a nurse and her liability insurer brought an action against her employer-physician's medical malpractice insurer. In a malpractice case against a physician and his employee-nurse, the physician's insurer refused to defend the employee-nurse. The physician was covered by a professional liability policy issued by the Medical Liability Mutual Insurance Co. (the insurer), which required payment by the insurer as follows:

To pay on behalf of the insured all sums which the insured shall becomed legally obligated to pay as damages because of injury or death resulting from rendering or failing to render, during the policy period, professional services by the insured, or by any person for whose acts or omissions the insured is legally responsible, performed in the practice of the insured's profession.[6]

The policy defined ''insured'' as ''the licensed phy-

REPORTS TO THE INSURER*

The following should be reported to the insurer:

1. Any incident involving an unexpected or unusual happening causing injury to a patient
2. Patient or family threat of suit
3. Bad outcome
4. Letter from an attorney on behalf of a patient
5. Any legal papers that are served

*This list is a general guide, not an all-inclusive list. Specific questions should be directed to the insurer.

sician or surgeon named in the declarations."[7] The court noted that a resolution of this controversy, as with other insurance disputes, necessitated an examination of the language of the policy to ascertain the extent of the coverage. The court held that there was no ambiguity and that the policy provisions had to be given their plain and ordinary meaning.

The issue before the court was the question of whether coverage existed for the nurse-employee. The court reviewed the entire insurance agreement and its provisions and noted that nowhere in the policy did it provide for the defense or indemnification of an *employee*. The policy was issued in the name of the physician only; no contractual relationship existed between Medical Mutual and the nurse. Furthermore, the court noted that the nurse's contention—that the policy agreed to indemnify the physician for liability for the acts of any person for whom he is legally responsible and that the policy must by implication afford such person a defense—required a rewriting of the clear, unambiguous language of the policy to defend only the insured.

CONDITIONS

The second part of the professional liability insurance policy contains the conditions of the contract, such as the obligations of the insurer and the insured. All conditions should be clearly set forth in the contract. Failure to uphold an obligation or to protect a right may result in a breach of the contract, possibly voiding the insurance policy or imposing liability on a party for any resulting damages.

One of the most important duties of the insured is to notify the insurer. The box above presents general items that should be reported to the insurer. The best practice is to ask questions about what and when to report directly to the insurance company.

EXCLUSIONARY CLAUSES

The final portion of the professional liability insurance policy consists of the exclusionary clauses. These provisions specify which acts are not covered under the policy and impose no liability on the insurer.

Policy provisions and coverage

Several aspects of the insurance policy are important beginning points. These include the issues of interpretation by the parties and by the court, the identity of the insured, the time period in which a claim will be covered, and the limits of the policy.

INTERPRETATION

The most frequent difficulty encountered by the courts in construing or interpreting insurance policy provisions and coverage is to determine the intent of the parties as reflected by the language. As Justice Holmes once said, "A word is not a crystal, transparent and unchanged, it is the skin of a living thought and may vary greatly in color and content according to the circumstances and the time in which it is used."[8] Thus the courts attempt to interpret an insurance contract in light of its purpose and the specific facts to which the contract is being applied. Any ambiguities are usually decided to benefit the insured.[9] As mentioned in the discussion of *National Union Fire Insurance Co.* when disputes arise, courts will use the plain and ordinary meaning of the words and terms in the contract itself, unless there are ambiguities.

INSURED'S IDENTITY

In individual liability insurance agreements, coverage is limited only to named individuals and is not extended for acts of unnamed individuals. However, if the insured is an institution, the insurer may cover the insured for liability arising from the acts or omissions of others acting under his or her direction.

A health care agency can be insured and obtain a policy that insures, as a group, all employees of that agency. Failure to know if the employers' policy covers nurses when legal responsibility is imposed for negligent acts is not a justifiable excuse and may expose the nurses personally to defend and satisfy any judgment rendered against them.

In the case of *Legler v. Meriwether*[10] a registered

nurse anesthetist and a physician were sued by an allegedly injured plaintiff. The question of negligence arose about the manner in which an anesthetic was administered while the plaintiff underwent an operation. The defendants called on the insurance company to defend them, since they had an insurance policy. The insurance company refused to defend the nurse. It was necessary for her to obtain her own counsel and defense at her expense.

The facts in the case were that the physician was one of four practicing partners. These partners were insured under a partnership liability insurance contract. The nurse was not named as an insured in the policy. The insurance agreement contained the following definition of insured:

> The unqualified word "Insured" includes the named insured and also includes any executive officer, director, or stockholder thereof while acting within the scope of his duties as such, and any organization or proprietor with respect to real estate management for the named insured. If the named insured is a partnership, the unqualified word "insured" also includes any partner therein, but only with respect to his liability as such.[11]

The nurse anesthetist testified that, during the employment interview, one of the physicians told her that she was included in the "group" liability policy: that the "group" would pay for liability insurance and would cover her in their "group" liability policy. The nurse argued in the case that the physician told her that she was covered by the insurance policy, and that this misrepresentation was authorized through an agent (the physician) of the insurance company. The nurse did not argue that she was a "named insured."

The court noted that the insurance contract in question was not a "group policy" but a policy issued to a partnership. The partnership policy by its terms (given above) did not purport to include as insured against malpractice exposure any employees of the partners, only the named partners. Moreover, the court held that the physician was not actually, or by implication, authorized by the insurance company to add employees' names as insureds under the policy.

Although most nurses are employed by institutions, not partnerships, this case reinforces the importance of determining whether an employee is covered by the institution's policy, such as in the case of a group policy, which may or may not necessitate the naming of individual insureds. In addition, nurses who are employees of physician groups, often organized as professional service corporations or as partnerships, should ascertain the exact language of the employer's insurance contract.

COVERAGE PERIOD: CLAIMS-MADE AND OCCURRENCE

The policy identifies the coverage period (the time period for which the insurer agrees to assume risks on behalf of the insured). The effectiveness of the insurance contract is limited to this specific time period and does not apply to acts or omissions occurring outside those dates.

There are two types of coverage periods: claims-made and occurrence.[12] Claims-made policies cover claims reported while the policy is in force for professional services rendered, either during the policy period or before it. The term *claim* is given a broad definition, including the filing of lawsuits, allegations by a patient or an attorney, notice received from a dissatisfied patient, or communication from the insured of an injury to a patient.[13] To ensure coverage, knowledge that a lawsuit may be asserted in the future must be given to the insurer during the policy period.[14]

An occurrence policy limits coverage to acts or omissions that are committed within the contract's policy period. Thus coverage is extended to any claims that result from professional services rendered while the policy is in force, even if not reported until sometime later.

Under an occurrence policy it is possible to have an alleged act of negligence by the insured occur within the policy period but of which neither the insured nor the insurer are notified or made aware until several years later. The intent of the policy is to provide coverage for all claims arising for occurrences during the policy period, regardless of when they are made.

An issue regarding claims-made policies arises when the insured retires and discontinues insurance coverage or changes coverage to an occurrence policy. When this happens the insured has no coverage for claims yet to be asserted. To protect the insured, insurance companies offer a "reporting endorsement" or "tail coverage policy," which preserves the coverage offered under the prior claims-made policy in the event that claims are ultimately asserted for acts or omissions previously committed during that policy period.

An issue with an occurrence policy arises when an injury results from a course of treatment that extends both within and outside the policy period. The *occurrence* within the context of the liability policy refers to the time at which the injurious effects of the negligent act or omission took place.[15]

If a question is raised by the insurer about its duty to provide coverage because of the timing of the occurrence, an action may be brought before a court either by the insurer or the insured to determine whether coverage should be afforded to the insured.

POLICY LIMITS

The insurer is liable only for damages totaling the maximal dollar amounts set in the policy. Those limits are usually stated as $X/$Y, with $X representing the dollar amount per occurrence or claim and $Y representing the aggregate dollar amount per policy period. The limits of liability for each claim apply regardless of the number of persons who sustain injury or the number of claims made or suits brought for loss resulting from any one occurrence.

Included in the policy limits are amounts for settlements and judgments. If the policy limits are $1,000,000/ $3,000,000, the insured has $1,000,000 available to satisfy a single judgment or settlement.

Duty to defend

The duty to defend must be a specific obligation undertaken by the insurer.[16] Most professional liability insurance companies accept this responsibility as the primary focus of their protection. In consideration of the premium paid by the insured, the insurer agrees to assume the obligation and to arrange for and pay expenses to defend certain lawsuits brought against the insured. These expenses are not limited by or included in the policy limits unless specifically set forth as such in the insurance contract. This duty is distinct from and independent of the insurer's duty to indemnify, which is discussed later.

The insurer's duty to defend is governed by the allegations set forth in the pleadings against the insured. If any allegations potentially fall within the terms of the policy coverage, the insurer's duty is triggered regardless of the truth or falsity of the allegations. If the facts or allegations are ambiguous, the insurer must still defend. Until such time as the allegations have been limited entirely to those outside the policy coverage, the duty of the insurer continues.

If the insurer assumes the duty to defend and it is later determined that the terms of the insurance policy do not include the asserted liability, the insurer can immediately give notice of such and deny liability coverage.[17]

EFFECTIVE REPRESENTATION

Most insurance contracts specify that the insurer has the right to designate counsel to represent the insured. The insurer's obligation (duty to defend) is met by employing an attorney on behalf of the insured. However, the insured is entitled to effective representation, and if a question arises regarding the legal services being provided, it should be communicated to the insurer. The appointed attorney actually has two clients, the insured and the insurer. Chapter 3 contains further information about selecting legal representation. In the case of *Smoot v. State Farm*[18] the attorney supplied by the insurer to defend the insured was held to be the agent of the insurer, and the insurer was liable for any legally culpable neglect or bad faith on the part of that attorney.

Although the insurer retains the right to select counsel to represent the insured, the insured retains the right to effective counseling and may take action to ensure and protect that right. There may be circumstances in which it is in the insured's best interest to retain a personal attorney. If a conflict of interest arises and the insurer and insured are taking diverse positions, the insured's attorney may need to withdraw from representation and both parties may need to get advice from another attorney.

SETTLEMENT

In most professional liability policies the insurer reserves the right to initiate compromise or settlement of claims or lawsuits. The terms of the insurance policy dictate whether the insurer may settle a claim without the consent of the insured or if the insured must give consent before the insurer may settle.

If the insurer refuses to accept a reasonable settlement offer, it may be liable for the full judgment rendered against the insured, even when the policy coverage limits are exceeded.[19] Certain factors are considered in determining if the insurer has acted appropriately in rejecting a settlement offer. The following determinations must be made:

1. The insurer took into account the interests of the insured and gave them the same considerations as its own interests.
2. A realistic evaluation of the case and a reckoning of the potential magnitude of the award were made by the insurer.
3. The insurer properly investigated the circumstances of the claim.
4. Reasonable consideration was given by the insured to the seriousness of the injuries involved.[20]

On the other hand, if the insured refuses to accept the proposed settlement and a judgment is ultimately rendered against her or him, the insurer's liability may be limited to the settlement offer. However, if the insurer fails to provide the insured the option of accepting or rejecting a settlement offer, the contract has been breached, and the insurer becomes liable for any resulting damages, including any excess over the policy limits.

APPEALS

The terms of the insurance policy determine whether there exists an obligation of the insurer to defend the insured further by appealing an adverse judgment. There are at least two perspectives on this question. For example, in one case the court held that under an insurance policy providing that the insurer would defend the insured against any suit, the insurer was obligated to take an appeal because the judgment was substantially above the limits of the policy.[21] The court also held that the insurer was liable for any consequential damages caused by breach of that duty, including the cost of appeal and reasonable attorney's fees.

The insurer's obligation to appeal tests the good faith and fair dealing of the insurer, who balances the rights of both insurer and insured. Therefore the other perspective to the question of appeal rests on the court's analysis of good faith and fair dealing. For example, in *Hawkeye Security Insurance Co. v. Indemnity Insurance Co. of North America*,[22] the insurer's refusal to appeal, despite the advice of counsel, did not constitute a breach of the insurer's legal duty to the insured, since the refusal to follow counsel's advice was not sufficient to sustain a finding of bad faith.

Duty of good faith

The insurance policy imposes an implied covenant of good faith and fairness on both insurer and insured. Each party consents to refrain from acts or omissions that could prevent the other from receiving any benefits of the contract. Violation of this good faith could expose a party to a breach of contract action and damages.

If an insurer acts in bad faith, the insured may be covered for any expenses incurred and even entitled to punitive or other damages. Bad faith is not simply a bad judgment or negligence but the conscious doing of wrong having the nature of fraud.[23] This could include rejecting the advice of counsel or statements by the insurer's agent that there was little or nothing to lose by refusing to settle.

Once undertaking the defense of an insured, the insurer may be liable if, in representing the insured, it acts in bad faith or in a negligent manner.[24] Some courts distinguish between bad faith and negligence when determining the liability of the insurer. Negligence refers to improperly conducting the defense of a case, failing to investigate the facts and interview witnesses carefully and prudently, failing to present competent and material evidence at the trial, or making improper stipulations.

Cancellation

Because an insurance policy is a voluntary contract, the parties may designate specific grounds and methods for cancellation of the policy. These provisions are strictly interpreted and therefore must be followed precisely to effect a cancellation. Generally, a clause in the policy indicates that a 30-day notice of cancellation must be given by either the insured or the insurer. At the end of the policy period either party may choose not to renew the policy.

Indemnification

Depending on the terms of the insurance policy, the insured may be entitled to indemnification. This is an action whereby the insured initially provides coverage and pays for any claims maintained against her or him. The insured is then able to seek recovery from the insurer for expenses and damages paid because of the insurer's obligation to make good any losses that he or she incurred as provided under the contract.

In addition, a nurse's employing organization may seek indemnification from the nurse for damages awarded against it in excess of the policy limits because of the nurse's acts or omissions. Although any negligence committed by an employee nurse is covered under the employer's liability policy, the employer is entitled to seek compensation for the damages paid for which it has no insurance coverage. Although this is permissible, it is rare because of the chilling effect it would produce in employer-employee relationships.

The nurse should pay particular attention to any indemnification clauses in either the individual professional liability policy or the institution's policy.

Payment of expenses

Although the insured is obligated to cooperate with the insurer when defending a claim, the insured is not required to act at his or her own expense; the insured need only contribute time and best efforts. The insurer will reimburse the insured for any expenses incurred. Some policies also provide for payment of lost wages.

Application for insurance

The application for insurance is a legal document. When any portion of the insurance application is falsified, the policy may be voided. This includes such practices as stating that a certificate is possessed when it is not and lying about being previously named in a malpractice action.

Notice to insurer

The insured is required to notify the insurer when he or she becomes aware that an injury occurred that is possibly attributable to the insured's professional acts or omissions. This enables the insurer to investigate all facts and circumstances promptly to gain all possible pertinent information. An advantage of early notification is that witnesses may be located more easily and quickly, while their recollections are still fresh. The insurance policy should state whether the notice requirement may be oral or must be written, and to whom it should be made.

Failure of the insured to notify or a delay in notification may void the insurer's obligation to provide coverage. In *INA Insurance Co.*[25] no justifiable reason for delay in notifying the insurer was found when it was revealed that the insured made no effort until 16 months after the accident and more than 3 months after the injured party commenced suit to ascertain whether coverage was available. In another case the insured delayed 6 months in notifying the insurer.[26] The insured tried to establish that this delay was reasonable because he believed the policy did not cover the accident, that he was not liable for the accident, and that he believed a suit would not be filed. These were classified unreasonable and the insurer was not obligated to defend because of the delay. The court noted that the insured had possession of the policy and ample opportunity to read it, was advised by the injured party's attorney to notify the insurer, and was repeatedly advised by his own attorney to bring him the policy to determine whether the accident was covered.

The prevailing majority rule, based on the traditional principles of contract law, is that unexcused delay in giving notice or forwarding legal papers to the insurer relieves the insurer from any obligations under the insurance policy.[27] However, the modern trend by courts is to place a burden on the insurer to prove prejudice resulting from the untimely notice before the insurer is relieved of the contractual obligations.[28]

When an insured has more than one insurance policy applicable to a claim, notification must be made to all insurers. It is then the obligation of the insurance companies to work out the details of defense and payment. Other issues relevant to multiple insurance policies are discussed further below.

In deciding what to report the nurse can be guided by professional judgment in assessing the facts. Examples of situations that require reporting include cases in which nursing judgment could be questioned or a bad outcome results from professional nursing services. Additionally, if an attorney on behalf of a patient sends a letter notifying of the intent to bring a claim, the insured should forward this letter immediately to the insurer.

Any time the insured becomes aware that a lawsuit has been initiated, the insurer must be notified immediately. It is imperative that the insured act promptly, since there are time constraints imposed by law when a lawsuit is filed.

Duty to cooperate

By virtue of the insurance contract the insured consents to cooperate with the insurer and offer whatever assistance is necessary in defending the claim. This assistance is required for investigating the occurrence, obtaining evidence, preparing a defense, and attending depositions and trial. A duty is imposed on the insured to refrain from voluntarily making any payments or settlements or admitting to or assuming any obligations.

The duty of cooperation also requires making a full, complete, and truthful disclosure of all facts. A breach of this duty occurs when the insured deliberately and willfully makes false statements or conceals information about matters material to the insured's liability or defense. The insurance policy may become void for such a breach of duty.[29] In one case the court held that an insured's misrepresentations to his insurer as to his beer-drinking activities before the accident and his failure to tell the insurer the truth in regard to such activities for 18 months, until just before trial, was a sufficiently material misrepresentation by the insured as to constitute a breach of the cooperation clause of the liability policy. The insurer was excused from liability because of that breach.[30]

Limitations of the policy

Generally, a professional liability insurance policy provides coverage only against negligence or malpractice claims. There are certain policies, however, that may or may not cover other types of claims. Coverage depends on the language of the policy. Usually questions arise about whether certain conduct—such as criminal acts, intentional torts, promises of cures, acts that exceed the scope of practice, or punitive damages—are covered by the policy. Each of these is discussed.

GUARANTEES, CRIMINAL OR INTENTIONAL ACTS

Coverage is not extended as to criminal acts because they are not within the scope of the insuring clause. Other acts that are alleged to be criminal in nature or intentional torts may be covered under a professional liability insurance policy. The rationale as to why these other acts are covered is that although they are of a criminal nature, they may lack specific intent to do harm. Also, if the policy's language states that "malpractice, error, and mistake" are covered, then acts other than malpractice can be included, including acts of a criminal nature.[31] However, most insurance policies specifically exclude from coverage any willful or unlawful acts of violence. Chapter 24 discusses criminal law and insurance, as well.

Professional liability insurance policies frequently contain clauses specifically excluding coverage for injuries intentionally caused by the insured. The language of the insurance policy should state whether allegations of libel and slander, and under what circumstances, are covered by the insurer. Courts have held coverage to be applicable when the allegations involved professional services rendered or were directly connected with the professional's practice.

For example, allegedly slanderous statements made by a physician during the course of a physicians' committee meeting seeking to upgrade services at the hospital were held by the court not to be outside the scope of professional liability endorsement.[32] However, in another case the insured, who was deputized by the Board of Medical Examiners to conduct an investigation into the conduct and competence of physicians, held an informal press conference with newspaper reporters at his professional offices. He made statements that were the subject of a subsequent slander action filed against him. The court held that the remarks were not embraced in his duty as an investigator and consequently did not constitute a "professional service" within the professional liability policy.[33] Thus the insurer was not obligated to pay damages because the alleged acts were outside the policy coverage.

Insurance policies typically have a clause that excludes coverage when an insured has guaranteed the results of professional services rendered. A guarantee is not the same as the customarily implied agreement to use the requisite standards of professional skill and care; it promises a cure or guarantees the proposed treatment to get a certain result. If this is the case, an insurer might not be obligated under the insurance contract.

EXCEEDING THE SCOPE OF PRACTICE

There is no obligation imposed on an insurer to provide coverage for a nurse acting outside the scope of the nurse practice act or license. Coverage is limited to losses incurred from acts or omissions arising out of the practice of *nursing*. Therefore it is important that the nurse functions within the parameters of the state statutes defining nursing. If allegations of practicing medicine without a license are asserted against the insured nurse, the insurer might not be required to defend those claims. This is an example of when the nurse may need to sue the insurers if they refuse to defend on the basis that the policy does not cover the nurse's action.

PUNITIVE DAMAGES

Historically, professional malpractice insurance policies have excluded coverage for punitive damages awarded against the insured. Recently there has been considerable movement away from the public argument against imposing a duty to indemnify when a claim is made for punitive damages. The courts are divided on this issue. Some hold that when the policy provisions make no distinction between actual and punitive damages, the contract terms encompass liability for punitive damages.[34] In deciding the insurer's obligation to pay punitive damages awarded against its insured, the courts closely examine the language of the insurance contract. When the policy provides payment of "all sums that the insured shall become legally obligated to pay as damages," some courts hold insurers liable for punitive damages because they are damages that the insured is "legally obligated to pay."[35] More courts are imposing a responsibility on the insurer to exclude expressly any punitive damages from coverage, if that is the intent.[36]

Policy changes

Once the insurance contract is entered into by the insurer and the insured, no changes can be made in the policy by one party without the written consent of the other party. This ensures that the insured will receive specific benefits in exchange for consideration (payment of premium), and new conditions may not be imposed without prior knowledge.

Multiple insurance policies

Nurses are often covered by more than one professional liability insurance policy, usually the employer's policy and an individual policy. Because more than one policy may exist, insurance policies usually contain clauses pertaining to multiple insurance coverage situations. Referred to as "other insurance" clauses, they are designed to determine which policy applies when there is a loss.

Usually the clause indicates which of the policies

provides "primary" coverage, and which policy provides "secondary" or "excess" coverage. The designation must be explicit either in the scheme of insurance established by the insured or in the insurance policy—or it may be determined by a court after a dispute arises between carriers.

There are three types of "other insurance" clauses. The "pro rata" clause provides that insurance carriers share the loss according to a rate or proportion established in the contract. Another type of other-insurance clause is the "excess" clause, which provides that an insurer's liability is limited to the amount by which the loss exceeds coverage provided by all other policies, up to the limit of the excess policy. Therefore an excess policy is not triggered until all other coverage is exhausted. However, if the insured has no primary insurance, the excess carrier becomes primarily liable up to the policy limit.

The third type of other-insurance clause is the "escape" clause. This policy attempts to eliminate the insurer's liability when other insurance protection is applicable.

Nurses and their insurers have litigated the issues of other-insurance clauses and which insurance policy applies, the nurse's or the employer's. The case of *Jones v. Medox, Inc.*[37] is illustrative and was a case of first impression in the District of Columbia. The case dealt with two policies, each of which had a different type of other-insurance clause. The issue before the court was to determine whether the pro rata clause in the policy issued by Globe Insurance (the insured nurse) and the excess clause in the policy issued by the Insurance Co. of North America (the insured nurse's employer) could be reconciled and interpreted to give effect to the intent of the contracting parties, or whether the clauses were irreconcilable and required the court to disregard the contractual language of the parties and impose a pro rata share of the loss on each insurance company.[38]

The court reviewed the majority and minority views held by other courts. The majority of the courts reconcile the pro rata clause and the excess clause by interpreting the policy containing the excess clause as secondary coverage when there is another insurance policy covering the same risk. The result is that the excess insurer is generally liable for the loss only to the extent that the insured's claim exceeds the pro rata policy's limits. On the other hand, the minority rule views the pro rata clause and the excess clause as conflicting, automatically requiring that each insurance company shoulder a pro rata share of the claim.

This case originated in a malpractice action initiated by a plaintiff who sustained injuries allegedly resulting from an injection administered by the nurse. The nurse, the hospital, and Medox (the nurse's employer, a corporation that provides temporary nursing personnel to hospitals) were sued. The case was settled for $100,000 in an agreement which provided that the insurance companies representing all defendants had to separately litigate their respective liabilities. In the event that this litigation were not concluded by a certain date, the settlement agreement provided that the nurse's insurer, Globe, had to pay the full amount of the settlement.

The litigation did not take place by the agreed date, and Globe paid the full amount of the settlement. Globe and Jones, the nurse, brought an action against the hospital and Medox and their insurers. The central dispute was between the nurse's insurer (Globe) and the nurse's employer's insurer (INA).

At the time of the injection, Jones was the sole insured under the Globe policy. The policy's limit was $1,000,000 and contained a pro rata other-insurance clause as follows:

> If the insured has other insurance against a loss covered by this policy . . . the company shall not be liable under this policy for a greater proportion of such loss than the applicable limit of liability . . . bears to the total applicable limit of liability of all valid and collectible insurance against such loss.

Jones was also covered under a provision of Medox's INA insurance policy under which Medox contracted with INA to pay liabilities incurred under stated circumstances by Medox's employees. This policy's limit was also $1,000,000 and the policy contained another type of other-insurance clause, the excess clause, which stated the following:

> The insurance afforded . . . shall be excess insurance over any other valid and collectible insurance.

The District of Columbia court adopted the majority view and determined that Globe's pro rata clause and INA's excess clause were not irreconcilable. The court noted that Globe's provision contemplated contribution from all other valid and collectible insurance. INA was not collectible insurance for this purpose because the INA's excess clause expressly stated that it would not pay if the claim is covered by any other valid and collectible insurance that does not exceed the policy limit of that other insurance.[39] Applying the clauses together, the court concluded that Globe was liable for any claim up to its policy limit, with INA liable for any excess.

Since the settlement was within the policy limit provided by Globe, INA was exonerated from any liability.

In another case involving other-insurance clauses, a nurse's insurer sued a hospital's insurer.[40] The hospital had an institutional insurance policy through INA. The policy contained an additional interest endorsement under which all employees were expressly included as insureds and were provided liability coverage of $500,000 per claim. However, the endorsement stated that the hospital itself would assume the risk for the first $100,000 of each claim. The endorsement also included a promise by the hospital to contract with ESIS, a subsidiary of INA, which would investigate, defend, and settle claims of the hospital's employees. Last, the endorsement contained an excess clause.

The nurse in this case was also insured by National Union Fire Insurance Co. (National) through the American Nurses' Association (ANA). The insurance was a contract between ANA, the insured, and National whereby National agreed to insure each association member for loss caused by professional negligence to the amount of $200,000 per claim. This policy also contained an excess clause.

The malpractice action in question involved the nurse's alleged negligence in nursing care of a patient in the hospital's postoperative recovery room. The case was settled for $375,000. While reserving their rights against each other, National contributed $150,000, INA contributed $125,000, and the hospital contributed $100,000 to the settlement payment.

The issue before the court was whether the hospital's agreement to "self-insure" for the first $100,000 of each claim was "other valid and collectible insurance" with respect to the other insurance policies. The lower court held that it was; the higher court reversed that, holding instead that there was no other insurance within the meaning of the hospital's agreement and that National was exclusively liable for that portion of the settlement.[41] Furthermore, they held that the balance of the settlement should be shared between National and INA on a prorated basis.

The court's reasoning included the determination that the concept of "self-insurance" was in fact no insurance and encompassed a failure to purchase obtainable insurance. The agreement of the hospital to assume responsiblity for the first $100,000 was in fact an agreement to indemnify employees for that sum. Therefore the employee-nurse had protection through indemnification, not insurance, for the first $100,000 but did have insurance for the next $400,000.

The court further reasoned that the meaning of the term "other insurance" was "another policy of insurance covering the same risks."[42] Hence, "other insurance" clauses by definition implicate other insurance policies and not uninsured assumptions of risk of loss. The court held that there was no other insurance within the intendment of the National policy covering the nurse's negligence up to the first $100,000 of the loss. For that portion of the loss National, as the only insurer, was primarily liable; the obligation for the balance of the loss was ordered prorated between INA and National.

This case in particular points out the importance of the nurse-employee knowing exactly what insurance coverage the employer has for employees. More important even would be checking to see if the employer is self-insuring for any amount of a claim.

Recommendations and trends

Nurses should ascertain before practicing nursing that they are adequately protected in all aspects of their professional practice, under either their employer's liability policy or their own individual policy. Whether to obtain insurance is a personal decision that depends on the individual nurse's situation. The decision should involve an exploration of the risks and benefits and a comparison of policies available in the insurance market.

The policy to select should provide coverage for the professional services that the nurse renders in a particular practice situation. For example, nurses in advanced practice will want to purchase insurance to cover that role. Nursing administrative, educative, and researcher functions may also require insurance coverage not routinely included in policies.

Given the recent trends in the insurance industry and malpractice litigation, including the range of tort reforms mentioned earlier, nurses may experience the unavailability of professional liability insurance or a dramatic increase in policy premiums.

Although this has not been an issue for most nurses, as it has been for physicians and others, nurse midwives recently have faced an insurance crisis. Insurance companies, concerned about the soaring losses that obstetricians have experienced, have refused to renew the policies protecting nurse midwives against malpractice claims.[43] Actually the insurance crisis is broader than professional liability, reaching into insurance for municipalities, school boards, day-care centers, roller-skating rinks, ski slopes, and many other areas.[44]

If availability of insurance or the dramatic increase in premiums becomes an issue, nurses have several options to consider. The options include entering agreements to self-insure with existing insurance companies, thereby possibly lowering the premiums; going "bare," that is, deciding to have no insurance; limiting one's practice to less risky areas; retiring or leaving the practice completely; and creating an insurance company through the professional nursing association.

Physicians and hospitals have tried all of these options. Nurse midwives, recently confronted with the crisis, first attempted to obtain other insurance when the insurer refused to continued the policy. The American Nurses' Association's insurer covered them for a while but then wrote an exclusion of nurse midwives into the policy on renewal. Nurse midwives then considered setting up their own insurance company and have lobbied Congress to make it possible to for them to do so quickly.

Insurance is a state-controlled and regulated entity—not under federal control. Given this, it could take years for a professional association insurance company to obtain approval in all states. Therefore nurse midwives and others have lobbied for federal legislation that allows insurance in one state to be available in other states and that standardizes state insurance laws, making the establishment of insurance companies easier for such groups as nurse midwives.[45]

Another arena of options, however, is available through state legislatures. For example, the state of West Virginia has taken steps to eject malpractice insurance companies from the state and replace them with a state-owned insurance system.[46] The state's move was based on its duty to protect the citizen's health, safety, and welfare, in that private malpractice insurers had recently notified thousands of physicians, nurses, lawyers, engineers, and others that their malpractice policies would not be renewed. The state legislature fears that this will cause so many physicians, clinics, and hospitals to cease work that "it would seriously cripple health care in the state."[47] An action for an injunction seeking to stop the malpractice insurance companies from cancelling of policies is pending an appeal.

The insurance crisis is an area of rapid change. The effects of it and the tort law system on the nursing profession needs in-depth study, exploration, and monitoring. Individual nurses and professional nursing associations must remain involved and aware.

Endnotes

1. R. KEETON, INSURANCE LAW 2, 3 (1971) (hereinafter cited as *Keeton*).
2. *But see, e.g., Duren v. Suburban Community Hospital,* 482 N.E.2d 1358 (Ohio 1985), where the court declared unconstitutional a statute limiting medical malpractice general damages not involving death to $200,000. The Ohio court refused to follow the precedent of three other state supreme courts holding similar limits on damages constitutional. *E.g., Fein v. Permanente Medical Group,* 695 P.2d 665 (Cal. 1985), which upheld a statute limiting noneconomic damages); *Johnson v. St. Vincent Hospital,* 404 N.E.2d 585 (Ind. 1980); and *Prendergast v. Nelson,* 256 N.W.2d 657 (Neb. 1977). *See, also,* Kelly, *Health Law Update: Fein v. Permanente Medical Group,* 3 IN BRIEF 1 (July 1985), publication of The American Association of Nurse Attorneys. The constitutionality of other tort reforms, such as the prelitigation or arbitration panels, have also been challenged. *See, e.g., Aldana v. Holub,* 381 So.2d 231 (Fla. 1980); *also State ex. Rel. Cardinal Glennon Memorial Hosp. v. Gaertner,* 583 S.W.2d 107 (Mo. 1979), in which the Supreme Courts of Florida and Missouri, respectively, held unconstitutional the requirements that medical malpractice cases be submitted to a review panel. *See also* Northrop, *Responding to the Malpractice Crisis* 80 A.J.N. 2245 (December 1980).
3. *See, e.g., New York Times,* April 13, 1986, at 50, col. 2, "Maryland Legislature Puts Ceiling on Personal Injury Awards." The new ceiling limits damages for pain and suffering (noneconomic damages) in personal injury awards to $350,000 in all types of professional and business negligence cases; the legislature also banned testimony from "hired guns," experts who spend more than 20% of their time in court and who are regarded more as advocates than objective witnesses.
4. *Marez v. Dairyland Insurance Co.,* 638 P.2d 286 (Colo. 1981).
5. *National Union Fire Insurance Co. Of Pittsburgh, Pa. v. Medical Liability Mutual Insurance Co.,* 446 N.Y.S.2d 480 (A.D. 1981).
6. *Id.* at 481.
7. *Id.*
8. *Towne v. Eisner,* 245 U.S. 418, 425 (1918), citing *Lamer v. United States,* 240 U.S. 60, 65.
9. *Benham v. World Airways, Inc.,* 296 F.Supp. 813 (D. Haw. 1969); *Baton Rouge Contracting Co. v. West Hatchie Drainage District of Tippah County,* 304 F.Supp. 580 (D. Miss, 1969), *aff'd,* 436 F.2d 976 (5th Cir. 1971); *Hodgins v. American Mutual Liability Insurance Co.,* 261 F.Supp. 129 (E.D. Pa. 1966).
10. 391 S.W.2d 599 (Mo. 1965).
11. *Id.*
12. Annot., 37 A.L.R. 4th 382 (1982); 7A APPELMAN, INSURANCE LAW AND PRACTICE 312 (1979) (hereinafter cited as *Annot/Appelman*).
13. *Manacare Corp. v. First State Inc. Co.,* 374 So.2d 1100 (Fla. App. 1979).
14. Annot/Appelman, *supra* note 12.
15. *Appalachian Insurance Co. v. Liberty Mutual Insurance Co.,* 676 F.2d 56 (3rd Cir. 1982); *See also American Motorists Insurance Co. v. E.R. Squibb & Sons, Inc.* 404 N.Y.S.2d 658 (N.Y. Sup. 1978) (coverage is predicated not on act that *might* give rise to ultimate liability, but on *result;* coverage is limited to conditions that result in bodily injury during policy period).
16. Annot, 65 A.L.R.3d 969 (1975).
17. *McGee v. United States Fidelity & Guaranty Co.,* 53 F.2d 953 (1st Cir. 1931).
18. *Smoot v. State Farm Mutual Automobile Insurance Co.,* 299 F.2d 525 (5th Cir. 1962).
19. *Canadian Universal Insurance Co. v. Employers Surplus Lines*

Insurance, 325 So.2d 29 (Fla. App. 1976), *cert. denied,* 336 So.2d 1180 (Fla. 1976).

20. *Glesby v. Hartford Accident & Indemnity Co.,* 44 P.2d 365 (Cal. 1935).
21. *See, e.g., Palmer v. Pacific Indemnity Co.,* 254 N.W.2d 52 (Mich. App. 1977); *Spitler v. State Auto Mutual, Inc.,* 400 N.E.2d 889 (Ohio 1980).
22. 260 F.2d 361 (10th Cir. 1958).
23. *Detenber v. American Universal Insurance Co.,* 371 F.2d 50 (6th Cir. 1967), *cert. denied,* 389 U.S. 987 (1967).
24. *Rova Farms Resort Inc. v. Investors Insurance Co. of America,* 323 A.2d 495 (N.J. 1974).
25. *INA Insurance Co. of Illinois v. City of Chicago,* 379 N.E.2d 34 (Ill. App. 1st Dist. 1978).
26. *Southern Guarantee Insurance Co. v. Thomas,*334 So.2d 879 (Ala. 1976).
27. *See, e.g., Members Mutual Insurance Co. v. Cutaia,* 576 S.W.2d 278 (Tex. 1972) (insured's failure to forward suit papers to the insurer relieved the insurer of liability for injury to third persons, despite lack of prejudice to the insurer).
28. *See, e.g., Johnson Controls, Inc. v. Bowes,* 409 N.E.2d 185 (Mass. 1980) (when an insurance company attempts to be relieved of its obligations under a policy on the grounds of untimely notice by the insured, the insurance company will be required to prove both that the notice provision was in fact breached and that the breach resulted in prejudice to its position). *See also Globe Indemnity Co., v. Blomfield,* 562 P.2d 1374 (Ariz. App. 1977); *Billington v. Interinsurance Exchange of Southern California,* 456 P.2d 982 (Cal. 1969).
29. *See, e.g., Williams v. Alabama Farm Bureau Mutual Casualty Insurance Co.,* 416 So.2d 744 (Ala. 1982).
30. *United States Fire Insurance Co. v. Watts,* 370 F.2d 405 (5th Cir. 1966).
31. *Sommer v. New Amsterdam Casualty Co.,* 171 F.Supp. 84 (E.D. Mo. 1959).
32. *St. Paul Fire and Marine Insurance Co. v. United States Fire Insurance Co.,* 655 F.2d 521 (3rd Cir. 1981).
33. *Buckner v. Physicians Protective Trust Fund,* 376 So.2d 461 (Fla. App. 1979).
34. *See, e.g., Skyline Harvestore Systems, Inc. v. Centennial Insurance,* 331 N.W.2d 106 (Iowa 1983); *Dayton Judson Corp. v. American Mutual Liability Insurance Co.,* 621 P.2d 1155 (Okla. 1980).
35. *Id.*
36. *Id.*
37. 430 A.2d 488 (D.C. App. 1981).
38. *Id.* at 489.
39. *Id.* at 494.
40. *American Nurses' Association v. Passaic General Hospital,* 471 A.2d 66 (N.J. Super. A.D. 1984).
41. *Id.* at 68.
42. *Id.* at 71, citing *Universal Underwriters Insurance Co. v. Marriott Homes, Inc.,* 238 So.2d 730 (Ala. 1970).
43. *See, e.g., New York Times,* June 13, 1985, at C3, col. 1, an article by Lawson entitled *Midwives Facing Loss of Insurance.*
44. *See, e.g., New York Times,* February 24, 1986, at 1, col. 1 and at D14, col. 1, an article by Nash entitled *Congress Looks at Liability Insurers; see, also, The Wall Street Journal,* January 21, 1986, Section 2, at 1, col. 1, an article entitled *Businesses Struggling to Adapt as Insurance Crises Spreads.*
45. The proposed legislation is an amendment to the 1981 Risk Retention Act and would allow nurse midwives to establish a mutual insurance company that could operate in all 50 states.
46. *New York Times,* May 2, 1986, at A1, col. 1, an article by Stevens entitled *Malpractice Insurers Stir Wrath of West Virginia.*
47. *Id.*

Additional Readings

Comment, *Is There a Solution to the Circular Riddle: The Effect of "Other Insurance" Clauses on the Public, the Courts, and the Insurance Industry*, 25 SOUTH DAKOTA L. REV. 37 (1980).

Klimon, *Nursing Professional Liability Insurance: An Analysis*, 3 NURS. ECON. 152 (May, June 1985).

Morris, *Conflicts of Interest in Defending Under Liability Insurance Policies: A Proposed Solution*, 1981 UTAH L. REV. 457 (1981).

Chapter 28

Quality assurance and documentation

Ann Baldwin Mech

During the past 10 years, much has been written about quality assurance in the health care industry. Spurred on by mandates from the federal government and private accrediting agencies, quality assurance programs have been implemented in many health care institutions.[1] Quality assurance in health care has come to mean not only the assessment of the quality of care provided at some point in time, but also the steps taken to improve that quality when it is necessary to do so.[2] Both the effectiveness of the care provided and the efficiency with which services are performed may be scrutinized through a quality assurance program.

Many other industries besides health care have a quality assurance program as an integral part of their operations. In manufacturing industries, quality assurance (or quality control as it is frequently called) involves pulling products off the assembly line and examining them to determine if they have been made according to specifications. If too few products are sampled, a valid picture of manufacturing techniques will not be obtained, and defects may slip by unnoticed. If too many products are torn apart for evaluation, a significant reduction in profits will occur.

Service industries, such as restaurants and hotels, also have their own quality assurance programs. Since their products are the services provided their customers, customer satisfaction with the service is very important. Therefore, quality assurance activities in service industries frequently seek to assess degree of customer satisfaction. Short questionnaires asking the customer to rate the food or the service on a scale from poor to excellent can be found on the back of restaurant checks and on tables in hotel rooms. Hotels may also have checklists which managers use when inspecting a room that has been prepared for a customer. These checklists address the cleaning and stocking of the room (for example, is the furniture free from dust; does the bathroom contain the proper number of towels and glasses?). Since the provision of health care is primarily a service, many components of health care quality assurance programs have been borrowed from other service industries.

This chapter will review the quality assurance programs in health care delivery and discuss documentation as a primary mode of achieving quality in health care. Standards utilized in hospitals and other health care agencies will be described. Nursing quality assurance activities will be outlined and described. Specific examples of nursing audits are included. The chapter concludes with a discussion of the contents of ideal records, what to include and what to avoid. Computers and the right to confidentiality will also be discussed.

Standards of practice

Whether the industry is one of manufacturing or service, the first step in a quality assurance program is an assessment of the state of the product or service being provided. Does the product or service meet the preset standards the industry believes are acceptable? There are many sources to which an industry can turn to determine what is or is not acceptable within the industry. Statutes and regulations from governmental entities, whether federal, state, or local, mandate many standards for industry. There are also private regulatory agencies and professional associations which serve the same function. For example, this text has emphasized standards of nursing practice.[3] What is the custom of the trade (what other members of the same industry do) is an extremely important source of acceptable practice. If an industry uses the products of another industry, brochures containing instructions for use that come with the product also serve as a source of standards.

Nurses, as professionals within the health care industry, can look to many of the above sources of standards to find what would be acceptable practice. Probably the most important source of a standard of practice would be the custom or accepted practice of what other reasonably prudent nurses in similar circumstances would do.[4] Similar circumstances might include consideration of the resources available to provide care (accessibility of equipment, numbers and levels of staff); the educational preparation of the staff; patient census, caseload, and acuity; and relevant factors from the nearby geographical region or community which may impact on the provision of care. In the past geographical region meant a small local area surrounding the place where the care was given.[5] Recent trends, however, have tended to expand the geographical region to a much broader area. In some cases courts have said that no regional differences exist in the way certain care should be provided, thus accepting what amounts to a national standard of care.[6]

Nursing practice acts of each state set bounds of practice for nurses licensed under those statutes and serve as a source of the standard of practice. Regulations promulgated by Medicare, Medicaid, and state health departments also govern nursing practice in hospitals and community settings and establish standards. Standards of practice from the American Nurses' Association and specialty nursing organizations (such as Association of Operating Room Nurses, American Public Health Association—Public Health Nursing Section, and the Association of Critical Care Nurses) can be utilized as guidelines for nursing practice and in development of nursing quality assurance programs.

Recent professional literature and continuing education programs can also be looked to as indicators of what is current and acceptable nursing practice.[7] Drug product literature and manufacturer's instructions on the safe and proper operation of medical equipment may function as a basis for standards of practice.[8] Finally standards of the Joint Commission on Accreditation of Hospitals (JCAH) have been cited in several leading court cases as evidence of the standard of care.[9]

Nursing quality assurance activities

There are many activities which nurses perform in their day-to-day practice which fall under the scope of quality assurance. Most, however, may not be thought of as traditional quality assurance activities. Materials from professional associations are available on quality assurance.[10] The major activities include development of policy and procedure, employee selection, and training, continuing education and certification, employee performance evaluation, and continuous monitoring activities. Each will be described below.

POLICY AND PROCEDURE DEVELOPMENT

In order to assure that nursing practice will be within acceptable limits, it is helpful to have guidelines to define those limits. Policies and procedures of a health care institution or agency function as those guidelines. If sufficiently specific as to who can perform an activity and how it should be carried out, a policy or procedure can be a helpful resource to nurses unfamiliar with a particular practice. A policy or procedure, if followed by all, will guarantee that an activity will be carried out each time in a standard and acceptable fashion. However, in order to be valid quality control devices, policies and procedures must be solidly based on accepted standards of practice. For hospitals the Joint Commission on Accreditation of Hospitals (JCAH) requires that certain policies and procedures be developed and gives guidance on what these policies and procedures should include.[11] For other health care agencies similar guidelines exist.[12]

EMPLOYEE SELECTION AND TRAINING

Job descriptions, setting out the duties of the job to be performed and the educational and experience requirements necessary for the person performing the job, serve as a quality control measure. By carefully selecting only personnel who are qualified to do a job, letting them know what is expected, and giving them some type of orientation and training in how to do what is expected, a nursing manager takes the first steps to assuring that nursing staff are adequately prepared for the jobs they have to do. So important are job descriptions and structured orientation and training programs to assuring acceptable quality of care, the JCAH has mandated that they be developed by nursing departments.[13]

CONTINUING EDUCATION AND CERTIFICATION

Because technology and practice in the health care industry are rapidly changing in response to new developments in the field of nursing research and practice, it is necessary for nurses to continue to learn in order to remain current in their practice. Acceptable practice can only be maintained if care givers are up-to-date in their knowledge and clinical skills. Nursing services are required by JCAH to provide educational programs so that staff may maintain competence in patient care.[14] Certification by the American Nurses' Association and various nursing specialty organizations is becoming more widespread. In the future, advanced certification may be among the requirements necessary for particular jobs within the field of nursing. Also, legal liability may fall upon a nurse who performs a function or operates a piece of equipment without adequate preparation.[15]

EMPLOYEE PERFORMANCE EVALUATION

Once employees are carefully selected and instructed in the job to be performed, and policies and procedures have been written to guide their performance, some type of regular and systematic evaluation must be conducted to determine if the care being rendered meets expected levels. Requirements for performance evaluation of nursing staff have been set by JCAH and other groups. Such evaluations must utilize written criteria based upon the individual's job description and be done at the end of the probationary period and at set intervals thereafter (yearly is recommended). When staff are obtained from outside agencies, the nursing department must either conduct its own evaluation of these nurses or receive verification of the performance of an acceptable evaluation by the outside agency.[16] The better practice would be to do both. Performance evaluations can be written reviews of practice, actual observation of a nurse giving care, or both. An example of an observational performance rating used in some institutions and agencies is the SLATER NURSING COMPETENCIES RATING SCALE, an 84-item scale of observable nursing actions.[17]

CONTINUOUS MONITORING ACTIVITIES

Also helpful in determining whether desired levels of care are being achieved are various continuous monitoring activities. Some of these monitors must be developed and performed by nurses themselves. Others are routinely conducted by nonnurses but nevertheless may yield data useful in a nursing quality assurance program. Findings of regular monitoring and evaluation activities can be used as a basis for planning educational programs to correct deficiencies in practice. Indeed, JCAH requires that monitoring activities be used to identify educational needs.[18] Continuous monitoring activities include environmental and equipment safety checks, infection control surveillance, incident reports and collaboration with risk management activities, and evaluations of care through nursing audits.

Surveillance by infection control nurses may yield important data or identify problems related to nosocomial infections that may require changes in practice to correct. If this is the case, inservice education efforts can be tailored to address the specific problem. Regular safety checks of the environment (such as operating room humidity) and of biomedical equipment are also required by JCAH, as is an organized safety education program.[19]

An incident reporting system and other risk management tools are useful ways of finding out about problems that may not come to light through routine monitoring activities. A smoothly functioning incident reporting system may also be required by the health care agency's insurance carrier, as an identifier of potentially compensable occurrences. Quality assurance programs and risk management programs often work together because program goals are similar. The topic of risk management is discussed in Chapter 26.

There are different viewpoints as to the admissibility of incident reports into evidence in malpractice cases. One view would hold that incident reports are relevant records kept in the ordinary course of business and are thus admissible in evidence.[20] Another argument states that since incident reports are prepared to identify and detail events that are or probably will be the subject of litigation, an incident report is an attorney's work product and therefore falls under the attorney-client privilege. As such, an incident report is neither discoverable in pretrial procedure nor admissible into evidence.[21]

Formal evaluations of care or audit may be conducted as part of a routine monitoring program or in response to a specific problem. There are several types of audits which may be employed in a particular agency or facility. Those types include the structure audit, process of care audit, outcome of care audit, and focused review audit. Each will be defined below, and an example will be given of how each would operate.

Structure Audit. A structure audit is an evaluation of the physical facility in which care is provided and of the resources necessary to provide that care. Such resources might include patient care equipment and supplies and numbers and levels of staff available. Structure audits are usually done concurrently, that is, an evaluation of resources at the current point in time. However, retrospective comparisons can be made. Structure audits are relatively easy to do, frequently consisting of a checklist. If criteria are specific, a structure audit can be performed by nonprofessionals, thus making it less expensive to do. One drawback to a structure audit, though, is that it does not directly evaluate professional practice. Having all the resources ideally necessary for providing care does not guarantee that good care will result. A sample of a structure audit is given in Fig. 4.

Process of Care Audit. A process or care audit is an evaluation of what health care professionals do to or for patients. It is a direct evaluation of professional practice. The SLATER NURSING COMPETENCIES RATING SCALE, mentioned before, is an example of a process audit. These audits can evaluate practice by observing it, by interviewing patients to determine their perceptions of it, and by reviewing the charts to see whether or not it is documented. Process of care audits can be conducted both concurrently and retrospectively. Results can tell if policies and procedures are being followed and if care is given according to accepted practice.

Process of care audits do not, however, say whether what is being done is effective in aiding the patient to reach the desired goals of care. Because the audit criteria address items involving professional practice, these audits may have to be performed by professional personnel. This, coupled with the fact that the audit itself may be lengthy, means that the process of care audit may be expensive to conduct. Also, establishing interrater reliability for observation sections of this type of audit may itself be a cumbersome procedure. Some sample process of care audit criteria are provided in Fig. 5.

Outcome of Care Audit. An outcome of care audit evaluates the results of care, that is, patient outcome at a given point in time. The outcomes evaluated are usually those of a particular patient population, often one having a common medical diagnosis or surgical procedure. However, the status of a patient population having a common nursing diagnosis could also be reviewed. This type of audit was very popular during the 1970s.

Outcome of care audits are usually retrospective chart reviews to determine if the patient population met desired health status or health knowledge outcomes following health care. Outcomes at discharge from the health care system and various points in-between are the most often evaluated, but interim outcomes can be studied as well. Criteria are specific and easily understood. Therefore, an initial chart review can be done by nonprofessionals, thus saving valuable professional time for consideration of deficiencies found on the first review. Since this is primarily a chart review, any deficiencies in documentation will hamper the ability to make valid judgments concerning the quality of patient care. It may be difficult to tell whether patients met expected outcomes if no outcome at all is recorded. A sample of an outcome audit is presented in Fig. 6.

Focused Review Audit. A focused review audit is not a type of audit per se but rather an approach to patient care evaluation. In 1979 JCAH began emphasizing the problem-focused approach to evaluation of care activities.[22] A focused review is a study of a previously identified problem (identified through various continuous monitoring activities) to determine the problem's extent, possible causes, and possible solutions. The study can be retrospective, concurrent, or prospective in nature. Criteria can be structure, process, or outcome, or any combination thereof. The key is flexibility, fitting the methodology to the characteristics of the problem. An advantage of a focused review is that it concentrates quality assurance efforts where they are needed: in solving quality of care problems. But the system for iden-

	Yes	No	Comments
1. Are medication rooms or storage cabinets locked?	_____	_____	____________________
2. Does the thermometer inside the medication refrigerator read between 38° and 42°F?	_____	_____	____________________
3. Do staff members know the location of the nearest fire extinguisher?	_____	_____	____________________

Fig. 4. Example of a structure audit.

Documentation	**Yes**	**No**	**N/A**	**Comments**
1. Does the nursing care plan document that learning needs have been identified and instruction has been planned or is being done?	_____	_____	_____	______________
Observation				
2. Are dressings changed as indicated in the directive/plan? (Date, time, and initials of personnel changing dressing should be visible on the dressing.)	_____	_____	_____	______________
Interview				
3. "When you ask a question or make comments, have you felt that the nurses listen to you and show an interest in what you say?"	_____	_____	_____	______________

Fig. 5. Example of a process of care audit.

TOPIC: Cholecystectomy without common bile duct exploration.

POPULATION: 30-65 Years Old
Elective Surgery

Screening Criteria	Data Retrieval Decision	Data Retrieval Notes	Variation Justification Yes	Variation Justification No	Reason
Systolic blood pressure is at least 90 mm Hg, and not more than 150 mm Hg (by third post-operative day)					
Surgical wounds are dry (by discharge)					

Fig. 6. Example of an outcome of care audit.

tifying problems, the continuous monitoring activities, must be strong or else serious deficiencies in care will remain hidden and uncorrected. One example of a focused review which documented the need for a dietician to do patient education is given in Fig. 7.

Whatever type of patient care evaluation is employed, it is important to remember that the criteria used to study patient care must have a valid basis in practice. Sources for identifying valid criteria can be the same as the sources for the standard of care: professional literature, statutes and regulations and standards from the various nursing organizations. When valid criteria are used in the evaluation phase, a practitioner can be certain that decisions made based on an audit result in better quality of care.

Documentation

The patient or client's record, regardless of the health care setting, is intended to be a complete and accurate reflection of the contact with the health care system. The record should contain the history and findings of an initial physical examination, nursing assessment, health status data, diagnostic tests performed and their results, therapy ordered and verification that it was carried out, response to the treatment (including any complications that may have occurred), and the practitioner's conclusions at the

DIETARY REFERRAL SURVEY

Clinic ______________________________

Total No. Charts Reviewed ______________ Name of Auditor: ______________

History Number	Primary Diagnosis	Was a Special Diet Ordered? (List Type of Diet)	Diet Instruction Given by Doctor, Nurse, Dietician	No Documentation of Diet Instructions

- Log kept of 2 weeks of clinic visits.
- All patients logged in but only additional information if patient had special diet ordered.

Fig. 7. Example of a focused review audit.

termination of treatment.[23] Documentation is an extremely important nursing activity. The many uses of records standards which exist regarding records, confidentiality, and the use of computers will be discussed below.

USES OF HEALTH CARE RECORDS

Records are used in a variety of ways. The primary use of the record is to facilitate patient care. No matter the health care setting, home or hospital, the record functions as a communication tool among health care providers to enhance continuity and coordinate the evaluation and treatment of the patient's condition. It is a record of the nursing process, assessment, planning, implementation, and evaluation of care. The record also documents communication between patient and health care provider, detailing the choices the patient has made as to treatment and health care decisions. The patient's record is used in the education and training of health care providers and is often integral to patient care rounds and morbidity and mortality conferences. Much data is also abstracted from records for research purposes as well. Public health agencies gather information from records in epidemiological surveillance of diseases.

Because of the essential nature of the record to actual provision of care, no quality assurance program could possibly assure an acceptable quality of care without including the patient's record within the scope of quality assurance efforts. If records are poorly kept, it may be impossible to determine what happened to the patient within the health care system and whether the standard of care was actually achieved. Indeed, many of the quality assurance evaluation methodologies are dependent upon adequate documentation in the patient's record. Likewise, accreditation bodies such as the JCAH place much emphasis on evaluating the completeness of the patient's record in determining accreditation status.

Increasingly, third-party payors such as Medicare and Blue Cross/Blue Shield are scrutinizing the patient's record to determine whether the services for which they have been billed have actually been performed. If documentation to that effect cannot be found, reimbursement may be denied. Third-party payors are also reviewing the record to determine if a particular course of therapy or even hospitalization itself was necessary. Professional Standards Review Organizations and Utilization Review Committees are actively involved in monitoring the length of stay in hospitals, length of services rendered, and the appropriateness of care. In home health agencies records must carefully document the homebound status of the patient in order to assure payment for services. In general, unless there is thorough documentation by the health care provider to justify treatment or hospitalization, a health care agency may loose a substantial amount of money as a result of denied reimbursement. This has become particularly relevant for hospitals now subject to the new Medicare reimbursement system, based on diagnostic related groups (DRGs).

The patient's record plays an important role in many legal proceedings. Documentation by nurses, who are with the patient more often than any other provider, may provide the court with valuable evidence regarding the patient's condition and the treatment given by the health care agency. The patient's record is involved in malpractice and many other legal actions.

The patient's record may be reviewed by the state medical examiner when the cause of the patient's death is under violent or suspicious circumstances and may be evidence in criminal proceedings. Nursing observations concerning the patient's state of mind or mental capacity while not determinative of the issue may lend support or may contradict other testimony on the issue in both criminal or civil cases. One example of this occurred in a Maryland case involving the probate of a will where the mental capacity of the testatrix when she drafted the will was at issue.[24] The nurse expressed an opinion that the patient was incompetent, based on the fact that the patient had just undergone a colostomy; was confused as to date and time; could not always carry out instructions as to colostomy care; and did not seem to accept the permanent nature of the colostomy itself, frequently asking when it would be reversed. The court determined that these facts alone would not support an allegation of lack of mental capacity and was, in fact, quite sympathetic to the patient's inability to adjust to such disfiguring surgery.

Documentation in the patient's record by nurses may be critical to proving whether malpractice, both nursing, medical, and corporate, has taken place. Often documentation is the only evidence to indicate whether the standard of care has been met in cases alleging professional negligence. Since several years may elapse between the occurrence of a negligent act and the filing of a malpractice suit, health care providers may forget important details surrounding the alleged negligent act and may be unable to establish through recollection alone that they acted in a reasonably prudent manner.

A defendant may lose a case on the fact of poor documentation alone.[25] An example of this occurred in a case where the husband of an automobile accident victim charged that negligence on the part of the patient's treating physician and the hospital nurses caused the victim's death from brain damage caused by fluid overload 7 days after the accident.[26] The plaintiff, the injured party, alleged that accurate records were not maintained, which was a violation of hospital policy in that input-output records were not correctly totaled, nurses notes did not agree with medication records, and that physician's written orders did not correspond with the written records of the care actually provided by nurses. The court held that the evidence presented did support the jury finding that the negligence of the nurses was a direct cause of the patient's death.

Similarly, in a wrongful death action involving a mother who died 3 hours following delivery, the expert nurse witness commented upon the poorly kept nurses' notes as support for the conclusion that the patient had been poorly monitored by the nursing staff.[27] Finally, in another case a patient was forced to have his new hip prosthesis removed as a result of postoperative infection in the surgical wound.[28] The infection probably developed following exposure to bath water when the wound reopened during the patient's whirlpool treatment. The nurses caring for the patient did not properly redress the wound, nor did they make any record of how the wound reopened. Since the physician did not know the circumstances under which the wound reopened, he did not order any measures to prevent infection. Had such measures been taken, the infection which resulted in loss of the prothesis might have been avoided.

Documentation of nursing assessments is one aspect of charting which has played an important role in malpractice litigation. In one case, a nurse noted under the "medication" section of the nursing care data sheet that the patient had been taking Lasix at home.[29] However, the attending physicians stated that they never reviewed this form, nor was it sent to the operating room when the patient went for surgery. During her operation, the patient experienced a cardiac arrest that resulted in extensive brain damage. It was determined that a potassium deficiency, a side effect of the Lasix therapy, caused the cardiac arrest. The physicians were able to avoid liability because the patient failed to tell them that she was taking any medications when she was asked. Had the physicians not questioned the patient as to her medication history and also failed to look at the nursing care data sheet, the verdict and patient care outcome might have been different.

In another case an emergency room nurse was sued for negligent taking or recording of the plaintiff patient's medical history when she failed to note that the patient had come to the emergency room because he had been struck in his eye by a small piece of metal.[30] The metal went undetected, and the patient ultimately lost his eye.

A nurses' professional judgment is increasingly recognized and valued by the judicial system, sometimes even when it contradicts a physician's judgment. For example, 8 days after a patient had knee surgery, nurses noted blistering near the operative site. The nurses recorded their observations in the patient's chart. The physician did not mention the blisters in his notes until 6 days later. The patient was subsequently awarded damages in a malpractice suit as a result of the pain and scarring she suffered as a result of the blisters. When asked during the trial why the blisters were not noted earlier, the physician said he did not consider them serious enough to note in his records. The physician was found liable for failing to adequately treat the patient's blisters. However, no liability was assessed against the nurses because they had evidence that they met their standard of care by recording their observations concerning the blisters, which turned out to be significant.[31]

In a case involving a patient who was mentally ill, a psychiatrist was found negligent for prematurely discharging a patient when nurses' notes indicated that he was still quite sick.[32] The patient had a long history of psychiatric disorders when he was admitted to a psychiatric unit with a diagnosis of schizophrenic reaction, acute paranoid type, and chronic drug abuse. Nursing documentation during the course of the patient's hospitalization noted delusions and restlessness in the patient. The patient resisted attempts to be medicated and had to be placed in restraints. In fact, the patient had been in and out of restraints up to the morning of his discharge. In spite of the nurses' comments, the patient's psychiatrist let him go home. A week after he was discharged, the patient set fire to himself. At the malpractice trial, the plaintiff's expert witness testified that the patient's premature discharge was an avoidable mistake, to which the court agreed. The court said that it was impossible to reconcile the attending physician's findings that the patient showed some improvement on the day of discharge with the statements in the notes by the nurse that the patient was worse. The court found that the necessity to use a straightjacket definitely did not indicate improvement.

STANDARDS FOR DOCUMENTATION

Standards governing documentation in the patient's health care record and when that documentation can be disclosed come from many different sources: federal and state statutes, the American Nurses' Association, the Joint Commission on Accreditation of Hospitals, other health care accreditation groups, and institutional policy and procedure. Important standards of documentation also exist in the principles of confidentiality and privileged communication.

American Nurses' Association Standards. Both the American Nurses' Association's (ANA) STANDARDS OF NURSING PRACTICE and the ANA's CODE FOR NURSES indicate that the nurse is responsible for documenting the nursing process. The CODE FOR NURSES states that the nurse is responsible for "data collection and assessment of health status of the client; determination of the nursing care plan directed toward designated goals; evaluation of the effectiveness of nursing care in achieving the goals of care; and subsequent reassessment and revision of the nursing care plan."[33] It would be prudent for developers of institutional policies and procedures concerning documentation to review ANA and JCAH standards, as well as applicable state nursing practice acts and Medicare and Medicaid regulations prior to drafting those policies and procedures.

Federal Conditions for Participation in Medicare. Federal legal standards for participation in Medicare require that adequate medical records be kept on every patient.[34] The medical records must contain sufficient information to justify the diagnosis and warrant the treatment and the end results. The medical record should contain the following information: identification data, chief complaint, present illness, medical history, family history, physical examination, provisional diagnosis, clinical laboratory reports, x-ray reports, consultations, medical and surgical treatment, tissue reports, progress notes, final diagnosis, discharge summary, autopsy findings.

Federal regulations require that home health agency clinical notes include a dated, written notation, by a member of the health team, of a contact with a patient. It should contain a description of signs and symptoms, treatment and/or drugs given, the patient's reaction, and any changes in physical or emotional condition. A home health agency clinical record is to contain identifying information, name of the physician, drug, diet, treatment, activity orders, signed and dated clinical notes (written the day service is rendered and incorporated no less often than weekly), progress notes, copies of summary reports sent to the physician, and a discharge summary.

Joint Commission Standards. The Joint Commission sets standards for documentation by nurses during the patient's hospitalization. JCAH states:

> The nursing process (assessment, planning, intervention, evaluation) shall be documented for each hospitalized patient

from admission through discharge. Each patient's nursing needs shall be assessed by a registered nurse at the time of admission or within the period established by nursing department/service policy. These assessment data shall be consistent with the medical plan of care and shall be available to all nursing personnel involved in the care of the patient.

A registered nurse must plan each patient's nursing care and, whenever possible, nursing goals should be mutually set with the patient and/or family. Goals shall be based on the nursing assessment and shall be realistic, measurable, and consistent with the therapy prescribed by the responsible medical practitioner. Patient education and patient family knowledge of self-care shall be given special consideration in the nursing plan. The instructions and counseling given to the patient must be consistent with that of the responsible medical practitioner. The plan of care must be documented and should reflect current standards of nursing practice. The plan shall include nursing measures that will facilitate the medical care prescribed and that will restore, maintain, or promote the patient's well-being. As appropriate, such measures should include physiological, psychosocial, and environmental factors; patient/family education; and patient discharge planning. The scope of the plan shall be determined by the anticipated needs of the patient and shall be revised as the needs of the patient change. Exceptions to the requirement for a care plan shall be defined in writing.

Documentation of nursing care shall be pertinent and concise and shall reflect the patient's status. Nursing documentation should address the patient's needs, problems, capabilities, and limitations. Nursing intervention and patient response must be noted. When a patient is transferred within or discharged from the hospital, a nurse shall note the patient's status in the medical record. As appropriate, patients who are discharged from the hospital requiring nursing care should receive instructions and individualized counseling prior to discharge, and evidence of the instructions and the patient's or family's understanding of these instructions should be noted in the medical record. Such instructions and counseling must be consistent with the responsible medical practitioner's instructions.

The nursing department/service is encouraged to standardize documentation of routine elements of care and repeated monitoring of, for example, personal hygiene, administration of medications, and physiological parameters.[35]

Confidentiality and Privileged Communications. The ANA also has set guidelines governing confidentiality of patient information. The CODE FOR NURSES states: "The Nurse safeguards the client's right to privacy by judiciously protecting information of a confidential nature."[36] The CODE also allows only limited exceptions to the rule that disclosure of patient information requires the patient's consent. Those exceptions are: disclosure to other members of the health team for purposes of patient care, disclosure for quality assurance activities, and disclosure in a court of law when a patient waives or lacks a statutory nurse-patient privilege of communication.[37] By privileged communication, it is meant the ability to keep from disclosure, even in a court of law, communications made as part of the nurse-patient relationship. The patient holds the privilege; it is only she or he who can waive it. Many states have statutes granting privilege to communications made between patient and various health care providers.[38] However, many of these statutes do not extend privilege to nurse-patient communications. Indeed, in some states not all patient-physician communications are privileged. For example, Florida gives a statutory privilege only to communications made between patient and psychotherapist.[39]

There are state laws addressing confidentiality and disclosure of patient information. These laws tend to vary in scope from state to state. Maryland's law lists 10 exceptions to the requirement of patient authorization for specific disclosure. These exceptions range from disclosure to governmental agencies acting within their statutory scope (e.g., public health agencies for epidemiological purposes), to researchers whose protocols have been approved by the institutional review board, and to third-party payors for billing purposes only.[40] In Maryland the patient also has a right to receive a copy of his or her health record within a reasonable time after making a written request, provided the patient pays the prevailing cost of copying it. If the patient's illness related to a psychiatric or psychological problem and the attending physician believes disclosure of the patient's record to be medically contraindicated the patient may receive a summary of the record, rather than the record itself.[41]

There are also federal laws concerning confidentiality of patient records. Medicare regulations prohibit disclosure without written consent of the patient.[42] Federal laws also exist for special confidentiality protection for records maintained as part of drug- or alcohol-abuse prevention and treatment programs assisted by the federal government. Federal law allows only three types of disclosure of these records without the patient's consent: to medical personnel in a true medical emergency; to researchers, financial audit, or program evaluation personnel, provided they do not identify individual patients; and upon court order after a request to the court showing good cause.[43]

DOCUMENTATION AS EVIDENCE IN MALPRACTICE LITIGATION

Documentary evidence often plays a crucial role in malpractice litigation. What is or is not documented frequently determines the outcome of the case. Attention to certain do's and don'ts can assure patients of quality care and provide nurses with a great deal of protection in the event of a lawsuit.

Accuracy. Health care providers should never falsify a record to cover up a negligent act. If the trier of fact (the judge or jury) discovers a falsification, doubt will be cast on the entire credibility of the witness or record. In one case, a nurse charted that a physician had delivered the patient's baby when in fact it was the nurse herself who had performed the delivery. One factor in the jury's finding in favor of the patient in a subsequent malpractice action was the fraudulent entry. According to the court, the jury was possibly persuaded that if the records were erroneous in one respect, they were erroneous in other respects too.[44]

Also, to avoid attempts to falsify, entries should be signed immediately following the last word in the entry, and lines should not be skipped between entries. In this way, someone else cannot later make additions to charting done by a practitioner.

Making Corrections. If an error in documentation is made, the incorrect section should be crossed through with a single line, marked "error," and initialed. The error should not be obliterated so that what was originally written cannot be read. In a recent malpractice case, a nurse had used whiteout erasure fluid to cover an erroneous entry. So important was the issue of whether the nurse was trying to hide something, x-rays were taken to determine what was beneath the whiteout.[45]

Completeness. Charting should be as complete and accurate as possible. While routine actions, such as changing a patient's bed linen, are not expected to be charted, the record should reflect the nursing process in discussing the patient's progress while in the health care facility or under the care of health services in the community.[46] If problems are identified, actions taken to resolve them and the patient's response should also be noted.[47] If a patient is unable to protect him- or herself from harm, nursing measures taken to protect the patient should be thoroughly documented (e.g., putting the bedrails up when a patient is confused or disoriented or in the community securing the aid of family members or significant others to watch the patient and calling a case conference to determine the patient's safety in the home). Measures taken to prevent complications also should be noted. This may provide evidence that the standard of care was met.

Objectivity. Charting should be objective. Statements such as "the patient's pulse has increased" are ambiguous. What was the pulse rate on a prior assessment? What is it now? If a conclusion is reached concerning the patient's condition, sufficient facts and symptoms should be charted to support the conclusion.

Date and Time. Each entry should be dated and timed, with the time reflecting as closely as possible the time the action actually occurred. This is especially true when documenting response to patient emergencies.[48] Block charting (e.g., 3 to 11 p.m., "Patient had a quiet evening") indicates a lack of attention paid to the patient.

Follow Through. The record should indicate that not only the nursing care plan but also the physician's orders for treatment were carried out. The reasons for any omissions in carrying out physician's orders should be documented, as well as should the action taken in response to the omission. If the patient's condition changes and the physician is notified, the record should indicate who was notified, at what time, and what the physician's response was. This would be true in hospital care as well as community care agencies. "In some situations, the chart may show that it was not the failure of the nurses to observe and report changes that occasioned the harm, but the ineffectiveness of the subsequent medical care. The chart can also serve to indicate who, among those responsible for the attention to the patient, failed to meet the standard of competent professional performance."[49]

Legibility and Permanency of Records. Finally, documentation must be permanent. Notes must not be written with anything that can easily be erased. For example, many facilities and health services prohibit the use of felt-tip pens if chart forms are carbonized. Writing must be legible. It does no good to document thoroughly if what is written can never be understood again. In addition, state laws and regulations must be consulted in developing agency policies regarding the length of time records should be kept. For example, agencies providing services to children will be required to maintain their records for a substantial period of time.

PAPER CHARTS AND COMPUTER RECORDS

At the beginning of the twentieth century, the patient's record consisted of an entry on the physician's ledger indicating the treatment prescribed and the fee charged. Today, the patient's record consists of many forms with multiple copies, and health care facilities are increasingly burdened with how to handle more and more paper. Storage and access to records is a concern. Papers are lost, and microfilming may be expensive. Additionally, coordination of the functions of various departments (e.g., laboratories, operating room, finance) within hospitals or coordination of multiple services in community agencies (e.g., physical therapy, nursing, social services) may be difficult if it is dependent upon a poorly working intra-organizational record and mail system.

Because of the concerns in dealing with paper records and because of the opportunities of new technology, more and more health care facilities are moving to the computerized patient record. Most often, computerization begins with business office and billing information and then moves to index classifications and medical abstracts, and finally to daily or regular charting itself.[50]

According to Miller and Beyda, computers offer decided benefits to the health care system.[51] Computers facilitate surveillance systems designed to protect public health, help to improve quality of care by making readily available protocols for diagnosis and treatment, make data easily accessible to researchers, and streamline operational and management systems within a facility. Along with these benefits, however, come some concerns, primarily related to confidentiality of patient information and the ease of access to changing notes and records.

While many institutions and agencies have developed policies dealing with maintaining confidentiality of the paper record, these policies may not satisfactorily transfer to maintaining confidentiality of the computer record. Breaches in confidentiality may come from both accidental release of information and intentional, unauthorized entry into the computer system.[52]

Procedures must be developed to ensure confidentiality of the computerized record. Only necessary data should be acquired and released. Not everyone in a health care facility needs to have access to all aspects of patient information. Identification and authorization codes or passwords can guarantee release of sensitive information to only those personnel who must have it.[53] Disciplinary procedures must be used against employees who survey and maliciously use information discovered. Only if these types of procedures are followed can the patient's right to privacy be protected in the computer age.

A Special Advisory Committee to the Secretary for the U.S. Department of Health and Human Services has issued a statement of principles regarding the use of computers as records. They include:

1. Collect only necessary information, which has lawful purposes
2. Use only data which are relevant, accurate, timely, and complete in making decisions
3. Give the data subject access to the information about self and a procedure by which to challenge and correct the information
4. Use data only for the purpose for which it was collected
5. Protect the data against unauthorized loss, alteration, or disclosure.[54]

These principles have been used by most health care providers in establishing new systems of data collection, particularly systems involving the use of computers. The fourth principle especially should be helpful in keeping nurses on track with what should be included in their notes. Chart only information pertaining to the patient's health care, not to their social life or other unrelated information. As computers represent a new ease of access to confidential information, health care providers must be vigilant in their protection efforts.

Recommendations and trends

Quality assurance programs and documentation will continue to grow in importance as legal issues in nursing practice. In all aspects of nursing practice, education, research, and administration, quality assurance and documentation are two methods of risk management. Following advice and information contained in this chapter will provide a framework for improved patient care and decreased exposure of the nurse to liability.

Changes in health care are rapid. The two topics of this chapter will strengthen the nurse's approach to these rapid developments. The new prospective payment plan for Medicare; the development of institutional ethics committees and infant bioethics committees; and the continuation of risk management programs, quality assurance programs, utilization review programs, and institutional review boards are only some of the areas in which health care institutions will change.

Quality of nursing care has not been thoroughly addressed. For example, no standards of nursing care exist specifically for home health nursing care.[55] In addition, no standards of nursing care exist for alternative health care delivery forms, such as health maintenance organizations, preferred provider organizations, ambulatory surgical centers, nurse-managed centers, nursing practice in nursing corporations or provider networks, and other managed-care programs.

Endnotes

1. 42 U.S.C. §1395y(g) (1982) (definition of utilization and quality control peer review); 42 U.S.C. §1301-1320c-12 (1982 and Supp. I 1983); Specific sections of interest are: 42 U.S.C. §1317 (1982) (health care financing administration, professional standards review relating to health care services); 42 U.S.C. §1320c (1982) (peer review of the utilization and quality of health care services); 42 U.S.C. §1320c-1 (1982 and Supp. I 1983) (utilization and quality control peer review organization defined); *See also* 42 C.F.R. §417.418 and 110.108(h) (1985) that contain qualifying

conditions for health maintenance organizations regarding quality assurance programs.

2. R. EGDAHL AND P. GERTMAN, QUALITY ASSURANCE IN HEALTH CARE 5 (1976).
3. Standards of Nursing Practice from the American Nurses' Association: STANDARDS FOR CONTINUING EDUCATION (1984); STANDARDS FOR NURSING SERVICES IN CAMP SETTINGS (1978); STANDARDS FOR ORGANIZED NURSING SERVICES (1982); STANDARDS FOR PROFESSIONAL NURSING EDUCATION (1984); STANDARDS OF CARDIOVASCULAR NURSING PRACTICE (1981); STANDARDS OF COMMUNITY HEALTH NURSING PRACTICE (1986); STANDARDS OF GERONTOLOGICAL NURSING PRACTICE (1976); STANDARDS OF MATERNAL-CHILD HEALTH NURSING PRACTICE (1983); STANDARDS OF MEDICAL-SURGICAL NURSING PRACTICE (1974); STANDARDS OF NEUROLOGICAL AND NEUROSURGICAL NURSING PRACTICE (1977); STANDARDS OF NURSING PRACTICE (1973); STANDARDS OF NURSING PRACTICE IN CORRECTIONAL FACILITIES (1985); STANDARDS OF ORTHOPEDIC NURSING PRACTICE (1978); STANDARDS OF PERIOPERATIVE NURSING PRACTICE (1981); STANDARDS OF PRACTICE FOR THE PERINATAL NURSE SPECIALIST (1984); STANDARDS OF PSYCHIATRIC–MENTAL HEALTH NURSING PRACTICE (1976); STANDARDS OF REHABILITATION NURSING PRACTICE (1977); STANDARDS OF SCHOOL NURSING PRACTICE (1983); STANDARDS OF UROLOGIC NURSING PRACTICE (1977).
4. *Blair v. Eblen,* 461 S.W.2d 370, 373 (Ky. 1970); *Downer v. Weilleux,* 322 A.2d 82, 88 (Me. 1974).
5. *Daigle v. St. Paul Fire and Marine Insurance Company,* 323 So.2d 186 (La. App. 1975).
6. *Shilkret v. Annapolis Emergency Hospital Association,* 349 A.2d 245 (Md. 1975).
7. *Halldin v. Peterson,* 159 N.W.2d 738 (Wisc. 1968).
8. *Julien v. Barker,* 272 P.2d 718 (Idaho 1954); *Mulder v. Parke Davis and Company,* 181 N.W.2d 882, 887 (Minn. 1970); *Holloway v. Hauver,* 322 A.2d 890 (Md. App. 1974).
9. *Darling v. Charlestown Community Memorial Hospital,* 211 N.E.2d 253 (Ill.) *cert. denied,* 383 U.S. 946 (1965); *Shilkret v. Annapolis Emergency Hospital Association,* 349 A.2d 345 (Md. 1975).
10. From the American Nurses' Association: GUIDELINES FOR REVIEW OF CARE AT THE LOCAL LEVEL (1976); A PLAN FOR IMPLEMENTATION OF THE STANDARDS OF NURSING PRACTICE (1975); NURSING QUALITY ASSURANCE MANAGEMENT/LEARNING SYSTEM QUALITY ASSURANCE WORKBOOK (1976). From the American Hospital Association: PERSPECTIVES IN HOSPITAL RISK MANAGEMENT (newsletter), American Society of Hospital Risk Management of the AHA. From the Joint Commission on Accreditation of Hospitals: QUALITY REVIEW BULLETIN (journal); and JCAH PERSPECTIVES (newsletter).
11. JOINT COMMISSION ON ACCREDITATION OF HOSPITALS, ACCREDITATION MANUAL FOR HOSPITALS 1985, 97, 99, 100, 187 (1984) (hereinafter cited *JCAH Manual*); *See also* ADVISORY PANEL ON PRIVACY AND CONFIDENTIALITY OF HOSPITAL MEDICAL RECORDS, AMERICAN HOSPITAL ASSOCIATION, GUIDELINES ON INSTITUTIONAL POLICIES FOR DISCLOSURE OF MEDICAL RECORD INFORMATION (1979), replacing AMERICAN HOSPITAL ASSOCIATION, HOSPITAL MEDICAL RECORDS: GUIDELINES FOR THEIR USE AND THE RELEASE OF MEDICAL INFORMATION (1972); and, *see,* J. BRUCE, PRIVACY AND CONFIDENTIALITY OF HEALTH CARE INFORMATION, (1984).
12. NATIONAL LEAGUE FOR NURSING/AMERICAN PUBLIC HEALTH ASSOCIATION, CRITERIA AND STANDARDS MANUAL FOR ACCREDITATION FOR HOME HEALTH AGENCIES AND COMMUNITY NURSING SERVICES (7th ed. 1980); NLN/APHA, POLICIES AND PROCEDURES FOR ACCREDITATION OF HOME HEALTH AGENCIES AND COMMUNITY NURSING SERVICES, (1980).
13. *JCAH Manual, supra* note 11, at 97, 99, 100, 187.
14. *Id.* at 99.
15. *Darling v. Charlestown Community Memorial Hospital,* 211 N.E.2d 253 (Ill.), *cert. denied,* 383 U.S. 946 (1965); Hemelt, *Your Legal Guide to Nursing Practice* 9 NURSING '79 57 (October 1979).
16. *JCAH Manual, supra* note 11, at 97.
17. D. SLATER, THE SLATER NURSING COMPETENCIES RATING SCALE (1967).
18. *JCAH Manual, supra* note 11, at 99.
19. *Id.* at 130-132, 136.
20. FED. R. EVID. 803 (6) Records of Regularly Conducted Activity; *Bernardi v. Community Hospital Association,* 443 P.2d 708 (Colo. 1968). *But see Leer v. Chicago, Milwaukee, St. Paul and Pacific Railway Co.,* 308 N.W.2d 305 (Minn. 1981), *overruling, Schmitt v. Emery,* 2 N.W.2d 413 (Minn. 1942) where the court held that statements made by other railroad employees to an investigator-employee of the railroad concerning the underlying accident were not protected from discovery by the attorney-client privilege.
21. MD. CTS. & JUD. PROC. CODE ANN. §9-108 (1984) (attorney-client privilege statute); *Sierra Vista Hospital v. Superior Court,* 56 Cal. Rptr. 387 (Cal. App. 1967).
22. *JCAH,* 5 QUALITY REV. BULL. 2 (June 1979).
23. *JCAH Manual, supra* note 11, at 63, 64; AMERICAN NURSES' ASSOCIATION, STANDARDS OF NURSING PRACTICE (1973) *supra* note 3.
24. *Giardina v. Wannen,* 179 A.2d 357 (Md. 1962).
25. Dean, *Medical Charts and Negligence* 10 FOCUS ON CRITICAL CARE 27 (February 1983) (hereinafter cited as *Dean*).
26. *Rogers v. Kasdan and Humana,* 612 S.W.2d 133 (Ky. 1981).
27. *Maslonka v. Hermann,* 414 A.2d 1350 (N.J. App. 1980), *rev'd.,* 428 A.2d 504 (N.J. 1981). The court reversed and remanded the case for trial on the finding that there was sufficient evidence from which a jury could find that doctors and nurses abandoned the patient and failed and neglected to provide her with professional care and treatment she required, and they were duty bound to provide, and that such abandonment was a proximate cause of death.
28. *St. Paul v. Prothro,* 590 S.W.2d 35 (Ark. 1979).
29. *Mackey v. Greenview Hospital,* 587 S.W.2d 249 (Ky. 1979).
30. *Bleiler v. Bodner,* 479 N.E.2d 230 (N.Y. 1985).
31. *Villetts v. Weilbaecher,* 377 So.2d 132 (La. 1979).
32. *Bell v. New York City Health and Hospitals Corp.,* 456 N.Y.S.2d 787 (A.D. 1982).
33. AMERICAN NURSES' ASSOCIATION, CODE FOR NURSES WITH INTERPRETIVE STATEMENTS 10 (1985).
34. 42 C.F.R. §405.1026(g) (1985) (medical records' content—hospitals); 42 C.F.R. §405.1032(d) (1985) (outpatient department);

42 C.F.R. §405.1033(d) (1985) (emergency services); 42 C.F.R. §405.1037 (1985) (psychiatric hospitals); 42 C.F.R. §405.1202, 1223, 1228, 1229 (1985) (home health agencies).
35. *JCAH Manual, supra* note 11, at 98, 99.
36. AMERICAN NURSES' ASSOCIATION, CODE FOR NURSES WITH INTERPRETIVE STATEMENTS 3 (1985).
37. *Id.* at 6, 7.
38. *See, e.g.,* N.Y. CIV. PRAC. LAW §4504 (McKinney 1986); *see also* PRIVACY PROTECTION STUDY COMMISSION, PERSONAL PRIVACY IN AN INFORMATION SOCIETY: THE REPORT OF THE PRIVACY PROTECTION STUDY COMMISSION 284 (1977).
39. FLA. STAT. ANN. §90.503 (West 1985).
40. MD. HEALTH-GEN. CODE ANN. §4-301 (Supp. 1986).
41. MD. HEALTH-GEN. CODE ANN. §4-302 (1982).
42. 45 C.F.R. §1026(a) (1985).
43. 42 U.S.C. §290ee-3, §290dd-3 (1982).
44. *Hyatt v. Groce,* 523 P.2d 320 (Kan. 1974).
45. *Ahrens v. Katz,* 595 F. Supp. 1108 (D. Ga. 1984).
46. Hershey and Lawrence, *The Influence of Charting Upon Liability Determinations* 3 J. NURS. ADMIN. 37 (March-April 1976) (hereinafter cited as *Hershey*).
47. *Dean, supra* note 25, at 28.
48. *Id.* at 27.
49. Hershey, *supra* note 46, at 37.
50. Miller and Beyda, *Computers, Medical Records, and the Right to Privacy,* 6 J. HEALTH, POLIT., POL. & LAW 464 (Fall 1981).
51. *Id.* at 468.
52. *Id.* at 478.
53. *Id.* at 479.
54. SPECIAL ADVISORY COMMITTEE TO THE SECRETARY, U.S. DEPT. OF HEALTH, EDUCATION & WELFARE, RECORDS, COMPUTERS AND RIGHTS OF CITIZENS (1973).
55. *But see* THE AMER. NURSE, May, 1986 at 14, which states that the Council of Community Health Nursing Practice is developing Home Health Nursing Standards.

Additional Readings

H. BENEDIKTER, FROM NURSING AUDIT TO MULTIDISCIPLINARY AUDIT (1977).

Cearlock, *The Development and Implementation of Nursing Audit in a Community Health Agency* 19 J. NURS. ED. 18 (October 1980).

Connelly, *Medical Records: How much patient access?* 10 LEG. ASP. MED. PRACT., 1 (January 1982).

Cushing, *Gaps in Documentation* 82 A.J.N. 1899 (December 1982).

Gardner, *Computers in Nursing* 9 QUALITY REV. BULL. 151 (May 1983).

Groatt and Reed, *Your Responsibility in Documenting Care.* 37 A.O.R.N. J. 1174 (May 1983).

E. HAYT, MEDICOLEGAL ASPECTS OF HOSPITAL RECORDS (2nd ed. 1977).

INTERNATIONAL MEDICAL INFORMATICS ASSOCIATION, DATA PROTECTION IN HEALTH INFORMATION SYSTEMS: CONSIDERATIONS AND GUIDELINES (1980).

M. MAYERS, R. NORLEY, AND A. WATSON, QUALITY ASSURANCE FOR PATIENT CARE: NURSING PERSPECTIVES (1977).

Migliozzi, *Quality Assurance in Occupational Health Nursing* 33 O.H.N. 63 (February 1985).

C. MILLER AND R. KNAPP, EVALUATING QUALITY OF CARE: ANALYTIC PROCEDURES AND MONITORING TECHNIQUES (1979).

OFFICE OF GENERAL COUNSEL, DEPARTMENT OF HEALTH AND HUMAN SERVICES, UNITED STATES, LEGAL OPINIONS ON THE CONFIDENTIALITY OF ALCOHOL AND DRUG ABUSE PATIENT'S RECORD (1980).

Bound
Periodicals

UNIT VI

The Nurse as Plaintiff

Chapter 29

Control of the practice of nurse practitioners, nurse midwives, nurse anesthetists, and clinical nurse specialists

Mary E. Kelly*

This chapter examines selected legal aspects of nurses in advanced practice. The term *nurse practitioner* is used to encompass the following: nurse practitioners, nurse midwives, nurse anesthetists, and clinical nurse specialists. An overview of various jurisdictions' approaches to authorizing advanced practice and challenges to that authority are first presented. Thereafter, prescriptive authority, hospital privileges and antitrust actions, and third-party reimbursement, are discussed. Where applicable, case law is analyzed.

History of selected nurse practitioners

Nurse anesthesia and midwifery, two fields generally considered to be expanded roles in nursing practice, may have developed before the regulation of nursing. Midwifery apparently began as a separate occupation[1]; in early years midwives were trained in apprenticeship programs without much formal education. As of 1910, approximately 50% of all births in the United States were attended by midwives, and in large cities, the percentage was often higher.[2]

In 1912, literature proposed training nurses as midwives,[3] and in 1926 the Frontier Nursing Service was formed to provide maternal and child health care in rural Kentucky. The Frontier results were impressive: during the first 1000 deliveries, no maternal deaths were reported and infant mortality was reduced from 36 per 10,000 births to 11 per 10,000 births.[4] The first educational program for nurse midwives opened in 1932; today, educational programs in nurse midwifery are available in programs throughout the United States.

Nurse anesthesia developed after the first demonstration of ether at Massachusetts General Hospital in 1846.[5] In 1906 a nurse anesthetist published a review of 14,000 surgical anesthetics that reported no deaths[6]. Nurses were well established as anesthetists by the 1920s.

The first reported clinical specialization conference occurred in 1936.[7] In that year, a group of nurses met to attempt to discern the future preparation of the clinical nurse specialists in psychiatric nursing.[8] The title clinical nurse specialists dates from 1938.

The nurse practitioner (NP) movement was initiated

*The author expresses gratitude to Sarah D. Cohn, M.S.N., J.D., for her contributions to the sections on prescriptive authority and third-party reimbursement.

in 1965 by Ford and Silver of the University of Colorado.[9] They referred to the nurses in their program as pediatric nurse associates or pediatric nurse practitioners. This and later programs expanded the scope of a registered nurse's practice in the areas of identification, assessment, and management of common acute and chronic illnesses and conditions. An influential report[10] helped convince Congress of the value of nurse practitioners as primary care providers, and federal funding for nurse practitioners began in 1971.

All of these roles may encompass functions that were formerly known as physician functions. Advanced nursing practice represents an area of overlap between the functions of the nursing and medical professions.

Legal regulation

As of 1984, more than 85,000 nurses held certification in one of 35 nursing specialties. These include 17,700 nurse anesthetists, 2300 nurse midwives, 3000 pediatric nurse practitioners, 14,700 critical care nurses, and more than 4000 family nurse practitioners.[11] Nurses in advanced practice are certified by the American Nurses' Association (ANA) and several specialty nursing organizations, such as the Nurses' Association of the American College of Obstetricians and Gynecologists (NAACOG) Certification Corporation and the American Association of Nurse Anesthetists. Over 2000 nurse practitioners annually enter the field.[12]

Some states have specific advanced practice laws authorizing nurse practitioner practice. Other nurse practitioners practice under authority of the state's nursing practice act (NPA). Many state laws require that nurse practitioners be certified by the applicable professional association. Chapter 23 discusses nurse practitioners as defendants.

SELECTED JURISDICTIONS' APPROACHES TO REGULATION

With the increase in the number and type of nurse practitioners, the legal system has exerted more explicit control. Some states, such as California[13] and Washington,[14] specifically authorize nurse practitioners. Washington[15] provides that the boards of nursing or other certified agency may make rules and regulations governing advanced practice. Some states, such as South Dakota,[16] require that regulations about nurse practitioners' practice be a collaborative effort between boards of nursing and medicine.

The Kentucky NPA[17] provides an example of a statute that explicitly regulates advanced registered nurse practitioners. The statute identifies several types of nurse practitioners but explicitly states that the act is not limited to these; the statute also directs advanced registered nurse practitioners to conform to the standards of the medical practice act and established medical protocol when they practice those acts "normally construed" as the practice of medicine.[18]

Some states include clinical specialists in the definition of advanced practice. For example, North Dakota, by regulation, defines three categories of advanced practitioners: nurse clinician, nurse practitioner, and clinical nurse specialist.[19]

In some states where nurse practitioners are not specifically mentioned in a statute, the definition of nursing practice has been broadened, and boards of nursing have been authorized to regulate various types of advanced nursing practice. For example, the Maryland NPA defines the practice of registered nursing as including "independent nursing functions or delegated medical functions and . . . any additional acts authorized by the Board. . . ."[20] The statute also authorizes the board to adopt rules and regulations for all of these functions.[21] Functions relating to the performance of delegated medical functions must be recognized jointly by the state boards of medical examiners and nurse examiners.[22] However, the statute does not define delegated medical functions.

A few states still explicitly regulate only nurse midwives and/or nurse anesthetists under practice acts,[23] although other types of nurse practitioners may be practicing. Connecticut[24] and Missouri[25] have no specific statutory provision for nurse practitioners. New York,[26] like Missouri, has expanded the definition of the practice of professional nursing to include acts of diagnosis and treatment without specifying certification requirements for nurse practitioners.

Nursing midwifery is apparently the only advanced nursing specialty that is regulated in some states outside the nurse practice act. For example, nurse midwives are regulated by the board of medicine in Indiana, New Jersey, Ohio, and Pennsylvania.[27]

This discussion illustrates that a major problem with present legislation is the lack of nationwide consistency in the method of defining and governing advance practice.[28] The ANA has warned against obtaining legislation to define the scope of advanced nursing practice because the legislative process is subject to input and political pressure from the medical profession, which seeks to control specialty nursing practice.[29] The statutes and regulations requiring joint recognition of medical functions, medical protocols, and physician supervision reflect this reality.

The ANA's position is that state NPAs should regulate nursing without reference to a specialized area of practice. Establishing the scope and qualifications for each area and certifying individuals as competent to practice a specific area of nursing are functions of a professional association. "The law should not provide for identifying clinical specialists . . . or require certification or other recognition for practice beyond the minimum qualifications established for the legal regulation."[30]

Others view specific statutory authority for advanced practice as protection against a charge of practicing illegal medicine.[31] The review of case law in a later section concerning challenges to nurse practitioner practice suggests that such charges will be unsuccessful, even in jurisdictions lacking a specific advanced practice regulation or statute.

SCOPE OF PRACTICE

States, by statute or regulation, may describe a scope of practice for the nurse practitioners who are authorized to practice. Scope of practice statements vary from the very detailed lists to the merely general description of function.

Idaho regulations provide an example of a scope of practice statement for nurse practitioners. Idaho was the first state to enact a statute authorizing nurses to diagnose and to treat patients under rules promulgated jointly by the boards of nursing and medicine and implemented by the board of nursing. The regulations provide that the nurse practitioner may perform the following acts:

1. Evaluate the physical and psychosocial health status through a comprehensive health history and physical examination. This may include the performance of pelvic examinations and Pap smears.
2. In consultation with the physician supervisor, initiate and interpret laboratory tests or other diagnoses and management of minor illnesses. Prior to consultation, laboratory tests may be ordered and interpreted (these are listed).
3. Diagnose and manage minor illnesses or conditions.
4. A nurse practitioner who is also a certified nurse midwife may perform uncomplicated deliveries.
5. Manage the health care of the stable chronically ill patient in accordance with the medical regimen initiated by a physician.
6. Institute appropriate care that might be required to stabilize a patient's condition in an emergency to potentially life-threatening situation until physician consultation can be obtained.
7. Perform certain acts of surgery that are the repair of minor lacerations, that is, no nerve, tendon, or major vessel involvement, after consultation with the supervising physician.[32]

PHYSICIAN SUPERVISION AND COLLABORATION REQUIREMENTS

Various nurse practitioner laws or regulations require physician supervision or collaboration. For example, Connecticut requires that a clinical practice relationship exist between "each certified nurse midwife and an obstetrician gynecologist" that is "based upon mutually agreed upon medical guidelines and protocol."[33] Direct physician supervision requirements are also imposed upon nurse practitioners who obtain admitting privileges in hospitals and, in some states, who seek reimbursement.

Such requirements are burdened by political reality. The medical profession provides powerful lobby resistance in the state legislatures to control and contain any statutory expansion of nursing practice.[34] In fact, the American Medical Association (AMA) has passed a resolution requiring development of a strategy to fight "incursions of nurse midwives, podiatrists, nurse practitioners, nurse anesthetists . . . into medical practice via prescribing privileges, independent practice, mandated third party reimbursement, or other expansion of their scope of practice."[35]

Although the resolution reaffirms AMA policy urging state medical associations to oppose such legislation, it also expands it to charge the AMA with providing staff support to help state societies resist expansions of practice by nonphysicians.[36] AMA's strategy is to systematically oppose and restrict legislation authorizing independent practice of medicine by nonphysicians, and to promote state legislators sympathetic to its goals. For the benefit of state and specialty societies, it will create a testimony and position paper exchange and compile reports on legislative status and histories concerning different allied health professionals throughout the states.

This resistance plan has come to fruition in the legislatures[37] and the medical boards and it is spilling into the courts. Court challenges to nursing board regulations and practice are discussed in the next section. The issue is the authority of the medical board to place restrictions on supervising physicians, which causes restrictions in nurse practitioner practice areas that are authorized "under the direction of a physician." Nursing board challenges to such medical regulations have had mixed success.

For example, in *Arkansas State Nurses' Association* (SNA) *v. Arkansas State Medical Board*[38] the Arkansas SNA brought a declaratory judgment action against the state medical board to invalidate medical board regulation 10 as an unauthorized and illegal attempt to regulate registered nurse practitioners. The lower court upheld the regulation; a majority of the Arkansas Supreme Court reversed in part.

By statute,[39] registered nurse practitioners (RNPs) are authorized to engage in the usual practice of registered nursing. They are also authorized, under the direction of a physician, to engage in other activities specified by the state board of nursing.

Medical regulation 10 provides that whenever a physician employs a RNP, the physician must file prescribed forms with the medical board setting forth his or her professional qualifications and experiences, in addition to those of the RNP, describing how the RNP's services are to be utilized and listing all other physicians to whom the RNP will be responsible in the absence of the employing physician. The second portion of the challenged provision provides:

> No physician licensed to practice medicine in the state of Arkansas shall employ more than two (2) licensed RNPs at any one time; nor shall such physician assume responsibility for collaborating with or directing the activities of more than two (2) RNPs at any one time. Violation of this regulation shall constitute malpractice within the meaning of the Arkansas Medical Practices Act and shall subject the violator to all penalties provided within.[40]

The regulation restricting the number of RNPs also extends to groups of two or more physicians working together.

A majority of the court found the regulation invalid insofar as it restricts the number of RNPs that may be employed by a physician or a group of physicians and declares that violation of the restriction is malpractice. The court reasoned that the legislature had not even attempted to delegate to the medical board the authority to define punishable malpractice. Instead, the legislature specified in the Medical Practices Act 16 instances of unprofessional conduct for which a physician's license may be revoked or suspended.

The matter of hiring too many RNPs, the court determined, does not fall within the malpractice statute by even the most liberal construction of the language. The medical board had no authority to create a nonstatutory basis for the revocation of a physician's license since the legislature never gave it that power.

The court further stated that this portion of regulation was clearly arbitrary on its face. If one physician could adequately supervise two RNPs, it was unreasonable to assume that a group of 10 physicians could not supervise more than two RNPs. The court agreed with the SNA's argument that the regulation's purpose was to restrict the number of RNPs that may be licensed.

One of the members of the medical board testified that the regulation was intended only to see that RNPs were adequately supervised. Without the regulation, the physician might hire 20 different RNPs in different areas of a city and let them practice while he was on the golf course.

The court rejected this claim, noting that the board already had specific authority to charge those who go to the golf course with gross negligence or ignorant malpractice and to discipline them. Citing the need for additional medical care in some parts of the state, the court noted that the effect of the regulation would be to discourage nurses from becoming RNPs since the regulation would limit the number of jobs available to them.

The court's decision does not characterize this portion of the regulation as an unauthorized and illegal attempt to regulate nursing. Perhaps this is because adopting that premise would require the court to invalidate the other challenged portion of the regulation, which requires a detailed disclosure to the medical board, in writing and on preprinted forms, concerning the qualifications and the duties of the RNP and the supervising physician. The fact that this portion was deemed reasonable infers that it is not an attempt to regulate RNPs.

Would the court's favorable ruling on that part of the regulation restricting the number of RNPs have been different if there was no need for additional medical care in parts of the state? There is a false security in advancing such a rationale to prove that RNPs are entitled to practice their profession.

While the court recognizes that the restriction on RNPs would discourage nurses from becoming RNPs, the court fails to see that the regulation's detailed disclosure requirements could ultimately have the same effect. The disclosure requirements will discourage physicians from supervising RNPs. Decreasing the number of supervising physicians, which the court cited in overturning the RNP restriction, in turn would limit the number of jobs available to RNPs. The result is the same: nurses are discouraged from becoming RNPs. When the need in certain areas of the state for medical care becomes less severe, will the court abandon its concern for discouraging nurses from becoming RNPs?

JUDICIAL AUTHORITY FOR ADVANCED PRACTICE UNDER THE NPA

A jurisdiction that lacks a specific statute or regulation authorizing expanded roles does not render advanced practice illegal. Court cases have so held.

Early cases first considered whether nurse anesthetists engaged in the practice of medicine. For example, in 1917, well before the enactment of statutes specifically authorizing advanced nursing practice, the Kentucky Court of Appeals rejected the view that a nurse anesthetist who administered anesthetics was practicing medicine. The court emphasized that she administered anesthetics solely to the patients of her employer-surgeon while under his direction. The court reasoned that the nurse anesthetist did not prescribe or treat the patient, either of which would have brought her conduct within the practice of medicine. That the nurse occasionally exercised her own judgment during a surgical emergency did not violate the medical practice act.[41]

In 1936, the Supreme Court of California used a similar analysis to reach the same conclusion about a nurse anesthetist employed by a hospital. The court reasoned that the care the nurse provided was neither diagnosis nor prescribing under the medical practice act. The court additionally noted that the nurse was subject to the orders of the surgeon in the operating room.[42]

The direct physician supervision factor continued to be cited by the courts as nursing practice advanced without corresponding amendments to NPAs. In 1961, prior to amendments to the NPA, the California Supreme Court recognized that the functions of nurses and physicians overlap. The court stated that so long as the licensed nurse acts under the direction of a licensed physician, the nurse is permitted to perform tasks that, without such supervision, would constitute the illegal practice of medicine.[43]

A more recent case suggests that state NPAs may obviate the need for direct supervision requirements in nurse practitioner practice. *Sermchief v. Gonzales*[44] upholds nurse practitioner practice even though no statute or regulation in Missouri specifically mentions nurse practitioners or provides for direct physician supervision. The court rejected the view that nurse practitioner practice was the illegal practice of medicine.

The court relied on the Missouri NPA,[45] which was revised in 1975 to broadly define professional nursing as:

> (T)he performance of any act which requires substantial specialized education, judgment and skill . . . including, but not limited to: . . . teaching health care and the prevention of illness . . . (a)ssessment, nursing diagnosis, nursing care, and counsel of persons who are ill, injured or experiencing alterations in normal health processes . . . (t)he administration of medications and treatments as prescribed by a person licensed in this state to prescribe. . . .[46]

The suit arose after the Missouri State Board of Registration for the Healing Arts, which regulates physicians in that state, threatened two certified family-planning nurse practitioners and their supervising physicians that it would require (1) the nurses to show why they were not practicing medicine without a license and (2) the physicians to show why they were not aiding and abetting the unauthorized practice of medicine. Malpractice was not an issue.

The physicians and nurses filed suit in state court seeking to prohibit the board from taking action (the board minutes reflected that it recommended criminal action against the nurses and license suspension or revocation for the physicians).[47] The nurse practitioners, who were licensed under the NPA as nurses, were providing the following services: breast and pelvic examinations, Pap smears, gonorrhea cultures and vaginal smears, vaginitis treatment, pregnancy testing, provision of contraceptives (including inserting IUDs, fitting diaphragms, and providing oral contraceptives), and counseling. These services were provided under standing orders and protocols that were mutually agreed upon by nurses and the five supervising physicians.

The lower court's ruling was unfavorable and was appealed to the Missouri Supreme Court; 35 nursing and other organizations filed briefs with the court advocating a decision favorable to one party or to the other party. The Missouri Supreme Court reversed the lower court's ruling, noting that the legislature's 1975 revision of the NPA substantially broadened the scope of nursing practice, and thus authorized the challenged activities of the family-planning nurse practitioners.

The court reasoned that a nurse acting under standing orders undertakes only a nursing diagnosis, as opposed to a medical diagnosis, when she or he finds or fails to find symptoms described by physician in such standing orders. The court warned that when the nurse reaches the limit of his or her knowledge, the limit of the standing orders is also reached, and referral to a physician must occur.

This case, reprinted in the Appendix and discussed in Chapter 23, is an important decision recognizing professional nursing autonomy. Nurse practitioners perform their services within the bounds of their skill and training; referrals to physicians are made once that limit is reached.

The requirement of a physician's direct supervision, found in several advanced practice statutes and regulations and reimbursement statutes, is unnecessary to the legality of advanced practice in Missouri and many other states, because the NPA recognizes professional nursing practice. If the intent of direct supervision language is to prevent charges of practicing medicine, the cases discussed later demonstrate that those challenges will be made, irrespective of this seemingly appeasing (to the medical profession) language.

Challenges to nurse practitioner practice

Sermchief, just discussed, is a strong judicial opinion supporting nurse practitioner practice as independent from the practice of medicine. The *Arkansas* case discussed earlier appears to be a mixed blessing for the present. A recent decision, *Bellegie, M.D. v. Texas Board of Nurse Examiners,*[48] is encouraging to nurse practitioners because it supports a nursing board's authority to adopt substantive rules and rejects claims that this authority violates the medical practice act.

The action was brought by two nurses, a physician, various Texas medical associations, the San Jainto Methodist Hospital, and the Texas Hospital Association and its Health Services Corporation to invalidate certain rules promulgated by the Board of Nurse Examiners in Texas. The lower court found in favor of the board. On appeal the matter was reversed for technical reasons; the appellate court clearly supports the validity of the rules.

The administrative rule[49] at issue concerns advanced nurse practitioners (ANPs). It provides that an ANP may act independently or in collaboration with health teams in the maintenance of mental and physical health, the prevention of illness, the management, observation, and counsel of the injured and ill, or the supervision of teaching of nursing.

The rule also requires the functions of the ANP to be clearly delineated in a written statement of policies that includes standard and emergency procedures. Those who manage the medical aspects of care must have written policies jointly developed and signed by the nurse practitioner and consulting physician. These policies are to be reviewed annually.

In addition, the rule authorizes an ANP, within the limitations of educational preparation and the written statement of policy, to assess the physical/mental status of a patient through history and physical examination, to perform simple laboratory tests, to formulate a health care plan, to recommend nonprescriptive measures for the relief of symptoms, and to refer deviations from normal to the appropriate health care professional. ANPs may also provide health education, initiate and maintain health records, evaluate health care provided, and modify it as needed.

The rule further states that ANPs may work collegially with other health care professionals and agencies to provide, and where appropriate, to coordinate services to individuals, families, and groups and to perform medical functions delegated by and done under the control and supervision of a licensed physician.

The plaintiffs successfully sought to have the lower court declare that there was no authority, express or implied, under the NPA for the board to create or regulate specialty practice and therefore the board was without authority to promulgate the rule. They also contended that the rule was not reasonably related to any specific statutory provision relating to the practice of nursing.

Further, the plaintiffs stated that the board did not have authority to enlarge the scope of practice of professional nursing beyond that provided by statute. They characterized the rule as an attempt to place restraints and proscriptions upon professional nurses. The plaintiffs also claimed the rule was vague and failed to give adequate notice as to what nursing conduct it permitted and what it proscribed, thereby violating their due process rights. They requested a declaration by the court of the rights, duties, and responsibilities of the advanced nurse practitioner and other duly licensed nurses and physicians with respect to various portions of the rule. On appeal, the matter was remanded for this determination.

The court of appeals held that as a matter of law the Texas Board of Nurse Examiners does have the statutory authority to make and issue the rule at issue. The court reasoned that the NPA clearly reflected the Texas legislature's intent that the board should have the authority to make the rules at issue. Moreover, the court concluded, the rules are reasonably related to the provisions of the NPA.

The appellate court further determined that the board had not enlarged the scope of professional nursing practice beyond that set forth in the statute.[50] In the court's view, the rule only authorizes acts that come within the definition of professional nursing. The rule also reflects the clear legislative intent to distinguish between nurses on the basis of nursing education. If any restrictions, burdens, or conditions have been placed upon plaintiffs, such restraints are within the board's statutory authority and the statutory provisions.

Finally, the court determined that the rule did not violate the due process rights of the plaintiffs. Moreover, the rule did not violate the medical practice act.

The issue is still pending in Louisiana. In *Louisiana State Medical Society v. Louisiana State Board of Nursing*,[51] the Louisiana State Medical Society filed two petitions with the defendant, the Louisiana State Board of Nursing, on Feb. 18, 1982. At issue was a nursing board rule establishing and defining the position of nurse practitioner.

Specifically, the rule authorizes nurse practitioners, under the direction of a physician, to develop a comprehensive health data base through the use of history and physical examination. The rule also provides that nurses may initiate or modify medical treatment when and to the extent authorized by the treating physician within an established plan of medical and nursing protocol. The rule also sets forth a variety of other functions.

The medical society complained that the rule allows for the illegal practice of medicine. In a petition to the board of nursing, the medical society asserted that the board exceeded its authority and asked that the board repeal the rule or amend it to incorporate the concept of physician supervision. The Louisiana State Nursing Association intervened, requesting that the phrase "under the direction of a physician" be deleted from the rule.

The nursing board dismissed the medical society's petition and declared the rule valid. In addition, it granted the state association's request to initiate rule-making proceedings to delete the phrase "under the direction of a physician" in the rule.

Thereafter, the Medical Society filed suit for an injunction in state court, asserting that the nursing board had exceeded its authority by promulgating rules that conflicted with the medical practice act. The nursing board contended that the medical society did not file its lawsuit in a timely fashion. The trial court overruled this objection, and the nursing board appealed. This was the sole issue on appeal, which the court resolved in favor of the medical society, and it remanded the case to the trial court for further proceedings. The case is now pending.

State board regulation of nurse midwives

In some states, the practices of midwifery and nurse midwifery are authorized under the medical practice act. In others, they are regulated by the NPA or a specific statute. Cases have considered whether the person acting outside the scope of the act violates that act. Some cases have resolved whether the board of nursing has jurisdiction over that person.

For example, in *Vicki Smith v. State Medical Licensing Board of Indiana,*[52] the plaintiff cared for a pregnant woman in Indiana, a state in which midwifery and nurse midwifery are practiced under the authority of the medical practice act.[53] Smith did not possess the required legal authorization to practice, but nevertheless she did uterine measurements, performed pelvic examinations and measurements, monitored fetal heartbeats, examined blood and urine specimens, and assisted women in childbirth. The opinion does not specify what training and qualifications Smith possessed.

The lower court issued a permanent injunction to restrain Smith from practicing medicine without a license. On appeal, this result was affirmed; the court held that the practices of midwifery and nurse midwifery are the limited practice of medicine in Indiana.

Leggett v. Tennessee Board of Nursing[54] reached a completely different result. There, a nurse without the state-prescribed qualifications to practice as a nurse midwife was practicing as a lay midwife. She did not claim to be a nurse midwife; however, she did deliver babies and used Pitocin on her patients. The Tennessee Board of Nursing revoked her license after concluding, following a hearing, that Leggett was practicing in an advanced nursing role without proper qualifications.

On appeal, the lower court overturned the license revocation; the Court of Appeals of Tennessee affirmed this ruling. The court determined that midwifery was not regulated by any statute in Tennessee and did not come under the jurisdiction of the board of nursing merely because a lay midwife is a nurse.

The court noted that Leggett did not practice as a nurse when she worked as a midwife. While she had improperly used Pitocin, which could not be administered by a non-nurse, the court reasoned the nurse could not be disciplined for something she did outside her nursing profession unless it affected the quality of the nursing care she rendered "when she is acting as a nurse."[55]

Leigh v. Board of Registration in Nursing[56] reached a different conclusion. There, a registered nurse who was not a nurse midwife held herself out to the public as a registered nurse with obstetrical training. The Massachusetts Supreme Court upheld the state nursing board's power to suspend her license for practicing nurse midwifery without certification and delivering babies without physician supervision in violation of state law. The court rejected the nurse's argument that she was only practicing lay midwifery and did not come under the nursing board's jurisdiction.

Prescriptive authority

Although some jurisdictions, as discussed below, provide nurse practitioners with limited prescriptive authority, the majority do not. The role of the nurse practitioner is greatly diminished without this authority. Although able to provide most of the patient's health care without physician presence or supervision, the authority to order treatment falls short of drug therapy. Clients of nurse practitioners then are subject to lengthy delays in treatment and needless gaps in the continuity of their care.

To maintain efficiency in their practice, nurse practitioners practicing without prescriptive authority have developed other means to obtain needed prescriptions for patients. The legal ramifications of these methods vary.

PRESCRIPTION PRACTICES WITHOUT STATUTORY AUTHORITY

Depending on the laws of the jurisdiction, nurse practitioner prescriptive methods include making a request of a physician for each prescription needed, utilizing presigned blank prescription forms, or telephoning prescriptions into a pharmacy using a supervising physician's name. Each of these methods has practical, and sometimes legal, problems.

The first method, which is legal in all jurisdictions, is to request a physician to do the prescribing. This procedure is time consuming and annoying for the nurse practitioner, the physician, and the patient who must wait. Further, it presumes, unrealistically, that a physician is always present when and where the nurse is practicing.

Second, nurse practitioners may use presigned prescription blanks. This has its problems, too. The blanks could be stolen, and in some states, the use of presigned blanks is explicitly illegal. In Rhode Island, for example, a physician who signs a blank prescription and gives it to anyone other than a duly licensed pharmacist is subject to a fine.[57]

Another example is South Carolina, where it is unlawful for a physician to issue a signed prescription blank. Both the signor and the recipient of the signed blank can be guilty of conspiracy to violate the statute and possession of a prescription document signed in blank by a person other than the person whose signature appears is a *prima facie* case of violation of the statute. A fine and/or a prison term are possible upon conviction; a first violation is a misdemeanor, whereas the second is a felony.[58]

Third, nurse practitioners, nurses, and unlicensed office personnel telephone prescriptions to pharmacies. Even though this method is widely used, its legality is unclear.

In the majority of states where there is no authority, the nurse practitioner, the supervising physician, and an employing agency, if any, are advised to agree on the types of medications and devices that may be prescribed by nurse practitioners and how these are to be prescribed, that is, whether to use presigned blanks or the telephone or to order from the pharmacy, and the like. The agreement should be written and incorporated into standing orders and protocols and annually updated.

In general, nurse practitioners are advised not to sign a physician's name on a prescription blank because this may be a violation of state or federal law. If presigned blank prescriptions are to be used, care must be taken to prevent loss or theft; in any event, nurse practitioners are cautioned against using presigned blanks to prescribe substances for which a provider number is required by the United States Bureau of Narcotics and Dangerous Drugs.

Specific policies and agreements, as well as careful documentation, will best protect against accusations that the nurse practitioner has violated state or federal drug laws or is practicing medicine without a license. These practices will demonstrate that the nurse practitioner was making a careful effort to practice efficiently where the law is unclear.

Nurse practitioners in states without prescriptive authority legislation must continue to make passage of authorizing legislation a priority. California, for example, is working toward authority for qualified nurse practitioners to furnish certain medications and permits all registered nurses to dispense certain medications.[59]

The proposed act provides that drugs or devices should be furnished to the patient in accordance with standardized procedures developed by a nurse and physician. Conditions for referral, periodic review, amount and type of physician supervision, the competency of the nurse, as well as a list of the drugs to be prescribed are included in the procedure or protocol.

STATE REQUIREMENTS FOR PRESCRIPTIVE AUTHORITY

The previous discussion demonstrates that legislation granting nurse practitioners prescriptive authority is the nurse's best protection. States regulate both the qualifications that a nurse must have to prescribe and the types of substances that may be prescribed.

States that grant prescriptive authority to nurses often require hours of pharmacology education and some prior clinical experience.[60] To renew prescriptive authority, nurses are sometimes required to participate in continuing education in pharmacology and drug therapy relevant to the nurse practitioner's certification.

Some states, such as New Hampshire, have amended their nurse practice acts to grant limited prescriptive authority.[61] Changes in the state's pharmacy act may need to accompany nurse practice act changes since pharmacy acts may define a "practitioner" (that person who may prescribe) in such a way as to exclude nurses.

Other jurisdictions have added nurses to the pharmacy definition of practitioner without concomitant changes in the nurse practice act. Vermont is one of these states[62]; rules and regulations written by the Vermont Board of Nursing authorize Vermont nurse practitioners to write and sign prescriptions for drugs covered under current protocols.[63] Some states, such as Utah, have passed prescriptive authority legislation that is separate from the nurse, medical, or pharmacy acts.[64]

Prescriptive authority statutes usually only list drugs or types of substances that nurse practitioners may *not* prescribe. The Washington statute, for example, prohibits the prescription of certain controlled substances.[65] In some states, administrative regulations specify the drugs that nurse practitioners can prescribe. For example, in Idaho, applications for prescription writing authority are limited to certain categories of drugs.[65a] Nurse practitioners may order refills for other drugs originally prescribed by the supervising physician for patients with stable chronic illness.[66]

The rules are clear in states granting nurse practitioners authority to write and to sign prescriptions. Legislative efforts to pass these laws in other jurisdictions must continue.

Hospital privileges

Some nurses practitioners need access to a licensed health facility where their patients can be admitted. Nurse anesthetists, nurse midwives, and other nurse practitioners are among those who must have hospital privileges to ensure good patient care. Thus, privileges are necessary to practice the full scope of their professions (both hospitals and other licensed health care facilities have privilege mechanisms; the term *hospital* used in this section includes other licensed facilities).

Nurse practitioners, including many nurse anesthetists, are employed by the hospital and, by the terms of employment, may use the facilities. Others, however, are self-employed or employed by physicians, and access to the hospital is not automatic. For many nurse practitioners, getting privileges has been no problem, but others have met resistance and refusal.[67]

OBTAINING HOSPITAL PRIVILEGES

If the decision by the facility is to grant privileges, reasonable restrictions may be placed on nurse practitioner practice, just as they may be placed on physician practice. A hospital, for example, may require that certain functions be performed only by a physician or, if done by the nurse practitioner, then only with physician consultation (such as the repair of a fourth-degree perineal laceration). Privileges extended may not be arbitrarily limited or withdrawn.[68]

Nurse practitioners and hospitals often differ on the meaning of privileges. For example, many nurse practitioners want to admit patients without a named supervising physician; yet many health care facilities demand that nurse practitioner patients be admitted under a physician's name or as a co-admission. This, the facilities argue, guarantees that there is a responsible physician named in case of emergency.

A nurse practitioner may view an admission under a physician's name as rendering the term "privileges" meaningless; nevertheless, privileges enable the nurse practitioner to write in the history and progress notes, write orders, and otherwise participate in or control the care the patient receives. Without privileges, the nurse practitioner may only visit the patient in the hospital during visiting hours. Legislative and judicial solutions to obtaining privileges have had some success.

STATUTORY REMEDIES

Nurse practitioners and other health care professionals face difficulties in obtaining hospital privileges, and legal remedies, particularly against private hospitals, are uncertain, expensive, and time consuming. Legislative solutions have been adopted in two jurisdictions that address nondiscrimination in granting hospital privileges.

The first was enacted in the District of Columbia in February 1984 as part of a statute that licenses health care facilities. The act provides that:

> The accordance and delineation of clinical privileges shall be determined on an individual basis and commensurate with an applicant's education, training, experience, and demonstrated current competence. . . . (T)he governing body, or designated persons so functioning, shall ensure that decisions on clinical privileges and staff membership are based on an objective evaluation of an applicant's credentials, free of anticompetitive intent or purpose.[69]

The act provides that various factors are not valid for consideration in the decision regarding privileges. These include the applicant's participation in a private group practice with members of a particular class of health professional or the applicant's willingness to send a certain amount of patients/clients who are in need of the services of a facility or agency to a particular facility or agency.[70]

Most important, the statute specifically bans any law—whether governmental or institutional—that prohibits certified registered nurse anesthetists, certified nurse midwives, and certified nurse practitioners, among others, from being accorded clinical privileges or being appointed to all categories of staff membership at any facility or agency that offers the kinds of services that can be performed by either members of these health professions or physicians.[71] The statute provides a procedure for processing of privilege applications and due process claims for rejection or other adverse decisions.

Ohio is the second jurisdiction to enact a law prohibiting discrimination in obtaining privileges at hospitals. The language is less strong than the Washington, D.C. statute. The Ohio statute requires the governing body of every hospital to establish and to apply standards and procedures in considering and acting upon applications for staff membership or professional privileges.[72]

The governing body of the hospital is prohibited from discriminating against persons solely on the basis of whether the person is certified to practice medicine, osteopathic medicine, podiatry, or dentistry.[73] A hospital that provides maternity services may not discriminate against a person ''solely on the basis that the person is certified to practice nurse-midwifery. An application from a nurse-midwife shall contain the name of a physician member of the hospital's medical staff who has agreed to direct and supervise the applicant. . . .''[74]

Both the District of Columbia and the Ohio statutes[75] provide that one aggrieved under the statute may bring a court action. The Supreme Court of Ohio, however, has partially and narrowly construed that statute.

Judicial Construction of the Ohio Law. The case involved a chiropractor who sued to gain access to a hospital after he was not permitted by a hospital to refer his patients for outpatient x-ray films. Apparently, however, he had not applied for privileges. The court also noted that the chiropractor had x-ray equipment of his own and therefore had not demonstrated that access to the hospital's services was essential. The statute, the court held, expressly protected only those named.[76]

Although this decision may make it more difficult for Ohio nurse practitioners, other than nurse midwives, to use the statute to obtain privileges, there are distinguishing facts. First, there was no application submitted. Second, access to the hospital's services for x-ray films, which the physician wanted, were not essential since he had access to these services with his own equipment. Most nurse practitioners' situations are different.

Another Ohio Supreme Court case, *Dooley v. Barberton Citizen's Hospital*,[77] demonstrates that it will strictly judge bylaw requirements that are unrelated to determining qualification and will hold them discriminatory. Damages may be obtained for the time period in which the practitioner sought staff privileges but was unable to surmount the illegally discriminatory practice requirements.

At issue were the hospital's original bylaws, which mandated a minimum 2-year residency for podiatrists. When a podiatrist with 12 years of experience applied for privileges, the hospital rejected him because he had not done a residency.

The court noted that less than 8% to 10% of the national podiatric graduates had participated in a 2-year residency at the time the rules were promulgated. In view of the fact that no 2-year residencies were available in the state, the hospital's rules were patently discriminatory against the class of podiatrists. Therefore, the rule was not reasonably related to whether the podiatrist was qualified.

JUDICIAL REMEDIES

A hospital may decide to deny an application without ever considering its merits. If the hospital does consider its merits, it may nevertheless reject the application. A hospital that grants privileges to nurse practitioners may refuse privileges to a particular applicant who does not possess the required qualifications. As long as those requirements are reasonable, they will be upheld.

A facility may refuse privileges to all nurse practitioners as a class or to all members of a particular type of nurse practitioner. This may be actionable.

The Due Process Claim for Summary Denials. Whether privileges can be obtained, and in what manner and nature, is determined by the bylaws and rules of the institution to which the nurse must apply and state and federal laws. Some hospital bylaws do not provide for privileges of any type for nonphysician personnel; if this is so, the hospital's view will be that the nurse practitioner's application need not be accepted or considered, unless its jurisdiction is Washington, D.C., where the law prohibits discriminatory bylaws that only give access to physicians.

The practitioner can also challenge the action, if the facility is a governmental entity or state action[78] exists, on the basis that the refusal to consider the application is the functional equivalent of denying the practitioner the right to practice his or her profession.[79] Since the practitioner has a property interest in his or her licensed profession, the action is a deprivation of property without due process of law.[80] In California,[81] these due process principles apply to private and public hospitals. Summary rejection of an application is arbitrary and capricious.

This argument has been successfully raised in cases involving physicians. The premise underlying the due process analysis, however, is equally applicable to many nurse practitioners.

The premise in the physician cases is that the continued existence of their profession, their property interest, requires access to the hospital. A denial of hospital privileges renders them unable to practice their profession, "since much of what a physician or surgeon must do can only be done in a hospital"[82]; thus, they are deprived of a property interest. This principle applies to nurse anesthetists, nurse midwives, nurse practitioners, and clinical specialists whose practices require the services of a hospital for the full scope of practicing their profession.

A New Jersey certified clinical nurse specialist in psychiatric nursing (Ms. Wrable) filed suit in state court after the hospital's chief executive officer (CEO) summarily rejected her application for nonphysician adjunct privileges and refused to allow her access to a client hospitalized there.[83] She also sought, among other claims, to compel the hospital to alter its bylaws to include members of her specialty.

The hospital bylaws defined staff eligibility as appropriately licensed physicians and dentists and the nonphysician adjunct staff as podiatrists. Since there was no category for Wrable, the CEO wrote her a rejection letter. The matter was not even considered by the medical staff committee or the board of trustees in accordance with usual application procedures. Although nonstaff consultations by psychiatrists had been allowed in the past, the CEO decided to discontinue them.

The hospital, in his view, could not supervise her performance since the department of medicine oversees psychiatrists and the department of nursing supervises nurses. The defense further contended that Wrable was not licensed to provide psychotherapy since the NPA did not authorize such activity. The defense also argued that tradition does permit privileges to nonphysicians.[84]

The court agreed that Wrable was not licensed to perform psychotherapy and that since there was no psychiatric department at the hospital, there was no way to supervise her hospital practice. The court also ruled that she could visit her clients during hospital visiting hours. The decision dismissing her case is being appealed. Among the issues are Ms. Wrable's right to have her application considered, as well as the sufficiency of her claims for intentional interference with business opportunities and antitrust violations.

Appealing a Denial After the Application is Considered. Generally, when an application for privileges is made, application materials, which may include proof of credentials, references, and professional liability insurance, must be submitted first to the department in which the nurse practitioner will practice, such as anesthesia for nurse anesthetists. The department then considers the credentials and votes to approve or disapprove the application. One or more other committees within the hospital may consider the application. The application and the recommendations are then reviewed by the governing body, such as the medical staff, which makes a final determination. This decision, if challenged, may be reviewed by the Board of Trustees.

While the "final" decision is made by the hospital governing body, which has the power to overturn a committee decision, the decision made in the original departmental committee is rarely overturned at higher levels, especially if it is negative. The Board of Trustees also generally upholds the decision of the governing body.

If the response is negative, an appeal through the procedures established by the bylaws is possible. The review must be procedurally fair and substantively rational.[85] After exhausting this review, the matter may be appealed to a court of law. The courts, however, are reluctant to substitute their judgment in area about which they know very little. The health facility has the expertise to make decisions based on the qualifications and competence of applicants. Public interest requires careful screening of applicants to protect the innocent from malpractice.[86]

Thus, the courts defer to the hospital committee who considered the application, and if the reasons for denial are reasonable, the action is upheld. Unless the application process or the review established by the bylaws was unfair procedurally, or the requirements are unreasonable, legal challenges to these decisions are rarely successful.[87]

ANTITRUST REMEDIES

When the facility refuses to grant privileges because of the class of practitioner, several actions may be taken. Even if all administrative appeals have been unsuccessful and the hospital has been scrupulous about following its own procedures in denying privileges, the nurse practitioner still may be able to take action.

First, a nurse practitioner may file a complaint with the Federal Trade Commission Bureau of Competition. The commission has discretion to investigate, but its resources are limited. The threat of a complaint, however, may cause the facility to reverse its decision.

Second, a nurse practitioner may choose to sue in federal court alleging antitrust violations of the Sherman and Clayton Acts, which prohibit restraints in trade and monopolies.[88] These acts are reviewed in Chapter 33. States also may have antitrust laws,[89] but some state courts have held they do not apply to staff privileges.[90] Certain immunities exist when the anticompetitive conduct is required by state law[91] or the business is insurance.[92] These suits are also quite costly and often extend over years, but the reward is treble damages (three times the damages proved).

The difficulty with federal antitrust actions is that the challenged activity must have a substantial impact on interstate commerce (commerce that extends outside the state in which the hospital is located). Otherwise, there is no jurisdiction for the court to hear the case. Many staff privilege cases involving other nonphysician providers have reached inconsistent conclusions on this issue.[93]

Another problem concerns the antitrust injury that must be alleged; the injury is to the marketplace, not the person. Thus, the loss of staff privileges must be shown to have a significant impact on competition in the relevant market,[94] and the injured party must be a participant in the same market as the alleged violators.[95]

Physicians may assert that the particular nurse practitioner does not compete in the same market that they do, and hence there is no antitrust injury. This was the position taken in *Bhan v. NME Hospitals, Inc.*,[96] where a nurse anesthetist brought an action alleging that the hospital's policy of allowing only anesthesiologists to perform anesthesia services in the hospital's operating rooms violated the federal antitrust laws. The Certified Registered Nurse Anesthetist (CRNA) alleged that the bulk of his practice was performed at the hospital under its contract with anesthesia services. When the contract expired, the hospital adopted a policy of allowing only physician anesthesiologists to perform anesthesia services in the hospital's operating room. Thus, he was precluded from practicing his profession at the hospital.

His complaint also alleged that the hospital administrator entered into negotiations, prior to the contract termination, with a physician anesthesiologist, named Sulk, and induced him to relocate to the hospital. An exclusive contract or the right to pick persons providing anesthesia was offered. This arrangement caused the hospital's existing physician anesthesiologist concern, and he contacted state physician anesthesiologist professional societies for help.

These organizations and Sulk combined to induce the administrator to recommend to the hospital board that they adopt an anesthesiologist-only policy and exclude nurse anesthetists from anesthesia practice. They allegedly were motivated by the fact that nurse anesthetists perform services at lower cost and with greater scheduling flexibility than do physician anesthesiologists, making them more attractive to consumers.

The defendants moved to dismiss the case on the ground that there was no antitrust injury since the nurse anesthetists do not compete with physician anesthesiologists. The district court dismissed the action with prejudice because the nurse anesthetist had no standing to sue.

The court of appeals reversed, noting that the sole issue was whether the nurse anesthetist was a proper party to bring the suit. This necessitated an inquiry into whether nurses and physicians are participants in a single market for anesthesia services or whether they each participate in their own markets. To determine if they participate in the same market, the test is the reasonable interchangeability of use or the cross-elasticity of demand between the services provided by nurse anesthetists and physician anesthesiologists.

The Ninth Circuit reviewed the lower court's decision that the legal restrictions on nurse anesthetists precluded any interchangeability of use since, under California law, a nurse anesthetist must act under the supervision and direction of, *inter alia*, a physician. The Ninth Circuit held, however, that the requirement of physician supervision does not end the inquiry, because a "*nurse anesthetist administering anesthesia under the supervision of a physician may still duplicate many of the services provided by the M.D. anesthesiologist.*"[97] Moreover, in California, the supervising physician need not be a physician anesthesiologist and might be any attending physician, dentist, or podiatrist.

In defining market products, the court reasoned, a product should not be excluded from a market simply because it requires additional input in order to be a reasonable substitute for other products in the market. The input required by the nurse anesthetist to match exactly many of the services of a physician anesthesiologist is the supervision of an attending physician. The nurse anesthetist alleged in his complaint that such supervision is attainable and common practice among the medical profession.

Although the legal restrictions create a functional distinction between the two groups, the court reasoned, they do not preclude the reasonable interchangeability of user or the cross-elasticity of demand that is sufficient to constrain the market power of physician anesthesiologists and thereby affect competition. The allegations of the complaint, the court held, were sufficient as a matter of law to show the nurse anesthetist was a proper party to bring the suit.

The court cautioned, however, that at this point in the lawsuit, it was not considering whether the nurse anesthetist would be able to introduce evidence to support his allegations or whether the restrictive arrangements might be upheld. With respect to this later aspect, the court was obliquely referring to the Supreme Court's decision in *Jefferson Parish Hospital District No. 2 v. Hyde.*[98] There, a contract between a group of anesthesiologists and a hospital that excluded other anesthesiologists was upheld based in part on the fact that the hospital had only a 30% share of the market (70% of patients were seen at other hospitals).

Another case, involving nurse midwives, is promising although still in the pretrial stages. The case may also raise implications for the current insurance cancellation crisis that nurse midwives are currently experiencing.

Two nurse midwives, who were partners of the plaintiff Nurse Midwifery Associates (NMA), a professional partnership for the provision of nurse-midwifery services, and their supervising physician brought an antitrust action against various physicians and an insurance company. The insurance company controlled 80% of the Tennessee medical malpractice market and was owned and operated by its physician policyholders. One of the defendant physicians was a member of the board of directors of the company.

NMA had entered into a separate agreement with a physician and his associates for medical supervision and services. Pursuant to the contractual arrangement, the nurse midwives applied for admitting privileges at the defendant hospitals; the physician sought renewal of his medical malpractice policy from the defendant insurance company.

The defendant physicians, the complaint alleged, entered into a conspiracy to prevent the nurse midwives from practicing in order to protect their lucrative obstetrics practice in Nashville. The defendants accomplished this by preventing the nurse midwives from obtaining privileges. They pressured the supervising physician and others not to collaborate with the plaintiffs. The defendants also brought concerted pressure on the insurance company to cancel the plaintiff supervising physician's medical malpractice insurance because of his contract with NMA.

Because of this action, the plaintiff supervising physician left Tennessee. The nurse midwives were unable to secure physician backup and went out of business. The court refused to apply the business of insurance exemption from antitrust liability to the insurance company or its board. The court was not convinced, based on the complaint, that denial of insurance under these circumstances, was the business of insurance. As of 1983, the parties were still in the discovery stage of litigation.[99] A Federal Trade Commission consent degree was entered against the physician-owned insurer that controlled 80% of the Tennessee medical malpractice insurance market.[100]

A settlement agreement such as this can be the result of tenacity in antitrust litigation. For example, chiropractors have achieved admitting privileges by such agreement. In *Wilk v. American Medical Association*,[101] an antitrust case brought by five chiropractors against the AMA and five other medical associations, charging a boycott of chiropractic services and denial of access to hospital facilities. The court of appeals ordered a new trial, and the case is still pending against four defendants. The fifth defendant, the Illinois State Medical Society, however, entered into a settlement agreement that allows chiropractors to practice on equal footing with medical physicians. The agreement allows them to obtain hospital privileges and requires medical physicians to cooperate with chiropractors regarding referrals and consultation.[102]

Relevant antitrust case law involving other nonphysician health care professionals appears to provide the nurse practitioner with a basis for challenging exclusionary practices of physicians and insurers. The success of these actions, of course, will depend on the ability to prove essential elements such as competition in the same market, agreements to restrain trade that have unreasonably limited competition in the market, and impact on interstate commerce.

Perhaps JCAH will soon require hospitals to include open staff privileges to nonphysicians. In 1984, the standards required that the medical staff be made of licensed physicians and dentists[103]; other provisions were made for podiatrists[104] and nurse anesthetists.[105] The 1985 standards provided that the medical staff includes licensed physicians and "*may* include other licensed individuals permitted by law and by the hospital to provide patient care services independently in the hospital."[106] The standards have a physician evaluation requirement "when non-physician members of the medical staff are granted privileges to admit patients to inpatient services."[107] Persons other than physicians "who are now permitted to provide patient care services independently may perform the history and physical examination, if granted such privileges and if the findings, conclusions, and assessment of risk are confirmed or endorsed by a qualified physician."[108]

Although somewhat restrictive, the standards do represent a change in the JCAH position on nonphysician staff privileges. JCAH requirements to establish a mechanism for privileges for nonphysicians, including nurse practitioners, would obviate the need for antitrust action against hospitals.

Third-party reimbursement

In recent years, nurses have been practicing independent of the role as employees of physicians and health facilities. Direct third-party reimbursement is important to independent practice because without it, patients may feel economically compelled to choose another provider's services whose costs may be reimbursed.

Indirect third-party reimbursement is also important for employees of hospitals and physicians, such as professional nurses, nurse midwives, clinical nurse specialists, and nurse anesthetists. Without it, some hospitals have refused to hire clinical nurse specialists for certain positions and hired other providers, such as social workers, whose services were reimbursable.[109] Reimbursement is also important statistically to employees so that their practice is valued as profitable and professional.

The ANA believes that the following aspects of role development for nurses are affected by reimbursement:

1. The development of innovative practice arrangements
2. The expansion of traditional practice settings
3. The relationship with professional colleagues
4. The image of nurses as revenue generators in the system
5. The degree of control over nursing practice[110]

THE SYSTEM

Third-party reimbursement for nursing services is governed by state and federal legislatures through state insurance codes and regulations. The system consists of public and private components. The public component includes Medicare, Medicaid, and the Civilian Health and Medical Programs of the Uniformed Services (CHAMPUS). The Health Care Financing Administration (HCFA) of the Department of Health and Human Services (HHS) administers Medicare and Medicaid; CHAMPUS is administered by the Department of Defense.

The private component consists of Blue Cross and Blue Shield and medical insurance companies. Blue Cross and Blue Shield have separate nonprofit corporations or plans located across the United States. These plans, respectively, provide hospital and physician service insurance coverage to subscribers. Commercial insurance companies, on the other hand, are typically organized for profit, and their boards of directors are not providers of health care services.[111]

Federal Law. Federal reimbursement is authorized by statute or regulation. CHAMPUS regulations provide direct reimbursement for the services of nurse midwives, who are licensed as required by the jurisdiction in which the care is given, and ACNM-certified nurse midwives, "independent of physician referral and supervision."[112] Reimbursement for the services of a registered nurse who does not possess the required qualifications may be authorized only where "the patient has been referred for care by a licensed physician and a licensed physician provided continuing supervision of the course of the care."[113] Nurse practitioners are also authorized to receive direct reimbursement for services.[114]

Medicare provides benefits to those 65 years and older and to the disabled. Indirect reimbursement may be obtained (billed through the physician or institution) for nursing services that are "rendered by a licensed health provider incident to or under the supervision" of a physician.[115]

Medicaid, which is a federally assisted, state-administered program, provides medical assistance to low-income persons who are aged, blind, or disabled and to families with dependent children. All states except Arizona participate and must comply with federal regulations. Regulations provide specific reimbursement for nurse practitioner services[116] and nurse midwives.[117]

State Law. Some state laws allow insurers to reimburse health care providers.[118] Although there is no state prohibition against reimbursement of nursing services, some private insurers have refused to reimburse; consequently state laws have been enacted to provide for either mandatory or optional reimbursement. Alaska,[119] for example, has a mandatory benefit law that mandates reimbursement; Maryland[120] has a mandatory option law that requires insurers to offer nurse reimbursement in insurance plans. Direct reimbursement is limited to nurse practitioners who work directly under the supervision of a physician.[121]

Required reimbursement for registered nurses without advanced training exists in some states. For example, Maryland provides that registered nurses can be reimbursed "for any service which is within the lawful scope of practice" of that licensed health care provider.[122] The services of certified nurse practitioners[123] and nurse midwives[124] are reimbursable under separate provisions. Reimbursed nurse practitioner services are subject to peer review by a committee appointed by the Board of Examiners of Nurses.[125] Policies may not require, as a condition of payment for nurse midwifery benefits, that the nurse midwife be employed by a physician or act pursuant to a physician's orders.[126]

Some states have free choice or equalization statutes requiring that insurers reimburse for services rendered by nonphysician providers if those same services would be covered when performed by a physician. For example, Minnesota's insurance statute provides that insurers must reimburse for nurse practitioner services within the scope of his or her practice, whether done by a physician or a nurse practitioner.[127] Such laws allow the consumer to choose a provider free from the penalty of discriminatory reimbursement policies. To the extent, however, that nurse practitioner services differ from physician services, they are not recoverable.[128]

Other states permit reimbursement. California, which does not require that all nurses be reimbursed, has the only provision that specifically proscribes any policy from prohibiting the insured, "upon referral by a licensed physician and surgeon from selecting . . . any registered nurse who possesses a master's degree in psychiatric-mental health nursing and two years supervised experience in psychiatric-mental health nursing . . . to perform services deemed necessary by the referring physician. . . ."[129] If the insured so elects, there must be reimbursement.[130]

RESTRICTIVE REIMBURSEMENT POLICIES

California's policy outlined above, that requires physician referral for reimbursement, is an example of a restriction on reimbursement. Other states limit direct reimbursement to nurse practitioners who work directly under the supervision of a physician.[131] Some states, such as Mississippi, condition reimbursement on physician supervision in the treatment of patients and the physician's participation in the billing process.[132]

These restrictive reimbursement policies requiring physician supervision hamper advanced practice by interposing physicians between nurse practitioners and their patients.[133] The ANA views this kind of physician involvement as relinquishing "part of the legal control of nursing practice to another profession and results in a superordinate-subordinate relationship that does not allow for flexible boundaries or evolution of roles."[134]

Obviously, physician supervision over advanced nursing practice is incompatible with professional independence. In addition, these policies hamper attempts to reduce health care costs by requiring the patient to see two providers.

The trend of prospective payment for services requires nurses to separate health care from medical care and "focus on the unique contibution they may bring to the health care arena."[135] The ANA recommends that:

> Nurses must be able to determine the cost of services they provide and must be aware of the effect (that change in financing structures) has on these services. . . . Nurses must think beyond collaboration to potential competition with physicians so that they can continue to provide the type of health care that the consumers need.[136]

Third- party legislative proposals should seek reimbursement for services of all registered nurses, and this should not be limited to a specific group of nurses. Moreover, "(t)here should be no association with or dependency upon other providers as a condition of reimbursement of nurses' services."[137]

Recommendations and trends

While nurse practitioners strive to make practice more efficient by seeking legislative changes, some insurers are substantially raising professional liability insurance premiums for physicians who have a collaborative relationship with a nurse practitioner. These premium increases, which are often not based on loss experience, are forcing some physicians to forego working with nurse practitioners despite their preference. Nurse midwives also have lost their malpractice insurance coverage.

The legal system, especially antitrust actions, may be a solution, but legislative efforts have a broader impact. Efforts must be made to eliminate direct physician supervision requirements in third-party reimbursement and advanced practice laws. The hallmark of a professional, as the *Sermchief* court noted, is knowing one's professional limitations. When these limits are reached, the professional nurse practitioner refers to the appropriate physician in accordance with the professional and legal duty to refer. The duty to refer obviates the need for direct physician supervision requirements. Nurse practitioner practice will retain its sound reputation by the cost-effective, high-quality nursing care and necessary referrals that its members provide.

Endnotes

1. Bullough, *The Current Phase in the Development of Nurse Practice Acts,* 28 ST. LOUIS UNIVERSITY LAW JOURNAL 365, 376 (1984) (hereinafter cited as *Bullough*).
2. Kobrin, *The American Midwife Controversy: A Crisis of Professionalization,* 40 BULLETIN OF THE HISTORY OF MEDICINE 350 (1966).
3. Tom, *The Evolution of Nurse-Midwifery: 1900-1960,* JOURNAL OF NURSE MIDWIFERY 4 (JULY/AUGUST 1982).
4. *Id.* at 8.
5. P. Starr, THE SOCIAL TRANSFORMATION OF AMERICAN MEDICINE 156 (1982).
6. McGaw, *A Review of over 14,000 Surgical Anesthetics,* SURGERY, GYNECOLOGY AND OBSTETRICS 795 (1906).
7. Peplau, *Specialization in Professional Nursing,* CLINICAL NURSE SPECIALIST: INTERPRETATIONS 19 (J. Riehl and J. McVay, eds., 1973).
8. *Id.*
9. Silver, Ford, and Stearly, *A Program to Increase Health Care for Children: the Pediatric Nurse Practitioner Program,* 39 PEDIATRICS 756 (May 1967).
10. DEPARTMENT OF HEALTH, EDUCATION AND WELFARE, EXTENDING THE SCOPE OF NURSING PRACTICE (1971).
11. Fickeissen, *Getting Certified,* 85 AMERICAN JOURNAL OF NURSING 265 (March 1985).
12. Hirsh & Studner, *The Nurse Practitioner in Action: Patients' Friend, Physicians' Foe?* 31 MED. TRIAL TECH. Q. 37, 38 (Summer 1984) (hereinafter cited as *Hirsh & Studner*).
13. CAL. BUS. & PROF. CODE §2834 (West 1986).
14. WASH. REV. CODE ANN. §74,42,010 (1985).
15. *See* WASH. REV. CODE Ann. §18.88.080 (1986) ("[t]he Board shall define by regulation what constitutes specialized and advanced levels of nursing practice as recognized by the medical and nursing professions").
16. S.D. CODIFIED LAWS ANN. §36-9A-5 (1985). This statute states that practice as a nurse practitioner or nurse midwife shall be subject to the joint control of the boards of nursing and medicine.
17. KY. REV. STAT. §314.011(6) (7).
18. *Id.*
19. *See, e.g.,* N. D. ADMIN. CODE §54-05-03 (1984).
20. MD. HEALTH OCC. CODE ANN. §7-101 (f)(2)(vi), (vii) (1986).
21. *Id.* at §7-205 (a) (3).
22. *Id.* at §7-205 (a) (3).
23. *See,* W. VA. CODE §30-7-15 (1980) (administration of anesthesia) and §30-15-1,2 (midwives under the Board of Examiners for Registered Professional Nurses).
24. CONN. GEN. STAT. ANN. §20-87 a-20-102 (West Supp. 1986).
25. MO. ANN. STAT. §335.016 (8) (a)-(e) (Vernon Supp. 1986).
26. *See, e.g.,* N.Y. EDUC. LAWS §6902 (McKinney 1985).
27. IND. CODE ANN. §25-22-5 5-5 (Burns 1985); N.J. STAT. ANN. §45: 10-2 (West 1978); OHIO REV. CODE ANN. §4731.30-32 (Baldwin 1984); PA. STAT. ANN. tit. 63 §171-176 (Purdon 1968).
28. Kelly, *Nurse Practitioner Challenges to the Orthodox Structure of Health Care Delivery: Regulation and Restraints on Trade,* 11 AMERICAN JOURNAL OF LAW AND MEDICINE 194, 201 (1985) (hereinafter cited as *Kelly*).
29. AMERICAN NURSES' ASSOC., THE NURSE PRACTICE ACT: SUGGESTED STATE LEGISLATION 26 (1981).
30. *Id.* at 3.
31. *Kelly, supra* note 28, at 202-203.

32. STATE OF IDAHO, BOARD OF NURSING, MINIMUM STANDARDS, RULES AND REGULATIONS, tit. 3, Ch. 4, (1984) Nurse Practitioners.
33. CONN. GEN. STAT. ANN. §20-86B (West Supp. 1986).
34. *Kelly, supra* note 28, at 201, citing *The Washington Post,* Oct. 31, 1985, at C3, col. 2 (physicians oppose proposal to delete physician-nurse collaboration requirements for advanced nurse practitioners).
35. THE NATIONAL COMMISSION FOR HEALTH CERTIFYING AGENCIES, 4 PROFESSIONAL REGULATION NEWS, 8 (December 1984).
36. *Id.*
37. *See, e.g., Kelly supra* note 28, at 201 citing *The Washington Post,* Oct. 31, 1985 at C3, col. 2 (physicians oppose proposal to delete physician-nurse collaboration requirements for advanced nurse practitioners).
38. 677 S.W.2d 293 (Ark. 1984).
39. ARK STAT. ANN. §72-746(e), 72-754(f) (1979).
40. *Arkansas State Nurses' Association v. Arkansas State Medical Board,* 677 S.W.2d 293, 295 (Ark. 1984).
41. *Frank v. South,* 194 S.W.2d 375 (Ky. 1971).
42. *Chalmers-Francis v. Nelson,* 57 P.2d 1312 (Cal. 1936).
43. *Magit v. Board of Medical Examiners,* 57 Cal. 2d 74 (1961).
44. 660 S.W. 2d 683 (Mo. banc 1983).
45. MO. REV. STAT. §335.016.8 (A)-(E) (1975). This section is still in effect in 1986.
46. *Id.*
47. Doyle & Meurer, *Missouri Legislation and Litigation: Practicing Medicine Without a License,* NURSE PRACTITIONER 41, 42 (June 1983).
48. 685 S.W.2d 431 (Tex. App. 1985).
49. Texas Administrative Rule 388.06.00, cite quoted in *Bellegie v. Texas Board of Nurse Examiners,* 685 SW2d 431, 432 (Tex. App. 1985).
50. TEX. REV. CIV. STAT. ANN art. 4518(1) (Supp 1986). This section provides that it is the duty of the board to prescribe and publish the minimum requirements and standards that prepare professional nurse practitioners. It further defines professional nursing as the "performance for compensation of any nursing act (a) in the observation, assessment, intervention, evaluation, rehabilitation, care and counsel and health teachings of persons who are ill, injured, infirm, or experiencing changes in normal health process; (b) in the maintenance of health or prevention of illness; (c) in the administration of medications or treatments as prescribed by licensed physician or dentist; (d) in the supervision or teaching of nurses; (e) in the administration supervision, evaluation of nursing practices, policies, and procedures. The foregoing shall not be deemed to include acts of medical diagnosis or prescription of therapeutic or corrective measures."
51. 484 So.2d 903 (La. App. 1986).
52. 459 N.E. 2d 401 (Ind. App. 1984).
53. IND. CODE ANN. §25-22.5.5-5 (1985).
54. 612 S.W. 2d 476 (Tenn. App. 1980).
55. *Id.* at 481.
56. 481 N.E.2d 1347 (Mass. 1985).

56a. *See generally,* Cohn, *Prescriptive Authority for Nurses,* 12 LAW, MEDICINE & HEALTH CARE 72 (1984).

57. R.I. GEN. LAWS §5-37-19 (1976).
58. S.C. CODE ANN. §44-53-395A (1),-(2),-13 (Law. Co-op 1979).
59. AB 4372, *reported in,* CALIFORNIA NURSE (April 1986), at 8, col. 1.
60. *See, e.g.,* WASH. ADMIN. CODE R. 308 -120-140 (2), (3), 450 (2) (a)- (c) (1983), which, among other things, requires a current year of clinical experience and 30 hours of pharmacology education, 8 of which must have been in the year before application for prescriptive authority; and for each renewal year, continuing education must be obtained.
61. N.H. REV. STAT. ANN. §326-B: 10(II) (1984). An advanced registered nurse practitioner who functions in collaboration with protocols established jointly with a collaborative physician may prescribe medications from the formulary for a specialty area that has been jointly agreed on by the state medical and nursing boards.
62. VT. STAT. ANN. tit. 26, §2022(7) (1985).
63. N.H. REV. STAT. ANN. §326-B:10(II) (1984). (*See* note 61.)
64. UTAH CODE ANN. §58-31a-2 (1985).
65. WASH. REV. CODE ANN. §18.88.280 (16) (1978).

65a. IDAHO STATE BOARD OF NURSING, MINIMUM STANDARDS RULES AND REGULATIONS, tit. 3, Ch. 4, §3-4.007.03 (Nurse Practitioners).

66. *Id.*
67. *Hirch & Studner, supra* note 12, at 56.
68. *See, e.g., Anton v. San Antonio Community Hospital,* 19 Cal. 3d 802 (1977)..
69. D.C. CODE ANN. §32-1307(a) (1986 Supp.).
70. *Id.* at §32-1307 (b)(4), (b)(6).
71. *Id.* at §32-1307 (c).
72. OHIO REV CODE Ann. §3701.351(A) (Page 1985).
73. *Id.* at §3701.351 (B).
74. *Id.* at (C) §3701.351.
75. *Id.* at (D) §3701.351.
76. *Fort Hamilton-Hughes Memorial Hospital Center v. Southard,* 466 N.E. 2d 903 (Ohio 1984).
77. 465 N.E. 2d 58 (Ohio 1984).
78. Chapter 5 thoroughly discusses the state action concept in the context of civil rights actions.
79. *Ezekial v. Winkley,* 20 Cal.3d 267, 273-74 (1977).
80. *Shaw v. Hospital Authority of Cobb County,* 507 F.2d 625 (5th Cir. 1975).
81. *Anton v. San Antonio Community Hospital,* 19 Cal.3d 802 (1977).
82. *Id.* at 824.
83. *Wrable v. Community Memorial Hospital,* 205 N.J. Super. 428 (1985), *Appeal pending* No. A-5401-84-T7 (App. Div. N.J. Sup. Ct. 1986).
84. Fickeissen, *Wrable loses Court Battle,* 15 NEW JERSEY NURSE, 1 at col. 4, (September/October 1985).
85. *Anton v. San Antonio Community Hospital,* 19 Cal.3d 802 (1977).
86. *Elam v. College Park Hospital,* 45 Cal. App.3d 507 (1975).
87. *See Shaw v. Hospital Authority of Cobb County,* 614 F.2d 946 (5th Cir. 1980), *cert. denied.* 449 U.S. 955 (1980).
88. 15 U.S.C. §1, 15 (1984).
89. *See, e.g.,* CAL. BUS. AND PROF. CODE §116600 (1984).
90. *Willis v. Santa Ana Community Hospital Association,* 58 Cal.2d 806 (1962) (California); *People v. Roth,* 420 N.E. 2d 929 (N.Y. 1981) (New York) *but see Cianci v. Superior Court,* 221 Cal. Rptr. 575 (Cal. 1985) (state antitrust laws apply to professionals).
91. *Parker v. Brown,* 317 U.S. 341 (1943).
92. 15 U.S.C. §1011 (1984).
93. For cases finding the jurisdictional element of impact on interstate

commerce, *see, e.g., Cardio-Medical Association v. Crozer-Chester Med. Ctr.*, 721 F.2d. 68 (3d. Cir. 1983); *McElhinney v. Medical Protective Co.*, 549 F.Supp 121 (E.D. Ky. 1982); remanded without opinion, 783 F.2d 439 (6th Cir. 1984); *Pontius v. Children's Hospital,* 552 F.Supp. 1352 (W.D.Pa. 1982). For cases reaching the opposite conclusion in staff privilege cases, *see, e.g., Wolf v. Jane Phillips Episcopal-Memorial Med. Ctr;* 513 F.2d 684 (10th Cir. 1975); *Capili v. Shott,* 620 F.2d 438 (4th Cir. 1980).

94. *Feldman v. Jackson Memorial Hosp.* 571 F. Supp. 1000 (S.D. Fla. 1983), *aff'd* 752 F.2d 647 (11th Cir.), *cert. den.* 105 S. Ct. 3504 (1985).
95. *See Associated General Contractors,* 459 U.S. 519, 538, 539 (1983).
96. 772 F.2d 1467 (9th Cir. 1985).
97. *Id.* at 1471 (emphasis added).
98. 466 U.S. 2 (1984).
99. *Nurse Midwifery Associates v. Hibbert,* 577 F. Supp. 1273 (D.Tenn. 1983).
100. *See* 48 FEDERAL REGISTER 27,089 (June 13, 1983) for the proposed consent agreement.
101. 719 F.2d 207 (7th Cir. 1983).
102. *Kelly, supra* note 28 at 218 & n. 143, citing an interview with plaintiff's counsel and *The Washington Post,* March 6, 1985, at A8, col. 5.
103. JCAH ACCREDITATION MANUAL FOR HOSPITALS 89 (1984).
104. *Id.*
105. *Id.* at 2.
106. *Id.* at 1.
107. *Id.* at 10.
108. *Id.*
109. Interview with Debbie Pedegra, R.N., M.S., certified psychiatric mental health clinical nurse specialist, May 29, 1986.
110. AMERICAN NURSES' ASSN., OBTAINING THIRD-PARTY REIMBURSEMENT: A NURSE'S GUIDE TO METHODS AND STRATEGIES, 1 (1984) (hereinafter cited as *ANA*).
111. *Id.*
112. 32 C.F.R. §199.12(c) (3) (iii) (d) (1) (1985).
113. *Id.* at (d) (1)-(2) (1983).
114. 32 C.F.R. §199.12(c) (3) (iii) (3) (1985).
115. Social Security Act, 42 U.S.C. §1395(x) (s) (2) (A) (1982).
116. 42 C.F.R. §440.60(a) (1984) (licensed practitioners generally).
117. 42 C.F.R. §440.165 (c), 441.21 (1985). Only maternity cycle services, including care during pregnancy, labor, birth, and up to 6 weeks postpartum are covered; interval gynecologist and family planning care are not reimbursed.
118. *See, e.g.,* S.D. CODIFIED LAWS ANN. §58-17-54 (Supp. 1984) (broad coverage for all licensed providers).
119. ALASKA STAT. §21.42.355 (1984).
120. MD. ANN. CODE art. 48A, §3545; 470-0 (1984); *id.* at §490A-1, A-2 (1985).
121. MD. ANN. CODE art. 48A, §354-S, 470-0 (Supp. 1985).
122. MD. ANN. CODE art. 48A, §470 (1983); *id.* at §470-0, 490A-1. A-2 (1985 Supp.).
123. MD. ANN. CODE. art. 48A, §3545, 470-0 (1984).
124. MD. ANN. CODE art. 48A §470M, 477R (1984).
125. *Id.*
126. MD. ANN. CODE art. 48A, §354N, 470M, 477R (1979) 490A-2 (1985).
127. MINN. STAT. §62a.15, subd. 3(a) (Supp. 1985).
128. *Kelly, supra* note 28, at 207.
129. CAL. INS. CODE §10176 (West Supp. 1986).
130. *See Kelly, supra* note 28, at 205 n.62, for citations to additional states that have either mandatory or optional benefit laws.
131. MD. ANN. CODE art. 48A §354-S, 470-0 (Supp. 1985).
132. MISS. CODE ANN. §83-41-213 (Supp. 1984).
133. *Kelly, supra* note 28, at 207.
134. M.E. SNYDER & C. LaBAR, ISSUES IN PROFESSIONAL NURSING PRACTICE: LEGAL AUTHORITY FOR PRACTICE 9 (1984).
135. *ANA, supra* note 110, at 7.
136. *Id.* at 8.
137. *Id.*

Additional Readings

AMERICAN NURSES' ASSN., OBTAINING THIRD-PARTY REIMBURSEMENT: A NURSE'S GUIDE TO METHODS AND STRATEGIES (1984).

Cohn, *Survey of Legislation on Third Party Reimbursement for Nurses,* 11 LAW, MEDICINE AND HEALTH CARE, 260 (1983).

FEDERAL TRADE COMMISSION, OFFICE OF POLICY PLANNING, ANTITRUST AND THE HEALTH PROFESSIONS (M. Pollard and R. Leibenluft, eds., 1981).

Greenlaw, *Sermchief v. Gonzales and the Debate of Advanced Nursing Practice Legislation,* 12 LAW, MEDICINE AND HEALTH CARE, 30 (February 1984).

Jenkins, *Exercising Nurse's Right to Fight for Clinical Privileges* 7 NURS. & HEALTH CARE 477 (November 1986).

Kelly, *Nurse Practitioner Challenges To The Orthodox Structure Of Health Care Delivery: Regulation And Restraints On Trade,* 11 AMERICAN JOURNAL OF LAW AND MEDICINE, 195 (1985).

M.E. SNYDER AND C. LaBAR, ISSUES IN PROFESSIONAL NURSING PRACTICE: LEGAL AUTHORITY FOR PRACTICE (1984).

Chapter 30

Employment claims

Katherine J. Pohlman

A review of the nursing and legal literature reveals that most focuses on nursing liability and professional negligence. Few authors focus on issues that involve the nurse as plaintiff, instead outlining areas of practice that expose the nurse to liability and the potential role of defendant. This phenomenon relates to the historically subordinate role of the nurse in the health care system. Despite the fact that nurses comprise the largest labor force within the health care delivery system, the profession is generally underrepresented in the decision-making and power-wielding levels of health care administration. However, the trend is changing.

Today, the nursing profession assumes more responsibility for decision making and exerts more influence on the delivery of health care. Individual nurses are asserting themselves and taking the initiative to protect their legal rights. In employment claim cases, the nurse is often the allegedly injured party, the plaintiff in the legal proceedings. The employment area presents many situations in which a nurse recognizes a wrong and files suit to enforce a freedom or right. Because many nurses are employees at will, by far the most frequent scenario is one which pits the nurse against the present or former employer.

The purpose of this chapter is to provide sufficient knowledge to enable a nurse to identify potential employment claims. The chapter reviews each employment claim. After identifying possible violations, a nurse should seek legal counsel before taking any further action. The box on pp. 488-489 outlines hypothetical fact situations and identifies in each the potential claim or claims available, the possible remedies, and the sources of protection, whether statutory or based on common law doctrines. Additional examples and cases appear throughout the chapter.

Express contracts

A nurse may enter into an express, written contract which binds her or him to deliver identified services for a specified period of time. Nursing faculty usually are under individual contracts. Collective express contracts are discussed below and in Chapter 31 on collective bargaining. Express contract terms dictate the mutually agreed upon duties and rights of each party. Where a nurse is a party to a contract and the other party breaches (fails to live up to the agreement), the nurse should seek legal counsel to assist in obtaining relief.

Interviewing and negotiating successfully in the nursing job market, according to one author, should include gathering facts, focusing on strengths, negotiating a realistic salary, looking for fringes and perks, choosing the correct timing, and being assertive, not apologetic.[1]

The conditions and terms of employment are often identified and formed during the hiring process. Questions during the interview often focus on experience, skills, aptitude, personality, attitude, and education. There are certain subjects which should not be included in an interview, including religion, age, sex and marital

SAMPLE EMPLOYMENT CLAIM SITUATIONS, POSSIBLE REMEDIES, AND NURSE'S RIGHTS

Situation 1

Terminated for refusing to participate in elective abortion where another staff member was available to assist (refusal based on religious grounds)

Issue: Wrongful discharge
Possible remedies: Reinstatement, back wages, damages
Rights: First Amendment, freedom of religion

Situation 2

Terminated for refusing to comply with supervisor's directive to administer medications without a physician's order

Issue: Wrongful discharge
Possible remedies: Reinstatement, back wages, damages
Rights: Public policy exception to the employment at will doctrine—refusal to perform illegal act

Situation 3

Terminated for reporting physician who administered experimental drugs without patient's consent or approved research protocol

Issue: Wrongful discharge
Possible remedies: Reinstatement, back wages, damages
Rights: Whistleblower exception to the employment at will doctrine—report of illegality (Federal Drug Administration regulates investigational drugs; American Nurses' Association Code for Nurses, Code of Ethics, supports reporting.)

Situation 4

Terminated for complying with summons for jury duty
Issue: Wrongful discharge
Possible remedies: Reinstatement, back wages, damages
Rights: Public policy exception to the employment at will doctrine—compliance with federal or state statutes

Situation 5

Denied annual cost-of-living raise for refusal to sign performance evaluation

Issue: Breach of implied contract
Possible remedies: Specific performance, retroactive wages
Rights: Breach of implied contract of good faith and fair dealing—support of claim from employee handbook, policy of annual raises

Situation 6

Terminated for reporting child abuse despite supervisor's directive not to report

Issue: Wrongful termination
Possible remedies: Reinstatement, back wages, damages
Rights: Whistleblower exception to employment at will doctrine—mandatory report of child abuse statute applicable to nurse

Situation 7

School nurse protected by express written contract terminated for refusal to submit to sexual advances by principal

Issue: Breach of contract, discrimination on the basis of sex, sexual harassment
Possible remedies: Reinstatement, damages, back wages
Rights: Contract exception to employment at will—express written contract; Title VII, Civil Rights Act of 1964

Situation 8

Pregnant nurse employee denied transfer that was then granted to male co-worker

Issue: Discrimination on the basis of sex, pregnancy
Possible remedies: Damages, back wages, injunctive relief
Rights: Title VII, Pregnancy Amendment, Civil Rights Act of 1964

Situation 9

Sixty-three–year–old nurse employee terminated after filing suit against employer who awarded promotion to younger, less-qualified co-worker

Issue: Wrongful termination, discrimination on the basis of age
Possible remedies: Reinstatement, back wages, damages, specific performance
Rights: Public policy exception to employment at will, age discrimination, Employment Act

Situation 10

Nurse employee suffered spontaneous abortion from exposure to ETO while employed in operating room

Issue: Tort—employer negligence for failure to disclose exposure and risks, worker's compensation
Possible remedies: Damages
Rights: Worker's compensation, right-to-know law

SAMPLE EMPLOYMENT CLAIM SITUATIONS, POSSIBLE REMEDIES, AND NURSE'S RIGHTS—cont'd

Situation 11

Nurse-employee permanently disabled after assault in employee parking lot—denied worker's compensation
Issue: Tort—employer negligence for failure to provide adequate security, worker's compensation
Possible remedies: Damages, disability
Rights: Worker's compensation

Situation 12

Former employer divulged inaccurate information about circumstances surrounding termination of nurse when contacted for reference by prospective employer
Issue: Violation of right of privacy, defamation
Possible remedies: Damages
Rights: Common law doctrine of defamation

Situation 13

Terminated for cohabitation with opposite sex co-worker
Issue: Wrongful termination, violation of right of privacy
Possible remedies: Reinstatement, back wages, damages
Rights: Constitutional right of privacy

Situation 14

Hispanic, qualified nurse employee denied promotion which was then granted to less-senior, less-qualified co-worker
Issue: Wrongful termination, discrimination on the basis of race, ethnic origin
Possible remedies: Reinstatement, back wages, damages
Rights: Contract exception to employment at will doctrine—implies contract of good faith, fair dealing; Title VII, Civil Rights Act of 1964

or family status, physical handicaps, criminal arrest record, and financial affairs. More about this area will be discussed later in the chapter.

Employment at will

Prior to the advanced role, a nurse rarely delivered services under a written, express contractual agreement. Although more nurses today enjoy this kind of protection, either independently or through union representation, the majority are still employees at will. The general rule in the American legal system presumes that employment for an indefinite period of time is "employment at will." Under this rule either the employee or employer can terminate the employment relationship without notice or cause. Recognizing that such equity often operates in theory only, state and federal statutes, as well as judicial opinions have developed exceptions to the rule in many jurisdictions. Consequently, in many situations where a nurse is an employee at will, an employer may terminate the nurse only for cause and after notice has been given.

Statutes and judicial decisions protecting employees terminated without notice or cause rely on various legal theories: public policy, contract, and tort. The later has been defined in other chapters. Each theory, as it applies to employment claims, is discussed below.

PUBLIC POLICY THEORY

Courts relying on public policy to support a finding that an employee was wrongfully terminated have found expressions of such policy in several sources, such as state law and professional codes of ethics. State courts vary in their willingness to recognize public policy statements from sources such as ethical codes. Courts are more likely to grant recovery to a nurse plaintiff where the plaintiff has refused to violate a state or federal law.

For example, a New Jersey physician, employed at will performing pharmaceutical research, refused to continue researching an antidiarrheal drug containing saccharin.[2] After being forced to resign, she filed suit, arguing that because of the questionable safety of saccharin, the research was unethical. She argued that the research violated state and federal regulatory law and the Hippocratic Oath, the American Medical Association's Standards of Ethics. The court denied her claim, relying on the controversial nature of saccharin, as opposed to its specific dangerousness. The court ruled that the Hippocratic Oath did not provide a clear mandate of public policy against experimentation. However, a strong dissent argued that other codes of medical ethics proscribe experimentation when a physician perceives an unreasonable threat to human health. "The integrity of codes of professional conduct . . . deserves judicial protection from undue economic pressure. Employers are a potential source of this pressure, for they can provide or withhold . . . job security and the means of enhancing a professional's reputation."[3]

In a similar case, a Colorado court reached the same result.[4] A head nurse refused to reduce her staff's overtime requests, maintaining that a reduction would jeopardize the health of the patients. In her suit for wrongful discharge, she relied on the preamble to the Colorado Nurse Practice Act. The court refused to accept the preamble as public policy, finding instead that it merely established a general standard of conduct.

Courts more often recognize a public policy exception to the at will doctrine that relies on an employee's refusal to perform an illegal act. For example, despite an x-ray technician's employment at will status, a New Jersey court allowed her to sue for breach of contract when she was terminated for refusing to perform a catheterization.[5] According to New Jersey law, only licensed nurses or medical doctors were authorized to perform the procedure. The court found the justification for limiting an employer's authority in that context more compelling than where discharge followed an employee's exercise of a statutory right or performance of a public obligation. Courts also consistently apply the public policy exception to order compensation for employees fired for complying with state or federal law.[6] For example, an employer cannot terminate a nurse because she responds to a summons for jury duty.

In another case a nurse anesthetist brought an action against a university hospital, chief nurse, and two physicians for wrongful discharge and wrongful interference with her employment contract.[7] The North Carolina court held that the hospital discharged the nurse in retaliation for her refusal to testify falsely or incompletely at a deposition for a medical malpractice trial. The court held that even if the contract was terminable at will, retaliation for telling the full truth in a deposition was against public policy.

Many states have codified another public policy exception to the at will doctrine. Referred to as "whistleblower" statutes, this protective legislation provides recourse for wrongful discharge following disclosure of alleged illegality. Such statutes rely on the theory that whistleblowing is in the public interest.

One such case involved a psychiatric head nurse terminated for providing information to a state agency, the Guardianship and Advocacy Commission, regarding a patient confined in the state hospital.[8] The nurse also testified on behalf of the patient at his commitment hearing. The hospital argued that it had discharged the nurse for her failure to support hospital programs, mistreatment of patients, insubordination, disruptive insults to superiors, and failure to mitigate damages by acceptance of a demotion. State legislation protected "reporters," including "employees of service providers." The court found that the hospital wrongfully discharged the nurse because she had provided information to the state agency. Finding the nurse's contract was one for personal services, the appeals court reversed the lower court's order to reinstate the nurse. The appeals court sent the case back to the lower court for a determination of the amount and type of damages (compensatory, punitive, or mitigating damages) due the nurse.

Much state legislation parallels federal statutory protection against wrongful discharge or retaliatory termination. Rather than enact general "just cause" protection, the federal and state statutes extend protection for special categories of claims or to particular classes of employees. Title VII of the Civil Rights Act of 1964 is the most well-known of the federal statutes that bar discrimination in the employment area.[9] Protection under Title VII is discussed in greater depth later in this chapter.

While individuals generally have a right to seek work, employers have the limited right to make employment decisions and place conditions on employment. When making employment decisions, employers must not discriminate against protected groups or participate in any proscribed behavior. In limited circumstances, employer defenses, such as business necessity or bona fide occupational qualification, may preclude liability for otherwise proscribed action. These also will be discussed later.

TORT AND CONTRACT THEORIES

A nurse must elect whether to base a wrongful termination claim on tort or contract theories of law. While the selection of theory is the attorney's responsibility, the nurse should know that the choice is important because the theories differ in significant respects. Actions based in tort benefit from a longer statute of limitations and may enable the nurse plaintiff to recover punitive damages. Even where no formal contract exists, some courts base recovery on employee contractual rights implied from sources such as oral assertions, employee handbooks, or continuing service.

In *Cleary* a California court defined a limitation on arbitrary or wrongful discharge of an employee based on two factors: length of service and the employer's express policy of dealing fairly with employees.[10] The court held that the existence of specific procedures for handling employee disputes revealed the employer's acceptance of responsibility to use good faith and fair dealing with respect to employees.

The same court expanded the *Cleary* principle further in *Pugh*.[11] Relying on the totality of the parties' relationships, the court found an implied promise to avoid arbitrary discharge. Those circumstances involved employer policies and assurances, commendations and promotions, absence of any direct employee criticism, and extended length of service by the employee. Proof of similar circumstances in a nurse's employment relationship supports a suit for wrongful termination.

Once an implied contract is found, courts enforce an implied covenant of good faith and fair dealing and provide the employee with protection similar to that provided by an explicit contract. In a Massachusetts case the employee alleged that his employer had discharged him to avoid awarding a commission due on a $5 million sale.[12] The court found that the employer had violated an implied covenant of good faith and fair dealing in a written employment contract that allowed discharge without cause.

According to a Montana court, probationary status does not prevent application of the implied covenant of good faith and fair dealing.[13] In that case, the employer had allowed the employee respiratory therapist to join the group insurance plan, a benefit available only to permanent staff. The court found that the employer's dismissal of the employee breached the implied covenant. An Arizona court reviewed the firing of a director of nursing after she sought a transfer back to a previously held nursing supervisor position.[14] The court held that the personnel manual can become terms of an employment contract and can limit an employer's ability to discharge employees.

Other torts defined elsewhere in this book arise in the nurse's employment setting. Discussed below, those torts include fraud, defamation and intentional infliction of emotional distress, and violations of both the right to privacy and confidentiality.

The nurse and labor relations

Two federal statutes apply to nurses in their employment situations: The National Labor Relations Act (NLRA) and The Federal Labor Standards Act (FLSA).[15] The following discussion presents an overview of both.

NATIONAL LABOR RELATIONS ACT

The National Labor Relations Act (NLRA) regulates union activities and collective bargaining. Chapter 31 discusses in detail the NLRA's application to nurse union members. The act also provides to all employees, whether union members or not, the right to engage in ''other concerted activities for the purpose of . . . mutual aid or protection.''[16] The NLRA prohibits an employer from retaliating against an employee who acts to further statutory rights or benefit fellow employees. The act also protects an employee acting solely on the behalf of other employees. The National Labor Relations Board (NLRB) hears claims brought under the NLRA. As in many areas governed by administrative agencies like the NLRB, the employee retains the right to review by a court.

The NLRB has the authority to order reinstatement of an employee wrongfully terminated, as it did in *Villa Care*.[17] Two nonunion nurses aides left their assigned workplace to report poor working conditions and request additional compensation. Both were subsequently discharged for refusing to work under inadequate staffing conditions. In its reinstatement decision, the NLRB found the walkout qualified for protection as ''concerted action.''

Just as the courts rely on public policy statements applying the at will exception, the NLRB considers various standards in determining whether the employee was acting ''for the purpose of mutual aid or protection.''[18] In another case the NLRB considered the American Nurses' Association (ANA) CODE FOR NURSES in its decision to order reinstatement.[19] A head nurse was fired for participating in preparing for the Joint Commission on Accreditation of Hospitals a report that documented inadequate patient care and working conditions. The court noted that the employer required that the nurse comply with the ANA CODE, which mandated that she act to improve standards of care and join with others to meet public health needs. Despite the fact that the report implemented the CODE in a manner outside the employee-employer relationship, the NLRB ordered the nurse reinstated.

Although the court ultimately found against the nurse, a New Jersey court considered the American Nurses' Association CODE FOR NURSES in its analysis of the public policy doctrine.[20] Discharged for her refusal to dialyze a terminally ill renal patient, the nurse relied on the ANA CODE to support her decision based on ''moral, medical and philosophical objections.''[21] The court ruled that although the CODE language supported appropriately noticed refusal, the right to refuse benefited the individual nurse rather than the public at large. The court continued its analysis, finding that even if the CODE constituted public policy, the state's interest in the preservation of life outweighs the nurse's right to refuse. The court held that the identification of public policy is a question of fact decided by the jury. Despite the unfavorable ruling, the court's willingness to consider the CODE leaves the door open for future cases.

The NLRB also protects the right of employees to bargain collectively, an area of increasing importance to nurses. The specifics of collective bargaining are discussed in Chapter 31 and are briefly mentioned here only as the basis of an employment claim. A 1974 NLRA amendment eliminated the nonprofit hospital exemption, granting hospital employees the right to unionize or bargain collectively.[22] Government hospitals remain exempt from the NLRA, as do specific categories of employees, including independent contractors, managerial employees, supervisors, and certain students.[23]

Once a majority of employees elect a bargaining representative or select a representative union, the NLRB requires that the employer engage in negotiations. The NLRB addressed the issue of bargaining units in health care facilities and concluded that groups of nurses within a facility cannot organize separately if they have a community of interests.[24] The federal court rejected that standard and found instead that the standard should allow separate organization only for those with disparate interests.[25]

The NLRA provides that with the employer's consent a union may require membership as a condition of employment. Some state courts interpret that language to mean employees must pay union dues but are not actually required to join the union. Others adopt an approach inconsistent with the NLRA. Codified in right to work laws, that approach prohibits unions and employers from requiring union membership or union dues as a condition of employment.[26]

The NLRA also protects the employee from unfair labor practices by the employer or union and defines those practices in detail. In one case, the court found unfair labor practices in management domination of a labor organization because the hospital ran the election and wrote the employee advisory committee bylaws.[27]

FEDERAL LABOR STANDARDS ACT

An additional source of protection for employee nurses is the federal legislation regulating conditions such as wages, overtime, and fringe benefits. Although most states have individual regulatory legislation, the Federal Labor Standards Act (FLSA) controls where state standards are lower or where no state statute exists.[28] The FLSA establishes employment requirements relating to minimum wage, overtime compensation, child labor, and equal pay. The Equal Pay Act of 1963 amended the FLSA and is discussed later in this chapter.[29] Although the FLSA covers all employees engaged in interstate commerce, it does exclude specific categories of workers. The exclusion for service establishment employees does not exempt hospital or nursing home employees.[30] The FLSA minimum wage and overtime compensation requirements therefore apply to many staff nurses. Salaried nurse management personnel fall within another FLSA exemption.

As with most federal legislation, a government agency administers the FLSA. The Wage and Hour Division of the Department of Labor investigates complaints and recommends changes in employment practices where necessary to obtain compliance. In most cases, an employee recovers back wages, the usual remedy, directly from an employer under supervision of the Wage and Hour Division. In other cases, the employee or the Department of Labor must seek relief in court.

Civil Rights Act of 1964

Other equal employment opportunity laws protect special categories of employees from discrimination based on individual characteristics. Title VII of the 1964 Civil Rights Act provides the most extensive protection. Title VII bars discrimination on the basis of race, color, religion, sex, national origin, and pregnancy, the latter added by a 1978 amendment.[31] Unlike the NLRA, which excludes certain classes of employees, Title VII covers virtually all ''persons,'' from hourly employees to executives.[32] Title VII applies to most employers and all aspects of employment, hiring to firing. One of the act's rare exceptions allows religious institutions to consider religion in employment decisions.[33] Two conditions, if present, allow the employer to discriminate: the business necessity and bona fide occupational qualification. These will be discussed later.

EQUAL EMPLOYMENT OPPORTUNITY COMMISSION

Created specifically to enforce Title VII, the Equal Employment Opportunity Commission (EEOC) investigates complaints and resolves violations through conciliation or court action, if required. There is a 180-day time limit within which one must file an EEOC complaint. If EEOC administrative remedies are unsatisfactory, a private individual may also file a lawsuit.

In certain circumstances, both avenues may be necessary to achieve a full remedy. In a race discrimination case, a federal appellate court found that litigation not only removed the barrier to job eligibility, but also secured for the plaintiff employee the desired position and back pay.[34] In that case, the State of Virginia refused to allow a black public health nurse to apply for a level C job, claiming the job required graduation from a nursing program accredited by the National League for Nursing. When the nurse filed suit in federal court, the State of Virginia claimed that the nurse's suit was unnecessary and frivolous because the state had removed the controversial job requirement after the nurse's EEOC complaint a year earlier. Finding that the state had refused to settle until the nurse filed suit, the court rejected the state's argument and awarded attorney's fees to the nurse.

However, as briefly mentioned earlier in this chapter, under specific circumstances an employer can consider or even require certain characteristics in employment decisions. These characteristics may be exempt from Title VII protection as "bona fide occupational qualifications" (BFOQ). For example, one court ruled that the ability to communicate in English constituted a bona fide occupational qualification for employment in a complex medical center and refused to find discrimination on the basis of national origin.[35] In a case brought by a male nurse, the court reached an opposite result. In *Backus* the court allowed the hospital to rely on patient preference to employ only female nurses in the obstetric department.[36] In its decision the court relied on the privacy rights of the patient and found that sex was a BFOQ. However, a higher federal court vacated the decision as moot when the male nurse voluntarily resigned from his position. The precedential value of this decision remains a question.

SEXUAL HARASSMENT

Sexual harassment by employers concerns many nurses. Prior to 1980, Title VII did not clearly include sexual harassment as discrimination on the basis of sex. Arguments rejecting protection against sexual harassment contended that adverse treatment of an employee because of her/his refusal to consent to sexual advances was not discrimination on the basis of gender. A legal fiction defined the two groups as those subjected to sexual advances and those who were not, maintaining neither group was by definition male or female.

While that categorization may be accurate, victims of discrimination no longer need rely on such twisted logic for protection. In 1980 the EEOC adopted guidelines that broadly define sexual harassment.[37] Since that time, the courts more readily impose liability on employers for behavior previously tolerated. The EEOC guidelines address sexual harassment that causes concrete economic detriment to the plaintiff or that creates an unproductive or offensive atmosphere in the workplace.

The guidelines identify and prohibit three separate types of harassment and provide the respective employer liability for each. The three categories include any conduct:

1. Where submission to sexual advances is implicitly or explicitly considered a condition of employment
2. Where submission is used as a basis for employment decisions
3. That effectively interferes with an employee's job performance, even if it merely creates an intimidating, offensive, or hostile atmosphere.[38]

The employer's liability parallels the continuum of harassment ranging from strict liability to liability conditioned on the employer's knowledge of the harassment. The guidelines also protect any employee denied employment advantages in favor of an employee that has submitted to sexual advances. In specifically defined circumstances, the guidelines impose liability on an employer for conduct of nonemployees, such as clients or customers.

In some cases affecting employment status courts use the *respondeat superior* theory to impose liability even when an employer has no knowledge of one employee's sexual harassment of another. In one case, the court held an employer liable for a supervisor's improper discharge of an employee, despite the employer's written policy prohibiting sexual harassment.[39] Even though the employee failed to utilize the grievance procedure to provide notice to the employer, the court applied the *respondeat superior* theory to impose liability.

Claims based on conduct that interferes with work performance require a greater showing to succeed. The court denied an employee's claim of sexual harassment in one case because the employee failed to demonstrate a sufficient relationship between her refusal of sexual advances and termination of her employment.[40]

Courts provide several types of relief for a nurse victimized by sexual harassment. Injunctive relief orders an employer to discontinue the activity or to take steps to prevent harassment by nonemployees. For employees terminated for refusal to submit to sexual harassment, a court awards back wages and/or reinstatement. Many states provide remedies under statutes that incorporate the federal legislation or provide substantially similar protection. Often state remedies are broader than federal[41]; some include punitive and/or compensatory damages.[42] Employees covered by a union contract that prohibits sexual harassment may seek relief through a grievance procedure, but that relief usually precludes recovery under federal or state statutes.

Other equal employment opportunity laws

A number of other statutes provide protection to special classes of individuals. Also enforced by the EEOC, the Age Discrimination in Employment Act prohibits discrimination against employees or applicants between the ages of 40 and 70 years.[43]

A *prima facie* case of age discrimination can be made out in at least three ways:

1. The plaintiff may produce evidence proving that he or she was a member of the protected group, he or she was discharged and replaced with a person outside the protected group, and he or she was qualified to do the job.
2. The plaintiff can show direct evidence of discriminatory intent.
3. The plaintiff can establish by statistical proof a pattern of discrimination.[44]

One case involved a 62-year-old day-shift nurse supervisor who alleged the hospital discharged her because of her age.[45] In this case the hospital administrator expressed surprise at the longevity of staff members, indicated the hospital needed "new blood," stated that the supervisor's "advanced age" caused her stress, failed to investigate fully the underlying incident, and stated he intended to recruit younger doctors and nurses. The court held that there was sufficient evidence to present questions to the jury. The case was reversed and remanded for trial.

Other employment issue statutes include the Labor Department's Office of Federal Contract Compliance Programs which enforces Section 503 of the 1973 Rehabilitation Act[46] and the 1972 and 1974 Vietnam Veterans Readjustment Assistance Acts.[47] Those acts require government contractors to employ and promote qualified handicapped persons and qualified veterans, respectively. Section 504 of the 1973 Rehabilitation Act prohibits discrimination against handicapped persons by entities that receive federal financial assistance.[48]

The U.S. Department of Health and Human Services (HHS) enforces Section 504 of the 1973 Rehabilitation Act as applied to hospitals. While receipt of Medicare and Medicaid funds usually establishes the applicability of Section 504 to hospital services, courts split on the applicability to employment decisions of those facilities. Most courts require receipt of federal funds specifically for employment before applying Section 504.[49] At least one court shares the HHS position and applies Section 504 based solely on receipt of general federal funds.[50]

The Equal Pay Act of 1963 (EPA),[51] which amended the FLSA discussed before, guarantees equal pay to male and female employees doing equal work. The act defines equal work as that which requires equal skill, effort, and responsibility and is performed under similar working conditions.[52] Due to the difficulty of demonstrating equality in those areas, the EPA is of limited effectiveness for nurses in addressing wage disparities between males and females. The courts presently utilize a case by case approach to determine equality of employment.

Comparable worth doctrine and nursing

The doctrine of comparable worth is part of the larger pay equity issue. Developed as a judicial doctrine to transcend the limitations of the equal work requirement of the EPA, comparable worth involves similar limitations because of the lack of any universal standard to measure the relative worth of jobs. Although a potential source of valuable protection for nurses, it has not been widely developed or accepted by courts.

In the 1980 landmark case of *Washington v. Gunther*[53] the Supreme Court ruled that employees may bring claims of sex-based wage discrimination under Title VII, as well as under the Equal Pay Act. That decision decreases an employee's burden by allowing suit for wage discrimination without satisfying the EPA, which specifically requires that members of the opposite sex hold equal, but higher paying jobs. In *Gunther* a wage survey determined the pay rates of prison guards and matrons. The plaintiff employees offered proof that males received 100% of those rates while females received 70%. The court found that, if substantiated, the facts supported a finding of intentional wage discrimination under Title VII. The court relied instead on the broad remedial purposes of Title VII to allow relief to victims of intentional discrimination not necessarily proscribed by the EPA.

Although the court based its decision on alternative grounds, the comparable worth issue involved was the type known as "common." The discrimination involved workers of one sex paid less than workers of the opposite sex in the same general job classification. "Common comparable worth'' contrasts with the ''pure'' type which involves workers in dissimilar job categories performing work of comparable worth to the employer. Brought by nurses, the *Lemmons* case involved the ''pure'' type of case.[54] In this case the court held that city nurses paid comparably to noncity nurses, but less than other city employees, were not entitled to relief under Title VII. The nurses failed to offer direct proof of intentional discrimination, a requirement after *Gunther*.

The EEOC has not yet provided comparable worth guidelines, as it did for sexual harassment, but it has outlined procedures for its specialists to follow when processing comparable worth cases. Many states have legislation that prohibits unequal compensation for jobs of comparable worth, either as an unfair labor practice or as independently discriminatory.[55]

However, similar barriers confront litigation under state statutes and federal legislation. Brought under a Washington statute that prohibits as unfair labor practice any discrimination by an employer on the basis of sex, the nurse plaintiffs in that case lost because they failed to prove discriminatory intent. In its ruling that the defendant had merely adopted market wages, the court reasoned that although past discrimination by other employers had influenced the defendant's pay scales that was insufficient to support the plaintiff's claim.[56] In a case based on constitutional rights and federal legislative protection, the defendant rebutted the employee's claim that they held sex-segregated job classifications and were paid less than male employees with jobs of similar skill, effort, and responsibility. Because the defendant showed the higher salaries were necessary to retain the male employees, the court refused to find discriminatory intent by the defendant's employer.

The future of the comparable worth doctrine remains uncertain. On April 11, 1985, the U.S. Civil Rights Commission voted to reject the concept of comparable worth.[57] Although advisory in nature, that opinion threatens the likelihood that comparable worth will ever gain acceptance equal to other protections against discrimination.

Issues for nurses in the workplace

In certain circumstances multiple statutes mandate inconsistent employer action, placing an employee's various rights in conflict. Tension between general workplace safety and individual worker health results when the Occupational Safety and Health Act (OSHA)[58] and Title VII require different results, as in protection of the pregnant worker. Title VII prohibits discrimination ''because of or on the basis of pregnancy, childbirth, or related medical conditions.''[59] In addition to proscribing employment decisions on the basis of pregnancy, the legislation protects specific employee benefits, such as insurance coverage, transfer, maternity leave, seniority, promotion, and reinstatement.[60]

Discussed in greater depth in Chapters 16 and 33, the Occupational Safety and Health Act orders the employer to provide a ''place of employment . . . free from recognized hazards that are causing or likely to cause death or serious physical harm to his employees.''[61] The Occupational Safety and Health Administration of the Department of Labor enforces the OSHA. In some states cooperative statutes or right to know laws require disclosure of hazards in the workplace.[62] Employers often utilize pre-employment screening to identify employees likely to be at risk in the particular workplace. If based on protected characteristics, selective screening violates Section 504 of the 1973 Rehabilitation Act and Title VII.

An employer's efforts to comply with OSHA may discriminate against both male and female employees. Exclusion of females from contact with fetotoxins fails to protect males from similar injury to reproductive capacity. In such cases, the courts consistently reject categorical exclusion of females as violative of a female's right to assume the risk of injury whenever men possess the right to choose.[63] To exclude employees of a particular sex from a job category, an employer must demonstrate that sex is a bona fide occupational qualification (BFOQ), as discussed earlier.[64] Courts construe the BFOQ narrowly, focusing on the worker's ability to perform the job, rather than on gender generalizations[65] or potential injury to a fetus.[66]

Worker's Compensation Act

Virtually all states, as well as the federal government, provide benefits to a nurse employee injured as a result of employment. Although statutes vary, most fall into one of two categories. One type of statute compensates only for injuries that result from a specific incident or accident. Another compensates for injuries that result from continuous trauma or exposure in the workplace.[67]

All states have a department of industrial relations, a worker's compensation appeals board, or some similar agency responsible for implementing worker's compensation legislation. Procedures for filing a claim vary accordingly. Enforced by the U.S. Department of Labor, the Federal Compensation Act protects federal employees injured in the course of employment.[68] Worker's compensation statutes also protect a nurse terminated for declining job performance caused by work-related injuries.[69] These laws are also discussed in Chapter 16.

Unemployment compensation

Under certain circumstances a nurse qualifies for unemployment benefits. Like worker's compensation, each state administers its own unemployment compensation program. Unlike worker's compensation or disability programs, an individual eligible for unemployment compensation must be able to work. Funded by a special tax on employers, the programs provide weekly benefits to those unemployed through no fault of their own. Unemployment compensation programs cover almost all employers except independent contractors, some newspaper and magazine vendors, and certain individuals employed by family members.

Unemployment compensation programs rarely award benefits to workers fired for misconduct or those that resign voluntarily. Cases interpreting misconduct vary widely. One court found misconduct where a nursing assistant was fired for violating a hospital rule against smoking in a patient's room.[70] Another court found a good faith error rather than misconduct when a nurse administered medications by intravenous push instead of intravenous drip.[71]

Each state requires that applicants satisfy specific requirements to qualify for compensation. Most require a minimum period of employment or minimum amount of earned wages prior to the time the individual becomes unemployed. The amount of wages earned during employment determines the level of unemployment benefits. Some states grant prorated benefits to those partially unemployed. Once a worker qualifies for benefits, most programs require specific job-seeking efforts to avoid disqualification and termination of benefits. Although a state often readjusts the amount according to benefits available under a different state's program, a worker's benefits continue even after relocation. Benefits usually continue for 26 weeks, at which time a worker must requalify for extended benefits under the state program or the special federal benefits sometimes available during periods of particularly high unemployment.

Nursing employment and right to privacy

Business necessity often affects an individual's legal rights in the employment setting. Rights sometimes limited in the workplace include:

1. First Amendment right to freedom of speech and religion
2. Fourth Amendment right to freedom from unreasonable search and seizure
3. Fifth Amendment right to freedom from self-incrimination

To be legal, limitations must be reasonably related to the employment purpose.

Although not expressly guaranteed by the U.S. Constitution, the Supreme Court recognized an independent constitutional right to privacy through interpretation of the three amendments listed above and the Third and Ninth Amendments.[72] Of particular significance to nurses in the employment context, that right to privacy guarantees freedom from unwarranted intrusions by others. Advanced electronic technology and increased social concern combine to make privacy interests in the workplace a complex issue. Common abuses of employee privacy fall into three categories:

1. Intrusive data gathering
2. Unfair use of information in employment decision making
3. Breach of confidentiality by release of protected data

Various state and federal statutes protect those privacy interests, and in some circumstances, additional constitutional safeguards apply.

Although a nurse may be most aware of these violations when applying for a position, information gathering violates an employee's privacy in various ways throughout the employment relationship. Intrusive methods of solicitation include personality and polygraph tests, which deny a worker the ability to control the release of information. Solicitation of specific types of information intrude into protected areas such as political and social activities, family relations, medical and psychiatric history, criminal and arrest background, or credit history. Unless the information relates to a recognized BFOQ, the solicitation of personal information violates Title VII.

Employer inquiries without the necessary employee consent violate privacy interests, perhaps even when an employee signs a blanket authorization required by the employer attempting to contact former employers, credit agencies, educational institutions, medical facilities, or social acquaintances. In addition to a claim against the employer for invasion of privacy, a nurse employee may have a claim against a third party for releasing information without consent. Itself a violation, intrusiveness causes greater harm when used in employment decisions or disseminated to unauthorized parties.

Misuse of information occurs whenever unauthorized or authorized information is used as the basis for an

NURSING EMPLOYMENT: SOURCES OF FEDERAL ASSISTANCE*

National Labor Relations Act:	National Labor Relations Board 1717 Pennsylvania Avenue, N.W. Washington, DC 20570 202-632-4950
Fair Labor Standards Act:	Department of Labor Wage and Hour Division 200 Constitution Avenue, N.W. Washington, DC 20210 202-523-8305
1964 Civil Rights Act:	Equal Employment Opportunity Commission 2401 E Street, N.W. Washington, DC 20507 202-634-6922
Age Discrimination in Employment Act:	Equal Employment Opportunity Commission (same as above)
1973 Rehabilitation Act, Section 503:	Department of Labor Office of Federal Contract Compliance Program 200 Constitution Avenue, N.W. Washington, DC 20210 202-523-9475
1974 Vietnam Veterans Readjustment Act:	Department of Labor Office of Federal Contract Compliance Program (same as above)
1973 Rehabilitation Act, Section 504:	Department of Health and Human Services 200 Independence Avenue, S.W. Washington, DC 20201 202-245-6296
Equal Pay Act of 1963:	Equal Employment Opportunity Commission 2401 E Street, N.W. Washington, DC 20210 202-523-8305
Occupational Safety & Health Act:	Department of Labor Occupational Safety and Health Administration 200 Constitution Avenue, N.W. Washington, DC 20210 202-523-9361
Federal Compensation Act:	Department of Labor 200 Constitution Avenue, N.W. Washington, DC 20210 202-523-7316
Federal Privacy Act of 1974:	United States Federal District Court (Location varies with jurisdiction)
Fair Credit Reporting Act, Federal Antitrust Laws, Federal Trade Commission Act:	Federal Trade Commission 6th St. and Pennsylvania Ave., N.W. Washington, D.C. 20580 202-523-3830

*Federal Government Locator (telephone, 202-655-4000).

adverse employment decision or is used in a manner to which the employee did not consent. Initial violations of privacy often lead to discrimination claims, discussed earlier in this chapter. Discrimination on the basis of personal information, such as credit or medical history, most often occurs at the application stage but exists in various forms throughout the employment relationship. Misuse of personnel file data, often generated during the provision of employee fringe benefits, constitutes a privacy violation when used collaterally as a basis for employment decisions. The harm inherent in any misuse multiplies when information is inaccurate.

Breach of confidentiality occurs when an employer discloses employee information to a third party without notice to or consent of the employee. Because it causes economic or personal harm to the employee, this abuse of privacy constitutes a significant violation, as in disclosures to credit agencies. When employment purposes require specific disclosures, statutory or employer policies should provide procedural safeguards.

Although violation of the right to privacy is itself a basis for a lawsuit, defamation may be the proper basis if the disclosure is inaccurate and dissemination to a third party causes harm to the employee's reputation. In some circumstances, a claim for defamation exists without a violation of the right to privacy. Defamation occurs when false or malicious statements communicated to a third party cause injury to an employee's fame, character, or reputation. This tort consists of two separate claims, slander for oral communication and libel for written communication. See Chapter 5 for more information.

Prospective employment inquiries and unfavorable performance evaluations carry the greatest potential for defamation by employers. Employer policies often outline specific procedural guarantees associated with performance evaluations. Internal grievance procedures usually provide a mechanism for appeal or remedy where an employer fails to comply with those provisions or where an employee objects to the contents of an evaluation. In certain circumstances an employee's claim constitutes a violation of one or more of the legal rights discussed in this chapter.

Heavily regulated by both state and federal legislation, protection of records and release of information safeguards an employee's privacy interest. The Federal Privacy Act of 1974 limits the federal government's acquisition of information about an individual to that which is "relevant and necessary to accomplish a purpose of the agency required to be accomplished by statute or by executive order of the President."[73]

Enacted to make government-held information public, the Freedom of Information Act (FOIA) seems in theory to conflict with the Privacy Act.[74] Although the statutes present a policy tension between dissemination and protection of information, in practice they work reasonably well. The Privacy Act allows government agencies to disclose information without an employee's consent if FOIA requires disclosure. The act also requires federal agencies to disclose information in an employee's personal record to that employee. Because of the power of the government as an employer, public sector employees enjoy greater protection in this area. In some cases, collective bargaining agreements or employer policies provide private employees with a right of access to employment records. Many state statutes and constitutions provide similar protections.[75]

Designed to protect all consumers, the Fair Credit Reporting Act[76] requires an employer to advise employees whenever it requests credit reports from outside parties or makes decisions based on that information. Consumer protection statutes in many states afford employees protection for credit records and medical records.[77]

Recommendations and trends

Protection of a nurse's legal rights involves consideration of many factors. The interplay of federal and state law requires complex analysis, best performed by an attorney experienced in this area. A health care professional should develop a basic understanding of available legal protections but should seek counsel if it is suspected that an employer has violated certain legal rights. Documentation of the facts and any related information, such as conversations with an employer, aids an attorney in evaluating the claim and formulating an opinion about the legal issues in question.

Major federal legislation affecting a nurse's rights in the employment setting are summarized on p. 497 (see box). The box also identifies the respective agency responsible for enforcement of those rights. In some cases, a nurse files suit directly in federal court without agency intervention. Because many state statutes provide similar protection, a nurse must seek legal counsel if the nurse believes rights are being violated. In the event of governmental reorganization, addresses and phone numbers may have changed since publication of this text.

Endnotes

1. Vance, *Getting What You Want: Negotiating Nursing Salaries* 3 NURS. ECON., 266 (September-October 1985).
2. *Pierce v. Ortho Pharmaceutical Corp.*, 417 A.2d 505 (N.J. Sup. 1980).
3. *Id.* at 515.
4. *Lampe v. Presbyterian Medical Center,* 590 P.2d 513 (Colo. App. 1978).
5. *O'Sullivan v. Mallon,* 390 A.2d 149 (N.J. Sup. 1978).
6. *Sheets v. Teddy's Frosted Foods, Inc.*, 427 A.2d 385 (Conn. 1980).
7. *Sides v. Duke Hospital,* 328 S.E.2d 818 (N.C. App. 1985), *review denied,* 335 S.E.2d 13 (N.C. 1985).
8. *Witt v. Forest Hospital,* 450 N.E.2d 811 (Ill. 1983).
9. 42 U.S.C. §2000e-20003-17 (1982 & Supp. I 1983).
10. *Cleary v. American Airlines,* 168 Cal. Rptr. 722 (Cal. App. 1980).

11. *Pugh v. See's Candies,* 171 Cal. Rptr. 917 (Cal. App. 1981).
12. *Fortune v. National Cash Register Co.,* 364 N.E.2d 1251 (Mass. 1977).
13. *Crenshaw v. Bozeman Deaconness Hospital,* 693 P.2d 487 (Mont. 1984).
14. *Liekvold v. Valley View Community Hospital,* 688 P.2d 201 (Ariz. App. 1983), *vacated* 688 P.2d 170 (Ariz. 1984). The highest court held that a genuine dispute as to material fact existed on the question of whether employer's policies manual was incorporated into and became part of terms of the employment contract, precluding summary judgment. They reversed and remanded the case.
15. 29 U.S.C. §141 through 187 (1982 & Supp. I 1983); 29 U.S.C. Sections 201-219 (1982 & Supp. I 1983).
16. 29 U.S.C. §157(a) (1982 & Supp. I 1983).
17. *Villa Care, Inc.,* 249 NLRB 705 (May 22, 1980).
18. 29 U.S.C. §157(a) (1982 & Supp. I 1983).
19. *Misercordia Hospital Medical Center v. NLRB,* 623 F.2d 808 (2nd Cir. 1980).
20. *Warthen v. Tom's River Community Memorial Hospital,* 488 A.2d 229 (N.J. Sup. App. Div. 1985).
21. *Id.* at 230.
22. 29 U.S.C. §141 through 187 (1982 & Supp I 1983).
23. *Cedars-Sinai Medical Center,* 223 NLRB 251 (1976).
24. *Newton-Wellesley,* 250 NLRB 409 (1980).
25. *Presbyterian/St. Luke's Medical Center v. NLRB,* 653 F.2d 450 (10th Cir. 1981).
26. Florida Const. Dec. of Rights, §6. Agency shop is outlined as violating the right to work provision. *Schermerhorn v. Retail Clerks International Ass'n., Local 1625, AFL-CIO,* 141 So.2d 269 (Fla. 1962), *aff'd.* 375 U.S. 96 (1963).
27. *Rideout Memorial Hospital,* 227 NLRB 1338 (1977).
28. 29 U.S.C. §201 through 219 (1982 & Supp. I 1983).
29. 29 U.S.C. §206(d) (1982 & Supp. I 1983).
30. 29 U.S.C. §213(a) (2) (1982 & Supp. I 1983).
31. 42 U.S.C. §2000e (1982 & Supp. I 1983).
32. *Id.*
33. 42 U.S.C. §2000e-2(e) (1982 & Supp. I 1983).
34. *Young v. Kenley,* 641 F.2d 192 (4th Cir. 1981).
35. *Garcia v. Rush-Presbyterian Medical Center,* 660 F.2d 1217 (7th Cir. 1981).
36. *Backus v. Baptist Medical Center,* 510 F. Supp. 1191 (E.D. Ark, 1981), *vacated,* 671 F.2d 1100 (8th Cir. 1982).
37. 29 C.F.R. §1604.11 (1985).
38. 29 C.F.R. §1604.11(a) (1985).
39. *Miller v. Bank of America,* 600 F.2d 211 (9th Cir. 1979).
40. *Fisher v. Flynn,* 598 F.2d 663 (1st Cir. 1979).
41. MASS. ANN. LAWS ch. 37 §2101 *et seq.* (Michie/Law. Co-op. 1985); MINN. STAT. ANN. §3.548 (101) *et seq.* (West 1985), COLO. REV. STAT. §24-34-301 *et seq.* (1982).
42. MASS. ANN. LAWS ch. 151B §5 (Michie/Law Co-op. 1985).
43. 29 U.S.C. §621-634 and 663(a) (1982 & Supp. I 1983).
44. *Id.*
45. *Buckley v. Hospital Corporation of America,* 758 F.2d 1525 (11th Cir. 1985).
46. 29 U.S.C. §793 (1982 & Supp. I 1983).
47. 38 U.S.C. §101 and 102 and scattered sections (1982); 38 U.S.C. §219, 241-245 and scattered sections (1982).
48. 29 U.S.C. §794 (1982 & Supp. I 1983).
49. *Tragester v. Libbie Rehabilitation Center,* 590 F.2d 87 (4th Cir. 1978), *cert. denied,* 442 U.S. 947 (1979).
50. *Jones v. Metropolitan Atlanta Rapid Transit Authority,* 681 F.2d 1376 (11th Cir. 1982), *cert. denied,* 465 U.S. 1099 (1984).
51. 29 U.S.C. §206(d) (1982 & Supp. I 1983).
52. *Id.*
53. 452 U.S. 161 (1981).
54. *Lemmons v. City of Denver,* 620 F.2d 228 (10th Cir. 1978), *cert. denied,* 449 U.S. 888 (1980).
55. MASS. ANN. LAWS ch. 149 §105A, 105B (Michie/Law. Co-op. 1985).
56. *Tacoma-Pierce County Public Health Employees Association v. Tacoma-Pierce County Health Department, City of Tacoma,* 586 P.2d 1215 (Wash. App. 1978).
57. Boston Globe, April 12, 1985 at 3, col. 2.
58. 29 U.S.C. §615-678 and scattered sections of 5, 15, 18, 29, 42 and 49 U.S.C. (1982).
59. 42 U.S.C. §2000e(k) (1982 & Supp. I 1983).
60. *Id.*
61. 29 U.S.C. §654 (1982 & Supp. I 1983).
62. CONN. GEN. STAT. ANN. §31N.40 (West 1985).
63. *Weeks v. Southern Bell Telephone and Telegraph Co.,* 408 F.2d 228 (5th Cir. 1969).
64. 42 U.S.C. §2000e-2(e) (1) (1982 & Supp. I 1983).
65. Furnish, *Prenatal Exposure to Fetally Toxic Work Environment: The Dilemma of the 1978 Pregnancy Amendment to Title VII of the Civil Rights Act of 1964* 66 IOWA L. REV., 63 (1980).
66. *Maclennan v. American Airlines, Inc.,* 440 F. Supp. 466, 471 (E.D. Va. 1977).
67. MASS. ANN. LAWS ch. 152 §1 (Michie/Law. Co-op. 1985); FLA. STAT. ANN. §440.151 (West 1985).
68. 5 U.S.C. §7902, 8101 (1982 & Supp. I 1983).
69. *In the Matter of the Claim of Griffin v. Worker's Compensation Board,* 436 N.Y.S.2d 441 (A.D. 3rd. Dept. 1981), where the court held that the employer violated the statute providing it is unlawful to discharge an employee because that employee claimed compensation.
70. *Selan v. Unemployment Compensation Board of Review,* 433 A.2d 1337 (Pa. 1981).
71. *Porter v. Department of Unemployment Security,* 430 A.2d 450 (Vt. 1981).
72. *Griswold v. Connecticut,* 381 U.S. 479 (1965).
73. 5 U.S.C. §552(a) (e) (1) (1982 & Supp. I 1983).
74. 5 U.S.C. §552 (1982).
75. MASS. ANN. LAWS ch. 214, §1B (Michie/Law. Co-op. 1985); FLA. CONST. art. I, §12; CAL. CONST. art. I, Section 1; CAL. CIV. CODE §1798 *et seq.* (West 1985).
76. 15 U.S.C. §1681d (1982 & Supp. I 1983).
77. R. SMITH, COMPILATION OF STATE AND FEDERAL PRIVACY LAWS (1981).

Additional Readings

C. BAKALY and W. ISAACSON, EMPLOYMENT AT WILL AND UNJUST DISMISSAL: THE LABOR ISSUES OF THE 80's (1983).

BUREAU OF NATIONAL AFFAIRS, THE COMPARABLE WORTH ISSUE (1981).

BUREAU OF NATIONAL AFFAIRS, WHITE COLLAR REPORT, (current ed.).

A. COOKE, COMPARABLE WORTH—THE PROBLEM AND STATES' APPROACH TO WAGE EQUITY (1983).

M. DICHTER and P. WEINER, EMPLOYMENT LITIGATION AND ITS ALTERNATIVES (1984).

Duldt, *Sexual Harassment in Nursing* 30 N.O., 237 (June 1982).

M. GIBSON, WORKER'S RIGHTS (1983).

M. MEYER, SEXUAL HARASSMENT AT WORK (1980).

Moskowitz and Moskowitz, *Protecting Your Job* 84 A.J.N., 55 (January 1984).

W. PEPPER and F. KENNEDY, SEX DISCRIMINATION IN EMPLOYMENT (1984).

Chapter 31

Collective bargaining

Cynthia E. Northrop*

While the preceding chapter discussed general employment claims aspects of labor law, this chapter will focus upon other aspects; that is, collective bargaining and labor-management relations. Generally, this chapter will review aspects of labor law as they relate to nurses who are employees and members of labor organizations.

Collective bargaining is a process involving contract negotiation and enforcement. It involves two phases: contract negotiation, or promise making, and contract administration, or promise checking.[1] The essence of collective bargaining is the promise, the exchange of rights and obligations that will determine the future relationship of the parties.[2] Once a collective bargaining agreement is reached, disputes which follow are most often handled through an arbitration and/or grievance process.

Historical perspective: nursing and unionization

The American Nurses' Association (ANA) first called attention to the need to improve the working conditions of nurses as early as 1914 when one of its presidents suggested that nurses' economic concerns be given greater consideration by the association.[3] Along with many other professional people, nurses first became interested in collective action in the 1930s. Most nurses, however, found a conflict between unionization and their ethical standards; and for this reason, as well as the legal constraints, few actually organized. Strike action in particular seemed contrary to nurses' responsibilities toward patients.[4]

Some nurses were joining unions, however, and in 1937 the ANA announced its policy that did not recommend union membership for nurses because of its conviction that "in their professional organization nurses had the instruments best fitted and equipped to improve every phase of their working and professional lives."[5] In that same year the ANA urged its affiliates, the state nurses' associations (SNA), to assume individual responsibility for improving the employment conditions of their own members.

The California Nurses' Association (CNA) was the first SNA to become involved in collective action. In 1943 it successfully secured a wage increase[6] and started to negotiate labor contracts with various hospitals and a few industrial plants in California.[7]

While the ANA in its early years had focused upon education goals and obtaining state licensure, at its 1946 convention it created the Economic Security Program, currently the Economic and General Welfare Program. This first program suggested to SNAs that they develop their own collective bargaining contracts, covering wages, hours, working conditions, and at least a three-step greivance procedure.[8] The ANA's convention resolutions in 1946 also indicated that the SNAs should be

*This author wishes to acknowledge and thank Pamela A. Ames, Director, Economic and General Welfare Program, American Nurses' Association, who developed the outline for this chapter.

the exclusive agents of their membership in the field of economic security and collective bargaining.

In 1950 the ANA adopted a no-strike provision and a neutrality clause which held that nurses should never strike and that they should maintain a neutral position in labor-management relations between their employers and non-nursing employees.[9] This was a voluntary relinquishment of the right to strike, as opposed to a legal mandate prohibiting striking. This was the ANA's stance until 1968, when it removed its self-imposed ban on strikes, adopting a more militant bargaining posture.[10]

By 1958, registered nurses (RNs) in a total of seven SNAs had written contracts with about 87 hospitals.[11] Also by 1958, Minnesota had the most comprehensive SNA program, with almost half of its 7,000 registered nurses covered by contracts in 22% of its hospitals.[12] CNA had about 2,000 RNs under collective bargaining agreements, representing 7% of the state's hospitals and about 10% of the total number of nurses in the state.[13]

With the 1974 amendments to the labor laws, the availability of collective bargaining for nurses changed. For example, only 38,000 of the 750,000 active RNs were organized in unions in 1971.[14] However, by 1977, 100,000 RNs had been organized by SNAs alone.[15] Other unions began representing employees in the health care industry as well.

Nurses have traditionally been reluctant to be involved in collective bargaining activities. This has changed over the last 10 years. The reasons are that collective bargaining is viewed as a process to control practice and achieve professional and economic goals. The women's movement has also had a great impact. In addition, nurses began assuming more responsibility and specializing more because of increased technology.

A collective voice can influence policy decisions.[16] The structure of collective bargaining can provide better communication, recourse to effective talks with management about time, position, and floating. Pro-union nurses usually feel that they are not listened to by management; anti-union nurses are more likely to feel that management listens to them. The less communication between management and staff, the higher the interest in organizing.[17]

Today, nurses are unionized not only through SNAs but through many other labor organizations, many of which are affiliated with the American Federation of Labor and Congress of Industrial Organizations (AFL-CIO). This large and diverse list includes the Service Employees International Union; Federation of Nurses and Health Professionals; American Association of University Professors; and Drug, Hospital and Health Care Employees Union (1199).

Laws governing collective bargaining

The laws which govern collective bargaining by nurses vary according to whether the nurses are public or private sector employees. Nurses who are federal government employees are part of the public sector, and the Civil Service Reform Act[18] governs their collective bargaining and other personnel matters. State or municipal government employee nurses are governed by state and local civil service laws.

Collective bargaining activities by nurses employed in the private sector (nongovernmental, proprietary, or nonprofit facilities) are governed by the National Labor Relations Act.[19] Each of these laws will be discussed.

PUBLIC SECTOR: FEDERALLY EMPLOYED NURSES

Federal employment is not contractual but rather appointive in nature.[20] The appointment becomes effective when an authorized official (usually a personnel officer) signs the proper form appointing the individual to the position. The appointed individual becomes a member of the federal civil service which includes all appointive positions in the executive, judicial, and legislative branches (except the uniformed services).[21]

Rights of federally employed nurses will vary depending on their appointment category, any special statuses, and any specific rules which apply to them because of their employment agency. As mentioned in Chapter 18, Nursing in Federal Employment, Title V of the UNITED STATES CODE, known as the Civil Service Reform Act of 1978, governs labor-management and personnel matters in the federal public sector. Title V created the civil service, the Office of Personnel Management,[22] the Merit System Protection Board, and Office of Special Counsel,[23] as well as the Federal Labor Relations Authority. All are important parts of the labor-management relationship in the federal government.

Federal employees have rights under this statute, including the right to take action for personnel decisions, such as adverse actions, performance-related actions, within-grade increase denials, reduction-in-force actions, and retirement-related actions.[24] The law prohibits certain personnel practices. These are listed in the box.

Beginning at Section 7101 of Title V, legal rights of federal employees who may be part of collective bargaining agreements or who wish to join a union are identified. When Congress passed this statute, it recognized

PROHIBITED FEDERAL PERSONNEL PRACTICES

A prohibited personnel practice is one which involves:

1. Discriminating
2. Soliciting or considering recommendations based on factors other than personal knowledge or records of job-related abilities or characteristics
3. Coercing the political activity of any person
4. Deceiving or willfully obstructing any person from competing for employment
5. Influencing any person to withdraw from job competition
6. Giving unauthorized preferred treatment or advantage to improve or injure the prospects of any particular person for employment
7. Engaging in nepotism (hiring or promoting relatives)
8. Taking reprisal for bona fide whistleblowing
9. Taking reprisal for exercising an appeal right
10. Discriminating on the basis of personal conduct that is not adverse to the performance of the employee, applicant, or others
11. Violating any law, rule, or regulation implementing or directly concerning merit system principles

Data from 5 U.S.C. §2302(b) (1982).

that statutory protection of the rights of federal employees to organize, bargain collectively, and participate in labor organizations of their choosing safeguards the public interest, contributes to the effective conduct of public business, and encourages the amicable settlement of disputes between employees and their employers involving conditions of employment.[25]

Federal Labor Relations Authority. Each federal employee has the right to form, join, or assist any labor organization or to refrain from any such activity freely and without fear of penalty or reprisal.[26] Congress created the Federal Labor Relations Authority (FLRA), an independent agency in the executive branch, made up of three members, to:

1. Determine the appropriateness of units for labor organization representation
2. Supervise or conduct elections to determine whether a labor organization has been selected as an exclusive representative by a majority of the employees in an appropriate unit
3. Prescribe criteria and resolve issues relating to the granting of national consultation rights
4. Prescribe criteria and resolve issues relating to determining compelling need for agency rules or regulations
5. Resolve issues relating to the duty to bargain in good faith
6. Prescribe criteria relating to the granting of consultation rights with respect to conditions of employment
7. Conduct hearings and resolve complaints of unfair labor practices
8. Resolve exceptions to arbitrator's awards
9. Take such other actions as are necessary and appropriate to effectively administer the provisions of the law[27]

Federal management rights are also addressed in the statute, including determining the mission, budget, organization, number of employees, and security practices of the agency, as well as hiring, assigning, directing, laying off, and retaining employees. These rights include the ability to suspend, remove, reduce in grade or pay, or take other disciplinary action against employees. Management assigns work, makes determinations with respect to contracting out, and fills positions.[28]

Federal employees may form or join a labor organization through petition to the FLRA and through a secret ballot election by a majority of the employees in an appropriate unit who cast valid ballots in the election.[29] Elections can be held at most once a year.[30] Exclusive recognition of a labor organization is achieved through this process.

The FLRA determines the appropriateness of labor organization units based upon criteria identified in the statute. The criteria include:

1. On an agency, plant, installation, functional, or other basis
2. If the determination ensures a clear and identifiable community of interests among the employees in the unit and will promote effective dealings with the agency involved.[31]

A union of federally employed nurses cannot include in its members management officials, supervisors, confidential employees, employees engaged in personnel work (except in other than a clerical capacity), employees engaged in administering the provisions of the civil service law, both professional employees and other employees (unless a majority of the professional employees vote for inclusion), and employees engaged in intelligence, investigative, or audit work.[32]

Once a labor organization has exclusive recognition it becomes the exclusive representative of employees and is entitled to negotiate collective bargaining agreements and is to be given the opportunity to represent the employee under other circumstances. The representative must be given the opportunity to be at:

1. Any formal discussion between one or more representatives of the agency and one or more employees in the unit or their representatives concerning any grievance or any personnel policy or practices or other general condition of employment
2. Any examination of an employee in the unit by a representative of the agency in connection with an investigation if the employee reasonably believes the examination may result in disciplinary action and the employee requests representation.[33]

Federal Unfair Labor Practices. The federal labor-management relations statute prohibits certain practices as unfair labor practices. The box lists selected unfair labor practices. Most notable among this list of practices is the prohibition against striking. All federal employees, including health care employees, are prohibited from striking. If a labor organization willfully and intentionally, with regard to any strike, work stoppage, or slowdown, violates Section 7116(b)(7) (listed in the box, no. 7 under "Labor Organization Unfair Labor Practices.") of this law, the FLRA shall revoke the exclusive recognition status of the labor organization, which then immediately ceases to be legally entitled and obligated to represent employees in the unit.[34] The only FLRA decision which has been issued concerning this unfair labor practice to date is the case of the air traffic controllers.[35]

The law specifies, as well, that an individual may not accept or hold a federal government position if that individual participates in a strike, asserts the right to strike, or is a member of an organization of employees that is known to assert the right to strike against the government.[36]

While reaching an impasse is not necessarily a sign of an unfair labor practice, if an impasse arises during negotiations, the law provides that the Federal Mediation and Conciliation Service assist the agency and labor organization in the resolution of the impasse.[37] If this service fails to resolve the impasse, the law provides that a Federal Service Impasses Panel, an entity within the FLRA, be convened to resolve the impasse.[38]

To be assured that disputes which arise between federal agencies and employees are settled fairly and expeditiously, the law requires that collective bargaining agreements contain procedures for settling grievances, including questions of arbitratability.[39]

FEDERAL UNFAIR LABOR PRACTICES*

Agency Unfair Labor Practices

1. Interfering with any employee in the exercise of any right under this law
2. Affecting membership in any labor organization by discrimination in connection with hiring, tenure, promotion, or other conditions of employment
3. Sponsoring, controling, or otherwise assisting any labor organization, other than to furnish, upon request, customary and routine services and facilities if the services and facilities are also furnished on an impartial basis to other labor organizations having equivalent status
4. Disciplining or discriminating against an employee for filing a complaint, affidavit, or petition or for giving any information/testimony under this law
5. Refusing to negotiate in good faith with a labor organization as required by this law
6. Failing to cooperate in impasse procedures and decisions as required by this law
7. Enforcing certain rules or regulations which are in conflict with any applicable collective bargaining agreement if the agreement was in effect before the date the rule or regulation was prescribed

Labor Organization Unfair Labor Practices

1. Interfering with any employee who exercises any right under this law
2. Causing an agency to discriminate against any employee in the exercise by the employee of any right under this law
3. Coercing or disciplining a member of the labor organization as punishment or reprisal or for the purpose of hindering or impeding the member's work performance or productivity as an employee or the discharge of the member's duties as an employee
4. Discriminating against an employee with regard to the terms or conditions of membership in the labor organization
5. Refusing to negotiate in good faith with an agency as required by this law
6. Failing to cooperate in impasse procedures and decisions as required by this law
7. Calling, condoning, or participating in a strike, work stoppage, or slowdown or picketing of an agency in a labor-management dispute if such picketing interferes with an agency's operations

Adapted from 5 U.S.C. §7116(a) and (b) (1982).

Thus far, the main points of the labor-management and employee relations law for federal employees have been presented. As one can imagine, personnel disputes of all kinds are possible and must be handled within a complex system. Nurses who are federal employees have the same rights and responsibilities as other federal employees and should seek legal advice on the interpretation and applicability of the civil service laws. Such advice can be obtained either through union representation or through seeking a lawyer's advice privately, depending on the nurse's situation.

PUBLIC SECTOR: LOCAL- AND STATE-EMPLOYED NURSES

As mentioned in the nurse executive chapter (Chapter 22), state labor and employment laws vary widely. Not all states have passed public sector bargaining laws. In those states which have, the laws set forth the particular policies for the state, county, or municipality where it is enacted.[40] For example, one state public sector law covers certain employees and excludes employees such as police, sheriffs, highway patrol, national guard, and teachers.[41]

Often state laws will follow the federal government labor-management laws and specify criteria for determining the bargaining units,[42] rights of the employees and employer, and unfair labor practices. State codes on unfair labor practices often parallel the National Labor Relations Act discussed below.[43] Limitations on the labor-management relationship are also included, such as a prohibition on the right to strike.[44]

PRIVATE SECTOR: NATIONAL LABOR RELATIONS ACT

Beginning in 1935, Congress has over the years passed laws pertaining to labor relations in private sector employment. In that year, Congress passed the National Labor Relations Act (NLRA), known as the Wagner Act.[45] Periodically, Congress has made amendments to this statute, the most important of these coming in 1947 (Taft-Hartley Act), 1959 (Landrum-Griffin Act), and, most relevant to the nursing profession, 1974 (Health Care Amendments).

The Wagner Act created the National Labor Relations Board (NLRB).[46] It is responsible for administering the NLRA, whose jurisdiction is limited to workers and employers in the private sector.[47] The NLRB performs two major functions:

1. It is responsible for the administration of the election process through which employees may exercise their right to select a labor organization to represent them in collective bargaining.
2. It administers the unfair labor practice provisions governing unlawful acts of employers and unions.[48]

The NLRB has five members, appointed by the President with advice and consent of the Senate. There is an office of the General Counsel of the Board which investigates unfair labor practices charges and prosecutes complaints. The administrative structure of the NLRB includes these two components and approximately 51 regional, subregional, and local offices. The administrative structure also includes administrative law judges who actually conduct the hearings and make recommendations to the NLRB.

The 1974 amendments to the NLRA, brought private, nonprofit health care institutions and their employees under the coverage of the act. The amendments were brought as a compromise between those who wanted to protect the public's right to receive uninterrrupted health care; health care institutions whose obligation it is to provide health services to the fullest extent possible; and health care employees who wanted the right to have the same voice in determining their wages, hours, and working conditions that other employees already were provided under the NLRA.[49]

Proprietary, private health care facilities have been covered by the NLRA since 1935; in 1947, Congress specifically excluded nonprofit, private health care facilities. In 1974 the amendments not only abolished this exclusion but created a series of rules specific to bargaining in health care facilities. These specific rules for health care bargaining activities include:

1. A 10-day notice requirement to the facility before engaging in a strike, picketing, or other concerted activity[50]
2. A requirement that the facility or the union must notify the other within 90 days of modification or termination of an existing collective bargaining agreement[51]
3. Mandatory mediation by the Federal Mediation and Conciliation Service, carrying certain notice requirements and power to appoint a board of inquiry in emergencies[52]

NLRA Representation Process. There are several ways in which a labor organization can become the employees' representative. An employer may voluntarily recognize a labor organization which has majority support among the employees. However, the most common method is through an election conducted under the jurisdiction of the NLRB. Another method is possible when an employer performs unfair labor practices of the type which make a fair election impossible, and the NLRB issues an order requiring the employer to bargain with the union. The election and certification process is outlined in the NLRA.[53]

Petitions. Petitions may be filed in the relevant regional offices of the NLRB. This office will answer any questions about the preparation of the petition upon request. The petition basically is requesting that the bargaining agent be certified by the NLRB. An employee, group of employees, or a labor organization, acting on behalf of the employees, may file the petition.

The petition must allege that a substantial number of employees wish to be represented by the bargaining agent for collective bargaining purposes. Such purposes include bargaining with respect to rates of pay, hours, or other conditions of employment.[54] The NLRB has determined that a substantial number of employees is 30%.

An employer may also file a petition if one or more unions have demanded recognition as representative of a unit of that employer's employees. The employer's petition must contain proof of the demands for recognition.

Employees, a group of employees, or labor organization may also file a decertification petition. This type of petition asserts that the currently certified bargaining representative no longer is such. The NLRB will not accept a decertification petition from an employer, supervisor, or confidential employee. Again, the NLRB has set 30% as the requisite minimum showing of interest and as the amount of support to show that a question concerning representation exists.

Yet, another petition authorized by the NLRA is the union-security deauthorization petition. This petition, if accepted, allows the NLRB to take a secret ballot of employees in a bargaining unit covered by a union-security agreement. This type of agreement involves clauses which provide for the protection of the union through determining membership and collection of dues and answering the question of whether the facility is an open shop or union shop, which will be defined later.[55]

Other petitions are also reviewed by the NLRB, including a petition to clarify the certification and to amend a certification. All of the petitions may raise questions of representation, the showing of interest, and unit appropriateness. If there has been an election within the previous year which led to the certification of an employee representative, the NRLB will dismiss the petition.[56]

The NLRA grants broad discretion to the NLRB to determine if a particular unit is appropriate.[57] This has become a question for nurses, as will be discussed further below. Generally, the NLRA provides that the NLRB will determine the appropriateness of a unit based upon:

1. Bargaining history[58]
2. Membership requirements of the union involved
3. Similarity in wage scales, hours of work, and working conditions and similarity and interdependence of functions of the employees wanting to be in the same unit[59]
4. ''Community of interest'' shared by the employees
5. Presence and extent of organization among the employees[60]
6. Employer's business operation organization and its relationship to the proposed unit[61]

In addition the NLRA prevents the Board from deciding that a unit combining professional with nonprofessional employees is appropriate, unless a majority of the professional employees vote for inclusion in the mixed unit.[62] For units in health care facilities there is an additional consideration: Congress' admonition that there not be an undue proliferation of units in the health care industry. As will be discussed further, courts have held that the NLRB erred in considering the appropriateness of a registered nurses' unit without addressing the question of proliferation of bargaining units in the health care industry, a problem about which Congress expressed its concern.[63]

Open Shop or Union Shop. The open shop clause provides that employees covered by the agreement may choose either to become members of the union or not to become members of the union; the union shop clause provides that as a condition of continued employment all employees covered by the agreement on its effective date shall remain members in good standing of the union.

Philosophical or Religious Objections. The collective bargaining agreement may also provide that nurses who, for philosophical reasons, do not wish to be members of the union will pay an agency fee equal to the amount of union dues to the union. The collective bargaining agreement should have a provision which exempts nurses who are members of a religious organization which prohibits union membership from paying union dues.

The NLRA provides that any employee who is a

member of and adheres to established teachings of a bona fide religion which objects to joining or supporting labor organizations shall not be required to join or financially support such an organization as a condition of employment, *except* that the employee may be required in a contract between employees and employer and a labor organization to pay sums equal to dues to a nonreligious, nonlabor organization, charitable fund.[64] However, this section indicates that if the objector-employee requests the labor organization to use the grievance or arbitration procedure on the objector-employee's behalf, the union is authorized to charge reasonable costs of using the procedures.

Religiously affiliated hospitals or other health care facilities have raised first amendment, constitutional challenges to the jurisdiction of the NLRB. Courts have held, however, that NLRB jurisdiction over the hospital did not violate either the establishment or free exercise clauses of the first amendment.[65]

Rights of Nurse Employees. An important provision of the NLRA is Section 157, which states that employees have the right to form, join, or assist labor organizations; to bargain collectively through representatives of their own choosing; and to engage in other concerted activities for the purpose of collective bargaining or other mutual aid or protection.[66] In addition employees have the right to strike.[67]

This basic right of nurse employees, covered by this act, also includes the right to refrain from any or all of such activities, except that such right may be affected by the collective bargaining agreement requiring membership in a labor organization as a condition of employment.[68]

Concerted Activity Other than Collective Bargaining. The NLRA also protects concerted activities of employees other than those those which involve collective bargaining.[69] As presented above and in the previous chapter, employees have the right to engage in concerted activities for the purpose of collective bargaining *or for other mutual aid or protection.*[70] Thus, even in the absence of an organizing campaign or a union contract, employers may not interfere with, restrain, or coerce nurses in the exercise of their right to engage in concerted activities.[71]

Until 1984, four requirements had evolved which were necessary in order to establish that an activity is a protected, concerted activity within the meaning of the NLRA:

1. There must be a work-related complaint or grievance.
2. The concerted activity must further some group interest.
3. A specific remedy or result must be sought through such activity.
4. The activity should not be unlawful or otherwise improper.[72]

Work-related complaints include the topics of wages, hours, and working conditions. For nurses work-related complaints can include patient care issues, such as safe staffing levels. In one case involving operating room (OR) nurses, the court found that the NLRB's decision that the hospital violated the NLRA was based upon substantial evidence.[73] The OR nurses began meeting together when they heard that the delivery room nurses were getting $3.00 an hour for on-call duty. These activities did not involve a union; the OR nurses formed their own group, approached the administration, and attempted to negotiate with the administration regarding the pay issue. The hospital responded by discharging two nurses, issuing warnings to one of them, threatening another nurse with extension of the probationary period or dismissal, suspending a nurse and refusing to allow her to work during the eighth month of pregnancy without also being on call, refusing to reassign the nurse to the operating room when she returned from maternity leave, warning one nurse not to be seen coming to work with another, and prohibiting the nurses from talking together on hospital premises during nonworking hours. It was established that all of these actions were protected, concerted activity.

In another case involving a nurse, a court found that there was ample evidence for the NLRB's decision that the hospital impliedly labeled as "disloyal" and threatened reprisals against a nurse who had contributed to a report critical of the hospital's operations.[74]

Furthering a group interest, one of the criteria for concerted action, does not necessarily mean that more than one employee must participate for it to be a protected activity. Furthering a group interest can involve a single nurse if the activity is one which would have the support of other nurses or relate to matters of mutual concern to all affected employees.[75]

In 1984 the NLRB abandoned the above four requirements and put in their place the following four:

1. The activity was engaged in with or on behalf of other employees.
2. The employer knew of the concerted nature of the employee's activity.
3. The activity was protected by the statute.
4. The employer's adverse employment action was

motivated by the employee's protected concerted activity.[76]

This NLRB decision represents a departure from the previous statutory analysis in that the new requirements include an employer's motivation. Judicial reaction to this NLRB decision has yet to be developed.

Organizing and Filing a Representation Petition. As the NLRA indicates, a nurse has the right to collectively bargain. The process begins with an organizing campaign, usually spearheaded by a committee of nurse employees in a particular health care facility. This committee plans the campaign, proposes the appropriate bargaining unit and works to obtain exclusive recognition for the chosen labor organization. Most often the decision to organize stems from multiple job problems, including inadequate staffing, lack of equipment and supplies, scheduling of work hours, and low salaries.[77]

The primary goal of the organizing activity is to obtain signed authorization cards from at least 30% of the nonsupervisory nurses involved, so that recognition can be obtained. Selecting an organization to represent them, meeting regularly, distributing information to potential union members, and other activities are undertaken. However, certain rules apply to health care facilities and the solicitation and distribution of materials. These are discussed next.

Employers are barred from seeing the signed authorization cards. The cards must be clearly written; signatures must be in writing, followed by the printed names. They should contain a date and may, if the organizers wish, indicate who solicited the card. This is particularly helpful if questions arise later about whether supervisors participated in the organizing activities.

Solicitation and Distribution Rules. Two sets of rules exist, depending on whether or not the organizers are employees of the facility. Nonemployees may assist in a campaign, but are barred from distributing literature and soliciting cards on private property. Nurses who are employee-organizers, generally, must:

1. Solicit and distribute material during their own free time
2. Avoid a disruption of patient care
3. Not solicit and distribute materials in immediate patient care areas (such as the patient's room and places where the patient receives actual treatment)

The health care employer may not discriminately apply rules regarding solicitation and distribution or ban distribution and solicitation.[78] The latter is an unfair labor practice, several of which will be discussed below. For example, a prohibition on nurses' solicitation in the lobby has been held to be an unfair labor practice.[79]

The U.S. Supreme Court has held that the freedom of employees to communicate with one another regarding self-organization on the job site is essential to their rights to bargain collectively.[80] In this case the Court said that the NLRB may adopt the rule, absent special circumstances, that employer's restriction on employee solicitation during nonworking time and in nonworking areas is presumptively unreasonable. Specifically, the Court held that a hospital's rule that there would be no soliciting in the cafeteria violated the employees' rights. The Court noted that the cafeteria was an area of the hospital to which patients infrequently went, and that it was a natural gathering place for employees.

The employer can also challenge the employees' activities. In one such case the nurses' union distributed NLRB publications with handwritten notes on them stating "vote, yes."[81] The court held that distribution of such literature improperly created the impression in the minds of voters that the NLRB favored unionization; therefore the election was held invalid. Where the employer offers specific evidence questioning the fairness of an election, the courts have ruled that the NLRB must give the employer a full evidentiary hearing on allegations that unions engaged in coercive conduct which tainted the representation election.[82]

PRIVATE SECTOR: THRESHOLD ISSUES

The NLRB and the courts have reviewed several issues which pertain to who may belong to a nursing union and whether nurses can maintain a union of only registered nurses or may be required to join unions of all health care professionals within a particular health care facility. These are threshold issues because they involve issues which must be clarified as part of the actual formation of a collective bargaining unit.

Nurses as Professional Employees. The NLRA defines a professional employee as:

1. Any employee engaged in work:
   a. Predominantly intellectual and varied in character as opposed to routine mental, manual, mechanical, or physical work
   b. Involving consistent exercise of discretion and judgment in its performance
   c. Of such a character that the output produced or the result accomplished cannot be standardized in relation to a given period of time
   d. Requiring knowledge of an advanced type of

field of science or learning customarily acquired by a prolonged course of specialized intellectual instruction and study in an institution of higher learning or hospital, as distinguished from a general academic education or from an apprenticeship or from training in the performance of routine mental, manual, or physical processes

2. Any employee, who:
   a. Has completed the courses of specialized intellectual instruction and study in number 1.(d) above
   b. Is performing related work under the supervision of a professional person to qualify to become a professional employee as defined in number 1. above[83]

This definition includes the registered nurse. Whether the nurse is full or part time is also an issue discussed by the NLRB. Generally, the part-time nurse-employee may be included in a bargaining unit.[84]

Nurses as Supervisors or Employees. A second and related threshold issue is the definition of nursing supervisor. As mentioned, only employees may collectively bargain; supervisors are an excluded group.[85] The NLRA defines a supervisor as:

> Any individual having authority, in the interest of the employer, to hire, transfer, suspend, lay off, recall, promote, discharge, assign, reward, or discipline other employees, or responsibility to direct them, or to adjust their grievances, or effectively to recommend such action; if in connection with the foregoing the exercise of such authority is not of a merely routine or clerical nature, but requires the use of independent judgment.[86]

There are many cases which have discussed whether nursing supervisors may be part of the nurse-employee's collective bargaining unit.[87] Cases have also discussed unit membership of nursing inservice directors, staff educators, nurse practitioners, assistant nursing supervisors, nurse coordinators, assistant nurse coordinators, charge nurses, head nurses, nursing faculty, infection control nurses, nurse epidemiologists, and hospital-employee health service nurses.

In some instances, supervisors and others listed above may be included, and, under other circumstances, they may be excluded from membership in the union.[88] The NLRB and court analysis is made on a case-by-case basis. Determination is made based upon the functions and content of the nursing role in question, not necessarily the job title. The key variable is whether the employee in question has "actual job responsibilities, authority and relationship to management."[89] The factors which are examined include differences in job classification, common educational background, uniform licensing examination, and separate administration of nurses within the facility.

In one case four occupational health nurses wished to form an all RN unit within the United Steelworkers of America. Their employer challenged the NLRB order directing the employer to bargain on the basis that the RNs were managerial employees and thus not covered by the NLRA.[90] In holding that the RNs were not managerial, the court reiterated that an employee is managerial "only if he represents management interests by taking or recommending discretionary actions that effectively control or implement employer policy."[91]

The court reviewed the nurses' primary responsibilities (treating employees' injuries, administering routine physical examinations, maintaining logs and records). The court noted that the nurses worked under a nursing supervisor and part-time physician. The nurses provide care 24 hours per day, 7 days a week; functioning, often, under standing orders left by the physician.

The court also reviewed what the nurses were *not* involved in, including that they did not have independent authority to purchase medical supplies or equipment, that they had to have requisitions approved by the supervisor, that they did not have authority to implement changes without approval, and that they did not participate in setting labor relations policies.

Nurses and Appropriate Bargaining Units: Community of Interest. This issue involves the debate over whether nurses should collectively bargain in units whose members are only registered nurses or whether nurses should bargain as part of a unit whose members may include other health professionals. The issue of membership with nonprofessionals has been specifically addressed by the NLRA, which states that mixed units (professional and nonprofessional employees) may only be appropriate bargaining units if a majority of the professional employees vote for inclusion in such a unit.[92]

Until recently, challenges by hospitals to petitions before the NLRB for separate RN units have been unsuccessful because the NRLB policy had been to approve all RN separate units, based upon the community of interests shared by RNs and by nursing's singular history of separate representation.[93]

The issue has arisen, however, as to whether RNs

can be a separate unit, to the exclusion of the other options.[94] The analysis of this issue rests upon the NLRB and, if challenged, by the court's interpretation of whether the Board's decision was based upon substantial evidence of the criteria for defining appropriate units. The NLRB has defined the RN's functions and skills as those which "share a close and substantial community of interest among themselves which is separate and distinct from that of other employees."[95]

Courts have held that the NLRB's responsibility is to choose an appropriate unit, but its decision need not be the *most* appropriate one.[96] Courts, generally, accord great respect to the expertise of the NLRB when its conclusions are rationally based on articulated facts and are consistent with the NLRA.[97]

Among the more recent cases, however, one court has held that the NLRB's decision approving an all RN separate unit was arbitrary and capricious.[98] This case represented a change in emphasis of the courts about the community of interest concept. In the legislative history of the NLRA's 1974 Health Care Amendments, Congress indicated that it did not intend that there be an undue proliferation of bargaining units in health care facilities.

In finding that the NLRB's decision was arbitrary and capricious, the court relied upon this legislative history, finding that the NLRB's presumption that nurses should be in a separate all RN unit contravened the strong congressional admonition to avoid a proliferation of bargaining units in the hospital industry.[99]

This court interjected a new analysis of the issue. First, it emphasized that it was not holding that separate bargaining units for RNs was inappropriate, but that the need for a separate unit had to be justified.[100] The court held that a separate unit for nurses could not be justified unless it could be proved that there was a "disparity of interests" between the nurses and other professionals included in the proposed unit. Therefore, this court's rule was that multiprofessional units are appropriate for nurses unless the nurses can demonstrate that their interests are so disparate with other professional groups that their interests will not be fairly represented.

However, the federal circuit courts have not taken a uniform approach to this question. In a more recent case, the Eleventh Circuit Court of Appeals held that the possibility of three bargaining units at a medical center, including an all nonprofessional employee unit, an all RN employee unit, and an all other professional employee unit, did not constitute undue proliferation of units in violation of Congress' directive.[101] But in other circuits the courts have held that the NLRB abused its discretion by applying its traditional presumption approach and certifying a nurses' unit without stating how its determination complied with Congress' admonition to more rigorously justify bargaining unit determinations in the health care field.[102] The NLRB must evaluate a claim of undue proliferation by the hospital in adequate and specific terms; to refuse to do so constitutes administrative error.[103]

Choice of Union. The choice of union is determined by the nurses involved. The choice of union should follow a systematic review of unions in the health care industry, evaluating the nurses' needs and how the union can meet those needs. O'Rourke and Barton suggest that a union be evaluated on dues structure, membership services, organizational structure (especially review of the union's bylaws and constitution), and reputation.[104]

Whether state nurses' associations (SNAs) may collectively bargain for nurse-employees has been another issue discussed by the courts because the membership of the association includes nurses who are supervisors, as defined by the NLRA.

The leading cases discussing this issue are *NLRB v. Annapolis Emergency Hospital Association*,[105] and *Sierra Vista Hospital, Inc. and California Nurses United*.[106] In the first case the court reviewed the NLRB's handling of a challenge by the hospital to the legality of the order certifying the SNA as the collective bargaining representative. The employer's challenge was based on the argument that the SNA was not a labor organization within the meaning of the NLRA because it was dominated and controlled by supervisory personnel. The SNA argued that it was a labor organization, noting that none of the employer's supervisors were on its board of directors and that it had delegated its collective bargaining activities to the professional chapter (individual, local unit).

In this complex case the court ultimately held that the NLRB's order could not be enforced because the NLRB may not certify a bargaining agent on the condition that it not bargain. The court held that the Board had exceeded its legal powers.

In the second case, a more clearly defined case, the NLRB held that the issue of nursing supervisor domination in the state nurses' association should be decided on a case-by-case basis during representation hearings. The Board held that the association could be certified as a labor organization, but could be disqualified if a conflict of interest existed.

A conflict of interest exists if:

1. The SNA is influenced by supervisors working in

the hospital which is the subject of the petition for recognition;

2. The SNA is influenced by supervisors working for third-parties

The NLRB declared in its opinion that the burden of proving a conflict of interest was substantial, including producing probative evidence substantiating a claim that supervisory participation in the affairs of the SNA presents a clear and present danger of interference with the bargaining process.

In subsequent cases courts have held that in determining whether an SNA is disqualified as a bargaining representative because its actions were controlled or influenced by persons occupying supervisory positions, the NLRB's inquiry should extend to all relevant circumstances. This includes a review of the governing structure and actual practice of the SNA as far as participation by supervisors was concerned.[107] In this ruling the court has indicated that limiting proof of supervisor involvement in the SNA to explicit supervisory interference was inadequate and that the NLRB needed to expand the evidence which it examined to make the determination.

PRIVATE SECTOR: CAMPAIGN AND ELECTION

The NLRB has held that any interference with, restraint of, or coercion of employees in the exercise of their right to organize during the critical period preceding the election is objectionable conduct which warrants setting aside the election.[108] The critical period is defined as that time between when the petition for representation is filed with the NLRB and the election.[109]

The goal of the Board is to maintain an environment in the workplace which is free of coercion and one which will assure a fair election. Sometimes referred to as "laboratory conditions," the NLRB's function has been defined by the courts as providing "a laboratory in which an experiment may be conducted under conditions as nearly ideal as possible, to determine the uninhibited desires of the employees."[110]

However, the employer need not remain neutral and silent during this period. Known as the "free speech provision" of the NLRA, Section 158(c) provides that *both* the employer and the union have a right to express their views regarding unionization. This expression can be "any views, argument, or opinion, or the dissemination thereof, whether written, printed, graphic, or visual form."[111] This expression is not considered an unfair labor practice as long as the expression contains no threat of reprisal, force, promise, or benefit.

"Laboratory conditions" where deemed disturbed, and new elections were ordered when the NLRB found that the employer threatened to discharge employees,[112] stated in advance an intention not to bargain in good faith,[113] threatened plant closings,[114] and made constant references to strikes and the consequences of strikes.[115] However, more recent NLRB cases have held that an employer cannot be penalized for accurate statements of law and facts.[116] Generally, the NLRB will set aside an election and/or find an unfair labor practice violation when the employer makes a pre-election statement which employees would reasonably interpret as threatening retaliation should they decide to bargain collectively.

The impact upon an election of pro-union activities of a hospital's charge nurses who were supervisory personnel was the topic of a recent case.[117] The court held that the charge nurses' activities did not constitute grounds for invalidating the election because the hospital employees were not misled into thinking that the hospital favored the union, were not coerced into voting in favor of the union because they feared future retaliation, and had no reason to believe that an adverse action would be taken against them if they did not support the union.

In another recent case, a potential wage increase around the time of an election was reviewed by a court.[118] The wage increase had been planned prior to the election, and the nurses knew that the employer had conducted a wage study prior to receiving a request for recognition from the SNA. The wage study had been conducted by an outside company. Even though the nurses knew about the study, no fixed date or dollar amount of the wage adjustment had been fixed. All of these factors were the basis of the court decision that withholding the wage increase did not constitute a violation of the NLRA.

Yet, in another case involving nurse employees, a court has found that announcement of a wage increase 2 weeks before the representation election and promises of benefits constituted unfair labor practices.[119] Surveillance of hospital employees' union activities and reporting those activities to the hospital security director has also been found to violate the NLRA.[120]

If a substantial increase in the size of the employee complement is expected with reasonable certainty in a relatively short time, an employer's plans for expansion of the work force can delay an election. For example, in one case the NLRB allowed a hospital 4 to 5 months to reach a representative complement in its registered nurse unit, where the hospital expected a five-fold increase in the number of registered nurses in that time.[121] The Board found that the hospital's plans for expansion were not speculative. At the time of the NLRB hearing, the hospital employed four RNs, but its budget provided for 29, hiring commitments had been made, and the hospital was involved in a recruitment campaign, expecting to hire 17 to 20 RNs within 5 months. All of these factors were the basis for the NLRB's decision to delay the election.

Duty of employer and representative to bargain in good faith

The elements of the duty to bargain in good faith are found in Section 158(d) of the NLRA.[122] This section contains a basic definition of collective bargaining:

> To bargain collectively is the performance of the mutual obligation of the employer and the representative of the employees to meet at reasonable times and confer in good faith with respect to wages, hours and other terms and conditions of employment, or the negotiation of an agreement, or any question arising thereunder, and the execution of a written contract incorporating any agreement reached if requested by either party . . .[123]

Many cases have dealt with the refusal of the employer to bargain. The refusal can be deemed an unfair labor practice. Examples of these cases will be discussed. However, an employer's refusal to bargain with an established union can be justified on at least two grounds: that the union no longer represents the majority of employees; or that the employer possesses a "good faith doubt" that the union continues to represent the majority of employees. This issue was discussed in a case involving a nurses' union.[124] In this case there was poor attendance at union meetings; employees told the hospital administration that there was a lack of interest and support; union members had resigned; and there was a high turnover of nurse-employees. After reviewing all the facts, however, the NLRB found that the hospital had failed to establish adequately its "good faith doubt" of the previously certified union majority.

Duty of fair representation

An individual nurse employee acquires legal rights under the collective agreement which can be enforced. While much of the discussion in this chapter has focused upon the union and employer relationship, the duty of fair representation exists between the employee and the labor organization and is based upon the collective agreement.[125] The duty is that the bargaining representative must act fairly toward all employees which are represented.

The duty has no explicit statutory origin, but was developed by the courts, which interpreted the duty as a mandate of Congress.[126] The rationale developed by the courts is that Congress would not have granted *exclusive power of representation* without requiring that those being represented be represented fairly.[127]

The duty of fair representation exists not only for private sector employees but also for public sector employees. The legal issues raised in litigation between unions and employees have dealt primarily with the duty owed by a union to an individual employee when it represents that employee in the grievance procedure or in arbitration. Courts have provided some direction as to what constitutes this duty:

1. A union must in good faith and in non-arbitrary manner, make decisions as to the merits of particular grievances
2. A union may not arbitrarily ignore a meritorious grievance or process it in a perfunctory manner[128]
3. A union must act fairly, impartially, and in good faith . . . without hostile discrimination[129]

In some jurisdictions the duty to avoid arbitrary and perfunctory conduct has been described in terms of a negligence standard. In these cases, the bargaining representative's action is evaluated using the "reasonable under the circumstances" standard.[130]

Before bringing suit, however the nurse-employee may be required to "exhaust" (proceed through) the grievance and arbitration procedures provided for in the collective bargaining agreement.[131] An action for breach of the fair representation duty has a 6-month statute of limitations.[132] Therefore, if in the situation, a nurse should immediately seek his or her own legal counsel.

Private sector: unfair labor practices

The NLRA lists unfair labor practices of both employers and labor organizations.[133] These have been summarized in the box on the facing page. Actually, the NLRB can regulate employer and union activity not only through Section 158 but also through the election process, discussed before.

Statements, promises, comments, and steps taken regarding employee benefits by the employer may violate the NLRA. Granting benefits during the organizing effort, however, is not always considered an unfair labor practice. Employers are permitted to give raises which are regularly and periodically granted or ones which em-

PRIVATE SECTOR UNFAIR LABOR PRACTICES

*Employer Unfair Labor Practices**

1. To interfere with, retrain, or coerce employees in the exercise of their right to organize (Section 157)
2. To dominate or interfere with the formation or administration of any labor organization or contribute financial or other support to it
3. To discriminate in regard to hire or tenure of employment or any term or condition of employment to encourage or discourage membership in any labor organization
4. To discharge or otherwise discriminate against an employee for filing charges or giving testimony under the NLRA
5. To refuse to bargain collectively with the employee's representative

Labor Organization Unfair Labor Practices†

1. To restrain or coerce employees in the exercise of their organizing rights
2. To cause an employer to discriminate against an employee
3. To refuse to bargain collectively with an employer
4. To engage in or encourage any individual employed by any person engaged in commerce or in an industry affecting commerce to engage in a strike or a refusal in the course of employment if it results in restraint of trade, ceasing to use, sell or otherwise deal in certain products, or other illegal acts
5. To require of employees covered by an agreement the payment, as a condition precedent to becoming a member of such organization, of a fee in an amount which the Board finds excessive or discriminatory under all circumstances
6. To cause an employer to pay or deliver or agree to pay or deliver any money or other thing of value, in the nature of an exation, for services which are not performed or not to be performed
7. To picket or threaten to picket any employer where an object thereof is forcing an employer to recognize or bargain with the labor organization or forcing the employees to accept or select such labor organization as their collective bargaining representative, unless such labor organization is currently certified as the representative of such employees

*Adapted from 29 U.S.C. §158(a) (1982).
†Adapted from 29 U.S.C. §158(b) (1982).

ployees normally expect to receive.[134] If the question arises, the NLRB will examine the benefits in terms of how they were connected to the unionization or whether they served the purpose of influencing the employees about unionization.

Employer promises are illegal if they could lead employees to believe that the benefit promised is conditioned upon the results of the election, even without an explicit, verbal statement to that effect by the employer. Threatening economic reprisals, such as a reduction in hours, to avoid unionization is prohibited.[135]

Postponing benefits, if they have the effect of punishing employees, can lead to an interference in the employee's rights.[136] Delaying expected wage increases until after an election has been interpreted as an unfair labor practice.[137] In one case the employer's chief executive officer told employees that the routine raise increases 2 weeks before the election had been suspended. The court upheld the NLRB's decision that this employer had created an impression that the suspension of wage increases was linked to the union.

An employer may not discharge an employee for exercising the right to organize.[138] The NLRB must be presented with a preponderance of the evidence that antiunion animus contributed to an employer's decision to discharge an employee. The employer avoids the unfair labor practice charge if the employer can prove, by a preponderance of evidence, that the discharge would have occurred, in any event, for reasons unrelated to the employee's union activities.[139] These cases are sometimes referred to as those which involve "mixed motive" discharges.[140]

Solicitation by the employer of grievances has been found to be an unfair labor practice.[141] Blacklisting former employees has also been deemed an unfair labor practice.[142] A hospital has been found to have committed an unfair labor practice when it dealt directly with employees rather than through the certified bargaining agent.[143] Another hospital made unilateral changes in nurses' wages and fringe benefits, and this was found to be an unfair labor practice.[144] Questioning job applicants as to their union sentiments is also a violation of the NLRA.[145]

In relation to trying to influence the right to strike, a hospital has been found to have committed an unfair labor practice when it granted a "compensatory day off" to all nurses who either did not strike, abandoned the strike, or were hired during the strike.[146]

Hospitals have charged unions with unfair labor practices, as well. One such case involved a challenge to the laboratory conditions just prior to an election.[147] This case involved a nurse who had started a rumor a day before the election that the hospital intended to rehire an unpopular supervisor after the election. The hospital refused to bargain on the basis that free and fair balloting has been precluded by the nurse's action. The court held that the election was valid. It determined that there was no evidence that the nurse's conduct was condoned or authorized by the union and that the conduct did not so "poison the environment of election" that the employees' choices could not be free.

In another case, however, a court would not enforce an NLRB order that the employer bargain because it found the order was not supported by substantial evidence. In this case a union representative made reckless and intentional misrepresentations about the employer's financial status. The union representative, during the election campaign, told employees that the employer had made a profit in the preceding fiscal year and in fact the employer had suffered a financial loss. The court denied the order to bargain because the ability of the employer to pay higher wages was of primary importance in the voting decision and such misrepresentation precluded the free choice of the employees.[148]

Contract provisions

Health care collective bargaining contracts have similar provisions to other union contracts, but they also have unique provisions which address the specific needs and interests of nurses. The box contains a list of provision topics found in the usual union contract in the health care industry. Those provisions of particular interest and importance to nurses will be discussed.

SAMPLE PROVISION HEADINGS OF NURSES' COLLECTIVE BARGAINING AGREEMENT

- Identification of the parties
  - Recognition of the union
- Contract termination, duration of the agreement
- Union security arrangements, open or union shop, membership and dues
- Management rights, union rights
- Wage and effort bargain
  - Hiring practices, orientation, hours, computation and rates of pay, scheduling, floating, transfers, overtime, shift differentials
  - Evaluations, performance appraisals, promotions
  - Disciplinary actions
- Patient care
  - Nurse-patient ratios, qualifications, assignments
  - Professional practice committees, standards of care
- Benefits
  - Paid holidays, vacation, sick leave, leaves of absence
  - Education, tuition reimbursement
  - Insurance, retirement, pension, disability, occupational safety and health, worker's compensation, unemployment compensation
- Job security
  - Job rights, seniority, lay-off and re-call, severance pay, on-the-job union representation
  - Due process, grievance and arbitration procedures
  - Strike, no-strike, lockout, no-lockout, wildcat and/or sympathy strikes.

HEALTH AND SAFETY

Nurses have employment rights under state and federal laws, for example, those rights created within state worker's compensation laws, which deal with health and safety. Occupational health and safety, federal laws, and state laws also provide nurses with employment protections. These laws were discussed in Chapter 30 and also in Chapter 15, Occupational Health Nurses. For example, the duty to inform employees of hazardous materials that are in the workplace environment is the employer's legal obligation (under OSHA and states with right to know laws).

However, the collective agreement can be another vehicle for providing workplace safety and for assuring a healthful work environment. Besides negotiating for sick leave benefits and medical benefits, nurses may wish to collectively bargain for environmental safety and healthful workplace practices.

STAFFING

A collective agreement can be negotiated to solve some of the concerns about inadequate number of staff available and inappropriate assignments. For example, the agreement may establish a special procedure for nurses regarding being assigned to a situation with inadequate number and type of staff. That procedure may involve formal documentation of the event, with copies of the documentation being distributed to the immediate nursing supervisor, the administrator, and the nurses' union representative. This documentation formalizes the process of tracking how often such assignments are made and what the reasons are for the shortage. Such information can become very important when it comes time to negotiate the next contract.[149]

As with any dispute under the collective agreement, it will involve grievance, arbitration, and possible NLRB administrative litigation. In a recent case the work of assigning second call for support personnel in an after hours adult OR in a specialized Hawaii hospital was awarded to RNs rather than OR technicians.[150] The decision of the NLRB to award the work assignment to the RNs was based on a comparison of the skills of the two groups, the employer's preference, and factors of economics and efficiency. The Board noted that the RN was qualified to do all duties of technician; but the technician was not qualified to perform all functions of the RN.

ORIENTATION AND EDUCATION

Nurses may negotiate for their particular and unique educational and orientation needs. Contracts can include allotment of time and payment of registration fees by the employer for continuing education in the nurses' practice areas. Inservice education can also be a part of the contract. The number per year, the choice of topics, and who participates are all decisions which the union can negotiate to be made by the nurses.

Orientation to the workplace can also be negotiated. Specifically, requiring the employer to orient and give internships in critical care areas for employees, may be items that are negotiable.

JOB SECURITY

Sharing control of the job and having a say in establishing the rules and policies which govern hiring, firing, evaluation, and promotion are important contract negotiation areas. The mechanisms for how jobs are announced, for example, requiring that job openings be posted, and participating in specifying job specifications and qualifications can be provided for in the collective agreement. The wages, seniority, and benefits for the work done are also important to have specified in the contract.

PROFESSIONAL PRACTICE COMMITTEES

The collective nursing contract may be unique in having a term creating a professional practice committee. There actually may be more than one committee created under the contract. For example, a nursing standards committee, a nursing care committee, an education committee, and a safety committee are just a few of the possibilities.

Portions of the contract dealing with these committees should:

1. Specify that the hospital or other health care facility agrees to recognize such committees
2. State the purpose and goals of the commitees
3. Give the membership criteria
4. Indicate how often the committees will meet

Sometimes the contract will require that agendas be distributed in advance. However, one caution about these committees is that they should not take the place of the collective bargaining or regular negotiation process. These committees are for the purpose of addressing patient care issues from the nurse-employee's perspective. Responses to these issues from the administration within a specified time period may also be part of the contract.

Contract enforcement

Once a contract has been negotiated and agreed upon, its enforcement becomes a matter of dealing with disputes among employers and employees based upon the terms of the contract. As listed on p. 510, contract provisions may provide for mechanisms for enforcing the bargaining agreement, including filing a grievance, and participating in arbitration. Other mechanisms include filing complaints with the NLRB; litigation; further negotiation among the parties; and, often the last resort, striking, picketing, or other concerted refusals to work.

In a recent case the NLRB petitioned a court to enforce an order it made requiring an employer to cease and desist from denying its employees sick leave benefits.[151] Evidence showed that the employees and employer negotiated sick leave benefits at the bargaining table and by mistake a clause dealing with sick leave was left out of the written contract. The court granted the NLRB's petition and ordered an enforcement of the NLRB order, saying that evidence supported the finding that the parties agreed to continue sick leave benefits according to previous practice. The fact that the contract had what is known as a "zipper clause," meaning that the written contract is the final agreement, did not dissuade the court from deciding that an item agreed to at the bargaining table and mistakenly omitted from the written contract could be denied by the employer.

As discussed previously, the duty to bargain and the duty of fair representation also are contract enforcement issues.[152] However, enforcing a collective bargaining agreement also involves the administration of the contract itself. That administration depends on the grievance procedures outlined in the contract and other provisions which deal with the contract's administration. Grievances, arbitration, and strikes will be discussed below.

GRIEVANCES

Generally, a grievance has been defined in union contracts as a dispute about wages, hours of work, and working conditions.[153] Grievances may first be settled between the individual employee and the supervisor; if this fails, then a formal grievance may be commenced. The grievance should be in writing. The box summarizes a sample, four-step grievance procedure found in many health care industry contracts. The exact wording of a contract should be checked and followed.

ARBITRATION

When a grievance cannot be settled through a process outlined in the contract, the contract usually provides that it be referred to arbitration. The grievance procedure's goal is voluntary settlement. However, when this fails, another process is available.[154] The decision to arbitrate can involve not only meritorious but also strategic considerations. A study by the Federal Mediation and Conciliation Service (FMCS) indicates that most often the issues of discipline and discharge, seniority, arbitratability, overtime, work assignment, job classification, and pay are arbitrated.[155]

THE NURSE'S RIGHT TO STRIKE

As mentioned, historically, nurses have refrained from striking. As one author put it, "a strike is industrial warfare and should not be taken lightly."[156] Also, as mentioned earlier, nurses who work for the federal government do not have a right to strike; nurses who work for other public sector employers may or may not have the right to strike, depending on state law.[157] A strike is still possible; however, it is illegal. In public or private employment, the nurse who participates in an illegal strike does so without legal protections and may face stiff penalties.

SAMPLE, FOUR-STEP GRIEVANCE PROCESS

Step 1. Employee and Immediate Supervisor

The employee orally discusses the grievance with the immediate supervisor. The union representative may be present. A reply to the grievance should come within 4 calendar days.

Step 2. Employee and Department Administrator

If the matter is not satisfactorily settled in Step 1, or a reply does not come within the time specified, the employee shall discuss (orally) the grievance with the department administrator. This discussion occurs within 10 calendar days of the employee–immediate supervisor discussion. The union representative may meet with the department administrator. The reply to the grievance shall be given within 4 calendar days.

Step 3. Written Grievance: Employee and Agency Administrator

If the grievance is not satisfactorily settled, or if a reply is not given in the requisite time, the grievance shall be written. A standard grievance form should be used; it should be dated and signed by the employee and the union representative. The written grievance should be submitted to the agency administrator within 7 calendar days after the Step 2 reply or time allotted. A meeting should be held where present are the employee, union representative, and agency administrator. A reply should be given within 10 calendar days after the meeting.

Step 4. Refer to Arbitration

If the grievance is not satisfactorily settled, or an answer is not given within the time specified, the union may give written notice to the employer within 10 calendar days after the Step 3 answer or time passage, requesting that the grievance be referred to an impartial arbitrator selected in the agreed manner.

Adapted from D. PETERSON, J. REZLER, K. REED, *Grievances: Forerunners to Arbitration*, ARBITRATION IN HEALTH CARE 23 (1981).

Nurse-employees who are within the coverage of the NRLA are governed by special provisions of that law when it comes to "any strike, picketing, or other concerted refusal to work at any health care institution."[158] This section requires the union to give at least 10 days notice to the health care institution; and before engaging in the stike, picketing, or other concerted refusal to work, the union must also notify the FMCS.

The union must include in its notice the date and time that the action will begin. Once the notice is given, the union and employer may extend it by written agreement. The employer's reaction might involve a move to "lock out" the employees. This is only permissible where the strike is an economic one versus the strike that involves an unfair labor practice.

An economic strike is a strike by employees in support of issues related to wages, hours, and working conditions or for any reason other than to protest an unfair labor practice of the employer. A work stoppage is considered an unfair labor practice strike when employees have struck in protest of an employer's conduct that is an unfair labor practice or when a strike is prolonged or aggravated because of such conduct. The ultimate decision as to whether a strike is purely economic or one which involves unfair labor practices rests with the NLRB and the courts.

In the unfair labor practice strike, the employer may not use "lockout." A "lockout" means that the employer may hire permanent replacements for the nurses who are out on strike and, thereby, lock them out. In at least one case where the NLRB found that the strike was prolonged by the hospital's unfair labor practices, its order that employees on strike be reinstated with back pay was upheld by a court.[159]

The FMCS role is to communicate promptly with the union and health care employer and use its efforts, by mediation and conciliation, to bring them to agreement.[160] If, in the opinion of the director of the FMCS, a threatened or actual strike or lockout affecting a health care institution will substantially interrupt the delivery of health care in the locality concerned, the director may establish within certain statutory time periods an impartial board of inquiry.[161]

The NLRB decisions and court cases on this topic stress that this notice provision is to be strictly interpreted. For example, several cases have held that nondisruptive, informational picketing was improper because the union had not given the notice.[162] However, spontaneous striking, not authorized by the union, does not require notice.[163] But, picketing by non–health care employees involved in construction and renovation of the hospital who set up a picketing gate partially on hospital property did not fall within the clause of the NLRA requiring 10 days prior notice to the FMCS before engaging in the picketing of the health care institution.[164]

Recommendations and trends

This chapter has reviewed the laws governing collective bargaining as they relate to nurses who are employed in the public sector (federal, state, or local employment) and in the private sector (employment in non-profit or proprietary health care facilities). The choice to exercise the right to bargain collectively is the nurse's to make. This choice should involve not only a review of applicable laws, but also consideration of professional and ethical viewpoints.

Whether a nurse is involved in a union or not, certain concerted efforts may be protected through the NLRA. Examples of such situations were given. Situations which present these issues should be taken to an attorney for review and application of the statutes and case law on the topic.

The economics of health care are assuming a larger role than in prior years. The impact of the cost containment measures upon nursing employment has yet to be fully realized. In 1983 the Massachusetts Nurses' Association sought declaratory and injunctive relief, citing that the new Massachusetts' hospital payment law was preempted by the Labor Management Relations Act.[165] The court held that the hospital payment law, which established a prospective reimbursement system for hospital costs, did not constitute an impermissible attempt to interfere with the balance of power in the collective bargaining process to give state hospitals and the state hospital association an advantage in contract negotiations relative to the nursing association.

This case, presenting rather novel legal issues, represents a reaching out for new interpretation and new protections for the employed nurse. This type of activity should continue; employment issues are most important to the everyday work life of the nurse.

Endnotes

1. Berkeley, *Arbitration: The Process and the Participants*, HEALTH CARE LABOR LAW 166 (I. Shepard and A.E. Doudera, eds. 1981).
2. *Id.*
3. L. FLANAGAN, ONE STRONG VOICE: THE STORY OF THE AMERICAN NURSES' ASSOCIATION 401 (1976).
4. French and Robinson, *Collective Bargaining by Nurses and Other Professionals: Anomaly or Trend?* 11 LABOR LAW J. 903, 904 (October 1960) (hereinafter cited as *French and Robinson*).
5. 37 A.J.N. 766 (July 1937).
6. Northrup, *Collective Bargaining by Professional Societies*, INSIGHTS INTO LABOR ISSUES 151, 152 (R. Lester and J. Shister, eds. 1948).
7. *Id.* at 152.
8. *French and Robinson, supra* note 7, at 904, citing the Washington State Nurses' Association's MANUAL ON CONFERENCE COMMITTEE.
9. *Id.*
10. E. BEAL, E. WICKERSHAM, P. KIENAST, THE PRACTICE OF COLLECTIVE BARGAINING 492 (5th ed. 1976).
11. *French and Robinson, supra* note 7, at 905.

12. Phillips, *The U.S. Nurse Today: An Economic Progress Report* 21 R.N. 17 (July 1958).
13. *Id.*
14. Donovon, *Is Nursing Ripe for a Union Explosion* 41 R.N. 41 (May 1978).
15. *More than 100,000 Registered Nurses are now Represented by SNAs for Collective Bargaining* 77 A.J.N. 381 (March 1977).
16. *See, e.g.* Publications of the American Nurses' Association: THE NATURE AND SCOPE OF ANA'S ECONOMIC & GENERAL WELFARE PROGRAM (1985); THE GRIEVANCE PROCEDURE (1985); ECONOMIC AND EMPLOYMENT ISSUES FOR REGISTERED NURSES (1985-84) (a series of 10 monographs examining complex cause and effect relationships between nurses and economic and employment issues for nurses, including salaries, issues in nursing education, hospital payment mechanisms, classification systems, collective bargaining, retirement income issues, third-party reimbursement, wage setting, evaluation, sex-based wage discrimination, and trends; ANA'S ECONOMIC & GENERAL WELFARE PROGRAM: DYNAMICS OF THE LOCAL UNIT (1981); ANA'S ECONOMIC & GENERAL WELFARE PROGRAM: A HISTORICAL PERSPECTIVE (1981); NURSES IN ACTION: A PUBLIC RELATIONS MANUAL (1977); ANA'S ECONOMIC & GENERAL WELFARE PROGRAM: ORGANIZING THE LOCAL UNIT (1975).
17. Godfrey, *Someone should represent nurses* 5 NURSING '76 73 (June 1976).
18. 5 U.S.C. §101 (1982).
19. 29 U.S.C. §151 (1982 and Supp. II 1984).
20. *Marbury v. Madison,* 1 Cranch 137 (1803).
21. 5 U.S.C. §2101(1) (1982).
22. The responsibilities of this office are found in 5 U.S.C. §4304 (1982).
23. Merit System Principles are found at 5 U.S.C. §2301 (1982) and include, in part, recruitment from qualified individuals to achieve a work force from all segments of society, selection and advancement determined solely on the basis of relative ability, knowledge, and skills, after fair and open competition assuring that all receive equal opportunity; fair and equitable treatment in all aspects of personnel management; equal pay for work of equal value; high standards of integrity, conduct, and concern for public interest; efficiency and effectiveness; protection against arbitrary action and whistleblowing.
24. *See, e.g.* 5 U.S.C. §7501 (Adverse Actions), 7701 (Appeals) (1982).
25. 5 U.S.C. §7101(a) (1982).
26. 5 U.S.C. §7102 (1982).
27. 5 U.S.C. §7105(a)(2) (1982).
28. 5 U.S.C. §7106(a) (1982).
29. 5 U.S.C. §7111 (1982).
30. 5 U.S.C. §7111(b)(2) (1982).
31. 5 U.S.C. §7112(a)(1) (1982).
32. 5 U.S.C. §7112(b) (1982).
33. 5 U.S.C. §7114(a)(2) (1982).
34. 5 U.S.C. §7120(f)(1) (1982).
35. *Professional Air Traffic Controllers Org., affiliated with MEBA, AFL-CIO (Federal Aviation Admin., Dept. of Transportation),* 7 FLRA No. 10 (1981) *enforced,* 685 F.2d 547 (D.C. Cir. 1982).
36. 5 U.S.C. §7311(3) and (4) (1982).
37. 5 U.S.C. §7119(a) (1982).
38. 5 U.S.C. §7119(c) (1982).
39. 5 U.S.C. §7121(a)(1) (1982).
40. *See, e.g.,* NEV. REV. STAT. §288.010 (1985) which is the public sector law for local governments.
41. *See, e.g.,* MO. ANN. STAT. §105.530 (Vernon Supp. 1986).
42. *See, e.g.,* ALASKA STAT. §23.40.090 (1984 and Supp. 1985), the Public Employment Relations Act which lists criteria for appropriate units, including factors of community of interest, wages, hours, and other working conditions of employees involved, history of collective bargaining, and desires of employees. Unnecessary fragmentation is to be avoided, according to this state statute.
43. *See, e.g* NEV. REV. STAT. §288.270 (1985).
44. *See, e.g.,* MO. ANN. STAT. §105.530 (Vernon Supp. 1986). This issue is discussed further later in the chapter.
45. 29 U.S.C. §141 (1982 and Supp. II 1984). The act was declared constitutional in *NLRB v. Jones & Laughlin Steel Corp.,* 301 U.S. 1 (1937). 29 C.F.R. §101, 102 (1985) contains the regulations relating to the NLRA.
46. 29 U.S.C. §153 (1982).
47. 29 U.S.C. §152 (2) (1982); excludes, for example, the following employers: the United States, state or political subdivision, thereof, and railways. 29 U.S.C. §152(3) (1982) excludes the following employees: agricultural laborers, domestic service employees, individuals employed by their parent or spouse, independent contractors, supervisors, and railway employees. In addition, case law has provided that managerial personnel and employees who assist and act in a confidential capacity to persons who exercise managerial functions (formulate, determine, and effectuate policies) within the field of labor relations are also excluded from coverage by the NLRA (this is known as the labor nexus test). (*See, e.g., Retail Clerks International Ass'n. v. NLRB,* 366 F.2d 642 (D.C. Cir. 1966), *cert. denied,* 386 U.S. 1017; *Ford Motor Co. (Chicago Branch),* 66 NLRB 1317 (1946); *Weyerhaeuser Co.,* 173 NLRB 1170 (1968).
48. 29 U.S.C. §153, 158, 159, 160, 161 (1982 and Supp. II 1984).
49. For more discussion of the legislative history and background of the 1974 Amendments, *see,* Shepard, *Health Care Institution Amendments to the National Labor Relations Act: An Analysis* 1 AM. J. LAW & MED. 41 (1975).
50. 29 U.S.C. §158(g) (1982).
51. 29 U.S.C. §158(d) (1982).
52. 29 U.S.C. §183 (1982).
53. 29 U.S.C. §159 (1982).
54. 29 U.S.C. §159(a) and (c)(1)(A) (1982).
55. 29 U.S.C. §157 and 158(a)(3) (1982).
56. 29 U.S.C. §159(c)(3) and (e)(2) (1982).
57. *See, e.g. Packard Motor Co. v. NLRB,* 330 U.S. 485, 491 (1947), where the court stated, the Board's decision, "if not final, is rarely to be disturbed."
58. *E.g.,* 29 U.S.C. §159(b)(2) (1982) prohibits the NLRB from deciding that a proposed unit is inappropriate because of prior establishment of a broader unit, unless a majority of the employees in the proposed unit vote against separate representation.
59. *NLRB v. Mercy Hospital Assoc.,* 606 F.2d 22 (2nd Cir. 1979), *cert. denied,* 445 U.S. 971 (1980).
60. 29 U.S.C. §159 (c)(5) (1982).
61. 29 U.S.C. §159 (1982).
62. 29 U.S.C. §159(b)(2) (1982).
63. *See, e.g., NLRB v. Frederick Memorial Hospital,* 691 F.2d 191 (4th Cir. 1982).

64. 29 U.S.C. §169 (1982).
65. *See, e.g., St. Elizabeth's Community Hospital v. NLRB,* 708 F.2d 1436 (9th Cir. 1983); *see also Tressler Lutheran Home for Children v. NLRB,* 677 F.2d 302 (3rd Cir. 1982) where First Amendment defense was not appropriate in proceeding claiming unfair labor practice against nursing home affiliated with a religion.
66. 29 U.S.C. §157 (1982).
67. 29 U.S.C. §163 (1982); *see also Crestline Memorial Hospital Assoc. v. NLRB,* 668 F.2d 243 (6th Cir. 1982), which involved a nurse's strike in Ohio.
68. 29 U.S.C. §157, 158(a)(3) (1982), but as discussed above, union-security clauses may be part of the collective bargaining agreement, which may allow nurses who object, philosophically, to pay an agency fee; or *see,* §169 which provides that nurses who object on religious grounds pay the amount of the dues to a charitable organization.
69. Concerted activities of supervisors is not covered by the NLRA. *See, e.g., NLRB v. St. Mary's Home, Inc.* 690 F.2d 1062 (4th Cir. 1982) where an LPN was properly classified as a supervisor under the NLRA and the Board was without jurisdiction over her claim of discriminatory discharge.
70. 29 U.S.C. §157 (1982).
71. 29 U.S.C. §158(a)(1) (1982).
72. *Shelley & Anderson Furniture Manufacturing, Inc. v. NLRB,* 497 F.2d 1200 (9th Cir. 1974); *see, e.g., East Chicago Rehabilitation Center v. NLRB,* 710 F.2d 397 (7th Cir. 1983), *cert. denied,* 465 U.S. 1065 (1984) where a spontaneous, 2-hour walkout by 17 nurse's aides at a nursing home constituted concerted activity protected by the NLRA. The court held also that the nurse's aides who had been fired for the walkout were entitled to reinstatement with back pay.
73. *NLRB v. St. Anne's Hospital,* 648 F.2d 67 (1st Cir. 1981).
74. *Misericordia Hospital Medical Center v. NLRB,* 623 F.2d 808 (2nd Cir. 1980).
75. *Alleluia Cushion Co.,* 221 NLRB 999 (1975); *Air Surrey Corp.,* 229 NLRB 1064 (1977).
76. *Meyers Industries, Inc.,* 268 NLRB 493 (1984).
77. K. O'ROURKE and S. BARTON, NURSE POWER, UNIONS AND THE LAW 126 (1981) (hereinafter cited as *O'Rourke and Barton).*
78. *See, e.g., NLRB v. St. Vincent's Hospital,* 729 F.2d 730 (11th Cir. 1984), where discipline of two employees for soliciting on behalf of the union in patient care areas was the result of discriminatory application of hospital policy.
79. *Eastern Maine Medical Center v. NLRB,* 658 F.2d 1 (1st Cir. 1981).
80. *Beth Israel Hospital v. NRLB,* 437 U.S. 483 (1978).
81. *Monmouth Medical Center v. NLRB,* 604 F.2d 820 (3rd Cir. 1979).
82. *See, e.g., Bay Medical Center v. NLRB,* 588 F.2d 1174 (6th Cir. 1978), *cert. denied,* 444 U.S. 827 (1979).
83. 29 U.S.C. §152(12) (1982).
84. *Anne Arundel General Hospital,* 217 N.L.R.B. 848 (1975).
85. *NLRB v. Bell Aerospace Co.,* 416 U.S. 267, 289 (1974).
86. 29 U.S.C. §152(11) (1982).
87. A case has also dealt with the issue of whether registered nurses in a nursing home were employees or supervisors. *See, NLRB v. American Medical Service Inc.,* 705 F.2d 1472 (7th Cir. 1983), where substantial evidence failed to support the NLRB's certification of a union consisting of 17 RNs employed at a nursing home because the record showed that the nurses were supervisors within the meaning of the NLRA since the RNs had authority to discharge and otherwise discipline other employees and had discretion over who worked when. The court held that the NLRB had improperly certified a unit of supervisors.
88. *See, e.g., NLRB v. Walker County Medical Center,* 722 F.2d 1535 (11th Cir. 1984), *reh'g. denied,* 726 F.2d 755 (11th Cir. 1984), where the court held that the NLRB's determination that assistant unit coordinators and charge nurses at the medical center were not supervisors was supported by substantial evidence; *Medical Center at Bowling Green v. NLRB,* 712 F.2d 1091 (6th Cir. 1983), where the Board's decision to allow unit directors (nurses) to vote in an election subject to challenge was appropriate.
89. *NLRB v. Bell Aerospace Co.,* 416 U.S. 267, 290 (1979).
90. *Noranda Aluminum, Inc. v. NLRB,* 751 F.2d 268 (8th Cir. 1984).
91. *Id.* at 269, quoting *Iowa Electric Light & Power Co. v. NLRB,* 717 F.2d 433, 434 (8th Cir. 1983), *cert. denied,* 466 U.S. 903 (1984), which quoted *NLRB v. Yeshiva University,* 444 U.S. 672, 683 (1980).
92. 29 U.S.C. §159(b)(1) (1982).
93. *See also* Cooper and Brent, *The Nursing Profession and the Right to Separate Representation* 58 CHI-KENT L. REV. 1053 (1982).
94. A related issue, whether LPNs could form an all LPN unit, has also been addressed by the courts. *See, e.g., NLRB v. Res-Care, Inc.,* 705 F.2d 1461 (7th Cir. 1983), where the court stated allowing seven LPNs to form their own collective bargaining unit, rather than merging them into the unit consisting of nurse's aides and other low-level workers, was not improper since thus allowing a maximum of two units in the health care facility could not be deemed an undue proliferation.
95. *Watonwan Memorial Hospital, Inc. v. NLRB,* 711 F.2d 848, 850 (8th Cir. 1983).
96. *Id. Kansas City Terminal Elevator Co. v. NLRB,* 697 F.2d 269, 270 (8th Cir. 1983).
97. *See, e.g., NLRB v. Yeshiva University,* 444 U.S. at 672, 691 (1980).
98. *NLRB v. St. Francis Hospital of Lynnwood,* 601 F.2d 404 (9th Cir. 1979).
99. *Id.* at 411-16.
100. *Id.* at 416, 419.
101. *NLRB v. Walker County Medical Center, Inc.,* 722 F.2d 1535 (11th Cir. 1984), *reh'g denied,* 726 F.2d 755 (1984).
102. *Beth Israel Hospital and Geriatric Center v. NLRB,* 688 F.2d 697 (10th Cir. 1982) *cert. dismissed,* 459 U.S. 1025 (1982), and *St. Anthony Hospital Systems v. NLRB,* 688 F.2d 697 (10th Cir. 1982). *See also Long Island Jewish-Hillside Medical Center v. NLRB,* 685 F.2d 29 (2nd Cir. 1982); *Vicksburg Hospital Inc. v. NLRB,* 653 F.2d 1070 (5th Cir. 1981), where combined service, maintenance, and technical employees unit was appropriate and not inconsistent with congressional mandate against undue proliferation. *But see Mary Thompson Hospital v. NLRB,* 621 F.2d 858 (7th Cir. 1980) where four licensed stationery engineers had been granted a separate bargaining unit. The court held that the NLRB had improperly relied exclusively on the traditional community of interest analysis and failed to expressly consider congressional admonition against undue proliferation of bargaining units in the health care industry.
103. *NLRB v. HMO International/California Medical Group Health Plan, Inc.,* 678 F.2d 806 (9th Cir. 1982).
104. *O'Rourke and Barton, supra* note 77, at 146.

105. 561 F.2d 524 (4th Cir. 1977).
106. 241 NLRB 107 (1979).
107. *See, e.g., NLRB and New York State Nurses' Association v. North Shore University Hospital,* 724 F.2d 269 (2nd Cir. 1983); *see also Kessler Institute for Rehabilitation v. NLRB,* 669 F.2d 138 (3rd Cir. 1982).
108. *Dal-Tex Optical Co.,* 137 NLRB 1782 (1962).
109. *Ideal Electric & Manufacturing Co.,* 134 NLRB 1275 (1961).
110. *General Shoe Corp.,* 77 NLRB 124, 127 (1948).
111. 29 U.S.C. §158(c) (1982).
112. *See, e.g., Montgomery Ward & Co.,* 232 NLRB 848 (1977).
113. *See, e.g., Plastronics, Inc.,* 233 NLRB 155 (1977).
114. *See, e.g., Royal Typewriter Co. v. NLRB,* 533 F.2d 1030 (8th Cir. 1976); *Paoli Chair Co.,* 231 NLRB 539 (1977).
115. *Thomas Products Co.,* 167 NLRB 732 (1967).
116. *St. Francis Hospital,* 263 NLRB 834 (1982).
117. *Wright Memorial Hospital v. NLRB,* 771 F.2d 400 (8th Cir. 1985).
118. *Bowling Green-Warren County Community Hospital Corp. v. NLRB,* 756 F.2d 41 (6th Cir. 1985).
119. *St. Francis Federation of Nurses and Health Professionals v. NLRB,* 729 F.2d 844 (D.C. Cir. 1984).
120. *NLRB v. St. Vincent's Hospital,* 729 F.2d 730 (11th Cir. 1984).
121. *St. John of God Hospital,* 260 NLRB 905 (1982).
122. 29 U.S.C. §158(d) (1982).
123. *Id.*
124. *Bellwood General Hospital, Inc. v. NLRB,* 627 F.2d 98 (7th Cir. 1980).
125. *Smith v. Evening News Assn.,* 371 U.S. 195 (1962); *Vaca v. Sipes,* 386 U.S. 171 (1967).
126. C. BERENDT, COLLECTIVE BARGAINING 200 (1984).
127. *Steele v. Louisville & Nashville R.R.,* 323 U.S. 192, 204 (1944); *Ford Motor Co. v. Huffman,* 345 U.S. 330 (1953).
128. *Vaca v. Sipes,* 386 U.S. 171, 194, 191 (1967); *see also Holodnak v. Avco Corp.,* 381 F. Supp. 191 (D. Conn. 1974), *aff'd. in part, rev'd. in part,* 514 F.2d 285 (2nd Cir. 1975), *cert. denied,* 423 U.S. 892 (1975); *De Arroyo v. Sindicato De Trabajadores Packinghouse AFL-CIO,* 425 F.2d 281 (1st Cir. 1970), *cert. denied,* 400 U.S. 877 (1970).
129. Steele *v. Louisville & Nashville RR,* 323 U.S. 192, 204 (1944).
130. *Foust v. International Brotherhood of Electrical Workers,* 572 F.2d 710 (10th Cir. 1978), *rev'd. in part,* 442 U.S. 42 (1979); *but see e.g., Ryan v. N.Y. Newspaper Printing Pressman's Union No. 2,* 590 F.2d 451 (2nd Cir. 1979), where the negligence standard was rejected.
131. *Vaca v. Sipes,* 386 U.S. at 171, 184 (1971).
132. *DelCostello v. Teamsters,* 462 U.S. 151 (1983).
133. 29 U.S.C. §158(a) (employer) and 158(b) (labor organization or its agents) (1982).
134. *Standards Coil Products, Inc.,* 99 NLRB 899, 903 (1952).
135. *Edgewood Nursing Center v. NLRB,* 581 F.2d 363 (3rd Cir. 1978).
136. *Sugardale Foods, Inc.,* 221 NLRB 1228 (1975).
137. *NLRB v. Porta Systems Corp.,* 625 F.2d 399 (2nd Cir. 1980).
138. *See, e.g., Presbyterian/St. Luke's Medical Center v. NLRB,* 723 F.2d 1468 (10th Cir. 1983), where a nurse was discharged in retaliation for her union activities. The court held that the evidence sustained the finding that the discharge was an unfair labor practice; *see also, NLRB v. American Geri-Care, Inc.,* 697 F.2d 56 (2nd Cir. 1982), where an employee was discharged because of testimony at NLRB hearing, and this was deemed an unfair labor practice.
139. *NLRB v. Transportation Management Corp.,* 103 S. Ct. 2469 (1983), *quoting, Mt. Healthy City School District Board of Education v. Doyle,* 429 U.S. 274 (1977) and *Wright Line,* 251 NLRB 1083 (1980), 662 F.2d 899 (1st Cir. 1981), *cert. denied,* 455 U.S. 989 (1982).
140. *See, e.g., Edgewood Nursing Center v. NLRB,* 581 F.2d 363 (3rd Cir. 1978) where nurse's second medication error was the employer's reason for terminating the employee, but the court found the underlying reason, union activity, the "real reason"; *but see Hubbard Regional Hospital v. NLRB,* 579 F.2d 1251 (1st Cir. 1978) where the bizarre manner in which the nurse prepared a sedated patient for transportation to surgery was bound to raise serious doubts with patients and other personnel as to the quality of nursing care at the hospital, and the events fell far short of proving that there was anti-union motivation on the part of the employer when it terminated the nurse's employment.
141. *Presbyterian/St. Luke's Medical Center,* 723 F.2d 1468 (10th Cir. 1983).
142. *See e.g. NLRB v. Mt. Desert Island Hospital,* 695 F.2d 634 (1st Cir. 1982).
143. *NLRB v. St. Mary's Home, Inc.,* 690 F.2d 1062 (4th Cir. 1982).
144. *See, e.g., N.T. Enloe Memorial Hospital v. NLRB,* 682 F.2d 790 (9th Cir. 1982).
145. *Eastern Maine Medical Center v. NLRB,* 658 F.2d 1 (1st Cir. 1981).
146. *NLRB v. Swedish Hospital Medical Center,* 619 F.2d 33 (9th Cir. 1980).
147. *NLRB v. Morgan Health Care Center, Inc.,* 618 F.2d 127 (1st Cir. 1980).
148. *LaCrescent Constant Care Center, Inc. v. NLRB,* 510 F.2d 1319 (8th Cir. 1975).
149. *See also* Note, *Nurses' Legal Dilemma: When Hospital Staffing Compromises Professional Standards* 18 U.S.F.L. Rev. 109 (Fall 1983).
150. *Hawaii Teamsters and Allied Workers Union, Local 996 IBT and Kopiolani Children's Medical Center,* 268 NLRB 160 (1984).
151. *NLRB v. Americana Healthcare Center,* 782 F.2d 941 (11th Cir. 1986).
152. Although the duty to bargain in good faith may also be a contract formation issue.
153. BUREAU OF LABOR STATISTICS, DEPT. OF LABOR, GRIEVANCE PROCEDURES 7 (1964); *see also* BUREAU OF NATIONAL AFFAIRS, BASIC PATTERNS IN UNION CONTRACTS (9th ed. 1979).
154. *See, generally,* 29 U.S.C. §158(d), 171, 173, 174, and 183 (1982) and 29 C.F.R. §1420 (1985).
155. D. PETERSON, J. REZLER & K. REED, ARBITRATION IN HEALTH CARE 26, 27 (1981).
156. M. HUTCHESON, R. SEBRIS, ST. RUMMAGE, D. PECK-GAINES, M. KILLEEN, EMPLOYER'S GUIDE TO STRIKE PLANNING AND PREVENTION 6 (1985).
157. As discussed above, *see, e.g.,* MO. ANN. STAT. §105.530 (Vernon Supp. 1986); *see also* ALASKA STAT. §23.40.200(b) (1984 & Supp. 1985), where hospital employees may not engage in strikes; NEV. REV. STAT. §288.230(2) (1985), where strikes against the state or any local government employer are illegal.
158. 29 U.S.C. §158(g) (1982).

159. *NLRB v. Windham Community Memorial Hospital*, 577 F.2d 805 (2nd Cir. 1978).
160. 29 C.F.R. §1420.1(a) (1985).
161. 29 U.S.C. §183 (1982) and 29 C.F.R. §1420.1(b) (1985).
162. *See, e.g., Orange Belt Painters, District Council of Painters (St. Joseph Hospital)*, 243 NLRB 609 (1979).
163. *See, e.g., East Chicago Rehabilitation Center v. NLRB*, 710 F.2d 397 (7th Cir. 1983), *cert. denied*, 465 U.S. 1065 (1984).
164. *Laborers' International Union of North America v. NLRB*, and *United Association of Journeymen and Apprentices of the Plumbing and Pipefitting Industry of the United States and Canada v. NLRB*, 567 F.2d 1006 (D.C. Cir. 1977).
165. *Massachusetts Nurses' Association v. Dukakis*, 570 F. Supp. 628 (D. Mass. 1983), *aff'd.*, 726 F.2d 41 (1st Cir. 1984).

Additional Readings

FEDERAL CIVIL SERVICE LAW AND PROCEDURE, A BASIC GUIDE (E. Bussey, ed. 1984).

Friss, *Work Force Policy Perspectives: Registered Nurses* 5 J. HEALTH POLIT., POL. & LAW 696 (Winter 1981).

C. GOODMAN, HANDBOOK ON PUBLIC PERSONNEL LAW (1978).

W. GOULD, STRIKES, DISPUTE PROCEDURES AND ARBITRATION, ESSAYS ON LABOR LAW (1985).

Levi, *Functional Redundancy and the Process of Professionalization: The Case of Registered Nurses in the United States* 5 J. HEALTH POLIT., POL. & LAW 333 (Summer 1980).

NATIONAL LABOR COMMITTEE, NATIONAL LAWYER'S GUILD, EMPLOYEE AND UNION MEMBER GUIDE TO LABOR LAW (R. Gibbs, P. Levy, D. Siegel, eds. 1985).

R. SMITH, WORK RIGHTS (1983).

UNIT VII

Nursing Businesses

Chapter 32

Expert nurse witnesses

Cynthia E. Northrop

In recent years nurses have increasingly served as expert witnesses in court and as consultants to attorneys. This development stems from changes in health care, law, and nursing. These changes include not only the increased use of advanced technology but the specialization of knowledge within the nursing profession. Historically, the profession of nursing has evolved into a separate and distinct body of knowledge from the profession of medicine. Hence, the increased need exists for nurses to serve as their own expert witnesses, setting their own standards of practice even in the courtroom. Chapters 2 and 4 discuss the distinction between negligence (ordinary) and malpractice (usually requires expert testimony) standards of care.

Nursing's accountability and responsibility has also changed. This is evidenced by a steady, although slow, increase in malpractice suits against nurses and the widespread practice of nurses of purchasing their own malpractice insurance. Nurses have also been leaders in the quality assurance and risk management movements, each movement having goals of improved services and practice.

This chapter will focus on issues related to the expert nurse witness. Following a discussion of when expert testimony is necessary, definitions of expert witness will be given. An expert will be distinguished from a lay witness. Qualifications of an expert, uses of expert witnesses, and recent cases involving nurses as expert witnesses will be presented. The chapter concludes with guidelines for effective expert testimony and consultation. Expert nurse witnesses may establish businesses of their own which involve consultation, case review, literature research, opinion development, and testimony.

Need for expert testimony

Not all legal cases need expert testimony. The use of an expert witness is often determined by the rules of legal procedure of the particular court and jurisdiction and the case law in a particular state. Many attorneys not only use expert nurse witnesses in the courtroom but usually consult with them long before getting to the courtroom about the facts of the cases. An expert witness's testimony usually is recorded initially as a deposition, an out-of-court statement made under oath in the presence of all parties. The attorney must give advanced notice, usually through the interrogatories, to the other party of whom he or she will use as an expert witness. These discovery tools, deposition and interrogatories, will be discussed further.

More often than merely serving as witnesses nurses are consultants to attorneys in the development of the case. This is especially true in the discovery or pretrial period of litigation, the time during which the parties sort out the pertinent facts and areas of agreement and disagreement. In addition many nurses have started their own businesses in litigation support services, including literature searches, record review, and location of expert testimony for health-related cases. Sometimes larger law firms employ nurses on a full-time basis to assist with case development. These nurses may also be paralegals whose responsibilities include not only reviewing medical records and gathering together standards of nursing practice, but also finding expert nurse witnesses and preparing initial legal forms.

Expert testimony becomes necessary only when the judge and/or jury needs it to make a decision that falls outside their knowledge and understanding. Generally, questions of common sense or common knowledge which are within a usual person's understanding do not require expert opinion.

A very early case, involving the question of whether nursing expert testimony was necessary to determine liability, stated that it was not necessary because six of the jurors were women and the issue in the case was care during labor and delivery.[1] In this case the plaintiff, the allegedly injured person, was in the hospital's labor room awaiting the birth of her first child. She was sedated and had made previous attempts to climb out of bed. At the end of a contraction, the nurse primarily responsible for the plaintiff's care temporarily left the room in order to check information concerning the plaintiff and to respond to a request for assistance from a physician. During the nurse's 5-minute absence, the plaintiff fell out of bed and was injured.

The hospital, the defendant in this case, claimed that the plaintiff needed to produce an expert witness to show that the nurse failed to meet the applicable standard of care. The majority of the Ohio Supreme Court rejected this claim and justified the result of the case (arrived at without expert testimony) on the basis that six members of the jury were women, that most were mothers and grandmothers, and that "they know probably as much if not more about childbirth than many witnesses who might be put on the witness stand."[2]

Using this approach, expert nurse testimony was not necessary to determine whether the nurse was negligent because the facts of the case involved common knowledge and the jury did not need assistance in making a decision. What occurred was within a lay person's knowledge and ability to decide the reasonableness of the action.

A jury is made up of lay persons who are citizens representing a cross section of the community. Therefore, when litigation involves questions of technology or complex issues, including health care delivery, the jury needs expert opinion. Expert nurse testimony and consultation may also be presented as part of the prelitigation requirements in the various states, for example, malpractice arbitration panels. These panels are examples of tort reform. Tort reforms specifically addressing the use of expert witnesses have been made. Recently, one state passed a law which limited the use of expert witnesses. As part of a tort reform package, the law bans testimony from experts who spend more than 20% of their time in court, and who are regarded more as advocates than objective witnesses.[3]

FEDERAL RULES OF EVIDENCE, used only in federal courts and jurisdictions, provide that expert opinion must "assist the trier-of-fact (judge and/or jury) to understand the evidence or to determine a fact in issue."[4] This is the standard (in the federal courts) which is applied to decide whether expert testimony is necessary. In a federal court case a plaintiff was granted damages because the court found that a registered nurse could testify as an expert concerning the safety precautions that were necessary to protect a patient under certain circumstances.[5]

In contrast to the labor and delivery case discussed above, another case involved a nurse who was caring for a woman during labor but who was found negligent for failing to notify the physician of the impending delivery.[6] The trial court issued the following instruction to the jury on the question of the appropriate standard of care required of a nurse in this situation:

> In determining whether a registered nurse used the learning, skill and conduct required of her, you are not permitted to arbitrarily set a standard of your own or determine this question from your personal knowledge. On questions of nursing expertise concerning the standard of care of a nurse, only those qualified as experts are permitted to testify. The standard of care is established by members of the same profession in the same or similar communities under like circumstances.[7]

Therefore, in cases where the judge and/or jury needs information in order to decide the import, impact, or implications of certain facts, expert testimony will be necessary. As discussed in Chapter 4, whether a nurse is held to a standard of negligence or malpractice varies among jurisdictions. In states which hold the nurse to a malpractice standard, expert nurse testimony is essential.

Definitions

An expert witness is an individual willing to testify in court who by education and experience has acquired knowledge of a particular subject or activity—not within the ken or realm of an ordinary person. BLACK'S LAW DICTIONARY defines an expert witness as a person who possesses special or peculiar knowledge acquired from practical experience, one who gives the results of reasoning which can be mastered only by special scientists, and one who has skilled experience or extensive knowledge in a calling or in any branch of learning.[8]

The expert witness in its purest form is one who has had no previous, personal contact with the specific case or litigation in question. The expert witness looks anew, objectively, without conflict of interest, at the situation and renders an opinion, makes a judgment, or provides an interpretation which usually pits what happened against what should have happened.

The lay witness or material witness, on the other hand, is one who testifies about what was personally observed. Because the lay witness actually participated in the situation that is being litigated, the lay witness can be subpoenaed. Usually, the expert witness must first agree to serve in the expert witness role and cannot be subpoenaed. Sometimes, however, once the expert decides to participate in a case, the expert may be subpoenaed.

The lay witness' observations are reachable by a subpoena in support of the judicial system's goal of getting at the truth. The lay witness is a participant in the event and should not be allowed to avoid telling what he or she knows. Nurses may be subpoenaed as lay witnesses if they participated or were involved with a case. The expert, on the other hand, is not a participant; other experts might be available, and one's opinion is deemed property and therefore an expert makes the decision whether to give it or not. Once the expert agrees, then the court may issue a subpoena. This practice, however, varies from state to state and is used for the convenience of the attorneys. If a subpoena is issued, the witness' presence is demanded and assured with certain penalties that attach should the witness not appear in court.

The areas of testimony which might need an expert are almost as diverse as the many possible topics of litigation. Expert nurse witnesses are needed in nursing malpractice litigation to establish the nursing standard of care. In this area of testimony the expert nurse witness provides the court and jury with information about the applicable standard of care and interprets and applies the standard to the situation being litigated. As thoroughly discussed in Chapter 4, malpractice is the failure to meet a standard of care which results in injuries. The standard is one of reasonableness.

The expert nurse witness examines the facts and basically asks—did the nurse act reasonably, given the circumstances? The expert nurse witness uses several sources for answering this question. For example, the expert's opinion is formed through reviewing policies and procedures which existed in the agency at the time of the incident and through nursing literature, educational programs, licensure laws, and statements of the professional associations regarding nursing practice standards and expectations. Many standards of care which an expert nurse witness would use to develop an opinion have been highlighted and discussed in this book.

In addition to interpreting and applying the nursing standard of care to malpractice litigation questions, the expert nurse witness may also provide testimony for other types of cases. Expert nurse witnesses have been involved in child abuse litigation; cases of child custody, divorce, and guardianship; adult or child protective service actions; competency assessment; probate actions; licensing investigations (both individual and institutional licensing); employment disputes; and actions for damages resulting from accidents. In the last type of litigation, the expert nurse witness may provide the jury with information about necessary nursing care in rehabilitation or home care and the costs of this care. The expert nurse witness is also used in various stages of litigation which will be discussed later in the chapter.

Qualifications

In order to serve as an expert nurse witness the nurse must be qualified as an expert. The criteria and process for qualifying as an expert vary among jurisdictions. When experts take the witness stand, they are usually asked two different sets of questions. The first set of questions regard the expert's background, education, experience, knowledge, and skills. In most instances, the judge assesses the answers to these questions and then decides whether the expert is qualified to continue to testify and render an opinion. Samples of the different types of questions will be given and discussed later in the chapter.

Most courts do not state specific criteria. For example, number of years of experience or education will not, generally, be specified (4 years of education versus 3 years of education or 6 years of experience versus 3 years of experience). The qualifications of an expert are examined on an individual basis and in relation to the evidentiary needs of the individual case. The trial court judge is the one who determines whether a witness can be an expert for a particular case. As will be described later, from various cases, however, a general idea of what qualifies an expert can be determined.

In *Dolan v. Galluzzo,* the court determined that a

podiatrist and not another physician should testify as to the standard of care of a podiatrist.[9] The court decided that in order to testify as an expert on the standard of care in a given school of medicine, the witness must be licensed in that school. The plaintiff was not entitled to establish the standard of care a podiatrist owes a patient by offering the testimony of a physician or surgeon or another expert other than a podiatrist. The court went on to say that a physician who is also licensed as a podiatrist may testify in a case involving a podiatrist.

The extension of this rule developed by the court in *Dolan*, and specifically discussed by the dissenting judge, is that the expert witness must be licensed in the field in which the standards of care are under examination. As a matter of fact, the dissenting judge commented that the majority's decision would not allow a physician to testify about nursing standards of care or to testify as to the standards for midwives because the physician was not licensed as a nurse or midwife. While licensure is a requirement in Illinois, it may not be required in other states.

The usual qualifications of an expert witness may include not only licensure in the area of practice being examined by the court, but also a strong knowledge base, based on education and experience. In addition, the most effective expert witness has good communication skills, both speaking and writing. The higher the education, the more extensive the experience, and the better the communication skills; the more credible, believable, and convincing the expert will be before the judge and jury. Qualifications of expert nurse witnesses in actual cases will be presented below.

SOURCES USED IN PREPARING EXPERT NURSE OPINION

1. Agency policy and procedure manuals
2. State Nurse Practice Act and regulations
3. American Nurses' Association Code for Nurses
4. American Nurses' Association Standards of Practice
5. Joint Commission on Accreditation of Hospitals Standards
6. Other accreditation standards
7. Agency licensing regulations
8. Specialty nursing group standards
9. Nursing textbooks and journals
10. Continuing education and education program curriculum

Uses of expert nurse witnesses

As mentioned before, the role of the expert nurse witness encompasses not only testimony in a court of law or during a deposition, but also advice and consultation throughout the litigation process. Given that most litigation is settled prior to court proceedings, involving an expert nurse witness in the early stages of litigation can be crucial in deciding to settle a case or to go to court. Early advice and consultation are almost more important than testimony in court.

If the opinion of the expert nurse witness is that no nursing malpractice occurred and it is believed that the jury will be persuaded by the opinion, then litigation will be unsuccessful, so is usually ended or settled. However, if it is the opinion of the expert nurse witness that nursing malpractice has occurred and that the jury will be persuaded by that testimony, then this will also encourage settlement prior to court proceedings.

When an attorney investigates a situation to determine whether to sue, an expert opinion is often sought. Similarly, when an attorney receives notice that a client is being sued, an expert opinion is sought to prepare the defense. Essential evidence which is reviewed by the expert in order to form an opinion is the medical record and statements of witnesses. The expert compares what happened in the situation to the standards of care expected for that situation. The box above lists material used most often by experts in arriving at their opinions. The expert opinion may be rendered verbally, initially, and usually is followed by a written statement of opinion, along with supporting data.

Before deciding to be an expert witness on a particular case, an interview should be held with the attorney, followed by a confirmation of the relationship of the expert to the case. This confirmation should be a written letter or contract which should indicate compensation, responsibilities, any deadlines, and other expectations. Following the initial interview, planning conferences will be held where materials are reviewed, other experts may attend and participate, and legal principles involved in the case are discussed. The expert's opinion is formed independently and objectively and should be prepared in writing.

In addition to consultation about cases, attorneys will also involve an expert nurse witness for the purpose of preparing for trial. For example, the expert witness may assist the attorney in developing questions for other witnesses, such as the defendant, the plaintiff, or other experts. These questions may appear in the tools of discovery—the interrogatories or depositions. As mentioned earlier, interrogatories are written questions exchanged between parties; depositions are out-of-court, under-oath statements of witnesses, including expert witnesses. Expert witnesses may also assist attorneys in preparing exhibits for use at trial. Expert witnesses also provide education and knowledge for attorneys who are not versed in health care issues.

The decision to use an expert's opinion is the attorney's. It is usual and expected that an expert will be paid a fee for rendering information and opinions about a case. As mentioned before, a contractual agreement should be established between the attorney and the expert. The contract is an agreement to provide a fee, on the part of the attorney, for a service, on the part of the expert. Experts establish their own fees based on their experience and education. Many experts charge differing fees based on time, effort, and extent of their involvement in the case. Researching the standard of care and preparing a written statement involve different time and effort than preparing and presenting courtroom testimony or a deposition. Expert witnesses should never make contingency fee arrangements (where a fee is based on the outcome of the case).

Providing expert testimony and consultation is an important service to the judicial system. Our legal system is one which is designed to redress wrongs and to compensate for injuries. But only wrongs and injuries which are the result of breaches of standards of care owed a patient should be compensated. Therefore, the expert nurse witness is crucial to the determination of nursing liability.

Cases involving expert nurse witnesses

Cases discussing the use, qualifications, and effectiveness of nurses as expert witnesses are few in number. The cases discussed in this section were selected for their importance in showing what qualifications expert nurse witnesses possessed and what areas of nursing testimony were deemed essential in determining liability in the cases.

In a case dealing with the care and treatment of decubitus ulcers of a nursing home patient, the expert nurse witness testified as to the usual and expected nursing care that should be rendered in such cases. The expert nurse witness was a professor of nursing, and the court declined to agree with the challenge to a nurse testifying about cause and treatment relationships launched by the defense. The court stated that the case involved primarily nursing problems and that the prevention, care, and treatment of decubitus ulcers were largely nursing duties.[10]

In a case involving the proper use by a physician of a needle in drawing a blood sample an expert nurse witness testified. The use of an unsterile needle resulted in a severely infected radial nerve. The court accepted the testimony of this expert nurse witness because she had graduated from an accredited school of nursing, held a license in the state, and had drawn blood and given intravenous injections over 2000 times. In addition, the defendant in the case testified that drawing blood was not a treatment exclusively within the professional skills of medical practice.[11]

The court questioned the qualifications of the expert nurse witness in a case dealing with diagnosis, causation, and permanency of a plaintiff's condition. The court decided that the expert nurse witness was attempting to testify about something beyond her expertise because she admitted that she was not an expert on hypoglycemia, that she had never rendered an opinion of the type being asked for in the case, and that her opinion was based on conversations with a physician at a conference.[12]

While providing expert testimony on a case involving the practice of using nurses' aides in helping convalescing patients take shower baths, the nurse's credentials were reviewed. In deciding that the nurse qualified as an expert, the court cited the nurse's training course, her certificate as a nurse's aide, the additional courses she had taken, her work experience, and her knowledge of standards in the area.[13]

A lower court held that an expert who is not a physician (one who is licensed to diagnose and prescribe treatment) may not give an opinion testimony as to the cause of a physical injury. In this case an expert nurse witness was presented to testify as to the relationship between an injury and the intravenous (IV) administration of undiluted potassium chloride. The higher court ruled that the expert nurse witness was qualified to testify in this case as to this causal relationship. Her qualifications included an associate degree in medicine, 3 years of hospital nurse's training, attendance at a university, currently in a pharmacy program, licensure as a registered nurse, experience as a staff nurse in acute care, nursing supervisor, coordinator of the intravenous therapy department, establisher of the IV program, President of the American Society of IV Therapy, consultant to pharmaceutical companies, and member of committees (U.S. Food and Drug Administration, Centers for Disease Control) which set standards and recommended national procedures for IV therapy.[14]

An expert nurse witness qualified in a case involving nurse's aides helping patients in the use of bedpans because she was licensed in three states, including the jurisdiction where she was testifying, was an assistant professor and had supervised students in four hospitals and a nursing home, had 14 years of nursing experience, and had a degree in nursing.[15] In another case an expert nurse witness qualified to testify about a nurse's failure to report to the physician the patient's history of a heart condition and medication the patient was taking in the hospital, her failure to take vital signs, and, when they were taken, her failure to record them in the patient's chart. This nurse witness was qualified on the basis of having graduated from a hospital school of nursing and 8 years of nursing experience in a hospital as charge nurse, in a physician's office and as "float" nurse in a hospital.[16]

In another case, one involving a psychiatric patient on suicide watch orders, three expert nurse witnesses qualified and testified as to the standard of psychiatric nursing practice. One expert nurse witness was chairperson of a university school of nursing, department of psychiatric and mental health nursing; another was supervisor of nursing in a hospital's department of psychiatry; the third was supervisor and faculty of psychiatric nursing. All were licensed as registered nurses. Each demonstrated extensive understanding and knowledge of psychiatric nursing standards. One had developed a model which is followed by many psychiatric nursing departments as a model of excellence.[17]

In another example, an expert nurse witness' testimony was challenged because it was deemed to exceed the field of nursing and invade the physician's field. The expert nurse witness testified that a nurse's duty in an intensive care unit (ICU) to a patient increased as the patient's partial thromboplastin time (PTT) value increased. The case involved the failure of an ICU nurse to observe a hematoma in a heparinized patient, to avoid blood pressure cuff trauma, and to recognize and respond properly to signs and symptoms of hemorrhage.

The defendant argued that testimony from an expert nurse witness regarding a PTT value was improper. The court stated that a nursing standard of care was at issue and that the expert nurse witness, who was an assistant professor of nursing with a specialty in cardiovascular nursing in ICUs, had precisely addressed the nursing issue. Although the court made this affirmation of the nurse's testimony, it also went on to say that if the testimony were disregarded, there was physician testimony offered in the case that could be used to find the same liability.[18]

In one case a registered nurse, who was an infection control practitioner, testified that authorities relied upon by the defendant in the case were considered obsolete and provided the jury with the most updated information available on the effects of herpes simplex viral strain.[19] The qualifications to testify which were reviewed by the court included 3 years experience in infection control; education at the Centers for Disease Control; seminars; conferences; and the responsibilities of the job, which included research and consultation to physicians and others. It was also noted that this expert nurse witness was prepared to access computer data bases on the topic of herpes simplex.

The lower court excluded the expert nurse witness's testimony, agreeing with the hospital defendant, that the nurse was not qualified to testify. However, the higher court reversed this decision, holding that this nurse qualified as an expert to provide rebuttal testimony to show that authorities used by the defense were outdated and to inform the jury of the most updated information available. The court commented, however, that the nurse would not qualify to make a diagnosis of the plaintiff's injury and causation.

These cases all involved issues in which nursing practice was involved. The expert nurse witnesses who qualified to testify were qualified on the basis of education, experience, licensure, and involvement in professional associations. Most had also contributed to the development of nursing standards and policies on an ongoing basis in their careers. Each state has different case law on this subject. The lawyer using an expert nurse witness should be familiar with the law in a particular state.

Preparation to present testimony or consultation

Deciding to be an expert witness or consultant on a case is a personal decision. As discussed before, a lay witness or material witness may have no choice but to participate in the case. If essential to the case, the lay witness will be issued a subpoena which if not followed will lead to judicial intervention. Preparation is often the same for an expert or lay witness and is an essential part of assuming the role and its responsibilities. This preparation begins through and with the attorney who is handling the case.

The box on p. 531, left, summarizes key points for effective testimony. The expert nurse witness must have the nursing knowledge and background to be an expert; the essential preparation for being an expert witness or

BEING AN EFFECTIVE EXPERT NURSE WITNESS

Preparation

Thorough, concise, well supported, and documented
Knowledgeable about reasonable, acceptable, and proper nursing practice

Presentation

Confident, authoritative, convincing
Professional appearance and impression

Opinion

Communicate directly with questioners, directing answers toward the judge and jury
Maintain composure; be relaxed
State opinion and do not change it; do not overtly react to other witnesses that may disagree
Avoid vague imprecise expressions such as "I think" or "I believe"; avoid superlatives such as "always" and "never"

APPROACHES TO ANSWERING QUESTIONS

1. When you know the answer, give it concisely and precisely, but do not answer more than you are asked. (For example, "Was Mrs. Jones on duty during the 3 to 11 shift?" "Yes, and she worked a double shift that same day.")
2. When it comes to giving your opinion, it is not always necessary to answer only "yes" or "no." It is often appropriate to say a few more words to explain your opinion.
3. Take time to allow the question to register and to prepare your answer. This allows the attorney to make appropriate objections before you answer. If an objection is made and overruled you must answer the question.
4. If you do not understand a question, ask for it to be repeated or clarified.
5. If you do not remember or know an answer, it is better to acknowledge this than make a mistake. If the answer involves exact time or number and you know the appropriate answer, state your recollection as an approximation.

consultant is to know what is expected in the legal process. The attorney can prepare the expert for participation in this legal process.

As mentioned, it is best to begin with a face-to-face discussion with the attorney about the issues in the case and to negotiate fees. At the conclusion of this first meeting the expert and the attorney decide if they will work well together and if both are committed to participating together in the endeavor. Following the first meeting, the expert independently forms an opinion based upon information provided by the attorney, the medical record, and other relevant documents and sources mentioned on p. 528. Several other meetings with the attorney are necessary to inform the attorney of the expert's opinion and to clarify the issues in the case.

If the attorney will be using the expert witness on the witness stand or in a deposition, preparation for this is essential. The expert witness should meet with the attorney prior to the court date or time of the deposition at least once to answer questions about what to expect. The box above, right, describes a general approach to the questioning process. A simulation of the conditions under questioning should be experienced prior to the actual event.

Actual questions that will be asked should be role played. The box on p. 532, top, lists sample questions the witness can expect from the attorney who called the witness. Direct examination takes place first and establishes the witness as an expert and states the opinion. Cross examination will follow and is intended to test the expert's qualifications, knowledge, and application of the standard of nursing care.

The attorney should also prepare the expert witness for the cross-examination by role playing potential and expected questions from the other attorney. The box on p. 532, left column, gives sample questions from cross-examination. These questions are often the most difficult to handle. Therefore, they should be discussed thoroughly prior to the situation.

A decision to serve as an expert nurse witness or consultant also needs to involve an examination of the level of knowledge about the nursing practice area that is the subject of the litigation. For example, the Maryland Nurses' Association Expert Nurse Witness and Consultation Service provides its members with the following list of questions to consider:

1. Have I read the State Nurse Practice Act and can I apply it in nursing situations?
2. Am I aware of how regulations may be promulgated and enforced and what regulations impact nursing practice in this state?
3. In my particular area of nursing practice, do I have working knowledge of the standards of care written by the American Nurses' Association and other professional organizations?

SAMPLE QUESTIONS: DIRECT EXAMINATION

Establishing the Witness as an Expert

Would you please state your name and address for the court?

What is your profession?
What is your educational background?
Where have you been employed?
Where are you currently employed?
What is your current position?
What is your nursing experience?
What is your nursing expertise or specialty?
What, if any, professional associations do you belong to?
Have you held any leadership positions in these groups?
What, if any, awards or certificates have you received?

Gaining the Expert's Opinion

Method 1: You've had an opportunity to review the medical records which are in evidence before the court and have heard the testimony of the plaintiff. What is your opinion as to the defendant's actions in this case? (Further questions would elicit the standard of care and explain the basis of the opinion.)

Method 2: The expert witness is given a hypothetical situation which is similar to the actual case and then asked to give an opinion.

SAMPLE QUESTIONS AND RESPONSES TO CROSS-EXAMINATION

Who told you to say that?
No one. I was told to tell the truth.
Are you being paid to testify?
Yes, I am being compensated for my time and work.
Have you discussed this case with anyone?
Yes, the lawyer.
Then your story is . . . ?
What I testified to is the truth, not a story.
That's just your opinion?
Yes, that is my opinion.
Do you find that reasonable people can disagree and that nursing is not an exact science?
Yes, my opinion is based on nursing knowledge and experience.
Do you have any first-hand knowledge of the facts in this case?
No, I do not. (Expert witnesses usually do not.)
You make a living by testifying, don't you?
Yes, nursing is a unique field of practice with its own standards of practice which require expert testimony.
Off the record, would you tell me why. . . ?
No.
(There are no off-the-record questions. Refer the opposition attorney to the attorney who called you to testify.)

4. Can I state what the applicable standard of care is in my area, state, or region, or nationally?
5. Have I explored with my employer the policies regarding serving as an expert witness? (e.g. working hours, possible conflicts)
6. Will I be reluctant to request a reasonable fee for participating in a case?
7. Does my schedule allow me to be available as an expert?
8. With planned educational experiences will I be an effective and clear communicator of nursing?
9. Is there anything in my past which might detract from my credibility?
10. Within the courtroom will the stressful situation in anyway inhibit my presentation?[20]

Referral services

Many state nurses' associations (SNAs), including Maryland, Massachusetts, Arizona, California, Washington, New Jersey and New York, have established services for referring to attorneys expert nurse witnesses and consultants. These SNAs refer individuals who voluntarily wish to serve as expert witnesses. Each service has its own requirements for participation, such as level of education, attendance at educational programs, submission of notarized resumes, and indication of prior experience as an expert witness. Some SNAs charge a finder's fee from the attorney when their service is used; others provide the service at no charge to the attorney. Legal counsel should review these SNA programs. Nurse attorneys are ideal resources for SNAs on establishing such programs.

Individual or groups of expert nurse witnesses may also form their own businesses. There are also other groups and businesses which utilize expert nurse witnesses or consultants. Many individual expert nurse witnesses advertise in TRIAL, the magazine for members (primarily plaintiff's attorneys) of the Association of Trial Lawyers of America (ATLA). In addition there is a Directory of Forensic Experts, provided by an association of forensic experts, where a nurse can be listed for a fee as an expert in a particular field.[21]

In advertising services as an expert nurse witness or consultant, the nurse should be guided by the American Nurses' Association, CODE FOR NURSES WITH INTERPRETIVE STATEMENTS, statement 10 and its interpretive statements.[22] Endorsing the use of registered nurse and symbols of academic degrees or other earned or honorary professional symbols of recognition in all ways that are legal and appropriate, the ANA CODE admonishes nurses from using any form of public or professional communication to make claims that are false, fraudulent, misleading, deceptive, or unfair. The earlier version of the ANA CODE listed acceptable forms of advertising, including professional cards and directory or publication listings, but prohibited endorsement of commercial products or services.[23]

Recommendations and trends

Encouraging the use and development of nurses as expert witnesses and consultants in effect advances the nursing profession. In particular, increasing the availability of expert nurse witnesses is a means of self-regulation, a hallmark of a profession. It is imperative that nurses speak about nursing even in the courtroom and that nurses evaluate nursing practice and apply nursing standards.

As more nurses gain experience in testifying, the areas of testimony and expertise will expand. Still common today is the physician testifying as to the nursing standard. This is slowly changing. Not only will nurses firmly place themselves as the ones who will and must judge nursing performance, but also nursing expertise will become valuable to court decisions in other areas. Already psychiatric clinical nurse specialists are providing expert testimony in family law disputes, such as child custody, and, as discussed in Chapter 13, public health nurses are providing expert testimony in cases of child abuse.

The expert nurse witness transmits nursing knowledge to the judge, jury, and legal system. Effectiveness of this communication may determine the outcome of a case. Tort reform measures may impact the future use of expert nurse witnesses. As mentioned before, at least one state has limited their use. This is certainly an area to continually assess.

Endnotes

1. *Jones v. Hawkes Hospital,* 196 N.E.2d 592 (Ohio 1964).
2. *Id.*
3. N.Y. Times, April 13, 1986, at 50, col. 2, entitled Maryland Legislature Puts Ceiling on Personal Injury Awards.
4. FED. R. EVID. 702 TESTIMONY BY EXPERTS. *See also* Bertelsman, *The Federal Rules of Evidence* TRIAL 55 (September 1985) and Bertelsman, *What You Think You Know (But Probably Don't) About the Federal Rules of Evidence: A Little Knowledge Can Be A Dangerous Thing* 8 N. KY L. REV. 81 (1981).
5. *Wooten v. United States,* 574 F. Supp. 200 (W.D. Tenn.), *aff'd.* 722 F.2d 743 (1982).
6. *Hyatt v. Groce,* 523 P.2d 320 (Kan. 1974).
7. *Id.*
8. BLACK'S LAW DICTIONARY 688 (4th ed. 1967).
9. *Dolan v. Galluzzo,* 396 N.E.2d 13 (Ill. 1979).
10. *Mellies v. National Heritage, Inc.,* 636 P.2d 215 (Kan. App. 1981). *See, also, Appeals Court Rules Nurse Can Be Expert Witness Re: Decubitus Care* 57 THE KANSAS NURSE 1 (1982).
11. *Avret v. McCormick,* 271 S.E.2d 832 (Ga. 1981).
12. *Leahy v. Kenosha Memorial Hospital,* 348 N.W.2d 607 (Wis. App. 1984).
13. *Biggs v. Cumberland County Hospital System, Inc.,* 317 S.E.2d 421 (N.C. App. 1984).
14. *Maloney v. Wake Hospital System,* 262 S.E.2d 680 (N.C. 1980).
15. *Page v. Wilson Memorial Hospital,* 262 S.E.2d 8 (N.C. App. 1980).
16. *Wood v. Rowland,* 592 P.2d 1332 (Colo. 1978).
17. *Pisel v. Stamford Hospital,* 430 A.2d 1 (Conn. 1980).
18. *Belmon v. St. Francis Cabrini Hospital,* 427 So.2d 541 (La. App. 1983).
19. *Carter v. St. Vincent Infirmary,* 690 S.W.2d 741 (Ark. App. 1985). The Arkansas court cited a Texas court which held similarly. *See, Johnson v. Hermann Hospital,* 659 S.W.2d 124 (Tex. Civ. App. 1983) and *Warren v. Hartnett,* 561 S.W.2d 860 (Tex. Civ. App. 1977).
20. MARYLAND NURSES' ASSOCIATION, EXPERT NURSE WITNESS SERVICE (Northrop and Mech, 1980).
21. *See also* the AMERICAN ACADEMY OF FORENSIC SCIENCES; and RESEARCH PUBLICATIONS, DIRECTORY OF EXPERT WITNESSES IN TECHNOLOGY (current ed.).
22. AMERICAN NURSES' ASSOCIATION, CODE FOR NURSES WITH INTERPRETIVE STATEMENTS 15 (1985). Code 10 states that the nurse participates in the profession's effort to protect the public from misinformation and misrepresentation and to maintain the integrity of nursing.
23. AMERICAN NURSES' ASSOCIATION, CODE FOR NURSES WITH INTERPRETIVE STATEMENTS (1976).

Additional Readings

W. ALTON, MALPRACTICE: A TRIAL LAWYER'S ADVICE FOR PHYSICIANS (1977).

Burgess and Laszlo, *The Professional as a Court Witness* J. EMER. NURS. 25 (March-April 1976).

Eccard, *A Revolution in White—New Approaches in Treating Nurses as Professionals* 30 VAND. L. R. 839 (1977).

Feder, *The Care and Feeding of Experts* TRIAL 49 (June 1985).

Josberger and Ries, *Nurse Experts* TRIAL 68 (June 1985).

Klimon, *Do you swear to tell the truth?* 3 NURS. ECON. 98 (March-April 1985).

T. KRAFT, USING EXPERTS IN CIVIL CASES (1977).

McCartney, *In the Witness Box: How to Give Nursing Testimony* 77 NURSING '77 89 (1977).

Northrop and Mech, *The Nurse As Expert Witness* 2 NURS. L. & ETHICS 1, 2, 6, 8, (March, 1981).

Perry, *If You're Called as an Expert Witness* 77 A. J. N. 458 (March 1977).

Scholin, *The Use of Nurses as Expert Witnesses* 19 HOUS. L. REV. 555 (1982).

Scully, *Are you Expert Enough to be an Expert Witness?* 82 NURS. LIFE 34 (July-August 1982).

Chapter 33

The nurse entrepreneur

Mary E. Kelly and Cynthia E. Northrop

The health care industry has become competitive with other big businesses; many health care business entities are on the Fortune 500 list.[1] Insurance companies, corporations, and hospitals are contracting with providers to provide preventive and curative health services on a competitive prospective payment system. This trend is spawning new business entities, such as urgicare centers, ambulatory surgery centers, and home health care agencies. New business relationships among health care providers are being created. In short, the health care market is an entrepreneur's dream come true.

Predictions are that by the year 2000, these new freestanding centers will encompass most traditional hospital health care; hospitals will become intensive care centers, aided by robotics for technical treatments and computers for diagnostic assessments and constant measurement of vital signs.[2] Computer programs such as these already exist for intensive care units (ICUs)[3] and programs are being developed for nursing care plans.[4] These trends suggest that nurses should begin shifting their focus from hospital based care and begin creating new systems of delivery for their unique holistic services. The entrepreneurial model—taking a creative idea, a vision, and actualizing it—may provide the vehicle.

This option enables the nurse to practice independently of traditional hospital and community health settings. More nurses are selecting entrepreneurial practice, as evidenced by the growth in nurse-managed centers, private nursing practice, nursing corporations and partnerships, and nurse-owned health care agencies. Nursing services currently offered include mental health and psychiatric counseling, geriatrics, and management of chronic illnesses.[5] Creative nurses are exploring other areas as well,[6] such as publishing companies, teaching corporations, computer software design for patient assessment and treatment, and direct contracts with hospitals to provide inpatient and follow-up care.

Nurse-managed centers have been described as "youngest members of a family that include visiting nurses associations, . . . [and] home health care agencies . . . ."[7] The American Nurses' Association's (ANA) position is that these centers provide a way for nursing to meet the health care needs of unserved and underserved populations, demonstrate the benefits of good nursing care, offer an alternative to traditional health care and demonstrate the positive effects of nurses controlling their practice in a cost-effective manner. This is certainly true of the other nurse entrepreneurial forms of practice.

Control over nursing practice and greater autonomy are hallmarks of the nurse's entrepreneurial practice. A major goal of this type of practice is to eliminate structural restrictions that often prevent nurses from contributing their specialized skills to primary care and other therapeutic modalities.[8] For example, some health care institutions compel nurse employees to concentrate on medical treatments and not on nursing practice. These institutions apparently value medical services more highly than nursing services because the prospective payment system allows recovery for medical rather than nursing services. Entrepreneurial practice provides a vehicle for nursing creativity.

This chapter provides an overview of considerations and decisions important to the nurse entrepreneur and an analysis of selected legal issues, including forms of business, employment relationships, and antitrust law.

Considerations in entrepreneurial practice

The nurse entrepreneur must first consider the feasibility of the business idea. Differences between existing products or services and the proposed idea should be scrutinized. The proposed idea will be more marketable and, therefore, more feasible if there is something that distinguishes it from those that are already available.

Feasibility also involves thinking about who will buy the product. The specific consumers of the proposed product or service (the market) should be identified. This market might include, for example, hospitals, schools, individuals, and organizations.

Other important considerations are the nurse entrepreneur's rationale for selecting the proposed idea and his or her qualifications to provide the proposed services or products. If necessary expertise is lacking, one solution is to develop a collaborating or consulting relationship with someone who is knowledgeable about the product or service.

The nurse entrepreneur should also be familiar with the steps necessary to develop a business plan. The basic process of setting up a nursing business includes the following business plan steps: (1) identify the purpose, skills, goals, and objectives; (2) identify potential consumers and their characteristics (marketing); (3) define the product or the service; (4) outline programs and services; (5) establish standards, policies, and criteria to evaluate programs and services; (6) develop the business budget, including proposed expenditures and income in detail for 6 months and generally for 2 years; and (7) locate initial funding sources.

The first step before forming the business is to develop and write the goals and objectives of the business. The written goals and objectives of the business must be consistent with the state nursing practice act, specifically, the legal scope of practice and any statutory limitations on professional businesses. Generally, the advice of an accountant, insurance agent, and nurse attorney will be beneficial.

Gaining support in the community for the nursing business is an important step. This can be done even before the business begins, and under some circumstances it may be imperative to develop this support before the business is formed. A marketing plan, including strategies for reaching the community, should be developed, evaluated, and updated. Methods of marketing can include speaking engagements, flyers, and personalized form letters on business stationery, with business cards included, directed to the potential consumer of the service. A marketing plan should consider these questions:

1. How will you inform consumers about the services or product?
2. How will the business be promoted?
3. What is the competition and how will you meet it?
4. What is the budget for the marketing activities?
5. Who are the prospective customers?
6. What will your fees be?
7. What is it about your service or product that will make the prospective customer want to purchase it?

Decisions in establishing a nursing business

Business enterprises involve a wide variety of activities. Determining the legal, economic, and social status of the enterprise is the beginning point. Sundry state and federal laws may impact upon enterprise activities. State laws are dominant in agency, fiduciary standards, partnerships, and corporation matters. Federal laws reign in aspects of the business dealing with securities, taxation, antitrust, and bankruptcy. In these areas state laws coexist with federal law.

Nurse entrepreneurs begin establishing their practices by selecting legal counsel. Decisions about location, finance, and form of business all generate materials that need to be reviewed with the attorney. Property purchases or leases may also involve real estate agents and escrow companies.

Financing the enterprise may necessitate expanding the capital or equity of the owner. If a loan is obtained, generally the borrower will execute a promissory note in which the borrower agrees to repay the indebtedness on specified terms. In some cases, a line of credit, which is an amount of money available to the nurse entrepreneur if needed, may be obtained from the bank. Depending on the type of business organization form selected, the indebtedness may be a personal obligation or an obligation of the business.

The bank will seek to secure its loan to the owner by taking a security interest in some or all of the assets of the nursing business. When this occurs, the bank becomes a secured creditor, and the owner of the business is the debtor, and a creditor-debtor relationship is established.

When a debtor defaults on the loan, fails to repay the indebtedness according to the terms of the promissory note, then the bank may foreclose and take over the assets of the nursing business. If prior to foreclosure, the owner liquidates the business or files bankruptcy proceedings, then the bank, as a secured creditor, would have a priority over unsecured creditors and equity owners for distribution of any assets.

Once the business is located and equipped, the activities of the business may begin. The nature of the business may necessitate hiring employees or independent contractors. The owner's legal relationship with the employee will be governed by principles of contract and agency law and by various federal and state labor, worker's compensation, and employment laws.

The legal relationship between the owner and employees also depends on whether there is a written contract and the terms to which the parties agree. Matters of compensation, fringe benefits and vacation time should be settled upon hiring the employee. The terms should be consistent with the state's labor law and employment codes. If the employee is hired to work on a creative project or the development of an invention, the contract should clearly state that the work is "work for hire" and should delineate the parties' respective rights in the final product. All employment contracts should be reviewed by legal counsel.

The employer should also ensure that adequate insurance coverage exists for any acts of negligence. The employer is liable for the negligent acts of employees, within the scope of their employment, under the legal doctrine of *respondeat superior.*

Getting clients and keeping them will determine the success or failure of the business. Each time the business and the client effect an exchange of services for fees or other compensation, a contractual relationship exists between them.

Inviting clients into the business location, or office, involves the undertaking of certain legal responsibilities for mishaps, such as injuries. Under tort laws the owner would be personally responsible if he or she failed to provide a safe environment and that failure led to the client's injury. Purchasing insurance allows the nurse entrepreneur to certain personal risks of loss arising from fire, theft, casualties, and acts of employees.

The advice of an accountant is helpful in terms of financial planning and setup. Consultation with an accountant may also be useful in establishing procedures for billing and collection of fees, whether directly from the consumer or through third parties, such as health insurance companies or the government. The final decisions regarding the fee schedule and collection policies, however, are the responsibility of the nurse owner.

Delivery of professional nursing services is regulated by the state nursing practice act. The state also regulates the actual business itself through various agencies. Clients may file complaints directly to the board of nursing regarding faulty nursing services they receive. Complaints also may be filed with the state's agencies that regulate business entities. Incompetent, unethical practices are disciplined through nursing law and regulations and may result in loss of the owner's business.

While the state nursing practice act is the cornerstone to planning an independent nursing practice, other governmental specifications and filings may be required. These may include not only health care delivery licensing and regulation laws, but local building, zoning, public health and sanitation, business licensing, and tax requirements.

This overview of decisions involved in establishing the nursing business gives an idea of the types and variety of laws and legal relationships involved. An enterprise does not operate in a vacuum, but is always in a state of continual evolvement. New community health needs will dictate new nursing services, which in turn will be impacted by a variety of laws. Categories of laws which affect enterprises are listed in the boxed material on p. 538.

Form of business

The nurse entrepreneur has three basic forms of business from which to choose. Those forms include:

1. Sole proprietorship
2. Partnership (general or limited)
3. Corporation (regular or professional)

There are other forms as well, including joint ventures, joint stock companies, syndicates, and business trusts. These later forms are variations of the basic three listed above. Each of these will be described, highlighting the advantages and disadvantages.

LAWS WHICH AFFECT BUSINESSES

- Contract laws
- Consumer laws
- Real property laws
- Torts and vicarious liability
- Agency law
- Laws of fiduciary standards
- Occupational licensing laws
- Partnership laws
- Corporation codes
- Taxation laws
- Securities and commercial laws
- Antitrust laws
- Bankruptcy laws
- Civil rights laws
- Labor laws
- Environmental, health, and safety laws

SOLE PROPRIETORSHIP

The sole proprietorship is an economic extension of the individual within the context of a selected business activity. This is the form of business chosen by the individual who wishes to establish a solo nursing practice. The resources of the proprietorship are the direct assets of the owner. The liabilities and obligations of the proprietorship are the direct, individual liabilities of the owner. This form of business is the simplest form, and in terms of frequency it is the predominant business form in the United States.

The solo practice involves the least cumbersome organization. From an income and tax standpoint the income of the practice is the income of the individual conducting the business. The business does not pay tax; the individual nurse pays a self-employment tax on the income from the practice.

PARTNERSHIP

A partnership is co-ownership of a business in that a partnership is an enterprise owned by two or more individuals. The partners typically enter into an agreement between or among themselves as to the degree of ownership and involvement in the business.

General Partnership. A general partnership does not require any legal formalities. In fact, a partnership can be inferred from the conduct of the individuals involved. Many partnerships, however, are formed under a written agreement that contractually provides an outline of the nature of the partnership, the rights and responsibilities of the partners, and the management and business of the partnership. Many partnership agreements also provide for the possibility of the partnership ending and set forth the terms of dissolution and liquidation of the partnership. A written partnership agreement is advisable.

Most states have a uniform partnership statute that sets forth minimum requirements and criteria for a partnership. These statutes also specify rules to govern the operation and the dissolution of the partnership in the absence of a formal agreement.

As a general rule, each partner is the agent of the partnership and is an agent of the other partners. This agency principle means that each partner is personally liable for the obligations of the partnership and the acts of the other partners, if those acts were within the scope of their partnership authority.

The disadvantage of the partnership is its lack of flexibility. Involving a new partner usually means that a new agreement will need to be written. Another disadvantage is that the partners' interests may be difficult to value and are not freely transferable like stock in a corporation (discussed below).

Like the corporation, the partnership is considered a separate taxable entity. The individual partners are assessed for the business's income and expenses according to the share of their ownership or according to the partnership agreement.

Limited Partnership. Another form of partnership, known as a limited partnership, is a creature of state statute. In order to be considered a limited partnership, the enterprise and its co-owners must strictly comply with state law and make all necessary state filings. If not filed, the enterprise will be considered a general partnership.

The limited partner usually is not involved in the management of the partnership. The advantage of the limited partnership is that it provides limited liability; unlike the general partner, the limited partner is liable only to the extent of his or her ownership interest. The limited partner is not personally liable for the obligations of the partnership, as is a general partner. Many entrepreneurs favor the limited partnership because of this limited liability, especially since the limited partnership, unlike the corporation, is not taxed as a separate business entity.

CORPORATIONS

Most state corporation statutes are enabling statutes, meaning that all persons complying with the statute may legally form a corporation. While the basic form of a corporation may be the same, there are special state corporation statutes for small corporations which function as partnerships, for banking institutions, insurance companies, and public utilities. Most relevant for the discussion here are the special statutes for incorporation of professional groups, such as lawyers, accountants, physicians, nurses, and others rendering professional services. These are discussed below.

The corporation, if formed in compliance with state corporation statutes, is recognized as a separate legal entity from its owners and managers. This is the feature that distinguishes corporations from general and limited partnerships. While the major advantage of the corporate form of business is that personal liability is limited, the drawback to the corporation is the potential for double taxation. The corporation may pay tax if it makes a profit; and when the corporation distributes a dividend—its profit—the shareholder pays income tax on the dividend. Professional tax and financial advice should be obtained by the nurse entrepreneur.

There are many types of corporations, including traditional, not-for-profit, professional, tax-exempt, and Subchapter S (or the closely held) corporation. The traditional corporation has the broadest powers and may engage in any type of legal activity. The members of the corporation generally file articles of incorporation and have bylaws which govern the operation of the business. Corporations must pay filing fees to the state, hold meetings at least annually, and submit annual reports to the state.

The not-for-profit corporation, unlike the regular corporation, is exempt from paying taxes. To achieve not-for-profit status and exemption from federal and state taxation, the corporation's scope of activities must meet the requirements of state and federal statutes, such as the Internal Revenue Code.[9] The not-for-profit status may make certain types of funding available to the nursing business, such as government grants and foundation donations.

Corporations and Professional Corporations. In the traditional corporation the owners are its shareholders, who generally have limited liability. In this form of business, there is a formal internal management structure, usually a board of directors, elected by the shareholders, who will have the primary responsibility for managing the enterprise. The directors usually elect officers and hire employees to conduct the day-to-day operation of the business. The officers and employees are agents of the corporation.

Professional service corporations are corporations formed under a special statute by members of a profession who provide a type of service to the public which may lawfully be rendered by a member of that profession. While in regular corporations personal civil liability[10] is limited, this principle does not apply to the professional service corporation.

In both the traditional and the professional corporation stockholders have the right to elect the board of directors, receive dividends when declared, and, if the corporation dissolves, receive their shares of any distribution. In the traditional corporation the shareholder may, generally, freely transfer his or her stock. Stock ownership in a professional corporation, however, is different; the stockholders must usually be professionals licensed in that state in the profession of the corporation.

Professional Nursing Corporations. In the following discussion the law concerning professional nursing corporations in New York and California is presented. Additional states are referenced.[11] Depending on the jurisdiction, there may or may not be state statutes specifically governing nursing corporations. California,[12] for example, has a separate statute governing nursing corporations, while New York[13] specifically mentions nurses in its general professional services corporations statute.

Other jurisdictions, such as Washington[14] and Maryland,[15] do not specifically mention nursing in their professional service corporation statutes, but the statutes, by their terms, authorize professional nursing corporations. Still other jurisdictions, such as Colorado,[16] allow physicians to form professional service corporations, but do not provide authority for nurses to do so.

New York. In New York nurses may form a professional service corporation under the same statute as physicians and lawyers.[17] The requirements of the statute range from general to specific items. For example, the statute requires that each report made or issued by a corporation practicing nursing shall bear the signature of one or more nurses who are in charge of such reports.[18]

By statute, the professional corporation differs from the general corporation in that shareholders, employees, or agents of the professional service corporation retain their personal liability. Each such person remains personally and fully liable and accountable for any negligent or wrongful act or misconduct committed by him or her or by any person under his or her direct supervision and control while rendering professional services.[19]

The name of the corporation formed under this type of corporate statute is usually followed by the abbreviation, P.C. meaning Professional Corporation.[20] Articles of incorporation, bylaws, and certain tax forms are required to be filed in order to effectuate a professional corporation. After articles of incorporation are approved by the state, a certificate of incorporation is issued, and the corporation may begin its business.

California. In addition to a professional corporation statute,[21] California has a nursing corporation statute. This statute provides that a nursing corporation is a corporation which is authorized to render professional services as defined in the Corporations Code, "so long as that corporation and its shareholders, officers, directors, and employees rendering professional services who are registered nurses are in compliance with the . . . Professional Corporation Act, the provisions of this article and all other statutes and regulations . . . pertaining to such corporation and the conduct of its affairs."[22]

The above quotation makes clear that the Nursing Corporation statute must be analyzed together with the Professional Corporations section of the Corporations Code. The Corporations Code defines professional services as any type of professional services which may be lawfully rendered only pursuant to license, certification, or registration authorized by California law.[23]

California requires that the professional corporation contain a specific statement concerning its status as a professional corporation in the articles of incorporation.[24] Unlike other professional corporations, however, the nursing corporation rendering professional services by registered nurses is not required to obtain a certificate of registration to perform professional nursing services.[25]

The name of the nursing corporation must contain the words "nursing" or "registered nursing," as well as "wording or abbreviations denoting corporate existence."[26] The statute also provides that with the exception of certain sections, which are explained below, each shareholder, director, and officer of a nursing corporation, except the assistant secretary and assistant treasurer, "shall be a licensed person as defined in Section 13401 of the Corporations Code."[27] Section 13401 defines a licensed person as someone licensed under the California Business and Professions Code or the Chiropractic Act "to render the same professional services as are . . . rendered by the professional corporation of which he or she intends to become an officer, director, shareholder, or employee."[28]

The exception[29] is that the following licensed persons may be shareholders, officers, directors, or professional employees of the nursing corporation so long as the sum of all shares owned by these persons does not exceed 49% of the total number of shares of the professional corporation: physicians; podiatrists; psychologists; optometrists; marriage, family, and child counselors; clinical social workers; and physician assistants.[30]

Shares of the capital stock in a professional corporation may be issued only to a licensed person, and if any shares are issued in violation of this restriction, they are void.[31] These shares may only be transferred to a licensed person or professional corporation, or the transfer is void.[32] The corporation must obtain the shares of a disqualified shareholder within 90 days of the disqualification, or it will be forced to stop rendering professional services.[33] A disqualified person is a licensed person who is an officer, director, shareholder, or employee of a professional corporation and who "for any reason" becomes legally disqualified, whether temporarily or permanently, to render the professional services which the professional corporation is rendering.[34]

In addition, the income in a nursing corporation which is attributable to professional services rendered while a shareholder is a disqualified person may not accrue to the benefit of the disqualified person or to his or her shares in the nursing corporation.[35] The Board of Registered Nursing is authorized to adopt and enforce regulations to carry out the nursing corporation statute, including regulations requiring (1) that the bylaws of a nursing corporation contain a provision that the capital stock owned by a disqualified person or deceased person shall be sold to the corporation or the remaining shareholders of the corporation within the time provided in the regulation and (2) that a nursing corporation shall provide adequate security by insurance or otherwise for claims against it by its patients arising out of the rendering of professional services.[36]

The professional corporation is subject to the rules and regulations adopted by the regulating governmental agency of the profession in which the corporation is engaged, and it is subject to its disciplinary powers.[37] In the case of the nursing corporation, the governmental agency is the Board of Registered Nursing.

Professional corporations in California may not be formed to violate any law or rule or regulation concerning fee splitting, kickbacks, or other similar practices by "physicians and surgeons or psychologists. . . ."[38] Any violation is grounds for suspension or revocation of the corporation's certificate and may be referred to the governmental agency regulating the profession in which the corporation is engaged.

Any attempted violation, whether indirect or direct, of the nursing corporation statute, the nurse practice act, or the professional corporation statute or any regulations under these laws is deemed unprofessional conduct under the nursing corporation statute.[39] In the conduct of its practice, the nursing corporation must observe the statutes and regulations to the same extent as a person holding a license as a registered nurse.

OTHER FORMS OF BUSINESS

Other forms of businesses exist through combinations or variations of the three business forms already discussed. The joint venture, for example, is a co-ownership of a business created for a specific purpose or for a limited period of time. The joint stock company is an unincorporated association that resembles a corporation. This company has articles, bylaws, and a board of directors; and its ownership is held through transferable shares. Since the company is unincorporated (it does not file with the state, and it is not recognized by the state), the owners of the joint stock company do not have the limited liabilities as shareholders of a general corporation.

The syndicate really is not a specific form of business but rather a cooperative business venture. Business trusts, on the other hand, are subject to trust law and are formed like other trusts under a trust agreement. The assets of the trust are held and managed by trustees set up under the agreement. The beneficiaries of the trust are the investors. Depending on state law, the beneficiaries may or may not be liable for the business debts of the trust.

The major models of nursing practice include independent practice, associations with other professionals, contractual arrangements with agencies for services, partnerships, corporations, consulting firms, joint appointments between educational institutions and health agencies, health agency–sponsored programs, interdisciplinary team practice, and university-based or sponsored nursing practices.[40]

As health care becomes more involved with sophisticated and creative business relationships, nurses will become involved in syndications, joint ventures, and the like. Professional advice will assist the nurse in the appropriate form of business.

Insurance

As mentioned, one of the ways in which owners or corporations shift their risks of legal liability is to purchase insurance for various purposes. The nurse entrepreneur should discuss insurance needs with an insurance agent, going over the needs of the business. The business property, real and personal, probably needs insurance to protect against fire, theft, and other damage. Insurance for general liability, health, disability, worker's compensation, automobile, and business interruption costs should be considered, depending on the needs of the business and its activities.

The professional nursing malpractice insurance policy should be reviewed to determine if it specifically covers independent practice. The policy may need clarification and require the insertion of new clauses to address coverage for independent practice.

Chapter 27 discusses professional liability insurance in detail and should be read in conjunction with this chapter. In addition the nurse entrepreneur may wish to consider life insurance and plans for retirement, especially participating in an individual retirement account or Keogh plan, whichever is applicable. The field of insurance is broad, yet complex. The nurse-owner may need one or more insurance representatives, one for life, health, and group insurance and one for commercial casualty insurance. As the business grows, nurse owners should consider formalizing risk management and quality assurance programs. Chapters 26 and 28 discuss these programs.

Employment policies

The issues with respect to employment policies are discussed in Chapter 30 on employment claims from the point of view of the employee and in Chapter 22, the nurse executive chapter more from the employer's point of view. From the point of view of the nurse-entrepreneur-employer, similar issues exist. Also, nurse-owners should explore Chapter 31, in which collective bargaining is discussed. Highlighted here, however, are issues such as avoiding violation of all discrimination laws and liability for wrongful discharge.

DISCRIMINATION

Federal law prohibits racial discrimination in the making and enforcing of private contracts. Hiring and termination policies, payment schedules, and employee benefit plans developed by the nurse-owner should be reviewed to determine gender, race, and age differences.

Title VII and the Age Discrimination in Employment Act prohibit private discriminatory conduct where an employer is engaged in an industry affecting commerce which has 15 or more employees for each working day in each of 20 or more calendar weeks in the current or preceding calendar year.[41] Private, tax-exempt membership clubs, the U.S. government, and corporations wholly owned by the U.S. government are expressly excluded from Title VII.[42]

In an age-discrimination suit, the plaintiff uses direct and circumstantial evidence to create inferences that the defendant employer's decision to terminate was based on the plaintiff's age. The plaintiff must show that his or her age is within the protected age group of between 40 and 70 years and that the employee was qualified for the position or was doing satisfactory work. Under some circumstances the plaintiff must also prove that his or her position was filled by a younger employee, unless the claim involves a reduction in the work force.[43]

The employer's defense generally is that termination was for nondiscriminatory, business-related reasons. The plaintiff employee then attacks these reasons as a pretext for discriminatory conduct.[44]

When racial, gender, or age differences exist in policies, payment schedules, or benefits, consider whether these differences are justifiable either as a business necessity or as a bona fide occupational qualification (BFOQ).[45] If they are not clearly justifiable under either of these legally accepted theories, they should be eliminated.

Business necessity is a judicially created defense for an employer. It requires the employer to show that the challenged rule or job criteria, which is claimed to have a disparate impact upon the protected class, has a "demonstrable relationship to successful performance of jobs for which [they were] used."[46]

Similarly, if sex is a BFOQ reasonably necessary to the normal operation of a particular business or enterprise, the employer may engage in discrimination on the basis of sex. The federal courts have uniformly held that the BFOQ defense is applied narrowly.[47]

Payment schedules and benefit plans also raise concerns about tax liability from both a civil and criminal context. Accountants and lawyers specializing in tax law must be consulted to provide the expertise to structure a legally and fiscally sound business practice.

WRONGFUL DISCHARGE

The employment agreement legally defines expectations between an employer and employee. For example, an employee agrees to provide services in exchange for a set salary or commission and other benefits. If the agreement does not provide otherwise, the employer, as a general rule, has been allowed to dismiss an employee summarily (without reason).

In recent years, the courts have developed the tort of wrongful discharge in response to an employer's reliance on the termination at will rule to discharge employees. Under this rule an employer has absolute discretion to discharge an employee without cause unless expressly limited by statute or contract.

The tort of wrongful discharge exists where one or both of the following exists:

1. Where the discharge has violated public policy
2. Where a contract is inferred from employer to employee communication that raises reasonable expectations that the discharge must be for good cause[48]

These two categories are examined next.

Public Policy Violations. There are three categories of cases of public policy violations:

1. Wrongful discharge for an employee's refusal to commit an unlawful act[49]
2. Wrongful discharge for exercising or attempting to exercise a legal right or privilege[50]
3. Wrongful discharge for whistleblowing[51]

The essential elements of the public policy type claim include protected conduct by the employee, whether statutory or otherwise, adverse action by the employer, and a causal connection between the two.[52] With respect to the first two categories outlined above, the employer must ensure that no employee assignment involves the violation of any law or interferes with the exercise of any legal right or privilege. These types of wrongful discharge claims are rather straightforward and, therefore, difficult to defend.

Courts, however, do not recognize liability where the employee refuses to carry out an assignment that is lawful but is merely objectionable on moral grounds. In *Warthen v. Toms River Community Memorial Hospital*,[53] the court rejected a wrongful discharge claim involving a nurse who was fired for failing to administer kidney dialysis to a terminally ill patient. The nurse argued, citing the *Code for Nurses*, that her discharge following her refusal to dialyze a terminally ill, double amputee patient was "in violation of public policy because of her 'moral, medical and philosophical objections' to performing the procedure."[54]

The court recognized that while a profession's code of ethics may contain an expression of public policy,[55] a code of ethics designed to serve only the interests of a profession would not be sufficient. The nurse attempted to justify her action by citing the section which states that the nurse provides services with respect for human dignity and the uniqueness of the client unrestricted by considerations of social or economic status, personal attributes, or the nature of the health problems.

In determining that this standard applied only to the individual nurse and not to the public at large and, therefore, was not a public policy, the court noted that preservation of human dignity should not be at the expense of the patient's life or contrary to the family's wishes. Since the record showed that the family requested dialysis and there was nothing to suggest that the patient had or would have requested otherwise, the ethical considerations cited by the nurse did not rise to the level of a public policy mandate "permitting a registered nursing professional to refuse to provide medical treatment to a terminally ill patient. . ."[56]

Thus, the court had "no hesitancy in concluding on this record that plaintiff was motivated by her own personal morals, precluding application of the public policy exception to the "at-will-employment doctrine."[57] This case points to the imperative that the patient's wishes with respect to treatment are controlling over the health care provider's personal moral views.

The last category, whistleblowing, involves an even more defensible position for the nurse entrepreneur because it raises questions of factual interpretation. For example, rather than characterizing the discharge as retaliation for whistleblowing, an employer may demonstrate that the employee was meddling in an internal dispute. This defense would not be applicable where a statute protects the employee's right to report an employer's violations of law, such as the Occupational Safety and Health Act.[58]

For example, in *Meierer v. E.I. du Pont de Nemours & Co.*[59] an occupational health nurse was fired from her job after she told her employer that she suspected possible health hazards in the plant. The employees complained to the nurse of recurrent cases of inflamed skin, ulcers of the nose and mouth, eye irritation, and fingernail and toenail cyanosis. Upon relaying these complaints to the employer, the nurse was told to ignore the situation because OSHA might learn of it, and she was ultimately fired.

The jury awarded the nurse a million dollars in damages for wrongful discharge. However, it rejected her claim of slander based on allegations that DuPont employees had made comments to local medical professionals about her abilities as a nurse.[60]

Contract Theories. The judicially recognized implied-in-fact contract doctrine has eroded the employment-at-will doctrine more effectively than the public policy category of wrongful discharge. Implied contracts to terminate employees for "just cause only" have been found in many employer policy and procedure statements.

For example, some courts have held that a policy statement alone can create a contract.[61] Other courts, however, have held that considerable reliance on policy statements and other employer representations are required to establish an implied contract.[62] To establish an implied contract to terminate for just cause only, the plaintiff employee may utilize statements in handbooks, performance appraisals, verbal or written inducements to transfer or to leave a job, and other employer communications, such as advertisements, interviews, officer speeches, termination interviews and documents, and benefit plans.[63]

In a wrongful discharge suit where an employee is attempting to prove an implied-in fact-contract, the employee must first create an inference from which a just-cause requirement for discharge can be found. Where jurisdictions recognize this type of contract, that inference must come from a reasonable expectation created by employer communications and employee reliance upon them.[64] In addition, the employee must prove that he or she was adequately performing the job so that just cause for termination is absent.

The employer's position in such cases often is that if a legitimate, nonfrivolous reason for termination exists, then the only issue for the jury is to decide whether the employer's decision was made in good faith.[65] Good faith includes acting and believing in the reasons for discharge, such as genuineness in dissatisfaction with employee performance.[66]

In public policy cases, the employer's defense will be to undermine the relationship between the discharge and the activity claimed to have caused it. In implied contract cases, the goal of the employer's defense is to reveal that communications were not relied on by the employee and, therefore, did not create expectations of termination for just cause.[67]

Careful and detailed documentation of employee performance, including date of notice of poor performance, strengthens the defense of the employer. In addition, documentation should also demonstrate the fact, if it exists, that the employee was not a team player, or was unreasonable or unfair to fellow workers. Notice of the employer's dissatisfaction with such conduct should be given as early as possible and be recorded. Employers want to demonstrate that the employee had more than adequate notice of poor performance and the opportunity to correct it.

The employee's attorney will seek, through the lawsuit, to obtain the following information: (1) employee file; (2) performance documents, and job description and expectations; (3) employer documents about employee complaints and investigations into the same; (4) personnel policies, employment handbooks, supervisory handbooks, and other documents about termination and discipline; (5) compensation documents, including employee benefits and career path; (6) documents and facts about reasons for plaintiff's termination, including information relied on for the discharge; and (7) the names of persons, particularly former employees whose terminations were not amicable, familiar with the reasons for the plaintiff's discharge, and the quality of work performed.[68]

Antitrust issues

The antitrust laws are procompetition and prohibit contracts, conspiracies, and combinations that restrain trade or commerce, including attempts to monopolize the sale of goods and services in commerce among the states.[69] These laws apply to anticompetitive activities which are actually in interstate commerce or which have a substantial effect upon interstate commerce.[70]

The nurse's business may occur within one state or be national or international. Regardless, the business activity may reach across state lines in terms of its effect. Thus, the jurisdictional issues for the nurse entrepreneur will most likely be whether his or her business activity has a substantial effect on interstate trade or commerce. International business and trade will involve obtaining special international advisors, attorneys, and accountants.

Contractual and business arrangements are analyzed by the courts as either *per se* violations of the law or under the "rule of reason" approach where the reasons behind the business activity are explored. When an activity is deemed a *per se* violation, it is automatically considered illegal because of its obviously severe anticompetitive effect. If the court concludes that an activity fails to warrant *per se* treatment, the court will examine the justification for the activity under the rule of reason analysis. Thus, the owner will urge the court to examine the reasons behind the business activity, using the rule of reason approach. The person claiming injury from the activity, on the other hand, will urge the court to determine that the activity was a *per se* violation.

Examples of business activities which the courts have held to be *per se* violations include price-fixing, tying arrangements, group boycotts, and concerted refusals to deal. An example of price-fixing is where a nurse entrepreneur becomes involved in setting fees with other competing nurse-owners for particular services.

Arizona v. Maricopa County Medical Society[71] is an example of a case involving price-fixing. There, a group of physicians formed a medical foundation which collectively developed a relative value scale and a maximum fee schedule for services to foundation subscribers. The Supreme Court held this pricing mechanism among hundreds of competitors was a *per se* violation of the federal antitrust laws. The Court distinguished the situation where a clinic offered complete medical coverage for a flat fee, and the cooperating physicians had a type of partnership agreement in which a price-fixing agreement among the physicians existed. This arrangement would be proper. Thus nurse entrepreneurs utilizing this arrangement avoid liability.

An example of a tying arrangement is where a seller of a product or perhaps a service conditions the sale of the product or service to an additional purchase of another product which the buyer might not necessarily want or need. In *Jefferson Parrish Hospital District No. 2 v. Hyde*[72] the Supreme Court reversed a lower court's determination that an exclusive service contract between the defendant hospital district and a specific group of anesthesiologists was a tying arrangement. The plaintiff was denied staff privileges because of the exclusive contract.

In applying the tying arrangement analysis, the Court assumed that the hospital had market power. The Court then addressed whether the hospital had committed a *per se* violation by tying the sale of general hospital services and operating room facilities (the tying service) to the sale of anesthesiologist services (the tied service).

The Court noted that tying arrangements need only be condemned if they restrain competition on the merits by forcing purchases that would not otherwise be made. Because patients could obtain the services of an anesthesiologist of their choice at another hospital, and there was no evidence that the hospital forced any such service on unwilling patients, the Court determined that the *per se* violation analysis was inapplicable. The Court concluded that without evidence that the hospital was using market power to force an unwanted exclusively contracted anesthesiologist upon patients, there was no basis to review the exclusive arrangement as *per se* unlawful.

The Court then examined the business activity under the rule of reason approach. The issue was whether the exclusive arrangement unreasonably restrained competition in the market in which anesthesiologists compete for exclusive contracts. There was no evidence, in the Court's view, that price, quality, supply, or demand for either general hospital services and operating room facilities or anesthesiologists' services had been adversely affected by the exclusive contract.

The Court reasoned that while it might be true that

the contract made it necessary for physicians not affiliated with the group to practice elsewhere, there had been no showing that the market as a whole had been affected by the contract. Consequently, the Court concluded, there was no showing of the kind of restraint on competition that is prohibited by the federal antitrust laws.

Group boycotts and refusals to deal are another example of *per se* antitrust violations that may be used against the nurse entrepreneur. The difficulty in obtaining staff privileges from hospital medical staffs makes nurse-managed centers attractive to the nurse practitioner. *Feminist Women's Health Center v. Mohammed,*[73] however, illustrates the potential difficulty that a nurse-managed center may encounter in attaining necessary physician backup.

There, a women's health and first trimester abortion clinic won the right to proceed to trial for injunctive and monetary relief against various physicians and the executive director of the Florida Board of Medical Examiners on charges that the physicians conspired to boycott the clinic, to fix the prices of abortions in the Tallahassee area, and to monopolize the market for providing women's health and abortion services in the area. The center employed a registered nurse, a nurse practitioner, 10 to 14 lay health workers, and an occasional laboratory technologist.

Physicians, hired on a part-time basis, performed abortions and, when possible, provided backup emergency services when patients developed postoperative complications. The defendant physicians included all members of the OB-GYN staff at the Tallahassee Memorial Hospital, which was the only hospital in the county that had complete OB-GYN facilities, and the executive director of the medical board.

From the outset, the clinic had difficulty recruiting physicians, and a resolution adopted by the OB-GYN staff at the hospital stated it would not approve the center if no member of the hospital staff were associated with it. Although two of the OB-GYN staff expressed interest about working at the center, one changed his mind after subsequent OB-GYN staff meetings and pressure from colleagues. The other, in keeping with another resolution of the OB-GYN staff against the center advertising services, conditioned his services on the clinic's promise not to advertise. Although the clinic agreed, the physician terminated his services after a newspaper interview with a center staff member was published emphasizing the relative inexpensiveness of the first trimester abortions at the clinic and the advantages of choosing a place run by women.

A subsequent OB-GYN staff meeting discussed the interview and the ethics of advertising and concluded that physicians should not be associated with organizations that advertise their medical services. Minutes from the staff meeting indicated that the physician formerly associated with the clinic stated that the local situation would collapse without support from obstetricians. The out-of-state physician employed by the clinic, who had attended the meeting, informed the clinic the next day that he could no longer work there until the advertising controversy was settled. Another staff physician informed a clinic member that the clinic should stop advertising and employees should stop giving speeches about it.

At the next monthly meeting of the OB-GYN staff, a letter was written to a private organization of physicians in the area which expressed the view that physicians in the private organization should not associate with organizations that advertise their medical services. A physician with the private organization left the clinic. Other OB-GYNs refused to accept any formal arrangements with the clinic because the OB-GYN staff would make their professional lives difficult, but one physician indicated he would accept emergencies.

Thereafter, the clinic hired residents. The OB-GYN staff sent a letter to the executive director of the medical board requesting appropriate corrective measures because the residents could not provide appropriate after care. The executive director examined the clinic's facilities and inquired about after care. A staff member indicated that the hospital would take care of complications. The hospital administrator, however, indicated that these arrangements were not formal and only covered emergencies.

The executive director contacted the resident employed at the clinic and indicated it was in his best interest to leave the clinic. The OB-GYN staff thereafter sent a letter to the residents who were working at the clinic and to the head of the residency program. The residents left the clinic. The clinic filed suit alleging various claims, including antitrust.

The facts of this case seem like a parade of horribles, but anticompetitive conduct in the health market is a reality. A successful antitrust action results in an award of money damages that is tripled (treble damages). The loss at the time a lawsuit is undertaken, however, may mean that the business usually has suffered substantially or has ended. In the clinic's case, profits actually increased during the difficulty. A recent settlement agreement between a group of chiropractors and the Illinois

Medical Society concerning staff privileges and access to other services suggests that antitrust actions may be a powerful tool for the nurse entrepreneur.[74] The value of these actions may be the potential for settlement agreements terminating anticompetitive and unprofessional conduct.

Conflicts of interest, fraud, and related matters

To the extent that the nurse entrepreneur receives reimbursement under Medicare and Medicaid, certain business conduct is proscribed.[75] These laws clearly prohibit the knowing and willful solicitation, receipt, offer, or payment of any remuneration in return for referring patients or customers, as well as the generating of business for the party furnishing the remuneration.

Remuneration includes kickbacks, bribes, and even rebates given or accepted directly or indirectly, overtly or covertly, in cash or kind.[76] For example, in *United States v. Hancock,*[77] two chiropractors challenged their convictions, claiming that payments were legitimate handling fees for the services of obtaining, packaging, and sending blood and tissue samples to a laboratory and then interpreting the results. The court rejected the argument, construing the payments as kickbacks.

In *United States v. Universal Trade and Industries,*[78] a conviction which rested in part on the testimony of a physician involved in the scheme who was given immunity was upheld against the operator of a laboratory. The operator offered the physician a kickback for each laboratory test that was done. The court noted that a kickback offered in return for ordering services is as much a violation as one offered for the referral of patients.

Even if the compensation is for services actually rendered, if this compensation is intended to induce the physician to use a particular laboratory for Medicare or Medicaid paid tests, there may be criminal liability. In *United States v. Greber*[79] the court concluded that if payment is intended to compensate for services performed and to induce a physician to use a particular laboratory facility, then the statute is violated.

Defendant Greber owned a company which provided physicians with diagnostic services, including monitoring equipment which needed to be later analyzed after the patient wore it all day. The government's proof was that the defendant paid to other physicians certain payments called "interpretation fees" for the physician's initial consultation services, as well as for explaining the test results to the patients. There was evidence that physicians received the fees even though Greber had actually evaluated the monitoring devices.

Although these cases do not involve nurses, the principles announced apply to all professionals involved in federal government reimbursement. Nurses who become involved in joint ventures designed to stimulate business must ensure that there are legitimate business reasons for the payment and that the payment is a reasonable value for the service provided. If the remuneration is related to the number of referrals of Medicare or Medicaid patients or the dollar value of the business generated, the government will be able to successfully contend that the statute has been violated.

Some states, such as California,[80] have enacted statutes prohibiting referrals to any organization in which the licensee or the licensee's immediate family has a significant beneficial interest unless a disclosure of the financial interest is made and the patient is informed that he or she is free to choose any organization for the purpose of obtaining the services ordered or requested by the licensee. A significant interest is 5% of the whole or $5,000.

This disclosure requirement applies to licensees who conduct their practice as members of the same professional corporation or partnership even if the services are rendered on the same physical premises or under the same professional corporation or partnership name. Where, however, the licensee is operating under a prepaid capitated contract with the Department of Health Services, the disclosure requirement does not apply.

California law also requires disclosure of financial interests of providers of services in the services to which they refer Medi-Cal (California's Medicaid program) recipients so that Medi-Cal may determine the extent to which conflicts of interest may exist.[81] In addition it is a misdemeanor for a person to refer or to recommend for profit another person to a physician, hospital, health related facility, or dispensary for any form of medical care or treatment of any ailment or physical condition.[82] The imposition of a fee or charge for any referral or recommendation creates a presumption that the referral or recommendation is for profit.

Liability issues in delivery of care

Several traditional business theories of liability may be applicable to the nurse entrepreneur who produces or sells a product or who owns a business facility that provides professional health services. These theories, corporate negligence and product liability, including breach of warranty and strict liability in tort, are next examined.

If the nurse entrepreneur is a seller or manufacturer of a product and that product causes injury to a consumer, potential product liability exists. Transactions in goods in most states are governed by the Uniform Commercial Code. Under this code these transactions in goods carry certain warranties, express and implied. These can be disclaimed under certain conditions. For example, the implied warranty of merchantability requires that the defendant be a merchant.[83] The implied warranty of fitness—that the product sold is fit for its intended use—requires that the defendant be a seller and that the buyer relied on the seller's skill or judgment in selecting the product for the buyer's use.[84]

Manufacturers, sellers, and retailers—those playing an integral part in the overall marketing or production enterprise[85]—may also be liable for defective products under the tort theory of strict liability. As noted in Chapter 2, most states have adopted some variation of the Restatement of Torts[86] definition of strict liability. In essence it provides that manufacturers or sellers of defective and unreasonably dangerous products are liable, without proof of negligence or fault, for injuries caused by such products to the user or consumer. There is an exception for unavoidably unsafe products, such as blood or drugs; liability for injuries caused by these products requires some element of fault: either constructive or actual knowledge of the defect that makes the product unreasonably dangerous.

Typically, hospitals and providers of health care have been able to argue successfully against application of strict liability and breach of warranty to injuries caused by defective products used by them in the care of patients.[87] Strict liability in tort requires that the defendant be a manufacturer, distributor, seller, or retailer—someone in the distribution chain—of the defective product. Similarly, breach of warranty theory requires some kind of transaction in goods, such as a sale or a lease by someone who is usually a merchant or seller. Health care providers maintain that they provide a service and that any products used in providing that service are incidentally used and not sold to the patient.

While strict liability has met with little success against health providers who provide only services and do not sell products, breach of warranty theories have met with more success where the hospital or provider could have found the defect by reasonable inspection.[88] Most courts, however, have held that the seller must be in the business of supplying the product to the consumer; and since a patient enters the hospital to be treated and not to buy a product, they have concluded that breach of warranty actions are improper in this context.[89]

A recent case, however, suggests that the breach of warranty theory may be more viable than earlier thought. In *Skelton v. Druid City Hospital Board,*[90] the appellate court held that the Uniform Commercial Code's definition of merchant is broad and does not exclude institutions such as hospitals which are businesses.

The court reasoned, in language that has application to home health care agencies, institutions, and professional corporations, that in the course of competition, hospitals hold themselves out to the public as having special knowledge regarding the provision of medical services to patients. Inherent in this presentation, the court noted, is a warranty that the hospital will sell, furnish, or supply patients with goods for use in the provision of medical services that are fit for their intended purpose. Even if the hospital were not a merchant, the court stated, it would nevertheless be liable because of the patient's reliance on its expertise to select and use a particular product.

The mere fact that the hospital did not sell the product—a suturing needle—which ultimately hurt the patient did not remove the hospital from breach of warranty. Since the hospital sterilized its needles and used them again, the transaction was more similar to a lease or rental of equipment than a sale, but the Uniform Commercial Code applies to transactions in goods not merely sales. Although the court recognized that the Uniform Commercial Code applies to merchants, it reasoned that liability was proper under warranty theory even though the hospital was not a merchant. Patients, the court reasoned, are rarely in a position to judge the quality of the medical supplies and other goods sold to them and used in their care. Many of those supplies are inherently dangerous. For this reason, the court concluded that the complete dependence of patients on the staff of a hospital to choose fit products for their care justifies the imposition of the implied warranty whether or not the hospital is a merchant.

Liability under negligence and contract principles of law also exists for the sale or manufacture of defective products that cause injury. The plaintiff would have to establish all the elements of a breach of contract or negligence action to recover under either theory.

Corporate negligence, a theory of liability applied to hospitals as businesses, could also be asserted against the nurse entrepreneur who maintains a business facility for health services. In *Darling v. Charleston Community Hospital,*[91] the Illinois Supreme Court imposed liability on the hospital and held it directly responsible for a patient's care.

Since that case, other jurisdictions, such as California,[92] have applied the doctrine. The rationale is that a corporate institution assumes the role of a comprehensive health center and takes responsibility for arranging and coordinating total health care. It charges patients for medical care and treatment and does far more than merely furnish facilities for treatment.

The doctrine of corporate negligence as applied to hospitals suggests that the nurse entrepreneur operating a health facility should ensure that agency policies are reasonable and proper, and that professional employees are continually assessed for competence through careful selection and review to avoid creating an unreasonable risk of injury to the patient. In addition, the nurse owner of a health facility should also ensure that safe and adequate equipment is provided for patients.

Recommendations and trends

Profound changes in the delivery and financing of health care are taking place. Hospitals and physicians are getting together to develop, own, and operate health care enterprises, including health maintenance organizations (HMOs), preferred provider groups, and free-standing ambulatory health care facilities.[93] Nurses are beginning to do the same, particularly in home health agencies.

Nurse entrepreneurs are also negotiating directly with those third parties who pay for health care; that is, insurance companies, self-insured employers, unions, HMOs, and governments. Nurse entrepreneurs are expanding their opportunities to other markets as well, such as the market for designing computer software for nursing care. Providing home postpartum care and teaching to new mothers and fathers is another example. The possibilities are endless; the capacity to imagine is the nurse entrepreneur's greatest asset.

Endnotes

1. Fortune 500.
2. Interview with various members of nursing 2020, July 25 1986.
3. Mandell, *Computers that Humanize Health Care,* XIV, Ms. p. 103, May 1986.
4. Interview with Laurie Avila, R.N. program systems designer, April 31, 1986.
5. *See, e.g.,* Durham & Hardin, *Nurse Psychotherapists' Experiences in Obtaining Individual Practice Privileges* 10 NURS. PRACTITIONER 62 (November 1985).
6. *E.g.,* as evidenced by the American Association of Nurses Practicing Independently, 21 Spruce Street, Dept. #1, Dansville, NY 14437, 716-335-8452, M.K. Norris, National Director.
7. *Nurse managed centers,* The American Nurse, vol. 16, no. 5, col. 2, at 1 (May 1984).
8. Baker, *Entrepreneurial Practice for Nurses: A Response to Hershey* 11 LAW MED. & HEALTH CARE 257 (December 1983).
9. *See* 15 U.S.C. §501 (1982) (IRS CODE).
10. Corporations may be responsible for the criminal acts of their agents, even where the agent is disobeying corporate or management policy. *See, e.g., United States v. Pomponio,* 429 U.S. 10 (1976); *Standard Oil Co. of Texas v. United States,* 307 F.2d 120 (1962); *see generally* Tigar, *Corporations' Liability for Criminal Acts* The National Law Journal, March 17, 1986, at 15, col. 4.
11. Northrop & Pohlman, *Professional Service Corporation Statute: A Comparison of Eight States* 2 IN BRIEF 18 (Summer, 1986).
12. *See, e.g.,* CAL. BUS. & PROF. CODE §2775-2781 (West Supp. 1986).
13. *See, e.g.,* N.Y. BUS. CORP. LAW §1504 (c) (McKinney 1985).
14. A professional service corporation in Washington means "any type of personal service to the public which requires as a condition precedent to the rendering of such service the obtaining of license or other legal authorization . . . *including but not by way of limitation,* certified public accountants, chiropractors, dentists, osteopaths, physicians, podiatrists, chiropodists, architects, veterinarians and attorneys at law." WASH. REV. CODE ANN. §18.100.030 (1) (Supp. 1986) (emphasis added).
15. In Maryland, "professional service means any personal service to the public which: (1) requires a license for its performance . . ." MD. CORPS. & ASS'NS. CODE ANN. §5-101 (e) (1985).
16. COLO. REV. STAT. §12-36-134 (1) (1984).
17. N.Y. BUS. CORP. §1501 (McKinney 1985).
18. *Id.* at §1504(c).
19. *Id.* at §1505(a).
20. *Id.* at §1512(b).
21. *See, e.g.,* CAL. CORP. CODE §13401-13410 (West 1967 & Supp. 1986).
22. *See, e.g.,* CAL. BUS. & PROF. CODE §2775-2781 (West Supp. 1986).
23. CAL. CORP. CODE §13101 (West Supp. 1986).
24. *Id.* at §13404 (West Supp. 1986).
25. *Id.* at §13401(b), 13404 (West Supp. 1986).
26. CAL. BUS. & PROF. CODE §2778 (West Supp. 1986).
27. *Id.* at §2779 (West Supp. 1986).
28. CAL. CORP. CODE §13410 (C) (West Supp. 1986).
29. The nursing corporation section concerning officers, directors, shareholders, and employees states that "[e]xcept as provided in §13401.5 and 13403 of the Corporations Code, each shareholder, director and officer of a nursing corporation . . . shall be a licensed person as defined in Section 13401 of the Corporations Code." CAL. BUS. & PROF. CODE §2779 (West Supp. 1986).
30. CAL. CORP. CODE §13401.5 (f) (1)-(7) (West Supp. 1986).
31. *Id.* at §13406 (West 1967).
32. *Id.* at §13407 (West 1967).
33. *Id.*
34. *Id.* at §13401 (d) (West Supp. 1986).
35. CAL. BUS. & PROF. CODE §2780 (West Supp. 1986).
36. *Id.* at §2781 (West Supp. 1986).
37. CAL. CORP. CODE at §13410 (West 1967).
38. *Id.* at §13408.5 (West Supp. 1986).
39. CAL. BUS. & PROF. CODE §2776, 2777 (West Supp. 1986).

40. A. JACOX & C. NOVIES, ORGANIZING FOR INDEPENDENT PRACTICE (1977).
41. 42 U.S.C. §2000e(b) (1982).
42. *Id.*
43. *See, e.g., Williams v. General Motors Corp.*, 656 F.2d 120 (5th Cir. 1981), *cert. denied,* 102 S. Ct. 1439 (1982).
44. Orth, *Trying An Age Discrimination Case* TRIAL 28 (June 1985).
45. See Chapter 30 for discussion of these defenses.
46. *Griggs v. Duke Power,* 401 U.S. 424, 431 (1971).
47. *Dothard v. Rawlinson,* 433 U.S. 321, 333-34 (1977).
48. Springer, *The Wrongful Discharge Case* TRIAL 38 (June 1985) (hereinafter cited as *Springer*).
49. *See, e.g., Tameny v. Atlantic Richfield Co.*, 164 Cal. Rptr. 839 (Cal. 1980) (refusal to participate in a price-fixing scheme); *Petermann v. Teamsters Local 396,* 344 P. 2d 25 (Cal. App. 1959) (refusal to commit perjury); *Trombetta v. Detroit, Toledo & Ironton R.R. Co.*, 265 N.W.2d 385 (Mich. App. 1978) (refusal to alter pollution control reports).
50. *See, e.g., Firestone Textile Co. Div. v. Meadows,* 666 S.W.2d 730 (Ky. 1983) (filing worker's compensation claim); *Nees v. Hocks,* 536 P.2d 512 (Or. 1975) (jury service).
51. *See, e.g., Sheets v. Teddy's Frosted Foods, Inc.*, 427 A.2d 385 (Conn. 1980) (complaints of poor quality and mislabeled food in violation of state law); *Petrik v. Monarch Printing Corp.*, 444 N.E. 2d 588 (Ill. App. 1982) (complaint of embezzlement of corporate funds and potential criminal violations by officers and employees).
52. *Springer, supra* note 48, at 40.
53. 488 A.2d 229 (N.J. App. Div. 1985), *cert. denied,* 501 A.2d 926 (N.J. 1985).
54. *Id* at 230.
55. *Id.* at 232, citing *Pierce v. Ortho Pharmaceutical Corp.*, 417 A.2d 505 (N.J. 1980).
56. *Id.* at 234.
57. *Id.*
58. 29 C.F.R. §1900 *et seq.* (1985).
59. Reported in The American Nurse, September, 1984, col. 1 at 16.
60. *Id.*
61. *See, e.g., Toussaint v. Blue Cross & Blue Shield,* 292 N.W.2d 880 (Mich. 1980).
62. *See, e.g., Weiner v. McGraw-Hill,* 443 N.E.2d 441 (N.Y. 1982).
63. *Springer, supra* note 48, at 41.
64. *See, e.g., Magnan v. Anaconda Indus., Inc.*, 479 A. 2d 781 (Conn. 1984); *Weiner v. McGraw-Hill,* 443 N.E.2d 441, 445 (N.Y. 1982); *Shah v. American Synthetic Rubber Corp.*, 655 S.W.2d 489, 491 (Ky. 1983); *Frasier v. Colonial Williamsburg Found.*, 574 F. Supp. 318, 320 (E.D. Va. 1983).
65. *Id.*
66. *See, e.g., Stern v. Vic Snyder, Inc.*, 473 A.2d 139, 143 (Pa. S. Ct. 1984) (all that is pertinent is genuineness of dissatisfaction in satisfaction contract).
67. *Springer, supra* note 48, at 43.
68. *Id.*
69. Sherman Act, 15 U.S.C. §1 (1982).
70. *Hospital Building Co. v. Board of Trustees of the Rex Hospital,* 425 U.S. 738 (1976), *later app.*, 691 F.2d 678 (4th Cir. 1982), *cert. denied,* 464 U.S. 890, 904 (1983), *reh. denied,* 464 U.S. 1003.
71. 457 U.S. 332 (1982).
72. 466 U.S. 2 (1984).
73. 586 F.2d 530 (5th Cir. 1979), *cert. denied,* 444 U.S. 924 (1979).
74. The case and the agreement are discussed in Chapter 29.
75. *See, e.g.,* 42 U.S.C. §1395nn(b) (Medicare) and 42 U.S.C. §1396n(b) (Medicaid) (1982).
76. *See generally* Sax, Physicians Face Government Crackdown on Fraud and Abuse 2 THE HEALTH LAWYER 3 (Fall 1985).
77. 604 F.2d 999 (7th Cir. 1979), *cert. denied,* 444 U.S. 991 (1979).
78. 695 F.2d 1151 (9th Cir. 1983).
79. 760 F.2d 68 (3rd Cir. 1985), *cert. denied,* 106 S. Ct. 396 (1985).
80. CAL. BUS. & PROF. CODE §654.2 (a), (b) (West Supp. 1986).
81. CAL. WELF. & INSTIT. CODE §14022 (West Supp. 1986).
82. CAL. HEALTH & SAFETY §445 (West Supp. 1986).
83. UNIFORM COMMERCIAL CODE §2-314.
84. *Id.*
85. *See, e.g., Silverhart v. Mt. Zion Hospital,* 98 Cal. Rptr. 187 (Cal. App. 1971).
86. RESTATEMENT (SECOND) OF TORTS §402a.
87. Annot., *Liability of Hospital or Medical Practitioner Under Doctrine of Strict Liability in Tort, Or Breach Of Warranty, For Harm Caused By Drug, Medical Instrument, Or Similar Device Used in Treating Patient* 54 ALR3d 258.
88. *See, e.g., Butler v. Northwestern Hospital of Minneapolis,* 278 N.W. 37 (Minn. 1938) (court affirmed judgment in favor of patient on breach of warranty theory where a clamp furnished by the hospital failed to close properly, and hot water intended for use in proctoclysis scalded patient; court noted one who furnishes an instrumentality for special use impliedly warrants it to be reasonably fit for the purpose for which it is furnished, and the defect could have been discovered).
89. *See, e.g., Chesire v. South Hampton Hospital Ass'n.*, 278 N.Y.S.2d 531 (1967); *Fisher v. Sibely Memorial Hospital,* 403 A.2d 1130 (D.C. App. 1979).
90. 459 So.2d 818 (Ala. 1984).
91. 211 N.E.2d 253 (Ill. 1965), *cert. denied,* 383 U.S. 946 (1966).
92. 183 Cal. Rptr. 156 (Cal. App.), *modified,* 133 Cal. App. 3d94 (1982).
93. Carpenter, *Joint Ventures in Competitive Contracting* 2 THE HEALTH LAWYER 3 (Fall 1984).

Additional Readings

AMERICAN NURSES' ASSOCIATION, GUIDELINES FOR APPOINTMENT OF NURSES FOR INDIVIDUAL PRACTICE (1978).

AMERICAN NURSES' ASSOCIATION, OBTAINING THIRD-PARTY REIMBURSEMENT: A NURSE'S GUIDE TO METHODS AND STRATEGIES (1984).

Archer and Fleshman, *Doing Our Own Thing: Community Health Nurses in Independent Practice,* 8 J. NURS. ADMIN 44 (November 1978).

Baker, *Entrepreneurial Practice for Nurses: A Response to Hershey,* 9 LAW, MED. & HEALTH CARE 257 (December 1983).

Braddock and Sawyer, *Becoming an Independent Consultant: Essentials to Consider* 3 NURS. ECON. 332 (November-December 1985).

Fortin and Rabinow, *Legal Implications of Nursing Diagnosis* 14 NURS. CLIN. N. AM. 553 (September 1979).

Hershey, *Entrepreneurial Practice for Nurses: An Assessment of the Issues,* 9 LAW, MED. & HEALTH CARE 253 (December 1983).

M. NEAL, NURSES IN BUSINESS (1982).

J. NORTON, REGULATION OF BUSINESS ENTERPRISES IN U.S.A. (1985).

SMALL BUSINESS ADMINISTRATION, CHECKLIST FOR GOING INTO BUSINESS (available free from any office of the SBA, or write the SBA at 1441 L Street, N.W., Washington, D.C. 10416.)

SMALL BUSINESS ADMINISTRATION, STARTING AN INDEPENDENT CONSULTING PRACTICE (1984).

R. SMITH, ENTREPRENEUR'S MARKETING GUIDE (1984).

Wriston, *Nurse Practitioner Reimbursement,* 6 J. HEALTH POLIT., POL. & LAW 444 (Fall 1981).

Appendix I

Nursing law glossary*

Compiled by Cynthia E. Northrop

absolute right Given to the person in whom it inheres the uncontrolled dominion over the object at all times and for all purposes.

ad litem For purposes of litigation.

administrative law Branch of law dealing with organs of government and their powers. (State Board of Nurse Examiners, for example.)

advanced directives Means by which competent adults indicate choices in health care treatment decisions. The means include, but are not limited to, verbal communication, power of attorney, living will, and trust agreements.

adversary Litigant opponent—the opposing party in a writ or action.

affiant Person who makes and subscribes an affidavit.

affidavit A declaration or statement of facts, made voluntarily, and confirmed by oath.

agency Includes every relation in which one person acts for or represents another by the latter's authority.

agent Person authorized by another to act for him.

allegation Charge or assertion that has not been proven.

appeal A complaint to a superior court to reverse or correct an injustice done or an alleged error committed by an inferior court.

appellant One taking an appeal.

appellate court That court in which judgments of trial courts are reviewed or appealed.

appellee Party against whom appeal is taken.

arbitrary and capricious Decision made without reason, at random, arising from will or caprice. A sudden, impulsive, and seemingly unmotivated change of mind; a sudden change or series of changes hard to predict.

arbitrator Neutral person chosen by both sides to decide disputed issues.

*Compiled from BLACK'S LAW DICTIONARY and cases and material presented in this book.

assault Threat to do bodily harm.

attorney general opinion Opinion of the attorney general, an attorney who is employed by the state or federal government, for the purpose of advising within the executive branch of government. The opinion is not law but is given credence should litigation arise on the issue discussed in an opinion.

audit A formal means of reviewing the status of a system, department, or activity. It is an examination with intent to verify, often in health care, the quality of nursing care.

battery Committing bodily harm.

binding arbitration Submission of disputed matters to final determination.

bona fide Good faith.

borrowed servant An employee temporarily under the control of another.

breach of contract Unjustified failure to perform the terms of a contract as agreed upon or when performance is due.

captain-of-the-ship doctrine Person in charge may be held responsible for all those under their supervision and makes the final decisions.

case law Decisions by the courts.

cause of action Averment of allegations or facts sufficient to cause defendant to respond to the allegations.

civil immunity Usually granted by legislation that requires a person to report a particular activity. (E.g., in reporting child abuse, one receives immunity from civil suits that might be available based upon breach of confidentiality by reporting.)

civil law Concerned with the legal rights and duties of private persons.

common law Derived from court decisions, judge-made law.

comparative negligence Doctrine of negligence of the plaintiff and defendant is compared and an apportionment of damages is made based on the acts the parties are found to have committed.

compensatory damages Amounts of money for proven loss.

confidentiality or confidential communication Communications passing between persons in a fiduciary relationship who have a duty not to reveal the information.

consent A voluntary act by which one person agrees to allow someone else to do something.

constitutional law Branch of law dealing with organization and function of governments.

contract A promissory agreement between two or more persons that creates, modifies, or destroys a legal relation. It is a legally enforceable promise between two or more persons to do or not to do something. There are two kinds of contracts, express (written) and implied (from behavior of parties).

contributory negligence The act or omission amounting to want of ordinary care on the part of the complaining party, which concurring with defendant's negligence, is the proximate cause of injury.

corporate negligence doctrine Means that a health care corporation as an entity is negligent. It is the failure of those entrusted with the task of providing the accommodations and facilities to carry out the purpose of the corporation and the failure to follow, in a given situation, the established standards of conduct to which the corporation should conform.

corroboration To strengthen, to add weight of credibility to a thing by additional and confirming facts or evidence.

criminal immunity Immunity from criminal prosecution granted through legislation (e.g., following a living will).

cross examination Examination of witnesses upon their evidence given in chief, to test its truth or credibility.

cruel and unusual punishment A prohibition found within the eighth amendment to the U.S. Constitution, this is usually the ground upon which a prisoner establishes a legal right to treatment and to reasonable and safe health care while imprisoned.

defamation A tort, civil wrong, in which one's reputation in the community is injured. Slander, the oral form, and libel, the written form, are both defamation.

defendant In a criminal case, the person accused of committing a crime. In a civil suit, the person against whom the suit is brought.

defense counsel Attorney who offers evidence as reasons in law or facts.

deliberate indifference That which a prisoner must show (in a lawsuit) was the manner in which health care was delivered to her or him. Usually a pattern of behavior directed toward one or more prisoners in delivering necessary prison or jail services. Constitutionally, prisoners are protected from services that reflect a deliberate indifference to their needs.

deposition An oral interrogation answering all manner of questions relating to the transaction at issue, given under oath and taken in writing before a judicial officer, such as a notary public.

direct examination The initial questions asked of a witness by the attorney who called the witness.

due care That degree of care or concern that would or should be exercised by an ordinary person in the same situation.

due process Certain procedural requirements to assure fairness; varies in application among academic, clinical, employment, and other settings.

employer One who selects the employee, pays a salary or wages, retains the power to dismiss, and can control the employee's conduct during working hours.

employment claims A variety of claims which are governed by laws which involve the employment context for nurses.

ethics The science relating to moral action or moral value.

evidence or evidentiary matter Any form of proof, or probative matter, presented by the act of the parties for the purpose of inducing belief in the minds of the court or jury as to their contention.

expert witness One who has special training, experience, skills, and knowledge in a relevant area, and whose testimony (the opinion) is allowed to be considered as evidence; nonexpert opinions are usually not admissible as evidence.

false imprisonment An intentional tort involving the act of placing someone in a bounded area that prevents the free exercise of power of movement.

fiduciary Position of trust.

foreseeability, doctrine of Individual is liable for all natural and proximate consequences of any negligent acts to another individual to whom a duty is owed.

fraud An intentional act that involves a perversion of truth. May include false representation, false, or misleading allegations, concealment, deception, or other means that serve to get advantage over another human being.

good samaritan law State laws that provide civil immunity from negligence lawsuits for individuals who stop and render care in an emergency.

guardian ad litem One appointed to prosecute or defend a suit on behalf of a person incapacitated by infancy or otherwise.

harm or injury Any wrong or damage done to another, either to person, to rights, or to property.

hearsay rule A rule of evidence that restricts the admissibility of evidence that is not the personal knowledge of the witness. Hearsay evidence is admissible only in certain circumstances under strict rules.

independent contractor Not an employee, but an individual who contracts for particular services with another.

indemnification An agreement under which a person who has compensated another for yet another's actions, can require that other person to compensate him or her for that compensation. (E.g., as the result of a lawsuit a hospital compensates an injured patient because of a nurse-employee's negligence; under an indemnification agreement, the hospital may seek compensation from the nurse for their outlay.)

informed consent One in which the patient has received sufficient information concerning the health care proposed, its incumbent risks, and the acceptable alternatives.

injunction A court order to stop a person from performing a specific act under the circumstances.

insurance A contract in which one party (insurer) agrees to compensate the other (insured) for a loss. The insurance policy is the written contract; the premium is the consideration; and, for example, the events insured against are the risks of practicing nursing.

international law The law that regulates the interaction among nations; the law of nations.

interrogatory Set of written questions, exchanged among parties through their attorneys as part of discovering the facts and issues in a case.

judge An officer who guides the court proceedings to ensure impartiality and who sees that the rules of evidence are observed. The trial judge determines the applicable law and instructs the jury. The appellate judge hears appeals and renders decisions about the correctness of actions of the trial judge, the law of the case, and/or the sufficiency of the evidence.

jurisdiction The court has the authority to hear the case.

law The sum total of man-made rules and regulations by which society is governed in a formal and legally binding manner.

lay witness One who testifies as to what was seen, heard, or otherwise observed. A material witness.

legal Permitted or authorized by law.

liability An obligation one has incurred or might incur through any act or failure to act, responsibility for conduct falling below a certain standard that is the causal connection to the plaintiff's injury.

license and licensure Permission granted by the state to conduct a certain activity that the state regulates and controls (e.g., nursing license issued by the state board of nursing; business license issued by a state department overseeing the conduct of businesses).

litigation A trial in court to determine legal issues and the rights and duties between parties.

mainstreaming Seeing that handicapped children are part of the regular school activities, including classroom and other activities.

malice The intentional doing of a wrongful act without just cause or excuse, with an intent to injure or under circumstances that the law will imply an evil intent.

malpractice Professional misconduct, improper discharge of professional duties, or a failure to meet the standard of care by a professional that results in harm to another.

military law Laws unique to the military; includes rules and regulations of the department of defense and all of its components.

minor and mature or emancipated minor Age of minority varies from state to state; generally, a person is a minor until the age of 18. However, state legislatures have passed laws that define circumstances under which a person under the age of 18 (a minor) may act as if they were adults (e.g., consent to treatment for pregnancy, alcohol, or drug abuse when married or living independently).

moral Normatively human, what is expected of humans, that which they ought to do.

mutual assent Clear understanding between or among parties considering an offer; known at law as a meeting of the minds.

negligence Failure to act as an ordinary prudent person which results in harm; conduct contrary to that of a reasonable person under specific circumstances.

negligence per se Failure to meet the standard of care outlined by statute.

outrageous conduct, doctrine of That conduct which is beyond all possible bounds of decency and is regarded as atrocious and utterly intolerable in a civilized community.

parens patria Duty of state to protect its citizens.

personal liability Each person is responsible for his or her own actions.

personal immunity Certain classes of individuals are granted immunity from a lawsuit, usually by legislative bodies. (E.g., nurses in the military have been granted personal immunity by Congress, the implication being that a patient injured by nursing negligence can only sue the government.)

plaintiff The person who brings a civil suit seeking damages or other legal relief.

policies Guidelines within which employees of an institution must operate.

precedent A previous adjudged decision that serves as authority in a similar case.

prima facie As far as can be judged from the first disclosure; on the first appearance. Such a case is presented when all the necessary elements of a valid cause of action are alleged to exist. The actual existence of such facts is then subject to proof and defense at trial.

privacy The right to be "left alone" to live in seclusion without being subjected to unwarranted or undesired publicity.

privileged communication Statements made to one in a position of trust, usually an attorney, physician, or spouse. Because of the confidential nature of the information, the law protects it from being revealed, even in court.

procedures Mode of proceeding by which a legal right is enforced. A series of steps outlined by the institution to accomplish a specific objective or task.

professional liability insurance Contract for insurance that provides compensation for losses due to professional liability (the liability connected with performance of a profession).

protocols Statements written and used by nurses, nurse midwives, nurse practitioners, nurse anesthetists, and clinical specialists that outline and authorize particular practice activities (e.g., prescriptive authority).

proximate cause Legal concept of cause and effect; the injury would not have occurred but for the particular cause; causal connection.

public health laws Legislation to protect and improve the good of the entire citizenry or public (e.g., laws requiring immunizations before school entrance).

public policy A principle of law that holds that no subject can lawfully do that which has a tendency to be injurious to the public or against the public good. Thus, certain classes of acts are said to be "against public policy" when the law refuses to enforce or recognize them, on the ground that they have a mischievous tendency, so as to be injurious to the interests of the state, apart from the illegality or immorality.

quality assurance A formal approach to assessing the status of health care delivery and activities directed to assuring that a quality level of care is delivered.

reasonable care That degree of skill and knowledge customarily used by a competent health practitioner or student of similar education and experience in treating and caring for the sick and injured in the community in which the individual is practicing.

records Written official documentary of what has happened to a particular patient during a specific period of time. An agency's business record.

res ipsa loquitur "The thing speaks for itself." A doctrine of law applicable to cases in which the defendant has exclusive control of the thing that caused the harm and where the harm ordinarily could not have occurred without negligent conduct. Normally, the plaintiff must prove the defendant's liability but when this doctrine is found to apply, the defendant must prove no responsibility for the harm.

respondeat superior "Let the master answer." The employer is responsible for the legal consequences of the acts of the servant or employee while the employee acts within the scope of the employment.

right Power, privilege, or faculty inherent in one person and incident upon another.

right-to-know law Occupational health and safety laws (federal and state) that provide that a worker has a right to know what toxic substances he or she is working with and the implications of such exposure.

risk The danger of hazard of a loss; the casualty contemplated in a contract of insurance.

rules and regulations Clear and concise statements mandating or prohibiting certain activity in an institution.

scope of practice Usually found in the state nursing practice act definitions, which contain a definition of nursing, either licensed practical or professional registered nursing practice.

standard of care Those acts performed or omitted that an ordinary prudent person in the defendant's position would have done or not done; a measure by which the defendant's conduct is compared to ascertain negligence or malpractice.

standards Criteria of measuring and conformity to established practice.

standing orders Medical orders, written, for use by nurses when a physician is not present.

statute of limitations A legal limit on the time one has to file a suit in civil matters, usually measured from the time the wrong occurred or was or should have been discovered.

statutes Legislative enactments; act of legislature declaring, commanding, or prohibiting something.

statutory law Enacted by a legislative group (e.g., Congress or State Legislature).

sovereign immunity The governmental type of immunity, granted or changed by the legislative branch.

subpeona A court order requiring one to come to court to give testimony; failure to appear results in punishment by the court.

suit Court proceeding in which one person seeks damages or other legal remedies from another.

terminable at will The legal concept in which, for example, a nurse who has no contract with a definite time frame may legally be discharged without cause. (E.g., at the will of the employer; however, the nurse may also terminate at will the work arrangement.)

testimony Oral statement of a witness, given under oath at trial.

tort A legal or civil wrong committed by one person against the person or property of another.

verdict The formal declaration of the jury of its findings.

waive To renounce or give up a privilege.

writ A writing issuing from a court ordering a sheriff or other officer of the law or some other person to perform an action desired by the court or authorizing an action to be done.

Appendix II

Legal research

Cynthia E. Northrop

Lawyers are trained to review factual situations, research the law, and prepare and argue an opinion for each legal issue raised. Similar to the nursing process (assess, plan, diagnose, implement, evaluate), a lawyer has been taught to examine issues using the following format:

1. *Identify the issue*. The issue is stated in precise legal terms. Generalizations are avoided.

2. *State the law*. In this step the rule and reasoning of law applicable to the issue is researched. All sources of law are reviewed: legislation, regulation, constitutions, case law, and common law. All views of courts and legislatures are considered. There are often "majority rules" or the general view and "minority rules," which only a few courts have expressed and followed. The underlying rationale for each rule of law is identified.

3. *Analyze: apply the law to the facts*. Here the facts of a particular situation are examined, weighing them in light of the rules of law. Logical inferences are drawn between the facts and the rules of law.

4. *Conclude*. Legal advice on each issue is stated clearly and explicitly. Often several solutions exist. Each is discussed but one position usually is selected; reasons are indicated.

In step 2 above, finding the law can be a time-consuming process. Legal research is uniquely part of a lawyer's skill and can be a voluminous task. To manage the task, several computerized systems are available to the lawyer. Whether by hand or by computer there are several sources to be tapped in researching a legal problem. There are basically three primary sources of law: constitutions, statutes and court decisions. An outline of legal reference materials is provided in the box on p. 556. This is provided as basic information for the reader but is not intended to supplant or replace seeking legal advice and professional legal research. After these sources are discussed, examples of citations and tips on reading a case are described.

There are several *statutes* that may help answer a legal concern. Each state has its own code of laws, as do many local jurisdictions, such as cities or counties within a state. There are often administrative codes or *regulations* within each state that compile the laws of the executive branch of government. The UNITED STATES CODE and the UNITED STATES STATUTES AT LARGE contain federal laws and the CODE OF FEDERAL REGULATIONS contain the regulations of the federal executive branch.

Decisions of various courts are located in many resources. Again, generally divided between state and federal courts, these previous decisions of courts may provide answers to current legal questions. The United States Supreme Court reports its decisions in a *Supreme Court Reporter*. West Publishing Company publishes case law in a National Reporter System. Each reporter is listed in the box on p. 556. The reporters are organized by geographic region and separate reports contain state and federal cases. Decisions of other judicial bodies, such as military courts, and administrative bodies, such as the Federal Trade Commission, have their own reporters.

Thus far primary sources of law have been men-

SELECTED LEGAL REFERENCE MATERIALS

Statutes, the Constitution of the United States, state constitutions

Federal Statutes: Statutes at Large, U.S. Code, U.S. Code Annotated, U.S. Code Service
State Statutes: Sessions Laws, Compiled Statutes, Revised Statutes, Codes, Annotated Codes
Municipal Ordinances, Rules of Administrative Bodies, Rules of Courts, Executive Orders

Court decisions

United States Supreme Court: Government Series Reports, Supreme Court Reporter
Other Federal Courts: Federal Cases (to 1880), Federal Reporter, Federal Supplement (1932 to date), Federal Rules Decisions
State Reports: National Reporter System, including Atlantic Reporter, North Eastern Reporter, North Western Reporter, Pacific Reporter, South Eastern Reporter, Southern Reporter, South Western Reporter, California Reporter, New York Supplement. (In addition each state has its own reporter.)
Selected Reports: e.g., American Law Reports, American Law Reports Federal, Military Justice Reporter
Special Subject Reports: e.g., Bankruptcy Reports, American Maritime Cases
Decisions of Administrative Bodies: e.g., Interstate Commerce Commission Decisions, Federal Trade Commission Decisions

tioned. There are, however, secondary sources of law. These include several digests, encyclopedias, books of words and phrases, textbooks, handbooks, forms, looseleaf services, dictionaries, and other index sources. There are also legal periodicals, generated by law schools and legal associations.

The law library is the most likely place to have all of these resources. However, local public libraries may also have selected legal materials, such as the state and federal codes and some legal periodicals.

When using a law library one is generally impressed by the tremendous number of different types of literature available. A thorough orientation to the library itself will provide a review of the number and types of materials available. Most law libraries have published guides that may include audio means of being oriented to the services of the library. Most law school librarians are specially trained in legal materials; many are lawyers themselves and most belong to an association of Law Librarians, which publishes many guidelines on organization of a law library and keeping current materials available.

In this book the endnotes and additional readings have referenced both primary and secondary legal materials and nursing and health care materials. Here are some examples of how to read the legal citations given in this book.

Example one: state statutes
MD. HEALTH GEN. CODE ANN. §18-205 (1982)

This is a citation to the Annotated Code of the State of Maryland. It cites to state legislation and includes annotations for applicable sections to secondary legal resources, such as law review articles that may have discussed the statute. As in many states, Maryland has a general code of law and a code of laws separated into special categories or subject-matters. In this example the special category is Health, Generally. The numbering indicates that the material will be found at Section 18-205 in that volume. The date is the date of publication of the subject-matter volume and supplements (looseleaf) are located in the back of that volume. This section is dated 1982, reflecting that no amendments or changes have been made by the state legislature since that time. The supplements must always be checked to see what the current law is.

Example two: federal statutes
42 U.S.C. §213(a) (1982 & Supp. I 1983)

This citation is to the UNITED STATES CODE (U.S.C.), which organizes all federal laws into fifty titles. This statute can be found in title 42 which is named The Public Health and Welfare and at Section 213(a). The latest publication of the U.S.C. is 1982. Supplements have been published in following years covering statutes passed up until January, 1987. Statutes since that time can be found in either a commercial publication, weekly loose-leaf service, known as the U.S. LAW WEEK, or in the UNITED STATES STATUTES AT LARGE. The supplements and main volumes are republished together every 6 years.

Example three: federal regulations
29 C.F.R. §2200 (1986)

The CODE OF FEDERAL REGULATION (C.F.R.) is arranged by topic into 50 titles. Some of the titles are similar to those of the federal statutes but not all the titles are the same. This reference is to title 29 and Section 2200. Regulations passed following publication of bound C.F.R. volumes can be found in the *Federal Register,* a publication printed several times a week, containing all federal administrative regulations, executive orders, and presidential proclamations. Any C.F.R. citation given in this book can be updated by checking the currently bound volume and the *Federal Register.*

Example four: state regulations

MASS. ADMIN. CODE tit. x, §x. (1986)

Not all states have published regulations. Those states that do follow the pattern of the federal regulations. Here the *Code of Massachusetts Regulations,* title x and section x is referenced. State regulations after this time can be found in the *Massachusetts Register,* the administrative register of that state. It is cited as Mass. Admin. Reg.

Example five: court decisions

As mentioned on p. 555, court decisions are made by various courts, including state and federal courts, highest to lowest levels. The following examples give a range of possibilities.

a. *Board of Curators of the University of Missouri v. Horowitz,* 435 U.S. 78 (1978).

This citation is to a United States Supreme Court decision, the highest court in the United States. The case can be found in volume 435 of the *United States Reports (U.S.)* at page 78. It was decided in 1978. Supreme Court decisions may also be found in the *Supreme Court Reporter* (Sup. Ct.).

b. *Nuttleman v. Case Western Reserve University,* 560 F. Supp. 1 (N.D. Ohio 1981), *aff'd* 708 F.2d 726.

This case is located in volume 560 of the *Federal Supplement* (F. Supp.) at page 1 and was affirmed by a higher court. That higher court's affirmation of the case can be found in the *Federal Reporter, Second series,* (F.2d) at volume 708 and page 726. The initial case was decided in 1981 by one of the federal district courts, the U.S. District Court for Ohio, Northern District; the Federal Circuit Court of Appeals affirmed (agreed with) the lower court's decision.

c. *Whittington v. Sowela Technical Institute,* 438 So. 2d 236 (La. 1983)

This is a decision of the highest court in Louisiana, found in the *Southern Reporter,* 2nd Series (So. 2d), at volume 438 and page 236. It was decided in 1983. The *Southern Reporter* is one of several reporters published by West Publishing Company as part of the National Reporter System. Others are listed in the box on p. 556.

Reading a case

Locating a court's opinion is only one step in understanding and using the law. Being prepared for how the opinion is presented and written is important to its understanding. As one approaches the case there are several items that should be noted first. Who are the parties? What are they seeking? Lawyers are taught to approach a case or "brief it" using the following format:

1. *Facts.* What is the general nature of the case? What are the essential facts leading to the controversy?
2. *Trial Court Decision.* What was decided by the lower court? What is the judicial history of the case?
3. *Issue.* What is the issue raised on appeal?
4. *Holding.* What did the higher court decide? What is the effect of its decision?
5. *Rationale.* What was the court's reasoning? Why did it arrive at its decision and how?

A landmark nursing case, *Sermchief v. Gonzales,* (660 S.W.2d 683 [Mo.banc 1983]) has been reprinted in Appendix III as an example of what a case looks like. Used with permission of West Publishing Company, this case can be found in the Southwestern Reporter, Second Series, volume 660 and at page 683. The case is presented, like many other cases, with the following sections:

1. Name of the case, which court decided the case, and the date the case was decided.
2. The West Publishing Company's Editor's summary note.
3. The keys that note what points of law were discussed in this particular case, which are indexed to other cases discussing the same legal points. (These are prepared by West Editor's, not the judges.)
4. Information about the lawyers who represented the parties in the case.
5. The court's official opinion begins on p. 684 of the case and is organized by legal issues presented by the case. (The court's opinion was written by Judge Welliver.)
6. On page 690 the names of the judges who concurred or agreed with the opinion rendered are noted, followed by the name of a judge who concurred in part of the opinion but excepted or did not agree with another part of the opinion and the name of a judge who was absent.

The substance of this important case has been discussed in several chapters in this text.

Not only are all the legal issues in one case indexed in a "key" system (established by West Publishing Company Editors) that cross-indexes the issues with all other issues in all other cases but all cases themselves are catalogued and must be checked by legal researchers through a system called "shepardizing." This system provides the legal researcher with the ability to find all cases that refer to a particular case or to trace the case and give its subsequent history as it is appealed and perhaps the initial decision overturned, altered, or supported. The system informs the legal researcher whether the case is still "good law" and whether the lower court's decision was affirmed (aff'd) or reversed (rev'd).

Other resources

As mentioned on p. 556, there are other legal research materials such as periodicals, newspapers, and other secondary sources. While these sources are not considered authoritative, they usually provide excellent overview, analysis, scholarly explorations of issues and comprehensive sources on the law. Legal texts and treatises provide exhaustive coverage of specific legal topics. For example, in this text the *Restatements of Law* have been referred to as a source of further information for the reader. Many legal periodicals such as St. Louis University Law Journal, cited as ST.LOUIS U.L.J., have been used in this text.

In addition, state and federal government manuals are excellent resources for detailed information on the executive branch of government. Texts are available that give more information about legal research itself. The reader may refer to:

1. J. JACOBSTEIN AND R. MERSKY, FUNDAMENTALS OF LEGAL RESEARCH (1977)
2. M. PRICE AND H. BITNER, EFFECTIVE LEGAL RESEARCH (4th ed. 1979)
3. HALT/AMERICANS FOR LEGAL REFORM, USING A LAW LIBRARY (1982)
4. M. COHEN, LEGAL RESEARCH IN A NUTSHELL (1978)

Lastly, the rules for legal citation that are uniformly accepted, used by lawyers and legal publishers, and generally followed in this text are contained in A UNIFORM SYSTEM OF CITATION published and distributed by The Harvard Law Review Association.

Appendix III

Sample case

Chaiyarat SERMCHIEF, et al., Appellants,

v.

Mario GONZALES, et al., Respondents,

and

State of Missouri, Intervenor-Respondent.

No. 64692.

Supreme Court of Missouri, En Banc.

Nov. 22, 1983.

Nurses and physicians brought petition for declaratory judgment and injunction that practices of nurses were authorized under nursing law and did not constitute unauthorized practice of medicine. The Circuit Court, St. Louis County, Milton A. Saitz, J., denied petition, and plaintiffs appealed directly to Supreme Court, alleging issue of validity of statutes. The Supreme Court, Welliver, J., held that services routinely provided by nurses and complained of by Board of Registration for the Healing Arts fell within legislative standard of "professional nursing."

Reversed and remanded.

1. Statutes ⚡181(1)

In construing statutes, court seeks to ascertain intent of lawmakers and to give effect to that intent.

2. Statutes ⚡188

Court normally accomplishes task of ascertaining legislative intent by attributing to words used in statute their plain and ordinary meaning.

3. Statutes ⚡184

For purposes of construing statute, legislative intent and meanings of words used in statute can be derived from general purposes of legislative enactment and by identification of problem sought to be remedied and circumstances and conditions existing at time of enactment.

4. Statutes ⚡212.5

Amended statute should be construed on theory that legislature intended to accomplish substantive change in law.

5. Physicians and Surgeons ⚡6(1)

Nursing Practice Act of 1975 substantially revised law affecting nursing profession by redefining term "professional nursing" to expand scope of authorized nursing practices, permitting nurses to assume responsibilities heretofore not considered to be within field so long as those responsibilities were consistent with nurse's specialized education, judgment and skill. V.A.M.S. §§ 335.011 et seq., 335.016, subd. 8; V.A. M.S. § 335.010, subd. 2 (Repealed).

6. Physicians and Surgeons ⚡6(1)

Acts of licensed nurses, who had postgraduate special training in field of obstetrics and gynecology, in taking of patient histories, breast and pelvic examinations, laboratory testing of PAP smears, gonorrhea cultures and blood serology, providing of, and giving of information about, oral contraceptives, condoms and intrauterine devices, dispensing of certain designated medications, counseling services and community education, done pursuant to written standing orders and protocols signed by physicians, were within "professional nursing" standard provided in amended statute and did not constitute unlawful practice of medicine, where nurses' diagnoses were within limits of nurses' respective knowledge and nurses referred patients to physicians upon reaching limits of their knowledge. V.A.M.S. §§ 334.155, 335.016, subd. 8.

Frank Susman, Roselee Adlin, Stephen G. Hamilton, Susan Schermer, St. Louis, for appellants.

Michael Wolff, St. Louis, Richard S. Brownlee, III, Jefferson City, Gene P. Schultz, St. Louis, Dara Klassel, Eve W. Paul, New York City, Elizabeth D. Badger, Kansas City, John Ashcroft, Atty. Gen., Sara Rittman, Asst. Atty. Gen., Jefferson City, Patricia M. Nagel, St. Louis, Paul L. Bradshaw, Jean Paul Bradshaw, Springfield, David J. Kornelis, Edward W. Kriss, Kansas City, Michael R. Nack, Clayton, Robert R. Northcutt, Dept. of Social Services, Jefferson City, for amicus curiae.

David Brydon, James Swearengen, Johnny K. Richardson, Mark W. Comley, Jefferson City, for respondents.

John Ashcroft, Atty. Gen., Paul M. Spinden, Asst. Atty. Gen., Jefferson City, for intervenor-respondent.

WELLIVER, Judge.

This is a petition for a declaratory judgment and injunction brought by two nurses and five physicians [1] employed by the East Missouri Action Agency (Agency) wherein the plaintiff-appellants ask the Court to declare that the practices of the Agency nurses are authorized under the nursing law of this state, § 335.016.8, RSMo 1978 [2] and that such practices do not constitute the unauthorized practice of medicine under Chapter 334 relating to the Missouri State Board of Registration For the Healing Arts (Board). The petition further requests that the Board be enjoined from taking any steps, either civil or criminal, to enforce the unauthorized practice of medicine provision of § 334.010 against these parties. The holding below was against appellants who make direct appeal to this Court alleging that the validity of the statutes is involved. Mo. Const. art. V, § 3. While the case may involve no more than application of the statutes, we retain jurisdiction because of the general interest in this matter. Mo. Const. art. V, § 4. We reverse.

I

The facts are simple and for the most part undisputed. The Agency is a federally tax exempt Missouri not-for-profit corporation that maintains offices in Cape Girardeau (main office), Flat River, Ironton, and Fredericktown. The Agency provides medical services to the general public in fields of family planning, obstetrics and gynecology. The services are provided to an area that includes the counties of Bollinger, Cape Girardeau, Perry, St. Francis, Ste. Genevieve, Madison, Iron and Washington. Some thirty-five hundred persons utilized these services during the year prior to trial. The Agency is funded from federal grants, Medicaid reimbursements and patient fees. The programs are directed toward the lower income segment of the population. Similar programs exist both statewide and nationwide.

Appellant nurses Solari and Burgess are duly licensed professional nurses in Missouri pursuant to the provisions of Chapter 335 and are employed by the Agency. Both nurses have had post-graduate special training in the field of obstetrics and gynecology. Appellant physicians are also employees of the Agency and duly licensed to practice medicine (the healing arts) pursuant to Chapter 334. Respondents are the members and the executive secretary of the Missouri State Board of Registration for the Healing Arts (Board) and as such are charged with the enforcement, implementation, and administration of Chapter 334.

The services routinely provided by the nurses and complained of by the Board included, among others, the taking of history; breast and pelvic examinations; laboratory testing of Papanicolaou (PAP) smears, gonorrhea cultures, and blood serology; the providing of and giving of information about oral contraceptives, condoms, and intrauterine devices (IUD); the dispensing of certain designated medications; and counseling services and community education. If the nurses determined the possibility of a condition designated in the standing orders or protocols that would contraindicate the use of contraceptives until further examination and evaluation, they would refer the patients to one of the Agency physicians. No act by either nurse is alleged to have caused injury or damage to any person. All acts by the nurses were done pursuant to

1. The physicians are joined for the reason that they are charged with aiding and abetting the unauthorized practice of medicine by the nurses.

2. All references are to RSMo 1978 unless otherwise indicated.

written standing orders and protocols signed by appellant physicians. The standing orders and protocols were directed to specifically named nurses and were not identical for all nurses.

The Board threatened to order the appellant nurses and physicians to show cause why the nurses should not be found guilty of the unauthorized practice of medicine and the physicians guilty of aiding and abetting such unauthorized practice. Appellants sought Court relief in this proceeding.

The trial can be capsulized by saying that the foregoing facts were either stipulated or agreed to by all parties. The appellants, in addition to the two nurses and the director of the Agency, called four witnesses who were permitted to express their opinion that the nurses' described acts were within § 335.016.8. The four witnesses called by appellants were, Phyllis Drennan, Dean of Nursing, University of Missouri-Columbia; Sallye Brown, Director of the Nurses Association of the American College of Obstetricians and Gynecologists; Sister Jeanne Meurer, Director of St. Louis University Graduate Program in Nurse Midwifery and Director of Nurse Midwifery, Department of Health and Hospitals, St. Louis; and Dr. Lawrence Kahn, Director of Nurse Practitioner Program, Washington University, St. Louis. Respondents called Dr. Hubert Ritter, Chairman of the obstetrics-gynecology (OBGYN) unit of St. Louis University; Dr. Raymond Ritter, a Cape Girardeau physician, practicing general and traumatic surgery and a former member of the Board of Healing Arts; and Dr. Kathleen LeVeck, a former nurse and 1980 graduate of St. Louis University Medical School, now in residency in OBGYN at St. Louis University Hospitals, all of whom expressed the view that the acts of the nurses were outside the contemplation of § 335.016.8 and constituted the practice of medicine prohibited by § 334.010. Virtually all of the admitted testimony of these seven witnesses consisted of their opinion of what the trial court described in its memorandum opinion as the ultimate issues for determination:

A. Does the conduct of plaintiff nurses Solari and Burgess constitute "Professional Nursing" as that term is defined in § 335.016.8, RSMo?

B. If the Court finds and concludes that any act or acts of plaintiff nurses Solari and Burgess does not or do not constitute(s) "professional nursing" and, constitutes the unauthorized practice of medicine under § 334.010, RSMo the Court must then determine if § 334.010, RSMo is unconstitutionally vague and uncertain on its face and, thus, is in violation of the specificity requirements of the Fifth and Fourteenth Amendments to the United States Constitution and of Article 1, § 10 of the Missouri Constitution.

All of appellants offers to prove the general practices of nursing, national or other recognized guidelines and standards for nursing, or the legislative intent with reference to the 1975 revision of the Nursing Practice Act, Chapter 335, were overruled by the trial court.

In our opinion the trial court correctly defined the issues of the case, both of which we deem to be matters of law to be determined by the Court. The trial court then made extensive findings of fact, the first nine denominated as stipulated and undisputed facts and the last nine denominated as controverted facts. The last nine findings are:

10. Pursuant to the standing orders and protocols (Joint Exhibits 3, 4 and 5), plaintiffs Burgess and Solari provided oral contraceptives, IUD's and vaginal medications to their patients.

11. Providing oral contraceptives, IUD's and vaginal medications is the administration of medications and treatments.

12. Plaintiffs Burgess and Solari administered these medications and treatments which were not prescribed by a person licensed in this state to prescribe such medications and treatments.

13. Plaintiffs Burgess and Solari performed pelvic examinations and based upon their findings, attempted to diag-

nose the existence or nonexistence of contraindications to the use of oral contraceptives, IUD's and vaginal medications, set out in their standing orders and protocols (Joint Exhibits 3, 4 and 5).

14. Graduation from a school of medicine or a school of osteopathy is a prerequisite for one to be capable of interpreting the results of a pelvic examination.

15. The State Board of Nursing regulations do not require professional nursing programs to include courses in pathology or physical diagnosis.

16. The acts of plaintiffs Burgess and Solari in utilizing the findings derived from pelvic examinations which they performed to attempt to diagnose the existence or nonexistence of contraindications to the use of oral contraceptives, IUD's and vaginal medications, require an individual to draw upon education, judgment and skill based upon knowledge and application of principles in addition to and beyond biological, physical, social and nursing sciences.

17. The acts of plaintiffs Burgess and Solari in administering oral contraceptives, IUD's and vaginal medications, without the same being prescribed by a person licensed in this state to prescribe such medications and treatments, require an individual to draw upon education, judgment and skill based upon knowledge and application of principles in addition to and beyond biological, physical, social and nursing sciences.

18. The conduct of plaintiffs Burgess and Solari in utilizing the findings derived from pelvic examinations which they performed to attempt to diagnose the existence or nonexistence of contraindications to the use of oral contraceptives, IUD's and vaginal medications, as described in their standing orders and protocols (Joint Exhibits 3, 4 and 5), constitutes medical diagnosis and not nursing diagnosis.

Findings 10, 13 and 15 appear to be undisputed in the record. Whether the acts referred to in findings 11, 12, 16, 17, and 18, all of which are admitted and undisputed, can be performed pursuant to standing orders and protocols signed by a licensed physician as opposed to, under supervision of a licensed physician, we deem to be a matter of law for determination by the court. Whether findings 14 and 16 are supported by substantial evidence is a question for consideration only if the Court determines as a matter of law that these findings are necessary to the interpretation of § 335.-016.8 and § 334.010 and § 334.155.

Following the findings the trial court stated that "[t]he preceding findings were arrived at by the Court after considering and weighing all of the evidence. In reaching its findings, the Court specifically found that the more credible evidence was presented by defendants' witnesses." This case being a court tried case, the decision must be reversed on appeal if "there is no substantial evidence to support it, . . . it is against the weight of the evidence, . . . it erroneously declares the law, or . . . it erroneously applies the law." *Murphy v. Carron,* 536 S.W.2d 30, 32 (Mo. banc 1976), and Rule 73.01. *Murphy* neither contemplated binding an appellate court by the co-mingling of law and fact nor by denominating as facts findings which are matters of law. In a case so hotly contested where both sides presented witnesses of such unquestionable professional stature, the broad labeling of one side's evidence as "more credible" tends to render the "specifically found credibility" suspect. We do no violence to the teachings of *Murphy* or Rule 73.01, but rather reaffirm the viability of both and proceed to decide the ultimate matters of law above defined.

II

The appeal of this case attracted amici briefs resembling a letter writing campaign directed at a legislative body.[3] The amici

3. Letters received in the Court were returned to the senders by the Clerk advising that they had not been read by the Court for the reason that justice requires that the Court limit its consideration to matters of record before the Court.

are listed in Appendix A to this opinion. It suffices to say that those briefs detailed the historical development of the nursing profession and the nurses expanding role in the delivery of health services, the reality of which both the Court and the public take notice. Many expressed their opinions as to how we should construe our Missouri statutes, a matter which we are obligated to do in accordance with long established rules of statutory construction. "[T]he construction of a statute is a question of law." *Staley v. Missouri Director of Revenue,* 623 S.W.2d 246, 248 (Mo. banc 1981).

In passing it might be noted that the volume of amici briefs, reflected both herein and in other cases pending before the Court, highlight the growing need for consideration by the Court of a rule relating to the filing of amici briefs in order that the Court may avoid the appearance of becoming victim to a bombardment of amici briefs.[4]

III

The statutes involved are:

> It shall be unlawful for any person not now a registered physician within the meaning of the law to practice medicine or surgery in any of its departments, or to profess to cure and attempt to treat the sick and others afflicted with bodily or mental infirmities, or engage in the practice of midwifery in this state, except as herein provided.

Section 334.010.

> This Chapter does not apply to dentists licensed and lawfully practicing their profession within the provisions of chapter 332, RSMo; *to nurses licensed and lawfully practicing their profession within the provisions of chapter 335, RSMo;* to optometrists licensed and lawfully practicing their profession within the provisions of chapter 336, RSMo; to pharmacists licensed and lawfully practicing their profession within the provisions of chapter 338, RSMo; to podiatrists licensed and lawfully practicing their profession within the provisions of chapter 330, RSMo; or to chiropractors licensed and lawfully practicing their profession within the provisions of chapter 331, RSMo.

Section 334.155, RSMo Supp.1982 (emphasis added).

> Definitions.—As used in sections 335.011 to 335.096, unless the context clearly

4. In the past the Court, almost without limitation, permitted the filing of briefs labeled "amicus curiae", when in most instances they were the briefs of advocates. The only reference to amici briefs in the current rules of this Court appears in the commentary following Canon 3 A(4) of the Missouri Code of Judicial Conduct: "An appropriate and often desirable procedure for a court to obtain the advice of a disinterested expert on legal issues is to invite him to file a brief *amicus curiae.*"

The federal courts and many states have adopted rules that limit the circumstances under which an interested third party may file a brief as an amicus curiae. These rules typically limit the filing of amici briefs to instances when all parties to the case consent to the filing or upon permission of the court after the amicus curiae demonstrates that facts or questions of law relevant to the case have not been adequately presented by the parties. *See, e.g.,* U.S. Supreme Court Rule 36:

> 2. A brief of an *amicus curiae* in a case before the Court for oral argument may be filed when accompanied by written consent of all parties to the case and presented within the time allowed for the filing of the brief of the party supported and if in support of neither party, within the time allowed for filing appellant's or petitioner's brief. Any such brief must identify the party supported, shall be as concise as possible, and in no event shall exceed 30 pages in length. No reply brief of an *amicus curiae* will be received.
> 3. When consent to the filing of a brief of an *amicus curiae* in a case before the Court for oral argument is refused by a party to the case, a motion for leave to file, accompanied by the proposed brief, complying with the 30-page limit, may be presented to the Court. No such motion shall be received unless submitted within the time allowed for the filing of an *amicus* brief on written consent. The motion shall concisely state the nature of the applicant's interest, set forth facts or questions of law that have not been, or reasons for believing that they will not adequately be, presented by the parties, and their relevancy to the disposition of the case; and it shall in no event exceed five pages in length. A party served with such motion may seasonably file an objection concisely stating the reasons for withholding consent.

requires otherwise, the following words and terms shall have the meanings indicated:

. . . .

(8) "Professional nursing" is the performance for compensation of any act which requires substantial specialized education, judgment and skill based on knowledge and application of principles derived from the biological, physical, social and nursing sciences, including, but not limited to:

(a) Responsibility for the teaching of health care and the prevention of illness to the patient and his family; or

(b) Assessment, nursing diagnosis, nursing care, and counsel of persons who are ill, injured or experiencing alterations in normal health processes; or

(c) The administration of medications and treatments as prescribed by a person licensed in this state to prescribe such medications and treatments; or

(d) The coordination and assistance in the delivery of a plan of health care with all members of the health team; or

(e) The teaching and supervision of other persons in the performance of any of the foregoing;

Section 335.016.8(a)–(e).

At the time of enactment of the Nursing Practice Act of 1975, the following statutes were repealed:

2. A person practices professional nursing who for compensation or personal profit performs, *under the supervision and direction of a practitioner authorized to sign birth and death certificates,* any professional services requiring the application of principles of the biological, physical or social sciences and nursing skills in the care of the sick, in the prevention of disease or in the conservation of health.

Section 335.010.2, RSMo 1969 (emphasis added).

Nothing contained in this chapter shall be construed as conferring any authority on any person to practice medicine or osteopathy or to undertake the treatment or cure of disease.

Section 335.190, RSMo 1969.

The parties on both sides request that in construing these statutes we define and draw that thin and elusive line that separates the practice of medicine and the practice of professional nursing in modern day delivery of health services. A response to this invitation, in our opinion, would result in an avalanche of both medical and nursing malpractice suits alleging infringement of that line and would hinder rather than help with the delivery of health services to the general public. Our consideration will be limited to the narrow question of whether the acts of these nurses were permissible under § 335.016.8 or were prohibited by Chapter 334.

[1–4] In analyzing this question, we are guided by well-established rules of statutory construction. Fundamentally, we seek to ascertain the intent of the lawmakers and to give effect to that intent. *Citizens Bank & Trust Company v. Director of Revenue,* 639 S.W.2d 833, 835 (Mo.1982); *State v. Kraus,* 530 S.W.2d 684, 685 (Mo. banc 1975). A court normally accomplishes this task by attributing to the words used in the statute their plain and ordinary meaning. *Bank of Crestwood v. Gravois Bank,* 616 S.W.2d 505, 510 (Mo. banc 1981); *Kieffer v. Kieffer,* 590 S.W.2d 915, 918 (Mo. banc 1979); *Beiser v. Parkway School District,* 589 S.W.2d 277, 280 (Mo. banc 1979); *State ex rel. Conservation Commission v. LePage,* 566 S.W.2d 208, 212 (Mo. banc 1978). Legislative intent and the meaning of words used in the statute also can be derived from the general purposes of the legislative enactment. *Eminence R–1 School District v. Hodge,* 635 S.W.2d 10, 13 (Mo.1982); *Bank of Crestwood* at 510. Further insight into the legislature's object can be gained by identifying the problems sought to be remedied and the circumstances and conditions existing at the time of enactment. *Kieffer* at 918; *State ex rel. Zoological Park Subdistrict of the City and County of St. Louis v. Jordan,* 521 S.W.2d 369, 372 (Mo.1975); *Mashak v. Poelker,* 367 S.W.2d 625, 626 (Mo.

banc 1963). An amended statute, such as § 335.016.8, should be construed on the theory that the legislature intended to accomplish a substantive change in the law. *City of Willow Springs v. Missouri State Librarian,* 596 S.W.2d 441, 444 (Mo. banc 1980); *Kilbane v. Director of the Department of Revenue,* 544 S.W.2d 9, 11 (Mo. banc 1976); *Gross v. Merchants-Produce Bank,* 390 S.W.2d 591, 597 (Mo.App.1965). Finally, "all provisions of a statute must be harmonized and every word, clause, sentence, and section thereof must be given some meaning." *Staley,* 623 S.W.2d at 250.

[5] The legislature substantially revised the law affecting the nursing profession with enactment of the Nursing Practice Act of 1975.[5] Perhaps the most significant feature of the Act was the redefinition of the term "professional nursing," which appears in § 335.016.8. Even a facile reading of that section reveals a manifest legislative desire to expand the scope of authorized nursing practices. Every witness at trial testified that the new definition of professional nursing is a broader definition than that in the former statute. A comparison with the prior definition vividly demonstrates this fact. Most apparent is the elimination of the requirement that a physician directly supervise nursing functions. Equally significant is the legislature's formulation of an open-ended definition of professional nursing. The earlier statute limited nursing practice to "services . . . in the care of the sick, in the prevention of disease or in the conservation of health." § 335.010.2, RSMo 1969. The 1975 Act not only describes a much broader spectrum of nursing functions, it qualifies this description with the phrase "including, but not limited to." We believe this phrase evidences an intent to avoid statutory constraints on the evolution of new functions for nurses deliverying health services. Under § 335.016.8, a nurse may be permitted to assume responsibilities heretofore not considered to be within the field of professional nursing so long as those responsibilities are consistent with her or his "specialized education, judgment and skill based on knowledge and application of principles derived from the biological, physical, social and nursing sciences." § 335.016.8.

[6] The acts of the nurses herein clearly fall within this legislative standard. All acts were performed pursuant to standing orders and protocols approved by physicians. Physician prepared standing orders and protocols for nurses and other paramedical personnel were so well established and accepted at the time of the adoption of the statute that the legislature could not have been unaware of the use of such practices. We see nothing in the statute purporting to limit or restrict their continued use.

Respondents made no challenge of the nurses' level of training nor the degree of their skill. They challenge only the legal right of the nurses to undertake these acts. We believe the acts of the nurses are precisely the types of acts the legislature contemplated when it granted nurses the right to make assessments and nursing diagnoses. There can be no question that a nurse un-

5. The impetus for the legislation was the ongoing expansion of nursing responsibilities. Several national commissions investigated the causes of and the implications of this phenomenon during the early 1970's. One committee concluded: "Professional nursing . . . is in a period of rapid and progressive change in response to the growth of biomedical knowledge, changes in patterns of demand for health services, and the evolution of professional relationships among nurses, physicians and other health professions." Secretary's Committee to Study Extended Roles for Nurses, Dep't. of Health, Education and Welfare, Pub. No. (HSM) 73-2037, "Extending the Scope of Nursing Practice: A Report of the Secretary's Committee to Study Extended Roles for Nurses" 8 (1971). *See also* National Comm'n for the Study of Nursing and Nursing Education, An Abstract for Action (1970); National Comm'n for the Study of Nursing and Nursing Education, From Abstract Into Action (1973). The broadening of nursing roles necessitated altering existing nursing practice laws to reflect the changes in a nurse's professional duties. At the time the Missouri legislature acted, thirty states had amended their laws regulating the nursing profession. *See* Comment, "Interpreting Missouri's Nursing Practice Act," 26 St. Louis U.L.J. 931, 931 n. 1 (1982). Forty states currently have broadened nursing practice statutes similar to § 335.016.8. *See infra* note 6.

dertakes only a nursing diagnosis, as opposed to a medical diagnosis, when she or he finds or fails to find symptoms described by physicians in standing orders and protocols for the purpose of administering courses of treatment prescribed by the physician in such orders and protocols.

The Court believes that it is significant that while at least forty states [6] have modernized and expanded their nursing practice laws during the past fifteen years neither counsel nor the Court have discovered any case challenging nurses' authority to act as the nurses herein acted.

The broadening of the field of practice of the nursing profession authorized by the legislature and here recognized by the Court carries with it the profession's responsibility for continuing high educational standards and the individual nurse's responsibility to conduct herself or himself in a professional manner. The hallmark of the professional is knowing the limits of one's professional knowledge. The nurse, either upon reaching the limit of her or his knowledge or upon reaching the limits prescribed for the nurse by the physician's standing orders and protocols, should refer the patient to the physician. There is no evidence that the assessments and diagnoses made by the nurses in this case exceeded such limits.

In preparing this opinion, the Court did considerable research and reading in medical libraries. We find nothing in our construction of the statutes that is incompatible with the history and development of the profession of nursing, the general standards of state and national nursing organizations and associations, the utilization of special nursing services by the Federal and State governments in the delivery of health services, or the utilization of nursing services by schools, factories, homes for the aging and our hospitals.

Having found that the nurses' acts were authorized by § 335.016.8, it follows that such acts do not constitute the unlawful practice of medicine for the reason that § 334.155 makes the provisions of Chapter 334 inapplicable "to nurses licensed and lawfully practicing their profession within the provisions of Chapter 335 RSMo."

This cause is reversed and remanded with instructions to enter judgment consistent with this opinion.

HIGGINS, GUNN and DONNELLY, JJ., and MORGAN, Senior Judge, concur.

RENDLEN, C.J., concurs in result.

BLACKMAR, J., concurs except as to Part II.

BILLINGS, J., not sitting.

6. Ala.Code § 34–21–1(3) (1975); Alaska Stat. § 08.68.410(8) (1983); Ariz.Rev.Stat.Ann. § 32–1601.5 (Supp.1983–84); Cal.Bus. & Prof. Code § 2725 (Supp.1983); Colo.Rev.Stat. § 12–38–104(10) (Supp.1982); Fla.Stat.Ann. § 464.-003(3)(a),–(c) (1981 & Supp.1983); Ga.Code Ann. § 43–26–1(3) (1982); Hawaii Rev.Stat. § 457–2(2) (1976); Idaho Code § 54–1402(b)(1) (1979); Ill.Ann.Stat. ch. 111, ¶ 3405, § 4 (Smith-Hurd Supp.1983–84); Ind.Code Ann. § 25–23–1–1(b) (1982); Iowa Code Ann. § 152.1.2 (West Supp.1983–84); Kan.Stat.Ann. § 65–1113(d) (1980); Ky.Rev.Stat. § 314.011(5) (1983); La.Rev.Stat.Ann. § 37:913(3) (West Supp.1983); Me.Rev.Stat.Ann. tit. 32, § 2102.2 (1978); Md.Health Occ.Code Ann. § 7–101(f) (Supp.1983); Mass.Ann.Laws ch. 112, § 80B (Michie/Law Co-op. Supp.1983); Mich.Comp. Laws Ann. § 333.17201(1)(a) (1980); Minn. Stat.Ann. § 148.171(3) (Supp.1983); Miss.Code

Appendix IV

Citations

Compiled by Cynthia E. Northrop

Nursing practice laws, child abuse, and adult/elder abuse state statutes

The first section number of each of the following statutes is listed below:

a. Nursing practice
b. Child abuse
c. Adult/elder abuse

Alabama
a. ALA. CODE §34-21-1 (1985)
b. ALA. CODE §26-14-1 (1975 & Supp. 1985)
c. ALA. CODE §38-9-1 (Supp. 1985)

Alaska
a. ALASKA STAT. §08.68.010 (1985)
b. ALASKA STAT. §47.17.010 (1985)
c. ALASKA STAT. §47.24.010 (1985)

Arizona
a. ARIZ. REV. STAT. ANN. §32-1601 (1976 & Supp. 1985)
b. ARIZ. REV. STAT. ANN. §13-3620 (Supp. 1985)
c. ARIZ. REV. STAT. §46-451 (Supp. 1985)

Arkansas
a. ARK. STAT. ANN. §72-726, 727, 745 (1979 & Supp. 1985)
b. ARK. STAT. ANN. §42-807 (1977 & Supp. 1985)
c. ARK. STAT. ANN. §59-1301 (Supp. 1985)

California
a. CAL. BUS. & PROF. CODE §2700 (West 1974 & Supp. 1985)
b. CAL. PENAL CODE §11165 (West 1982 & Supp. 1985)
c. CAL. WELF. & INST. CODE §15600 (West Supp. 1985)

Colorado
a. COLO. REV. STAT. §12-38-101 (Supp. 1985)
b. COLO. REV. STAT. §19-10-101 (1978 & Supp. 1985)
c. COLO. REV. STAT. §26-3.1-101 (Supp. 1985)

Connecticut
a. CONN. GEN. STAT. ANN. §20-87a (West Supp. 1985)
b. CONN. GEN. STAT. ANN. §17-38, 38a, 38b, 38c (West Supp. 1985)
c. CONN. GEN. STAT. ANN. §46a-14 (West Supp. 1985)

Delaware
a. DEL. CODE ANN. tit. 24, §1901 (Supp. 1985)
b. DEL. CODE ANN. tit. 16, §901 (1983 & Supp. 1985)
c. None

District of Columbia
a. D.C. CODE ANN. §2-1701.1 (RN); 2-1702.1 (PN) (1981)
b. D.C. CODE ANN. §6-2101 (1981 & Supp. 1985)
c. D.C. CODE ANN. §6-2501 (Supp. 1985)

Florida
a. FLA. STAT. ANN. §464.001 (West Supp. 1985)
b. FLA. STAT. ANN. §415.501 (West Supp. 1985)
c. FLA. STAT. ANN. §415.101 (West Supp. 1985)

Georgia
a. GA. CODE ANN. §43-26-1 (RN); 43-26-30 (LPN) (1984)
b. GA. CODE ANN. §19-7-5 (1982)
c. GA. CODE ANN. §30-5-4 (Supp. 1985)

Hawaii
a. HAWAII REV. STAT. §457-1 (1976 & Supp. 1985)
b. HAWAII REV. STAT. §350 (1976 & Supp. 1985)

c. HAWAII REV. STAT. §349C (Supp. 1985)

Idaho

a. IDAHO CODE §54-1401 (1979 & Supp. 1985)
b. IDAHO CODE §16-1601 (Supp. 1985)
c. IDAHO CODE §39-5201 (Supp. 1985)

Illinois

a. ILL. ANN. STAT. ch. 111, §3405 (Smith-Hurd Supp. 1985)
b. ILL. ANN. STAT. ch. 23, §2051 (Smith-Hurd Supp. 1985)
c. ILL. ANN. STAT. ch. 23, §6301; 6501 (Smith-Hurd Supp. 1985)

Indiana

a. IND. CODE ANN. §25-23-1-1 (Burns Supp. 1985)
b. IND. CODE ANN. §31-6-11-1 (Burns 1980 & Supp. 1985)
c. IND. CODE ANN. §4-27-7-1 (Burns Supp. 1985)

Iowa

a. IOWA CODE ANN. §152.1 (West Supp. 1985)
b. IOWA CODE ANN. §232.67; 235A (West 1985)
c. IOWA CODE ANN. §235B (West 1985)

Kansas

a. KAN. STAT. ANN. §65-1113 (1980 & Supp. 1985)
b. KAN. STAT. ANN. §38-716 (1981 & Supp. 1985)
c. KAN. STAT. ANN. §60-3101 (1983 & Supp. 1985)

Kentucky

a. KY. REV. STAT. §314.011 (1983)
b. KY. REV. STAT. §199.335 (1985)
c. KY. REV. STAT. §209.010 (1985)

Louisiana

a. LA. REV. STAT. ANN. §37:911 (RN) (West Supp. 1985); 37:961 (PN) (West 1974 & Supp. 1985)
b. LA. REV. STAT. ANN. §14-403 (West 1974 & Supp. 1985)
c. LA. REV. STAT. ANN. §14-403.2 (West Supp. 1985)

Maine

a. ME. REV. STAT. ANN. tit. 32, §2101 (RN); 2251 (PN) (1978 & Supp. 1985)
b. ME. REV. STAT. ANN. tit. 22, §4001 (Supp. 1985)
c. ME. REV. STAT. ANN. tit. 22, §3470 (Supp. 1985)

Maryland

a. MD. HEALTH OCC. CODE ANN. §7-300 (1986)
b. MD. FAM. LAW CODE ANN. §5-901 (1984 & Supp. 1985)
c. MD. FAM. LAW CODE ANN. §14-201 (1984 & Supp. 1985)

Massachusetts

a. MASS. ANN. LAWS ch. 112, §74 (RN); 74A (PN) (Michie/Law Co-op 1985)
b. MASS. ANN. LAWS ch. 119, §51-A (Michie/Law Co-op Supp. 1985)
c. MASS. ANN. LAWS ch. 209A, §1 (Michie/Law Co-op 1981 & Supp. 1985)

Michigan

a. MICH. COMP. LAWS ANN. §333.17201 (West 1980)
b. MICH. COMP. LAWS ANN. §722.621 (West Supp. 1985)
c. MICH. COMP. LAWS ANN. §400.11a (West Supp. 1985)

Minnesota

a. MINN. STAT. ANN. §148.171 (RN) (West Supp. 1985); 148.29 (LPN) (West 1970 & Supp. 1985)
b. MINN. STAT. ANN. §626.556 (West 1983 & Supp. 1985)
c. MINN. STAT. ANN. §626.557 (West 1983 & Supp. 1985)

Mississippi

a. MISS. CODE ANN. §73-15-1 (Supp. 1985)
b. MISS. CODE ANN. §43-21-353 (Supp. 1985)
c. MISS. CODE ANN. §43-45-1 (Supp. 1985)

Missouri

a. MO. ANN. STAT. §335.011 (Vernon Supp. 1986)
b. MO. ANN. STAT. §210.110 (Vernon 1983 & Supp. 1986)
c. MO. ANN. STAT. §660.250 (Vernon Supp. 1986)

Montana

a. MONT. CODE ANN. §37-8-101 (1985)
b. MONT. CODE ANN. §41-3-101 (1985)
c. MONT. CODE ANN. §53-5-201 (1985)

Nebraska

a. NEB. REV. STAT. §71-1132.04 (1979)
b. NEB. REV. STAT. §28-707 (1979 & Supp. 1985)
c. NEB. REV. STAT. §28-711 (1979 & Supp. 1985)

Nevada

a. NEV. REV. STAT. §632.010 (1985)
b. NEV. REV. STAT. §200.508 (1985)
c. NEV. REV. STAT. §200.5091 (1985)

New Hampshire

a. N.H. REV. STAT. ANN. §326-B (1984)
b. N.H. REV. STAT. ANN. §169-C (Supp. 1985)
c. N.H. REV. STAT. ANN. §161-D (Supp. 1985)

New Jersey

a. N.J. STAT. ANN. §45:11 (West 1978 & Supp. 1985)
b. N.J. STAT. ANN. §9:6-8.8 (West 1976 & Supp. 1985)

c. N.J. STAT. ANN. §52:27G (West Supp. 1985, institutionalized elderly ombudsman program)

New Mexico

a. N.M. STAT. ANN. §61-3-1 (1986)
b. N.M. STAT. ANN. §32-1-15 (Supp. 1985)
c. None

New York

a. N.Y. EDUC. LAW §6900 (McKinney 1985)
b. N.Y. SOC. SERV. LAW §411 (McKinney Supp. 1986)
c. N.Y. SOC. SERV. LAW §473 (McKinney Supp. 1986)

North Carolina

a. N.C. GEN. STAT. §90.171.19 (1985)
b. N.C. GEN. STAT. §7A-543 (1981 & Supp. 1985)
c. N.C. GEN. STAT. §108A-99 (Supp. 1985)

North Dakota

a. N.D. CENT. CODE §43-12.1 (1978 & Supp. 1985)
b. N.D. CENT. CODE §50-25.1 (1982 & Supp. 1985)
c. N.D. CENT. CODE §14-07.1-01 (1981 & Supp. 1985)

Ohio

a. OHIO REV. CODE ANN. §4723.01 (Baldwin 1984)
b. OHIO REV. CODE ANN. §2151.411 (Baldwin 1978 & Supp. 1984)
c. OHIO REV. CODE ANN. §5101.60 (Baldwin 1984)

Oklahoma

a. OKLA. STAT. ANN. tit. 59, §567 (West 1971 & Supp. 1985)
b. OKLA. STAT. ANN. tit. 21, §845 (West Supp. 1985)
c. OKLA. STAT. ANN. tit. 43A, §801 (West Supp. 1985)

Oregon

a. OR. REV. STAT. §678.010 (1983)
b. OR. REV. STAT. §418.740 (1983)
c. OR. REV. STAT. §410.610 (1983)

Pennsylvania

a. PA. STAT. ANN. tit. 63, §211 (Professional nursing); 651 (PN) (Purdon 1968 & Supp. 1985)
b. PA. STAT. ANN. tit. 11, §2201 (Purdon Supp. 1985)
c. PA. STAT. ANN. tit. 35, §10181 (Purdon Supp. 1985)

Rhode Island

a. R.I. GEN. LAWS §5-34-1 (Supp. 1985)
b. R.I. GEN. LAWS §40-11-1 (1984 & Supp. 1985)
c. R.I. GEN. LAWS §42-66-1 (1984 & Supp. 1985)

South Carolina

a. S.C. CODE ANN. §40-33-10 (Law. Co-op. 1977 & Supp. 1984)
b. S.C. CODE ANN. §20-7-480 (Law. Co-op. 1985)
c. S.C. CODE ANN. §43-29-10 (Law. Co-op. 1985)

South Dakota

a. S.D. CODIFIED LAWS ANN. §36-9 (Supp. 1984 & Interim Supp. 1985)
b. S.D. CODIFIED LAWS ANN. §26-10 (Supp. 1984 & Interim Supp. 1985)
c. S.D. CODIFIED LAWS ANN. §25-10 (Domestic Abuse) (Supp. 1983 & Interim Supp. 1985)

Tennessee

a. TENN. CODE ANN. §63-7-101 (Supp. 1985)
b. TENN. CODE ANN. §37-1-401 (1984 & Supp. 1985)
c. TENN. CODE ANN. §14-25-101 (1980 & Supp. 1985)

Texas

a. TEX. REV. CIV. STAT. art. 4513 (RN); art. 4528c (LVN) (Vernon Supp. 1986)
b. TEX. FAM. CODE ANN. §34.01 (Vernon 1975 & Supp. 1985)
c. TEX. HUM. RES. CODE ANN. §48.001 (Vernon Supp. 1985)

Utah

a. UTAH CODE ANN. §58-31-1 (Supp. 1985)
b. UTAH CODE ANN. §78-3b-1 (Supp. 1985)
c. UTAH CODE ANN. §55-19-1 (Supp. 1985)

Vermont

a. VT. STAT. ANN. tit. 26, §1571 (Supp. 1984)
b. VT. STAT. ANN. tit. 33, §681 (Supp. 1984)
c. VT. STAT. ANN. tit. 18, §1150 (1982 & Supp. 1984)

Virgin Islands, U.S.

a. V.I. CODE ANN. tit. 27, §91 (Supp. 1984)
b. V.I. CODE ANN. tit. 5, §2532 (Supp. 1984)
c. None

Virginia

a. VA. CODE §54-367.1 (1982 & Supp. 1985)
b. VA. CODE §63.1-248.1 (1980 & Supp. 1985)
c. VA. CODE §63.1-55.1 (1980 & Supp. 1985)

Washington

a. WASH. REV. CODE §18.88.005 (1983 & Supp. 1984)
b. WASH. REV. CODE §26.44.010 (1983 & Supp. 1984)
c. WASH. REV. CODE §74.34 (Supp. 1984)

West Virginia

a. W. VA. CODE §30-7 (RN) (1980 & Supp. 1985), 30-7A (PN) (1980)
b. W. VA. CODE §49-6A-1 (1980 & Supp. 1985)
c. None

Wisconsin

a. WIS. STAT. ANN. §441 (West 1974 & Supp. 1985)
b. WIS. STAT. ANN. §48.981 (West Supp. 1985)
c. WIS. STAT. ANN. §55 (West Supp. 1985)

Wyoming

a. WYO. STAT. §33-21-119 (Supp. 1985)
b. WYO. STAT. §14-3-201 (1977 & Supp. 1985)
c. WYO. STAT. §35-20-101 (Supp. 1985)

Index

T

U

V